THE CANADIAN WOMEN'S MOVEMENT, 1960-1990:
A GUIDE TO ARCHIVAL RESOURCES

LE MOUVEMENT CANADIEN DES FEMMES, 1960-1990 :
GUIDE DE RESSOURCES ARCHIVISTIQUES

THE CANADIAN WOMEN'S MOVEMENT, 1960-1990:
A GUIDE TO ARCHIVAL RESOURCES

Edited by
MARGARET FULFORD
Directrice de la rédaction

LE MOUVEMENT CANADIEN DES FEMMES, 1960-1990 :
GUIDE DE RESSOURCES ARCHIVISTIQUES

Canadian Women's Movement Archives
Archives canadiennes du mouvement des femmes

ECW PRESS

Copyright © Canadian Women's Movement Archives/Archives canadiennes du mouvement des femmes and ECW PRESS, 1992

All rights reserved.

CANADIAN CATALOGUING IN PUBLICATION DATA

Main entry under title:

The Canadian Women's Movement, 1960-1990:
A Guide to Archival Resources

Includes bibliographical references.
ISBN 1-55022-156-6

1. Feminism — Canada — Archival resources.
I. Fulford, Margaret, 1960–

Z7963.F44C3 1992   305.42   C92-095255-0

Design and imaging by ECW Type & Art, Oakville, Ontario.
Distributed by General Publishing Co. Limited
30 Lesmill Road, Toronto, Ontario M3B 2T6.

Published by ECW PRESS,
1980 Queen Street East, Toronto, Ontario M4L 1J2.

TABLE OF CONTENTS / TABLE DES MATIÈRES

Acknowledgements 6
Remerciements 7
Introduction (English) 8
Introduction (français) 14
The Canadian Women's Movement Archives 21
Les Archives canadiennes du mouvement des femmes 24
How to Use This Guide 27
L'utilisation du Guide 29

Part I: Records Held by Archives / *Partie I :* Fonds détenus par des archives

    National Organizations/Groupes pancanadiens 33
    Yukon 60
    Northwest Territories/Territoires du Nord-Ouest 61
    British Columbia/Colombie-Britannique 63
    Alberta 78
    Saskatchewan 90
    Manitoba 100
    Ontario 111
    Québec 155
    New Brunswick/Nouveau-Brunswick 166
    Prince Edward Island/Île-du-Prince-Édouard 170
    Nova Scotia/Nouvelle-Écosse 171
    Newfoundland and Labrador/Terre-Neuve et Labrador 177

Part II: Records Held by Groups / *Partie II :* Fonds détenus par des groupes

    National Organizations/Groupes pancanadiens 181
    Yukon 195
    Northwest Territories/Territoires du Nord-Ouest 197
    British Columbia/Colombie-Britannique 198
    Alberta 213
    Saskatchewan 221
    Manitoba 227
    Ontario 233
    Québec 257
    New Brunswick/Nouveau-Brunswick 283
    Prince Edward Island/Île-du-Prince-Édouard 289
    Nova Scotia/Nouvelle-Écosse 292
    Newfoundland and Labrador/Terre-Neuve et Labrador 298

Name Index/Index des noms 303
Subject Index/Index des sujets 335
Appendix: Addresses and Entry Numbers for Archives /
    Annexe : Adresses et numéros de notices des archives 371
List of Illustrations / Liste des reproductions 379

ACKNOWLEDGEMENTS

This guide was made possible by a generous grant from the Canadian Studies Research Tools programme of the Social Sciences and Humanities Research Council of Canada.

The collective of the Canadian Women's Movement Archives and the board of the Women's Information Centre of Toronto came up with the idea for this guide and contributed in countless ways to its becoming a reality. I am especially grateful to Johanne Pelletier, who supervised the project on behalf of the collective and board. Her knowledge of both archival and women's issues was essential to the project's success, and her ideas are reflected throughout this book. Her support and good humour were also much appreciated. I thank Jane Abray, Nancy Adamson, Karen Dubinsky, Janice Hill, Beth McAuley, and Anne Molgat for their valuable suggestions, encouragement, and generous assistance throughout the project.

Many thanks are due to staff members Susan Shea (Research Assistant) and Darleen Degrieck (Clerical Assistant) — not only for the great skill, care, and creativity they brought to their work, but also for their enthusiasm and commitment to the project.

We thank Jack David, Paul Davies, and Don McLeod at ECW PRESS for their interest in the project, their encouragement, and all their excellent work on this book.

Many others worked on various aspects of the project. We especially appreciate translator/editor Doreen Bédard-Bull's assistance with the French parts of the book.

This guide would not have been possible without the generous co-operation of archivists across Canada who patiently responded to numerous requests for information and shared their expertise and their interest in the records of the women's movement.

Equally important were the hundreds of organizations which demonstrated their commitment to preserving the records of the women's movement by taking the time to fill in our detailed questionnaire.

Finally, we thank the many friends, family members, and colleagues who offered assistance, advice, and encouragement, especially Bob Fulford, Rebecca Green, Franca Iacovetta, and Sharon Larade.

Margaret Fulford
Project Archivist

REMERCIEMENTS

La publication de ce guide a été rendue possible grâce à un généreux octroi du Conseil de recherches en sciences humaines du Canada, dans le cadre de son programme Études canadiennes : outils de recherche.

La collective des Archives canadiennes du mouvement des femmes, de concert avec le conseil du Women's Information Centre of Toronto, ont conçu ce projet et ont contribué à sa réalisation de mille et une façons. Je désire exprimer ma gratitude tout particulièrement à Johanne Pelletier, qui a supervisé le projet au nom de la collective et du conseil. Son appréciation des questions archivistiques aussi bien que féministes s'est révélée essentielle au succès de nos travaux et ses idées ont trouvé leur application à travers tout le guide. Enfin, son appui et sa bonne humeur m'ont rendu la tâche beaucoup plus agréable. Un merci tout particulier à Jane Abray, Nancy Adamson, Karen Dubinsky, Janice Hill, Beth McAuley et Anne Molgat. Leurs suggestions, leur encouragement et leur assistance dans toutes les phases du projet m'ont été d'un précieux secours.

Mes remerciements vont aussi à Susan Shea, assistante à la recherche, et à Darleen Degrieck, préposée au travail de bureau, non seulement pour l'habileté, le soin et la créativité déployés dans l'exercice de leurs fonctions, mais aussi pour l'enthousiasme et le zèle dont elles ont fait preuve dans la mise à exécution de ce projet.

J'aimerais remercier au nom de toute l'équipe Jack David, Paul Davies et Don McLeod, de ECW PRESS, pour l'intérêt qu'ils ont manifesté envers ce projet et pour leur excellent travail.

Plusieurs autres personnes ont collaboré de diverses manières à ce projet. Nous tenons à souligner tout spécialement l'assistance que nous a fournie Doreen Bédard-Bull, traductrice et réviseure, dans la réalisation de la partie française de cet ouvrage.

Ce guide n'aurait pas été possible sans la généreuse collaboration d'archivistes à travers le Canada qui ont répondu avec patience aux innombrables demandes de renseignements que nous leur avons adressées et qui ont bien voulu partager leur expertise avec nous en s'intéressant de près aux documents du mouvement des femmes.

D'égale importance, soulignons le vif intérêt pour la sauvegarde de documents féministes manifesté par des centaines d'organismes qui ont pris le temps de remplir notre questionnaire détaillé.

Enfin, nous nous devons de mentionner la collaboration, les conseils et l'encouragement de nombreux amies et amis, membres de famille et collègues, en particulier de Bob Fulford, Rebecca Green, Franca Iacovetta et Sharon Larade.

Margaret Fulford
Archiviste/Directrice de projet

INTRODUCTION

During the three decades covered by this guide, the Canadian women's movement grew phenomenally. In the 1960s, established women's organizations lobbied for and then advised the Royal Commission on the Status of Women, which was set up in 1967. By the time the commission reported in 1970, radical women's groups emerging from campus and left-wing organizations had dramatically transformed Canadian feminism. The number of women's groups rose remarkably in the 1970s and continued to grow during the 1980s.

As the women's movement has achieved increasing importance in Canadian society, feminist scholars have shown a burgeoning interest in the archival resources which document the movement, and activists have seen that preserving the movement's history allows them to learn from past experiences, evaluate strategies, and recognize achievements.

Veronica Strong-Boag, writing in *Archivaria* in 1978, criticized Canadian archives for neglecting records relating to women in favour of those relating to "political, military, diplomatic, and economic elites" dominated by men. She concluded that "existing holdings should be reappraised for their value for women's history and additions must be made to present collections."[1] Feminist scholars like Strong-Boag have recognized that archival appraisal is inherently political. With limited resources, archivists must constantly make decisions as to what records will be collected, and where resources will be allocated to make collections more accessible to researchers; politics inevitably plays a role in such decisions. In addition to urging archives to collect more women's records, feminists have stressed the need for improved access to existing resources.

A number of guides have been published in response to this need, beginning in 1974 with *Some Sources for Women's History in the Public Archives of Canada*.[2] Other guides to individual repositories have included *Sources for Women's History at the Provincial Archives of Alberta* (1980, revised 1989)[3] and the 1991 guide to the holdings of the National Archives of Canada, *Women's Archives Guide: Manuscript Sources for the History of Women*.[4] Several regional surveys covering more than one archival institution were conducted in the late 1970s.[5] The "archival bibliography" *Planting the Garden*, listing sources for the history of women in Manitoba, was published in 1987.[6] In 1990 les Archives nationales du Québec published *Guide sommaire : Archives des femmes au Québec*, which lists about 200 collections in Quebec.[7] Guides such as these are part of a growing support structure for feminist research, provided by interested archivists, librarians, academics, and publishers.

While earlier guides have dealt with women's history in general, this one focuses on the women's movement as a distinct aspect of women's history. Rather than covering a particular region or repository, it has a national scope and covers records held by many different archives and organizations.

This guide came about because the Canadian Women's Movement Archives/Archives canadiennes du mouvement des femmes (CWMA/ACMF) saw the need for a national, bilingual guide dealing specifically with the contemporary women's movement. The CWMA/ACMF, founded in 1977 to preserve the history of the movement, has collected the records of a broad spectrum of post-1960 women's groups. (For more information on the CWMA/ACMF, see the history

---

1 Veronica Strong-Boag, "Raising Clio's Consciousness: Women's History and Archives in Canada," *Archivaria*, no. 6 (Summer 1978), pp. 73-74.

2 Heather Rielly and Marilyn Hindmarch, *Some Sources for Women's History in the Public Archives of Canada*, National Museum of Man Mercury Series, History Division, Paper no. 5 (Ottawa: National Museums of Canada, 1974).

3 Jean E. Dryden, *Some Sources for Women's History at the Provincial Archives of Alberta*, Provincial Archives of Alberta Occasional Paper no. 2 (Alberta Culture, Historical Resources Division, 1980); Merrily K. Aubrey, *Sources for Women's History at the Provincial Archives of Alberta*, Provincial Archives of Alberta Occasional Paper no. 2, rev. ed. (Alberta Culture and Multiculturalism, Historical Resources Division, 1989).

4 Joanna Dean and David Fraser, *Women's Archives Guide: Manuscript Sources for the History of Women* (Ottawa: National Archives of Canada, 1991).

5 Veronica Strong-Boag, "Canadian Committee on Women's History," *Canadian Newsletter of Research on Women* 5, no. 1 (February 1976): 40-47 [includes a survey of archival holdings in Ontario]; Marie Lavigne and Jennifer Stoddart, "Rapport sur les archives au Québec," *Canadian Newsletter of Research on Women* 5, no. 3 (October 1976): 87-89; Eliane Leslau Silverman and Rodney Anne Muir, "Archival Holdings in Canadian Women's History: Alberta, Manitoba, and Saskatchewan," *Canadian Newsletter of Research on Women* 6, no. 1 (February 1977): 127-130; Margaret Conrad, "Report on the Archival Resources of the Atlantic Provinces on the Subject of Women's History," *Canadian Newsletter of Research on Women* 7, no. 2 (July 1978): 103-112; Linda Louise Hale, *Selected Bibliography of Manuscripts and Pamphlets Pertaining to Women Held in Archives, Libraries, Museums, and Associations in British Columbia*, Canadian Women's History Series no. 9 (Toronto: Ontario Institute for Studies in Education, 1978).

6 Mary Kinnear and Vera Fast, *Planting the Garden: An Annotated Archival Bibliography of the History of Women in Manitoba* (Winnipeg: University of Manitoba Press, 1987).

7 Madeleine Lamothe, Ghislaine Fecteau, and Pierrette Lalancette, *Guide sommaire : Archives des femmes au Québec* (Québec: Archives nationales du Québec, 1990).

of the organization on page 21.) In 1985/86, funded by the Secretary of State, the CWMA/ACMF undertook a preliminary survey that revealed the existence of a wealth of material, much of it in the offices of women's organizations. It became apparent that compiling a comprehensive guide would require much more time. The 1985/86 survey became a pilot project for the present guide.

In 1989 the Canadian Studies Research Tools programme of the Social Sciences and Humanities Research Council of Canada awarded the CWMA/ACMF a grant to produce a guide to the records of the women's movement; the two-year project began in 1990. Because records in archival repositories represented only a fraction of the material available, one goal was to encourage researchers to consult records in the offices of current organizations as well as holdings of archives. Another goal was to reflect the diversity of Canadian feminist organizing in terms of ideology, region, race, ethnicity, religion, language, class, and sexual orientation.

An important aspect of the project was outreach to women's organizations. Records dating from the 1960s or later tend to be seen as less "archival" than earlier records. Many organizations have never been approached by archives interested in acquiring their records, and activists often do not see their own records as historically valuable.. The material we sent to groups was designed to be accessible to people who were not familiar with archival concepts and terminology, and it encouraged them to see their work as part of contemporary history, recognize the value of their records, and preserve them.

This is not a complete guide to the records of the women's movement. Even with unlimited time and money, it would be impossible to produce a complete guide to the records of a vast, living, constantly changing movement. Nonetheless, by listing even a fraction of the movement's records, this guide gives a sense of the rich history of the movement since 1960, and the breadth and strength of the movement today.

Like the movement itself, the records this guide attempts to capture are in constant motion. The guide includes active, semi-active, and inactive records located in archives and offices of many kinds. As groups are founded, undergo changes, or disband, records are created, change hands, are destroyed, or are preserved. Such a state of flux means that this guide cannot be definitive; it differs in this way from guides which deal only with defunct organizations whose records have been preserved by archives and are unlikely to grow.

The records of the women's movement have certain characteristics which were taken into consideration in conceiving this project. The questionnaire sent to women's groups allowed for the prevalence of specific types of records among feminist groups: for instance, log-books, briefs, petitions, grant applications, graphic materials such as posters, and non-paper records such as buttons, banners, and T-shirts. The questionnaire also took into account organizations' concerns about confidentiality. Because many records are created by women's committees within larger organizations or are donated to archives by individual members, efforts were made to locate women's movement records within collections for larger organizations and within personal collections. The detailed Name Index was compiled to provide access to the records of groups known by more than one name. The Subject Index accommodates researchers' interest in specific women's issues; it also reflects the increasing prevalence of organizations which deal with a specific issue rather than the overall status of women.

The CWMA/ACMF defines as part of the women's movement "any organization having as one of its principal goals the improvement of women's social, economic, or political condition." This encompasses not only autonomous groups but also feminist committees within institutions such as political parties, unions, ethnocultural organizations, universities, and churches. It also includes many lesbian and gay organizations, trade unions whose members are mostly women, and organizations focused on specific "women's issues" such as child care or birth control. It does not encompass all women's groups — for instance, charities run by women are not included. While such groups are important to women's history, they are not part of the movement as the CWMA/ACMF defines it.

Government departments, royal commissions, and advisory councils are not within the scope of the guide. Government records fall within the acquisition mandate of federal and provincial archives, and information about these records is available in a variety of descriptive tools produced by these repositories.

We date the contemporary women's movement, sometimes called the "second wave," from 1960, the year Voice of Women was founded and, conveniently, the beginning of a decade. We include groups formed or functioning after 1960; for groups existing both before and after 1960, we list pre-1960 records as well, in order to give a picture of the organization's history.

The guide does not include the personal papers of individual feminists; this reflects the CWMA/ACMF's focus on organizations rather than individuals. However, individual activists have often preserved records of groups in which they were involved, so we identify group records located within personal collections in archives. For example, Muriel Duckworth's papers, at the Public Archives of Nova Scotia, include records from Voice of Women, of which she was the national president from 1967 to 1971.

The guide has two parts: Part I lists records held by archives, and Part II lists records held by organizations. Each part begins with a section listing the records of national organizations, followed by sections for groups in each province or territory, from west to east. Within a geographical section, the entries are arranged alphabetically by the name of the organization.

To gather data for Part I, we wrote to over 400 archival repositories. A few are in-house archives within organizations such as the Canadian Nurses Association and la Centrale de l'enseignement du Québec. Such organizations are included in Part I (archives' holdings) rather than Part II (organizations' holdings) if they were defined as archives by the *Directory of Canadian Archives*.[1]

Eighty archives reported relevant holdings. The entries for these are based mostly on archival finding aids and correspondence with archivists; with a few exceptions, we did not actually visit the repositories. The guide reflects the considerable diversity in the way archives arrange and describe their holdings. It lists archival holdings of about 800 collections, representing about 650 groups and ranging in size from one item to many linear metres.

Because we were unable in most cases to examine the records, we relied on finding aids or other descriptive tools provided by responding archives. It was difficult to determine whether certain groups fell within our guidelines, because the administrative histories or biographical notes available reflected varying levels of description. In some cases, the only information available was the name of the group, plus what little could be gleaned from books or articles.

Most of the archives whose holdings appear in the guide reported between one and five relevant collections; there are nineteen archives for which the guide includes more than five collections. The CWMA/ACMF has by far the largest number of relevant collections, 300 of which are listed in the guide. Because the CWMA/ACMF's holdings are extensive and have few finding aids, it was not possible to list all its records in the guide. The CWMA/ACMF's holdings include records of over 2,000 organizations; it also holds approximately 800 posters, 250 sound recordings, 450 buttons, and 1,300 photographs. The CWMA/ACMF's periodical collection includes 800 titles, about 75 of them on microfilm. CWMA/ACMF collections were examined individually and the 300 most significant were described for the guide. Determining a collection's significance was necessarily a subjective process, guided by our knowledge of the history of the women's movement. Factors included how large a collection was, what types of records it contained, when they were created, whether the group was defunct, what records of the group had been located elsewhere, and how well similar groups were represented in the guide. Many small collections were left out, especially material from the last decade.

To compile data for Part II, we sent questionnaires to about 3,000 current organizations. Many groups had moved or disbanded since 1988, when FEM-DIRECT, the CWMA/ACMF's computerized directory of Canadian women's groups, was produced. We updated and expanded FEM-DIRECT, using published and unpublished lists, and ended up with a mailing list of over 4,000, which we cut by over 1,000 groups in order to stay within our budget. In choosing which groups to retain, we gave priority to those regions which would be least well represented among the archives' holdings in Part I. For instance, because archives' holdings of women's movement records are much stronger in Ontario than in Atlantic Canada, we cut the Ontario part of the mailing list drastically, and left the Atlantic Canada part intact. Like the mail survey, the telephone follow-up emphasized the regions which would be less well represented in Part I. The survey and follow-up also emphasized the kinds of groups which are under-represented in archives' holdings. For example, because business and professional women's clubs are well represented in Part I, they were a low priority for Part II. Native women's organizations, on the other hand, are under-represented in archives, so they were a high priority for Part II. The collections located for Part II compensate to some extent for gaps in Part I.

The questionnaire to groups listed specific types of records and asked respondents to check off which types they had and for what years. In addition to the types of records common to most organizations (such as minutes, correspondence, and reports), the questionnaire also listed records which are particularly common in women's groups. Since respondents might not know anything about archives, it provided definitions of basic archival concepts such as "records," and it used vocabulary which would be accessible to those unfamiliar with archival terminology. An information sheet on how to preserve records was also included.

About 600 completed questionnaires were returned (around 20 per cent of those mailed). The questionnaire worked well: respondents found it clear and accessible, and it generated enthusiasm for preserving the records of the women's movement. It seems to have worked best for groups which use the types of records listed, and less well for those with different approaches to record keeping. (Not many respondents filled in the space for "other types not listed here.") The questionnaire did not always work well for women's committees within larger organizations such as unions. It asked them to describe only the records of their own committee, not those of the whole organization; but some committees did not conceive of their records as being distinct from those of the organization as a whole. For instance, a women's committee within a union reported that its records could not be identified and listed separately, because women's issues had been addressed within various projects, and the committee's records were mixed with other records of those projects.

Some groups chose not to have their records listed in the guide because of concerns about confidentiality — even though it would be up to them to decide which records (if any) to show to whom. (Some groups prefer not even to keep records, so as to protect members' confidentiality. A support and information group for gay men and lesbians wrote to us,

---

1 *Directory of Canadian Archives* (Ottawa: Canadian Council of Archives, 1990).

"We deliberately chose not to keep any records whatsoever as a guarantee of client confidentiality. Except for an agreed statement of purposes, no records exist.")

The guide lists the records of a particular organization under the name of the organization, not under the name of the collection, which may be different. (For instance, the Voice of Women records in the Muriel Duckworth collection at the Public Archives of Nova Scotia are listed under "Voice of Women," not under "Duckworth.") Some of these "organizations" are actually committees within larger organizations; while the larger organization's records are not listed in the guide, the committee's records should be examined in the context of the larger organization's records. (For example, the entry for "Newfoundland and Labrador Federation of Labour. Women's Committee" lists only the records of the Women's Committee, not all the records within the Newfoundland and Labrador Federation of Labour collection. But researchers interested in the committee may need to consult other records of the federation as well.)

The name at the head of an entry is the latest name used by the group during the period covered by the records. Because a reader may know the organization by a different name, the Name Index lists all the variations we know: acronyms, earlier names, and alternate forms of the name. In some cases it also includes the title of a periodical published by the group or the title of a conference the group organized. For a spectacular example, consider the entry headed "Vancouver Status of Women." Readers can find it listed in the Name Index under the original name, British Columbia Status of Women Action and Coordinating Council (or simply Status of Women Action and Coordinating Council), or its subsequent name, British Columbia Status of Women Council (or simply Status of Women Council), or under the title of its periodical, Kinesis, or under one of the acronyms used by the group at various times: VSW, BCSWACC, SWACC, BCSWC, or SWC. (Luckily, not all organizations have used this many names.)

The Subject Index uses headings found in the *Canadian Feminist Thesaurus*, whose feminist vocabulary, useful cross references, and bilingualism made it well suited to our purposes.[1]

Most entries were written in either English or French, according to the language of the records in question. For bilingual groups, identical entries usually appear in both languages. In some cases, although the group is bilingual, the records are entirely in one language, so an entry is included for that language only. Since we didn't actually see most of the collections, we weren't always sure of their language; in the case of bilingual organizations, researchers would be well advised to confirm the language of the records in advance.

Each entry begins with some information about the organization which created the records: name, location, dates of existence, and a brief description. The information about the groups came from various sources: questionnaires filled in by organizations; archival finding aids and correspondence with archivists; pamphlets and other documents in which organizations describe themselves; and books and articles. (When the source is a finding aid or other secondary source, this is indicated in the entry.) Often these sources differ; two documents published by a group may give two different founding dates, and the questionnaire filled in by the group may give a third. The differences among sources can sometimes be attributed to incorrect information. At other times, these differences simply reflect varying approaches to the information; for instance, the founding of a women's centre might be defined as the first meeting of the organizing committee, or the organization's incorporation, or the centre's official opening. Rather than do exhaustive research, we accepted that such inconsistencies and errors were bound to appear. We used our time and resources to locate and describe as many collections as we could, rather than create perfect entries on a much smaller number of collections. This is a guide to the *records* of women's groups; it should not be used as a guide to the groups themselves.

The rest of the entry concerns the records: types and years, physical condition, any restrictions on access, whether there is a finding aid, and where the records are located. Where some of this information was not applicable or was unavailable, it has been omitted from the entry. An entry lists records by or about the organization in question. In devising a format for the entries, we borrowed ideas from other thematic guides such as *A Guide to Labour Records and Resources in British Columbia*.[2]

Some entries list each type of record, with precise dates (e.g., "brief, 1974; photograph, 1976"), while others contain more general information (e.g., "correspondence, miscellaneous records, 1972-1985"). The level of description in an entry depends on the information available. The subject matter of a document is not specified — for example, "minutes," not "minutes of the finance committee." The entries also do not specify whether documents are originals or copies. Titles are provided for periodicals whose names differ from those of the organizations publishing them. Titles of other documents are not given.

Rules for archival description and cataloguing have been used to make the entries as consistent, accurate, and clear as possible. We consulted the *Rules for Archival Description* (RAD);[3] the

---

1   Canadian Women's Indexing Group, *The Canadian Feminist Thesaurus* (Toronto: Ontario Institute for Studies in Education, 1990).
2   Louise May, comp., *A Guide to Labour Records and Resources in British Columbia* (Vancouver: University of British Columbia Library, Special Collections Division, 1985).
3   Bureau of Canadian Archivists, Planning Committee on Descriptive Standards, *Rules for Archival Description* (Ottawa: Bureau of Canadian Archivists, 1990); *Report of the Textual Records Working Group to the Bureau of Canadian Archivists Planning Committee on Descriptive Standards* (Draft, January 1991).

Anglo-American Cataloguing Rules, Second Edition (AACR2);[1] and *Archives, Personal Papers, and Manuscripts: A Cataloging Manual for Archival Repositories, Historical Societies, and Manuscript Libraries*.[2] We drew on all three in compiling rules to accommodate the needs of a thematic guide reflecting a wide range of descriptive practices. The principal source for the content and format of the entries was RAD — specifically, the General Rules for Description and the Appendices (1990) and the Report of the Textual Records Working Group (Draft, January 1991). Because RAD's chapters on Choice of Access Points and Headings for Corporate Bodies were not yet available, AACR2 was used to determine what forms of an organization's name would appear in the entry's heading and in the Name Index. To describe a group of records which formed part of a larger collection, we used the rule for relationship complexity from *Archives, Personal Papers, and Manuscripts*.

The archives and organizations which supplied information for this guide used varying terminology for record types. For the most part we retained the terminology used by respondents, sometimes editing for simplification (for instance, we changed "receipts, ledgers, and bank statements" to "financial records").

Wherever possible, we expressed the physical extent of archives' holdings according to the *Rules for Archival Description*, providing the metric linear extent of textual records and indicating separately the number of posters, photographs, sound recordings, and three-dimensional objects such as buttons (for example, "6 cm of text, 1 sound recording, 8 photographs"). However, the guide reflects the varying descriptive practices of the archives responding to our survey; for instance, some archives indicated the number of photographs, while others included an unspecified number of photographs within a linear measurement. As a result, indications of physical extent are approximate.

The description of physical extent in Part II (records held by current organizations) balances the need for archival standardization with the context in which the records are created and stored. Rather than imposing archival linear measurement on organizations holding their own records, our questionnaire encouraged them to use everyday language (e.g., "3 filing cabinets" or "2 boxes").

Not all archives responded to our survey, and those that did may not always have been aware of all their relevant holdings. Finding aids may not reveal the records of a women's group within a personal collection or the records of a women's committee within a larger organization's collection; and many collections do not have finding aids at all. Sometimes a collection was omitted from the guide because no name could be identified for the creating group. For instance, in one collection, a group from the mid-1960s is identified only as "a small group of married women with children [who] met informally to discuss their experiences as graduate students or as staff members at the University of Toronto."[3] Some groups were omitted because they appeared not to fit our definition of the women's movement; however, information about such groups may sometimes be located through the records of related organizations. For instance, while local Women's Institutes are not included, Women's Institutes are included at the national and provincial levels. Many organizations which did not fall within our guidelines are affiliated with local Councils of Women, and some information about them may be found among the records of Councils of Women listed in this guide.

The guide includes some periodicals held by archives (including rare-book libraries), but it does not include the many periodicals held by women's studies libraries or general libraries. The guide lists only a fraction of the Canadian feminist newsletters and other periodicals in existence. Researchers trying to locate periodicals should consult the CWMA/ACMF's extensive collection (only about a fifth of whose 800 titles are included in the guide), as well as other archives and libraries.

Researchers should also be aware that a good deal of information about non-governmental organizations will be found in government records, which are not included in this guide. At the Provincial Archives of Alberta, for instance, records of the premier's office contain information on women's organizations from 1967 to 1971;[4] and the Doris Lewis Rare Book Room at the University of Waterloo has copies of the briefs presented to the Royal Commission on the Status of Women.[5]

Collections for branches of national organizations such as the Canadian Federation of University Women often contain some records of the larger organization. In cases where a finding aid lists the records of the larger organization as a discrete section or subgroup within the collection, the records of the larger organization are given a separate entry in this guide; in other cases, they are not specifically listed here. Similarly, a collection for a national or provincial organization may contain some branch records not listed separately.

A group's records may contain information about another group with which it had a relationship. In a few cases such

---

1   Joint Steering Committee for Revision of AACR, *Anglo-American Cataloguing Rules*, 2nd ed. rev. (Ottawa: Canadian Library Association, 1988).
2   Stephen L. Hensen, *Archives, Personal Papers, and Manuscripts: A Cataloging Manual for Archival Repositories, Historical Societies, and Manuscript Libraries* (Washington: Library of Congress, 1983).
3   "Study of Forty-Two Women Who Have Children and Who Are in Graduate Programmes at the University of Toronto," in the Germaine T. Warkentin collection, University of Toronto Archives.
4   Aubrey, *Sources for Women's History*, p. 86.
5   Susan Bellingham, "Women's Studies Collections in the University of Waterloo Library," in *Women's Collections: Libraries, Archives, and Consciousness*, ed. Suzanne Hildebrand (New York: Haworth Press, 1986), p. 132.

INTRODUCTION

records form a subgroup within a collection and are given a separate entry in this guide; but usually (if they are identified at all in the finding aid), they consist of just a few documents on each of many groups, so in most cases they aren't listed here. For instance, dozens of women's groups are mentioned in the finding aid for the Planned Parenthood Saskatchewan collection at the Saskatchewan Archives Board in Regina, e.g., "Saskatoon Women's Health Collective, 1980, 1 mm ... University of Regina Women's Centre, 1980, 1 mm." Researchers will sometimes find such information within collections through a detailed finding aid; but in most cases, researchers will have to examine the collections themselves to uncover such hidden information.

Group records within personal collections may remain hidden unless there is a detailed finding aid (e.g., the CWMA/ACMF has sound recordings of interviews with individual feminists, but as there is no finding aid to show what groups these women belonged to, the sound recordings are not listed in this guide).

Because certain finding aids list only textual records, some records in other media (such as photographs and posters) have been omitted from the guide. (Archives may have separate finding aids for certain types of records.[1])

For groups which existed before as well as after 1960, we probably missed some pre-1960 records, as some respondents to our survey may not have understood that we were interested in pre-1960 records in such cases.

Information about access restrictions is provided where available (however, such restrictions are subject to change). Researchers should always contact an archives prior to visiting, to confirm that the collection is accessible and enquire about making an appointment. Researchers interested in consulting records held by a women's organization should write or phone to ask for the organization's permission. Having the records listed in the guide does not oblige an organization to show its records to researchers; each organization will determine what records to show, to whom, and for what purposes.

As the following pages show, there exists a wealth of archival resources on the women's movement. Many records have been preserved by the CWMA/ACMF, gay and lesbian archives, and individual activists; without the pioneering efforts of the CWMA/ACMF and other grass-roots archives, many of these would have been lost. Public archives and university archives have shown an increasing interest in women's movement records, and the scope of their acquisitions in this area has begun to encompass more aspects of the diverse women's movement. Access to existing resources has been improved by a number of published guides and in-house finding aids. Feminists in northern Alberta have developed an innovative response to "the problem of women and women's organizations being under-represented and difficult to locate in archival collections": the Northern Alberta Women's Archives Project acts as a liaison between the Provincial Archives of Alberta and potential donors, encouraging women to donate their records and fostering "archival methods which are sensitive to the lives of women."[2]

A great deal remains to be done. Archivists should encourage groups to preserve their own records and show them how to do it. More resources should be provided to grass-roots archives. Groups should be able to preserve their records in a variety of ways, such as deposit in community or provincial archives, or preservation by the group itself. It is especially important that such options be available to groups in communities traditionally left out of many archives' holdings, such as gay and lesbian and ethnocultural organizations. Archives should be collecting records of a much broader spectrum of women's groups, including sound recordings and visual media, and designing finding aids which improve access to women's records. Preserving the history of the women's movement is an important task that requires ongoing cooperation among activists, archivists, and scholars.

While this guide cannot provide a complete picture of the Canadian women's movement since 1960, it does reveal a strong, diverse, dynamic movement. The guide is designed to facilitate and stimulate research into the rich past and present of the women's movement; we hope that it will also inspire both archives and organizations to preserve the movement's records.

— Margaret Fulford

---

1   Examples include: *A Descriptive Inventory of the Sound Recordings at the Canadian Women's Movement Archives/Archives canadiennes du mouvement des femmes* (Toronto: Canadian Women's Movement Archives, 1988); Alan V. Miller, comp., *Our Own Voices: A Directory of Lesbian and Gay Periodicals, 1890-1990, Including the Complete Holdings of the Canadian Gay Archives*, Canadian Gay Archives Publication no. 12 (Toronto, 1991).

2   Northern Alberta Women's Archives Project, *Recovering Women's History* (pamphlet), 1990.

INTRODUCTION

Au cours des trois décennies représentées par ce guide, le mouvement des femmes a connu une croissance phénoménale au Canada. Dans les années 60, les groupements de femmes établis au pays ont fait campagne pour obtenir la création de la Commission royale d'enquête sur le statut de la femme et, après sa formation en 1967, ont déposé des mémoires auprès de la Commission. Lorsque celle-ci a soumis son rapport en 1970, les groupes féministes radicaux sortant des campus universitaires et des organisations de gauche avaient transformé le féminisme canadien de façon dramatique. Les regroupements de femmes se sont multipliés durant les années 70 et ont continué à s'accroître durant les années 80.

À mesure que le mouvement des femmes prenait de l'importance dans la société canadienne, les chercheuses féministes manifestaient un intérêt croissant pour les ressources archivistiques du mouvement; de même, le grand courant des activistes se rendait compte de l'importance de retracer l'historique du mouvement quand il s'agit de tirer des leçons du passé, d'évaluer des stratégies et de couronner les succès.

En 1978, Veronica Strong-Boag, écrivant dans la revue Archivaria, critiquait la tendance des archives canadiennes à négliger les documents se rapportant aux femmes en faveur de ceux qui concernent les élites politiques, militaires, diplomatiques et économiques dominées par les hommes. L'auteure invite les archivistes à réévaluer les fonds existants en fonction de leur valeur pour l'histoire des femmes et de compléter les collections actuelles.[1] Des féministes averties comme Strong-Boag reconnaissent que le tri des archives est un exercice essentiellement politique. Disposant de ressources limitées, les archivistes doivent constamment déterminer quelles pièces collectionner et à quels fonds appliquer les instruments de recherche qui en faciliteront l'accès. La politique joue un rôle inévitable dans pareilles décisions. En plus d'insister sur la nécessité d'accorder aux femmes une place équitable dans les archives, les féministes ont aussi souligné le besoin d'améliorer la communicabilité des ressources disponibles.

Un certain nombre d'ouvrages de référence ont été publiés pour combler ces lacunes, à commencer par *Some Sources for Women's History in the Public Archives of Canada*, paru en 1974.[2] Par la suite, d'autres répertoires ont été préparés pour des collections particulières, dont *Sources for Women's History at the Provincial Archives of Alberta* (1980, révisé en 1989)[3] et le *Guide des archives sur les femmes : Sources manuscrites sur l'histoire des femmes* (1991), répertoire de documents pertinents déposés aux Archives nationales du Canada.[4] Quelques inventaires régionaux regroupant plus d'une institution archivistique ont été préparés vers la fin des années 70.[5] La « bibliographie archivistique » *Planting the Garden*, sur l'histoire des femmes au Manitoba, a été publiée en 1987.[6] En 1990, les Archives nationales du Québec publiaient le répertoire *Guide sommaire : Archives des femmes au Québec*, qui identifie quelque 200 collections conservées dans cette province.[7] De tels travaux font partie d'une structure de soutien grandissante édifiée par les archivistes, les bibliothécaires, les universitaires et les maisons d'édition pour venir en aide aux chercheuses féministes.

Tandis que les ouvrages précédents traitent de l'histoire des femmes en général, le présent guide met l'accent sur le mouvement des femmes en tant qu'aspect distinct de leur histoire. Au lieu de s'adresser à une région ou à un dépôt d'archives en particulier, il se veut d'une portée nationale,

---

1 STRONG-BOAG, Veronica, « Raising Clio's Consciousness : Women's History and Archives in Canada », *Archivaria*, n° 6 (Été 1978), pp. 73-74.
2 RIELLY, Heather, et HINDMARCH, Marilyn, *Some Sources for Women's History in the Public Archives of Canada*, Musée national de l'Homme, Collection Mercure, Division de l'histoire, dossier n° 5 (Ottawa : Musées nationaux du Canada, 1974.)
3 DRYDEN, Jean E., *Some Sources for Women's History at the Provincial Archives of Alberta*, Archives provinciales de l'Alberta, dossier hors série n° 2 (Alberta Culture, Historical Resources Division, 1980); AUBREY, Merrily K., *Sources for Women's History at the Provincial Archives of Alberta*, Archives provinciales de l'Alberta, dossier hors série n° 2, éd. rév. (Alberta Culture and Multiculturalism, Historical Resources Division, 1989).
4 DEAN, Joanna, et FRASER, David, *Guide des archives sur les femmes : Sources manuscrites sur l'histoire des femmes* (Ottawa : Archives nationales du Canada, 1991).
5 STRONG-BOAG, Veronica, « Canadian Committee on Women's History », *Recherches sur la femme : Bulletin d'information canadien* 5, n° 1 (février 1976) : 40-47 (comprend une revue des dépôts d'archives en Ontario); LAVIGNE, Marie et STODDART, Jennifer, « Rapport sur les archives au Québec », *Recherches sur la femme : Bulletin d'information canadien* 5, n° 3 (octobre 1976) : 87-89; LESLAU SILVERMAN, Eliane, et MUIR, Rodney Anne, « Archival Holdings in Canadian Women's History : Alberta, Manitoba, and Saskatchewan », *Recherches sur la femme : Bulletin d'information canadien* 6, n° 1 (février 1977) : 127-130; CONRAD, Margaret, « Report on the Archival Resources of the Atlantic Provinces on the Subject of Women's History », *Recherches sur la femme : Bulletin d'information canadien* 7, n° 2 (juillet 1978) : 103-112; HALE, Linda Louise, *Selected Bibliography of Manuscripts and Pamphlets Pertaining to Women Held in Archives, Libraries, Museums, and Associations in British Columbia*, Canadian Women's History Series no. 9 (Toronto : Institut d'études pédagogiques de l'Ontario, 1978).
6 KINNEAR, Mary et FAST, Vera, *Planting the Garden : An Annotated Archival Bibliography of the History of Women in Manitoba* (Winnipeg : University of Manitoba Press, 1987).
7 LAMOTHE, Madeleine, FECTEAU, Ghislaine et LALANCETTE, Pierrette, *Guide sommaire : Archives des femmes au Québec* (Québec : Archives nationales du Québec, 1990).

répertoriant les documents appartenant à nombre de dépôts et organisations.

Si ce guide a vu le jour, c'est que les Archives canadiennes du mouvement des femmes/Canadian Women's Movement Archives (ACMF/CWMA) ont découvert le besoin d'un guide national bilingue sur le mouvement contemporain des femmes. L'ACMF/CWMA, fondé en 1977 dans le but de préserver l'histoire de ce mouvement, a collectionné les documents d'un grand éventail de groupements féminins remontant à 1960. (Pour plus de renseignements sur l'ACMF/CWMA, voir l'historique de l'organisation à la page 24). En 1985-86, grâce à un octroi du Secrétariat d'État, l'ACMF/CWMA entreprenait un sondage préliminaire qui révélait l'existence d'un matériel archivistique abondant dont une grande partie se trouvait dans les bureaux d'organismes féminins. Il était évident que la compilation d'un inventaire détaillé prendrait du temps. Le sondage initial devint le projet-pilote du guide actuel.

En 1989, dans le cadre de son programme « Études canadiennes : outils de recherche », le Conseil de recherches en sciences humaines du Canada accordait à l'ACMF/CWMA un octroi pour la publication d'un guide sur les archives du mouvement des femmes. Ce projet de deux ans débuta en 1990. Comme les documents contenus dans les collections d'archives dûment constituées représentent seulement une fraction du matériel disponible, un des buts du projet était d'encourager les chercheuses et chercheurs à consulter les dossiers tenus dans les bureaux en plus de ceux des dépôts d'archives. Un autre objectif était de refléter la diversité du féminisme canadien du point de vue idéologie, région, race, ethnicité, religion, langue, classe sociale et orientation sexuelle.

Un aspect important du projet consistait à rejoindre les groupements de femmes. Les documents datant des années 60 à nos jours tendent à être considérés comme moins « archivistiques » que les documents antérieurs. Un grand nombre de groupements n'ont jamais été pressentis par des archivistes intéressés à faire l'acquisition de leurs documents et, très souvent, les activistes elles-mêmes ne perçoivent pas la valeur historique de leurs propres collections. Les formules de demande que nous avons envoyées aux divers groupes étaient conçues pour être accessibles aux personnes étrangères aux concepts et à la terminologie archivistiques et pour encourager les récipiendaires à voir le potentiel historique de leur travail, à reconnaître la valeur de leurs documents et à les conserver.

Ce guide n'est pas un répertoire archivistique complet du mouvement des femmes. Même avec un temps et des moyens illimités, il serait impossible de faire un inventaire exhaustif de tous les documents d'un mouvement qui, en raison de son ampleur et de sa vitalité, évolue continuellement. Cependant, en énumérant même une fraction de ces documents, ce guide donne une idée de la riche histoire du mouvement depuis 1960 et témoigne de sa portée et de sa force actuelles.

Comme le mouvement lui-même, la documentation que ce guide tente de décrire est, elle aussi, en constante évolution. Le guide fait mention d'archives courantes, intermédiaires et inertes conservées dans une grande diversité de dépôts et de bureaux. Suivant la formation, la transformation ou la dissolution de groupements, une documentation peut se créer, changer de mains, être détruite ou préservée. Ces mouvements fréquents signifient que la publication de ce guide ne peut constituer un répertoire définitif, à l'encontre d'autres guides qui s'adressent seulement à des organismes disparus dont les archives sont conservées dans une collection et demeureront tout probablement inchangées.

Les documents du mouvement des femmes présentent des caractéristiques dont il a fallu tenir compte dans l'élaboration de ce projet. Notre questionnaire permettait de spécifier certains types de documents utilisés fréquemment par les groupements de femmes, notamment : journaux de bord, mémoires, pétitions, demandes de subventions, matériel graphique tel qu'affiches, et documents tels que macarons, bannières et t-shirts. Le questionnaire respectait également le désir de confidentialité de certaines répondantes. Étant donné qu'un grand nombre de documents sont créés par des comités siégeant au sein d'organisations plus vastes ou sont donnés privément à des archives par des membres, nous nous sommes efforcées de repérer les documents relatifs au mouvement des femmes à l'intérieur des archives de grandes organisations et de celles de collections personnelles. L'Index des noms permet de retrouver les documents de groupements connus sous plus d'une apellation. Quant à l'Index des sujets, il a pour objet de faciliter la recherche sur des questions précises d'intérêt féminin; il reflète également le nombre croissant des mouvements féministes qui concentrent leurs efforts sur un domaine en particulier plutôt que sur le statut de la femme en général.

L'ACMF/CWMA définit comme faisant partie du mouvement des femmes « tout organisme dont l'un des principaux objectifs consiste à améliorer la condition sociale, économique ou politique de la femme ». Cette définition englobe non seulement les groupes autonomes mais aussi les comités féministes au sein d'institutions telles que partis politiques, syndicats, organismes ethnoculturels, universités et églises. Elle comprend aussi des groupements gais et lesbiens, les syndicats dont la majorité des membres sont des femmes et les organismes qui se soucient de « questions féminines » comme la garde des enfants et la limitation des naissances. Par contre, elle ne s'applique pas à tous les groupements de femmes; elle n'inclut pas, par exemple, les sociétés de bienfaisance dirigées par des femmes. Bien que ces groupements aient leur importance dans l'histoire des femmes, ils ne font pas partie du mouvement des femmes tel que défini par l'ACMF/CWMA.

Les ministères du gouvernement, les commissions royales et les conseils consultatifs n'entrent pas non plus dans le cadre de référence de cet ouvrage. Les documents créés par les gouvernements tombent sous le mandat des archives fédérales

INTRODUCTION

et provinciales et l'information qu'ils contiennent peut être obtenue par l'intermédiaire des divers instruments de recherche produits par ces corps d'archives.

Il est convenu de considérer que la naissance du mouvement contemporain des femmes, appelé parfois « la deuxième vague », remonte à 1960, année de la fondation de la Voix des femmes et, par une heureuse coïncidence, le début d'une décennie. Sont inclus dans ce guide les groupements formés ou fonctionnant après cette date; y figurent également les groupements en existence avant et après 1960. Dans ce dernier cas, les documents qui précèdent 1960 sont aussi compilés, car on ne saurait autrement retracer l'histoire de ces organismes.

Le présent guide ne fait pas mention des papiers personnels de féministes individuelles, en accord avec l'importance accordée par l'ACMF/CWMA aux organisations plutôt qu'aux individus. Cependant, il est souvent arrivé que des activistes aient conservé privément des archives de groupements auxquels elles appartenaient; en conséquence, nous identifions comme tels les documents d'organismes qui se trouvent dans les collections personnelles. Ainsi, les papiers de Muriel Duckworth, déposés aux archives publiques de la Nouvelle-Écosse, comprennent des documents provenant de la Voix des femmes, dont elle était présidente nationale de 1967 à 1971.

Le guide se compose de deux parties. La Partie I fait l'inventaire des fonds détenus par les archives et la Partie II, celui des fonds détenus par les organismes. Chacune des parties commence par une section dressant la liste des fonds se rapportant aux organismes nationaux, suivie de sections concernant les groupements de chaque province ou territoire d'ouest en est. Au sein d'une division géographique, les notices sont classées par ordre alphabétique d'après le nom de l'organisme.

Pour établir le répertoire de la Partie I, nous avons communiqué avec plus de 400 dépôts d'archives. Certains fonds sont conservés sur place par des associations, comme c'est le cas pour l'Association des infirmières et infirmiers du Canada et la Centrale de l'enseignement du Québec. Ces organismes figurent dans la Partie I (Fonds détenus par des archives) plutôt que dans la Partie II (Fonds détenus par des groupes) lorsque leurs fonds sont classés en tant qu'archives par l'*Annuaire des services d'archives canadiens*.[1]

Quatre-vingt dépôts ont rapporté des documents pertinents. Les notices décrivant ces documents sont basées principalement sur des instruments de recherche et sur une correspondance avec les archivistes; à peu d'exceptions près, nous n'avons pas examiné les collections sur place. Le guide reflète donc la grande diversité des méthodes de classement et de description des dépôts d'archives. Il compile quelque 800 collections, représentant environ 650 groupements et variant en quantité d'un seul document à plusieurs mètres linéaires.

Comme nous avons été incapables de consulter les documents dans la plupart des cas, nous nous en sommes remises aux instruments de recherche et aux descriptions fournies par les archivistes. Il a été parfois difficile de déterminer si certains groupes entraient ou non dans notre cadre de référence, car l'historique ou les notes biographiques des instruments de recherche ne fournissent pas toujours un niveau de description uniforme. Dans certains cas, les seuls renseignements disponibles étaient le nom du groupe et les quelques bribes d'information glanées dans des livres ou des articles.

La plupart des dépôts d'archives dont les fonds figurent dans ce guide ont rapporté entre une et cinq collections pertinentes; dix-neuf dépôts inclus dans notre inventaire comprennent plus de cinq collections. L'ACMF/CWMA possède de loin le plus grand nombre de collections pertinentes, dont 300 sont inscrites dans cet ouvrage. Étant donné le nombre considérable de fonds détenus par l'ACMF/CWMA et le peu d'instruments de recherche qui les accompagnent, il n'a pas été possible d'inventorier tous ces documents dans ce guide. Les fonds conservés par l'ACMF/CWMA contiennent des documents de plus de 2 000 organismes, sans compter environ 800 affiches, 250 enregistrements sonores, 450 macarons et 1 300 photos. De plus, la collection de périodiques de l'ACMF/CWMA comprend 800 titres, dont environ 75 sur microfilm. Les collections de l'ACMF/CWMA ont été examinées individuellement et nous avons retenu ici les 300 plus importantes. Déterminer l'importance d'une collection s'est révélé une opération nécessairement subjective, soumise à notre connaissance de l'histoire du mouvement des femmes. Nous nous sommes posé plusieurs questions. Quelle est l'ampleur de la collection ? Quels types de documents contient-elle ? À quelle date ces documents remontent-ils ? Le groupe existe-t-il encore ? Quels documents du groupe ont-ils été repérés en d'autres endroits ? Les groupes de même nature sont-ils bien représentés dans le guide ? Au bout du compte, nous avons écarté maintes petites collections, surtout celles dont le matériel ne précède pas la dernière décennie.

Pour recueillir les données servant à la Partie II, nous avons envoyé des questionnaires à 3 000 organismes actuellement en existence. Très souvent, ces organismes avaient déménagé ou s'étaient dispersés depuis 1988, année où FEM-DIRECT, le répertoire informatisé de l'ACMF/CWMA sur les groupes de femmes, a été compilé. Nous avons mis à jour et complété FEM-DIRECT à l'aide de listes publiées et non publiées, produisant une liste d'envoi de plus de 4 000 noms, dont nous avons retranché plus d'un millier de noms pour rester dans les limites de notre budget. En faisant le choix des groupes à retenir, nous avons accordé la préférence aux régions les moins bien représentées dans les fonds d'archives de la Partie I. Ainsi, parce que ces fonds étaient beaucoup plus volumineux en Ontario que dans les provinces atlantiques, nous avons fait des

---

1 *Annuaire des services d'archives canadiens* (Ottawa : Conseil canadien des archives, 1990).

coupures draconiennes dans la liste d'envoi de l'Ontario et laissé intacte la liste du Canada atlantique. À l'instar de notre enquête postale, notre suivi téléphonique a mis l'accent sur les régions à faible représentation dans la Partie I. L'enquête et le suivi ont également fait cas des types de groupements que l'on retrouve rarement dans la Partie I. Par exemple, étant donné que les cercles de femmes d'affaires et de profession sont très bien représentés dans la Partie I, leur ordre de priorité est peu élevé dans la Partie II. Les groupes de femmes autochtones, par contre, ne figurent pas de façon importante dans les archives; nous avons donc cherché à augmenter leur représentation dans la Partie II. Jusqu'à un certain point, la place accordée aux collections de la Partie II rétablit l'équilibre avec la Partie I.

Le questionnaire spécifiait les types de documents pertinents et demandait aux répondantes de cocher ceux qu'elles avaient en leur possession et de les dater par années. En plus du genre de documents communs à la plupart des organismes, tels que procès-verbaux, correspondance et rapports, le questionnaire mentionnait aussi des archives particulièrement courantes dans les groupes féminins. Et comme les répondantes ne connaissaient peut-être pas grand-chose à l'archivage, le formulaire d'enquête offrait une définition d'éléments archivistiques de base — telle que celle de « document » — , tout en utilisant un vocabulaire accessible à celles qui n'étaient pas familières avec la terminologie du métier. Une feuille de renseignements sur la façon de conserver les documents était également incluse dans l'envoi.

Environ 600 questionnaires complétés nous ont été retournés (soit à peu près 20 % du nombre posté). Le questionnaire a bien fonctionné : les répondantes l'ont trouvé clair et facile à comprendre et il a engendré de l'enthousiasme pour la conservation de documents d'archives touchant le mouvement des femmes. Il semble avoir été le plus efficace pour les groupes qui emploient les types de documents spécifiés et moins bien assorti aux groupes qui utilisent des approches différentes dans la tenue de documents. (Peu de répondantes ont rempli l'espace réservé aux « autres documents non mentionnés ci-dessus ».) Le questionnaire n'a pas toujours été bien interprété par des comités féminins faisant partie d'organisations plus vastes comme, par exemple, les syndicats. Il demandait à ces comités de décrire uniquement leurs propres documents; mais, dans l'esprit de certains comités, ces documents ne se distinguaient pas de ceux de l'organisation mère. C'est ainsi que le comité féminin d'un syndicat nous laissait savoir que ses documents ne pouvaient être identifiés et répertoriés séparément parce que les questions touchant les femmes avaient été traitées dans le cadre de projets divers et que lesdits documents faisaient partie des dossiers de ces projets.

Par ailleurs, certains groupes n'ont pas voulu dévoiler la teneur de leurs archives pour des raisons de confidentialité — même s'ils étaient libres de montrer (ou non) leurs documents à qui bon leur semblait. (Pour les mêmes raisons, certains groupes préfèrent ne pas tenir de dossiers du tout. Un groupe d'appui et d'information pour gais et lesbiennes nous a écrit : « Nous avons délibérément choisi de ne garder aucun document afin de garantir la confidentialité de notre clientèle. Sauf pour une déclaration d'entente sur nos objectifs, nous n'avons pas de documents. »)

La liste des documents d'un organisme quelconque paraît sous le nom de cet organisme, et non sous le nom de la collection, laquelle peut porter un nom différent. (Par exemple, les documents se rapportant à la Voix des femmes dans la collection Muriel Duckworth aux Archives publiques de la Nouvelle-Écosse sont classés sous l'entrée « Voix des femmes » et non sous « Duckworth ».) Certains de ces « organismes » sont en réalité des comités siégeant au sein d'organisations plus grandes; bien que les fonds d'archives de ces organisations ne soient pas inscrits dans notre répertoire, les documents de leurs comités doivent être examinés en fonction des archives de l'organisation mère. (Par exemple, l'entrée pour « L'Alliance des professeurs de Montréal. Comité de la condition féminine » n'énumère que les documents du comité et non pas tous ceux de l'Alliance. Mais les chercheuses et chercheurs qui s'intéressent au comité doivent peut-être examiner aussi d'autres documents de cette organisation.)

Le nom de l'entrée est le dernier nom porté par le groupe durant la période représentée par ses documents. Étant donné qu'une lectrice puisse connaître l'organisme par un nom différent de celui de l'entrée, l'Index des noms énumère toutes les variations connues : sigles, désignations antérieures ou autres formes du nom. L'Index inclut parfois le titre d'un périodique publié par le groupe ou le titre d'un congrès organisé par le groupe. Un bon exemple est celui de l'entrée « Association féminine d'éducation et d'action sociale ». Comme cet organisme est né de la fusion de deux groupes antérieurs et qu'il publie un périodique, il peut être repéré dans l'Index des noms par son nom actuel (ci-devant), par son sigle AFÉAS, par ses noms antérieurs : Union catholique des femmes rurales ou Cercles d'économie domestique et par son périodique *Femmes d'ici*.

L'Index des sujets s'inspire, pour ses entrées, du *Thésaurus féministe du Canada*, dont le vocabulaire féministe, les renvois utiles et le format bilingue convenaient admirablement à nos besoins.[1]

La plupart des notices ont été rédigées soit en anglais, soit en français, suivant la langue des documents en question. Les notices des groupes bilingues paraissent habituellement dans les deux langues. Dans les cas où les documents d'un groupe bilingue sont entièrement unilingues, l'entrée a été faite seule-

---

1 GROUPE D'ANALYSE DE DOCUMENTS FÉMINISTES CANADIENS, *Le Thésaurus féministe du Canada* (Toronto : Institut d'études pédagogiques de l'Ontario, 1990).

ment dans la langue des documents. Puisque nous n'avons pas vu nous-mêmes la plupart des collections, nous n'étions pas toujours sûres de leur langue d'écriture ; lorsqu'il s'agit d'organismes bilingues, les chercheuses et chercheurs feraient bien de vérifier d'avance la langue des documents.

Chaque notice débute par des renseignements sur l'organisme qui a créé les documents : son nom, la ville où il se trouve, la durée de son existence et une brève description de ses fonctions. Cette information nous est parvenue de différentes sources : questionnaires remplis par les organismes ; instruments de recherche archivistiques et correspondance avec des archivistes ; dépliants et autres documents dans lesquels les organismes se décrivent ; et, enfin, livres et articles. (Si la source est un instrument de recherche ou une autre source secondaire, l'entrée en fait mention.) Très souvent, ces sources diffèrent ; deux documents publiés par un groupe peuvent donner deux dates de fondation différentes et le questionnaire rempli par ce groupe peut même en donner une troisième. Cette disparité peut être le résultat d'informations erronées, mais elle peut aussi refléter des interprétations différentes. Ainsi, la date de formation d'un centre de femmes peut être considérée, selon les unes ou les autres, comme remontant à la première réunion du comité d'organisation, ou à son incorporation ou encore à son ouverture officielle. Au lieu de procéder à des recherches exhaustives, nous avons accepté le fait que de telles contradictions étaient inévitables. Nous avons préféré employer notre temps et nos ressources à repérer et à décrire autant de collections que possible plutôt qu'à créer des références scrupuleusement exactes pour un petit nombre d'entrées. Ce guide se veut un répertoire de *documents d'archives* et non un ouvrage de référence sur les groupements féministes.

Quant au reste de la notice, il est consacré aux documents : types, années, état du matériel, restrictions de communicabilité, existence ou absence d'instruments de recherche et lieu de conservation. Lorsque cette information n'était pas pertinente ou disponible, elle a été omise. La notice affiche les documents créés par un organisme ou au sujet de cet organisme. En établissant le format des entrées, nous nous sommes inspirées d'autres guides thématiques tels que *A Guide to Labour Records and Resources in British Columbia*.[1]

Certaines notices mentionnent chaque type de document et leurs dates exactes (p. ex., « mémoire, 1974 ; photo, 1976 »), tandis que d'autres contiennent une information plus générale (p. ex., « correspondance, documents divers, 1972-1985 »).

Le niveau de description d'une notice dépend des renseignements disponibles. Le sujet traité par un document n'est pas spécifié (p. ex., « procès-verbal » et non « procès-verbal du comité de finances »). Les notices ne précisent pas non plus si les documents sont des originaux ou des copies. Les titres de périodiques sont donnés lorsque leur nom diffère de celui de l'organisme qui les publie. Quant aux titres des autres documents, ils ne sont pas fournis.

Nous avons suivi les règles de la description archivistique et du catalogage pour rédiger nos notices de façon aussi uniforme, aussi exacte et aussi claire que possible. À cette fin, nous avons consulté les *Règles pour la description des documents d'archives*[2] ; les *Règles de catalogage anglo-américaines*, deuxième édition[3] ; et les *Archives, Personal Papers, and Manuscripts : A Cataloging Manual for Archival Repositories, Historical Societies, and Manuscript Libraries*.[4] Nous avons eu recours aux trois ouvrages pour établir une série de règles susceptibles de répondre aux besoins d'un guide thématique reflétant une grande diversité de pratiques descriptives. Nous nous sommes surtout inspirées du premier ouvrage pour le contenu et le format des notices — plus précisément les Règles générales et les Appendices (1990) et le Rapport du groupe de travail sur les documents textuels (Version préliminaire, janvier 1991). Les chapitres traitant du « Choix des catégories d'accès » et des « Vedettes de personnes morales » n'étant pas encore publiés, nous avons utilisé les *Règles de catalogage anglo-américaines* pour déterminer sous quelles formes le nom d'un organisme doit figurer dans le titre de la notice et dans l'Index des noms. Pour décrire un ensemble d'archives formant partie d'une plus grande collection, nous avons suivi la règle sur la complexité des rapports recommandée dans *Archives, Personal Papers, and Manuscripts*.

Les dépôts d'archives et les organismes qui nous ont fait parvenir des renseignements n'employaient pas toujours les mêmes termes pour définir les types de documents. La plupart du temps, nous avons retenu la terminologie utilisée par les répondants et répondantes, la simplifiant à l'occasion (ainsi, « reçus, grands livres et relevés de compte » sont devenus « documents financiers »).

Chaque fois que cela était possible, nous avons exprimé la quantité des pièces d'une collection en mètres linéaires d'espace occupé dans le cas d'archives textuelles, indiquant séparément le nombre d'affiches, de photos, d'enregistrements sonores et d'objets à trois dimensions comme les macarons (p. ex., « 6 cm de texte, 1 enregistrement sonore, 8 photos »). Cependant, le guide traduit les diverses pratiques

---

1 MAY, Louise, *A Guide to Labour Records and Resources in British Columbia* (Vancouver : University of British Columbia Library, Special Collections Division, 1985).

2 BUREAU CANADIEN DES ARCHIVISTES, Comité de planification sur les normes de description, *Règles pour la description des documents d'archives* (Ottawa : Bureau canadien des archivistes, 1990) ; *Rapport du groupe de travail sur les documents textuels présenté au Comité de planification sur les normes de description du Bureau canadien des archivistes* (Version préliminaire, janvier 1991).

3 *Règles de catalogage anglo-américaines*, 2e éd., révision de 1988 (Montréal : ASTED, 1990).

4 HENSEN, Stephen L., *Archives, Personal Papers, and Manuscripts : A Cataloging Manual for Archival Repositories, Historical Societies, and Manuscript Libraries* (Washington : Library of Congress, 1983).

descriptives des dépôts répondants; ainsi, certains d'entre eux ont indiqué le nombre de photos détenues, tandis que d'autres les ont rapportées en mesures linéaires sans spécifier leur nombre. En conséquence, les indications de quantité ne sont qu'approximatives.

La description, dans la Partie II, de l'espace occupé par les documents actuellement détenus combine le besoin de normalisation archivistique avec le contexte dans lequel les documents sont créés puis entreposés. Au lieu d'imposer des mesures linéaires aux organismes qui détiennent leurs propres fonds d'archives, notre questionnaire a encouragé les dépositaires à se servir d'expressions courantes (p. ex., « 3 classeurs » ou « 2 boîtes »).

Ce ne sont pas tous les dépôts d'archives qui ont répondu à notre questionnaire et parmi ceux qui l'ont fait, il s'est peut-être trouvé des personnes qui n'étaient pas toujours conscientes de la présence de documents pertinents. Les instruments de recherche ne révèlent pas nécessairement l'existence de fonds appartenant à un groupement dans une collection personnelle ni celle de documents émanant d'un comité siégeant au sein d'une plus grande organisation. Et nombre de collections ne possèdent aucun instrument de recherche. Il est arrivé qu'une collection soit mise de côté, faute de pouvoir identifier par son nom le groupe dont elle émanait. Ainsi, dans une collection, un groupe du milieu des années 60 est identifié simplement comme « un petit groupe de femmes mariées et mères de famille [qui] se rencontraient sans cérémonie pour discuter de leurs expériences en tant qu'étudiantes diplômées ou membres du personnel de l'Université de Toronto »[1]. En outre, nous avons écarté certains groupes du guide parce qu'ils ne semblaient pas entrer dans notre définition du mouvement des femmes; toutefois, des données concernant ces groupes peuvent quelquefois être retrouvées dans les archives d'organismes apparentés. Par exemple, bien que les Instituts féminins locaux ne soient pas inclus, les Instituts national et provinciaux le sont. De nombreux groupements qui ne répondaient pas à nos critères sont affiliés aux Conseils des femmes de leur localité et certaines données à leur sujet peuvent être retracées parmi les archives des Conseils des femmes représentés dans ce guide.

Notre inventaire comprend quelques périodiques conservés dans les fonds d'archives (y compris les réserves d'ouvrages rares dans les bibliothèques), mais il n'inclut pas les nombreux périodiques détenus par les bibliothèques spécialisées en études des femmes ni ceux des bibliothèques générales. Le guide ne mentionne qu'une fraction des bulletins et autres périodiques féministes en existence au Canada. Les chercheuses et chercheurs qui tentent de repérer des périodiques devraient consulter la vaste collection de l'ACMF/CWMA (dont environ un cinquième seulement des 800 titres détenus figure dans ce guide), ainsi que d'autres archives et bibliothèques.

De même, les personnes à la recherche d'information doivent se rappeler qu'un grand nombre de renseignements sur des organismes non gouvernementaux peuvent être extraits de documents gouvernementaux, lesquels ne sont pas répertoriés dans ce guide. Aux archives provinciales de l'Alberta, par exemple, les documents du bureau du premier ministre contiennent des renseignements sur les mouvements de femmes de 1967 à 1971[2] et la réserve des livres rares de la salle Doris Lewis à l'Université de Waterloo renferme des exemplaires de mémoires présentés à la Commission royale d'enquête sur le statut de la femme.[3]

Par ailleurs, les collections concernant les filiales d'associations telles que la Fédération canadienne des diplômées des universités contiennent souvent des documents qui se rapportent à l'organisation mère. Lorsqu'un instrument de recherche identifie les documents de l'organisation mère comme une section ou un sous-fonds distincts au sein de la collection, ces documents ont fait l'objet d'une entrée à part; autrement, ils ne sont pas inscrits en tant que tels dans ce guide. Pareillement, le fonds d'un organisme national ou provincial peut contenir des documents de filiales qui ne font pas l'objet d'une mention séparée.

La collection d'un groupe peut contenir de l'information sur d'autres groupes avec lesquels il a eu des liens. Dans quelques cas, ces documents forment un sous-fonds au sein de la collection et sont inscrits séparément dans le guide; mais la plupart du temps (si toutefois ils sont identifiés dans l'instrument de recherche), ils ne constituent que quelques documents concernant chacun des groupes et ne sont pas répertoriés dans cet ouvrage. C'est ainsi que des dizaines de groupements de femmes sont mentionnés dans l'instrument de recherche élaboré pour la collection Planned Parenthood Saskatchewan au conseil des archives de cette province à Regina (p. ex., « Saskatoon Women's Health Collective, 1980, 1 mm . . . University of Regina Women's Centre, 1980, 1 mm »). Les chercheuses et chercheurs trouveront parfois ce genre d'information dans un fonds à l'aide d'un instrument de recherche mais, la plupart du temps, il leur faudra examiner les collections elles-mêmes pour découvrir l'information cachée.

De même, les documents d'organismes dissimulés dans les collections personnelles peuvent demeurer cachés à moins

---

[1] « Study of Forty-Two Women Who Have Children and Who Are in Graduate Programmes at the University of Toronto », dans la collection Germaine T. Warkentin, archives de l'Université de Toronto.
[2] AUBREY, *Sources for Women's History*, p. 86.
[3] BELLINGHAM, Susan, « Women's Studies Collections in the University of Waterloo Library » dans *Women's Collections : Libraries, Archives, and Consciousness*, édité par Suzanne Hildebrand (New York : Haworth Press, 1986), p. 132.

qu'il n'existe un instrument de recherche détaillé qui permette de les découvrir (l'ACMF/CWMA possède des enregistrements d'interviews personnelles avec des féministes, mais comme il n'y a pas d'instrument de recherche qui indique à quels organismes ces femmes appartenaient, ces enregistrements ne peuvent être classés dans notre inventaire).

Parce que certains instruments de recherche ne font mention que de documents textuels, des pièces d'archives provenant d'autres médias (telles que photos et affiches) ne figurent pas dans ce guide. (Des archives peuvent être dotées d'instruments de recherche différents suivant le type de documents recherchés.[1])

Il se peut que des archives antérieures à 1960, se rapportant aux groupements qui existaient avant et après cette date, aient été omises dans notre répertoire, car certains répondants et répondantes n'ont peut-être pas compris que ces archives étaient admissibles dans leur cas.

Des indications sur la communicabilité des archives sont fournies chaque fois qu'elles sont disponibles. (Notons que les restrictions d'accès sont sujettes à changement.) Les personnes qui font des recherches doivent toujours communiquer avec les dépôts d'archives avant une visite, afin de confirmer la communicabilité des documents et de prendre rendez-vous. Pareillement, les personnes qui désirent consulter des documents détenus par un organisme indépendant doivent solliciter la permission de cet organisme. Le fait que ces fonds sont répertoriés dans le guide n'oblige pas un organisme à ouvrir ses dossiers pour fins de recherche; il appartient à chaque organisme de déterminer quels documents montrer, à qui et à quelles fins.

Comme l'indiquent les pages suivantes, les ressources archivistiques du mouvement des femmes sont d'une grande richesse. Une bonne partie de ces ressources a été préservée par l'ACMF/CWMA, par les archives des mouvements gais et lesbiens et par des activistes individuelles. Sans les efforts de l'ACMF/CWMA et d'autres archives communautaires, ces documents auraient été perdus à jamais. Les conservateurs et conservatrices d'archives publiques et universitaires ont témoigné un intérêt croissant pour les documents du mouvement des femmes et la portée de leurs acquisitions dans ce domaine s'étend de plus en plus à des aspects plus variés du mouvement. D'autre part, la publication de divers répertoires et instruments de recherches a amélioré l'accès aux ressources existantes. Dans le nord de l'Alberta, des féministes ont trouvé un moyen ingénieux de régler « le problème de la sous-représentation des femmes et groupements de femmes dans les collections d'archives et de la difficulté de localiser ces documents » : elles ont formé un comité (Northern Alberta Women's Archives Project) qui sert d'agent de liaison entre les archives provinciales de l'Alberta et des donatrices éventuelles en encourageant les femmes à léguer leurs archives et en promouvant des « méthodes archivistiques réceptives à l'existence de la femme ».[2]

Il reste encore beaucoup à faire. Les archivistes doivent encourager les groupements à conserver leurs documents et leur montrer comment faire. Un plus grand nombre de ressources doivent être mises à la disposition des archives communautaires. Les groupements devraient avoir accès à différents moyens de conservation : par exemple, remettre leurs documents à un dépôt communautaire ou à des archives provinciales ou bien les conserver sur place si tel est leur choix. Il est particulièrement important que de telles options soient offertes à des groupements formés dans des communautés traditionnellement écartées de maintes collections archivistiques, tels que les groupes gais et lesbiens et les regroupements ethnoculturels. Les dépôts d'archives devraient collectionner des documents, y compris les enregistrements sonores et les médias visuels, provenant d'un éventail beaucoup plus large de groupements féminins et élaborer des instruments de recherche aptes à faciliter l'accès à ces documents. Préserver l'histoire du mouvement des femmes est une oeuvre considérable qui exige une collaboration constante entre les activistes, les archivistes et les universitaires.

Bien que ce répertoire ne puisse fournir une image complète de l'histoire du mouvement des femmes au Canada depuis 1960, il révèle la force, la diversité et le dynamisme du mouvement. Cet ouvrage est conçu pour faciliter et stimuler la recherche dans le passé et le présent plein de promesses du mouvement des femmes; nous espérons qu'il saura également inspirer les conservateurs et conservatrices d'archives et les membres d'organismes féministes à préserver les documents du mouvement pour la postérité.

— Margaret Fulford

---

1 Les exemples comprennent : *A Descriptive Inventory of the Sound Recordings at the Canadian Women's Movement Archives / Archives canadiennes du mouvement des femmes* (Toronto : Archives canadiennes du mouvement des femmes, 1988); MILLER, Alan V., *Our Own Voices : A Directory of Lesbian and Gay Periodicals, 1890-1990, Including the Complete Holdings of the Canadian Gay Archives*, Canadian Gay Archives Publication no. 12 (Toronto, 1991).
2 NORTHERN ALBERTA WOMEN'S ARCHIVES PROJECT, *Recovering Women's History* (dépliant), 1990. (Traduction libre)

THE CANADIAN WOMEN'S MOVEMENT ARCHIVES/ LES ARCHIVES CANADIENNES DU MOUVEMENT DES FEMMES

In 1972 a Toronto-based feminist newspaper, *The Other Woman*, began collecting information on the growing women's movement in Canada. Following the demise of the newspaper in the spring of 1977, the material was reorganized and filed for permanent storage. In July, Pat Leslie sent a letter to women's organizations across Canada introducing them to the newly founded Women's Archives and asking them to support it by sending copies of their material and by encouraging individuals and other women's organizations to save their records. In her letter Pat urged groups to remember that ". . . the past *and* the future lies also in every letter written to a friend. Everything speaking about and to feminism is precious to us all!"

Thus began what was to become the Canadian Women's Movement Archives. Its founding mother was Pat Leslie. A member of *The Other Woman* collective, Pat was the driving force behind its decision to collect and preserve material from groups and publications across Canada. When *The Other Woman* ceased publication in 1977, Pat took its records into her home, organized them, and continued to expand them. She explained the need for such an archives in a 1985 interview: ". . . it quickly became clear to me that public archives, with few exceptions, have not been noted for their preservation of materials from groups working for social change. An independent archive on the grass-roots organizing of the women's liberation movement is more than it seems at first. . . . The archives is . . . about putting women back into history, the way we see ourselves, and through our own eyes."[1]

By 1982 it became clear to Pat that the material she was collecting was too much for one woman to handle. She and other women also recognized that this valuable resource should be made more available to the women's community and to researchers. At the same time the Women's Information Centre of Toronto (WIC) was looking for a long-term project to take on.[2]

WIC was founded in 1972 as the incorporated body of Women's Place, a Toronto women's centre. In subsequent years, Women's Place and WIC sponsored a variety of Toronto women's groups and services, among them Interval House, the first Toronto shelter for battered women; Times Change, a women's employment centre; the Toronto Women's Bookstore; and the Toronto Rape Crisis Centre. When Women's Place closed in 1975, WIC carried on, assisting in the founding of the Metro Toronto Women's Credit Union; the Women's Fundraising Coalition, an organization which raised money for women's groups; and the Women's Calendar of Events in *Broadside* (a feminist periodical). In 1981, WIC sponsored *Tales of Tomorrow*, a film about aging by feminist producer Barbara Martineau. By 1982, WIC had exhausted itself and the Women's Archives had outgrown Pat Leslie's basement. The two organizations came together.

In the years that followed, the newly created Canadian Women's Movement Archives set about defining itself, developed a collection policy, established processing guidelines, and expanded its collection. By 1985, the Archives had come to see itself as "an independent, non-profit, community-based, collectively run archives and resource centre, dedicated to collecting and preserving archival material from the contemporary (post-1960) Canadian women's movement."[3] It had also, in classic collective fashion, held a pot-luck dinner to discuss how to define the women's movement.

In 1985, thanks to a grant from the Secretary of State, the Archives embarked on what became the pilot project for this guide. As that project evolved, the Archives began to grapple with the difficulty of running a "national" organization out of Toronto and the implications of being a bilingual organization with a largely unilingual board. It officially changed its name to the Canadian Women's Movement Archives/Archives canadiennes du mouvement des femmes, began producing its material in both French and English, and committed itself to providing service in either official language. It hired bilingual staff and set out to develop a network of contacts in both archives and feminist organizations across the country.

This network was built upon and expanded in the years that followed, as the Archives produced FEM-DIRECT, a computerized directory of Canadian feminist groups, and began laying the groundwork for this guide. Our various projects also

---

1 Eve Zaremba, "CWMA: Collective Collections," *Broadside*, March 1985, p. 5.
2 Ibid., pp. 4-5.
3 Anne Molgat, "Canadian Women's Movement Archives/Archives canadiennes du mouvement des femmes," *CCWH Newsletter/Bulletin du CCHF*, Fall 1988, p. 1.

generated a number of donations of records. Some of these donations were included in "Graphic Feminism," an exhibition of graphic art from the Ontario women's movement mounted at A Space gallery in Toronto. A national version of this exhibition was subsequently shown in several cities. With financial assistance from several small foundations, the Archives produced inventories of its sound recordings and its holdings from lesbian organizations.

◆ ◆ ◆

The CWMA/ACMF has collected the records of the contemporary, or "second wave," Canadian women's movement, beginning in 1960 with the founding of Voice of Women. We have defined as part of the women's movement any group having as one of its principal goals the improvement of women's social, economic, or political condition. While we have collected the records of any women's group fitting this definition, we have focused on the grass-roots women's movement, as opposed to the institutional. By "institutional" we mean feminism which operates within traditional institutions (political parties, government, churches, etc.) and which calls for more opportunities for women within those institutions. By "grass-roots" we mean feminism which is community based and emphasizes collective organizing and reaching out to "the woman on the street." Our focus on grass-roots feminism came about partly as a result of our own experiences as activists and our familiarity with the grass-roots women's movement, partly out of our belief that it is the grass-roots women's movement that initiates many of those ideas which make their way into institutional feminism, and partly because the records of institutional feminism find their way into mainstream or institutional archives more often and more easily than do those of grass-roots feminism.

Our definition of the archival record is broad, including just about anything produced by the women's movement. The holdings are not limited to textual records such as minutes, correspondence, and financial records, but include photographs, slides, posters, sound recordings, buttons, dance cards, postcards, business cards, T-shirts, banners, and two original brass plaques from the Toronto Morgentaler Clinic, complete with anti-choice graffiti. In addition, we have the most extensive collection of Canadian feminist periodicals, newspapers, magazines, and newsletters in existence. The number of groups represented in the Archives continues to grow and has now reached well over 2,000.

Records have found their way into the Archives in many different ways. When organizations close their doors, a phenomenon which has been happening with alarming frequency of late, they may donate the records of their group to the CWMA/ACMF. Sometimes one organization has been holding the records of other local organizations, and so the Archives receives a donation from several groups at once. Sometimes groups just run out of room and decide to pass along records not regularly used. Some feminist groups have donated their records on an ongoing basis — the Women's Press, Women Healthsharing, and *Fireweed*, for example. One staff member, while travelling across the country promoting the Archives and urging women's groups to keep their records, developed the "manila envelope" method of depositing records. She asked each group to tape a manila envelope next to their garbage can and before they discarded records to think about whether the CWMA/ACMF might be interested in them. A number of groups became adept at routing their material to us in this way, and records that might otherwise have been lost were preserved. Many individual women have also donated material they had been saving for years — usually when they decided to move and couldn't take the records with them. Material has occasionally arrived in garbage bags, and it has sometimes come anonymously. However it arrives, and in whatever quantity, the material is always welcomed.

◆ ◆ ◆

Like most community-based groups, the Archives has had a precarious existence. For most of its life, it has been entirely self-funded, relying on donations from individuals, yard sales, various special events, and the sale of items such as postcards, T-shirts, sweatshirts, posters, and buttons. While we have received several much-appreciated grants, the availability of such project funding has been limited.

By the summer of 1991, the CWMA/ACMF's collective and the WIC board realized that they could no longer maintain the functions of an independent archives. The CWMA/ACMF had become too successful, requiring staff and funds which were beyond our ability to provide. Our primary concerns were to ensure the long-term survival and accessibility of the Archives, to have the Collection continue to grow, and to have it maintained in a manner consistent with our operating principles. After careful consideration of several options, we decided to place the CWMA/ACMF Collection at the University of Ottawa. We have every confidence in the university's ability to maintain what is, in our opinion, the finest collection of records from the contemporary Canadian women's movement, and we look forward to seeing it grow. We wish them well.

We have operated as a collective, under the auspices of the Women's Information Centre of Toronto. The size of the collective has varied from four to eight over the years. We are, or were, historians, librarians, archivists, computer programmers, employees of women's organizations, students, and teachers; all of us have been and remain active in the women's movement. Like all collectives, we shared the work: policy making, acquisitions, processing, providing reference service, outreach, fund raising, and all the other tasks associated with maintaining an archives. We are: Jane Abray (1989-present), Nancy Adamson (1982-present), Pat Baker (1989), Joan Berger (1990-1991), Megan Davies (1986-1987), Jeannette

THE CANADIAN WOMEN'S MOVEMENT ARCHIVES/LES ARCHIVES CANADIENNES DU MOUVEMENT DES FEMMES

Dowson (1985-1986), Karen Dubinsky (1988-present), Linda Galen (1987-1988), Debbie Green (1985-1988), Janice Hill (1990-1991), Luanne Karn (1984-1988), Andrea Knight (1982-1984), Wiesia Kolasinska (1982-1984), Pat Leslie (1982-1984), Beth McAuley (1990-present), Anne Molgat (1985-present), Kathy Moules (1990-1991), Johanne M. Pelletier (1988-present), Margaret Shepherd (1988-1990), Tori Smith (1985-1987), Miriam Ticoll (1986-1989), Lorna Weir (1982-1985).

The Archives owes its existence to these women, to the women who donated money, to those who gave items to our book and yard sales, to those who bought T-shirts and postcards and posters, to the organizations who donated their records and gave us free subscriptions to their periodicals and free copies of their publications, to the activists and researchers who used the Archives, to the foundations and government departments who gave us grants, to the individuals and groups who bought FEM-DIRECT, to Archives staff, and to the extended family of Canadian feminists who make the Canadian women's movement the vital and powerful force it continues to be. Thank you all.

— CWMA/ACMF Collective and WIC Board of Directors

LES ARCHIVES CANADIENNES DU MOUVEMENT DES FEMMES / THE CANADIAN WOMEN'S MOVEMENT ARCHIVES

En 1972, un journal féministe de Toronto, *The Other Woman*, entreprenait de collectionner des documents ayant trait au mouvement alors grandissant du féminisme canadien. Lorsque le journal dut abandonner ses opérations au printemps de 1977, le matériel accumulé fut réorganisé et classé pour être entreposé en permanence. Dès juillet, Pat Leslie, ancien membre de la défunte équipe journalistique, envoyait à tous les regroupements féminins du Canada une lettre leur annonçant la récente formation des Archives des femmes et sollicitant leur appui en faisant parvenir au nouveau centre d'archives des exemplaires de leur documentation. Dans sa lettre, Pat encourageait les membres de ces organismes à conserver leurs documents et leur rappelait que « ... même une lettre écrite à une amie peut révéler le passé *et* l'avenir. *Tout* ce qui touche au féminisme doit nous tenir à coeur à nous toutes! »

C'est ainsi que furent fondées, sous l'égide de Pat Leslie, les Archives canadiennes du mouvement des femmes. En tant que membre de la collective *The Other Woman*, Pat avait joué un rôle majeur dans la décision de collectionner et de préserver le matériel provenant de groupements et de publications à travers le pays. Lorsque *The Other Woman* cessa d'être publié en 1977, Pat rapporta tous les dossiers chez elle pour les organiser tout en continuant d'élargir la collection. Dans une entrevue donnée en 1985, elle explique pourquoi la tenue de telles archives lui paraissait nécessaire : « ... je me suis vite rendu compte qu'à très peu d'exceptions près les documents émanant de mouvements voués à l'action sociale ne figurent pas dans les archives publiques. La tenue indépendante d'archives sur les organismes qui militent en faveur de la libération de la femme est plus importante qu'elle ne le paraît de prime abord... Ces archives réintègrent, en quelque sorte, la femme dans l'histoire, en lui donnant le visage que nous, les femmes, voyons à travers nos propres yeux ».[1]

Vers 1982, il était devenu évident qu'une seule personne ne pouvait suffire à la tâche, tant le matériel amassé était considérable. Par ailleurs, Pat et d'autres collègues avaient reconnu la nécessité de rendre cette précieuse ressource plus accessible à la communauté des femmes ainsi qu'aux chercheuses et chercheurs. Au même moment, le Women's Information Centre of Toronto (WIC) était en quête d'un projet à long terme sur lequel il pouvait concentrer ses énergies.[2]

Le WIC avait été fondé en 1972 en tant qu'organisme incorporé faisant corps avec Women's Place (centre torontois pour femmes). Au cours des années qui suivirent, les deux organismes mirent sur pied un nombre varié d'institutions et de services féminins de Toronto, dont Interval House, le premier abri de cette ville pour femmes victimes de violence; un centre d'emploi pour femmes, Times Change; la librairie pour femmes Toronto Women's Bookstore; et le Toronto Rape Crisis Centre, un centre secours-détresse pour victimes de viol. Quand Women's Place ferma ses portes en 1975, le WIC continua son oeuvre de soutien, aidant à la fondation d'une coopérative de crédit pour femmes dans la région torontoise (Metro Toronto Women's Credit Union), à la formation d'une coalition de collecte de fonds pour groupements féminins (Women's Fundraising Coalition); et publiant un calendrier des événements d'intérêt féminin dans le périodique *Broadside*. En 1981, le WIC commandita un film sur le vieillissement, *Tales of Tomorrow*, produit par la cinéaste féministe Barbara Martineau. En 1982, le WIC avait épuisé ses ressources et les Archives des femmes ne tenaient plus dans le sous-sol de Pat Leslie. Le moment était opportun pour les deux entreprises de se fusionner.

Durant la période qui suivit la création des Archives canadiennes du mouvement des femmes, le nouvel organisme chercha à se définir, à établir une politique de collecte et de traitement des documents et à développer ses collections. À compter de 1985, les Archives avaient acquis une identité propre et se considéraient comme « un centre indépendant d'archives et de ressources gérées collectivement, ayant un but non lucratif, fondé sur une orientation communautaire et visant à collectionner et à conserver le matériel archivistique relié au mouvement contemporain (à partir de 1960) des femmes canadiennes »[3]. Dans un geste typique marquant son engagement à l'action collective, l'organisme avait organisé un

---

1 ZAREMBA, Eve, « CWMA : Collective Collections », *Broadside*, mars 1985, p. 5. (Traduction libre)
2 Ibid., pp. 4-5.
3 MOLGAT, Anne, « Canadian Women's Movement Archives/Archives canadiennes du mouvement des femmes », *CCWH Newsletter/Bulletin du CCHF*, automne 1988, p. 1. (Traduction libre)

souper pot-pourri pour tenter de définir « le mouvement des femmes ».

En 1985, grâce à un octroi du Secrétariat d'État, les Archives ont entrepris ce qui devait devenir le projet-pilote menant à ce guide. Une fois le projet lancé, les Archives se sont retrouvées aux prises avec la difficulté d'administrer un organisme « national », donc bilingue, à partir de Toronto et avec un conseil plus ou moins unilingue. L'organisme a donc changé son nom pour devenir officiellement Canadian Women's Movement Archives/Archives canadiennes du mouvement des femmes; il a commencé à publier son matériel en français et en anglais, et s'est engagé à fournir ses services dans l'une ou l'autre des langues officielles. Pour ce faire, il lui a fallu embaucher un personnel bilingue et établir un réseau de contacts auprès d'archives et de groupes de femmes d'un bout à l'autre du pays.

Ce réseau s'est étendu avec les années alors que les Archives produisaient FEM-DIRECT, répertoire informatisé de groupements féministes canadiens, et qu'elles jetaient les bases qui devaient mener à la publication de ce guide. Nos divers projets ont entraîné le don de plusieurs archives permanentes dont quelques-unes ont, par la suite, fait partie d'une exposition d'arts graphiques du mouvement des femmes de l'Ontario, « Graphic Feminism », montée à la galerie torontoise A Space. Une version nationale de cette exposition a fait le tour de plusieurs villes peu de temps après. Avec l'aide financière de différentes petites fondations, les Archives ont dressé et publié des inventaires de leurs enregistrements sonores et de documents d'organisations lesbiennes.

◆ ◆ ◆

L'ACMF/CWMA collectionne les documents relatifs au mouvement contemporain, ou « seconde vague », des femmes canadiennes à partir de 1960, année de la fondation de la Voix des femmes. Nous avons défini comme faisant partie du mouvement des femmes tout groupe dont l'un des principaux objectifs consiste à améliorer la condition sociale, économique ou politique de la femme. Bien que nous ayons collectionné les documents de tout groupement de femmes répondant à cette définition, nous avons concentré nos efforts sur le féminisme communautaire plutôt qu'institutionnel. Par « institutionnel », nous entendons le féminisme qui s'exprime au sein d'institutions traditionnelles (partis politiques, gouvernement, églises, etc.) et qui revendique l'avancement de la femme à l'intérieur de ces institutions. Par « communautaire », nous entendons le féminisme originant dans la communauté et qui met l'accent sur l'organisation collective et le recrutement de « la femme ordinaire ». L'attention particulière que nous accordons au féminisme communautaire est le résultat de nos propres expériences en tant d'activistes et de notre connaissance plus intime de cette forme d'action. Mais cette attention est aussi due au fait que, d'une part, nous sommes d'avis que ce genre de féminisme initie plusieurs des idées reprises plus tard par le féminisme institutionnel et que, d'autre part, les documents du féminisme institutionnel trouvent leur place plus facilement dans les archives de corps publics ou d'institutions que ceux des mouvements féministes communautaires.

Notre définition de ce qui constitue une pièce archivistique est très large, incluant à peu près tout ce que produit le mouvement des femmes. Nos archives ne se limitent pas aux textes écrits, tels que procès-verbaux, correspondance et états financiers, mais comprennent également des photos, diapositives, affiches, enregistrements, macarons, carnets « de bal », cartes postales, cartes d'affaires, t-shirts, bannières et deux plaques de bronze de la clinique Morgentaler de Toronto garnies de graffiti anti-choix. De plus, nous possédons la plus vaste collection de périodiques, journaux, revues et bulletins du mouvement féministe canadien en existence. Le nombre d'organismes représentés dans les Archives continue de s'accroître et va maintenant chercher dans les 2 000.

Les pièces à collection parviennent aux Archives de diverses façons. Lorsque, par exemple, un organisme ferme ses portes — phénomène par trop fréquent hélas! ces derniers temps — il peut faire don de ses dossiers à l'ACMF/CWMA. Il arrive parfois qu'une seule association détienne les documents d'autres organismes locaux; dans ce cas, les Archives reçoivent un don de plusieurs groupes à la fois. Quelquefois encore, certains groupes manquent d'espace pour l'entreposage de dossiers peu usités et décident de nous les confier. Par ailleurs, certains groupes féministes ont pris l'habitude de nous remettre leurs dossiers de façon régulière : c'est le cas, entre autres, de Women's Press, Women Healthsharing et de *Fireweed*. Une membre de notre personnel, en voyage à travers le pays pour faire connaître les Archives et encourager les groupements de femmes à conserver leurs documents, a inventé le système de « l'enveloppe de papier brun » comme instrument d'archivage. En vertu de ce système, chaque groupe est prié de suspendre une enveloppe de papier brun près de la corbeille à papier et de se demander, avant d'y jeter des documents, si ceux-ci n'intéresseraient pas les Archives. Plusieurs organismes se sont servis de ce système avec succès et nous ont ainsi envoyé du matériel qui, autrement, aurait disparu. Un grand nombre de femmes nous ont également fait parvenir individuellement des documents qu'elles gardaient depuis des années — souvent lors d'un déménagement qui empêche le transfert de ces papiers. De temps en temps, le matériel nous est arrivé entassé dans des sacs à ordures et quelquefois, il nous a été envoyé anonymement. Qu'importe! Quels que soient l'emballage des documents et leur quantité, nous sommes toujours heureuses de les recevoir.

◆ ◆ ◆

À l'instar de tous les groupements d'action communautaire, les Archives ont connu une existence précaire. La plupart du temps, elles ont dû se suffire à elles-mêmes, en comptant sur les dons de toutes et chacune, les ventes-débarras, les événements spéciaux et la vente d'articles tels que cartes postales, t-shirts, pulls de survêtement et macarons. Bien que les octrois reçus pour l'exécution de projets aient été fort appréciés, la disponibilité de telles sommes demeure limitée.

Dès l'été de 1991, la collective ACMF/CWMA, de concert avec le conseil du WIC, avait reconnu qu'elle ne pouvait plus fonctionner comme centre d'archivage indépendant. Le projet avait pris une ampleur trop considérable, nécessitant un personnel et des fonds bien au-delà de ses moyens. Les objectifs primordiaux de notre organisme ont toujours été la conservation permanente et la communicabilité de nos archives, ainsi que l'expansion continue de la collection et son maintien selon des méthodes compatibles avec nos buts et principes. Après avoir examiné soigneusement plusieurs options, nous avons décidé de confier la collection de l'ACMF/CWMA à l'Université d'Ottawa. Nous avons la confiance absolue que l'Université saura maintenir ce qui, à notre avis, constitue la meilleure documentation en existence sur le mouvement contemporain des femmes canadiennes et nous avons hâte de voir grandir la collection. Bon succès aux archivistes qui ont pris la relève!

Notre groupement fonctionne sous les auspices du Women's Information Centre de Toronto. Nous formons une collective dont le nombre de membres a varié de quatre à huit au cours des années. Nous sommes, ou nous étions, des historiennes, bibliothécaires, archivistes, informaticiennes, employées d'organismes féminins, étudiantes et enseignantes; toutes, nous avons pris, et nous prenons encore, une part active au mouvement des femmes. Comme dans toutes les collectives, nous nous sommes partagé les tâches : formulation de politiques, acquisitions, traitement de documents, services de référence, action sociale, collecte de fonds et tous autres travaux reliés à la tenue d'archives. Nous sommes : Jane Abray (1989–), Nancy Adamson (1982–), Pat Baker (1989), Joan Berger (1990-1991), Megan Davies (1986-1987), Jeannette Dowson (1985-1986), Karen Dubinsky (1988–), Linda Galen (1987-1988), Debbie Green (1985-1988), Janice Hill (1990-1991), Luanne Karn (1984-1988), Andrea Knight (1982-1984), Wiesia Kolasinska (1982-1984), Pat Leslie (1982-1984), Beth McAuley (1990–), Anne Molgat (1985–), Kathy Moules (1990-1991), Johanne M. Pelletier (1988–), Margaret Shepherd (1988-1990), Tori Smith (1985-1987), Miriam Ticoll (1986-1989), Lorna Weir (1982-1985).

Les Archives doivent leur existence à ces femmes, aux femmes qui ont puisé à même leurs fonds, à celles qui ont fourni des articles pour nos ventes de livres et de bric-à-brac, à celles qui ont acheté des t-shirts, des cartes postales et des affiches, aux organismes qui nous ont fait don de leurs dossiers et nous ont offert des abonnements et des exemplaires gratuits de leurs publications, aux activistes et chercheuses qui ont utilisé les Archives, aux fondations et ministères gouvernementaux qui nous ont accordé des octrois, aux personnes et groupements qui ont acheté FEM-DIRECT, au personnel des Archives et, enfin, à la grande famille des féministes canadiennes qui prêtent au mouvement des femmes la vitalité et la force dont il continue de faire preuve. Un grand merci à vous toutes.

— La Collective ACMF/CWMA et le Conseil d'administration du WIC

HOW TO USE THIS GUIDE

This guide is designed to help researchers locate records of the Canadian women's movement since 1960. If you are interested in viewing a collection listed here, contact the organization or archives which holds the records in advance. Many collections can be viewed only with permission or have other access restrictions; these should be confirmed ahead of time. The guide describes holdings as they were when we surveyed the archives and organizations; further records may have been added since then, and organizations may have moved or disbanded.

Part I lists records held by archives, and Part II lists records held by organizations. Each part is divided into sections: the first section is for the records of national groups, and this is followed by sections for groups in each province or territory, from west to east. Within a section, each entry lists records of a particular group; the entries are in alphabetical order by the name of the group. An entry appears in either French or English, according to the probable language of the records listed; for a bilingual collection, there are two entries with identical information, one in French and one in English.

Researchers may want to locate records for an individual province, a specific organization, or a particular type of group. For example, if you are interested in the Saskatchewan women's movement, you can browse through the two sections for Saskatchewan (one section in Part I and one in Part II).

To locate records of a specific group, look in the Name Index. For example, the guide has two entries for the records of Mount Saint Vincent University. The Name Index will direct you to these entries whether you look under the university's present name (*Mount Saint Vincent University*), or its earlier name (*Sisters of Charity. Mount Saint Vincent College* or simply *Mount Saint Vincent College*), or the name of its women's studies institute (*Institute for the Study of Women*), or the institute's acronym (*ISW*), or the name of the journal it publishes (*Atlantis*).

Use the Subject Index to find all the entries related to a particular subject. You might be interested in a certain kind of organization (e.g., *bookstores* or *coalitions*), or in organizations dealing with a particular issue (e.g., *abortion* or *employment*), or in organizations for a certain group of women (e.g., *clerical workers* or *immigrant women*).

The following example shows how the entries work. Please note that not all entries contain every element of information found in this example; information was omitted if it was not applicable or not available.

(1) 77. **New Democratic Party. Rosemary Brown Leadership Campaign Committee**

(2) ✣ Vancouver, B.C. Formed 1975. Disbanded 1975.

(3) This committee supported Rosemary Brown's campaign for the leadership of the New Democratic Party. Women's issues figured prominently in the campaign.

(4) LOCATION OF RECORDS: University of Toronto Archives. (See Appendix for address.)

(5) COLLECTION NAME: Forms part of: Marianne Holder collection (UTA B88-0075/004).

(6) RECORDS: Minutes, procedures, speeches, clippings, bulletins, itinerary, flyers, pamphlets, songsheet, 1975.

(7) AMOUNT: 1 cm.

(8) CONDITION: Good.

(9) ACCESS: No restrictions.

(10) FINDING AID: Box list available for Holder collection.

(1) **Entry Number.** Each entry has a number; the indexes refer to entry numbers, not page numbers.
Name of Organization. In some cases the group's location or other information has been added in parentheses to distinguish the group from another with a similar name. The group is listed in the Name Index under other names as well — e.g., another form of the present name, or a name it had at an earlier date.

(2) **Group's location and dates of existence:** where the group is or was located, when it was formed, and when it disbanded, if known.

(3) **Description of Group.**

(4) **Location of Records:** the archives or organization which holds the records. Addresses and phone numbers for archives are listed in the Appendix; if an organization holds the records, its address is included in the entry.

(5) **Collection Name.** An archival collection has a name

(and often a number). You will need the collection name (which may be different from the name which heads the entry) to locate the records at the archives.

(6) **Records:** the types of records (with their dates, where known). The level of precision varies, depending on the source of the information. For instance, *minutes, 1970-1974, 1976-1980* means there are minutes for every year from 1970 to 1980 except 1975; but sometimes the information is less precise: *minutes, 1970-1980* may mean there are records for every year from 1970 to 1980, or it may mean that the minutes start in 1970 and end in 1980, but with gaps for some years in between.

(7) **Amount:** the physical extent of the collection. For archival holdings, this is usually the linear extent: for instance, *15 cm* means that if the files were standing in a filing cabinet, their depth from front to back would be 15 centimetres. Sometimes a separate measurement is given for non-textual records — e.g., *9 cm of text, 2 posters, 1 sound recording*. For records held by organizations, the amount is usually expressed in everyday terms — e.g., *1 filing cabinet*.

(8) **Condition:** the physical condition of the records. Condition is expressed by one of three terms, whichever best describes most of the records:

— *Good* (records in similar condition to when they were created)
— *Fair* (e.g., paper yellowing or a little musty, but can still be handled and read with no problem)
— *Poor* (e.g., damaged by water, mouldy, badly stained, paper so fragile that it's falling apart).

(9) **Access.** *Restricted* collections may be closed to researchers or may be viewed only under specific circumstances — e.g., only after a certain date or only with the permission of the donor. *No restrictions* means the records are open to researchers (i.e., there are no restrictions apart from the overall regulations which apply to all the archives' holdings). There may be restrictions on reproduction or quotation; these are not listed in this guide.

(10) **Finding Aid.** An archival collection may be described in a finding aid — e.g., a guide, an inventory, a list of boxes, or a list of files. Finding aids range from a brief overall description to a detailed list of documents.

Uncertain dates are enclosed in brackets. For example:
[1967?] means probably 1967
[ca. 1967] means approximately 1967
[197-] means in the 1970s
[197-?] means probably in the 1970s

L'UTILISATION DU GUIDE

Ce guide est conçu pour faciliter la recherche de documents concernant le mouvement canadien des femmes depuis 1960. Les personnes qui désirent consulter une collection inscrite dans ce répertoire doivent communiquer avec l'organisme ou le dépôt qui détient les documents. Dans bien des cas, l'examen d'une collection est soumis à l'obtention d'une permission ou à des restrictions de communicabilité; il faut donc vérifier d'avance les conditions d'accès. Les fonds répertoriés dans ce guide sont décrits tels qu'ils étaient au moment de notre sondage. Il se peut que, depuis ce temps, d'autres documents y aient été déposés ou que des organismes aient déménagé ou aient été dissous.

La Partie I fait la liste des fonds détenus par les dépôts d'archives, tandis que la Partie II fait celle des fonds détenus par les organismes. Chaque partie est divisée en sections : la première section contient les documents de groupements nationaux et les autres revoient ceux de chaque province ou territoire allant de l'ouest vers l'est. À l'intérieur d'une section, chaque notice énumère les documents d'un groupe particulier; les notices sont classées par ordre alphabétique d'après le nom du groupe. La notice est rédigée soit en français, soit en anglais, suivant la langue probable des documents inventoriés, à moins que la collection ne soit bilingue, dans quel cas le guide affiche deux entrées identiques, l'une en français et l'autre en anglais.

Le guide permet aux chercheuses et chercheurs de repérer des documents s'adressant à une seule province, ou à un organisme spécifique ou à un regroupement de type particulier. Disons, par exemple, qu'on soit à la recherche d'informations sur le mouvement des femmes en Saskatchewan : on peut parcourir les deux sections consacrées à cette province (l'une dans la Partie I et l'autre dans la Partie II).

Les documents relatifs à un groupe spécifique se retrouvent en consultant l'Index des noms. Prenons l'exemple du Groupe de recherche multidisciplinaire féministe, groupe qui fonctionne sous les auspices de l'Université Laval. L'Index des noms renvoie au nom du groupe lui-même (*Groupe de recherche multidisciplinaire féministe*), au nom de l'université dont il dépend (*Université Laval. Groupe de . . .*), à son sigle (*GREMF*) et au nom de sa revue (*Recherches féministes*).

L'Index des sujets, comme son nom l'indique, permet de retrouver toutes les notices traitant d'un même sujet. Celui-ci peut être un certain type d'organisme (p. ex. *librairie* ou *coalition*), ou des organismes poursuivant la même cause (p. ex. *avortement* ou *emploi*), ou des organismes regroupant la même catégorie de femmes (p. ex., *employée de bureau* ou *immigrante*).

L'exemple suivant montre comment fonctionne le système des notices. Prière de noter que les notices ne contiennent pas toutes chaque élément d'information représenté dans l'exemple. Un ou plusieurs éléments sont omis s'ils ne sont pas applicables ou s'ils sont inconnus.

(1) **596.** *Centre de planning familial du Québec*

(2) ✢ Montréal (Québec). Groupe fondé 1967. Dissous 1972.

(3) Le centre a fondé une clinique de planning familial, s'est impliqué dans le débat sur l'avortement et a fait des recherches sur les aspects sociaux et psychologiques de la sexualité.

(4) LIEU DE CONSULTATION : Université du Québec à Montréal, Service des archives. (Voir Annexe pour l'adresse.)

(5) NOM DU FONDS : Fonds du Centre de planning familial du Québec (113P).

(6) MATÉRIEL : Règlements de régie interne, documents financiers, procès-verbaux, dossiers de comités, dossiers de projets, coupures de presse, documents divers.

(7) QUANTITÉ : Env. 1 m.

(8) ÉTAT : Bon.

(9) ACCÈS : Aucune restriction.

(10) INSTRUMENT DE RECHERCHE : « Répertoire numérique simple du fonds du Centre de planning familial ».

(1) **Numéro d'entrée.** Chaque entrée porte un numéro : les index renvoient à des numéros d'entrées et non à des numéros de pages.

Nom de l'organisme. Dans certains cas, la ville d'origine du groupe ou d'autres renseignements ont été ajoutés entre parenthèses pour distinguer ce groupe d'un autre de nom analogue. Le groupe figure dans l'Index des noms sous d'autres noms également, c'est-à-dire sous une autre forme de son nom actuel ou sous une désignation antérieure.

(2) **Nom du lieu et dates d'existence du groupe :** l'endroit où le groupe est ou était situé; sa date de formation et celle de sa dissolution, si elles sont connues.

(3) **Description du groupe.**

(4) **Lieu de consultation :** le dépôt ou l'organisme qui détient le fonds. Les adresses et numéros de téléphone des dépôts d'archives sont inscrits dans l'Annexe; quant aux adresses des organismes, elles sont données dans les notices correspondantes.

(5) **Nom du fonds.** Un fonds d'archives porte un nom (et souvent aussi un numéro). On aura besoin du nom du fonds (lequel peut être différent du nom de l'entrée) pour repérer les documents qu'il contient.

(6) **Matériel :** le type de documents (ainsi que leur date, si elle est connue). Le niveau de description varie selon la source d'information. Ainsi, *procès-verbaux, 1970-1974, 1976-1980* signifie qu'il y a des procès-verbaux pour chaque année sauf 1975. Cependant, cette information n'est pas toujours aussi précise : *procès-verbaux, 1970-1980* peut vouloir dire que chaque année est documentée entre 1970 et 1980, ou que la tenue de procès-verbaux remonte à 1970 et se termine en 1980 mais qu'il peut y avoir des écarts d'années dans cet intervalle.

(7) **Quantité :** l'espace occupé par la collection. Les archives se mesurent généralement en mètres linéaires; par exemple, *15 cm* veut dire que si les dossiers étaient rangés dans un classeur, l'espace qu'ils occuperaient en profondeur serait de 15 centimètres. Quelquefois, on exprime autrement les documents non textuels — p. ex., *9 cm de texte, 2 affiches, 1 enregistrement sonore*. Quant aux documents conservés sur les lieux d'un organisme, leur quantité est habituellement exprimée en termes de tous les jours — p. ex., *1 classeur*.

(8) **État :** condition matérielle des documents. L'état est caractérisé par l'un des trois termes suivants (le terme choisi est celui qui décrit le mieux la majorité des documents) :
— *Bon* (documents qui sont dans le même état que lorsqu'ils ont été créés)
— *Assez bon* (p. ex., papier jauni ou légèrement moisi, mais qui peut se manier et être lu sans difficulté)
— *Médiocre* (p. ex., papier endommagé par l'eau, moisi, couvert de taches ou si fragile qu'il s'effrite).

(9) **Accès.** Des *restrictions* peuvent interdire l'accès à certaines collections ou n'en permettre l'examen que dans des conditions déterminées. *Aucune restriction* signifie que les documents sont disponibles pour fins de recherche (c'est-à-dire qu'ils ne sont soumis à aucune restriction en dehors des règles générales qui s'appliquent à la consultation d'archives). Il peut exister des restrictions quant à la reproduction ou à la citation de documents; ces restrictions ne sont toutefois pas mentionnées dans ce guide.

(10) **Instrument de recherche.** Un fonds d'archives peut être décrit dans un instrument de recherche comme, par exemple, un guide, un inventaire, une liste de boîtes ou une liste de dossiers. Les instruments de recherche fournissent une information qui varie d'une description sommaire à une liste détaillée des documents contenus dans un fonds.

Les dates incertaines sont incluses entre parenthèses. Par exemple :
[1967?] signifie en 1967 probablement
[ca 1967] signifie vers 1967
[197-] signifie dans les années 1970
[197-?] signifie dans les années 1970 probablement

PART I: RECORDS HELD BY ARCHIVES
PARTIE I : FONDS DÉTENUS PAR DES ARCHIVES

NATIONAL ORGANIZATIONS / GROUPES PANCANADIENS

1. *Abortion Caravan*

✢ Formed 1970. Disbanded 1970.

This group of women travelled across Canada and demonstrated in Ottawa in May 1970. The group (also known as the Abortion Cavalcade) advocated abortion on demand and the removal of abortion from the Criminal Code.

LOCATION OF RECORDS: Canadian Women's Movement Archives Collection, Morisset Library Special Collections, University of Ottawa. (See Appendix for address.)

COLLECTION NAME: Abortion Caravan; SR 10/1B.

RECORDS: Proposal, brief, speech, pamphlet, clippings, press release, photographs, poster, 1970; sound recording, 1971.

AMOUNT: 4 mm of text, 1 sound recording, 2 photographs, 1 poster.

CONDITION: Fair.

ACCESS: No restrictions.

2. *Amalgamated Clothing and Textile Workers Union / Travailleurs amalgamés du vêtement et du textile*

[Renseignements en français, notice 90.]

[See also entry # 695 (in Part II), which lists other records of this organization.]

✢ Don Mills, Ont. Formed 1976.

The Amalgamated Clothing and Textile Workers Union (ACTWU) is a trade union which aims to improve the lives of Canadian workers. The majority of its members are women.

LOCATION OF RECORDS: National Archives of Canada. (See Appendix for address.)

COLLECTION NAME: Amalgamated Clothing and Textile Workers Union, Textile Division (MG 28, I 219).

RECORDS: **The National Archives of Canada has recently published a guide to many of its collections related to women. Rather than reproduce this information in detail, our entries for National Archives collections include only the name and number of the collection and the name of the group whose records it contains. For more information (the types of records and their dates, descriptions of the groups, etc.), we invite readers to consult:**

Women's Archives Guide: Manuscript Sources for the History of Women / Joanna Dean and David Fraser. Ottawa: National Archives of Canada, 1991.

"Post-Confederation Sources for the History of Women in Canada" (Finding Aid No. 1069) [an unpublished thematic guide (1984), available at the National Archives of Canada].

3. *Archives canadiennes du mouvement des femmes / Canadian Women's Movement Archives*

[For English entry, see # 35.]

✢ Toronto (Ont.). Groupe fondé 1977.

Les Archives canadiennes du mouvement des femmes (ACMF) recueillent et répertorient les documents retraçant l'évolution du mouvement contemporain (1960-) des femmes au Canada. L'ACMF est un organisme administré par le Women's Information Centre of Toronto. [Voir aussi Women's Information Centre of Toronto (559).]

LIEU DE CONSULTATION : Fonds des Archives canadiennes du mouvement des femmes, Collections spéciales de la Bibliothèque Morisset, Université d'Ottawa. (Voir Annexe pour l'adresse.)

NOM DU FONDS : Archives canadiennes du mouvement des femmes.

MATÉRIEL : Procès-verbaux, 1982-1992; correspondance, 1977-1992; rapports, coupures de presse, dépliants, photographies, enregistrements sonores, instruments de recherche, 1980-1992; journaux de bord, 1984-1992; listes d'envoi, 1986-1992; demandes de subvention, 1981-1984; dossiers administratifs, dossiers de projets, affiches, macaron, T-shirts, documents divers.

QUANTITÉ : Env. 4 m.

ÉTAT : Bon.

ACCÈS : Aucune restriction.

4. *Association canadienne pour la santé, l'éducation physique et la récréation. Comité athlétique féminin / Canadian Association for Health, Physical Education, and Recreation. Women's Athletic Committee*

[For English entry, see # 17.]

Fonds (a)

LIEU DE CONSULTATION : Archives nationales du Canada. (Voir Annexe pour l'adresse.)

NOM DU FONDS : Fait partie du fonds de l'Association canadienne pour la santé, l'éducation physique et la récréation (MG 28, I 153).

MATÉRIEL : **Les Archives nationales du Canada ont récemment publié un guide à plusieurs de leurs fonds d'archives sur les femmes. Plutôt que de reproduire en détail ces renseignements, nos notices sur les fonds des Archives nationales du Canada n'incluent que le nom du fonds, sa cote et le nom du groupe auquel les documents se rapportent. Pour de plus amples renseignements (types et années des documents, des-**

BRIEF OF THE ABORTION CARAVAN, MAY 1970

We women are not here to beg male politicians for our rights. We are here to tell you what our needs are, and to find out whether you are prepared to act. We demand answers on behalf of all the women in this country who are today wondering if they are pregnant; for all the women who can only worry about their futures since they cannot plan them. Women must find answers <u>today</u> and every month. We cannot wait for the male politicians' months and years of useless discussions. We want answers <u>today</u> to our demands. We will get more answers this week and next week and next month from our local hospitals and doctors.

THE PRINCIPLES OF WOMEN'S RIGHTS TO ABORTION

Get Your Laws Off Our Backs!
We women will have control of our bodies. We can no longer put up with the present situation where our entire lives are controlled by the medical profession and the politicians and lawmakers - all men. Trudeau's "Just Society" has no place in the wombs of the women of Canada. No one should make a decision for a woman about how to control her body or when and how she will have her children. It is <u>her</u> future, her very life, as well as that of her children, that is being decided, and a truly 'just' society must recognize the basic human rights of fifty percent of the people.

We have been given a reformed abortion law. This law has done nothing but give the doctors the right to do as <u>they</u> wish. If these men think that young girls should be punished for being pregnant they can say no to an abortion. If <u>they</u>, who have never been pregnant or missed one menstrual period in their lives, think that an aboriton is more 'traumatic' than bearing an unwanted child, they can say no. If these doctors are too busy making thousands of dollars a month from women patients, and have not got room in their schedules for a woman with <u>no</u> money, they can say no to an abortion. And no woman can even be considered for the abortion board unless she can find a doctor, and in most cases two psychiatrists, who will take her case to the board. <u>Nineteen women out of twenty</u> who want abortions are refused by their doctors before they even get to the hospital board.

Therapeutic abortion boards, that is, a half-dozen little male gods who sit at a table once a month, can say yes or no to the desperation and aspirations of thousands of women in every city of this country. What blatant male supremist arrogance! We demand immediate repeal of all abortion laws by this government and <u>we</u> are going to rid ourselves of those hospital boards.

We Have No Rights Without Birth Control
Women do not even have the possibility of control of our lives without access to birth control. Our training for jobs is irrelevant when we cannot plan when and how we will be able to work. Therefore, we are forced to marry to support ourselves rather than to plan our lives according to our individual interests. There must be totally

Excerpt from a 1970 brief entitled: / Extrait d'un mémoire de 1970 intitulé :
"Abortion Caravan Demands"
Abortion Caravan
CWMA Collection / Fonds de l'ACMF

criptions des groupes, etc.), nous vous recommandons de consulter : *Guide des archives sur les femmes : Sources manuscrites sur l'histoire des femmes/ Joanna Dean et David Fraser*. Ottawa : Archives nationales du Canada, 1991.

« Sources postérieures à la Confédération sur l'histoire de la femme au Canada » (Instrument de recherche n° 1069) [un guide thématique inédit (1984), disponible aux Archives nationales du Canada].

Fonds (b)

LIEU DE CONSULTATION : Archives nationales du Canada.

NOM DU FONDS : Fait partie du fonds de l'Union sportive interuniversitaire canadienne féminine (MG 28, I 312).

MATÉRIEL : Voir la note sur les fonds des Archives nationales du Canada, notice 4.

5. *Association canadienne pour le droit à l'avortement / Canadian Abortion Rights Action League*

[For English entry, see # 16.]

✣ Toronto (Ont.). Groupe fondé 1973.

L'Association canadienne pour le droit à l'avortement (ACDA) s'appelait à ses débuts l'Association canadienne pour l'abrogation de la loi sur l'avortement (ACALA). L'ACDA a lutté pour l'abrogation des articles du Code criminel ayant trait à l'avortement et pour la mise sur pied, à travers le Canada, de services d'avortement et de contraception complets. [Voir aussi Childbirth by Choice Trust (718).]

Fonds (a)

LIEU DE CONSULTATION : Fonds des Archives canadiennes du mouvement des femmes, Collections spéciales de la Bibliothèque Morisset, Université d'Ottawa. (Voir Annexe pour l'adresse.)

NOM DU FONDS : Canadian Abortion Rights Action League.

MATÉRIEL : Documents d'assemblées générales annuelles, 1977, 1980-1984 ; statuts et règlements, 1979-1980 ; bulletins, 1975-1976, 1979-1990 ; exposé de position, 1972 ; rapports, 1979, 1982-1983, 1988 ; énoncés de politiques, 1978, 1982-1983 ; correspondance, 1975-1977, 1979-1989 ; analyse, 1977 ; listes de membres, 1976-1977 ; affiches, 1983 ; invitation, 1986 ; enquête, 1989 ; mémoires, soumission, objectifs, coupures de presse, communiqués de presse, circulaires d'information, formules de protestation, dépliants, notes biographiques, tracts, questionnaire, notes, autocollant.

QUANTITÉ : 24 cm de texte, 2 affiches.

ÉTAT : Bon.

ACCÈS : Aucune restriction.

Fonds (b)

LIEU DE CONSULTATION : Archives nationales du Canada. (Voir Annexe pour l'adresse.)

NOM DU FONDS : Fait partie du fonds June Callwood (MG 31, K 24).

MATÉRIEL : Voir la note sur les fonds des Archives nationales du Canada, notice 4.

6. *Association des adjoints administratifs / Association of Administrative Assistants*

[For English entry, see # 12.]

✣ Toronto (Ont.). Groupe fondé 1951.

Connu à ses débuts sous le nom d'« Association of Private Secretaries », cet organisme a été incorporé en 1952 et rebaptisé « Association of Administrative Assistants or Private Secretaries ». L'un de ses buts était d'accroître les options des adjointes et adjoints administratifs en matière d'éducation. À ses débuts cet organisme n'oeuvrait qu'à Toronto ; mais au cours des années 1950, des filiales ont été fondées dans d'autres villes canadiennes, surtout en Ontario. L'association a adopté sa désignation actuelle en 1976. (Source : instrument de recherche des Archives publiques de l'Ontario, 1990.)

LIEU DE CONSULTATION : Archives publiques de l'Ontario. (Voir Annexe pour l'adresse.)

NOM DU FONDS : Association of Administrative Assistants - Association des Adjoints Administratifs Papers (F 1288).

MATÉRIEL : Lettres patentes, statuts et règlements, 1952-1979 ; procès-verbaux, 1951-1987 ; listes de membres, 1956-1983 ; documents financiers, 1959-1974 ; correspondance, 1963-1985 ; documents de comités, 1969-1981 ; rapports, 1963-1967 ; bulletins, 1974-1981 ; brochures, documents divers.

QUANTITÉ : Env. 1,5 m.

ÉTAT : Bon.

ACCÈS : Ce fonds ne pourra être consulté avant le 1er janvier 1993.

INSTRUMENT DE RECHERCHE : « Preliminary Inventory of the Papers of the Association of Administrative Assistants ».

7. *Association des femmes progressistes conservatrices / Progressive Conservative Women's Association*

[For English entry, see # 84.]

✣ Ottawa (Ont.).

LIEU DE CONSULTATION : Archives nationales du Canada. (Voir Annexe pour l'adresse.)

NOM DU FONDS : Fait partie du fonds du Parti progressiste conservateur du Canada (MG 28, IV 2).

MATÉRIEL : Voir la note sur les fonds des Archives nationales du Canada, notice 4.

8. *Association des infirmières et infirmiers du Canada / Canadian Nurses Association*

[For English entry, see # 28.]

✣ Ottawa (Ont.). Groupe fondé 1908.

L'Association des infirmières et infirmiers du Canada est une fédération d'associations provinciales et territoriales qui, en tant que porte-parole des membres de cette profession, joue un rôle d'influence dans les questions relatives au travail infirmier. L'association s'appelait à ses débuts l'Association canadienne nationale des infirmières diplômées, devenue par la suite l'Association des infirmières canadiennes (AIC). Elle publie une revue professionnelle, *L'Infirmière canadienne*, fondée en 1905. (Source : *Guide des collections historiques de l'Association des infirmières et infirmiers du Canada*. — Ottawa : Association des infirmières et infirmiers du Canada, 1987.)

Fonds (a)

LIEU DE CONSULTATION : Archives de l'Association des infirmières et infirmiers du Canada. (Voir Annexe pour l'adresse.)

MATÉRIEL : Procès-verbaux, rapports, documents de congrès, documents d'assemblées annuelles, périodiques, correspondance, notes historiques, discours, extraits, photographies, vidéocassettes, productions de diapositives sonores, transparents pour rétroprojecteur, enregistrements sonores, documents divers, 1905-1991.

QUANTITÉ : Env. 15 m de texte, 11 bobines de microfilm.

ACCÈS : Les recherchistes seront priés d'utiliser des microfilms au lieu de certains originaux ; accès restreint quant aux rapports des dix dernières années.

INSTRUMENT DE RECHERCHE : *Guide des collections historiques de l'Association des infirmières et infirmiers du Canada*.

Fonds (b)
LIEU DE CONSULTATION : Archives nationales du Canada. (Voir Annexe pour l'adresse.)
NOM DU FONDS : Association des infirmières et des infirmiers du Canada (MG 28, I 248).
MATÉRIEL : Voir la note sur les fonds des Archives nationales du Canada, notice 4.

9. *Association des universités et collèges du Canada. Comité spécial sur le rapport de la Commission royale d'enquête sur la situation de la femme / Association of Universities and Colleges of Canada. Special Committee on the Report of the Royal Commission on the Status of Women*

[For English entry, see # 14.]

✣ Groupe fondé 1971. Dissous.

LIEU DE CONSULTATION : Fonds des Archives canadiennes du mouvement des femmes, Collections spéciales de la Bibliothèque Morisset, Université d'Ottawa. (Voir Annexe pour l'adresse.)
NOM DU FONDS : Association of Universities and Colleges of Canada.
MATÉRIEL : Document de référence, commentaires, 1971; correspondance, 1971-1972.
QUANTITÉ : 1 cm.
ÉTAT : Assez bon.
ACCÈS : Aucune restriction.

10. *Association des universités et collèges du Canada. Comité sur la situation de la femme dans les universités / Association of Universities and Colleges of Canada. Committee on the Status of Women in Universities*

[For English entry, see # 13.]

✣ Groupe fondé [ca 1975].

LIEU DE CONSULTATION : Fonds des Archives canadiennes du mouvement des femmes, Collections spéciales de la Bibliothèque Morisset, Université d'Ottawa. (Voir Annexe pour l'adresse.)
NOM DU FONDS : Association of Universities and Colleges of Canada.
MATÉRIEL : Rapport, 1977.
QUANTITÉ : 1 pièce.
ÉTAT : Bon.
ACCÈS : Aucune restriction.

11. *Association for the Review of Canadian Abortion Laws*

✣ Ottawa, Ont. Formed 1966.

LOCATION OF RECORDS: National Archives of Canada. (See Appendix for address.)
COLLECTION NAME: Association for the Review of Canadian Abortion Laws (MG 28, I 350).
RECORDS: Please see the note about National Archives of Canada collections, in entry # 2.

12. *Association of Administrative Assistants / Association des adjoints administratifs*

[Renseignements en français, notice 6.]

✣ Toronto, Ont. Formed 1951.

Originally called the Association of Private Secretaries, this organization was incorporated in 1952 as the Association of Administrative Assistants or Private Secretaries. One of its aims was to increase educational opportunities for administrative assistants. It began in Toronto as a local organization; but during the 1950s, branches were established in other Canadian cities (predominantly in Ontario). The association adopted its present name in 1976. (Source: Archives of Ontario finding aid, 1990.)

LOCATION OF RECORDS: Archives of Ontario. (See Appendix for address.)
COLLECTION NAME: Association of Administrative Assistants - Association des Adjoints Administratifs Papers (F 1288).
RECORDS: Letters patent, constitution, by-laws, 1952-1979; minutes, 1951-1987; membership lists, 1956-1983; financial records, 1959-1974; correspondence, 1963-1985; committee records, 1969-1981; reports, 1963-1967; newsletters, 1974-1981; brochures, miscellaneous records.
AMOUNT: Approx. 1.5 m.
CONDITION: Good.
ACCESS: Closed until January 1, 1993.
FINDING AID: "Preliminary Inventory of the Papers of the Association of Administrative Assistants."

13. *Association of Universities and Colleges of Canada. Committee on the Status of Women in Universities / Association des universités et collèges du Canada. Comité sur la situation de la femme dans les universités*

[Renseignements en français, notice 10.]

✣ Formed [ca. 1975].

LOCATION OF RECORDS: Canadian Women's Movement Archives Collection, Morisset Library Special Collections, University of Ottawa. (See Appendix for address.)
COLLECTION NAME: Association of Universities and Colleges of Canada.
RECORDS: Report, 1977.
AMOUNT: 1 item.
CONDITION: Good.
ACCESS: No restrictions.

14. *Association of Universities and Colleges of Canada. Special Committee on the Report of the Royal Commission on the Status of Women / Association des universités et collèges du Canada. Comité spécial sur le rapport de la Commission royale d'enquête sur la situation de la femme*

[Renseignements en français, notice 9.]

✣ Formed 1971. Disbanded.

LOCATION OF RECORDS: Canadian Women's Movement Archives Collection, Morisset Library Special Collections, University of Ottawa. (See Appendix for address.)

NATIONAL ORGANIZATIONS / GROUPES PANCANADIENS

COLLECTION NAME: Association of Universities and Colleges of Canada.
RECORDS: Background paper, comments, 1971; correspondence, 1971-1972.
AMOUNT: 1 cm.
CONDITION: Fair.
ACCESS: No restrictions.

15. Body Politic

✢ Toronto, Ont. Formed 1971. Disbanded 1987.

The *Body Politic* (sometimes referred to as TBP) was a gay and lesbian newspaper. From 1975 on, the newspaper was owned by Pink Triangle Press, a non-profit corporation whose other projects included a typesetting company called Pink Type. The *Body Politic* Free the Press Fund was established after charges were laid against the newspaper in 1978. Although the collective which put out the *Body Politic* disbanded in 1987, Pink Triangle Press continued to exist. (Source: Canadian Gay Archives finding aid, 1988.)

Collection (a)

LOCATION OF RECORDS: Canadian Gay Archives. (See Appendix for address.)
COLLECTION NAME: 82-002 / 003 / 009 / 019 / 031, 83-002 / 009 / 010 / 023, 84-003 / 009 / 013 / 024 / 026, 85-002 / 007 / 008 / 017, 86-001 / 003 / 012 / 021 / 032, 87-004 / 011, 88-004.
RECORDS: Records of the *Body Politic*, Pink Triangle Press, Pink Type, and the *Body Politic* Free the Press Fund (correspondence, financial records, 1971-1987; minutes, 1973-1987; by-laws, leases, incorporation records, 1972-1979; list of directors and members, 1976-1977; photographs, 1971-1982; subscription records, 1971-1985; annual reports, 1977-1980; datebooks, calendars, daily journals, incoming-mail logs, 1976-1980; appointment book, 1987; subject files, 1971-1980; grant applications, 1978-1984; mailing list, 1976-1977; survey records, 1972, 1981, 1985, 1987; distribution records, 1971-1984, 1986-1987; production manual, 1985; sound recordings [interviews], 1972-1983, 1986; video recording, 1979; production files, editorial files, background files, manuscripts, reports, fund-raising records, legal records, graphics, posters, art work, administrative files, advertising files, promotional material, buttons, banners, T-shirts, rubber stamps, miscellaneous records).
AMOUNT: 38.21 m.
FINDING AID: "Inventory of the Records of the *Body Politic* and Pink Triangle Press"; index to photographs available for 1971 to 1978.

Collection (b)

LOCATION OF RECORDS: Canadian Gay Archives.
COLLECTION NAME: The Body Politic (88-023, 88-029, 89-053).
RECORDS: Sound recording, drawing, [198-]; correspondence, legal records, 1983-1984; miscellaneous records, 1982-1986.

Collection (c)

LOCATION OF RECORDS: Canadian Gay Archives.
COLLECTION NAME: Pink Triangle Press (88-053, 89-009, 90-095).
RECORDS: Miscellaneous records.

Collection (d)

LOCATION OF RECORDS: Canadian Gay Archives.
COLLECTION NAME: Lynnie Johnston (83-018).
RECORDS: Photographs, 1978-1981.
AMOUNT: 46 photographs.

Collection (e)

LOCATION OF RECORDS: Canadian Gay Archives.
COLLECTION NAME: Forms part of: Chris Bearchell collection (84-017, 85-009).
RECORDS: Interviews, 1979, 1983; miscellaneous records, 1978-1985.

Collection (f)

LOCATION OF RECORDS: Canadian Gay Archives.
COLLECTION NAME: Forms part of: Gillian Rodgerson collection (89-023).
RECORDS: Notes, miscellaneous records, 1983-1986.

Collection (g)

LOCATION OF RECORDS: Canadian Women's Movement Archives Collection, Morisset Library Special Collections, University of Ottawa. (See Appendix for address.)
COLLECTION NAME: SR 11/12.
RECORDS: Sound recording (interview), 1976.
AMOUNT: 1 sound recording.
ACCESS: Restricted; conditional access negotiable.

16. Canadian Abortion Rights Action League / Association canadienne pour le droit à l'avortement

[Renseignements en français, notice 5.]

✢ Toronto, Ont. Formed 1973.

The Canadian Abortion Rights Action League (CARAL) was originally called the Canadian Association for Repeal of the Abortion Law. CARAL has lobbied for the repeal of Criminal Code sections dealing with abortion and has advocated the establishment of comprehensive contraception and abortion services throughout Canada. [See also Childbirth by Choice Trust (718).]

Collection (a)

LOCATION OF RECORDS: Canadian Women's Movement Archives Collection, Morisset Library Special Collections, University of Ottawa. (See Appendix for address.)
COLLECTION NAME: Canadian Abortion Rights Action League.
RECORDS: Records of annual general meetings, 1977, 1980-1984; constitutions, by-laws, 1979-1980; newsletters, 1975-1976, 1979-1990; position paper, 1972; reports, 1979, 1982-1983, 1988; policy statements, 1978, 1982-1983; correspondence, 1975-1977, 1979-1989; critique, 1977; membership lists, 1976-1977; posters, 1983; invitation, 1986; survey, 1989; briefs, submission, statement of purpose, clippings, press releases, information sheets, protest forms, pamphlets, biographical notes, flyers, questionnaire, notes, sticker.
AMOUNT: 24 cm of text, 2 posters.
CONDITION: Good.
ACCESS: No restrictions.

Collection (b)

LOCATION OF RECORDS: National Archives of Canada. (See Appendix for address.)
COLLECTION NAME: Forms part of: June Callwood collection (MG 31, K 24).
RECORDS: Please see the note about National Archives of Canada collections, in entry # 2.

17. Canadian Association for Health, Physical Education, and Recreation. Women's Athletic Committee / Association canadienne pour la santé, l'éducation physique et la récréation. Comité athlétique féminin

[Renseignements en français, notice 4.]

Collection (a)

LOCATION OF RECORDS: National Archives of Canada. (See Appendix for address.)
COLLECTION NAME: Forms part of: Canadian Association for Health, Physical Education, and Recreation collection (MG 28, I 153).

RECORDS: Please see the note about National Archives of Canada collections, in entry # 2.

Collection (b)

LOCATION OF RECORDS: National Archives of Canada.

COLLECTION NAME: Forms part of: Canadian Women's Intercollegiate Athletic Union collection (MG 28, I 312).

RECORDS: Please see the note about National Archives of Canada collections, in entry # 2.

18. Canadian Coalition against Media Pornography / Coalition canadienne contre la pornographie dans les médias

[Renseignements en français, notice 40.]

✣ Ottawa, Ont. Formed 1983. Disbanded 1989.

LOCATION OF RECORDS: National Archives of Canada. (See Appendix for address.)

COLLECTION NAME: Canadian Coalition against Media Pornography (MG 28, I 459).

RECORDS: Please see the note about National Archives of Canada collections, in entry # 2.

19. Canadian Committee on the Status of Women / Comité canadien sur la situation de la femme

[Renseignements en français, notice 46.]

Collection (a)

LOCATION OF RECORDS: National Archives of Canada. (See Appendix for address.)

COLLECTION NAME: Forms part of: Margaret MacLellan collection (MG 31, E 17).

RECORDS: Please see the note about National Archives of Canada collections, in entry # 2.

Collection (b)

LOCATION OF RECORDS: National Archives of Canada.

COLLECTION NAME: Forms part of: Dorothy Eva Flaherty collection (MG 31, K 25).

RECORDS: Please see the note about National Archives of Canada collections, in entry # 2.

20. Canadian Committee on Women's History / Comité canadien de l'histoire des femmes

[Renseignements en français, notice 45.]

✣ Formed 1975.

LOCATION OF RECORDS: National Archives of Canada. (See Appendix for address.)

COLLECTION NAME: Canadian Committee on Women's History (MG 28, I 57).

RECORDS: Please see the note about National Archives of Canada collections, in entry # 2.

21. Canadian Congress for Learning Opportunities for Women / Congrès canadien pour la promotion des études chez la femme

[Renseignements en français, notice 48.]

[See also entry # 707 (in Part II), which lists other records of this organization.]

✣ Toronto, Ont. Formed 1973.

The Canadian Congress for Learning Opportunities for Women (CCLOW) is a national organization which promotes learning opportunities for women. It promotes networking, identifies barriers, publicizes critical issues, organizes conferences, and publishes a periodical, *Women's Education des femmes*. CCLOW was originally called the Canadian Committee on Learning Opportunities for Women.

Collection (a)

LOCATION OF RECORDS: Saskatchewan Archives Board, Regina. (See Appendix for address.)

COLLECTION NAME: Canadian Congress for Learning Opportunities for Women (R-1035).

RECORDS: Correspondence, minutes, reports, information sheets, miscellaneous records, [ca. 1978]-1983.

AMOUNT: 90 cm.

FINDING AID: Guide no. GR 141.

Collection (b)

LOCATION OF RECORDS: Canadian Women's Movement Archives Collection, Morisset Library Special Collections, University of Ottawa. (See Appendix for address.)

COLLECTION NAME: Canadian Congress for Learning Opportunities for Women.

RECORDS: Agendas, 1981-1986; invitation, 1980; press releases, 1981, 1985; proposals, 1976-1978; briefs, 1979-1980, 1984; presentation, 1981; flyers, 1978-1979, 1983-1984, 1987-1988, 1991; pamphlets, 1981, [ca. 1990]; conference programme, 1984; project outline, 1977; membership list, 1987; mailing lists, 1980-1982; seminar materials, 1973, 1975, 1977; periodicals, 1978-1987; statement of purpose, minutes, correspondence, reports, survey, questionnaires, working paper, project files, publications list, advertisements, clipping, form.

AMOUNT: 18.5 cm.

CONDITION: Good.

ACCESS: No restrictions.

22. Canadian Federation of Business and Professional Women's Clubs / Fédération canadienne des clubs de femmes de carrières libérales et commerciales

[Renseignements en français, notice 52.]

✣ Ottawa, Ont. Formed 1930.

The federation (also known as CFBPWC) is an umbrella organization for business and professional women's clubs throughout Canada.

Collection (a)

LOCATION OF RECORDS: National Archives of Canada. (See Appendix for address.)

COLLECTION NAME: Canadian Federation of Business and Professional Women's Clubs (MG 28, I 55).

RECORDS: Please see the note about National Archives of Canada collections, in entry # 2.

Collection (b)

LOCATION OF RECORDS: National Archives of Canada.

COLLECTION NAME: Forms part of: Dorothy Heneker collection (MG 30, C 128).

RECORDS: Please see the note about National Archives of Canada collections, in entry # 2.

Collection (c)

LOCATION OF RECORDS: National Archives of Canada.

COLLECTION NAME: Forms part of: Charlotte Elizabeth Whitton collection (MG 30, E 256).

RECORDS: Please see the note about National Archives of Canada collections, in entry # 2.

Collection (d)

LOCATION OF RECORDS: Saskatchewan Archives Board, Regina. (See Appendix for address.)

COLLECTION NAME: Forms part of: Ruth S. McGill Papers.

RECORDS: Incorporation documents, 1930; constitution, by-laws, regulations, 1947-1963; organization history, [ca. 1930]-1945; minutes, agendas, 1962-1965; correspondence, 1956-1964; newsletters, [ca. 1961]-1965; membership records, 1935-1965; briefs, 1953-1963; reports, 1935-1964; publications, 1941-1962; speeches, [ca. 1944]-1964; financial records, resolutions, press releases, 1962-1964; convention records, 1948-1964; clippings, [ca. 1933]-1965; rosters, 1946-1965; pamphlets, brochures, [ca. 1955]-1965; procedures, miscellaneous records.

AMOUNT: 44 cm.

ACCESS: No restrictions.

FINDING AID: "A Checklist of the Papers of Ruth S. McGill" (Guide no. GR 351).

23. Canadian Federation of University Women / Fédération canadienne des femmes diplômées des universités

[Renseignements en français, notice 53.]

✤ Ottawa, Ont. Formed 1919.

The Canadian Federation of University Women (CFUW) is a federation of university women's clubs (clubs for women university graduates). CFUW's goals include encouraging women scholars and safeguarding the rights of women. (Source: *The Canadian Encyclopedia*. — Edmonton: Hurtig Publishers, 1985.)

Collection (a)

LOCATION OF RECORDS: National Archives of Canada. (See Appendix for address.)

COLLECTION NAME: Canadian Federation of University Women (MG 28, I 196).

RECORDS: Please see the note about National Archives of Canada collections, in entry # 2.

Collection (b)

LOCATION OF RECORDS: National Archives of Canada.

COLLECTION NAME: Forms part of: Miriam Sheridan collection (MG 31, K 27).

RECORDS: Please see the note about National Archives of Canada collections, in entry # 2.

Collection (c)

LOCATION OF RECORDS: National Archives of Canada.

COLLECTION NAME: Forms part of: Marion Creelman Savage collection (MG 30, C 92).

RECORDS: Please see the note about National Archives of Canada collections, in entry # 2.

Collection (d)

LOCATION OF RECORDS: National Archives of Canada.

COLLECTION NAME: Forms part of: Margaret MacLellan collection (MG 31, E 17).

RECORDS: Please see the note about National Archives of Canada collections, in entry # 2.

Collection (e)

LOCATION OF RECORDS: National Archives of Canada.

COLLECTION NAME: Forms part of: Ruth Marion (Rolph) Bell collection (MG 31, K 22, volumes 1-7).

RECORDS: Please see the note about National Archives of Canada collections, in entry # 2.

Collection (f)

LOCATION OF RECORDS: National Archives of Canada.

COLLECTION NAME: Forms part of: Gladys Harvey collection (MG 31, K 26).

RECORDS: Please see the note about National Archives of Canada collections, in entry # 2.

Collection (g)

LOCATION OF RECORDS: National Archives of Canada.

COLLECTION NAME: Forms part of: Dorothy Eva Flaherty collection (MG 31, K 25).

RECORDS: Please see the note about National Archives of Canada collections, in entry # 2.

24. Canadian Lesbian and Gay Rights Coalition / Coalition canadienne pour les droits des lesbiennes et gais

[Renseignements en français, notice 41.]

✤ Ottawa, Ont. Formed 1975. Disbanded 1980.

The Canadian Lesbian and Gay Rights Coalition (CLGRC) was a coalition of lesbian and gay organizations. CLGRC's primary objectives were "the removal of all federal legislation which permits, condones, or encourages discrimination against homosexuals" and "the implementation of legislatively guaranteed civil rights for gay people." (Source: CLGRC statement of principles, 1978.) Until 1978 the coalition was called the National Gay Rights Coalition / Coalition nationale pour les droits des homosexuels (NGRC/CNDH). The coalition held annual conferences.

Collection (a)

LOCATION OF RECORDS: Canadian Gay Archives. (See Appendix for address.)

COLLECTION NAME: Canadian Lesbian and Gay Rights Coalition; CLGRC Reference Material; Conf.: Celebration '79: 7th Annual Conference for Lesbians and Gay Men; Conf.: National Conference of Lesbians and Gay Men. 8th Annual. Celebration '80. Calgary; National Gay Rights Coalition; Conf.: National Gay Conf. 3rd Annual, Ottawa, 1975; Conf.: National Gay Conf. 5th Annual. Saskatoon, 1977; Conf.: National Gay Conf. 6th Annual. Halifax '78 (vertical files).

RECORDS: Conference records, statements of principles, financial records, press releases, agenda, newsletters, membership lists, clippings, correspondence, resolutions, flyers, pamphlets, stickers, brief, annual report, chronology, address, fact sheet, form, petition, position paper, workshop material, questionnaire, proposal, 1975-1980.

AMOUNT: Approx. 10 cm.

CONDITION: Good.

Collection (b)

LOCATION OF RECORDS: Canadian Gay Archives.

COLLECTION NAME: Forms part of: Douglas Whitfield collection (88-050).

RECORDS: Conference records, 1979-1980.

Collection (c)

LOCATION OF RECORDS: Canadian Women's Movement Archives Collection,

Morisset Library Special Collections, University of Ottawa. (See Appendix for address.)
COLLECTION NAME: Conf.: National Gay Coalition Conference, June 1978, Halifax, N.S.
RECORDS: Conference records, 1978.
AMOUNT: 1 cm.
ACCESS: Restricted; conditional access negotiable.

25. Canadian Library Association. Gay Interest Group

✣ Formed 1980. Disbanded.

The Gay Interest Group (GIG) of the Canadian Library Association (CLA) works to develop communication among gay men and lesbians working in or using Canadian libraries and to facilitate access to sources of information for lesbians and gay men.

LOCATION OF RECORDS: Canadian Gay Archives. (See Appendix for address.)
COLLECTION NAME: Canadian Library Association. Gay Interest Group (vertical file); A.E. Millward (90-074); John R. Smith (91-106); some records form part of: Jim Thomas collection (89-133).
RECORDS: Minutes, correspondence, reports, clippings, resource sheets, announcements, bibliographies, press releases, membership forms, flyers, miscellaneous records, 1979-1989.

26. Canadian Mental Health Association. Women and Mental Health Committee

✣ Toronto, Ont.

The Canadian Mental Health Association (CMHA), established in 1918, is dedicated to the promotion of mental health.

LOCATION OF RECORDS: Griffin-Greenland Collection on the History of Canadian Psychiatry, Queen Street Mental Health Centre. (See Appendix for address.)
COLLECTION NAME: Forms part of: Canadian Mental Health Association collection (box 19, folder 9).
RECORDS: Report, 1987.
AMOUNT: 124 pages.
CONDITION: Good.
ACCESS: The report can be examined with the permission of the general director of the CMHA.

27. Canadian Native Sisterhood Organization

✣ Kingston, Ont.

This group of Native women prisoners at the Penitentiary for Women published a periodical, *Native Sisterhood*.

LOCATION OF RECORDS: Canadian Women's Movement Archives Collection, Morisset Library Special Collections, University of Ottawa. (See Appendix for address.)
COLLECTION NAME: Native Sisterhood.
RECORDS: Periodical (*Native Sisterhood*), 1972.
AMOUNT: 1 item.
ACCESS: No restrictions.

28. Canadian Nurses Association / Association des infirmières et infirmiers du Canada

[Renseignements en français, notice 8.]

✣ Ottawa, Ont. Formed 1908.

The Canadian Nurses Association (CNA) is a federation of provincial and territorial nursing associations. Its goals include speaking for Canadian nurses and providing leadership on issues related to the working lives of nurses. The association was originally called the Canadian National Association of Trained Nurses (CNATN). It publishes a professional journal, *The Canadian Nurse*, which was founded in 1905. (Source: *Guide to the Historical Collections of the Canadian Nurses Association*. — Ottawa: Canadian Nurses Association, 1987.)

Collection (a)

LOCATION OF RECORDS: Canadian Nurses Association Archives. (See Appendix for address.)
RECORDS: Minutes, reports, convention records, records of annual meetings, periodicals, correspondence, historical notes, speeches, abstracts, photographs, videotapes, slide-sound productions, overhead transparencies, sound recordings, miscellaneous records, 1905-1991.
AMOUNT: Approx. 15 m of text, 11 reels of microfilm.
ACCESS: Researchers will be asked to use microfilm in place of some originals; reports are restricted for the most recent ten years.
FINDING AID: *Guide to the Historical Collections of the Canadian Nurses Association*.

Collection (b)

LOCATION OF RECORDS: National Archives of Canada. (See Appendix for address.)
COLLECTION NAME: Canadian Nurses Association (MG 28, I 248).
RECORDS: Please see the note about National Archives of Canada collections, in entry # 2.

29. Canadian Organization for the Rights of Prostitutes

[See also entry # 712 (in Part II), which lists other records of this organization.]

✣ Toronto, Ont. Formed 1983.

The Canadian Organization for the Rights of Prostitutes (CORP) campaigns for the decriminalization of prostitution and for an end to the stigmatization of prostitutes. CORP's goals are to have prostitution seen as work and to have prostitutes recognized as independent business people.

LOCATION OF RECORDS: Canadian Women's Movement Archives Collection, Morisset Library Special Collections, University of Ottawa. (See Appendix for address.)
COLLECTION NAME: SR 31/1.
RECORDS: Sound recording (interview), 1986.
AMOUNT: 1 sound recording.
ACCESS: No restrictions.

30. Canadian Rape Crisis Centres / Centres canadiens de viol

[Renseignements en français, notice 39.]

✣ Formed [1975?].

This was a national network of sexual assault centres.

LOCATION OF RECORDS: Canadian Women's Movement Archives Collection, Morisset Library Special Collections, University of Ottawa. (See Appendix for address.)
COLLECTION NAME: Canadian Rape Crisis Centres.

RECORDS: Minutes, 1977-1978; correspondence, contact list, 1975; submission, newsletters, 1978; manuals, position papers, flyers.
AMOUNT: 15 cm.
CONDITION: Good.
ACCESS: No restrictions.

31. Canadian Research Institute for the Advancement of Women / Institut canadien de recherches sur les femmes

[Renseignements en français, notice 64.]

[See also entry # 713 (in Part II), which lists other records of this organization.]

✣ Ottawa, Ont. Formed 1976.

This organization, also known as CRIAW, encourages, co-ordinates, and disseminates research into women's experience and works to ensure an equal place for women and women's experience in the body of knowledge and research about Canada.

Collection (a)

LOCATION OF RECORDS: Public Archives of Nova Scotia. (See Appendix for address.)
COLLECTION NAME: Forms part of: Muriel Duckworth collection (MG 1, volumes 2905-2906).
RECORDS: Statement of aims, constitution and by-laws, programme, 1976; minutes, agendas, financial records, 1976-1981; reports, 1976, [ca. 1980]; records of annual general meetings, 1978-1981; conference records, 1983; annual reports, 1979-1981; correspondence, 1975-1983; press releases, 1976-1984; study, proposals, 1981; position papers, 1979-1980; membership and mailing lists, research papers, pamphlets, miscellaneous records.
FINDING AID: Finding aid available for Muriel Duckworth collection.

Collection (b)

LOCATION OF RECORDS: Northwest Territories Archives. (See Appendix for address.)
COLLECTION NAME: Canadian Research Council for the Advancement of Women / Institut canadien de recherches sur les femmes (13th : 1989 : Yellowknife) (N91-008).
RECORDS: Sound recordings (conference proceedings), 1989.
AMOUNT: 32 items.
ACCESS: No restrictions.
FINDING AID: Conference programme and list of cassettes available.

32. Canadian Textile and Chemical Union / Syndicat canadien des travailleurs du textile et de la chimie

[Renseignements en français, notice 88.]

✣ Brantford, Ont.

LOCATION OF RECORDS: National Archives of Canada. (See Appendix for address.)
COLLECTION NAME: Forms part of: Frank and Libbie Park collection (MG 31, K 9, volume 29 / 419-30/441).
RECORDS: Please see the note about National Archives of Canada collections, in entry # 2.

33. Canadian Textile Council / Conseil canadien du textile

[Renseignements en français, notice 49.]

✣ Formed [1952?].

LOCATION OF RECORDS: National Archives of Canada. (See Appendix for address.)
COLLECTION NAME: Forms part of: Madeleine Parent and R. Kent Rowley collection (MG 31, B 19, volumes 3-4, 15-16).
RECORDS: Please see the note about National Archives of Canada collections, in entry # 2.

34. Canadian Women's Coalition to Repeal the Abortion Laws

✣ Toronto, Ont. Formed 1972. Disbanded [ca. 1974].

The coalition (also called CWCRAL) demanded the repeal of sections of the Criminal Code dealing with abortion. It also advocated sex education and access to birth control.

Collection (a)

LOCATION OF RECORDS: University of Toronto Archives. (See Appendix for address.)
COLLECTION NAME: Forms part of: Marianne Holder collection (UTA B88-0075/006).
RECORDS: Proposals, correspondence, 1973; periodicals (*Spokeswoman*, 1972-1973); brief, 1972; petition, pamphlet, flyers, policy statements, conference records, questionnaire, [ca. 1973].
AMOUNT: 2 cm.
CONDITION: Good.
ACCESS: No restrictions.
FINDING AID: Box list available for Holder collection.

Collection (b)

LOCATION OF RECORDS: Canadian Women's Movement Archives Collection, Morisset Library Special Collections, University of Ottawa. (See Appendix for address.)
COLLECTION NAME: Canadian Women's Coalition to Repeal the Abortion Laws.
RECORDS: Periodicals (*Spokeswoman*, 1972-1973); pamphlet, 1972; clippings, 1973; brief, flyers.
AMOUNT: 5 mm.
CONDITION: Fair.
ACCESS: No restrictions.

35. Canadian Women's Movement Archives / Archives canadiennes du mouvement des femmes

[Renseignements en français, notice 3.]

✣ Toronto, Ont. Formed 1977.

The Canadian Women's Movement Archives (CWMA) collects material from the contemporary (post-1960) Canadian women's movement. The CWMA is administered by the Women's Information Centre of Toronto. [See also Women's Information Centre of Toronto (559).]

LOCATION OF RECORDS: Canadian Women's Movement Archives Collection, Morisset Library Special Collections, University of Ottawa. (See Appendix for address.)
COLLECTION NAME: Canadian Women's Movement Archives.
RECORDS: Minutes, 1982-1992; correspondence, 1977-1992; reports, clippings, pamphlets, photographs, sound recordings, finding aids, 1980-1992; log-books, 1984-1992; mailing lists, 1986-1992; grant applications, administrative files, project files, posters, button, T-shirts, miscellaneous records.

AMOUNT: Approx. 4 m.
CONDITION: Good.
ACCESS: No restrictions.

COLLECTION NAME: Forms part of: Charlotte Elizabeth Whitton collection (MG 30, E 256).
RECORDS: Please see the note about National Archives of Canada collections, in entry # 2.

36. Canadian Women's Music and Cultural Festival

✢ Winnipeg, Man. Formed 1984. Disbanded [198-].

The Canadian Women's Music and Cultural Festival, a non-profit organization, produced the Canadian Women's Festival / Festival des femmes canadiennes. The organization aimed "to promote the status of women in the Canadian cultural arena, with particular emphasis on those performers who are largely unrecognized by the general public." (Source: Canadian Women's Music and Cultural Festival proposal, 1986.)

LOCATION OF RECORDS: Canadian Women's Movement Archives Collection, Morisset Library Special Collections, University of Ottawa. (See Appendix for address.)
COLLECTION NAME: Canadian Women's Music and Cultural Festival.
RECORDS: Minutes, financial records, clippings, 1985-1986; pamphlets, flyers, 1984-1986; programmes, 1984-1985; report, tickets, 1985; membership list, proposals, notes, 1986; button, 1984; correspondence, order form, posters, cap.
AMOUNT: 5 cm of text, 3 posters, 1 button, 1 cap.
CONDITION: Good.
ACCESS: No restrictions.

37. Canadian Women's Press Club

✢ Formed 1904.

The Canadian Women's Press Club (CWPC) was an association of women writers, mainly journalists. In 1971 it opened its membership to men and changed its name to the Media Club of Canada. (Source: *The Canadian Encyclopedia*. — Edmonton: Hurtig Publishers, 1985.)

Collection (a)
LOCATION OF RECORDS: National Archives of Canada. (See Appendix for address.)
COLLECTION NAME: Media Club of Canada (MG 28, I 232).
RECORDS: Please see the note about National Archives of Canada collections, in entry # 2.

Collection (b)
LOCATION OF RECORDS: National Archives of Canada.
COLLECTION NAME: Forms part of: Kathleen Blake "Kit" Coleman collection (MG 29, D 112).
RECORDS: Please see the note about National Archives of Canada collections, in entry # 2.

Collection (c)
LOCATION OF RECORDS: National Archives of Canada.
COLLECTION NAME: Forms part of: Henry Burton and Abbie Lyon Sharman collection (MG 30, C 224).
RECORDS: Please see the note about National Archives of Canada collections, in entry # 2.

Collection (d)
LOCATION OF RECORDS: National Archives of Canada.
COLLECTION NAME: Forms part of: Olha Woycenko collection (MG 30, D 212).
RECORDS: Please see the note about National Archives of Canada collections, in entry # 2.

Collection (e)
LOCATION OF RECORDS: National Archives of Canada.

38. Centre international MATCH / MATCH International Centre

[For English entry, see # 70.]

[Voir aussi la notice 717 (dans la partie II) pour autres documents de ce groupe.]

✢ Ottawa (Ont.). Groupe fondé 1976.

Le Centre international MATCH est un organisme féministe en développement qui a pour but d'établir un réseau d'échange entre les femmes du Canada et celles des pays en voie de développement. L'organisme veut éliminer la violence faite aux femmes globalement, entre autres objectifs.

LIEU DE CONSULTATION : Archives nationales du Canada. (Voir Annexe pour l'adresse.)
NOM DU FONDS : Fait partie du fonds Ruth Marion (Rolph) Bell (MG 31, K 22, tomes 9-10).
MATÉRIEL : Voir la note sur les fonds des Archives nationales du Canada, notice 4.

39. Centres canadiens de viol / Canadian Rape Crisis Centres

[For English entry, see # 30.]

✢ Groupe fondé [1975?].

Les Centres canadiens de viol constituaient un réseau national de centres contre les agressions sexuelles.

LIEU DE CONSULTATION : Fonds des Archives canadiennes du mouvement des femmes, Collections spéciales de la Bibliothèque Morisset, Université d'Ottawa. (Voir Annexe pour l'adresse.)
NOM DU FONDS : Canadian Rape Crisis Centres.
MATÉRIEL : Procès-verbaux, 1977-1978; correspondance, liste de contacts, 1975; soumission, bulletins, 1978; manuels, exposés de position, tracts.
QUANTITÉ : 15 cm.
ÉTAT : Bon.
ACCÈS : Aucune restriction.

40. Coalition canadienne contre la pornographie dans les médias / Canadian Coalition against Media Pornography

[For English entry, see # 18.]

✢ Ottawa (Ont.). Groupe fondé 1983. Dissous 1989.

LIEU DE CONSULTATION : Archives nationales du Canada. (Voir Annexe pour l'adresse.)
NOM DU FONDS : Coalition canadienne contre la pornographie dans les médias (MG 28, I 459).
MATÉRIEL : Voir la note sur les fonds des Archives nationales du Canada, notice 4.

NATIONAL ORGANIZATIONS / GROUPES PANCANADIENS

41. Coalition canadienne pour les droits des lesbiennes et gais / Canadian Lesbian and Gay Rights Coalition

[For English entry, see # 24.]

✣ Ottawa (Ont.). Groupe fondé 1975. Dissous 1980.

La Coalition canadienne pour les droits des lesbiennes et gais (CCDLG) était une coalition d'organismes lesbiens et gais. Les principaux objectifs de la CCDLG étaient : « le retrait de toutes lois fédérales qui permettent, approuvent ou encouragent la discrimination envers les lesbiennes et hommes gais » et « la formulation de droits civiques pour tout(e) homosexuel(le), garantis par la loi ». (Source : déclaration de principes de la CCDLG, 1978.) Jusqu'en 1978, la coalition s'appelait la Coalition nationale pour les droits des homosexuels/National Gay Rights Coalition (CNDH/NGRC). La coalition a tenu des congrès annuels.

Fonds (a)

LIEU DE CONSULTATION : Canadian Gay Archives. (Voir Annexe pour l'adresse.)

NOM DU FONDS : Canadian Lesbian and Gay Rights Coalition; CLGRC Reference Material; Conf.: Celebration '79: 7th Annual Conference for Lesbians and Gay Men; Conf.: National Conference of Lesbians and Gay Men. 8th Annual. Celebration '80. Calgary; National Gay Rights Coalition; Conf.: National Gay Conf. 3rd Annual, Ottawa, 1975; Conf.: National Gay Conf. 5th Annual. Saskatoon, 1977; Conf.: National Gay Conf. 6th Annual. Halifax '78 (vertical files).

MATÉRIEL : Documents de congrès, déclarations de principes, documents financiers, communiqués de presse, ordre du jour, bulletins, listes de membres, coupures de presse, correspondance, résolutions, tracts, dépliants, autocollants, mémoire, rapport annuel, historique, discours, feuille de renseignements, formulaire, pétition, exposé de position, matériel pour ateliers, questionnaire, proposition, 1975-1980.

QUANTITÉ : Env. 10 cm.

ÉTAT : Bon.

Fonds (b)

LIEU DE CONSULTATION : Canadian Gay Archives.

NOM DU FONDS : Fait partie du fonds Douglas Whitfield (88-050).

MATÉRIEL : Documents de congrès, 1979-1980.

Fonds (c)

LIEU DE CONSULTATION : Fonds des Archives canadiennes du mouvement des femmes, Collections spéciales de la Bibliothèque Morisset, Université d'Ottawa. (Voir Annexe pour l'adresse.)

NOM DU FONDS : Conf.: National Gay Coalition Conference, June 1978, Halifax, N.S.

MATÉRIEL : Documents de congrès, 1978.

QUANTITÉ : 1 cm.

ACCÈS : Avec restriction. Accès conditionnel négociable.

42. Coalition des associations de femmes canadiennes : Le Congrès international sur la paix / Coalition of Canadian Women's Groups: International Peace Conference

[For English entry, see # 43.]

✣ Halifax (N.-É.). Groupe fondé 1984. Dissous 1985.

Cette coalition a organisé un congrès intitulé « La Sécurité : une question d'urgence : les alternatives des femmes pour négocier la paix », qui a eu lieu à Halifax en 1985. Des représentantes de vingt-six organisations nationales de femmes ont participé à la coalition, qui a été inaugurée à l'invitation de la Voix des femmes. [Voir aussi La Voix des femmes/Voice of Women (93).]

LIEU DE CONSULTATION : Public Archives of Nova Scotia. (Voir Annexe pour l'adresse.)

NOM DU FONDS : Women's International Peace Conference (MG 20, volumes 1750-1757).

MATÉRIEL : Documents de congrès (enregistrements sonores, programmes, invitations, documents financiers, documents divers), 1984-1985.

QUANTITÉ : 1,8 m.

ACCÈS : Aucune restriction.

INSTRUMENT DE RECHERCHE : Instrument de recherche disponible.

43. Coalition of Canadian Women's Groups: International Peace Conference / Coalition des associations de femmes canadiennes : Le Congrès international sur la paix

[Renseignements en français, notice 42.]

✣ Halifax, N.S. Formed 1984. Disbanded 1985.

This coalition organized the Women's International Peace Conference, held in Halifax in 1985. The conference's title was "The Urgency for True Security: Women's Alternatives for Negotiating Peace." The coalition (initiated by Voice of Women) was made up of representatives of twenty-six national women's organizations. [See also Voice of Women/La Voix des femmes (92).]

LOCATION OF RECORDS: Public Archives of Nova Scotia. (See Appendix for address.)

COLLECTION NAME: Women's International Peace Conference (MG 20, volumes 1750-1757).

RECORDS: Conference records (sound recordings, programmes, invitations, financial records, miscellaneous records), 1984-1985.

AMOUNT: 1.8 m.

ACCESS: No restrictions.

FINDING AID: Finding aid available.

44. Comité canadien d'action sur le statut de la femme / National Action Committee on the Status of Women

[For English entry, see # 71.]

[Voir aussi la notice 720 (dans la partie II) pour autres documents de ce groupe.]

✣ Toronto (Ont.). Groupe fondé 1971.

Le Comité canadien d'action sur le statut de la femme (CCA) est le plus grand organisme de femmes au Canada, regroupant plus de 450 associations et groupes autonomes de tous les coins du pays. Ses priorités sont de susciter les contacts et la collaboration entre les groupes de femmes, de favoriser des changements politiques et législatifs et de sensibiliser le public aux problèmes des femmes. À ses débuts, le CCA portait le nom de National Ad Hoc Action Committee on the Status of Women. Son nom actuel a été adopté en 1972. [Voir aussi Évaluation-Médias/MediaWatch (727).]

Fonds (a)

LIEU DE CONSULTATION : Fonds des Archives canadiennes du mouvement des femmes, Collections spéciales de la Bibliothèque Morisset, Université d'Ottawa. (Voir Annexe pour l'adresse.)

NOM DU FONDS : National Action Committee on the Status of Women.

MATÉRIEL : Statuts et règlements, 1978, 1983-1984, 1986-1988; documents d'assemblées annuelles, 1974-1990; coupures de presse, 1973-1990; correspondance, 1971-1991; rapports, 1971, 1976-1980, 1982, 1985-1989; procès-verbaux, 1971-1978, 1980-1981, 1984-1989; périodiques (*La Revue Statut de la femme/Status of Women News*, 1973-1985; *Action féministe/Feminist Action*, 1985-1991; *Action Bulletin Action*, 1985-1990; *À

PART I: RECORDS HELD BY ARCHIVES / PARTIE I : FONDS DÉTENUS PAR DES ARCHIVES

Buttons / Macarons
CWMA Collection / Fonds de l'ACMF

NATIONAL ORGANIZATIONS / GROUPES PANCANADIENS

l'*action*/*Action Now*, 1990-1991; *Bulletin*, 1975; *CCA Memo*/*NAC Memo*, 1975-1985; *NAC Housing Newsletter*, 1987-1989, 1991); documents de travail, 1982-1983, 1985-1986; propositions, 1977, 1979-1980, 1985, 1987-1989; mémoires, 1975, 1978, 1980-1981, 1984-1987; soumissions, 1972-1973, 1975, 1986; communications, 1977-1980, 1983, 1986-1987; énoncés de politiques, 1979-1980, 1984-1989; documents financiers, 1977-1978, 1985-1988; index des résolutions, 1987-1988; index des recommandations, 1978; exposés de position, 1986, 1988; discours, 1977, 1980; présentation radiophonique, 1989; demande de subvention, 1985; articles, 1979, 1983, 1986-1989; documents de congrès, 1972; ordres du jour, 1973, 1976-1977, 1982, 1988-1989; billets, 1985-1986, 1988-1989; communiqués de presse, 1973, 1976, 1978-1981, 1985-1989; directives, 1981; listes de membres, 1980, 1986-1989; invitations, 1984, 1986-1987; T-shirt, questionnaire-réponses, 1988; circulaires d'information, 1973, 1985; avis de convocation, 1983, 1987; publicité, brochures, tracts, notes, questionnaires, formulaires, listes d'envoi, règlements, manuel, affiches, macarons, documents divers.

QUANTITÉ : 1,74 m de texte, 4 affiches, 1 T-shirt, 8 macarons.
ACCÈS : Aucune restriction.

Fonds (b)

LIEU DE CONSULTATION : Archives nationales du Canada. (Voir Annexe pour l'adresse.)
NOM DU FONDS : Fait partie du fonds Dorothy Flaherty (MG 31, K 25).
MATÉRIEL : Voir la note sur les fonds des Archives nationales du Canada, notice 4.

Fonds (c)

LIEU DE CONSULTATION : Archives nationales du Canada.
NOM DU FONDS : Fait partie du fonds Ruth Marion (Rolph) Bell (MG 31, K 22, tomes 8-9).
MATÉRIEL : Voir la note sur les fonds des Archives nationales du Canada, notice 4.

Fonds (d)

LIEU DE CONSULTATION : Archives nationales du Canada.
NOM DU FONDS : Fait partie du fonds Elsie Gregory MacGill (MG 31, K 7, tome 10).
MATÉRIEL : Voir la note sur les fonds des Archives nationales du Canada, notice 4.

Fonds (e)

LIEU DE CONSULTATION : Region of Peel Archives. (Voir Annexe pour l'adresse.)
NOM DU FONDS : Fait partie du fonds Helen Tucker (91.0058, série 5, boîte 1).
MATÉRIEL : Documents divers, 1973-1975.
QUANTITÉ : 2 cm.
ACCÈS : Avec certaines restrictions.
INSTRUMENT DE RECHERCHE : Instrument de recherche : fonds Helen Tucker disponible.

45. Comité canadien de l'histoire des femmes / Canadian Committee on Women's History

[For English entry, see # 20.]

✢ Groupe fondé 1975.

LIEU DE CONSULTATION : Archives nationales du Canada. (Voir Annexe pour l'adresse.)
NOM DU FONDS : Comité canadien de l'histoire des femmes (MG 28, I 57).
MATÉRIEL : Voir la note sur les fonds des Archives nationales du Canada, notice 4.

46. Comité canadien sur la situation de la femme / Canadian Committee on the Status of Women

[For English entry, see # 19.]

Fonds (a)

LIEU DE CONSULTATION : Archives nationales du Canada. (Voir Annexe pour l'adresse.)
NOM DU FONDS : Fait partie du fonds Margaret MacLellan (MG 31, E 17).
MATÉRIEL : Voir la note sur les fonds des Archives nationales du Canada, notice 4.

Fonds (b)

LIEU DE CONSULTATION : Archives nationales du Canada.
NOM DU FONDS : Fait partie du fonds Dorothy Eva Flaherty (MG 31, K 25).
MATÉRIEL : Voir la note sur les fonds des Archives nationales du Canada, notice 4.

47. Communications Union Canada / Syndicat des communications Canada

[Renseignements en français, notice 89.]

✢ Formed 1946. Disbanded 1980.

LOCATION OF RECORDS: National Archives of Canada. (See Appendix for address.)
COLLECTION NAME: Communications Union Canada (MG 28, I 329).
RECORDS: Please see the note about National Archives of Canada collections, in entry # 2.

48. Congrès canadien pour la promotion des études chez la femme / Canadian Congress for Learning Opportunities for Women

[For English entry, see # 21.]

[Voir aussi la notice 721 (dans la partie II) pour autres documents de ce groupe.]

✢ Toronto (Ont.). Groupe fondé 1973.

Le Congrès canadien pour la promotion des études chez la femme (CCPEF) est un organisme national qui vise à promouvoir les possibilités d'études pour les femmes. Il favorise la création de réseaux, identifie les obstacles, fait connaître les problèmes cruciaux, organise des congrès et publie un périodique, *Women's Education des femmes*. Le CCPEF s'appelait à ses débuts Canadian Committee on Learning Opportunities for Women.

Fonds (a)

LIEU DE CONSULTATION : Saskatchewan Archives Board, Regina. (Voir Annexe pour l'adresse.)
NOM DU FONDS : Canadian Congress for Learning Opportunities for Women (R-1035).
MATÉRIEL : Correspondance, procès-verbaux, rapports, circulaires d'information, documents divers, [ca 1978]-1983.
QUANTITÉ : 90 cm.
INSTRUMENT DE RECHERCHE : Guide no. GR 141.

Fonds (b)

LIEU DE CONSULTATION : Fonds des Archives canadiennes du mouvement des femmes, Collections spéciales de la Bibliothèque Morisset, Université d'Ottawa. (Voir Annexe pour l'adresse.)
NOM DU FONDS : Canadian Congress for Learning Opportunities for Women.
MATÉRIEL : Ordres du jour, 1981, 1986; invitation, 1980; communiqués de presse, 1981, 1985; propositions, 1976-1978; mémoires, 1979-1980, 1984; communication, 1981; tracts, 1978-1979, 1983-1984, 1987-1988, 1991; dépliants, 1981, [ca 1990]; programme de congrès, 1984;

ébauche de projet, 1977; liste de membres, 1987; listes d'envoi, 1980-1982; matériel pour séminaires, 1973, 1975, 1977; périodiques, 1978-1987; objectifs, procès-verbaux, correspondance, rapports, enquête, questionnaires, document préparatoire, dossiers de projets, liste de publications, publicité, coupure de presse, formulaire.

QUANTITÉ : 18,5 cm.

ÉTAT : Bon.

ACCÈS : Aucune restriction.

49. Conseil canadien du textile / Canadian Textile Council

[For English entry, see # 33.]

✣ Groupe fondé [1952?].

LIEU DE CONSULTATION : Archives nationales du Canada. (Voir Annexe pour l'adresse.)

NOM DU FONDS : Fait partie du fonds Madeleine Parent et R. Kent Rowley (MG 31, B 19, tomes 3-4, 15-16).

MATÉRIEL : Voir la note sur les fonds des Archives nationales du Canada, notice 4.

50. Documentation sur la recherche féministe / Resources for Feminist Research

[For English entry, see # 85.]

[Voir aussi la notice 726 (dans la partie II) pour autres documents de ce groupe.]

✣ Toronto (Ont.). Groupe fondé 1972.

Resources for Feminist Research/Documentation sur la recherche féministe (RFR/DRF) est un périodique canadien sur la recherche féministe internationale. Jusqu'en 1979, cette revue portait le nom de *Canadian Newsletter of Research on Women/Recherches sur la femme : Bulletin d'information canadien*.

LIEU DE CONSULTATION : Fonds des Archives canadiennes du mouvement des femmes, Collections spéciales de la Bibliothèque Morisset, Université d'Ottawa. (Voir Annexe pour l'adresse.)

NOM DU FONDS : Resources for Feminist Research/Documentation sur la recherche féministe.

MATÉRIEL : Brouillons d'articles (pour le numéro de mars 1983, « Être Lesbienne »), [ca 1982]; proposition, 1981; correspondance, questionnaires, formulaires, tracts, dépliants, affiches.

QUANTITÉ : 5 cm de texte, 2 affiches.

ACCÈS : Aucune restriction.

51. Federated Women's Institutes of Canada

✣ Ottawa, Ont. Formed 1919.

LOCATION OF RECORDS: National Archives of Canada. (See Appendix for address.)

COLLECTION NAME: Federated Women's Institutes of Canada (MG 28, I 316).

RECORDS: Please see the note about National Archives of Canada collections, in entry # 2.

52. Fédération canadienne des clubs de femmes de carrières libérales et commerciales / Canadian Federation of Business and Professional Women's Clubs

[For English entry, see # 22.]

✣ Ottawa (Ont.). Groupe fondé 1930.

La fédération est une organisation-cadre qui regroupe des clubs de femmes d'affaires et de professionnelles à travers le Canada.

Fonds (a)

LIEU DE CONSULTATION : Archives nationales du Canada. (Voir Annexe pour l'adresse.)

NOM DU FONDS : Fédération canadienne des clubs de femmes de carrières libérales et commerciales (MG 28, I 55).

MATÉRIEL : Voir la note sur les fonds des Archives nationales du Canada, notice 4.

Fonds (b)

LIEU DE CONSULTATION : Archives nationales du Canada.

NOM DU FONDS : Fait partie du fonds Dorothy Heneker (MG 30, C 128).

MATÉRIEL : Voir la note sur les fonds des Archives nationales du Canada, notice 4.

Fonds (c)

LIEU DE CONSULTATION : Archives nationales du Canada.

NOM DU FONDS : Fait partie du fonds Charlotte Elizabeth Whitton (MG 30, E 256).

MATÉRIEL : Voir la note sur les fonds des Archives nationales du Canada, notice 4.

Fonds (d)

LIEU DE CONSULTATION : Saskatchewan Archives Board, Regina. (Voir Annexe pour l'adresse.)

NOM DU FONDS : Fait partie du fonds Ruth S. McGill.

MATÉRIEL : Constitution en société, 1930; statuts et règlements, 1947-1963; historique de l'association, [ca 1930]-1945; procès-verbaux, ordres du jour, 1962-1965; correspondance, 1956-1964; bulletins, [ca 1961]-1965; dossiers des membres, 1935-1965; mémoires, 1953-1963; rapports, 1935-1964; publications, 1941-1962; discours, [ca 1944]-1964; documents financiers, résolutions, communiqués de presse, 1962-1964; documents de congrès, 1948-1964; coupures de presse, [ca 1933]-1965; listes, 1946-1965; dépliants, brochures, [ca 1955]-1965; procédures, documents divers.

QUANTITÉ : 44 cm.

ACCÈS : Aucune restriction.

INSTRUMENT DE RECHERCHE : « A Checklist of the Papers of Ruth S. McGill » (Guide no. GR 351).

53. Fédération canadienne des femmes diplômées des universités / Canadian Federation of University Women

[For English entry, see # 23.]

✣ Ottawa (Ont.). Groupe fondé 1919.

La Fédération canadienne des femmes diplômées des universités est une fédération de clubs dont les membres sont des diplômées d'universités. La fédération se propose, entre autres buts, d'encourager le haut-savoir chez les femmes et de sauvegarder les droits des femmes. (Source : *The Canadian Encyclopedia*. — Edmonton : Hurtig Publishers, 1985.)

Fonds (a)

LIEU DE CONSULTATION : Archives nationales du Canada. (Voir Annexe pour l'adresse.)

NOM DU FONDS : Fédération canadienne des femmes diplômées des universités (MG 28, I 196).

MATÉRIEL : Voir la note sur les fonds des Archives nationales du Canada, notice 4.

Fonds (b)

LIEU DE CONSULTATION : Archives nationales du Canada.

NOM DU FONDS : Fait partie du fonds Miriam Sheridan (MG 31, K 27).

MATÉRIEL : Voir la note sur les fonds des Archives nationales du Canada, notice 4.

Fonds (c)

LIEU DE CONSULTATION : Archives nationales du Canada.

NOM DU FONDS : Fait partie du fonds Marion Creelman Savage (MG 30, C 92).

MATÉRIEL : Voir la note sur les fonds des Archives nationales du Canada, notice 4.

Fonds (d)

LIEU DE CONSULTATION : Archives nationales du Canada.

NOM DU FONDS : Fait partie du fonds Margaret MacLellan (MG 31, E 17).

MATÉRIEL : Voir la note sur les fonds des Archives nationales du Canada, notice 4.

Fonds (e)

LIEU DE CONSULTATION : Archives nationales du Canada.

NOM DU FONDS : Fait partie du fonds Ruth Marion (Rolph) Bell (MG 31, K 22, tomes 1-7).

MATÉRIEL : Voir la note sur les fonds des Archives nationales du Canada, notice 4.

Fonds (f)

LIEU DE CONSULTATION : Archives nationales du Canada.

NOM DU FONDS : Fait partie du fonds Gladys Harvey (MG 31, K 26).

MATÉRIEL : Voir la note sur les fonds des Archives nationales du Canada, notice 4.

Fonds (g)

LIEU DE CONSULTATION : Archives nationales du Canada.

NOM DU FONDS : Fait partie du fonds Dorothy Eva Flaherty (MG 31, K 25).

MATÉRIEL : Voir la note sur les fonds des Archives nationales du Canada, notice 4.

54. Fédération des femmes médecins du Canada / Federation of Medical Women of Canada

[For English entry, see # 57.]

✥ Ottawa (Ont.). Groupe fondé 1924.

LIEU DE CONSULTATION : Archives nationales du Canada. (Voir Annexe pour l'adresse.)

NOM DU FONDS : Fédération des femmes médecins du Canada (MG 28, I 324).

MATÉRIEL : Voir la note sur les fonds des Archives nationales du Canada, notice 4.

55. Fédération nationale des femmes canadiennes-françaises

✥ Ottawa (Ont.). Groupe fondé 1914.

La Fédération nationale des femmes canadiennes-françaises (FNFCF) (appellée auparavant la Fédération des femmes canadiennes-françaises ou FFCF) poursuit, entre autres, les buts suivants : sensibiliser les milieux minoritaires aux problèmes collectifs spécifiques des femmes francophones et impliquer les femmes francophones dans une action communautaire propre à améliorer leur condition.

Fonds (a)

LIEU DE CONSULTATION : Centre de recherche en civilisation canadienne-française, Université d'Ottawa. (Voir Annexe pour l'adresse.)

NOM DU FONDS : Fédération nationale des femmes canadiennes-françaises.

MATÉRIEL : Constitution en société, statuts et règlements, notes historiques, rapports annuels, plans d'action, documents d'assemblées générales, documents de colloques, documents de congrès, documents administratifs, dossiers d'information, coupures de presse, photographies, enregistrements sonores, rubans, tampons, clef, affiches, broches, documents divers, 1914-1986.

QUANTITÉ : 11 m de texte, 770 photographies, 68 enregistrements sonores.

ACCÈS : Accessible.

INSTRUMENT DE RECHERCHE : « Répertoire numérique détaillé du fonds de la Fédération nationale des femmes canadiennes-françaises ».

Fonds (b)

LIEU DE CONSULTATION : Archives nationales du Canada. (Voir Annexe pour l'adresse.)

NOM DU FONDS : Fédération des femmes canadiennes-françaises (MG 28, I 231).

MATÉRIEL : Voir la note sur les fonds des Archives nationales du Canada, notice 4.

56. Fédération nationale des femmes libérales du Canada / Women's Liberal Federation of Canada

[For English entry, see # 98.]

✥ Groupe fondé 1928. Dissous 1970.

LIEU DE CONSULTATION : Archives nationales du Canada. (Voir Annexe pour l'adresse.)

NOM DU FONDS : Fait partie du fonds du Parti libéral du Canada (MG 28, IV 3).

MATÉRIEL : Voir la note sur les fonds des Archives nationales du Canada, notice 4.

57. Federation of Medical Women of Canada / Fédération des femmes médecins du Canada

[Renseignements en français, notice 54.]

✥ Ottawa, Ont. Formed 1924.

LOCATION OF RECORDS: National Archives of Canada. (See Appendix for address.)

COLLECTION NAME: Federation of Medical Women of Canada (MG 28, I 324).

RECORDS: Please see the note about National Archives of Canada collections, in entry # 2.

58. Feminist News Service

✥ Formed 1974. Disbanded [ca. 1976].

The Feminist News Service (FNS) distributed monthly newsletters about Canadian women to subscribing organizations and individuals. FNS grew out of a conference for journalists writing for feminist publications (the Women's Press Conference, held in Saskatoon in 1974). FNS was initially called the Ad Hoc Committee for a Feminist Information Network. Its French name was le Service d'information féministe.

LOCATION OF RECORDS: Canadian Women's Movement Archives Collection, Morisset Library Special Collections, University of Ottawa. (See Appendix for address.)

COLLECTION NAME: Feminist News Service.

RECORDS: Conference records, 1974-1975; correspondence, 1974-1976; newsletters (*Feminist News Service*, 1975-1976); press release, paste-ups, 1975; pamphlet, 1976; policy statement, style guide, mailing list, articles, clippings, reading lists, questionnaire, flyers, photographs, button.

AMOUNT: 15 cm of text, 28 photographs, 1 button.

CONDITION: Good.

ACCESS: No restrictions.

59. Feminist Party of Canada

✤ Toronto, Ont. Formed 1979. Disbanded 1982.

The founders of the Feminist Party of Canada (FPC) believed that other political parties had failed to respond adequately to women's concerns and that "women's full participation in the political arena [would] bring a new perspective and new direction to government." (Source: FPC flyer, 1979.) The party's French name was le Parti féministe du Canada.

LOCATION OF RECORDS: Canadian Women's Movement Archives Collection, Morisset Library Special Collections, University of Ottawa. (See Appendix for address.)

COLLECTION NAME: Feminist Party of Canada.

RECORDS: Statement of principles, organization history, booklet, pamphlet, press release, 1979; newsletters, 1979-1982; flyers, 1979-1981; clippings, 1979-1980; agenda, correspondence, 1980; membership forms, membership card, petition, information sheets, posters, button.

AMOUNT: 3 cm of text, 2 posters, 1 button.

CONDITION: Good.

ACCESS: No restrictions.

60. Feminist Publications of Ottawa

[See also entry # 732 (in Part II), which lists other records of this organization.]

✤ Ottawa, Ont. Formed 1976. Disbanded 1980.

Feminist Publications of Ottawa (FPO) published the newspaper *Upstream: An Ottawa Women's Publication*. In 1978 the newspaper became a national publication, changing its name to *Upstream: A Canadian Women's Publication*. FPO organized the Feminist Print Media Conference, held in Ottawa in 1980.

LOCATION OF RECORDS: Canadian Women's Movement Archives Collection, Morisset Library Special Collections, University of Ottawa. (See Appendix for address.)

COLLECTION NAME: Upstream.

RECORDS: Conference records, 1980; newspapers (*Upstream*, 1976-1980); correspondence, poster, 1978; publicity material.

AMOUNT: 15 cm of text, 1 poster.

CONDITION: Good.

ACCESS: No restrictions.

61. Fireweed: A Quarterly Journal

✤ Toronto, Ont. Formed 1978.

This journal was originally called *Fireweed: A Women's Literary and Cultural Journal*; the present name was adopted in 1980. The foreword to the first issue described *Fireweed* as a "feminist journal devoted to stimulating dialogue, knowledge, and creativity among women" and stated that the journal's collective was "committed to an editorial policy of diversity."

LOCATION OF RECORDS: Canadian Women's Movement Archives Collection, Morisset Library Special Collections, University of Ottawa. (See Appendix for address.)

COLLECTION NAME: Fireweed.

RECORDS: Periodicals (*Fireweed*, 1978-1991); manuscripts, 1978-1980; editorial comments on submissions, subscription forms, 1979-1981; organization history, notes, review, 1978; correspondence, 1978-1982; minutes, administrative notes, 1978-1979; financial records, 1980-1981; flyers, 1978, 1981, 1983, 1989, 1991; invitations, 1990; photographs, subscription lists, posters, advertisements, articles, abstract, biographical information, lists of contributors, interview, book cover, programme, forms, tickets, announcement.

AMOUNT: 62 cm of text, 19 photographs, 5 posters.

CONDITION: Good.

ACCESS: No restrictions.

62. Groupe marxiste révolutionnaire / Revolutionary Marxist Group

[For English entry, see # 86.]

✤ Groupe fondé 1973. Dissous 1977.

Le Groupe marxiste révolutionnaire (GMR) était un organisme trotskyste. Le GMR avait formé une commission des femmes. [Voir aussi Revolutionary Workers League (87).]

LIEU DE CONSULTATION : Fonds des Archives canadiennes du mouvement des femmes, Collections spéciales de la Bibliothèque Morisset, Université d'Ottawa. (Voir Annexe pour l'adresse.)

NOM DU FONDS : Revolutionary Marxist Group.

MATÉRIEL : Rapports, 1973-1974, 1977, 1979; articles, 1973, 1976, 1981; correspondance, 1977-1978; rapports de congrès, 1974-1975, 1979; questionnaires, 1977; tracts, 1975; documents préparatoires, 1974-1977, 1979.

QUANTITÉ : 8 cm.

ÉTAT : Bon.

ACCÈS : Aucune restriction.

63. Indian Rights for Indian Women

✤ Edmonton, Alta. Formed 1971. Disbanded.

Indian Rights for Indian Women (IRIW) campaigned against inequities in the Indian Act, under which Indian women who married non-Indians lost their legal status as Indians, as did their children.

Collection (a)

LOCATION OF RECORDS: Provincial Archives of Alberta. (See Appendix for address.)

COLLECTION NAME: National Committee on Indian Rights for Indian Women (83.328/126, box 5).

RECORDS: Correspondence, 1973-1974.

AMOUNT: 1 cm.

ACCESS: No restrictions.

Collection (b)

LOCATION OF RECORDS: Canadian Women's Movement Archives Collection, Morisset Library Special Collections, University of Ottawa. (See Appendix for address.)

COLLECTION NAME: Indian Rights for Indian Women Newsletter.

RECORDS: Newsletters, 1979-1980.

AMOUNT: 3 mm.

ACCESS: No restrictions.

64. Institut canadien de recherches sur les femmes / Canadian Research Institute for the Advancement of Women

[For English entry, see # 31.]

[Voir aussi la notice 739 (dans la partie II) pour autres documents de ce groupe.]

✣ Ottawa (Ont.) Groupe fondé 1976.

L'institut, appellé aussi l'ICREF, a pour mission de coordonner, de stimuler et de diffuser des travaux de recherche sur la réalité vécue par les femmes et d'assurer à celles-ci et à leurs expériences une place équitable dans l'ensemble des connaissances et de la recherche concernant le Canada.

Fonds (a)

LIEU DE CONSULTATION : Public Archives of Nova Scotia. (Voir Annexe pour l'adresse.)

NOM DU FONDS : Fait partie du fonds Muriel Duckworth (MG 1, volumes 2905-2906).

MATÉRIEL : Objectifs, statuts et règlements, programme, 1976; procès-verbaux, ordres du jour, documents financiers, 1976-1981; rapports, 1976, [ca 1980]; documents d'assemblées générales annuelles, 1978-1981; documents de congrès, 1983; rapports annuels, 1979-1981; correspondance, 1975-1983; communiqués de presse, 1976-1984; étude, propositions, 1981; exposés de position, 1979-1980; listes de membres et d'envoi, documents de recherche, dépliants, documents divers.

INSTRUMENT DE RECHERCHE : Instrument de recherche : fonds Muriel Duckworth disponible.

Fonds (b)

LIEU DE CONSULTATION : Northwest Territories Archives. (Voir Annexe pour l'adresse.)

NOM DU FONDS : Canadian Research Council for the Advancement of Women/Institut canadien de recherches sur les femmes (13th : 1989 : Yellowknife) (N91-008).

MATÉRIEL : Enregistrements sonores (actes de congrès), 1989.

QUANTITÉ : 32 pièces.

ACCÈS : Aucune restriction.

INSTRUMENT DE RECHERCHE : Liste de cassettes et programme de congrès disponibles.

65. League for Socialist Action

✣ Formed [196-?]. Disbanded 1977.

The League for Socialist Action (LSA) was a Trotskyist revolutionary Marxist group which had a women's commission. In 1977 LSA merged with the Revolutionary Marxist Group to become the Revolutionary Workers League. LSA's French name was la Ligue socialiste ouvrière (LSO). [See also Revolutionary Marxist Group/Groupe marxiste révolutionnaire (86), Revolutionary Workers League (87), and Toronto Women's Caucus (508).]

Collection (a)

LOCATION OF RECORDS: Canadian Women's Movement Archives Collection, Morisset Library Special Collections, University of Ottawa. (See Appendix for address.)

COLLECTION NAME: League for Socialist Action.

RECORDS: Background papers, 1972-1973, 1975-1976; conference records, brief, 1970; correspondence, 1977; reports, position papers.

AMOUNT: 5 cm.

CONDITION: Good.

ACCESS: No restrictions.

Collection (b)

LOCATION OF RECORDS: Canadian Gay Archives. (See Appendix for address.)

COLLECTION NAME: League for Socialist Action (89-002); some records form part of: Chris Bearchell collection (83-016) and Walter Davis collection (83-001).

RECORDS: Miscellaneous records.

66. League of Canadian Poets. Feminist Caucus

✣ Formed [1982?].

The Feminist Caucus of the League of Canadian Poets works to increase the participation and recognition of women in Canadian poetry.

LOCATION OF RECORDS: Canadian Women's Movement Archives Collection, Morisset Library Special Collections, University of Ottawa. (See Appendix for address.)

COLLECTION NAME: League of Canadian Poets — Feminist Caucus — Montreal.

RECORDS: Statement of goals, mailing lists, correspondence, worksheets, newsletter, 1982.

AMOUNT: 1 cm.

CONDITION: Good.

ACCESS: No restrictions.

67. Lesbian Conference (1981: Vancouver, B.C.). Organizing Committee

✣ Vancouver, B.C. Formed 1980. Disbanded 1981.

This committee organized the 1981 Lesbian Conference, also called "Lesbian Power: Organizing for the '80s." The objectives of the conference were to begin building a national network of lesbian organizations, to strengthen lesbian organizations in each region of Canada, and to celebrate lesbianism.

Collection (a)

LOCATION OF RECORDS: Canadian Women's Movement Archives Collection, Morisset Library Special Collections, University of Ottawa. (See Appendix for address.)

COLLECTION NAME: Lesbian Conference — Bi-national Meetings (1981).

RECORDS: Minutes, correspondence, 1980-1981; report, clippings, questionnaire, press releases, workshop materials, songsheets, pamphlets, flyers, invitations, ticket, poster, 1981.

AMOUNT: 3 cm of text, 1 poster.

CONDITION: Good.

ACCESS: Restricted; conditional access negotiable.

Collection (b)

LOCATION OF RECORDS: Canadian Gay Archives. (See Appendix for address.)

COLLECTION NAME: Conf.: 1981 Lesbian Conference (vertical file).

RECORDS: Conference records, 1981.

AMOUNT: 1.5 cm.

CONDITION: Good.

68. Liberal Party of Canada. National Women's Liberal Commission / Parti libéral du Canada. Commission libérale féminine nationale

[Renseignements en français, notice 81.]

[See also entry # 741 (in Part II), which lists other records of this organization.]

✣ Ottawa, Ont. Formed 1928.

The National Women's Liberal Commission (NWLC) represents and promotes the interests of women within the Liberal Party of Canada and

encourages the active participation of women at all levels of the party.
LOCATION OF RECORDS: National Archives of Canada. (See Appendix for address.)
COLLECTION NAME: Forms part of: Liberal Party of Canada collection (MG 28, IV 3).
RECORDS: Please see the note about National Archives of Canada collections, in entry # 2.

69. Makara Publishing and Design Co-operative

✢ Vancouver, B.C. Formed 1973. Disbanded.

The Pacific Women's Graphic Arts Co-operative Association, also called the Ad Company, was a feminist graphic-arts company. In 1975 it began publishing *Makara*, a "general-interest, alternative Canadian magazine" produced by a collective of women artists, writers, and graphic technicians. The organization then changed its name to Makara Publishing and Design Co-operative.

LOCATION OF RECORDS: Canadian Women's Movement Archives Collection, Morisset Library Special Collections, University of Ottawa. (See Appendix for address.)
COLLECTION NAME: Pacific Women's Graphic Arts Co-operative Association — Vancouver; Makara Publishing and Design — Vancouver.
RECORDS: Periodicals (*Makara*, 1975-1978); sound recording (interview), press release, 1976; correspondence, 1975, 1979-1980; calendar, 1975; organization history, 1977; pamphlets, invitation, T-shirt, poster.
AMOUNT: 7 cm of text, 1 sound recording, 1 T-shirt, 1 poster.
CONDITION: Good.
ACCESS: No restrictions.

70. MATCH International Centre / Centre international MATCH

[Renseignements en français, notice 38.]

[See also entry # 742 (in Part II), which lists other records of this organization.]

✢ Ottawa, Ont. Formed 1976.

MATCH International Centre is a feminist development organization which matches the resources and needs of Canadian women with those of women in developing countries. The organization's goals include eliminating violence against women globally.

LOCATION OF RECORDS: National Archives of Canada. (See Appendix for address.)
COLLECTION NAME: Forms part of: Ruth Marion (Rolph) Bell collection (MG 31, K 22, volumes 9-10).
RECORDS: Please see the note about National Archives of Canada collections, in entry # 2.

71. National Action Committee on the Status of Women / Comité canadien d'action sur le statut de la femme

[Renseignements en français, notice 44.]

[See also entry # 744 (in Part II), which lists other records of this organization.]

✢ Toronto, Ont. Formed 1971.

The National Action Committee on the Status of Women (NAC) is the largest women's organization in Canada, representing over 450 non-governmental associations from all regions of the country. Its priorities are to promote co-operation among women's groups, advocate political and legislative reforms, and sensitize the public to women's issues. NAC was originally called the National Ad Hoc Action Committee on the Status of Women. The present name was adopted in 1972. [See also MediaWatch/Évaluation-Médias (743).]

Collection (a)

LOCATION OF RECORDS: Canadian Women's Movement Archives Collection, Morisset Library Special Collections, University of Ottawa. (See Appendix for address.)
COLLECTION NAME: National Action Committee on the Status of Women.
RECORDS: Constitutions, 1978, 1983-1984, 1986-1988; records of annual meetings, 1974-1990; clippings, 1973-1990; correspondence, 1971-1991; reports, 1971, 1976-1980, 1982, 1985-1989; minutes, 1971-1978, 1980-1981, 1984-1989; periodicals (*Status of Women News/La Revue Statut de la femme*, 1973-1985; *Feminist Action/Action féministe*, 1985-1991; *Action Bulletin Action*, 1985-1990; *Action Now/À l'action*, 1990-1991; *Bulletin*, 1975; *NAC Memo/CCA Memo*, 1975-1985; *NAC Housing Newsletter*, 1987-1989, 1991); discussion papers, 1982-1983, 1985-1986; proposals, 1977, 1979-1980, 1985, 1987-1989; briefs, 1975, 1978, 1980-1981, 1984-1987; submissions, 1972-1973, 1975, 1986; presentations, 1977-1980, 1983, 1986-1987; policy statements, 1979-1980, 1984-1989; financial records, 1977-1978, 1985-1988; index to resolutions, 1987-1988; index to recommendations, 1978; position papers, 1986, 1988; speeches, 1977, 1980; radio presentation, 1989; grant application, 1985; articles, 1979, 1983, 1986-1989; convention records, 1972; agendas, 1973, 1976-1977, 1982, 1988-1989; tickets, 1985-1986, 1988-1989; press releases, 1973, 1976, 1978-1981, 1985-1989; guidelines, 1981; membership lists, 1980, 1986-1989; invitations, 1984, 1986-1987; T-shirt, questionnaire responses, 1988; information sheets, 1973, 1985; notices of meetings, 1983, 1987; advertisement, brochures, flyers, notes, questionnaires, forms, mailing lists, by-laws, manual, posters, buttons, miscellaneous records.
AMOUNT: 1.74 m of text, 4 posters, 1 T-shirt, 8 buttons.
ACCESS: No restrictions.

Collection (b)

LOCATION OF RECORDS: National Archives of Canada. (See Appendix for address.)
COLLECTION NAME: Forms part of: Dorothy Flaherty collection (MG 31, K 25).
RECORDS: Please see the note about National Archives of Canada collections, in entry # 2.

Collection (c)

LOCATION OF RECORDS: National Archives of Canada.
COLLECTION NAME: Forms part of: Ruth Marion (Rolph) Bell collection (MG 31, K 22, volumes 8-9).
RECORDS: Please see the note about National Archives of Canada collections, in entry # 2.

Collection (d)

LOCATION OF RECORDS: National Archives of Canada.
COLLECTION NAME: Forms part of: Elsie Gregory MacGill collection (MG 31, K 7, volume 10).
RECORDS: Please see the note about National Archives of Canada collections, in entry # 2.

Collection (e)

LOCATION OF RECORDS: Region of Peel Archives. (See Appendix for address.)
COLLECTION NAME: Forms part of: Helen Tucker collection (91.0058, series 5, box 1).
RECORDS: Miscellaneous records, 1973-1975.
AMOUNT: 2 cm.
ACCESS: Some restrictions apply.
FINDING AID: Finding aid available for Helen Tucker collection.

NATIONAL ORGANIZATIONS / GROUPES PANCANADIENS

72. National Council of Jewish Women of Canada

[See also entry # 747 (in Part II), which lists other records of this organization.]

✣ Downsview, Ont. Formed 1897.

The main activities of the National Council of Jewish Women of Canada (NCJW) are education, service, and social action. While its priorities are the protection of human rights and the preservation of Jewish life, NCJW is also concerned with women's issues such as family planning, abortion, child care, pornography, and affirmative action. Its French name is le Conseil des femmes juives du Canada.

LOCATION OF RECORDS: Canadian Jewish Congress, National Archives. (See Appendix for address.)

COLLECTION NAME: National Council of Jewish Women.

RECORDS: Miscellaneous records, 1916-1975.

AMOUNT: 9 m.

73. National Council of Women of Canada

✣ Ottawa, Ont. Formed 1893.

The National Council of Women of Canada (NCWC) is a federation of local and provincial councils of women. NCWC has lobbied on many women's and social issues (for instance, it lobbied for the establishment of the Royal Commission on the Status of Women). In 1967 NCWC donated the Lady Aberdeen Memorial Library (a women's studies collection) to the University of Waterloo Library. NCWC's French name is le Conseil national des femmes du Canada (CNFC).

Collection (a)

LOCATION OF RECORDS: National Archives of Canada. (See Appendix for address.)

COLLECTION NAME: National Council of Women of Canada (MG 28, I 25).

RECORDS: Please see the note about National Archives of Canada collections, in entry # 2.

Collection (b)

LOCATION OF RECORDS: National Archives of Canada.

COLLECTION NAME: Forms part of: Olha Woycenko collection (MG 30, D 212).

RECORDS: Please see the note about National Archives of Canada collections, in entry # 2.

Collection (c)

LOCATION OF RECORDS: National Archives of Canada.

COLLECTION NAME: Forms part of: Marion Creelman Savage collection (MG 30, C 92).

RECORDS: Please see the note about National Archives of Canada collections, in entry # 2.

Collection (d)

LOCATION OF RECORDS: National Archives of Canada.

COLLECTION NAME: Forms part of: Margaret MacLellan collection (MG 31, E 17).

RECORDS: Please see the note about National Archives of Canada collections, in entry # 2.

Collection (e)

LOCATION OF RECORDS: National Archives of Canada.

COLLECTION NAME: Forms part of: Dorothy Eva Flaherty collection (MG 31, K 25).

RECORDS: Please see the note about National Archives of Canada collections, in entry # 2.

Collection (f)

LOCATION OF RECORDS: National Archives of Canada.

COLLECTION NAME: Forms part of: John Campbell Hamilton Gordon, Seventh Earl of Aberdeen and Lady Ishbel Aberdeen collection (MG 27, I B 5).

RECORDS: Please see the note about National Archives of Canada collections, in entry # 2.

Collection (g)

LOCATION OF RECORDS: Doris Lewis Rare Book Room, University of Waterloo Library. (See Appendix for address.)

COLLECTION NAME: Forms part of: Lady Aberdeen collection (WA18).

RECORDS: Correspondence, notes, library accessions list, minutes, leaflet, clippings, miscellaneous records, 1895-1968.

FINDING AID: "Finding Aid No. 18."

Collection (h)

LOCATION OF RECORDS: Doris Lewis Rare Book Room, University of Waterloo Library.

COLLECTION NAME: Forms part of: Elizabeth Smith Shortt collection (WA10).

RECORDS: Correspondence, 1913-1914, 1917, 1919-1926, 1931, 1948, 1952; meeting notes, 1913; handbook, 1914; reports, 1919-1920; pamphlet, 1920; leaflets, clippings.

FINDING AID: "Finding Aid No. 10."

Collection (i)

LOCATION OF RECORDS: Glenbow Museum Archives. (See Appendix for address.)

COLLECTION NAME: Forms part of: Calgary Local Council of Women collection (M5841, box 17, files 182-230; M6802, box 31, files 320-323; M7222, box 32, files 329-333; M7653, box 35, files 368-371).

RECORDS: Constitution, by-laws, 1955, 1962, 1967; handbooks, 1964-1968; yearbooks, 1937-1938, 1941, 1952-1953, 1956-1971, 1973, 1975-1977, 1980-1982; records of annual meetings, 1939-1952, 1959-1964, 1966-1974, 1977, 1982; committee membership lists, 1954-1955; resolutions, 1949-1952, 1958-1964, 1966-1982; correspondence, reports, 1949-1952, 1958-1959, 1965-1967, 1970-1977; submissions, 1962-1977; newsletters, 1949, 1958-1984; biographical notes, 1964-1965, 1973; clippings, 1963-1964; minutes, 1978; press releases, 1979; work plans, 1980-1984; songsheet, pamphlets, briefs, miscellaneous records.

AMOUNT: 62 files.

ACCESS: No restrictions.

FINDING AID: "Calgary Local Council of Women Papers, 1919-1985."

Collection (j)

LOCATION OF RECORDS: Provincial Archives of New Brunswick. (See Appendix for address.)

COLLECTION NAME: Forms part of: Council of Women collection (MC626).

RECORDS: Resolutions, 1969-1974; lists of officers, 1966-1967; handbook, 1964; organization history, 1920-1950; biographical notes, 1957-1958; speeches, 1958, 1976; notes for article, 1978; records of meetings, 1956, 1961, 1974, 1978; correspondence, 1958, 1961, 1967, 1969; financial records, 1950-1958; report, 1958; yearbooks, 1926, 1957-1977; aims and objectives, miscellaneous records.

ACCESS: No restrictions.

FINDING AID: Inventory available.

Collection (k)

LOCATION OF RECORDS: University of Guelph Library, Archives and Special Collections. (See Appendix for address.)

COLLECTION NAME: Forms part of: Courtice Family Papers (X4A MS A363).

RECORDS: Miscellaneous records, [before 1924].

FINDING AID: On-line finding aid available for Courtice collection.

Collection (l)

LOCATION OF RECORDS: University of Guelph Library, Archives and Special Collections.

COLLECTION NAME: Forms part of: Hoodless Family Papers (XR1 MS A001).

PART I: RECORDS HELD BY ARCHIVES / PARTIE I : FONDS DÉTENUS PAR DES ARCHIVES

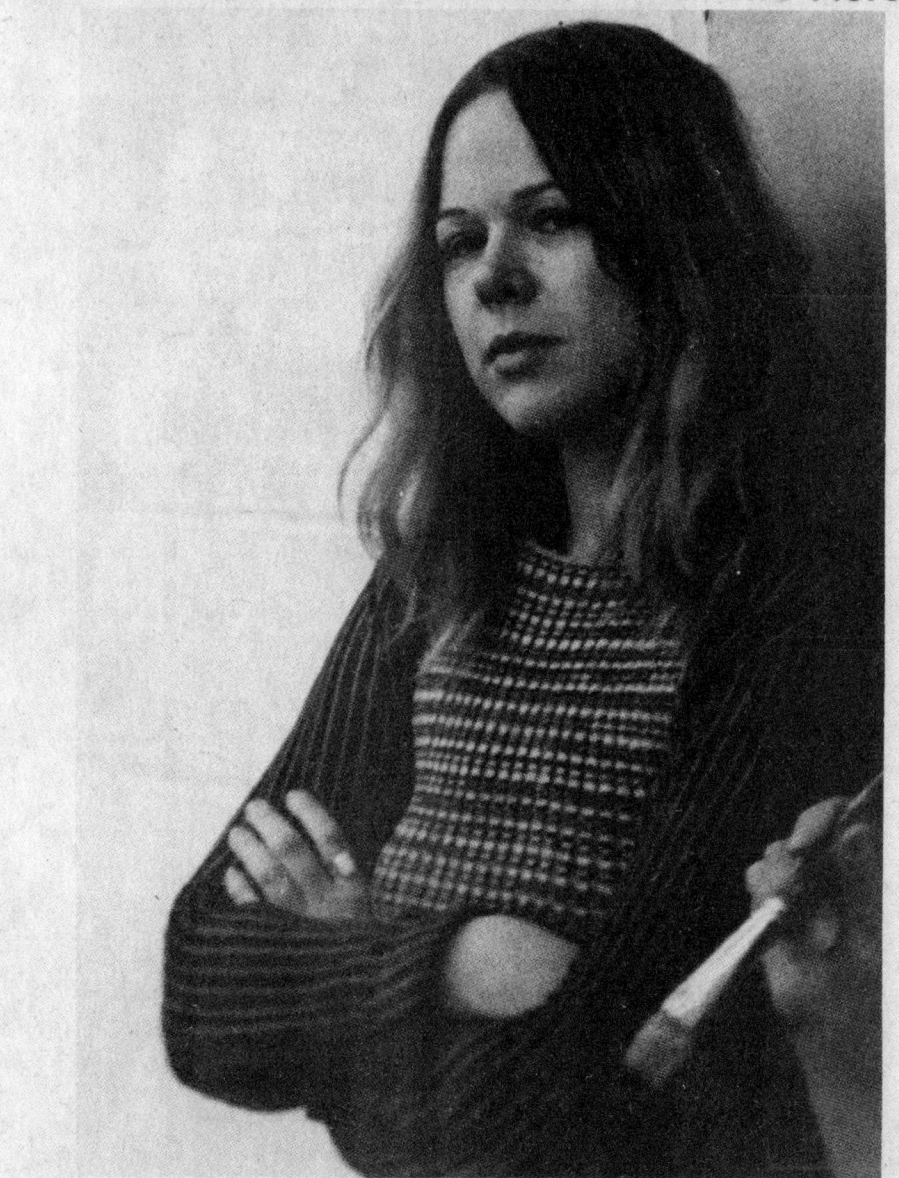

Newspaper / Journal, 1972
The Other Woman
Photographer unknown / Photographe inconnue
CWMA Collection / Fonds de l'ACMF

NATIONAL ORGANIZATIONS / GROUPES PANCANADIENS

RECORDS: Miscellaneous records, [before 1911].
FINDING AID: Finding aid available for Hoodless collection.

74. National Council of Young Men's Christian Associations. Task Force on the Status of Women in the YMCA

✢ Toronto, Ont. Formed [1977?].

LOCATION OF RECORDS: National Archives of Canada. (See Appendix for address.)
COLLECTION NAME: Forms part of: Ruth Marion (Rolph) Bell collection (MG 31, K 22).
RECORDS: Please see the note about National Archives of Canada collections, in entry # 2.

75. New Democratic Party. Federal Women's Committee / Nouveau Parti démocratique. Comité fédéral féminin

[Renseignements en français, notice 79.]

LOCATION OF RECORDS: National Archives of Canada. (See Appendix for address.)
COLLECTION NAME: Forms part of: Marjorie Mann collection (MG 32, G 12).
RECORDS: Please see the note about National Archives of Canada collections, in entry # 2.

76. New Democratic Party. Participation of Women Committee. Task Force on Older Women in Canada

✢ Ottawa, Ont. Formed 1982. Disbanded 1983.

LOCATION OF RECORDS: University of Toronto Archives. (See Appendix for address.)
COLLECTION NAME: Forms part of: Marianne Holder collection (UTA B88-0075/005).
RECORDS: Outline of procedures, questionnaires, 1982; correspondence, 1980-1983; report, 1983; agenda, notes, clippings.
AMOUNT: 1 cm.
CONDITION: Good.
ACCESS: No restrictions.
FINDING AID: Box list available for Holder collection.

77. New Democratic Party. Rosemary Brown Leadership Campaign Committee

✢ Vancouver, B.C. Formed 1975. Disbanded 1975.

This committee supported Rosemary Brown's campaign for the leadership of the New Democratic Party. Women's issues figured prominently in the campaign.

LOCATION OF RECORDS: University of Toronto Archives. (See Appendix for address.)
COLLECTION NAME: Forms part of: Marianne Holder collection (UTA B88-0075/004).
RECORDS: Minutes, procedures, speeches, clippings, bulletins, itinerary, flyers, pamphlets, songsheet, 1975.
AMOUNT: 1 cm.
CONDITION: Good.
ACCESS: No restrictions.
FINDING AID: Box list available for Holder collection.

78. New Democratic Party. Women's Liberation Caucus

✢ Formed 1970. Disbanded.

The NDP Women's Liberation Caucus (also called the NDP Women's Liberation Movement) was an unofficial group within the New Democratic Party. The group worked to elicit support for women's liberation within the party and to increase awareness of women's issues both inside and outside the party.

LOCATION OF RECORDS: Canadian Women's Movement Archives Collection, Morisset Library Special Collections, University of Ottawa. (See Appendix for address.)
COLLECTION NAME: NDP Women's Liberation Caucus.
RECORDS: Correspondence, article, 1970; resolutions, policy statements, flyers, educational material, [197-].
AMOUNT: 2 cm.
CONDITION: Good.
ACCESS: No restrictions.

79. Nouveau Parti démocratique. Comité fédéral féminin / New Democratic Party. Federal Women's Committee

[For English entry, see # 75.]

LIEU DE CONSULTATION : Archives nationales du Canada. (Voir Annexe pour l'adresse.)
NOM DU FONDS : Fait partie du fonds Marjorie Mann (MG 32, G 12).
MATÉRIEL : Voir la note sur les fonds des Archives nationales du Canada, notice 4.

80. The Other Woman

✢ Toronto, Ont. Formed 1972. Disbanded 1977.

The Other Woman (sometimes referred to as TOW) was a collectively run periodical which addressed women's issues from a feminist, anti-capitalist perspective. [See also Women's Information Centre of Toronto (559).]

Collection (a)

LOCATION OF RECORDS: Canadian Women's Movement Archives Collection, Morisset Library Special Collections, University of Ottawa. (See Appendix for address.)
COLLECTION NAME: The Other Woman; SR 11/1-15.
RECORDS: Periodicals (*The Other Woman*, 1972-1977); manuscripts, 1974-1977; sound recordings (interviews), layouts, reports, 1974-1976; financial records, correspondence, 1972-1977; minutes, 1973-1977; mailing list, schedules, 1974-1975; grant applications, 1975-1976; agreements, 1976-1977; order forms, 1972, 1974, 1976-1977; briefs, press release, 1975; distribution lists, advertisements, clipping, proposal, 1976; poster, 1973; subscription forms, list of back issues, layout instructions, flyers, organization history, notes, policy statement, pamphlet, booklets, guidelines, catalogue, photographs, T-shirt, rubber stamp.
AMOUNT: 96 cm of text, 18 sound recordings, 1 poster, 7 photographs, 1 T-shirt, 1 rubber stamp.
CONDITION: Good.
ACCESS: No restrictions.

Collection (b)

LOCATION OF RECORDS: Canadian Gay Archives. (See Appendix for address.)
COLLECTION NAME: The Other Woman.
RECORDS: Periodicals (*The Other Woman*, 1972-1977).

Collection (c)

LOCATION OF RECORDS: Thomas Fisher Rare Book Library, University of Toronto. (See Appendix for address.)

COLLECTION NAME: Forms part of: F.M. Denison collection.
RECORDS: Periodicals (*The Other Woman*, 1972-1975).
ACCESS: No restrictions.

81. Parti libéral du Canada. Commission libérale féminine nationale / Liberal Party of Canada. National Women's Liberal Commission

[For English entry, see # 68.]

[Voir aussi la notice 756 (dans la partie II) pour autres documents de ce groupe.]

✣ Ottawa (Ont.). Groupe fondé 1928.

La Commission libérale féminine nationale (CLFN) est chargée de représenter et de promouvoir les intérêts des femmes au sein du Parti libéral du Canada et d'encourager les femmes à participer activement à ses activités, à tous les échelons.

LIEU DE CONSULTATION : Archives nationales du Canada. (Voir Annexe pour l'adresse.)
NOM DU FONDS : Fait partie du fonds du Parti libéral du Canada (MG 28, IV 3).
MATÉRIEL : Voir la note sur les fonds des Archives nationales du Canada, notice 4.

82. Parti progressiste conservateur du Canada. Bureau des femmes / Progressive Conservative Party of Canada. Women's Bureau

[For English entry, see # 83.]

✣ Ottawa (Ont.).

LIEU DE CONSULTATION : Archives nationales du Canada. (Voir Annexe pour l'adresse.)
NOM DU FONDS : Fait partie du fonds du Parti progressiste conservateur du Canada (MG 28, IV 2).
MATÉRIEL : Voir la note sur les fonds des Archives nationales du Canada, notice 4.

83. Progressive Conservative Party of Canada. Women's Bureau / Parti progressiste conservateur du Canada. Bureau des femmes

[Renseignements en français, notice 82.]

✣ Ottawa, Ont.

LOCATION OF RECORDS: National Archives of Canada. (See Appendix for address.)
COLLECTION NAME: Forms part of: Progressive Conservative Party of Canada collection (MG 28, IV 2).
RECORDS: Please see the note about National Archives of Canada collections, in entry # 2.

84. Progressive Conservative Women's Association / Association des femmes progressistes conservatrices

[Renseignements en français, notice 7.]

✣ Ottawa, Ont.

LOCATION OF RECORDS: National Archives of Canada. (See Appendix for address.)
COLLECTION NAME: Forms part of: Progressive Conservative Party of Canada collection (MG 28, IV 2).
RECORDS: Please see the note about National Archives of Canada collections, in entry # 2.

85. Resources for Feminist Research / Documentation sur la recherche féministe

[Renseignements en français, notice 50.]

[See also entry # 762 (in Part II), which lists other records of this organization.]

✣ Toronto, Ont. Formed 1972.

Resources for Feminist Research/Documentation sur la recherche féministe (RFR/DRF) is a Canadian journal of international feminist research. Until 1979 it was called the *Canadian Newsletter of Research on Women/Recherches sur la femme : Bulletin d'information canadien*.

LOCATION OF RECORDS: Canadian Women's Movement Archives Collection, Morisset Library Special Collections, University of Ottawa. (See Appendix for address.)
COLLECTION NAME: Resources for Feminist Research/Documentation sur la recherche féministe.
RECORDS: Drafts of articles, [ca. 1982] (for "The Lesbian Issue," published March 1983); proposal, 1981; correspondence, questionnaires, forms, flyers, pamphlets, posters.
AMOUNT: 5 cm of text, 2 posters.
ACCESS: No restrictions.

86. Revolutionary Marxist Group / Groupe marxiste révolutionnaire

[Renseignements en français, notice 62.]

✣ Formed 1973. Disbanded 1977.

The Revolutionary Marxist Group (RMG) was a Trotskyist organization which had a women's commission. [See also Revolutionary Workers League (87).]

LOCATION OF RECORDS: Canadian Women's Movement Archives Collection, Morisset Library Special Collections, University of Ottawa. (See Appendix for address.)
COLLECTION NAME: Revolutionary Marxist Group.
RECORDS: Reports, articles, correspondence, conference reports, questionnaires, flyers, background papers, [197-].
AMOUNT: 8 cm.
CONDITION: Good.
ACCESS: No restrictions.

87. Revolutionary Workers League

✣ Formed 1977.

The Revolutionary Workers League (RWL) is a Trotskyist revolutionary Marxist group which was formed when the League for Socialist Action and the Revolutionary Marxist Group merged. In the late 1970s, RWL had several women's and lesbian and gay subgroups. [See also League for Socialist Action (65) and Revolutionary Marxist Group/Groupe marxiste révolutionnaire (86).]

LOCATION OF RECORDS: Canadian Women's Movement Archives Collection, Morisset Library Special Collections, University of Ottawa. (See Appendix for address.)
COLLECTION NAME: Revolutionary Workers League.

RECORDS: Minutes, 1977-1979; correspondence, 1978; policy statements, 1977-1978; background papers, 1977-1980; reports, 1978-1980; articles, 1977, 1979; pamphlets, flyers.
AMOUNT: 11 cm.
CONDITION: Good.
ACCESS: No restrictions.

88. Syndicat canadien des travailleurs du textile et de la chimie / Canadian Textile and Chemical Union

[For English entry, see # 32.]

✣ Brantford (Ont.).

LIEU DE CONSULTATION : Archives nationales du Canada. (Voir Annexe pour l'adresse.)

NOM DU FONDS : Fait partie du fonds Frank et Libbie Park (MG 31, K 9, tome 29 / 419-30/441).

MATÉRIEL : Voir la note sur les fonds des Archives nationales du Canada, notice 4.

89. Syndicat des communications Canada / Communications Union Canada

[For English entry, see # 47.]

✣ Groupe fondé 1946. Dissous 1980.

LIEU DE CONSULTATION : Archives nationales du Canada. (Voir Annexe pour l'adresse.)

NOM DU FONDS : Syndicat des communications Canada (MG 28, I 329).

MATÉRIEL : Voir la note sur les fonds des Archives nationales du Canada, notice 4.

90. Travailleurs amalgamés du vêtement et du textile / Amalgamated Clothing and Textile Workers Union

[For English entry, see # 2.]

[Voir aussi la notice 766 (dans la partie II) pour autres documents de ce groupe.]

✣ Don Mills (Ont.). Groupe fondé 1976.

Le syndicat des Travailleurs amalgamés du vêtement et du textile (TAVT) vise à améliorer la vie des ouvrières et ouvriers canadiens. La majorité de ses membres sont des femmes.

LIEU DE CONSULTATION : Archives nationales du Canada. (Voir Annexe pour l'adresse.)

NOM DU FONDS : Travailleurs amalgamés du vêtement et du textile, Division du textile (MG 28, I 219).

MATÉRIEL : Voir la note sur les fonds des Archives nationales du Canada, notice 4.

91. United Church of Canada. Committee to Consider the Report of the Royal Commission on the Status of Women

✣ Formed 1972. Disbanded 1972.

This committee grew out of the committee which produced the United Church's brief to the Royal Commission.

LOCATION OF RECORDS: Canadian Women's Movement Archives Collection, Morisset Library Special Collections, University of Ottawa. (See Appendix for address.)

COLLECTION NAME: United Church of Canada. Committee to Consider the Report of the Royal Commission on the Status of Women.
RECORDS: Reports, 1972.
AMOUNT: 11 pages.
CONDITION: Good.
ACCESS: No restrictions.

92. Voice of Women / La Voix des femmes

[Renseignements en français, notice 93.]

✣ Ottawa, Ont. Formed 1960.

Voice of Women (VOW) opposes war and violence and promotes peace and disarmament. A national women's organization with provincial and local branches, VOW lobbies all levels of government and organizes educational campaigns, meetings, and conferences. (Source: *The Canadian Encyclopedia*. — Edmonton: Hurtig Publishers, 1985.) [See also Coalition of Canadian Women's Groups: International Peace Conference/Coalition des associations de femmes canadiennes : Le Congrès international sur la paix (43).]

Collection (a)

LOCATION OF RECORDS: National Archives of Canada. (See Appendix for address.)

COLLECTION NAME: Voice of Women (MG 28, I 218).

RECORDS: Please see the note about National Archives of Canada collections, in entry # 2.

Collection (b)

LOCATION OF RECORDS: Doris Lewis Rare Book Room, University of Waterloo Library. (See Appendix for address.)

COLLECTION NAME: Forms part of: Voice of Women / Jo Davis Papers (GA81).

RECORDS: Correspondence, 1960-1965, 1969, 1971-1972; survey results, 1962; clippings, 1960-1991; notes, 1990-1991; subject files, records of annual meetings, briefs, constitution and by-laws, organization history, membership records, minutes, newsletters, press releases, speeches, financial records, miscellaneous records, 1960-1963.

FINDING AID: "Voice of Women / Jo Davis Papers, 1959-1990."

Collection (c)

LOCATION OF RECORDS: Public Archives of Nova Scotia. (See Appendix for address.)

COLLECTION NAME: Forms part of: Muriel Duckworth collection (MG 1, volumes 2900-2903).

RECORDS: Organization histories, 1962, 1967; minutes, 1961-1979, 1981-1985; records of annual general meetings, 1961-1971, 1976, 1978; correspondence, 1960-1986; conference records, 1983-1985; constitutions, statement of purpose, membership and mailing lists, lists of officers, miscellaneous records.

FINDING AID: Finding aid available for Muriel Duckworth collection.

Collection (d)

LOCATION OF RECORDS: University of British Columbia Library, Special Collections-Manuscripts. (See Appendix for address.)

COLLECTION NAME: Forms part of: British Columbia Voice of Women collection (files 7-1, 2-(2-3), 7-(4-9), 10-(3-4), 11-(18-21), 13-(12-14), 14-(9-13), 15-9, 16-(3-4), 17-(17-18), 18-1, 18-14).

RECORDS: Minutes, 1967-1983; newsletters, 1960-1985; records of annual meetings, 1970-1979; press releases, 1968-1979; briefs, 1963-1977; financial records, 1969-1970; clippings, leaflets, 1982-1983; radio transcript, 1979; statement of policy, resolutions, 1976; correspondence, reports, organization history, notices, publications, miscellaneous records.

AMOUNT: Approx. 500 items.
ACCESS: No restrictions.

International Women's Day march / Manifestation de la Journée internationale des femmes, Toronto, 1987
Photograph by / Photo prise par Johanne M. Pelletier
Photo #1190; acc. #99
CWMA Collection / Fonds de l'ACMF

NATIONAL ORGANIZATIONS / GROUPES PANCANADIENS

FINDING AID: Inventory and addenda available for British Columbia Voice of Women collection.

Collection (e)

LOCATION OF RECORDS: British Columbia Archives and Records Service. (See Appendix for address.)

COLLECTION NAME: Forms part of: Hilary Brown collection (Add.MSS. 1074).

RECORDS: Conference records, 1968-1969; minutes, 1965-1969; press releases, 1965-1971; newsletters, 1960-1974; reports, circulars, correspondence, policy statements, submissions, briefs, miscellaneous records.

ACCESS: No restrictions.

FINDING AID: Finding aid available.

Collection (f)

LOCATION OF RECORDS: Region of Peel Archives. (See Appendix for address.)

COLLECTION NAME: Forms part of: Helen Tucker collection (91.0058, series 6, box 8).

RECORDS: Miscellaneous records, 1960-1987.

AMOUNT: 1 cm.

ACCESS: Some restrictions apply.

FINDING AID: Finding aid available for Tucker collection.

Collection (g)

LOCATION OF RECORDS: McMaster University Library, William Ready Division of Archives and Research Collections. (See Appendix for address.)

COLLECTION NAME: Forms part of: Claire Culhane Papers.

RECORDS: Correspondence.

FINDING AID: Finding aid available for Claire Culhane collection.

Collection (h)

LOCATION OF RECORDS: Canadian Women's Movement Archives Collection, Morisset Library Special Collections, University of Ottawa. (See Appendix for address.)

COLLECTION NAME: Voice of Women.

RECORDS: Newsletters, 1962, 1967-1969, 1973, 1975-1977, 1981, 1984, 1986-1989; correspondence, [196-]; reports, organization history, clippings, resolutions, flyers.

AMOUNT: 4 cm.

CONDITION: Fair.

ACCESS: No restrictions.

93. *La Voix des femmes / Voice of Women*

[For English entry, see # 92.]

✣ Ottawa (Ont.). Groupe fondé 1960.

La Voix des femmes est un organisme de femmes national doté de sections provinciales et locales. Il s'oppose à la guerre et à la violence et il favorise la paix et le désarmement. La Voix des femmes fait des représentations aux gouvernements et organise des campagnes éducatives, des réunions et des congrès. (Source : *The Canadian Encyclopedia*. — Edmonton : Hurtig Publishers, 1985.) [Voir aussi Coalition des associations de femmes canadiennes : Le Congrès international sur la paix/Coalition of Canadian Women's Groups: International Peace Conference (42).]

Fonds (a)

LIEU DE CONSULTATION : Archives nationales du Canada. (Voir Annexe pour l'adresse.)

NOM DU FONDS : Voix des femmes (MG 28, I 218).

MATÉRIEL : Voir la note sur les fonds des Archives nationales du Canada, notice 4.

Fonds (b)

LIEU DE CONSULTATION : Doris Lewis Rare Book Room, University of Waterloo Library. (Voir Annexe pour l'adresse.)

NOM DU FONDS : Fait partie du fonds Voice of Women/Jo Davis (GA81).

MATÉRIEL : Correspondance, 1960-1965, 1969, 1971-1972; sondage, 1962; coupures de presse, 1960-1991; notes, 1990-1991; dossiers-matière, documents d'assemblées annuelles, mémoires, statuts et règlements, historique de l'association, dossiers des membres, procès-verbaux, bulletins, communiqués de presse, discours, documents financiers, documents divers, 1960-1963.

INSTRUMENT DE RECHERCHE : « Voice of Women/Jo Davis Papers, 1959-1990 ».

Fonds (c)

LIEU DE CONSULTATION : Public Archives of Nova Scotia. (Voir Annexe pour l'adresse.)

NOM DU FONDS : Fait partie du fonds Muriel Duckworth (MG 1, volumes 2900-2903).

MATÉRIEL : Historiques de l'association, 1962, 1967; procès-verbaux, 1961-1979, 1981-1985; documents d'assemblées générales annuelles, 1961-1971, 1976, 1978; correspondance, 1960-1986; documents de congrès, 1983-1985; statuts et règlements, objectifs, listes de membres et d'envoi, listes des membres du comité de direction, documents divers.

INSTRUMENT DE RECHERCHE : Instrument de recherche : fonds Muriel Duckworth disponible.

Fonds (d)

LIEU DE CONSULTATION : University of British Columbia, Special Collections-Manuscripts. (Voir Annexe pour l'adresse.)

NOM DU FONDS : Fait partie du fonds British Columbia Voice of Women (dossiers 7-1, 2-(2-3), 7-(4-9), 10-(3-4), 11-(18-21), 13-(12-14), 14-(9-13), 15-9, 16-(3-4), 17-(17-18), 18-1, 18-14).

MATÉRIEL : Procès-verbaux, 1967-1983; bulletins, 1960-1985; documents d'assemblées annuelles, 1970-1979; communiqués de presse, 1968-1979; mémoires, 1963-1977; documents financiers, 1969-1970; coupures de presse, tracts, 1982-1983; transcription radiophonique, 1979; énoncé de politique, résolutions, 1976; correspondance, rapports, historique de l'association, avis, publications, documents divers.

QUANTITÉ : Env. 500 pièces.

ACCÈS : Aucune restriction.

INSTRUMENT DE RECHERCHE : Inventaire et documents annexes de la collection British Columbia Voice of Women disponibles.

Fonds (e)

LIEU DE CONSULTATION : British Columbia Archives and Records Service. (Voir Annexe pour l'adresse.)

NOM DU FONDS : Fait partie du fonds Hilary Brown (Add.MSS. 1074).

MATÉRIEL : Documents de congrès, 1968-1969; procès-verbaux, 1965-1969; communiqués de presse, 1965-1971; bulletins, 1960-1974; rapports, circulaires, correspondance, énoncés de politiques, soumissions, mémoires, documents divers.

ACCÈS : Aucune restriction.

INSTRUMENT DE RECHERCHE : Instrument de recherche disponible.

Fonds (f)

LIEU DE CONSULTATION : Region of Peel Archives. (Voir Annexe pour l'adresse.)

NOM DU FONDS : Fait partie du fonds Helen Tucker (91.0058, série 6, boîte 8).

MATÉRIEL : Documents divers, 1960-1987.

QUANTITÉ : 1 cm.

ACCÈS : Avec certaines restrictions.

INSTRUMENT DE RECHERCHE : Instrument de recherche : fonds Helen Tucker disponible.

Fonds (g)

LIEU DE CONSULTATION : McMaster University Library, William Ready Division of Archives and Research Collections. (Voir Annexe pour l'adresse.)

NOM DU FONDS : Fait partie du fonds Claire Culhane.

MATÉRIEL : Correspondance.
INSTRUMENT DE RECHERCHE : Instrument de recherche : fonds Claire Culhane disponible.

Fonds (h)
LIEU DE CONSULTATION : Fonds des Archives canadiennes du mouvement des femmes, Collections spéciales de la Bibliothèque Morisset, Université d'Ottawa. (Voir Annexe pour l'adresse.)
NOM DU FONDS : Voice of Women.
MATÉRIEL : Bulletins, 1962, 1967-1969, 1973, 1975-1977, 1981, 1984, 1986-1989; correspondance, [196-]; rapports, historique de l'association, coupures de presse, résolutions, tracts.
QUANTITÉ : 4 cm.
ÉTAT : Assez bon.
ACCÈS : Aucune restriction.

94. *The Waffle. Women's Caucus*
✣ Formed 1969. Disbanded [ca. 1975].

The Waffle, which was established in 1969, was a left-wing movement within the New Democratic Party (NDP). The Waffle Women's Caucus aimed to convince Waffle and NDP members to work for improvements in the situation of women (especially working-class women) and to pass convention resolutions essential to women.

LOCATION OF RECORDS: Canadian Women's Movement Archives Collection, Morisset Library Special Collections, University of Ottawa. (See Appendix for address.)
COLLECTION NAME: Waffle Women's Caucus (New Democratic Party).
RECORDS: Position papers, 1971, 1974; conference records, 1972, 1974; policy statements, report, 1974; flyer.
AMOUNT: 1.5 cm.
CONDITION: Good.
ACCESS: No restrictions.

95. *Women and Film*
✣ Toronto, Ont. Formed 1972. Disbanded [197-].

This group organized the Women and Film/Femme et le film festival, held in Toronto in 1973. This festival of films made by women subsequently toured Canada.

LOCATION OF RECORDS: Canadian Women's Movement Archives Collection, Morisset Library Special Collections, University of Ottawa. (See Appendix for address.)
COLLECTION NAME: Women and Film Festival — Toronto, 1973; SR 14/1.
RECORDS: Catalogue, schedules, guide, outline, contact list, press release, posters, sound recording (lecture), 1973; correspondence, [197-].
AMOUNT: 1 cm of text, 3 posters, 1 sound recording.
CONDITION: Good.
ACCESS: No restrictions.

96. *Women Healthsharing*
✣ Toronto, Ont. Formed 1978.

Women Healthsharing is a feminist collective which does research, writing, and advocacy related to women's health issues. Its main activity is publishing a national magazine, *Healthsharing: A Canadian Women's Health Quarterly*. The organization is sometimes called Women Healthsharing: A Resource and Writing Collective.

LOCATION OF RECORDS: Canadian Women's Movement Archives Collection, Morisset Library Special Collections, University of Ottawa. (See Appendix for address.)
COLLECTION NAME: Healthsharing.
RECORDS: Correspondence, log-books, financial records, 1979-1985; periodicals (*Healthsharing: A Canadian Women's Health Quarterly*, 1979-1991); questionnaires, [ca. 1982]; clippings, job description, 1981; raffle ticket, 1986; flyers, proposal, invitations.
AMOUNT: 1.15 m.
CONDITION: Good.
ACCESS: No restrictions.

97. *Women in Canadian Sociology / Anthropology*
✣ Downsview, Ont. Formed [1974?]. Disbanded.

Women in Canadian Sociology/Anthropology was based at York University. The group was originally called Women in Canadian Sociology. Its French name was Femmes et sociologie/anthropologie canadiennes (and earlier, Femmes et sociologie canadiennes).

LOCATION OF RECORDS: Canadian Women's Movement Archives Collection, Morisset Library Special Collections, University of Ottawa. (See Appendix for address.)
COLLECTION NAME: Women in Canadian Sociology/Anthropology Bulletin (York University).
RECORDS: Newsletters, 1974-1977.
AMOUNT: 5 mm.
CONDITION: Fair.
ACCESS: No restrictions.

98. *Women's Liberal Federation of Canada / Fédération nationale des femmes libérales du Canada*

[Renseignements en français, notice 56.]
✣ Formed 1928. Disbanded 1970.

LOCATION OF RECORDS: National Archives of Canada. (See Appendix for address.)
COLLECTION NAME: Forms part of: Liberal Party of Canada collection (MG 28, IV 3).
RECORDS: Please see the note about National Archives of Canada collections, in entry # 2.

99. *Women's Press*
✣ Toronto, Ont. Formed 1972.

The Women's Press (also known as the Canadian Women's Educational Press) is a feminist publishing house. It was founded when a group within the Toronto Women's Liberation Movement formed a socialist-feminist collective to publish feminist fiction, non-fiction, and children's books. In its early years, the press appears occasionally to have been called the Women's Education Press, the Canadian Women's Press, or the Canadian Women's Cooperative Press. Following a 1988 dispute over a proposed policy on racism, some members departed to form the Second Story Press. (Source: Canadian Women's Movement Archives finding aid, 1990.) [See also Toronto Women's Liberation Movement (509).]

LOCATION OF RECORDS: Canadian Women's Movement Archives Collection, Morisset Library Special Collections, University of Ottawa. (See Appendix for address.)
COLLECTION NAME: Canadian Women's Educational Press; SR 8/11, 11/11.
RECORDS: Statements of aims and purposes, 1978, 1986; organization histories, 1973-1975; manuscripts, 1972-[198-]; minutes, 1972-1982;

financial records, 1972-1983; log-books, 1974-1980; correspondence, 1972-1990; contracts, 1973-1981; contact list, 1972; grant application, 1974; guidelines, 1988; sound recordings (interviews), 1976, 1980; speech, 1975; library accession register, [197-]; rental agreements, 1972, 1976-1978, 1980, 1982; questionnaire, 1973; photographs, proposals, production records, book covers, graphics, layouts, catalogues, reports, advertisements, clippings, flyers, guest book, manual, permits, pamphlets, posters, press releases, notes, miscellaneous records.
AMOUNT: 8 m of text, 610 photographs, 22 posters, 2 sound recordings.
CONDITION: Good.
ACCESS: No restrictions.
FINDING AID: "Inventory: The Canadian Women's Educational Press, 1970-1988."

100. Women's Research Centre

✣ Vancouver, B.C. Formed 1973.

The centre does "action research — research which is not distanced, which is rooted in women's description of their experience, and which is intended to promote action to change women's situation." (Source: Women's Research Centre pamphlet, 1990.)

LOCATION OF RECORDS: Canadian Women's Movement Archives Collection, Morisset Library Special Collections, University of Ottawa. (See Appendix for address.)
COLLECTION NAME: Women's Research Centre — Vancouver.
RECORDS: Minutes, 1977-1978; interviews, abstract, 1978; reports, 1974, 1977-1981, 1985; study, 1982; questionnaire, research paper, 1977; briefs, 1977, 1981, 1983; kits, 1985-1987; guides, 1986, 1990; book, 1990; correspondence, 1974, 1977-1978, 1982; lists of publications, flyers, subscriptions, position papers, clipping, pamphlets, notes, button.
AMOUNT: 22 cm of text, 1 button.
CONDITION: Good.
ACCESS: No restrictions.

101. Young Women's Christian Association of Canada

✣ Toronto, Ont. Formed 1893.

Collection (a)

LOCATION OF RECORDS: National Archives of Canada. (See Appendix for address.)
COLLECTION NAME: Young Women's Christian Association of Canada (MG 28, I 198).
RECORDS: Please see the note about National Archives of Canada collections, in entry # 2.

Collection (b)

LOCATION OF RECORDS: National Archives of Canada.
COLLECTION NAME: Forms part of: Mabel Geldard-Brown collection (MG 30, E 497).
RECORDS: Please see the note about National Archives of Canada collections, in entry # 2.

YUKON

102. Victoria Faulkner Women's Centre
✣ Whitehorse, Yukon. Formed 1974.

The Victoria Faulkner Women's Centre fosters friendship and the sharing of skills and information. It was originally called simply the Women's Centre.

LOCATION OF RECORDS: Yukon Archives. (See Appendix for address.)
COLLECTION NAME: Forms part of: Eleanor Millard collection and Victoria Anna Belle Faulkner collection.
RECORDS: Pamphlets, 1975; miscellaneous records.
AMOUNT: Approx. 1 file.
ACCESS: No restrictions.
FINDING AID: Finding aids available for Millard and Faulkner collections.

103. Whitehorse Business and Professional Women's Club
✣ Whitehorse, Yukon. Formed 1957.

An affiliate of the Canadian Federation of Business and Professional Women's Clubs, the Whitehorse club has been active in promoting the interests of Yukon women. (Source: Yukon Archives finding aid.)

LOCATION OF RECORDS: Yukon Archives. (See Appendix for address.)
COLLECTION NAME: Whitehorse Business and Professional Women's Club.
RECORDS: Constitution, by-laws, minutes, correspondence, membership lists, clippings, photographs, programmes, sketches, blueprints, miscellaneous files, 1957-1980.
AMOUNT: 1.25 m.
CONDITION: Good.
ACCESS: No restrictions.
FINDING AID: Partial file list available.

104. Yukon Child Care Association
✣ Whitehorse, Yukon.

This association represents child-care centres throughout the Yukon.

LOCATION OF RECORDS: Yukon Archives. (See Appendix for address.)
COLLECTION NAME: Forms part of: Eleanor Millard collection.
RECORDS: Brief, 1975; position paper, 1976; miscellaneous records.
AMOUNT: Approx. 1 file.
ACCESS: No restrictions.
FINDING AID: "Eleanor Millard — Finding Aid."

NORTHWEST TERRITORIES / TERRITOIRES DU NORD-OUEST

105. Northern Women's Coalition

This group organized the Northern Women's Coalition Conference, entitled "Women in Action," held in Yellowknife in 1983.

LOCATION OF RECORDS: Canadian Women's Movement Archives Collection, Morisset Library Special Collections, University of Ottawa. (See Appendix for address.)

COLLECTION NAME: Conf.: Northern Women's Coalition Conference, Yellowknife, N.W.T., February 1983.

RECORDS: Conference proceedings, 1983.

AMOUNT: 1 cm.

CONDITION: Good.

ACCESS: No restrictions.

BREAD + ROSES, Vancouver, B.C.

Strategies for the Women's Movement: summary of December 1, 1980 meeting

1) What is the women's movement?
- the women's movement consists of all those women who fight back against women's oppression and who struggle for women's rights. This includes not only those women who are involved in groups which are clearly part of the women's movement like the Women's Health Collective and SORWUC ; but as well women who are involved in many other struggles like trade unions, anti-rascism etc.

-women's groups tend to be organized around specific issues or areas of concern. The groups are generally small enough so that there is accountability amongst members. Through these groups we are exploring new organizational forms and developing methods of work which are necessary if we are to work together in the long term revolutionary struggle

-we have a rich experience as a movement. We have taken up many diffferent issues, frequently redefining them as political questions for the first time (the ways in which people conduct their "personal" lives, the role of reproduction in the economic and social structure) We have worked in many different areas. Over the last ten years, the women's movement has had an effect on the way women think.

- as well as the ongoing organizing we have done, the women's movement has been characterized by "ad hocness". This has meant, amongst other things, that we have learned to validate our experiences enough so that if we want to organize around something we can go ahead and do it, and we have reasonably effective communication networks amongst ourselves

2) Objectives
- We need to develop more effective communication within the women's movement and particularly with the "world out there".

We have to increase our ability to develop tactics; to mobilize for individual events as well as to develop more long term strategies for where we work and how. One example of such a strategic question would be how we should deal with the question of nuclear energy. Do we work within existing anti-nuke groups and if so, how, or do we organize on our own?
We need to organize so that we can combat the attack from the right We have to be able to priorize where we place our energies.

3) Questions to be dealt with

) How do we, within the women's movement, establish our points of unity? How do we struggle over differences? What forms will leadership take? In what ways are we accountable to each other?

b) What is the relationship of the women's movement to women who are open to the ideas of the women's movement? How do we integrate new women? How are we to relate to women who are involved in the struggles of the women's movement but with whom the "women's movement" is not in contact? (Women in trade unions, caucuses etc.) What is the relationship of the women's movement to the left?

Excerpt from minutes / Extrait de procès-verbal, 1980
Bread and Roses
CWMA Collection / Fonds de l'ACMF

BRITISH COLUMBIA / COLOMBIE-BRITANNIQUE

106. *Amalgamated Clothing and Textile Workers Union. Local 178*

✣ Vancouver, B.C. Formed 1936.

Local 178 received its original charter from the Journeymen Tailors' Union in 1876. In 1936 it joined the Amalgamated Clothing Workers Union and formed the Amalgamated Clothing and Textile Workers Union. (Source: University of British Columbia Library finding aid, 1988.)

LOCATION OF RECORDS: University of British Columbia Library, Special Collections-Manuscripts. (See Appendix for address.)

COLLECTION NAME: Amalgamated Clothing and Textile Workers' Union, Local 178 (M9).

RECORDS: Charter, 1898; printed material, [196-]-[197-].

AMOUNT: 26 cm.

ACCESS: No restrictions.

107. *Archives Collective*

✣ Vancouver, B.C.

The Archives Collective collects records of various gay and lesbian organizations, most of them located in Vancouver, as well as other records related to the gay and lesbian community. (Source: University of British Columbia Library finding aid, 1988.)

LOCATION OF RECORDS: University of British Columbia Library, Special Collections-Manuscripts. (See Appendix for address.)

COLLECTION NAME: Archives Collective (M28).

RECORDS: Miscellaneous records, 1975-1985.

AMOUNT: 53 cm.

108. *Association of University and College Employees. Local 1*

✣ Vancouver, B.C. Formed 1973. Disbanded 1985.

Local 1 of the Association of University and College Employees (AUCE) represented library workers and support staff at the University of British Columbia. (Source: University of British Columbia Library finding aid, 1988.)

LOCATION OF RECORDS: University of British Columbia Library, Special Collections-Manuscripts. (See Appendix for address.)

COLLECTION NAME: Association of University and College Employees, Local 1 (M34).

RECORDS: Office files, 1973-1978; minutes, correspondence, 1973-1981; grievance-committee records, 1973-1979; office log, financial records, 1979; convention records, 1976-1977, 1979-1982; miscellaneous records.

AMOUNT: 1.9 m.

ACCESS: Closed. Open only with written permission of union executive.

FINDING AID: Inventory available.

109. *Bread and Roses (Vancouver, B.C.)*

✣ Vancouver, B.C. Formed 1980. Disbanded 1982.

Bread and Roses was a socialist-feminist organization which aimed to build the women's movement by holding discussions, distributing information, and initiating action.

LOCATION OF RECORDS: Canadian Women's Movement Archives Collection, Morisset Library Special Collections, University of Ottawa. (See Appendix for address.)

COLLECTION NAME: Bread and Roses (Vancouver, B.C.).

RECORDS: Minutes, 1980-1982; policy statement, outline of report, 1981; reports, flyer, notes.

AMOUNT: 2.5 cm.

CONDITION: Good.

ACCESS: No restrictions.

110. *B.C. Committee to Defend Dr Morgentaler*

✣ Vancouver, B.C. Formed 1973. Disbanded.

This committee demanded an end to criminal proceedings against Dr Henry Morgentaler (arrested on abortion charges). [See also Toronto Committee to Defend Dr Morgentaler (500).]

LOCATION OF RECORDS: Canadian Women's Movement Archives Collection, Morisset Library Special Collections, University of Ottawa. (See Appendix for address.)

COLLECTION NAME: B.C. Committee to Defend Dr Morgentaler — Vancouver.

RECORDS: Testimonials, flyers, 1973; clipping, 1974.

AMOUNT: 1 mm.

CONDITION: Good.

ACCESS: No restrictions.

111. British Columbia Federation of Women

[See also entry # 791 (in Part II), which lists other records of this organization.]

✣ Vancouver, B.C. Formed 1974. Disbanded [198-].

The British Columbia Federation of Women (BCFW) was an umbrella organization for women's groups in B.C.; its objective was to bring about women's liberation through fundamental social change. BCFW's Rights of Lesbians Subcommittee published *Waves*, a lesbian-feminist newsletter. [See also International Women's Day Committee (Vancouver, B.C.) (136).]

Collection (a)

LOCATION OF RECORDS: Canadian Women's Movement Archives Collection, Morisset Library Special Collections, University of Ottawa. (See Appendix for address.)

COLLECTION NAME: British Columbia Federation of Women.

RECORDS: Minutes, 1979-1981; newsletters (*B.C. Federation of Women Newsletter*, 1974-1975, 1977-1981; *Waves*, 1978-1979); financial records, 1978-1980; correspondence, 1976-1981; clippings, 1974-1976; convention records, 1977-1980; committee membership list, [1978?]; poster, 1979; research paper, 1986; photographs, 1981; constitution, handbooks, pamphlets, flyers, policy proposals, resolutions, reports, brief, questionnaire, contact lists, notes, sticker, sweatshirt, buttons.

AMOUNT: 9 cm of text, 1 poster, 3 photographs, 2 buttons, 1 sweatshirt.

CONDITION: Good.

ACCESS: No restrictions.

Collection (b)

LOCATION OF RECORDS: University of British Columbia Library, Special Collections-Manuscripts. (See Appendix for address.)

COLLECTION NAME: Forms part of: Vancouver Status of Women collection (M660: box 1, files 27a, 27b, 28; box 23, files 27-28; box 33, file 44; box 39, file 3).

RECORDS: Newsletters, conference material, miscellaneous records.

AMOUNT: 7 files.

ACCESS: No restrictions.

FINDING AID: Inventory available for Vancouver Status of Women collection.

Collection (c)

LOCATION OF RECORDS: University of British Columbia Library, Special Collections-Manuscripts.

COLLECTION NAME: Forms part of: Vancouver Women in Focus Society collection (M663: box 5, files 2-7).

RECORDS: Minutes, reports, membership records, resolutions, financial records, communiqués, miscellaneous records.

AMOUNT: 6 files.

ACCESS: No restrictions.

FINDING AID: Inventory available for Vancouver Women in Focus Society collection.

Collection (d)

LOCATION OF RECORDS: Canadian Gay Archives. (See Appendix for address.)

COLLECTION NAME: British Columbia Federation of Women. The Rights of Lesbians Subcommittee (vertical file); Waves.

RECORDS: Newsletters (*Waves*, 1978-1979); correspondence, 1976; policy statement, [before 1977]; flyer, 1979; annual report, [1980?]; pamphlet, 1982; workshop manual, poster, 1981.

Collection (e)

LOCATION OF RECORDS: McMaster University Library, William Ready Division of Archives and Research Collections. (See Appendix for address.)

COLLECTION NAME: Forms part of: Claire Culhane Papers.

RECORDS: Correspondence.

FINDING AID: Finding aid available for Claire Culhane collection.

112. British Columbia New Democratic Party. Vancouver Women's Committee

✣ Vancouver, B.C.

LOCATION OF RECORDS: University of British Columbia Library, Special Collections-Manuscripts. (See Appendix for address.)

COLLECTION NAME: Vancouver Women's Committee of the New Democratic Party (B.C.) (M664).

RECORDS: Minute book, correspondence, lists of names, miscellaneous records, 1961-1963.

AMOUNT: 2 cm.

113. British Columbia New Democratic Party. Women's Rights Committee

[See also entry # 793 (in Part II), which lists other records of this organization.]

✣ Vancouver, B.C. Formed 1971.

The Women's Rights Committee (WRC) develops policy related to women's issues and encourages women to participate in the political process. In 1979 WRC established the Task Force on Older Women in British Columbia. The committee has also been called the Standing Committee on Women's Rights. It publishes a newsletter, *Priorities*. (Source: University of British Columbia Library finding aid, 1985.)

LOCATION OF RECORDS: University of British Columbia Library, Special Collections-Manuscripts. (See Appendix for address.)

COLLECTION NAME: New Democratic Party of B.C. Women's Rights Committee.

RECORDS: Minutes, agendas, correspondence, reports, press releases, financial records, mailing lists, printed materials, pamphlets, submissions, briefs, summary briefs, recommendations, newsletters, publications, notes, registration forms, clippings, sound recordings (hearings), resource files, posters, art work, buttons, T-shirt, miscellaneous records, 1973-1984.

AMOUNT: 1.6 m.

ACCESS: No restrictions.

FINDING AID: Inventory available.

114. British Columbia Provincial Co-operative Commonwealth Federation. Women's Council. Vancouver Branch

✣ Vancouver, B.C. Disbanded 1961.

The Co-operative Commonwealth Federation (CCF), a socialist party founded in 1932, was the predecessor of the New Democratic Party.

LOCATION OF RECORDS: University of British Columbia Library, Special Collections-Manuscripts. (See Appendix for address.)

COLLECTION NAME: British Columbia Provincial C.C.F. Women's Council (Vancouver Branch) (M82).

RECORDS: Minute book, 1958-1961.

AMOUNT: 2.5 cm.

ACCESS: No restrictions.

115. British Columbia Voice of Women

✣ Formed 1960.

This is the British Columbia section of Voice of Women (VOW), a national organization which opposes war and violence. VOW lobbies all levels of government and organizes educational campaigns, meetings, and conferences. (Source: *The Canadian Encyclopedia*. — Edmonton: Hurtig Publishers, 1985.)

Collection (a)

LOCATION OF RECORDS: University of British Columbia Library, Special Collections-Manuscripts. (See Appendix for address.)

COLLECTION NAME: British Columbia Voice of Women collection; some correspondence and clippings form part of: Lille d'Easum collection (files 10-1, 11-1, 14-19).

RECORDS: Organization histories, 1960-1978; constitutions, by-laws, 1964-1974; minutes, 1964-1981, 1985-1987; financial records, 1974-1976; records of annual meetings, 1965-1979; newsletters (*The B.C. Voice*, 1964-1985); correspondence, 1961-1987; scrapbooks, 1964-1979; reports, 1960-1986; conference records, 1978, 1985; bibliographies, 1981-1982, 1984; ephemera, 1965-1970; briefs, 1967, 1970-1971; subject files, membership applications, leaflets, clippings, speeches, announcements, brochures, printed material, sound recordings, slides, miscellaneous records.

AMOUNT: 3 m.

ACCESS: No restrictions.

FINDING AID: Preliminary inventory and addenda available for British Columbia Voice of Women collection; inventory available for Lille d'Easum collection.

Collection (b)

LOCATION OF RECORDS: British Columbia Archives and Records Service. (See Appendix for address.)

COLLECTION NAME: Forms part of: Hilary Brown collection (Add.MSS. 1074).

RECORDS: Minutes, 1964-1978; reports, 1966-1975; newsletters, 1961-1968, 1970-1978; circulars, memoranda, miscellaneous records.

ACCESS: No restrictions.

FINDING AID: File list available.

Collection (c)

LOCATION OF RECORDS: Public Archives of Nova Scotia. (See Appendix for address.)

COLLECTION NAME: Forms part of: Muriel Duckworth collection (MG 1, volume 2900, # 11).

RECORDS: Minutes, 1966-1980.

FINDING AID: Finding aid available for Muriel Duckworth collection.

116. British Columbia Voice of Women. Nanaimo Branch

✣ Nanaimo, B.C.

LOCATION OF RECORDS: University of British Columbia Library, Special Collections-Manuscripts. (See Appendix for address.)

COLLECTION NAME: Forms part of: British Columbia Voice of Women collection (files 10-2a, 12-9).

RECORDS: Minutes, 1979.

AMOUNT: 2 items.

ACCESS: No restrictions.

FINDING AID: Inventory and addenda available for British Columbia Voice of Women collection.

117. British Columbia Voice of Women. North Shore Branch

LOCATION OF RECORDS: University of British Columbia Library, Special Collections-Manuscripts. (See Appendix for address.)

COLLECTION NAME: Forms part of: British Columbia Voice of Women collection (file 12-10).

RECORDS: Newsletters (*The North Shore Voice*, 1967-1969).

AMOUNT: 13 items.

ACCESS: No restrictions.

FINDING AID: Inventory and addenda available for British Columbia Voice of Women collection.

118. British Columbia Voice of Women. Parksville-Qualicum Branch

LOCATION OF RECORDS: University of British Columbia Library, Special Collections-Manuscripts. (See Appendix for address.)

COLLECTION NAME: Forms part of: British Columbia Voice of Women collection (files 12-[11-12]).

RECORDS: Scrapbooks, 1960-1969.

AMOUNT: 2 items.

ACCESS: No restrictions.

FINDING AID: Inventory and addenda available for British Columbia Voice of Women collection.

119. British Columbia Voice of Women. Powell River Branch

✣ Powell River, B.C.

LOCATION OF RECORDS: University of British Columbia Library, Special Collections-Manuscripts. (See Appendix for address.)

COLLECTION NAME: Forms part of: British Columbia Voice of Women collection (file 8-4).

RECORDS: Reports, minutes, workshop records, 1974-1977.

AMOUNT: 16 items.

ACCESS: No restrictions.

FINDING AID: Inventory and addenda available for British Columbia Voice of Women collection.

120. British Columbia Voice of Women. Vancouver Branch

✣ Vancouver, B.C.

LOCATION OF RECORDS: University of British Columbia Library, Special Collections-Manuscripts. (See Appendix for address.)

COLLECTION NAME: Forms part of: British Columbia Voice of Women collection (files 8-1, 10-2, 12-13, 13-15, 14-14, 15-10).

RECORDS: Records of annual meetings, briefs, press releases, pamphlets, newsletters, notices, clippings, printed material, correspondence, 1966-1981.

AMOUNT: 95 items.

ACCESS: No restrictions.

FINDING AID: Inventory and addenda available for British Columbia Voice of Women collection.

121. British Columbia Voice of Women. Victoria Branch

✣ Victoria, B.C.

LOCATION OF RECORDS: University of British Columbia Library, Special Collections-Manuscripts. (See Appendix for address.)

COLLECTION NAME: Forms part of: British Columbia Voice of Women collection (files 14-15, 18-14).

RECORDS: Newsletter, 1985; recommendations.

AMOUNT: 3 items.

ACCESS: No restrictions.

FINDING AID: Inventory and addenda available for British Columbia Voice of Women collection.

122. British Columbia Women's Abortion Law Repeal Coalition

✣ Vancouver, B.C. Formed 1971.

LOCATION OF RECORDS: Canadian Women's Movement Archives Collection, Morisset Library Special Collections, University of Ottawa. (See Appendix for address.)
COLLECTION NAME: B.C. Women's Abortion Law Repeal Coalition.
RECORDS: Newsletters, 1971; flyer.
AMOUNT: 3 items.
CONDITION: Fair.
ACCESS: No restrictions.

123. Business and Professional Women's Clubs of British Columbia and Yukon

✣ Formed 1948.

This is a federation of about twenty business and professional women's clubs.

LOCATION OF RECORDS: British Columbia Archives and Records Service. (See Appendix for address.)
COLLECTION NAME: Business and Professional Women's Club of British Columbia and Yukon (82-036; 87-047).
RECORDS: Scrapbook, 1967-1975; minutes.
AMOUNT: 3 volumes.
ACCESS: As of 1991, these records have yet to be arranged and described, and they are not yet available to researchers.

124. Canadian Women's Press Club. Vancouver Chapter

✣ Vancouver, B.C. Formed 1909.

One of the goals of the Canadian Women's Press Club (CWPC) was to promote journalism as a profession for women. Many Vancouver women journalists were members. (Source: City of Vancouver Archives finding aid.)

LOCATION OF RECORDS: City of Vancouver Archives. (See Appendix for address.)
COLLECTION NAME: Add. MSS. 396
RECORDS: Minutes, 1917-1929; correspondence, 1927; constitution, membership lists, 1923-1937; scrapbooks, 1912-1927; 1930-1969; reports, 1913-1920; publications.
AMOUNT: 43 cm.
FINDING AID: Preliminary inventory available.

125. Child Care Federation

✣ Vancouver, B.C. Formed 1973. Disbanded.

LOCATION OF RECORDS: Canadian Women's Movement Archives Collection, Morisset Library Special Collections, University of Ottawa. (See Appendix for address.)
COLLECTION NAME: Ragamuffin; Growing Pains.
RECORDS: Newsletters (*Ragamuffin*, 1974; *Growing Pains*, 1974-1975).
AMOUNT: 3 items.
CONDITION: Fair.
ACCESS: No restrictions.

126. Child Care Occupation Forces

✣ Vancouver, B.C. Disbanded [197-].

This organization lobbied the provincial government for child-care services which would be responsive to the needs of parents and children.

LOCATION OF RECORDS: Canadian Women's Movement Archives Collection, Morisset Library Special Collections, University of Ottawa. (See Appendix for address.)
COLLECTION NAME: Child Care Occupation Forces.
RECORDS: Proposals, 1973.
AMOUNT: 1 mm.
CONDITION: Good.
ACCESS: No restrictions.

127. Chilliwack Business and Professional Women's Club

✣ Chilliwack, B.C. Formed 1947. Disbanded 1982.

The club organized lectures and social activities, lobbied for women's rights, and promoted charitable causes.

LOCATION OF RECORDS: Chilliwack Archives, Chilliwack Museum and Historical Society. (See Appendix for address.)
COLLECTION NAME: Chilliwack Business and Professional Women's Club (Add. MSS. 637).
RECORDS: Constitution and by-laws, 1951, 1959; minutes, 1978-1982; photographs, 1957-1958, 1960-1979; scrapbooks, 1947-1981; correspondence, 1976-1982; newsletters, annual reports, 1981-1982; financial statement, 1976; membership list, [ca. 1980]; workshop materials, 1981; agendas, 1979-1981; press releases, handbooks, brochures, crest, napkin, notes.
AMOUNT: 85 cm.
ACCESS: No restrictions.
FINDING AID: "Chilliwack Business and Professional Women's Club: An Inventory of Its Papers Held by the Chilliwack Museum and Historical Society."

128. Chilliwack Council of Women

✣ Chilliwack, B.C. Formed 1927. Disbanded 1982.

Affiliated with the National Council of Women of Canada, the Chilliwack council was an umbrella organization of clubs and associations in the Chilliwack area.

LOCATION OF RECORDS: Chilliwack Archives, Chilliwack Museum and Historical Society. (See Appendix for address.)
COLLECTION NAME: Chilliwack Council of Women (Add. MSS. 232); one minute book is filed in Add. MSS. 263.
RECORDS: Correspondence, 1968-1982; minutes, 1927-1932, 1934-1983; financial records, 1927-1960; printed material, 1959-1980; programme, 1977; brief, 1968; resolutions, 1968-1969; scrapbooks, membership and attendance records, by-laws, photograph, display cards.
AMOUNT: 86 cm.
ACCESS: No restrictions.
FINDING AID: "The Collection of Chilliwack Council of Women, 1927-1983."

129. Concerned Aboriginal Women

✣ Vancouver, B.C. Formed 1981. Disbanded.

This group of Native women occupied the Vancouver office of the Department of Indian Affairs in July 1981. The group demanded an independent inquiry into the department's activities.

BRITISH COLUMBIA / COLOMBIE-BRITANNIQUE

Demonstration to protest discrimination against women in the Indian Act /
manifestation contre la discrimination envers les femmes dans la Loi sur les Indiens, 1973
Photographer unknown / Photographe inconnue
Uncatalogued photograph / Photographie non répertoriée
CWMA Collection / Fonds de l'ACMF

LOCATION OF RECORDS: Canadian Women's Movement Archives Collection, Morisset Library Special Collections, University of Ottawa. (See Appendix for address.)
COLLECTION NAME: Concerned Aboriginal Women.
RECORDS: Statement of aims, correspondence, 1981.
AMOUNT: 2 mm.
CONDITION: Good.
ACCESS: No restrictions.

130. Douglas College. Women's Studies Programme

✣ New Westminster, B.C. Disbanded.

LOCATION OF RECORDS: Douglas College Archives. (See Appendix for address.)
COLLECTION NAME: Douglas College. Women's Studies.
RECORDS: Minutes, correspondence, clippings, reports, 1973-1975.
AMOUNT: 60 cm.

131. Downtown Eastside Women's Centre

✣ Vancouver, B.C. Formed 1973.

This is a drop-in centre for women living and working in the area. (Source: City of Vancouver Archives finding aid.)

LOCATION OF RECORDS: City of Vancouver Archives. (See Appendix for address.)
COLLECTION NAME: Downtown Eastside Women's Centre (Add.MSS 412).
RECORDS: Interviews, 1978-1979.
AMOUNT: 42 pages.
ACCESS: No restrictions.
FINDING AID: Preliminary inventory available.

132. Feminist Lesbian Action Group

✣ Victoria, B.C. Formed 1977. Disbanded 1982.

The objectives of the Feminist Lesbian Action Group (FLAG) were to create a support group for lesbians, dispel myths about lesbians, engender public awareness of discrimination, and challenge discriminatory laws.

LOCATION OF RECORDS: Canadian Women's Movement Archives Collection, Morisset Library Special Collections, University of Ottawa. (See Appendix for address.)
COLLECTION NAME: Feminist Lesbian Action Group — Victoria, B.C; SR 40/1-3.
RECORDS: Correspondence, 1977-1980; sound recordings (workshop, panel discussion), conference records, mailing list, notes, 1979; newsletters, 1978-1981; clippings, 1977-1979; booklet, 1977; receipts, 1978; statement of purpose, advertisement, press releases, articles, notes, minutes, position papers.
AMOUNT: 16 cm of text, 3 sound recordings.
CONDITION: Good.
ACCESS: Restricted; conditional access negotiable.

133. Gay Alliance toward Equality (Vancouver, B.C.)

✣ Vancouver, B.C. Formed 1971. Disbanded.

The Gay Alliance toward Equality (GATE) lobbied for the inclusion of sexual orientation in human-rights legislation.

LOCATION OF RECORDS: Canadian Gay Archives. (See Appendix for address.)
COLLECTION NAME: Gay Alliance toward Equality (Vancouver) (82-005, 88-040).
RECORDS: Administrative records, correspondence, publications, briefs, posters, sound recordings, photographs, artifacts, subject files, press releases, submissions, conference material, flyers, brochures, constitution, miscellaneous records, 1971-1980; newsletters (*Gay Tide*, 1973-1980).
AMOUNT: 2.55 m.

134. Images: West Kootenay Women's Paper

[See also entry # 816 (in Part II), which lists other records of this organization.]

✣ Nelson, B.C. Formed 1972.

Images is a news journal featuring women's writing, art work, and photography. *Images* was originally published by the West Kootenay Status of Women Council.

Collection (a)

LOCATION OF RECORDS: Selkirk College Library, Archives and Local History Collection. (See Appendix for address.)
COLLECTION NAME: Newsletter; Images.
RECORDS: Periodicals, 1973-1974.
ACCESS: No restrictions.

Collection (b)

LOCATION OF RECORDS: Canadian Women's Movement Archives Collection, Morisset Library Special Collections, University of Ottawa. (See Appendix for address.)
COLLECTION NAME: Images.
RECORDS: Periodicals, 1973-1991.
ACCESS: No restrictions.

135. International Women's Day Coalition of Marxist-Leninists and Progressives

✣ Vancouver, B.C. Formed [1977?].

This organization (often referred to as the IWD Coalition of Marxist-Leninists and Progressives) advocated rights for women in such areas as maternity leave, day care, and marital law. Its position was that "only the leadership of the proletarian party can ensure success in the struggle for the liberation of women." (Source: IWD Coalition pamphlet, 1977.)

LOCATION OF RECORDS: Canadian Women's Movement Archives Collection, Morisset Library Special Collections, University of Ottawa. (See Appendix for address.)
COLLECTION NAME: International Women's Day Coalition of Marxist-Leninists and Progressives — Vancouver.
RECORDS: Proposal, position statements, reports, guidelines, clipping, 1977; minutes, booklets, correspondence, songsheets.
AMOUNT: 5 mm.
CONDITION: Good.
ACCESS: No restrictions.

136. International Women's Day Committee (Vancouver, B.C.)

✣ Vancouver, B.C. Formed [1978?].

This committee appears to have grown out of the Vancouver International Women's Day Organizing Committee, which was formed on the initiative of the British Columbia Federation of Women. [See also British Columbia Federation of Women (111, 791).]

LOCATION OF RECORDS: Canadian Women's Movement Archives Collection, Morisset Library Special Collections, University of Ottawa. (See Appendix for address.)
COLLECTION NAME: International Women's Day (Vancouver, B.C.).
RECORDS: Booklets, 1978-1979; posters, 1981-1982, 1986; songsheets, 1980; newsletter, 1981; correspondence, 1978, 1986; minutes, clippings, flyers, brochures, historical information.
AMOUNT: 7 mm of text, 3 posters.
CONDITION: Good.
ACCESS: No restrictions.

137. *Ishtar Women's Centre and Transition House*
✢ Aldergrove, B.C. Formed 1973.

This organization provides temporary accommodation to women in crisis and their children, a drop-in centre, and counselling services.
LOCATION OF RECORDS: Canadian Women's Movement Archives Collection, Morisset Library Special Collections, University of Ottawa. (See Appendix for address.)
COLLECTION NAME: Ishtar Women's Centre and Transition House.
RECORDS: Newsletters (*Ishtar News*, 1974-1976); pamphlet.
AMOUNT: 5 mm.
ACCESS: No restrictions.

138. *Kaslo Women's Group*
✢ Kaslo, B.C. Formed 1976. Disbanded 1980.

This group ran the Kaslo Women's Centre, did consciousness raising and community education, and took a stand on local political issues.
LOCATION OF RECORDS: Kootenay Lake Archives. (See Appendix for address.)
COLLECTION NAME: Kaslo Women's Group.
RECORDS: Minutes, correspondence, 1976-1980.
AMOUNT: 5 cm.
CONDITION: Good.
ACCESS: No restrictions.

139. *Kitimat Business and Professional Women's Club*
✢ Kitimat, B.C. Formed [1957?]. Disbanded [197-?].

This club awarded scholarships to female students, formed a study group on the Royal Commission on the Status of Women, and engaged in various social, educational, and charitable activities.
LOCATION OF RECORDS: Kitimat Centennial Museum. (See Appendix for address.)
COLLECTION NAME: Kitimat Business and Professional Women's Club (982.102.1, 982.109.2, 982.109.3).
RECORDS: Scrapbooks, 1960-1976; ledger, 1957-1977; organization history, correspondence, list, [197-].
AMOUNT: 223 pages.
CONDITION: Good.
ACCESS: No restrictions.

140. *Lesbian and Feminist Mothers Political Action Group*
✢ Vancouver, B.C. Formed 1979. Disbanded [198-].

This group (also known as LAFMPAG) worked to increase feminist support for mothers and children.

LOCATION OF RECORDS: Canadian Women's Movement Archives Collection, Morisset Library Special Collections, University of Ottawa. (See Appendix for address.)
COLLECTION NAME: Lesbian and Feminist Mothers Political Action Group.
RECORDS: Correspondence, 1983; book excerpt, [ca. 1982].
AMOUNT: 2 items.
CONDITION: Good.
ACCESS: Restricted; conditional access negotiable.

141. *North Shore Women's Centre*
[See also entry # 829 (in Part II), which lists other records of this organization.]
✢ North Vancouver, B.C. Formed 1976.

The North Shore Women's Centre does public education on women's issues, with the goal of improving the status of women. The centre offers an information and referral service, resource materials, lecture series, and space for women's events.
LOCATION OF RECORDS: Simon Fraser University Archives. (See Appendix for address.)
COLLECTION NAME: North Shore Women's Centre.
RECORDS: Minutes, 1974-1985; correspondence, 1973-1985; log, 1979-1984; subject files, 1976-1987; financial records, 1980-1985.
AMOUNT: 2.44 m.

142. *Office and Technical Employees' Union. Local 378*
✢ Vancouver, B.C. Formed [ca. 1921].

The B.C. Electric Employees' Association was an independent union which operated from the 1920s until 1955, when it became Local 378 of the Office Employees' International Union (OEIU). In 1964 the union's name was changed to the Office and Professional [or Technical] Employees' Union (OTEU). (Source: University of British Columbia Library finding aid, 1988.)
LOCATION OF RECORDS: University of British Columbia Library, Special Collections-Manuscripts. (See Appendix for address.)
COLLECTION NAME: Office and Technical Employees' Union, Local 378 (M485).
RECORDS: Minutes, 1921-1978; correspondence, negotiations, records of meetings, agreements, financial records, bulletins, notes, reports, proposals, forms, constitutions, by-laws, amendments, guidelines, discussion paper, clippings, pamphlets, manuals, submissions, recommendations, lay-off lists, work schedules, job analyses, application forms, notices, grievance reports, employment applications, certification records, job descriptions, booklets, posters, survey, resolutions, publications, floor plans, instructions, maps, diagrams, questionnaires, information sheets, newsletters, lists of employees, petitions, certificates of training, applications for strike authorization, job classifications, permits, lists, tables, charts, press releases, résumés, articles, job notices, conference records, work assignment sheets, record of employment, applications for affiliation, worksheets, rules and regulations, printed material, information sheets, duty sign-up sheets, time slips, brief, course descriptions, salary scales, wage rates, voting lists, arbitration records, strike-vote records, attendance lists, chronology, address lists, membership applications, election records, photographs, statistical information, miscellaneous records, 1929-1982.
AMOUNT: 12.7 m.
ACCESS: No restrictions.
FINDING AID: Inventory available.

143. Port Coquitlam Area Women's Centre

[See also entry # 833 (in Part II), which lists other records of this organization.]

✥ Port Coquitlam, B.C. Formed 1975.

The centre promotes feminism and provides a safe space for women in the area. It offers drop-in services, support groups, counselling, and a library.

LOCATION OF RECORDS: Simon Fraser University Archives. (See Appendix for address.)

COLLECTION NAME: Port Coquitlam Area Women's Centre.

RECORDS: Constitution, 1975; membership records, 1979; records of meetings, 1975-1983; committee records, 1975-1979; correspondence, 1974-1984; financial records, [198-]; policies and procedures, miscellaneous records, 1975-1984.

AMOUNT: 3.35 m.

144. Press Gang

[See also entry # 834 (in Part II), which lists other records of this organization.]

✥ Vancouver, B.C. Formed [ca. 1970].

Until 1990 Press Gang Printers and Press Gang Publishers were the same organization (a feminist, anti-capitalist printing and publishing company). Since 1990, Press Gang Printers has been a separate company.

LOCATION OF RECORDS: Canadian Women's Movement Archives Collection, Morisset Library Special Collections, University of Ottawa. (See Appendix for address.)

COLLECTION NAME: Press Gang; SR 11/6B-11/7A.

RECORDS: Sound recording (interview), 1976; calendars, 1971, 1975, 1978-1979; article, 1980; pamphlets, 1984; press release, 1986; posters, catalogues, flyers, invitations, bookmarks, stickers, postcard, ticket, T-shirt, button.

AMOUNT: 4 cm of text, 1 sound recording, 14 posters, 1 T-shirt, 1 button.

ACCESS: No restrictions.

145. Provincial Council of Women of British Columbia

✥ Formed 1921.

The provincial council represents local councils of women throughout British Columbia. It has taken an interest in a variety of women's issues and other social issues.

Collection (a)

LOCATION OF RECORDS: British Columbia Archives and Records Service. (See Appendix for address.)

COLLECTION NAME: Provincial Council of Women (British Columbia) (Add.MSS. 1961).

RECORDS: Minutes, 1919-1945, 1947-1961; history of resolutions, 1919-1969; resolutions, 1921, 1928, 1937-1961; submissions, 1947, 1954-1959, 1970; annual reports, 1944-1961; radio transcripts, 1958-1959; correspondence, 1905-1910, 1925-1942, 1945-1953; committee records, 1925-1936, 1944-1945, 1949-1961; lists of officers, 1947-1961; pledge, 1954; scrapbook, 1894-1920; proceedings of meeting, 1894; organization histories, 1953, 1969; memorial-service records, 1955; clippings, 1895, 1950, 1967; programme, 1895; handbook, 1906; scroll, 1969; constitution and standing orders, photographs, miscellaneous records.

AMOUNT: 1.1 m.

ACCESS: No restrictions.

FINDING AID: File list available.

Collection (b)

LOCATION OF RECORDS: University of British Columbia Library, Special Collections-Manuscripts. (See Appendix for address.)

COLLECTION NAME: Forms part of: Vancouver Council of Women collection (files 10-3, 11-[8-9], 12-[6-10], 13-[1-11, 13], 16-[1-2]).

RECORDS: Correspondence, 1959-1971; minutes, 1963-1964; resolutions, 1959, 1963-1964; newsletters, 1964-1967; miscellaneous records, 1959-1972; letterhead.

AMOUNT: Approx. 22 files.

ACCESS: No restrictions.

FINDING AID: Inventory available for Vancouver Council of Women collection.

146. Service, Office, and Retail Workers' Union of Canada. Local 4 (Bank and Finance Workers)

✥ Vancouver, B.C. Formed 1976. Disbanded 1986.

The Service, Office, and Retail Workers' Union of Canada (SORWUC) was a feminist, member-controlled union founded in Vancouver in 1972. It sought to organize workers in occupations often ignored by unions, such as restaurant and office work. In 1976 SORWUC began organizing bank workers and established Local 2, the United Bank Workers (UBW). Local 2 was shut down in 1978; but in 1981, Local 4 (the Bank and Finance Workers) was established to carry on the work of Local 2. Local 4 later began to organize restaurant workers as well. SORWUC disbanded in 1986. (Source: University of British Columbia Library finding aid, 1989.) [See also Service, Office, and Retail Workers' Union of Canada. Local 7 (1073).]

Collection (a)

LOCATION OF RECORDS: University of British Columbia Library, Special Collections-Manuscripts. (See Appendix for address.)

COLLECTION NAME: Service Office and Retail Workers' Union: Local 2 United Bank Workers; Local 4 Bank and Finance Workers.

RECORDS: Legal records, financial records, correspondence, minutes, research material, newsletters, bulletins, press releases, mailing lists, paste-ups, layout, clippings, membership forms, membership lists, dues-authorization forms, certification application forms, sign-up sheets, contract proposals, model contracts, negotiations, contract drafts, constitution, by-laws, organization histories, rules of order, agendas, reports, flyers, brochures, pamphlets, notes, evaluation sheets, personnel manual, research contracts, statistics, voters' lists, poster, miscellaneous records, 1972-1984.

AMOUNT: 8.8 m.

ACCESS: Restricted until September 1, 1992.

FINDING AID: Inventory available.

Collection (b)

LOCATION OF RECORDS: National Archives of Canada. (See Appendix for address.)

COLLECTION NAME: Forms part of: Eileen Tallman Sufrin collection (MG 31, B 31, volume 1).

RECORDS: Please see the note about National Archives of Canada collections, in entry # 2.

147. SFU Co-op Family

✥ Burnaby, B.C. Formed 1968.

The SFU Co-op Family (also referred to as the Louis Riel University Family Co-op) was a day-care centre run collectively by students at Simon Fraser University (SFU). The co-op grew out of a sit-in at the SFU Board of Governors' meeting room.

LOCATION OF RECORDS: Canadian Women's Movement Archives Collection, Morisset Library Special Collections, University of Ottawa. (See Appendix for address.)

COLLECTION NAME: Simon Fraser University. The Louis Riel University Family Co-op.
RECORDS: Essay, excerpt from essay, 1969.
AMOUNT: 2 mm.
CONDITION: Good.
ACCESS: No restrictions.

148. Simon Fraser University. Women's Studies Program

✤ Burnaby, B.C. Formed [197-].

Simon Fraser University has minor, certificate, and master's programmes in women's studies. The goals of the Women's Studies Program include exploring women's experiences and achievements and developing new criteria and methods for appraising the status of women.

LOCATION OF RECORDS: Simon Fraser University Archives. (See Appendix for address.)
COLLECTION NAME: Women's Studies Program.
RECORDS: Publications, agendas, minutes, 1986-1991; correspondence, 1972; miscellaneous records, 1982-1989.
AMOUNT: 4.26 m.
ACCESS: Miscellaneous records, 1982-1989 restricted.

149. Society for Political Action by Gays

✤ Vancouver, B.C. Disbanded [198-].

The Society for Political Action by Gays (SPAG) was also known as the Society for Political Action for Gay People.

LOCATION OF RECORDS: Canadian Gay Archives. (See Appendix for address.)
COLLECTION NAME: Society for Political Action by Gays (83-004).
RECORDS: Administrative files, correspondence, subject files, legal files, buttons, newsletters, miscellaneous records, 1978-1983.
AMOUNT: 20 cm.

150. Tamitik Status of Women

✤ Kitimat, B.C. Formed 1975.

Tamitik Status of Women runs a women's centre and works to rectify injustices, especially those which affect women.

Collection (a)

LOCATION OF RECORDS: Kitimat Centennial Museum. (See Appendix for address.)
COLLECTION NAME: Tamitik Status of Women.
RECORDS: Newsletters, 1989-1990.
ACCESS: No restrictions.

Collection (b)

LOCATION OF RECORDS: Canadian Women's Movement Archives Collection, Morisset Library Special Collections, University of Ottawa. (See Appendix for address.)
COLLECTION NAME: Tamitik Status of Women.
RECORDS: Organization history, 1985; minutes, 1977-1978; announcement, flyer, newsletter, 1986; clippings.
AMOUNT: 3 mm.
CONDITION: Good.
ACCESS: No restrictions.

151. University of British Columbia. Academic Women's Association

✤ Vancouver, B.C. Formed 1976.

The Academic Women's Association of the University of British Columbia (AWA) is open to women academic staff at the university. AWA promotes equal opportunities for women to participate fully in the university. (Source: University of British Columbia Library finding aid, 1988.)

LOCATION OF RECORDS: University of British Columbia Library, University Archives. (See Appendix for address.)
COLLECTION NAME: Academic Women's Association.
RECORDS: Constitution, 1976; minutes, notices of meetings, reports, correspondence, questionnaires, printed material, membership records, legal records, miscellaneous records, 1976-1985.
AMOUNT: 32.5 cm.
ACCESS: No restrictions.
FINDING AID: "Academic Women's Association — An Inventory."

152. University of British Columbia. Women's Office

✤ Vancouver, B.C. Formed 1971. Disbanded 1976.

The Women's Office at the University of British Columbia (UBC) was run by "a group of women students concerned with providing women with the support needed to realize our full potential as future professionals." (Source: Women's Office flyer, 1975.) The Women's Office operated a drop-in centre and a library. When the group was evicted by UBC's Student Administration Committee in 1976, the Women's Office moved its audio-visual library (called Women in Focus) to a new location off campus. [See also Vancouver Women in Focus Society (159).]

LOCATION OF RECORDS: Canadian Women's Movement Archives Collection, Morisset Library Special Collections, University of Ottawa. (See Appendix for address.)
COLLECTION NAME: University of British Columbia. Women's Office.
RECORDS: Press releases, 1974, 1976; catalogue, 1974; correspondence, 1976; flyer, 1975; mission statement, booklets, evaluation.
AMOUNT: 4 mm.
CONDITION: Good.
ACCESS: No restrictions.

153. University of Victoria. Faculty Association. Status of Women Committee

✤ Victoria, B.C. Formed 1971.

The Status of Women Committee of the University of Victoria Faculty Association (UVFA) has examined the following issues, among others: pay equity, hiring policy, day care, pension-plan equity, and the establishment of a women's studies programme.

LOCATION OF RECORDS: University of Victoria Archives. (See Appendix for address.)
COLLECTION NAME: Forms part of: University of Victoria Faculty Association collection (Accession #84-20-3).
RECORDS: Correspondence, reports, 1971-1975; statistical data, 1975; questionnaires, notes, 1971-1976.
ACCESS: Correspondence closed. Access to other records requires permission of Faculty Association executive.
FINDING AID: "Inventory of the Records of the University of Victoria Faculty Association."

154. University of Victoria. President's Advisory Committee on Equal Rights and Opportunities

✣ Victoria, B.C. Formed 1977.

This committee was charged with examining aspects of equal rights and opportunities for women and men at the university, identifying areas of concern and need, and making specific recommendations.

LOCATION OF RECORDS: University of Victoria Archives. (See Appendix for address.)

COLLECTION NAME: Forms part of: University of Victoria Faculty Association collection (Accession #84-20-3).

RECORDS: Minutes, correspondence, 1977-1981; agendas, lists of subcommittees, 1977-1978; reports, 1978-1979.

ACCESS: Correspondence closed. Access to other records requires permission of Faculty Association executive.

FINDING AID: "Inventory of the Records of the University of Victoria Faculty Association."

155. University of Victoria. Women's Action Group

✣ Victoria, B.C. Formed 1973.

The University of Victoria Women's Action Group (WAG) was founded to act in the interests of all women in the university community. Its activities have included lobbying for the establishment of women's studies courses. (Source: University of Victoria Archives finding aid, 1991.)

LOCATION OF RECORDS: University of Victoria Archives. (See Appendix for address.)

COLLECTION NAME: University of Victoria. Women's Action Group (Accession #80-3).

RECORDS: Correspondence, 1974-1978; minutes, mission statement, report, 1974-1975; membership lists and forms, 1974-1976; policy statements, 1974; pamphlets, announcements, 1975-1978; financial records, 1973-1974, 1977-1978; notes, 1975-1976; newsletters, 1976-1977; press releases, clippings, 1977-1978; course outlines, 1974-1977.

AMOUNT: 14 cm.

ACCESS: No restrictions.

FINDING AID: "University of Victoria. Women's Action Group: Inventory."

156. Vancouver Business and Professional Women's Club

✣ Vancouver, B.C. Formed 1922.

One of the club's early projects was a loan fund to help women complete their education. (Source: City of Vancouver Archives finding aid.)

LOCATION OF RECORDS: City of Vancouver Archives. (See Appendix for address.)

COLLECTION NAME: Vancouver Business and Professional Women's Club (Add.MSS 799).

RECORDS: Minutes, scrapbooks, correspondence, publications, 1946-1984.

AMOUNT: 107 cm.

ACCESS: No restrictions.

FINDING AID: Preliminary inventory available.

157. Vancouver Council of Women

✣ Vancouver, B.C. Formed 1894.

The Vancouver Council of Women (VCW) was established by seventeen local women's groups. It has spoken out on issues affecting women in the workplace and in the home. (Source: City of Vancouver Archives finding aid.)

Collection (a)

LOCATION OF RECORDS: University of British Columbia Library, Special Collections-Manuscripts. (See Appendix for address.)

COLLECTION NAME: Vancouver Council of Women (M657).

RECORDS: Minutes, 1910-1951, 1953-1964, 1967-1969, 1972, 1977-1986; correspondence, 1916-1931, 1943-1970, 1979-1986; correspondence summary, 1961-1963; correspondence lists, 1951-1953, 1960-1961; membership lists, 1902-1917, 1941-1945, 1951-1954, 1962-1965, 1967-1968; lists of officers, 1912-1916, 1951-1954, 1971-1981; attendance records, 1971-1981; lists of delegates, 1946-1948; affiliation records, 1950-1952, 1957-1963; reports, 1927-1928, 1962-1968; financial records, 1966-1968, 1976-1986; constitutions, by-laws, 1955, 1964, 1969; records of annual meetings, 1945-1967; convention records, 1917; conference records, pamphlets, 1958; briefs, 1947-1954; radio scripts, 1958-1959; notices of meetings, 1946-1949, 1979-1986; clippings, 1951-1964, 1980-1985; history and memorabilia, 1894-1954; workshop records, 1965; resolutions, 1955-1969; photographs, [1954?]; newsletter, 1957; printed material, 1963-1970; committee files, project files, subject files, scrapbooks, draft of organization history, miscellaneous records.

AMOUNT: 3 m.

ACCESS: No restrictions.

FINDING AID: Inventory available.

Collection (b)

LOCATION OF RECORDS: City of Vancouver Archives. (See Appendix for address.)

COLLECTION NAME: Vancouver Council of Women (Add.MSS 438).

RECORDS: Account of activities, 1894-1968; certificate, 1986; photographs.

AMOUNT: 5 cm.

ACCESS: No restrictions.

FINDING AID: Preliminary inventory available.

158. Vancouver Status of Women

✣ Vancouver, B.C. Formed 1971.

This organization was originally called the British Columbia Status of Women Action and Coordinating Council (BCSWACC or simply SWACC); by 1972 the name had changed to the British Columbia Status of Women Council (BCSWC or SWC); and in 1973 the organization became Vancouver Status of Women (VSW). One of the original aims of the council, whose members represented a wide range of women's organizations, was to promote the implementation of the recommendations of the Royal Commission on the Status of Women. VSW has published the feminist newspaper *Kinesis* since 1974.

Collection (a)

LOCATION OF RECORDS: University of British Columbia Library, Special Collections-Manuscripts. (See Appendix for address.)

COLLECTION NAME: Vancouver Status of Women (M660).

RECORDS: Minutes, correspondence, financial records, grant applications, reports, briefs, periodicals, press releases, subject files, office files, research papers, 1971-1978.

AMOUNT: 15.2 m.

ACCESS: No restrictions.

FINDING AID: Inventory available.

Collection (b)

LOCATION OF RECORDS: Canadian Women's Movement Archives Collection, Morisset Library Special Collections, University of Ottawa. (See Appendix for address.)

COLLECTION NAME: Status of Women Action and Coordinating Council of B.C.; Vancouver Status of Women.

RECORDS: Periodicals (*SWACC Newsletter*, 1971; *Status of Women Newsletter*, 1972-1973; *Kinesis*, 1974-1991); brief, booklet, organization history, 1972; press release, 1977; reports, 1972-1974, 1976-1979, 1985; handbooks, 1975, 1981; minutes, 1972, 1980-1981; financial records, 1981; guides, 1975-1976, 1986; correspondence, pamphlets, fact sheets, flyers, lists of publications, posters, photograph.
AMOUNT: 66 cm of text, 2 posters, 1 photograph.
CONDITION: Good.
ACCESS: No restrictions.

159. Vancouver Women in Focus Society

✢ Vancouver, B.C. Formed 1974.

This organization, often referred to simply as Women in Focus, was originally part of the Women's Office at the University of British Columbia. The members of Women in Focus work co-operatively to produce, distribute, and support women's arts and media. The organization also operates an audio-visual library. [See also University of British Columbia. Women's Office (152).]

LOCATION OF RECORDS: University of British Columbia Library, Special Collections-Manuscripts. (See Appendix for address.)
COLLECTION NAME: Vancouver Women in Focus Society (M663).
RECORDS: Correspondence, newsletters, grant applications, catalogues, contracts, distribution files, jury submission forms, release forms, sales and rental records, publicity material, biographical information, bibliographies, surveys, printed material, office files, financial records, scripts, research materials, miscellaneous records, 1974-1986.
AMOUNT: 2 m.
ACCESS: No restrictions.
FINDING AID: Inventory available.

160. Vancouver Women's Bookstore

[See also entry # 854 (in Part II), which lists other records of this organization.]

✢ Vancouver, B.C. Formed 1973.

The bookstore provides books, periodicals, and music by, for, and about women. It also carries non-sexist books for children.

LOCATION OF RECORDS: Canadian Women's Movement Archives Collection, Morisset Library Special Collections, University of Ottawa. (See Appendix for address.)
COLLECTION NAME: Vancouver Women's Bookstore; SR 11/5B - 11/6A.
RECORDS: Sound recording (interview), interview transcript, 1976; posters, [1973?], 1983; correspondence, 1971; catalogue, [197-]; flyers, bookmarks, booklet.
AMOUNT: 5 mm of text, 1 sound recording, 2 posters.
CONDITION: Fair.
ACCESS: No restrictions.

161. Vancouver Women's Caucus

✢ Vancouver, B.C. Formed 1968. Disbanded.

This group began as the Women's Caucus at Simon Fraser University, which demanded that the campus health services provide birth control; in 1969 the group moved off campus. The activities of the caucus included demonstrations, discussions, and abortion counselling; it dealt with issues such as jobs, education, and society's responsibility for children. In 1969 it founded the feminist newspaper *The Pedestal* (later known for a brief period as *Women Can*).

LOCATION OF RECORDS: Canadian Women's Movement Archives Collection, Morisset Library Special Collections, University of Ottawa. (See Appendix for address.)
COLLECTION NAME: Vancouver Women's Caucus; Simon Fraser University. Women's Caucus; The Pedestal.
RECORDS: Booklets, 1969-1971, 1975; research paper, press release, 1969; organization history, proposal, 1970; correspondence, 1969-1970; periodicals (*Women's Caucus News*, 1969; *The Pedestal*, 1969-1975; *Women Can*, 1974); discussion papers, reports, subscription form, position statements, brief, fact sheet, schedule, posters, photograph, flyer.
AMOUNT: 9.5 cm of text, 2 posters, 1 photograph.
CONDITION: Good.
ACCESS: No restrictions.

162. Vancouver Women's Health Collective

[See also entry # 855 (in Part II), which lists other records of this organization.]

✢ Vancouver, B.C. Formed 1972.

The Vancouver Women's Health Collective (VWHC) operates a resource centre on women's health. VWHC's goal is to provide women with the information they need to make good choices about their health care. The group's French name is le Collectif de la santé des femmes de Vancouver.

LOCATION OF RECORDS: Canadian Women's Movement Archives Collection, Morisset Library Special Collections, University of Ottawa. (See Appendix for address.)
COLLECTION NAME: Vancouver Women's Health Collective.
RECORDS: Description of organization, 1976; newsletters (*Vancouver Women's Health Collective Newsletter*, 1973-1974; *Wicca*, 1975; *Healthmatters*, 1985-1987); calendar, 1980; clippings, 1977-1978, 1983, 1988; correspondence, training materials, publications list, information sheets, information packages, coupon, form, guide, phone list, schedules, photograph, T-shirt.
AMOUNT: 3.5 cm of text, 1 T-shirt, 1 photograph.
CONDITION: Good.
ACCESS: No restrictions.

163. Victoria Business and Professional Women's Club

[See also entry # 857 (in Part II), which lists other records of this organization.]

✢ Victoria, B.C. Formed 1921.

The Victoria Business and Professional Women's Club (BPWC) works for the improvement of economic and social conditions for women and girls. It also encourages women to participate in the business of government. Until 1930 the group was called Kumtuks.

LOCATION OF RECORDS: British Columbia Archives and Records Service. (See Appendix for address.)
COLLECTION NAME: Victoria Business and Professional Women's Club (80-161; 81-060).
RECORDS: Minutes, reports, briefs, by-laws, publications, miscellaneous records, 1921-1979.
AMOUNT: Approx. 4 boxes.
ACCESS: As of 1991, these records have yet to be arranged and described, and they are not yet available to researchers.

164. Victoria Council of Women

✢ Victoria, B.C. Formed 1894.

The council is made up of about twenty local women's organizations. It has lobbied on a variety of social issues, including some women's issues. It was originally called the Victoria and Vancouver Island Local Council of Women.

LESBIANS BELONG IN THE WOMEN'S MOVEMENT

Vancouver Women's Caucus

Vancouver, B.C. - 1972

There are a lot of lesbians in women's liberation in Vancouver and other cities in Canada. There are a lot more lesbains (thousands more) who are not a part of the movement, some who have never been in contact with women's liberation, others who have chosen not to come to the movement because "they will give it a bad name', or will not be accepted. That's right;

Anyone in women's liberation has faced lesbian-baiting on some level from "you're a bunch of lesbians"-"what you need is a good fuck" to "women's Liberation loosens women up for men". It is important for all women's Liberationists to think about those attacks, now often we have been intimidated or defensive when we hear them, or remember when we first heard them. We have to think about that and realize that when we ligitimize womenás liberation through our relationships to men we're saying to lesbians that they do give women's liberation a bad name.

What the hell is that - a bad name? What is lesbianism? It's love between women, one form of the sisterhood most of us have discovered to be powerful. It is loving women without putting any limitations on that love.

As lesbians, we have understood our sexuality in a way that is despised, feared and ridiculed by this society. And not just by some abstract society but by the people we grew up with. Most heavily by our families. People we work with, friends and even, it must painfully be admitted, sometimes by ourselves.

For without the personal support and the social and political understanding of the women's movement, many lesbians accept society's defintion of themselves as 'different', 'sinful', 'sick' or 'perverted' - to be 'saved', 'cured' or made 'normal'.

Most are alone and isolated, having made an individual rebellion which puts them in for all kinds of shit. Psychological and social guilt which male dominated religions heap on lesbians, and which gets us even if we're not believers. And fear. Fear of losing jobs, fear of being found out by family, not just because of rejection but because parents agonize and mutilate themselves trying to find out where they failed. Because even if we don't feel guilt, they do.

And friends. The experience of being cut off from them. Friendship turned to pity and fear. The assumption that because you are a lesbian you are going to exploit other women sexually. That, of course, comes from straight women's experience that sexuality usually means exploitation. But that assumption lays a male role on lesbians, denying us our humanity.

To the degree that the fucked-up roles of 'butch' and 'femme' really exist amoung lesbians, it is because the only models of sexual relationships lesbians see are the dominant-submissive, agressive-passive, dickjane ones that stifle all womens,and for that matter all men's human growth. A growing number of lesbians both in and out of the movement are struggling with and are rejecting those sex roles. We are building relationships in which those polarities, those limitations are broken.

Feminism has much to give us as lesbians, as we have much to give our sisiters in the women's movement.

Excerpt from a 1972 document entitled: / Extrait d'un document de 1972 intitulé :
"Lesbians Belong in the Women's Movement"
Vancouver Women's Caucus
CWMA Collection / Fonds de l'ACMF

LOCATION OF RECORDS: British Columbia Archives and Records Service. (See Appendix for address.)
COLLECTION NAME: Local Council of Women, Victoria (79-139; 81-140; 81-141).
RECORDS: Correspondence, scrapbooks, essay, pamphlets, clippings, miscellaneous records.
AMOUNT: 3 boxes.
ACCESS: As of 1991, these records have yet to be arranged and described, and they are not yet available to researchers.

165. *Victoria Status of Women Action Group*

[See also entry # 858 (in Part II), which lists other records of this organization.]

✢ Victoria, B.C. Formed 1971.

The Victoria Status of Women Action Group (SWAG) fosters public knowledge of the rights and status of women and promotes the full participation of women in social, economic, and political life. It offers educational programmes, a drop-in centre, and a library.

LOCATION OF RECORDS: Canadian Women's Movement Archives Collection, Morisset Library Special Collections, University of Ottawa. (See Appendix for address.)
COLLECTION NAME: Victoria Status of Women Action Group; Status of Women Action Group (Victoria, B.C.).
RECORDS: Photographs, [197-?]; newsletters, 1979-1990; report, 1976; press release, workshop material, pamphlets, flyers.
AMOUNT: 6 cm of text, 66 photographs.
ACCESS: No restrictions.

166. *Victoria Women's Centre*

✢ Victoria, B.C. Formed 1972. Disbanded [197-?].

The Victoria Women's Centre provided a drop-in centre, a library, a counselling service, consciousness-raising groups, and courses. The centre appears to have been known at times as A Room of One's Own, the Women's Centre and Transition House, and simply the Women's Centre.

LOCATION OF RECORDS: Canadian Women's Movement Archives Collection, Morisset Library Special Collections, University of Ottawa. (See Appendix for address.)
COLLECTION NAME: Victoria Women's Centre.
RECORDS: Organization history, [1975?]; correspondence, 1975-1976; resource material, 1972; newsletters (*Sister*, 1973; *Sisters*, 1974; *Surfacing*, 1974; *Women's Centre and Transition House Newsletter*, 1974; *Victoria B.C. Women's Centre Newsletter*, 1975; *Lysistrata*, 1975-1976); photographs, report, flyer.
AMOUNT: 4 cm of text, 9 photographs.
CONDITION: Good.
ACCESS: No restrictions.

167. *Western Canadian Women's News Service*

✢ Vancouver, B.C. Formed 1974. Disbanded 1976.

The Western Canadian Women's News Service (WCWN) published feminist news packages, which it distributed each month to the media and to women's groups in British Columbia and the Yukon.

Collection (a)

LOCATION OF RECORDS: Canadian Women's Movement Archives Collection, Morisset Library Special Collections, University of Ottawa. (See Appendix for address.)
COLLECTION NAME: Western Canadian Women's News Service.
RECORDS: News packages, guides, 1974-1975; reports, 1974-1976; position paper, speech, correspondence, article, 1974; outline, 1975; resource material, kit, 1976; story, questionnaire, index.
AMOUNT: 7 cm.
CONDITION: Good.
ACCESS: No restrictions.

Collection (b)

LOCATION OF RECORDS: Thomas Fisher Rare Book Library, University of Toronto. (See Appendix for address.)
COLLECTION NAME: Forms part of: F.M. Denison collection — Manuscript Collection 51, Box 9.
RECORDS: News packages, 1975.
AMOUNT: 1 cm.
ACCESS: No restrictions.

168. *A Woman's Place (Vancouver, B.C.)*

✢ Vancouver, B.C. Disbanded [1973?].

Among other activities, this women's centre produced resources on women's health.

LOCATION OF RECORDS: Canadian Women's Movement Archives Collection, Morisset Library Special Collections, University of Ottawa. (See Appendix for address.)
COLLECTION NAME: A Woman's Place (Vancouver, B.C.).
RECORDS: Booklet, 1972; newsletters, 1972-1973; questionnaires, [1972?].
AMOUNT: 1.6 cm.
CONDITION: Good.
ACCESS: No restrictions.

169. *Women against Pornography (Victoria, B.C.)*

✢ Victoria, B.C. Formed [198-?]. Disbanded [1985?].

Women against Pornography (WAP) was a feminist collective which opposed pornography and defended women's rights. WAP also aimed to expose myths surrounding prostitution, and it published newsletters or bad-trick sheets for prostitutes.

LOCATION OF RECORDS: Canadian Women's Movement Archives Collection, Morisset Library Special Collections, University of Ottawa. (See Appendix for address.)
COLLECTION NAME: Women against Pornography (Victoria, B.C.).
RECORDS: Photographs, article, press release, 1983; advertisements, 1981; log, 1982; fact sheet, evaluation form, 1984; clippings, 1983-1984; briefs, reports, policy statement, discussion papers, script, newsletters, booklet, bibliography, pamphlet, flyers, banner.
AMOUNT: 4.5 cm of text, 3 photographs, 1 banner.
CONDITION: Good.
ACCESS: No restrictions.

170. *Women Rally for Action*

✢ Port Coquitlam, B.C. Formed 1976. Disbanded 1976.

Women Rally for Action (WRA) was a provincial lobbying group which organized a 1976 demonstration in Victoria.

LOCATION OF RECORDS: Canadian Women's Movement Archives Collection, Morisset Library Special Collections, University of Ottawa. (See Appendix for address.)

COLLECTION NAME: Women Rally for Action.
RECORDS: Organization history, report, brief, pamphlet, accounts of meetings, analysis, song, position paper, 1976.
AMOUNT: 1.5 cm.
CONDITION: Good.
ACCESS: No restrictions.

171. Women's Centre (Vancouver, B.C.)

✣ Vancouver, B.C. Formed (197-). Disbanded [197-].

The Women's Centre was a collectively run drop-in centre where women could meet and exchange information.

LOCATION OF RECORDS: Canadian Women's Movement Archives Collection, Morisset Library Special Collections, University of Ottawa. (See Appendix for address.)
COLLECTION NAME: Women's Centre (Vancouver, B.C.).
RECORDS: Flyer, 1972; calendar, correspondence, 1973; proposal, newsletter.
AMOUNT: 5 mm.
CONDITION: Fair.
ACCESS: No restrictions.

172. Women's International League for Peace and Freedom. Vancouver Branch

✣ Vancouver, B.C. Formed 1920.

The Women's International League for Peace and Freedom (WILPF) was founded in 1915 by suffragists who wanted to end World War I and prevent further wars. The Vancouver branch of WILPF was the first in Canada. It was also the only Canadian branch to survive the decline of WILPF during and after World War II. (However, WILPF began to expand again in Canada in the 1970s.) (Source: University of British Columbia Library finding aid, 1988.)

LOCATION OF RECORDS: University of British Columbia Library, Special Collections-Manuscripts. (See Appendix for address.)
COLLECTION NAME: Women's International League for Peace and Freedom.
RECORDS: Correspondence, 1949-1988; project files, 1948-1987; conference records, 1952-1953, 1956, 1959, 1962, 1965, 1968, 1971, 1977; printed material, reference material, photographs, miscellaneous records.
AMOUNT: 42 cm.
ACCESS: No restrictions.
FINDING AID: Inventory available.

173. Women's Labour History Project

[See also entry # 871 (in Part II), which lists other records of this organization.]

✣ Vancouver, B.C. Formed 1978.

The Women's Labour History Project (WLHP) researches the history of women and work and the history of working-class women and family and community life. It creates photographic, sound, and video archives and produces videotapes about women's labour history. WLHP is also known as the Western Women's Labour History Project of B.C.

LOCATION OF RECORDS: British Columbia Archives and Records Service. (See Appendix for address.)
COLLECTION NAME: Women's Labour History Project (TAPE 215:3-4; 2062:2; 3587-3629; 4271:1-28).
RECORDS: Sound recordings (interviews), 1979, 1982, 1986.
AMOUNT: 84 tape reels, 28 cassettes.
ACCESS: No restrictions.
FINDING AID: Summaries and list of interviewees available.

174. Women's Liberation Alliance (Vancouver, B.C.)

✣ Vancouver, B.C. Formed 1970. Disbanded [197-].

The Women's Liberation Alliance (WLA) was an action-oriented organization created to combat the oppression of women. WLA's demands included equal educational opportunities, paid maternity leave, abortion on demand, and free twenty-four-hour child-care centres.

Collection (a)

LOCATION OF RECORDS: University of British Columbia Library, Special Collections-Manuscripts. (See Appendix for address.)
COLLECTION NAME: Forms part of: Vancouver Status of Women collection (M660, box 13, files 45-64).
RECORDS: Minutes, conference material, publications, financial reports, miscellaneous records, [197-].
AMOUNT: 20 files.
ACCESS: No restrictions.
FINDING AID: Inventory available for Vancouver Status of Women collection.

Collection (b)

LOCATION OF RECORDS: Canadian Women's Movement Archives Collection, Morisset Library Special Collections, University of Ottawa. (See Appendix for address.)
COLLECTION NAME: Women's Liberation Alliance — Vancouver; SR 20/1.
RECORDS: Brief, clippings, correspondence, press release, newsletters, 1971; manifesto, constitution, sound recording (debate), reading lists, questionnaire, flyers, schedule, invitations.
AMOUNT: 1.5 cm of text, 1 sound recording.
CONDITION: Good.
ACCESS: No restrictions.

175. Women's Self-Help Clinic (Vancouver, B.C.)

✣ Vancouver, B.C. Formed 1972.

The Women's Self-Help Clinic (also called the Wednesday Night Health Group) was a group of women who met to discuss women's health issues.

LOCATION OF RECORDS: Canadian Women's Movement Archives Collection, Morisset Library Special Collections, University of Ottawa. (See Appendix for address.)
COLLECTION NAME: Women's Self-Help Clinic — Vancouver.
RECORDS: Organization history, 1972; information sheets, [197-].
AMOUNT: 2 mm.
CONDITION: Fair.
ACCESS: No restrictions.

176. Women's Studies Association of British Columbia

LOCATION OF RECORDS: Simon Fraser University Archives. (See Appendix for address.)
COLLECTION NAME: Women's Studies Association of B.C.
RECORDS: Conference records, minutes, 1974-1980; correspondence, 1978-1980; constitution, by-laws, membership records, publications, newsletters.
AMOUNT: 91 cm.

177. Women's Study Group (Vancouver, B.C.)

✣ Vancouver, B.C. Formed [197-].

This was a socialist-feminist study and discussion group.

LOCATION OF RECORDS: Canadian Women's Movement Archives Collection,

Morisset Library Special Collections, University of Ottawa. (See Appendix for address.)
COLLECTION NAME: Women's Socialist-Feminist Study Group, Vancouver.
RECORDS: Essay, 1974; minutes, summaries, 1977, 1980; notes, 1980; discussion paper, mailing lists.
AMOUNT: 1.3 cm.
CONDITION: Good.
ACCESS: No restrictions.

178. Working Women's Association

✢ Vancouver, B.C. Formed 1971. Disbanded [197-].

The Working Women's Association (WWA) worked for the unionization of women workers.
LOCATION OF RECORDS: Canadian Women's Movement Archives Collection, Morisset Library Special Collections, University of Ottawa. (See Appendix for address.)
COLLECTION NAME: Working Women's Association — Vancouver.
RECORDS: Correspondence, 1972; newsletter, 1973; booklets, flyers.
AMOUNT: 1 cm.
CONDITION: Good.
ACCESS: No restrictions.

179. Young Women's Christian Association (Vancouver, B.C.)

[See also entry # 873 (in Part II), which lists other records of this organization.]

✢ Vancouver, B.C. Formed [1897?].

The YWCA of Vancouver works to foster self-reliance and mutual support among women. It offers physical-education and health programmes, temporary accommodation, and a wide range of other services for women and children. The YWCA operates Munroe House (founded in 1979), which provides second-stage housing for battered women.
LOCATION OF RECORDS: University of British Columbia Library, Special Collections-Manuscripts. (See Appendix for address.)
COLLECTION NAME: Vancouver Young Women's Christian Association.
RECORDS: Minutes, 1903-1938, 1941-1970; financial records, 1922-1941, 1952-1969; reports, 1924-1949, 1956-1963; correspondence, 1975-1976; building records, 1928, 1950, 1952-1959, 1963, 1965-1969; printed material, 1905-1938, 1940-1974; board and committee membership lists, 1941-1958, 1966; lists of presidents, 1923-1948; clippings, 1902-1974; photo albums, 1940, 1947, 1967, 1969; scrapbooks, 1923-1933, 1942-1978; proclamations, 1968, 1972; citations, 1956-1958; guest books, 1965, 1971; subject files, 1939-1977; photographs, miscellaneous records.
AMOUNT: 3.2 m.
ACCESS: No restrictions.
FINDING AID: Inventory available.

ALBERTA

180. *Academic Women's Association (University of Alberta)*

✣ Edmonton, Alta. Formed 1975.

The Academic Women's Association was established to implement the recommendations of the University of Alberta's Senate Task Force on the Status of Women. It promotes collegiality among academic women and equal opportunities for women in university affairs.

LOCATION OF RECORDS: University of Alberta Archives. (See Appendix for address.)

COLLECTION NAME: Academic Women's Association (81-120; 87-29).

RECORDS: Constitution, by-laws, 1976-1979; minutes, financial records, 1975-1982; organization histories, 1975, 1977; reports, correspondence, 1975-1980, 1985-1986; committee records, 1974-1978, 1980-1982; project files, 1975-1981; notices of meetings, 1977-1981; agendas, sound recordings, 1978-1979; video recordings, 1976, 1978; miscellaneous records.

FINDING AID: Inventory available.

181. *Alberta Community Health Nurses Society*

LOCATION OF RECORDS: Provincial Archives of Alberta. (See Appendix for address.)

COLLECTION NAME: Alberta Community Health Nurses Society (83.106 S, 87.50 SE).

RECORDS: Newsletters, 1985-1986; constitution and by-laws, minutes, correspondence, reports, membership lists, miscellaneous records, 1961-1982.

AMOUNT: 31 cm.

ACCESS: No restrictions.

182. *Alberta Native Women's Conference (1st: 1968: Edmonton, Alta.). Planning Committee*

✣ Formed 1967. Disbanded 1968.

The committee planned the First Alberta Native Women's Conference, held in Edmonton in 1968. The conference's theme was "Native Women: Yesterday, Today, and Tomorrow."

LOCATION OF RECORDS: Canadian Women's Movement Archives Collection, Morisset Library Special Collections, University of Ottawa. (See Appendix for address.)

COLLECTION NAME: Conf.: "Alberta Native Women's 1st Conference," Edmonton, 1968.

RECORDS: Conference report, 1968.
AMOUNT: 3 mm.
CONDITION: Fair.
ACCESS: No restrictions.

183. *Alberta Provincial Council of Women*

The Alberta Provincial Council of Women is an umbrella organization for local councils of women throughout the province.

Collection (a)

LOCATION OF RECORDS: Glenbow Museum Archives. (See Appendix for address.)

COLLECTION NAME: Forms part of: Calgary Local Council of Women collection (M5841, box 15, files 157-181; M7222, box 32, file 328; M7653, box 35, files 364-367).

RECORDS: Constitution, by-laws, standing rules, 1958-1965; records of annual meetings, 1958-1974; committee records, 1966-1975; correspondence, 1966-1974, 1977-1979; programmes, invitations, 1939, 1966; conference records, 1968; reports, 1968-1972; clippings, 1959-1972; circular letters, 1979-1983; minutes, 1977-1978, 1982; press releases, 1977-1980; resolutions, miscellaneous records.

AMOUNT: 30 files.

ACCESS: No restrictions.

FINDING AID: "Calgary Local Council of Women Papers, 1919-1985."

Collection (b)

LOCATION OF RECORDS: City of Red Deer Archives. (See Appendix for address.)

COLLECTION NAME: Forms part of: Ethel Isabella Taylor Papers.

RECORDS: Minutes, correspondence, reports, membership records, constitution, by-laws, notes, 1958, 1960-1969, 1973-1974.

ACCESS: No restrictions.

FINDING AID: "The Papers of Ethel Isabella Taylor, 1908-1989."

184. *Alberta Status of Women Action Committee*

[See also entry # 878 (in Part II), which lists other records of this organization.]

✣ Edmonton, Alta. Formed 1976.

Through public education, lobbying, and networking, the Alberta Status of Women Action Committee (ASWAC) contributes to the work of improving the social, political, economic, and emotional situation of women.

Collection (a)

LOCATION OF RECORDS: Canadian Women's Movement Archives Collection, Morisset Library Special Collections, University of Ottawa. (See Appendix for address.)

COLLECTION NAME: Alberta Status of Women Action Committee.

RECORDS: Newsletters, 1980-1991; by-laws, 1979; reports, 1976, 1978, 1982-1983; financial records, press releases, background paper, 1982; minutes, 1981; conference materials, 1978, 1981-1982; handbook, list of member organizations, 1983; correspondence, 1975, 1982-1984; clippings, 1975; poster, 1976; notes, 1989; pamphlets, flyers.

AMOUNT: 8 cm of text, 1 poster.

CONDITION: Good.

ACCESS: No restrictions.

Collection (b)

LOCATION OF RECORDS: Glenbow Museum Archives. (See Appendix for address.)

COLLECTION NAME: Forms part of: Irma Wright collection (6542).

RECORDS: Minutes, conference records, correspondence, 1976-1979.

AMOUNT: 1 file.

ACCESS: No restrictions.

FINDING AID: "Irma Wright, Collector."

185. Alberta Women's Institutes

✣ Formed 1915.

This is a rural homemakers' organization with branches throughout the province.

LOCATION OF RECORDS: Provincial Archives of Alberta. (See Appendix for address.)

COLLECTION NAME: Alberta Women's Institutes.

RECORDS: Historical notes, [ca. 1920]; annual convention reports, 1915-1963; minutes, 1909-1912, 1915-1933, 1963-1977; correspondence, 1909-1917; financial records, 1909-1912, 1920, 1922-1956; organization history, 1949; biographical sketches, book of remembrance, miscellaneous records.

AMOUNT: Approx. 1.5 m.

ACCESS: No restrictions.

FINDING AID: Inventories available.

186. Alberta Women's Liberal Association

✣ Formed 1937. Disbanded 1970.

The Alberta Women's Liberal Association (AWLA) aimed to encourage women in Alberta to take an active role in Canadian politics. Many local Women's Liberal Clubs belonged to AWLA, which was affiliated with the National Women's Liberal Association. (Source: Glenbow Museum Archives finding aid.)

LOCATION OF RECORDS: Glenbow Museum Archives. (See Appendix for address.)

COLLECTION NAME: Alberta Women's Liberal Association Papers (M1725, M6090).

RECORDS: Historical information, correspondence, constitutions, by-laws, minutes, membership lists, reports, notices, policy papers, convention records, biographical information, speeches, newsletters, clippings, leaflets, scrapbooks, songsheets, 1932-1979.

AMOUNT: 5 document boxes.

ACCESS: No restrictions.

FINDING AID: "Alberta Women's Liberal Association Papers, 1932-1979."

187. Calgary Birth Control Association

✣ Calgary, Alta. Formed 1971.

The Calgary Birth Control Association (CBCA) was founded when the Calgary Abortion Information Centre and an inactive Planned Parenthood group amalgamated. (Source: Glenbow Museum Archives finding aid.)

LOCATION OF RECORDS: Glenbow Museum Archives. (See Appendix for address.)

COLLECTION NAME: Calgary Birth Control Association Fonds.

RECORDS: Constitution, by-laws, minutes, correspondence, financial records, annual reports, briefs, publicity files, 1971-1980.

AMOUNT: 5 m.

ACCESS: Subject to approval of CBCA.

188. Calgary Housewives Association

✣ Calgary, Alta. Formed 1975. Disbanded 1987.

The Calgary Housewives Association grew out of a conference about women in the home, held in Banff in 1975. The association gave homemakers an opportunity to discuss their goals and develop a sense of worth and dignity. (Source: Glenbow Museum Archives finding aid.)

LOCATION OF RECORDS: Glenbow Museum Archives. (See Appendix for address.)

COLLECTION NAME: Calgary Housewives Association Fonds.

RECORDS: Minutes, conference records, newsletters, related material, 1969-1988.

AMOUNT: 12.5 cm.

ACCESS: No restrictions.

FINDING AID: Inventory available.

189. Calgary Local Council of Women

✣ Calgary, Alta. Formed 1894.

The Calgary Local Council of Women has had between twenty-nine and fifty-one member organizations, including feminist groups and women's social and service clubs. (Source: Glenbow Museum Archives finding aid, 1987.)

Collection (a)

LOCATION OF RECORDS: Glenbow Museum Archives. (See Appendix for address.)

COLLECTION NAME: Calgary Local Council of Women (5841, 6802, 7222, 7453, 7653).

RECORDS: Constitution and by-laws, 1965-1968; annual reports, 1950-1976, 1981-1982; records of annual meetings, 1939-1979, 1983-1985; yearbooks, 1925-1933, 1938-1944, 1946-1949, 1951-1952, 1959-1960, 1962, 1964-1971, 1981-1982; minutes, 1919-1938, 1942-1982; agendas, 1958-1966, 1977-1978; committee files, 1950-1984; attendance records, 1920-1931, 1958-1975, 1977-1978, 1980-1981; resolutions, 1950-1985; correspondence, 1938-1943, 1947-1981; financial records, 1951-1962, 1964-1982; project files, 1950-1978, 1981-1985; conference records, 1934, 1963, 1966-1974, 1977-1979; newsletters, 1970-1974, 1978-1983; briefs, 1978-1982; speeches, biographical sketches, 1950-1979; invitations, 1958-1964, 1970, 1972-1979; clippings, 1939-1978; scrapbooks, 1933-1934, 1952-1980; press releases, 1979; executive lists, 1980-1985; reports, 1972; submissions, proposals, 1965-1978; place card, luncheon ticket, historical information, photographs, notes.

AMOUNT: 36 document boxes, 1 oversize box, 12 oversize items.

ACCESS: No restrictions.

FINDING AID: "Calgary Local Council of Women Papers, 1919-1985."

Collection (b)

LOCATION OF RECORDS: Glenbow Museum Archives.

COLLECTION NAME: Forms part of: Aileen Alexander Hackett Fish collection (file 117).

RECORDS: Newsletters, speech, notes, clippings, 1970-1976.

AMOUNT: 1 file.

ACCESS: No restrictions.

FINDING AID: "Aileen Alexander Hackett Fish Papers, 1913-1977."

Collection (c)

LOCATION OF RECORDS: Glenbow Museum Archives.

COLLECTION NAME: Forms part of: Irma Wright collection (box 1, file 2).

RECORDS: Annual report, membership records, correspondence, miscellaneous records, 1970-1979.

AMOUNT: 1 file.

ACCESS: No restrictions.

FINDING AID: "Irma Wright, Collector."

190. Calgary Status of Women Action Committee

[See also entry # 881 (in Part II), which lists other records of this organization.]

✢ Calgary, Alta. Formed 1974.

The principal aim of this committee (also known as CSWAC or SWAC) is to strengthen the social, political, and economic status of women. Public education and advocacy are CSWAC's main activities.

Collection (a)

LOCATION OF RECORDS: Glenbow Museum Archives. (See Appendix for address.)

COLLECTION NAME: Calgary Status of Women Action Committee Fonds.

RECORDS: Charter, minutes, personnel records, financial records, committee files, correspondence, project files, by-laws, newsletters, grant applications, miscellaneous records, [197-]-[198-].

AMOUNT: 2.5 m.

ACCESS: No restrictions.

FINDING AID: "Calgary Status of Women Action Committee Papers, 1974-1978."

Collection (b)

LOCATION OF RECORDS: Glenbow Museum Archives.

COLLECTION NAME: Forms part of: Irma Wright collection (files 4-13).

RECORDS: Correspondence, 1972-1978; financial report, 1977; newsletter, 1974; conference and workshop records, 1975-1976; press releases, 1976-1978; membership records, 1976-1977; records of meetings, reports, by-laws, miscellaneous records.

AMOUNT: 10 files.

ACCESS: No restrictions.

FINDING AID: "Irma Wright, Collector."

191. Calgary Women's Emergency Shelter Association

[See also entry # 882 (in Part II), which lists other records of this organization.]

✢ Calgary, Alta. Formed 1974.

Also known as CWES, this association offers shelter to abused women and children in crisis, counselling, public education, outreach programmes, and a child-support programme. The shelter is also known as the Senator Patrick Burns Family Shelter; it was originally called Oasis.

LOCATION OF RECORDS: Glenbow Museum Archives. (See Appendix for address.)

COLLECTION NAME: Calgary Women's Emergency Shelter (5976).

RECORDS: Minutes, 1975-1977; reports, 1974-1978; correspondence, 1974-1979; financial records, clippings, 1974-1975; staff policy manual, [ca. 1974]; construction contracts, 1976; agreements, 1977-1978.

AMOUNT: 1 document box.

ACCESS: No restrictions.

FINDING AID: "Calgary Women's Emergency Shelter Papers, 1971-78."

192. Canadian Federation of Business and Professional Women's Clubs. Calgary Local

✢ Calgary, Alta. Formed 1927.

The Calgary Local of the Canadian Federation of Business and Professional Women's Clubs (CFBPWC) was called the Current Event Club until 1929. It promotes the equality of women with men and stimulates interest in government business and elections. (Source: Glenbow Museum Archives finding aid.)

LOCATION OF RECORDS: Glenbow Museum Archives. (See Appendix for address.)

COLLECTION NAME: Canadian Federation of Business and Professional Women's Clubs, Calgary Local Fonds.

RECORDS: By-laws, historical sketches, minutes, convention proceedings, committee records, membership lists, correspondence, financial statements, newsletters, publications, scrapbooks, clippings, photographs, miscellaneous records, 1927-1990.

AMOUNT: 2 m of text, 61 photographic prints, 5 negatives.

ACCESS: No restrictions.

FINDING AID: Inventory available.

193. Canadian Women's Press Club. Calgary Branch

✢ Calgary, Alta. Formed 1912. Disbanded 1974.

The Calgary branch of the Canadian Women's Press Club (CWPC) was a club for women journalists. It disbanded during the Second World War but was revived in 1950. In 1971 the CWPC opened its membership to men and became the Media Club of Canada. (Source: Glenbow Museum Archives finding aid, 1978.)

LOCATION OF RECORDS: Glenbow Museum Archives. (See Appendix for address.)

COLLECTION NAME: Media Club of Canada, Calgary Branch Fonds.

RECORDS: Minutes, 1960-1974; membership lists, 1961-1971; reports, 1959-1965, 1968; correspondence, 1959-1973; financial statements, 1961-1965; radio script, 1958; constitution, by-laws, regulations, newsletters, clippings, scrapbooks, guest books, miscellaneous records.

AMOUNT: 56 cm of text, 2 photographic negatives.

ACCESS: No restrictions.

FINDING AID: "Canadian Women's Press Club. Calgary Branch Papers, 1950-1972."

194. Canadian Women's Press Club. Edmonton Branch

✢ Edmonton, Alta. Formed 1908.

The Edmonton branch of the Canadian Women's Press Club (CWPC) aimed to promote its members in the profession of journalism and to foster good will among women writers. In 1971, the CWPC admitted men and changed its name to the Media Club of Canada. (Source: Provincial Archives of Alberta finding aid, 1988.)

LOCATION OF RECORDS: Provincial Archives of Alberta. (See Appendix for address.)

COLLECTION NAME: Canadian Women's Press Club. Edmonton Branch (75.161 SE); Media Club of Canada (74.56 S).
RECORDS: Book, 1917; minutes, correspondence, reports, photographs, clippings, 1904-1969.
AMOUNT: 1.05 m.
ACCESS: No restrictions.
FINDING AID: Inventory available for Media Club of Canada collection.

195. Desk and Derrick Club of Calgary
✣ Calgary, Alta. Formed 1951.

The club was established to provide an educational forum for women in the petroleum and allied industries, in order to increase their scope of activities within these industries. (Source: Glenbow Museum Archives finding aid.)

LOCATION OF RECORDS: Glenbow Museum Archives. (See Appendix for address.)
COLLECTION NAME: Desk and Derrick Club of Calgary Papers (6070, 6249, 6446).
RECORDS: Bulletins (*Black Gold*), programmes, menus, songsheet, notes, membership records, articles, correspondence, clippings, certificates, speech (organization history), scrapbooks, handbook, leaflets, photographs, 1950-1989.
AMOUNT: 1.76 m of text, 13 photographic prints.
ACCESS: Bulletins restricted to club members and researchers authorized by the current Desk and Derrick executive.
FINDING AID: "Desk and Derrick Club of Calgary Papers, 1950-1981."

196. Edmonton Business and Professional Women's Club
✣ Edmonton, Alta.

LOCATION OF RECORDS: Provincial Archives of Alberta. (See Appendix for address.)
COLLECTION NAME: Edmonton Business and Professional Women's Club (87.53 S; 87.284 S).
RECORDS: Administrative records, minutes, scrapbooks, publications, 1933-1980; financial records, 1970-1980.
AMOUNT: 2.4 m.
ACCESS: No restrictions.

197. Edmonton Local Council of Women
✣ Edmonton, Alta. Formed 1908.

The Edmonton Local Council of Women (ELCW) is made up of various Edmonton women's organizations. It has examined many issues affecting the status of women. (Source: Provincial Archives of Alberta finding aid, 1988.)

LOCATION OF RECORDS: Provincial Archives of Alberta. (See Appendix for address.)
COLLECTION NAME: Edmonton Local Council of Women.
RECORDS: Minutes, 1908-1913, 1964-1982; correspondence, 1909-1915, 1962-1982; reports, 1910-1916, 1962-1977, 1984-1987; scrapbook, 1955-1963; yearbook, 1967; agendas, records of annual meetings, 1910-1916; notices, 1962-1967; financial records, 1964-1982; newsletters, executive lists, 1964-1982; clippings, 1984-1987; constitutions, by-laws, miscellaneous records.
AMOUNT: 72 cm.
ACCESS: No restrictions.
FINDING AID: Inventory available for some records.

198. Edmonton Women's Centre
✣ Edmonton, Alta.

LOCATION OF RECORDS: Provincial Archives of Alberta. (See Appendix for address.)
COLLECTION NAME: Forms part of: Options for Women collection (79.135 S).
RECORDS: Miscellaneous records, [197-].
ACCESS: No restrictions.

199. Edmonton Women's Coalition
✣ Edmonton, Alta. Formed 1977. Disbanded.

The coalition aimed to foster public awareness of the oppression of women and to fight that oppression. International Women's Day actions were among the coalition's priorities.

LOCATION OF RECORDS: Canadian Women's Movement Archives Collection, Morisset Library Special Collections, University of Ottawa. (See Appendix for address.)
COLLECTION NAME: Edmonton Women's Coalition.
RECORDS: Minutes, 1978; constitution.
AMOUNT: 3 mm.
CONDITION: Good.
ACCESS: No restrictions.

200. Edmonton Women's Place
✣ Edmonton, Alta. Formed [ca. 1973]. Disbanded [197-?].

The Edmonton Women's Place Society worked for two years to establish this women's centre, which opened in 1975. Edmonton Women's Place (EWP) provided information and referral services and offered workshops, study groups, and self-help groups.

LOCATION OF RECORDS: Canadian Women's Movement Archives Collection, Morisset Library Special Collections, University of Ottawa. (See Appendix for address.)
COLLECTION NAME: Edmonton Women's Place.
RECORDS: Minutes, correspondence, 1975; newsletters (*Everywoman*, 1975-1976); flyers.
AMOUNT: 1.3 cm.
CONDITION: Good.
ACCESS: No restrictions.

201. Elizabeth Fry Society of Calgary
[See also entry # 892 (in Part II), which lists other records of this organization.]
✣ Calgary, Alta. Formed 1965.

This organization (also known as E-Fry) aims to provide assistance to women in conflict with the law and to help with the rehabilitation of female offenders. Public education, social work, counselling, and advocacy are some of its activities. It used to be called the Elizabeth Fry Society of Alberta.

LOCATION OF RECORDS: Glenbow Museum Archives. (See Appendix for address.)
COLLECTION NAME: Elizabeth Fry Society of Calgary Fonds.
RECORDS: Minutes, 1965-1985; correspondence, 1966-1987; financial records, 1969-1971, 1982-1986; lists of members and officers, 1966-1973; reports, 1977-1987; annual reports, 1979-1990; programme records, 1973-1976, 1981-1986; committee records, 1968-1983; manual, 1981-1982; handbook, 1986; public-relations records, 1980-1987;

workshop files, 1979-1985; appointment book, 1988; newsletters, 1977-1984; constitution and by-laws, organization history, statistics.
AMOUNT: 1.18 m.
ACCESS: No restrictions.

202. Every Woman's Place (Edmonton, Alta.)

✤ Edmonton, Alta. Formed 1981. Disbanded [198-].

This women's centre (also known as EWP) had a library, organized support groups, and published directories of local resources. The centre also housed several other women's groups.

LOCATION OF RECORDS: Canadian Women's Movement Archives Collection, Morisset Library Special Collections, University of Ottawa. (See Appendix for address.)
COLLECTION NAME: Every Woman's Place (Edmonton, Alta.).
RECORDS: Minutes, 1981-1982; organization history, report, 1983; newsletters, 1983-1984, 1986; resource directories, 1983-1984; information package, 1981; calendars, correspondence, clippings, 1982; press releases, 1982-1984; flyers, pamphlets, proposal, questionnaire, poster, buttons, stickers, membership card.
AMOUNT: 3 cm of text, 1 poster, 3 buttons.
CONDITION: Good.
ACCESS: No restrictions.

203. Faculty Women's Club (University of Alberta)

✤ Edmonton, Alta. Formed 1933.

The Faculty Women's Club (also called the Faculty Women's Association) at the University of Alberta is primarily a social organization. The club's oral-history projects have documented the history of women at the university.

LOCATION OF RECORDS: University of Alberta Archives. (See Appendix for address.)
COLLECTION NAME: Faculty Women's Club.
RECORDS: Sound recordings (oral history), 1981-1983, 1985; minutes, 1933-1970, 1975-1976, 1983; membership records, 1933-1943, 1946-1965, 1968-1983; constitutions, 1944, 1956-1964; reports, 1933-1943, 1951-1969, 1975-1976, 1986; correspondence, 1960-1966, 1968-1970, 1975-1978, 1980-1987; organization history, 1983; programmes, 1967, 1983; financial records, 1944-1962, 1983; notes for speech, 1984; publicity material, 1961-1967; photographs, miscellaneous records.
ACCESS: No restrictions.
FINDING AID: Inventories available.

204. Farm Women's Union of Alberta. Hillside Local

LOCATION OF RECORDS: Provincial Archives of Alberta. (See Appendix for address.)
COLLECTION NAME: Forms part of: Winifred Ross collection (77.113 S).
RECORDS: Correspondence, newsletters, bulletins, 1949-1970.
ACCESS: No restrictions.
FINDING AID: Inventory available for Winifred Ross collection.

205. Farm Women's Union of Alberta. Sunniebend Local

✤ Formed 1927. Disbanded 1965.

This group became a local of the Farm Women's Union of Alberta in 1949; prior to that, it was the Sunniebend local of the United Farm Women of Alberta. (Source: Glenbow Museum Archives finding aid.)

LOCATION OF RECORDS: Glenbow Museum Archives. (See Appendix for address.)
COLLECTION NAME: Farm Women's Union of Alberta, Sunniebend Local Fonds.
RECORDS: Minutes, membership rolls, financial records, scrapbook, 1927-1965.
AMOUNT: 13 cm of text, 1 reel of microfilm.
ACCESS: No restrictions.
FINDING AID: Inventory available.

206. Fédération nationale des femmes canadiennes-françaises (Alberta)

Il s'agit de la section albertaine de la Fédération nationale des femmes canadiennes-françaises (FNFCF) (appelée auparavant la Fédération des femmes canadiennes-françaises ou FFCF). La FNFCF poursuit, entre autres, les buts suivants : sensibiliser les milieux minoritaires aux problèmes collectifs spécifiques des femmes francophones et impliquer les femmes francophones dans une action communautaire propre à améliorer leur condition.

LIEU DE CONSULTATION : Provincial Archives of Alberta. (Voir Annexe pour l'adresse.)
NOM DU FONDS : La Fédération des femmes canadiennes-françaises.
MATÉRIEL : Rapports, procès-verbaux, correspondance, renseignements biographiques, album de photos, évaluations, documents administratifs, documents divers, 1927-1987.
QUANTITÉ : 2 m.
ACCÈS : Aucune restriction.
INSTRUMENT DE RECHERCHE : Inventaires disponibles.

207. Femmes d'aujourd'hui

✤ Edmonton (Alb.).

En 1988, le nom de l'organisme est devenu Entre Femmes.

LIEU DE CONSULTATION : Provincial Archives of Alberta. (Voir Annexe pour l'adresse.)
NOM DU FONDS : Femmes d'aujourd'hui (85.207).
MATÉRIEL : Documents administratifs, documents financiers, 1983-1985.
QUANTITÉ : 2 cm.
ACCÈS : Aucune restriction.

208. Grande Prairie Women's Place

✤ Grande Prairie, Alta. Formed [197-]. Disbanded.

LOCATION OF RECORDS: Canadian Women's Movement Archives Collection, Morisset Library Special Collections, University of Ottawa. (See Appendix for address.)
COLLECTION NAME: Grande Prairie Women's Place Newsletter; She Ain't Heavy — Grande Prairie, Alta.
RECORDS: Newsletters (*She Ain't Heavy*, 1975-1976; *Grande Prairie Women's Place Newsletter*, [197-]).
AMOUNT: 4 items.
CONDITION: Good.
ACCESS: No restrictions.

209. Groupe de concertation des Franco-Albertaines

✣ Groupe fondé 1984.

Ce groupe, composé de représentantes de sept organismes de femmes francophones, s'est réuni à Edmonton pour discuter de questions d'intérêt commun, organiser un congrès provincial et entreprendre une étude sur les besoins des femmes francophones en Alberta. (Source : instrument de recherche des Glenbow Museum Archives.)

LIEU DE CONSULTATION : Glenbow Museum Archives. (Voir Annexe pour l'adresse.)
NOM DU FONDS : Fonds du Groupe de concertation des Franco-Albertaines.
MATÉRIEL : Procès-verbaux, correspondance, listes de membres, actes de congrès, demandes de subvention, documents financiers, 1984-1986.
QUANTITÉ : 12.5 cm.
ACCÈS : Aucune restriction.
INSTRUMENT DE RECHERCHE : Inventaire disponible.

210. La Leche League Alberta / Northwest Territories

The purpose of La Leche League is "to offer encouragement, information, and support to women who wish to breast feed their babies.... La Leche League Alberta/Northwest Territories co-ordinates the activities of the local branches within this geographic area." (Source: Glenbow Museum Archives finding aid.)

LOCATION OF RECORDS: Glenbow Museum Archives. (See Appendix for address.)
COLLECTION NAME: La Leche League Alberta/Northwest Territories Fonds.
RECORDS: Correspondence, reports, membership lists, workshop and resource materials, financial records, photographs, 1973-1989.
AMOUNT: 2 m of text, 4 photographic prints, 1 negative.
ACCESS: No restrictions.

211. La Leche League International. Calgary Branch

✣ Calgary, Alta. Formed [ca. 1966].

LOCATION OF RECORDS: Glenbow Museum Archives. (See Appendix for address.)
COLLECTION NAME: La Leche League (6046).
RECORDS: By-laws, organizational plan, 1974-1978; minutes, 1976-1981; correspondence, 1977-1981; membership lists, attendance records, 1976-1980; workshop materials, 1975-1981; invitations, clipping, 1981; job lists.
AMOUNT: 1 document box.
ACCESS: No restrictions.
FINDING AID: "La Leche League Papers, 1974-1981."

212. National Council of Jewish Women of Canada. Calgary Branch

✣ Calgary, Alta.

The main activities of the National Council of Jewish Women of Canada (NCJW) are education, service, and social action. While its priorities are the protection of human rights and the preservation of Jewish life, NCJW is also concerned with women's issues such as family planning, abortion, child care, pornography, and affirmative action.

LOCATION OF RECORDS: Glenbow Museum Archives. (See Appendix for address.)
COLLECTION NAME: Forms part of: Calgary Jewish Community Council collection.
RECORDS: Miscellaneous records, [195-]-[196-].
AMOUNT: Approx. 1 m.

213. On Our Way

✣ Edmonton, Alta. Formed 1972. Disbanded [1974?].

On Our Way was a monthly feminist newspaper.

LOCATION OF RECORDS: Canadian Women's Movement Archives Collection, Morisset Library Special Collections, University of Ottawa. (See Appendix for address.)
COLLECTION NAME: On Our Way.
RECORDS: Newspapers, 1972-1974.
AMOUNT: 3 cm.
CONDITION: Fair.
ACCESS: No restrictions.

214. Options for Women (Edmonton, Alta.)

✣ Edmonton, Alta.

Local Options for Women councils were established to provide a feminist communications network which would work to improve the status of women. (Source: Provincial Archives of Alberta finding aid, 1988.)

LOCATION OF RECORDS: Provincial Archives of Alberta. (See Appendix for address.)
COLLECTION NAME: Options for Women (79.135 S).
RECORDS: Minutes, correspondence, publications, miscellaneous records, 1968-1978.
AMOUNT: 1.2 m.
ACCESS: No restrictions.

215. Red Deer Local Council of Women

✣ Red Deer, Alta.

LOCATION OF RECORDS: City of Red Deer Archives. (See Appendix for address.)
COLLECTION NAME: Forms part of: Ethel Isabella Taylor Papers.
RECORDS: Constitution and by-laws, 1955; annual reports, 1961-1967; minutes, reports, membership lists, resolutions, [196-]-[197-]; correspondence, 1962-1968, 1970; clippings, pamphlets.
AMOUNT: 4 boxes.
ACCESS: No restrictions.
FINDING AID: "The Papers of Ethel Isabella Taylor, 1908-1989."

216. Red Deer University Women's Club

✣ Red Deer, Alta.

University women's clubs are local organizations of women university graduates. The local clubs belong to the Canadian Federation of University Women.

LOCATION OF RECORDS: City of Red Deer Archives. (See Appendix for address.)
COLLECTION NAME: Red Deer University Women's Club.
RECORDS: Minute books, 1947-1952, 1955-1974; certificate, 1967; handbook, 1971-1973; scrapbook, 1947-1972; guest book, 1965-1973; brief, 1970; miscellaneous records.
ACCESS: No restrictions.
FINDING AID: Inventory available.

PART I: RECORDS HELD BY ARCHIVES / PARTIE I : FONDS DÉTENUS PAR DES ARCHIVES

Photographer unknown / Photographe inconnue
Photo #790
CWMA Collection / Fonds de l'ACMF

217. Riverside Villa Association

✤ Calgary, Alta. Formed 1970.

The association runs two half-way houses which offer a recovery programme for women alcoholics. (Source: Glenbow Museum Archives finding aid, 1981.)

LOCATION OF RECORDS: Glenbow Museum Archives. (See Appendix for address.)

COLLECTION NAME: Riverside Villa Association (6129).

RECORDS: Minutes, 1974-1979; by-laws, annual reports, records of annual meetings, 1974-1981; reports, 1975-1978; membership lists, 1976-1978; financial records, 1974-1978, 1981; correspondence, 1974-1979; staff policy handbook, outlines of staff duties, 1972-1976; clippings, 1976-1977; newsletters (*Villa Vignettes*, 1978); floor plan, [ca. 1977]; historical sketches, pamphlet, invitations, admission form, application form, programme outline, staff schedule, photographs.

AMOUNT: 1 document box.

ACCESS: No restrictions.

FINDING AID: "Riverside Villa Association Papers, 1970-1981."

218. Second Wreath

✤ Edmonton, Alta. Formed [1984?].

Second Wreath (or Druhyi Vinok) organized the 1985 Second Wreath Conference in Edmonton. The conference commemorated the 100th anniversary of the Ukrainian women's movement and explored issues relating to ethnicity and feminism. Second Wreath also organized a seminar series and published a newsletter.

LOCATION OF RECORDS: Canadian Women's Movement Archives Collection, Morisset Library Special Collections, University of Ottawa. (See Appendix for address.)

COLLECTION NAME: Second Wreath (Edmonton, Alta.).

RECORDS: Conference records, correspondence, 1985; position paper, 1984; newsletters (*Vinok*, 1985); flyer.

AMOUNT: 5 mm.

CONDITION: Good.

ACCESS: No restrictions.

219. Source

✤ Edmonton, Alta. Formed 1974. Disbanded.

Source was an Alberta women's newsletter.

LOCATION OF RECORDS: Canadian Women's Movement Archives Collection, Morisset Library Special Collections, University of Ottawa. (See Appendix for address.)

COLLECTION NAME: Source: Alberta Women's Newsletter.

RECORDS: Newsletters (*Source*, 1974).

AMOUNT: 5 mm.

CONDITION: Good.

ACCESS: No restrictions.

220. United Farm Women of Alberta

✤ Formed 1915. Disbanded.

Women were permitted to join the United Farmers of Alberta in 1913; two years later, a separate women's organization was formed: the United Farm Women of Alberta (UFWA). The UFWA worked to improve the status of women, especially rural women. (Source: Provincial Archives of Alberta finding aid, 1988.) The organization Women of Unifarm grew out of the UFWA. [See also Women of Unifarm (911).]

Collection (a)

LOCATION OF RECORDS: Provincial Archives of Alberta. (See Appendix for address.)

COLLECTION NAME: Forms part of: Winifred Ross collection (71.420 S, 77.113 S); sound recording: 72.404.

RECORDS: Sound recording (interview), [after 1964]; minutes, convention records, reports, bulletins, newsletters, correspondence, literature, 1920-1967.

ACCESS: No restrictions.

FINDING AID: Inventory available for Winifred Ross collection.

Collection (b)

LOCATION OF RECORDS: Provincial Archives of Alberta.

COLLECTION NAME: Forms part of: United Farm Women of Alberta collection (69.193/2 SE; 75.181 SE).

RECORDS: Organization history, 1934; speech, 1924.

AMOUNT: 2 items.

ACCESS: No restrictions.

221. United Farm Women of Alberta. County of Red Deer Local

✤ Disbanded.

LOCATION OF RECORDS: Provincial Archives of Alberta. (See Appendix for address.)

COLLECTION NAME: Forms part of: United Farm Women of Alberta collection (77.282 S).

RECORDS: Minutes, 1963-1969.

ACCESS: No restrictions.

222. United Farm Women of Alberta. Horn Hill Local

✤ Horn Hill, Alta. Disbanded.

LOCATION OF RECORDS: Provincial Archives of Alberta. (See Appendix for address.)

COLLECTION NAME: Forms part of: United Farm Women of Alberta collection (77.282 S).

RECORDS: Minutes, 1929-1966.

ACCESS: No restrictions.

223. University of Alberta. Association of the Academic Staff at the University of Alberta. Committee on Employment Conditions of Full Time Women Faculty

✤ Edmonton, Alta.

LOCATION OF RECORDS: University of Alberta Archives. (See Appendix for address.)

COLLECTION NAME: Forms part of: Association of the Academic Staff at the University of Alberta collection (Accession no. 73-162, AASUA/7/7, Status of Women).

RECORDS: Report, 1975; related material.

FINDING AID: Finding aid available for Association of the Academic Staff at the University of Alberta collection.

224. University of Alberta. Campus Day Care Committee

✣ Edmonton, Alta. Formed 1975.

The Campus Day Care Committee was composed of academic staff, non-academic staff, graduate students, and representatives of the Students' Union. It was also called the Day Care Centre Committee, and it later became the University and Community Day Care Society.

LOCATION OF RECORDS: University of Alberta Archives. (See Appendix for address.)
COLLECTION NAME: Forms part of: Academic Women's Association collection (Accession no. 81-120, box 3).
RECORDS: Correspondence, pledges, reports, minutes, 1975-1979.
AMOUNT: 1 box.
FINDING AID: Inventory available for Academic Women's Association collection.

225. University of Alberta. Office of the Dean of Women

✣ Edmonton, Alta. Formed 1911.

The Office of the Dean of Women was originally called the Office of the Advisor to Women Students. During the 1960s and '70s, the office dealt with many women's organizations and women's issues. In 1977 the Office of the Dean of Women and the Office of the Dean of Men amalgamated to become the Office of the Dean of Students.

LOCATION OF RECORDS: University of Alberta Archives. (See Appendix for address.)
COLLECTION NAME: Office of the Dean of Women (Acc. no. 77-63).
RECORDS: Subject files, correspondence, administrative records, financial records, reports, minutes, clippings, speeches, miscellaneous records, 1948-1975.
AMOUNT: 13 boxes.
ACCESS: Official records of the university are restricted for twenty-five years from the date of creation. Permission to view the records must be obtained from the unit which created them.
FINDING AID: Inventory available.

226. University of Alberta. President's Interim Advisory Committee on Women's Issues

✣ Edmonton, Alta. Formed 1984. Disbanded 1985.

This committee advised the president of the University of Alberta on those matters concerning women at the university which were not addressed by specific bodies.

LOCATION OF RECORDS: University of Alberta Archives. (See Appendix for address.)
COLLECTION NAME: Forms part of: Office of the Vice-President (Academic) collection (Acc. no. 89-26, box 9).
RECORDS: Miscellaneous records, 1984-1985.
ACCESS: Official records of the university are restricted for twenty-five years from the date of creation. Permission to view the records must be obtained from the unit which created them.

227. University of Alberta. Senate. Task Force on the Status of Women

✣ Edmonton, Alta. Formed [ca. 1973].

The original purpose of this task force (established by the University of Alberta Senate) was to review the status and career patterns of women employees at the university.

Collection (a)
LOCATION OF RECORDS: University of Alberta Archives. (See Appendix for address.)
COLLECTION NAME: Forms part of: Senate collection (Acc. no. 82-113, box 4, #114-117; Acc. no. 89-74, box 1, #1-28).
RECORDS: Reports, correspondence, minutes, questionnaires, recommendations, articles, miscellaneous records, 1972-1988.
ACCESS: Official records of the university are restricted for twenty-five years from the date of creation. Permission to view the records must be obtained from the unit which created them.
FINDING AID: Inventories available for Senate collection.

Collection (b)
LOCATION OF RECORDS: University of Alberta Archives.
COLLECTION NAME: Forms part of: Academic Women's Association collection (Acc. no. 81-120, box 2).
RECORDS: Reviews, correspondence, briefs, petition, 1974-1978.
ACCESS: Official records of the university are restricted for twenty-five years from the date of creation. Permission to view the records must be obtained from the unit which created them.
FINDING AID: Inventory available for Academic Women's Association collection.

Collection (c)
LOCATION OF RECORDS: University of Alberta Archives.
COLLECTION NAME: Forms part of: Office of the Vice-President (Academic) collection (Acc. no. 89-26, box 8).
RECORDS: Miscellaneous records, 1979-1988.
ACCESS: Official records of the university are restricted for twenty-five years from the date of creation. Permission to view the records must be obtained from the unit which created them.

228. University of Alberta. Women's Program and Resource Centre

✣ Edmonton, Alta. Formed 1981.

The Women's Program and Resource Centre offer courses and resources in women's studies. They operate within the Faculty of Extension at the University of Alberta.

LOCATION OF RECORDS: University of Alberta Archives. (See Appendix for address.)
COLLECTION NAME: Forms part of: Office of the Vice-President (Academic) collection (Acc. no. 87-118, box 4, University/Community Special Projects Fund Advisory Committee, # 60).
RECORDS: Miscellaneous records, 1984-1986.
ACCESS: Official records of the university are restricted for twenty-five years from the date of creation. Permission to view the records must be obtained from the unit which created them.

229. University Women's Club of Calgary

✣ Calgary, Alta. Formed 1923.

The University Women's Club of Calgary (UWC) aims to stimulate its members' interest and participation in public affairs. UWC's areas of interest have included day care, continuing education for women, and marriage and taxation laws affecting women. (Source: Glenbow Museum Archives finding aid, 1988.)

LOCATION OF RECORDS: Glenbow Museum Archives. (See Appendix for address.)

COLLECTION NAME: University Women's Club of Calgary (M2055; M7890; and RCT-820).
RECORDS: Constitution and amendments, 1923-1972; annual reports, 1924-1944, 1949-1986; minutes, 1923-1940, 1944-1985; membership records, 1923-1983, 1986-1987; correspondence, 1950-1983; newsletters, 1955-1987; financial records, 1943-1982; briefs, 1953-1977, 1984-1985; archives inventories, 1949, 1971, 1978; notes for organization history, 1943-1978; programme cards, 1931-1978; award, 1967; clippings, 1958-1966; duty rosters, 1980-1987; programmes, 1970-1986; questionnaire, 1981; scholarship applications, 1983-1986; conference materials, 1984-1985; scrapbooks, 1972-1981; sound recordings, 1978, 1985; songsheets, miscellaneous records.
AMOUNT: 13 document boxes, 2 sound recordings.
FINDING AID: "University Women's Club of Calgary Papers, 1923-1987."

230. University Women's Club of Edmonton

✣ Edmonton, Alta. Formed 1909.

Originally called the Alberta Women's Association, the University Women's Club of Edmonton (UWCE) was a founding member of the Canadian Federation of University Women. The club promotes educational interests and improvement in the status of women. (Source: Provincial Archives of Alberta finding aid, 1988.)

Collection (a)

LOCATION OF RECORDS: Provincial Archives of Alberta. (See Appendix for address.)
COLLECTION NAME: University Women's Club of Edmonton.
RECORDS: Minutes, 1909-1984; subject files, 1909-1969; correspondence, 1945-1984; reports, 1952-1984; clippings, membership records, 1945-1983; financial records, 1956-1982; briefs, 1972-1979; newsletters, 1962-1982; conference records, 1966-1984; photographs, negatives, slides, 1976-1983; constitution, scrapbook, miscellaneous records.
AMOUNT: 4.63 m.
ACCESS: No restrictions.
FINDING AID: Inventory available for some records.

Collection (b)

LOCATION OF RECORDS: University of Alberta Archives. (See Appendix for address.)
COLLECTION NAME: Some records form part of: the President's Papers (68-1 3/2/11/1-3; 68-1 3/3/11/1-2; 68-1 3/4/9/1-34); other records have the following accession numbers: 74-104; 82-155-75; 83-96-5; 88-21-51.
RECORDS: Organization history, 1973; correspondence, 1928-1931, 1938, [between 1945 and 1949]; photograph, 1920; miscellaneous records, 1971-1986.

231. Voice of Alberta Native Women's Society

✣ Formed 1968. Disbanded [before 1984].

The society (also called VANWS) grew out of the first Alberta Native Women's Conference, held in 1968. VANWS organized the Alberta Native Women's Second Annual Conference in 1969 and the First National Native Women's Conference in 1971, both held in Edmonton.

LOCATION OF RECORDS: Canadian Women's Movement Archives Collection, Morisset Library Special Collections, University of Ottawa. (See Appendix for address.)
COLLECTION NAME: Voice of Alberta Native Women's Society; Conf.: National Native Women's Conference (1st: 1971: Edmonton, Alta.).
RECORDS: Conference reports, 1969, 1971.
AMOUNT: 1.6 cm.
CONDITION: Good.
ACCESS: No restrictions.

232. Voice of Women (Calgary, Alta.)

[See also entry # 906 (in Part II), which lists other records of this organization.]

✣ Calgary, Alta. Formed 1960.

The Calgary branch of the national organization Voice of Women (VOW) is concerned with peace issues and women's issues.

Collection (a)

LOCATION OF RECORDS: Glenbow Museum Archives. (See Appendix for address.)
COLLECTION NAME: Voice of Women, Calgary Branch Fonds.
RECORDS: Correspondence, newsletters, press releases, reports, news clippings, 1961-1970.
AMOUNT: 18.5 cm.
ACCESS: No restrictions.

Collection (b)

LOCATION OF RECORDS: Glenbow Museum Archives.
COLLECTION NAME: Forms part of: Helen and Mort Freeman collection.
RECORDS: Miscellaneous records.
ACCESS: No restrictions.

233. Voice of Women. Edmonton Branch

✣ Edmonton, Alta.

Voice of Women (VOW) is a national organization which opposes war and violence and promotes peace and disarmament. VOW lobbies all levels of government and organizes educational campaigns, meetings, and conferences. (Source: *The Canadian Encyclopedia*. — Edmonton: Hurtig Publishers, 1985.)

LOCATION OF RECORDS: Provincial Archives of Alberta. (See Appendix for address.)
COLLECTION NAME: Canadian Voice of Women for Peace (Edmonton) (88.297 S).
RECORDS: Minutes, correspondence, newsletters, 1960-1987.
AMOUNT: 2 m.
ACCESS: No restrictions.

234. Women for Political Action (Calgary, Alta.)

✣ Calgary, Alta. Formed 1972. Disbanded 1974.

Women for Political Action aimed to increase politicians' awareness of issues concerning women and to bring about greater involvement of women in politics at all levels. (Source: Glenbow Museum Archives finding aid.)

Collection (a)

LOCATION OF RECORDS: Glenbow Museum Archives. (See Appendix for address.)
COLLECTION NAME: Women for Political Action Fonds.
RECORDS: Correspondence, meeting notices, newsletters, 1972-1974.
AMOUNT: 4 cm.
ACCESS: No restrictions.

Collection (b)

LOCATION OF RECORDS: Glenbow Museum Archives.

COLLECTION NAME: Forms part of: Irma Wright collection (box 1, file 3).
RECORDS: Newsletters, meeting notices, questionnaire responses, miscellaneous records, 1972-1973.
AMOUNT: 1 file.
ACCESS: No restrictions.
FINDING AID: "Irma Wright, Collector."

235. Women in Scholarship, Engineering, Science, and Technology (University of Alberta)

[See also entry # 908 (in Part II), which lists other records of this organization.]

✤ Edmonton, Alta. Formed 1982.

Women in Scholarship, Engineering, Science, and Technology (WISEST) works to increase the proportion of women in decision-making roles, especially in engineering and the sciences. WISEST encourages girls to consider careers in the sciences and in engineering, and it provides support to women in these fields at the University of Alberta. WISEST has also been known as the Task Force on Women in Scholarship, Engineering, Science, and Technology.

LOCATION OF RECORDS: University of Alberta Archives. (See Appendix for address.)
COLLECTION NAME: Forms part of: Office of the Vice President (Research) collection (85-48; 87-90).
RECORDS: Records of meetings, miscellaneous records, 1983-1985.
ACCESS: Official records of the university are restricted for twenty-five years from the date of creation. Permission to view the records must be obtained from the unit which created them.

236. Women's Liberation (Edmonton, Alta.)

✤ Edmonton, Alta. Disbanded.

LOCATION OF RECORDS: Canadian Women's Movement Archives Collection, Morisset Library Special Collections, University of Ottawa. (See Appendix for address.)
COLLECTION NAME: Women's Liberation Newsletter, Edmonton, Alta.
RECORDS: Newsletter, 1971.
AMOUNT: 1 item.
CONDITION: Fair.
ACCESS: No restrictions.

237. Women's Place (Lethbridge, Alta.)

✤ Lethbridge, Alta. Formed [1973?]. Disbanded.

Women's Place was a drop-in centre which offered courses, a lending library, and a referral service.

LOCATION OF RECORDS: Canadian Women's Movement Archives Collection, Morisset Library Special Collections, University of Ottawa. (See Appendix for address.)
COLLECTION NAME: Women's Place — Lethbridge.
RECORDS: Newsletters (Up, 1974-1976); proposal, 1973; form, 1978; information sheet, [197-].
AMOUNT: 3 cm.
ACCESS: No restrictions.

238. Young Women's Christian Association of Calgary

[See also entry # 914 (in Part II), which lists other records of this organization.]

✤ Calgary, Alta. Formed 1907.

The original purpose of the YWCA of Calgary was to provide accommodation for single women arriving in the city. The YWCA's many other services have included physical education, summer camps, and co-operative housing for unmarried mothers. The YWCA Women's Resource Centre opened in 1973, closed in 1976, and reopened in 1979. The resource centre provides an information and referral service and works to improve the status of women. (Sources: Glenbow Museum Archives finding aids, 1980, 1982.) The YWCA Women's Resource Centre publishes a quarterly feminist journal founded in 1986, *Perspective: A Women's Journal*. The journal's goals are to tell women's stories and to validate women's experiences. [See also YWCA Banff Community Resource Centre (917).]

Collection (a)

LOCATION OF RECORDS: Glenbow Museum Archives. (See Appendix for address.)
COLLECTION NAME: Young Women's Christian Association of Calgary (5419, 6274).
RECORDS: Minutes, 1907-1946, 1953-1970; records of annual meetings, 1961-1974; financial statements, 1953, 1965-1969; correspondence, 1929-1932, 1937, 1942-1949, 1967-1971; reports, 1927-1930, 1966-1971, 1976; residence records, 1968-1971; conference records, 1965, 1969-1971; committee membership lists, 1907-1971; board membership lists, 1930-1939; outline of procedures, 1942; outlines of policies, 1951-1967; booklets, 1956-1965; speeches, 1960-1970; bequests, 1966-1967; proposal, 1966; newsletters, 1965-1971; manuals, resource kits, 1967-1970; miscellaneous records.
AMOUNT: 11 document boxes, 1 oversize box.
ACCESS: No restrictions.
FINDING AID: "Young Women's Christian Association of Calgary Papers, 1907-1976."

Collection (b)

LOCATION OF RECORDS: Glenbow Museum Archives.
COLLECTION NAME: Y.W.C.A. Women's Resource Centre (5826).
RECORDS: Proposals, lists of procedures, lists of resources, scrapbooks, statistics summaries, 1973-1976; reports, 1974-1977; programme information, 1973-1975; miscellaneous records.
AMOUNT: 1 document box, 1 oversize box.
ACCESS: No restrictions.
FINDING AID: "Y.W.C.A. Women's Resource Centre Papers, 1882-1976."

239. Young Women's Christian Association of Edmonton

[See also entry # 915 (in Part II), which lists other records of this organization.]

✤ Edmonton, Alta. Formed 1907.

Services provided by the YWCA of Edmonton have included a women's residence, a fitness centre, child-care services, and a library. (Source: *Women's Resource Directory for Edmonton, Alberta*. — Edmonton: Every Woman's Place, 1984.)

Collection (a)

LOCATION OF RECORDS: Provincial Archives of Alberta. (See Appendix for address.)
COLLECTION NAME: Young Women's Christian Association, Edmonton Branch.
RECORDS: Minutes, 1907-1980; financial records, 1929-1978; reports, 1938-1975; scrapbook, 1928-1959; booklets, 1957, 1961-1964; speech, 1947; programme files, personnel files, 1949-1970; correspondence, [ca. 1942], 1953-1975; residence guest registers, 1948-1949,

1954-1970; conference programme, 1959; clippings, 1937-1940, [ca. 1942]; photographs, miscellaneous records.

AMOUNT: Approx. 6 m.

ACCESS: No restrictions.

FINDING AID: Inventory available for some records.

Collection (b)

LOCATION OF RECORDS: Provincial Archives of Alberta.

COLLECTION NAME: Forms part of: Cora Taylor Watt Casselman collection (70.154 S, box 3, items no. 138-142).

RECORDS: Organization history, 1957; guest book, 1953; notes, speeches, clippings, miscellaneous records, [ca. 1945]-[ca. 1960].

ACCESS: No restrictions.

FINDING AID: Inventory available for Cora Taylor Watt Casselman collection.

240. *Zonta Club of Edmonton*

✣ Edmonton, Alta.

The Zonta Club of Edmonton is a branch of Zonta International, a service organization of business and professional women. One of the goals of Zonta International is improving the status of women.

LOCATION OF RECORDS: Provincial Archives of Alberta. (See Appendix for address.)

COLLECTION NAME: Zonta Club of Edmonton (77.49 SE).

RECORDS: Pamphlets, scrapbooks, organization history, 1953-1976.

AMOUNT: 3 cm.

ACCESS: No restrictions.

SASKATCHEWAN

241. Business and Professional Women's Club of Moose Jaw

✣ Moose Jaw, Sask. Formed 1947.

This club was established to improve the status of women in business and the professions, encourage a spirit of co-operation, and provide educational and recreational activities for women. (Source: Saskatchewan Archives Board finding aid.)

Collection (a)

LOCATION OF RECORDS: Moose Jaw Public Library, Archives Department. (See Appendix for address.)

COLLECTION NAME: Moose Jaw Business and Professional Women's Club (Acc. 1.89).

RECORDS: Minutes, scrapbooks, reports, correspondence, membership lists, miscellaneous records, 1947-1986.

AMOUNT: 64.5 cm.

Collection (b)

LOCATION OF RECORDS: Saskatchewan Archives Board, Regina. (See Appendix for address.)

COLLECTION NAME: Business and Professional Women's Club of Moose Jaw (R-877).

RECORDS: Minutes, reports, financial records, resolutions, by-laws, miscellaneous records, 1947-1983.

AMOUNT: 26 cm.

FINDING AID: Guide no. GR 329.

Collection (c)

LOCATION OF RECORDS: Saskatchewan Archives Board, Regina.

COLLECTION NAME: Forms part of: Saskatchewan Business and Professional Women's Clubs collection (R-141, #41; R-856, #7).

RECORDS: Correspondence, lists of officers and members, installation ceremony, rules of order, by-laws, 1947, 1954-1955, 1958, 1962-1966, 1971-1980.

ACCESS: No restrictions.

FINDING AID: "An Inventory of the Records of the Saskatchewan Business and Professional Women's Clubs" (Guide no. GR 216).

242. Business and Professional Women's Club of Regina

✣ Regina, Sask. Formed 1933.

The Business and Professional Women's Club of Regina was formed "to promote the interests of business and professional women, to encourage a spirit of co-operation and fellowship, and to extend educational opportunities to women." (Source: Saskatchewan Archives Board finding aid.)

Collection (a)

LOCATION OF RECORDS: Saskatchewan Archives Board, Regina. (See Appendix for address.)

COLLECTION NAME: Business and Professional Women's Club of Regina (R-770, R-106, R-1177).

RECORDS: Membership lists, handbooks, newsletters, reports, photographs, correspondence, conference records, speeches, miscellaneous records, 1930-1983.

AMOUNT: 1.6 m.

ACCESS: No restrictions.

FINDING AID: Guide no. GR 194.

Collection (b)

LOCATION OF RECORDS: Saskatchewan Archives Board, Regina.

COLLECTION NAME: Forms part of: Ruth S. McGill collection.

RECORDS: Bulletins, financial records, 1964-1966; resolutions, 1962; organization history, 1933-[ca. 1959].

AMOUNT: 9 mm.

ACCESS: No restrictions.

FINDING AID: "A Checklist of the Papers of Ruth S. McGill" (Guide no. GR 351).

Collection (c)

LOCATION OF RECORDS: Saskatchewan Archives Board, Regina.

COLLECTION NAME: Forms part of: Saskatchewan Business and Professional Women's Clubs collection (R-141, #58, #29; R-856, #12).

RECORDS: Correspondence, lists of officers and members, by-laws, newsletters, annual reports, notices of meetings, directory, miscellaneous records, 1952-1955, 1960-1981; organization history.

ACCESS: No restrictions.

FINDING AID: "An Inventory of the Records of the Saskatchewan Business and Professional Women's Clubs" (Guide no. GR 216).

243. Canadian Congress for Learning Opportunities for Women. Regina Chapter

✣ Regina, Sask. Formed 1980.

The Canadian Congress for Learning Opportunities for Women (CCLOW) works for the improvement of learning opportunities for women. The Regina chapter maintains an information network on learning opportunities for women in Regina.

Collection (a)

LOCATION OF RECORDS: Saskatchewan Archives Board, Regina. (See Appendix for address.)

COLLECTION NAME: Canadian Congress on Learning Opportunities for Women. Regina Chapter (R-275).

RECORDS: Correspondence, minutes, 1977-1981; brief, 1982.

AMOUNT: 5 cm.

ACCESS: No restrictions.

Collection (b)

LOCATION OF RECORDS: Saskatchewan Archives Board, Regina.

COLLECTION NAME: Forms part of: Canadian Congress for Learning Opportunities for Women collection (R-1035).

RECORDS: Minutes, reports, briefs.

FINDING AID: Guide no. GR 141.

244. Coalition to Answer Anita Bryant (Saskatoon, Sask.)

✢ Saskatoon, Sask. Formed 1978. Disbanded [1978?].

The coalition was formed to oppose a campaign by Anita Bryant (an American singer and evangelist) against rights for lesbians and gay men and against reproductive choice. The coalition organized counter-rallies during Bryant's 1978 tour of Western Canada. [See also Coalition to Stop Anita Bryant (Toronto, Ont.) (373).]

LOCATION OF RECORDS: Canadian Women's Movement Archives Collection, Morisset Library Special Collections, University of Ottawa. (See Appendix for address.)

COLLECTION NAME: Coalition to Answer Anita Bryant — Saskatoon.

RECORDS: Notes, correspondence, clippings, flyers, 1978.

AMOUNT: 1 cm.

CONDITION: Good.

ACCESS: Restricted; conditional access negotiable.

245. Community Women's Centre (Regina, Sask.)

✢ Regina, Sask. Formed [197-].

The Community Women's Centre (CWC) was a drop-in centre for women.

Collection (a)

LOCATION OF RECORDS: Canadian Women's Movement Archives Collection, Morisset Library Special Collections, University of Ottawa. (See Appendix for address.)

COLLECTION NAME: Community Women's Centre Newsletter — Regina, Sask.

RECORDS: Newsletters, 1973-1974.

AMOUNT: 5 mm.

CONDITION: Good.

ACCESS: No restrictions.

Collection (b)

LOCATION OF RECORDS: Saskatchewan Archives Board, Regina. (See Appendix for address.)

COLLECTION NAME: Community Women's Centre Newsletter.

RECORDS: Newsletters, 1974.

246. Fédération nationale des femmes canadiennes-françaises. Section Willow Bunch

✢ Willow Bunch (Sask.).

La Fédération nationale des femmes canadiennes-françaises (FNFCF) (appelée auparavant la Fédération des femmes canadiennes-françaises ou FFCF) poursuit, entre autres, les buts suivants : sensibiliser les milieux minoritaires aux problèmes collectifs spécifiques des femmes francophones et impliquer les femmes francophones dans une action communautaire propre à améliorer leur condition.

LIEU DE CONSULTATION : Saskatchewan Archives Board, Regina. (Voir Annexe pour l'adresse.)

NOM DU FONDS : Fédération des femmes canadiennes-françaises, Willow Bunch (Micro. R-9.50).

MATÉRIEL : Documents divers, 1967-1990.

QUANTITÉ : 31 m de microfilm.

247. Kipichisichakanisik Women's Peace Camp

✢ Cole Bay, Sask. Formed 1983. Disbanded [198-].

This camp was established by a group of women opposed to the testing of cruise missiles in Canada. The group supported Aboriginal rights to land which was being used as an air-weapons range.

LOCATION OF RECORDS: Canadian Women's Movement Archives Collection, Morisset Library Special Collections, University of Ottawa. (See Appendix for address.)

COLLECTION NAME: Kipichisichakanisik Women's Peace Camp.

RECORDS: Newsletters, 1983-1984; organization history, 1983; pamphlets.

AMOUNT: 2 mm.

CONDITION: Good.

ACCESS: No restrictions.

248. Moose Jaw Co-operative Commonwealth Federation Women's Club

✢ Moose Jaw, Sask. Disbanded.

The Co-operative Commonwealth Federation (CCF), a socialist party founded in 1932, was the predecessor of the New Democratic Party.

LOCATION OF RECORDS: Saskatchewan Archives Board, Saskatoon. (See Appendix for address.)

COLLECTION NAME: Moose Jaw Co-operative Commonwealth Federation Women's Club (S-A546).

RECORDS: Minutes, 1942-1963.

AMOUNT: 4 cm.

ACCESS: No restrictions.

249. Moose Jaw Council of Women

✢ Moose Jaw, Sask.

LOCATION OF RECORDS: Moose Jaw Public Library, Archives Department. (See Appendix for address.)

COLLECTION NAME: Moose Jaw Council of Women (Boxes 23a, 23b, 23c, 67a, 67b).

RECORDS: Minutes, 1916-1931, 1953-1959, 1962-1967, 1970-1972; financial records, 1923-1956; reports, 1962-1967; scrapbooks, 1933-1967; organization histories, miscellaneous records.

AMOUNT: 55 cm.

250. Planned Parenthood Saskatchewan

✢ Formed 1971.

The Family Planning Association of Saskatchewan was established to promote the provision and use of family-planning services in the province. The association's name was changed to Planned Parenthood Saskatchewan in 1976. (Source: Saskatchewan Archives Board finding aid.)

LOCATION OF RECORDS: Saskatchewan Archives Board, Regina. (See Appendix for address.)

COLLECTION NAME: Planned Parenthood Saskatchewan (R-1274, R-891).

RECORDS: Minutes, reports, financial records, 1970-1982; surveys, [ca. 1971]-1982; statistics, 1970-1980; conference records, [ca. 1966]-1980; constitution, [ca. 1978]; correspondence, 1972-1982; mailing lists, 1978-1980; invitations, 1976-1979; subject files, clippings, articles, bibliographies, briefs, submissions, brochures, pamphlets, news releases, committee records, order forms, membership forms, job applications, job descriptions, evaluations, newsletters, graphics, miscellaneous records.

AMOUNT: 6 m.

ACCESS: No restrictions.

FINDING AID: "A Checklist of the Records of Planned Parenthood Saskatchewan" (Guide no. GR 342).

251. Prince Albert Business and Professional Women's Club

✣ Prince Albert, Sask.

LOCATION OF RECORDS: Saskatchewan Archives Board, Regina. (See Appendix for address.)

COLLECTION NAME: Forms part of: Saskatchewan Business and Professional Women's Clubs collection (R-141, #53; R-856, #8)

RECORDS: Correspondence, lists of members, miscellaneous records, 1946-1954, 1960-1981.

ACCESS: No restrictions.

FINDING AID: "An Inventory of the Records of the Saskatchewan Business and Professional Women's Clubs" (Guide no. GR 216).

252. Provincial Council of Women of Saskatchewan

✣ Formed 1919.

Collection (a)

LOCATION OF RECORDS: Saskatchewan Archives Board, Regina. (See Appendix for address.)

COLLECTION NAME: Provincial Council of Women of Saskatchewan (R-1185.1, R-E1865).

RECORDS: Organization histories, 1955, 1984; minutes, reports, financial records, resolutions, miscellaneous records, 1971-1987.

AMOUNT: 5.5 cm.

ACCESS: No restrictions.

Collection (b)

LOCATION OF RECORDS: Saskatchewan Archives Board, Regina.

COLLECTION NAME: Forms part of: J.M. and G.S. Telford Papers (R-382, part II).

RECORDS: Miscellaneous records, 1952-1964.

AMOUNT: 1 file.

ACCESS: No restrictions.

FINDING AID: "An Inventory of the Papers of Mr and Mrs J.M. Telford" (Guide no. GR 189).

Collection (c)

LOCATION OF RECORDS: Saskatchewan Archives Board, Saskatoon. (See Appendix for address.)

COLLECTION NAME: Saskatchewan Provincial Council of Women (S-B83).

RECORDS: Correspondence, minutes, reports, financial records, organization history, scrapbooks, miscellaneous records.

AMOUNT: 6.08 m.

ACCESS: No restrictions.

Collection (d)

LOCATION OF RECORDS: National Archives of Canada. (See Appendix for address.)

COLLECTION NAME: Forms part of: Louise Lucas collection (MG 27, III D 6).

RECORDS: Please see the note about National Archives of Canada collections, in entry # 2.

253. Regina Council of Women

✣ Regina, Sask. Formed 1895.

Local Councils of Women belong to the National Council of Women of Canada, which has lobbied on behalf of various women's causes. The original purpose of the Regina Council of Women was "to promote the welfare of the community through the co-operation of women of varied talents and many faiths." Until about 1945, it was known as the Local Council of Women of Regina. (Source: Saskatchewan Archives Board finding aid.)

Collection (a)

LOCATION OF RECORDS: Saskatchewan Archives Board, Regina. (See Appendix for address.)

COLLECTION NAME: Regina Council of Women; a few items are in the pamphlet files "Woman — Societies and clubs" and "Woman — Legal status, laws, etc."

RECORDS: Minutes, 1895-1986; organization histories, 1955, 1965, 1974, 1980; booklets, 1915, 1926, 1945; correspondence, reports, photographs, briefs, newsletters, financial statements, clippings, scrapbooks, directories, student essay, list of members, roster, attendance records, miscellaneous records.

AMOUNT: Approx. 2.9 m.

ACCESS: No restrictions.

FINDING AID: Guide no. GR 63.

Collection (b)

LOCATION OF RECORDS: Saskatchewan Archives Board, Regina.

COLLECTION NAME: Forms part of: Ruth S. McGill collection.

RECORDS: Building construction records, 1944-1946; organization history, 1945; clippings, miscellaneous records.

AMOUNT: 1.8 cm.

ACCESS: No restrictions.

FINDING AID: "A Checklist of the Papers of Ruth S. McGill" (Guide no. GR 351).

Collection (c)

LOCATION OF RECORDS: Saskatchewan Archives Board, Regina.

COLLECTION NAME: Forms part of: J.M. and G.S. Telford Papers (R-382, parts II, VIII, XIX).

RECORDS: Organization histories, 1945, 1955; reports, correspondence, newsletters, lists of officers, resolutions, minutes, miscellaneous records, 1951-1971.

ACCESS: No restrictions.

FINDING AID: "An Inventory of the Papers of Mr and Mrs J.M. Telford" (Guide no. GR 189).

254. Regina Status of Women Co-ordinating Committee

✣ Regina, Sask. Formed 1972.

This committee organized a conference called "Woman Today," held in Regina in 1973.

LOCATION OF RECORDS: Canadian Women's Movement Archives Collection, Morisset Library Special Collections, University of Ottawa. (See Appendix for address.)

COLLECTION NAME: Conf.: "Woman Today," Regina Status of Women Co-ordinating Committee, June, 1973.
RECORDS: Conference report, 1973.
AMOUNT: 4 mm.
CONDITION: Good.
ACCESS: No restrictions.

255. Regina Transition Women's Society

✣ Regina, Sask. Formed [197-].

The Regina Transition Women's Society operates Transition House, which provides crisis housing for women with children.

LOCATION OF RECORDS: Saskatchewan Archives Board, Regina. (See Appendix for address.)
COLLECTION NAME: Regina Transition Women's Society (R-E593).
RECORDS: Brief, 1979.
AMOUNT: 1 item.
ACCESS: No restrictions.

256. Regina Voice of Women

✣ Regina, Sask. Formed 1961.

Regina Voice of Women (a branch of the national organization Voice of Women) provides a forum in which women can work against war and promote peace. (Source: Saskatchewan Archives Board finding aid.)

Collection (a)

LOCATION OF RECORDS: Saskatchewan Archives Board, Regina. (See Appendix for address.)
COLLECTION NAME: Regina Voice of Women (R-138; R-138.1; R-464).
RECORDS: Minutes, correspondence, newsletters, clippings, publications, submissions, notices, pamphlets, photographs, miscellaneous records, 1958-1988.
AMOUNT: 1.18 m.
FINDING AID: Guide no. GR 448.

Collection (b)

LOCATION OF RECORDS: National Archives of Canada. (See Appendix for address.)
COLLECTION NAME: Forms part of: Evelyn Cherry collection (MG 31, D 173).
RECORDS: Please see the note about National Archives of Canada collections, in entry # 2.

257. Regina Women's Liberation Movement

✣ Regina, Sask. Formed 1970. Disbanded [197-].

The Regina Women's Liberation Movement lobbied to improve the situation of working women. It appears also to have been called the Women's Liberation Group of Regina.

Collection (a)

LOCATION OF RECORDS: Saskatchewan Archives Board, Regina. (See Appendix for address.)
COLLECTION NAME: * D H108 24.
RECORDS: Brief, 1972.
AMOUNT: 1 item.
ACCESS: No restrictions.

Collection (b)

LOCATION OF RECORDS: Canadian Women's Movement Archives Collection, Morisset Library Special Collections, University of Ottawa. (See Appendix for address.)
COLLECTION NAME: Regina Women's Liberation Movement; Women's Liberation Group of Regina.
RECORDS: Brief, pamphlet, 1972.
AMOUNT: 2 items.
CONDITION: Fair.
ACCESS: No restrictions.

258. Regina Women's Network

✣ Regina, Sask.

LOCATION OF RECORDS: Saskatchewan Archives Board, Regina. (See Appendix for address.)
COLLECTION NAME: Regina Women's Network (R-1026).
RECORDS: Correspondence, financial records, news releases, 1983-1984; minutes, clippings, 1982; briefs, submissions, 1983; brochures, pamphlets, [ca. 1983]-1985; constitution, by-laws, [ca. 1982]; contracts, 1985; miscellaneous records, 1982-1985.
AMOUNT: 20 cm.
ACCESS: No restrictions.
FINDING AID: "A Checklist of the Records of the Regina Women's Network" (Guide no. GR 380).

259. Regina Young Women's Christian Association

[See also entry # 936 (in Part II), which lists other records of this organization.]

✣ Regina, Sask. Formed 1910.

The Regina YWCA works to improve the status of women. It operates a shelter for abused women (the Isobel Johnson Shelter) and offers child-care and residential services.

LOCATION OF RECORDS: Saskatchewan Archives Board, Regina. (See Appendix for address.)
COLLECTION NAME: Young Women's Christian Association of Regina.
RECORDS: Minutes, 1910-1960; reports, 1910-1981; photographs, 1910-1986; committee records, 1911-1988; conference records, 1932-1958; directory, 1943-1952; speeches, 1954-1968; correspondence, 1942-1976; financial statements, 1941-1970; pension-plan records, 1958-1980; scrapbooks, 1937-1984; posters, 1969-1982; clippings, 1938; professional staff records, 1959-1983; diary, [ca. 1973]; publicity and promotion records, 1911-1973, 1983-1986; prospectus, 1910-1912; sound recording, 1977; guest books, 1962-1970; newsletters, 1956-1957; manuals, [ca. 1975]; film, [ca. 1977]; publications, volunteer records, miscellaneous records.
AMOUNT: Approx. 90 cm of text, 279 photographic prints, 297 negatives, 3 sound recordings, 1 film.
ACCESS: No restrictions.
FINDING AID: "A Checklist of the Records of the Young Women's Christian Association of Regina."

260. Saskatchewan Action Committee, Status of Women

[See also entry # 937 (in Part II), which lists other records of this organization.]

✣ Regina, Sask. Formed 1973.

This organization (also known as SAC) brings women together to work toward economic, social, and political justice. Education and lobbying are its main activities. SAC has also been called the Status of Women Society.

Collection (a)
LOCATION OF RECORDS: Saskatchewan Archives Board, Saskatoon. (See Appendix for address.)
COLLECTION NAME: Status of Women Society (S-B104).
RECORDS: Minutes, correspondence, briefs, conference reports, newsletters, pamphlets, clippings, photographs, 1967-1978.
AMOUNT: 50 cm.
ACCESS: No restrictions.
FINDING AID: Guide no. GS 152.

Collection (b)
LOCATION OF RECORDS: Saskatchewan Archives Board, Saskatoon.
COLLECTION NAME: Forms part of: Mary Helen Richards collection (S-A229).
RECORDS: Miscellaneous records.
ACCESS: No restrictions.

Collection (c)
LOCATION OF RECORDS: Saskatchewan Archives Board, Regina. (See Appendix for address.)
COLLECTION NAME: Saskatchewan Action Committee, Status of Women (R-F61).
RECORDS: Newsletters, 1973-1976.
ACCESS: No restrictions.

261. Saskatchewan Business and Professional Women's Clubs

✢ Formed 1944.

This is a federation of business and professional women's clubs throughout Saskatchewan. It is affiliated with the Canadian Federation of Business and Professional Women's Clubs.

LOCATION OF RECORDS: Saskatchewan Archives Board, Regina. (See Appendix for address.)
COLLECTION NAME: Saskatchewan Business and Professional Women's Clubs (R-141, R-461, R-856).
RECORDS: Minutes, 1950-1980; correspondence, 1947-1980; financial records, 1949-1958, 1964-1975; conference records, 1947, 1949, 1951, 1954, 1956-1957, 1959, 1961, 1964-1978; submissions, 1951, [1967?], 1971-1977; nomination records, 1959-1966, 1968-1970; by-laws, regulations, 1972-1980; rosters, 1972-1978; publicity material, 1976-1978; lists of officers and members, organization histories, reports, constitutions, clippings, pamphlets, handbooks, newsletters, miscellaneous records.
AMOUNT: 2.4 m.
ACCESS: No restrictions.
FINDING AID: "An Inventory of the Records of the Saskatchewan Business and Professional Women's Clubs" (Guide no. GR 216).

262. Saskatchewan Health-Care Auxiliaries Association

The association was originally called the Saskatchewan Hospital Auxiliaries Association; the name was changed in 1977.

LOCATION OF RECORDS: Saskatchewan Archives Board, Saskatoon. (See Appendix for address.)
COLLECTION NAME: Saskatchewan Hospital Auxiliaries Association (S-B27); Saskatchewan Health-Care Auxiliaries Association (S-A673).
RECORDS: Minutes, reports, accounts, programmes, publications, miscellaneous records, 1938-1988.
AMOUNT: 3.97 m.
FINDING AID: Guide no. GS 126.

263. Saskatchewan Native Women's Movement

✢ Regina, Sask. Formed [before 1975]. Disbanded [ca. 1982].

The Saskatchewan Native Women's Movement (SNWM) worked to create unity among Native women in Saskatchewan, promote their interests, and foster their social, political, and economic development at the community level. SNWM had locals throughout the province.

LOCATION OF RECORDS: Canadian Women's Movement Archives Collection, Morisset Library Special Collections, University of Ottawa. (See Appendix for address.)
COLLECTION NAME: Iskwew: Saskatchewan Native Women's Movement Newsletter.
RECORDS: Newsletters (*Iskwew: Saskatchewan Native Women's Movement Newsletter*, 1975).
AMOUNT: 3 mm.
CONDITION: Good.
ACCESS: No restrictions.

264. Saskatchewan Provincial Council of the Canadian Federation of University Women

✢ Formed 1973.

The Canadian Federation of University Women (CFUW) is made up of university women's clubs (local organizations of women university graduates). The Saskatchewan Provincial Council is composed of the Saskatchewan national officers and two representatives from each club in the province. It deals with issues such as education, women's rights, and human rights. (Source: Saskatchewan Archives Board finding aid.)

LOCATION OF RECORDS: Saskatchewan Archives Board, Regina. (See Appendix for address.)
COLLECTION NAME: Saskatchewan Provincial Council of the Canadian Federation of University Women (Tape R-7880 to 7882; R-638.1; R-638).
RECORDS: Sound recordings, 1977, 1979; minutes, reports, newsletters, correspondence, briefs, by-laws, photographs, biographical information, miscellaneous records, 1973-1985.
AMOUNT: 8 cm of text, 3 sound recordings.
ACCESS: No restrictions.
FINDING AID: Guide no. GR 262.

265. Saskatchewan Teachers' Federation. Saskatoon Women Teachers' Local

✢ Saskatoon, Sask. Formed 1918. Disbanded 1981.

The Saskatoon Women Teachers' Association (SWTA) campaigned for equal pay for women teachers and opposed discrimination against married women teachers. In 1949 it became the Saskatoon Women Teachers' Local of the Saskatchewan Teachers' Federation (STF). (Source: Saskatchewan Archives Board finding aid.) [See also Saskatchewan Teachers' Federation. Women in Education Advisory Committee (939).]

LOCATION OF RECORDS: Saskatchewan Archives Board, Saskatoon. (See Appendix for address.)
COLLECTION NAME: Saskatoon Women Teachers' Association (S-B141).
RECORDS: Minutes, correspondence, accounting records, scrapbooks, 1918-1968.
AMOUNT: 60 cm.
ACCESS: No restrictions.
FINDING AID: Guide no. GS 153.

266. Saskatchewan Tradeswomen

✣ Regina and Saskatoon, Sask. Formed 1977. Disbanded [1986?].

Saskatchewan Tradeswomen was an association of women who were interested in non-traditional occupations and were working or training in the trades or technologies. The association promoted public awareness of women working in trades, produced educational materials, and published the periodical *Women in Trades News*.

LOCATION OF RECORDS: Canadian Women's Movement Archives Collection, Morisset Library Special Collections, University of Ottawa. (See Appendix for address.)
COLLECTION NAME: Saskatchewan Tradeswomen.
RECORDS: Minutes, 1980-1985; periodicals (*Women in Trades News: A Saskatchewan Tradeswomen's Quarterly*, 1979-1983, 1985); booklet, 1985; pamphlet, logo design, letterhead design.
AMOUNT: 3 cm.
CONDITION: Good.
ACCESS: No restrictions.

267. Saskatchewan Women's Institutes

[See also entry # 941 (in Part II), which lists other records of this organization.]

✣ Saskatoon, Sask. Formed 1911.

The Saskatchewan Women's Institutes (SWI) is a voluntary educational organization with branches in rural communities throughout Saskatchewan. SWI works toward the equality of women and the improvement of rural communities. Until 1971 it was called the Association of Homemakers' Clubs of Saskatchewan.

Collection (a)
LOCATION OF RECORDS: Saskatchewan Archives Board, Regina. (See Appendix for address.)
COLLECTION NAME: Women's Institutes of Saskatchewan (R-E2320); Saskatchewan Women's Institutes (R-E2449).
RECORDS: Newsletters, 1971, 1976; convention programme and registration form, 1986; clippings.
AMOUNT: 3 mm.

Collection (b)
LOCATION OF RECORDS: University of Saskatchewan Archives. (See Appendix for address.)
COLLECTION NAME: Saskatchewan Homemakers Clubs/Saskatchewan Women's Institute (RG 11 s.3).
RECORDS: Miscellaneous records, 1911-1986.
AMOUNT: 4.41 m.
ACCESS: No restrictions.

268. Saskatchewan Working Women

✣ Saskatoon, Sask. Formed 1979. Disbanded [198-].

Saskatchewan Working Women (SWW) had the following objectives: to unite women in the labour movement, encourage women to become unionized, improve women's working conditions, and promote equal opportunity for women.

LOCATION OF RECORDS: Canadian Women's Movement Archives Collection, Morisset Library Special Collections, University of Ottawa. (See Appendix for address.)
COLLECTION NAME: Saskatchewan Working Women.
RECORDS: Constitution, clipping, statement of expenses, 1980; by-laws, 1979; newsletters (*Saskatchewan Working Women Newsletter*, 1980-1982; *Working Woman*, 1980); convention records, 1979-1982; correspondence, agendas, 1980-1982; membership lists, 1979, 1981; discussion paper, speech, study, 1982; press releases, 1980-1981; proposal, 1981; minutes, flyers, questionnaire, guidelines, resolutions, membership forms, rules of order, position paper, notices of meetings, invitation, contact list, button.
AMOUNT: 19 cm of text, 1 button.
CONDITION: Good.
ACCESS: No restrictions.

269. Saskatchewan Working Women. Regina Chapter

✣ Regina, Sask. Formed 1979. Disbanded [198-].

LOCATION OF RECORDS: Saskatchewan Archives Board, Regina. (See Appendix for address.)
COLLECTION NAME: Saskatchewan Working Women, Regina Chapter (R-666).
RECORDS: Minutes, correspondence, miscellaneous records, 1978-1982.
AMOUNT: 12.5 cm.
FINDING AID: Guide no. GR 223.

270. Saskatoon Business and Professional Women's Club

✣ Saskatoon, Sask. Formed 1947.

Collection (a)
LOCATION OF RECORDS: Saskatchewan Archives Board, Saskatoon. (See Appendix for address.)
COLLECTION NAME: Saskatoon Business and Professional Women's Club (S-B99).
RECORDS: Minutes, 1947-1963; annual reports, history, lists of officers, by-laws, constitution.
AMOUNT: 10 cm.
ACCESS: No restrictions.

Collection (b)
LOCATION OF RECORDS: Saskatchewan Archives Board, Regina. (See Appendix for address.)
COLLECTION NAME: Forms part of: Saskatchewan Business and Professional Women's Clubs collection (R-141, #63, #29).
RECORDS: Correspondence, lists of officers, by-laws, miscellaneous records, 1952-1966, 1969-1972; organization history.
ACCESS: No restrictions.
FINDING AID: "An Inventory of the Records of the Saskatchewan Business and Professional Women's Clubs" (Guide no. GR 216).

271. Saskatoon Local Council of Women

✣ Saskatoon, Sask. Formed 1916.

Collection (a)
LOCATION OF RECORDS: Saskatchewan Archives Board, Saskatoon. (See Appendix for address.)
COLLECTION NAME: Saskatoon Local Council of Women (S-B82).
RECORDS: Minute books, 1916-1919, 1926-1942, 1946-1966; minutes and reports, 1919-1967; accounts, 1917-1941; newsletters, 1947-1964; briefs, 1944-1964; constitution, clippings, correspondence, 1926-1963.
AMOUNT: 1.75 m.
ACCESS: No restrictions.

Collection (b)
LOCATION OF RECORDS: Saskatchewan Archives Board, Saskatoon.
COLLECTION NAME: Forms part of: Jessie Caldwell collection (S-A632).
RECORDS: Miscellaneous records.
ACCESS: No restrictions.

Flyer / Tract, 1979
Saskatoon Women's Liberation
CWMA Collection / Fonds de l'ACMF

272. Saskatoon Women for Abortion Law Repeal

✣ Saskatoon, Sask. Formed [1971?]. Disbanded [1976?].

Saskatoon Women for Abortion Law Repeal (SWALR) held the view that women must take the leadership role in the struggle for abortion rights.

LOCATION OF RECORDS: Canadian Women's Movement Archives Collection, Morisset Library Special Collections, University of Ottawa. (See Appendix for address.)

COLLECTION NAME: Saskatoon Women for Abortion Law Repeal.

RECORDS: Brief, 1974; poster, 1973; clippings, press releases, list of files, flyer.

AMOUNT: 5 mm of text, 1 poster.

CONDITION: Good.

ACCESS: No restrictions.

273. Saskatoon Women's Liberation

✣ Saskatoon, Sask. Formed [196-?]. Disbanded [198-].

Saskatoon Women's Liberation challenged societal values and structures which perpetuated the oppression of women. It published the *Saskatoon Women's Liberation Newsletter* and *Prairie Woman*. It ran the Saskatoon Women's Centre (or Saskatoon Women's Resource Centre). In 1978 it co-sponsored the Prairie Women's Socialist-Feminist Conference.

Collection (a)

LOCATION OF RECORDS: Saskatchewan Archives Board, Saskatoon. (See Appendix for address.)

COLLECTION NAME: Saskatoon Women's Centre (S-B112).

RECORDS: Office files, publications, clippings, 1970-1975.

AMOUNT: 7.75 m.

ACCESS: Restricted.

Collection (b)

LOCATION OF RECORDS: Canadian Women's Movement Archives Collection, Morisset Library Special Collections, University of Ottawa. (See Appendix for address.)

COLLECTION NAME: Saskatoon Women's Liberation; Saskatoon Women's Centre; Prairie Women's Socialist-Feminist Conference (1978: Saskatoon, Sask.); SR 27/1-3.

RECORDS: Newsletters (*Saskatoon Women's Liberation Newsletter*, 1973-1975, 1977; *Prairie Woman: A Newsletter of Saskatoon Women's Liberation*, 1977-1981); organization history, [1977?]; proposed constitution, 1978; correspondence, 1970, 1973, 1975, 1977, 1979; press release, clippings, 1974; flyers, [1970 or 1971], 1978-1979; conference records, sound recordings (conference proceedings), 1978; button, 1975; position papers, policy statements, pamphlet, poster, brief, notes.

AMOUNT: 6 cm of text, 3 sound recordings, 1 poster, 1 button.

CONDITION: Fair.

ACCESS: No restrictions.

Collection (c)

LOCATION OF RECORDS: Saskatchewan Archives Board, Regina. (See Appendix for address.)

COLLECTION NAME: Saskatoon Women's Liberation Newsletter (R-F62).

RECORDS: Newsletters, 1970-1975.

ACCESS: No restrictions.

274. Spadina Childcare Co-operative Association

✣ Saskatoon, Sask.

LOCATION OF RECORDS: Saskatchewan Archives Board, Saskatoon. (See Appendix for address.)

COLLECTION NAME: Spadina Childcare Co-operative Association (S-A476).

RECORDS: Minutes, newsletters, circulars, agreements, reports, correspondence, 1974-1980.

AMOUNT: 6 cm.

ACCESS: No restrictions.

275. Swift Current Business and Professional Women's Club

✣ Swift Current, Sask.

LOCATION OF RECORDS: Saskatchewan Archives Board, Regina. (See Appendix for address.)

COLLECTION NAME: Forms part of: Saskatchewan Business and Professional Women's Clubs collection (R-141, #67).

RECORDS: Correspondence, lists of officers and members, 1948-1954, 1960-1966.

ACCESS: No restrictions.

FINDING AID: "An Inventory of the Records of the Saskatchewan Business and Professional Women's Clubs" (Guide no. GR 216).

276. Swift Current Council of Women

✣ Swift Current, Sask. Formed 1916.

LOCATION OF RECORDS: Saskatchewan Archives Board, Regina. (See Appendix for address.)

COLLECTION NAME: Swift Current Council of Women (Micro. R-2.917).

RECORDS: Minutes, 1965-1986; scrapbooks, 1942-1981; miscellaneous records, 1920-1981; photographs.

AMOUNT: 62 m of microfilm.

ACCESS: No restrictions.

277. United Action Committee for Abortion Reform

✣ Regina, Sask. Formed 1974.

This committee, which was formed at a conference on abortion, was composed of representatives of feminist and left-wing organizations.

LOCATION OF RECORDS: Canadian Women's Movement Archives Collection, Morisset Library Special Collections, University of Ottawa. (See Appendix for address.)

COLLECTION NAME: United Action Committee for Abortion Reform, Regina.

RECORDS: Brief, correspondence, 1974.

AMOUNT: 1 mm.

CONDITION: Poor.

ACCESS: No restrictions.

278. University of Saskatchewan. Committee on the Status of Women

✣ Saskatoon, Sask.

LOCATION OF RECORDS: University of Saskatchewan Archives. (See Appendix for address.)

COLLECTION NAME: Forms part of: Presidential Records Series V (R.W. Begg): President's Committees — Status of Women (RG 1 s.5 [II.1.L.v-ix], vols. 39-40); University Studies Group — Review of the Status of Women (RG 1 s.5 [II.1.R.xvii], vol. 45).

RECORDS: Correspondence, minutes, reports, publications, conference records, related material, 1975-1980.

AMOUNT: 9 files.

ACCESS: No restrictions.

279. University Women's Club (Moose Jaw, Sask.)

✣ Moose Jaw, Sask.

University women's clubs are local organizations of women university graduates. The clubs belong to the Canadian Federation of University Women.

LOCATION OF RECORDS: Moose Jaw Public Library, Archives Department. (See Appendix for address.)
COLLECTION NAME: University Women's Club, Moose Jaw (Boxes 66, 71-73).
RECORDS: Correspondence, 1969-1976, 1979-1983; financial records, 1960-1982; constitution and by-laws, 1967, 1973; reports, 1973-1980; minutes, 1976-1980; publications, 1977-1980.
AMOUNT: 48 cm.

280. University Women's Club of Regina

✣ Regina, Sask. Formed 1915.

This is an organization of women university graduates in Regina. Its original goals included the stimulation of intellectual activity in women and the promotion of their social welfare. (Source: University Women's Club of Regina: A History/Jean Larmour. — Regina: University Women's Club of Regina, 1985.)

Collection (a)
LOCATION OF RECORDS: Saskatchewan Archives Board, Regina. (See Appendix for address.)
COLLECTION NAME: University Women's Club of Regina.
RECORDS: Minutes, reports, correspondence, photographs, resolutions, financial statements, membership lists, newsletters, clippings, bulletins, programmes, membership cards, catalogue, organization history, miscellaneous records, [ca. 1915]-1989.
AMOUNT: Approx. 2.5 m.
ACCESS: No restrictions.
FINDING AID: Guide no. GR 158.

Collection (b)
LOCATION OF RECORDS: Saskatchewan Archives Board, Regina.
COLLECTION NAME: Forms part of: Ruth S. McGill collection.
RECORDS: Bulletins, 1942-1945; membership lists, 1931-1947; programmes, 1941-1947; miscellaneous records, [ca. 1947].
AMOUNT: 1.5 cm.
ACCESS: No restrictions.
FINDING AID: "A Checklist of the Papers of Ruth S. McGill" (Guide no. GR 351).

281. University Women's Club (Saskatoon, Sask.)

✣ Saskatoon, Sask. Formed 1918.

Collection (a)
LOCATION OF RECORDS: Saskatchewan Archives Board, Saskatoon. (See Appendix for address.)
COLLECTION NAME: University Women's Club, Saskatoon (S-B41, S-A589).
RECORDS: Minutes, correspondence, accounting records, publications, reports, programmes, agenda, briefs, membership lists, newsletters, clippings, printed items, photographs, 1918-1988.
AMOUNT: 4.64 m.
ACCESS: No restrictions.

Collection (b)
LOCATION OF RECORDS: Saskatchewan Archives Board, Saskatoon.
COLLECTION NAME: Forms part of: Jessie Caldwell collection (S-A632).
RECORDS: Miscellaneous records.
ACCESS: No restrictions.

282. University Women's Club (Swift Current, Sask.)

✣ Swift Current, Sask. Formed 1930.

LOCATION OF RECORDS: Saskatchewan Archives Board, Regina. (See Appendix for address.)
COLLECTION NAME: University Women's Club, Swift Current (R-643, Micro. R-2.49).
RECORDS: Minutes, 1930-1978; scrapbook, 1931-1970.
AMOUNT: 10 cm of text, 20 m of microfilm.
ACCESS: No restrictions.

283. Women and Drug Use Society of Saskatoon

✣ Saskatoon, Sask. Formed [197-]. Disbanded [ca. 1981].

LOCATION OF RECORDS: Saskatchewan Archives Board, Saskatoon. (See Appendix for address.)
COLLECTION NAME: Women and Drug Use Society of Saskatoon (S-A466).
RECORDS: Minutes, correspondence, mailing lists, financial records, manuscripts for booklet, 1977-1980.
AMOUNT: 11 cm.
ACCESS: No restrictions.

284. Women's Action Collective on Health

✣ Regina, Sask. Formed [ca. 1976]. Disbanded.

The members of the Women's Action Collective on Health (WACH) "initially came together to struggle against the critical abortion situation in Saskatchewan." They continued meeting "with an objective of developing an analysis of women's oppression in capitalist society." (Source: WACH statement, 1977.) WACH co-sponsored the Prairie Women's Socialist-Feminist Conference, held in Saskatoon in 1978.

LOCATION OF RECORDS: Canadian Women's Movement Archives Collection, Morisset Library Special Collections, University of Ottawa. (See Appendix for address.)
COLLECTION NAME: Women's Action Collective on Health; Conf.: Prairie Women's Socialist-Feminist Conference (1978: Saskatoon, Sask.); SR 27/1-3.
RECORDS: Brief, 1976; organization history, position statement, 1977; correspondence, conference records, sound recordings (conference proceedings), 1978; flyers.
AMOUNT: 7 mm of text, 3 sound recordings.
CONDITION: Good.
ACCESS: No restrictions.

285. Yorkton Business and Professional Women's Club

✣ Yorkton, Sask.

Collection (a)
LOCATION OF RECORDS: Saskatchewan Archives Board, Regina. (See Appendix for address.)
COLLECTION NAME: Yorkton Business and Professional Women's Club (R-855).
RECORDS: Minutes, 1957-1982; ledgers, 1954-1983.
AMOUNT: 6 cm.

Collection (b)
LOCATION OF RECORDS: Saskatchewan Archives Board, Regina.
COLLECTION NAME: Forms part of: Saskatchewan Business and Professional Women's Clubs collection (R-141, #74, #29).
RECORDS: Correspondence, lists of officers, miscellaneous records, 1946-1972; organization history.

ACCESS: No restrictions.
FINDING AID: "An Inventory of the Records of the Saskatchewan Business and Professional Women's Clubs" (Guide no. GR 216).

286. Yorkton Women's Advisory Committee
✢ Yorkton, Sask. Formed [1987?]. Disbanded 1988.

This committee conducted a survey to determine whether there was a need for a women's resource centre in Yorkton.

LOCATION OF RECORDS: Canadian Women's Movement Archives Collection, Morisset Library Special Collections, University of Ottawa. (See Appendix for address.)
COLLECTION NAME: Yorkton Women's Advisory Committee.
RECORDS: Report, questionnaire, correspondence, 1988.
AMOUNT: 5 mm.
CONDITION: Good.
ACCESS: No restrictions.

287. Young Women's Christian Association, Saskatoon
✢ Saskatoon, Sask. Formed 1910.

Originally established to provide accommodation for young women, the YWCA has also offered physical-education programmes, summer camps, and classes. (Source: Saskatchewan Archives Board finding aid.)

LOCATION OF RECORDS: Saskatchewan Archives Board, Saskatoon. (See Appendix for address.)
COLLECTION NAME: Young Women's Christian Association, Saskatoon (S-A553); Saskatoon YWCA (S-A661).
RECORDS: Minutes, financial records, building and renovation records, correspondence, publications, photographs, clippings, 1910-1980.
AMOUNT: 3 m.
ACCESS: No restrictions.
FINDING AID: Guide no. GS 97.

MANITOBA

288. Affirm (Winnipeg, Man.)
✣ Winnipeg, Man.

This is the Winnipeg branch of Affirm, an organization for lesbians and gay men in the United Church of Canada.

LOCATION OF RECORDS: Manitoba Gay/Lesbian Archive. (See Appendix for address.)
COLLECTION NAME: Forms part of: Fay McNaught collection.
RECORDS: Miscellaneous records, 1984-1990.

289. Brandon Council of Women
✣ Brandon, Man. Formed 1952.

This federation of local women's organizations has promoted the election of women to civic office, among other activities. (Source: *Planting the Garden: An Annotated Archival Bibliography of the History of Women in Manitoba*/Mary Kinnear and Vera Fast. — Winnipeg: University of Manitoba Press, 1987.)

LOCATION OF RECORDS: Brandon University Archives. (See Appendix for address.)
COLLECTION NAME: Brandon Council of Women (M80-23).
RECORDS: Minutes, reports, correspondence, clippings, scrapbooks, photographs, resolutions, miscellaneous records, 1956-1973.

290. Business and Professional Women's Club (Flin Flon, Man.)
✣ Flin Flon, Man. Disbanded [198-].

LOCATION OF RECORDS: Flin Flon Community Archives. (See Appendix for address.)
COLLECTION NAME: Business and Professional Women's Club.
RECORDS: Minutes, scrapbooks, photographs, miscellaneous records, 1948-1978.
AMOUNT: Approx. 2 drawers of a filing cabinet.

291. Business and Professional Women's Club of Winnipeg
✣ Winnipeg, Man. Formed 1924.

Originally called the Professional and Business Women's Club of Winnipeg, the club adopted its present name in 1954. It encourages the promotion of women in business and the professions and organizes social and cultural activities. (Source: Provincial Archives of Manitoba finding aid, 1988.)

Collection (a)
LOCATION OF RECORDS: Provincial Archives of Manitoba. (See Appendix for address.)
COLLECTION NAME: Business and Professional Women's Club of Winnipeg (P4225-P4236, D307 f. 6 and P4648).
RECORDS: Legal registrations, 1932-1958; minutes, 1952-1986; correspondence, 1961-1981; financial records, 1927-1983; records of annual meetings, 1971, 1973-1978; newsletters, publications, scrapbooks, reports, speeches, seminar information, charter, by-laws, membership rosters, presentations, resolutions, miscellaneous records.
AMOUNT: 3.2 m.
ACCESS: No restrictions.
FINDING AID: Inventory and file lists available.

Collection (b)
LOCATION OF RECORDS: University of Manitoba Libraries, Department of Archives and Special Collections. (See Appendix for address.)
COLLECTION NAME: Forms part of: Nan Shipley collection (MSS 21).
RECORDS: Correspondence, 1974-1975.
AMOUNT: 2 items.
ACCESS: No restrictions.

292. Canadian Women's Press Club. Winnipeg Branch
✣ Winnipeg, Man. Formed 1907.

The Canadian Women's Press Club (CWPC), founded in 1904, was an association of women journalists and other women writers. In 1971 the CWPC began admitting men and changed its name to the Media Club of Canada. (Source: *The Canadian Encyclopedia*. — Edmonton: Hurtig Publishers, 1985.)

LOCATION OF RECORDS: Provincial Archives of Manitoba. (See Appendix for address.)
COLLECTION NAME: Canadian Women's Press Club: Winnipeg Branch (MG 10 A1); Canadian Women's Press Club Collection, Still Images Section.
RECORDS: Minutes, membership lists, accounts, clippings, correspondence, reports, newsletters, photographs, books, 1906-1973.
AMOUNT: 1.2 m.
ACCESS: No restrictions.
FINDING AID: Inventory available.

293. Consulting Committee on the Status of Women with Disabilities

✣ Winnipeg, Man. Formed 1986. Disbanded 1990.

The committee (also known as CCSWD) worked to improve the status of women with disabilities. CCSWD was concerned with the need for information by and about women with disabilities, and it addressed the issue of access to women's organizations and services. (Source: Provincial Archives of Manitoba finding aid.)

LOCATION OF RECORDS: Provincial Archives of Manitoba. (See Appendix for address.)

COLLECTION NAME: Consulting Committee on the Status of Women with Disabilities (P4743-P4747).

RECORDS: Administrative files, subject files, newsletters, Braille resource guide, 1986-1990.

AMOUNT: 69 cm.

ACCESS: No restrictions.

FINDING AID: Inventory and file list available.

294. Council of Women of Winnipeg

✣ Winnipeg, Man. Formed 1894.

A non-sectarian, non-partisan federation of Winnipeg women's organizations, the council takes "action in respect to the welfare and general progress" of the community. Pay equity is one of the issues the council has addressed. (Source: Provincial Archives of Manitoba finding aid, 1988.)

LOCATION OF RECORDS: Provincial Archives of Manitoba. (See Appendix for address.)

COLLECTION NAME: Council of Women of Winnipeg (P 3586-3607).

RECORDS: Constitution, by-laws, 1916-1974; minutes, 1894-1983; correspondence, 1932-1980; financial records, 1937-1983; reports, 1918, 1933-1983; resolutions, briefs, 1899-1984; subject files, 1922-1984; publications, scrapbooks, clippings, 1894-1976; miscellaneous records.

AMOUNT: 2.54 m.

ACCESS: No restrictions.

FINDING AID: Inventory and file list available.

295. Council on Homosexuality and Religion

✣ Winnipeg, Man. Formed 1979.

The council has lobbied for greater acceptance of homosexuality among religious denominations. It has also published material on homosexuality and religion.

LOCATION OF RECORDS: Manitoba Gay/Lesbian Archive. (See Appendix for address.)

COLLECTION NAME: Council on Homosexuality and Religion.

RECORDS: Miscellaneous records, 1977-1991.

AMOUNT: Approx. 3 m.

296. Day Nursery Centre

✣ Winnipeg, Man. Formed 1909.

The Mothers' Association Day Nursery was established to provide day care for the children of working women. In 1954 its name was changed to the Day Nursery Centre. (Source: Provincial Archives of Manitoba finding aid, 1986.)

LOCATION OF RECORDS: Provincial Archives of Manitoba. (See Appendix for address.)

COLLECTION NAME: Day Nursery Centre (P884-916); the photographs have been transferred to the Still Images Collection.

RECORDS: Programme, 1914-1915; list of members, 1915; minutes, 1950-1980; constitution, 1959, 1976; by-laws, 1954-1966; manuals, 1955-1967, 1977; reports, 1942-1981; correspondence, 1942-1980; staff-structure chart, 1953; briefs, speeches, 1958-1976; building records, 1971-1972; office diaries, 1977-1979; press clippings, 1914, 1951-1964; job description, 1978; staff files, financial records, 1956-1981; attendance registers, message books, 1972-1980; photographs, miscellaneous records.

AMOUNT: 4 m of text, 2 photographs.

ACCESS: Certain files are restricted.

FINDING AID: Inventory and file list available.

297. Flin Flon Graduate Nurses Association

✣ Flin Flon, Man. Disbanded [197-].

LOCATION OF RECORDS: Flin Flon Community Archives. (See Appendix for address.)

COLLECTION NAME: Flin Flon Graduate Nurses Association.

RECORDS: Minutes, scrapbooks, miscellaneous records, [194-]-[197-].

298. Gay Christian Week

✣ Winnipeg, Man. Formed 1977.

This group produced a radio programme of the same name. The group (also called Gay Week) later became the Winnipeg Gay Media Collective.

LOCATION OF RECORDS: Manitoba Gay/Lesbian Archive. (See Appendix for address.)

COLLECTION NAME: Gay Christian Week.

RECORDS: Scripts, sound recordings, miscellaneous records, 1977-1982.

AMOUNT: Approx. 2 m.

299. Gays for Equality (Winnipeg, Man.)

✣ Winnipeg, Man. Formed 1972.

Gays for Equality (GFE) was founded at the University of Manitoba and was originally called the Campus Gay Club. GFE's activities have included counselling and referral, public education, and lobbying.

Collection (a)

LOCATION OF RECORDS: Manitoba Gay/Lesbian Archive. (See Appendix for address.)

COLLECTION NAME: Gays for Equality.

RECORDS: Minutes, photographs, videotapes, membership lists, posters, miscellaneous records, 1972-1991.

AMOUNT: Approx. 5 m.

Collection (b)

LOCATION OF RECORDS: Canadian Gay Archives. (See Appendix for address.)

COLLECTION NAME: Gays for Equality (83-024, 85-005, 86-010, 87-018).

RECORDS: Administrative files, correspondence, briefs, publications, miscellaneous records, 1972-[1987?].

Collection (c)

LOCATION OF RECORDS: Canadian Gay Archives.

COLLECTION NAME: Forms part of: Chris Vogel collection (89-117).

RECORDS: Miscellaneous records, 1988-1989.

PART I: RECORDS HELD BY ARCHIVES / PARTIE I : FONDS DÉTENUS PAR DES ARCHIVES

Flyer / Tract, 1972
Cross-Canada Abortion Conference
Manitoba Abortion Action Coalition
CWMA Collection / Fonds de l'ACMF

300. Home Economists in Business — Winnipeg

✤ Winnipeg, Man. Formed 1981.

Home Economists in Business (HEIB) — Winnipeg works to increase recognition of home economics as a profession and to facilitate communication and co-operation among home economists in business. (Source: Provincial Archives of Manitoba finding aid, 1989.)

LOCATION OF RECORDS: Provincial Archives of Manitoba. (See Appendix for address.)

COLLECTION NAME: Home Economists in Business — Winnipeg (P4640); slides and photographs have been transferred to the Still Images Section.

RECORDS: Constitution, by-laws, minutes, 1981-1988; publicity material, reports, memoranda, position papers, 1983-1988; newsletters, 1983-1989; slides, photographs.

AMOUNT: 20 cm.

ACCESS: No restrictions.

FINDING AID: Inventory and file list available.

301. International Ladies Garment Workers Union. Local 286

✤ Winnipeg, Man.

Local 286 of the International Ladies Garment Workers Union (ILGWU) was formed in the late 1970s when four locals merged: Local 216 (for cloak workers, established around 1934); Local 237 (for workers in dress and sportswear factories, formed a year later); Local 304 (for outerwear and knitwear workers, formed in 1941); and Local 319 (for cutters, formed in 1967). (Source: Provincial Archives of Manitoba finding aid, 1984.)

LOCATION OF RECORDS: Provincial Archives of Manitoba. (See Appendix for address.)

COLLECTION NAME: International Ladies Garment Workers Union, Local 286 (P 271-P 286).

RECORDS: Minutes, 1940-1978; agreements, 1935-1980; dues books, 1954-1981; legal files, 1954-1970; miscellaneous records, 1934-1981; photographs, posters.

AMOUNT: 2 m of text, 70 photographs, 2 posters.

ACCESS: No restrictions.

FINDING AID: Inventory available.

302. Lake Agazzis Amazon Guild

✤ Winnipeg, Man. Formed 1989.

This is a group for lesbians seeking emotional and spiritual growth through social and political networking.

LOCATION OF RECORDS: Manitoba Gay/Lesbian Archive. (See Appendix for address.)

COLLECTION NAME: Lake Agazzis Amazon Guild.

RECORDS: Minutes, correspondence, membership lists, mailing lists, 1989-1990; posters, 1989.

AMOUNT: 5 cm.

ACCESS: The records are restricted for fifteen years after being deposited.

303. Lesbian Mothers Support Group

✤ Winnipeg, Man. Formed 1985. Disbanded 1989.

This group provided emotional and legal support to lesbian mothers.

LOCATION OF RECORDS: Manitoba Gay/Lesbian Archive. (See Appendix for address.)

COLLECTION NAME: Lesbian Mothers Support Group.

RECORDS: Correspondence, membership lists, petitions, scrapbooks, reports, briefs, pamphlets, flyers, press releases, posters, banners, 1985-1990.

AMOUNT: 20 cm.

CONDITION: Good.

304. Manitoba Abortion Action Coalition

✤ Winnipeg, Man.

This coalition hosted the Cross-Canada Abortion Conference, held in Winnipeg in 1972. It appears also to have been called the Abortion Coalition Committee.

Collection (a)

LOCATION OF RECORDS: Provincial Archives of Manitoba. (See Appendix for address.)

COLLECTION NAME: Forms part of: Linda Taylor collection (P2633, file 1).

RECORDS: Minutes, 1972-1974.

AMOUNT: 1 file.

ACCESS: No restrictions.

FINDING AID: File list available for Taylor collection.

Collection (b)

LOCATION OF RECORDS: Canadian Women's Movement Archives Collection, Morisset Library Special Collections, University of Ottawa. (See Appendix for address.)

COLLECTION NAME: Conf.: "Cross-Canada Abortion Conference," Manitoba, 1972.

RECORDS: Conference records, 1972.

AMOUNT: 3 mm.

CONDITION: Fair.

ACCESS: No restrictions.

305. Manitoba Action Committee on the Status of Women

[See also entry # 964 (in Part II), which lists other records of this organization.]

✤ Winnipeg, Man. Formed 1967.

The Manitoba Action Committee on the Status of Women (MACSW) aims to improve attitudes to women, raise issues affecting women, and promote equality. It works to achieve these aims through political action, public education, and personal growth. MACSW was originally called the Manitoba Committee on the Status of Women, then became the Manitoba Volunteer Committee on the Status of Women, and finally adopted its present name in 1971. Its French name is le Comité d'action manitobain sur le statut de la femme. [See also Parkland Status of Women (979).]

LOCATION OF RECORDS: Provincial Archives of Manitoba. (See Appendix for address.)

COLLECTION NAME: Manitoba Action Committee on the Status of Women (P 263-266, P4234A).

RECORDS: Correspondence, minutes, constitution, reports, briefs, information packets, contracts of employment, newsletters, pamphlets, news and press releases, mailing lists, membership lists, volunteer lists, research notes, terms of reference, resolutions, discussion transcripts, organizational material, historical sketch, 1967-1983.

AMOUNT: 65 cm.

ACCESS: No restrictions.

FINDING AID: Inventory and file list available for P 263-266; inventory available for P4234A.

306. Manitoba Association of Licensed Practical Nurses

✣ Winnipeg, Man. Formed 1944.

The first action of this association was to negotiate a wage increase for its members. (Source: Provincial Archives of Manitoba finding aid, 1989.)

LOCATION OF RECORDS: Provincial Archives of Manitoba. (See Appendix for address.)

COLLECTION NAME: Manitoba Association of Licensed Practical Nurses (P4561-P4576).

RECORDS: Minutes, 1944-1988; correspondence, 1965-1986; reports, motions, 1966-1984; reviews, submissions, 1969-1984; financial records, 1944-1984; personnel files, [195-]-[198-].

AMOUNT: 4.4 m.

ACCESS: Written permission from the association's president or executive director is required to view certain records.

FINDING AID: Inventory and file list available.

307. Manitoba Association of Social Workers

✣ Winnipeg, Man. Formed 1930.

The Manitoba Association of Social Workers (MASW) began as the Manitoba Branch of the Canadian Association of Social Workers. Its objectives include improving members' salaries and working conditions. (Source: Provincial Archives of Manitoba finding aid, 1989.)

Collection (a)

LOCATION OF RECORDS: Provincial Archives of Manitoba. (See Appendix for address.)

COLLECTION NAME: Manitoba Association of Social Workers (P4509-P4515).

RECORDS: Minutes, reports, correspondence, policy papers, briefs, newsletters, miscellaneous records, 1956-1986.

AMOUNT: 2 m.

ACCESS: No restrictions.

FINDING AID: Inventory and file list available.

Collection (b)

LOCATION OF RECORDS: Provincial Archives of Manitoba.

COLLECTION NAME: Forms part of: Darlene Germscheid Papers (P 241, #6).

RECORDS: By-laws, financial statement, 1975; minutes, 1976; report, correspondence, newsletter, information sheet.

ACCESS: No restrictions.

FINDING AID: Inventory and file list available for Germscheid collection.

308. Manitoba Federation of Labour. Women's Committee

[See also entry # 967 (in Part II), which lists other records of this organization.]

✣ Winnipeg, Man. Formed [1975?].

The Manitoba Federation of Labour (MFL) Women's Committee works to develop an awareness of women's issues within the trade-union movement and in society at large. It also lobbies the provincial government on women's issues. Prior to 1985, it was known as the MFL Equal Rights and Opportunities Committee.

LOCATION OF RECORDS: Provincial Archives of Manitoba. (See Appendix for address.)

COLLECTION NAME: Forms part of: Manitoba Federation of Labour collection (P 431, #10).

RECORDS: Miscellaneous records, 1977-1979.

AMOUNT: 5 mm.

ACCESS: Restricted.

FINDING AID: Finding aid available for Manitoba Federation of Labour collection.

309. Manitoba Organization of Nurses' Associations. Local 1

✣ Winnipeg, Man. Formed 1964.

Local 1 of the Manitoba Organization of Nurses' Associations (MONA) represents Municipal Hospital and City of Winnipeg Public Health nurses in contract negotiations and other aspects of labour relations. The organization was formed when nurses withdrew from Local 500 of the Canadian Union of Public Employees and reorganized as the Winnipeg Civic Registered Nurses Association, which became Local 1 of MONA. (Source: Provincial Archives of Manitoba finding aid, 1985.)

LOCATION OF RECORDS: Provincial Archives of Manitoba. (See Appendix for address.)

COLLECTION NAME: Winnipeg Civic Registered Nurses Association (P331).

RECORDS: Minute books, 1964-1980.

AMOUNT: 5 cm.

ACCESS: No restrictions.

FINDING AID: Inventory available.

310. Manitoba Provincial Organization of Business and Professional Women's Clubs

✣ Formed 1953.

The organization's aim is "to promote the development and recognition of the abilities of women in business, the professions, and industry throughout Manitoba and to encourage member clubs to participate in provincial projects." (Source: Provincial Archives of Manitoba finding aid.)

LOCATION OF RECORDS: Provincial Archives of Manitoba. (See Appendix for address.)

COLLECTION NAME: Manitoba Organization of Business and Professional Women's Clubs (MG 10 A 19).

RECORDS: Minutes, workshop material, conference records, seminar material, resolutions, publicity material, miscellaneous records, 1930-1978.

AMOUNT: 30 cm.

ACCESS: No restrictions.

FINDING AID: Inventory and file list available.

311. Manitoba Society of Occupational Therapists

✣ Winnipeg, Man. Formed 1961.

The society (also known as MSOT) is affiliated with the Canadian Association of Occupational Therapists.

LOCATION OF RECORDS: Provincial Archives of Manitoba. (See Appendix for address.)

COLLECTION NAME: Manitoba Society of Occupational Therapists (P4558-P4560).

RECORDS: Constitution, by-laws, 1962-1986; annual reports, 1959-1987; minutes, 1973-1986; correspondence, 1960-1986; financial reports, 1966-1984; subject files, 1964-1986; newsletters, publications, 1954-1988; miscellaneous records.

AMOUNT: 91 cm.

ACCESS: No restrictions.

FINDING AID: Inventory and file list available.

312. Manitoba Teachers' Society

[See also entry # 969 (in Part II), which lists other records of this organization.]

✣ Winnipeg, Man. Formed 1919.

Through political action, professional activities, and collective bargaining, the Manitoba Teachers' Society (MTS) works to promote education and safeguard the welfare of teachers. It was known as the Manitoba Teachers' Federation until 1942.

LOCATION OF RECORDS: Provincial Archives of Manitoba. (See Appendix for address.)

COLLECTION NAME: Manitoba Teachers' Society (P3235-P3346).

RECORDS: Records of annual general meetings, 1920-1930, 1932-1933, 1951-1972; certification records, [ca. 1949]-1967; collective agreements, [ca. 1950]-[ca. 1970]; committee records, 1940-1981; submissions, briefs, 1954-1970; arbitration files, 1953-1974; legal records, 1953-1975; subject files, correspondence, newsletters, reports, recommendations, miscellaneous records.

AMOUNT: 33.6 m.

ACCESS: Restricted.

FINDING AID: Inventory and file list available.

313. Manitoba Women's Institute

✣ Formed 1910.

The Manitoba Women's Institute, which has branches throughout the province, is a rural women's organization whose interests include home economics, adult education, leadership, and personal improvement. The organization has lobbied on various social issues, including women's issues such as family law. (Source: *The Great Human Heart: A History of the Manitoba Women's Institute, 1910-1980*. — Manitoba Women's Institute, 1980.)

LOCATION OF RECORDS: Provincial Archives of Manitoba. (See Appendix for address.)

COLLECTION NAME: Manitoba Women's Institute (P574-584, MG 10 C 8, P4584-4593).

RECORDS: Minutes, correspondence, financial records, reports, resolutions, convention records, publicity materials, newsletters, publications, clippings, scrapbooks, historical files, miscellaneous records, 1910-1988.

AMOUNT: 13.4 m.

ACCESS: No restrictions.

FINDING AID: Finding aids available.

314. Mother's Allowance Group (Winnipeg, Man.)

✣ Winnipeg, Man.

The Mother's Allowance Group also had an extension called Incentives. (Source: Provincial Archives of Manitoba finding aid.)

LOCATION OF RECORDS: Provincial Archives of Manitoba. (See Appendix for address.)

COLLECTION NAME: Forms part of: Darlene Germscheid Papers (P 241, #7).

RECORDS: Minutes, 1971; clippings, memoranda, reports, briefs, reference material, [ca. 1969]-[ca. 1971].

ACCESS: No restrictions.

FINDING AID: Inventory and file list available for Germscheid collection.

315. National Council of Jewish Women of Canada. Winnipeg Section

[See also entry # 972 (in Part II), which lists other records of this organization.]

✣ Winnipeg, Man. Formed 1897.

The main activities of the National Council of Jewish Women of Canada (NCJW) are education, service, and social action. While its priorities are the protection of human rights and the preservation of Jewish life, NCJW is also concerned with women's issues such as family planning, abortion, child care, pornography, and affirmative action.

LOCATION OF RECORDS: Jewish Historical Society of Western Canada. (See Appendix for address.)

COLLECTION NAME: National Council of Jewish Women, Winnipeg (MG 2 B9).

RECORDS: Minutes, 1925-1947, 1955, 1961-1979; correspondence, 1951-1952, 1955-1958, 1961-1962, 1967-1969, 1971-1974, 1978; financial records, 1939-1940, 1944-1948, 1951, 1954, 1960-1974, 1977; by-laws, 1932-1938, 1950-1952, 1955, 1969; conference records, 1950; briefs, 1963, 1965; handbook, 1956; press releases, 1955; letters patent, 1974; scripts of plays, notices of events, resolution, reports, questionnaires, bulletins, membership lists, clippings, miscellaneous records.

ACCESS: The archival holdings of the Jewish Historical Society of Western Canada are housed by special agreement at the Provincial Archives of Manitoba. Written permission of the Society is required to view the records.

FINDING AID: Finding Aid No. 4.

316. Planned Parenthood Manitoba

✣ Winnipeg, Man. Formed 1934.

The Winnipeg Birth Control Society (WBCS) was established by members of five women's groups in order to disseminate birth-control information to married women despite legal sanctions. In 1953 WBCS changed its name to the Family Planning Association of Winnipeg; in 1977 it became Planned Parenthood Manitoba. (Source: Provincial Archives of Manitoba finding aid, 1988.)

Collection (a)

LOCATION OF RECORDS: Provincial Archives of Manitoba. (See Appendix for address.)

COLLECTION NAME: Planned Parenthood Manitoba (P3933-P3961 D307 f. 1); the photographs have been transferred to the Still Images Section.

RECORDS: Constitution, by-laws, 1972-1984; records of annual meetings, 1970-1985; minutes, 1967-1985; correspondence, 1965-1985; financial records, 1969-1985; subject files, 1962-1985; scrapbooks, poster, photographs, miscellaneous records.

AMOUNT: 3.625 m.

ACCESS: Minutes and job applications restricted.

FINDING AID: Inventory and file list available.

Collection (b)

LOCATION OF RECORDS: Provincial Archives of Manitoba.

COLLECTION NAME: Forms part of: Social Planning Council of Winnipeg collection (MG 10 B 20, P730-731).

RECORDS: Records of annual meetings, 1934-1935, 1938, 1955-1959; annual reports, 1936-1965, 1967; committee records, 1934, 1951, 1957; financial records, 1936-1958; correspondence, historical information, articles, pamphlets, reports, notes, conference records, submissions, clippings, minutes, publications, speeches, petition, newsletters, statistics, map, miscellaneous records.

ACCESS: Restricted.

FINDING AID: Inventory and file list available for Social Planning Council of Winnipeg collection.

317. Prostitutes and Other Women for Equal Rights (Winnipeg, Man.)

✣ Winnipeg, Man.

This organization, also known as POWER, provides services for women working as prostitutes in Winnipeg. These services include a drop-in centre, a medical programme, and a court-support programme. POWER was originally called the Association for the Safety of Prostitutes (ASP). The new name was adopted around 1986.

LOCATION OF RECORDS: Canadian Women's Movement Archives Collection, Morisset Library Special Collections, University of Ottawa. (See Appendix for address.)

COLLECTION NAME: Prostitutes and Other Women for Equal Rights (POWER).

RECORDS: Newsletters, 1986-1989; correspondence, 1988-1989; notice, 1986; poster, 1989; invitation, 1988; flyers, 1986, 1988.

AMOUNT: 2 mm of text, 1 poster.

CONDITION: Good.

ACCESS: No restrictions.

318. Provincial Council of Women of Manitoba

✢ Winnipeg, Man.

Collection (a)

LOCATION OF RECORDS: Provincial Archives of Manitoba. (See Appendix for address.)

COLLECTION NAME: Provincial Council of Women of Manitoba (MG 10 C 44).

RECORDS: Constitution, by-laws, 1971; minutes, correspondence, reports, financial statements, briefs, notices of meetings, resolutions, 1949-1980; cash book, 1956-1975; scrapbook, 1949-1955; clippings, 1969-1978.

AMOUNT: 2.1 m.

ACCESS: No restrictions.

FINDING AID: Box list available.

Collection (b)

LOCATION OF RECORDS: Provincial Archives of Manitoba.

COLLECTION NAME: Forms part of: Beatrice Alice Brigden collection (MG 14 C 19, box 4).

RECORDS: Miscellaneous records, 1960-1965.

ACCESS: No restrictions.

FINDING AID: Inventory and box list available for Brigden collection.

319. Sexual Orientation Lobby

✢ Winnipeg, Man. Formed [ca. 1983]. Disbanded [ca. 1986].

This organization lobbied for the inclusion of sexual orientation in both federal and provincial human-rights legislation.

LOCATION OF RECORDS: Manitoba Gay/Lesbian Archive. (See Appendix for address.)

COLLECTION NAME: Sexual Orientation Lobby.

RECORDS: Miscellaneous records, [ca. 1983]-[ca. 1986].

AMOUNT: Approx. 1 m.

320. Sexual Orientation Lobby of Manitoba

✢ Winnipeg, Man. Formed [ca. 1985]. Disbanded 1987.

The Sexual Orientation Lobby of Manitoba lobbied for the inclusion of sexual orientation in Manitoba's human-rights legislation.

LOCATION OF RECORDS: Manitoba Gay/Lesbian Archive. (See Appendix for address.)

COLLECTION NAME: Sexual Orientation Lobby of Manitoba.

RECORDS: Correspondence, miscellaneous records, [ca. 1985]-1987.

AMOUNT: Approx. 2 m.

321. Soroptimist Club of Winnipeg

✢ Winnipeg, Man. Formed 1943.

The Soroptimist Club of Winnipeg (also called Soroptimist International of Winnipeg) is the Winnipeg branch of an international service organization of professional and executive women. Soroptimist's goals include advancing the status of women. The Winnipeg club sponsored the Second Mile Club, a centre for elderly women. (Source: Provincial Archives of Manitoba finding aid, 1986.)

LOCATION OF RECORDS: Provincial Archives of Manitoba. (See Appendix for address.)

COLLECTION NAME: Soroptimist Club of Winnipeg (P957-963); Soroptimist International of Winnipeg (P2876-P2878). The photographs and logo cut have been transferred to the Still Images Section.

RECORDS: Constitution, by-laws, regulations, minutes, membership rosters, guest books, reports, committee records, convention records, conference records, printed materials, scrapbooks, correspondence, instructions, directories, publicity materials, newsletters, clippings, photographs, logo cut, miscellaneous records, 1943-1985.

AMOUNT: 1.38 m.

ACCESS: No restrictions.

FINDING AID: Inventory and file lists available.

322. Soroptimist Federation of the Americas. Western Canada Region

✢ Formed [193-].

Soroptimist is an international service organization of professional and executive women. Its aims include advancing the status of women. This regional division has a fellowship committee which helps women to undertake graduate studies. (Source: Provincial Archives of Manitoba finding aid, 1986.)

LOCATION OF RECORDS: Provincial Archives of Manitoba. (See Appendix for address.)

COLLECTION NAME: Soroptimist Federation of Americas, Inc. Western Canada Region (P2587-2595); photographs and slides have been transferred to the Still Images Section.

RECORDS: Minutes, 1932, 1969-1980, 1984; correspondence, 1970-1984; financial records, 1937-1977; membership records, 1932-1980; conference reports, 1933-1953, 1981, 1984; committee records, 1950-1984; slides, miscellaneous records.

AMOUNT: 1.28 m.

ACCESS: No restrictions.

FINDING AID: Inventory and file list available.

323. University of Manitoba. Women's Studies Committee

✢ Winnipeg, Man. Formed 1973.

This committee was established to supervise courses in women's studies offered by the Faculty of Arts at the University of Manitoba. The committee has since developed a programme offering a major in women's studies.

LOCATION OF RECORDS: Canadian Women's Movement Archives Collection, Morisset Library Special Collections, University of Ottawa. (See Appendix for address.)

COLLECTION NAME: University of Manitoba. Women's Studies.

RECORDS: Minutes, correspondence, 1986-1987; course descriptions, 1982; contact list, 1986; enrolment information, 1987; pamphlets, biographical information, notice.

AMOUNT: 3 mm.
CONDITION: Good.
ACCESS: No restrictions.

324. University Women's Club of Winnipeg

✢ Winnipeg, Man. Formed 1909.

University women's clubs are local organizations of women university graduates. The clubs belong to the Canadian Federation of University Women, whose goals include encouraging women scholars and safeguarding women's rights. The Winnipeg club was established to work for the advancement of education, civic reform, and individual development. (Sources: *The Canadian Encyclopedia.* — Edmonton: Hurtig Publishers, 1985; Provincial Archives of Manitoba finding aid.)

LOCATION OF RECORDS: Provincial Archives of Manitoba. (See Appendix for address.)
COLLECTION NAME: University Women's Club of Winnipeg (MG 10 C58).
RECORDS: Minutes, membership lists, 1909-1977; reports, 1914-1978; correspondence, 1914-1958; financial records, 1914-1973; committee records, 1934-1977; scrapbooks, 1909-1973; miscellaneous records, 1909-1975; photographs.
AMOUNT: 3.96 m.
ACCESS: Written permission from the club's president (or, in her absence, the vice-president) is required to consult the records.
FINDING AID: Inventory and box list available.

325. Voice of Women. Manitoba Branch

✢ Winnipeg, Man. Formed 1961.

Voice of Women (VOW) opposes war and advocates disarmament. The activities of the Manitoba branch have included demonstrations, letter campaigns, and briefs to governments. (Source: Provincial Archives of Manitoba finding aid.)

Collection (a)

LOCATION OF RECORDS: Provincial Archives of Manitoba. (See Appendix for address.)
COLLECTION NAME: Voice of Women — Manitoba Branch (P 1017-1020).
RECORDS: Minutes, 1961-1980; financial records, 1963-1967; correspondence, 1961-1982; briefs, submissions, reports, publicity, scrapbooks, clippings, 1960-1985.
AMOUNT: 46.5 cm.
ACCESS: No restrictions.
FINDING AID: Inventory and file list available.

Collection (b)

LOCATION OF RECORDS: Provincial Archives of Manitoba.
COLLECTION NAME: Forms part of: Myrtle Anderson Wells collection (P 388-P 389).
RECORDS: Correspondence, newsletters, scrapbooks, lists, financial information, photographs, speech, 1960-1984.
AMOUNT: 9.5 cm.
ACCESS: No restrictions.
FINDING AID: Inventory available for Wells collection.

Collection (c)

LOCATION OF RECORDS: Provincial Archives of Manitoba.
COLLECTION NAME: Forms part of: Beatrice Alice Brigden collection (MG 14 C 19, boxes 3-4).
RECORDS: Minutes, newsletters, correspondence, reports, financial records, miscellaneous records, 1961-1970.
ACCESS: No restrictions.
FINDING AID: Inventory and box list available for Brigden collection.

326. Winnipeg Association of Non-Teaching Employees

✢ Winnipeg, Man. Formed 1980.

The Winnipeg Association of Non-Teaching Employees (WANTE) is the bargaining unit for non-managerial and non-teaching employees of Winnipeg School Division Number I. (Source: Provincial Archives of Manitoba finding aid, 1987.)

LOCATION OF RECORDS: Provincial Archives of Manitoba. (See Appendix for address.)
COLLECTION NAME: Winnipeg Association of Non-Teaching Employees (WANTE) (P2644A-2647); the photographs have been transferred to the Still Images Section.
RECORDS: Constitution and by-laws, minutes, reports, financial records, records of collective-agreement negotiations, correspondence, [ca. 1980]-[ca. 1984]; membership applications, 1980-1981; photographs.
AMOUNT: 44 cm of text, 3 photographs.
ACCESS: Restricted.
FINDING AID: Inventory and file list available.

327. Winnipeg Council of Self-Help

✢ Winnipeg, Man. Formed 1970. Disbanded 1979.

Originally called the Winnipeg Council of Self-Help Groups, this was a network of citizens' groups which aimed to improve the conditions of life for people living in poverty and enable them to take action on their own behalf. An important aspect of the council's work was representing women living on mother's allowances. In 1974 the name was changed to the Winnipeg Council of Self-Help to reflect the fact that individuals, rather than groups, then constituted its members. (Source: Provincial Archives of Manitoba finding aid, 1985.)

Collection (a)

LOCATION OF RECORDS: Provincial Archives of Manitoba. (See Appendix for address.)
COLLECTION NAME: Winnipeg Council of Self-Help, Inc. (P839-845).
RECORDS: Minutes, studies, 1971-1976; newsletters (*Orbit*, 1971-1976); financial records, 1971-1978; address lists, 1970-1974; objectives and history, 1970-1971; policies and procedures, 1970-1976; briefs, 1971-1975; grant applications, 1974-1976; reports, 1974, 1976; membership files, committee files, miscellaneous records.
AMOUNT: 90 cm.
ACCESS: No restrictions.
FINDING AID: Inventory and file list available.

Collection (b)

LOCATION OF RECORDS: Provincial Archives of Manitoba.
COLLECTION NAME: Forms part of: Darlene Germscheid Papers (P 244, #7).
RECORDS: Reports, 1973-1975; constitution, position papers, publicity material, clipping, newsletter, excerpt from thesis, miscellaneous records, [ca. 1969]-[ca. 1975].
ACCESS: No restrictions.
FINDING AID: Inventory and file list available for Germscheid collection.

328. Winnipeg Gay Community Health Centre

✢ Winnipeg, Man. Formed 1983. Disbanded 1987.

LOCATION OF RECORDS: Manitoba Gay/Lesbian Archive. (See Appendix for address.)
COLLECTION NAME: Winnipeg Gay Community Health Centre.
RECORDS: Minutes, related material, 1983-1987.
AMOUNT: Approx. 1 m.

329. Winnipeg Gay / Lesbian Youth
✣ Winnipeg, Man. Formed [ca. 1982].

This group used to be called Winnipeg Gay Youth. It became Winnipeg Gay/Lesbian Youth in 1985.

LOCATION OF RECORDS: Manitoba Gay/Lesbian Archive. (See Appendix for address.)
COLLECTION NAME: Winnipeg Gay Youth.
RECORDS: Miscellaneous records, [ca. 1982]-1990.
AMOUNT: Approx. 2 m.

330. Winnipeg Women School Administrators Club
✣ Winnipeg, Man. Formed [ca. 1938].

Primarily a professional organization, this club also engages in social and charitable activities. It was originally known as the Women Principals Club, and later as the Women Principals and Supervisors Club. (Source: Provincial Archives of Manitoba finding aid, 1989.)

LOCATION OF RECORDS: Provincial Archives of Manitoba. (See Appendix for address.)
COLLECTION NAME: Winnipeg Women School Administrators Club (P4352A).
RECORDS: Financial records, 1938-1972; minutes, correspondence, lists, 1949-1986; membership cards and lists, 1963-1971.
AMOUNT: 15 cm.
ACCESS: No restrictions.
FINDING AID: Inventory available.

331. Winnipeg Women's Health Collective
✣ Winnipeg, Man.

LOCATION OF RECORDS: Provincial Archives of Manitoba. (See Appendix for address.)
COLLECTION NAME: Forms part of: Linda Taylor collection (P2638, file 9).
RECORDS: Records of grants, 1974.
AMOUNT: 1 file.
ACCESS: No restrictions.
FINDING AID: File list available for Taylor collection.

332. Winnipeg Women's Liberation
✣ Winnipeg, Man. Disbanded.

This group published the monthly *Winnipeg Women's Liberation Newsletter*. The group's office was at A Woman's Place. [See also A Woman's Place (Winnipeg, Man.) (333).]

Collection (a)

LOCATION OF RECORDS: Provincial Archives of Manitoba. (See Appendix for address.)
COLLECTION NAME: Forms part of: Linda Taylor collection (P2642, files 4-9).
RECORDS: Correspondence, newsletters, miscellaneous records, 1971-1978.
AMOUNT: 6 files.
ACCESS: No restrictions.
FINDING AID: File list available for Taylor Collection.

Collection (b)

LOCATION OF RECORDS: Canadian Women's Movement Archives Collection, Morisset Library Special Collections, University of Ottawa. (See Appendix for address.)
COLLECTION NAME: Winnipeg Women's Liberation Newsletter.
RECORDS: Newsletters, 1974-1978.
AMOUNT: 4 cm.
ACCESS: No restrictions.

333. A Woman's Place (Winnipeg, Man.)
✣ Winnipeg, Man. Disbanded [197-].

A Woman's Place was a referral and resource centre for women. [See also Winnipeg Women's Liberation (332).]

Collection (a)

LOCATION OF RECORDS: Provincial Archives of Manitoba. (See Appendix for address.)
COLLECTION NAME: Forms part of: Linda Taylor collection (P2638, file 10; P2640, files 11-16).
RECORDS: Records of grants, 1974-1975; financial record, 1971; journal, 1973; newsletters, 1973-1974; correspondence, manual, miscellaneous records, [197-].
AMOUNT: 7 files.
ACCESS: No restrictions.
FINDING AID: File list available for Taylor collection.

Collection (b)

LOCATION OF RECORDS: Canadian Women's Movement Archives Collection, Morisset Library Special Collections, University of Ottawa. (See Appendix for address.)
COLLECTION NAME: A Woman's Place — Winnipeg.
RECORDS: Handbooks, 1972, 1975; clipping, newsletter, 1974; correspondence, 1974-1975; position statements, 1975.
AMOUNT: 1.3 cm.
CONDITION: Good.
ACCESS: No restrictions.

334. Women in Trades Association (Winnipeg, Man.)
✣ Winnipeg, Man. Formed 1977. Disbanded [198-?].

This association (sometimes referred to as the Manitoba Women in Trades Association or WIT) assisted women working in trades or interested in going into the field, by promoting public awareness of women in trades, exchanging information, identifying the problems of women in trades, and making recommendations to the appropriate authorities. WIT organized the National Conference of Women in Trades, held in Winnipeg in 1980.

LOCATION OF RECORDS: Canadian Women's Movement Archives Collection, Morisset Library Special Collections, University of Ottawa. (See Appendix for address.)
COLLECTION NAME: Women in Trades Association — Winnipeg; Women in Trades — National Conference, 1980.
RECORDS: Conference records, 1980; newsletters, 1978-1982; correspondence, 1978-1979, 1982; workshop material, 1982; press releases, 1978-1979; membership form, announcement, pamphlets, button.
AMOUNT: 2 cm of text, 1 button.
CONDITION: Good.
ACCESS: No restrictions.

335. Women into Rail Committee
✣ Winnipeg, Man. Formed 1980. Disbanded.

The Women into Rail Committee was formed to support complaints filed before the Canadian Human Rights Commission by three Manitoba women. The women charged Canadian National Railways with sex discrimination for refusing to hire them as switch-men and car-men. The committee also pressed for an affirmative-action programme at the company.

LOCATION OF RECORDS: Canadian Women's Movement Archives Collection, Morisset Library Special Collections, University of Ottawa. (See Appendix for address.)
COLLECTION NAME: Women into Rail — Winnipeg.
RECORDS: Newsletter, flyer, correspondence, 1980.
AMOUNT: 8 pages.
CONDITION: Good.
ACCESS: No restrictions.

336. Women's Building (Winnipeg, Man.)

✣ Winnipeg, Man. Formed 1978. Disbanded [198-].

The Women's Building was owned by the Winnipeg Women's Cultural and Education Centre, a non-profit corporation. The building housed various women's organizations and businesses.

LOCATION OF RECORDS: Canadian Women's Movement Archives Collection, Morisset Library Special Collections, University of Ottawa. (See Appendix for address.)
COLLECTION NAME: The Women's Building — Winnipeg.
RECORDS: Newsletters (*Harpies*, 1979-1981); constitution, by-laws, 1978; clippings, 1979; press releases, 1979, 1983; announcements, 1982; posters, 1979, 1982; brief, correspondence, fact sheet, membership form.
AMOUNT: 2 cm of text, 3 posters.
CONDITION: Good.
ACCESS: No restrictions.

337. Women's Inter-Church Council of Canada. Winnipeg Branch

✣ Winnipeg, Man.

The Women's Inter-Church Council of Canada (WICC), an ecumenical Christian organization, promotes spiritual development, women's concerns, and human rights.

LOCATION OF RECORDS: Provincial Archives of Manitoba. (See Appendix for address.)
COLLECTION NAME: Women's Inter-Church Council (P 857-863).
RECORDS: Minutes, 1933-1985; constitution, by-laws, 1949, 1974, 1976; financial records, 1948-1982; reports, 1943-1982; correspondence, publicity material, printed material, posters, audio-visual presentation.
AMOUNT: 87.5 cm.
FINDING AID: File list available.

338. Women's Model Parliament

✣ Winnipeg, Man. Formed [1970?].

This group organized annual model-parliament sessions, at which women from many parts of Manitoba debated issues affecting women.

LOCATION OF RECORDS: Legislative Library of Manitoba. (See Appendix for address.)
COLLECTION NAME: Women's Model Parliament.
RECORDS: Proceedings of sessions, 1972-1976, 1979, 1981.
ACCESS: No restrictions.

339. Young Women's Christian Association of Thompson

[See also entry # 991 (in Part II), which lists other records of this organization.]

✣ Thompson, Man. Formed 1969.

The YWCA of Thompson aims to enrich the lives of women through leadership. It offers counselling, recreational activities, courses, and residential facilities.

LOCATION OF RECORDS: Provincial Archives of Manitoba. (See Appendix for address.)
COLLECTION NAME: Young Women's Christian Association of Thompson (P 988-1013).
RECORDS: Constitution, by-laws, 1973, 1977; minutes, reports, 1965-1985; correspondence, 1969-1982; financial records, 1972-1979; project files, programme files, 1971-1983; desk diaries, 1971-1984; staff files, 1973-1982; historical information, lists, supply inventories, directories, handbooks, newsletters, clippings, pamphlets.
AMOUNT: 3.16 m.
ACCESS: Desk diaries and staff files restricted.
FINDING AID: Inventory and file list available.

340. Young Women's Christian Association (Winnipeg, Man.)

✣ Winnipeg, Man. Formed 1897.

The main concern of the YWCA in Winnipeg has been the welfare of women. The YWCA's services have included Osborne House, a shelter for battered women and their children. In 1989 the YWCA and the YMCA merged to become the YM-YWCA. [See also Osborne House (977).]

LOCATION OF RECORDS: Provincial Archives of Manitoba. (See Appendix for address.)
COLLECTION NAME: Young Women's Christian Association (P3848-3927 D306 f. 8).
RECORDS: Constitution, by-laws, 1904-1981; records of annual meetings, 1939-1985; minutes, 1897-1986; correspondence, 1954-1985; financial records, 1965-1985; subject files, 1908-1986; posters, photographs, painting, flags, plaques, film.
AMOUNT: 10.35 m.
ACCESS: No restrictions.
FINDING AID: Inventory and file list available

PART I: RECORDS HELD BY ARCHIVES / PARTIE I : FONDS DÉTENUS PAR DES ARCHIVES

Photograph by / Photo prise par Eleanor Gelms [ca. 1972]
CWMA Collection / Fonds de l'ACMF

ONTARIO

341. Abortion and Contraception Committee of Toronto

✣ Toronto, Ont. Formed 1974. Disbanded [197-?].

The Abortion and Contraception Committee of Toronto (ACCT) was a coalition of agencies and individuals involved in abortion and contraception counselling and education. ACCT organized the Politics of Contraception Conference, held in 1976.

LOCATION OF RECORDS: Canadian Women's Movement Archives Collection, Morisset Library Special Collections, University of Ottawa. (See Appendix for address.)

COLLECTION NAME: Abortion and Contraception Committee (Toronto, Ont.); SR 32/1-3.

RECORDS: Conference proceedings, 1974, 1976; sound recordings (conference proceedings), poster, clipping, 1976; correspondence, 1975; flyers, 1976-1977; mailing list.

AMOUNT: 6 mm of text, 3 sound recordings, 1 poster.

CONDITION: Good.

ACCESS: No restrictions.

342. Action Day Care

✣ Toronto, Ont. Formed 1979. Disbanded [198-].

Action Day Care was an organization of parents, child-care workers, and interested groups and individuals who believed that day care should be free and accessible to all children.

LOCATION OF RECORDS: Canadian Women's Movement Archives Collection, Morisset Library Special Collections, University of Ottawa. (See Appendix for address.)

COLLECTION NAME: Action Day Care.

RECORDS: Correspondence, newsletters, 1980-1984; policy statement, minutes, clipping, 1980; brief, report, labour-negotiation records, 1981; position paper, 1982; handbook, 1983; proposal, memorial-service programme, press release, 1984; flyers, petitions, diagram, poster, button, T-shirt.

AMOUNT: 2 cm of text, 1 poster, 1 button, 1 T-shirt.

CONDITION: Good.

ACCESS: No restrictions.

343. Action for Women's Rights in the U.S.S.R.

✣ Toronto, Ont. Formed 1975. Disbanded [197-?].

This was a group of women concerned with women's rights in the Soviet Union and the defense of Soviet women political prisoners.

LOCATION OF RECORDS: Canadian Women's Movement Archives Collection, Morisset Library Special Collections, University of Ottawa. (See Appendix for address.)

COLLECTION NAME: Action for Women's Rights in the U.S.S.R.

RECORDS: Speech, press release, 1975; correspondence, 1975-1976; membership list, pamphlets, manuscript of article, flyers.

AMOUNT: 3 mm.

CONDITION: Good.

ACCESS: No restrictions.

344. Amazon Press

✣ Toronto, Ont. Formed [197-?]. Disbanded 1976.

Amazon Press printed women's literature and children's books and did printing jobs for other women's organizations. Originally called the Women's Lib Type Press, it was renamed A Women's Press and then became Amazon Press (also known as the Amazon Community Press).

LOCATION OF RECORDS: Canadian Women's Movement Archives Collection, Morisset Library Special Collections, University of Ottawa. (See Appendix for address.)

COLLECTION NAME: Amazon Press.

RECORDS: Minutes, reports, agreements, 1976; inventory, 1977; financial records, 1976-1977; grant application, 1975; correspondence, pamphlet, flyers, proposal, layouts, photographs.

AMOUNT: 2 cm of text, 10 photographs.

CONDITION: Fair.

ACCESS: No restrictions.

345. The Anna Project

✣ Toronto, Ont. Formed 1983. Disbanded [1986?].

The Anna Project produced *This Is for You Anna*, a play which explored women's responses to violence.

LOCATION OF RECORDS: Canadian Women's Movement Archives Collection,

Morisset Library Special Collections, University of Ottawa. (See Appendix for address.)
COLLECTION NAME: The Anna Project.
RECORDS: Minutes, correspondence, 1983-1984; grant application, poster, 1985; press releases, 1984-1986; reports, scripts and revisions, research notes, tour itineraries, clippings, programmes, flyers, invitation, ticket.
AMOUNT: 4 cm of text, 1 poster.
CONDITION: Good.
ACCESS: No restrictions.

346. *Association des lesbiennes et des gais de l'Outaouais / Association of Lesbians and Gays of Ottawa*

[For English entry, see # 347.]

[Voir aussi la notice 996 (dans la partie II) pour autres documents de ce groupe.]

✣ Ottawa (Ont.). Groupe fondé 1971.

L'Association des lesbiennes et des gais de l'Outaouais (ALGO) vise à développer une prise de conscience positive à l'endroit des lesbiennes et des gais par l'éducation publique et l'action politique, sociale et juridique. Elle publie un périodique, GO Info. Auparavant, l'organisme s'appelait Gais de l'Outaouais (GO).

LIEU DE CONSULTATION: Canadian Gay Archives. (Voir Annexe pour l'adresse.)
NOM DU FONDS: Gays of Ottawa (82-017, 88-041).
MATÉRIEL: Dossiers administratifs, mémoires, correspondance, publications, coupures de presse, photographies, dossiers juridiques, statuts et règlements, rapports, dépliants, tracts, procès-verbaux, documents divers, 1969-1981; périodiques (GO Info, 1972-1980, 1982-1990).
QUANTITÉ: 3,08 m.

347. *Association of Lesbians and Gays of Ottawa / Association des lesbiennes et des gais de l'Outaouais*

[Renseignements en français, notice 346.]

[See also entry # 997 (in Part II), which lists other records of this organization.]

✣ Ottawa, Ont. Formed 1971.

The Association of Lesbians and Gays of Ottawa (ALGO) works to develop a positive awareness of lesbians and gay men through public education and political, social, and legal action. It publishes a periodical, GO Info. The organization used to be known as Gays of Ottawa (GO).

LOCATION OF RECORDS: Canadian Gay Archives. (See Appendix for address.)
COLLECTION NAME: Gays of Ottawa (82-017, 88-041).
RECORDS: Administrative files, briefs, correspondence, publications, clippings, photographs, legal files, constitution and by-laws, reports, pamphlets, flyers, minutes, miscellaneous records, 1969-1981; periodicals (GO Info, 1972-1980, 1982-1990).
AMOUNT: 3.08 m.

348. *Association of Women Teaching at Queen's*

✣ Kingston, Ont. Formed 1974.

This association was established to represent all women teaching at Queen's University. It worked for the implementation of the recommendations of the 1974 Report of the Principal's Committee on the Status of Women at Queen's.

LOCATION OF RECORDS: Canadian Women's Movement Archives Collection, Morisset Library Special Collections, University of Ottawa. (See Appendix for address.)
COLLECTION NAME: Association of Women Teaching at Queen's.
RECORDS: Correspondence, 1974-1975; brief, report, 1975.
AMOUNT: 3 cm.
CONDITION: Good.
ACCESS: No restrictions.

349. *Battered Women's Advocacy Clinic*

✣ London, Ont. Formed 1981.

The Battered Women's Advocacy Clinic (BWAC) provides legal and emotional counselling for women. It offers a referral service, information, and advice related to matters such as housing, welfare, legal aid, day care, and careers.

LOCATION OF RECORDS: D.B. Weldon Library — Regional Collection, University of Western Ontario. (See Appendix for address.)
COLLECTION NAME: Battered Women's Advocacy Clinic.
RECORDS: Minutes, miscellaneous records, 1981-1989.
AMOUNT: 1 box.
CONDITION: Good.
ACCESS: No restrictions.
FINDING AID: Regional Collection manuscript catalogue.

350. *Better End All Vicious Erotic Repression*

✣ Toronto, Ont. Formed 1978. Disbanded.

Commonly known as BEAVER, this was an organization of prostitutes, strippers, topless performers, and pornography actresses. BEAVER advocated the decriminalization of prostitution.

LOCATION OF RECORDS: Canadian Women's Movement Archives Collection, Morisset Library Special Collections, University of Ottawa. (See Appendix for address.)
COLLECTION NAME: Better End All Vicious Erotic Repression (BEAVER).
RECORDS: Clippings, 1978-1979; pamphlet, 1979; flyers, business card.
AMOUNT: 2 mm.
CONDITION: Fair.
ACCESS: No restrictions.

351. *Birth Control and V.D. Information Centre*

✣ Toronto, Ont. Formed 1969.

Originally called the Birth Control Centre, this organization provides medical services, counselling, information, and community education. Its focus is the reproductive health of women.

LOCATION OF RECORDS: Canadian Women's Movement Archives Collection, Morisset Library Special Collections, University of Ottawa. (See Appendix for address.)
COLLECTION NAME: Birth Control and V.D. Information Centre.
RECORDS: Newsletter, 1970; list of contacts, [ca. 1970]; invitation, 1975; photographs, 1979; pamphlets, flyers, poster.
AMOUNT: 5 mm of text, 9 photographs, 1 poster.
CONDITION: Good.
ACCESS: No restrictions.

352. *Bisexual, Lesbian, and Gay Alliance at York*

[See also entry # 1001 (in Part II), which lists other records of this organization.]

✣ Downsview, Ont. Formed [1971?].

The Bisexual, Lesbian, and Gay Alliance at York (BLGAY) operates under the auspices of the York Student Federation. BLGAY provides a comfortable meeting place for gay, lesbian, bisexual, and gay-positive people at York University; offers a support network for people coping with their sexual orientation; and works to enhance awareness in the York community of the need for bisexual, lesbian, and gay rights. It was previously known as the Gay Alliance at York (GAY), and then as the Lesbian and Gay Alliance at York (LGAY).

LOCATION OF RECORDS: Canadian Gay Archives. (See Appendix for address.)
COLLECTION NAME: Lesbian and Gay Alliance at York (88-035).
RECORDS: Flyers, clippings, memorabilia, photograph.
AMOUNT: 5 files.

353. Brampton Women's Centre

✤ Brampton, Ont. Disbanded [198-].

The Brampton Women's Centre (BWC) offered programmes and courses addressing a variety of women's issues. The centre also provided an information and referral service.

Collection (a)
LOCATION OF RECORDS: Brampton Public Library, Local History Collection, Chinguacousy Resource Branch. (See Appendix for address.)
COLLECTION NAME: Brampton Women's Centre (P-1973-3, Pnd-7Pf).
RECORDS: Pamphlet, 1979; clippings, brochures.
ACCESS: No restrictions.

Collection (b)
LOCATION OF RECORDS: Canadian Women's Movement Archives Collection, Morisset Library Special Collections, University of Ottawa. (See Appendix for address.)
COLLECTION NAME: Brampton Women's Centre Newsletter.
RECORDS: Newsletters, 1975-1980.
AMOUNT: 1 cm.
ACCESS: No restrictions.

354. Branching Out: Lesbian Productions (Toronto, Ont.)

✤ Toronto, Ont. Formed 1983. Disbanded [198-].

This group produced social and cultural events for the lesbian community of Toronto, including the 1984 Lesbian Sexuality Conference. Until 1984 or 1985 the group was called Branching Out: Lesbian Culture Resource Centre.

LOCATION OF RECORDS: Canadian Women's Movement Archives Collection, Morisset Library Special Collections, University of Ottawa. (See Appendix for address.)
COLLECTION NAME: Branching Out: Lesbian Culture Resource Centre.
RECORDS: Minutes, 1983; conference materials, grant application, 1984; press release, poster, 1985; flyers, dance cards.
AMOUNT: 1.5 cm of text, 1 poster.
CONDITION: Good.
ACCESS: Restricted; conditional access negotiable.

355. Breaking the Silence: A Feminist Quarterly

✤ Ottawa, Ont. Formed 1982. Disbanded 1990.

Breaking the Silence was originally published by the Feminist Caucus of the School of Social Work at Carleton University; its editorial collective later became autonomous. Until 1985 the name of the publication was *Breaking the Silence: A Feminist Newsmagazine on Social Issues*.

LOCATION OF RECORDS: Canadian Women's Movement Archives Collection, Morisset Library Special Collections, University of Ottawa. (See Appendix for address.)
COLLECTION NAME: Breaking the Silence.
RECORDS: Minutes, 1983-1984, 1986-1988; correspondence, 1982-1988; reports, 1982-1984; grant applications, 1982, 1984-1985, 1987; proposals, 1981; clippings, 1982-1983; periodicals (*Breaking the Silence*, 1982-1990); questionnaire, flyer, style guides, photographs.
AMOUNT: 8 cm of text, 29 photographs.
CONDITION: Good.
ACCESS: No restrictions.

356. Broadside

✤ Toronto, Ont. Formed 1978. Disbanded 1989.

Broadside (sometimes called *Broadside: A Feminist Review*) was a monthly feminist newspaper including news, arts reviews, and feature articles on a wide range of women's issues. While the organization was formed in 1978, the newspaper's first issue appeared in 1979.

LOCATION OF RECORDS: Canadian Women's Movement Archives Collection, Morisset Library Special Collections, University of Ottawa. (See Appendix for address.)
COLLECTION NAME: Broadside.
RECORDS: Minutes, correspondence, financial records, subscription records, production records, newspapers, miscellaneous records, 1978-1989.
AMOUNT: Approx. 7 m.
ACCESS: As of 1992, most of the collection has not yet been processed.

357. Brunswick Four

✤ Toronto, Ont. Formed 1974. Disbanded.

The Brunswick Four (later called the Brunswick Four Minus One) was a group of women who were the targets of an anti-lesbian incident at a Toronto tavern. The women, who were charged with creating a disturbance, alleged that they had been assaulted by the police.

Collection (a)
LOCATION OF RECORDS: Canadian Women's Movement Archives Collection, Morisset Library Special Collections, University of Ottawa. (See Appendix for address.)
COLLECTION NAME: Brunswick Four.
RECORDS: Correspondence, press release, clippings, excerpt from report, poster, 1974; photographs.
AMOUNT: 5 mm of text, 1 poster, 3 photographs.
CONDITION: Good.
ACCESS: Restricted; conditional access negotiable.

Collection (b)
LOCATION OF RECORDS: Canadian Gay Archives. (See Appendix for address.)
COLLECTION NAME: Brunswick Four (vertical file).
RECORDS: Correspondence, contact lists, pamphlet, sample letter, posters, 1974.
AMOUNT: 2 mm of text, 2 posters.
CONDITION: Good.

358. A Bunch of Feminists

✤ Toronto, Ont. Formed [1989 or 1990].

A Bunch of Feminists — a group of women artists, writers, activists, and community workers — came together following the massacre of fourteen women in Montreal on December 6, 1989. The group organized Healing Images, an art exhibition and symposium held in Toronto in 1990. The purpose of Healing Images was to engage artists and the broader community

PART I: RECORDS HELD BY ARCHIVES / PARTIE I : FONDS DÉTENUS PAR DES ARCHIVES

Photographer unknown / Photographe inconnue
Photo #102; acc. #0109
Donated by / Don de Breaking the Silence
CWMA Collection / Fonds de l'ACMF

in the creation and discussion of images and ideas about violence against women.

LOCATION OF RECORDS: Canadian Women's Movement Archives Collection, Morisset Library Special Collections, University of Ottawa. (See Appendix for address.)

COLLECTION NAME: A Bunch of Feminists.

RECORDS: Sound recordings (poetry readings, panel discussions), slides, flyers, press release, calendar of events, list of participants, pamphlet, clipping, poster, 1990; correspondence, 1991.

AMOUNT: 2 mm of text, 4 sound recordings, 24 slides, 1 poster.

ACCESS: As of 1992, the collection has not yet been processed.

359. Business and Professional Women's Clubs of Ontario

✣ Formed [ca. 1932].

This is an umbrella association of business and professional women's clubs throughout the province. The goals of the local clubs include promoting the interests of business and professional women and encouraging education, training, and equal status for women. (Source: Archives of Ontario finding aid, 1990.)

Collection (a)

LOCATION OF RECORDS: Archives of Ontario. (See Appendix for address.)

COLLECTION NAME: Business and Professional Women's Clubs of Ontario Papers (F 207).

RECORDS: Constitutions, by-laws, handbooks, minutes, correspondence, financial records, lists of executives, membership lists, rosters, reports, briefs, newsletters (*Ontario Messenger*), clippings, scrapbooks, organization histories, resolutions, manuals, speeches, questionnaires, press releases, pamphlets, brochures, agendas, flyers, forms, reference materials, miscellaneous records, 1948-1989.

AMOUNT: 3.5 m.

CONDITION: Good.

ACCESS: No restrictions.

FINDING AID: "Preliminary Inventory of the Business and Professional Women's Clubs of Ontario."

Collection (b)

LOCATION OF RECORDS: Archives of Ontario.

COLLECTION NAME: Kay Marks Papers (F 212).

RECORDS: Reports, minutes, agendas, correspondence, newsletters, programmes, financial records, booklets, briefs, 1957-1970.

AMOUNT: 20 cm.

ACCESS: No restrictions.

FINDING AID: "Inventory of the Kay Marks Papers: Business and Professional Women's Clubs of Ontario."

Collection (c)

LOCATION OF RECORDS: National Archives of Canada. (See Appendix for address.)

COLLECTION NAME: Forms part of: Elsie Gregory MacGill collection (MG 31, K 7).

RECORDS: Please see the note about National Archives of Canada collections, in entry # 2.

360. Campus and Community Co-operative Day Care Centre

✣ Toronto, Ont. Formed 1969.

The centre was founded by parents (mostly students and staff at the University of Toronto) who belonged to the Toronto Women's Liberation Movement. Having unsuccessfully lobbied the university for a day-care centre, the group organized a sit-in. This led to the establishment of the centre (which has also been known as the Women's Liberation Campus Community Cooperative Daycare Centre, the Campus Co-operative Community Day Care Centre, and the Sussex-Devonshire Day Care Centres). [See also Toronto Women's Liberation Movement (509).]

LOCATION OF RECORDS: Canadian Women's Movement Archives Collection, Morisset Library Special Collections, University of Ottawa. (See Appendix for address.)

COLLECTION NAME: Campus and Community Co-operative Day Care Centre.

RECORDS: Organization history, 1977; handbooks, 1971-1972; position paper, clippings, 1972-1973; petition, 1983; brief, [between 1969 and 1973]; flyers, pamphlets.

AMOUNT: 1 cm.

CONDITION: Fair.

ACCESS: No restrictions.

361. Canadian Federation of University Women. Thunder Bay Chapter

✣ Thunder Bay, Ont. Formed [ca. 1925].

The Canadian Federation of University Women (CFUW) is an organization of women university graduates. The Thunder Bay chapter (previously the Port Arthur and Fort William chapter) encourages women to further their education and engage in cultural pursuits.

LOCATION OF RECORDS: Chancellor Paterson Library Archives, Lakehead University. (See Appendix for address.)

COLLECTION NAME: Canadian Federation of University Women Collection.

RECORDS: Scrapbook, financial reports, correspondence, video recording, photographs, minutes, charter, membership lists, reports, miscellaneous records, 1925-1990.

AMOUNT: 4 boxes.

CONDITION: Good.

ACCESS: Permission of archivist required.

362. Canadian Women's Press Club. Ottawa Branch

✣ Ottawa, Ont.

Collection (a)

LOCATION OF RECORDS: National Archives of Canada. (See Appendix for address.)

COLLECTION NAME: Canadian Women's Press Club, Ottawa Branch (MG 28 I 69).

RECORDS: Please see the note about National Archives of Canada collections, in entry # 2.

Collection (b)

LOCATION OF RECORDS: National Archives of Canada.

COLLECTION NAME: Forms part of: Media Club of Canada collection (MG 28, I 232).

RECORDS: Please see the note about National Archives of Canada collections, in entry # 2.

363. Canadian Women's Press Club. Toronto Branch

✣ Toronto, Ont.

LOCATION OF RECORDS: National Archives of Canada. (See Appendix for address.)

COLLECTION NAME: Forms part of: Kate Scott Aitken collection (MG 30, D 206).

RECORDS: Please see the note about National Archives of Canada collections, in entry # 2.

364. Cayenne: A Socialist Feminist Bulletin

✣ Toronto, Ont. Formed 1984. Disbanded 1989.

Cayenne was a quarterly publication of socialist-feminist news, opinion, and debate. It was founded by the former editors of the newsletter of the International Women's Day Committee in Toronto. [See also Toronto Socialist Feminist Action (505, 1085).]

LOCATION OF RECORDS: Canadian Women's Movement Archives Collection, Morisset Library Special Collections, University of Ottawa. (See Appendix for address.)
COLLECTION NAME: Cayenne.
RECORDS: Subscription records, 1984-1988; correspondence, 1983-1988; financial records, 1985-1988; minutes, 1986; periodicals (*Cayenne: A Socialist Feminist Bulletin*, 1984-1988); graphics, art work.
AMOUNT: 15 cm.
CONDITION: Good.
ACCESS: No restrictions.

365. Centre for Women (Sheridan College. Brampton Campus)

✣ Brampton, Ont. Formed 1980.

The Centre for Women is a meeting place and resource library for women at Sheridan College's Brampton campus. The centre sponsors films, discussion groups, guest lectures, and other events.

LOCATION OF RECORDS: Canadian Women's Movement Archives Collection, Morisset Library Special Collections, University of Ottawa. (See Appendix for address.)
COLLECTION NAME: Sheridan College. Brampton Campus. Centre for Women.
RECORDS: Correspondence, reports, 1980-1982; mission statement, presentations, 1980-1981; press releases, 1982; pamphlets, clippings, survey, bulletin, agenda, notes, flyers.
AMOUNT: 4 cm.
CONDITION: Good.
ACCESS: No restrictions.

366. Chatham Business and Professional Women's Club

✣ Chatham, Ont. Formed 1932.

LOCATION OF RECORDS: Archives of Ontario. (See Appendix for address.)
COLLECTION NAME: Chatham Business and Professional Women's Club Papers (F 215).
RECORDS: Minutes, 1937-1941, 1950-1959, 1966-1976; account books, 1942-1961; scrapbooks, 1935-1974; membership lists, clippings, correspondence, financial statements, reports, pamphlets.
AMOUNT: 25 cm.
CONDITION: Good.
ACCESS: No restrictions.
FINDING AID: "Inventory of the Chatham Business and Professional Women's Club."

367. Citizen's Organization to Repeal Prostitution-Related Laws

✣ Toronto, Ont. Formed 1987.

The Citizen's Organization to Repeal Prostitution-Related Laws (CORPL), a coalition of organizations and individuals, was established to support prostitutes in their struggle to protect their rights.

LOCATION OF RECORDS: Canadian Gay Archives. (See Appendix for address.)
COLLECTION NAME: Forms part of: Gillian Rodgerson collection (89-023).
RECORDS: Constitution, correspondence, brochures, information sheets, 1987.

368. Clearinghouse for Feminist Media

✣ Ancaster, Ont. Formed 1972. Disbanded 1976.

The Clearinghouse for Feminist Media published newsletters which listed feminists involved in writing, publishing, and the media. The newsletters also included bibliographies.

LOCATION OF RECORDS: Canadian Women's Movement Archives Collection, Morisset Library Special Collections, University of Ottawa. (See Appendix for address.)
COLLECTION NAME: Clearinghouse for Feminist Media.
RECORDS: Newsletters, 1972-1976.
AMOUNT: 1 cm.
ACCESS: No restrictions.

369. Clementyne's Café

✣ Toronto, Ont. Formed 1974. Disbanded 1975.

Clementyne's Café was to be a restaurant and café for women; however, it never opened. Some of the organizers became involved in another café, the Three of Cups. [See also the Three of Cups (495).]

LOCATION OF RECORDS: Canadian Women's Movement Archives Collection, Morisset Library Special Collections, University of Ottawa. (See Appendix for address.)
COLLECTION NAME: Clementyne's Café.
RECORDS: Correspondence, flyers, 1975; ballots.
AMOUNT: 1 cm.
CONDITION: Good.
ACCESS: No restrictions.

370. Coalition des femmes de l'Ontario / Ontario Women's Action Coalition

[For English entry, see # 460.]

✣ Toronto (Ont.). Groupe fondé 1990.

La Coalition des femmes de l'Ontario (CFO) est un organisme réunissant des groupes féministes de toute la province ayant pour but d'aider les femmes à changer la société. La coalition fournit de l'information, favorise l'échange entre groupes et joue un rôle de défense et de lobby au niveau provincial.

LIEU DE CONSULTATION : Fonds des Archives canadiennes du mouvement des femmes, Collections spéciales de la Bibliothèque Morisset, Université d'Ottawa. (Voir Annexe pour l'adresse.)
NOM DU FONDS : Ontario Women's Action Coalition.
MATÉRIEL : Enregistrements sonores, bulletins, 1990-1992; procès-verbaux, correspondance, documents financiers, demandes de subvention, listes de membres, listes d'envoi, mémoires, actes de congrès, communiqués de presse, 1989-1992; statuts et règlements, macaron, bannière, 1990.
QUANTITÉ : Env. 75 cm de texte, env. 50 enregistrements sonores, 1 macaron, 1 bannière.
ÉTAT : Bon.
ACCÈS : Jusqu'à cette date (1992), la collection n'a pas été classée.

371. Coalition for Lesbian and Gay Rights in Ontario

[See also entry # 1011 (in Part II), which lists other records of this organization.]

✣ Toronto, Ont. Formed 1975.

The Coalition for Lesbian and Gay Rights in Ontario (CLGRO) works toward feminism and lesbian and gay liberation by engaging in the public struggle for full human rights and by strengthening co-operative networks for lesbian and gay activism. Until 1987 it was called the Coalition for Gay Rights in Ontario (CGRO). Its French name is la Coalition pour les droits des lesbiennes et des hommes gais en Ontario.

LOCATION OF RECORDS: Canadian Gay Archives. (See Appendix for address.)

COLLECTION NAME: Coalition for Gay Rights in Ontario (82-016, 83-012, 84-001, 84-020, 86-005, 86-028, 87-010, 89-006, 89-027); Coalition for Lesbian and Gay Rights in Ontario (90-032, 90-119, 91-167); some records form part of: Russell Martin collection (84-022) and Chris Bearchell collection (83-016).

RECORDS: Minutes, correspondence, reports, publications, posters, conference records, briefs, newsletters, notices, mock-ups of newsletter, financial records, questionnaires, photographs, sound recordings, miscellaneous records, 1973-1991.

372. Coalition for the Week of Survival and Disarmament

✣ Toronto, Ont. Formed 1981. Disbanded [198-].

This was a feminist coalition of local peace, women's, and social-justice groups which organized Survival and Disarmament Week, held in 1981.

LOCATION OF RECORDS: Canadian Women's Movement Archives Collection, Morisset Library Special Collections, University of Ottawa. (See Appendix for address.)

COLLECTION NAME: Survival and Disarmament Week — April 12-17, 1981 — Toronto.

RECORDS: Statement of purpose, report, flyer, [1981?]; minutes, 1980-1981; correspondence, conference records, 1981; educational materials.

AMOUNT: 3 mm.
CONDITION: Good.
ACCESS: No restrictions.

373. Coalition to Stop Anita Bryant (Toronto, Ont.)

✣ Toronto, Ont. Formed 1977. Disbanded [1978?].

This coalition organized demonstrations to protest a campaign against lesbian and gay rights led by Anita Bryant (an American singer and evangelist). The coalition appears also to have been called the Southern Ontario Coalition to Stop Anita Bryant. [See also Coalition to Answer Anita Bryant (Saskatoon, Sask.) (244).]

Collection (a)

LOCATION OF RECORDS: Canadian Gay Archives. (See Appendix for address.)
COLLECTION NAME: Coalition to Stop Anita Bryant (vertical file).
RECORDS: Organization history, position paper, 1977; press releases, correspondence, 1977-1978; financial records, rental application, 1978; chant sheets, flyers, clippings, contact list, announcement of meeting.
AMOUNT: 1.5 cm.
CONDITION: Good.

Collection (b)

LOCATION OF RECORDS: Canadian Women's Movement Archives Collection, Morisset Library Special Collections, University of Ottawa. (See Appendix for address.)
COLLECTION NAME: Coalition to Stop Anita Bryant — Toronto.
RECORDS: Correspondence, 1977; minutes, 1978; statement of purpose, instructions, photocopy of photograph, poster, flyers.

AMOUNT: 5 mm of text, 1 poster.
CONDITION: Fair.
ACCESS: Restricted; conditional access negotiable.

374. Committee against the Deportation of Immigrant Women

✣ Toronto, Ont. Formed [ca. 1977]. Disbanded [197-?].

The Committee against the Deportation of Immigrant Women (CADIW) was formed to oppose discrimination, harassment, and deportation faced by immigrant women, particularly women from the Caribbean. CADIW did some of its work in collaboration with the Immigrant Women's Committee of Women against Violence against Women. [See also Women against Violence against Women (Toronto, Ont.) (540).]

LOCATION OF RECORDS: Canadian Women's Movement Archives Collection, Morisset Library Special Collections, University of Ottawa. (See Appendix for address.)

COLLECTION NAME: Committee against the Deportation of Immigrant Women.

RECORDS: Position paper, 1978; clippings, flyers, correspondence, 1977-1978; agenda, [1977 or 1978].

AMOUNT: 4 mm.
CONDITION: Good.
ACCESS: No restrictions.

375. Committee for a Socialist Women's Conference

✣ Toronto, Ont. Formed 1974. Disbanded 1975.

This committee was struck to organize an international conference to be held in Toronto during International Women's Year (1975).

LOCATION OF RECORDS: Canadian Women's Movement Archives Collection, Morisset Library Special Collections, University of Ottawa. (See Appendix for address.)

COLLECTION NAME: Committee for a Socialist Women's Conference.
RECORDS: Minutes, correspondence, 1974; flyers, 1974-1975.
AMOUNT: 1 mm.
CONDITION: Good.
ACCESS: No restrictions.

376. Committee to Establish Ontario Federation of Women

✣ Toronto, Ont. Formed 1979. Disbanded [1979?].

In response to funding cutbacks to Toronto women's groups, the Committee to Establish Ontario Federation of Women made plans to establish a network linking women's groups throughout the province. Several meetings were held to decide on a structure and guidelines for the federation; but the Ontario Federation of Women never actually materialized.

LOCATION OF RECORDS: Canadian Women's Movement Archives Collection, Morisset Library Special Collections, University of Ottawa. (See Appendix for address.)

COLLECTION NAME: Ontario Federation of Women.
RECORDS: Statement of purpose, correspondence, agenda, organization history, flyer, 1979; articles.
AMOUNT: 2 cm.
CONDITION: Good.
ACCESS: No restrictions.

Flyer, [1977 or 1978] / Tract, [1977 ou 1978]
Committee against the Deportation of Immigrant Women
CWMA Collection / Fonds de l'ACMF

377. Community Homophile Association of Toronto

✣ Toronto, Ont. Formed 1971. Disbanded [ca. 1981].

The activities of the Community Homophile Association of Toronto (CHAT) included a weekly Women's Drop-in, a Lesbian Collective, women's dances, and Gay Pride Week celebrations.

Collection (a)
LOCATION OF RECORDS: Canadian Gay Archives. (See Appendix for address.)
COLLECTION NAME: Community Homophile Association of Toronto (82-001, 82-023).
RECORDS: Administrative records, correspondence, subject files, briefs, photographs, artifacts, membership records, financial records, publications, posters, miscellaneous records, 1970-1981; newsletters (*Back Chat Newsletter*, 1971-1974, 1976; *CHAT Newsletter*, 1977).
AMOUNT: 3.6 m.

Collection (b)
LOCATION OF RECORDS: Canadian Women's Movement Archives Collection, Morisset Library Special Collections, University of Ottawa. (See Appendix for address.)
COLLECTION NAME: Community Homophile Association of Toronto.
RECORDS: Correspondence, 1973, 1975; article, 1975; newsletters (*CHAT Newsletter*, 1976-1977; *Back Chat Newsletter*, 1971-1974, 1976); drafts of articles, recommendation, pamphlet, flyers.
AMOUNT: 5 mm.
CONDITION: Good.
ACCESS: Restricted; conditional access negotiable.

378. Community Resources for Women

✣ Kitchener-Waterloo, Ont. Formed 1978. Disbanded 1987.

Community Resources for Women (CRW) was an inter-agency network which promoted co-operation and information sharing among organizations serving women. CRW held meetings and workshops, produced directories, and published a newsletter. (Source: Kitchener Public Library finding aid.)

LOCATION OF RECORDS: Grace Schmidt Room of Local History, Kitchener Public Library. (See Appendix for address.)
COLLECTION NAME: Community Resources for Women (MC 73).
RECORDS: Minutes, correspondence, clippings, membership lists, workshop information, questionnaires, evaluations, newsletters, grant information, 1978-1987.
FINDING AID: Finding aid available.

379. Concerned Women (Sault Ste Marie, Ont.)

✣ Sault Ste Marie, Ont. Formed 1974. Disbanded.

Concerned Women, which emerged from a political discussion group, addressed issues of concern to women.

LOCATION OF RECORDS: Canadian Women's Movement Archives Collection, Morisset Library Special Collections, University of Ottawa. (See Appendix for address.)
COLLECTION NAME: Concerned Women — Sault Ste. Marie, Ontario.
RECORDS: Report, 1975; newsletters (*Concerned Women Newsletter*, 1974-1976; *Superior Woman*, 1976-1977; *Concerned Woman*, 1978).
AMOUNT: 2 cm.
CONDITION: Good.
ACCESS: No restrictions.

380. Cora: The Feminist Bookmobile

✣ Toronto, Ont. Formed 1973. Disbanded [1975?].

This travelling bookstore and library was also known as the Women's Bookmobile or the Women's Liberation Bookmobile. A group of women, travelling in a bus, brought feminist literature to towns throughout Ontario.

LOCATION OF RECORDS: Canadian Women's Movement Archives Collection, Morisset Library Special Collections, University of Ottawa. (See Appendix for address.)
COLLECTION NAME: Cora: The Feminist Bookmobile.
RECORDS: Clippings, flyers, 1973-1975; organization history, permits, financial records, 1974; correspondence, 1973-1974; photographs, parking tickets, poem.
AMOUNT: 3 cm of text, 4 photographs.
CONDITION: Fair.
ACCESS: No restrictions.

381. Council of Business and Professional Women's Clubs of Metropolitan Toronto

✣ Formed [before 1963]. Disbanded [after 1975].

This umbrella organization "appears to have acted as a co-ordinating body between the various clubs in the area." (Source: Archives of Ontario finding aid, 1990.) [See also Toronto Business and Professional Women's Club (498).]

LOCATION OF RECORDS: Archives of Ontario. (See Appendix for address.)
COLLECTION NAME: Forms part of: Toronto Business and Professional Women's Club collection (F 2085).
RECORDS: Minutes, correspondence, programmes, 1962-1963, 1969-1973.
AMOUNT: 1.3 cm.
CONDITION: Good.
ACCESS: No restrictions.
FINDING AID: "Inventory of the Toronto Business and Professional Women's Club."

382. Day Care Organizing Committee

✣ Toronto, Ont. Formed [1972?]. Disbanded [1974?].

This committee (also known as DCOC) lobbied for legislation to establish non-profit, parent-controlled day-care centres. The committee published a newspaper, *Day Care for Everyone*.

LOCATION OF RECORDS: Canadian Women's Movement Archives Collection, Morisset Library Special Collections, University of Ottawa. (See Appendix for address.)
COLLECTION NAME: Day Care Organizing Committee — Toronto.
RECORDS: Minutes, brief, 1972; newspapers (*Day Care for Everyone*, 1972-1974); handbook.
AMOUNT: 1 cm.
CONDITION: Good.
ACCESS: No restrictions.

383. Day Care Reform Action Alliance

✣ Toronto, Ont. Formed 1974. Disbanded [197-].

This organization was largely made up of parents and staff from Toronto day-care centres. It opposed provincial day-care legislation proposed in 1974, and it advocated non-profit, high-quality day care.

LOCATION OF RECORDS: Canadian Women's Movement Archives Collection,

THE ~~CONTINUING~~ ADVENTURES OF CORA, THE BOOKMOBILE

by ellen, typed by judy, revised by boo

approved
about
Norwood
Fall 74
2 pages

The Women's Movement is alive and well in rural Ontario.

How did we get started?
We have had the idea for two years. Judith and ellen started saving money in September, 1973. The bus was bought in the spring of 1974, after a winter of hard work, advance publicity, and fund-raising. We painted Cora (named after E Cora Hind- pioneer suffragist, grain expert, and journalist), put in shelves, display racks, and a children's corner. On the first of May Cora was on the road (at 35 miles per hour- with a tailwind). We received an OFY grant at the end of June, and four more women joined us- Wanda, Marcia, Scamp and Boo. The bookmobile has been going steadily since May, and will continue year-round, except ~~for the~~ during the cold winter months.

ADVENTURES AND ESCAPADES

Clinton: Boo and ellen got thrown out of a pool hall, because "there was no women's washroom"

Wingham: Most of the women who came on the bus were over sixty. One octagenarian woman, to an older man: "I've worked all my life, and now I haven't a penny. You worked all your life and have three pensions- You're retired- I'm just tired."
A middle aged woman had been running a pig farm for five years. She said that women make the best pig-farmers "It's like running a giant maternity ward."

Orillia: Women in the town tried to organize a strike of waitresses and cleaning women over the long weekend (they get $1.65/hr.). The bosses found out about it and bought them off by raising their wages by 5¢.

Owen Sound: A woman's Centre is starting.

London: A gay club is starting.

Midland: We were part of a sidewalk sale, and a friendly lesbian brought us a picnic lunch.
An older woman stood outside the bus and kept men off by telling them "You can't come in- this is for us" She never came in herself.
The librariabn didn't like women's liberation- she was into Bahai - "If you love a man, you will be happy to serve him".

Sarnia: When we arrived at the Women"s Fair, the IODE left in disgust. The rest of the groups were extremely friendly.

We learned a lot this summer- about women's lives that are different from ours. We learned how to talk with women froma many different backgrounds. We learned how little organizind has been done in small towns- and how much women are doing it for themselves. We learned how to keep smiling, and still befirm about our beliefs. We learned that it wasn't as exciting as we had imagined- mostly hard work. We found that ~~the problems of~~ rural women are finding the strength to reach out to each other when faced with incredible social pressures to conform. We will be on the road again by next April. If you want us to visit you, or have money or books to donate, writeto us at: 195 Seaton St. Toronto.

Excerpts from a 1974 document entitled: / Extraits d'un document de 1974 intitulé :
"The Adventures of Cora, the Bookmobile"
Cora: The Feminist Bookmobile
CWMA Collection / Fonds de l'ACMF

Morisset Library Special Collections, University of Ottawa. (See Appendix for address.)

COLLECTION NAME: Day Care Reform Action Alliance.

RECORDS: Brief, petition, position papers, educational materials, flyers, 1974; agendas, 1974-1975; clipping, 1976; newsletters (*Good Daycare*, 1975-1976).

AMOUNT: 1.5 cm.

CONDITION: Good.

ACCESS: No restrictions.

384. Dignity Toronto Dignité

✤ Toronto, Ont. Formed [1978?].

This is the Toronto branch of Dignity Canada Dignité, an organization for lesbian and gay Catholics and their friends.

LOCATION OF RECORDS: Canadian Gay Archives. (See Appendix for address.)

COLLECTION NAME: Dignity Toronto (89-068, 89-118, 89-132, 90-120, 90-121); some records form part of: Don St. Jean collection (89-121).

RECORDS: Newsletters, correspondence, miscellaneous records, 1978-1989.

385. Dovercourt NDP. Women's Action Committee

✤ Toronto, Ont. Formed 1980.

The Women's Action Committee was established within the Dovercourt NDP (a local organization of New Democratic Party members) to familiarize members with issues affecting working-class and immigrant women; to increase women's involvement in NDP policy discussions and decision making within the riding (Dovercourt); and to support local strikes and demonstrations affecting women.

LOCATION OF RECORDS: Canadian Women's Movement Archives Collection, Morisset Library Special Collections, University of Ottawa. (See Appendix for address.)

COLLECTION NAME: Dovercourt NDP Women's Action Committee.

RECORDS: Correspondence, 1981-1982; newsletter, minutes, contact lists, notes, [198-].

AMOUNT: 5 mm.

CONDITION: Good.

ACCESS: No restrictions.

386. Durham International Women's Day Committee

✤ Disbanded.

The committee organized annual International Women's Day events for Oshawa, Whitby, Newcastle, Ajax, Pickering, and Port Perry.

LOCATION OF RECORDS: Canadian Women's Movement Archives Collection, Morisset Library Special Collections, University of Ottawa. (See Appendix for address.)

COLLECTION NAME: Durham International Women's Day Committee.

RECORDS: Minutes, newsletters, clippings, press releases, correspondence, miscellaneous records, [ca. 1983]-[ca. 1988].

AMOUNT: 1 box.

ACCESS: As of 1992, the collection has not yet been processed.

387. Elizabeth Fry Society of Kingston

[See also entry # 1022 (in Part II), which lists other records of this organization.]

✤ Kingston, Ont. Formed 1949.

The Elizabeth Fry Society of Kingston (also called E. Fry) is a community organization which addresses the needs of women who are or have been in conflict with the law (or who may be at risk of being so).

LOCATION OF RECORDS: National Archives of Canada. (See Appendix for address.)

COLLECTION NAME: Forms part of: Flora Isabel MacDonald collection (MG 32, B 26).

RECORDS: Please see the note about National Archives of Canada collections, in entry # 2.

388. Elizabeth Fry Society. Ottawa Branch

✤ Ottawa, Ont.

Collection (a)

LOCATION OF RECORDS: National Archives of Canada. (See Appendix for address.)

COLLECTION NAME: Forms part of: Margaret MacLellan collection (MG 31, E 17).

RECORDS: Please see the note about National Archives of Canada collections, in entry # 2.

Collection (b)

LOCATION OF RECORDS: National Archives of Canada.

COLLECTION NAME: Forms part of: Dorothy Eva Flaherty collection (MG 31, K 25).

RECORDS: Please see the note about National Archives of Canada collections, in entry # 2.

389. Family Benefits Work Group

✤ Toronto, Ont. Formed 1978. Disbanded [198-].

The Family Benefits Work Group (FBWG) was made up of single mothers on social assistance and professionals working in social services. FBWG lobbied for changes to welfare legislation.

LOCATION OF RECORDS: Canadian Women's Movement Archives Collection, Morisset Library Special Collections, University of Ottawa. (See Appendix for address.)

COLLECTION NAME: Family Benefits Work Group.

RECORDS: Minutes, 1978-1979, 1982-1983; correspondence, 1978-1983; newsletters (*Mothers Organizing Mothers*, 1979-1981; *Family Benefits Work Group Newsletter*, 1982-1984); grant application, 1978; briefs, recommendations, pamphlet, 1979; clippings, press releases, 1978-1979; organization history, [ca. 1980]; questionnaire, annual report, financial report, 1983; membership form, 1984; membership lists, notes, notices of meetings, agendas, policy outline, fact sheets, songsheet, flyers.

AMOUNT: 6.5 cm.

CONDITION: Good.

ACCESS: No restrictions.

390. Federated Women's Institutes of Ontario

✤ Formed 1919.

This is an association of rural homemakers, with branches throughout Ontario.

LOCATION OF RECORDS: Archives of Ontario. (See Appendix for address.)

COLLECTION NAME: Federated Women's Institutes of Ontario (RG 16, Series 16-87).

RECORDS: Minutes, lists of board members and officials, correspondence, subject files, historical and background files, maps, photographs, miscellaneous records, 1901-1976.

AMOUNT: 1.83 m.

FINDING AID: File list available.

391. Fly by Night Lounge

✣ Toronto, Ont. Formed 1979. Disbanded 1980.

This bar for women held live performances by feminist musicians.

LOCATION OF RECORDS: Canadian Women's Movement Archives Collection, Morisset Library Special Collections, University of Ottawa. (See Appendix for address.)
COLLECTION NAME: Fly by Night (Women's Bar).
RECORDS: Correspondence, articles, 1979; flyers, T-shirt.
AMOUNT: 2 mm of text, 1 T-shirt.
CONDITION: Good.
ACCESS: No restrictions.

392. Friends of Hagar

✣ Toronto, Ont. Formed 1974. Disbanded [1979?].

The Friends of Hagar published a Christian feminist newsletter of the same name. The newsletter had close ties with the Movement for Christian Feminism, which helped to publish it. [See also Movement for Christian Feminism (444).]

Collection (a)

LOCATION OF RECORDS: Anglican Church of Canada, General Synod Archives. (See Appendix for address.)
COLLECTION NAME: The Friends of Hagar.
RECORDS: Newsletters (*The Friends of Hagar*, 1974-1979); correspondence, articles, speeches, reports, mailing lists, minutes, miscellaneous records.

Collection (b)

LOCATION OF RECORDS: Canadian Women's Movement Archives Collection, Morisset Library Special Collections, University of Ottawa. (See Appendix for address.)
COLLECTION NAME: The Friends of Hagar.
RECORDS: Newsletters (*The Friends of Hagar*, 1975-1978).
AMOUNT: 1 cm.
CONDITION: Good.
ACCESS: No restrictions.

393. Gay Alliance toward Equality (Toronto, Ont.)

✣ Toronto, Ont. Formed 1973. Disbanded.

The Gay Alliance toward Equality (GATE) lobbied for full civil and human rights for lesbians and gay men. GATE also held educational forums and social events, and it organized the Fourth Annual Gay Conference for Lesbians and Gay Men in Canada and Quebec, held in 1976. GATE had a lesbian caucus.

Collection (a)

LOCATION OF RECORDS: Canadian Gay Archives. (See Appendix for address.)
COLLECTION NAME: Gay Alliance toward Equality (Toronto) (82-029, 85-019).
RECORDS: Constitutional material, minutes, correspondence, flyers, briefs, petitions, newsletters, 1972-1980; conference records, 1976.
AMOUNT: 27 cm.

Collection (b)

LOCATION OF RECORDS: Canadian Women's Movement Archives Collection, Morisset Library Special Collections, University of Ottawa. (See Appendix for address.)
COLLECTION NAME: Gay Alliance toward Equality (Toronto, Ont.).
RECORDS: Brief, notes, 1973; conference records, photographs, calendar of events, 1976; press releases, 1973-1974; background paper, 1977; article, 1978; sticker, 1974; newsletters (*Gay Rising*, 1975-1978; *Lesbian Caucus of the Gay Alliance toward Equality Bulletin*, [197-]); statement of purpose, correspondence, flyers, invitations, speech, proposal, letterhead, pamphlets.
AMOUNT: 1.5 cm of text, 9 photographs.
CONDITION: Good.
ACCESS: Restricted; conditional access negotiable.

394. Gay Community Calendar

✣ Toronto, Ont. Formed 1977.

The Gay Community Calendar runs 923-GAYS, a recorded message providing information on Toronto events of interest to gay men and lesbians.

LOCATION OF RECORDS: Canadian Gay Archives. (See Appendix for address.)
COLLECTION NAME: 923-GAYS (84-007, 91-244).
RECORDS: Scripts, 1980-1983; miscellaneous records.

395. Gay Women Unlimited

✣ Toronto, Ont. Formed 1976. Disbanded [197-].

Gay Women Unlimited was a social and support group for lesbians.

LOCATION OF RECORDS: Canadian Women's Movement Archives Collection, Morisset Library Special Collections, University of Ottawa. (See Appendix for address.)
COLLECTION NAME: Gay Women Unlimited — Toronto.
RECORDS: Calendars of events, flyers, 1976.
AMOUNT: 1 mm.
CONDITION: Fair.
ACCESS: Restricted; conditional access negotiable.

396. Gays and Lesbians against the Right Everywhere

✣ Toronto, Ont. Formed [1981?]. Disbanded [198-].

Gays and Lesbians against the Right Everywhere (GLARE) engaged in educational work, cultural activities, and demonstrations to oppose attacks against lesbians and gays by right-wing organizations.

LOCATION OF RECORDS: Canadian Gay Archives. (See Appendix for address.)
COLLECTION NAME: Gays and Lesbians against the Right Everywhere (86-023).
RECORDS: Minutes, financial records, correspondence, administrative files, flyers, notices, questionnaires, booklets, clippings, briefs, miscellaneous records, 1981-1984.
AMOUNT: 13 cm.

397. Gays and Lesbians in Health Care

✣ Toronto, Ont. Formed 1980.

Gays and Lesbians in Health Care (GLHC) was established to support gay and lesbian health-care workers, promote health in the gay and lesbian community, and educate the public about the health concerns of gay men and lesbians. It was originally called Gays in Health Care.

LOCATION OF RECORDS: Canadian Gay Archives. (See Appendix for address.)
COLLECTION NAME: Forms part of: David A. Whaley collection (87-009).
RECORDS: Articles, notes, miscellaneous records.

398. George Brown College. Advisory Committee for Equity

✣ Toronto, Ont. Formed 1981.

The committee's original name was the Affirmative Action Advisory Committee (AAAC). Reporting to the president of George Brown College, the committee succeeded the Women's Advisor position established in 1976. The committee's concerns have included employment opportunities, sexual harassment, curriculum development, and child care. In 1990 the committee was renamed the Advisory Committee for Equity (ACE). It also addresses the concerns of disabled, visible-minority, and Native people.

LOCATION OF RECORDS: George Brown College Archives. (See Appendix for address.)
COLLECTION NAME: Office of the President. President's Office. Affirmative Action Advisory Committee (A.A.A.C.) (90-56; 90-57; Serials 0 3.1, 0 3.2).
RECORDS: Minutes, posters, brochures, flyers, booklets, informational material, 1982-1990; reports, 1983-1988; newsletters, 1983-1990.
AMOUNT: 7 cm.
ACCESS: No restrictions.

399. Group for Equal Rights at McMaster

✣ Hamilton, Ont. Formed 1971. Disbanded [197-?].

The Group for Equal Rights at McMaster (GERM) was composed of faculty, staff, and students at McMaster University. It investigated the status of women at McMaster and recommended steps to enable fuller participation by women in the university community. [See also McMaster University. Senate. Equal Rights Review and Co-ordinating Committee (437).]

LOCATION OF RECORDS: Canadian Women's Movement Archives Collection, Morisset Library Special Collections, University of Ottawa. (See Appendix for address.)
COLLECTION NAME: Group for Equal Rights at McMaster.
RECORDS: Correspondence, minutes, 1971-1972; petition, reports, clipping, 1971; briefs, membership list, pamphlet.
AMOUNT: 7 cm.
CONDITION: Good.
ACCESS: No restrictions.

400. Guelph Business and Professional Women's Club

✣ Guelph, Ont. Formed 1928. Disbanded 1975.

LOCATION OF RECORDS: Archives of Ontario. (See Appendix for address.)
COLLECTION NAME: Guelph Business and Professional Women's Club Papers (F 227).
RECORDS: Minutes, 1933-1936, 1940-1956, 1963-1976; financial records, 1934-1957; convention records, 1943-1944; programmes, 1940-1954, 1965-1970; membership lists, correspondence, reports, clippings.
AMOUNT: 29 cm.
CONDITION: Good.
ACCESS: No restrictions.
FINDING AID: "Inventory of the Guelph Business and Professional Women's Club."

401. Guelph Council for International Women's Year

✣ Guelph, Ont. Formed [1975?]. Disbanded [1975?].

The council organized the Women and Health Conference and the Nellie McClung Conference, both held in Guelph in 1975.

LOCATION OF RECORDS: Canadian Women's Movement Archives Collection, Morisset Library Special Collections, University of Ottawa. (See Appendix for address.)
COLLECTION NAME: Guelph Council for International Women's Year.
RECORDS: Conference reports, pamphlet, notice, clipping, flyer, press release, 1975.
AMOUNT: 3 mm.
CONDITION: Good.
ACCESS: No restrictions.

402. Guelph Women's Centre

✣ Guelph, Ont.

LOCATION OF RECORDS: Canadian Women's Movement Archives Collection, Morisset Library Special Collections, University of Ottawa. (See Appendix for address.)
COLLECTION NAME: Guelph Women's Centre.
RECORDS: Newsletters (*Virago*, 1972-1975); flyers.
AMOUNT: 1 cm.
ACCESS: No restrictions.

403. Hamilton and District Local Council of Women

✣ Hamilton, Ont.

Collection (a)

LOCATION OF RECORDS: Hamilton Public Library, Special Collections. (See Appendix for address.)
COLLECTION NAME: Hamilton and District Local Council of Women.
RECORDS: Miscellaneous records.
ACCESS: As of 1992, the collection has not yet been processed.

Collection (b)

LOCATION OF RECORDS: Archives of Ontario. (See Appendix for address.)
COLLECTION NAME: Forms part of: Provincial Council of Women of Ontario Papers (F 7981, Series F).
RECORDS: Miscellaneous records, 1949-1951.
AMOUNT: 1 file.
ACCESS: No restrictions.
FINDING AID: "Inventory of the Provincial Council of Women of Ontario Papers."

404. Holly Near Concert Organizing Committee

✣ Ottawa, Ont. Formed 1982. Disbanded 1982.

The committee organized a 1982 Ottawa concert by American feminist singer Holly Near.

LOCATION OF RECORDS: Canadian Women's Movement Archives Collection, Morisset Library Special Collections, University of Ottawa. (See Appendix for address.)
COLLECTION NAME: Holly Near Concert Organizing Committee (Ottawa, 1982).
RECORDS: Correspondence, publicity material, clipping, contract, notes, press release, pamphlets, flyers, 1982; biographical information, guidelines, contact list.
AMOUNT: 2 cm.
CONDITION: Good.
ACCESS: No restrictions.

405. Hour a Day Study Club

✣ Windsor, Ont. Formed 1934.

The Hour a Day Study Club (originally called the Mother's Club) is an organization of Black women in Windsor. The club's motto is "Working Together for Community Betterment." The club organized the Fourth National Congress of Black Women in Canada/Quatrième Congrès national des femmes noires du Canada, held in Windsor in 1977. The congress (called "Impetus: The Black Woman/Nouvel essor : La Femme noire") brought together Black women from across Canada to discuss their current status, common concerns, and achievements.

LOCATION OF RECORDS: North American Black Historical Museum. (See Appendix for address.)
COLLECTION NAME: Hour a Day Study Club.
RECORDS: Conference records, 1977; organization history, constitution, report of meetings, list of guest speakers, list of recipients of scholarships.

406. Identity

✣ Toronto, Ont. Formed 1975. Disbanded.

Identity was a Toronto newsletter which published articles on lesbianism and feminism.

LOCATION OF RECORDS: Canadian Women's Movement Archives Collection, Morisset Library Special Collections, University of Ottawa. (See Appendix for address.)
COLLECTION NAME: Identity.
RECORDS: Newsletters, 1975.
AMOUNT: 2 items.
CONDITION: Good.
ACCESS: No restrictions.

407. International Women's Week Coalition (Kingston, Ont.)

✣ Kingston, Ont.

Each year this ad hoc coalition organizes a week of activities (such as workshops, speakers, marches, and dances) to celebrate International Women's Day.

LOCATION OF RECORDS: Canadian Women's Movement Archives Collection, Morisset Library Special Collections, University of Ottawa. (See Appendix for address.)
COLLECTION NAME: International Women's Week Coalition (Kingston, Ont.).
RECORDS: Minutes, posters, flyers, 1986-1987; workshop materials, 1987, 1990; membership list, correspondence, background paper, 1987; button, 1986; booklet.
AMOUNT: 5 mm of text, 1 button, 2 posters.
CONDITION: Good.
ACCESS: No restrictions.

408. Jane Doe Study Group

✣ Windsor, Ont. Formed 1972. Disbanded [197-].

This group was originally called the Socialist Women's Group (SWG). During its first year of existence, SWG became the Socialist Women's Caucus (SWC) of the Labour Centre and organized the Open Women's Group. SWC held discussions, supported striking workers, and established a day-care centre. In 1973, it became a study group with an emphasis on Marxism and the women's movement; it was then renamed the Jane Doe Study Group.

LOCATION OF RECORDS: Canadian Women's Movement Archives Collection, Morisset Library Special Collections, University of Ottawa. (See Appendix for address.)
COLLECTION NAME: Jane Doe Study Group (Windsor, Ont.).
RECORDS: Organization history, [1973?].
AMOUNT: 1 item.
CONDITION: Good.
ACCESS: No restrictions.

409. K-W Woman's Place

✣ Kitchener-Waterloo, Ont. Formed 1973. Disbanded [1976?].

K-W Woman's Place (sometimes called simply the Woman's Place or the Women's Place) was a women's centre which offered courses, discussions, lectures, and social events. [See also Lesbian Collective (Waterloo, Ont.) (419).]

LOCATION OF RECORDS: Canadian Women's Movement Archives Collection, Morisset Library Special Collections, University of Ottawa. (See Appendix for address.)
COLLECTION NAME: K-W Woman's Place.
RECORDS: Organization history, discussion paper, booklet, conference report, 1975; clipping, 1974; correspondence, 1975-1976; newsletters (*Woman's Place Newsletter*, 1974; *Woman's Place*, 1975; *Strength*, 1975-1976); flyer.
AMOUNT: 2 cm.
CONDITION: Good.
ACCESS: No restrictions.

410. Kincardine Women's Study Group

✣ Kincardine, Ont. Formed [1980?]. Disbanded 1988.

"A group of concerned women focusing on women's issues and awareness through education," the Kincardine Women's Study Group organized a series of public lectures and workshops. (Source: Study Group flyer.) The group was initially called Kincardine Women Alive.

LOCATION OF RECORDS: Canadian Women's Movement Archives Collection, Morisset Library Special Collections, University of Ottawa. (See Appendix for address.)
COLLECTION NAME: Kincardine Women's Study Group.
RECORDS: Membership lists, 1981, 1983; grant application, 1981; financial statement, 1982; correspondence, 1978, 1981; clippings, tickets, 1980-1982; flyers, workshop materials.
AMOUNT: 1 cm.
CONDITION: Fair.
ACCESS: No restrictions.

411. Kingston Women's Centre

✣ Kingston, Ont. Formed 1972. Disbanded [1977?].

The Kingston Women's Centre appears to have grown out of the Kingston Women's Liberation Movement (which began in 1969). Planning for the centre began in 1972, and it opened the following year. The centre had consciousness-raising groups, study groups, and action groups for various issues. With the Queen's Feminist Socialist Study Group, the centre co-sponsored a 1977 conference called the Women in Revolution Weekend.

LOCATION OF RECORDS: Canadian Women's Movement Archives Collection, Morisset Library Special Collections, University of Ottawa. (See Appendix for address.)
COLLECTION NAME: Kingston Women's Centre.

RECORDS: Organization histories, 1971, 1973; newsletters, 1973-1976; conference materials, 1976-1977; questionnaire, [1975?]; articles, flyers, poster.
AMOUNT: 5 cm of text, 1 poster.
CONDITION: Fair.
ACCESS: No restrictions.

412. Kitchener-Waterloo Business and Professional Women's Club

✤ Kitchener-Waterloo, Ont. Formed 1929. Disbanded 1971.

The club's objectives included the improvement of women's economic, employment, and social conditions. The club was involved in various community services. (Source: Kitchener Public Library finding aid.)

LOCATION OF RECORDS: Grace Schmidt Room of Local History, Kitchener Public Library. (See Appendix for address.)
COLLECTION NAME: Kitchener-Waterloo Business and Professional Women's Club (MC 62).
RECORDS: Minutes, 1929-1939, 1950-1955, 1964-1971; correspondence, 1932-1951; clippings, 1949-1967; membership lists, miscellaneous records.
FINDING AID: Finding aid available.

413. Kitchener-Waterloo Women's Coalition for Repeal of the Abortion Laws

✤ Kitchener-Waterloo, Ont.

LOCATION OF RECORDS: Canadian Women's Movement Archives Collection, Morisset Library Special Collections, University of Ottawa. (See Appendix for address.)
COLLECTION NAME: Kitchener-Waterloo Women's Coalition for Repeal of the Abortion Laws.
RECORDS: Newsletter, press release, 1972.
AMOUNT: 2 items.
ACCESS: No restrictions.

414. Kitchener-Waterloo Young Women's Christian Association

[See also entry # 1036 (in Part II), which lists other records of this organization.]

✤ Kitchener-Waterloo, Ont. Formed 1905.

Originally called the Young Women's Christian Association of Berlin, the Kitchener-Waterloo YWCA provides services for women and children in response to current needs. Its services have included temporary housing, child care, and a physical-education programme.

LOCATION OF RECORDS: Doris Lewis Rare Book Room, University of Waterloo Library. (See Appendix for address.)
COLLECTION NAME: Young Women's Christian Association of Kitchener-Waterloo.
RECORDS: Minutes, 1905-1985; constitution, by-laws, 1913, 1959, 1966, 1969, 1971; financial records, 1905-1980; reports, 1941-1949, 1951-1983; lists of board members, attendance sheets, 1906-1909, 1923-1943, 1946-1951, 1955-1957, 1959-1960, 1962-1965, 1967-1968, 1972, 1977-1978; personnel records, 1940-[198-]; directories, 1943-1980; photographs, clippings, correspondence, organization histories, project files, committee files, policy statements, residence records, physical-plant records, recommendations, speech, advertisements, miscellaneous records.

AMOUNT: 9.15 m.
ACCESS: Restrictions on some financial, camp, personnel, and committee records.
FINDING AID: Finding aid available.

415. Leila Khaled Collective

✤ Toronto, Ont. Formed 1970. Disbanded [197-].

The Leila Khaled Collective was formed by members of the Toronto Women's Liberation Movement (TWLM) who left TWLM to focus on solidarity with struggles against imperialism. (Source: *Feminist Organizing for Change: The Contemporary Women's Movement in Canada* / Nancy Adamson, Linda Briskin, and Margaret McPhail. — Toronto: Oxford University Press, 1988.) Collective members were involved in organizing the 1971 Indochinese Women's Conference, which was hosted by TWLM. [See also Toronto Women's Liberation Movement (509).]

LOCATION OF RECORDS: Canadian Women's Movement Archives Collection, Morisset Library Special Collections, University of Ottawa. (See Appendix for address.)
COLLECTION NAME: Leila Khaled Collective.
RECORDS: Position paper, [1970 or 1971]; notes.
AMOUNT: 2 mm.
CONDITION: Fair.
ACCESS: No restrictions.

416. Lesbian and Gay Community Appeal of Toronto

[See also entry # 1040 (in Part II), which lists other records of this organization.]

✤ Toronto, Ont. Formed 1980.

The Lesbian and Gay Community Appeal of Toronto (LGCA) provides funding to lesbian and gay groups and individuals for projects in areas such as health, culture, and politics. LGCA produces "Fruit Cocktail," a lesbian and gay musical-comedy revue. LGCA was originally called the Gay Community Appeal of Toronto.

Collection (a)
LOCATION OF RECORDS: Canadian Gay Archives. (See Appendix for address.)
COLLECTION NAME: Encore Entertainments (83-011).
RECORDS: Stage manager's prompt book, flyers, programme, posters, 1983.
AMOUNT: 40 cm.

Collection (b)
LOCATION OF RECORDS: Canadian Gay Archives.
COLLECTION NAME: Lesbian and Gay Community Appeal of Toronto (89-135).
RECORDS: Programmes, notices, posters, newsletters, 1983-1989.
AMOUNT: 7 cm.

417. Lesbian and Gay History Group of Toronto

✤ Toronto, Ont. Formed 1980. Disbanded [ca. 1983].

This group was founded to discover, record, and analyse the history of lesbians and gay men. Its Oral History Project documented lesbian and gay Toronto history.

LOCATION OF RECORDS: Canadian Gay Archives. (See Appendix for address.)
COLLECTION NAME: Lesbian and Gay History Group of Toronto (83-025).
RECORDS: Oral-history records, newsletter production records, brief, articles, miscellaneous records, 1980-1983.
AMOUNT: 20 cm.

418. Lesbian and Gay Pride Day Committee (Toronto, Ont.)

✣ Toronto, Ont.

This committee organizes annual local events to celebrate Lesbian and Gay Pride Day.

Collection (a)

LOCATION OF RECORDS: Canadian Gay Archives. (See Appendix for address.)
COLLECTION NAME: Lesbian and Gay Pride Day Committee (84-028, 87-016, 88-013, 88-042, 89-037, 89-050).
RECORDS: Flyers, banners, videotapes, posters, minutes, booklets, artifacts, buttons, programmes, miscellaneous records, 1982-1989.

Collection (b)

LOCATION OF RECORDS: Canadian Gay Archives.
COLLECTION NAME: Kyle Rae (87-022).
RECORDS: Miscellaneous records, 1981-1987.
AMOUNT: 78 cm.

419. Lesbian Collective (Waterloo, Ont.)

✣ Waterloo, Ont. Formed [1974 or 1975]. Disbanded [1975?].

The Lesbian Collective was "open to all women interested in the issues facing gay women." It held social and cultural events and had a library. The collective met at K-W Woman's Place. (Source: Lesbian Collective flyer, 1975.) [See also K-W Woman's Place (409).]

Collection (a)

LOCATION OF RECORDS: Canadian Women's Movement Archives Collection, Morisset Library Special Collections, University of Ottawa. (See Appendix for address.)
COLLECTION NAME: Lesbian Collective (Waterloo, Ont.).
RECORDS: Correspondence, 1975; flyers, booklet.
AMOUNT: 3 mm.
CONDITION: Good.
ACCESS: Restricted; conditional access negotiable.

Collection (b)

LOCATION OF RECORDS: Canadian Gay Archives. (See Appendix for address.)
COLLECTION NAME: Lesbian Collective — Waterloo (vertical file).
RECORDS: Correspondence, 1975; press releases, flyers.
AMOUNT: 2 mm.
CONDITION: Good.

420. Lesbian Dance Committee

✣ Toronto, Ont. Formed 1986.

The Lesbian Dance Committee (LDC) represents a number of local feminist and lesbian and gay groups in Toronto. Proceeds from dances organized by LDC are distributed among these groups. LDC was originally called the Lesbian Dance Council.

LOCATION OF RECORDS: Canadian Women's Movement Archives Collection, Morisset Library Special Collections, University of Ottawa. (See Appendix for address.)
COLLECTION NAME: Lesbian Dance Committee — Toronto.
RECORDS: Minutes, financial statement, 1986; flyers, 1986-1989; policy statement, notes.
AMOUNT: 1 cm.
CONDITION: Good.
ACCESS: Restricted; conditional access negotiable.

421. Lesbian / Lesbienne

✣ Formed 1979. Disbanded 1982.

The newsletter *Lesbian/Lesbienne* (L/L) was established to provide a forum for lesbians across Canada. Although some articles were published in French, L/L was an anglophone organization based in Ontario. The newsletter was produced by women in Kitchener-Waterloo, Guelph, and Toronto.

LOCATION OF RECORDS: Canadian Women's Movement Archives Collection, Morisset Library Special Collections, University of Ottawa. (See Appendix for address.)
COLLECTION NAME: Lesbian/Lesbienne.
RECORDS: Newsletters (*Lesbian/Lesbienne*, 1979-1982); minutes, financial records, 1980-1982; correspondence, 1979-1982; policy statements, 1981; advertisements, drafts of articles, translations, 1981-1982; proposal, 1982; clipping, paper, 1979; mailing lists, notes, flyers, sign, questionnaires, paste-ups, graphics, booklet, resource list, button.
AMOUNT: 16 cm of text, 1 sign, 1 button.
CONDITION: Good.
ACCESS: Restricted; conditional access negotiable.

422. Lesbian Mothers' Defence Fund (Toronto, Ont.)

✣ Toronto, Ont. Formed 1978. Disbanded 1987.

A resource for lesbians facing child-custody battles, the Lesbian Mothers' Defence Fund (LMDF) was founded by members of the Toronto organization Wages for Housework. LMDF provided referrals to lawyers, financial assistance, and emotional support; the group also published a newsletter (*Grapevine*) and did public speaking. Affiliated organizations were established in Montreal, Calgary, and Vancouver. [See also Wages for Housework Committee (Toronto, Ont.) (528).]

LOCATION OF RECORDS: Canadian Women's Movement Archives Collection, Morisset Library Special Collections, University of Ottawa. (See Appendix for address.)
COLLECTION NAME: Lesbian Mothers' Defence Fund — Toronto.
RECORDS: Constitution, 1978; correspondence, 1984-1988; clippings, 1982, 1984-1985; newsletters (*Grapevine*, 1979-1985, 1987); financial records, 1984-1985; brief, 1984; permit, 1986; minutes, organization history, log-books, flyers, pamphlets, questionnaire, contact list, mailing lists, notes, button.
AMOUNT: 12 cm of text, 1 button.
CONDITION: Good.
ACCESS: Restricted; conditional access negotiable.

423. Lesbian Organization of Kitchener

✣ Kitchener, Ont. Formed [197-]. Disbanded [198-].

The Lesbian Organization of Kitchener (LOOK) offered telephone counselling, organized dances and film screenings, produced radio shows, and lobbied local government.

LOCATION OF RECORDS: Canadian Women's Movement Archives Collection, Morisset Library Special Collections, University of Ottawa. (See Appendix for address.)
COLLECTION NAME: Lesbian Organization of Kitchener.
RECORDS: Minutes, 1981-1982; report, 1983; presentation, telephone tree, 1982; correspondence, 1978; ticket, 1981; logo design, flyers.
AMOUNT: 5 mm.
CONDITION: Fair.
ACCESS: Restricted; conditional access negotiable.

424. Lesbian Organization of Toronto

✣ Toronto, Ont. Formed 1976. Disbanded 1980.

The activities of the Lesbian Organization of Toronto (LOOT) included discussions, dances, counselling services, a newsletter, a telephone line, and political action. LOOT seems briefly to have been called the Toronto Lesbian Organization. It co-organized the 1979 Toronto conference "A Fine Kettle of Fish: Lesbians and Feminists in the Women's Movement." (The other organizers were Women against Violence against Women and the International Women's Day Committee.) LOOT also organized the 1979 Bi-national Lesbian Conference/Conférence lesbienne bi-nationale. [See also Political Lesbians of Toronto (474).]

Collection (a)

LOCATION OF RECORDS: Canadian Women's Movement Archives Collection, Morisset Library Special Collections, University of Ottawa. (See Appendix for address.)

COLLECTION NAME: Lesbian Organization of Toronto; SR 23/1-3.

RECORDS: Minutes, correspondence, 1976-1979; newsletters (*Lesbian Organization of Toronto Newsletter*, 1977-1979; *Lesbian Perspective*, 1979-1980; *Lavender Sheets*, 1980); sound recordings (meetings, conference proceedings, oral history), 1978-1979, 1988-1990; financial records, 1975, 1978-1980; photographs, press release, buttons, conference records, 1976, 1979; historical information, 1976, 1978; layouts, 1979-1980; manuscripts, 1978-1979; floor plan, 1974; evaluation, speech, 1978; news release, questionnaire, 1980; policy statements, 1977; contact lists, notices of meetings, flyers, membership lists, membership cards, list of rules, graphics, notes, mailing list, articles, advertisement, calendars, schedules, lottery tickets, graffiti, ticket stub, T-shirt.

AMOUNT: 40 cm of text, 40 photographs, 59 sound recordings, 1 T-shirt, 2 buttons.

CONDITION: Good.

ACCESS: Restricted; conditional access negotiable. As of 1992, most of the sound recordings have not yet been processed.

Collection (b)

LOCATION OF RECORDS: Canadian Gay Archives. (See Appendix for address.)

COLLECTION NAME: Lesbian Organization of Toronto (84-005, 89-154); Conf.: Bi-National Lesbian Conference, Toronto, May 19-21, 1979 (vertical file).

RECORDS: Reference and research material, 1975-1978; correspondence, 1977, 1979-1980; bibliographies, [after 1975], 1978; interview, 1978; calendar, 1977; clipping, 1981; conference records, 1979; newsletters (*Lesbian Organization of Toronto Newsletter*, 1977-1979; *Lesbian Perspective*, 1979-1980; *Lavender Sheets*, 1980); poster, [ca. 1977]; flyers, notes, notebook, account of meeting, organization history, programmes, questionnaire, letterhead, logos, membership cards, lottery tickets, pamphlets, miscellaneous records.

AMOUNT: Approx. 16 cm.

Collection (c)

LOCATION OF RECORDS: Canadian Gay Archives.

COLLECTION NAME: Forms part of: Coalition for Gay Rights in Ontario collection (84-020).

RECORDS: Statistics, 1977-1979; procedures, 1977; flyer.

AMOUNT: 2 mm.

425. Lesbians against the Right

✣ Toronto, Ont. Formed 1981. Disbanded [198-].

At their first meeting, the members of Lesbians against the Right (LAR) defined themselves as "women-identified women who work together to fight the right wing...from a lesbian perspective." LAR organized political, social, and cultural events. (Source: manuscript of LAR leaflet, [1982?].)

LOCATION OF RECORDS: Canadian Women's Movement Archives Collection, Morisset Library Special Collections, University of Ottawa. (See Appendix for address.)

COLLECTION NAME: Lesbians against the Right.

RECORDS: Minutes, financial records, speeches, 1981-1983; organization history, pamphlet, permits, news release, 1981; photographs, proposal, layout material, questionnaire, 1982; notes, workshop and discussion material, 1981-1982; manuscript of leaflet, [1982?]; buttons, 1981, 1983; flyers, report, correspondence, information sheet, article, tickets, membership lists, contact list, outline of pamphlet, case study, song booklet, invitation, banner.

AMOUNT: 20 cm of text, 8 photographs, 1 banner, 2 buttons.

CONDITION: Good.

ACCESS: Restricted; conditional access negotiable.

426. Lesbians of Ottawa Now

✣ Ottawa, Ont. Formed 1976. Disbanded 1979.

Lesbians of Ottawa Now (LOON) hosted the 1976 National Lesbian Conference/Conférence nationale de lesbiennes and the 1978 Ontario Lesbians' Conference.

Collection (a)

LOCATION OF RECORDS: Canadian Women's Movement Archives Collection, Morisset Library Special Collections, University of Ottawa. (See Appendix for address.)

COLLECTION NAME: Conf.: "Lesbian Conf.", 2nd Ontario, May 1978, Ottawa; Conf.: "Lesbian Conf.", 1st National, October 1976, Ottawa.

RECORDS: Conference records, 1976, 1978.

AMOUNT: 1.5 cm.

CONDITION: Good.

ACCESS: Restricted; conditional access negotiable.

Collection (b)

LOCATION OF RECORDS: Canadian Gay Archives. (See Appendix for address.)

COLLECTION NAME: Conf.: National Lesbian Conference, 3rd Annual, Ottawa, October 9-11, 1976; Lesbians of Ottawa Now (vertical files).

RECORDS: Conference records, 1976, 1978.

AMOUNT: 7 mm.

427. Local Council of Women (London, Ont.)

✣ London, Ont. Formed 1894.

The council co-ordinates the interests of certain women's groups in London.

LOCATION OF RECORDS: D.B. Weldon Library — Regional Collection, University of Western Ontario. (See Appendix for address.)

COLLECTION NAME: Local Council of Women.

RECORDS: Minutes, related records, 1894, 1917-1968.

AMOUNT: 3 reels of microfilm.

CONDITION: Good.

ACCESS: No restrictions.

FINDING AID: Regional Collection manuscript catalogue.

428. Local Council of Women (Weston, Ont.)

✣ Weston, Ont.

LOCATION OF RECORDS: Archives of Ontario. (See Appendix for address.)

COLLECTION NAME: Forms part of: Provincial Council of Women of Ontario Papers (F 798, Series F).

RECORDS: Minutes, constitution and by-laws, financial records, correspondence, resolutions, scrapbooks, 1931-1964.
AMOUNT: 10 cm.
ACCESS: No restrictions.
FINDING AID: "Inventory of the Provincial Council of Women Papers."

429. London Lesbian Collective

✣ London, Ont. Formed 1977. Disbanded [1978?].

The goals of the London Lesbian Collective (LLC) were to develop a strong and active lesbian community in London and to nurture a positive self-image for lesbians. LLC held social events and published a newsletter.

Collection (a)

LOCATION OF RECORDS: Canadian Women's Movement Archives Collection, Morisset Library Special Collections, University of Ottawa. (See Appendix for address.)
COLLECTION NAME: London Lesbian Collective.
RECORDS: Policy statement, [1977?]; newsletters, correspondence, 1977-1978; clippings, 1978; organization history, notes.
AMOUNT: 3 cm.
CONDITION: Good.
ACCESS: Restricted; conditional access negotiable.

Collection (b)

LOCATION OF RECORDS: Canadian Gay Archives. (See Appendix for address.)
COLLECTION NAME: London Lesbian Collective.
RECORDS: Newsletters, 1977-1978; poster, 1977.

430. London Status of Women Action Group

✣ London, Ont. Formed 1978.

The London Status of Women Action Group (LSWAG) works to improve the status of women through education and political action. It publishes a monthly newsletter, *Matrix*.

LOCATION OF RECORDS: Canadian Women's Movement Archives Collection, Morisset Library Special Collections, University of Ottawa. (See Appendix for address.)
COLLECTION NAME: London Status of Women Action Group.
RECORDS: Newsletters (*Matrix*, 1984-1991); briefs, 1981, 1983; minutes, correspondence, budget, poster, 1985; profiles of committees, membership form, flyers, button.
AMOUNT: 10 cm of text, 1 poster, 1 button.
CONDITION: Good.
ACCESS: No restrictions.

431. London Women's Liberation

✣ London, Ont. Formed 1970. Disbanded [197-].

This organization grew out of several short-lived feminist groups active in London in 1969 and 1970: the Birth Control Group; two abortion rights groups, People for a Sane Society and Abortion Action; and a group of women in the Student Christian Movement. London Women's Liberation held consciousness-raising sessions, published a newsletter, and did public speaking.

LOCATION OF RECORDS: Canadian Women's Movement Archives Collection, Morisset Library Special Collections, University of Ottawa. (See Appendix for address.)
COLLECTION NAME: London Women's Liberation.
RECORDS: Organization history, [ca. 1971]; newsletters, 1970-1971; correspondence, 1969-1971; flyers, 1968-1970; proposal, 1972; membership lists, position papers, list of committees, songsheet.
AMOUNT: 1 cm.
CONDITION: Fair.
ACCESS: No restrictions.

432. London Women's Resource Centre

✣ London, Ont. Formed 1973. Disbanded [197-?].

The London Women's Resource Centre (LWRC) promoted the improvement of women's position in society. LWRC organized discussions, lectures, and films; it also had a lending library.

LOCATION OF RECORDS: Canadian Women's Movement Archives Collection, Morisset Library Special Collections, University of Ottawa. (See Appendix for address.)
COLLECTION NAME: London Women's Resource Centre.
RECORDS: Constitution, [ca. 1973]; newsletters (*Women's Centre Review*, 1973-1977); proposal, flyers.
AMOUNT: 4.5 cm.
CONDITION: Fair.
ACCESS: No restrictions.

433. McMaster Faculty Association. Committee to Study the Status of Women Faculty at McMaster

✣ Hamilton, Ont. Formed 1971. Disbanded [197-].

The committee examined the status of women faculty at McMaster University, especially with regard to salaries.

LOCATION OF RECORDS: Canadian Women's Movement Archives Collection, Morisset Library Special Collections, University of Ottawa. (See Appendix for address.)
COLLECTION NAME: McMaster Faculty Association. Committee to Study the Status of Women Faculty at McMaster.
RECORDS: Brief, 1971; correspondence, 1971-1972.
AMOUNT: 3 mm.
CONDITION: Good.
ACCESS: No restrictions.

434. McMaster Homophile Association

✣ Hamilton, Ont. Formed 1973. Disbanded [1977?].

The McMaster Homophile Association (MHA), at McMaster University, was originally known as the Hamilton McMaster Gay Liberation Movement, and subsequently as the Hamilton McMaster Homophile Association.

LOCATION OF RECORDS: Canadian Gay Archives. (See Appendix for address.)
COLLECTION NAME: McMaster Homophile Association (82-013).
RECORDS: Administrative files, correspondence, reports, publications, newsletters, miscellaneous records, 1973-1977.
AMOUNT: 26 cm.

435. McMaster Student Social Work Association. Sub-committee to Celebrate International Women's Year

✣ Hamilton, Ont. Formed 1975. Disbanded 1975.

This committee organized a one-day celebration at McMaster University in March 1975. The activities included a conference, a concert, and a dance.

LOCATION OF RECORDS: Canadian Women's Movement Archives Collection, Morisset Library Special Collections, University of Ottawa. (See Appendix for address.)
COLLECTION NAME: McMaster Student Social Work Association. Sub-committee to Celebrate International Women's Year.
RECORDS: Minutes, correspondence, flyers, 1975.
AMOUNT: 5 mm.
CONDITION: Good.
ACCESS: No restrictions.

436. McMaster University. Faculty of Humanities Council. Sub-committee to Encourage Qualified Women Students to Proceed to Honours and Graduate Study in the Humanities

✣ Hamilton, Ont. Formed [1971?]. Disbanded.

LOCATION OF RECORDS: Canadian Women's Movement Archives Collection, Morisset Library Special Collections, University of Ottawa. (See Appendix for address.)
COLLECTION NAME: McMaster University. Faculty of Humanities Council. Sub-committee to Encourage Qualified Women Students to Proceed to Honours and Graduate Study in the Humanities.
RECORDS: Minutes, 1971; correspondence, [1972?].
AMOUNT: 2 items.
CONDITION: Good.
ACCESS: No restrictions.

437. McMaster University. Senate. Equal Rights Review and Co-ordinating Committee

✣ Hamilton, Ont. Formed 1971. Disbanded.

The Equal Rights Review and Co-ordinating Committee of Senate was established in response to a petition from the Group for Equal Rights at McMaster. The committee's mandate was to ensure that McMaster University provided equal rights and opportunities to women. [See also Group for Equal Rights at McMaster (399).]

LOCATION OF RECORDS: Canadian Women's Movement Archives Collection, Morisset Library Special Collections, University of Ottawa. (See Appendix for address.)
COLLECTION NAME: McMaster University Equal Rights Review Committee.
RECORDS: Terms of reference, reports, agendas, minutes, 1971; correspondence, 1971-1972.
AMOUNT: 1 cm.
CONDITION: Good.
ACCESS: No restrictions.

438. Mama Quilla II

✣ Toronto, Ont. Formed 1978. Disbanded 1982.

Mama Quilla II was a feminist rock band composed of seven women. The band's concerts included benefits for feminist, lesbian and gay, and other causes. Mama Quilla II released a record in 1982.

LOCATION OF RECORDS: Canadian Women's Movement Archives Collection, Morisset Library Special Collections, University of Ottawa. (See Appendix for address.)
COLLECTION NAME: Mama Quilla II.
RECORDS: Clippings, 1979-1982; press release, 1981; record sleeve, 1982; correspondence, 1981-1982; lyric sheets, lists of performances, posters, flyers, profiles of members, contract, budget, lists of fees and conditions, photographs, play-lists, letterhead, sticker.
AMOUNT: 7 cm of text, 98 photographs, 16 posters.
CONDITION: Fair.
ACCESS: No restrictions.

439. March 8th Coalition

✣ Toronto, Ont. Formed 1977.

The March 8th Coalition is made up of Toronto women's organizations which together plan events for International Women's Day. It has occasionally been referred to as the Coalition for International Women's Day or the International Women's Day Coalition. [See also Toronto Socialist Feminist Action (505, 1085) and Women's Liberation Working Group (Toronto, Ont.) (562).]

LOCATION OF RECORDS: Canadian Women's Movement Archives Collection, Morisset Library Special Collections, University of Ottawa. (See Appendix for address.)
COLLECTION NAME: March 8th Coalition; SR 4/1-2.
RECORDS: Minutes, 1978, 1981-1986; agendas, 1980-1983; correspondence, 1978-1983, 1986; policy statements, 1979-1983; proposals, 1978, 1981-1986, 1989; financial records, 1981-1983, 1986; reports, 1979, 1986; contact lists, 1980-1982; historical information, speeches, stickers, 1982-1983; notes, 1978-1987, 1989; sound recordings (meeting), floor plan, press kit, 1983; press releases, 1980-1981, 1983-1985, 1989; pamphlets, 1978-1982, 1984-1986; flyers, 1978-1987, 1989-1990; programmes, 1979-1980, 1982-1983, 1985-1986, 1989; leaflets, 1978-1983, 1985-1987; booklets, 1982, 1984-1985, 1989; clippings, 1979, 1981-1983, 1987; maps, 1985-1986; lyric sheets, 1978-1981, 1983; schedules, pledge forms, 1981-1982; questionnaires, 1982; instructions, 1980; buttons, 1979-1990; posters.
AMOUNT: 30 cm of text, approx. 20 posters, 14 buttons, 2 sound recordings.
CONDITION: Good.
ACCESS: No restrictions.

440. May 28th Coalition for Abortion Rights

✣ Toronto, Ont. Formed 1977. Disbanded [1977?].

The coalition organized a demonstration to protest obstacles facing women in need of abortions in Toronto.

LOCATION OF RECORDS: Canadian Women's Movement Archives Collection, Morisset Library Special Collections, University of Ottawa. (See Appendix for address.)
COLLECTION NAME: May 28th Coalition for Abortion Rights.
RECORDS: Correspondence, notes, fact sheets, flyers, 1977.
AMOUNT: 2 mm.
CONDITION: Good.
ACCESS: No restrictions.

441. Metro Toronto Women's Credit Union

✣ Toronto, Ont. Formed 1975. Disbanded 1981.

The credit union was founded in response to discriminatory policies of other financial institutions. As a feminist alternative to such institutions, the credit union was dedicated to helping women accumulate and manage money. It was sponsored by the Women's Information Centre. [See also Women's Information Centre of Toronto (559).]

LOCATION OF RECORDS: Canadian Women's Movement Archives Collection, Morisset Library Special Collections, University of Ottawa. (See Appendix for address.)
COLLECTION NAME: Metro Toronto Women's Credit Union; SR 11/14.
RECORDS: By-laws, notices of meetings, press release, sound recording (interview), 1976; newsletters, 1976-1981; clippings, 1975, 1977, 1979; correspondence, 1975-1976, 1979; calendar, 1978; agendas, 1977; reports, 1976, 1978, 1980; minutes, 1976, 1980; financial records, debate, brochures, balloon, stickers, photographs.
AMOUNT: 3.5 cm of text, 1 sound recording, 2 photographs, 1 balloon.
CONDITION: Fair.
ACCESS: No restrictions.

442. Metropolitan Community Church of Toronto

✣ Toronto, Ont. Formed 1973.

The Metropolitan Community Church (MCC) of Toronto is a gay-positive, ecumenical Christian church.

LOCATION OF RECORDS: Canadian Gay Archives. (See Appendix for address.)
COLLECTION NAME: Wayne Hagen (82-031).
RECORDS: Minutes, reports, promotional material, correspondence, books, brochures, photographs, sound recordings, miscellaneous records, 1971-1978.
AMOUNT: 26 cm.

443. Mother Led Union

✣ Toronto, Ont. Formed 1974. Disbanded [198-?].

The Mother Led Union (MLU) was a local organization of single mothers which lobbied for improvements to social assistance and other social services.

LOCATION OF RECORDS: Canadian Women's Movement Archives Collection, Morisset Library Special Collections, University of Ottawa. (See Appendix for address.)
COLLECTION NAME: Mother Led Union.
RECORDS: Minutes, correspondence, 1974; newsletters, 1975; bulletin, 1976; statements of objectives, drafts of articles, brief, clippings, flyers, button.
AMOUNT: 2 cm of text, 1 button.
CONDITION: Good.
ACCESS: No restrictions.

444. Movement for Christian Feminism

✣ Toronto, Ont. Formed 1975. Disbanded.

The Movement for Christian Feminism (MCF) was an ecumenical project which examined how feminism could enrich and strengthen Christianity. MCF made contact with women in the churches and the women's movement and produced resources on feminism and Christianity. MCF helped to publish the newsletter *The Friends of Hagar*. [See also Friends of Hagar (392).]

Collection (a)

LOCATION OF RECORDS: Anglican Church of Canada, General Synod Archives. (See Appendix for address.)
COLLECTION NAME: Movement for Christian Feminism.
RECORDS: Minutes, proposal, reports, financial records, miscellaneous records, [197-].

Collection (b)

LOCATION OF RECORDS: Canadian Women's Movement Archives Collection, Morisset Library Special Collections, University of Ottawa. (See Appendix for address.)
COLLECTION NAME: Movement for Christian Feminism.
RECORDS: Organization history, report, minutes, notes, 1978; notice, registration form, 1975; list of events, 1975-1978; programme, 1976; correspondence, 1978-1980; conference records, 1979; clipping, 1977; position paper, thesis, bibliography, research paper, article, agenda, programme description, workshop records, pamphlets, flyers.
AMOUNT: 1.5 cm.
CONDITION: Good.
ACCESS: No restrictions.

445. Nellie's

✣ Toronto, Ont. Formed 1974.

Nellie's is an emergency shelter for women with or without children. The organization is incorporated under the name Women's Hostels. It also runs a second-stage housing programme.

Collection (a)

LOCATION OF RECORDS: Canadian Women's Movement Archives Collection, Morisset Library Special Collections, University of Ottawa. (See Appendix for address.)
COLLECTION NAME: Nellie's.
RECORDS: Minutes, 1985-1987; correspondence, 1977-1978, 1986; reports, 1976, 1979, 1984; policy statement, 1978; by-law, 1979; policy manual, 1985; clippings, 1973-1974, 1976-1980, 1983-1984; financial records, 1985-1986; notices, 1979-1980; ticket stub, 1980; position papers, membership list, fact sheet, pamphlet, flyers, posters, button.
AMOUNT: 3 cm of text, 3 posters, 1 button.
CONDITION: Good.
ACCESS: No restrictions.

Collection (b)

LOCATION OF RECORDS: National Archives of Canada. (See Appendix for address.)
COLLECTION NAME: Forms part of: June Callwood collection (MG 31, K 24, volumes 13-14).
RECORDS: Please see the note about National Archives of Canada collections, in entry # 2.

446. New College. Women's Studies Programme

✣ Toronto, Ont. Formed 1971.

New College is part of the University of Toronto (U of T). The women's studies programme was originally administered by the university but is now administered by the college. New College courses form the core of the programme and are supplemented by cross-listed courses from various U of T departments. (A separate women's studies programme is offered by another college at U of T, Scarborough College.) [See also Women's Studies Student Union (New College) (573).]

LOCATION OF RECORDS: Canadian Women's Movement Archives Collection, Morisset Library Special Collections, University of Ottawa. (See Appendix for address.)
COLLECTION NAME: University of Toronto. Women's Studies.
RECORDS: Minutes, 1972, 1982-1984; syllabuses, 1971-1976, 1981-1990; correspondence, 1971-1973, 1975-1977, 1983-1984, 1986, 1988-1990; reports, 1977-1978, 1983, 1985; newsletters (*Women's Studies Newsletter*, 1982-1986); brochures, 1973-1990; guidelines, 1981-1983, 1986; lecture outlines, 1981-1984, 1986; tests, 1981-1983; programme review, 1983; posters, 1983, 1989; pamphlets, 1985-1986, 1989; press

releases, 1973; order forms, questionnaires, survey results, financial records, 1972; lecture, 1974; journal, 1980; reading lists, bibliographies, course evaluations, student assignments, grading records, class lists, notes, essays, essay outline, presentation, schedules, proposals, flyers, clippings, educational material.
AMOUNT: 38 cm of text, 2 posters.
CONDITION: Good.
ACCESS: No restrictions.

447. New Feminists
✣ Toronto, Ont. Formed 1969. Disbanded [1973?].

This organization was formed by radical feminists and lesbians who split off from the Toronto Women's Liberation Movement. (Source: *Feminist Organizing for Change: The Contemporary Women's Movement in Canada*/Nancy Adamson, Linda Briskin, and Margaret McPhail. — Toronto: Oxford University Press, 1988.) The New Feminists organized demonstrations, did public speaking, and published a newsletter, *The New Feminist*. [See also Toronto Women's Liberation Movement (509) and Toronto Women's Caucus (508).]

Collection (a)
LOCATION OF RECORDS: Nellie Langford Rowell Library, York University. (See Appendix for address.)
COLLECTION NAME: Forms part of: Broadsides — WG.
RECORDS: Constitution, membership lists, brief, minutes, correspondence, flyer, eviction notice, agenda, article, songsheets, 1970; newsletters (*The New Feminist*, 1969-1973); reading list.
CONDITION: Fair.
ACCESS: No restrictions.

Collection (b)
LOCATION OF RECORDS: Canadian Women's Movement Archives Collection, Morisset Library Special Collections, University of Ottawa. (See Appendix for address.)
COLLECTION NAME: New Feminists.
RECORDS: Newsletters (*The New Feminist*, 1969-1973); organization history, clippings, 1970; correspondence, 1971; interview, 1972.
AMOUNT: 3 cm.
CONDITION: Good.
ACCESS: No restrictions.

Collection (c)
LOCATION OF RECORDS: Thomas Fisher Rare Book Library, University of Toronto. (See Appendix for address.)
COLLECTION NAME: Forms part of: F.M. Denison collection.
RECORDS: Newsletters (*The New Feminist*, 1969-1973).
AMOUNT: 14 items.
ACCESS: No restrictions.

448. New Left Caucus. Knitting Circle
✣ Toronto, Ont. Formed [ca. 1969]. Disbanded.

The New Left Caucus (NLC), established on the University of Toronto campus in 1969, was committed to developing a "mass revolutionary student movement." (Source: *Long Way from Home: The Story of the Sixties Generation in Canada*/Myrna Kostash. — Toronto: James Lorimer, 1980, p. 96.) The Knitting Circle of the New Left Caucus was a group of women who wrote a position paper criticizing attitudes within NLC to women and women's liberation.

LOCATION OF RECORDS: Canadian Women's Movement Archives Collection, Morisset Library Special Collections, University of Ottawa. (See Appendix for address.)
COLLECTION NAME: New Left Caucus, the Knitting Circle of.
RECORDS: Position paper, [ca. 1969].
AMOUNT: 8 pages.
CONDITION: Fair.
ACCESS: No restrictions.

449. New Left Committee. Women's Liberation Front
✣ Toronto, Ont. Formed [196-]. Disbanded.

LOCATION OF RECORDS: Canadian Women's Movement Archives Collection, Morisset Library Special Collections, University of Ottawa. (See Appendix for address.)
COLLECTION NAME: Women's Liberation Front of the New Left Committee.
RECORDS: Annotated bibliography, 1967.
AMOUNT: 4 pages.
CONDITION: Fair.
ACCESS: No restrictions.

450. Niagara Women's Magazine
✣ St Catharines, Ont. Formed [1975?]. Disbanded 1976.

Niagara Women's Magazine was a feminist publication for the Niagara region. It was originally called *Niagara Women This Year*.

LOCATION OF RECORDS: Canadian Women's Movement Archives Collection, Morisset Library Special Collections, University of Ottawa. (See Appendix for address.)
COLLECTION NAME: Niagara Women's Magazine.
RECORDS: Periodicals, 1975-1976.
AMOUNT: 1 cm.
CONDITION: Fair.
ACCESS: No restrictions.

451. Northern Women's Centre
✣ Thunder Bay, Ont. Formed 1973.

This organization is also known as the Northwestern Ontario Women's Centre. The *Northern Woman Journal* began as part of the Northern Women's Centre but moved away from the centre in October 1975. The centre hosted the First National Conference of Women's Centres in 1975. [See also Northern Woman Journal (1051).]

LOCATION OF RECORDS: Canadian Women's Movement Archives Collection, Morisset Library Special Collections, University of Ottawa. (See Appendix for address.)
COLLECTION NAME: Northern Women's Centre; Conf.: National Women's Centres Conference (March 1975, Thunder Bay, Ont.).
RECORDS: Periodicals (*Northern Woman Journal*, 1973-1976); conference records, 1975, 1980, 1987; correspondence, 1975; handbook, 1976; lecture, 1987; article, 1990; questionnaire, pamphlets, organization histories, flyers.
AMOUNT: 5 cm.
CONDITION: Good.
ACCESS: No restrictions.

452. October 25th Women's Action Coalition
✣ Toronto, Ont. Formed 1975. Disbanded 1975.

Originally called the May 10th March Committee, this group organized a feminist demonstration in Toronto during International Women's Year (1975). The demonstration dealt with equal pay for work of equal value, child care, marriage and property laws, birth control, and abortion. After the demonstration in May, the group changed its name to the October 25th Women's Action Coalition and attempted unsuccessfully to organize another demonstration for October.

LOCATION OF RECORDS: Canadian Women's Movement Archives Collection, Morisset Library Special Collections, University of Ottawa. (See Appendix for address.)

COLLECTION NAME: May 10th March Committee; October 25th Toronto Women's Action Coalition.

RECORDS: Minutes, correspondence, grant application, log, mailing list, press release, songsheet, notes, flyers, 1975.

AMOUNT: 1.5 cm.

CONDITION: Good.

ACCESS: No restrictions.

453. Ontario Association of Registered Nursing Assistants

✢ Toronto, Ont. Formed 1958.

The Ontario Association of Registered Nursing Assistants (OARNA) was originally called the Association of Certified Nursing Assistants. It grew out of the Sub-committee on Nursing Assistants of the Registered Nurses Association of Ontario (RNAO). (Source: Archives of Ontario finding aid, 1987.)

LOCATION OF RECORDS: Archives of Ontario. (See Appendix for address.)

COLLECTION NAME: Ontario Association of Registered Nursing Assistants Papers (F 897).

RECORDS: Minutes, correspondence, circulars, brochures, historical information, reports, constitution and by-laws, news bulletins, leaflets, book, 1953-1985.

ACCESS: No restrictions.

FINDING AID: "Inventory of the Ontario Association of Registered Nursing Assistants Papers."

454. Ontario Coalition for Abortion Clinics

✢ Toronto, Ont. Formed 1982.

The Ontario Coalition for Abortion Clinics (OCAC) was established to press for the legalization of free-standing abortion clinics (i.e., clinics outside of hospitals).

LOCATION OF RECORDS: Canadian Women's Movement Archives Collection, Morisset Library Special Collections, University of Ottawa. (See Appendix for address.)

COLLECTION NAME: Ontario Coalition for Abortion Clinics; SR 3/1.

RECORDS: Minutes, clippings, 1982-1983; correspondence, 1983-1989; article, tickets, 1988; press releases, 1983, 1987-1988; flyers, 1982-1990; mailing lists, 1978, 1982-1983; affidavit, list of names, 1982; press kit, outreach package, placards, sound recording (meeting), 1983; policy statements, forms, petitions, advertisement, newsletters, position papers, posters, photograph, book of coupons, dollar bill, T-shirts, buttons.

AMOUNT: 14 cm of text, 3 posters, 7 placards, 1 photograph, 1 sound recording, 2 T-shirts, 7 buttons.

CONDITION: Good.

ACCESS: No restrictions.

455. Ontario Coalition for Better Child Care

✢ Toronto, Ont. Formed [1981?].

The members of the Ontario Coalition for Better Child Care include child-care advocacy groups, parents, child-care centres, trade-union locals, and women's organizations. The coalition lobbies the provincial and federal governments for improvements to the child-care system. It used to be called the Ontario Coalition for Better Day Care.

LOCATION OF RECORDS: Canadian Women's Movement Archives Collection, Morisset Library Special Collections, University of Ottawa. (See Appendix for address.)

COLLECTION NAME: Ontario Coalition for Better Day Care — Toronto.

RECORDS: Minutes, 1982-1985; correspondence, 1982-1987; financial records, educational materials, 1983; proposal, 1985; newsletters, 1982-1988; poster, 1986; button, 1990; article, [after 1981]; petition, conference records, briefs, pamphlets, flyers.

AMOUNT: 3 cm of text, 1 poster, 1 button.

CONDITION: Good.

ACCESS: No restrictions.

456. Ontario Committee on the Status of Women

✢ Toronto, Ont. Formed 1972.

The Ontario Committee on the Status of Women (OCSW) was founded to press for the implementation of the recommendations of the Royal Commission on the Status of Women. OCSW's activities have included lobbying government and supporting women who sought equal pay and better working conditions.

LOCATION OF RECORDS: Canadian Women's Movement Archives Collection, Morisset Library Special Collections, University of Ottawa. (See Appendix for address.)

COLLECTION NAME: Ontario Committee on the Status of Women.

RECORDS: Briefs, 1972-1974, 1976-1980; membership lists, position papers, 1972-1973; mailing list, 1974; handbook, minutes, 1972; newsletters, 1972-1989; bulletin, 1973; membership forms, 1975, 1980; press releases, correspondence, clippings, flyers, notices of meetings, notes, registration form, contact list, reports, songsheet, pamphlet, lists of publications, questionnaire.

AMOUNT: 21 cm.

CONDITION: Fair.

ACCESS: No restrictions.

457. Ontario New Democratic Party. Women's Committee

✢ Toronto, Ont.

The Ontario New Democratic Party Women's Committee (ONDP Women's Committee) works to increase the participation of women in the party, develop policy recommendations, and "participate with women outside the Party in areas of mutual interest." (Source: ONDP Women's Committee constitution, 1980.) The committee was originally called the Provincial Committee on Women's Issues.

Collection (a)

LOCATION OF RECORDS: University of Toronto Archives. (See Appendix for address.)

COLLECTION NAME: Forms part of: Marianne Holder collection (UTA B88-0075).

RECORDS: Minutes, correspondence, photographs, report, conference records, financial records, constitution, newsletters, newsletter production records, membership lists, resolutions, recommendations, policy background papers, notices of meetings, notes, flyers, button, miscellaneous records, 1974-1983.

AMOUNT: Approx. 35 cm.

CONDITION: Good.

ACCESS: No restrictions.

FINDING AID: Box list available for Holder collection.

Collection (b)

LOCATION OF RECORDS: Queen's University Archives. (See Appendix for address.)

COLLECTION NAME: Forms part of: Co-operative Commonwealth Federation-New Democratic Party collection.

RECORDS: Correspondence, 1960-1965; subject files, [196-]; miscellaneous records, 1972-1974.

AMOUNT: Approx. 8 files.

458. Ontario Psychological Association. Task Force on the Status of Women in Psychology in Ontario

✢ Toronto, Ont. Formed 1976.

This task force was established by the Ontario Psychological Association to examine the 1976 report of the Canadian Psychological Association's Task Force on the Status of Women in Canadian Psychology, and to adapt that task force's findings to Ontario.

Collection (a)

LOCATION OF RECORDS: Archives of Ontario. (See Appendix for address.)

COLLECTION NAME: Forms part of: Ontario Psychological Association Papers (F 1383, box 21, files 6-7).

RECORDS: Miscellaneous records, 1976-1979.

AMOUNT: 2 files.

ACCESS: No restrictions on these particular files.

FINDING AID: "Inventory of the Ontario Psychological Association, 1946-1983, Papers."

Collection (b)

LOCATION OF RECORDS: Canadian Women's Movement Archives Collection, Morisset Library Special Collections, University of Ottawa. (See Appendix for address.)

COLLECTION NAME: Ontario Psychological Association. Task Force on the Status of Women in Psychology in Ontario.

RECORDS: Report, 1977.

AMOUNT: 1 cm.

CONDITION: Good.

ACCESS: No restrictions.

459. Ontario Women's Abortion Law Repeal Coalition

✢ Toronto, Ont. Formed 1971. Disbanded [197-].

The purpose of this coalition was to unite women and organizations supporting repeal of the abortion laws, in order to ensure that all women have easy, immediate access to abortion in the early months of pregnancy. The coalition, originally called the Ontario Women for an Abortion Law Repeal Coalition, organized the Ontario Women's Abortion Action Conference, held in Toronto in 1971.

LOCATION OF RECORDS: Canadian Women's Movement Archives Collection, Morisset Library Special Collections, University of Ottawa. (See Appendix for address.)

COLLECTION NAME: Ontario Women's Abortion Law Repeal Coalition.

RECORDS: Policy statement, contact list, newsletter, notes, statement of objectives, 1971; correspondence, 1971-1972; brief, 1972; guidelines, petition, announcement, flyers.

AMOUNT: 5 mm.

CONDITION: Good.

ACCESS: No restrictions.

460. Ontario Women's Action Coalition / Coalition des femmes de l'Ontario

[Renseignements en français, notice 370.]

✢ Toronto, Ont. Formed 1990.

The Ontario Women's Action Coalition (OWAC) is a province-wide coalition of feminist groups dedicated to helping women organize for social change. OWAC provides information, facilitates communication, and does advocacy and lobbying at the provincial level.

LOCATION OF RECORDS: Canadian Women's Movement Archives Collection, Morisset Library Special Collections, University of Ottawa. (See Appendix for address.)

COLLECTION NAME: Ontario Women's Action Coalition.

RECORDS: Sound recordings, newsletters, 1990-1992; minutes, correspondence, financial records, grant applications, membership lists, mailing lists, briefs, conference proceedings, press releases, 1989-1992; constitution, button, banner, 1990.

AMOUNT: Approx. 75 cm of text, approx. 50 sound recordings, 1 button, 1 banner.

CONDITION: Good.

ACCESS: As of 1992 the collection has not yet been processed.

461. Operation Family Rights

✢ Toronto, Ont. Formed [1973?]. Disbanded [197-].

Operation Family Rights (OFR) was an organization of women receiving social assistance. OFR lobbied for improvements to the social-assistance system.

LOCATION OF RECORDS: Canadian Women's Movement Archives Collection, Morisset Library Special Collections, University of Ottawa. (See Appendix for address.)

COLLECTION NAME: Operation Family Rights Newsletter.

RECORDS: Newsletters, 1973.

AMOUNT: 2 items.

CONDITION: Good.

ACCESS: No restrictions.

462. Organized Working Women (Toronto Area)

✢ Toronto, Ont. Formed 1976.

Organized Working Women (Toronto Area) (OWW) is an association open to women who are covered by a bona fide collective-bargaining unit, organizing committee, or union. Its purpose is "to unite women as women and as unionists in order to work vigorously within our unions." (Source: OWW pamphlet, [ca. 1978].) OWW has published a newspaper, *Union Woman*, and has organized a number of conferences, including Daycare and the Union Movement (1980) and Technology and the Working Woman (1982).

LOCATION OF RECORDS: Canadian Women's Movement Archives Collection, Morisset Library Special Collections, University of Ottawa. (See Appendix for address.)

COLLECTION NAME: Organized Working Women.

RECORDS: Constitution, 1976; minutes, financial statements, 1977-1979; periodicals (*Organized Working Women Newsletter*, 1976-1977, 1979; *Union Woman*, 1977-1985, 1987); correspondence, 1976-1980, 1983; resolutions, 1979-1980; agendas, 1977-1978; membership lists, 1979, 1985; clippings, 1978, 1982, 1985-1986; press release, 1977; proceedings, 1976-1977, 1979-1980; booklet, 1985; photographs, 1980-1981; conference records, 1980-1985; organization history, flyers, reports, briefs,

policy statement, fact sheet, programme, newspaper production guidelines, posters, buttons.
AMOUNT: 14 cm of text, 3 posters, 2 photographs, 3 buttons.
CONDITION: Good.
ACCESS: No restrictions.

463. OtherWise: A Feminist Newspaper at U of T

✣ Toronto, Ont. Formed 1984. Disbanded [1990?].

OtherWise was a feminist newspaper at the University of Toronto, run by a collective of women.

LOCATION OF RECORDS: Canadian Women's Movement Archives Collection, Morisset Library Special Collections, University of Ottawa. (See Appendix for address.)
COLLECTION NAME: OtherWise.
RECORDS: Minutes, correspondence, financial records, 1984-1985; clipping, 1985; production schedule, 1986; periodicals (*OtherWise: A Feminist Newspaper at U of T*, 1984-1987, 1990); guidelines, interviews, contact lists, articles, distribution records, flyers, notes, press release.
AMOUNT: 7 cm.
CONDITION: Good.
ACCESS: No restrictions.

464. Ottawa Coalition for Reproductive Choice

✣ Ottawa, Ont. Formed 1983. Disbanded 1983.

This coalition of groups and individuals (also known as OCRC) advocated the repeal of Section 251 of the Criminal Code and supported the Morgentaler Clinic in Toronto.

LOCATION OF RECORDS: Canadian Women's Movement Archives Collection, Morisset Library Special Collections, University of Ottawa. (See Appendix for address.)
COLLECTION NAME: Ottawa Coalition for Reproductive Choice.
RECORDS: Minutes, statement of principles, mailing list, correspondence, press release, flyers, ticket, notes, 1983.
AMOUNT: 2 cm.
CONDITION: Good.
ACCESS: No restrictions.

465. Ottawa Local Council of Women

✣ Ottawa, Ont.

Collection (a)

LOCATION OF RECORDS: National Archives of Canada. (See Appendix for address.)
COLLECTION NAME: Ottawa Local Council of Women (MG 28, I 32).
RECORDS: Please see the note about National Archives of Canada collections, in entry # 2.

Collection (b)

LOCATION OF RECORDS: Doris Lewis Rare Book Room, University of Waterloo Library. (See Appendix for address.)
COLLECTION NAME: Forms part of: Elizabeth Smith Shortt Collection (WA10).
RECORDS: Correspondence, 1914, 1916; clippings, 1913-1916, 1923; notes.
FINDING AID: "Finding Aid No. 10."

466. Ottawa Women's Centre

[See also entry # 1061 (in Part II), which lists other records of this organization.]

✣ Ottawa, Ont. Formed 1972. Disbanded 1980.

The Ottawa Women's Centre, also known as the Women's Centre of Ottawa-Carleton, was committed to the struggle for the liberation of women. The centre provided various services, resources, and activities in support of this aim. The centre's French name was le Centre des femmes d'Ottawa. [See also Chez nous (1008) and Ottawa Women's Information and Referral Service (1062).]

LOCATION OF RECORDS: Canadian Women's Movement Archives Collection, Morisset Library Special Collections, University of Ottawa. (See Appendix for address.)
COLLECTION NAME: Ottawa Women's Centre.
RECORDS: Newsletters, 1972-1977; correspondence, 1973, 1975; proposal, 1972; flyers.
AMOUNT: 2.5 cm.
ACCESS: No restrictions.

467. Ottawa Women's Liberation Committee

✣ Ottawa, Ont. Formed [1969?]. Disbanded.

The Ottawa Women's Liberation Committee demanded reproductive rights, day-care centres, equal opportunities in education, and equality in the work force.

LOCATION OF RECORDS: Canadian Women's Movement Archives Collection, Morisset Library Special Collections, University of Ottawa. (See Appendix for address.)
COLLECTION NAME: Ottawa Women's Liberation Committee.
RECORDS: Proposal, 1969; newsletter (*Women's Liberation Newsletter*, [1970?]).
AMOUNT: 2 items.
CONDITION: Good.
ACCESS: No restrictions.

468. Parents' Information Bureau

✣ Kitchener, Ont. Formed [ca. 1930]. Disbanded [ca. 1976].

The Parents' Information Bureau was a birth-control clinic. In 1937 a nurse employed by the clinic was tried for distributing birth-control information and contraceptive devices. (Source: University of Waterloo Library finding aid.)

Collection (a)

LOCATION OF RECORDS: Doris Lewis Rare Book Room, University of Waterloo Library. (See Appendix for address.)
COLLECTION NAME: Parents' Information Bureau (GA58).
RECORDS: Correspondence, leaflet, legal agreement, application card, instructions, price lists, report, clippings, form letters, poem, biographical material, speeches, publications, miscellaneous records, 1930-1976.
AMOUNT: 91 cm.
FINDING AID: Finding aid available.

Collection (b)

LOCATION OF RECORDS: Doris Lewis Rare Book Room, University of Waterloo Library.
COLLECTION NAME: Dorothea Palmer (WA17).
RECORDS: Legal records, correspondence, 1936-1937; research materials, pamphlets, clippings, miscellaneous records, [193-].
AMOUNT: 1.17 m.
FINDING AID: "Finding Aid No. 17."

Collection (c)
LOCATION OF RECORDS: Archives of Ontario. (See Appendix for address.)
COLLECTION NAME: Forms part of: Planned Parenthood Ontario Papers (F 825, Series B, MU 4468, A.R. Kaufman).
RECORDS: Correspondence, photographs, [1976?]; pamphlet, 1936-1937; organization history.
ACCESS: No restrictions.
FINDING AID: "Inventory of the Planned Parenthood Ontario Papers."

469. Pauline McGibbon Cultural Centre

✣ Toronto, Ont. Formed 1975. Disbanded 1981.

Originally called the Women's Cultural Centre, this centre for women in the arts held events featuring music, drama, visual arts, poetry, and lectures. [See also Women's Cultural Building Collective (554).]

LOCATION OF RECORDS: Canadian Women's Movement Archives Collection, Morisset Library Special Collections, University of Ottawa. (See Appendix for address.)
COLLECTION NAME: Pauline McGibbon Cultural Centre.
RECORDS: Clippings, 1976, 1979-1980, 1982; correspondence, 1976-1977, 1980; publicity material, motions, flyers.
AMOUNT: 1 cm.
CONDITION: Fair.
ACCESS: No restrictions.

470. Peterborough Women's Committee

✣ Peterborough, Ont. Formed 1977. Disbanded 1987.

The Peterborough Women's Committee operated a resource centre which housed a library of material about women.

LOCATION OF RECORDS: Trent University Archives. (See Appendix for address.)
COLLECTION NAME: Peterborough Women's Committee Papers (88-023).
RECORDS: Subject files, library catalogues, library circulation records, reports, clippings, directory, correspondence.
AMOUNT: 2 m.
ACCESS: No restrictions.
FINDING AID: "Peterborough Women's Committee Papers."

471. Peterborough Women's Place

✣ Peterborough, Ont. Formed 1973. Disbanded [1975?].

This women's centre was devoted to obtaining and securing rights for women. Its goal was to bring together women of all ages and backgrounds, in order to share ideas and find practical solutions to difficulties faced by women.

LOCATION OF RECORDS: Canadian Women's Movement Archives Collection, Morisset Library Special Collections, University of Ottawa. (See Appendix for address.)
COLLECTION NAME: Peterborough Women's Place.
RECORDS: Correspondence, grant application, 1973; mailing list, 1974; terms of reference, report, flyer, articles, calendar of activities, newsletters.
AMOUNT: 1 cm.
CONDITION: Good.
ACCESS: No restrictions.

472. Planned Parenthood Ontario

[See also entry # 1065 (in Part II), which lists other records of this organization.]

✣ Toronto, Ont. Formed 1972.

Planned Parenthood Ontario (PPO) promotes responsible sexuality and reproductive choice through public education and advocacy.

LOCATION OF RECORDS: Archives of Ontario. (See Appendix for address.)
COLLECTION NAME: Planned Parenthood Ontario Papers (F 825).
RECORDS: Articles, correspondence, newsletters, questionnaires, clippings, briefs, forms, minutes, reports, conference material, seminar material, publicity material, financial records, miscellaneous records, 1972-1980.
AMOUNT: 2.7 m.
ACCESS: No restrictions.
FINDING AID: "Inventory of the Planned Parenthood Ontario Papers."

473. Planned Parenthood Society of Hamilton

[See also entry # 1066 (in Part II), which lists other records of this organization.]

✣ Hamilton, Ont. Formed 1931.

The Planned Parenthood Society of Hamilton (PPSH) is dedicated to creating a community where responsible and healthy sexual behaviour is practised and supported. PPSH was originally known as the Maternal Health Clinic, and subsequently as the Birth Control Society of Hamilton.

LOCATION OF RECORDS: Hamilton Public Library, Special Collections. (See Appendix for address.)
COLLECTION NAME: Planned Parenthood Society of Hamilton.
RECORDS: Minute books, annual reports, correspondence, financial statements, 1933-1971; speeches, photographs, clippings, scrapbooks, constitution, by-laws, miscellaneous records.
FINDING AID: Finding aid available.

474. Political Lesbians of Toronto

✣ Toronto, Ont. Formed 1979. Disbanded.

Political Lesbians of Toronto (PLOT) was a lesbian-feminist discussion group committed to radical social, economic, and political change. PLOT was a splinter group from the Lesbian Organization of Toronto. [See also Lesbian Organization of Toronto (424).]

LOCATION OF RECORDS: Canadian Women's Movement Archives Collection, Morisset Library Special Collections, University of Ottawa. (See Appendix for address.)
COLLECTION NAME: Political Lesbians of Toronto.
RECORDS: Drafts of articles, 1979; clippings, 1979-1980.
AMOUNT: 1 mm.
CONDITION: Good.
ACCESS: Restricted; conditional access negotiable.

475. Political Lesbians United about the Media

✣ Toronto, Ont.

Political Lesbians United about the Media (PLUM) presented a brief to the Canadian Radio-Television and Telecommunications Commission criticizing the media's portrayal of lesbians.

LOCATION OF RECORDS: Canadian Gay Archives. (See Appendix for address.)
COLLECTION NAME: Political Lesbians United about the Media (PLUM) (vertical file).
RECORDS: Brief, 1980.
AMOUNT: 1 item.
CONDITION: Good.

PART I: RECORDS HELD BY ARCHIVES / PARTIE I : FONDS DÉTENUS PAR DES ARCHIVES

International Women's Day march / Manifestation de la Journée internationale des femmes, Toronto, 1982
Photograph by / Photo prise par Nancy L. Adamson
Photo #571
CWMA Collection / Fonds de l'ACMF

476. Provincial Council of Women of Ontario

[See also entry # 1069 (in Part II), which lists other records of this organization.]

✣ Formed 1923.

The Provincial Council of Women of Ontario (PCWO) is a network of local councils of women throughout the province.

Collection (a)

LOCATION OF RECORDS: Archives of Ontario. (See Appendix for address.)
COLLECTION NAME: Provincial Council of Women of Ontario (F 798).
RECORDS: Minutes, agendas, notices, correspondence, briefs, resolutions, nomination papers, lists of officers, reports, speeches, presentations, publicity material, constitutions, financial records, procedure manual, mailing lists, project files, visitors' registers, yearbooks, reference material, miscellaneous records, 1926-1973.
AMOUNT: 2.65 m.
ACCESS: No restrictions.
FINDING AID: "Inventory of the Provincial Council of Women of Ontario Papers."

Collection (b)

LOCATION OF RECORDS: Archives of Ontario.
COLLECTION NAME: Forms part of: Anastazja Kozlowski Papers (POL:0012), in the Multicultural History Society of Ontario Papers (F 1405).
RECORDS: Miscellaneous records, 1960-1967.
ACCESS: No restrictions.
FINDING AID: "Inventory to the Multicultural History Society of Ontario Papers."

477. Queen's Homophile Association. Conference Steering Committee

✣ Kingston, Ont.

The committee organized a 1976 conference at Queen's University entitled "The Not-So-Invisible Woman: Lesbian Perspectives in the Gay Movement."

Collection (a)

LOCATION OF RECORDS: Canadian Women's Movement Archives Collection, Morisset Library Special Collections, University of Ottawa. (See Appendix for address.)
COLLECTION NAME: Conf.: Lesbian Conference, 1st Ontario, May 1976, Kingston.
RECORDS: Conference records, 1976.
AMOUNT: 5 mm.
ACCESS: Restricted; conditional access negotiable.

Collection (b)

LOCATION OF RECORDS: Canadian Gay Archives. (See Appendix for address.)
COLLECTION NAME: Conf.: The Not-So-Invisible Woman: Lesbian Perspectives in the Gay Movement, Kingston, May 22-24, 1976 (vertical file).
RECORDS: Conference records, 1976.
AMOUNT: 4 items.

478. Queen's University. Women's Studies Programme. Lesbian Speakers Series Committee

✣ Kingston, Ont. Formed 1989.

This committee (also known as the Ad Hoc Lesbian Speakers Series Committee) organized a series of guest lectures which explored ways to increase the visibility of lesbians and counteract homophobia within the Women's Studies Programme at Queen's University and in women's studies generally.

LOCATION OF RECORDS: Canadian Women's Movement Archives Collection, Morisset Library Special Collections, University of Ottawa. (See Appendix for address.)
COLLECTION NAME: Queen's University. Lesbian Speakers Series Committee.
RECORDS: Report, 1990.
AMOUNT: 5 mm.
CONDITION: Good.
ACCESS: Restricted; conditional access negotiable.

479. Queen's University. Women's Study Action Committee

✣ Kingston, Ont. Disbanded.

The Women's Study Action Committee was concerned with the position of women at Queen's University and in society generally.

LOCATION OF RECORDS: Canadian Women's Movement Archives Collection, Morisset Library Special Collections, University of Ottawa. (See Appendix for address.)
COLLECTION NAME: Queen's University. Women's Study Action Committee.
RECORDS: Brief, 1972.
AMOUNT: 6 pages.
CONDITION: Fair.
ACCESS: No restrictions.

480. Radio Free Women

✣ Toronto, Ont. Formed 1973. Disbanded [before 1977].

Radio Free Women (RFW) attempted to establish a non-profit community radio station, in order to produce non-sexist programmes and give women opportunities in radio production. RFW (sometimes called Radio Free Women/Radio Libres Femmes) produced programmes for a station at the University of Toronto.

LOCATION OF RECORDS: Canadian Women's Movement Archives Collection, Morisset Library Special Collections, University of Ottawa. (See Appendix for address.)
COLLECTION NAME: Radio Free Women.
RECORDS: Clippings, press releases, 1973-1974; minutes, 1974; pamphlet, article, flyer.
AMOUNT: 2 mm.
CONDITION: Good.
ACCESS: No restrictions.

481. Rape Crisis Centre (Hamilton)

✣ Hamilton, Ont. Formed 1975.

The Rape Crisis Centre (Hamilton) provides support and counselling to victims and educates the public about sexual assault. In 1976 the centre organized the "One Day Awareness Conference."

LOCATION OF RECORDS: Canadian Women's Movement Archives Collection, Morisset Library Special Collections, University of Ottawa. (See Appendix for address.)
COLLECTION NAME: Rape Crisis Centre (Hamilton).
RECORDS: Funding application, clipping, 1979; conference records, 1976; pamphlets.
AMOUNT: 2.5 cm.
CONDITION: Good.
ACCESS: No restrictions.

482. Redlight Theatre

✣ Toronto, Ont. Formed 1974. Disbanded [197-?].

This theatre company produced plays by and about women and gave women opportunities to work in the technical, administrative, and artistic areas of theatre.

LOCATION OF RECORDS: Canadian Women's Movement Archives Collection, Morisset Library Special Collections, University of Ottawa. (See Appendix for address.)
COLLECTION NAME: Redlight Theatre.
RECORDS: Organization history, interview, [ca. 1976]; press releases, flyers, 1974-1976; programme, correspondence, 1975; clipping, 1974; posters.
AMOUNT: 1 cm of text, 1 poster.
CONDITION: Good.
ACCESS: No restrictions.

483. Regional Lesbian Conference (Ontario). Coordinating Committee

✣ Toronto, Ont.

This committee organized the 1983 Regional Lesbian Conference for Ontario.

LOCATION OF RECORDS: Canadian Women's Movement Archives Collection, Morisset Library Special Collections, University of Ottawa. (See Appendix for address.)
COLLECTION NAME: Conf.: "Lesbian Conf.", Ontario, 1983.
RECORDS: Conference records, 1983.
AMOUNT: 2 cm.
ACCESS: Restricted; conditional access negotiable.

484. Revolutionary Prostitutes League

✣ Toronto, Ont. Formed 1978. Disbanded.

The Revolutionary Prostitutes League demanded an end to the oppression of prostitutes by the police and the state. The organization did public education about issues such as the distinction between legalizing and decriminalizing prostitution.

LOCATION OF RECORDS: Canadian Women's Movement Archives Collection, Morisset Library Special Collections, University of Ottawa. (See Appendix for address.)
COLLECTION NAME: Revolutionary Prostitutes League.
RECORDS: Statements of demands, flyers.
AMOUNT: 5 mm.
CONDITION: Good.
ACCESS: No restrictions.

485. Ryerson Polytechnical Institute. Employment and Educational Equity Office

✣ Toronto, Ont.

The office implements the employment and educational equity programme established at Ryerson Polytechnical Institute in 1984.

LOCATION OF RECORDS: Ryerson Polytechnical Institute Archives. (See Appendix for address.)
RECORDS: Reports, 1986, 1988, 1990-1991; newsletters, 1987-1988; pamphlet, 1987; notices, 1986; census, 1990; clippings, photographs, related material.

486. Ryerson Polytechnical Institute. Office of Harassment Prevention Services

✣ Toronto, Ont. Formed 1990.

The Office of Harassment Prevention Services (within the Department of Campus Safety and Security Services at Ryerson Polytechnical Institute) provides information about the issue of harassment and offers an advisory service to parties involved in incidents which appear to constitute harassment. The Ryerson Harassment Policy, in addition to addressing sexual harassment, recognizes other forms of harassment related to prohibited grounds for discrimination in the Ontario Human Rights Code.

LOCATION OF RECORDS: Ryerson Polytechnical Institute Archives. (See Appendix for address.)
RECORDS: Reports, handbook, policy and procedures, 1991; correspondence, clippings, pamphlets, related material.

487. Sappho Sound

✣ Toronto, Ont. Formed [1977?]. Disbanded [1978?].

Sappho Sound was a collectively run company, which produced concerts. It provided exposure for women musicians and training and employment for women in concert production.

LOCATION OF RECORDS: Canadian Women's Movement Archives Collection, Morisset Library Special Collections, University of Ottawa. (See Appendix for address.)
COLLECTION NAME: Sappho Sound.
RECORDS: Minutes, poster, correspondence, 1977-1978; financial records, contracts, programme, 1978; ticket, 1977; description of organization, position paper, mailing lists, time sheets, letterhead design, flyers.
AMOUNT: 10 cm of text, 1 poster.
CONDITION: Good.
ACCESS: No restrictions.

488. Sarnia-Lambton Status of Women Committee

✣ Sarnia, Ont.

This committee opened the Women's Centre in Sarnia in 1975.

LOCATION OF RECORDS: Canadian Women's Movement Archives Collection, Morisset Library Special Collections, University of Ottawa. (See Appendix for address.)
COLLECTION NAME: Sarnia Women's Centre.
RECORDS: Newsletters (*Sarnia-Lambton Status of Women Newsletter*, 1976; *The Women's Forum*, 1974-1977); correspondence.
AMOUNT: 5 mm.
CONDITION: Fair.
ACCESS: No restrictions.

489. Service Employees' Union. Local 268

✣ Thunder Bay, Ont. Formed 1974. Disbanded [197-].

Local 268 of the Service Employees' Union was formed to demand better wages and benefits for workers at the Port Arthur Clinic, a medical facility employing about ninety women. The union represented the workers during a two-year strike.

LOCATION OF RECORDS: Canadian Women's Movement Archives Collection, Morisset Library Special Collections, University of Ottawa. (See Appendix for address.)
COLLECTION NAME: Service Employees' Union. Local 268.

RECORDS: Correspondence, 1975; press release, summary of demands, organization history, [1975?]; workshop materials.
AMOUNT: 2 mm.
CONDITION: Good.
ACCESS: No restrictions.

490. Soroptimist International of Toronto

✣ Toronto, Ont. Formed 1934.

The original goal of Soroptimist International of Toronto (which has also been called the Toronto Soroptimist Club) was to help older business and professional women who were in financial need during the Depression. This business and professional women's service organization has since undertaken a variety of projects helping women in need. It also sponsored the Venture Club of Toronto, which existed from 1944 to 1981 and which had similar goals. (Source: Archives of Ontario finding aid, 1986.)

Collection (a)

LOCATION OF RECORDS: Archives of Ontario. (See Appendix for address.)
COLLECTION NAME: Soroptimist International of Toronto Papers (F 1181); the photographs have been transferred to the Picture Collection.
RECORDS: Minutes, annual reports, financial records, subject files, scrapbooks, photographs, bulletins, publicity material, miscellaneous records, 1933-1986.
AMOUNT: 4.5 m.
FINDING AID: "Inventory of the Soroptimist International of Toronto Papers."

Collection (b)

LOCATION OF RECORDS: National Archives of Canada. (See Appendix for address.)
COLLECTION NAME: Forms part of: Kate Scott Aitken collection (MG 30, D 206).
RECORDS: Please see the note about National Archives of Canada collections, in entry # 2.

491. Southern Ontario Association of Unitarian-Universalist Women

The Southern Ontario Association of Unitarian-Universalist Women (SOAUUW) is a branch of the Unitarian Universalist Women's Federation (UUWF), which was established "to identify, as a religiously motivated group, the Unitarian Universalist women's concern for all women as persons and to eradicate the traditional image of women as sex symbols and male dependents." (Source: SOAUUW report, 1971.)

LOCATION OF RECORDS: Canadian Women's Movement Archives Collection, Morisset Library Special Collections, University of Ottawa. (See Appendix for address.)
COLLECTION NAME: Unitarian Universalist Women's Federation.
RECORDS: Conference report, 1971.
AMOUNT: 1 mm.
CONDITION: Good.
ACCESS: No restrictions.

492. Students' Administrative Council (University of Toronto). Women's Commission

✣ Toronto, Ont. Formed 1973.

The Students' Administrative Council (SAC) at the University of Toronto established the Women's Committee in 1973; the Women's Commission, established in 1974/75, replaced the committee. The SAC Women's Commission disseminates information on issues concerning women and conducts research into areas potentially affecting the status of women at the university.

LOCATION OF RECORDS: Canadian Women's Movement Archives Collection, Morisset Library Special Collections, University of Ottawa. (See Appendix for address.)
COLLECTION NAME: University of Toronto. Students' Administrative Council. Women's Commission.
RECORDS: Minutes, 1977; notes, 1984; clippings, 1973, 1980; conference records, 1973; correspondence, 1980; organization history, drawings, pamphlets, flyers, petition.
AMOUNT: 5 mm.
CONDITION: Good.
ACCESS: No restrictions.

493. Take Back the Night Committee (Toronto, Ont.)

✣ Toronto, Ont. Formed 1980.

This committee was established to organize a "Take Back the Night" march in Toronto, as part of an international movement protesting violence against women. The committee worked in co-operation with the Toronto Rape Crisis Centre. [See also Toronto Rape Crisis Centre (504).]

LOCATION OF RECORDS: Canadian Women's Movement Archives Collection, Morisset Library Special Collections, University of Ottawa. (See Appendix for address.)
COLLECTION NAME: Take Back the Night Demonstrations — 1980 — Toronto.
RECORDS: Minutes, press releases, 1980; flyers, agendas, reports, [ca.1980].
AMOUNT: 4 mm.
CONDITION: Good.
ACCESS: No restrictions.

494. Task Force on Violence in Lesbian Relationships

✣ Toronto, Ont. Formed 1985. Disbanded [1986?].

The purpose of this task force was to provide resources about non-consensual violence (i.e., physical, sexual, or mental abuse) in lesbian relationships. The group was also referred to as the Task Force on Lesbians in Violent Relationships and as the Violence in Lesbian Relationships Political Action Group.

LOCATION OF RECORDS: Canadian Women's Movement Archives Collection, Morisset Library Special Collections, University of Ottawa. (See Appendix for address.)
COLLECTION NAME: Task Force on Violence in Lesbian Relationships.
RECORDS: Minutes, 1985-1986; survey, correspondence, financial records, 1986; resource material.
AMOUNT: 2 cm.
CONDITION: Fair.
ACCESS: Restricted; conditional access negotiable.

495. The Three of Cups

✣ Toronto, Ont. Formed 1975. Disbanded 1978.

The Three of Cups was a women's café. Concerts were sometimes held at the Three of Cups. [See also Clementyne's Café (369).]

Collection (a)

LOCATION OF RECORDS: Canadian Women's Movement Archives Collection, Morisset Library Special Collections, University of Ottawa. (See Appendix for address.)

COLLECTION NAME: Three of Cups — Toronto; SR 11/1-2A, 11/3.
RECORDS: Minutes, newsletters, 1976-1978; sound recordings (interview, concert), 1976; correspondence, questionnaire, 1978; contracts, membership lists, 1977; financial records, ticket stubs, flyers, poster, membership card, rubber stamp, slide.
AMOUNT: 4 cm of text, 2 sound recordings, 1 poster, 1 rubber stamp, 1 slide.
CONDITION: Good.
ACCESS: No restrictions.

Collection (b)

LOCATION OF RECORDS: Canadian Gay Archives. (See Appendix for address.)
COLLECTION NAME: Three of Cups (vertical file).
RECORDS: Newsletters, 1976-1977; flyers, 1977-1978; poster.

496. Toronto and Area Council of Women

✣ Toronto, Ont. Formed 1893.

Originally called the Local Council of Women of Toronto, this federation of local women's organizations has dealt with a range of social issues, including women's issues. (Source: Archives of Ontario finding aid, 1991.)

Collection (a)

LOCATION OF RECORDS: Archives of Ontario. (See Appendix for address.)
COLLECTION NAME: Toronto and Area Council of Women Papers (F 805).
RECORDS: Minutes, 1903-1938, 1941-1973, 1975-1977, 1980-1982, 1984-1987; bulletins (*The Councillor*, 1953-1978, 1982, 1984-1990); directories, 1930-1951, 1953-1990; attendance registers, 1935-1938, 1941-1955; annual reports, 1925-1926, 1932, 1935-1937, 1963-1964, 1966; drafts of reports, 1932-1984; resolutions, briefs, 1975-1989; scrapbooks, [195-]-[196-]; financial records, 1936-1975; committee reports, 1969-1974; correspondence, 1965-1968; organization history, 1978; press releases, 1893-1901; constitution, by-laws, standing rules, miscellaneous records.
AMOUNT: 2.44 m.
ACCESS: No restrictions.
FINDING AID: "Inventory of the Toronto and Area Council of Women Papers."

Collection (b)

LOCATION OF RECORDS: Thomas Fisher Rare Book Library, University of Toronto. (See Appendix for address.)
COLLECTION NAME: Forms part of: F.M. Denison collection.
RECORDS: Annual reports, 1903, 1911-1912, 1915-1916.
ACCESS: No restrictions.

497. Toronto Area Gays

✣ Toronto, Ont. Formed [1975].

Toronto Area Gays (TAG) established a telephone line offering peer counselling.

LOCATION OF RECORDS: Canadian Gay Archives. (See Appendix for address.)
COLLECTION NAME: Forms part of: Peter Zorzi collection (88-031).
RECORDS: Membership records, correspondence, financial records, logbooks, miscellaneous records, 1975-1986.
FINDING AID: "What We Did, and Why We Did It (from the Cheap Seats at the Revolution: A Monologue on TAG in the 1970s, with Entertaining Supplementary Harangues)."

498. Toronto Business and Professional Women's Club

✣ Toronto, Ont. Formed 1910.

This club was originally called the Canadian Business Women's Club. Its goals include improving the status of business and professional women. (Source: Archives of Ontario finding aid, 1990.) [See also Council of Business and Professional Women's Clubs of Metropolitan Toronto (381).]

Collection (a)

LOCATION OF RECORDS: Archives of Ontario. (See Appendix for address.)
COLLECTION NAME: Toronto Business and Professional Women's Club Papers (F 2085).
RECORDS: By-laws, rules of procedure, 1959, [ca. 1975]; minutes, 1962-1974; annual reports, 1972-1975; register of directors, 1949-1969; attendance records, 1972-1974; rosters, 1951-1954, 1956-1962, 1964-1970; legal agreement, 1949; pamphlets, 1965-1971; membership lists, correspondence, reports, financial records, notices, agendas, clippings, newsletters.
AMOUNT: 69 cm.
CONDITION: Good.
ACCESS: No restrictions.
FINDING AID: "Inventory of the Toronto Business and Professional Women's Club."

Collection (b)

LOCATION OF RECORDS: National Archives of Canada. (See Appendix for address.)
COLLECTION NAME: Forms part of: Kate Scott Aitken collection (MG 30, D 206).
RECORDS: Please see the note about National Archives of Canada collections, in entry # 2.

Collection (c)

LOCATION OF RECORDS: National Archives of Canada.
COLLECTION NAME: Forms part of: Elsie Gregory MacGill collection (MG 31, K 7).
RECORDS: Please see the note about National Archives of Canada collections, in entry # 2.

499. Toronto Centre for Lesbian and Gay Studies

✣ Toronto, Ont. Formed 1988.

The Toronto Centre for Lesbian and Gay Studies (TCLGS) is committed to fostering lesbian and gay studies throughout Canada, with a focus on Canadian, historical, and minority subjects. The centre holds lectures and offers awards.

LOCATION OF RECORDS: Canadian Women's Movement Archives Collection, Morisset Library Special Collections, University of Ottawa. (See Appendix for address.)
COLLECTION NAME: Toronto Centre for Lesbian and Gay Studies.
RECORDS: Minutes, agendas, flyers, correspondence, 1988-1990; press releases, plan, 1989-1990; proposals, incorporation records, 1988; newsletters (*centre/fold*, 1989-1990); mailing list, [1989?]; newsletter material, 1989; invitation, poster, 1990.
AMOUNT: 2 cm of text, 1 poster.
CONDITION: Good.
ACCESS: Restricted; conditional access negotiable.

500. Toronto Committee to Defend Dr Morgentaler

✣ Toronto, Ont. Formed [1973 or 1974]. Disbanded.

The committee worked to bring about the freedom of Dr Henry Morgentaler (arrested on abortion charges). It also advocated the removal of abortion from the Criminal Code. [See also B.C. Committee to Defend Dr Morgentaler (110).]

LOCATION OF RECORDS: Canadian Women's Movement Archives Collection,

Morisset Library Special Collections, University of Ottawa. (See Appendix for address.)
COLLECTION NAME: Toronto Committee to Defend Dr Morgentaler.
RECORDS: Correspondence, press releases, 1974-1975; fact sheet, flyers, declaration, 1974; pamphlets, 1975; clipping.
AMOUNT: 5 mm.
CONDITION: Good.
ACCESS: No restrictions.

501. Toronto Gay Action

✣ Toronto, Ont. Formed 1971. Disbanded [ca. 1973].

Toronto Gay Action (TGA) worked toward an end to all legal and social discrimination against gay men and lesbians.

LOCATION OF RECORDS: Canadian Gay Archives. (See Appendix for address.)
COLLECTION NAME: Toronto Gay Action (89-058).
RECORDS: Minutes, correspondence, financial records, briefs, subject files, press releases, clippings, flyers, 1971-1972.
AMOUNT: 7 cm.

502. Toronto Gay Community Council

✣ Toronto, Ont. Formed 1981.

The council (also known as TGCC) promotes the exchange of ideas and information and works for legal reform and gay-positive policing. TGCC established an Advisory Committee on Police, and it sponsored the 1982 conference "Doing It!: Lesbian and Gay Liberation in the '80s."

Collection (a)

LOCATION OF RECORDS: Canadian Gay Archives. (See Appendix for address.)
COLLECTION NAME: Toronto Gay Community Council (89-024; vertical file).
RECORDS: Minutes, 1981-1983; correspondence, 1982-1984; press statement, financial statement, agenda, 1982; submissions, 1981-1982; reports, 1982-1983; description of organization, telephone list, flyers, posters.
AMOUNT: 4 cm of text, 2 posters.
CONDITION: Good.

Collection (b)

LOCATION OF RECORDS: Canadian Women's Movement Archives Collection, Morisset Library Special Collections, University of Ottawa. (See Appendix for address.)
COLLECTION NAME: Toronto Gay Community Council.
RECORDS: Conference records, correspondence, 1982; minutes, 1981-1982; paper airplane, instructions.
AMOUNT: 6 cm.
CONDITION: Good.
ACCESS: Restricted; conditional access negotiable.

503. Toronto Lesbian Network

✣ Toronto, Ont. Formed 1982. Disbanded [198-].

The Toronto Lesbian Network was established to share information and resources and to publicize cultural and political events.

LOCATION OF RECORDS: Canadian Women's Movement Archives Collection, Morisset Library Special Collections, University of Ottawa. (See Appendix for address.)
COLLECTION NAME: Toronto Lesbian Network.
RECORDS: Minutes, 1982; contact list, flyer.
AMOUNT: 1 mm.
CONDITION: Good.
ACCESS: Restricted; conditional access negotiable.

504. Toronto Rape Crisis Centre

✣ Toronto, Ont. Formed 1973.

The Toronto Rape Crisis Centre (TRCC) opened in 1974 with two objectives: to provide "support and assistance to victims of rape and sexual assault" and to undertake "community education and rape prevention." (Source: TRCC pamphlet.) TRCC organized the 1982 Toronto conference "Fighting Back." [See also Take Back the Night Committee (Toronto, Ont.) (493).]

LOCATION OF RECORDS: Canadian Women's Movement Archives Collection, Morisset Library Special Collections, University of Ottawa. (See Appendix for address.)
COLLECTION NAME: Toronto Rape Crisis Centre.
RECORDS: Newsletters, 1976-1980; correspondence, 1974-1975, 1981, 1983, 1985; booklets, 1974, 1976, 1978-1980; flyers, 1981-1990; press release, 1977; bibliographies, 1977, 1979; tickets, 1983, 1986; conference records, 1982; contact lists, briefs, clippings, guidelines, pamphlets, educational material, posters, T-shirts, buttons.
AMOUNT: 17 cm of text, 4 posters, 2 T-shirts, 8 buttons.
CONDITION: Good.
ACCESS: No restrictions.

505. Toronto Socialist Feminist Action

[See also entry # 1085 (in Part II), which lists other records of this organization.]

✣ Toronto, Ont. Formed 1978.

Toronto Socialist Feminist Action (TSFA) was originally called the International Women's Day Committee (IWDC); it changed its name in 1989. IWDC was formed by women who had taken part in organizing the 1978 International Women's Day events in Toronto; from 1979 to 1984, it played a leadership role in the March 8th Coalition. IWDC made outreach to women in unions a priority. (Source: *Feminist Organizing for Change: The Contemporary Women's Movement in Canada* / Nancy Adamson, Linda Briskin, and Margaret McPhail. — Toronto: Oxford University Press, 1988.) TSFA is now an independent, multi-issue, socialist-feminist organization. It publishes a newsletter, *Rebel Girls' Rag: A Forum of Women's Resistance*. [See also March 8th Coalition (439) and Cayenne: A Socialist Feminist Bulletin (364).]

LOCATION OF RECORDS: Canadian Women's Movement Archives Collection, Morisset Library Special Collections, University of Ottawa. (See Appendix for address.)
COLLECTION NAME: International Women's Day Committee — Toronto; Toronto Socialist Feminist Action; SR 9/1-2.
RECORDS: Minutes, 1977-1985; basis-of-unity statements, 1978-1986; reports, speeches, 1977-1986; correspondence, 1978-1987; financial records, 1980-1985; proposals, 1977-1978, 1981-1984; notes, 1977-1978, 1980-1987; newsletters (*International Women's Day Committee Newsletter*, 1978-1986; *Rebel Girls' Rag: A Forum of Women's Resistance*, 1987-1991); buttons, 1978, 1981, 1983-1984; conference records, telephone lists, 1982-1983; pamphlets, 1981-1983; news release, announcement, policy statements, 1981; briefs, photographs, 1981, 1983; educational material, 1981-1982; leaflets, 1980-1981; historical information, 1980, 1982; sign, circular, 1977; grant application, 1985; paper, 1982; sound recordings (meetings), 1979, 1983; clippings, flyers, articles, presentation, letterhead, mailing lists, membership lists, posters, statement of support.
AMOUNT: 53 cm of text, 1 sign, 4 posters, 16 photographs, 4 buttons, 2 sound recordings.
CONDITION: Good.
ACCESS: No restrictions.

506. Toronto West Business and Professional Women's Club

Until 1984 the club was called the Lakeshore Business and Professional Women's Club.

LOCATION OF RECORDS: Archives of Ontario. (See Appendix for address.)

COLLECTION NAME: Forms part of: Business and Professional Women's Clubs of Ontario collection (Series F 207-9).

RECORDS: Minutes, clippings, pamphlets, reports, agendas, miscellaneous records, 1949-1984.

AMOUNT: 16.5 cm.

ACCESS: No restrictions.

FINDING AID: "Preliminary Inventory of the Business and Professional Women's Clubs of Ontario."

507. Toronto Women's Bookstore

✣ Toronto, Ont. Formed 1972.

The bookstore began as Let Us Out Books, which was part of a women's centre, the Women's Place; the store moved out of the centre in 1974. The Toronto Women's Bookstore was incorporated in 1975. [See also the Women's Place (Toronto, Ont.) (566).]

LOCATION OF RECORDS: Canadian Women's Movement Archives Collection, Morisset Library Special Collections, University of Ottawa. (See Appendix for address.)

COLLECTION NAME: Toronto Women's Bookstore; SR 11/4.

RECORDS: Organization history, 1976; correspondence, 1975, 1983-1986, [1987?], 1991; sound recording (meeting), mail-order lists, agenda, 1974; newsletters, 1981-1982; reading list, 1984; notice, 1985; button, 1983; log, presentation, photographs, notes, financial records, clippings, press releases, catalogues, questionnaire, bibliographies, posters, pamphlets, bookmarks, announcement, flyers, business card, ticket stub, rubber stamp.

AMOUNT: 4.5 cm of text, 1 sound recording, 2 posters, 6 photographs, 1 rubber stamp, 1 button.

CONDITION: Good.

ACCESS: No restrictions.

508. Toronto Women's Caucus

✣ Toronto, Ont. Formed 1970. Disbanded [1972?].

Abortion rights were the main concern of the Toronto Women's Caucus (TWC), which was formed by women who withdrew from the New Feminists. TWC was influenced by the League for Socialist Action (a Trotskyist group). (Source: *Feminist Organizing for Change: The Contemporary Women's Movement in Canada*/Nancy Adamson, Linda Briskin, and Margaret McPhail. — Toronto: Oxford University Press, 1988.) TWC published *Velvet Fist: A Women's Liberation Newspaper*. [See also New Feminists (447) and League for Socialist Action (65).]

Collection (a)

LOCATION OF RECORDS: Canadian Women's Movement Archives Collection, Morisset Library Special Collections, University of Ottawa. (See Appendix for address.)

COLLECTION NAME: Toronto Women's Caucus; SR 10/1B.

RECORDS: Periodicals (*Velvet Fist: A Women's Liberation Newspaper*, 1970-1972); sound recording, minutes, correspondence, 1971; discussion papers, agenda, 1972; clippings, flyers, 1970-1972; reading list, 1970.

AMOUNT: 4 cm of text, 1 sound recording.

CONDITION: Fair.

ACCESS: No restrictions.

Collection (b)

LOCATION OF RECORDS: Thomas Fisher Rare Book Library, University of Toronto. (See Appendix for address.)

COLLECTION NAME: Forms part of: F.M. Denison collection.

RECORDS: Periodicals (*Velvet Fist: A Women's Liberation Newspaper*, 1970-1972).

ACCESS: No restrictions.

509. Toronto Women's Liberation Movement

✣ Toronto, Ont. Formed 1968. Disbanded [1972?].

The Toronto Women's Liberation Movement (TWLM) was formed by the University of Toronto Women's Caucus of the Student Union for Peace Action. In 1969 and 1970, some members split off from TWLM to form the New Feminists and the Leila Khaled Collective. (Source: *Feminist Organizing for Change: The Contemporary Women's Movement in Canada*/Nancy Adamson, Linda Briskin, and Margaret McPhail. — Toronto: Oxford University Press, 1988.) TWLM's activities included discussion groups, a newsletter, abortion referrals, public speaking, and a sit-in to establish a day-care centre. The group was also known as the Toronto Women's Liberation Group or Toronto Women's Liberation Front. TWLM hosted the 1971 Indochinese Women's Conference. [See also New Feminists (447), Leila Khaled Collective (415), Campus and Community Co-operative Day Care Centre (360), and Women's Press (99).]

Collection (a)

LOCATION OF RECORDS: Canadian Women's Movement Archives Collection, Morisset Library Special Collections, University of Ottawa. (See Appendix for address.)

COLLECTION NAME: Toronto Women's Liberation Movement.

RECORDS: Newsletters, 1969-1972; newspapers (*Bellyful*, 1972); mailing lists, 1969-1970; conference records, 1971; briefs, proposals, articles, fact sheets, correspondence, pamphlets, flyers, clippings, financial statement, form.

AMOUNT: 9 cm.

CONDITION: Fair.

ACCESS: No restrictions.

Collection (b)

LOCATION OF RECORDS: Thomas Fisher Rare Book Library, University of Toronto. (See Appendix for address.)

COLLECTION NAME: Forms part of: F.M. Denison collection.

RECORDS: Periodicals (*Bellyful*, 1972).

AMOUNT: 4 items.

ACCESS: No restrictions.

510. Toronto Women's Network

✣ Toronto, Ont. Formed 1975. Disbanded [197-?].

Through the Toronto Women's Network, local feminist organizations exchanged information and formed ad hoc coalitions around common interests. It was sometimes called the Toronto Feminist Network.

LOCATION OF RECORDS: Canadian Women's Movement Archives Collection, Morisset Library Special Collections, University of Ottawa. (See Appendix for address.)

COLLECTION NAME: Toronto Women's Network.

RECORDS: Minutes, correspondence, 1975; articles, announcements of meetings, 1975-1976; contact lists.

AMOUNT: 1 cm.

CONDITION: Good.

ACCESS: No restrictions.

511. Trent Lesbian and Gay Collective

[See also entry # 1087 (in Part II), which lists other records of this organization.]

✣ Peterborough, Ont. Formed 1972.

The Trent Lesbian and Gay Collective (TLGC) offers support, social events, and political activities to lesbians and gay men at Trent University and elsewhere in Peterborough. Originally known as the Trent Homophile Association (THA), it became Gays of Trent and Peterborough (GTP) and then Gays and Lesbians of Trent and Peterborough (GLTP).

LOCATION OF RECORDS: Canadian Gay Archives. (See Appendix for address.)
COLLECTION NAME: Gays and Lesbians of Trent and Peterborough (86-006).
RECORDS: Miscellaneous records, 1976-1986.

512. Union culturelle des Franco-Ontariennes

[Voir aussi la notice 1088 (dans la partie II) pour autres documents de ce groupe.]

✣ Ottawa (Ont.). Groupe fondé 1936.

Parmi ses objectifs, l'Union culturelle des Franco-Ontariennes (UCFO) vise à améliorer le statut socio-économique des femmes par la formation, l'information et la revendication. Jusqu'en 1969 l'UCFO portait le nom de l'Union catholique des fermières.

LIEU DE CONSULTATION : Centre de recherche en civilisation canadienne-française, Université d'Ottawa. (Voir Annexe pour l'adresse.)
NOM DU FONDS : Union culturelle des Franco-Ontariennes.
MATÉRIEL : Statuts et règlements, documents de congrès, procès-verbaux, historique, rapports, dossiers des comités, photographies, sceau, insignes, documents divers, 1936-1987.
QUANTITÉ : 6 m de texte, 393 photographies.
ACCÈS : Accessible lorsque le fonds sera organisé, traité et décrit.

513. Unitarian Universalist Association. Gay Caucus. Toronto Branch

✣ Toronto, Ont. Formed 1974.

The Unitarian Universalist Gay Caucus (UUGC) was founded in Washington in 1971. The Toronto branch was active in the mid-1970s. In the 1980s, it was restructured as Unitarian Universalist Lesbians and Gays.

LOCATION OF RECORDS: Canadian Gay Archives. (See Appendix for address.)
COLLECTION NAME: Forms part of: Elgin Ferguson Blair collection (84-011).
RECORDS: Correspondence, 1975-1976; miscellaneous records.

514. University of Toronto. Advisory Committee to the Status of Women Officer

✣ Toronto, Ont. Formed 1985.

The position of Status of Women Officer (reporting to the president of the University of Toronto) was created in 1984. The Advisory Committee to the Status of Women Officer is composed of faculty, administrative staff, and students.

LOCATION OF RECORDS: Canadian Women's Movement Archives Collection, Morisset Library Special Collections, University of Ottawa. (See Appendix for address.)
COLLECTION NAME: University of Toronto. Advisory Committee to the Status of Women Officer.
RECORDS: Minutes, correspondence, 1988-1989; clippings, 1984, 1989; guidelines, invitation, flyers, 1989; pamphlet, 1990.
AMOUNT: 2 cm.
CONDITION: Good.
ACCESS: No restrictions.

515. University of Toronto. Committee on Sexual Harassment

✣ Toronto, Ont. Formed 1982. Disbanded.

The Committee on Sexual Harassment at the University of Toronto lobbied for a policy dealing with sexual and gender harassment at the university.

LOCATION OF RECORDS: Canadian Women's Movement Archives Collection, Morisset Library Special Collections, University of Ottawa. (See Appendix for address.)
COLLECTION NAME: University of Toronto. Committee on Sexual Harassment.
RECORDS: Minutes, survey form, 1982.
AMOUNT: 5 mm.
CONDITION: Good.
ACCESS: No restrictions.

516. University of Toronto. Gays and Lesbians at the University of Toronto

✣ Toronto, Ont. Formed [ca. 1983].

Gays and Lesbians at the University of Toronto (GLAUT) grew out of the organization Gays at the University of Toronto. GLAUT organizes Lesbian and Gay Awareness Week events, among other activities. [See also University of Toronto. Gays at the University of Toronto (517).]

LOCATION OF RECORDS: Canadian Gay Archives. (See Appendix for address.)
COLLECTION NAME: Gays and Lesbians at the University of Toronto (90-107).
RECORDS: Legal records, 1990.

517. University of Toronto. Gays at the University of Toronto

✣ Toronto, Ont. Formed 1976. Disbanded [ca. 1981].

Primarily a student organization, Gays at the University of Toronto aimed to give a sense of community to gay men and lesbians on campus. [See also University of Toronto. Gays and Lesbians at the University of Toronto (516).]

LOCATION OF RECORDS: Canadian Gay Archives. (See Appendix for address.)
COLLECTION NAME: Gays at the University of Toronto (83-013).
RECORDS: Correspondence, minutes, clippings, flyers, miscellaneous records, 1979-1981.

518. University of Toronto. Homophile Association

✣ Toronto, Ont. Formed 1969. Disbanded [ca. 1973].

One goal of the University of Toronto Homophile Association (UTHA) was to inform the University of Toronto community and the general public about homosexuality, by initiating discussions, combatting stereotypes, and distributing literature.

LOCATION OF RECORDS: Canadian Gay Archives. (See Appendix for address.)
COLLECTION NAME: University of Toronto Homophile Association (82-006).
RECORDS: Constitution, minutes, correspondence, newsletters, flyers, miscellaneous records, poster, 1968-1973.
AMOUNT: 20 cm of text, 1 poster.

519. University of Toronto. Lesbian and Gay Academic Society

✣ Toronto, Ont. Formed 1975.

The Lesbian and Gay Academic Society at the University of Toronto (LGAS) was originally called the Gay Academic Union. LGAS provides a forum in which to discuss topics of special interest to lesbians and gay men.

Collection (a)

LOCATION OF RECORDS: Canadian Gay Archives. (See Appendix for address.)

COLLECTION NAME: Lesbian and Gay Academic Society at the University of Toronto (84-027, 85-006).

RECORDS: Sound recordings (lectures), 1984-1985.

AMOUNT: 2 sound recordings.

Collection (b)

LOCATION OF RECORDS: Canadian Women's Movement Archives Collection, Morisset Library Special Collections, University of Ottawa. (See Appendix for address.)

COLLECTION NAME: SR 19/1-2.

RECORDS: Sound recordings (lectures), 1984-1985.

AMOUNT: 2 sound recordings.

ACCESS: No restrictions.

520. University of Toronto. Sexual Education Centre

✛ Toronto, Ont. Formed 1977.

The University of Toronto Sexual Education Centre (SEC) was established by students to provide peer counselling, a referral service, and educational programmes related to human sexuality and relationships. The centre has provided birth-control information and supported freedom of choice regarding sexual orientation. SEC's attempts to offer pregnancy counselling in the early 1980s resulted in conflict and controversy over the issue of abortion.

LOCATION OF RECORDS: Canadian Women's Movement Archives Collection, Morisset Library Special Collections, University of Ottawa. (See Appendix for address.)

COLLECTION NAME: University of Toronto. Sexual Education Centre.

RECORDS: Proposal, 1977; minutes, 1980, 1982-1984; diaries, 1983-1984; financial records, notes, 1982-1984; petition, statistics, button, press release, 1983; clippings, 1977, 1979-1982, 1984; reports, 1979, 1982, 1984; correspondence, 1977-1978, 1983-1984; staff list, 1982; telephone lists, 1984; policy statements, information packages, training materials, guidelines, questionnaires, flyers, lectures, research paper, agreement, letterhead, application form.

AMOUNT: 10 cm of text, 1 button.

CONDITION: Good.

ACCESS: No restrictions.

521. University of Toronto. Status of Women Committee

✛ Toronto, Ont. Formed 1980. Disbanded.

The University of Toronto Status of Women Committee (UTSWC) was an umbrella organization for women's groups at the university. The committee worked toward improving the status of women on campus. It began as an ad hoc committee opposed to the sexism in a newspaper published by engineering students.

LOCATION OF RECORDS: Canadian Women's Movement Archives Collection, Morisset Library Special Collections, University of Ottawa. (See Appendix for address.)

COLLECTION NAME: University of Toronto. Status of Women Committee.

RECORDS: Correspondence, minutes, brochure, 1980.

AMOUNT: 5 mm.

ACCESS: No restrictions.

522. University of Toronto. Women's Centre

✛ Toronto, Ont. Formed 1984.

The Women's Centre at the University of Toronto organizes social, cultural, and educational events, with the goal of improving the condition of women at the university. The organization was originally called the Coalition for a Women's Centre at U of T.

LOCATION OF RECORDS: Canadian Women's Movement Archives Collection, Morisset Library Special Collections, University of Ottawa. (See Appendix for address.)

COLLECTION NAME: University of Toronto. Coalition for a Women's Centre; University of Toronto. Women's Centre at U of T.

RECORDS: Correspondence, 1984-1990; financial records, mailing list, application, 1984; clippings, 1984, 1986, 1988-1989; flyers, 1984-1991; notices, appendix, 1985; policy statement, report, 1988; newsletters (*That Time of the Month*, 1986-1988); press releases, 1984, 1988; position papers, statements of principles, list of supporters, guidelines, minutes, business card, petition, pamphlets, survey, invitation, posters, buttons.

AMOUNT: 3.5 cm of text, 2 buttons, 2 posters.

CONDITION: Good.

ACCESS: No restrictions.

523. University of Toronto. Women's Coalition

✛ Toronto, Ont. Formed [before 1982]. Disbanded.

The University of Toronto Women's Coalition (UTWC) organized various feminist activities on campus, including a 1982 Take Back the Night march.

LOCATION OF RECORDS: Canadian Women's Movement Archives Collection, Morisset Library Special Collections, University of Ottawa. (See Appendix for address.)

COLLECTION NAME: University of Toronto. Women's Coalition.

RECORDS: Minutes, 1982-1983; membership list, map, brochure, 1982; posters, flyers.

AMOUNT: 5 mm of text, 2 posters.

CONDITION: Good.

ACCESS: No restrictions.

524. University of Western Ontario. University Students' Council. Women's Issues Commission

[See also entry # 1093 (in Part II), which lists other records of this organization.]

✛ London, Ont. Formed 1971.

As part of the students' council at the University of Western Ontario, the Women's Issues Commission (WIC) acts as an advocate for women students, operates a women's centre, provides an information and referral service, and organizes discussions, lectures, and film screenings.

LOCATION OF RECORDS: D.B. Weldon Library — Regional Collection, University of Western Ontario. (See Appendix for address.)

COLLECTION NAME: Women's Issues Commission (University of Western Ontario).

RECORDS: Correspondence, newspaper and magazine articles, studies, pamphlets, 1971-1982.

AMOUNT: Half a box.

CONDITION: Good.

ACCESS: No restrictions.

FINDING AID: Regional Collection manuscript catalogue; basic listing.

525. University Women's Club of North York

✢ North York, Ont. Formed 1951.

The University Women's Club of North York (UWCNY) was the first suburban club in the Canadian Federation of University Women. (Source: Archives of Ontario finding aid, 1981.)

Collection (a)

LOCATION OF RECORDS: Archives of Ontario. (See Appendix for address.)

COLLECTION NAME: University Women's Club of North York Papers (F 1220).

RECORDS: Minutes, annual reports, 1951-1976; membership records, 1952-1977; constitution, 1975; newsletters, 1974-1978; organization history, 1972; conference records, 1970; conference reports, 1954-1955, 1960, 1962-1963, 1965-1966, 1969, 1971; clippings, guides, resolutions, miscellaneous records.

AMOUNT: 1.07 m.

ACCESS: No restrictions.

FINDING AID: "Inventory of the University Women's Club of North York Papers."

Collection (b)

LOCATION OF RECORDS: University of Toronto Archives. (See Appendix for address.)

COLLECTION NAME: Forms part of: Germaine T. Warkentin collection (UTA B78-0004).

RECORDS: Conference records, 1966.

AMOUNT: 5 mm.

CONDITION: Good.

ACCESS: No restrictions.

FINDING AID: File list available for Warkentin collection.

526. University Women's Club of Ottawa

✢ Ottawa, Ont. Formed 1910.

Collection (a)

LOCATION OF RECORDS: National Archives of Canada. (See Appendix for address.)

COLLECTION NAME: University Women's Club of Ottawa (MG 28 I 101).

RECORDS: Please see the note about National Archives of Canada collections, in entry # 2.

Collection (b)

LOCATION OF RECORDS: National Archives of Canada.

COLLECTION NAME: Forms part of: Miriam Sheridan collection (MG 31, K 27).

RECORDS: Please see the note about National Archives of Canada collections, in entry # 2.

527. Wages Due Lesbians

✢ Toronto, Ont. Formed [197-]. Disbanded [1978?].

Wages Due Lesbians (also known simply as Wages Due) was a group of lesbians who belonged to the Wages for Housework Committee. The group's policies were similar to those of the Wages for Housework Committee, but Wages Due emphasized the rights of lesbian mothers. [See also Wages for Housework Committee (Toronto, Ont.) (528).]

Collection (a)

LOCATION OF RECORDS: Canadian Women's Movement Archives Collection, Morisset Library Special Collections, University of Ottawa. (See Appendix for address.)

COLLECTION NAME: Wages Due Lesbians.

RECORDS: Report, clippings, testimony, conference records, 1976; manual, 1977; press release, 1978; position papers, correspondence, speeches, policy statements, bibliography, flyers, posters.

AMOUNT: 2 cm of text, 2 posters.

CONDITION: Good.

ACCESS: Restricted; conditional access negotiable.

Collection (b)

LOCATION OF RECORDS: Canadian Gay Archives. (See Appendix for address.)

COLLECTION NAME: Wages Due Lesbians (Toronto) (vertical file).

RECORDS: Press releases, correspondence, clippings, 1978-1979; discussion paper and reply, grant application, 1978; policy statements, speech, 1976; information package, 1977; newsletters, 1977-1978; flyers, notes, brief, poster, list of publications.

AMOUNT: 2 cm of text, 1 poster.

528. Wages for Housework Committee (Toronto, Ont.)

✢ Toronto, Ont. Formed [1973?]. Disbanded [198-].

The Wages for Housework Committee (WFH) was the Toronto branch of an international organization which demanded that governments pay wages for housework. It saw a connection between women's unpaid labour in the home and the low wages they received in paid employment. [See also Waitresses' Action Committee (529), Wages Due Lesbians (527), and Lesbian Mothers' Defence Fund (Toronto, Ont.) (422).]

Collection (a)

LOCATION OF RECORDS: Canadian Women's Movement Archives Collection, Morisset Library Special Collections, University of Ottawa. (See Appendix for address.)

COLLECTION NAME: Wages for Housework.

RECORDS: Newsletters (*Wages for Housework Campaign Bulletin*, 1976-1979, 1981); clippings, 1975-1979, 1983; briefs, 1976-1977; speeches, 1975-1977; songbook, essay, 1975; correspondence, 1977, 1985; reports, flyers, pamphlets, leaflets, policy statement, notes, press releases, organization histories, handbooks, notebooks, booklet, stickers, reading list, button, miscellaneous records.

AMOUNT: 21 cm of text, 1 button.

CONDITION: Good.

ACCESS: No restrictions.

Collection (b)

LOCATION OF RECORDS: Canadian Gay Archives. (See Appendix for address.)

COLLECTION NAME: Wages for Housework Committee (Toronto) (vertical file).

RECORDS: Correspondence, 1976-1977; press releases, 1977, 1979; brief, 1977; clippings, speech, 1976; list of publications, flyers, fact sheets, miscellaneous records.

AMOUNT: 1 cm.

529. Waitresses' Action Committee

✢ Toronto, Ont. Formed [1976?]. Disbanded [197-].

The Waitresses' Action Committee opposed proposals to freeze the minimum wage for workers earning tips. Some of its members also belonged to the Wages for Housework Committee. [See also Wages for Housework Committee (Toronto, Ont.) (528).]

LOCATION OF RECORDS: Canadian Women's Movement Archives Collection, Morisset Library Special Collections, University of Ottawa. (See Appendix for address.)

COLLECTION NAME: Waitresses' Action Committee.

RECORDS: Correspondence, 1976-1978; report, 1976; article, clippings, submission, 1977; press releases, 1977-1978; petition, 1978; log, notes, briefs, position paper, mailing lists, flyers.

AMOUNT: 4 cm.
CONDITION: Fair.
ACCESS: No restrictions.

530. West Algoma Council of Women

LOCATION OF RECORDS: Thunder Bay Historical Museum Society. (See Appendix for address.)
COLLECTION NAME: West Algoma Council of Women (E 11).
RECORDS: Minute books, 1914-1960; correspondence, 1894-[196-].
AMOUNT: 7 minute books, 13 cm of correspondence.
ACCESS: No restrictions.

531. Weston Business and Professional Women's Club

✣ Weston, Ont.

LOCATION OF RECORDS: Archives of Ontario. (See Appendix for address.)
COLLECTION NAME: Forms part of: Business and Professional Women's Clubs of Ontario collection (Series F 207-10).
RECORDS: Minutes, 1948-1961; annual reports, 1952-1956; correspondence, 1948-1958.
AMOUNT: 6 cm.
ACCESS: No restrictions.
FINDING AID: "Preliminary Inventory of the Business and Professional Women's Club of Ontario."

532. Windsor Local Council of Women

✣ Windsor, Ont. Formed 1934.

Representing a number of women's groups in the Windsor area, the council aims to strengthen women's role in community activities and policy making. Until 1935 it was called the Border Cities Local Council of Women. (Source: Municipal Archives — Windsor Public Library finding aid.)

LOCATION OF RECORDS: Municipal Archives — Windsor Public Library. (See Appendix for address.)
COLLECTION NAME: Windsor Local Council of Women (MS 19).
RECORDS: Minutes, 1934-1972; reports, 1935-1975; constitution, by-laws, resolutions, 1934-1966; membership lists, executive lists, 1944-1978; correspondence, 1934-1974; financial records, 1937-1967; briefs, project files, 1935-1968; bulletins, 1937-1977; clippings, [ca. 1949]-1950; photographs, [ca. 1950]-1975; sound recording, miscellaneous records.
ACCESS: No restrictions.
FINDING AID: Inventory available.

533. Windsor Woman

✣ Windsor, Ont. Formed 1972. Disbanded.

Windsor Woman was a women's liberation newspaper.

LOCATION OF RECORDS: Canadian Women's Movement Archives Collection, Morisset Library Special Collections, University of Ottawa. (See Appendix for address.)
COLLECTION NAME: Windsor Woman.
RECORDS: Newspapers (Windsor Woman, 1972-1973).
AMOUNT: 1 cm.
CONDITION: Fair.
ACCESS: No restrictions.

534. Witches against Nuclear Technology

✣ Toronto, Ont. Formed [197-]. Disbanded.

Witches against Nuclear Technology (also known as Witches ANT) performed anti-nuclear guerrilla theatre. [See also Women against Nuclear Technology (539).]

LOCATION OF RECORDS: Canadian Women's Movement Archives Collection, Morisset Library Special Collections, University of Ottawa. (See Appendix for address.)
COLLECTION NAME: Witches: Anti-nuclear Theatre.
RECORDS: Scripts, flyers, article, notes.
AMOUNT: 1 cm.
CONDITION: Fair.
ACCESS: No restrictions.

535. Womanpower, Inc.

✣ London, Ont. Formed 1974.

Womanpower, Inc. provides free career and vocational counselling services and resources for women. It offers special programmes for groups with particular needs, such as sole-support mothers, immigrant women, and women over forty.

LOCATION OF RECORDS: D.B. Weldon Library — Regional Collection, University of Western Ontario. (See Appendix for address.)
COLLECTION NAME: Womanpower, Inc.
RECORDS: Registration forms, clippings, brochures, articles, miscellaneous records, 1974-[199-].
AMOUNT: 13 boxes.
CONDITION: Fair.
ACCESS: No restrictions.
FINDING AID: Regional Collection manuscript catalogue.

536. Womanspirit Art Research and Learning Centre

✣ London, Ont. Formed 1978. Disbanded 1986.

This was a studio, gallery, and research and resource centre for the creation, display, study, documentation, and retention of feminist or women's art.

LOCATION OF RECORDS: D.B. Weldon Library — Regional Collection, University of Western Ontario. (See Appendix for address.)
COLLECTION NAME: Womanspirit Art Research and Learning Centre; the slides have been transferred to the Slide Library, Visual Arts Department, University of Western Ontario.
RECORDS: Slides, sound recordings (interviews), correspondence, financial records, artists' files, 1978-1986.
AMOUNT: 22 boxes.
CONDITION: Good.
ACCESS: Correspondence restricted for five years; financial records restricted for fifty years.
FINDING AID: Regional Collection manuscript catalogue.

537. Women after Rights

✣ Toronto, Ont. Formed [197-]. Disbanded.

Women after Rights (WAR) lobbied the Ontario government for financial assistance to sole-support mothers furthering their education.

LOCATION OF RECORDS: Canadian Women's Movement Archives Collection, Morisset Library Special Collections, University of Ottawa. (See Appendix for address.)

COLLECTION NAME: Women after Rights — Toronto.
RECORDS: Brief, response, agenda, notes, 1976.
AMOUNT: 3 mm.
CONDITION: Good.
ACCESS: No restrictions.

538. *Women against Free Trade*

✣ Toronto, Ont. Formed 1988. Disbanded 1988.

This was a coalition of Toronto feminist groups opposed to the free-trade agreement between Canada and the United States.

LOCATION OF RECORDS: Canadian Women's Movement Archives Collection, Morisset Library Special Collections, University of Ottawa. (See Appendix for address.)
COLLECTION NAME: Women against Free Trade.
RECORDS: Minutes, policy statements, briefs, background papers, reports, pamphlets, flyers, 1988.
AMOUNT: 2 cm.
CONDITION: Good.
ACCESS: No restrictions.

539. *Women against Nuclear Technology*

✣ Toronto, Ont. Formed [1979?]. Disbanded.

Women against Nuclear Technology (WANT) was a feminist group which participated in anti-nuclear protests. [See also Witches against Nuclear Technology (534).]

LOCATION OF RECORDS: Canadian Women's Movement Archives Collection, Morisset Library Special Collections, University of Ottawa. (See Appendix for address.)
COLLECTION NAME: Women against Nuclear Technology — Toronto.
RECORDS: Agendas, flyers, notes, layout, mailing lists, 1979; minutes, pamphlets, speeches, petitions, press releases, resource list, notes, membership list, articles, cue cards.
AMOUNT: 1 cm.
CONDITION: Good.
ACCESS: No restrictions.

540. *Women against Violence against Women (Toronto, Ont.)*

✣ Toronto, Ont. Formed 1977. Disbanded [198-].

Women against Violence against Women (WAVAW) was "a radical feminist group committed to identifying and combatting violence against women in all its forms," including rape, battering, sexist advertising, and pornography. (Source: WAVAW flyer, 1983.) Another Toronto group with the same name was established in 1986. [See also the Committee against the Deportation of Immigrant Women (374).]

LOCATION OF RECORDS: Canadian Women's Movement Archives Collection, Morisset Library Special Collections, University of Ottawa. (See Appendix for address.)
COLLECTION NAME: Women against Violence against Women — Toronto; SR 7/1-6.
RECORDS: Minutes, 1977-1978, 1980-1983; correspondence, 1977-1978, 1981-1983; sound recordings (meetings), 1977-1978; clippings, press releases, 1977-1979; flyers, 1978-1984; layouts, 1977, 1979; contact lists, 1978-1979; calendar, 1977; notes, 1980, 1982-1983; policy statements, telephone lists, educational material, sign, button, posters.
AMOUNT: 9 cm of text, 5 posters, 1 sign, 1 button, 6 sound recordings.
CONDITION: Good.
ACCESS: No restrictions.

541. *Women and Children's Health Centre (Toronto, Ont.)*

✣ Toronto, Ont. Formed [before 1974]. Disbanded [197-].

This health centre, which was run collectively by women, provided non-sexist health care for women and children. In addition to the services provided by most medical clinics, the centre offered pre- and post-natal classes, abortion referral, and self-help clinics. It was also called the Women's Health Centre.

LOCATION OF RECORDS: Canadian Women's Movement Archives Collection, Morisset Library Special Collections, University of Ottawa. (See Appendix for address.)
COLLECTION NAME: Women and Children's Health Centre.
RECORDS: Position paper, 1974; organization history, flyer, notes, stickers, poster, photograph.
AMOUNT: 2 mm of text, 1 photograph, 1 poster.
CONDITION: Good.
ACCESS: No restrictions.

542. *Women Back into Stelco Committee*

✣ Hamilton, Ont. Formed 1979. Disbanded [198-].

The Women Back into Stelco Committee demanded that 10 per cent of steel workers hired by Stelco be women. The committee stated that 10 per cent of those applying to Stelco since 1961 had been women and pointed out that Stelco had hired women in wartime.

LOCATION OF RECORDS: Canadian Women's Movement Archives Collection, Morisset Library Special Collections, University of Ottawa. (See Appendix for address.)
COLLECTION NAME: Women Back into Stelco Committee — Hamilton.
RECORDS: Pamphlet, poster, article, 1980; press release, 1979; position paper, flyer, telegram.
AMOUNT: 2 mm of text, 1 poster.
CONDITION: Good.
ACCESS: No restrictions.

543. *Women for Political Action (Toronto, Ont.)*

✣ Toronto, Ont. Formed 1972. Disbanded [198-].

Women for Political Action (WPA) sought equal representation for women at all levels of government. It held public meetings, ran candidates in federal elections, and conducted research. WPA was not affiliated with a particular political party.

LOCATION OF RECORDS: Canadian Women's Movement Archives Collection, Morisset Library Special Collections, University of Ottawa. (See Appendix for address.)
COLLECTION NAME: Women for Political Action — Toronto.
RECORDS: Newsletters, 1972-1981; clippings, 1972-1978; correspondence, 1972-1973, 1975-1976, 1980; conference records, 1973, 1975, 1981; agendas, 1973, 1981; educational material, 1977-1980; by-laws, 1981; contact list, promotional material, 1973; brief, 1974; financial records, [197-]; campaign literature, 1972, 1974; press releases, 1972-1973; flyers, 1973-1981; membership card, 1973-1974; meeting notes, policy statements, grant applications, questionnaires, business card.
AMOUNT: 10 cm.
CONDITION: Fair.
ACCESS: No restrictions.

544. Women for Survival

☩ Toronto, Ont. Formed 1980. Disbanded [198-].

This organization was "concerned about nuclear proliferation and the destruction of the environment." It demanded that nuclear power plants be phased out. (Source: Women for Survival pamphlet.)

LOCATION OF RECORDS: Canadian Women's Movement Archives Collection, Morisset Library Special Collections, University of Ottawa. (See Appendix for address.)
COLLECTION NAME: Women for Survival — Toronto.
RECORDS: Membership list, 1980; minutes, 1980-1981; agenda, invitation, flyers, brochure, button.
AMOUNT: 5 mm of text, 1 button.
CONDITION: Good.
ACCESS: No restrictions.

545. Women in Crisis — Sioux, Hudson, North

☩ Sioux Lookout, Ont. Formed [1983?].

Women in Crisis — Sioux, Hudson, North (WICSHN) provides shelter, counselling, and other services to battered women and their children. Services for Native women are available. The organization has also been called the Sioux-Hudson Steering Committee to Examine Violence against Women and the Sioux-Hudson Transition House Steering Committee.

LOCATION OF RECORDS: Canadian Women's Movement Archives Collection, Morisset Library Special Collections, University of Ottawa. (See Appendix for address.)
COLLECTION NAME: Women in Crisis — Sioux, Hudson, North.
RECORDS: Minutes, correspondence, 1983; proposal, [1983?].
AMOUNT: 5 mm.
CONDITION: Good.
ACCESS: No restrictions.

546. Women in Trades Association of Toronto

☩ Toronto, Ont. Formed 1980. Disbanded.

The Women in Trades Association of Toronto (WIT) was a support and information network for women training or working in non-traditional occupations.

LOCATION OF RECORDS: Canadian Women's Movement Archives Collection, Morisset Library Special Collections, University of Ottawa. (See Appendix for address.)
COLLECTION NAME: Women in Trades Association of Toronto.
RECORDS: Correspondence, subject files, financial records, newsletters, photographs, conference records, clippings, miscellaneous records.
AMOUNT: Approx. 1.4 m.
ACCESS: As of 1992, most of the collection has not yet been processed.

547. Women (Trent University)

☩ Peterborough, Ont. Formed 1975. Disbanded 1976.

"Women" was an informal support group and social group for lesbians at Trent University.

LOCATION OF RECORDS: Canadian Gay Archives. (See Appendix for address.)
COLLECTION NAME: Lesbian group (Peterborough), 1975-1976 (vertical file).
RECORDS: Drafts of posters, announcement, [1975 or 1976]; note.
AMOUNT: 2 mm.
CONDITION: Good.

548. Women's Action for Peace

☩ Toronto, Ont. Formed [1982?]. Disbanded 1984.

Women's (sometimes spelled Womyn's) Action for Peace saw a connection between militarism and the oppression of women in patriarchal society. It advocated disarmament and non-hierarchical alternatives to power structures controlled by men. The group engaged in non-violent civil disobedience to protest the manufacture of cruise missiles.

LOCATION OF RECORDS: Canadian Women's Movement Archives Collection, Morisset Library Special Collections, University of Ottawa. (See Appendix for address.)
COLLECTION NAME: Women's Action for Peace.
RECORDS: Correspondence, financial records, notes, mailing lists, flyers, 1983-1984; minutes, press releases, photographs, statements of unity, programme, evaluation, 1983; proposal, speech, legal-defence handbook, button, 1984; membership lists, report, clippings, songsheets, map.
AMOUNT: 10 cm of text, 8 photographs, 1 button.
CONDITION: Good.
ACCESS: No restrictions.

549. Women's Art Mobile

☩ Toronto, Ont. Formed [after 1973]. Disbanded [197-].

The Women's Art Mobile (WAM) was an exhibition of work by forty-six women artists. Organized mainly by students at the Ontario College of Art, the exhibition toured Southern Ontario.

LOCATION OF RECORDS: Canadian Women's Movement Archives Collection, Morisset Library Special Collections, University of Ottawa. (See Appendix for address.)
COLLECTION NAME: Women's Art Mobile.
RECORDS: Report, [197-].
AMOUNT: 14 pages.
CONDITION: Good.
ACCESS: No restrictions.

550. Women's Centre (Ryerson Polytechnical Institute)

☩ Toronto, Ont. Formed 1980.

The Women's Centre at Ryerson Polytechnical Institute offers a referral service, a library, seminars, lectures, and International Women's Day events.

LOCATION OF RECORDS: Ryerson Polytechnical Institute Archives. (See Appendix for address.)
COLLECTION NAME: RSU — Women's Centre/Issues.
RECORDS: Clippings, pamphlets, flyers, [198-]-1991.
AMOUNT: 1.5 cm.
CONDITION: Good.

551. Women's Centre (University of Waterloo)

☩ Waterloo, Ont. Formed 1981.

The Women's Centre, also known as the Women's Resource Centre, is run by a volunteer collective, under the auspices of the Federation of Students at the University of Waterloo.

LOCATION OF RECORDS: Canadian Women's Movement Archives Collection, Morisset Library Special Collections, University of Ottawa. (See Appendix for address.)
COLLECTION NAME: University of Waterloo. Women's Resource Centre.
RECORDS: Agendas, 1983; poster, 1987; minutes, flyer, brochure, job descriptions, correspondence.

AMOUNT: 5 mm of text, 1 poster.
CONDITION: Good.
ACCESS: No restrictions.

552. Women's Coalition (Toronto, Ont.)

✢ Toronto, Ont. Formed 1970. Disbanded.

This coalition of Ontario women's organizations recommended that the Ontario Human Rights Code be amended to include the word "sex" in the phrase "race, creed, colour, nationality, ancestry, or place of origin." While it was usually called simply the Women's Coalition, it was also referred to as the Women's Coalition for Inclusion of the Word "Sex" in the Ontario Human Rights Code.

LOCATION OF RECORDS: Canadian Women's Movement Archives Collection, Morisset Library Special Collections, University of Ottawa. (See Appendix for address.)
COLLECTION NAME: Women's Coalition — Sex in the Human Rights Code.
RECORDS: Brief, speech, 1970; correspondence, 1971; flyers, 1970-1971.
AMOUNT: 3 mm.
CONDITION: Good.
ACCESS: No restrictions.

553. Women's Communications Centre

✢ Toronto, Ont. Formed 1972. Disbanded [197-?].

Originally called the Women's Communication Centre, this resource centre taught film, radio, and video production to women. By 1975 it was attempting to form a national network of women's communication centres.

LOCATION OF RECORDS: Canadian Women's Movement Archives Collection, Morisset Library Special Collections, University of Ottawa. (See Appendix for address.)
COLLECTION NAME: Women's Communications Centre.
RECORDS: Organization history, 1973; correspondence, questionnaires, summary of survey results, 1975; notes, flyer.
AMOUNT: 8 mm.
CONDITION: Fair.
ACCESS: No restrictions.

554. Women's Cultural Building Collective

✢ Toronto, Ont. Formed 1981. Disbanded.

Discussion about founding the Women's Cultural Building Collective began when the Pauline McGibbon Cultural Centre closed in 1981. The collective's aim was to provide a forum for women artists and expand the audience for their work. [See also Pauline McGibbon Cultural Centre (469).]

LOCATION OF RECORDS: Canadian Women's Movement Archives Collection, Morisset Library Special Collections, University of Ottawa. (See Appendix for address.)
COLLECTION NAME: Women's Cultural Building.
RECORDS: Minutes, membership list, reference material, 1982; grant applications, press release, correspondence, publicity material, programmes, tickets, sample questionnaire, button, 1983; clippings, 1983, 1985; posters.
AMOUNT: 1 cm of text, 12 posters, 1 button.
CONDITION: Good.
ACCESS: No restrictions.

555. Women's Emergency Centre (Woodstock, Ont.)

[See also entry # 1106 (in Part II), which lists other records of this organization.]

✢ Woodstock, Ont. Formed 1976.

The Women's Emergency Centre provides shelter and support to abused women.

LOCATION OF RECORDS: Woodstock Public Library, Local History Collection. (See Appendix for address.)
COLLECTION NAME: Women's Emergency Centre.
RECORDS: Minutes, 1975-1977; newsletters, miscellaneous records, 1974-1980.
AMOUNT: 1 box.
ACCESS: No restrictions.

556. Women's Fund

✢ Toronto, Ont. Formed 1977. Disbanded.

Until 1979 this organization was called the Women's Fund-Raising Coalition. Its purpose was to establish a permanent fund which would provide assistance to a wide range of women's services and projects. [See also Women's Information Centre of Toronto (559).]

LOCATION OF RECORDS: Canadian Women's Movement Archives Collection, Morisset Library Special Collections, University of Ottawa. (See Appendix for address.)
COLLECTION NAME: Women's Fundraising Coalition.
RECORDS: Minutes, 1977; notices, 1977, 1979; financial records, 1979; button, 1983; statements of objectives, correspondence, flyers, posters.
AMOUNT: 6 mm of text, 3 posters, 1 button.
CONDITION: Good.
ACCESS: No restrictions.

557. Women's Habitat

✢ Etobicoke, Ont. Formed 1975.

Women's Habitat is an emergency shelter for women and their children. Many of the residents are women seeking refuge from violent husbands.

LOCATION OF RECORDS: Canadian Women's Movement Archives Collection, Morisset Library Special Collections, University of Ottawa. (See Appendix for address.)
COLLECTION NAME: Women's Habitat.
RECORDS: Minutes, reports, financial records, 1978-1981; by-laws, 1976, 1978, 1980; organization histories, 1978-1979; labour-negotiation records, 1979-1980; board membership lists, 1978, 1981; newsletters, 1975, 1979-1980; resolution, 1980; policy statements, guidelines, clippings, employment contract, membership form, flyers.
AMOUNT: 7 cm.
CONDITION: Good.
ACCESS: No restrictions.

558. Women's Health Interaction

[See also entry # 1107 (in Part II), which lists other records of this organization.]

✢ Ottawa, Ont. Formed 1983.

Women's Health Interaction (WHI) does community education on women's health issues, particularly women's reproductive health and women and medicinal drugs. WHI is a partner of Inter Pares, a group working in international development. In 1985, WHI produced *Side Effects: A Play about Women and Pharmaceuticals*. WHI's French name is Interaction femmes-santé.

LOCATION OF RECORDS: Canadian Women's Movement Archives Collection, Morisset Library Special Collections, University of Ottawa. (See Appendix for address.)
COLLECTION NAME: Women's Health Interaction.
RECORDS: Minutes, correspondence, 1985, 1987-1988; proposal, script, handbook, copyright and royalties agreement, press kit, clippings, questionnaire, 1985; newsletters (*Interaction*, 1986-1988); pamphlets, flyers, booklet, postcard, button.
AMOUNT: 4 cm of text, 1 button.
CONDITION: Good.
ACCESS: No restrictions.

559. Women's Information Centre of Toronto

✢ Toronto, Ont. Formed 1972.

A number of Toronto women's organizations have been administered by the Women's Information Centre of Toronto (WIC) or began as projects initiated by WIC. These organizations include the Women's Place, the Metro Toronto Women's Credit Union, *The Other Woman*, and the Women's Fund. Since 1983 WIC has administered the Canadian Women's Movement Archives/Archives canadiennes du mouvement des femmes. [See also the Women's Place (Toronto, Ont.) (566), Metro Toronto Women's Credit Union (441), The Other Woman (80), Women's Fund (556), and Canadian Women's Movement Archives/Archives canadiennes du mouvement des femmes (35).]

LOCATION OF RECORDS: Canadian Women's Movement Archives Collection, Morisset Library Special Collections, University of Ottawa. (See Appendix for address.)
COLLECTION NAME: Women's Information Centre of Toronto.
RECORDS: Financial records, 1972-1981; newsletters, 1974-1976; correspondence, kit, minutes, miscellaneous records, [197-].
AMOUNT: Approx. 24 cm.
ACCESS: No restrictions.

560. Women's Information Line

✢ Toronto, Ont. Formed 1985. Disbanded [1986?].

The Women's Information Line (WIL) acquainted newcomers with the Toronto women's movement and provided information on support groups for women.

LOCATION OF RECORDS: Canadian Women's Movement Archives Collection, Morisset Library Special Collections, University of Ottawa. (See Appendix for address.)
COLLECTION NAME: Women's Information Line — Toronto.
RECORDS: Correspondence, financial records, 1985-1986; membership list, 1986; agreement, flyers, 1985; agenda, poster.
AMOUNT: 5 mm of text, 1 poster.
ACCESS: No restrictions.

561. Women's Involvement Programme (Toronto, Ont.)

✢ Toronto, Ont. Formed [1972?]. Disbanded.

The Women's Involvement Programme produced "Liberation Media," a series of videotapes on women's issues.

LOCATION OF RECORDS: Canadian Women's Movement Archives Collection, Morisset Library Special Collections, University of Ottawa. (See Appendix for address.)
COLLECTION NAME: Women's Involvement Programme (Toronto, Ont.).
RECORDS: Grant application, 1972; organization history, catalogue, pamphlet, [197-].

AMOUNT: 1 mm.
CONDITION: Good.
ACCESS: No restrictions.

562. Women's Liberation Working Group (Toronto, Ont.)

✢ Toronto, Ont. Formed 1984. Disbanded [1984?].

The March 8th Coalition established this group to develop a proposal for an ongoing feminist coalition in Toronto. It was originally called the Follow-up Committee, March 8 1984 Coalition. [See also March 8th Coalition (439).]

LOCATION OF RECORDS: Canadian Women's Movement Archives Collection, Morisset Library Special Collections, University of Ottawa. (See Appendix for address.)
COLLECTION NAME: Women's Liberation Working Group — Toronto.
RECORDS: Statement of principles, proposals, correspondence, minutes, agenda, organization history, notes, contact lists, flyer, 1984; mailing lists, clipping.
AMOUNT: 2.5 cm.
CONDITION: Good.
ACCESS: No restrictions.

563. Women's Media Alliance of Toronto

✢ Toronto, Ont. Formed 1981.

The Women's Media Alliance of Toronto (WMA) — a feminist collective of women working in film, video, performance, and visual art — was established to provide support to women working in these areas, exchange information and ideas, and make the public more aware of women's art.

LOCATION OF RECORDS: Canadian Women's Movement Archives Collection, Morisset Library Special Collections, University of Ottawa. (See Appendix for address.)
COLLECTION NAME: Women's Media Alliance.
RECORDS: Minutes, correspondence, 1981-1984; financial records, 1981-1985; reports, posters, 1983-1984; organization history, research notes, 1983; grant applications, 1981, 1983; invitation, 1984; membership lists, mailing lists, flyers, pamphlet.
AMOUNT: 15 cm of text, 2 posters.
CONDITION: Good.
ACCESS: No restrictions.

564. Women's Network Steering Committee (Hamilton, Ont.)

✢ Hamilton, Ont. Formed 1977. Disbanded.

This committee grew out of the Women's Movement Development Project Committee (WMDP), which studied the feasibility of forming a network to meet the needs of women and women's organizations in Hamilton. WMDP was founded in 1977; in 1978 it was dissolved and reborn as the Women's Network Steering Committee (or Steering Committee for a Women's Network).

LOCATION OF RECORDS: Canadian Women's Movement Archives Collection, Morisset Library Special Collections, University of Ottawa. (See Appendix for address.)
COLLECTION NAME: Women's Movement Development Project.
RECORDS: Minutes, report, notice, statement of objectives, 1978; correspondence, 1978-1979; programme, agenda.
AMOUNT: 4 mm.
CONDITION: Good.
ACCESS: No restrictions.

565. Women's Perspective Collective

✣ Toronto, Ont. Formed 1982. Disbanded [198-].

The Women's Perspective Collective (or simply the Women's Collective) began as a committee within an art gallery, the Partisan Gallery. The collective organized the May 1983 women's art exhibition "Women's Perspective '83." Later that year the collective separated from the Partisan Gallery; the autonomous group organized exhibitions and exchanged information.

LOCATION OF RECORDS: Canadian Women's Movement Archives Collection, Morisset Library Special Collections, University of Ottawa. (See Appendix for address.)

COLLECTION NAME: Women's Perspective Collective.

RECORDS: Minutes, 1982-1984; proposals, report, clippings, invitation, financial records, 1983; correspondence, flyers, posters, 1983-1984; newsletters, 1984-1985; membership list, buttons.

AMOUNT: 2.5 cm of text, 3 posters, 2 buttons.

CONDITION: Good.

ACCESS: No restrictions.

566. The Women's Place (Toronto, Ont.)

✣ Toronto, Ont. Formed 1971. Disbanded.

The Women's Place was a feminist organizing centre whose activities included liberation workshops, consciousness-raising groups, speaking engagements, and a library. The Women's Place was administered by the Women's Information Centre of Toronto. [See also Women's Information Centre of Toronto (559) and Toronto Women's Bookstore (507).]

LOCATION OF RECORDS: Canadian Women's Movement Archives Collection, Morisset Library Special Collections, University of Ottawa. (See Appendix for address.)

COLLECTION NAME: Women's Place — Toronto.

RECORDS: Log-books, financial records, notes, 1972-1975; newsletters, correspondence, 1972-1976; minutes, proposals, grant applications, 1973-1975; policy statements, reports, 1972-1973; clippings, 1972-1974; article, periodical, 1971; historical information, 1972; handbook, 1973; speech, conference records, guidelines, office procedures, résumés, 1974; educational material, announcements, flyers, schedules, poster, questionnaire, pamphlets, floor plans, fact sheets, inventory lists, registration forms, book lists, referral lists, photographs.

AMOUNT: 50 cm of text, 4 photographs, 1 poster.

CONDITION: Good.

ACCESS: No restrictions.

567. The Women's Place (Windsor, Ont.)

✣ Windsor, Ont. Formed 1972. Disbanded [197-?].

The Women's Place was a women's centre whose projects included research into the situation of working women.

LOCATION OF RECORDS: Canadian Women's Movement Archives Collection, Morisset Library Special Collections, University of Ottawa. (See Appendix for address.)

COLLECTION NAME: Women's Place (Windsor, Ont.).

RECORDS: Report, 1973; newsletters, 1974-1975; organization histories, interviews, policy statements, correspondence, flyers, [197-].

AMOUNT: 1 cm.

CONDITION: Good.

ACCESS: No restrictions.

568. Women's Regale

✣ Brantford, Ont. Formed 1975. Disbanded 1975.

The purpose of the Women's Regale was to compile historical information on women in Brantford and Brant County who had contributed to the advancement of women.

LOCATION OF RECORDS: Canadian Women's Movement Archives Collection, Morisset Library Special Collections, University of Ottawa. (See Appendix for address.)

COLLECTION NAME: Women's Regale (Brantford, Ont.).

RECORDS: Educational materials, 1975.

AMOUNT: 6 cm.

CONDITION: Good.

ACCESS: No restrictions.

569. Women's Resource Centre (St Catharines, Ont.)

✣ St Catharines, Ont. Formed 1973. Disbanded [198-?].

The centre began as part of the Young Women's Christian Association (YWCA), but it subsequently became autonomous. In its early years the centre held consciousness-raising sessions.

LOCATION OF RECORDS: Canadian Women's Movement Archives Collection, Morisset Library Special Collections, University of Ottawa. (See Appendix for address.)

COLLECTION NAME: Women's Resource Centre (St Catharines, Ont.).

RECORDS: Notes, flyer, pamphlet, [197-]; newsletters (*Women's News*, 1973-1977).

AMOUNT: 3 cm.

CONDITION: Good.

ACCESS: No restrictions.

570. Women's Resource Centre (Timmins, Ont.)

✣ Timmins, Ont. Formed 1975. Disbanded [1978?].

The Women's Resource Centre (WRC) aimed to increase women's status, well-being, and participation in life outside the home. The organization's official name was Women's Resource Centre Association of Timmins/Association Aid'Elle de Timmins.

LOCATION OF RECORDS: Canadian Women's Movement Archives Collection, Morisset Library Special Collections, University of Ottawa. (See Appendix for address.)

COLLECTION NAME: Women's Resource Centre (Timmins, Ont.).

RECORDS: Minutes, directory, bulletin, clippings, 1976; newsletters (*Womantalk*, 1976-1978); telephone list, 1975; reports, guidelines, correspondence, constitution and by-laws, statement of objectives.

AMOUNT: 3.5 cm.

CONDITION: Good.

ACCESS: No restrictions.

571. Women's Self-Defence Centre

✣ Toronto, Ont. Formed 1974. Disbanded [ca. 1976].

The centre offered short-term training in basic self-defence techniques for women. The courses took women's size and strength into account and helped women overcome fear and lack of confidence.

LOCATION OF RECORDS: Canadian Women's Movement Archives Collection, Morisset Library Special Collections, University of Ottawa. (See Appendix for address.)

COLLECTION NAME: Women's Self-Defence Centre.

RECORDS: Correspondence, grant applications, financial records, responsi-

Notes on Consciousness-Raising

"An organization might stir the waters; a raised consciousness can change the tide." --Susan Dworkin.

One definition of C-R:

"The process of transforming the hidden, individual fears of women into a shared awareness of the meaning of them as social problems, the release of anger, anxiety, the struggle of proclaiming the painful and transforming it into the political--this process is consciousness-raising." --Juliet Mitchell.

I An Overview, by a member of the St. Catharines Women's Resource Centre

The weekly consciousness-raising sessions I have attended this winter have had a cathartic effect on me. I feel as if I have been freed from antiquated restrictions, restraints and inhibitions and I am now more myself. And it feels good!

It has always been difficult for me to speak out and give my opinions in a large group situation. This was most likely a result of being from a home in which good communication was lacking and also as a result of being afraid to be aggressive because I am a woman.

Now, because of C-R, I don't feel as much trepidation when I am speaking in front of a group. This was the result of the mechanics of a C-R group, ie., communication, and also the supportive nature of the group which boosts one's confidence tremendously.

The women in our C-R sessions are friends, real friends. We share problems, experiences, successes and failures openly and without guilt or fear of rejection. There is a feeling of trust and security within the group stemming from an underlying philosophy in C-R of honesty. It is probably the only group that I have been in that does not thrive on dissidence and one-up-manship. To be honest with yourself and others means excluding the ego. I believe this has been accomplished at most of our sessions because of the intimacy and frankness that seem to pervade the room.

I have also come to realize the universality of "A Woman's Problem". We are actually microcosms of macrocosms. Sisterhood meant very little to me before I attended C-R. It was a very detached and vague concept in my mind. Now I feel the common bond and see the similarities every time I walk into a C-R session, or see a woman in the street, or think about my mother. Sisterhood is Powerful!

Excerpt from a 1975 document entitled: / Extrait d'un document de 1975 intitulé :
"Notes on Consciousness-Raising"
Women's Resource Centre (St Catharines, Ontario)
CWMA Collection / Fonds de l'ACMF

bility waivers, 1974-1975; class register, 1976; lists of prospective teachers and classes, outreach information, 1974; notices of meetings, course evaluations, sign-in books, press releases, course outline, registration list, guidelines, notes.
AMOUNT: 11 cm.
CONDITION: Good.
ACCESS: No restrictions.

572. Women's Services Network (Toronto, Ont.)
✢ Toronto, Ont. Disbanded 1987.

Through the Women's Services Network (WSN), women working in services for women met to share information and discuss common concerns. WSN was sometimes called the Toronto Women's Services Network. The Toronto Abortion Committee was a subcommittee of WSN.

LOCATION OF RECORDS: Canadian Women's Movement Archives Collection, Morisset Library Special Collections, University of Ottawa. (See Appendix for address.)
COLLECTION NAME: Women's Services Network — Toronto.
RECORDS: Minutes, 1983-1985; correspondence, 1983-1984, 1987; announcements, 1983-1987; flyer, 1983; basis of unity, pamphlet, clipping.
AMOUNT: 5 mm.
CONDITION: Good.
ACCESS: No restrictions.

573. Women's Studies Student Union (New College)
✢ Toronto, Ont. Formed 1980.

The Women's Studies Student Union (WSSU) represents students in the women's studies programme at New College, which is part of the University of Toronto. WSSU organizes course evaluations, social events, discussions, and guest lectures. [See also New College. Women's Studies Programme (446).]

LOCATION OF RECORDS: Canadian Women's Movement Archives Collection, Morisset Library Special Collections, University of Ottawa. (See Appendix for address.)
COLLECTION NAME: University of Toronto. Women's Studies Student Union.
RECORDS: Course evaluations, pamphlets, flyers, poster, [198-].
AMOUNT: 4 cm of text, 1 poster.
CONDITION: Good.
ACCESS: No restrictions.

574. Women's Writing Collective
✢ Toronto, Ont. Formed [1976?]. Disbanded.

The Women's Writing Collective created links among women who wanted to write and provided them with encouragement, constructive criticism, and an opportunity to share their writing. It sponsored a series of poetry readings by women writers called the Women's Writing Salon or the Women's Poetry Salon.

LOCATION OF RECORDS: Canadian Women's Movement Archives Collection, Morisset Library Special Collections, University of Ottawa. (See Appendix for address.)
COLLECTION NAME: Women's Writing Collective; Women's Writing Salon.
RECORDS: Newsletter, correspondence, clippings, notes, 1978; reading lists, contact lists, anthology, flyers, pamphlet, notice.
AMOUNT: 1 cm.
CONDITION: Good.
ACCESS: No restrictions.

575. York University. Committee on Women's Programmes
✢ North York, Ont. Formed [197-].

A group of York University faculty formed the York Women's Studies Committee, which later became the York Committee on Women's Programmes. The committee (which came to include students and staff as well as faculty) worked for the creation of the York Women's Centre in 1975. [See also York Women's Centre (580, 1115).]

LOCATION OF RECORDS: Nellie Langford Rowell Library, York University. (See Appendix for address.)
COLLECTION NAME: Forms part of: Broadsides — YC.
RECORDS: Correspondence, 1974-1975; membership lists, 1975.
AMOUNT: 5 mm.
CONDITION: Good.
ACCESS: No restrictions.

576. York University. Harbinger Community Services
✢ Downsview, Ont. Formed [197-]. Disbanded.

Harbinger Community Services at York University was a community health centre offering information and education in the areas of sexuality, birth control, pregnancy, venereal disease, and drugs. It also offered women's self-help groups and a lesbian drop-in service.

LOCATION OF RECORDS: Canadian Women's Movement Archives Collection, Morisset Library Special Collections, University of Ottawa. (See Appendix for address.)
COLLECTION NAME: Harbinger Community Service, York University.
RECORDS: Correspondence, grant application, brief, 1975; report, 1974; notes, [1976?]; questionnaire, [ca. 1977]; flyers, pamphlets, educational materials.
AMOUNT: 1.5 cm.
CONDITION: Good.
ACCESS: No restrictions.

577. York University. Office of the Advisor to the University on the Status of Women
✢ North York, Ont. Formed 1975.

Originally called the Office of the Advisor to the President on the Status of Women, this office was established to oversee the implementation of the Report of the Senate Task Force on the Status of Women at York University.

LOCATION OF RECORDS: Nellie Langford Rowell Library, York University. (See Appendix for address.)
COLLECTION NAME: Forms part of: Broadsides — ED6.
RECORDS: Reports, 1977, 1985; newsletters (*The Second Decade/La Deuxième décennie*, 1986-1991); pamphlets, 1989-1990; brief.
AMOUNT: 6 cm.
CONDITION: Good.
ACCESS: No restrictions.

578. York University. Presidential Committee to Review the Salaries of Full-Time Faculty Women
✢ North York, Ont. Formed 1975. Disbanded [1976?].

The committee was established in pursuance of the recommendations of the Report of the Senate Task Force on the Status of Women at York University.

LOCATION OF RECORDS: Nellie Langford Rowell Library, York University. (See Appendix for address.)
COLLECTION NAME: Forms part of: Broadsides — ED6.
RECORDS: Correspondence, 1975; report, 1976.

AMOUNT: 1 cm.
CONDITION: Good.
ACCESS: No restrictions.

579. York University. Senate Task Force on the Status of Women

✣ North York, Ont. Formed [ca. 1974]. Disbanded [1975?].

The task force's mandate was to study the status of all women at York University and to report to the Senate.

LOCATION OF RECORDS: Nellie Langford Rowell Library, York University. (See Appendix for address.)
COLLECTION NAME: Forms part of: Broadsides — ED6.
RECORDS: Reports, summary of recommendations, clippings, 1975.
AMOUNT: 3 cm.
CONDITION: Fair.
ACCESS: No restrictions.

580. York Women's Centre

[See also entry # 1115 (in Part II), which lists other records of this organization.]

✣ North York, Ont. Formed 1975.

A centre for women's activities and information at York University, the York Women's Centre offers referral services, peer counselling, and educational forums. The organization has also been referred to as the York Women's Group. [See also York University. Committee on Women's Programmes (575).]

LOCATION OF RECORDS: Nellie Langford Rowell Library, York University. (See Appendix for address.)
COLLECTION NAME: Forms part of: Broadsides — YC.
RECORDS: Minutes, 1975-1978; correspondence, 1975-1978, 1986; funding application, brief, 1976; membership lists, 1976-1977; reports, 1976-1978, 1987; newsletters, 1975, 1983-1984, 1987; clippings, 1976-1977, 1989; ballot, 1977; pamphlets, 1976, [1989?]; flyers.
AMOUNT: 6 cm.
CONDITION: Good.
ACCESS: No restrictions.

581. Young Women's Christian Association of Metropolitan Toronto

[See also entry # 1116 (in Part II), which lists other records of this organization.]

✣ Toronto, Ont. Formed 1873.

The YWCA of Metropolitan Toronto works to create better lives for women through education, pre-employment counselling, fitness and recreation programmes, affordable housing, crisis shelters, and advocacy. It was once called the Young Women's Christian Guild of Toronto. The YWCA ran Stop 158 (a hostel for young women) and the Women's Resource Centre. [See also Nellie Langford Rowell Library (1049).]

Collection (a)
LOCATION OF RECORDS: Archives of Ontario. (See Appendix for address.)
COLLECTION NAME: Young Women's Christian Association (F 794).
RECORDS: Minutes, 1873-1971; annual reports, 1874-1972; newsletters, 1961-1972; financial records, 1940-1973; scrapbooks, 1933-1963; photographs, [192-]-[196-]; sound recordings, 1966, 1968, 1970; correspondence, clippings, reference material, historical information, leases, position papers, staff lists, phonograph records, films, trowel, miscellaneous records.

AMOUNT: 2.9 m.
ACCESS: Microfilm copies must be used when available.
FINDING AID: "Inventory of the Records of the Young Women's Christian Association."

Collection (b)
LOCATION OF RECORDS: Canadian Women's Movement Archives Collection, Morisset Library Special Collections, University of Ottawa. (See Appendix for address.)
COLLECTION NAME: Young Women's Christian Association — Toronto.
RECORDS: Correspondence, 1972-1973, 1979, 1984-1989; newsletters (*Your YW*, 1980; *YWCA Access*, 1983-1987); resource lists, 1975, 1977-1982; brochures, 1978, 1980, 1983, 1985-1987; directories, 1976, 1980, 1985-1987; educational material, 1972-1975, 1977, 1979; minutes, 1974-1975, 1986; flyers, 1973, 1976, 1979, 1981-1988; clippings, 1973, 1986-1987; policy statements, 1975, 1981; reports, 1972, 1976; interview, research papers, 1972; booklet, 1975; workshop material, 1974; article, 1978; petition, T-shirt, 1986; press release, 1983; membership lists, 1981; poster, bookmark, guides, historical information, bibliographies.
AMOUNT: 26 cm of text, 1 poster, 1 T-shirt.
ACCESS: No restrictions.

582. Young Women's Christian Association of Peterborough Victoria and Haliburton

[See also entry # 1117 (in Part II), which lists other records of this organization.]

✣ Peterborough, Ont. Formed 1891.

The YWCA of Peterborough Victoria and Haliburton works to improve the status of women, offering shelters for abused women and children, a resource centre for low-income tenants, and a variety of programmes designed to empower women. Until 1990 it was called the Peterborough YWCA.

LOCATION OF RECORDS: Trent University Archives. (See Appendix for address.)
COLLECTION NAME: Young Women's Christian Association Papers (85-001).
RECORDS: Minutes, 1908-1912, 1919-1978, 1980; reports, correspondence, 1919-1978, 1980; financial reports, 1920-1979; programmes, 1960-1966, 1971, 1976-1980; booklets, 1941, 1955; scrapbooks, legal documents, photographs, pamphlets, historical notes, clippings, songbook, miscellaneous records.
AMOUNT: 1 m.
ACCESS: No restrictions.
FINDING AID: "Young Women's Christian Association Papers" (Finding Aid 196).

583. Young Women's Christian Association of St Thomas-Elgin

[See also entry # 1118 (in Part II), which lists other records of this organization.]

✣ St Thomas, Ont. Formed 1902.

The YWCA of St Thomas-Elgin works to improve the status of women. Its services include support groups, a shelter for abused women and children, and a work-orientation programme.

LOCATION OF RECORDS: St Thomas-Elgin Public Library, Local History Section (George Thorman Room). (See Appendix for address.)
COLLECTION NAME: Young Women's Christian Association.
RECORDS: Scrapbooks containing clippings, [196-]-[198-].
AMOUNT: 5 items.

QUÉBEC

584. Alliance des professeurs de Montréal. Comité de la condition féminine

✣ Montréal (Québec). Groupe fondé 1973.

Le comité avait comme mandat de sensibiliser les membres de l'Alliance à la situation de la femme dans la société et plus précisément dans son milieu de travail.

LIEU DE CONSULTATION : Université Laval, Division des archives. (Voir Annexe pour l'adresse.)

NOM DU FONDS : Fait partie du fonds de l'Alliance des professeurs de Montréal (P250/12/8/2).

MATÉRIEL : Projet de comité, listes de membres, procès-verbaux, documents de travail, annonces d'assemblées ou de rencontres, rapport d'activités, annonces, 1972-1976.

ÉTAT : Bon.

ACCÈS : Aucune restriction sur la consultation des documents portant sur la condition féminine. N.B. : Le fonds de l'Alliance des professeurs de Montréal sera transféré au Service des archives de l'Université de Montréal.

INSTRUMENT DE RECHERCHE : « Répertoire numérique du fonds de l'Alliance des professeurs de Montréal » (publication n° 5).

585. Alliance des professeurs de Montréal. Comité des droits de la femme

✣ Montréal (Québec). Groupe fondé 1968.

Le comité a organisé des campagnes d'information et de sensibilisation et a présenté un mémoire à la Commission royale d'enquête sur la situation de la femme au Canada. Il a également étudié la question des valeurs à enseigner pour favoriser l'émergence d'une société plus juste pour les femmes.

LIEU DE CONSULTATION : Université Laval, Division des archives. (Voir Annexe pour l'adresse.)

NOM DU FONDS : Fait partie du fonds de l'Alliance des professeurs de Montréal (P250/12/8/1).

MATÉRIEL : Listes des membres, procès-verbaux, études, bibliographies, mémoires, bulletin, communiqué de presse, 1968.

ÉTAT : Bon.

ACCÈS : Aucune restriction sur la consultation des documents portant sur la condition féminine. N.B. : Le fonds de l'Alliance des professeurs de Montréal sera transféré au Service des archives de l'Université de Montréal.

INSTRUMENT DE RECHERCHE : « Répertoire numérique du fonds de l'Alliance des professeurs de Montréal » (publication n° 5).

586. Association des femmes diplômées des universités (Montréal, Québec)

✣ Montréal (Québec). Groupe fondé 1948.

L'Association des femmes diplômées des universités (AFDU) s'appelait à ses débuts l'Association des femmes universitaires du Québec. Elle a entrepris un grand nombre d'activités visant à améliorer le statut de la femme.

LIEU DE CONSULTATION : Université de Montréal, Service des archives. (Voir Annexe pour l'adresse.)

MATÉRIEL : Correspondance, procès-verbaux, travaux et études, documents financiers, dossiers de documentation, mémoires, documents de comités, rapports, spicilèges, cahier de coupures de journaux, photographies, 1949-1980.

QUANTITÉ : 6,42 m.

ACCÈS : La correspondance et les procès-verbaux sont communicables dix ans après leur création sauf pour consultation par les membres du Conseil d'administration de l'Association ou par toute autre personne mandatée à cette fin.

INSTRUMENT DE RECHERCHE : « Répertoire numérique (provisoire) du Fonds de l'Association des femmes diplômées des universités » (P 107).

587. Association des femmes diplômées des universités (Québec)

✣ Québec (Québec). Groupe fondé [avant 1949].

L'association vise à stimuler l'intérêt des femmes diplômées pour les questions d'intérêt public, leur fournir l'occasion d'être des agentes de changement, favoriser les contacts sociaux entre elles, promouvoir l'enseignement supérieur et la recherche chez les femmes et améliorer le statut de la femme. L'association est affiliée à la Fédération canadienne des femmes diplômées des universités.

LIEU DE CONSULTATION : Université Laval, Division des archives. (Voir Annexe pour l'adresse.)

NOM DU FONDS : Fonds de l'Association des femmes diplômées des universités (Québec) (P219).

MATÉRIEL : Constitution, statuts, règlements, procès-verbaux, rapports annuels, rapports d'activités, rapports financiers, listes des membres, correspondance, imprimés, 1948-1985.

QUANTITÉ : 2,7 m.
ÉTAT : Bon.
ACCÈS : Aucune restriction. Le fonds n'est pas encore traité à cette date (1991), ce qui rend sa consultation difficile.

588. Association féminine d'éducation et d'action sociale

[Voir aussi la notice 1131 (dans la partie II) pour autres documents de ce groupe.]

✣ Montréal (Québec). Groupe fondé 1966.

L'Association féminine d'éducation et d'action sociale (AFÉAS) est un corps intermédiaire de pression qui pilote d'importants dossiers pour l'avancement de la condition féminine. L'AFÉAS représente les intérêts de ses plus de 30,000 membres de toutes les régions du Québec auprès des différents paliers de gouvernements. L'AFÉAS est née du fusionnement de l'Union catholique des femmes rurales et des Cercles d'économie domestique.

LIEU DE CONSULTATION : Archives nationales du Québec, Centre d'archives de Montréal. (Voir Annexe pour l'adresse.)
NOM DU FONDS : Association féminine d'éducation et d'action sociale.
MATÉRIEL : Procès-verbaux, correspondance, rapports, résolutions, listes des membres, historiques, constitution, revues, bulletins, mémoires, documents de congrès, ordres du jour, documents d'assemblées générales annuelles, recommandations, photographies, documents divers, 1938-1979.
QUANTITÉ : 12,69 m de texte, 2 photographies.
INSTRUMENT DE RECHERCHE : « Répertoire des manuscrits du fonds de l'AFÉAS ».

589. Association féminine d'éducation et d'action sociale. Section Rouyn-Noranda

✣ Rouyn-Noranda (Québec). Groupe fondé 1972.

La section Rouyn-Noranda de l'Association féminine d'éducation et d'action sociale (AFÉAS) a pour buts de participer à l'éducation de ses membres et de faire de l'action sociale pour améliorer la situation des femmes et de la société en général. (Source : instrument de recherche des Archives nationales du Québec.)

LIEU DE CONSULTATION : Archives nationales du Québec, Centre d'archives de l'Abitibi-Témiscamingue. (Voir Annexe pour l'adresse.)
NOM DU FONDS : Association féminine d'éducation et d'action sociale, section Rouyn-Noranda (P164).
MATÉRIEL : Photographies, 1926-1976.
QUANTITÉ : 17 photos.

590. Association pour la planification familiale de Montréal / Family Planning Association of Montreal

[For English entry, see # 601.]

✣ Montréal (Québec). Groupe fondé 1964. Dissous.

L'association était membre de la Fédération de la planification familiale du Canada. Elle s'est associée avec le Lakeshore Unitarian Church afin de créer un centre de planification familiale à Pointe-Claire. (Source : instrument de recherche des Archives nationales du Québec, 1990.) [Voir aussi Lakeshore Unitarian Church. Family Planning Advisory Service (612).]

LIEU DE CONSULTATION : Archives nationales du Québec, Centre d'archives de Montréal. (Voir Annexe pour l'adresse.)
NOM DU FONDS : Association pour la planification familiale de Montréal (P99).
MATÉRIEL : Ordres du jour, 1966-1969; procès-verbaux, 1964, 1966-1970; correspondance, 1966-1978; rapports financiers, 1966-1967; bulletins, 1966-1973; articles de journaux, 1966-1973; constitution, feuillets publicitaires, dépliant, discours, documents divers.
QUANTITÉ : 11 cm.
INSTRUMENT DE RECHERCHE : « Répertoire du fonds de l'Association pour la planification familiale de Montréal » (Instrument de recherche # 6003005).

591. Association pour les droits des gai(e)s du Québec

✣ Montréal (Québec). Groupe fondé 1976.

Un comité des femmes a été formé au sein de l'Association pour les droits des gai(e)s du Québec (ADGQ) en 1981.

LIEU DE CONSULTATION : Canadian Gay Archives. (Voir Annexe pour l'adresse.)
NOM DU FONDS : Association pour les droits des gai(e)s du Québec (82-024); « Congress : National de tous les gai(e)s du Québec : 1st (Montreal), Oct. 15-16, 1977 » (dossier vertical).
MATÉRIEL : Dossiers administratifs, brochures, mémoires, correspondance, communiqués de presse, documents annexes, 1976-1982; documents de congrès, 1977; bulletin (À propos, 1987); affiche, 1982.
QUANTITÉ : 13 cm.

592. La Centrale

[For English entry, see # 593.]

✣ Montréal (Québec). Groupe fondé 1973.

Connue d'abord sous le nom de Galerie Powerhouse/Powerhouse Gallery, La Centrale est une galerie sans but lucratif, dirigée par les artistes et qui monte des expositions d'art contemporain produit par des femmes. À ses débuts, l'organisme a regroupé des femmes artistes pour discuter de leur art; ce groupe de femmes (issu de l'organisme « the Flaming Apron ») a monté sa première exposition en 1973 et a ouvert une galerie en 1974. L'organisme a changé de nom en 1990. [Voir aussi the Flaming Apron (609).]

LIEU DE CONSULTATION : Fonds des Archives canadiennes du mouvement des femmes, Collections spéciales de la Bibliothèque Morisset, Université d'Ottawa. (Voir Annexe pour l'adresse.)
NOM DU FONDS : Powerhouse Gallery; SR 11/15.
MATÉRIEL : Enregistrement sonore (entrevue), 1976; calendrier, entrevue, 1983; communiqués de presse, 1983-1991; bulletins, 1975-1983; dépliants, 1979, 1983; correspondance, 1974, 1983; affiches, annonces, tracts.
QUANTITÉ : 14 cm de texte, 21 affiches, 1 enregistrement sonore.
ÉTAT : Bon.
ACCÈS : Aucune restriction.

593. La Centrale

[Renseignements en français, notice 592.]

✣ Montreal, Quebec. Formed 1973.

La Centrale (originally known as Powerhouse Gallery/Galerie Powerhouse) is a non-profit, artist-run gallery which exhibits the work of contemporary women artists. It began as a discussion group for women artists; this group (which emerged from an organization called the Flaming Apron) held its first exhibition in 1973 and opened a gallery in 1974. The organization changed its name in 1990. [See also the Flaming Apron (609).]

LOCATION OF RECORDS: Canadian Women's Movement Archives Collection,

Morisset Library Special Collections, University of Ottawa. (See Appendix for address.)
COLLECTION NAME: Powerhouse Gallery; SR 11/15.
RECORDS: Sound recording (interview), 1976; calendar, interview, 1983; press releases, 1983-1991; newsletters, 1975-1983; pamphlets, 1979, 1983; correspondence, 1974, 1983; posters, announcements, flyers.
AMOUNT: 14 cm of text, 21 posters, 1 sound recording.
CONDITION: Good.
ACCESS: No restrictions.

594. Centrale de l'enseignement du Québec. Comité de la condition féminine

✣ Québec et Montréal (Québec). Groupe fondé 1973.

Ce comité, siégeant au sein de la Centrale de l'enseignement du Québec (CEQ), s'appelait lors de sa mise sur pied, le Comité Laure-Gaudreault. En 1980, le comité a adopté le nom de Comité CEQ de la condition féminine. Les objectifs du comité comprennent les suivants : susciter la formation de comités de la condition des femmes dans les syndicats CEQ et favoriser la présence des femmes aux instances décisionnelles du CEQ.

LIEU DE CONSULTATION : Centrale de l'enseignement du Québec, Centre de documentation. (Voir Annexe pour l'adresse.)
NOM DU FONDS : Comité CEQ de la condition féminine.
MATÉRIEL : Décisions, 1976-1977; procès-verbaux, 1973-1979, 1982-1985; rapports d'étapes, 1974-1976; historique du comité, documents divers.
QUANTITÉ : 1 boîte.

595. Centre de la femme nouvelle / New Woman Centre

[For English entry, see # 627.]

✣ Montréal (Québec). Groupe fondé 1974. Dissous [197-].

Le centre avait pour tâche de promouvoir une qualité de vie équitable pour la femme dans tous ses domaines d'activité. Il offrait les principaux services suivants : un service de secours, un service d'information et de référence, des programmes d'éducation populaire et d'organisation communautaire. Le Centre de la femme nouvelle a été établi par des anciennes employées du YWCA Women's Centre, à la suite d'un conflit entre celles-ci et la Young Women's Christian Association. [Voir aussi YWCA Women's Centre (Montreal, Quebec) (638).]

LIEU DE CONSULTATION : Fonds des Archives canadiennes du mouvement des femmes, Collections spéciales de la Bibliothèque Morisset, Université d'Ottawa. (Voir Annexe pour l'adresse.)
NOM DU FONDS : New Woman Centre.
MATÉRIEL : Rapport, 1976; bulletin, 1974; correspondance, 1974-1975; coupure de presse, 1977; tracts.
QUANTITÉ : 3 cm.
ÉTAT : Assez bon.
ACCÈS : Aucune restriction.

596. Centre de planning familial du Québec

✣ Montréal (Québec). Groupe fondé 1967. Dissous 1972.

Le centre a fondé une clinique de planning familial, s'est impliqué dans le débat sur l'avortement et a fait des recherches sur les aspects sociaux et psychologiques de la sexualité.

LIEU DE CONSULTATION : Université du Québec à Montréal, Service des archives. (Voir Annexe pour l'adresse.)
NOM DU FONDS : Fonds du Centre de planning familial du Québec (113P).
MATÉRIEL : Règlements de régie interne, documents financiers, procès-verbaux, dossiers de comités, dossiers de projets, coupures de presse, documents divers.
QUANTITÉ : Env. 1 m.
ÉTAT : Bon.
ACCÈS : Aucune restriction.
INSTRUMENT DE RECHERCHE : « Répertoire numérique simple du fonds du Centre de planning familial ».

597. Committee for the Feminist Symposium, Montreal 1973

✣ Montreal, Quebec. Formed [1972 or 1973]. Disbanded 1973.

The committee organized the Feminist Symposium/Symposium féministe, held at McGill University. The conference's theme was "A change is about to come/Au seuil d'un jour nouveau."

LOCATION OF RECORDS: Canadian Women's Movement Archives Collection, Morisset Library Special Collections, University of Ottawa. (See Appendix for address.)
COLLECTION NAME: Conf.: "Feminist Symposium," June 1973, Montreal.
RECORDS: Conference records, 1973.
AMOUNT: 2 mm.
CONDITION: Fair.
ACCESS: No restrictions.

598. Conseil des femmes de Montréal / Montreal Council of Women

[For English entry, see # 621.]

✣ Montréal (Québec). Groupe fondé 1893.

LIEU DE CONSULTATION : Archives nationales du Canada. (Voir Annexe pour l'adresse.)
NOM DU FONDS : Conseil des femmes de Montréal (MG 28, I 164).
MATÉRIEL : Voir la note sur les fonds des Archives nationales du Canada, notice 4.

599. École des hautes études commerciales. Groupe femmes, gestion et entreprises

✣ Montréal (Québec). Groupe fondé 1981.

Le Groupe femmes, gestion et entreprises a été mis sur pied par des professeures de l'École des hautes études commerciales. Il vise à promouvoir, réaliser et diffuser des recherches et des interventions susceptibles de contribuer à l'avancement des femmes dans les entreprises.

LIEU DE CONSULTATION : École des hautes études commerciales, Service des archives. (Voir Annexe pour l'adresse.)
NOM DU FONDS : Fonds du Groupe femmes, gestion et entreprises (E010).
MATÉRIEL : Rapports d'activités, documents de colloques, rapports de recherche, 1982-1990.
QUANTITÉ : 24 pièces.
ÉTAT : Bon.
INSTRUMENT DE RECHERCHE : La description à la pièce est disponible par le truchement du Fichier informatique des archives historiques.

600. Église catholique. Diocèse de Sainte-Anne-de-la-Pocatière. Service de la condition des femmes dans l'Église et la société

✣ La Pocatière (Québec). Groupe fondé 1984.

Dans le diocèse de La Pocatière, le Service de la condition des femmes a été créé en 1988, mais un comité diocésain se penchait déjà sur cette problématique depuis 1984. Les objectifs du service comprennent les suivants : promouvoir la place et le rôle des femmes dans l'Église et dans la société et susciter des actions qui favorisent la reconnaissance de la dignité et de l'égalité des femmes et des hommes.

LIEU DE CONSULTATION : Archives de l'Évêché de Sainte-Anne-de-la-Pocatière. (Voir Annexe pour l'adresse.)

NOM DU FONDS : Service de la condition des femmes dans l'Église et la société (306.122).

MATÉRIEL : Correspondance, comptes rendus des réunions, documents divers, 1984-1990; photographies, 1990.

QUANTITÉ : Env. 1 m.

ACCÈS : Aucune restriction à date.

601. Family Planning Association of Montreal / Association pour la planification familiale de Montréal

[Renseignements en français, notice 590.]

✣ Montreal, Quebec. Formed 1964. Disbanded.

The Family Planning Association of Montreal co-operated with the Lakeshore Unitarian Church to establish a family-planning centre in Pointe-Claire. The association belonged to the Family Planning Federation of Canada. (Source: Archives nationales du Québec finding aid, 1990.) [See also Lakeshore Unitarian Church. Family Planning Advisory Service (612).]

LOCATION OF RECORDS: Archives nationales du Québec, Centre d'archives de Montréal. (See Appendix for address.)

COLLECTION NAME: Association pour la planification familiale de Montréal (P99).

RECORDS: Agendas, 1966-1969; minutes, 1964, 1966-1970; correspondence, 1966-1978; financial reports, 1966-1967; newsletters, newspaper articles, 1966-1973; constitution, leaflets, pamphlet, speech, miscellaneous records.

AMOUNT: 11 cm.

FINDING AID: "Répertoire du fonds de l'Association pour la planification familiale de Montréal" (Instrument de recherche # 6003005).

602. Fédération canadienne des clubs de femmes de carrières libérales et commerciales. Club de Shawinigan

✣ Shawinigan (Québec). Groupe fondé 1959.

Le but du club est d'encourager l'esprit de coopération parmi les femmes de carrières et de professions.

LIEU DE CONSULTATION : Archives nationales du Québec, Centre d'archives de la Mauricie et des Bois-Francs. (Voir Annexe pour l'adresse.)

NOM DU FONDS : Fédération canadienne des clubs de femmes de carrières libérales et commerciales (04T-P42).

MATÉRIEL : Correspondance, procès-verbaux, rapports, mémoires, documents divers, 1966-1976.

QUANTITÉ : 32 cm.

ACCÈS : Aucune restriction.

603. Fédération des femmes du Québec

[Voir aussi la notice 1203 (dans la partie II) pour autres documents de ce groupe.]

✣ Montréal (Québec). Groupe fondé 1966.

La Fédération des femmes du Québec (FFQ) s'est donné pour mission de travailler solidairement, dans une perspective féministe, à l'accès des femmes à l'égalité dans tous les secteurs d'activité : social, politique, économique, juridique, familial et culturel. La fédération comprend une centaine d'associations membres à travers le Québec.

LIEU DE CONSULTATION : Archives nationales du Canada. (Voir Annexe pour l'adresse.)

NOM DU FONDS : Fait partie du fonds Thérèse Casgrain (MG 32, C 25).

MATÉRIEL : Voir la note sur les fonds des Archives nationales du Canada, notice 4.

604. Fédération des femmes du Québec. Conseil régional de Québec

✣ Québec (Québec). Groupe fondé 1968.

Le conseil régional de Québec (CRQ) respecte les objectifs de la Fédération des femmes du Québec (FFQ), mais en tenant compte d'abord des priorités régionales. (Source : *Guide sommaire* : Archives des femmes au Québec/Madeleine Lamothe, Ghislaine Fecteau et Pierrette Lalancette. — Québec : Archives nationales du Québec, 1990.)

LIEU DE CONSULTATION : Archives nationales du Québec, Centre d'archives de Québec et de Chaudière-Appalaches. (Voir Annexe pour l'adresse.)

NOM DU FONDS : Conseil régional de Québec de la Fédération des femmes du Québec.

MATÉRIEL : Historique, statuts et règlements, procès-verbaux et documents annexes, correspondance, états financiers, rapports annuels, rapports d'activités, documents administratifs, mémoires, bulletins internes, coupures de presse, documents divers, 1966-1990.

QUANTITÉ : 96 cm.

ACCÈS : Accessible.

INSTRUMENT DE RECHERCHE : « Répertoire sommaire du Conseil régional de Québec de la Fédération des femmes du Québec ».

605. Fédération nationale des femmes canadiennes-françaises. Section Rouyn-Noranda

✣ Rouyn-Noranda (Québec). Groupe fondé 1936. Dissous.

La Fédération nationale des femmes canadiennes-françaises (FNFCF) vise à sensibiliser les milieux minoritaires aux problèmes collectifs spécifiques des femmes francophones et à impliquer les femmes francophones dans une action communautaire propre à améliorer leur condition. (Source : dépliant de la FNFCF [siège social].) La FNFCF s'appelait auparavant la Fédération des femmes canadiennes-françaises (FFCF).

LIEU DE CONSULTATION : Archives nationales du Québec, Centre d'archives de l'Abitibi-Témiscamingue. (Voir Annexe pour l'adresse.)

NOM DU FONDS : Fonds de la Fédération des femmes canadiennes-françaises, section Rouyn-Noranda (08-Y,P63).

MATÉRIEL : Règlements, 1979; listes des membres, 1936-1946, 1953-1979; procès-verbaux, 1936-1947, 1952-1979; documents financiers, 1955-1982; liste des présences, 1969-1976; correspondance, 1965-1981; rapports, 1960-1976; dossiers de projets, 1966, 1979; communiqués de presse, 1963-1970; coupures de presse, 1961-1981; contes, [1979?]; diplôme, 1976; rubans, 1946, 1961; texte de prière, texte de chansons, tableaux, timbres de caoutchouc (étampes), épinglettes, carte d'identification, photographies, documents divers.

INSTRUMENT DE RECHERCHE : Inventaire sommaire n° 800065-VV-MF.

606. Fédération nationale Saint-Jean-Baptiste

✣ Montréal (Québec). Groupe fondé 1907.

La fédération, qui est issue de la section féminine de la Société Saint-Jean-Baptiste de Montréal, est devenue autonome en 1912. Elle s'exerce dans les domaines de la charité, de l'éducation et de la vie économique, familiale et sociale. Une des initiatives de la fédération a été de réunir en associations des employées de bureau et de magasin, des ouvrières, des institutrices et des femmes d'affaires, afin de promouvoir les intérêts matériels et moraux des femmes qui travaillent. (Source : *Guide sommaire : Archives des femmes au Québec*/Madeleine Lamothe, Ghislaine Fecteau et Pierrette Lalancette. — Québec : Archives nationales du Québec, 1990.)

Fonds (a)

LIEU DE CONSULTATION : Archives nationales du Québec, Centre d'archives de Montréal. (Voir Annexe pour l'adresse.)

NOM DU FONDS : Fédération nationale Saint-Jean-Baptiste.

MATÉRIEL : Charte, buts de la fédération, statuts et règlements, demandes de constitution en société, historiques, renseignements sur la fédération, correspondance, procès-verbaux, rapports d'activités, listes, bulletins de vote, bilans, contrats, permis, documents financiers, requêtes, enquêtes, pétitions, mémoires, souscriptions, programmes, plaidoiries, baux, assurances, coupures de presse, discours, imprimés, documents iconographiques, documents divers, 1903-1977.

QUANTITÉ : 10,61 m.

ACCÈS : Accessible.

INSTRUMENT DE RECHERCHE : « Répertoire des manuscrits et des imprimés du fonds de la Fédération nationale Saint-Jean-Baptiste ».

Fonds (b)

LIEU DE CONSULTATION : Archives nationales du Canada. (Voir Annexe pour l'adresse.)

NOM DU FONDS : Fait partie du fonds Florence Fernet-Martel (MG 30, C 106).

MATÉRIEL : Voir la note sur les fonds des Archives nationales du Canada, notice 4.

607. Feminist Communication Collective

✣ Montreal, Quebec. Formed [197-]. Disbanded.

The Feminist Communication Collective published a newsletter of the same name for Montreal feminists.

Collection (a)

LOCATION OF RECORDS: Canadian Women's Movement Archives Collection, Morisset Library Special Collections, University of Ottawa. (See Appendix for address.)

COLLECTION NAME: Feminist Communication Collective.

RECORDS: Newsletters, 1973-1975, 1977.

AMOUNT: 1.5 cm.

CONDITION: Good.

ACCESS: No restrictions.

Collection (b)

LOCATION OF RECORDS: Thomas Fisher Rare Book Library, University of Toronto. (See Appendix for address.)

COLLECTION NAME: Forms part of: F.M. Denison collection.

RECORDS: Newsletters, 1974-1975, 1977.

AMOUNT: 1.5 cm.

ACCESS: No restrictions.

608. Féministes lesbiennes de Montréal / Lesbian Feminists of Montreal

[For English entry, see # 614.]

✣ Montréal (Québec). Groupe fondé [1977?].

Les Féministes lesbiennes de Montréal ont entrepris, parmi d'autres activités, de mettre sur pied des groupes de discussion.

LIEU DE CONSULTATION : Canadian Gay Archives. (Voir Annexe pour l'adresse.)

NOM DU FONDS : Lesbian Feminists of Montreal Newsletter.

MATÉRIEL : Bulletins, 1977.

QUANTITÉ : 2 pièces.

609. The Flaming Apron

✣ Montreal, Quebec. Disbanded [197-].

The Flaming Apron was a non-profit store which sold women's craft work. It also organized consciousness-raising groups and skills exchanges. [See also La Centrale (593).]

LOCATION OF RECORDS: Canadian Women's Movement Archives Collection, Morisset Library Special Collections, University of Ottawa. (See Appendix for address.)

COLLECTION NAME: The Flaming Apron.

RECORDS: Correspondence, 1973; flyer.

AMOUNT: 3 pages.

CONDITION: Good.

ACCESS: No restrictions.

610. Front de libération des femmes québécoises

[For English entry, see # 611.]

✣ Montréal (Québec). Groupe fondé 1970. Dissous 1971.

Le Front de libération des femmes québécoises (FLF) avait trois objectifs : la libération des femmes, le socialisme et la libération du Québec.

LIEU DE CONSULTATION : Fonds des Archives canadiennes du mouvement des femmes, Collections spéciales de la Bibliothèque Morisset, Université d'Ottawa. (Voir Annexe pour l'adresse.)

NOM DU FONDS : Front de libération des femmes québécoises.

MATÉRIEL : Manifeste, 1971; historique de l'association.

QUANTITÉ : 2 pièces.

ÉTAT : Assez bon.

ACCÈS : Aucune restriction.

611. Front de libération des femmes québécoises

[Renseignements en français, notice 610.]

✣ Montreal, Quebec. Formed 1970. Disbanded 1971.

Le Front de libération des femmes québécoises (FLF) had three objectives: women's liberation, socialism, and the liberation of Quebec.

LOCATION OF RECORDS: Canadian Women's Movement Archives Collection, Morisset Library Special Collections, University of Ottawa. (See Appendix for address.)

COLLECTION NAME: Front de libération des femmes québécoises.

RECORDS: Manifesto, 1971; organization history.

AMOUNT: 2 items.

CONDITION: Fair.

ACCESS: No restrictions.

612. Lakeshore Unitarian Church. Family Planning Advisory Service

✢ Pointe-Claire, Quebec. Disbanded.

Lakeshore Unitarian Church established the Family Planning Advisory Service in co-operation with the Family Planning Association of Montreal. [See also Family Planning Association of Montreal/Association pour la planification familiale de Montréal (601).]

LOCATION OF RECORDS: Archives nationales du Québec, Centre d'archives de Montréal. (See Appendix for address.)
COLLECTION NAME: Forms part of: Association pour la planification familiale de Montréal collection (P99).
RECORDS: Minutes, 1966-1967; financial document, equipment list, 1967; report, 1967-1968; correspondence, miscellaneous records.
AMOUNT: 27 items.
FINDING AID: "Répertoire du fonds de l'Association pour la planification familiale de Montréal" (Instrument de recherche # 6003005).

613. Lesbian and Gay Friends of Concordia

✢ Montreal, Quebec. Formed [ca. 1974].

This organization at Concordia University was originally called Gay Friends of Concordia.

LOCATION OF RECORDS: Canadian Gay Archives. (See Appendix for address.)
COLLECTION NAME: Lesbian and Gay Friends of Concordia (83-008).
RECORDS: Administrative files, correspondence, newsletters, miscellaneous records, 1978-1980.
AMOUNT: 10 cm.

614. Lesbian Feminists of Montreal / Féministes lesbiennes de Montréal

[Renseignements en français, notice 608.]

✢ Montreal, Quebec. Formed 1977. Disbanded [197-?].

Lesbian Feminists of Montreal organized discussion groups, among other activities.

LOCATION OF RECORDS: Canadian Gay Archives. (See Appendix for address.)
COLLECTION NAME: Lesbian Feminists of Montreal Newsletter.
RECORDS: Newsletters, 1977.
AMOUNT: 2 items.

615. Lesbian Studies Coalition of Concordia

[See also entry # 1218 (in Part II), which lists other records of this organization.]

✢ Montreal, Quebec. Formed 1987.

This organization at Concordia University (also known as LSCC or "Lez Studs") opposes heterosexism in education and advocates the establishment of a degree-granting programme in lesbian studies. It is also committed to fighting racism, sexism, classism, and other forms of oppression. The coalition's French name is les Études lesbiennes de Concordia.

LOCATION OF RECORDS: Canadian Gay Archives. (See Appendix for address.)
COLLECTION NAME: Lesbian Studies Coalition of Concordia (91-040).
RECORDS: Conference proceedings, publication, 1988.

616. Lesbiennes de Montréal / Montreal Gay Women

[For English entry, see # 622.]

✢ Montréal (Québec).

Les Lesbiennes de Montréal ont organisé la deuxième Conférence nationale annuelle de lesbiennes (appelée aussi la Conférence de lesbiennes de Montréal), qui a eu lieu en 1975.

LIEU DE CONSULTATION: Fonds des Archives canadiennes du mouvement des femmes, Collections spéciales de la Bibliothèque Morisset, Université d'Ottawa. (Voir Annexe pour l'adresse.)
NOM DU FONDS: Montreal Gay Women; Conf.: Lesbian Conference, 2nd Annual National, January 1975, Montreal.
MATÉRIEL: Documents de congrès, 1975.
ÉTAT: Assez bon.
ACCÈS: Avec restriction. Accès conditionnel négociable.

617. Ligue des droits et libertés. Office des droits des femmes

✢ Montréal (Québec). Groupe fondé 1978.

La Ligue des droits de l'homme a été fondée en 1963. Elle est devenue la Ligue des droits et libertés en 1978 (la même année que l'établissement de son Office des droits des femmes).

LIEU DE CONSULTATION: Université du Québec à Montréal, Service des archives. (Voir Annexe pour l'adresse.)
NOM DU FONDS: Fait partie du fonds de la Ligue des droits et libertés (24P).
MATÉRIEL: Documents concernant la condition féminine et l'Office des droits des femmes (procès-verbaux, correspondance, documents divers), 1963-1985.
QUANTITÉ: 50 cm.
ÉTAT: Bon.
ACCÈS: Aucune restriction.
INSTRUMENT DE RECHERCHE: « Répertoire numérique simple du fonds de la Ligue des droits et libertés » (Publication n° 20).

618. Long Time Coming

✢ Montreal, Quebec. Formed 1973. Disbanded 1977.

Long Time Coming was a periodical by and for Montreal lesbians. It included articles, poems, stories, and announcements of upcoming events.

Collection (a)

LOCATION OF RECORDS: Canadian Gay Archives. (See Appendix for address.)
COLLECTION NAME: Conf.: Montreal Lesbian Conference, Montreal, January 19-20, 1974; Long Time Coming (Montreal) (vertical files).
RECORDS: Periodicals (Long Time Coming, 1973-1976); conference programme, 1974; press releases, 1975-1976; flyers, [197-].

Collection (b)

LOCATION OF RECORDS: Canadian Women's Movement Archives Collection, Morisset Library Special Collections, University of Ottawa. (See Appendix for address.)
COLLECTION NAME: Long Time Coming.
RECORDS: Periodicals (Long Time Coming, 1973-1975); press releases, 1975-1976.
AMOUNT: 5 cm.
CONDITION: Good.
ACCESS: No restrictions.

619. McGill University. Committee for Teaching and Research on Women

✣ Montreal, Quebec. Formed 1976.

The McGill Committee for Teaching and Research on Women (MCTRW) advocated the establishment of a centre for teaching and research on women at McGill University and provided a forum for discussion of issues relating to women's studies and the position of women at the university.

Collection (a)

LOCATION OF RECORDS: McGill University Archives. (See Appendix for address.)
COLLECTION NAME: McGill Committee for Teaching and Research on Women.
RECORDS: Sound recordings, speeches, newsletters.

Collection (b)

LOCATION OF RECORDS: McGill University Archives.
COLLECTION NAME: Forms part of: Margaret Gillett collection.
RECORDS: Miscellaneous records, 1976.

620. McGill Women's Union

✣ Montreal, Quebec. Formed [ca. 1975].

The McGill Women's Union is a student organization which maintains a women's drop-in centre and library and organizes a variety of events and services for women at McGill University.

LOCATION OF RECORDS: Canadian Women's Movement Archives Collection, Morisset Library Special Collections, University of Ottawa. (See Appendix for address.)
COLLECTION NAME: McGill Women's Union; SR 24/1-4.
RECORDS: Sound recordings (conference proceedings), 1976; programme, 1975; constitution, clippings, correspondence, advertisement, 1982; information sheet, tickets, 1981; pamphlets, 1981-1983; T-shirts, 1982, [1984 or 1985]; sticker, information card, letterhead.
AMOUNT: 3 mm of text, 4 sound recordings, 2 T-shirts.
CONDITION: Fair.
ACCESS: No restrictions.

621. Montreal Council of Women / Conseil des femmes de Montréal

[Renseignements en français, notice 598.]

✣ Montreal, Quebec. Formed 1893.

LOCATION OF RECORDS: National Archives of Canada. (See Appendix for address.)
COLLECTION NAME: Montreal Council of Women (MG 28, I 164).
RECORDS: Please see the note about National Archives of Canada collections, in entry # 2.

622. Montreal Gay Women / Lesbiennes de Montréal

[Renseignements en français, notice 616.]

✣ Montreal, Quebec.

Montreal Gay Women organized the Second Annual National Lesbian Conference (also called the Montreal Lesbian Conference), held in 1975.

LOCATION OF RECORDS: Canadian Women's Movement Archives Collection, Morisset Library Special Collections, University of Ottawa. (See Appendix for address.)
COLLECTION NAME: Montreal Gay Women; Conf.: Lesbian Conference, 2nd Annual National, January 1975, Montreal.
RECORDS: Conference records, 1975.
AMOUNT: 2 mm.
CONDITION: Fair.
ACCESS: Restricted; conditional access negotiable.

623. Montreal Women's Liberation

✣ Montreal, Quebec. Formed 1969. Disbanded [197-].

The activities of Montreal Women's Liberation (MWL) included consciousness-raising groups, an abortion committee, and a welfare committee. MWL was sometimes referred to as the Women's Liberation Movement.

LOCATION OF RECORDS: Canadian Women's Movement Archives Collection, Morisset Library Special Collections, University of Ottawa. (See Appendix for address.)
COLLECTION NAME: Montreal Women's Liberation.
RECORDS: Newsletters, 1970-1971; clipping, 1970; correspondence, 1974; organization history, proposals, policy statements, discussion paper, recommendations, notes.
AMOUNT: 1.5 cm.
CONDITION: Good.
ACCESS: No restrictions.

624. Montreal Young Women's Christian Association

✣ Montreal, Quebec. Formed 1874.

[See also YWCA Women's Centre (Montreal, Quebec) (638).]

LOCATION OF RECORDS: National Archives of Canada. (See Appendix for address.)
COLLECTION NAME: Montreal Young Women's Christian Association (MG 28 I 240).
RECORDS: Please see the note about National Archives of Canada collections, in entry # 2.

625. Naches

[Renseignements en français, notice 626.]

✣ Montreal, Quebec. Formed 1977.

Naches was a group for Jewish gays and lesbians in Montreal. It organized discussions, social events, religious services, and holiday celebrations.

LOCATION OF RECORDS: Canadian Gay Archives. (See Appendix for address.)
COLLECTION NAME: Naches (87-012).
RECORDS: Newsletters, 1978-1983; correspondence, 1977-1980, 1982; press release, 1978; programme, 1982; list of library holdings, 1979.
AMOUNT: 2 cm.

626. Naches

[For English entry, see # 625.]

✣ Montréal (Québec). Groupe fondé 1977.

Naches était un organisme regroupant des lesbiennes et gais juifs de Montréal. Il a organisé des discussions, des événements sociaux, des services religieux et des célébrations de fêtes.

LIEU DE CONSULTATION: Canadian Gay Archives. (Voir Annexe pour l'adresse.)
NOM DU FONDS: Naches (87-012).

On Jan 19 and 20 there was a lesbian conference in Montreal. It was, for me, the first conference of any kind that I'd ever attended in my whole life. The conference was more than a political experience, it was also an emotional experience.

Before the workshops began, we just sat and chatted. And lesbians just kept arriving and arriving. The vibrations were very good; everyone was friendly and wanted to meet their sisters from Ottawa and Hamilton and Waterloo and Montreal and New York State and everywhere else. You could just sit back and feel the collective energies of about a hundred lesbians in two rooms. The feeling was good; it was a combination of solidarity as lesbians and strength as a group.

My first workshop was Lesbianism and Society. A group of three of us broke off to discuss Lesbians and Politics. This was the most interesting of all my discussions. Basically, our conclusion was that the consciousness of society and of other lesbians would have to be raised before we could be accepted by straights as a positive alternative to their society. Speaking to straight school, church or social groups seems to be one of the best ways to achieve this. They can see for themselves that we look like other women, simply because we are women, and as varied and individual as straight women are.

Excerpt from a personal account of a conference / Extrait d'un compte rendu personnel
National Lesbian Conference / Conférence nationale de lesbiennes, 1975
Montreal Gay Women / Lesbiennes de Montréal
CWMA Collection / Fonds de l'ACMF

QUÉBEC

MATÉRIEL: Bulletins, 1978-1983; correspondance, 1977-1980, 1982; communiqué de presse, 1978; programme, 1982; liste de livres de bibliothèque, 1979.
QUANTITÉ: 2 cm.

627. New Woman Centre / Centre de la femme nouvelle

[Renseignements en français, notice 595.]

✣ Montreal, Quebec. Formed 1974. Disbanded [197-].

The centre's purpose was to promote equality of opportunity in all aspects of women's lives. Its services included crisis intervention, information and referral, education, and community organizing. The New Woman Centre was founded by former staff of the YWCA Women's Centre following a dispute between staff and the YWCA. [See also YWCA Women's Centre (Montreal, Quebec) (638).]

LOCATION OF RECORDS: Canadian Women's Movement Archives Collection, Morisset Library Special Collections, University of Ottawa. (See Appendix for address.)
COLLECTION NAME: New Woman Centre.
RECORDS: Report, 1976; newsletter, 1974; correspondence, 1974-1975; clipping, 1977; flyers.
AMOUNT: 3 cm.
CONDITION: Fair.
ACCESS: No restrictions.

628. Nouveau Parti démocratique du Québec. Comité féminin

✣ Montréal (Québec). Groupe fondé 1965.

Le Nouveau Parti démocratique du Canada, né en 1961, est la continuation de la Co-operative Commonwealth Federation et de son aile québécoise, le Parti social démocratique. Le Nouveau Parti démocratique du Québec (NPD-Q) a abordé des questions diverses concernant les femmes et a mis sur pied un Comité féminin. (Source : instrument de recherche du Service des archives de l'Université du Québec à Montréal.)

LIEU DE CONSULTATION: Université du Québec à Montréal, Service des archives. (Voir Annexe pour l'adresse.)
NOM DU FONDS: Fait partie du fonds du Nouveau Parti démocratique du Québec (39P).
MATÉRIEL: Documents ayant trait au Comité féminin et au mouvement des femmes (correspondance, rapports, documents divers), 1963-1980.
QUANTITÉ: 10 cm.
ÉTAT: Bon.
ACCÈS: Aucune restriction.
INSTRUMENT DE RECHERCHE: « Répertoire numérique détaillé du fonds du Nouveau Parti démocratique du Québec ».

629. Organisation marxiste-léniniste du Canada En Lutte!. Comité de la condition féminine

✣ Montréal (Québec). Groupe dissous.

Le groupe En Lutte! a été fondé en 1972 et le premier numéro du journal En Lutte! a été lancé en 1973. En 1979, le groupe a adopté le nom d'Organisation marxiste-léniniste du Canada En Lutte!. La plupart de ses membres étaient des Québécois. Au tournant des années 80, le groupe s'est rapproché du mouvement féministe. Des débats sur le féminisme ont eu lieu au sein de l'organisme avant sa dissolution en 1982. (Source : instrument de recherche du Service des archives de l'Université du Québec à Montréal, 1987.)

Fonds (a)

LIEU DE CONSULTATION: Université du Québec à Montréal, Service des archives. (Voir Annexe pour l'adresse.)
NOM DU FONDS: Fait partie du fonds de l'Organisation marxiste-léniniste du Canada En Lutte! (38P13a).
MATÉRIEL: Articles, notes de travail, communiqués, comptes-rendus, correspondance, résolutions, discours, procès-verbaux et documents annexes, rapports, notes, bilans, plans de travail, déclaration, étude, textes divers, 1974-1982.
QUANTITÉ: 168 pièces.
ACCÈS: Les archives du Comité de la condition féminine sont consultables sans restriction.
INSTRUMENT DE RECHERCHE: « Répertoire numérique simple du fonds de l'Organisation marxiste-léniniste du Canada En Lutte! » (Publication n° 30).

Fonds (b)

LIEU DE CONSULTATION: Université du Québec à Montréal, Service des archives.
NOM DU FONDS: Fait partie du fonds Charles-Gagnon (124P).
MATÉRIEL: Documents divers, 1970-1982.
QUANTITÉ: 20 cm.
ÉTAT: Bon.
ACCÈS: L'autorisation écrite de Charles Gagnon (le donateur) est nécessaire pour consulter ces documents.
INSTRUMENT DE RECHERCHE: « Répertoire numérique simple du fonds Charles-Gagnon ».

630. Parti communiste ouvrier. Comité des femmes

✣ Montréal (Québec).

L'objectif du parti était d'organiser une révolution prolétarienne au Canada afin d'y instaurer le socialisme et ensuite le communisme. À ses débuts, le parti était connu sous le nom de Ligue communiste (marxiste-léniniste) du Canada. Né en 1975, le parti a été dissous en 1983.

LIEU DE CONSULTATION: Université du Québec à Montréal, Service des archives. (Voir Annexe pour l'adresse.)
NOM DU FONDS: Fait partie du fonds du Parti communiste ouvrier (47P).
MATÉRIEL: Documents ayant trait au Comité des femmes et au mouvement des femmes, 1974-1982.
QUANTITÉ: 20 cm.
ÉTAT: Bon.
ACCÈS: Aucune restriction.
INSTRUMENT DE RECHERCHE: « Répertoire numérique simple du fonds du Parti communiste ouvrier » (Publication n° 35).

631. Stop Rape Week Committee

✣ Montreal, Quebec. Formed 1984. Disbanded 1985.

The committee's purpose was to increase public awareness about rape and related issues such as pornography, sexual harassment, militarization, and incest. The committee organized workshops, demonstrations, lectures, and films in the week around International Women's Day in 1985. The committee was affiliated with the McGill Women's Union, the Concordia Women's Collective, and Dawson New School.

LOCATION OF RECORDS: Canadian Women's Movement Archives Collection, Morisset Library Special Collections, University of Ottawa. (See Appendix for address.)
COLLECTION NAME: Stop Rape Week Committee — Montreal.
RECORDS: Photographs, pamphlets, clipping, correspondence, flyers, 1985.

AMOUNT: 3 mm of text, 5 photographs.
CONDITION: Good.
ACCESS: No restrictions.

632. Université Laval. Comité d'étude sur la condition féminine

✣ Québec (Québec). Groupe fondé 1979. Dissous [1980?].

Le Cabinet du recteur de l'Université Laval a formé le Comité d'étude sur la condition féminine à l'Université Laval à la suite de la publication par le Conseil du statut de la femme du rapport *Pour les Québécoises : égalité et indépendance*. Le mandat du comité était d'analyser *Pour les Québécoises*, en dégager les recommandations pouvant avoir une incidence sur l'Université Laval et formuler des recommandations susceptibles d'améliorer la condition des femmes à l'Université. Le rapport du comité, intitulé *L'Université Laval au féminin*, contient 185 recommandations. [Voir aussi Université Laval. Comité pour l'Université Laval au féminin (633).]

LIEU DE CONSULTATION : Université Laval, Division des archives. (Voir Annexe pour l'adresse.)
NOM DU FONDS : Fait partie du fonds du Cabinet du recteur (U502/31/2 [Bu 163.14]).
MATÉRIEL : Rapport, [1980?].
QUANTITÉ : 1,7 cm.
ÉTAT : Bon.
ACCÈS : Aucune restriction.

633. Université Laval. Comité pour l'Université Laval au féminin

✣ Québec (Québec). Groupe fondé 1981. Dissous 1987.

Le comité a été mis sur pied pour veiller à l'application des recommandations du rapport du Comité d'étude sur la condition féminine à l'Université Laval. Ses activités consistaient surtout à sensibiliser la communauté universitaire aux problèmes de discrimination sexuelle et au sexisme sur le campus et de conseiller les directeurs des unités de l'Université. En 1987, le comité a été remplacé par une coordonnatrice à la condition féminine et un comité des responsables de la condition féminine. [Voir aussi Université Laval. Comité d'étude sur la condition féminine (632).]

LIEU DE CONSULTATION : Université Laval, Division des archives. (Voir Annexe pour l'adresse.)
NOM DU FONDS : Fait partie du fonds du Cabinet du recteur (U502/31/2 [Bu 163.17]).
MATÉRIEL : Étude, 1982; dépliants, 1983.
QUANTITÉ : 5 mm.
ÉTAT : Bon.
ACCÈS : Aucune restriction.

634. Université Laval. Groupe gai

✣ Québec (Québec). Groupe fondé 1977.

Les buts du Groupe gai de l'Université Laval (GGUL) sont les suivants : faciliter l'échange social entre les personnes gaies (hommes et femmes) de la communauté universitaire; favoriser l'échange et la diffusion de l'information pertinente au sujet de l'homosexualité; et appuyer les personnes et les groupes subissant des attaques policières et judiciaires.

LIEU DE CONSULTATION : Université Laval, Division des archives. (Voir Annexe pour l'adresse.)
NOM DU FONDS : Fonds du Groupe gai de l'Université Laval (P318).
MATÉRIEL : Fondation et constitution, procès-verbaux, documents financiers, listes des membres, dossiers divers, 1978-1988.
QUANTITÉ : 35 cm.
ÉTAT : Bon.
ACCÈS : Jusqu'au 20 juin 1996, toute consultation du fonds requiert l'autorisation écrite du conseil d'administration du GGUL. Certains dossiers sont fermés à la consultation pendant quatre-vingts ans à moins d'une autorisation écrite du conseil d'administration.
INSTRUMENT DE RECHERCHE : Listes d'envoi des documents disponibles.

635. *A Woman's Place* (Montreal, Quebec)

✣ Montreal, Quebec. Formed [197-]. Disbanded [197-].

A Woman's Place (also called A Women's Place) was a women's centre.

LOCATION OF RECORDS: Canadian Women's Movement Archives Collection, Morisset Library Special Collections, University of Ottawa. (See Appendix for address.)
COLLECTION NAME: Women's Place Newsletter, Montreal.
RECORDS: Newsletters, 1973.
AMOUNT: 5 items.
CONDITION: Good.
ACCESS: No restrictions.

636. *Women's Collective Press*

✣ Montreal, Quebec. Formed [1975?]. Disbanded.

The Women's Collective Press (WCP) was a student organization at McGill University which produced a feminist newspaper of the same name.

LOCATION OF RECORDS: Canadian Women's Movement Archives Collection, Morisset Library Special Collections, University of Ottawa. (See Appendix for address.)
COLLECTION NAME: Women's Collective Press.
RECORDS: Newspapers, 1975-1976; correspondence, flyer, 1976.
AMOUNT: 1.5 cm.
CONDITION: Poor.
ACCESS: No restrictions.

637. *Women's Liberation Study Group* (Montreal, Quebec)

✣ Montreal, Quebec. Disbanded.

LOCATION OF RECORDS: Canadian Women's Movement Archives Collection, Morisset Library Special Collections, University of Ottawa. (See Appendix for address.)
COLLECTION NAME: Women's Liberation Study Group.
RECORDS: Position papers, [ca. 1970].
AMOUNT: 3 mm.
CONDITION: Fair.
ACCESS: No restrictions.

638. *YWCA Women's Centre* (Montreal, Quebec)

✣ Montreal, Quebec. Disbanded.

The YWCA Women's Centre (also called the Women's Information Centre) was part of the Montreal Young Women's Christian Association. The centre offered counselling and information on a wide range of women's concerns (including abortion). The centre's overall goal was to help girls and women in their efforts toward personal fulfilment and social change. [See also Montreal Young Women's Christian Association (624) and New Woman Centre/Centre de la femme nouvelle (627).]

LOCATION OF RECORDS: Canadian Women's Movement Archives Collection, Morisset Library Special Collections, University of Ottawa. (See Appendix for address.)

COLLECTION NAME: YWCA Women's Centre, Montreal.
RECORDS: Reports, 1972-1974; newsletters, 1974-1976; proposal, 1971; statement of objectives, 1972; chart, flyer.
AMOUNT: 1 cm.
CONDITION: Poor.
ACCESS: No restrictions.

NEW BRUNSWICK / NOUVEAU-BRUNSWICK

639. Association des femmes chefs de famille. (Moncton, N.-B.)

✢ Moncton (N.-B.) Groupe fondé 1974. Dissous 1982.

L'idée d'un regroupement de femmes chefs de famille est née lors d'un colloque provincial sur le statut de la femme en 1974; un comité exécutif provincial a été nommé en 1975; et une association permanente a été créée en 1976. L'association a offert les services suivants à ses membres : réunions mensuelles, cours, conférences, activités sociales, bulletin mensuel et autres services.

LIEU DE CONSULTATION : Centre d'études acadiennes, Université de Moncton. (Voir Annexe pour l'adresse.)

NOM DU FONDS : Association des femmes chefs de famille (205, P205).

MATÉRIEL : Rapports, 1973-1982; procès-verbaux, documents financiers, 1976-1982; annuaire, 1978; avis de convocation, 1974-1977; correspondance, 1974-1982; dossier de presse, 1976; mémoires, 1973-1980; notes historiques, liste de cours, programme, 1981; ordres du jour, 1977-1982; statistiques, 1978-1982; statuts et règlements, enquête, études, fiches, formulaires, liste d'adresse, liste des membres, liste des participantes, notes de cours, organigrammes, dépliants, photographies, plans d'action, questionnaires, articles de revue, bibliographie, bulletins d'information, cartes de remerciement, communiqués de presse, conférences.

QUANTITÉ : 1,7 m.

ACCÈS : Restrictions sur les dossiers du personnel.

640. Canadian Federation of University Women. Sackville Club

✢ Sackville, N.B.

Clubs belonging to the Canadian Federation of University Women (CFUW) are local organizations of women university graduates. CFUW's goals include encouraging women scholars and safeguarding the rights of women. (Source: *The Canadian Encyclopedia*. — Edmonton: Hurtig Publishers, 1985.)

LOCATION OF RECORDS: Mount Allison University Archives. (See Appendix for address.)

COLLECTION NAME: Canadian Federation of Women — Sackville Club (7931).

RECORDS: Minutes, 1947-1950, 1956-1989; constitution and by-laws, 1940-1967, 1978; reports, 1948-1989; correspondence, 1947-1985, 1988-1989; financial records, 1949-1978; membership lists, 1947-1978; resolutions, 1963-1989; clippings, handbook, newsletters, miscellaneous records.

FINDING AID: Preliminary inventory available.

641. Coalition pour la réforme des droits de la personne du Nouveau-Brunswick / New Brunswick Coalition for Human Rights Reform

[For English entry, see # 648.]

✢ Fredericton (N.-B.).

La coalition a pour but de réduire la discrimination et la violence dirigée contre les personnes gaies et bisexuelles. Elle veut faire adopter des modifications au Code des droits de la personne du Nouveau-Brunswick et à la Loi canadienne sur les droits de la personne.

LIEU DE CONSULTATION : Canadian Gay Archives. (Voir Annexe pour l'adresse.)

NOM DU FONDS : New Brunswick Coalition for Human Rights Reform (91-039).

MATÉRIEL : Mémoires, brochures, papier à lettres à en-tête, macarons, documents divers, 1988-1991.

QUANTITÉ : 1 boîte.

642. Conference '80: Women and the Economy (1980: Fredericton, N.B.). Provincial Organizing Committee

✢ Formed 1979. Disbanded [1980?].

LOCATION OF RECORDS: Canadian Women's Movement Archives Collection, Morisset Library Special Collections, University of Ottawa. (See Appendix for address.)

COLLECTION NAME: Conf.: "Women and the Economy," New Brunswick, 1980.

RECORDS: Conference records, 1980.

AMOUNT: 7 mm.

CONDITION: Good.

ACCESS: No restrictions.

643. Equal Times

✣ Fredericton, N.B. Formed [197-]. Disbanded [197-].

Equal Times was a feminist newspaper.

LOCATION OF RECORDS: Canadian Women's Movement Archives Collection, Morisset Library Special Collections, University of Ottawa. (See Appendix for address.)
COLLECTION NAME: Equal Times (New Brunswick).
RECORDS: Newspapers, 1975.
AMOUNT: 2 cm.
CONDITION: Fair.
ACCESS: No restrictions.

644. Fredericton Lesbians and Gays

✣ Fredericton, N.B. Formed 1979.

Fredericton Lesbians and Gays (FLAG) is dedicated to the well-being of lesbians, bisexuals, and gay men in New Brunswick.

LOCATION OF RECORDS: Canadian Gay Archives. (See Appendix for address.)
COLLECTION NAME: Stephen Dopp (86-017).
RECORDS: Miscellaneous records, [before 1987].
AMOUNT: 7 cm.

645. Fredericton Women's Centre

✣ Fredericton, N.B. Formed [197-]. Disbanded.

This drop-in centre provided support, a referral service, and educational programmes.

LOCATION OF RECORDS: Canadian Women's Movement Archives Collection, Morisset Library Special Collections, University of Ottawa. (See Appendix for address.)
COLLECTION NAME: Fredericton Women's Centre.
RECORDS: Newsletters, 1975; flyers.
AMOUNT: 5 mm.
CONDITION: Good.
ACCESS: No restrictions.

646. Liberté Égalité Sororité : Femmes acadiennes de Moncton

✣ Moncton (N.-B.). Groupe fondé [197-]. Dissous.

Liberté Égalité Sororité : Femmes acadiennes de Moncton s'appelait aussi LES FAM.

LIEU DE CONSULTATION : Fonds des Archives canadiennes du mouvement des femmes, Collections spéciales de la Bibliothèque Morisset, Université d'Ottawa. (Voir Annexe pour l'adresse.)
NOM DU FONDS : LES FAM.
MATÉRIEL : Bulletins, 1975.
QUANTITÉ : 3 pièces.
ÉTAT : Bon.
ACCÈS : Aucune restriction.

647. Moncton Council of Women

✣ Moncton, N.B. Formed 1918.

LOCATION OF RECORDS: Provincial Archives of New Brunswick. (See Appendix for address.)
COLLECTION NAME: Forms part of: Council of Women collection (MC626).
RECORDS: Minutes, 1946-1976; executive lists, 1936-1978; lists of affiliated societies, 1920-1980; financial records, 1956-1963, 1971; resolutions, 1936-1958; annual reports, 1946-1948, 1973-1976; scrapbooks, 1942-1975; agenda books, 1956-1959; radio talk, 1939; conference programme, 1974; constitution, by-laws, correspondence, organization history, biographies, interviews, committee files, project files, clippings, handbook, speeches, photographs, miscellaneous records.
ACCESS: No restrictions.
FINDING AID: Inventory available for Council of Women collection.

648. New Brunswick Coalition for Human Rights Reform / Coalition pour la réforme des droits de la personne du Nouveau-Brunswick

[Renseignements en français, notice 641.]

✣ Fredericton, N.B.

The coalition's goal is to reduce discrimination and violence against gay men, lesbians, and bisexual people. It lobbies for amendments to the New Brunswick Human Rights Code and the Canadian Human Rights Act.

LOCATION OF RECORDS: Canadian Gay Archives. (See Appendix for address.)
COLLECTION NAME: New Brunswick Coalition for Human Rights Reform (91-039).
RECORDS: Briefs, brochures, letterhead, buttons, miscellaneous records, 1988-1991.
AMOUNT: 1 box.

649. New Brunswick Native Indian Women's Council

✣ Fredericton, N.B. Formed 1981.

The council, which was founded at a 1981 Native Indian Women's Conference, works on behalf of all Native women in New Brunswick.

LOCATION OF RECORDS: Canadian Women's Movement Archives Collection, Morisset Library Special Collections, University of Ottawa. (See Appendix for address.)
COLLECTION NAME: New Brunswick Native Indian Women's Council.
RECORDS: Conference records, 1984-1985; correspondence, financial records, 1985; contract, 1978; constitution and by-laws, position papers, resolutions, basis of unity.
AMOUNT: 1 cm.
CONDITION: Good.
ACCESS: No restrictions.

650. New Brunswick Women's Institutes

✣ Formed 1913.

The New Brunswick Women's Institutes (NBWI) is the provincial organization representing local Women's Institutes in rural communities throughout the province. (Women's Institutes are associations of homemakers.) Educational and charitable activities are the organization's priorities. NBWI has provided scholarships to young women and held lectures dealing with women's issues.

LOCATION OF RECORDS: Provincial Archives of New Brunswick. (See Appendix for address.)
COLLECTION NAME: New Brunswick Women's Institute Records (MC492).
RECORDS: Minute books, 1922-1980.
AMOUNT: 20 volumes.
ACCESS: No restrictions.

Bulletin / Newsletter, 1975
Liberté Égalité Sororité : Femmes acadiennes de Moncton
Fonds de l'ACMF / CWMA Collection

651. Provincial Council of Women of New Brunswick

LOCATION OF RECORDS: Provincial Archives of New Brunswick. (See Appendix for address.)

COLLECTION NAME: Forms part of: Council of Women collection (MC626).

RECORDS: Constitution, by-laws, 1957, 1961; records of meetings, 1959-1966; budget, list of officers, 1961-1962; notice of nominations, 1965-1966; correspondence, 1958, 1961-1964, 1967; reports, 1947-1948, 1963; miscellaneous records.

ACCESS: No restrictions.

FINDING AID: Inventory available for Council of Women collection.

652. *Women's Atlantic Council*

✣ Fredericton, N.B. Formed 1959. Disbanded [ca. 1962].

The aims of the Women's Atlantic Council included developing members' knowledge of economic and social processes in the Atlantic provinces and extending this knowledge among all women in the region. The council was affiliated with the Atlantic Provinces Economic Council (APEC).

LOCATION OF RECORDS: Provincial Archives of New Brunswick. (See Appendix for address.)

COLLECTION NAME: Women's Atlantic Council Records (MC 1074).

RECORDS: Minutes, 1959-1962; reports, 1959-1960; constitution, correspondence, questionnaire, miscellaneous records.

AMOUNT: 5 cm.

ACCESS: No restrictions.

PRINCE EDWARD ISLAND / ÎLE-DU-PRINCE-ÉDOUARD

653. Canadian Federation of University Women. Charlottetown Branch

[See also entry # 1303 (in Part II), which lists other records of this organization.]

✣ Charlottetown, P.E.I. Formed 1955.

The Charlottetown branch of the Canadian Federation of University Women (CFUW) encourages advanced study and research by women and works to improve the status of women. It holds guest lectures and raises funds for scholarships for female students.

LOCATION OF RECORDS: Public Archives of Prince Edward Island. (See Appendix for address.)

COLLECTION NAME: Canadian Federation of University Women Fonds (3977).

RECORDS: Annual reports, constitution, by-laws, minutes, correspondence, conference reports, briefs, 1955-1984.

ACCESS: Restricted.

654. Charlottetown Business and Professional Women's Club

[See also entry # 1306 (in Part II), which lists other records of this organization.]

✣ Charlottetown, P.E.I. Formed 1949.

The Charlottetown Business and Professional Women's Club works for improvement in the status of women in Canada and around the world. The club's activities include fund raising and networking.

LOCATION OF RECORDS: Public Archives of Prince Edward Island. (See Appendix for address.)

COLLECTION NAME: P.E.I. Business and Professional Women's Clubs (3027).

RECORDS: Organization history, 1979; minutes, 1960-1977; constitution, by-laws, [ca. 1971]; correspondence, 1952-1976; reports, 1950-1973; financial records, 1951-1976; programme material, 1952-1974; seminar material, brief, 1967; clippings, 1960-1977; resolutions, 1967-1968; newsletters (*The Charlottetown Business and Professional Women's Club Newsletter*, 1952; *The Busy Women's Bulletin*, 1957-1975); scrapbook, songs, miscellaneous records.

AMOUNT: 2 boxes.

ACCESS: No restrictions.

FINDING AID: Accession listing available.

655. A Women's Newsletter

✣ Charlottetown, P.E.I. Formed 1974. Disbanded.

A Women's Newsletter provided information about women's activities in Prince Edward Island and other parts of Canada.

LOCATION OF RECORDS: Canadian Women's Movement Archives Collection, Morisset Library Special Collections, University of Ottawa. (See Appendix for address.)

COLLECTION NAME: A Women's Newsletter, Charlottetown, P.E.I.

RECORDS: Newsletters (*A Women's Newsletter*, 1974-1976).

AMOUNT: 1 cm.

CONDITION: Fair.

ACCESS: No restrictions.

656. Zonta Club (Charlottetown, P.E.I.)

✣ Charlottetown, P.E.I. Formed 1962.

The Zonta Club is a chapter of Zonta International, a service organization of women in business and the professions. Charitable activities have been the club's focus. It has also sponsored scholarships for women, and it presented a brief to the Royal Commission on the Status of Women. (Sources: Public Archives of Prince Edward Island finding aids.)

LOCATION OF RECORDS: Public Archives of Prince Edward Island. (See Appendix for address.)

COLLECTION NAME: Zonta Club (Charlottetown) Fonds (4057).

RECORDS: Minutes, correspondence, newsletters, annual reports, conference information, project information, 1962-1987.

ACCESS: The most recent five years are closed to all but club members.

FINDING AID: Accession listing available.

NOVA SCOTIA / NOUVELLE-ÉCOSSE

657. Association des Acadiennes de la Nouvelle-Écosse

[Voir aussi la notice 1316 (dans la partie II) pour autres documents de ce groupe.]

✥ Halifax (N.-É.). Groupe fondé 1984.

L'Association des Acadiennes de la Nouvelle-Écosse (AANE) vise à regrouper les femmes acadiennes de la Nouvelle-Écosse afin de travailler à leur plein épanouissement. Elle fonctionne au sein de la Fédération acadienne de la Nouvelle-Écosse (FANE), un groupe de pression et de développement communautaire. [Voir aussi Société Madeleine LeBlanc (1341).]

LIEU DE CONSULTATION : Centre acadien de l'Université Sainte-Anne. (Voir Annexe pour l'adresse.)
NOM DU FONDS : MG 8 FANE, volume 2.
MATÉRIEL : Correspondance, rapports, études, 1975-1982.
QUANTITÉ : 25 cm.

658. Atlantic Provinces Political Lesbians for Equality

✥ Halifax, N.S. Disbanded.

This organization was commonly referred to as APPLE.

Collection (a)

LOCATION OF RECORDS: Canadian Women's Movement Archives Collection, Morisset Library Special Collections, University of Ottawa. (See Appendix for address.)
COLLECTION NAME: Lesbian Canada Lesbienne; The Sisters' Lightship.
RECORDS: Newsletters (*Lesbian Canada Lesbienne*, 1977; *The Sisters' Lightship*, 1978).
AMOUNT: 2 items.
ACCESS: No restrictions.

Collection (b)

LOCATION OF RECORDS: Canadian Gay Archives. (See Appendix for address.)
RECORDS: Newsletters (*Lesbian Canada Lesbienne*, 1977; *The Sisters' Lightship*, 1978); poster, 1977.
AMOUNT: 3 items.

659. Canadian Federation of University Women. Cape Breton Branch

✥ Sydney, N.S. Formed 1967.

Branches of the Canadian Federation of University Women (CFUW) are local organizations of women university graduates. CFUW's goals include encouraging women scholars and safeguarding the rights of women. (Source: *The Canadian Encyclopedia*. — Edmonton: Hurtig Publishers, 1985.)

LOCATION OF RECORDS: Beaton Institute, University College of Cape Breton. (See Appendix for address.)
COLLECTION NAME: Canadian Federation of University Women, Cape Breton Branch (MG 14, 57).
RECORDS: Minutes, 1967-1970, 1982-1987; resolutions, 1974-1981; correspondence, 1968-1971, 1974-1980; reports, 1965-1967; newsletters, journals, 1981-1987; scrapbooks, 1967-1977, 1980-1981; organization history, clippings, booklet, miscellaneous records.
AMOUNT: 54.4 cm.
ACCESS: No restrictions.
FINDING AID: Inventory available.

660. Canadian Federation of University Women. Halifax Branch

✥ Halifax, N.S. Formed [1936?].

The Halifax Branch of the Canadian Federation of University Women (CFUW) is an association of women university graduates which encourages advanced study and research by women and advocates improvement of the status of women. (Source: *Halifax/Dartmouth/Metro Women's Directory*. — Halifax: Halifax City Regional Library, 1990.) The club has also been known as the University Women's Club of Halifax.

LOCATION OF RECORDS: Public Archives of Nova Scotia. (See Appendix for address.)
COLLECTION NAME: University Women's Club of Halifax (MG 20, Volumes 494-495, 956); Canadian Federation of University Women. Halifax Branch (MG 20, volumes 1658, 1866-1867, 3097-3098).
RECORDS: Constitution, by-laws, 1976, 1980; minutes, 1970-1987; reports, 1956-1960, 1967-1970, 1972-1973, 1975-1988; briefs, submissions, 1970-1982; financial records, 1936-1989; membership lists, 1953-1954, 1958-1967, 1969-1973, 1975-1986; newsletters, 1975-1988; conference records, 1972, 1982-1985, 1987-1988; clippings, 1976-1978; handbook, 1973-1975; sound recordings, slides, 1977; thesis, 1976; correspondence, membership cards, bulletins, notices of meetings, brochures, questionnaires, honorary-membership certificate, miscellaneous records.
AMOUNT: 1.32 m.
ACCESS: No restrictions.
FINDING AID: File lists available.

PART I: RECORDS HELD BY ARCHIVES / PARTIE I : FONDS DÉTENUS PAR DES ARCHIVES

Newsletter / Bulletin, 1978
Atlantic Provinces Political Lesbians for Equality
Artist unknown / Artiste inconnue
CWMA Collection / Fonds de l'ACMF

661. Canadian Research Institute for the Advancement of Women — Nova Scotia

[See also entry # 1318 (in Part II), which lists other records of this organization.]

✣ Halifax, N.S. Formed 1976.

This organization (also known as CRIAW — Nova Scotia) promotes the advancement of women through feminist and woman-centred research. It encourages information exchange among academic women, activists, women's groups, and concerned individuals and disseminates its research results through publications and conferences.

LOCATION OF RECORDS: Public Archives of Nova Scotia. (See Appendix for address.)
COLLECTION NAME: Forms part of: Muriel Duckworth collection (MG 1, volume 2906).
RECORDS: Minutes, agendas, 1977-1983; conference papers, 1979, 1981; membership and mailing lists.
FINDING AID: Finding aid available for Muriel Duckworth collection.

662. Cape Breton Transition House

✣ Sydney, N.S. Formed 1981.

The Cape Breton Transition House is a refuge for battered women and their children. From 1986 to 1988, it conducted a research project involving interviews with residents and statistical analysis of data compiled by the organization.

LOCATION OF RECORDS: Beaton Institute, University College of Cape Breton. (See Appendix for address.)
COLLECTION NAME: Cape Breton Transition House (MG 14, 185).
RECORDS: Research papers, 1988.
AMOUNT: 83 pages.
ACCESS: No restrictions.
FINDING AID: Inventory available.

663. Citizens' Day Care Action Committee

✣ Halifax, N.S. Formed 1971. Disbanded.

This committee was composed of parents, interested citizens, educators, and representatives of day-care centres and social and health agencies. It advocated good day-care services for all children, regardless of their parents' ability to pay.

LOCATION OF RECORDS: Canadian Women's Movement Archives Collection, Morisset Library Special Collections, University of Ottawa. (See Appendix for address.)
COLLECTION NAME: Citizens' Day Care Action Committee — Halifax.
RECORDS: Brief, 1972.
AMOUNT: 1 item.
CONDITION: Good.
ACCESS: No restrictions.

664. Gay Alliance for Equality (Halifax, N.S.)

✣ Halifax, N.S. Formed 1972. Disbanded [ca. 1987].

The Gay Alliance for Equality (GAE) had members throughout Nova Scotia. GAE's activities included a civil-rights committee and a telephone line.

LOCATION OF RECORDS: Canadian Gay Archives. (See Appendix for address.)
COLLECTION NAME: Gay Alliance for Equality (84-018).
RECORDS: Briefs, publications, miscellaneous records, 1971-1984.
AMOUNT: 13 cm.

665. Halifax Club of Business and Professional Women

✣ Halifax, N.S. Formed [1936?].

The club aims "to develop and train women in business, the professions, and industry" and "to work toward the improvement of economic, employment, and social conditions for women." (Source: *Halifax/Dartmouth/Metro Women's Directory*. — Halifax: Halifax City Regional Library, 1990.)

LOCATION OF RECORDS: Public Archives of Nova Scotia. (See Appendix for address.)
COLLECTION NAME: Halifax Club of Business and Professional Women.
RECORDS: Minutes, 1936-1976; financial records, 1936-1973; membership book, 1970-1971; roll books, 1936-1937, 1956-1957; scrapbook, 1944; correspondence, list of deceased members, organization histories, newsletter, miscellaneous records.
AMOUNT: 2.53 m.
ACCESS: No restrictions.

666. Halifax Local Council of Women

✣ Halifax, N.S. Formed 1894.

The Halifax Local Council of Women is concerned with various women's issues and other social issues, including child abuse, pornography, and battered women. (Source: *Halifax/Dartmouth/Metro Women's Directory*. — Halifax: Halifax City Regional Library, 1990.)

LOCATION OF RECORDS: Public Archives of Nova Scotia. (See Appendix for address.)
COLLECTION NAME: Halifax Local Council of Women (MG 20, No. 204).
RECORDS: Reports, minutes, correspondence, membership lists, financial records, scrapbook, histories, constitutions, handbooks, medals, photographs, programmes, menus, miscellaneous records, [189-]-1981.
AMOUNT: 1.51 m.
ACCESS: No restrictions.

667. Halifax Young Women's Christian Association

[See also entry # 1327 (in Part II), which lists other records of this organization.]

✣ Halifax, N.S. Formed 1874.

The mandate of the Halifax YWCA is to further the development of women and their families. It offers a residence, child care, employment training, adult education, and physical education. [See also A Woman's Place (Halifax, N.S.) (677).]

LOCATION OF RECORDS: Public Archives of Nova Scotia. (See Appendix for address.)
COLLECTION NAME: Young Women's Christian Association, Halifax (MG 20, volumes 776-780, 1243, 1889).
RECORDS: Scrapbooks (containing clippings, notices, pictures, programmes, financial statements, miscellaneous records), 1912-1961; programmes, 1981-1987; leaflets, brochures, 1979-1983; course information, pamphlets, newsletters.
AMOUNT: 48 cm.
ACCESS: No restrictions.
FINDING AID: File lists available.

668. Indian Brook Women's Group

LOCATION OF RECORDS: Beaton Institute, University College of Cape Breton. (See Appendix for address.)
COLLECTION NAME: Forms part of: Women Unlimited collection (MG 14, 168 — C. 2.).

RECORDS: Correspondence, posters, photographs, 1985.
AMOUNT: 2 files.
ACCESS: No restrictions.
FINDING AID: Finding aids available for Women Unlimited collection.

669. Margaret Beaton Foundation for Women

✤ Formed 1983.

This foundation was established to initiate programmes to improve the lives of women living on or below the poverty line. (Source: Beaton Institute finding aid.)

LOCATION OF RECORDS: Beaton Institute, University College of Cape Breton. (See Appendix for address.)
COLLECTION NAME: Margaret Beaton Foundation for Women (MG 10, 6).
RECORDS: Proposal, brief, 1983.
AMOUNT: 12 pages.
FINDING AID: Finding aid available.

670. Mount Saint Vincent University

[See also entry # 1331 (in Part II), which lists other records of this organization.]

✤ Halifax, N.S. Formed 1873.

Mount Saint Vincent University's primary concern has been the education of women. It began as an academy established by the Sisters of Charity. In 1925 it gained the right to grant its own degrees, making it the only independent women's college in the British Commonwealth. In 1966, Mount Saint Vincent College became Mount Saint Vincent University. Male students have been admitted since 1967, but about 85 per cent of the students are women. The Institute for the Study of Women (ISW) at Mount Saint Vincent University was established in 1981 to do research which aims to improve women's lives and promote equality for women. ISW publishes the journal *Atlantis*.

LOCATION OF RECORDS: Mount Saint Vincent University Archives. (See Appendix for address.)
COLLECTION NAME: Mount Saint Vincent University.
RECORDS: Minutes, correspondence, financial records, newsletters, clippings, photographs, pamphlets, miscellaneous records.
AMOUNT: Approx. 180 square m.
FINDING AID: "MSVU Archival Holdings" (a listing of files by broad subdivision; key words in the names of files can be searched by computer).

671. New Glasgow Local Council of Women

✤ New Glasgow, N.S. Formed 1898.

Until 1931 the New Glasgow council was called the East Pictou Local Council of Women.

LOCATION OF RECORDS: Public Archives of Nova Scotia. (See Appendix for address.)
COLLECTION NAME: New Glasgow Local Council of Women.
RECORDS: Minutes, 1898-1935, 1939-1977; roll-call book, 1951-1966; organization history, 1898-1942; citation, 1971; dues record book, 1947-1972.
AMOUNT: 45 cm of text, 3 reels of microfilm.
ACCESS: No restrictions.

672. Nova Scotia Home Economics Association. Cape Breton Branch

✤ Formed [195-].

The Nova Scotia Home Economics Association was founded to promote and encourage home economists and to improve their status. The association has been active in Cape Breton since the 1950s. (Source: Beaton Institute finding aid.)

LOCATION OF RECORDS: Beaton Institute, University College of Cape Breton. (See Appendix for address.)
COLLECTION NAME: Nova Scotia Home Economics Association. Cape Breton Branch.
RECORDS: Minutes, records of annual meetings, reports, financial records, certificate and membership forms, constitution and by-laws, convention records, correspondence, journals, mailing list, meeting announcements, membership lists, newsletters, photographs, programmes, stationery, annual reports, clippings, miscellaneous records, 1953-1984.
AMOUNT: 33 cm.

673. Nova Scotia Women's Action Committee

✤ Halifax, N.S. Formed [197-]. Disbanded [198-].

The Nova Scotia Women's Action Committee (NSWAC) took political action toward achieving the full and equal participation of women in all aspects of Nova Scotia society.

Collection (a)

LOCATION OF RECORDS: Public Archives of Nova Scotia. (See Appendix for address.)
COLLECTION NAME: Nova Scotia Women's Action Committee (MG 20, volumes 1345-1347); two files form part of: A Woman's Place collection (MG 20, vol. 1262, folders 23-24).
RECORDS: Correspondence, reports, clippings, 1975-1981; newsletters, 1974-1982; financial records, 1977-1979; personnel records, 1977-1978; press releases, announcements, 1978; by-laws, list of contacts, telephone list, working paper, pamphlets, brochures, notices, pictures, typing stencils, agenda, questionnaire, notes, miscellaneous records.
AMOUNT: 69 cm.
ACCESS: No restrictions.
FINDING AID: Finding aids available.

Collection (b)

LOCATION OF RECORDS: Dalhousie University Archives. (See Appendix for address.)
COLLECTION NAME: Nova Scotia Women's Action Committee.
RECORDS: Correspondence, minutes, reports, miscellaneous records, 1976-1978.
AMOUNT: 60 cm.
ACCESS: No restrictions.

Collection (c)

LOCATION OF RECORDS: Canadian Women's Movement Archives Collection, Morisset Library Special Collections, University of Ottawa. (See Appendix for address.)
COLLECTION NAME: Nova Scotia Women's Action Committee.
RECORDS: Constitution, 1976; minutes, membership lists, 1976-1977; correspondence, 1976-1978; position paper, questionnaire, 1978; notes, 1975-1978; flyers, 1980-1981; mailing lists, clippings, brief, press release, poster.
AMOUNT: 2 cm of text, 1 poster.
CONDITION: Good.
ACCESS: No restrictions.

674. Reel Life

✣ Halifax, N.S. Formed 1973. Disbanded [197-?].

Reel Life organized feminist film festivals, distributed women's films, and took films and other women's resources to smaller communities in Nova Scotia and New Brunswick.

LOCATION OF RECORDS: Canadian Women's Movement Archives Collection, Morisset Library Special Collections, University of Ottawa. (See Appendix for address.)

COLLECTION NAME: Reel Life.

RECORDS: Newsletters, 1974-1975, 1978; handbook, flyer, 1975; questionnaire.

AMOUNT: 1 cm.

CONDITION: Good.

ACCESS: No restrictions.

675. Voice of Women (Halifax, N.S.)

✣ Halifax, N.S.

The Halifax branch of Voice of Women (VOW) is sometimes referred to as Nova Scotia Voice of Women or Voice of Women Nova Scotia. Activities of the Halifax branch have included public speaking and lobbying.

LOCATION OF RECORDS: Public Archives of Nova Scotia. (See Appendix for address.)

COLLECTION NAME: Forms part of: Muriel Duckworth collection (MG 1, volume 2900, # 9-10, 30, 32).

RECORDS: Minutes, 1960-1985; membership lists, 1965-1969; accounts, 1962-1970.

FINDING AID: Finding aid available for Muriel Duckworth collection.

676. Westville Local Council of Women

✣ Westville, N.S. Formed [before 1943].

LOCATION OF RECORDS: Public Archives of Nova Scotia. (See Appendix for address.)

COLLECTION NAME: Forms part of: New Glasgow Local Council of Women collection (MG 20, vol. 1030, # 10-12).

RECORDS: Minute books, 1942-1959; account book, 1971-1975.

AMOUNT: 3 items.

ACCESS: No restrictions.

677. A Woman's Place (Halifax, N.S.)

✣ Halifax, N.S. Formed 1977. Disbanded [1983?].

A Woman's Place (also known as AWP or Forrest House) was a women's centre. The Halifax YWCA initiated the centre and owned the house in which it was located. [See also Halifax Young Women's Christian Association (667, 1327) and Women's Information, Resource, and Referral Service (Halifax, N.S.) (682).]

LOCATION OF RECORDS: Public Archives of Nova Scotia. (See Appendix for address.)

COLLECTION NAME: A Woman's Place (MG 20, volumes 1260-1263, 1343-1344, 1498, 1551-1552, 1563-1564).

RECORDS: Minutes, correspondence, 1977-1982; log-books, newsletters, 1977-1981; reports, 1977-1980; financial records, 1974-1983; building restoration records, 1977; appointment books, 1979-1980; telephone log, 1977-1978; notes, 1981-1982; inventory, 1981; log-book form, 1980-1981; administrative structure, 1980; staff manual, 1978; clippings, photographs, press releases, organization history, calendars, programmes, grant applications, personnel records, flyers, committee membership lists, posters, questionnaires, resource list, lists of volunteers, handbooks, pamphlet, mailing lists, publicity lists, recommendations, miscellaneous records.

AMOUNT: 2 m.

ACCESS: Restricted.

FINDING AID: "A Woman's Place Collection."

678. Women Now

✣ Formed 1977. Disbanded.

Women Now was a feminist group founded in industrial Cape Breton. It conducted a feasibility study into the reproductive health needs of women, and it applied for and implemented a Health and Welfare demonstration grant for the Family Planning Resource Team in Sydney.

LOCATION OF RECORDS: Beaton Institute, University College of Cape Breton. (See Appendix for address.)

COLLECTION NAME: Forms part of: Women Unlimited collection (MG 14, 168 — C. 1.).

RECORDS: Miscellaneous records, 1977-[ca. 1980].

AMOUNT: 2 cm.

ACCESS: No restrictions.

FINDING AID: Finding aids available for Women Unlimited collection.

679. Women Unlimited

✣ Sydney, N.S. Formed 1983.

Women Unlimited promotes the economic, cultural, social, and educational interests of women; initiates programmes for women's physical and mental welfare; and promotes peace and sisterhood. (Source: Beaton Institute finding aid.)

LOCATION OF RECORDS: Beaton Institute, University College of Cape Breton. (See Appendix for address.)

COLLECTION NAME: Women Unlimited (MG 14, 168).

RECORDS: Minutes, 1983; correspondence, 1975-1986; bulletins, newsletters, 1981-1986; pamphlets, committee lists, 1985-1987; petitions, 1985; reports, 1984-1986; evaluations, press releases, certificate of incorporation, 1986; grant proposals, 1983-1984; conference records, 1983-1985; magazines, booklets, kits, 1976-1986; book lists, information sheet, essays, clippings, work book, miscellaneous records.

AMOUNT: 70 cm.

ACCESS: No restrictions.

FINDING AID: Finding aids available.

680. Women's Centre (Halifax, N.S.)

✣ Halifax, N.S. Formed 1973.

The Women's Centre was also called the Women's Recreational, Educational, and Cultural Centre.

LOCATION OF RECORDS: Canadian Women's Movement Archives Collection, Morisset Library Special Collections, University of Ottawa. (See Appendix for address.)

COLLECTION NAME: Halifax Women's Centre; Women's Centre Newsletter — Halifax.

RECORDS: Newsletters, 1974-1975; correspondence, 1975; pamphlet, flyer.

AMOUNT: 2 mm.

CONDITION: Good.

ACCESS: No restrictions.

681. Women's Health Education Network

The Women's Health Education Network (WHEN) promotes health awareness and disease prevention among women in Nova Scotia.

LOCATION OF RECORDS: Canadian Women's Movement Archives Collection, Morisset Library Special Collections, University of Ottawa. (See Appendix for address.)

COLLECTION NAME: Women's Health Education Network — WHEN, Nova Scotia.

RECORDS: Correspondence, 1981, 1984; report, manual, 1982; conference records, 1984-1985, 1987; questionnaire, 1981; periodicals (*The Monthly*, 1980-1984; *Vitality*, 1984-1991; *Now at WHEN/New at WHEN*, 1981-1984); statement of purpose, pamphlets.

AMOUNT: 6.5 cm.

CONDITION: Good.

ACCESS: No restrictions.

682. Women's Information, Resource, and Referral Service (Halifax, N.S.)

✢ Halifax, N.S. Formed 1982. Disbanded 1985.

The Women's Information, Resource, and Referral Service (WIRRS) evolved out of the women's centre A Woman's Place. The goals of WIRRS were to provide direct, supportive services for women and to upgrade volunteers' skills. (Source: Public Archives of Nova Scotia finding aid.) [See also A Woman's Place (Halifax, N.S.) (677).]

LOCATION OF RECORDS: Public Archives of Nova Scotia. (See Appendix for address.)

COLLECTION NAME: Women's Information, Resource, and Referral Service (Halifax) (MG 20, volumes 1531-1532, 1825-1827, 3099-3101).

RECORDS: Minutes, 1981-1984; correspondence, financial records, 1981-1985; by-laws, employee contracts, 1982-1984; leases, evaluations, personnel records, outline of organization, telephone and drop-in report forms, resource lists, 1982-1983; schedules, message books, 1983-1984; counselling request forms, 1981; publicity material, 1983-1985; mailing list, workshop evaluation, 1984; photographs, [ca. 1982]; guidelines, 1983; reports, bibliographies, press releases, pamphlets, brochures, posters, grant applications, handbooks, library borrowing records, evaluation forms, statistics, surveys, questionnaires, miscellaneous records.

AMOUNT: 1 m.

ACCESS: Restricted.

FINDING AID: Inventory available.

683. Zonta Club (Halifax, N.S.)

✢ Halifax, N.S.

The Zonta Club is part of an international service organization of business and professional women whose projects are designed to meet community needs and improve the status of women. (Source: *Halifax/Dartmouth/Metro Women's Directory*. — Halifax: Halifax City Regional Library, 1990.)

LOCATION OF RECORDS: Public Archives of Nova Scotia. (See Appendix for address.)

COLLECTION NAME: Zonta Club (Halifax) (MG 20, volumes 378-385, 647, 791, 1243, 1508, 1525).

RECORDS: Minutes, 1951-1969, 1981-1983; correspondence, 1952-1966, 1968-1969, 1983-1984; scrapbooks, 1952-1969, 1972-1984; financial records, 1981-1983; membership directories, 1980-1983; clipping, 1982; newsletters, reports, list of members, organization history, miscellaneous records.

AMOUNT: 1.3 m.

ACCESS: No restrictions.

FINDING AID: File list available.

NEWFOUNDLAND AND LABRADOR / TERRE-NEUVE ET LABRADOR

684. Ladies Coldstorage Workers Union

✢ St John's, Nfld. Formed [1939?]. Disbanded.

This union was made up entirely of women. Its members did coldstorage work in the fishing industry and sorted and cleaned blueberries. The union had a connection with the Longshoremen's Protective Union (LSPU).

LOCATION OF RECORDS: Centre for Newfoundland Studies Archives, Memorial University of Newfoundland. (See Appendix for address.)

COLLECTION NAME: Forms part of: Longshoremen's Protective Union (St John's, Nfld.) collection (COLL-40).

RECORDS: Roll books, 1951-1967.

AMOUNT: 3 items.

ACCESS: For use of bona fide researchers.

FINDING AID: Inventory available for Longshoremen's Protective Union collection.

685. Local Council of Women (St John's, Nfld.)

✢ St John's, Nfld. Formed 1966. Disbanded 1977.

The Local Council of Women (LCW) was made up of various women's organizations in St John's. LCW worked on a variety of women's issues and other social issues. To mark International Women's Year (1975), it produced a radio series and book, *Remarkable Women of Newfoundland and Labrador*.

Collection (a)

LOCATION OF RECORDS: Provincial Archives of Newfoundland and Labrador. (See Appendix for address.)

COLLECTION NAME: Local Council of Women, St John's (P8/B/49).

RECORDS: Minutes, 1966-1977; annual reports, 1968-1976; newsletters, 1972-1973; briefs, reports, 1972-1974; clippings, 1974-1976, 1978; correspondence, 1975-1978; pamphlets, book, manuscript, galleys, paste-up, 1976; sales records, 1976-1977; sound recordings, 1975-1976; by-laws, miscellaneous records.

AMOUNT: 4 boxes.

ACCESS: No restrictions.

FINDING AID: Index available.

Collection (b)

LOCATION OF RECORDS: Canadian Women's Movement Archives Collection, Morisset Library Special Collections, University of Ottawa. (See Appendix for address.)

COLLECTION NAME: Local Council of Women (St John's, Nfld.).

RECORDS: By-laws, 1968; minutes, 1974-1975; membership lists, 1973-1974; newsletter (*LCW Newsletter*, 1972); correspondence, 1973; brief.

AMOUNT: 6 mm.

CONDITION: Good.

ACCESS: No restrictions.

686. Memorial University of Newfoundland. Women's Association

✢ St John's, Nfld. Formed 1966.

The Women's Association of Memorial University of Newfoundland (WAMUN) is a social, educational, and charitable organization open to women staff, faculty, and graduate students and to wives of staff, faculty, and graduate students.

LOCATION OF RECORDS: Centre for Newfoundland Studies Archives, Memorial University of Newfoundland. (See Appendix for address.)

COLLECTION NAME: Women's Association of Memorial University of Newfoundland (COLL-052).

RECORDS: Minutes, 1969-1981; financial records, 1972-1976.

AMOUNT: 8 cm.

CONDITION: Good.

ACCESS: No restrictions.

687. Newfoundland and Labrador Federation of Labour. Women's Committee

✢ St John's, Nfld.

The federation's mandate is to promote the interests of its member unions and of the workers of Newfoundland and Labrador.

LOCATION OF RECORDS: Provincial Archives of Newfoundland and Labrador. (See Appendix for address.)

COLLECTION NAME: Forms part of: Newfoundland and Labrador Federation of Labour collection (P8/B/47, boxes 32 and 41).

RECORDS: Miscellaneous records, 1978-1980.

AMOUNT: 4 files.

ACCESS: No restrictions.

688. Newfoundland Outport Nursing and Industrial Association

✣ St John's, Nfld. Formed 1924.

The original purpose of the Newfoundland Outport Nursing and Industrial Association (NONIA) was to raise money through knitting and weaving, in order to pay the salaries of nurses in outport communities. Since 1934, when the government absorbed the nursing section of NONIA, this non-profit organization has provided women in outport communities with opportunities to make money through knitting. (Source: "NONIA: A Newfoundland Tradition" / Jeannie House. — *Newfoundland Lifestyle*.)

LOCATION OF RECORDS: Newfoundland Historical Society. (See Appendix for address.)
COLLECTION NAME: NONIA.
RECORDS: Clippings, 1963, 1966, 1969-1970, 1972, 1976, 1979-1982, 1984-1986, 1988; historical notes, booklet.
AMOUNT: 24 items.
ACCESS: No restrictions.

689. St John's Status of Women Council

[See also entry # 1364 (in Part II), which lists other records of this organization.]

✣ St John's, Nfld. Formed 1972.

The St John's Status of Women Council (SJSWC) was originally called the Newfoundland Status of Women Council (NSWC). It was established to improve the status of women and promote the recommendations of the Royal Commission on the Status of Women. SJSWC runs the Women's Centre. It also sponsors Iris Kirby House, a battered women's shelter providing crisis intervention, counselling, advocacy, and referral. Iris Kirby House was founded in 1981; until 1983 it was called Transition House. SJSWC co-sponsored the Women's Health Education Project of Newfoundland and Labrador, which operated from 1981 to 1984.

LOCATION OF RECORDS: Canadian Women's Movement Archives Collection, Morisset Library Special Collections, University of Ottawa. (See Appendix for address.)
COLLECTION NAME: Newfoundland Status of Women Council; St John's Status of Women Council; Women's Health Education Project of Newfoundland and Labrador.
RECORDS: Newsletters (*Newfoundland Status of Women Council Newsletter*, 1972-1985; *St John's Status of Women Council Newsletter*, 1984-1985, 1989; *Web*, 1985-1989; *Spokes/Women*, 1989; *Hatch*, 1982-1983); correspondence, 1972-1976; historical information, agenda, 1982; handbooks, 1975-1976, 1980, 1983; briefs, notice, 1985; reports, 1984; clippings, 1975, 1987; conference records, 1984, 1986; buttons, 1990; pamphlets, flyers.
AMOUNT: 41.5 cm of text, 2 buttons.
CONDITION: Good.
ACCESS: No restrictions.

690. Single Moms Centre

✣ Corner Brook, Nfld. Formed 1983.

The Single Moms Centre (also known simply as Single Moms) began as a support group for unmarried mothers. The centre, which opened in 1984, offers counselling, information and referral, discussions, films, and presentations by local resource people.

LOCATION OF RECORDS: Canadian Women's Movement Archives Collection, Morisset Library Special Collections, University of Ottawa. (See Appendix for address.)
COLLECTION NAME: Single Moms Centre (Corner Brook, Nfld.).
RECORDS: Correspondence, 1983-1984; newsletters, 1985; press release, clippings, 1983; evaluation, 1984; pamphlet.
AMOUNT: 1 cm.
CONDITION: Good.
ACCESS: No restrictions.

691. *Women and the Constitution Conference* (1984: St John's, Nfld.). Organizing Committee

LOCATION OF RECORDS: Canadian Women's Movement Archives Collection, Morisset Library Special Collections, University of Ottawa. (See Appendix for address.)
COLLECTION NAME: Conf.: Women and the Constitution (St John's, Nfld., 1984).
RECORDS: Conference report, 1984.
AMOUNT: 5 mm.
CONDITION: Good.
ACCESS: No restrictions.

692. *Young Women's Christian Association* (St John's, Nfld.)

✣ St John's, Nfld.

In the early 1970s, the YWCA in St John's offered courses in women's studies and had a committee on the status of women. In the mid-1970s, the YWCA and the YMCA merged to become the St John's YM-YWCA.

LOCATION OF RECORDS: Centre for Newfoundland Studies Archives, Memorial University of Newfoundland. (See Appendix for address.)
COLLECTION NAME: Forms part of: Dorothy Inglis collection (COLL-70).
RECORDS: Albums containing clippings, correspondence, reports, minutes, agenda, 1973-1974.
AMOUNT: 2 albums.
ACCESS: No restrictions.

693. Zonta Club of St John's

✣ St John's, Nfld. Formed 1951. Disbanded 1970.

The Zonta Club of St John's was a branch of Zonta International, a service organization of business and professional women dedicated to "improving the status of women and encouraging high ethical standards in business." The St John's club provided financial aid, educational training, and volunteer service to the community. (Source: Centre for Newfoundland Studies finding aid.)

LOCATION OF RECORDS: Centre for Newfoundland Studies Archives, Memorial University of Newfoundland. (See Appendix for address.)
COLLECTION NAME: Zonta Club of St John's (COLL-095).
RECORDS: Minutes, 1951-1970; reports, 1952-1970; correspondence, 1951-1972; financial statements, 1951-1969; constitution, organization, membership records, miscellaneous records.
AMOUNT: 32 cm.
CONDITION: Good.
ACCESS: No restrictions.
FINDING AID: "Inventory of the Records of the Zonta Club of St John's."

PART II: RECORDS HELD BY GROUPS
PARTIE II : FONDS DÉTENUS PAR DES GROUPES

NATIONAL ORGANIZATIONS / GROUPES PANCANADIENS

694. *Alliance nationale des lesbiennes / National Lesbian Forum*

[For English entry, see # 751.]

✤ Regina (Sask.). Groupe fondé 1988.

Le but de l'Alliance nationale des lesbiennes (ANL) est de travailler avec d'autres organismes féministes, gais et lesbiens à travers le Canada pour gagner un soutien et sensibiliser le grand public.

LIEU DE CONSULTATION : Alliance nationale des lesbiennes. [*Adresse postale* : C.P. 482, Regina (Sask.) S4P 3A2. *Téléphone* : (306) 522-8307.]

MATÉRIEL : Correspondance, documents financiers, 1988-1991; listes de membres, listes d'envoi, 1989; tracts, bulletins, 1988-1989.

QUANTITÉ : Env. 1 tiroir de classeur.

ÉTAT : Bon.

ACCÈS : Permission requise. Listes de membres et listes d'envoi confidentielles.

695. *Amalgamated Clothing and Textile Workers Union / Travailleurs amalgamés du vêtement et du textile*

[Renseignements en français, notice 766.]

[See also entry # 2 (in Part I), which lists other records of this organization.]

✤ Don Mills, Ont. Formed 1976.

The Amalgamated Clothing and Textile Workers Union (ACTWU) is a trade union which aims to improve the lives of Canadian workers. The majority of its members are women.

LOCATION OF RECORDS: Amalgamated Clothing and Textile Workers Union. [*Address:* 15 Gervais Dr., Suite 601, Don Mills, Ont. M3C 1Y8. *Telephone:* (416) 441-1806. *Fax:* (416) 441-9680.]

RECORDS: Constitution, minutes, financial records, conference proceedings, 1976-1991; correspondence, reports, briefs, pamphlets, flyers, press releases, 1989-1991; newsletters (*Action*, 1988-1991; *Labor Unity*, 1976-1991); membership lists, mailing lists, books, photographs, films.

AMOUNT: 4 filing cabinets.

CONDITION: Good.

ACCESS: Permission required. Membership lists, mailing lists, and some reports closed.

696. *Arab Canadian Women's Network*

✤ Toronto, Ont. Formed 1985.

The Arab Canadian Women's Network (ACWN) provides a forum for Canadian women of Arab origin to discuss issues of common concern and acquaint the broader community with these issues. ACWN works to create links with like-minded sister organizations in the Middle East and Canada.

LOCATION OF RECORDS: Arab Canadian Women's Network. [*Address:* 106 Duplex Ave., Toronto, Ont. M5P 2A7. *Telephone:* (416) 483-6467. *Fax:* (416) 483-5732.]

RECORDS: Constitution, pamphlets, 1985; correspondence, press releases, 1991; membership lists, 1990-1991; flyers, 1985-1986; minutes.

AMOUNT: 1 file.

CONDITION: Good.

ACCESS: Permission required. Membership records may be closed.

697. *Association canadienne des sociétés Elizabeth Fry / Canadian Association of Elizabeth Fry Societies*

[For English entry, see # 705.]

✤ Ottawa (Ont.). Groupe fondé 1969.

L'Association canadienne des sociétés Elizabeth Fry (ACSEF) est une fédération de dix-neuf sociétés autonomes qui travaillent avec et pour les femmes touchées par le système de justice, et tout particulièrement celles qui ont des démêlés avec la justice. L'ACSEF encourage les réformes qui peuvent améliorer la condition des femmes à tous les échelons du système de justice pénale.

LIEU DE CONSULTATION : Association canadienne des sociétés Elizabeth Fry. [*Adresse* : 600 - 251, rue Bank, Ottawa (Ont.) K2P 1X3. *Téléphone* : (613) 238-2422. *Télécopieur* : (613) 233-4051.]

MATÉRIEL : Statuts et règlements, 1978; procès-verbaux, correspondance, 1977-1991; documents financiers, rapports, mémoires, actes de congrès, dépliants, tracts, bulletins, 1978-1991.

QUANTITÉ : 1 classeur.

ÉTAT : Assez bon.

ACCÈS : Permission requise.

698. Association canadienne pour la promotion des services de garde à l'enfance / Canadian Day Care Advocacy Association

[For English entry, see # 708.]

✣ Ottawa (Ont.). Groupe fondé 1982.

L'Association canadienne pour la promotion des services de garde à l'enfance travaille pour des services de garde de qualité, accessibles à tous, à prix abordable, sans but lucratif.

LIEU DE CONSULTATION : Association canadienne pour la promotion des services de garde à l'enfance. [*Adresse* : 323, rue Chapel, 3e étage, Ottawa (Ont.) K1N 7Z2. *Téléphone* : (613) 594-3196. *Télécopieur* : (613) 237-5969.]

MATÉRIEL : Statuts et règlements, procès-verbaux, correspondance, documents financiers, demandes de subvention, dossiers concernant la clientèle, listes de membres, listes d'envoi, albums de coupures, rapports, dépliants, communiqués de presse, affiches, macarons, T-shirts, 1982-1991; bulletins (*Vision*, *Bulletin*).

QUANTITÉ : 20 reliures à feuilles mobiles.

ÉTAT : Bon.

699. Association canadienne pour l'avancement des femmes, du sport et de l'activité physique / Canadian Association for the Advancement of Women and Sport and Physical Activity

[For English entry, see # 704.]

✣ Gloucester (Ont.). Groupe fondé 1982.

L'Association canadienne pour l'avancement des femmes, du sport et de l'activité physique (ACAFS) est un organisme féministe qui milite en faveur de l'adoption de réformes progressistes au profit des femmes et à l'accroissement des possibilités de participation qui leur sont offertes dans le sport et l'activité physique. Auparavant, l'organisme était connu sous le nom de l'Association canadienne pour l'avancement des femmes et du sport.

LIEU DE CONSULTATION : Association canadienne pour l'avancement des femmes, du sport et de l'activité physique. [*Adresse* : 1600, promenade James Naismith, Gloucester (Ont.) K1B 5N4. *Téléphone* : (613) 748-5793.]

MATÉRIEL : Statuts et règlements, documents financiers, 1982-1991; procès-verbaux, correspondance, dépliants, 1983-1991; actes de congrès, 1982-1990; demandes de subvention, rapports, mémoires, communiqués de presse, affiche, T-shirt, bulletins (*Action*, *Starting Line*, *Bulletin*), thèses, manuel.

QUANTITÉ : 1 classeur, 1 boîte.

ÉTAT : Bon.

ACCÈS : Permission requise.

700. Association des infirmières et infirmiers autochtones du Canada / Indian and Inuit Nurses of Canada

[For English entry, see # 737.]

✣ Ottawa (Ont.). Groupe fondé 1974.

L'Association des infirmières et infirmiers autochtones du Canada (AIIAC) est un organisme national de spécialistes autochtones de la santé qui vise à améliorer les soins de santé chez les autochtones. Une grande partie du travail de cet organisme se fait auprès des femmes autochtones. L'AIIAC était connue de 1974 à 1983 sous le nom d'Infirmières et infirmiers diplômés d'origine indienne du Canada (IIDOIC).

LIEU DE CONSULTATION : Association des infirmières et infirmiers autochtones du Canada. [*Adresse* : 55, rue Murray, 4e étage, Ottawa (Ont.) K1N 5M3. *Téléphone* : (613) 230-1864.]

MATÉRIEL : Statuts et règlements, procès-verbaux, correspondance, journaux de bord, documents financiers, demandes de subvention, dossiers concernant la clientèle, listes de membres, listes d'envoi, rapports, mémoires, actes de congrès, dépliants, affiches, macarons, T-shirts, bulletins, livres, photographies, enregistrements sonores, [197-]-1991.

ÉTAT : Bon.

ACCÈS : Permission requise.

701. Association for Women's Equity in the Canadian Forces

✣ Ottawa, Ont. Formed 1985.

This association (also known as AWECF) promotes equality of opportunity and improved conditions of service for women in the Canadian Armed Forces. It opposes harassment and other barriers which discriminate against women or restrict them. AWECF's French name is l'Association pour l'équité à l'égard des femmes dans les forces canadiennes.

LOCATION OF RECORDS: Association for Women's Equity in the Canadian Forces. [**Mailing Address:** Box 8791, Alta Vista Terminal, Ottawa, Ont. K1G 3J1. **Telephone:** (613) 748-1483.]

RECORDS: Constitution, briefs, press releases, 1985; minutes, reports, conference proceedings, 1988; correspondence, log-books, financial records, membership lists, scrapbooks, clippings, sound recordings, 1985-1991; grant applications, 1987; mailing lists, 1985-1990; newsletters, 1987, 1990.

AMOUNT: Approx. 1 filing cabinet.

CONDITION: Fair.

ACCESS: Permission required.

702. Association nationale de la femme et du droit / National Association of Women and the Law

[For English entry, see # 745.]

✣ Ottawa (Ont.). Groupe fondé 1975.

L'Association nationale de la femme et du droit (ANFD) vise à promouvoir l'égalité sociale et juridique des femmes. [Voir aussi Revue Femmes et droit/Canadian Journal of Women and the Law (763).]

LIEU DE CONSULTATION : Association nationale de la femme et du droit. [*Adresse* : 1, rue Nicholas, suite #604, Ottawa (Ont.) K1N 7B7. *Téléphone* : (613) 238-1544.]

MATÉRIEL : Statuts et règlements, 1975-1991; procès-verbaux, 1982-1991; correspondance, 1989-1991; documents financiers, listes de membres, rapports, mémoires, 1981-1991; demandes de subvention, 1983-1991; listes d'envoi, communiqués de presse, affiches, 1987-1991; actes de congrès, 1981, 1983, 1985, 1987; dépliants, 1985-1991; bulletins, 1977-1987.

QUANTITÉ : 4 classeurs.

ÉTAT : Bon.

ACCÈS : Permission requise. Listes des membres confidentielles.

703. Les Cahiers de la femme / Canadian Woman Studies

[For English entry, see # 715.]

✣ Downsview (Ont.). Groupe fondé 1978.

Canadian Woman Studies/Les Cahiers de la femme (CWS/CF) est une publication trimestrielle créée dans le but de rendre la documentation et la recherche

NATIONAL ORGANIZATIONS / GROUPES PANCANADIENS

actuelles, sur toute une gamme de sujets féministes, accessibles au plus grand nombre de femmes possible. De 1978 à 1980, son nom anglais était *Canadian Women's Studies*.

LIEU DE CONSULTATION : Cahiers de la femme. [*Adresse* : 212 Founders College, York University, 4700, rue Keele, Downsview (Ont.) M3J 1P3. *Téléphone* : (416) 736-5356.]

MATÉRIEL : Procès-verbaux, correspondance, demandes de subvention, 1989-1991; mémoires, 1989; affiches, 1987-1988; périodiques (*Canadian Woman Studies/Les Cahiers de la femme*, 1987-1991); documents financiers, 1984-1991; listes d'envoi, dépliants, tracts.

QUANTITÉ : 2 classeurs.

ACCÈS : Permission requise. Dossiers concernant le personnel confidentiels.

704. Canadian Association for the Advancement of Women and Sport and Physical Activity / Association canadienne pour l'avancement des femmes, du sport et de l'activité physique

[Renseignements en français, notice 699.]

✣ Gloucester, Ont. Formed 1982.

The Canadian Association for the Advancement of Women and Sport and Physical Activity (CAAWS) is a feminist organization which advocates progressive changes of benefit to women and enhanced participation by women in sport and physical activity. It used to be called the Canadian Association for the Advancement of Women and Sport.

LOCATION OF RECORDS: Canadian Association for the Advancement of Women and Sport and Physical Activity. [*Address*: 1600 James Naismith Dr., Gloucester, Ont. K1B 5N4. *Telephone*: (613) 748-5793.]

RECORDS: Constitution, financial records, 1982-1991; minutes, correspondence, pamphlets, 1983-1991; conference proceedings, 1982-1990; grant applications, reports, briefs, press releases, poster, T-shirt, newsletters (*Action, Starting Line, Bulletin*), theses, handbook.

AMOUNT: 1 filing cabinet, 1 box.

CONDITION: Good.

ACCESS: Permission required.

705. Canadian Association of Elizabeth Fry Societies / Association canadienne des sociétés Elizabeth Fry

[Renseignements en français, notice 697.]

✣ Ottawa, Ont. Formed 1969.

The Canadian Association of Elizabeth Fry Societies (CAEFS) is a federation of nineteen autonomous societies which work with, and on behalf of, women involved in the justice system, especially those in conflict with the law. CAEFS advocates reforms to improve the situation of women at all levels of the criminal justice system.

LOCATION OF RECORDS: Canadian Association of Elizabeth Fry Societies. [*Address*: 600 - 251 Bank St., Ottawa, Ont. K2P 1X3. *Telephone*: (613) 238-2422. *Fax*: (613) 233-4051.]

RECORDS: Constitution, 1978; minutes, correspondence, 1977-1991; financial records, reports, briefs, conference proceedings, pamphlets, flyers, newsletters, 1978-1991.

AMOUNT: 1 filing cabinet.

CONDITION: Fair.

ACCESS: Permission required.

706. Canadian Child Day Care Federation / Fédération canadienne des services de garde à l'enfance

[Renseignements en français, notice 729.]

✣ Ottawa, Ont. Formed 1987.

The Canadian Child Day Care Federation (CCDCF) works to improve the quality of child-care services.

LOCATION OF RECORDS: Canadian Child Day Care Federation. [*Address*: 120 Holland Ave., Suite 401, Ottawa, Ont. K1Y 0X6. *Telephone*: (613) 729-5289. *Fax*: (613) 729-3159.]

RECORDS: Constitution, 1988, 1991; minutes, newsletters, 1987-1991; correspondence, financial records, grant applications, 1983-1991; client records, membership lists, mailing lists, scrapbooks, reports, flyers, press releases, 1985-1991; briefs, 1990-1991; conference proceedings, T-shirts, banners, 1989-1991; pamphlets, 1986-1991; posters, sound recordings, 1989; videotapes, 1991; clippings, photographs, miscellaneous records.

AMOUNT: Approx. 3 filing cabinets.

CONDITION: Good.

ACCESS: Permission required.

707. Canadian Congress for Learning Opportunities for Women / Congrès canadien pour la promotion des études chez la femme

[Renseignements en français, notice 721.]

[See also entry # 21 (in Part I), which lists other records of this organization.]

✣ Toronto, Ont. Formed 1973.

The Canadian Congress for Learning Opportunities for Women (CCLOW) is a national organization which promotes learning opportunities for women. It facilitates networking, identifies barriers, publicizes critical issues, organizes conferences, and publishes a periodical, *Women's Education des femmes*. CCLOW was originally called the Canadian Committee on Learning Opportunities for Women.

LOCATION OF RECORDS: Canadian Congress for Learning Opportunities for Women. [*Address*: 47 Main St., Toronto, Ont. M4E 2V6. *Telephone*: (416) 699-1909. *Fax*: (416) 699-2145.]

RECORDS: Constitution, mailing lists, pamphlets, press releases, 1979-1991; minutes, correspondence, 1978-1991; financial records, grant applications, reports, 1977-1991; membership lists, clippings, 1987-1991; briefs, 1979-1990; conference proceedings, 1981, 1984, 1989; flyers, 1988-1991; T-shirts, 1989-1991; periodicals (*Minerva*, 1988-1989; *Women's Education des femmes*, 1982-1991); books, 1983, 1991; photographs, 1982-1991; sound recordings, 1990.

AMOUNT: 8 filing cabinets, 12 boxes.

CONDITION: Good.

ACCESS: Permission required. Personnel records and some financial records restricted.

708. Canadian Day Care Advocacy Association / Association canadienne pour la promotion des services de garde à l'enfance

[Renseignements en français, notice 698.]

✣ Ottawa, Ont. Formed 1982.

The Canadian Day Care Advocacy Association (CDCAA) works for accessible, affordable, non-profit, high-quality child care.

LOCATION OF RECORDS: Canadian Day Care Advocacy Association. [*Address*:

323 Chapel St., 3rd Floor, Ottawa, Ont. K1N 7Z2. **Telephone:** (613) 594-3196. **Fax:** (613) 237-5969.]

RECORDS: Constitution, minutes, correspondence, financial records, grant applications, client records, membership lists, mailing lists, scrapbooks, reports, pamphlets, press releases, posters, buttons, T-shirts, 1982-1991; newsletters (*Vision, Bulletin*).

AMOUNT: 20 binders.

CONDITION: Good.

709. Canadian Ethnocultural Council. Women's Committee / Conseil ethnoculturel du Canada. Comité des femmes

[Renseignements en français, notice 723.]

✣ Ottawa, Ont. Formed [1985?].

The Women's Committee of the Canadian Ethnocultural Council (CEC) works to improve the conditions of life for immigrant women and women who belong to ethnic or visible minorities. It is committed to fighting against the sexism, racism, poverty, and violence experienced by these women. CEC is a coalition of thirty-seven national ethnocultural organizations.

LOCATION OF RECORDS: Canadian Ethnocultural Council. Women's Committee. [*Address:* 251 Laurier Ave., Suite 1100, Ottawa, Ont. K1P 5J6. **Telephone:** (613) 230-3867. **Fax:** (613) 230-8051.]

RECORDS: Minutes, correspondence, grant applications, membership lists, briefs, 1985-1991.

AMOUNT: 6 filing cabinets.

CONDITION: Fair.

ACCESS: Permission required.

710. Canadian Farm Women's Network

✣ Formed 1985.

This network (also known as CFWN) facilitates sharing, support, education, and advocacy on behalf of farm women. It has members in six provinces.

LOCATION OF RECORDS: Canadian Farm Women's Network. [*Address:* Zelma GMB #36, Allan, Sask. S0K 0C0. **Telephone:** (306) 257-3911. **Fax:** (306) 257-3911.]

RECORDS: Constitution, banners, 1991; minutes, 1986-1991; correspondence, financial records, newsletters, 1988-1991; grant applications, 1989-1991; scrapbooks, clippings, 1985-1991; conference proceedings, 1985, 1987, 1989; photographs.

AMOUNT: 1 box.

CONDITION: Good.

ACCESS: Permission required.

711. Canadian Journal of Women and the Law / Revue Femmes et droit

[Renseignements en français, notice 763.]

✣ Ottawa, Ont. Formed 1984.

The *Canadian Journal of Women and the Law* (CJWL) provides in-depth analysis of legal issues of concern to women. Although it is published by the National Association of Women and the Law, the journal maintains full editorial independence. [See also National Association of Women and the Law/Association nationale de la femme et du droit (745).]

LOCATION OF RECORDS: Canadian Journal of Women and the Law. [*Address:* 575 King Edward Ave., Ottawa, Ont. K1N 6N5. **Telephone:** (613) 564-5617. **Fax:** (613) 564-9800.]

RECORDS: Constitution, minutes, correspondence, financial records, grant applications, client records, membership lists, mailing lists, periodicals, 1985-1991; pamphlets, 1990.

AMOUNT: 4 filing cabinets.

CONDITION: Good.

ACCESS: Permission required. Referee reports confidential.

712. Canadian Organization for the Rights of Prostitutes

[See also entry # 29 (in Part I), which lists other records of this organization.]

✣ Toronto, Ont. Formed 1983.

The Canadian Organization for the Rights of Prostitutes (CORP) campaigns for the decriminalization of prostitution and for an end to the stigmatization of prostitutes. CORP's goals are to have prostitution seen as work and to have prostitutes recognized as independent business people.

LOCATION OF RECORDS: Canadian Organization for the Rights of Prostitutes. [*Mailing Address:* Box 1143, Station F, Toronto, Ont. M4Y 2T8. **Telephone:** (416) 964-0150.]

RECORDS: Constitution, 1983; minutes, correspondence, photographs, 1986-1991; petitions, 1983-1991; scrapbooks, press releases, clippings, 1987-1991; conference proceedings, 1988-1991; pamphlets, flyers, buttons, 1985-1991; newsletters (*Stiletto*, 1990-1991).

AMOUNT: Approx. 1 filing cabinet.

CONDITION: Good.

ACCESS: Permission required.

713. Canadian Research Institute for the Advancement of Women / Institut canadien de recherches sur les femmes

[Renseignements en français, notice 739.]

[See also entry # 31 (in Part I), which lists other records of this organization.]

✣ Ottawa, Ont. Formed 1976.

This organization, also known as CRIAW, encourages, co-ordinates, and disseminates research into women's experience and works to ensure an equal place for women and women's experience in the body of knowledge and research about Canada.

LOCATION OF RECORDS: Canadian Research Institute for the Advancement of Women. [*Address:* 151 Slater St., Suite 408, Ottawa, Ont. K1P 5H3. **Telephone:** (613) 563-0681. **Fax:** (613) 563-0682.]

RECORDS: Minutes, correspondence, photographs, 1976-1991; grant applications, 1978-1991; conference proceedings, 1982-1987; T-shirts, sweatshirts, 1986; banners, 1990; publications, 1981-1991; sound recordings, 1989; videotapes, 1989-1990; financial records, membership lists, reports, pamphlets, flyers, posters.

AMOUNT: Approx. 2 filing cabinets.

CONDITION: Good.

ACCESS: Permission required. Personnel files closed.

714. Canadian Teachers' Federation / Fédération canadienne des enseignantes et des enseignants

[Renseignements en français, notice 728.]

✣ Ottawa, Ont. Formed 1920.

The goal of the Canadian Teachers' Federation (CTF) is to promote the quality of education and the status of teachers. The federation has a Women and Education department.

LOCATION OF RECORDS: Canadian Teachers' Federation. [*Address:* 110 Argyle Ave., Ottawa, Ont. K2P 1B4. *Telephone:* (613) 232-1505. *Fax:* (613) 232-1886.]

RECORDS: Correspondence, financial records, grant applications, membership lists, reports, briefs, pamphlets, press releases, posters, buttons, newsletters, 1978-1991.

AMOUNT: 3 filing cabinets.

ACCESS: Permission required. Briefs, publications, and reports are accessible.

715. Canadian Woman Studies / Les Cahiers de la femme

[Renseignements en français, notice 703.]

✣ Downsview, Ont. Formed 1978.

Canadian Woman Studies/Les Cahiers de la femme (CWS/CF) is a feminist quarterly founded with the purpose of making current writing and research on a wide variety of feminist topics available to as many women as possible. From 1978 to 1980 its name in English was *Canadian Women's Studies*.

LOCATION OF RECORDS: Canadian Woman Studies. [*Address:* 212 Founders College, York University, 4700 Keele St., Downsview, Ont. M3J 1P3. *Telephone:* (416) 736-5356.]

RECORDS: Minutes, correspondence, grant applications, 1989-1991; briefs, 1989; posters, 1987-1988; periodicals (*Canadian Woman Studies/Les Cahiers de la femme*, 1987-1991); financial records, 1984-1991; mailing lists, pamphlets, flyers.

AMOUNT: 2 filing cabinets.

ACCESS: Permission required. Personnel files closed.

716. Candida Research and Information Foundation (Canada)

✣ Toronto, Ont. Formed 1984.

This foundation (also known as CRIF or the Candida Foundation) works for prevention of and recovery from Candida and other immune-deficiency disorders. It provides information, promotes research, facilitates self-help, and advocates the right to choose in health care.

LOCATION OF RECORDS: Candida Research and Information Foundation. [*Address:* 598 St Clair Ave., Toronto, Ont. M6C 1A6. *Telephone:* (416) 656-0047.]

RECORDS: Minutes, correspondence, financial records, membership lists, mailing lists, scrapbooks, pamphlets, flyers, clippings, 1984-1991; client records, 1984-1988, [1989?]; newsletters, 1985-1991; videotapes, 1991; constitution, log-books, grant applications, studies, miscellaneous records.

AMOUNT: Approx. 3 filing cabinets.

CONDITION: Good.

ACCESS: Permission required. Access may be difficult because of reorganization. Client files, financial records, and grant files accessible at organization's discretion.

717. Centre international MATCH / MATCH International Centre

[For English entry, see # 742.]

[Voir aussi la notice 38 (dans la partie I) pour autres documents de ce groupe.]

✣ Ottawa (Ont.). Groupe fondé 1976.

Le Centre international MATCH est un organisme féministe en développement qui a pour but d'établir un réseau d'échange entre les femmes du Canada et celles des pays en voie de développement. L'organisme veut éliminer la violence faite aux femmes globalement, entre autres objectifs.

LIEU DE CONSULTATION : Centre international MATCH. [*Adresse :* 1102 - 200, rue Elgin, Ottawa (Ont.) K2P 1L5. *Téléphone :* (613) 238-1312. *Télécopieur :* (613) 238-6867.]

MATÉRIEL : Statuts et règlements, 1977; procès-verbaux, correspondance, documents financiers, demandes de subvention, listes de membres, listes d'envoi, rapports, dépliants, tracts, communiqués de presse, affiches, bulletins, vidéocassettes, 1986-1991.

ÉTAT : Bon.

ACCÈS : Permission requise.

718. Childbirth by Choice Trust

✣ Toronto, Ont. Formed 1982.

The Childbirth by Choice Trust does public education about abortion, reproductive rights, and contraception. It maintains a library and produces and distributes pro-choice literature. It is affiliated with the Canadian Abortion Rights Action League (CARAL). [See also Canadian Abortion Rights Action League/Association canadienne pour le droit à l'avortement (16).]

LOCATION OF RECORDS: Childbirth by Choice Trust. [*Address:* 344 Bloor St. W., #306, Toronto, Ont. M5S 3A7. *Telephone:* (416) 961-1507. *Fax:* (416) 961-5771.]

RECORDS: Constitution, 1981, 1988; minutes, financial records, 1983-1991; correspondence, 1982-1991; membership lists, pamphlets, flyers.

AMOUNT: 7 filing cabinets.

CONDITION: Fair.

ACCESS: Internal organization files closed. Public information files open.

719. Chinese Canadian National Council. Women's Issues Committee

✣ Toronto, Ont. Formed 1979.

The Women's Issues Committee of the Chinese Canadian National Council (CCNC) was formed to address women's issues and develop a national network among Chinese-Canadian Women. It does grass-roots mobilization against sexism and racism.

LOCATION OF RECORDS: Chinese Canadian National Council. Women's Issues Committee. [*Address:* 386 Bathurst St., 2nd Floor, Toronto, Ont. M5T 2S6. *Telephone:* (416) 868-1777. *Fax:* (416) 868-1781.]

RECORDS: Minutes, 1979-1991; briefs, 1988; flyers, pamphlets, 1991; newsletters, 1990-1991; correspondence, financial records, grant applications, membership lists, mailing lists, reports, posters, books, clippings, photographs.

AMOUNT: 1 filing cabinet.

CONDITION: Fair.

ACCESS: Permission required.

720. Comité canadien d'action sur le statut de la femme / National Action Committee on the Status of Women

[For English entry, see # 744.]

[Voir aussi la notice 44 (dans la partie I) pour autres documents de ce groupe.]

✣ Toronto (Ont.). Groupe fondé 1971.

Le Comité canadien d'action sur le statut de la femme (CCA) est le plus grand organisme de femmes au Canada, regroupant plus de 450 associations et groupes autonomes de tous les coins du pays. Ses priorités sont de susciter les contacts et la collaboration entre les groupes de femmes, de favoriser des changements politiques et législatifs et de sensibiliser le public aux problèmes des femmes. À ses débuts, le CCA portait le nom de National Ad Hoc Action Committee on the Status of Women. Son nom actuel a été adopté en 1972. [Voir aussi Évaluation-Médias/MediaWatch (727).]

LIEU DE CONSULTATION : Comité canadien d'action sur le statut de la femme. [*Adresse* : 57, promenade Mobile, Toronto (Ont.) M4A 1H5. *Téléphone* : (416) 759-5252. *Télécopieur* : (416) 759-5370.]

MATÉRIEL : Procès-verbaux, correspondance, journaux de bord, rapports, actes de congrès, demandes de subvention, enregistrements sonores, listes de membres, pétitions, dépliants, mémoires, communiqués de presse, T-shirts, bannières, périodiques, documents financiers, tracts, affiches, macarons, photographies, 1971-1991.

QUANTITÉ : 8 classeurs, 144 boîtes.

ACCÈS : Permission requise. Les dossiers qui ne sont pas courants sont entreposés hors du lieu de consultation.

721. Congrès canadien pour la promotion des études chez la femme / Canadian Congress for Learning Opportunities for Women

[For English entry, see # 707.]

[Voir aussi la notice 48 (dans la partie I) pour autres documents de ce groupe.]

✣ Toronto (Ont.). Groupe fondé 1973.

Le Congrès canadien pour la promotion des études chez la femme (CCPEF) est un organisme national qui vise à promouvoir les possibilités d'études pour les femmes. Il favorise la création de réseaux, identifie les obstacles, fait connaître les problèmes cruciaux, organise des congrès et publie un périodique, *Women's Education des femmes*. Le CCPEF s'appelait à ses débuts Canadian Committee on Learning Opportunities for Women.

LIEU DE CONSULTATION : Congrès canadien pour la promotion des études chez la femme. [*Adresse* : 47, rue Main, Toronto (Ont.) M4E 2V6. *Téléphone* : (416) 699-1909. *Télécopieur* : (416) 699-2145.]

MATÉRIEL : Statuts et règlements, listes d'envoi, dépliants, communiqués de presse, 1979-1991 ; procès-verbaux, correspondance, 1978-1991 ; documents financiers, demandes de subvention, rapports, 1977-1991 ; listes de membres, coupures de presse, 1987-1991 ; mémoires, 1979-1990 ; actes de congrès, 1981, 1984, 1989 ; tracts, 1988-1991 ; T-shirts, 1989-1991 ; périodiques (*Minerva*, 1988-1989 ; *Women's Education des femmes*, 1982-1991) ; livres, 1983, 1991 ; photographies, 1982-1991 ; enregistrements sonores, 1990.

QUANTITÉ : 8 classeurs, 12 boîtes.

ÉTAT : Bon.

ACCÈS : Permission requise. Restrictions pour certains documents financiers et pour les documents concernant le personnel.

722. Congress of Black Women of Canada

✣ Formed 1973.

This organization promotes the rights of Black women in Canada. It provides a network of solidarity among Black women and does lobbying, advocacy, and education. It began holding ad hoc conferences in 1973 and became a national organization in 1980.

LOCATION OF RECORDS: Congress of Black Women of Canada. [*Address:* 3736 Regina Ave., Saskatoon, Sask. S4S 0H6. *Telephone:* (306) 584-2594.]

RECORDS: Constitution, 1980; minutes, 1973-1974, 1977, 1980-1991; correspondence, 1973-1991; financial records, grant applications, membership lists, briefs, pamphlets, 1980-1991; mailing lists, 1977-1991; reports, 1974-1991; conference proceedings, 1973-1974, 1976-1977, 1980-1991; T-shirts, 1984, 1986, 1988, 1990; newsletters (*Congress News*, 1984-1986).

AMOUNT: Approx. 4 boxes.
CONDITION: Good.
ACCESS: Permission required.

723. Conseil ethnoculturel du Canada. Comité des femmes / Canadian Ethnocultural Council. Women's Committee

[For English entry, see # 709.]

✣ Ottawa (Ont.). Groupe fondé [1985?].

Le Comité des femmes du Conseil ethnoculturel du Canada (CEC) vise à améliorer la condition de vie des femmes immigrantes ou membres de minorités ethniques ou visibles. Le comité lutte contre le sexisme, le racisme, la pauvreté et la violence vécus par ces femmes. Le CEC est une coalition de trente-sept organismes ethnoculturels nationaux.

LIEU DE CONSULTATION : Conseil ethnoculturel du Canada. Comité des femmes. [*Adresse* : 251, av. Laurier ouest, suite 1100, Ottawa (Ont.) K1P 5J6. *Téléphone* : (613) 230-3867. *Télécopieur* : (613) 230-8051.]

MATÉRIEL : Procès-verbaux, correspondance, demandes de subvention, listes de membres, mémoires, 1985-1991.

QUANTITÉ : 6 classeurs.

ÉTAT : Assez bon.

ACCÈS : Permission requise.

724. Conseil œcuménique des chrétiennes du Canada / Women's Inter-Church Council of Canada

[For English entry, see # 771.]

✣ Toronto (Ont.). Groupe fondé 1919.

Les buts du Conseil œcuménique des chrétiennes du Canada sont de promouvoir le développement spirituel de même que les questions qui touchent les femmes et les droits de la personne. Le conseil a produit du matériel éducatif sur des sujets tels que la violence faite aux femmes. À ses débuts, l'organisme était connu sous le nom de the Federated Women's Missionary Boards of Canada ; par la suite, il est devenu the Inter-Board Committee of the Women's Missionary Societies of Canada.

LIEU DE CONSULTATION : Conseil œcuménique des chrétiennes du Canada. [*Adresse* : 77, rue Charles ouest, Toronto (Ont.) M5S 1K5. *Téléphone* : (416) 922-6177.]

MATÉRIEL : Statuts et règlements, procès-verbaux, correspondance, documents financiers, rapports, bulletins, 1989-1991.

QUANTITÉ : 2 classeurs.

ÉTAT : Bon.

725. DisAbled Women's Network Canada / Réseau d'action des femmes handicapées du Canada

[Renseignements en français, notice 759.]

✣ Toronto, Ont. Formed 1985.

The purpose of the DisAbled Women's Network Canada (DAWN Canada) is to be the voice of women with disabilities in Canada. DAWN offers support, information, and resources to disabled women.

LOCATION OF RECORDS: DisAbled Women's Network Canada. [*Address:* 658 Danforth Ave., Suite 203, Toronto, Ont. M4J 1L1. *Telephone:* (416) 406-1080/1081. *Fax:* (416) 406-1082.]

RECORDS: Constitution, briefs, pamphlets, 1986-1991; minutes, correspondence, financial records, grant applications, membership lists, mailing lists, petitions, reports, conference proceedings, flyers, press releases, posters, 1985-1991; newsletters (*Thriving*, 1990); books, clippings, photographs, sound recordings.
AMOUNT: 4 filing cabinets.
CONDITION: Fair.
ACCESS: Permission required. Personnel files closed.

726. Documentation sur la recherche féministe / Resources for Feminist Research

[For English entry, see # 762.]

[Voir aussi la notice 50 (dans la partie I) pour autres documents de ce groupe.]

✣ Toronto (Ont.). Groupe fondé 1972.

Resources for Feminist Research/Documentation sur la recherche féministe (RFR/DRF) est un périodique canadien sur la recherche féministe internationale. Jusqu'en 1979, cette revue portait le nom de *Canadian Newsletter of Research on Women/Recherches sur la femme : Bulletin d'information canadien*.

LIEU DE CONSULTATION : Documentation sur la recherche féministe. [*Adresse* : Ontario Institute for Studies in Education, 252, rue Bloor ouest, Toronto (Ont.) M5S 1V6. *Téléphone* : (416) 923-6641. *Télécopieur* : (416) 926-4725.]

MATÉRIEL : Statuts et règlements, procès-verbaux, correspondance, documents financiers, demandes de subvention, listes d'abonnement, listes d'envoi, communiqués de presse, affiches, coupures de presse, [1985?]-1991; périodiques (RFR/DRF, 1972-1990).

ÉTAT : Bon.

ACCÈS : Permission requise. Procès-verbaux des réunions du comité de rédaction confidentiels.

727. Évaluation-Médias / MediaWatch

[For English entry, see # 743.]

✣ Toronto (Ont.). Groupe fondé 1983.

Évaluation-Médias vise à améliorer les images des femmes dans les médias. Il fournit des outils de sensibilisation et d'information sur les médias, soutient l'action des femmes qui travaillent dans les médias et revendique des changements en exerçant des pressions auprès des gouvernements et de l'industrie. Son nom officiel est Évaluation nationale des images des femmes dans les médias. L'organisme est issu d'un sous-comité du Comité canadien d'action sur le statut de la femme. [Voir aussi Comité canadien d'action sur le statut de la femme/ National Action Committee on the Status of Women (44, 720).]

LIEU DE CONSULTATION : Évaluation-Médias. [*Adresse* : 517, rue Wellington, suite 204, Toronto (Ont.) M5V 1G1. *Téléphone* : (416) 408-2065.]

MATÉRIEL : Statuts et règlements, 1983, 1988; procès-verbaux, demandes de subvention, 1986-1991; correspondance, vidéocassettes, 1983-1991; documents financiers, dossiers concernant la clientèle, communiqués de presse, coupures de presse, bulletins, 1985-1991; listes de membres, 1988-1991; rapports, mémoires, 1981-1991; actes de congrès, affiches, bannières, 1987; dépliants, 1984, 1987, 1989; T-shirts, 1990.

QUANTITÉ : 4 classeurs, 6 boîtes.

ÉTAT : Assez bon.

ACCÈS : Permission requise. Dossiers concernant le personnel et correspondance interne confidentiels.

728. Fédération canadienne des enseignantes et des enseignants / Canadian Teachers' Federation

[For English entry, see # 714.]

✣ Ottawa (Ont.). Groupe fondé 1920.

Le but de la Fédération canadienne des enseignantes et des enseignants (FCE) est de promouvoir la qualité d'éducation et le statut des enseignantes et des enseignants. La fédération possède un service chargé de promouvoir la situation de la femme en éducation.

LIEU DE CONSULTATION : Fédération canadienne des enseignantes et des enseignants. [*Adresse* : 110, av. Argyle, Ottawa (Ont.) K2P 1B4. *Téléphone* : (613) 232-1505. *Télécopieur* : (613) 232-1886.]

MATÉRIEL : Correspondance, documents financiers, demandes de subvention, listes de membres, rapports, mémoires, dépliants, communiqués de presse, affiches, macarons, bulletins, 1978-1991.

QUANTITÉ : 3 classeurs.

ACCÈS : Permission requise. Les mémoires, publications et rapports sont accessibles.

729. Fédération canadienne des services de garde à l'enfance / Canadian Child Day Care Federation

[For English entry, see # 706.]

✣ Ottawa (Ont.). Groupe fondé 1987.

Le but de la fédération est d'améliorer la qualité des services de garde à l'enfance.

LIEU DE CONSULTATION : Fédération canadienne des services de garde à l'enfance. [*Adresse* : 120, av. Holland, suite 401, Ottawa (Ont.) K1Y 0X6. *Téléphone* : (613) 729-5289. *Télécopieur* : (613) 729-3159.]

MATÉRIEL : Statuts et règlements, 1988, 1991; procès-verbaux, bulletins, 1987-1991; correspondance, documents financiers, demandes de subvention, 1983-1991; dossiers concernant la clientèle, listes de membres, listes d'envoi, albums de coupures, rapports, tracts, communiqués de presse, 1985-1991; mémoires, 1990-1991; actes de congrès, T-shirts, bannières, 1989-1991; dépliants, 1986-1991; affiches, enregistrements sonores, 1989; vidéocassettes, 1991; coupures de presse, photographies, documents divers.

QUANTITÉ : Env. 3 classeurs.

ÉTAT : Bon.

ACCÈS : Permission requise.

730. Fédération nationale des syndicats d'infirmières/infirmiers / National Federation of Nurses' Unions

[For English entry, see # 750.]

✣ Ottawa (Ont.). Groupe fondé [198-].

La Fédération nationale des syndicats d'infirmières/infirmiers (FNSII) est le groupe d'encadrement de six syndicats provinciaux d'infirmières et d'infirmiers.

LIEU DE CONSULTATION : Fédération nationale des syndicats d'infirmières/ infirmiers. [*Adresse* : 275, rue Slater, #405, Ottawa (Ont.) K1P 5H9. *Téléphone* : (613) 233-1018. *Télécopieur* : (613) 233-3892.]

MATÉRIEL : Statuts et règlements, procès-verbaux, correspondance, documents financiers, demandes de subvention, listes de membres, listes d'envoi, rapports, mémoires, actes de congrès, dépliants, tracts, communiqués de presse, affiches, macarons, bannières, coupures de presse, photographies, enregistrements sonores, vidéocassettes, films, 1976-1991; bulletins, 1982-1988.

QUANTITÉ : 3 classeurs.
ÉTAT : Bon.
ACCÈS : Permission requise. Restriction partielle à cause des limitations du personnel.

731. Fédération pour le planning des naissances du Canada / Planned Parenthood Federation of Canada

[For English entry, see # 758.]

✣ Ottawa (Ont.). Groupe fondé 1964.

La Fédération pour le planning des naissances du Canada s'est donné pour mission de promouvoir la sexualité saine et le planning des naissances par la diffusion de l'information appropriée et l'assurance de services adéquats pour tous les Canadiens et Canadiennes. À ses débuts, l'organisme s'appelait la Fédération de la planification familiale du Canada.

LIEU DE CONSULTATION : Fédération pour le planning des naissances du Canada. [*Adresse :* 1, rue Nicholas, suite 430, Ottawa (Ont.) K1N 7B7. *Téléphone :* (613) 238-4474. *Télécopieur :* (613) 238-1162.]

MATÉRIEL : Documents divers, 1986-1991.

ACCÈS : Permission requise.

732. Feminist Publications of Ottawa

[See also entry # 60 (in Part I), which lists other records of this organization.]

✣ Ottawa, Ont. Formed 1976. Disbanded 1980.

Feminist Publications of Ottawa (FPO) published the newspaper *Upstream: An Ottawa Women's Publication.* In 1978 the newspaper became a national publication, changing its name to *Upstream: A Canadian Women's Publication.* FPO organized the Feminist Print Media Conference, held in Ottawa in 1980.

LOCATION OF RECORDS: Women's Place. [*Address:* 241 Bruyère St., Ottawa, Ont. K1N 5E5. *Telephone:* (613) 789-2155. *Fax:* (613) 789-2745.]

RECORDS: Minutes, correspondence, financial records, grant applications, mailing lists, press releases, résumés, distribution records, 1976-1980; posters, 1978; periodicals (*Upstream*, 1976-1980); rubber stamps.

AMOUNT: 3 drawers of a filing cabinet.

733. Fonds d'action et d'éducation juridiques pour les femmes / Women's Legal Education and Action Fund

[For English entry, see # 772.]

✣ Toronto (Ont.). Groupe fondé 1985.

Le Fonds d'action et d'éducation juridiques pour les femmes (FAEJ) est un organisme national qui soutient la cause de l'égalité des femmes au Canada par le biais de poursuites judiciaires et d'éducation juridique, en utilisant la Charte canadienne des droits et libertés.

LIEU DE CONSULTATION : Fonds d'action et d'éducation juridiques pour les femmes. [*Adresse :* 489, rue College, #403, Toronto (Ont.) M6G 1A5. *Téléphone :* (416) 963-9654. *Télécopieur :* (416) 963-8455.]

MATÉRIEL : Statuts et règlements, procès-verbaux, correspondance, documents financiers, demandes de subvention, dossiers concernant la clientèle, listes de membres, listes d'envoi, rapports, mémoires, dépliants, tracts, communiqués de presse, T-shirts, 1985-1991; affiches, 1988-1990; bulletins, 1986-1991; vidéocassettes, 1989; coupures de presse, photographies, enregistrements sonores, livres.

QUANTITÉ : Env. 50 classeurs.

ÉTAT : Bon.

ACCÈS : Permission requise. Restrictions pour les documents juridiques.

734. Gallerie Publications

✣ North Vancouver, B.C. Formed 1987.

This organization publishes a quarterly magazine on contemporary women's art. It also maintains a registry of women artists and publishes artists' books.

LOCATION OF RECORDS: Gallerie Publications. [*Address:* 2901 Panorama Dr., North Vancouver, B.C. V7G 2A4. *Telephone:* (604) 929-8706. *Fax:* (604) 929-3247.]

RECORDS: Correspondence, financial records, grant applications, membership lists, mailing lists, scrapbooks, pamphlets, flyers, press releases, 1987-1991; periodicals (*Gallerie Women's Art*, 1988-1990; *Gallerie: Women Artists' Monographs*, 1990-1991; *Gallerie: Artists' News*, 1990-1991); T-shirts, 1990; clippings, 1988.

AMOUNT: 2 filing cabinets.

CONDITION: Good.

ACCESS: Permission required. Access depends on researcher's purpose, references, etc.

735. Growing Room Collective

✣ Vancouver, B.C. Formed 1975.

The Growing Room Collective publishes *Room of One's Own*, a feminist literary journal for women's poetry and fiction. The organization is also called the West Coast Feminist Literary Magazine Society.

LOCATION OF RECORDS: Growing Room Collective. [*Mailing Address:* P.O. Box 46160, Station G, Vancouver, B.C. V6R 4G5.]

RECORDS: Periodicals (*Room of One's Own*, 1975-1991); financial records, grant applications, mailing lists, 1975-1991.

AMOUNT: 1 drawer of a filing cabinet.

CONDITION: Good.

ACCESS: Permission required.

736. Herizons

✣ Winnipeg, Man. Formed 1979.

Herizons is a national feminist magazine. *Herizons* suspended publication in 1987 due to lack of funding; it resumed publishing in the spring of 1992, following a subscription campaign. Until 1982 it was called the *Manitoba Women's Newspaper*.

LOCATION OF RECORDS: Herizons. [*Mailing Address:* P.O. Box 128, Winnipeg, Man. R3C 2G1. *Telephone:* (204) 774-6225.]

RECORDS: Constitution, 1983; minutes, correspondence, financial records, grant applications, client records, subscription lists, donor lists, mailing lists, pamphlets, flyers, press releases, 1979-1987, 1991; petitions, 1986-1987; scrapbooks, 1981-1987, 1991; reports, 1982-1987; posters, 1986; periodicals (*Manitoba Women's Newspaper*, 1979-1982; *Herizons*, 1982-1987); clippings, 1981; photographs, 1982; television commercial, 1984.

AMOUNT: Approx. 12 boxes.

CONDITION: Good.

ACCESS: Permission required.

737. Indian and Inuit Nurses of Canada / Association des infirmières et infirmiers autochtones du Canada

[Renseignements en français, notice 700.]

✣ Ottawa, Ont. Formed 1974.

Indian and Inuit Nurses of Canada (IINC), also known as Native Nurses, is a national organization of Native health professionals which works to improve health-care services for Native people. Native women's health concerns are a large part of IINC's work. Until 1983 it was called Registered Nurses of Canadian Indian Ancestry (RNCIA).

LOCATION OF RECORDS: Indian and Inuit Nurses of Canada. [*Address:* 55 Murray St., 4th Floor, Ottawa, Ont. K1N 5M3. *Telephone:* (613) 230-1864.]

RECORDS: Constitution, minutes, correspondence, log-books, financial records, grant applications, client records, membership lists, mailing lists, reports, briefs, conference proceedings, pamphlets, posters, buttons, T-shirts, newsletters, books, photographs, sound recordings, [197-]-1991.

CONDITION: Good.

ACCESS: Permission required.

738. Infant Feeding Action Coalition Canada

✢ Toronto, Ont. Formed 1979.

The Infant Feeding Action Coalition Canada (INFACT) promotes maternal and infant health by protecting breast feeding and by fostering appropriate mother and infant nutrition. INFACT does lobbying, research, and education.

LOCATION OF RECORDS: Infant Feeding Action Coalition Canada. [*Address:* 10 Trinity Sq., Toronto, Ont. M5G 1B1. *Telephone:* (416) 595-9819. *Fax:* (416) 598-1432.]

RECORDS: Newsletters, 1980-1991; constitution, minutes, correspondence, financial records, grant applications, membership lists, mailing lists, petitions, reports, briefs, conference proceedings, pamphlets, flyers, press releases, banners, clippings.

AMOUNT: 2 filing cabinets, 4 boxes.

CONDITION: Good.

739. Institut canadien de recherches sur les femmes / Canadian Research Institute for the Advancement of Women

[For English entry, see # 713.]

[Voir aussi la notice 64 (dans la partie I) pour autres documents de ce groupe.]

✢ Ottawa (Ont.). Groupe fondé 1976.

L'institut, appelé aussi l'ICREF, a pour mission de coordonner, de stimuler et de diffuser des travaux de recherche sur la réalité vécue par les femmes et d'assurer à celles-ci et à leurs expériences une place équitable dans l'ensemble des connaissances et de la recherche concernant le Canada.

LIEU DE CONSULTATION : Institut canadien de recherches sur les femmes. [*Adresse :* 151, rue Slater, suite 408, Ottawa (Ont.) K1P 5H3. *Téléphone :* (613) 563-0681. *Télécopieur :* (613) 563-0682.]

MATÉRIEL : Procès-verbaux, correspondance, photographies, 1976-1991; demandes de subvention, 1978-1991; actes de congrès, 1982-1987; T-shirts, sweat-shirts, 1986; bannières, 1990; publications, 1981-1991; enregistrements sonores, 1989; vidéocassettes, 1989-1990; documents financiers, listes de membres, rapports, dépliants, tracts, affiches.

QUANTITÉ : Env. 2 classeurs.

ÉTAT : Bon.

ACCÈS : Permission requise. Dossiers concernant le personnel confidentiels.

740. Iranian Woman Publications of Canada

✢ Toronto, Ont. Formed 1986.

IranianWoman, a quarterly journal, aims to inform and educate Iranian women in Canada, help them adjust to Canadian culture, and preserve Iranian culture.

LOCATION OF RECORDS: Iranian Woman Publications of Canada. [*Address:* 238 Davenport Rd., #334, Toronto, Ont. M5R 1J6. *Telephone:* (416) 920-5228.]

RECORDS: Constitution, correspondence, log-books, financial records, client records, mailing lists, conference proceedings, pamphlets, banners, 1986-1991; periodicals (*Iranian Woman*, 1986-1991).

AMOUNT: Approx. 8 filing cabinets.

CONDITION: Good.

741. Liberal Party of Canada. National Women's Liberal Commission / Parti libéral du Canada. Commission libérale féminine nationale

[Renseignements en français, notice 756.]

[See also entry # 68 (in Part I), which lists other records of this organization.]

✢ Ottawa, Ont. Formed 1928.

The National Women's Liberal Commission (NWLC) represents and promotes the interests of women within the Liberal Party of Canada and encourages the active participation of women at all levels of the party.

LOCATION OF RECORDS: Liberal Party of Canada. National Women's Liberal Commission. [*Address:* 200 - 200 Laurier Ave. W., Ottawa, Ont. K1P 6M8. *Telephone:* (613) 237-0740. *Fax:* (613) 235-7208.]

RECORDS: Constitution, minutes, correspondence, financial records, membership lists, mailing lists, scrapbooks, reports, conference proceedings, 1989-1991.

AMOUNT: 1 filing cabinet.

CONDITION: Good.

ACCESS: Permission required.

742. MATCH International Centre / Centre international MATCH

[Renseignements en français, notice 717.]

[See also entry # 70 (in Part I), which lists other records of this organization.]

✢ Ottawa, Ont. Formed 1976.

MATCH International Centre is a feminist development organization which matches the resources and needs of Canadian women with those of women in developing countries. The organization's goals include eliminating violence against women globally.

LOCATION OF RECORDS: MATCH International Centre. [*Address:* 1102 - 200 Elgin St., Ottawa, Ont. K2P 1L5. *Telephone:* (613) 238-1312. *Fax:* (613) 238-6867.]

RECORDS: Constitution, 1977; minutes, correspondence, financial records, grant applications, membership lists, mailing lists, reports, pamphlets, flyers, press releases, posters, newsletters, videotapes, 1976-1991.

CONDITION: Good.

ACCESS: Permission required.

743. MediaWatch / Évaluation-Médias

[Renseignements en français, notice 727.]

✢ Toronto, Ont. Formed 1983.

MediaWatch works to improve media images of women. It provides resources to foster media literacy, supports women working in the media, and presses for change through political and industry lobbying. Its official name is the National Watch on Images of Women in the Media. MediaWatch grew out of a subcommittee of the National Action Committee on the Status of Women. [See also National Action Committee on the Status of Women/Comité canadien d'action sur le statut de la femme (71, 744).]

LOCATION OF RECORDS: MediaWatch. [*Address:* 517 Wellington St., Suite 204, Toronto, Ont. M5V 1G1. *Telephone:* (416) 408-2065.]

RECORDS: Constitution, 1983, 1988; minutes, grant applications, 1986-1991; correspondence, videotapes, 1983-1991; financial records, client records, press releases, clippings, newsletters, 1985-1991; membership lists, 1988-1991; reports, briefs, 1981-1991; conference proceedings, posters, banners, 1987; pamphlets, 1984, 1987, 1989; T-shirts, 1990.

AMOUNT: 4 filing cabinets, 6 boxes.

CONDITION: Fair.

ACCESS: Permission required. Personnel and internal correspondence files closed.

744. National Action Committee on the Status of Women / Comité canadien d'action sur le statut de la femme

[Renseignements en français, notice 720.]

[See also entry # 71 (in Part I), which lists other records of this organization.]

✣ Toronto, Ont. Formed 1971.

The National Action Committee on the Status of Women (NAC) is the largest women's organization in Canada, representing over 450 non-governmental associations from all regions of the country. Its priorities are to promote co-operation among women's groups, advocate political and legislative reforms, and sensitize the public to women's issues. NAC was originally called the National Ad Hoc Action Committee on the Status of Women. The present name was adopted in 1972. [See also MediaWatch/Évaluation-Médias (743).]

LOCATION OF RECORDS: National Action Committee on the Status of Women. [*Address:* 57 Mobile Dr., Toronto, Ont. M4A 1H5. *Telephone:* (416) 759-5252. *Fax:* (416) 759-5370.]

RECORDS: Minutes, correspondence, log-books, reports, conference proceedings, grant applications, sound recordings, membership lists, petitions, pamphlets, briefs, press releases, T-shirts, banners, periodicals, financial records, flyers, posters, buttons, photographs, 1971-1991.

AMOUNT: 8 filing cabinets, 144 boxes.

ACCESS: Permission required. Non-current records are stored off-site.

745. National Association of Women and the Law / Association nationale de la femme et du droit

[Renseignements en français, notice 702.]

✣ Ottawa, Ont. Formed 1975.

The National Association of Women and the Law (NAWL) promotes the equality of women in law and society. [See also Canadian Journal of Women and the Law/Revue Femmes et droit (711).]

LOCATION OF RECORDS: National Association of Women and the Law. [*Address:* 1 Nicholas St., Suite #604, Ottawa, Ont. K1N 7B7. *Telephone:* (613) 238-1544.]

RECORDS: Constitution, 1975-1991; minutes, 1982-1991; correspondence, 1989-1991; financial records, membership lists, reports, briefs, 1981-1991; grant applications, 1983-1991; mailing lists, press releases, posters, 1987-1991; conference proceedings, 1981, 1983, 1985, 1987; pamphlets, 1985-1991; newsletters, 1977-1987.

AMOUNT: 4 filing cabinets.

CONDITION: Good.

ACCESS: Permission required. Membership lists closed.

746. National Coaching School for Women

✣ Gloucester, Ont. Formed 1987.

The National Coaching School for Women (NCSW), under the auspices of the Canadian Interuniversity Athletic Union (CIAU), works to empower women coaches and athletes. NCSW promotes the advancement of women within existing coaching systems and works to develop feminist curricula.

LOCATION OF RECORDS: National Coaching School for Women. [*Address:* c/o Canadian Interuniversity Athletic Union, 1600 James Naismith Dr., Gloucester, Ont. K1B 5N4. *Telephone:* (613) 748-5619. *Fax:* (613) 748-5764.]

RECORDS: Constitution, 1991; minutes, correspondence, financial records, client records, membership lists, mailing lists, scrapbooks, reports, conference proceedings, pamphlets, flyers, press releases, posters, T-shirts, banners, clippings, photographs, 1987-1991.

AMOUNT: 1 filing cabinet.

CONDITION: Fair.

ACCESS: Permission required.

747. National Council of Jewish Women of Canada

[See also entry # 72 (in Part I), which lists other records of this organization.]

✣ Downsview, Ont. Formed 1897.

The main activities of the National Council of Jewish Women of Canada (NCJW) are education, service, and social action. While its priorities are the protection of human rights and the preservation of Jewish life, NCJW is also concerned with women's issues such as family planning, abortion, child care, pornography, and affirmative action. Its French name is le Conseil des femmes juives du Canada.

LOCATION OF RECORDS: National Council of Jewish Women of Canada. [*Address:* 1110 Finch Ave. W., #518, Downsview, Ont. M3J 2T2. *Telephone:* (416) 665-8251. *Fax:* (416) 665-8702.]

RECORDS: Grant applications, pamphlets, press releases, posters, T-shirts, booklets, clippings, photographs, videotapes, 1981-1991; briefs, 1991; newsletters (*New Edition*).

CONDITION: Good.

ACCESS: Permission required. Many records are confidential and closed to researchers.

748. National Eating Disorder Information Centre

✣ Toronto, Ont. Formed 1986.

The National Eating Disorder Information Centre (NEDIC) provides support, information, and resources related to eating disorders and weight preoccupation.

LOCATION OF RECORDS: National Eating Disorder Information Centre. [*Address:* 200 Elizabeth St., CWI-328, Toronto, Ont. M5G 2C4. *Telephone:* (416) 340-4156/4188. *Fax:* (416) 340-5888.]

RECORDS: Minutes, 1987-1991; correspondence, financial records, grant applications, client records, membership lists, mailing lists, scrapbooks, reports, pamphlets, flyers, clippings, photographs, 1986-1991; conference proceedings, press releases, 1989-1991; posters, buttons, sound recordings, 1988-1991; T-shirts, banners, 1990-1991; newsletters.

AMOUNT: 2 filing cabinets.

CONDITION: Good.

ACCESS: Permission required. Client files and files deemed confidential closed.

749. National Farmers Union. Women's Advisory Committee

✢ Saskatoon, Sask. Formed 1969.

The Women's Advisory Committee encourages the participation of women in decision making, policy formulation, and all other activities of the National Farmers Union (NFU).

LOCATION OF RECORDS: National Farmers Union. Women's Advisory Committee. [*Address:* c/o Current President Nettie Wiebe, 250-C 2nd Ave. S., Saskatoon, Sask. S7K 2M1. *Telephone:* (306) 369-2993. *Fax:* (306) 664-6226.]

RECORDS: Constitution, 1969; minutes, correspondence, financial records, grant applications, membership lists, mailing lists, reports, briefs, pamphlets, flyers, press releases, posters, buttons, T-shirts, banners, clippings, photographs, 1969-1991; conference proceedings, sound recordings, videotapes.

AMOUNT: Approx. 6 filing cabinets.

CONDITION: Fair.

ACCESS: Permission required. Some files may be closed.

750. National Federation of Nurses' Unions / Fédération nationale des syndicats d'infirmières/infirmiers

[Renseignements en français, notice 730.]

✢ Ottawa, Ont. Formed [198-].

The National Federation of Nurses' Unions (NFNU) is the umbrella organization for six provincial nurses' unions.

LOCATION OF RECORDS: National Federation of Nurses' Unions. [*Address:* 275 Slater St. #405, Ottawa, Ont. K1P 5H9. *Telephone:* (613) 233-1018. *Fax:* (613) 233-3892.]

RECORDS: Constitution, minutes, correspondence, financial records, grant applications, membership lists, mailing lists, reports, briefs, conference proceedings, pamphlets, flyers, press releases, posters, buttons, banners, clippings, photographs, sound recordings, videotapes, films, 1976-1991; newsletters, 1982-1988.

AMOUNT: 3 filing cabinets.

CONDITION: Good.

ACCESS: Permission required. Some restrictions due to limited staff.

751. National Lesbian Forum / Alliance nationale des lesbiennes

[Renseignements en français, notice 694.]

✢ Regina, Sask. Formed 1988.

The goal of the National Lesbian Forum (NLF) is to work with other feminist, lesbian, and gay organizations across Canada to build support for lesbians and public awareness of lesbian issues.

LOCATION OF RECORDS: National Lesbian Forum. [*Mailing Address:* Box 482, Regina, Sask. S4P 3A2. *Telephone:* (306) 522-8307.]

RECORDS: Correspondence, financial records, 1988-1991; membership lists, mailing lists, 1989; flyers, newsletters, 1988-1989.

AMOUNT: Approx. 1 drawer of a filing cabinet.

CONDITION: Good.

ACCESS: Permission required. Membership lists and mailing lists closed.

752. National Organization of Immigrant and Visible Minority Women of Canada / Organisation nationale des femmes immigrantes et des femmes appartenant à une minorité visible du Canada

[Renseignements en français, notice 754.]

✢ Ottawa, Ont. Formed 1986.

The purpose of this organization (also known as NOIVMWC) is to ensure equality for immigrant and visible-minority women, through lobbying, networking, and advocacy.

LOCATION OF RECORDS: National Organization of Immigrant and Visible Minority Women of Canada. [*Address:* 251 Bank St., #506, Ottawa, Ont. K2P 1X3. *Telephone:* (613) 232-0689. *Fax:* (613) 238-8735.]

RECORDS: Constitution, minutes, correspondence, financial records, grant applications, membership lists, mailing lists, reports, briefs, conference proceedings, pamphlets, flyers, press releases, newsletters, clippings, 1986-1991; videotapes, 1991.

AMOUNT: Approx. 3 filing cabinets.

CONDITION: Good.

ACCESS: Permission required.

753. Native Women's Association of Canada

✢ Ohawaken, Ont. Formed 1974.

The goal of the Native Women's Association of Canada (NWAC) is to enhance, promote, and foster the social, economic, cultural, and political well-being of First Nations and Métis women. NWAC is an aggregate of Native women's organizations which functions as a "Grandmother's Lodge."

LOCATION OF RECORDS: Native Women's Association of Canada. [*Mailing Address:* P.O. Box 185, Ohawaken, Ont. N0A 1M0. *Telephone:* (613) 236-6057. *Fax:* (613) 235-4957.]

RECORDS: Constitution, 1983-1991; minutes, correspondence, log-books, financial records, grant applications, membership lists, mailing lists, reports, press releases, books, clippings, photographs, videotapes, 1974-1991; pamphlets, 1990; newsletters, 1990-1991.

AMOUNT: 12 filing cabinets, 25 boxes.

CONDITION: Good.

ACCESS: Permission required. Records are not for public viewing.

754. Organisation nationale des femmes immigrantes et des femmes appartenant à une minorité visible du Canada / National Organization of Immigrant and Visible Minority Women of Canada

[For English entry, see # 752.]

✢ Ottawa (Ont.). Groupe fondé 1986.

Le but de l'organisme, appellée aussi ONFIFAMVC, est d'assurer l'égalité des femmes immigrantes ou appartenant à une minorité visible au Canada. Ses activités comprennent le lobbying, le travail en réseau et l'appui de causes pertinentes.

LIEU DE CONSULTATION : Organisation nationale des femmes immigrantes et des femmes appartenant à une minorité visible du Canada. [*Adresse :* 251, rue Bank, #506, Ottawa (Ont.) K2P 1X3. *Téléphone :* (613) 232-0689. *Télécopieur :* (613) 238-8735.]

MATÉRIEL : Statuts et règlements, procès-verbaux, correspondance, documents financiers, demandes de subvention, listes de membres, listes d'envoi, rapports, mémoires, actes de congrès, dépliants, tracts, communiqués de presse, bulletins, coupures de presse, 1986-1991; vidéocassettes, 1991.

QUANTITÉ : Env. 3 classeurs.
ÉTAT : Bon.
ACCÈS : Permission requise.

755. Organizational Society for the Spouses of Military Members

✢ Ottawa, Ont. Formed [1985?].

The Organizational Society for the Spouses of Military Members (OSSOMM) speaks out on behalf of the spouses of military personnel. OSSOMM works to improve the lives of military families; it does public education and lobbying on issues such as pensions, unemployment insurance, health plans, domestic violence, and common-law spousal rights.

LOCATION OF RECORDS: Organizational Society for the Spouses of Military Members. [*Address:* c/o L. Laliberte, Pothier and Gahrns, 305 - 116 Albert, Ottawa, Ont. *Telephone:* (613) 235-6299.]

RECORDS: Constitution, [1985?]; minutes, newsletters, 1985-1991; correspondence, membership lists, mailing lists, reports, briefs, pamphlets, flyers, press releases, thesis.

AMOUNT: 3 filing cabinets.

CONDITION: Good.

ACCESS: Permission required. Membership lists and mailing lists may be closed.

756. Parti libéral du Canada. Commission libérale féminine nationale / Liberal Party of Canada. National Women's Liberal Commission

[For English entry, see # 741.]

[Voir aussi la notice 81 (dans la partie I) pour autres documents de ce groupe.]

✢ Ottawa (Ont.). Groupe fondé 1928.

La Commission libérale féminine nationale (CLFN) est chargée de représenter et de promouvoir les intérêts des femmes au sein du Parti libéral du Canada et d'encourager les femmes à participer activement à ses activités, à tous les échelons.

LIEU DE CONSULTATION : Parti libéral du Canada. Commission libérale féminine nationale. [*Adresse :* 200 - 200 av. Laurier, Ottawa (Ont.) K1P 6M8. *Téléphone :* (613) 237-0740. *Télécopieur :* (613) 235-7208.]

MATÉRIEL : Statuts et règlements, procès-verbaux, correspondance, documents financiers, listes de membres, listes d'envoi, albums de coupures, rapports, actes de congrès, 1989-1991.

QUANTITÉ : 1 classeur.

ÉTAT : Bon.

ACCÈS : Permission requise.

757. Pauktuutit: Inuit Women's Association of Canada

✢ Ottawa, Ont. Formed 1984.

Pauktuutit: Inuit Women's Association of Canada (IWA) is committed to improving the quality of life for all Inuit women in Canada by fostering a greater awareness of their needs. The association operates in Inuktitut and English.

LOCATION OF RECORDS: Pauktuutit: Inuit Women's Association of Canada. [*Address:* 804 - 200 Elgin St., Ottawa, Ont. K2P 1L5. *Telephone:* (613) 238-3977. *Fax:* (613) 238-1787.]

RECORDS: Constitution, 1984-1991; minutes, correspondence, financial records, grant applications, membership lists, mailing lists, reports, briefs, conference proceedings, press releases, photographs, 1985-1991; buttons, 1986; T-shirts, 1991; newsletters (*Suvaguuq*, 1985, 1990-1991), books, 1985-1990; videotapes, 1990.

AMOUNT: 4 filing cabinets.

CONDITION: Good.

ACCESS: Permission required.

758. Planned Parenthood Federation of Canada / Fédération pour le planning des naissances du Canada

[Renseignements en français, notice 731.]

✢ Ottawa, Ont. Formed 1964.

The mission of the Planned Parenthood Federation of Canada (PPFC) is to promote healthy sexuality and birth planning by assuring adequate education and services for all Canadians. It was originally called the Family Planning Federation of Canada.

LOCATION OF RECORDS: Planned Parenthood Federation of Canada. [*Address:* 1 Nicholas St., Suite 430, Ottawa, Ont. K1N 7B7. *Telephone:* (613) 238-4474. *Fax:* (613) 238-1162.]

RECORDS: Miscellaneous records, 1986-1991.

ACCESS: Permission required.

759. Réseau d'action des femmes handicapées du Canada / DisAbled Women's Network Canada

[For English entry, see # 725.]

✢ Toronto (Ont.). Groupe fondé 1985.

Le Réseau d'action des femmes handicapées du Canada est un porte-parole des femmes handicapées au Canada. L'organisme offre un soutien, des informations et des ressources aux femmes handicapées.

LIEU DE CONSULTATION : Réseau d'action des femmes handicapées du Canada. [*Adresse :* 658, av. Danforth, suite 203, Toronto (Ont.) M4J 1L1. *Téléphone :* (416) 406-1080/1081. *Télécopieur :* (416) 406-1082.]

MATÉRIEL : Statuts et règlements, mémoires, dépliants, 1986-1991; procès-verbaux, correspondance, documents financiers, demandes de subvention, listes de membres, listes d'envoi, pétitions, rapports, actes de congrès, tracts, communiqués de presse, affiches, 1985-1991; bulletins (*Thriving*, 1990); livres, coupures de presse, enregistrements sonores.

QUANTITÉ : 4 classeurs.

ÉTAT : Assez bon.

ACCÈS : Permission requise. Dossiers concernant le personnel confidentiels.

760. Réseau d'action en milieu urbain / Urban Core Support Network

[For English entry, see # 767.]

✢ Toronto (Ont.). Groupe fondé 1971.

Le Réseau d'action en milieu urbain est une association canadienne de personnes qui désirent combattre la pauvreté urbaine (et la pauvreté rurale liée), en particulier celle des célibataires et des familles monoparentales. Un sous-réseau s'occupe spécialement de services pour femmes. À ses débuts, l'organisme s'appelait the Skid Row National Coalition Committee. Cet organisme est subventionné par les églises ; ses membres oeuvrent activement dans les programmes religieux et communautaires.

LIEU DE CONSULTATION : Réseau d'action en milieu urbain. [*Adresse :* 315, rue Dundas est, Toronto (Ont.) M5A 2A2. *Téléphone :* (416) 363-7655.]

MATÉRIEL : Procès-verbaux, correspondance, listes de membres, listes d'envoi, dépliants, bulletins, 1971-1991.

QUANTITÉ : 2 classeurs, 6 boîtes.

ACCÈS : Permission requise.

761. Réseau national d'Action éducation femmes

✣ Ottawa (Ont.). Groupe fondé 1983.

Le but du Réseau national d'Action éducation femmes (AEF) est de promouvoir l'éducation chez les femmes francophones par la diffusion d'information. Ses dossiers principaux sont l'alphabétisation, la reconnaissance des acquis et l'étude du profil des femmes francophones.

LIEU DE CONSULTATION: Réseau national d'Action éducation femmes. [*Adresse*: 50, rue Vaughan, Ottawa (Ont.) K1G 4N1. *Téléphone*: (613) 741-9978. *Télécopieur*: (613) 741-3805.]

MATÉRIEL: Statuts et règlements, procès-verbaux, correspondance, journaux de bord, documents financiers, demandes de subvention, dossiers concernant la clientèle, pétitions, albums de coupures, rapports, mémoires, coupures de presse, 1983-1991; listes de membres, listes d'envoi, livres, 1988-1991; dépliants, communiqués de presse, 1985-1991; affiches, macarons, 1991; bannières, 1990; bulletins (*Le Bulletin*, 1987-1991; *Info*, 1989-1990); photographies, 1990-1991.

QUANTITÉ: 4 classeurs.

ÉTAT: Assez bon.

ACCÈS: Permission requise.

762. Resources for Feminist Research / Documentation sur la recherche féministe

[Renseignements en français, notice 726.]

[See also entry # 85 (in Part I), which lists other records of this organization.]

✣ Toronto, Ont. Formed 1972.

Resources for Feminist Research/Documentation sur la recherche féministe (RFR/DRF) is a Canadian journal of international feminist research. Until 1979 it was called the *Canadian Newsletter of Research on Women/Recherches sur la femme : Bulletin d'information canadien*.

LOCATION OF RECORDS: Resources for Feminist Research. [*Address:* Ontario Institute for Studies in Education, 252 Bloor St. W., Toronto, Ont. M5S 1V6. *Telephone:* (416) 923-6641. *Fax:* (416) 926-4725.]

RECORDS: Constitution, minutes, correspondence, financial records, grant applications, subscription lists, mailing lists, press releases, posters, clippings, [1985?]-1991; periodicals (RFR/DRF, 1972-1990).

CONDITION: Good.

ACCESS: Permission required. Minutes of editorial board meetings closed.

763. Revue Femmes et droit / Canadian Journal of Women and the Law

[For English entry, see # 711.]

✣ Ottawa (Ont.). Groupe fondé 1984.

La *Revue Femmes et droit* (RFD) (autrefois appelée la *Revue juridique La Femme et le droit*) vise à faire une analyse en profondeur des questions d'ordre juridique intéressant les femmes. La revue est publiée par l'Association nationale de la femme et du droit, mais elle est totalement indépendante sur le plan de la rédaction. [Voir aussi Association nationale de la femme et du droit/National Association of Women and the Law (702).]

LIEU DE CONSULTATION: Revue Femmes et droit. [*Adresse*: 575, av. King Edward, Ottawa (Ont.) K1N 6N5. *Téléphone*: (613) 564-5617. *Télécopieur*: (613) 564-9800.]

MATÉRIEL: Statuts et règlements, procès-verbaux, correspondance, documents financiers, demandes de subvention, dossiers concernant la clientèle, listes de membres, listes d'envoi, périodiques, 1985-1991; dépliants, 1990.

QUANTITÉ: 4 classeurs.

ÉTAT: Bon.

ACCÈS: Permission requise. Les rapports des arbitres sont confidentiels.

764. Rites Magazine

✣ Toronto, Ont. Formed 1984. Disbanded 1992.

Rites was a national periodical covering the lesbian and gay liberation movement, feminism, and the labour movement. *Rites* also featured poetry and fiction by lesbians and gay men.

LOCATION OF RECORDS: *Rites* disbanded shortly before this book went to press. For information on the location of the records, please contact the Canadian Gay Archives. (See Appendix for address.)

RECORDS: Periodicals (*Rites*, 1984-1991); minutes, 1988-1991; correspondence, 1990-1991, financial records, 1987-1991; grant applications, 1984-1991; membership lists, mailing lists.

CONDITION: Good.

ACCESS: Permission required. Mailing lists closed.

765. Society for Canadian Women in Science and Technology

✣ Vancouver, B.C. Formed 1981.

This organization, also known as SCWIST, provides a forum for the exchange of ideas and information about women and girls in mathematics and science. It encourages equal opportunity for women in scientific, technological, and engineering careers and does public education to improve attitudes. Its French name is la Société des Canadiennes dans les sciences et les technologies.

LOCATION OF RECORDS: Society for Canadian Women in Science and Technology. [*Mailing Address:* P.O. Box 2184, Vancouver, B.C. V6B 3V7.]

RECORDS: Constitution, 1984; minutes, correspondence, financial records, grant applications, membership lists, mailing lists, scrapbooks, reports, pamphlets, posters, buttons, T-shirts, newsletters, 1981-1991; conference proceedings, 1983; books, 1989; videotapes, 1990.

AMOUNT: Approx. 3 filing cabinets.

CONDITION: Good.

ACCESS: Permission required.

766. Travailleurs amalgamés du vêtement et du textile / Amalgamated Clothing and Textile Workers Union

[For English entry, see # 695.]

[Voir aussi la notice 90 (dans la partie I) pour autres documents de ce groupe.]

✣ Don Mills (Ont.). Groupe fondé 1976.

Le syndicat des Travailleurs amalgamés du vêtement et du textile (TAVT) vise à améliorer la vie des ouvrières et ouvriers canadiens. La majorité de ses membres sont des femmes.

LIEU DE CONSULTATION: Travailleurs amalgamés du vêtement et du textile. [*Adresse*: 15, promenade Gervais, suite 601, Don Mills (Ont.) M3C 1Y8. *Téléphone*: (416) 441-1806. *Télécopieur*: (416) 441-9680.]

MATÉRIEL: Statuts et règlements, procès-verbaux, documents financiers, actes de congrès, 1976-1991; correspondance, rapports, mémoires, dépliants, tracts, communiqués de presse, 1989-1991; bulletins (*Action*, 1988-1991; *Labor Unity*, 1976-1991); listes de membres, listes d'envoi, livres, photographies, films.

QUANTITÉ: 4 classeurs.

ÉTAT: Bon.

ACCÈS: Permission requise. Listes de membres et d'envoi et certains rapports confidentiels.

767. Urban Core Support Network / Réseau d'action en milieu urbain

[Renseignements en français, notice 760.]

✣ Toronto, Ont. Formed 1971.

The Urban Core Support Network (UCSN) is a national association of activists working to combat inner-city poverty (and related rural poverty), particularly the poverty of single people and single-parent families. A sub-network focuses specifically on services for women. The organization's original name was the Skid Row National Coalition Committee. UCSN is funded by churches; its members are church and community-based activists.

LOCATION OF RECORDS: Urban Core Support Network. [*Address:* 315 Dundas St. E., Toronto, Ont. M5A 2A2. *Telephone:* (416) 363-7655.]

RECORDS: Minutes, correspondence, membership lists, mailing lists, pamphlets, newsletters, 1971-1991.

AMOUNT: 2 filing cabinets, 6 boxes.

ACCESS: Permission required.

768. The Womanist

✣ Ottawa, Ont. Formed 1988.

The Womanist is a national feminist newspaper published by Catalyst Research and Communications.

LOCATION OF RECORDS: The Womanist. [*Address:* c/o Catalyst Research and Communications, 541 Sussex Dr., Suite 201, Ottawa, Ont. K1N 6Z6. *Telephone:* (613) 233-2621. *Fax:* (613) 236-7118.]

RECORDS: Periodicals (The Womanist, 1988-1991); minutes, correspondence, log-books, financial records, client records, membership lists, mailing lists, reports, pamphlets, flyers, press release, articles, photographs, graphics, 1988-1991.

AMOUNT: 14 filing-cabinet drawers, 5 boxes.

CONDITION: Good.

ACCESS: Permission required. Financial records and authors' files closed.

769. Women in Trades, Technology, and Operations — National Network

✣ Winlaw, B.C. Formed 1988.

Also known as the WITT National Network, this organization encourages, trains, and promotes women in trades, technologies, and operations. The network's French name is le Réseau national WITT. (Although the group operates primarily in English, many of its publications have been translated into French.)

LOCATION OF RECORDS: Women in Trades, Technology, and Operations — National Network. [*Address:* R.R. #1, Winlaw, B.C. V0G 2J0. *Telephone:* (604) 226-7624. *Fax:* (604) 226-7624.]

RECORDS: Minutes, correspondence, financial records, grant applications, mailing lists, reports, briefs, 1988-1991; conference proceedings, 1988; newsletters, 1989-1991; constitution, books, clippings, photographs, slide show, sound recordings, videotapes.

AMOUNT: 12 filing-cabinet drawers.

CONDITION: Good.

ACCESS: Permission required.

770. Women's Art Resource Centre

✣ Toronto, Ont. Formed 1985.

The Women's Art Resource Centre (WARC) supports women artists through education and the provision of resources. WARC organizes lectures, workshops, and studio visits and publishes Matriart, a feminist art journal.

LOCATION OF RECORDS: Women's Art Resource Centre. [*Address:* 394 Euclid Ave., Suite 308, Toronto, Ont. M6G 2S9. *Telephone:* (416) 324-8910. *Fax:* (416) 324-8268.]

RECORDS: Minutes, 1985; correspondence, 1988-1991; financial records, grant applications, client records, membership lists, flyers, 1985-1991; periodicals (WARC, 1990; Matriart, 1990-1991); press releases, posters, clippings, photographs, sound recordings, videotapes, 1986-1991; buttons, 1990.

AMOUNT: 8 filing cabinets.

CONDITION: Good.

ACCESS: Permission required. Mailing lists and financial records restricted.

771. Women's Inter-Church Council of Canada / Conseil œcuménique des chrétiennes du Canada

[Renseignements en français, notice 724.]

✣ Toronto, Ont. Formed 1919.

The Women's Inter-Church Council of Canada (WICC) promotes spiritual development, women's concerns, and human rights. This Christian organization has produced educational materials dealing with issues such as violence against women. The organization was originally known as the Interim Committee of the Federated Women's Missionary Boards of Canada and was later called the Inter-Board Committee of the Women's Missionary Societies of Canada.

LOCATION OF RECORDS: Women's Inter-Church Council of Canada. [*Address:* 77 Charles St. W., Toronto, Ont. M5S 1K5. *Telephone:* (416) 922-6177.]

RECORDS: Constitution, minutes, correspondence, financial records, reports, newsletters, 1989-1991.

AMOUNT: 2 filing cabinets.

CONDITION: Good.

772. Women's Legal Education and Action Fund / Fonds d'action et d'éducation juridiques pour les femmes

[Renseignements en français, notice 733.]

✣ Toronto, Ont. Formed 1985.

The Women's Legal Education and Action Fund (LEAF) is a national organization which promotes equality for Canadian women, through legal action and public education based primarily on the Canadian Charter of Rights and Freedoms.

LOCATION OF RECORDS: Women's Legal Education and Action Fund. [*Address:* 489 College St., #403, Toronto, Ont. M6G 1A5. *Telephone:* (416) 963-9654. *Fax:* (416) 963-8455.]

RECORDS: Constitution, minutes, correspondence, financial records, grant applications, client records, membership lists, mailing lists, reports, briefs, pamphlets, flyers, press releases, T-shirts, 1985-1991; posters, 1988-1990; newsletters, 1986-1991; videotapes, 1989; clippings, photographs, sound recordings, books.

AMOUNT: Approx. 50 filing cabinets.

CONDITION: Good.

ACCESS: Permission required. Restrictions on legal documents.

YUKON

773. Association for the Prevention of Community and Family Violence

✢ Whitehorse, Yukon. Formed 1988.

The Association for the Prevention of Community and Family Violence (APCFV) was formed through the amalgamation of two earlier committees: the Ad Hoc Committee on Family Violence and the Ad Hoc Committee on the Treatment of Child Sexual Abuse. APCFV advocates the development of a co-ordinated response to community and family violence, in the areas of investigation, assessment, treatment, education, and training of professionals and para-professionals.

LOCATION OF RECORDS: Association for the Prevention of Community and Family Violence. [*Address:* c/o #4 Hospital Road, Whitehorse, Yukon Y1A 3H8. *Telephone:* (403) 667-8346.]

RECORDS: Constitution, minutes, correspondence, financial records, grant applications, membership lists, mailing lists, reports, briefs, press releases, 1982-1991.

CONDITION: Good.

ACCESS: Permission required.

774. Dawson Shelter Society

✢ Dawson City, Yukon. Formed 1987.

This organization offers shelter, support, and information to women and children in crisis. It also does public education.

LOCATION OF RECORDS: Dawson Shelter Society. [*Mailing Address:* Box 784, Dawson City, Yukon Y0B 1G0. *Telephone:* (403) 993-5086.]

RECORDS: Constitution, 1988; minutes, financial records, pamphlets, photographs, 1988-1991; correspondence, log-books, grant applications, client records, membership lists, mailing lists, scrapbooks, reports, posters, newsletters, clippings, 1987-1991, banners, 1990-1991.

AMOUNT: 2 filing cabinets.

CONDITION: Good.

ACCESS: Permission required. Client files closed.

775. Women's Business Network

✢ Whitehorse, Yukon. Formed 1989.

The Women's Business Network (WBN) fosters the participation of women in all aspects of business and economic activity in the Yukon. WBN provides opportunities for women to develop skills, make business contacts, and exchange information.

LOCATION OF RECORDS: Women's Business Network. [*Mailing Address:* P.O. Box 3941, Whitehorse, Yukon Y1A 5M6. *Telephone:* (403) 668-3600.]

RECORDS: Constitution, minutes, correspondence, financial records, membership applications, membership lists, mailing lists, scrapbooks, newsletters, 1989-1991; clippings, photographs, 1989.

AMOUNT: 1 filing cabinet.

CONDITION: Good.

ACCESS: Permission required. Access provided at discretion of executive.

776. Yukon Indian Women's Association

✢ Whitehorse, Yukon. Formed 1974.

The Yukon Indian Women's Association (YIWA) focuses on community organizing to improve the lives of Yukon Native women. At the local level, YIWA focuses on self-awareness, training, and employment. At the territorial level, it focuses on human-rights legislation, the Child Welfare Act, and fetal alcohol syndrome. At the national level, YIWA focuses on Indian self-government, child custody, sexual harassment, and sexual abuse.

LOCATION OF RECORDS: Yukon Indian Women's Association. [*Address:* 11 Nisutlin Drive, Whitehorse, Yukon Y1A 3S4. *Telephone:* (403) 667-6162. *Fax:* (403) 668-6577.]

RECORDS: Constitution, 1974-1975; minutes, correspondence, log-books, financial records, grant applications, mailing lists, conference proceedings, 1974-1991; books, 1980; posters, [198-]; pamphlets, flyers, buttons.

AMOUNT: Approx. 3 filing cabinets.

ACCESS: Permission of the executive required.

777. Yukon Status of Women Council

✢ Whitehorse, Yukon. Formed 1973.

The Yukon Status of Women Council advocates reforms to improve political, economic, legal, social, and educational opportunities for women in the Yukon. The council publishes *The OptiMSt*, a quarterly feminist newspaper founded in 1973 and produced by a volunteer collective.

PART II: RECORDS HELD BY GROUPS / PARTIE II : FONDS DÉTENUS PAR DES GROUPES

Collection (a)

LOCATION OF RECORDS: Yukon Status of Women Council. [*Address:* 206 - 302 Steele St., Whitehorse, Yukon Y1A 2C5. *Telephone:* (403) 667-4637.]

RECORDS: Constitution, minutes, correspondence, membership lists, mailing lists, reports, briefs, conference proceedings, pamphlets, flyers, press releases, 1973-1991; financial records, grant applications, [1973?]-1991; newsletters, [1988?]-1989.

AMOUNT: 6 filing-cabinet drawers.

CONDITION: Good.

ACCESS: Open.

Collection (b)

LOCATION OF RECORDS: The OptiMSt. [*Address:* c/o 206 - 302 Steele St., Whitehorse, Yukon Y1A 2C5. *Telephone:* (403) 667-4637.]

RECORDS: Records of *The OptiMSt* (correspondence, financial records, mailing lists, 1973-1991; flyers, 1989-1991; periodicals [*The OptiMSt*, 1973-1991]).

AMOUNT: Approx. 2 drawers of a filing cabinet.

CONDITION: Good.

ACCESS: Open.

NORTHWEST TERRITORIES / TERRITOIRES DU NORD-OUEST

778. Canadian Congress for Learning Opportunities for Women (Fort Smith, N.W.T.)

✤ Fort Smith, N.W.T. Formed 1979.

The Northwest Territories network of the Canadian Congress for Learning Opportunities for Women (CCLOW) works to achieve social, political, and economic equality for women through improved learning opportunities.

LOCATION OF RECORDS: Canadian Congress for Learning Opportunities for Women. [*Mailing Address:* Box 772, Fort Smith, N.W.T. X0E 0P0. *Telephone:* (403) 872-7212/3003. *Fax:* (403) 872-2150.]

RECORDS: Constitution, minutes, correspondence, financial records, grant applications, membership lists, mailing lists, petitions, scrapbooks, reports, briefs, pamphlets, flyers, press releases, T-shirts, 1989-1991.

CONDITION: Good.

ACCESS: Permission required.

779. Coppermine Women's Group

✤ Coppermine, N.W.T. Formed 1985.

This group provides a voice for women in Coppermine. It has held demonstrations, monitored the legal system, and worked to establish a day-care centre. Violence against women has been an ongoing concern of the group.

LOCATION OF RECORDS: Coppermine Women's Group. [*Mailing Address:* Box 316, Coppermine, N.W.T. X0E 0E0. *Telephone:* (403) 982-3406. *Fax:* (403) 982-3060.]

RECORDS: Constitution, 1985; minutes, correspondence, financial records, 1985-1991; grant applications, [1988 or 1989].

AMOUNT: Approx. 2 boxes.

CONDITION: Good.

ACCESS: Permission required.

780. Public Service Alliance of Canada. Yellowknife Regional Women's Committee

✤ Yellowknife, N.W.T. Formed 1990.

This committee works to promote the advancement of women in the Public Service Alliance of Canada (PSAC), in the rest of the labour movement, and in society in general.

LOCATION OF RECORDS: Public Service Alliance of Canada. Yellowknife Regional Women's Committee. [*Address:* c/o Dianne Strilaeff - Union of Northern Workers, Suite 215, 5112 - 52nd St., Yellowknife, N.W.T. X1A 1T6. *Telephone:* (403) 873-5670. *Fax:* (403) 920-4448.]

RECORDS: Minutes, correspondence, financial records, membership lists, mailing lists, posters, 1990-1991; briefs, 1990; press releases, 1991.

AMOUNT: A third of a filing-cabinet drawer.

CONDITION: Good.

ACCESS: Permission required.

781. Women's Resource Centre (Hay River, N.W.T.)

✤ Hay River, N.W.T. Formed 1985.

The Women's Resource Centre promotes equal status for women in the Northwest Territories and works to eliminate family violence. It operates a shelter for battered women and a counselling centre. The organization was originally known as the Hay River Women's Centre or Hay River Women's Coalition.

LOCATION OF RECORDS: Women's Resource Centre. [*Mailing Address:* Box 276, Hay River, N.W.T. X0E 0R0. *Telephone:* (403) 874-3311. *Fax:* (403) 874-3252.]

RECORDS: By-laws, 1987; minutes, 1987-1991; correspondence, log-books, financial records, grant applications, client records, membership lists, mailing lists, petitions, photograph albums, reports, pamphlets, press releases, clippings, photographs, 1988-1991; conference proceedings, 1989; flyers, videotapes, 1990; newsletters (*Women's Free Press*, 1989-1991); handbooks, research papers, bibliography.

AMOUNT: 4 filing cabinets, 4 boxes.

CONDITION: Good.

ACCESS: Permission required. Client and personnel files closed.

782. Young Women's Christian Association of Yellowknife

✤ Yellowknife, N.W.T. Formed 1966.

The YWCA of Yellowknife provides a variety of services for women, including Alison McAteer House (a shelter for abused women founded in 1986), residential services, day care, and a resource centre.

LOCATION OF RECORDS: Young Women's Christian Association of Yellowknife. [*Address:* 5004-54th St., Yellowknife, N.W.T. X1A 2R6. *Telephone:* (403) 920-2777. *Fax:* (403) 873-9406.]

RECORDS: Constitution, minutes, correspondence, log-books, financial records, grant applications, client records, membership lists, mailing lists, reports, briefs, pamphlets, press releases, posters, T-shirts, banners, clippings, photographs, 1983-1991.

AMOUNT: 3 filing cabinets.

CONDITION: Fair.

ACCESS: Permission required. Client files and logs closed.

BRITISH COLUMBIA / COLOMBIE-BRITANNIQUE

783. Alliance of Women against Racism Etcetera
✣ Vancouver, B.C. Formed 1987.

The Alliance of Women against Racism Etcetera (AWARE) provides workshops on unlearning racism. The workshops are offered in the workplace, in educational institutions, and elsewhere in the community.

LOCATION OF RECORDS: Alliance of Women against Racism Etcetera. [*Address:* 5 - 2023 Grant St., Vancouver, B.C. V5L 2Z2. *Telephone:* (604) 251-4356.]
RECORDS: Constitution, 1991; mailing lists, 1987-1991; pamphlets, 1990.
AMOUNT: 15 cm.
CONDITION: Good.
ACCESS: Permission required. Mailing lists confidential.

784. Amata Transition House Society
✣ Quesnel, B.C. Formed 1977.

This shelter offers safety, advocacy, and therapy to women and children in crisis.

LOCATION OF RECORDS: Amata Transition House Society. [*Address:* 693 McLean St., Quesnel, B.C. V2J 2P7. *Telephone:* (604) 992-3385. *Fax:* (604) 992-2657.]
RECORDS: Constitution, minutes, correspondence, log-books, financial records, grant applications, client records, membership lists, mailing lists, petitions, scrapbooks, reports, briefs, conference proceedings, pamphlets, posters, 1977-1991.
AMOUNT: 5 filing cabinets.
CONDITION: Fair.
ACCESS: Permission required. Client files closed.

785. Aquelarre: Latin American Women's Cultural Society
✣ Vancouver, B.C. Formed 1988.

Aquelarre, a periodical, promotes the expression and understanding of the cultural identity of Latin American women in Canada. It also contributes to the integration and successful settlement of Latin American women.

LOCATION OF RECORDS: Aquelarre: Latin American Women's Cultural Society. [*Mailing Address:* P.O. Box 65535, Station F, Vancouver, B.C. V5N 5K6. *Telephone:* (604) 251-6678.]
RECORDS: Minutes, correspondence, log-books, grant applications, client records, mailing lists, reports, pamphlets, flyers, press releases, T-shirts, clippings, photographs, sound recordings, 1988-1991; periodicals (*Aquelarre*, 1989-1991); constitution.
AMOUNT: 1 filing cabinet.
CONDITION: Good.
ACCESS: Permission required.

786. Atira Transition House
✣ White Rock, B.C. Formed 1981.

This is a transition house for women and children who are confronting abuse in their homes.

LOCATION OF RECORDS: Atira Transition House. [*Mailing Address:* Box 39582, White Rock, B.C. V4B 5G4. *Telephone:* (604) 531-9151.]
RECORDS: Correspondence, financial records, clippings, 1983-1991; constitution, 1983; log-books, client records, 1987-1991; minutes, 1981-1991; buttons, 1987; grant applications, membership lists, mailing lists, scrapbooks, reports, pamphlets.
AMOUNT: 2 filing cabinets.
CONDITION: Good.
ACCESS: Permission required. Client files and staff log-books closed.

787. Aurora House
✣ Vancouver, B.C. Formed 1973.

Aurora House provides an intensive residential treatment programme for women dealing with addiction.

LOCATION OF RECORDS: Aurora House. [*Address:* 2036 W. 13th Ave., Vancouver, B.C. V6J 2H7. *Telephone:* (604) 733-9191. *Fax:* (604) 733-8957.]
RECORDS: Constitution, 1973-1991; minutes, correspondence, 1975-1991; log-books, 1990-1991; financial records, grant applications, client records, 1984-1991; reports, pamphlets, 1988-1991; photographs, 1989-1991; film, 1985.
AMOUNT: 4 filing cabinets.
CONDITION: Good.
ACCESS: Permission required. Client files closed.

788. Battered Women's Support Services
✣ Vancouver, B.C. Formed 1979.

This organization promotes services for battered women and provides educational resources on battering.

LOCATION OF RECORDS: Battered Women's Support Services. [*Mailing Address:* P.O. Box 1098, Station A, Vancouver, B.C. V6C 2T1. (*Street Address:* 757 West Hastings.) *Telephone:* (604) 687-1868. *Fax:* (604) 687-1864.]

RECORDS: Minutes, correspondence, financial records, 1981-1991; grant applications, pamphlets, 1987-1991; scrapbooks, reports, T-shirts, logbooks, client records, membership lists, mailing lists, banners, newsletters, 1989-1991; books, clippings, photographs.

AMOUNT: Approx. 4 filing cabinets.

CONDITION: Good.

ACCESS: Permission required. Client files closed. Access to all other files subject to collective approval.

789. BOA Magazine and Productions

✣ Vancouver, B.C. Formed 1986.

This group publishes BOA, a "'zine" by and for women, and organizes cultural events such as poetry evenings and art shows. The group has also been known as Bevy of Anarchist Feminists/Bande d'anarchistes féministes.

LOCATION OF RECORDS: BOA Magazine and Productions. [*Address:* c/o Spartacus Books, 311 West Hastings, Vancouver, B.C.]

RECORDS: Mailing lists, posters, periodicals, 1986-1991; flyers, 1986; clippings, 1991.

AMOUNT: Half a drawer of a filing cabinet.

CONDITION: Good.

ACCESS: Permission required.

790. B.C. and Yukon Association of Women's Centres

✣ Formed 1986.

This association co-ordinates the exchange of information between member centres, lobbies on their behalf, and organizes an annual conference.

LOCATION OF RECORDS: B.C. and Yukon Association of Women's Centres. [*Address:* 507 Hall St., Nelson, B.C. V1L 1Z1. *Telephone:* (604) 352-9916.]

RECORDS: Minutes, correspondence, financial records, grant applications, membership lists, reports, conference proceedings, 1986-1991; briefs, 1988, 1990-1991; flyers, 1991; newsletters (*Newsflash*, 1986-1991); constitution.

AMOUNT: 3 boxes.

CONDITION: Good.

ACCESS: Permission required. Some restrictions.

791. British Columbia Federation of Women

[See also entry # 111 (in Part I), which lists other records of this organization.]

✣ Vancouver, B.C. Formed 1974. Disbanded [198-].

The British Columbia Federation of Women (BCFW) was an umbrella organization for women's groups in B.C.; its objective was to bring about women's liberation through fundamental social change. BCFW's Rights of Lesbians Subcommittee published *Waves*, a lesbian-feminist newsletter. [See also International Women's Day Committee (Vancouver, B.C.) (136).]

LOCATION OF RECORDS: Simon Fraser University Women's Centre. [*Address:* c/o Simon Fraser Student Society, Burnaby, B.C. V5A 1S6. *Telephone:* (604) 291-3670.]

RECORDS: Newsletters, financial records, miscellaneous records.

AMOUNT: 2 boxes.

ACCESS: Available on request.

792. British Columbia Government Employees' Union. Provincial Executive Women's Committee

✣ Burnaby, B.C. Formed 1976.

This committee promotes awareness of women's issues within the union (also known as BCGEU). It encourages the participation of women at all levels of the union and makes recommendations for the elimination of systemic barriers to women's full participation.

LOCATION OF RECORDS: British Columbia Government Employees' Union. Provincial Executive Women's Committee. [*Address:* 4911 Canada Way, Burnaby, B.C. V5G 3W3. *Telephone:* (604) 291-9611. *Fax:* (604) 294-5092.]

RECORDS: Minutes, correspondence, reports, briefs, conference proceedings, pamphlets, posters, 1976-1991.

CONDITION: Good.

ACCESS: Permission required.

793. British Columbia New Democratic Party. Women's Rights Committee

[See also entry # 113 (in Part I), which lists other records of this organization.]

✣ Vancouver, B.C. Formed 1971.

The Women's Rights Committee (WRC) develops policy related to women's issues and encourages women to participate in the political process. In 1979 WRC established the Task Force on Older Women in British Columbia. The committee has also been called the Standing Committee on Women's Rights. It publishes a newsletter, *Priorities*. (Source: University of British Columbia Library finding aid, 1985.)

LOCATION OF RECORDS: British Columbia New Democratic Party. Women's Rights Committee. [*Address:* 3110 Boundary Rd., Burnaby, B.C. V5M 4A2. *Telephone:* (604) 430-8600.]

RECORDS: Minutes, correspondence, financial records, membership lists, 1973-1991; handbook, 1990; newsletters (*Priorities*, 1973-1991); conference proceedings, pamphlets, press releases, photographs.

CONDITION: Good.

ACCESS: Permission required. Possible restrictions subject to vote by committee.

794. British Columbia Nurses' Union

✣ Burnaby, B.C. Formed 1981.

The British Columbia Nurses' Union (BCNU) works for the advancement of the social, economic, and overall welfare of nurses and allied personnel. BCNU grew out of the Labour Relations Division of the Registered Nurses Association of B.C.

LOCATION OF RECORDS: British Columbia Nurses' Union. [*Address:* 100 - 4259 Canada Way, Burnaby, B.C. V5G 1H1. *Telephone:* (604) 433-2268. *Fax:* (604) 433-7945.]

RECORDS: Constitution, 1981-1990; briefs, 1984-1991; newsletters (*BCNU Reports*, 1981-1990; *BCNU Update*, 1991; *Slate*, 1990-1991); financial records, membership lists, reports, pamphlets, press releases, posters, buttons, T-shirts, banners, photographs, videotapes.

CONDITION: Good.

ACCESS: Permission required. In *camera* records of council, grievance records, some other records closed.

795. British Columbia Women's Housing Coalition

✣ Vancouver, B.C. Formed 1988.

The British Columbia Women's Housing Coalition (also known as "B.C. WoHoCo") is a coalition of individuals and groups which does lobbying and networking to promote affordable and appropriate housing for women.

LOCATION OF RECORDS: British Columbia Women's Housing Coalition. [*Address:* 314 Powell St., Vancouver, B.C. V6M 1P1. *Telephone:* (604) 682-6679. *Fax:* (604) 683-6649.]

RECORDS: Minutes, mailing lists, reports, conference proceedings, pamphlets.

AMOUNT: 1 drawer of a filing cabinet.

CONDITION: Good.

ACCESS: Permission required.

796. Canadian Abortion Rights Action League. Fraser Valley Chapter

✣ Surrey, B.C. Formed 1985.

The Fraser Valley Chapter of the Canadian Abortion Rights Action League (CARAL) works to keep abortion out of the Criminal Code and promotes access to reproductive services, through lobbying, fund raising for court challenges, and education.

LOCATION OF RECORDS: Canadian Abortion Rights Action League. Fraser Valley Chapter. [*Address:* 241 - 15087 - 16th Ave., Surrey, B.C. V4A 6G3. *Telephone:* (604) 888-2720.]

RECORDS: Constitution, minutes, correspondence, financial records, membership lists, mailing lists, reports, conference proceedings, pamphlets, press releases, posters, buttons, T-shirts, banners, 1985-1991; film, 1986.

AMOUNT: 1 drawer of a filing cabinet.

CONDITION: Good.

ACCESS: Permission required. Membership lists closed with some exceptions.

797. Canadian Federation of University Women — Kelowna

✣ Kelowna, B.C. Formed 1960.

Previously known as the Kelowna University Women's Club, this branch of the Canadian Federation of University Women (CFUW) promotes the education of women and stimulates women's interest in public affairs.

LOCATION OF RECORDS: Canadian Federation of University Women — Kelowna. [*Address:* 2515 Dunsmuir Rd., Kelowna, B.C. V1W 2S2. *Telephone:* (604) 860-2433.]

RECORDS: Constitutions, 1960, 1991; minutes, correspondence, financial records, membership lists, scrapbooks, 1960-1991; conference proceedings, pamphlets, banners, newsletters, clippings, photographs.

AMOUNT: 4 boxes.

CONDITION: Good.

ACCESS: Permission required.

798. Canadian Federation of University Women. Nelson Branch

✣ Nelson, B.C. Formed 1967.

The Nelson branch of the Canadian Federation of University Women (CFUW) encourages advanced study and research by women university graduates. It prepares studies and briefs, sponsors educational events, promotes women as candidates for elected or appointed positions, and offers scholarships.

LOCATION OF RECORDS: Canadian Federation of University Women. Nelson Branch. [*Mailing Address:* Box 41, Nelson, B.C. V1L 5P7. *Telephone:* (604) 352-7158.]

RECORDS: Constitution, financial records, membership lists, scrapbooks, reports, pamphlets, flyers, press releases, 1967-1991; minutes, 1980-1991; briefs, 1990; clippings, 1967; newsletters, photographs.

AMOUNT: Approx. 1 filing cabinet.

CONDITION: Good.

ACCESS: Permission required.

799. Canadian Federation of University Women. Parksville / Qualicum Beach Club

✣ Qualicum Beach, B.C. Formed 1982.

This branch of the Canadian Federation of University Women (CFUW) is sometimes called the University Women's Club of Parksville/Qualicum Beach. It promotes the continuing education of women and encourages women university graduates to take an interest in public affairs.

LOCATION OF RECORDS: Canadian Federation of University Women. Parksville/Qualicum Beach Club. [*Mailing Address:* Box 1766, Qualicum Beach, B.C. V0R 2T0.]

RECORDS: Constitution, minutes, correspondence, log-books, financial records, membership lists, mailing lists, scrapbooks, reports, briefs, conference proceedings, pamphlets, press releases, 1982-1991; grant applications, 1990-1991; newsletters, books, clippings, photographs.

AMOUNT: 1 drawer of a filing cabinet.

CONDITION: Good.

ACCESS: Permission required.

800. Central Valley Transition House Society

✣ Mission, B.C. Formed 1982.

Originally called the Mission Transition House Society, this organization offers shelter, support, and advocacy to battered women in Mission and Matsqui.

LOCATION OF RECORDS: Central Valley Transition House Society. [*Mailing Address:* Box 3044, Mission, B.C. V2V 4J3. *Telephone:* (604) 826-7800 or 852-6008.]

RECORDS: Constitution, [1983?]; minutes, correspondence, log-books, financial records, 1982-1991; grant applications, membership lists, mailing lists, reports, press releases, 1983-1991; client records, pamphlets, 1984-1991.

AMOUNT: 4 filing cabinets.

CONDITION: Good.

ACCESS: Permission required. Client files closed.

801. Chetwynd Women's Resource Society

✣ Chetwynd, B.C. Formed [1982?].

The Chetwynd Women's Resource Society (previously called the Chetwynd Women's Council) runs a drop-in centre and works to improve the status of women and enhance public awareness of women's issues.

LOCATION OF RECORDS: Chetwynd Women's Resource Society. [*Mailing Address:* Box 626, Chetwynd, B.C. V0C 1J0. *Telephone:* (604) 788-3793.]

RECORDS: Constitution, minutes, correspondence, log-books, financial records, grant applications, client records, membership lists, mailing lists, scrapbooks, reports, briefs, pamphlets, flyers, press releases, banners, 1982-1991; newsletters (*Nikamo Ishwewak (Singing Women)*, 1982-1990; *Chetwynd Women's Centre Newsletter*, 1990-1991); clippings, photographs.

AMOUNT: 3 filing cabinets.
CONDITION: Good.
ACCESS: Permission required. Client and personnel files closed.

802. Chimo Personal Distress Intervention Service

✣ Richmond, B.C. Formed 1973.

The Chimo Personal Distress Intervention Service (also known as the Richmond Crisis Centre) runs Nova House, a transition house for battered women, and offers various other crisis-intervention services.

LOCATION OF RECORDS: Chimo Personal Distress Intervention Service. [*Address:* 7120 Westminster Highway, Richmond, B.C. V6X 1A1. *Telephone:* (604) 273-8661. *Fax:* (604) 273-8663.]

RECORDS: Constitution, minutes, correspondence, financial records, grant applications, clippings, 1973-1991; client records, 1991; membership lists, press releases, 1978-1991; reports, 1974-1991; pamphlets, photographs.

AMOUNT: 1 filing cabinet.
CONDITION: Fair.
ACCESS: Permission required. Client files closed.

803. DisAbled Women's Network (Fort St John, B.C.)

✣ Fort St John, B.C. Formed 1990.

The DisAbled Women's Network (DAWN) of Fort St John provides support and information to women who have physical, mental, or emotional disabilities, whether visible or invisible. It also promotes positive images of disabilities.

LOCATION OF RECORDS: DisAbled Women's Network. [*Address:* c/o Women's Resource Centre, 10343 - 100 Ave., Fort St John, B.C. V1J 1Y8. *Telephone:* (604) 787-1121.]

RECORDS: Minutes, correspondence, 1990-1991; financial records, grant applications, membership lists, scrapbooks, reports, conference proceedings, pamphlets, clippings, 1991; newsletters, 1990.

CONDITION: Good.
ACCESS: Permission required.

804. Douglas College. Women's Centre

✣ New Westminster, B.C. Formed 1981.

The Douglas College Women's Centre runs a resource centre and offers workshops, lectures, and film series.

LOCATION OF RECORDS: Douglas College. Women's Centre. [*Mailing Address:* P.O. Box 2503, New Westminster, B.C. V3L 5B2. *Telephone:* (604) 527-5400. *Fax:* (604) 527-5095.]

RECORDS: Minutes, correspondence, reports, 1981-1991; client records, membership lists, mailing lists, 1989-1991; briefs, 1986-1991.

AMOUNT: 2 filing cabinets, 1 bookshelf.
CONDITION: Fair.
ACCESS: Permission required. Client files closed.

805. Entre Nous Femmes Housing Society

✣ Vancouver, B.C. Formed 1983.

This non-profit society, also known as ENF Housing Society, develops and manages safe, affordable housing for female-led single-parent families.

LOCATION OF RECORDS: Entre Nous Femmes Housing Society. [*Address:* 1656 Adanac St., Vancouver, B.C. V5L 2C6. *Telephone:* (604) 251-1213.]

RECORDS: Minutes, correspondence, financial records, grant applications, client records, membership lists, mailing lists, reports, pamphlets, clippings, photographs, 1985-1991; constitution, 1985; conference proceedings, 1988-1990.

CONDITION: Good.
ACCESS: Permission required. Client files closed.

806. Everywoman's Health Centre Society

✣ Vancouver, B.C. Formed 1988.

This organization manages a free-standing abortion clinic. In addition to performing abortions, the clinic provides counselling and related health care. The organization also does lobbying.

LOCATION OF RECORDS: Everywoman's Health Centre Society. [*Address:* 2005 East 44th Ave., Vancouver, B.C. V5P 1N1. *Telephone:* (604) 322-6692.]

RECORDS: Constitution, minutes, correspondence, financial records, client records, membership lists, mailing lists, scrapbooks, reports, briefs, pamphlets, press releases, clippings, photographs, 1988-1991.

AMOUNT: 10 filing cabinets.
CONDITION: Good.
ACCESS: Permission required. Client and personnel files, *in camera* minutes closed.

807. Fernie Women's Resource and Drop-in Centre

✣ Fernie, B.C. Formed 1980.

This women's centre seeks to support and empower women; it offers an information and referral service, workshops, films, lectures, and political activities.

LOCATION OF RECORDS: Fernie Women's Resource and Drop-In Centre. [*Mailing Address:* Box 2054, Fernie, B.C. V0B 1M0. *Telephone:* (604) 423-4819. *Fax:* (604) 423-4065.]

RECORDS: Correspondence, financial records, grant applications, log-books, 1980-1991; constitution, 1980; minutes, 1978-1991; pamphlets, 1985-1991; newsletters, 1983-1991; membership lists, mailing lists, petitions, reports, briefs, conference proceedings, press releases, clippings, photographs, videotapes.

AMOUNT: 4 boxes.
CONDITION: Good.
ACCESS: Permission required.

808. First Mature Women's Network Society

✣ Vancouver, B.C. Formed 1983.

Often referred to as the Mature Women's Network (MWN), this is a social and support network for women in their forties, fifties, or sixties.

LOCATION OF RECORDS: First Mature Women's Network Society. [*Address:* 411 Dunsmuir St., 2nd Floor, Vancouver, B.C. V6B 1X4. *Telephone:* (604) 681-3986.]

RECORDS: Constitution, 1983; minutes, correspondence, financial records, grant applications, membership lists, mailing lists, scrapbooks, reports, conference proceedings, pamphlets, press releases, newsletters, books, clippings, photographs, 1983-1991.

AMOUNT: 1 filing cabinet.
CONDITION: Good.
ACCESS: Permission required.

809. Fort St John Women's Resource Centre

✣ Fort St John, B.C. Formed 1981.

This centre works to improve women's social, economic, and political condition.

LOCATION OF RECORDS: Fort St John Women's Resource Centre. [*Address:* #102 - 10343 - 100th Ave., Fort St John, B.C. V1J 1Y8. *Telephone:* (604) 787-1121.]

RECORDS: Constitution, 1981; minutes, correspondence, log-books, financial records, grant applications, mailing lists, reports, briefs, conference proceedings, pamphlets, flyers, press releases, 1981-1991; membership lists, newsletters, 1989-1991; scrapbooks, 1986-1991; petitions, 1990; client records, clippings, photographs.

AMOUNT: 1 storage room.

CONDITION: Good.

ACCESS: Permission required. Client files and some grant applications closed.

810. Gay / Lesbian Outreach

✣ Langley, B.C. Formed 1987.

Gay/Lesbian Outreach (GLO) provides support and alternative services to the local gay and lesbian community. GLO was formed through the merging of the Langley Gay/Lesbian Support Group (established in 1986) and the Lower Fraser Valley Lesbian Support Network. GLO is sponsored by Langley Family Services (LFS).

LOCATION OF RECORDS: Gay/Lesbian Outreach. [*Address:* c/o Langley Family Services, 5339 - 207th St., Langley, B.C. V3A 2E6. *Telephone:* (604) 534-7921. *Fax:* (604) 534-9884.]

RECORDS: Philosophy and mandate, 1987; minutes, 1986-1988, 1990; correspondence, 1987-1991; mailing lists, 1988-1989; scrapbooks, clippings, 1986-1988; pamphlets, press releases, newsletters, workshop presentation, 1988; miscellaneous records.

AMOUNT: 13 cm.

CONDITION: Good.

ACCESS: Permission required.

811. Golden Women's Resource Centre

✣ Golden, B.C. Formed 1979.

Also known as the Golden Women's Centre Society, this organization promotes women's equality and addresses issues affecting the status of women. It operates safe homes, an information and referral service, and a resource library.

LOCATION OF RECORDS: Golden Women's Resource Centre. [*Mailing Address:* Box 2343, Golden, B.C. V0A 1H0. *Telephone:* (604) 344-5317.]

RECORDS: Constitution, grant applications, membership lists, reports, 1982-1991; minutes, correspondence, financial records, petitions, press releases, 1979-1991; mailing lists, conference proceedings, 1990; posters, 1981-1991.

AMOUNT: 2 filing cabinets, 8 boxes.

CONDITION: Good.

ACCESS: Permission required.

812. Greater Victoria Women's Shelter Society

✣ Victoria, B.C. Formed 1986.

The Greater Victoria Women's Shelter Society provides second-stage housing for women and children in need. It also provides housing for women with special needs.

LOCATION OF RECORDS: Greater Victoria Women's Shelter Society. [*Address:* 306 - 620 View St., Victoria, B.C. *Telephone:* (604) 361-1994.]

RECORDS: Constitution, 1986; minutes, financial records, 1986-1991; grant applications, 1988.

AMOUNT: Half a drawer of a filing cabinet.

CONDITION: Good.

813. Health Sciences Association of British Columbia

✣ Vancouver, B.C. Formed 1971.

The Health Sciences Association of British Columbia (HSA) is a trade union for health-care professionals. Eighty-five per cent of HSA's members are women. HSA's Equality of Rights Committee (ERC) deals with women's and human-rights issues.

LOCATION OF RECORDS: Health Sciences Association of British Columbia. [*Address:* #303 - 3680 East Hastings St., Vancouver, B.C. V5K 2A9. *Telephone:* (604) 299-2707. *Fax:* (604) 299-0306.]

RECORDS: Constitution, minutes, correspondence, financial records, membership lists, mailing lists, reports, briefs, conference proceedings, pamphlets, flyers, press releases, posters, buttons, T-shirts, banners, newsletters, 1971-1991; clippings, photographs, videotapes.

AMOUNT: 2 filing cabinets.

CONDITION: Good.

ACCESS: Permission required.

814. Herspectives

✣ Squamish, B.C. Formed 1989.

Herspectives (also known as HER) is a periodical committed to presenting the writing of feminists who could not get their work published in the mainstream press. *Herspectives* is solely supported by its subscribers.

LOCATION OF RECORDS: Herspectives. [*Mailing Address:* Box 2047, Squamish, B.C. V0N 3G0. *Telephone:* (604) 892-5723.]

RECORDS: Correspondence, subscription lists, mailing lists, newsletters, 1989-1991; banners.

AMOUNT: 1 box.

CONDITION: Good.

ACCESS: Permission required.

815. Hotel, Restaurant, Culinary Employees, and Bartenders Union. Local 40

✣ Burnaby, B.C. Formed 1900.

The Hotel, Restaurant, Culinary Employees, and Bartenders Union (HERE) represents workers in British Columbia and the Yukon.

LOCATION OF RECORDS: Hotel, Restaurant, Culinary Employees, and Bartenders Union. Local 40. [*Address:* 4853 E. Hastings St., Burnaby, B.C. V5C 2L1. *Telephone:* (604) 291-8211. *Fax:* (604) 291-2676.]

RECORDS: Constitution, minutes, correspondence, log-books, financial records, client records, membership lists, mailing lists, petitions, scrapbooks, reports, briefs, conference proceedings, pamphlets, flyers, press releases, posters, buttons, T-shirts, banners, newsletters (*Mixer News*), books, clippings, photographs, sound recordings, videotapes.

ACCESS: Permission required. Records related to health care and certain grievances are closed.

816. Images: West Kootenay Women's Paper

[See also entry # 134 (in Part I), which lists other records of this organization.]

✥ Nelson, B.C. Formed 1972.

Images is a news journal featuring women's writing, art work, and photography. *Images* was originally published by the West Kootenay Status of Women Council.

LOCATION OF RECORDS: Images: West Kootenay Women's Paper. [*Mailing Address:* Box 736, Nelson, B.C. V1N 5R4. *Telephone:* (604) 352-3177.]

RECORDS: Minutes, 1977-1988, 1991; financial records, 1986-1991; grant applications, 1976; periodicals (*Images: West Kootenay Women's Paper*, 1972-1991).

CONDITION: Good.

ACCESS: Permission required.

817. Island Gay Society

✥ Victoria, B.C. Formed 1979.

The Island Gay Society (IGS) provides lesbian and gay people with a supportive meeting place and fights discrimination based on sexual orientation. Forty per cent of the members are women, and resources addressing the specific concerns of lesbians are provided. The group was originally called the Society for Homosexual Awareness, Research, and Education (SHARE); in 1981 it became the Island Gay Community Centre Society (IGCC); the present name was adopted around 1985.

LOCATION OF RECORDS: Island Gay Society. [*Mailing Address:* Box 695, Station E, Victoria, B.C. V8W 2P9. *Telephone:* (604) 361-4900.]

RECORDS: Constitution, financial records, 1981-1991; minutes, correspondence, 1979-1991; petitions, 1987; briefs, 1985; conference proceedings, 1986-1987, 1990; buttons, 1986; newsletters (*Centrefold; Target; IGS Newsletter*), membership lists, mailing lists, reports, pamphlets, posters, clippings.

AMOUNT: 1 filing cabinet.

CONDITION: Good.

ACCESS: Permission required. Membership records closed.

818. Kamloops and District Elizabeth Fry Society

✥ Kamloops, B.C. Formed 1974.

This volunteer agency provides assistance, education, and counselling to women and youth in conflict with the law. It used to be called the Kamloops Branch of the Elizabeth Fry Society of British Columbia.

LOCATION OF RECORDS: Kamloops and District Elizabeth Fry Society. [*Address:* #201 - 156 Victoria St., Kamloops, B.C. V2C 1Z7. *Telephone:* (604) 374-2119.]

RECORDS: Constitution, membership lists, 1988-1991; minutes, 1978-1991; correspondence, reports, 1972-1991; financial records, grant applications, scrapbooks, press releases, clippings, photographs, 1974-1991; conference proceedings, 1989; newsletters, 1985; client records, mailing lists, pamphlets, flyers, posters, buttons, T-shirts, banners.

AMOUNT: 8 filing cabinets.

CONDITION: Fair.

ACCESS: Permission required.

819. Kamloops Sexual Assault Counselling Centre

✥ Kamloops, B.C. Formed 1982.

The Kamloops Sexual Assault Counselling Centre (KSACC) provides client-centred support services to victims of sexual assault, child abuse (sexual or physical), battering, or sexual harassment. Until 1983 it was called the Thompson Nicola Rape Crisis Centre.

LOCATION OF RECORDS: Kamloops Sexual Assault Counselling Centre. [*Address:* #204 - 750 Cottonwood Ave., Kamloops, B.C. V2B 3X2. *Telephone:* (604) 376-0179.]

RECORDS: Constitution, minutes, correspondence, log-books, financial records, grant applications, client records, membership lists, mailing lists, reports, briefs, conference proceedings, pamphlets, press releases, books, clippings, photographs, newsletters, 1982-1991.

CONDITION: Good.

ACCESS: Permission required.

820. Kate Booth House

✥ Vancouver, B.C. Formed 1985.

Kate Booth House (under the auspices of the Salvation Army) is an emergency shelter for women and their children who are fleeing domestic violence. The shelter provides referral, counselling, education, and follow-up support.

LOCATION OF RECORDS: Kate Booth House. [*Mailing Address:* P.O. Box 35361, Station E, Vancouver, B.C. V6M 4G5. *Telephone:* (604) 872-0772.]

RECORDS: Minutes, correspondence, log-books, financial records, client records, scrapbooks, policy manual, conference proceedings, 1985-1991.

AMOUNT: 2 filing cabinets.

CONDITION: Good.

ACCESS: Permission required. Client files closed.

821. Kelowna Women's Resource Centre

✥ Kelowna, B.C. Formed 1985.

The Kelowna Women's Resource Centre works to improve the status of women through lobbying, public education, and various services for women.

LOCATION OF RECORDS: Kelowna Women's Resource Centre. [*Address:* 347 Leon Ave., Kelowna, B.C. V1Y 8C7. *Telephone:* (604) 762-2355.]

RECORDS: Constitution, minutes, correspondence, log-books, financial records, client records, membership lists, conference proceedings, pamphlets, 1985-1991; petitions, flyers, press releases, posters, buttons, 1990-1991; reports, 1988-1991; newsletters (*Perspectives*, 1989-1991; *She Mail*, 1991); mailing lists, T-shirts, books, clippings, photographs, sound recordings.

CONDITION: Good.

ACCESS: Permission required.

822. Lesbia News

✥ Victoria, B.C. Formed 1989.

Lesbia News is a newsletter for lesbian feminists of Vancouver Island and the Gulf Islands. It aims to build a sense of community and stimulate grass-roots writing.

LOCATION OF RECORDS: Lesbia News. [*Mailing Address:* P.O. Box 5339, Station B, Victoria, B.C. V8R 6S4.]

RECORDS: Newsletters (*Lesbia News*, 1989-1991); financial records, 1989-1991; photographs, 1990; subscription lists.

AMOUNT: 1 drawer of a filing cabinet.

CONDITION: Good.

823. Maiya House

✥ Lantzville, B.C. Formed 1989.

Maiya House is a residence for chemically dependent women. It offers a treatment programme, advocacy for its clients, and community education.

LOCATION OF RECORDS: Maiya House. [*Address:* 6731 Aulds Rd., Lantzville, B.C. V0R 2H0. *Telephone:* (604) 390-2100. *Fax:* (604) 390-2141.]

RECORDS: Constitution, minutes, correspondence, log-books, financial records, grant applications, client records, membership lists, mailing lists, scrapbooks, reports, flyers, press releases, clippings, photographs, 1989-1991; newsletters, 1991.

AMOUNT: Approx. 2 filing cabinets.

CONDITION: Good.

ACCESS: Permission required. Client files (with names deleted) available only under supervision.

824. Malaspina College. Faculty Association. Status of Women Committee

✥ Nanaimo, B.C. Formed 1989.

The Status of Women Committee of the Malaspina College Faculty Association (MCFA) works to increase the number and status of female faculty members. It also does advocacy on behalf of female students.

LOCATION OF RECORDS: Malaspina College. Faculty Association. Status of Women Committee. [*Address:* 900 - 5th St., Nanaimo, B.C. V9R 5S5. *Telephone:* (604) 753-3245.]

RECORDS: Reports, 1989-1991.

AMOUNT: 1 file.

CONDITION: Good.

ACCESS: Permission required.

825. Marguerite Dixon House

✥ Burnaby, B.C.

Marguerite Dixon House is a battered women's shelter operated by the Life Line Society.

LOCATION OF RECORDS: Marguerite Dixon House. [*Telephone:* (604) 299-2488. *Fax:* (604) 299-6650.]

RECORDS: Minutes, 1986-1991; correspondence, 1988-1991; log-books, client records.

AMOUNT: 1 drawer of a filing cabinet.

CONDITION: Good.

ACCESS: Permission required. Client files and log-books closed.

826. Mavis McMullen Housing Society

✥ Vancouver, B.C. Formed 1987.

The Mavis McMullen Housing Society works to provide older women and single mothers with secure, affordable housing which offers a sense of community, in Vancouver's downtown east side.

LOCATION OF RECORDS: Mavis McMullen Housing Society. [*Address:* 430 East Cordova St., Vancouver, B.C. V6A 1L6. *Telephone:* (604) 253-9333.]

RECORDS: Constitution, 1987; minutes, correspondence, financial records, grant applications, client records, membership lists, mailing lists, scrapbooks, reports, 1987-1991.

AMOUNT: 2 filing cabinets, approx. 4 boxes.

CONDITION: Good.

827. Mizpah Transition House

✥ Dawson Creek, B.C. Formed 1972.

Mizpah Transition House provides safe shelter, advocacy, and support for women in need. It is administered by South Peace Community Resources.

LOCATION OF RECORDS: Mizpah Transition House. [*Mailing Address:* Box 713, Dawson Creek, B.C. V1G 1C6. *Telephone:* (604) 782-9174. *Fax:* (604) 782-4068.]

RECORDS: Constitution, minutes, correspondence, log-books, financial records, grant applications, client records, membership lists, mailing lists, scrapbooks, reports, briefs, conference proceedings, pamphlets, flyers, press releases, posters, 1982-1991; clippings, photographs.

AMOUNT: 3 filing cabinets.

CONDITION: Good.

ACCESS: Permission required. Client files and journal closed.

828. Nanaimo Women's Resources Society

✥ Nanaimo, B.C. Formed 1979.

This organization oversees an outreach programme, "Hiring Opportunities for Women," and has been working to establish a women's centre.

LOCATION OF RECORDS: Nanaimo Women's Resources Society. [*Address:* 285 Prideaux St., Room #219, Nanaimo, B.C. V9R 2N2. *Telephone:* (604) 753-0633.]

RECORDS: Financial records, 1987-1990; grant applications, 1985, 1987-1991; reports, 1979-1991; constitution, minutes, correspondence, membership lists, conference proceedings, pamphlets, flyers, posters, T-shirts.

AMOUNT: Approx. 10 boxes.

CONDITION: Good.

ACCESS: Permission required.

829. North Shore Women's Centre

[See also entry # 141 (in Part I), which lists other records of this organization.]

✥ North Vancouver, B.C. Formed 1976.

The North Shore Women's Centre does public education on women's issues, with the goal of improving the status of women. The centre offers an information and referral service, resource materials, lecture series, and space for women's events.

LOCATION OF RECORDS: North Shore Women's Centre. [*Address:* 103 - 145 West 15th St., North Vancouver, B.C. V7M 1R9. *Telephone:* (604) 984-6009.]

RECORDS: Constitution, 1976; minutes, financial records, clippings, 1976-1991; correspondence, 1985-1991; log-books, press releases, 1990-1991; grant applications, 1978-1991; client records, 1980-1991; mailing lists, 1987-1991; scrapbooks, photographs, 1987-1990; reports, 1984-1991; briefs, 1985; pamphlets, 1988; posters, 1991; newsletters (*Nellie*, 1990-1991; *North Shore Women's News*, 1988-1990; *North Shore Women*, 1981-1985); videotapes, 1987-1988; conference proceedings.

AMOUNT: 1 filing cabinet, 20 boxes.

CONDITION: Good.

ACCESS: Permission required.

830. Penticton and Area Women's Centre

✥ Penticton, B.C. Formed 1986.

This centre's services include advocacy, referral, education, and a lending library.

LOCATION OF RECORDS: Penticton and Area Women's Centre. [*Address:* 319 Main St., Penticton, B.C. V2A 5K6. *Telephone:* (604) 493-6822.]

RECORDS: Minutes, financial records, grant applications, membership lists, mailing lists, scrapbooks, reports, clippings, 1986-1991; correspondence, 1985-1991; log-books, 1988-1991; briefs, 1989; conference proceedings, 1991; press releases, 1989-1991; banners, 1990; newsletters (*Womanews*, 1989-1991).

AMOUNT: 4 filing cabinets.

CONDITION: Fair.

831. Planned Parenthood Association of British Columbia

✣ Vancouver, B.C. Formed 1963.

The Planned Parenthood Association of British Columbia (PPABC) has twenty-one birth-control and women's health clinics and provides education about sexuality to schools, churches, and community groups. Until the early 1970s, it was called the Family Planning Association of B.C.

LOCATION OF RECORDS: Planned Parenthood Association of British Columbia. [*Address:* 305 - 2902 West Broadway, Vancouver, B.C. V6K 2G8. *Telephone:* (604) 731-4252. *Fax:* (604) 731-4698.]

RECORDS: Constitution, 1961; minutes, 1961-1991; financial records, client records, 1983-1991; newsletters (*About Us*, 1985-1991); grant applications, membership lists, reports, pamphlets, videotapes.

AMOUNT: 6 filing cabinets, 1 storage room.

CONDITION: Good.

ACCESS: Permission required. Client files closed.

832. Port Alberni Women's Resources Society

✣ Port Alberni, B.C. Formed 1980.

The Port Alberni Women's Resources Society (PAWRS) promotes the equality of women through the following services: a shelter, a drop-in centre, education, advocacy, and counselling.

LOCATION OF RECORDS: Port Alberni Women's Resources Society. [*Address:* 3151 3rd Ave., Port Alberni, B.C. V9Y 4C7. *Telephone:* (604) 724-7111.]

RECORDS: Constitution, 1980; minutes, financial records, grant applications, 1980-1991; correspondence, 1985-1991; log-books, membership lists, 1989-1991; mailing lists, 1990; conference proceedings, 1988-1991; scrapbooks, reports, briefs, pamphlets, newsletter.

AMOUNT: 3 filing cabinets.

CONDITION: Fair.

ACCESS: Permission required. Client files closed.

833. Port Coquitlam Area Women's Centre

[See also entry # 143 (in Part I), which lists other records of this organization.]

✣ Port Coquitlam, B.C. Formed 1975.

The centre promotes feminism and provides a safe space for women in the area. It offers drop-in services, support groups, counselling, and a library.

LOCATION OF RECORDS: Port Coquitlam Area Women's Centre. [*Address:* 2420 Mary Hill Rd., Port Coquitlam, B.C. V3C 3B1. *Telephone:* (604) 941-6311.]

RECORDS: Constitution, minutes, correspondence, log-books, financial records, grant applications, membership lists, mailing lists, reports, pamphlets, press releases, banners, 1988-1991; newsletters (*Women Today*, 1988-1991); books, 1989; videotapes.

AMOUNT: 2 filing cabinets.

CONDITION: Fair.

834. Press Gang

[See also entry # 144 (in Part I), which lists other records of this organization.]

✣ Vancouver, B.C. Formed [ca. 1970].

Until 1990 Press Gang Printers and Press Gang Publishers were the same organization (a feminist, anti-capitalist printing and publishing company). Since 1990, Press Gang Printers has been a separate company.

LOCATION OF RECORDS: Press Gang. [*Address:* 603 Powell St., Vancouver, B.C. V6A 1H2. *Telephone:* (604) 253-1224.]

RECORDS: Minutes, correspondence, log-books, financial records, client records, 1970-1991; mailing lists, 1990-1991; scrapbooks, pamphlets, flyers, posters, banners, clippings, photographs.

AMOUNT: Approx. 4 filing cabinets.

CONDITION: Fair.

ACCESS: Permission required.

835. Prince Rupert Transition House

✣ Prince Rupert, B.C. Formed 1980.

This organization (previously known as the Maud Bevan Transition House) provides shelter and support for victims of family violence.

LOCATION OF RECORDS: Prince Rupert Transition House. [*Mailing Address:* Box 907, Prince Rupert, B.C. V8J 3B4. *Telephone:* (604) 627-8588.]

RECORDS: Constitution, 1980; minutes, correspondence, membership lists, 1980-1991; financial records, grant applications, reports, pamphlets, flyers, 1981-1991; scrapbooks, briefs, clippings, photographs.

AMOUNT: 1 filing cabinet, 8 boxes.

CONDITION: Good.

ACCESS: Permission required. Client files and log-books closed.

836. Richmond Women's Resource Centre Association

✣ Richmond, B.C. Formed 1974.

This association works to improve the status of women through education, advocacy, and a variety of services.

LOCATION OF RECORDS: Richmond Women's Resource Centre Association. [*Address:* 8240 General Currie Rd., Richmond, B.C. V6Y 1M1. *Telephone:* (604) 270-6182 or 276-9617. *Fax:* (604) 278-6902.]

RECORDS: Constitution, 1976; minutes, correspondence, log-books, financial records, grant applications, membership lists, mailing lists, petitions, scrapbooks, reports, briefs, conference proceedings, pamphlets, flyers, press releases, buttons, T-shirts, banners, clippings, photographs, videotapes, 1976-1991; newsletters (*Freespace*).

AMOUNT: 4 filing cabinets.

CONDITION: Fair.

ACCESS: Permission required. Surveys on dating violence closed.

837. Rural Women's Seminar Society

✣ Cranbrook, B.C. Formed 1985.

The Rural Women's Seminar Society (RWS) organizes seminars throughout B.C. which bring rural women together to share knowledge and experience and learn new skills.

LOCATION OF RECORDS: Rural Women's Seminar Society. [*Address:* 200 - 42 - 8th Ave. S., Cranbrook, B.C. V1C 2W9. *Telephone:* (604) 426-1535. *Fax:* (604) 426-1546.]

RECORDS: Constitution, 1985; financial records, grant applications, membership lists, mailing lists, reports, press releases, posters, photographs, 1985-1990; T-shirts, 1987, 1990; banners, 1987.

AMOUNT: 1 drawer of a filing cabinet.
CONDITION: Good.
ACCESS: Permission required.

838. Second Stage Program (Victoria, B.C.)
✣ Victoria, B.C.

The Second Stage Program runs a transition house called Barner House and offers day care, low-income housing, family-violence services, and counselling to families. The Second Stage Program grew out of the Bishop Cridge Centre for the Family (previously the B.C. Protestant Orphanage).

LOCATION OF RECORDS: Second Stage Program. [*Mailing Address:* P.O. Box 5755, Station B, Victoria, B.C. V8R 6S8. *Telephone:* (604) 380-3073.]
RECORDS: Financial records, grant applications, client records, reports, pamphlets, 1989-1991.
AMOUNT: 1 drawer of a filing cabinet.
CONDITION: Good.
ACCESS: Permission required. Client files, staff files, and some other records closed.

839. Sexual Assault Recovery Anonymous
✣ Surrey, B.C. Formed 1983.

Sexual Assault Recovery Anonymous (SARA) runs self-help groups for adults and adolescents who were sexually abused as children. SARA also provides educational materials for the prevention of sexual abuse.

LOCATION OF RECORDS: Sexual Assault Recovery Anonymous. [*Mailing Address:* P.O. Box 16, Surrey, B.C. V3T 4W4. *Telephone:* (604) 584-2626/2888.]
RECORDS: Constitution, 1983; minutes, correspondence, financial records, grant applications, client records, membership lists, mailing lists, pamphlets, flyers, press releases, posters, buttons, books, clippings, photographs, sound recordings, videotapes, 1983-1991; newsletters (*Linkages*, 1991).
AMOUNT: 5 filing cabinets.
CONDITION: Good.
ACCESS: Permission required. Client files, membership lists, and minutes closed.

840. Simon Fraser University. Employment Equity Advisory Committee
✣ Burnaby, B.C. Formed 1988.

This committee advises Simon Fraser University's employment-equity coordinator with respect to the university's employment-equity programme for women, visible minorities, Native people, and people with disabilities.

LOCATION OF RECORDS: Simon Fraser University. Employment Equity Advisory Committee. [*Address:* c/o President's Office, Burnaby, B.C. V5A 1S6. *Telephone:* (604) 291-4557. *Fax:* (604) 291-3449.]
RECORDS: Minutes, correspondence, reports, 1988-1991; pamphlets, 1989-1991; posters, 1990.
AMOUNT: 2 drawers of a filing cabinet.
CONDITION: Good.

841. Simon Fraser University. Public Interest Research Group
✣ Burnaby, B.C. Formed 1967.

The Simon Fraser University Public Interest Research Group (SFUPIRG) is a student organization which does social research and advocacy, focusing on environmental and women's issues. The Women's Economic Agenda, a subgroup which is no longer active, published the *B.C. Women's Resource Guide*.

LOCATION OF RECORDS: Simon Fraser University. Public Interest Research Group. [*Address:* T.C. 304, Burnaby, B.C. V5A 1S6. *Telephone:* (604) 291-4360.]
RECORDS: Constitution, minutes, correspondence, financial records, grant applications, membership lists, mailing lists, petitions, reports, briefs, conference proceedings, pamphlets, flyers, press releases, posters, buttons, banners, 1967-1991; clippings, photographs, videotapes.
AMOUNT: 6 filing-cabinet drawers.
CONDITION: Good.
ACCESS: Permission required.

842. Simon Fraser University. Women's Centre
✣ Burnaby, B.C. Formed 1974.

The Simon Fraser University Women's Centre provides a lounge, a library, a meeting space, and programming for women. The centre is part of the Simon Fraser Student Society (SFSS).

LOCATION OF RECORDS: Simon Fraser University. Women's Centre. [*Address:* c/o Simon Fraser Student Society, Burnaby, B.C. V5A 1S6. *Telephone:* (604) 291-3670.]
RECORDS: Minutes, 1977, 1980-1983, 1987-1991; correspondence, 1975-1976, 1980, 1982-1984, 1986, 1990; log-books, 1975, 1979-1980, 1983, 1985-1986, 1989-1991; financial records, 1974-1975, 1984-1991; membership lists, 1988-1991; newsletters, 1974-1975, 1981-1982; photographs, 1990; scrapbooks, reports, conference proceedings.
AMOUNT: 2 shelves of a filing cabinet.
CONDITION: Good.

843. Terrace Sexual Assault Centre
✣ Terrace, B.C. Formed 1980.

The Terrace Sexual Assault Centre offers a crisis line, accompaniment, counselling, and advocacy.

LOCATION OF RECORDS: Terrace Sexual Assault Centre. [*Address:* #4 - 3238 Kalum St., Terrace, B.C. V8G 1V4. *Telephone:* (604) 635-4042.]
RECORDS: Constitution, minutes, correspondence, log-books, financial records, grant applications, client records, membership lists, mailing lists, scrapbooks, reports, conference proceedings, pamphlets, flyers, press releases, posters, clippings, 1980-1991.
AMOUNT: 2 filing cabinets.
CONDITION: Good.

844. Terrace Women's Resource Centre
✣ Terrace, B.C. Formed 1980.

This drop-in centre offers information, referral, resources, and advocacy.

LOCATION OF RECORDS: Terrace Women's Resource Centre. [*Address:* 4542 Park Ave., Terrace, B.C. V6G 1V4. *Telephone:* (604) 638-0228.]
RECORDS: Constitution, minutes, correspondence, log-books, financial records, grant applications, membership lists, mailing lists, reports, 1975-1991; newsletters (*Tamarack*, 1975-1991); pamphlets, press releases, buttons, T-shirts, books, clippings, photographs.
AMOUNT: 2 filing cabinets, 1 storage room.
CONDITION: Good.
ACCESS: Permission required.

845. United Fishermen and Allied Workers Union. Women's Rights Committee

✢ Vancouver, B.C. Formed 1979.

The Women's Rights Committee (WRC) of the United Fishermen and Allied Workers Union (UFAWU) works to foster equality and improve women's working conditions.

LOCATION OF RECORDS: United Fishermen and Allied Workers Union. Women's Rights Committee. [*Address*: 160 - 111 Victoria Dr., Vancouver, B.C. V5L 4C4. *Telephone*: (604) 255-8771. *Fax*: (604) 255-3162.]

RECORDS: Minutes, correspondence, 1979-1991; reports, briefs, conference proceedings, photographs.

ACCESS: Permission required.

846. Urban Images for Native Indian Women

✢ Vancouver, B.C. Formed 1984.

Urban Images offers programmes to prepare Native women to secure employment in an urban environment and to participate fully in society. The organization was formed as the result of a study by the Ad Hoc Committee of Native Indian Women.

LOCATION OF RECORDS: Urban Images for Native Indian Women. [*Address*: Suite 1 - 245 East Broadway, Vancouver, B.C. V5T 1W4. *Telephone*: (604) 875-9211. *Fax*: (604) 872-1845.]

RECORDS: Constitution, minutes, correspondence, log-books, financial records, grant applications, client records, membership lists, mailing lists, reports, 1985-1991; pamphlets, flyers, posters, T-shirts, banners, clippings, photographs, sound recordings, videotapes, 1991.

AMOUNT: Approx. 6 filing cabinets.

CONDITION: Good.

ACCESS: Permission required. Client files closed.

847. Vancouver Association of Women and the Law

✢ Vancouver, B.C.

The Vancouver Association of Women and the Law (VAWL) is a branch of the National Association of Women and the Law (NAWL), which was founded in 1975 to improve the legal status of women in Canada.

LOCATION OF RECORDS: Vancouver Association of Women and the Law. [*Mailing Address*: Box No. 48665, Bentall Centre, Vancouver, B.C. V7X 1A3.]

RECORDS: Minutes, correspondence, financial records, grant applications, client records, membership lists, mailing lists, petitions, scrapbooks, conference proceedings, T-shirts.

AMOUNT: 3 boxes.

CONDITION: Good.

848. Vancouver Charter of Rights Coalition

✢ Vancouver, B.C. Formed 1985. Disbanded [1987?].

This coalition, also known as CORC, worked to advance women's equality through public education about the Canadian Charter of Rights and Freedoms.

LOCATION OF RECORDS: West Coast LEAF Association. [*Address*: 301 - 207 W. Hastings St., Vancouver, B.C. V6B 1H7. *Telephone*: (604) 684-8772. *Fax*: (604) 684-4543.]

RECORDS: Correspondence, grant applications, membership lists, reports, briefs, conference proceedings, pamphlets, 1985-1987.

CONDITION: Fair.

849. Vancouver Island Haven Society

✢ Nanaimo, B.C. Formed 1978.

The Vancouver Island Haven Society operates Haven House, a shelter for women undergoing transition in their family life, especially abused women. The society also offers counselling, information and referral, and a Native liaison training programme.

LOCATION OF RECORDS: Vancouver Island Haven Society. [*Mailing Address*: P.O. Box 311, Nanaimo, B.C. V9R 5L3. *Telephone*: (604) 756-0616/2452.]

RECORDS: Constitution, 1981-1982; minutes, correspondence, log-books, financial records, grant applications, client records, reports, press releases, 1981-1991; mailing lists, 1985, 1989, 1991; scrapbooks, clippings, 1978-1991; conference proceedings, pamphlets.

AMOUNT: Approx. 5 filing cabinets.

CONDITION: Good.

ACCESS: Permission required. Client files, employee files, and minutes of staff meetings closed.

850. Vancouver Lesbian Centre

✢ Vancouver, B.C. Formed 1984.

The Vancouver Lesbian Centre (VLC), known until 1990 as Vancouver Lesbian Connection, offers an information and referral service, peer counselling, a library, and self-help groups. VLC is committed to fighting discrimination based on sexual orientation.

LOCATION OF RECORDS: Vancouver Lesbian Centre. [*Mailing Address*: Box 6951, Station F, Vancouver, B.C. V5W 5L4. (*Street Address*: 876 Commercial Dr.) *Telephone*: (604) 254-8458.]

RECORDS: Constitution, correspondence, photographs, 1984-1991; minutes, log-books, financial records, 1987-1991; grant applications, pamphlets, press releases, posters, clippings, 1986-1991; mailing lists, buttons, banners, 1991.

AMOUNT: 2 filing cabinets.

ACCESS: Permission required.

851. Vancouver Life Skills Society

✢ Vancouver, B.C. Formed 1977.

The Vancouver Life Skills Society gives parents (mostly mothers) access to community resources and opportunities to develop parenting skills. It operates South Vancouver Family Place, a drop-in centre for women and children.

LOCATION OF RECORDS: Vancouver Life Skills Society. [*Address*: 7595 Victoria Dr., Vancouver, B.C. V5P 3Z6. *Telephone*: (604) 325-5213.]

RECORDS: Constitution, 1977; minutes, financial records, grant applications, membership lists, 1977-1991; reports, books, 1989; banners, 1984; correspondence, pamphlets, press releases.

AMOUNT: 1 filing cabinet, 2 bookshelves.

CONDITION: Fair.

ACCESS: Permission required.

852. Vancouver Rape Relief and Women's Shelter

✢ Vancouver, B.C. Formed 1973.

Vancouver Rape Relief and Women's Shelter (also known simply as Rape Relief) aids victims of sexist violence through a crisis line, a transition house, public education, protests, and community organizing toward women's liberation.

PART II: RECORDS HELD BY GROUPS / PARTIE II : FONDS DÉTENUS PAR DES GROUPES

Victoria Status of Women Action Group, [197-?]
Photographer unknown / Photographe inconnue
Photo #244
CWMA Collection / Fonds de l'ACMF

LOCATION OF RECORDS: Vancouver Rape Relief and Women's Shelter. [*Address:* 77 East 20th Ave., Vancouver, B.C. V5V 1L7. *Telephone:* (604) 872-8212. *Fax:* (604) 876-8450.]

RECORDS: Constitution, 1973; minutes, correspondence, financial records, grant applications, membership lists, mailing lists, scrapbooks, reports, briefs, conference proceedings, pamphlets, flyers, press releases, posters, buttons, T-shirts, banners, clippings, photographs, videotapes, films, 1973-1991; newsletters, 1982-1984.

ACCESS: Permission required. Client files and certain other files closed.

853. Vancouver Society on Immigrant Women

✢ Vancouver, B.C. Formed 1982.

The activities of the Vancouver Society on Immigrant Women (VSIW) include research, networking, workshops, and lobbying. Until 1985 it was called the British Columbia Task Force on Immigrant Women.

LOCATION OF RECORDS: Vancouver Society on Immigrant Women. [*Address:* 2524 Cypress St., Vancouver, B.C. V6J 3N2. *Telephone:* (604) 731-9108.]

RECORDS: Constitution, 1985; minutes, correspondence, log-books, financial records, grant applications, client records, membership lists, mailing lists, petitions, scrapbooks, reports, briefs, conference proceedings, pamphlets, flyers, press releases, banners, books, photographs, sound recordings, videotapes, 1982-1991; newsletters, 1982-1990.

AMOUNT: 2 filing cabinets.

CONDITION: Good.

ACCESS: Permission required.

854. Vancouver Women's Bookstore

[See also entry # 160 (in Part I), which lists other records of this organization.]

✢ Vancouver, B.C. Formed 1973.

The bookstore provides books, periodicals, and music by, for, and about women. It also carries non-sexist books for children.

LOCATION OF RECORDS: Vancouver Women's Bookstore. [*Address:* 315 Cambie St., Vancouver, B.C. V6B 2N4. *Telephone:* (604) 684-0523.]

RECORDS: Minutes, correspondence, log-books, financial records, flyers, catalogues, 1973-1991; posters, 1983; banners.

AMOUNT: 3 filing cabinets.

CONDITION: Fair.

ACCESS: Permission required. Log-books and minutes closed.

855. Vancouver Women's Health Collective

[See also entry # 162 (in Part I), which lists other records of this organization.]

✢ Vancouver, B.C. Formed 1972.

The Vancouver Women's Health Collective (VWHC) operates a resource centre on women's health. VWHC's goal is to provide women with the information they need to make good choices about their health care. The group's French name is le Collectif de la santé des femmes de Vancouver.

LOCATION OF RECORDS: Vancouver Women's Health Collective. [*Address:* #302 - 1720 Grant St., Vancouver, B.C. V5L 4G1. *Telephone:* (604) 255-8284.]

RECORDS: Constitution, 1973; minutes, log-books, grant applications, 1983-1991; correspondence, 1988-1991; briefs, press releases, 1986-1991; newsletters (*Healthmatters*, 1985-1987); books, 1978; photographs, 1973-1991; talks, 1978-1985; financial records, mailing lists, scrapbooks, conference proceedings, pamphlets, flyers, posters, banners, clippings.

AMOUNT: 1 filing cabinet.

CONDITION: Good.

ACCESS: Permission required.

856. Vernon Women's Transition House Society

✢ Vernon, B.C. Formed 1977.

The Vernon Women's Transition House Society (VWTH) operates a transition house for women and their children. It also offers second-stage housing, support groups, and a live-in programme for single mothers (the Lifeline Program). Until 1979 the organization was called Vernon Women's Forum Society.

LOCATION OF RECORDS: Vernon Women's Transition House Society. [*Mailing Address:* Box 625, Vernon, B.C. V1T 6M6. *Telephone:* (604) 542-1122.]

RECORDS: Constitution, minutes, correspondence, log-books, financial records, grant applications, client records, membership lists, mailing lists, scrapbooks, reports, pamphlets, flyers, press releases, clippings, photographs, videotapes, 1977-1991.

CONDITION: Fair.

ACCESS: Permission required. Client files closed.

857. Victoria Business and Professional Women's Club

[See also entry # 163 (in Part I), which lists other records of this organization.]

✢ Victoria, B.C. Formed 1921.

The Victoria Business and Professional Women's Club (BPWC) works for the improvement of economic and social conditions for women and girls. It also encourages women to participate in the business of government. Until 1930 the group was called Kumtuks.

LOCATION OF RECORDS: Victoria Business and Professional Women's Club. [*Mailing Address:* Box 5621, Station B, Victoria, B.C. V8R 1H0.]

RECORDS: Constitution, minutes, correspondence, log-books, membership lists, scrapbooks, reports, 1969-1991; menus, programmes, photographs, sound recordings, songbooks.

AMOUNT: 3 boxes.

CONDITION: Good.

858. Victoria Status of Women Action Group

[See also entry # 165 (in Part I), which lists other records of this organization.]

✢ Victoria, B.C. Formed 1971.

The Victoria Status of Women Action Group (SWAG) fosters public knowledge of the rights and status of women and promotes the full participation of women in social, economic, and political life. It offers educational programmes, a drop-in centre, and a library.

LOCATION OF RECORDS: Victoria Status of Women Action Group. [*Mailing Address:* P.O. Box 484, Station E, Victoria, B.C. V8W 2N8. *Telephone:* (604) 381-1012.]

RECORDS: Constitution, minutes, financial records, membership lists, briefs, conference proceedings, pamphlets, flyers, clippings, 1971-1991; correspondence, 1977-1991; log-books, 1982-1991; grant applications, 1981-1991; mailing lists, petitions, press releases, T-shirts, photographs, 1989-1991; reports, [198-]-1991; posters, 1988-1991; banners, 1990-1991; newsletters (*Times Feminist*, 1971-1991); books, 1986, 1990; videotapes, 1983, 1989.

CONDITION: Fair.

ACCESS: Permission required. Minutes of internal steering committee and financial records closed.

859. Victoria Women's Sexual Assault Centre

✣ Victoria, B.C. Formed 1982.

The Victoria Women's Sexual Assault Centre (WSAC) provides crisis-intervention services and counselling to survivors of sexual assault and childhood sexual abuse. WSAC also works for the prevention of sexual assault.

LOCATION OF RECORDS: Victoria Women's Sexual Assault Centre. [*Address:* 306 - 620 View St., Victoria, B.C. V8W 1J6. *Telephone:* (604) 383-5545. *Fax:* (604) 383-6112.]

RECORDS: Constitution, minutes, correspondence, log-books, financial records, grant applications, client records, scrapbooks, reports, pamphlets, flyers, posters, T-shirts, banners, sound recordings, videotapes, manuals, 1983-1991.

AMOUNT: 10 filing-cabinet drawers.

CONDITION: Good.

ACCESS: The board of directors will consider written requests to see the records. Client files closed.

860. Wednesday Nite Live

✣ Kelowna, B.C. Formed 1989.

Wednesday Nite Live grew out of an annual retreat held by women of the First United Church in Kelowna. The group explores issues related to women's spirituality.

LOCATION OF RECORDS: Wednesday Nite Live. [*Address:* First United Church, Kelowna, 721 Bernard Ave., Kelowna, B.C. V1Y 6P6. *Telephone:* (604) 762-3314.]

RECORDS: Programme designs, records of liturgies and rituals, 1984-1991.

861. West Coast Domestic Workers Association

✣ Vancouver, B.C. Formed [ca. 1987].

The West Coast Domestic Workers Association (WCDWA or DWA) aims to improve working conditions and ensure that domestic workers are treated fairly by employers, employment agencies, and branches of government.

LOCATION OF RECORDS: West Coast Domestic Workers Association. [*Address:* #309 - 119 West Pender St., Vancouver, B.C. V6B 1S5. *Telephone:* (604) 669-4482.]

RECORDS: Constitutions, 1986, 1990; minutes, correspondence, financial records, grant applications, client records, membership lists, 1989-1991; reports, 1990; briefs, 1989; newsletters (*Nannies' Voice*; *West Coast Domestic Workers' Newsletter*); petitions, photograph albums, pamphlets, flyers, posters, buttons, banners, handbooks, clippings, photographs, sound recordings.

AMOUNT: 3 filing cabinets.

CONDITION: Good.

ACCESS: Permission required from steering committee. Client files closed.

862. West Coast LEAF Association

✣ Vancouver, B.C. Formed 1985.

The West Coast LEAF Association is a branch of the Women's Legal Education and Action Fund (LEAF). It works to advance the status of women by sponsoring test cases using equality-rights guarantees in the Canadian Charter of Rights and Freedoms and human-rights legislation. It also does public education.

LOCATION OF RECORDS: West Coast LEAF Association. [*Address:* 301 - 207 W. Hastings St., Vancouver, B.C. V6B 1H7. *Telephone:* (604) 684-8772. *Fax:* (604) 684-4543.]

RECORDS: Minutes, correspondence, 1985-1991; financial records, grant applications, pamphlets, 1986-1991; client records, membership lists, mailing lists, reports, press releases, clippings, photographs, sound recordings, 1987-1991; briefs, conference proceedings, posters, 1988-1991; T-shirts, 1988; newsletters (*Leaflet*, 1988-1991); constitution, banners.

AMOUNT: Approx. 3 filing cabinets.

CONDITION: Good.

ACCESS: Permission required. Client files closed.

863. West Coast Women and Words Society

✣ Vancouver, B.C. Formed 1982.

West Coast Women and Words Society provides a network for women writers, runs a summer school and writing retreat called West Word, and holds public readings and discussions. The group was originally called Women and Words/Les Femmes et les mots (which was also the name of a conference it organized in 1983).

LOCATION OF RECORDS: West Coast Women and Words Society. [*Mailing Address:* P.O. Box 65563, Station F, Vancouver, B.C. V5N 5K5. (*Street Address:* #210 - 640 W. Broadway.) *Telephone:* (604) 872-8014.]

RECORDS: Constitution, 1982-1988; minutes, correspondence, financial records, grant applications, membership lists, mailing lists, scrapbooks, reports, flyers, press releases, posters, clippings, photographs, sound recordings, 1982-1991; log-books, 1985-1991; conference proceedings, videotapes, 1983; pamphlets, 1988; books, 1985; newsletters.

AMOUNT: Approx. 3 filing cabinets.

CONDITION: Fair.

ACCESS: Permission required.

864. West Kootenay Women's Association

✣ Nelson, B.C. Formed 1972.

The West Kootenay Women's Association (WKWA) promotes women's right to social, economic, and physical control of their lives. WKWA operates the Nelson and District Women's Centre (previously the Nelson Women's Centre) and helps organize the annual West Kootenay Women's Festival.

LOCATION OF RECORDS: West Kootenay Women's Association. [*Address:* 507 Hall St., Nelson, B.C. V1L 1Z1. *Telephone:* (604) 352-9916/3177.]

RECORDS: Constitution, minutes, correspondence, log-books, financial records, grant applications, membership lists, mailing lists, petitions, scrapbooks, reports, briefs, conference proceedings, pamphlets, flyers, press releases, posters, T-shirts, banners, newsletters, clippings, photographs, 1972-1991.

AMOUNT: Approx. 3 filing cabinets.

ACCESS: Permission required. Some records may be restricted.

865. Westcoast Women Futures Community Economic Development Society

✣ Vancouver, B.C. Formed 1988.

The Westcoast Women Futures Community Economic Development Society (also known simply as Women Futures) works with women's groups, community organizations, and co-operatives to demystify economics, create strategies for community economic development, and increase women's participation in economic development. The group began as a project of the Women Skills Development Society.

LOCATION OF RECORDS: Westcoast Women Futures Community Economic Development Society. [*Address:* #217 - 1956 West Broadway, Vancouver, B.C. V6J 1Z2. *Telephone:* (604) 737-1338.]

RECORDS: Constitution, minutes, correspondence, financial records, grant applications, mailing lists, reports, briefs, conference proceedings, buttons, 1988-1991; book, 1988.

AMOUNT: 5 filing-cabinet drawers.

CONDITION: Good.

ACCESS: Permission required.

866. *Women and Work Research and Education Society*

✣ Burnaby, B.C. Formed 1983.

This organization does research and education on women and work, especially women's health issues related to work. The organization grew out of the Women Skills Development Society and the Micro Tech Research Group.

LOCATION OF RECORDS: Women and Work Research and Education Society. [*Address:* 4340 Carson St., Burnaby, B.C. V5J 2X9. *Telephone:* (604) 430-0458.]

RECORDS: Constitution, minutes, correspondence, financial records, grant applications, membership lists, mailing lists, 1982-1991; newsletters (*The Clerical Voice*, 1988-1990).

AMOUNT: 2 filing cabinets.

CONDITION: Fair.

ACCESS: Permission required.

867. *Women Educating in Self-Defense Training*

✣ Vancouver, B.C. Formed 1978.

Women Educating in Self-Defense Training (WEST) offers Wenlido, a self-defence programme for women and their children. The organization was called Wen-Do WEST until 1985.

LOCATION OF RECORDS: Women Educating in Self-Defense Training. [*Address:* 2349 St Catherines St., Vancouver, B.C. V5T 3X8. *Telephone:* (604) 876-6390.]

RECORDS: Constitution, financial records, 1985-1991; minutes, correspondence, reports, pamphlets, flyers, posters, sound recordings, 1978-1991; membership lists, 1986-1991; mailing lists, 1989-1991; scrapbooks, clippings, photographs, 1974-1991; T-shirts, banners, 1979-1991; newsletters (*Women's Strength News*, 1986-1991; *Wen-Do Newsletter*, 1980-1985); videotapes, 1983-1991.

AMOUNT: 1 filing cabinet.

CONDITION: Fair.

ACCESS: Permission required. Instructors' files may only be used with permission of instructor.

868. *Women in Music*

✣ Vancouver, B.C. Formed 1990.

Women in Music (also called WIM or Society for Women in Music) grew out of the B.C. Chapter of the Association of Canadian Women Composers (ACWC). WIM unites women musicians and their supporters, holds concerts and discussions, and encourages composition, performance, production, promotion, and appreciation.

LOCATION OF RECORDS: Women in Music. [*Address:* 1208 Nootka St., Vancouver, B.C. V5K 4E7. *Telephone:* (604) 255-4388.]

RECORDS: Constitution, pamphlets, newsletters, 1991; minutes, correspondence, financial records, grant applications, flyers, press releases, clippings, photographs, sound recordings, 1988-1991; posters, interviews, scores, 1988; videotapes, 1990.

AMOUNT: 2 drawers of a filing cabinet, sound recordings.

CONDITION: Good.

ACCESS: Permission required.

869. *Women in Need Society*

✣ Trail, B.C. Formed 1980.

The Women in Need Society (WINS) provides a safe environment and support to battered women and their children through a transition house, a crisis line, and support groups.

LOCATION OF RECORDS: Women in Need Society. [*Mailing Address:* Box 153, Trail, B.C. V1R 4L5. *Telephone:* (604) 364-2326.]

RECORDS: Minutes, correspondence, financial records, grant applications, scrapbooks, [1980?]-1991; photographs, [1982?]-1991.

AMOUNT: 8 boxes.

CONDITION: Good.

ACCESS: Permission required. Client records and records of crisis calls closed.

870. *Women's Employment and Training Coalition*

✣ New Westminster, B.C. Formed 1985.

The Women's Employment and Training Coalition (WETC) is a network of groups involved with women's employment and training issues in the Lower Mainland. WETC works to improve women's access to high-quality education and training.

LOCATION OF RECORDS: Women's Employment and Training Coalition. [*Address:* c/o The Women's Centre, Douglas College, P.O. Box 2503, New Westminster, B.C. V3L 5B2. *Telephone:* (604) 527-5148.]

RECORDS: Minutes, correspondence, membership lists, mailing lists, reports, briefs, 1985-1991; pamphlets, 1990.

AMOUNT: 1 drawer of a filing cabinet.

CONDITION: Fair.

ACCESS: Permission required.

871. *Women's Labour History Project*

[See also entry # 173 (in Part I), which lists other records of this organization.]

✣ Vancouver, B.C. Formed 1978.

The Women's Labour History Project (WLHP) researches the history of women and work and the history of working-class women and family and community life. It creates photographic, sound, and video archives and produces videotapes about women's labour history. WLHP is also known as the Western Women's Labour History Project of B.C.

LOCATION OF RECORDS: Women's Labour History Project. [*Address:* 2534 Cambridge St., Vancouver, B.C. V5K 1L4. *Telephone:* (604) 254-5210.]

RECORDS: Constitution, 1985; minutes, financial records, mailing lists, briefs, press releases, posters, 1985-1991; correspondence, grant applications, scrapbooks, pamphlets, flyers, clippings, photographs, sound recordings, videotapes, 1978-1991; newsletters (*Women's Labour History in B.C.*, 1981).

AMOUNT: 10 filing cabinets.

ACCESS: Permission required. Correspondence, financial records, grant applications, and mailing lists closed.

872. Women's Resources Centre (University of British Columbia)

✢ Vancouver, B.C. Formed 1973.

The Women's Resources Centre (WRC) of the Centre for Continuing Education at the University of British Columbia was originally established as a life-planning centre for women in transition. WRC now provides counselling, personal-development programmes, and career planning to the community at large, as well as programmes meeting the special needs of women.

LOCATION OF RECORDS: Women's Resources Centre. [*Address:* Centre for Continuing Education, University of British Columbia, 1144 Robson St., Vancouver, B.C. V6E 1B2. *Telephone:* (604) 685-3934.]

RECORDS: Minutes, financial records, membership lists, mailing lists, scrapbooks, pamphlets, flyers, press releases, clippings, photographs, 1973-1991; grant applications, 1986-1991.

AMOUNT: 3 filing cabinets.

CONDITION: Fair.

ACCESS: Permission required. Minutes, financial records, and membership lists closed.

873. Young Women's Christian Association (Vancouver, B.C.)

[See also entry # 179 (in Part I), which lists other records of this organization.]

✢ Vancouver, B.C. Formed [1897?].

The YWCA of Vancouver works to foster self-reliance and mutual support among women. It offers physical-education and health programmes, temporary accommodation, and a wide range of other services for women and children. The YWCA operates Munroe House (founded in 1979), which provides second-stage housing for battered women.

Collection (a)

LOCATION OF RECORDS: Young Women's Christian Association. [*Address:* 580 Burrard St., Vancouver, B.C. V6C 2K9. *Telephone:* (604) 683-2531. *Fax:* (604) 684-9171.]

RECORDS: Constitution, minutes, correspondence, log-books, financial records, grant applications, client records, membership lists, mailing lists, petitions, scrapbooks, reports, briefs, conference proceedings, pamphlets, flyers, press releases, posters, buttons, newsletters, clippings, photographs, sound recordings, videotapes, 1983-1991; T-shirts, banners.

CONDITION: Fair.

ACCESS: Permission required. Client files closed.

Collection (b)

LOCATION OF RECORDS: Munroe House. [*Address:* 580 Burrard St., Vancouver, B.C. V6C 2K9. *Telephone:* (604) 683-2531.]

RECORDS: Records of Munroe House (minutes, correspondence, log-books, financial records, grant applications, client records, scrapbooks, reports, briefs, pamphlets, flyers, press releases, 1979-1991; newsletters [*Voices*, 1990-1991]; programme review, clippings, photographs, sound recordings, videotapes).

CONDITION: Good.

ACCESS: Permission required. Certain files may be closed.

ALBERTA

874. Abortion by Choice Society of Alberta

✣ Edmonton, Alta. Formed 1983.

Abortion by Choice (ABC) works to improve access to abortion services through lobbying and education. It is a member of the Canadian Abortion Rights Action League.

LOCATION OF RECORDS: Abortion by Choice Society of Alberta. [*Mailing Address:* P.O. Box 4098, Edmonton, Alta. T6E 4S8. *Telephone:* (403) 429-6015.]

RECORDS: Constitution, 1983; buttons, T-shirts, 1990; banners, 1988; newsletters, 1989-1991; videotapes, 1991; minutes, correspondence, financial records, membership lists, mailing lists, petitions, briefs, conference proceedings, pamphlets, flyers, press releases, posters, clippings.

AMOUNT: Approx. 1 filing cabinet.

CONDITION: Fair.

ACCESS: Permission required. Mailing, membership, and contributors' lists closed.

875. Alberta Association of Midwives

✣ Calgary, Alta. Formed 1986.

The Alberta Association of Midwives (AAM) works to obtain legal status for midwifery in Alberta, establish midwifery education and training, set standards for midwives, respond to public demand for midwifery care, and educate the public, health-care professionals, and the government about midwifery issues. AAM grew out of two midwifery organizations which joined together: the Western Nurse Midwives Association and the Alberta Council and Register of Domiciliary Midwives Association.

LOCATION OF RECORDS: Alberta Association of Midwives. [*Mailing Address:* P.O. Box 1177, Station G, Calgary, Alta. T3A 3G3. *Telephone:* (403) 274-1447.]

RECORDS: Constitution, 1986; minutes, correspondence, log-books, briefs, 1984-1991; financial records, membership lists, mailing lists, pamphlets, flyers, press releases, posters, 1986-1991; scrapbooks, [197-]-1991; reports, [198-]-1991; T-shirts, 1989; newsletters, 1989-1991; books, clippings, photographs, sound recordings, videotapes.

AMOUNT: Approx. 2 filing cabinets.

CONDITION: Fair.

876. Alberta Coalition against Pornography

✣ Calgary, Alta. Formed 1983.

The Alberta Coalition against Pornography (ACAP) promotes awareness of pornography's pervasiveness and negative social effects. It also promotes legislative reform. ACAP used to be called the Calgary Coalition against Pornography.

LOCATION OF RECORDS: Alberta Coalition Against Pornography. [*Address:* #304, 223 - 12th Ave. S.W., Calgary, Alta. T2R 0G9. *Telephone:* (403) 264-6778. *Fax:* (403) 269-2012.]

RECORDS: Constitution, minutes, log-books, financial records, grant applications, client records, newsletters, 1983-1991; correspondence, 1985-1991; mailing lists, petitions, scrapbooks, reports, briefs, conference proceedings, pamphlets, flyers, press releases, posters, buttons, photographs, sound recordings, videotapes.

AMOUNT: 1 filing cabinet, 1 closet.

CONDITION: Good.

ACCESS: Permission required. Client files and some personal correspondence closed.

877. Alberta Farm Women's Network

✣ Edmonton, Alta. Formed [1984?].

This is a network of individual women and five organizations. It shares information and responds to government policies related to agriculture.

LOCATION OF RECORDS: Alberta Farm Women's Network. [*Address:* 9623 - 83rd St., Edmonton, Alta. T6C 3A3. *Telephone:* (403) 347-0660 or 465-6211. *Fax:* (403) 465-6937.]

RECORDS: Minutes, correspondence, financial records, grant applications, membership lists, mailing lists, pamphlets, press releases, 1984-1991; newsletters, 1986-1991; constitution.

AMOUNT: 1 filing cabinet.

CONDITION: Good.

ACCESS: No restrictions.

878. Alberta Status of Women Action Committee

[See also entry # 184 (in Part I), which lists other records of this organization.]

✣ Edmonton, Alta. Formed 1976.

Through public education, lobbying, and networking, the Alberta Status of Women Action Committee (ASWAC) contributes to the work of improving the social, political, economic, and emotional situation of women.

LOCATION OF RECORDS: Alberta Status of Women Action Committee. [*Mailing Address:* Box 1573, Edmonton, Alta. T5J 2N7. *Telephone:* (403) 421-0306. *Fax:* (403) 425-3293.]

RECORDS: Constitution, minutes, correspondence, financial records, grant applications, membership lists, mailing lists, petitions, scrapbooks, reports, briefs, conference proceedings, pamphlets, flyers, press releases, posters, T-shirts, banners, 1976-1991; newsletters, clippings, photographs, 1980-1991.
AMOUNT: 2 filing cabinets, 24 boxes, 4 bookcases.
CONDITION: Good.

879. *Association des groupes de femmes francophones de l'Alberta*

✣ Edmonton (Alb.). Groupe fondé 1990.

Les objectifs de l'Association des groupes de femmes francophones de l'Alberta (AGFFA) sont de rassembler et de soutenir les groupes locaux de femmes francophones de l'Alberta et de travailler en collaboration avec tous les organismes, francophones et anglophones, qui favorisent le développement des femmes en Alberta.

LIEU DE CONSULTATION : Association des groupes de femmes francophones de l'Alberta. [*Adresse* : 100, 8925 - 82 Ave., Edmonton (Alb.) T6C 0Z2. *Téléphone* : (403) 469-4401. *Télécopieur* : (403) 469-3997.]
MATÉRIEL : Statuts et règlements, procès-verbaux, correspondance, documents financiers, demandes de subvention, listes d'envoi, rapports, communiqués de presse, bannières, 1990-1991; bulletins (*Des Yeux au coeur*, 1991).
QUANTITÉ : 1 classeur.
ÉTAT : Bon.

880. *Calgary Society for Women Plus*

✣ Calgary, Alta. Formed 1986.

Through peer counselling and other services, the Calgary Society for Women Plus (sometimes called simply Women Plus) helps formerly battered women reintegrate themselves and their children into the community.

LOCATION OF RECORDS: Calgary Society for Women Plus. [*Address:* 303, 501 - 18th Ave. S.W., Calgary, Alta. T2S 0C7. *Telephone:* (403) 228-0293.]
RECORDS: Minutes, financial records, 1986-1991; press releases, 1989-1991; newsletters, 1991; constitution, client records, membership lists, volunteer lists, pamphlets, posters, buttons.
AMOUNT: Approx. 2 drawers of a filing cabinet.
CONDITION: Good.
ACCESS: Permission required.

881. *Calgary Status of Women Action Committee*

[See also entry # 190 (in Part I), which lists other records of this organization.]

✣ Calgary, Alta. Formed 1974.

The principal aim of this committee (also known as CSWAC or SWAC) is to strengthen the social, political, and economic status of women. Public education and advocacy are CSWAC's main activities.

LOCATION OF RECORDS: Calgary Status of Women Action Committee. [*Address:* 319, 223 - 12th Ave. S.W., Calgary, Alta. T2R 0G9. *Telephone:* (403) 262-1873.]
RECORDS: Constitution, minutes, correspondence, financial records, grant applications, membership lists, mailing lists, briefs, conference proceedings, pamphlets, flyers, press releases, posters, buttons, T-shirts, banners, 1974-1991; newsletters (*Calgary Women's Newspaper*, 1974-1981; *Status of Women Action Committee*, 1982-1991); photographs, 1981, 1986.
AMOUNT: 3 filing cabinets.

CONDITION: Good.
ACCESS: Permission required.

882. *Calgary Women's Emergency Shelter Association*

[See also entry # 191 (in Part I), which lists other records of this organization.]

✣ Calgary, Alta. Formed 1974.

Also known as CWES, this association provides shelter to abused women and children in crisis, counselling, public education, outreach programmes, and a child-support programme. The shelter is also known as the Senator Patrick Burns Family Shelter; it was originally called Oasis.

LOCATION OF RECORDS: Calgary Women's Emergency Shelter Association. [*Mailing Address:* P.O. Box 52051, Edmonton Trail N.E., Calgary, Alta. T2E 8K9. *Telephone:* (403) 232-8717/8723. *Fax:* (403) 237-7728.]
RECORDS: Constitution, minutes, scrapbooks, 1974-1991; correspondence, log-books, financial records, grant applications, client records, membership lists, mailing lists, pamphlets, fact sheets, newsletters, clippings, photographs, 1984-1991; buttons.
AMOUNT: 9 filing cabinets.
CONDITION: Good.
ACCESS: Permission required. Client and personnel files closed.

883. *Calgary Women's Health Collective*

✣ Calgary, Alta. Formed 1984.

The Calgary Women's Health Collective (WHC) offers mental-health counselling provided by counsellors specializing in issues of particular concern to women. A non-profit, feminist organization, WHC has a sliding fee scale.

LOCATION OF RECORDS: Calgary Women's Health Collective. [*Address:* 316, 223 - 12th Ave. S.W., Calgary, Alta. T2R 0G9. *Telephone:* (403) 265-9590.]
RECORDS: Constitution, 1988; minutes, 1984-1985; financial records, 1984-1991; grant applications, membership lists, 1984-1987; correspondence, briefs, pamphlets, flyers.
AMOUNT: Approx. 1 filing cabinet.
CONDITION: Good.
ACCESS: Permission required.

884. *Celebration of Women in the Arts*

✣ Edmonton, Alta. Formed 1983.

Celebration of Women in the Arts (CWA) is dedicated to the advancement of women in film, dance, music, theatre, visual arts, and literature. It sponsors events and does advocacy on behalf of women artists in Alberta. CWA grew out of a 1983 conference of Canadian women artists.

LOCATION OF RECORDS: Celebration of Women in the Arts. [*Address:* 905 - 10136 100th St., Edmonton, Alta. T5J 0P1. *Telephone:* (403) 424-0287.]
RECORDS: Constitution, minutes, correspondence, financial records, grant applications, membership lists, flyers, press releases, posters, postcards, 1983-1991; conference proceedings, 1983; pamphlets, 1990; mailing lists, buttons, T-shirts, clippings, photographs.
AMOUNT: Approx. 2 drawers of a filing cabinet, 4 shelves.
CONDITION: Good.

885. *Central Alberta Immigrant Women's Association*

✣ Red Deer, Alta. Formed 1990.

This organization works to raise awareness of issues affecting immigrant women and to help immigrant women achieve their full potential as members of Canadian society.

ALBERTA

LOCATION OF RECORDS: Central Alberta Immigrant Women's Association. [*Address:* 112, 4818 Gaetz Ave., Red Deer, Alta. T4N 4A3. *Telephone:* (403) 341-3553.]

RECORDS: Constitution, membership lists, 1991; minutes, log-books, 1990-1991.

AMOUNT: 1 filing cabinet.

CONDITION: Good.

ACCESS: Permission required. Client files closed.

886. Central Alberta Women's Emergency Shelter

✣ Red Deer, Alta. Formed 1982.

This shelter (also known as CAWES) is an emergency refuge for women (with or without children) who are being physically, sexually, emotionally, or psychologically abused, are in crisis, or are transient or homeless.

LOCATION OF RECORDS: Central Alberta Women's Emergency Shelter. [*Mailing Address:* P.O. Box 561, Red Deer, Alta. T4N 5G1. *Telephone:* (403) 346-5643. *Fax:* (403) 341-3510.]

RECORDS: Constitution, 1982; minutes, correspondence, log-books, financial records, grant applications, client records, membership lists, reports, buttons, clippings, 1983-1991; T-shirts, newsletters, 1989-1991; pamphlets, [198-].

AMOUNT: 10 filing cabinets.

CONDITION: Good.

ACCESS: Permission required. Client files closed.

887. Changing Together: A Centre for Immigrant Women

✣ Edmonton, Alta. Formed 1984.

This centre offers a drop-in space, language training, discussion groups, employment counselling, and workshops.

LOCATION OF RECORDS: Changing Together: A Centre for Immigrant Women. [*Address:* Room 209 - 10010 - 107A Ave., Edmonton, Alta. T5H 4H8. *Telephone:* (403) 421-0175.]

RECORDS: Constitution, 1984; newsletters, 1984-1991; minutes, correspondence, log-books, financial records, grant applications, client records, membership lists, mailing lists, petitions, scrapbooks, reports, pamphlets, press releases, photographs.

AMOUNT: 6 filing cabinets.

CONDITION: Good.

ACCESS: Permission required. Client files closed for approx. four years.

888. Crossroads

✣ Fairview, Alta. Formed 1985.

Crossroads is a women's shelter and centre which assists women and children in crisis and helps provide skills which may prevent crisis situations. Crossroads provides accommodation, food and clothing, transportation, a crisis line, and educational programmes. Until 1989 it was called the Fairview and District Women's Centre.

LOCATION OF RECORDS: Crossroads. [*Mailing Address:* Box 1194, Fairview, Alta. T0H 1L0. *Telephone:* (403) 835-2120.]

RECORDS: Constitution, correspondence, pamphlets, 1985-1991; minutes, log-books, financial records, grant applications, client records, membership lists, reports, briefs, conference proceedings, press releases, posters, clippings, photographs, 1986-1991; scrapbook, mailing lists, 1988-1991; newsletters (*Crossroads Update,* 1986-1991; *Volunteer Newsletter,* 1991); videotapes, 1989; flyers.

AMOUNT: 6 filing cabinets.

CONDITION: Good.

ACCESS: Permission required. Client and employee files closed.

889. Crowsnest Pass Women's Resources and Crisis Centre Society

✣ Blairmore, Alta. Formed 1984.

This organization runs a drop-in, information, and referral centre for women of all ages. The centre's services include assistance to women in times of need or crisis.

LOCATION OF RECORDS: Crowsnest Pass Women's Resources and Crisis Centre Society. [*Mailing Address:* Box 1207, Blairmore, Alta. T0K 0E0. *Telephone:* (403) 562-8000/8500.]

RECORDS: Constitution, minutes, correspondence, log-books, financial records, grant applications, client records, membership lists, mailing lists, scrapbooks, reports, pamphlets, posters, newsletters, clippings, photographs, videotapes, 1984-1991; briefs, 1987-1991; press releases, 1988-1991.

AMOUNT: 2 drawers of a filing cabinet.

CONDITION: Good.

ACCESS: Permission required. Client files closed.

890. Edmonton Women and AIDS Project

✣ Edmonton, Alta. Formed 1990.

The Edmonton Women and AIDS Project, under the auspices of the AIDS Network of Edmonton, works to increase awareness about women and HIV/AIDS through workshops and information booths at conferences.

LOCATION OF RECORDS: Edmonton Women & Aids Project. [*Address:* c/o Aids Network of Edmonton Office, 2nd Floor, 10704 - 108 St., Edmonton, Alta. T5H 3A3. *Telephone:* (403) 424-4767. *Fax:* (403) 424-5659.]

RECORDS: Minutes, financial records, mailing lists, 1990-1991; display banner, 1990.

AMOUNT: 1 box.

CONDITION: Good.

ACCESS: Permission required.

891. Edmonton Women's Health Collective

✣ Edmonton, Alta. Formed 1984.

The Edmonton Women's Health Collective provides information related to women's health from a feminist perspective.

LOCATION OF RECORDS: Edmonton Women's Health Collective. [*Mailing Address:* P.O. Box 4134, Edmonton, Alta. T6E 4T2.]

RECORDS: Minutes, financial records, membership lists, mailing lists, 1984-1990; grant applications, 1984; banners, 1990.

AMOUNT: 1 drawer of a filing cabinet.

CONDITION: Fair.

ACCESS: Permission required.

892. Elizabeth Fry Society of Calgary

[See also entry # 201 (in Part I), which lists other records of this organization.]

✣ Calgary, Alta. Formed 1965.

This organization (also known as E-Fry) aims to provide assistance to women in conflict with the law and to help with the rehabilitation of female offenders. Public education, social work, counselling, and advocacy are some of its activities. It was originally called the Elizabeth Fry Society of Alberta.

LOCATION OF RECORDS: Elizabeth Fry Society of Calgary. [*Address:* 204, 1009 - 7th Ave. S.W., Calgary, Alta. T2P 1A8. *Telephone:* (403) 294-0737. *Fax:* (403) 262-0285.]

RECORDS: Constitution, minutes, correspondence, log-books, grant applications, client records, membership lists, mailing lists, petitions, scrapbooks, reports, briefs, conference proceedings, clippings, 1987-1991; newsletters, 1983-1991; book, 1991; pamphlets, flyers, press releases, posters.

AMOUNT: 6 boxes.
CONDITION: Good.
ACCESS: Permission required.

893. Fort McMurray Sexual Assault Centre

✤ Fort McMurray, Alta. Formed 1987.

The Fort McMurray Sexual Assault Centre (SAC) aims to reduce the incidence of sexual assault and alleviate the trauma of victims. SAC's activities include public education, counselling, and support groups for adults molested as children.

LOCATION OF RECORDS: Fort McMurray Sexual Assault Centre. [*Address:* 107 - 10012 Franklin Ave., Fort McMurray, Alta. T9H 2E4. *Telephone:* (403) 791-6708. *Fax:* (403) 791-0088.]

RECORDS: Constitution, 1987; minutes, correspondence, log-books, financial records, grant applications, client records, membership lists, mailing lists, pamphlets, 1987-1991; flyers, press releases, posters, buttons, banners.

AMOUNT: 2 filing cabinets.
CONDITION: Good.
ACCESS: Permission required. Access depends on board approval.

894. Gay and Lesbian Academics, Students, and Staff (University of Calgary)

✤ Calgary, Alta. Formed 1988.

Gay and Lesbian Academics, Students, and Staff (GLASS) provides educational information pertaining to gay and lesbian issues. It is affiliated with the Students' Union at the University of Calgary. GLASS has previously been known as the Gay Students Association and the Gay Students Society.

LOCATION OF RECORDS: Gay and Lesbian Academics, Students, and Staff. [*Mailing Address:* Box 47, MacEwan Hall, University of Calgary, 2500 University Drive N.W., Calgary, Alta. T2N 1N4.]

RECORDS: Constitution, 1988-1991; minutes, pamphlets, banners, 1990-1991; log-books, financial records, membership lists, mailing lists, press releases, clippings, 1989-1991.

AMOUNT: Approx. 2 drawers of a filing cabinet.
CONDITION: Good.
ACCESS: Permission required. Membership lists closed.

895. Grande Cache Transition House

✤ Grande Cache, Alta. Formed 1985.

Grande Cache Transition House is an emergency shelter for abused women and their children. It also does community education.

LOCATION OF RECORDS: Grande Cache Transition House. [*Mailing Address:* Box 1242, Grande Cache, Alta. T0E 0Y0. *Telephone:* (403) 827-5055.]

RECORDS: Constitution, minutes, correspondence, financial records, client records, 1985-1991; grant applications, 1991; scrapbooks, 1989; pamphlets, 1988; press releases, 1989-1990; photographs, 1986-1990; membership lists.

AMOUNT: Approx. 2 filing cabinets.
CONDITION: Good.
ACCESS: Permission required. Client files closed.

896. Lesbian Information Line

✤ Calgary, Alta. Formed 1979.

The Lesbian Information Line (LIL) was originally known as the Womyn's Social and Recreational Collective of Calgary (or simply the Womyn's Collective). LIL provides support and information to lesbian and bisexual women and to the lesbian, gay, and bisexual community. It offers telephone lines, a drop-in service, peer counselling, support groups, a lending library, and social events.

LOCATION OF RECORDS: Lesbian Information Line. [*Address:* #211, 223 - 12th Ave. S.W., Calgary, Alta. T2R 0G9. *Telephone:* (403) 265-9458.]

RECORDS: Constitutions, 1979, 1990; minutes, log-books, 1986-1991; correspondence, 1990; financial records, 1982-1991; grant applications, membership lists, 1987-1991; pamphlets, 1987, 1989, 1991; periodicals (*Lavender Times*, 1987-1990; *LIL Newsletter*, 1990-1991); banners.

AMOUNT: Approx. 2 drawers of a filing cabinet.
CONDITION: Good.
ACCESS: Permission required. Peer-counselling log-book closed.

897. Lloydminster Interval Home

✤ Lloydminster, Alta. Formed 1980.

Lloydminster Interval Home (also known simply as Interval Home or IH) provides temporary, safe accommodation for women and their children experiencing family violence or other crises. It also offers counselling, referral, and support groups.

LOCATION OF RECORDS: Lloydminster Interval Home. [*Mailing Address:* Box 1523, Lloydminster, Alta. S9V 1K5. *Telephone:* (403) 875-0966.]

RECORDS: Constitution, minutes, correspondence, log-books, financial records, grant applications, client records, membership lists, mailing lists, clippings, photographs, 1980-1991; scrapbooks, 1989-1991; reports, newsletters, 1982-1991; briefs, 1990-1991; pamphlets, flyers, 1985; press releases, 1989; T-shirts, 1991; sound recordings, 1990.

AMOUNT: 1 filing cabinet.
CONDITION: Good.
ACCESS: Permission required. Client files closed.

898. Medicine Hat Women's Shelter

✤ Medicine Hat, Alta. Formed 1980.

This shelter offers a safe, supportive environment for battered women or women in crisis and their children. It also provides women with resources to facilitate decisions about their future.

LOCATION OF RECORDS: Medicine Hat Women's Shelter. [*Address:* 631 Prospect Dr. S.W., Medicine Hat, Alta. T1A 4C2. *Telephone:* (403) 529-1091 or 527-8223.]

RECORDS: Constitution, minutes, correspondence, financial records, grant applications, reports, 1980-1991; log-books, client records, 1982-1991; scrapbooks, photographs, 1983-1991; pamphlets, posters, 1988-1991; press releases, clippings, 1985-1991; newsletters, 1984-1990.

AMOUNT: 3 filing cabinets, 7 boxes.
CONDITION: Good.
ACCESS: Permission required. Client files, personnel files, and financial records closed.

899. National Council of Jewish Women of Canada. Edmonton Section

✣ Edmonton, Alta. Formed 1947.

The main goals of the Edmonton section of the National Council of Jewish Women of Canada (NCJW) are education, service, and social action. While the priorities of NCJW are the protection of human rights and the preservation of Jewish life, it is also concerned with women's issues such as family planning, abortion, child care, pornography, and affirmative action.

LOCATION OF RECORDS: National Council of Jewish Women of Canada. Edmonton Section. [*Address:* 7200 - 156 St., Edmonton, Alta. T5R 1X3. *Telephone:* (403) 439-3977. *Fax:* (403) 439-3970.]

RECORDS: Minutes, pamphlets, press releases, 1987-1991; correspondence, 1986-1991; log-books, financial records, 1954-1991; membership lists, 1982-1991; scrapbooks, 1988-1990; photographs, 1988-1991; videotapes, 1989-1990.

AMOUNT: 1 filing cabinet, 2 boxes.

ACCESS: Permission required.

900. Providing Assistance, Counselling, and Education

✣ Grande Prairie, Alta. Formed 1981.

More commonly known as PACE, this organization works with victims of sexual abuse (both children and adult survivors). It offers a crisis line, counselling, and public education.

LOCATION OF RECORDS: Providing Assistance, Counselling, and Education. [*Address:* # 201, 10118 - 101st Ave., Grande Prairie, Alta. T8V 0Y2. *Telephone:* (403) 539-6692.]

RECORDS: Minutes, correspondence, financial records, grant applications, client records, membership lists, mailing lists, scrapbooks, reports, conference proceedings, pamphlets, flyers, press releases, newsletters, 1981-1991; clippings, photographs.

CONDITION: Good.

ACCESS: Permission required. Some files closed.

901. Rainbow Harbour Women's Association

✣ Edmonton, Alta. Formed 1990.

This association works to empower women through social and emotional support and practical services such as a clothing exchange and a babysitting registry.

LOCATION OF RECORDS: Rainbow Harbour Women's Association. [*Mailing Address:* Box 42051, Lee Ridge P.O., Edmonton, Alta. T6K 4C4. *Telephone:* (403) 461-5677.]

RECORDS: Constitution, minutes, correspondence, financial records, grant applications, client records, membership lists, mailing lists, petitions, scrapbooks, reports, flyers, photographs, 1990-1991.

AMOUNT: 1 drawer of a filing cabinet.

CONDITION: Good.

ACCESS: Permission required. Client files closed.

902. Reproductive Health Clinic

✣ Edmonton, Alta. Formed 1988.

The Reproductive Health Clinic (RHC) at the Royal Alexandra Hospital provides counselling, education, and clinical services in the areas of sexuality, contraception, sexually transmitted diseases, infertility, and abortion.

LOCATION OF RECORDS: Reproductive Health Clinic. [*Address:* Royal Alexandra Hospital, 10240 Kingsway Ave., Edmonton, Alta. T5H 3V9. *Telephone:* (403) 477-4111.]

RECORDS: Minutes, correspondence, client records, scrapbooks, 1988-1991; grant applications, posters, 1989; pamphlets, photographs.

CONDITION: Good.

ACCESS: Permission required. Client files closed.

903. Rocky Mountain House Women's Committee

✣ Rocky Mountain House, Alta. Formed 1985.

The Rocky Mountain House (RMH) Women's Committee works to increase understanding of women's issues and promotes action on these issues. It was originally called the Rocky Mountain House (RMH) Women's Conference Committee.

LOCATION OF RECORDS: Rocky Mountain House Women's Committee. [*Mailing Address:* P.O. Box 2037, Rocky Mountain House, Alta. T0M 1T0. *Telephone:* (403) 845-4544.]

RECORDS: Financial records, grant applications, 1987-1991; programme attendance records, membership lists, 1985-1991; petitions, 1991; scrapbooks, conference programmes, clippings, 1985; photographs, 1987; minutes, correspondence, miscellaneous records.

AMOUNT: 1 drawer of a filing cabinet.

CONDITION: Good.

ACCESS: Permission required.

904. St Albert Stop Abuse in Families Society

✣ St Albert, Alta. Formed 1987.

The St Albert Stop Abuse in Families (SAIF) Society provides crisis intervention, counselling, advocacy, referral, and support to individuals experiencing family abuse. It also educates professionals working in this area and the general public about family abuse. Until 1988 it was known as the St Albert Prevention of Family Violence Committee.

LOCATION OF RECORDS: St Albert Stop Abuse in Families Society. [*Address:* 219, 86 McKenney Ave., Mission Ridge Shopping Centre, St Albert, Alta. T8N 2T7. *Telephone:* (403) 460-2195.]

RECORDS: By-laws, grant applications, 1988-1991; minutes, correspondence, financial records, membership lists, books, 1987-1991; client records, mailing lists, reports, pamphlets, clippings, photographs, 1989-1991; scrapbooks, banners, newsletters, videotapes, 1990-1991.

AMOUNT: 1 drawer of a filing cabinet.

CONDITION: Good.

ACCESS: Permission required. Client files closed.

905. University of Calgary. Women's Studies Programme

✣ Calgary, Alta. Formed 1983.

The Women's Studies Programme at the University of Calgary offers a major and a minor in women's studies. The programme's activist and academic perspective is designed to relate to students' own lives and to prepare them for careers in a variety of fields.

LOCATION OF RECORDS: University of Calgary. Women's Studies Programme. [*Address:* Faculty of General Studies, SS302, Calgary, Alta. T2N 1N4. *Telephone:* (403) 220-7246. *Fax:* (403) 282-6716.]

RECORDS: Correspondence, 1985-1991.

CONDITION: Good.

ACCESS: Permission required.

906. Voice of Women (Calgary, Alta.)

[See also entry # 232 (in Part I), which lists other records of this organization.]

✣ Calgary, Alta. Formed 1960.

The Calgary branch of the national organization Voice of Women (VOW) is concerned with peace issues and women's issues.

LOCATION OF RECORDS: Voice of Women. [*Address:* 1717 2nd Ave. N.W., Calgary, Alta. T2N 0G3. *Telephone:* (403) 283-0859.]

RECORDS: Constitution, minutes, correspondence, financial records, membership lists, scrapbooks, reports, briefs, conference proceedings, pamphlets, press releases, banners, 1960-1991; books, 1960-1988; T-shirts, photographs, films.

AMOUNT: 1 filing cabinet.

CONDITION: Fair.

ACCESS: Permission required.

907. Wellspring Women's Association

✣ Whitecourt, Alta. Formed 1983.

The Wellspring Women's Association (WWA) offers temporary shelter to battered women, emotionally abused women, and women in transition. WWA also offers a resource and referral centre, counselling, and a crisis line.

LOCATION OF RECORDS: Wellspring Women's Association. [*Mailing Address:* Box 681, Whitecourt, Alta. T7S 1N7. *Telephone:* (403) 778-6209.]

RECORDS: Minutes, correspondence, financial records, grant applications, reports, 1983-1991; log-books, press releases, clippings, 1984-1991; membership lists, mailing lists, 1991.

AMOUNT: 1 filing cabinet.

CONDITION: Good.

ACCESS: Permission required. Client and employee files closed.

908. Women in Scholarship, Engineering, Science, and Technology (University of Alberta)

[See also entry # 235 (in Part I), which lists other records of this organization.]

✣ Edmonton, Alta. Formed 1982.

Women in Scholarship, Engineering, Science, and Technology (WISEST) works to increase the proportion of women in decision-making roles, especially in engineering and the sciences. WISEST encourages girls to consider careers in engineering and the sciences, and it provides support to women in these fields at the University of Alberta. WISEST has also been known as the Task Force on Women in Scholarship, Engineering, Science, and Technology.

LOCATION OF RECORDS: Women in Scholarship, Engineering, Science and Technology. [*Address:* Dept. of Chemistry, University of Alberta, Edmonton, Alta. T6G 2G2. *Telephone:* (403) 492-4969/1842. *Fax:* (403) 492-8231.]

RECORDS: Grant applications, mailing lists, 1985-1991; membership lists, 1982-1991; conference proceedings, 1986; posters, 1984-1986; buttons, 1990; T-shirts, 1991; newsletters, 1986-1991.

AMOUNT: 1 filing cabinet.

CONDITION: Good.

909. Women of Colour Collective

✣ Calgary, Alta. Formed 1987.

This collective does anti-racist public education, provides support to its members, and lobbies for non-racist, non-sexist, and economically inclusive legislation and policies.

LOCATION OF RECORDS: Women of Colour Collective. [*Address:* 319, 223 - 12th Ave. S.W., Calgary, Alta. T2R 0G9. *Telephone:* (403) 262-1873.]

RECORDS: Minutes, correspondence, 1987-1991; grant applications, flyers, press releases, posters, 1989-1990; membership lists, briefs, 1990; newsletters (*Critical Creations*, 1990); pamphlets, 1987.

AMOUNT: Half a drawer of a filing cabinet.

CONDITION: Good.

ACCESS: Permission required.

910. Women of the Métis Nation Alliance

✣ Stony Plain, Alta. Formed 1986.

Women of the Métis Nation Alliance (WMN) is a provincial organization representing Métis women on issues that affect them politically, legally, economically, socially, or culturally. Through programme development and lobbying, WMN works to raise the status of Métis women.

LOCATION OF RECORDS: Women of the Métis Nation Alliance. [*Mailing Address:* P.O. Box 818, Stony Plain, Alta. T0E 2G0. *Telephone:* (403) 484-7989. *Fax:* (493) 489-9681.]

RECORDS: Constitution, newsletters, 1989; minutes, correspondence, membership lists, mailing lists, reports, clippings, 1987-1991; log-books, buttons, videotapes, 1990; financial records, grant applications, 1988-1991; client records, petitions, posters, 1991; scrapbooks, pamphlets, press releases, photographs, 1989-1991; books, 1987.

CONDITION: Good.

ACCESS: Permission required. Training programme and client files closed.

911. Women of Unifarm

✣ Edmonton, Alta.

Women of Unifarm is a support, lobby, and information group which works for equal legal and economic rights for farm women. It also deals with various other social and agricultural issues. Women of Unifarm grew out of the United Farm Women of Alberta. [See also United Farm Women of Alberta (220).]

LOCATION OF RECORDS: Women of Unifarm. [*Address:* 14815 - 119th Ave., Edmonton, Alta. T5L 4W2. *Telephone:* (403) 451-5912. *Fax:* (403) 453-2669.]

RECORDS: Constitution, 1991; minutes, correspondence, financial records, grant applications, membership lists, mailing lists, petitions, reports, briefs, conference proceedings, pamphlets, press releases, photographs, 1970-1991; scrapbooks.

AMOUNT: 2 filing cabinets.

CONDITION: Fair.

ACCESS: Permission required. Organization reserves the right to close some files.

912. Women's Collective and Resource Centre (University of Calgary)

✣ Calgary, Alta. Formed 1990.

The Women's Collective and Resource Centre (WCRC) seeks to provide opportunities for women at the University of Calgary to achieve their full potential.

LOCATION OF RECORDS: Women's Collective and Resource Centre. [*Address:* University of Calgary, Box 5, 251 M.S.C., 2500 University Dr. N.W., Calgary, Alta. T2N 1N4. *Telephone:* (403) 289-9401.]

RECORDS: Constitution, briefs, grant applications, mailing lists, reports,

press releases, 1990; minutes, correspondence, financial records, membership lists, 1990-1991; pamphlets, posters, 1991; newsletters, articles.
AMOUNT: 2 filing cabinets.
CONDITION: Good.
ACCESS: Permission required. Membership lists closed.

913. *Women's Resource Society of Fort McMurray*
✣ Fort McMurray, Alta. Formed 1987.

This organization operates a resource centre and provides women with opportunities to empower themselves.

LOCATION OF RECORDS: Women's Resource Society of Fort McMurray. [**Mailing Address:** Box 5072, Fort McMurray, Alta. T9H 3G2. **Telephone:** (403) 743-2121.]

RECORDS: By-laws, 1987; minutes, correspondence, financial records, grant applications, membership lists, reports, clippings, 1987-1991; log-books, petitions, sound recordings, 1991; conference proceedings, 1988-1991; pamphlets, T-shirts, 1990; press releases, photographs, 1989-1991; posters, buttons, banners, article, 1990-1991; newsletters (*The Source*, 1989-1991).

AMOUNT: 1 filing cabinet, 1 box.
CONDITION: Good.

914. *Young Women's Christian Association of Calgary*
[See also entry # 238 (in Part I), which lists other records of this organization.]

✣ Calgary, Alta. Formed 1907.

The original purpose of the YWCA of Calgary was to provide accommodation for single women arriving in the city. The YWCA's many other services have included physical education, summer camps, and co-operative housing for unmarried mothers. The YWCA Women's Resource Centre opened in 1973, closed in 1976, and reopened in 1979. The resource centre provides an information and referral service and works to improve the status of women. (Sources: Glenbow Museum Archives finding aids, 1980, 1982.) The YWCA Women's Resource Centre publishes a quarterly feminist journal founded in 1986, *Perspective: A Women's Journal*. The journal's goals are to tell women's stories and to validate women's experiences. [See also YWCA Banff Community Resource Centre (917).]

LOCATION OF RECORDS: Perspective: A Women's Journal. [*Address:* #305, 223 - 12th Ave. S.W., Calgary, Alta. T2R 0G9. *Telephone:* (403) 266-3878.]

RECORDS: Records of *Perspective: A Women's Journal* (by-laws, 1988; minutes, 1987-1991; correspondence, financial records, grant applications, 1985-1991; mailing lists, 1991; periodicals, 1986-1991; paper, 1989; interview transcripts, 1988-1989; calendar).

AMOUNT: 1 bookcase.
CONDITION: Fair.
ACCESS: Permission required.

915. *Young Women's Christian Association of Edmonton*
[See also entry # 239 (in Part I), which lists other records of this organization.]

✣ Edmonton, Alta. Formed 1907.

Services provided by the YWCA of Edmonton have included a women's residence, a fitness centre, child-care services, and a library. (Source: *Women's Resource Directory for Edmonton, Alberta*. — Edmonton: Every Woman's Place, 1984.)

LOCATION OF RECORDS: Young Women's Christian Association of Edmonton. [*Address:* 10305 - 100th Ave., Edmonton, Alta. T5J 3C8. *Telephone:* (403) 423-9922.]

RECORDS: Constitution, 1907-1991; sound recordings, 1988; minutes, correspondence, financial records, grant applications, client records, membership lists, mailing lists, scrapbooks, reports, briefs, pamphlets, flyers, press releases, posters, T-shirts, banners, newsletters (*Y-Week; Contact*), books, photographs.

CONDITION: Good.
ACCESS: Permission required. Client files closed.

916. *Young Women's Christian Association of Lethbridge and District*
✣ Lethbridge, Alta. Formed 1951.

The YWCA of Lethbridge and District provides services to women and children and works to improve the status of women. Its services include child care and a shelter for abused women and children.

LOCATION OF RECORDS: Young Women's Christian Association of Lethbridge and District. [*Address:* 604 - 8th St. S., Lethbridge, Alta. T1J 2K1. *Telephone:* (403) 329-0088. *Fax:* (403) 327-9112.]

RECORDS: Constitutions, 1951, 1988; correspondence, 1985-1991; client records, 1986-1991; scrapbooks, clippings, [195-]; pamphlets, [198-]-[199-]; T-shirts, [199-]; photographs, [197-]-1990; minutes, financial records, grant applications, membership lists, mailing lists, press releases.

AMOUNT: 2 filing cabinets, 2 shelf units.
CONDITION: Fair.
ACCESS: Permission required. Client files closed.

917. *YWCA Banff Community Resource Centre*
✣ Banff, Alta. Formed 1988.

The YWCA Banff Community Resource Centre is affiliated with the Young Women's Christian Association of Calgary. The centre offers an information and referral service, family-planning and crisis counselling, and educational workshops. [See also Young Women's Christian Association of Calgary (238, 914).]

LOCATION OF RECORDS: YWCA Banff Community Resource Centre. [**Mailing Address:** Box 520, Banff, Alta. T0L 0C0. **Telephone:** (403) 762-4511. **Fax:** (403) 762-2602.]

RECORDS: Minutes, correspondence, financial records, grant applications, client records, reports, pamphlets, clippings, photographs, 1988-1991.

AMOUNT: 2 drawers of a filing cabinet.
CONDITION: Fair.
ACCESS: Permission required. Records confidential.

PART II: RECORDS HELD BY GROUPS / PARTIE II : FONDS DÉTENUS PAR DES GROUPES

Demonstration on child care / Manifestation concernant la garde d'enfants, Toronto, 1980
Photographer unknown / Photographe inconnue
Photo #114
CWMA Collection / Fonds de l'ACMF

SASKATCHEWAN

918. Aboriginal Women's Council of Saskatchewan

✤ Prince Albert, Sask. Formed 1972.

The Aboriginal Women's Council of Saskatchewan (AWCS) serves as a forum in which Aboriginal women can deal with issues of concern to themselves and their children. AWCS promotes equal opportunities for Aboriginal women and works to offset stereotyping and discrimination against Aboriginal people.

LOCATION OF RECORDS: Aboriginal Women's Council of Saskatchewan. [*Address:* 62 - 17th St. W., Prince Albert, Sask. S6V 3X3. **Telephone:** (306) 763-6005. **Fax:** (306) 922-6034.]

RECORDS: Minutes, financial records, 1987-1991; correspondence, newsletters, 1972-1991; pamphlets, T-shirts, 1991; constitution, grant applications, client records, mailing lists.

CONDITION: Good.

ACCESS: Permission required.

919. Battlefords' and Area Sexual Assault Centre

✤ North Battleford, Sask. Formed 1980.

This centre provides support, counselling, and a crisis line to those who have been sexually assaulted and their families and friends. It was known as the Battlefords' and Area Rape Crisis Centre until 1984.

LOCATION OF RECORDS: Battlefords' and Area Sexual Assault Centre. [*Address:* 1211 - 98 St., North Battleford, Sask. S9A 0L8. **Telephone:** (306) 445-0055.]

RECORDS: Minutes, correspondence, financial records, grant applications, client records, membership lists, scrapbooks, pamphlets, press releases, posters, clippings, newsletters, 1980-1991; conference proceedings, 1981-1991; buttons, banners, 1989-1991; photographs, 1984; videotapes, 1985.

CONDITION: Good.

ACCESS: Permission required. Client files closed.

920. Congress of Black Women of Canada. Regina Chapter

✤ Regina, Sask. Formed 1980.

The Regina chapter of the Congress of Black Women of Canada (CBWC) is dedicated to improving the welfare of Black women and their families and to bringing due recognition to the role of Black women in Canadian society. Issues of concern to the organization include human rights, racism, housing, health, child development, education, and pensions.

LOCATION OF RECORDS: Congress of Black Women of Canada. Regina Chapter. [*Address:* 79 Murphy Crescent, Regina, Sask. S4X 1S6. **Telephone:** (306) 585-4295, 924-0771, or 949-8193. **Fax:** (306) 585-4878.]

RECORDS: Constitution, 1980; minutes, correspondence, financial records, membership lists, mailing lists, reports, flyers, 1980-1991; grant applications, posters, 1982-1991; briefs, 1982-1985, 1988-1991.

AMOUNT: 8 filing cabinets.

CONDITION: Good.

ACCESS: Permission required.

921. Equality for Gays and Lesbians Everywhere — Regina

✤ Regina, Sask. Formed 1988.

Commonly known as EGALE — Regina, this organization lobbies for the inclusion of sexual orientation as prohibited grounds of discrimination in provincial and federal human-rights legislation. It also does public education.

LOCATION OF RECORDS: Equality for Gays and Lesbians Everywhere — Regina. [*Mailing Address:* Box 195, Regina, Sask. S4P 2Z6. **Telephone:** (306) 522-8307.]

RECORDS: Minutes, correspondence, financial records, reports, briefs, 1988-1991; mailing lists, 1989-1991; pamphlets, 1990; press releases, newsletters, photographs, 1989-1990; banners, 1989; clippings, 1988-1990.

AMOUNT: 1 filing cabinet.

CONDITION: Good.

ACCESS: Permission required. Membership and mailing lists closed.

922. Fédération nationale des femmes canadiennes-françaises (Gravelbourg, Sask.)

✤ Gravelbourg (Sask.). Groupe fondé 1968.

La Fédération nationale des femmes canadiennes-françaises (FNFCF) vise à valoriser la femme, favoriser son autonomie financière et l'égalité juridique et reconnaître l'importance de la famille, de la femme collaboratrice et de la spiritualité. La FNFCF s'appelait auparavant la Fédération des femmes canadiennes-françaises (FFCF).

LIEU DE CONSULTATION : Fédération nationale des femmes canadiennes-françaises. [*Adresse postale* : C.P. 367, Gravelbourg (Sask.) S0H 1X0. *Téléphone* : (306) 648-3233.]

MATÉRIEL : Statuts et règlements, procès-verbaux, correspondance, journaux de bord, documents financiers, demandes de subvention, dossiers con-

cernant la clientèle, listes de membres, pétitions, albums de coupures, rapports, communiqués de presse, 1968-1991; bannières, 1990.
QUANTITÉ: 2 tiroirs de classeur.
ÉTAT: Bon.

923. Integrity Regina

✢ Regina, Sask. Formed 1984.

This is the Regina chapter of Integrity, an international organization of gay and lesbian Anglicans and their friends. The Regina chapter was called the Gay Religious Group of Regina until 1989.

LOCATION OF RECORDS: Integrity Regina. [*Mailing Address:* P.O. Box 4031, Regina, Sask. S4P 3R9. *Telephone:* (306) 569-2974.]

RECORDS: Constitution, 1989; minutes, financial records, membership lists, reports, 1984-1991; correspondence, 1988-1991; pamphlets, 1988.

AMOUNT: 2 boxes.
CONDITION: Good.
ACCESS: Permission required.

924. Iskwew

✢ Prince Albert, Sask. Formed 1988.

Sponsored by the Prince Albert Co-operative Health Centre, Iskwew (also known as Women Helping Women) is a project designed to meet the needs of abused women and their children. The services, offered in English and Cree, include mutual-help groups, networking, public education, and advocacy.

LOCATION OF RECORDS: Iskwew. [*Address:* c/o Co-operative Health Centre, 110 - 8th St. E., Prince Albert, Sask. S6V 0V7. *Telephone:* (306) 953-6229. *Fax:* (306) 953-2919.]

RECORDS: Minutes, log-books, financial records, grant applications, client records, scrapbooks, reports, 1988-1991; correspondence, articles, 1989-1991; pamphlets, posters, buttons, 1988; press releases, 1988-1990; banner, 1991; photographs, 1988-1989; clippings.

AMOUNT: 1 filing cabinet.
CONDITION: Good.
ACCESS: Permission required. Client files closed.

925. La Ronge Native Women's Council

✢ La Ronge, Sask. Formed 1973.

The La Ronge Native Women's Council (LRNWC) runs an emergency shelter for battered women and their children. LRNWC also provides support services to Native people, promotes a better understanding of Native women, and works toward the elimination of stereotyping and discrimination against Native people. Until 1988 it was called the La Ronge Native Women's Organization.

LOCATION OF RECORDS: La Ronge Native Women's Council. [*Mailing Address:* Box 888, La Ronge, Sask. S0J 1L0. *Telephone:* (306) 425-3900. *Fax:* (306) 425-4922.]

RECORDS: Constitution, minutes, correspondence, financial records, client records, reports, 1986-1991; grant applications, 1973-1991; pamphlets, buttons, T-shirts, 1991; press releases, 1990-1991.

AMOUNT: 3 filing cabinets.
ACCESS: Permission required.

926. Lesbian/Gay Pride Planning Committee (Regina, Sask.)

✢ Regina, Sask. Formed 1989.

This committee organizes annual events to celebrate lesbian and gay pride.

LOCATION OF RECORDS: Lesbian/Gay Pride Planning Committee. [*Mailing Address:* Box 482, Regina, Sask. S4P 3A2. *Telephone:* (306) 522-8307.]

RECORDS: Minutes, correspondence, 1990-1991; financial records, posters, clippings, photographs, 1989-1991.

AMOUNT: 1 box.
CONDITION: Good.
ACCESS: Permission required.

927. Moose Jaw Transition House

✢ Moose Jaw, Sask. Formed [197-].

The Moose Jaw Transition House provides short-term housing and other services to women and their children fleeing family violence, marriage breakdown, or other personal crises.

LOCATION OF RECORDS: Moose Jaw Transition House. [*Mailing Address:* P.O. Box 1866, Moose Jaw, Sask. S6H 7N6. *Telephone:* (306) 693-6511.]

RECORDS: Minutes, 1977-1991; correspondence, log-books, financial records, client records, 1979-1991; scrapbooks, pamphlets, clippings, 1981-1991; posters, T-shirts, 1988-1991; buttons, 1987-1991; videotapes, 1989-1991.

AMOUNT: Approx. 3 filing cabinets, 2 boxes.
CONDITION: Good.
ACCESS: Permission required. Client files closed.

928. North East Crisis Intervention Centre

✢ Melfort, Sask. Formed 1984.

The North East Crisis Intervention Centre (NECIC) provides support services to victims of family and personal violence. It also promotes positive social change. It was originally called the Melfort Sexual Assault and Information Centre.

LOCATION OF RECORDS: North East Crisis Intervention Centre. [*Mailing Address:* P.O. Box 2066, Melfort, Sask. S0E 1A0. *Telephone:* (306) 752-9464.]

RECORDS: Correspondence, financial records, grant applications, client records, scrapbooks, reports, clippings, photographs, 1984-1991; minutes, membership lists, mailing lists, pamphlets.

CONDITION: Good.
ACCESS: Permission required. Client files closed.

929. One Sky

✢ Saskatoon, Sask. Formed 1973.

One Sky (also known as the Saskatchewan Cross-Cultural Centre) is a development education centre, library, and bookstore which specializes in issues relating to developing countries, women, and Native people.

LOCATION OF RECORDS: One Sky. [*Address:* 136 Avenue F South, Saskatoon, Sask. S7M 1S8. *Telephone:* (306) 652-1571. *Fax:* (306) 652-8377.]

RECORDS: Constitution, minutes, financial records, grant applications, reports, pamphlets, 1973-1991; newsletters, 1981-1991; membership lists, mailing lists.

AMOUNT: Approx. 1 filing cabinet.
CONDITION: Good.
ACCESS: Permission required.

930. Perceptions: The Gay and Lesbian Newsmagazine of the Prairies

✣ Saskatoon, Sask. Formed 1984.

Perceptions provides lesbians and gay men of the prairies with news of events that affect their lives.

LOCATION OF RECORDS: Perceptions: The Gay and Lesbian Newsmagazine of the Prairies. [*Mailing Address:* P.O. Box 8581, Saskatoon, Sask. S7K 6K7. *Telephone:* (306) 244-1930.]

RECORDS: Periodicals (*Perceptions*, 1984-1991); minutes, correspondence, 1984-1991; mailing lists.

AMOUNT: 1 filing cabinet.

CONDITION: Good.

ACCESS: Permission required.

931. Photographers Gallery

✣ Saskatoon, Sask. Formed 1971.

The Photographers Gallery holds photographic exhibitions by contemporary Canadian photographers, runs photography workshops and classes, has a library and permanent collection, and publishes a quarterly magazine, *Blackflash*. Many of its programmes deal with women's issues, and *Blackflash* often profiles the work of Canadian women photographers.

LOCATION OF RECORDS: Photographers Gallery. [*Address:* 12 - 23rd St. E., 2nd Floor, Saskatoon, Sask. S7K 0H5. *Telephone:* (306) 244-8018. *Fax:* (306) 665-6568.]

RECORDS: Constitution, minutes, correspondence, financial records, grant applications, client records, membership lists, mailing lists, scrapbooks, reports, briefs, pamphlets, flyers, press releases, posters, T-shirts, 1971-1991; periodicals (*Blackflash*, 1984-1991); newsletters, [197-]-1991; clippings, photographs, videotapes.

AMOUNT: 1 storage room, 4 filing cabinets, 2 shelves.

ACCESS: Permission required.

932. Planned Parenthood Regina

✣ Regina, Sask. Formed 1986.

Planned Parenthood Regina (PPR) promotes an informed understanding of human sexuality and the adoption of birth planning as a means of improving the quality of life.

LOCATION OF RECORDS: Planned Parenthood Regina. [*Address:* 201 - 1808 Smith St., Regina, Sask. S4P 2N4. *Telephone:* (306) 522-0902.]

RECORDS: Constitution, minutes, correspondence, log-books, financial records, grant applications, client records, membership lists, mailing lists, reports, briefs, pamphlets, press releases, T-shirts, banners, newsletters, clippings, photographs, 1986-1991.

AMOUNT: 1 filing cabinet.

CONDITION: Good.

ACCESS: Permission required. Client files closed.

933. Planned Parenthood Saskatoon Centre

✣ Saskatoon, Sask. Formed 1971.

Planned Parenthood Saskatoon Centre (PPSC) supports universal access to reliable information and services which enhance sexual health and family planning.

LOCATION OF RECORDS: Planned Parenthood Saskatoon Centre. [*Mailing Address:* Box 8355, Saskatoon, Sask. S7K 6C6. *Telephone:* (306) 244-7989.]

RECORDS: Constitution, minutes, 1971-1991; correspondence, financial records, client records, 1980-1991; grant applications, 1985; membership lists, press releases, 1985-1991; mailing lists, 1989-1991; reports, 1984-1991; briefs, 1990; newsletters (*Planned Parenthood Newsletter*, 1990; *The Planner*, 1985); sound recordings, 1981; videotapes, 1986; pamphlets, posters.

CONDITION: Fair.

ACCESS: Permission required. Client files closed.

934. Provincial Association of Transition Houses of Saskatchewan

✣ Saskatoon, Sask. Formed 1984.

The Provincial Association of Transition Houses of Saskatchewan (PATHS) represents transition and interval houses, safe homes, shelters, agencies working in the field of family violence, and concerned individuals. Networking, public education, and advocacy are the association's main activities.

LOCATION OF RECORDS: Provincial Association of Transition Houses of Saskatchewan. [*Address:* 307 - 135 21st St. E., Saskatoon, Sask. S7K 0B4. *Telephone:* (306) 652-6175.]

RECORDS: Constitution, 1987-1991; minutes, grant applications, membership lists, mailing lists, 1985-1991; correspondence, financial records, 1984-1991; briefs, 1985, 1987-1991; conference proceedings, pamphlets, posters, 1989-1991; manual, 1990; books.

AMOUNT: 2 filing cabinets.

CONDITION: Good.

ACCESS: Permission required.

935. Regina Women's Community Centre and Sexual Assault Line

✣ Regina, Sask. Formed 1975.

The Regina Women's Community Centre and Sexual Assault Line works toward a non-violent, equitable society by empowering women who have suffered various forms of abuse and by doing community education and advocacy. It was originally called simply the Regina Women's Community Centre; in 1977 it was renamed the Regina Women's Community Centre and Rape Crisis Line; and in 1983 the present name was adopted.

LOCATION OF RECORDS: Regina Women's Community Centre and Sexual Assault Line. [*Address:* #306 - 2505 - 11th Ave., Regina, Sask. S4P 0K6. *Telephone:* (306) 522-2777.]

RECORDS: Minutes, log-books, 1975-1991; financial records, 1984-1991; grant applications, 1985-1991; client records, 1988-1991; membership lists, mailing lists, 1987-1991; buttons, 1983; banners, 1990; newsletters, 1988-1989; constitution, correspondence, reports, briefs, conference proceedings, pamphlets, flyers, press releases, posters, clippings.

AMOUNT: 5 filing cabinets.

CONDITION: Good.

ACCESS: Permission required. Client files closed.

936. Regina Young Women's Christian Association

[See also entry # 259 (in Part I), which lists other records of this organization.]

✣ Regina, Sask. Formed 1910.

The Regina YWCA works to improve the status of women. It operates a shelter for abused women (the Isobel Johnson Shelter) and offers child-care and residential services.

LOCATION OF RECORDS: Regina Young Women's Christian Association. [*Address:* 1940 McIntyre St., Regina, Sask. S4P 2R3. *Telephone:* (306) 525-2141. *Fax:* (306) 522-7688.]

RECORDS: Minutes, 1985-1986, 1988-1991; financial records, 1970-1991; grant applications, 1988-1991; constitution, 1985; correspondence, log-books, client records, membership lists, scrapbooks, reports, flyers, press releases, posters, buttons, T-shirts, banners, clippings, photographs.

AMOUNT: 1 storage room.

CONDITION: Fair.

ACCESS: Permission required. Client files closed.

937. Saskatchewan Action Committee, Status of Women

[See also entry # 260 (in Part I), which lists other records of this organization.]

✣ Regina, Sask. Formed 1973.

This organization (also known as SAC) brings women together to work toward economic, social, and political justice. Education and lobbying are its main activities. SAC has also been called the Status of Women Society.

LOCATION OF RECORDS: Saskatchewan Action Committee, Status of Women. [*Address:* 2343 Cornwall St., Regina, Sask. S4P 2L4. *Telephone:* (306) 525-8329. *Fax:* (306) 757-4548.]

RECORDS: Constitution, 1979-1991; grant applications, 1985-1991; membership lists, mailing lists, 1989-1991; reports, 1986-1991; briefs, 1983-1991; press releases, 1987-1991; newsletters (*Network of Saskatchewan Women*, 1972-1991; *Action*, 1990-1991); scrapbooks, clippings, [198-].

AMOUNT: Approx. 6 filing cabinets.

CONDITION: Fair.

938. Saskatchewan Interfacing Law and Sociology

✣ Saskatoon, Sask. Formed 1981.

Saskatchewan Interfacing Law and Sociology (SILS) does research in the combined areas of sociology and law. Its main project deals with battered women and family law, with a view to developing strategies for the women and groups involved in the family-law process.

LOCATION OF RECORDS: Saskatchewan Interfacing Law and Sociology. [*Address:* 1106 Osler St., Saskatoon, Sask. S7N 0T7. *Telephone:* (306) 242-7369.]

RECORDS: Minutes, reports, 1981-1988; correspondence, 1981-1990; grant applications, 1981-1986; mailing lists, 1981-1987; conference proceedings, 1986-1987; videotapes, 1987.

AMOUNT: Approx. 1 filing cabinet.

CONDITION: Fair.

ACCESS: Permission required. Data collected directly from clients closed.

939. Saskatchewan Teachers' Federation. Women in Education Advisory Committee

✣ Saskatoon, Sask. Formed 1976.

This committee, also known as WIE, promotes personal and professional growth and mutual support among women teachers. It organizes conferences and advises the Saskatchewan Teachers' Federation (STF) on women's issues. [See also Saskatchewan Teachers' Federation. Saskatoon Women Teachers' Local (265).]

LOCATION OF RECORDS: Saskatchewan Teachers' Federation. Women in Education Advisory Committee. [*Address:* 2317 Arlington Ave., Saskatoon, Sask. S7J 2H8. *Telephone:* (306) 373-1660. *Fax:* (306) 374-1122.]

RECORDS: Constitution, 1976-1990; minutes, grant applications, conference proceedings, clippings, 1975-1991; correspondence, financial records, reports, 1976-1991; mailing lists, 1980; briefs, discussion papers, policy papers, 1977-1979, 1982-1983, 1985-1986; pamphlets, 1977-1991; books, 1988; seminar programmes, 1985, 1987, 1989.

CONDITION: Good.

ACCESS: Permission required.

940. Saskatchewan Women's Agricultural Network

✣ Saskatoon, Sask. Formed 1985.

The main activities of the Saskatchewan Women's Agricultural Network (SWAN) are networking, advocacy, and education. SWAN is a member of the Canadian Farm Women's Network.

LOCATION OF RECORDS: Saskatchewan Women's Agricultural Network. [*Mailing Address:* Box 9738, Saskatoon, Sask. S7K 7G5. *Telephone:* (306) 257-3911. *Fax:* (306) 257-3911.]

RECORDS: Constitution, 1985; minutes, correspondence, financial records, grant applications, membership lists, mailing lists, scrapbooks, reports, newsletters, clippings, photographs, 1985-1991; briefs, 1990; buttons, 1988; T-shirts, banners, 1988-1991.

AMOUNT: 3 boxes.

CONDITION: Good.

ACCESS: Permission required.

941. Saskatchewan Women's Institutes

[See also entry # 267 (in Part I), which lists other records of this organization.]

✣ Saskatoon, Sask. Formed 1911.

The Saskatchewan Women's Institutes (SWI) is a voluntary educational organization with branches in rural communities throughout Saskatchewan. SWI works toward the equality of women and the improvement of rural communities. Until 1971 it was called the Association of Homemakers' Clubs of Saskatchewan.

LOCATION OF RECORDS: Saskatchewan Women's Institutes. [*Address:* Room 137, Kirk Hall, University of Saskatchewan, Saskatoon, Sask. S7N 0W0. *Telephone:* (306) 966-5566.]

RECORDS: Minutes, conference proceedings, 1972-1991; correspondence, 1989-1991; financial records, 1984-1991; grant applications, 1988-1991; books, 1911-1988; newsletters (*Second Penny*, 1964-1991; *Brown Envelope*, 1988-1991); membership lists, mailing lists, pamphlets, buttons, photographs.

AMOUNT: Approx. 3 shelves.

CONDITION: Good.

ACCESS: Permission required. Financial records closed, except with permission of president.

942. Saskatchewan Women's Resources

✣ Regina, Sask. Formed 1984.

Saskatchewan Women's Resources provides services to women's organizations wishing to improve their effectiveness. It offers board or staff members assistance with organizational development, evaluation, research, and skill development.

LOCATION OF RECORDS: Saskatchewan Women's Resources. [*Address:* 2398 Scarth St., Regina, Sask. S4P 2J7. *Telephone:* (306) 522-2656.]

RECORDS: Minutes, correspondence, log-books, financial records, grant applications, client records, membership lists, mailing lists, reports, 1984-1991; handbooks.

AMOUNT: 3 filing cabinets.

CONDITION: Good.

ACCESS: Permission required. Client files closed.

SASKATCHEWAN

943. Saskatoon Abortion Rights Association
✣ Saskatoon, Sask. Formed 1983.

Through education, lobbying, and public action, the Saskatoon Abortion Rights Association (SARA) works to improve women's access to abortion services and to ensure women's right to choose in all aspects of reproductive health.

LOCATION OF RECORDS: Saskatoon Abortion Rights Association. [*Mailing Address:* Box 7586, Saskatoon, Sask. S7K 4R4.]

RECORDS: Minutes, correspondence, financial records, membership lists, mailing lists, petitions, scrapbooks, reports, briefs, conference proceedings, pamphlets, flyers, press releases, posters, buttons, T-shirts, banners, 1983-1991; videotapes, 1982; newsletters, clippings, photographs, sound recordings.

AMOUNT: 1 filing cabinet.

CONDITION: Good.

ACCESS: Permission required. Tribunal testimony and letters which identify individuals closed.

944. Saskatoon Interval House
✣ Saskatoon, Sask. Formed 1973.

This emergency shelter offers safe accommodation, counselling, and other services to abused women, with or without children. It was originally sponsored by the Women Alone Society, which has since disbanded.

LOCATION OF RECORDS: Saskatoon Interval House. [*Telephone:* (306) 244-0185.]

RECORDS: Correspondence, log-books, financial records, grant applications, client records, membership lists, pamphlets, press releases, posters, buttons, clippings, 1973-1991; by-laws, scrapbooks, photographs.

CONDITION: Good.

ACCESS: Permission required. Client files closed.

945. Saskatoon Sexual Assault and Information Centre
✣ Saskatoon, Sask. Formed 1975.

This centre provides information and support to victims of sexual assault and works to increase public awareness of this crime. It used to be known as the Saskatoon Rape Crisis Centre.

LOCATION OF RECORDS: Saskatoon Sexual Assault and Information Centre. [*Address:* 302 - 115 2nd Ave. N., Saskatoon, Sask. S7K 2B1. *Telephone:* (306) 244-2294.]

RECORDS: Minutes, correspondence, financial records, grant applications, membership lists, reports, 1975-1991; client records, 1989-1991; mailing lists, 1985-1991; constitution, briefs, pamphlets, posters.

CONDITION: Fair.

ACCESS: Permission required. Client files closed.

946. Saskatoon Women's Charities
✣ Saskatoon, Sask. Formed 1987.

Saskatoon Women's Charities (SWC) is comprised of a number of Saskatoon organizations which provide services to women. SWC works to make these services more accessible, avoid duplication of space and resources, and increase public awareness of the individual and collective work of the agencies. SWC used to be called the Saskatoon Women's Service Coalition.

LOCATION OF RECORDS: Saskatoon Women's Charities. [*Address:* #307 - 135 - 21st St. E., Saskatoon, Sask. S7K 0B4. *Telephone:* (306) 934-4606.]

RECORDS: Constitution, 1988; minutes, correspondence, membership lists, mailing lists, reports, 1987-1991; financial records, 1988-1991; grant applications, 1988-1990.

AMOUNT: 1 drawer of a filing cabinet.

CONDITION: Good.

947. Saskatoon Women's Network
✣ Saskatoon, Sask. Formed 1983.

The Saskatoon Women's Network (SWN) provides working women, including homemakers, with an opportunity to make business and social contacts. It holds workshops and other educational events, promotes networking, and provides a comfortable environment for sharing common concerns.

LOCATION OF RECORDS: Saskatoon Women's Network. [*Mailing Address:* Box 8504, Saskatoon, Sask. S7K 6K5. *Telephone:* (306) 933-3393.]

RECORDS: Constitution, 1983; minutes, 1983-1991; financial records, scrapbooks, 1986-1991; membership lists, mailing lists, pamphlets, newsletters, clippings, photographs.

ACCESS: Permission required.

948. Southwest Crisis Services
✣ Swift Current, Sask. Formed 1984.

Southwest Crisis Services co-ordinates services to victims of personal and family violence, providing shelter and undertaking research and education. The organization grew out of the Swift Current Sexual Assault and Information Centre and the Southwest Action Group for Battered Women.

LOCATION OF RECORDS: Southwest Crisis Services. [*Mailing Address:* Box 1102, Swift Current, Sask. S9H 3X3. *Telephone:* (306) 778-3386.]

RECORDS: Constitution, 1984; minutes, correspondence, financial records, 1984-1991; client records, membership lists, reports, 1985-1991; banners, 1991; grant applications, pamphlets, press releases, T-shirts, clippings, photographs.

AMOUNT: 2 filing cabinets.

CONDITION: Good.

ACCESS: Permission required. Client and personnel files closed.

949. University of Saskatchewan. Women's Centre
✣ Saskatoon, Sask. Formed 1983.

The University of Saskatchewan Women's Centre promotes women's social, personal, and political autonomy by offering support to women on campus and providing information and referral on women's issues. The centre is part of the University of Saskatchewan Students' Union (USSU) and is sometimes called the USSU Women's Centre. It has a connection to an earlier organization, the Women's Directorate, which existed from 1971 to 1979.

LOCATION OF RECORDS: University of Saskatchewan. Women's Centre. [*Address:* Room 65, Place Riel, Saskatoon, Sask. S7N 0W0. *Telephone:* (306) 966-6980.]

RECORDS: Constitution, correspondence, log-books, 1983-1991; minutes, financial records, posters, 1986-1991; grant applications, 1989; membership lists, 1987-1991; mailing lists, pamphlets, press releases, 1989-1991; petitions, 1990; reports, clippings, photographs, 1971-1991; buttons, T-shirts, 1988-1991; newsletters (*Womynews*, 1989-1990).

AMOUNT: 1 filing cabinet.

CONDITION: Good.

950. University of Saskatchewan. Women's Studies Research Unit

✣ Saskatoon, Sask. Formed 1986.

The Women's Studies Research Unit (WSRU) at the University of Saskatchewan promotes scholarly research by, for, and about women. WSRU helps researchers develop proposals and obtain grants, promotes gender equity, and encourages interdisciplinary research.

LOCATION OF RECORDS: University of Saskatchewan. Women's Studies Research Unit. [*Address:* 200 Kirk Hall, Saskatoon, Sask. S7N 0W0. *Telephone:* (306) 966-7524.]

RECORDS: Constitution, 1986; minutes, correspondence, membership lists, reports, flyers, newsletters, 1986-1991; financial records, 1987-1991; briefs, 1991; conference proceedings, book, 1988; press releases, 1987-1988; grant applications.

AMOUNT: 1 filing cabinet.

CONDITION: Good.

ACCESS: Permission required. Confidential material will not be released without the permission of the parties involved and the membership.

951. Women in Science Network (University of Saskatchewan)

✣ Saskatoon, Sask. Formed 1990.

The Women in Science Network (WISN) provides a forum for the exchange of ideas, concerns, and suggestions among women working in science at the University of Saskatchewan. Its goal is to develop a network of all women working in science at the university, in order to facilitate all aspects of professional growth.

LOCATION OF RECORDS: Women in Science Network. [*Address:* University of Saskatchewan, Dept. of Crop Science and Pl. Ecology, Saskatoon, Sask. S7N 0W0. *Telephone:* (306) 966-8584. *Fax:* (306) 966-5015.]

RECORDS: Minutes, membership lists, 1990-1991; correspondence, 1990; financial records, 1991.

AMOUNT: 1 drawer of a filing cabinet.

CONDITION: Good.

ACCESS: Permission required.

952. Women Working Together

✣ Lloydminster, Sask. Formed 1991.

This group studies and addresses issues relating to women. Its activities include workshops and organizational development.

LOCATION OF RECORDS: Women Working Together. [*Address:* c/o Border City Métis Society, 4608 - 50th St., Lloydminster, Sask. S9V 1B8. *Telephone:* (306) 825-8855.]

RECORDS: Minutes, correspondence, grant applications, membership lists, mailing lists, 1991.

AMOUNT: 1 file.

CONDITION: Good.

ACCESS: Permission of committee members required.

953. Working for Women

✣ Saskatoon, Sask. Formed 1980.

Working for Women helps women overcome barriers to personal and economic independence. Most of the organization's programmes focus on improving women's employment opportunities.

LOCATION OF RECORDS: Working for Women. [*Address:* # 203 - 315 - 22nd St. E., Saskatoon, Sask. S7K 0G6. *Telephone:* (306) 665-2802.]

RECORDS: By-laws, minutes, correspondence, scrapbooks, reports, 1980-1991; videotapes, 1986; briefs, pamphlets, press releases.

AMOUNT: Approx. 6 filing cabinets.

CONDITION: Good.

ACCESS: Permission required. Client files closed.

954. Young Women's Christian Association of Prince Albert

✣ Prince Albert, Sask. Formed 1912.

The YWCA of Prince Albert operates a shelter for women and children, offers courses for educational and personal development, and provides a variety of other practical services for women.

LOCATION OF RECORDS: Young Women's Christian Association of Prince Albert. [*Address:* 1895 Central Ave. "B" W., Prince Albert, Sask. S6V 4W8. *Telephone:* (306) 763-8571.]

RECORDS: Constitutions, 1983, 1987; minutes, [196-]-1991; correspondence, log-books, financial records, client records, conference proceedings, 1983-1991; membership lists, 1986-1991; mailing lists, 1988-1991; scrapbooks, [195-]-1990; reports, 1983-1990; briefs, press releases, posters, 1988-1990; flyers, 1986-1990; clippings, photographs, [195-]-1991; organization history, 1912-1987; grant applications, petitions, pamphlets.

AMOUNT: 3 filing cabinets, 1 bookcase, 12 boxes.

ACCESS: Permission required.

MANITOBA

955. Brandon University. Status of Women Organization
✣ Brandon, Man. Formed 1986.

The Brandon University Status of Women Organization (BUSWO) promotes gender equality on campus through the discussion of women's issues, support of women's rights, and promotion of women's studies.

LOCATION OF RECORDS: Brandon University. Status of Women Organization. [*Address:* Brandon, Man. R7A 6A9. *Telephone:* (204) 727-9635. *Fax:* (204) 726-4573.]

RECORDS: Constitution, 1986; minutes, correspondence, financial records, grant applications, membership lists, mailing lists, reports, 1986-1991; briefs, 1989-1990; conference proceedings, videotapes, 1987, 1990.

AMOUNT: Approx. 1 drawer of a filing cabinet.

CONDITION: Good.

ACCESS: Permission required.

956. Congress of Black Women of Canada. Manitoba Chapter
✣ Winnipeg, Man. Formed 1981.

This organization was established to enhance the consciousness, education, and rights of Black women in Manitoba, through networking, education, and working toward constructive change affecting Black women.

LOCATION OF RECORDS: Congress of Black Women of Canada. Manitoba Chapter. [*Mailing Address:* P.O. Box 315, St Vital, Winnipeg, Man. R2M 5C8.]

RECORDS: Constitution, minutes, correspondence, financial records, grant applications, membership lists, mailing lists, scrapbooks, reports, briefs, conference proceedings, pamphlets, flyers, posters, buttons, T-shirts, banners, newsletters, books, photographs, videotapes.

AMOUNT: 2 drawers of a filing cabinet.

CONDITION: Good.

957. December 6th Women's Memorial Committee
✣ Winnipeg, Man. Formed 1989.

This committee works toward ending violence against women and making women full and equal members of society. It is creating a memorial garden on the grounds of the Manitoba Legislature to celebrate the lives and rights of Manitoba women.

LOCATION OF RECORDS: December 6th Women's Memorial Committee. [*Mailing Address:* Sherbrook Westminster, P.O. Box 26033, Winnipeg, Man. R3C 2B0. *Telephone:* (204) 477-4498.]

RECORDS: Minutes, correspondence, financial records, membership lists, clippings, 1989-1991; mailing lists, 1991; petitions, 1990-1991; press releases, posters, buttons, T-shirts, sweatshirts, photographs, 1990.

AMOUNT: One drawer of a filing cabinet.

CONDITION: Good.

ACCESS: Permission required.

958. Fort Garry Women's Resource Centre
✣ Winnipeg, Man. Formed 1983.

This resource centre (also known as FGWRC) provides women with information, referrals, counselling, opportunities for personal growth, and links with other agencies.

LOCATION OF RECORDS: Fort Garry Women's Resource Centre. [*Address:* 1910 Pembina Highway, Winnipeg, Man. R3T 4S5. *Telephone:* (204) 269-6836.]

RECORDS: By-laws, 1983-1984; minutes, 1984-1991; client records, 1986-1991; banners, 1989-1990; newsletters (*Making Waves*, 1989-1991); correspondence, financial records, grant applications, membership lists, mailing lists, reports, pamphlets, flyers, press releases, posters, clippings, photographs.

AMOUNT: Approx. 4 filing cabinets.

CONDITION: Good.

ACCESS: Permission required. Client files closed.

959. Herstory
✣ Winnipeg, Man. Formed 1988.

Herstory is a programme developed by women of the Augustine United Church in order to share stories of personal and spiritual growth. The women tell their life stories and record them for possible publication.

LOCATION OF RECORDS: Herstory. [*Address:* c/o Augustine United Church, 444 River Ave., Winnipeg, Man. R3L 0C7. *Telephone:* (204) 284-2250.]

RECORDS: Sound recordings, 1988-1991.

AMOUNT: 15 sound recordings.

CONDITION: Good.

ACCESS: Permission required. Tapes available only with consent of storytellers.

960. Immigrant Women's Association of Manitoba

✣ Winnipeg, Man. Formed 1983.

The Immigrant Women's Association of Manitoba (IWAM) promotes the full integration of immigrant women as equal partners in society, through workshops, settlement education, and other services. IWAM also has chapters in Thompson, Brandon, and Portage la Prairie.

LOCATION OF RECORDS: Immigrant Women's Association of Manitoba. [*Address:* 201 - 323 Portage Ave., Winnipeg, Man. R3B 2C1. *Telephone:* (204) 943-8612.]

RECORDS: Constitution, 1983; minutes, correspondence, financial records, 1989-1991; membership lists, mailing lists, briefs, 1983-1991; pamphlets, 1988; T-shirts, 1990; client records.

CONDITION: Good.

ACCESS: Permission required. Client files closed. No access to clients' or members' names.

961. Immigrant Women's Association of Manitoba. Thompson Chapter

✣ Thompson, Man. Formed 1984.

LOCATION OF RECORDS: Immigrant Women's Association of Manitoba. Thompson Chapter. [*Mailing Address:* P.O. Box 1153, Thompson, Man. R8N 1N9. *Telephone:* (204) 677-4205.]

RECORDS: Constitution, minutes, correspondence, financial records, membership lists, conference proceedings, pamphlets, 1985-1991; newsletters.

CONDITION: Good.

ACCESS: Permission required.

962. Indigenous Women's Collective of Manitoba

✣ Winnipeg, Man. Formed 1985.

The collective plays a leading role in representing Native women and their children in Manitoba. Its main activity is government lobbying.

LOCATION OF RECORDS: Indigenous Women's Collective of Manitoba. [*Address:* 120 - 388 Donald St., Winnipeg, Man. R3B 2J4. *Telephone:* (204) 944-8709. *Fax:* (204) 949-1336.]

RECORDS: Minutes, correspondence, log-books, financial records, grant applications, membership lists, mailing lists, petitions, scrapbooks, reports, briefs, conference proceedings, pamphlets, flyers, press releases, posters, buttons, T-shirts, banners, clippings, 1985-1991; constitution, sound recordings, videotapes, films.

AMOUNT: 1 room.

CONDITION: Good.

ACCESS: Permission required. Some records may be restricted.

963. Lundar / Eriksdale / Ashern Wife Abuse Committee

✣ Ashern, Man. Formed 1975.

This committee (also known as the LEA Wife Abuse Committee) provides front-line intervention and transportation for women and their children who have been victims of family violence. It also does advocacy and public education.

LOCATION OF RECORDS: Lundar/Eriksdale/Ashern Wife Abuse Committee. [*Mailing Address:* Box 628, Ashern, Man. R0C 0E0. *Telephone:* (204) 768-3016.]

RECORDS: Constitution, 1984; minutes, financial records, client records, 1984-1991; correspondence, grant applications, 1986-1991; membership lists, mailing lists, 1991; reports, 1988-1991; briefs, 1989-1991; pamphlets, 1987-1991.

AMOUNT: 1 filing cabinet.

CONDITION: Good.

ACCESS: Permission required. Client files closed.

964. Manitoba Action Committee on the Status of Women

[See also entry # 305 (in Part I), which lists other records of this organization.]

✣ Winnipeg, Man. Formed 1967.

The Manitoba Action Committee on the Status of Women (MACSW) aims to improve attitudes toward women, raise issues affecting women, and promote equality. It works to achieve these aims through political action, public education, and personal growth. MACSW was originally called the Manitoba Committee on the Status of Women, then became the Manitoba Volunteer Committee on the Status of Women, and finally adopted its present name in 1971. Its French name is le Comité d'action manitobain sur le statut de la femme. [See also Parkland Status of Women (979).]

LOCATION OF RECORDS: Manitoba Action Committee on the Status of Women. [*Address:* 16 - 222 Osborne St. S., Winnipeg, Man. R3L 1Z3. *Telephone:* (204) 453-3879.]

RECORDS: Constitution, minutes, correspondence, grant applications, membership lists, mailing lists, reports, briefs, conference proceedings, pamphlets, press releases, posters, T-shirts, banners, clippings, photographs, sound recordings, videotapes, 1971-1991; financial records, 1984-1991; newsletters (*Action*, 1973-1991).

AMOUNT: Approx. 8 filing cabinets.

CONDITION: Good.

ACCESS: Permission required. Membership lists closed.

965. Manitoba Child Care Association

✣ Winnipeg, Man. Formed 1974.

The Manitoba Child Care Association (MCCA) works to promote and advance child care as a profession and as a service. MCCA is a non-profit organization funded by its members.

LOCATION OF RECORDS: Manitoba Child Care Association. [*Address:* 364 McGregor St., Winnipeg, Man. R2W 4X3. *Telephone:* (204) 586-8587. *Fax:* (204) 589-5613.]

RECORDS: Constitution, minutes, correspondence, financial records, 1974-1991; grant applications, 1981-1991; client records, membership lists, mailing lists, pamphlets, flyers, press releases, photographs, 1984-1991; scrapbooks, briefs, clippings, 1977-1991; reports, 1975-1991; newsletters (*Child Care Focus*, 1975-1991); videotapes, 1989.

AMOUNT: 5 filing cabinets, 20 boxes.

CONDITION: Good.

ACCESS: Permission required. Member files closed.

966. Manitoba Coalition for Reproductive Choice

✣ Winnipeg, Man. Formed 1982.

The Manitoba Coalition for Reproductive Choice (CRC) works for the recognition of abortion as a regular medical service funded by medicare and available to all Canadian women. Public education and political action are CRC's main activities.

LOCATION OF RECORDS: Manitoba Coalition for Reproductive Choice. [*Mailing Address:* P.O. Box 51, Station L, Winnipeg, Man. R3H 0Z4. *Telephone:* (204) 453-7774.]

RECORDS: Constitution, 1982; minutes, correspondence, log-books, financial records, membership lists, mailing lists, petitions, scrapbooks, flyers, press releases, posters, buttons, T-shirts, banners, 1982-1991; grant applications, pamphlets, 1984-1991; reports, briefs, newsletters, 1989-1991; photographs, 1989; sound recordings, 1990; videotapes, 1990-1991; clippings.

AMOUNT: Approx. 1 filing cabinet, 9 shelves.

CONDITION: Fair.

ACCESS: Permission required.

967. Manitoba Federation of Labour. Women's Committee

[See also entry # 308 (in Part I), which lists other records of this organization.]

✣ Winnipeg, Man. Formed [1975?].

The Manitoba Federation of Labour (MFL) Women's Committee works to develop an awareness of women's issues within the trade-union movement and in society at large. It also lobbies the provincial government on women's issues. Prior to 1985, it was known as the MFL Equal Rights and Opportunities Committee.

LOCATION OF RECORDS: Manitoba Federation of Labour. Women's Committee. [*Address:* 101 - 275 Broadway Ave., Winnipeg, Man. R3C 4M6. *Telephone:* (204) 947-1400. *Fax:* (204) 943-4276.]

RECORDS: Minutes, correspondence, financial records, grant applications, membership lists, mailing lists, petitions, reports, briefs, conference proceedings, pamphlets, press releases, posters, buttons, 1975-1991; newsletters (*UnionWomen*, 1985-1991); videotapes, 1991.

AMOUNT: Approx. 1 filing cabinet.

ACCESS: Permission required.

968. Manitoba Homebirth Network

✣ Winnipeg, Man. Formed 1987.

The Manitoba Homebirth Network (MHN) provides support and educational materials to parents and other individuals interested in home birth and midwifery.

LOCATION OF RECORDS: Manitoba Homebirth Network. [*Address:* c/o 1119 Manitoba Ave., Winnipeg, Man. R2X 0K6.]

RECORDS: Constitution, minutes, correspondence, financial records, membership lists, mailing lists, petitions, scrapbooks, banners, newsletters, clippings, 1987-1991; press releases, 1989-1990; T-shirts, 1990-1991.

AMOUNT: Approx. 1 drawer of a filing cabinet.

CONDITION: Good.

ACCESS: Permission required.

969. Manitoba Teachers' Society

[See also entry # 312 (in Part I), which lists other records of this organization.]

✣ Winnipeg, Man. Formed 1919.

Through political action, professional activities, and collective bargaining, the Manitoba Teachers' Society (MTS) works to promote education and safeguard the welfare of teachers. It was known as the Manitoba Teachers' Federation until 1942.

LOCATION OF RECORDS: Manitoba Teachers' Society. [*Address:* 191 Harcourt St., Winnipeg, Man. R3J 3H2. *Telephone:* (204) 888-7961. *Fax:* (204) 831-0877.]

RECORDS: Constitution, pamphlets, 1980-1991; minutes, [192-]-1991; correspondence, 1975-1991; financial records, [193-]-1991; client records, 1960-1991; mailing lists, 1990-1991; reports, 1950-1991; briefs, 1940-1991; membership lists, 1984-1991; newsletters (*The Manitoba Teacher*, 1919-1991; *Update*, 1981-1991); books, 1969; conference proceedings, press releases, banners, clippings, journals.

AMOUNT: Approx. 10 filing cabinets.

CONDITION: Fair.

ACCESS: Permission required. Client files closed.

970. Mentoring Artists for Women's Art

✣ Winnipeg, Man. Formed 1984.

This organization supports women visual artists and encourages their professional development. It was originally called Manitoba Artists for Women's Art and was part of Plug in Gallery. In 1990 it became independent and changed its name to Mentoring Artists for Women's Art (MAWA).

LOCATION OF RECORDS: Mentoring Artists for Women's Art. [*Address:* 175 McDermot Ave., 3rd Floor, Winnipeg, Man. R3B 0S1. *Telephone:* (204) 949-9490.]

RECORDS: Constitution, minutes, correspondence, financial records, grant applications, membership lists, mailing lists, petitions, reports, pamphlets, flyers, press releases, posters, photographs, newsletters, 1984-1991; magazines (*in versions*, 1990-1991).

AMOUNT: 2 filing cabinets.

CONDITION: Good.

ACCESS: Permission required. Personnel files and Advisory Program Evaluations closed indefinitely.

971. Minnedosa and Area Committee on Wife Abuse

✣ Minnedosa, Man. Formed 1983.

This committee provides abused women and their children with safe emergency accommodation, information, resources, and peer support.

LOCATION OF RECORDS: Minnedosa and Area Committee on Wife Abuse. [*Mailing Address:* Box 711, Minnedosa, Man. R0J 1E0. *Telephone:* (204) 867-2942.]

RECORDS: Constitution, 1983; minutes, correspondence, financial records, grant applications, membership lists, mailing lists, scrapbooks, reports, conference proceedings, pamphlets, press releases, clippings, 1983-1991; videotapes, 1985; photographs.

AMOUNT: 1 filing cabinet.

CONDITION: Good.

ACCESS: Permission required.

972. National Council of Jewish Women of Canada. Winnipeg Section

[See also entry # 315 (in Part I), which lists other records of this organization.]

✣ Winnipeg, Man. Formed 1897.

The main activities of the National Council of Jewish Women of Canada (NCJW) are education, service, and social action. While its priorities are the protection of human rights and the preservation of Jewish life, NCJW is also concerned with women's issues such as family planning, abortion, child care, pornography, and affirmative action.

LOCATION OF RECORDS: National Council of Jewish Women of Canada. Winnipeg Section. [*Address:* 1588 Main St., Winnipeg, Man. R2V 1Y3. *Telephone:* (204) 339-7291.]

RECORDS: Constitution, minutes, correspondence, financial records, grant applications, membership lists, scrapbooks, reports, briefs, conference proceedings, pamphlets, flyers, press releases, posters, banners, newsletters, books, clippings, photographs.

AMOUNT: 4 filing cabinets, approx. 8 boxes.
CONDITION: Good.
ACCESS: Permission required. Membership lists and financial information closed.

973. Native Women's Transition Centre (Winnipeg, Man.)
✣ Winnipeg, Man. Formed 1979.

This centre (also known as NWTC) offers a residential programme for Native women and their children. Counselling, life-skills programmes, and child care are provided.

LOCATION OF RECORDS: Native Women's Transition Centre. [*Address:* 105 Aikens St., Winnipeg, Man. *Telephone:* (204) 586-8487.]
RECORDS: Constitution, 1979; minutes, correspondence, 1979-1991; log-books, client records, 1986-1991; financial records, grant applications, 1981-1991; briefs, 1989-1991; press releases, 1991; T-shirts, banners, 1990; membership lists, mailing lists, reports, pamphlets, clippings, photographs.
AMOUNT: 1 closet, 3 filing cabinets.
CONDITION: Fair.
ACCESS: Permission required. Client files closed.

974. Northern Women's Resource Service
✣ Flin Flon, Man. Formed 1989.

The Northern Women's Resource Service (NWRS) is committed to improving the social, economic, and political status of women, through services such as information, support, and advocacy.

LOCATION OF RECORDS: Northern Women's Resource Service. [*Mailing Address:* Box 266, Flin Flon, Man. R8A 1M9. *Telephone:* (204) 687-3346. *Fax:* (204) 687-3322.]
RECORDS: Constitution, 1990-1991; minutes, 1986-1991; correspondence, log-books, financial records, grant applications, client records, membership lists, mailing lists, petitions, reports, pamphlets, press releases, banners, 1989-1991; conference proceedings, 1990; newsletters, 1991.
AMOUNT: 2 filing cabinets.
CONDITION: Good.
ACCESS: Permission required. Client information closed unless cleared by client.

975. Nurse-Midwives Association of Manitoba
✣ Winnipeg, Man. Formed 1989.

This association (also known as NMAM) works toward improvements in the nursing care of mothers and their newborn children, the legalization of nurse-midwifery in Manitoba, and the development of standards of practice and education for nurse-midwifery in the province.

LOCATION OF RECORDS: Nurse-Midwives Association of Manitoba. [*Mailing Address:* Norwood Post Office, P.O. Box 83, Winnipeg, Man. R2H 3B8.]
RECORDS: Constitution, 1990; minutes, 1989-1991; correspondence, financial records, membership lists, mailing lists, scrapbooks, reports, press releases, clippings, 1989; newsletters, 1990-1991.
AMOUNT: 1 filing cabinet.
CONDITION: Good.
ACCESS: Permission required. Membership registration certificates closed.

976. Original Women's Network
✣ Winnipeg, Man. Formed 1985.

The Original Women's Network (OWN) runs a resource centre for all Aboriginal women (Métis, status, and non-status) in Manitoba. OWN recognizes achievements, provides communication and support services, facilitates the development of skills, and promotes the visibility of Aboriginal women and their contributions to Canadian society.

LOCATION OF RECORDS: Original Women's Network. [*Address:* 356A Stella Ave., Winnipeg, Man. R2W 2T9. *Telephone:* (204) 582-2383. *Fax:* (204) 582-6468.]
RECORDS: Constitution, minutes, correspondence, financial records, grant applications, membership lists, mailing lists, reports, pamphlets, flyers, banners, clippings, photographs, sound recordings, videotapes, 1985-1991.
AMOUNT: 3 filing cabinets.
CONDITION: Good.
ACCESS: Permission required.

977. Osborne House
✣ Winnipeg, Man. Formed 1974.

Osborne House offers shelter, safety, and support to battered women and their children. Osborne House is part of the YM-YWCA (until 1989, the YWCA). [See also Young Women's Christian Association (Winnipeg, Man.) (340).]

LOCATION OF RECORDS: Osborne House. [*Address:* 100 - 290 Vaughan St., Winnipeg, Man. R3B 2N8. *Telephone:* (204) 942-7373. *Fax:* (204) 956-1212.]
RECORDS: Minutes, correspondence, log-books, financial records, grant applications, client records, mailing lists, scrapbooks, reports, conference proceedings, pamphlets, press releases, books, clippings, photographs, 1985-1991; newsletters, 1986-1991.
AMOUNT: 10 filing cabinets.
CONDITION: Good.
ACCESS: Permission required. Minutes, correspondence, log-books, financial records, client records, membership lists, mailing lists, and reports closed.

978. Parkland Crisis Centre
✣ Dauphin, Man. Formed 1982.

The Parkland Crisis Centre (PCC), known as the Dauphin Crisis Centre until 1987, offers temporary housing and advocacy to women and children in crisis, including victims of violence.

LOCATION OF RECORDS: Parkland Crisis Centre. [*Address:* 31 - 1st Ave. S.W., Dauphin, Man. R7N 3C8. *Telephone:* (204) 638-8707.]
RECORDS: Constitution, 1982; minutes, financial records, client records, reports, 1982-1991; pamphlets, 1991; banners, 1990.
AMOUNT: 4 filing cabinets.
CONDITION: Good.
ACCESS: Permission required. Client files closed.

979. Parkland Status of Women
✣ Dauphin, Man. Formed 1981.

Parkland Status of Women (PSW) is a voluntary organization which works to improve attitudes to women, raise issues affecting women, and promote equality. PSW is a branch of the Manitoba Action Committee on the Status of Women (MACSW). [See also Manitoba Action Committee on the Status of Women (305, 964).]

LOCATION OF RECORDS: Parkland Status of Women. [*Mailing Address:* Box 23, Dauphin, Man. R7N 2T9. *Telephone:* (204) 638-3599.]

RECORDS: Correspondence, financial records, grant applications, membership lists, scrapbooks, briefs, press releases, T-shirts, banners, 1981-1991; clippings, photographs.

AMOUNT: Approx. 1 filing cabinet.

CONDITION: Good.

ACCESS: Permission required.

980. Selkirk Cooperative on Abuse against Women

✣ Selkirk, Man. Formed 1986.

The Selkirk Cooperative on Abuse against Women (SCOAAW) operates Nova House, a shelter for women and children in crisis, and provides services to abused women and children.

LOCATION OF RECORDS: Selkirk Cooperative on Abuse against Women. [*Mailing Address:* Box 337, Selkirk, Man. R1A 2B3. *Telephone:* (204) 482-7882. *Fax:* (204) 482-8483.]

RECORDS: Constitution, 1986; minutes, correspondence, log-books, financial records, grant applications, client records, 1986-1991; membership lists, mailing lists, scrapbooks, reports, pamphlets, press releases, newsletters, 1987-1991; petitions, 1989-1990; conference proceedings, posters, 1989-1991; photographs, 1988-1991; flyers.

AMOUNT: 1 filing cabinet.

CONDITION: Good.

ACCESS: Permission required. Client files closed.

981. Serena Manitoba

✣ Winnipeg, Man. Formed 1977.

Serena Manitoba (a branch of Serena Canada) provides information about natural family planning and fertility awareness to couples and individuals. It grew out of an earlier organization, the Natural Family Planning Centre.

LOCATION OF RECORDS: Serena Manitoba. [*Address:* Room 545 Wolseley West, 99 Cornish Ave., Winnipeg, Man. R3C 1A2. *Telephone:* (204) 783-0091.]

RECORDS: Constitution, minutes, correspondence, log-books, financial records, grant applications, client records, membership lists, mailing lists, reports, pamphlets, flyers, press releases, 1977-1991.

ACCESS: Permission required. Client and personnel files closed. Access to other records decided upon request.

982. Snow Lake Centre on Family Violence

✣ Snow Lake, Man. Formed 1984.

The Snow Lake Centre on Family Violence (also called the Snow Lake Crisis and Resource Centre) provides crisis-intervention services for victims of family violence. It also does public education.

LOCATION OF RECORDS: Snow Lake Centre on Family Violence. [*Mailing Address:* Box 838, Snow Lake, Man. R0B 1M0. *Telephone:* (204) 358-7141.]

RECORDS: Minutes, correspondence, financial records, grant applications, client records, membership lists, scrapbooks, reports, pamphlets, press releases, posters, 1984-1991; clippings.

AMOUNT: 2 filing cabinets.

CONDITION: Good.

ACCESS: Permission required. Client files closed.

983. Swan Valley Crisis Centre

✣ Swan River, Man. Formed 1984.

The Swan Valley Crisis Centre provides safe homes, a transition house, a crisis line, counselling, and other services for victims of family violence. Until 1991 it was called the Swan River Committee on the Abuse of Women.

LOCATION OF RECORDS: Swan Valley Crisis Centre. [*Mailing Address:* Box 2354, Swan River, Man. R0L 1Z0. *Telephone:* (204) 734-9369.]

RECORDS: Constitution, 1984; minutes, financial records, 1984-1991; correspondence, client records, 1985-1991; membership lists, 1988-1991; pamphlets, 1988.

AMOUNT: 1 filing cabinet

CONDITION: Good.

ACCESS: Permission required. Client files closed.

984. The Pas Committee for Women in Crisis

✣ The Pas, Man. Formed 1982.

This committee runs Aurora House, an emergency shelter for women in crisis, and provides a referral service, counselling, support, and advocacy. It used to be called Isquway House.

LOCATION OF RECORDS: The Pas Committee for Women in Crisis. [*Mailing Address:* Box 3779, The Pas, Man. R9A 1S4. *Telephone:* (204) 623-7427. *Fax:* (204) 623-3901.]

RECORDS: Constitution, 1983-1991; minutes, correspondence, 1982-1991; log-books, financial records, 1984; client records, 1990; reports, 1989.

AMOUNT: 2 filing cabinets.

CONDITION: Fair.

ACCESS: Permission required. Client, employee, and legal files closed.

985. Thompson Crisis Centre

✣ Thompson, Man. Formed 1977.

The Thompson Crisis Centre (TCC) operates an emergency shelter (North Win House or NWH) and second-stage housing for abused women and children, a crisis line, and public-education and advocacy services. Originally called the Thompson Rape Crisis Centre, the organization changed its name to the Thompson Women's Crisis Centre and then to the Thompson Crisis Centre. The centre offers services in English, Cree, and Saulteaux.

LOCATION OF RECORDS: Thompson Crisis Centre. [*Mailing Address:* Box 1226, Thompson, Man. R8N 1P1. *Telephone:* (204) 677-9668. *Fax:* (204) 677-9042.]

RECORDS: Constitution, grant applications, 1980-1991; minutes, 1985-1991; correspondence, log-books, membership lists, mailing lists, scrapbooks, pamphlets, 1986-1991; financial records, 1987-1991; client records, 1981-1991; reports, 1985, 1987-1990; conference proceedings, 1983-1984, 1987, 1990; briefs, press releases, posters, buttons, T-shirts, banners, newsletters, clippings, photographs, sound recordings, videotapes, films.

CONDITION: Good.

ACCESS: Permission required.

986. Winnipeg Gay / Lesbian Resource Centre

✣ Winnipeg, Man. Formed 1988.

The Winnipeg Gay/Lesbian Resource Centre (WGLRC) provides information, peer counselling, referrals, a library, and public education. The centre also houses the Manitoba Gay/Lesbian Archive. WGLRC's parent organization is the Manitoba Institute on Society and Sexuality (MISS).

LOCATION OF RECORDS: Winnipeg Gay/Lesbian Resource Centre. [*Mailing Address:* P.O. Box 1661, Winnipeg, Man. R3C 2Z6. *Telephone:* (204) 474-0212 or 284-5208. *Fax:* (204) 474-0212.]

RECORDS: Constitution, 1988; minutes, correspondence, log-books, financial records, grant applications, client records, membership lists, mailing lists, petitions, reports, briefs, pamphlets, flyers, press releases, posters, banners, clippings, photographs, 1988-1991; newsletters (*The Alternative*, 1991); sound recordings, 1990.

AMOUNT: Approx. 7 boxes.

CONDITION: Fair.

ACCESS: Permission required. Restrictions determined by research interview.

987. *Women's Employment Counselling Service*

✣ Winnipeg, Man. Formed 1977.

The Women's Employment Counselling Service (WECS) provides employment counselling on an individual or group basis.

LOCATION OF RECORDS: Women's Employment Counselling Service. [*Address:* 503 - 352 Donald St., Winnipeg, Man. R3B 2H8. *Telephone:* (204) 949-5319. *Fax:* (204) 944-9918.]

RECORDS: Constitution, minutes, correspondence, 1977-1991; reports, 1984-1991.

CONDITION: Good.

ACCESS: Permission required. Client files closed.

988. *Women's Health Clinic (Winnipeg, Man.)*

✣ Winnipeg, Man. Formed 1981.

The Women's Health Clinic (WHC) promotes a feminist vision of holistic health care for women. WHC offers direct and self-help health care related to pre-menstrual syndrome, menopause, weight preoccupation, birth control, unplanned pregnancy, and other women's health issues.

LOCATION OF RECORDS: Women's Health Clinic. [*Address:* Third Floor, 419 Graham Ave., Winnipeg, Man. R3C 0M3. *Telephone:* (204) 947-1517.]

RECORDS: Financial records, grant applications, client records, membership lists, reports, pamphlets, press releases, 1981-1991; posters, 1983-1991; T-shirts, 1987-1991; banners, 1985-1991; newsletters (*Womanly Times*, 1983-1991); minutes, correspondence, mailing lists, photographs.

AMOUNT: Approx. 1 room.

CONDITION: Fair.

ACCESS: Permission required. Clients' medical charts closed unless special permission given.

989. *Women's Health Research Foundation of Canada*

✣ Winnipeg, Man. Formed 1983.

The Women's Health Research Foundation of Canada (WHRF) works for the improvement of women's health and quality of life. It does public education, sponsors events, and raises funds to support women's health research. While WHRF hopes eventually to have a national scope, it currently operates only in Manitoba. It was called the Women's Health Research Foundation of Manitoba until 1984.

LOCATION OF RECORDS: Women's Health Research Foundation of Canada. [*Mailing Address:* Box 24079, Winnipeg, Man. R3N 2B1. (*Street Address:* 1853 Grant Ave.) *Telephone:* (204) 488-4541.]

RECORDS: By-laws, minutes, financial records, 1983-1991; correspondence, grant applications, clippings, 1985-1991; mailing lists, pamphlets, photographs, 1988-1991; reports, 1989-1991; conference proceedings, 1988-1990; press releases, videotapes, 1988-1989; cookbooks, 1989; speeches, 1991.

AMOUNT: 1 filing cabinet.

CONDITION: Good.

ACCESS: Permission required. Membership files, unpublished research information, some minutes closed.

990. *Women's Post Treatment Centre*

✣ Winnipeg, Man. Formed 1985.

This centre provides counselling for women dealing with addiction issues who need to resolve the trauma of childhood sexual abuse. It also does public education and provides training for professionals.

LOCATION OF RECORDS: Women's Post Treatment Centre. [*Address:* 246 Toronto St., Winnipeg, Man. R3G 1S2. *Telephone:* (204) 783-5460.]

RECORDS: Constitution, minutes, correspondence, log-books, financial records, grant applications, client records, membership lists, mailing lists, scrapbooks, reports, briefs, pamphlets, books, clippings, photographs, sound recordings, 1985-1991; programme descriptions, job descriptions.

AMOUNT: 4 filing cabinets, 6 boxes.

CONDITION: Good.

ACCESS: Permission required. Client files closed.

991. *Young Women's Christian Association of Thompson*

[See also entry # 339 (in Part I), which lists other records of this organization.]

✣ Thompson, Man. Formed 1969.

The YWCA of Thompson aims to enrich the lives of women through leadership. It offers counselling, recreational activities, courses, and residential facilities.

LOCATION OF RECORDS: Young Women's Christian Association of Thompson. [*Address:* 39 Nickel Rd., Thompson, Man. R8N 0Y5. *Telephone:* (204) 778-6341. *Fax:* (204) 778-5308.]

RECORDS: Constitution, minutes, correspondence, log-books, financial records, grant applications, client records, membership lists, mailing lists, petitions, scrapbooks, reports, briefs, conference proceedings, press releases, buttons, T-shirts, banners, clippings, photographs, 1983-1991.

AMOUNT: 1 filing cabinet.

CONDITION: Good.

ACCESS: Permission required.

ONTARIO

992. Action on Women's Addictions: Research and Education / AWARE à Kingston

[Renseignements en français, notice 999.]

✣ Kingston, Ont. Formed 1985.

Action on Women's Addictions: Research and Education (AWARE) is a community-based group of women concerned with the problems of women addicted to prescription medications, alcohol, tobacco, and other substances.

LOCATION OF RECORDS: Action on Women's Addictions: Research and Education. [*Mailing Address:* P.O. Box 86, Kingston, Ont. K7L 4V6. *Telephone:* (613) 545-0117.]

RECORDS: Constitution, 1985; minutes, financial records, grant applications, membership lists, 1985-1991; correspondence, mailing lists, reports, briefs, conference proceedings, pamphlets, 1987-1991; flyers, clippings, 1989-1991; press releases, 1988-1991.

AMOUNT: 2 filing cabinets, 3 bookshelves.

CONDITION: Good.

ACCESS: Permission required.

993. AIDS Committee of Ottawa. Women's Project / Comité du SIDA d'Ottawa. Comité ELLES

[Renseignements en français, notice 1016.]

✣ Ottawa, Ont. Formed 1990.

The Women's Project of the AIDS Committee of Ottawa (ACO) works to reduce the rate of HIV infection in women through prevention education and offers a community of support to women who have HIV or AIDS and their loved ones. It also disseminates information about women and AIDS to women's groups and individual women.

LOCATION OF RECORDS: AIDS Committee of Ottawa. Women's Project. [*Address:* 267 Dalhousie St., Ottawa, Ont. K1N 7E3. *Telephone:* (613) 238-5014. *Fax:* (613) 238-3425.]

RECORDS: Minutes, correspondence, grant applications, 1990-1991; logbooks, membership lists, mailing lists, reports, clippings, photographs, videotapes, 1991; articles.

AMOUNT: 1 filing cabinet.

CONDITION: Good.

ACCESS: Permission required.

994. AIDS Committee of Toronto. Women and AIDS Project

✣ Toronto, Ont. Formed 1989.

The Women and AIDS Project, under the auspices of the AIDS Committee of Toronto (ACT), is concerned with AIDS education, support, and prevention as they relate to the specific needs of women.

LOCATION OF RECORDS: AIDS Committee of Toronto. Women and AIDS Project. [*Address:* 464 Yonge St., 2nd Floor, Toronto, Ont. M4Y 1W9. *Telephone:* (416) 926-0063. *Fax:* (416) 926-0386.]

RECORDS: Constitution, minutes, correspondence, financial records, grant applications, membership lists, mailing lists, petitions, reports, conference proceedings, pamphlets, flyers, press releases, posters, buttons, T-shirts, banners, books, clippings, photographs, sound recordings, 1989-1991.

AMOUNT: 2 filing cabinets.

CONDITION: Good.

ACCESS: Permission required. Client files closed.

995. Amethyst Women's Addiction Centre

✣ Ottawa, Ont. Formed 1979.

The centre treats women who are addicted to drugs or alcohol. It also does public education and has a children's drug-abuse prevention programme.

LOCATION OF RECORDS: Amethyst Women's Addiction Centre. [*Address:* 488 Wilbrod St., Ottawa, Ont. K1N 6M8. *Telephone:* (613) 563-0363. *Fax:* (613) 565-2175.]

RECORDS: Minutes, financial records, grant applications, client records, clippings, photographs, 1979-1991; membership lists, press releases, 1985-1991; reports, 1984-1991; briefs, flyers, T-shirts, 1990-1991; pamphlets, 1989-1991; buttons, 1988; banners, 1985; newsletters (*Amethyst Matters*, 1990-1991); books, 1984; videotapes, 1989; by-laws, correspondence, mailing lists.

AMOUNT: 5 filing cabinets.

CONDITION: Good.

ACCESS: Permission required. Client files closed.

PART II: RECORDS HELD BY GROUPS / PARTIE II : FONDS DÉTENUS PAR DES GROUPES

Demonstration, Parliament Hill / Manifestation, Colline du parlement, [197-]
Photographer unknown / Photographe inconnue
Photo #P110; acc. #0109
Donated by / Don de Breaking the Silence
CWMA Collection / Fonds de l'ACMF

996. Association des lesbiennes et des gais de l'Outaouais / Association of Lesbians and Gays of Ottawa

[For English entry, see # 997.]

[Voir aussi la notice 346 (dans la partie I) pour autres documents de ce groupe.]

✣ Ottawa (Ont.). Groupe fondé 1971.

L'Association des lesbiennes et des gais de l'Outaouais (ALGO) vise à développer une prise de conscience positive à l'endroit des lesbiennes et des gais par l'éducation publique et l'action politique, sociale et juridique. Elle publie un périodique, *GO Info*. Auparavant, l'organisme portait le nom Gais de l'Outaouais (GO).

LIEU DE CONSULTATION : Association des lesbiennes et des gais de l'Outaouais. [*Adresse postale* : C.P. 2919, Succursale D, Ottawa (Ont.) K1P 5W9.]

MATÉRIEL : Procès-verbaux, 1981-1991; périodiques (*GO Info*, 1971-1991); statuts et règlements, journaux de bord, documents financiers, listes de membres.

QUANTITÉ : 4 classeurs.

ÉTAT : Assez bon.

ACCÈS : Permission requise. Listes de membres confidentielles.

997. Association of Lesbians and Gays of Ottawa / Association des lesbiennes et des gais de l'Outaouais

[Renseignements en français, notice 996.]

[See also entry # 347 (in Part I), which lists other records of this organization.]

✣ Ottawa, Ont. Formed 1971.

The Association of Lesbians and Gays of Ottawa (ALGO) works to develop a positive awareness of lesbians and gay men through public education and political, social, and legal action. It publishes a periodical, *GO Info*. The organization used to be known as Gays of Ottawa (GO).

LOCATION OF RECORDS: Association of Lesbians and Gays of Ottawa. [*Mailing Address*: Box 2919, Station D, Ottawa, Ont. K1P 5W9.]

RECORDS: Minutes, 1981-1991; periodicals (*GO Info*, 1971-1991); constitution, log-books, financial records, membership lists.

AMOUNT: 4 filing cabinets.

CONDITION: Fair.

ACCESS: Permission required. Membership lists confidential.

998. Association of Ontario Midwives

✣ Toronto, Ont. Formed 1984.

The Association of Ontario Midwives (AOM) promotes midwifery as an integral part of the health-care system and is the regulatory body for the profession in Ontario. It was formed through the amalgamation of the Ontario Association of Midwives (founded in 1979) and the Ontario Nurse-Midwives Association (founded in 1974).

LOCATION OF RECORDS: Association of Ontario Midwives. [*Mailing Address:* P.O. Box 85, Station C, Toronto, Ont. M6J 3M7. *Telephone:* (416) 538-4389.]

RECORDS: Constitution, minutes, press releases, 1984-1991; financial records, 1979-1991; petitions, 1983-1986; reports, pamphlets, 1989-1991; briefs, 1983-1986, 1989; newsletters (*Issue*, 1980-1984; *Association of Ontario Midwives Newsletter*, 1984-1991).

AMOUNT: 2 filing cabinets.

CONDITION: Good.

ACCESS: Permission required. Records of complaints and hearings closed.

999. AWARE à Kingston / Action on Women's Addictions: Research and Education

[For English entry, see # 992.]

✣ Kingston (Ont.). Groupe fondé 1985.

AWARE à Kingston est un groupe communautaire de femmes qui s'impliquent dans les problèmes de femmes souffrant de dépendance aux médicaments, à l'alcool, au tabac et à d'autres drogues.

LIEU DE CONSULTATION : AWARE à Kingston. [*Adresse postale* : C.P. 86, Kingston (Ont.) K7L 4V6. *Téléphone* : (613) 545-0117.]

MATÉRIEL : Statuts et règlements, 1985; procès-verbaux, documents financiers, demandes de subvention, listes de membres, 1985-1991; correspondance, listes d'envoi, rapports, mémoires, actes de congrès, dépliants, 1987-1991; tracts, coupures de presse, 1989-1991; communiqués de presse, 1988-1991.

QUANTITÉ : 2 classeurs, 3 étagères.

ÉTAT : Bon.

ACCÈS : Permission requise.

1000. Bay Centre for Birth Control

✣ Toronto, Ont. Formed 1973.

The Bay Centre for Birth Control (BCBC) offers family-planning and abortion counselling and referral. It is part of the Regional Women's Health Centre (RWHC) at Women's College Hospital.

LOCATION OF RECORDS: Bay Centre for Birth Control. [*Address:* 790 Bay St., Toronto, Ont. M5G 1N9. *Telephone:* (416) 323-6010.]

RECORDS: Client records, 1973-1991; pamphlets, 1990-1991; books, 1991; photographs, 1990; minutes.

CONDITION: Good.

ACCESS: Permission required. Client files closed.

1001. Bisexual, Lesbian, and Gay Alliance at York

[See also entry # 352 (in Part I), which lists other records of this organization.]

✣ Downsview, Ont. Formed [1971?].

The Bisexual, Lesbian, and Gay Alliance at York (BLGAY) operates under the auspices of the York Student Federation. BLGAY provides a comfortable meeting place for gay, lesbian, bisexual, and gay-positive people at York University; offers a support network for people coping with their sexual orientation; and works to enhance awareness in the York community of the need for bisexual, lesbian, and gay rights. It was previously known as the Gay Alliance at York (GAY), and then as the Lesbian and Gay Alliance at York (LGAY).

LOCATION OF RECORDS: Bisexual, Lesbian, and Gay Alliance at York. [*Address:* York University, 4700 Keele St., Room 447, Student Centre, Downsview, Ont. M3J 1P3. *Telephone:* (416) 736-2100, ext. 20494.]

RECORDS: Constitution, buttons, banners, 1990; minutes, correspondence, financial records, clippings, 1990-1991; membership lists, pamphlets, 1991.

AMOUNT: 1 file.

CONDITION: Good.

ACCESS: Membership lists closed.

1002. Business and Professional Women's Club of Ottawa

✣ Ottawa, Ont. Formed 1933.

This club seeks to improve the economic and social status of women. It lobbies the government and encourages women to participate in the business of government. The club's French name is l'Association des femmes d'affaires et professionnelles d'Ottawa.

LOCATION OF RECORDS: Business and Professional Women's Club of Ottawa. [*Mailing Address:* P.O. Box 1292, Station B, Ottawa, Ont. K1P 5R3.]

RECORDS: Constitution, minutes, correspondence, financial records, membership lists, mailing lists, petitions, reports, briefs, conference proceedings, pamphlets, press releases, newsletters, books, clippings, photographs.

AMOUNT: Approx. 11 boxes.

CONDITION: Fair.

ACCESS: Permission required.

1003. Cambodian Women's Group of Ontario

✣ Toronto, Ont. Formed 1987.

This group helps Cambodian women to adapt and integrate into Canadian society. The group provides support and organizes educational and social activities. It is affiliated with the Canadian Cambodian Association of Ontario.

LOCATION OF RECORDS: Cambodian Women's Group of Ontario. [*Address:* 1111 Finch Ave. W., Suite 300, Downsview, Ont. M3J 2E5. *Telephone:* (416) 736-0138/0629. *Fax:* (416) 736-9454.]

RECORDS: Minutes, correspondence, grant applications, client records, mailing lists, pamphlets, flyers, photographs, 1987-1991; financial records, reports, 1990-1991.

AMOUNT: 1 filing cabinet.

CONDITION: Good.

ACCESS: Permission required from group's president.

1004. Carleton University. Institute of Women's Studies

✣ Ottawa, Ont. Formed 1970.

This institute offers undergraduate programmes in women's studies. It developed out of the Interfaculty Committee on Women's Studies, which became the Institute of Women's Studies (IWS) in 1987.

LOCATION OF RECORDS: Carleton University. Institute of Women's Studies. [*Address:* Room 330, Paterson Hall, Ottawa, Ont. K1S 5B6. *Telephone:* (613) 788-6645.]

RECORDS: Constitution, minutes, correspondence, financial records, mailing lists, reports, pamphlets, posters, 1972-1991; newsletters, 1987-1990; videotapes.

AMOUNT: 1 filing cabinet.

CONDITION: Good.

ACCESS: Permission required. Personnel and student files closed.

1005. Carleton University. Status of Women Office

✣ Ottawa, Ont. Formed 1981.

The Status of Women Office represents women at Carleton University. It makes policy recommendations, develops programming on women's issues, and advises women on their rights within the university.

LOCATION OF RECORDS: Carleton University. Status of Women Office. [*Address:* Ottawa, Ont. K1S 5B6. *Telephone:* (613) 788-5622. *Fax:* (613) 788-5604.]

RECORDS: Minutes, correspondence, reports, clippings, 1981-1991; financial records, pamphlets, 1983-1991; grant applications, 1985-1991; conference proceedings, 1984-1991; newsletters, 1984-1990.

AMOUNT: 2 filing cabinets.

CONDITION: Good.

ACCESS: Permission required.

1006. Centre d'aide aux agressées sexuelles d'Ottawa / Sexual Assault Support Centre of Ottawa

[For English entry, see # 1076.]

✣ Ottawa (Ont.). Groupe fondé 1983.

Le Centre d'aide aux agressées sexuelles d'Ottawa offre des services d'orientation aux femmes qui ont été victimes de violence sexuelle. Cet organisme vise également à sensibiliser la population générale, les écoles, les universités et d'autres organismes aux problèmes de l'assaut sexuel, de l'inceste et des autres formes de violence sexuelle faite aux femmes.

LIEU DE CONSULTATION : Centre d'aide aux agressées sexuelles d'Ottawa. [*Adresse postale :* C.P. 4441, Succursale E, Ottawa (Ont.) K1S 5B4. *Téléphone :* (613) 725-2160 or 234-2266.]

MATÉRIEL : Procès-verbaux, journaux de bord, documents financiers, demandes de subvention, 1982-1991; documents divers, 1989.

QUANTITÉ : 3 classeurs.

ÉTAT : Assez bon.

ACCÈS : Permission requise. Restrictions pour les journaux de bord et les procès-verbaux des réunions.

1007. Centre des femmes de Sudbury / Sudbury Women's Centre

[For English entry, see # 1081.]

✣ Sudbury (Ont.). Groupe fondé 1981.

Le centre est un organisme bilingue, ayant pour objectif l'amélioration du statut de la femme dans le Nord de l'Ontario par la sensibilisation du public, la revendication et l'action politique.

LIEU DE CONSULTATION : Centre des femmes de Sudbury. [*Adresse :* 258, rue Victoria, Sudbury (Ont.) P3C 1K4. *Téléphone :* (705) 673-1916.]

MATÉRIEL : Statuts et règlements, procès-verbaux, correspondance, journaux de bord, documents financiers, demandes de subvention, listes de membres, listes d'envoi, pétitions, albums de coupures, rapports, mémoires, actes de congrès, dépliants, tracts, communiqués de presse, bannières, coupures de presse, photographies, 1981-1991; affiches, macarons, T-shirts, 1985-1991; bulletins, 1982-1991.

QUANTITÉ : 6 classeurs.

ÉTAT : Assez bon.

ACCÈS : Permission requise. Documents financiers et documents annexes confidentiels.

1008. Chez nous

[Renseignements en français, notice 1009.]

✣ Ottawa, Ont. Formed 1978. Disbanded 1980.

Chez nous was a club for women; it offered its members a pleasant place for socializing and organizing. Chez nous was run by the Ottawa Women's Centre. [See also Ottawa Women's Centre (466, 1061).]

LOCATION OF RECORDS: Women's Place. [*Address:* 241 Bruyère St., Ottawa, Ont. K1N 5E5. *Telephone:* (613) 789-2155. *Fax:* (613) 789-2745.]

RECORDS: Minutes, correspondence, 1978-1979; financial records, 1978-1980; pamphlets, press releases, 1979.

AMOUNT: Approx. 20 cm.

CONDITION: Good.

1009. Chez nous

[For English entry, see # 1008.]

✣ Ottawa (Ont.). Groupe fondé 1978. Dissous 1980.

Chez nous était un club de femmes qui offrait à ses membres un endroit chaleureux où elles pouvaient se réunir, discuter et établir des plans d'action. Chez nous était marrainé par le Centre des femmes d'Ottawa (Ottawa Women's Centre). [Voir aussi Ottawa Women's Centre (466, 1061).]

LIEU DE CONSULTATION: Place aux femmes. [*Adresse*: 241, rue Bruyère, Ottawa (Ont.) K1N 5E5. *Téléphone*: (613) 789-2155. *Télécopieur*: (613) 789-2745.]

MATÉRIEL: Procès-verbaux, correspondance, 1978-1979; documents financiers, 1978-1980; dépliants, communiqués de presse, 1979.

QUANTITÉ: Env. 20 cm.

ÉTAT: Bon.

1010. The Circle

✣ London, Ont. Formed 1990.

The Circle is a women's spirituality group which operates out of Brescia College. It holds workshops and public rituals and runs the Circle Resource Centre.

LOCATION OF RECORDS: The Circle. [*Address*: 1285 Western Rd., Brescia College, London, Ont. N6G 1H2. *Telephone*: (519) 432-8353. *Fax*: (519) 679-6489.]

RECORDS: Constitution, financial records, membership lists, mailing lists, scrapbooks, 1990-1991; newsletters, books, photographs, 1991; flyers.

AMOUNT: 1 drawer of a filing cabinet.

CONDITION: Fair.

1011. Coalition for Lesbian and Gay Rights in Ontario

[See also entry # 371 (in Part I), which lists other records of this organization.]

✣ Toronto, Ont. Formed 1975.

The Coalition for Lesbian and Gay Rights in Ontario (CLGRO) works toward feminism and lesbian and gay liberation by engaging in the public struggle for full human rights and by strengthening co-operative networks for lesbian and gay activism. Until 1987 it was called the Coalition for Gay Rights in Ontario (CGRO). Its French name is la Coalition pour les droits des lesbiennes et des hommes gais en Ontario.

LOCATION OF RECORDS: Coalition For Lesbian and Gay Rights in Ontario. [*Mailing Address*: Box 822, Station A, Toronto, Ont. M5W 1G3. *Telephone*: (416) 533-6824.]

RECORDS: Constitution, minutes, correspondence, newsletters, 1975-1991; financial records, 1988-1991; briefs, 1975, 1978, 1981, 1986; buttons, 1983, 1991; banners, 1989; grant applications, membership lists, mailing lists, reports, pamphlets, flyers, press releases, books, photographs, videotapes.

CONDITION: Fair.

ACCESS: Permission required.

1012. Coalition of Visible Minority Women (Ontario)

✣ Toronto, Ont. Formed 1983.

This coalition, also called CVMW (Ontario), has worked to build a support system for visible-minority women in the fight against racism and sexism. It also works to enhance and build language skills for foreign-trained nurses wishing to return to the nursing profession in Canada.

LOCATION OF RECORDS: Coalition of Visible Minority Women (Ontario). [*Address*: 579 St Clair Ave. W., Suite 203, Toronto, Ont. M6C 1A3. *Telephone*: (416) 651-5071.]

RECORDS: Minutes, correspondence, financial records, grant applications, client records, membership lists, mailing lists, reports, 1983-1991; clippings, 1988-1991; pamphlets.

AMOUNT: 2 filing cabinets.

CONDITION: Good.

ACCESS: Permission required.

1013. Collectif des femmes francophones du nord-est ontarien

✣ Sudbury (Ont.). Groupe fondé 1988.

Les buts de l'organisme sont de favoriser l'avancement et l'autonomie des femmes francophones par le biais de l'éducation sous toutes ses formes et de faciliter l'accès des femmes francophones aux études post-secondaires.

LIEU DE CONSULTATION: Collectif des femmes francophones du nord-est ontarien. [*Adresse postale*: S.S. 1, B.P. 1, site 5., Sudbury (Ont.) P3E 2C7. (*Indication de rue*: 1204, ch. du Lac Ramsey.) *Téléphone*: (705) 675-1151, poste 3402.]

MATÉRIEL: Statuts et règlements, procès-verbaux, correspondance, documents financiers, demandes de subvention, dossiers concernant la clientèle, listes de membres, listes d'envoi, pétitions, albums de coupures, rapports, dépliants, communiqués de presse, 1988-1991; mémoires, 1989; articles, 1989-1990; coupures de presse, 1989-1991.

QUANTITÉ: 1 classeur.

ÉTAT: Bon.

ACCÈS: Permission requise.

1014. La Collective (Université d'Ottawa) / The Collective (University of Ottawa)

[For English entry, see # 1015.]

✣ Ottawa (Ont.). Groupe fondé 1985.

La Collective veut bâtir et maintenir la solidarité dans la communauté des femmes de l'Université d'Ottawa. De plus, elle participe au développement du Programme en études des femmes. Auparavant, elle était connue sous les noms suivants: la Collective en études des femmes et la Collective des étudiantes en études des femmes. [Voir aussi Université d'Ottawa. Programme en études des femmes/University of Ottawa. Women's Studies Programme (1090).]

LIEU DE CONSULTATION: La Collective. [*Adresse*: Université d'Ottawa. Programme en études des femmes, 143 Séraphin-Marion, Ottawa (Ont.) K1N 6N5. *Téléphone*: (613) 564-4019. *Télécopieur*: (613) 564-7461.]

MATÉRIEL: Statuts et règlements, 1985; procès-verbaux, 1987-1991; documents financiers, 1985-1991; listes de membres, pétitions, 1991; bulletins (Digression, 1986-1987; Encrelle/Print Her, 1987-1989; Journal féministe/The Feminist Newspaper, 1990); photographies, 1989-1990; macarons.

QUANTITÉ: 1 tiroir de classeur.

ÉTAT: Bon.

ACCÈS: Permission requise.

1015. The Collective (University of Ottawa) / La Collective (Université d'Ottawa)

[Renseignements en français, notice 1014.]

✣ Ottawa, Ont. Formed 1985.

The Collective works to build and maintain solidarity in the women's community at the University of Ottawa. It also participates in the development of the Women's Studies Programme. In the past it has been known as the Women's Studies Collective and as the Women's Studies Student Collective. [See also University of Ottawa. Women's Studies Programme/Université d'Ottawa. Programme en études des femmes (1091).]

LOCATION OF RECORDS: The Collective. [*Address:* University of Ottawa, Women's Studies Programme, 143 Séraphin-Marion, Ottawa, Ont. K1N 6N5. *Telephone:* (613) 564-4019. *Fax:* (613) 564-7461.]

RECORDS: Constitution, 1985; minutes, 1987-1991; financial records, 1985-1991; membership lists, petitions, 1991; newsletters (*Digression*, 1986-1987; *Print Her/Encrelle*, 1987-1989; *The Feminist Newspaper/Journal féministe*, 1990); photographs, 1989-1990; buttons.

AMOUNT: 1 drawer of a filing cabinet.

CONDITION: Good.

ACCESS: Permission required.

1016. Comité du SIDA d'Ottawa. Comité ELLES / AIDS Committee of Ottawa. Women's Project

[For English entry, see # 993.]

✣ Ottawa (Ont.). Groupe fondé 1990.

Le Comité ELLES (éducation, liaison, lumière et services) du Comité du SIDA d'Ottawa (CSO) a pour mission de réduire le taux d'infection par le VIH chez les femmes par l'éducation préventive. Le comité offre également un appui communautaire aux femmes atteintes du VIH ou du SIDA et un soutien à leurs familles et à leurs amies et amis. Finalement, le groupe veut offrir de l'information sur les femmes et le SIDA aux groupes de femmes et aux femmes individuelles.

LIEU DE CONSULTATION : Comité du SIDA d'Ottawa. Comité ELLES. [*Adresse :* 267, rue Dalhousie, Ottawa (Ont.) K1N 7E3. *Téléphone :* (613) 238-5014. *Télécopieur :* (613) 238-3425.]

MATÉRIEL : Procès-verbaux, correspondance, demandes de subvention, 1990-1991; journaux de bord, listes de membres, listes d'envoi, rapports, coupures de presse, photographies, vidéocassettes, 1991; articles.

QUANTITÉ : 1 classeur.

ÉTAT : Bon.

ACCÈS : Permission requise.

1017. The Company of Sirens

✣ Toronto, Ont. Formed 1985.

The Company of Sirens is a theatre company which develops and produces plays by women and educates the public about women's issues through theatre.

LOCATION OF RECORDS: The Company of Sirens. [*Address:* 296 Brunswick Ave., Toronto, Ont. M5S 2M7. *Telephone:* (416) 975-9642.]

RECORDS: Correspondence, grant applications, photographs, pamphlets, flyers, 1985-1991; posters, 1986-1991; scrapbooks, 1990-1991; T-shirts, banners, clippings, sound recordings.

AMOUNT: Approx. 2 filing cabinets.

CONDITION: Good.

1018. Constance Hamilton Housing Co-operative

✣ Toronto, Ont. Formed 1981.

The Constance Hamilton Housing Co-operative provides long-term, affordable, safe housing for independent women.

LOCATION OF RECORDS: Constance Hamilton Housing Co-operative. [*Address:* 70A Lambert Lodge Ave., Toronto, Ont. M6G 3X3. *Telephone:* (416) 532-8860.]

RECORDS: Constitution, 1981; minutes, correspondence, financial records, client records, membership lists, reports, 1981-1991; banners, clippings, photographs, videotapes.

AMOUNT: 2 filing cabinets, 2 shelves.

CONDITION: Fair.

ACCESS: Permission required. Members' files and *in camera* board minutes closed.

1019. DisAbled Women's Network, Toronto

✣ Toronto, Ont. Formed 1986.

The DisAbled Women's Network, Toronto (DAWN Toronto) fights for the rights of women with disabilities, through advocacy, education, and an information and referral service.

LOCATION OF RECORDS: DisAbled Women's Network, Toronto. [*Address:* 160 The Esplanade, #601, Toronto, Ont. M5A 3T2. *Telephone:* (416) 368-1331.]

RECORDS: Constitution, minutes, correspondence, membership lists, mailing lists, 1986-1991; financial records, briefs, 1988-1991; pamphlets, 1987-1988; flyers, press releases, 1991; buttons, 1988; banners, 1986; photographs, 1987; newsletters (*The Dawning*, 1991); clippings.

AMOUNT: 4 filing cabinets.

CONDITION: Fair.

ACCESS: Permission required. Mailing lists and all records related to sexual assault permanently closed.

1020. Dryden Aboriginal Women's Resource Centre

✣ Dryden, Ont. Formed 1971.

This resource centre works to meet the needs of women and Native families, through drop-in services, workshops, and a clothing and furniture depot. Until 1991 it was known as the Dryden Native Women's Resource Centre.

LOCATION OF RECORDS: Dryden Aboriginal Women's Resource Centre. [*Mailing Address:* P.O. Box 575, Dryden, Ont. P8N 2Z3. *Telephone:* (807) 223-6100.]

RECORDS: Constitution, 1990; minutes, correspondence, log-books, financial records, grant applications, membership lists, mailing lists, scrapbooks, reports, briefs, conference proceedings, pamphlets, flyers, press releases, posters, clippings, photographs, 1971-1991; banners, 1991; videotapes.

AMOUNT: Approx. 2 filing cabinets.

CONDITION: Good.

ACCESS: Permission required.

1021. Elizabeth Fry Society. Hamilton Branch

✣ Hamilton, Ont. Formed 1970.

The Hamilton branch of the Elizabeth Fry Society is a community-based correctional agency which addresses the particular concerns of women. It provides counselling, housing, education, and preventative services, and it does advocacy on behalf of individuals involved in the criminal-justice system.

LOCATION OF RECORDS: Elizabeth Fry Society. Hamilton Branch. [*Address:* 627 Main St. E., 2nd Floor., Hamilton, Ont. L8M 1J5. *Telephone:* (416) 527-3097.]

RECORDS: Minutes, correspondence, log-books, grant applications, reports, clippings, photographs, 1970-1991; financial records, 1980-1991; client records, 1974-1991; membership lists, petitions, 1985-1991; mailing lists, 1988-1991; newsletters (*Turning Point*, 1970-1991); sound recordings, 1984-1991; briefs, conference proceedings, pamphlets, flyers, press releases, posters.

AMOUNT: 10 filing cabinets.

CONDITION: Good.

ACCESS: Permission required. Client files closed.

1022. Elizabeth Fry Society of Kingston

[See also entry # 387 (in Part I), which lists other records of this organization.]

✣ Kingston, Ont. Formed 1949.

The Elizabeth Fry Society of Kingston (also called E. Fry) is a community organization which addresses the needs of women who are or have been in conflict with the law (or who may be at risk of being so).

LOCATION OF RECORDS: Elizabeth Fry Society of Kingston. [*Address:* #501 - 837 Princess St., Kingston, Ont. K7L 1G8. *Telephone:* (613) 544-1744. *Fax:* (613) 544-0676.]

RECORDS: Constitution, 1961; minutes, correspondence, 1984-1991; scrapbooks, 1959-1978; briefs, 1976-1988; slides, 1986-1987; newsletters, 1981-1991; log-books, financial records, grant applications, client records, membership lists, mailing lists, reports, conference proceedings, pamphlets, flyers, press releases, buttons, T-shirts, records of research projects.

AMOUNT: 20 filing cabinets.

CONDITION: Good.

ACCESS: Permission required. Client files closed.

1023. Elizabeth Fry Society of Toronto

✣ Toronto, Ont. Formed 1952.

The Elizabeth Fry Society of Toronto helps women in conflict with the law, through a half-way house for women coming out of prison, counselling (individual and group), and visits to incarcerated women.

LOCATION OF RECORDS: Elizabeth Fry Society of Toronto. [*Address:* 215 Wellesley St. E., Toronto, Ont. M4X 1G1. *Telephone:* (416) 924-3708. *Fax:* (416) 924-3367.]

RECORDS: Constitution, minutes, correspondence, financial records, grant applications, client records, briefs, newsletters, books, photographs, 1952-1991; membership lists, [ca. 1980]-1991; mailing lists, scrapbooks, reports, 1988-1991; buttons, 1985, 1991; T-shirts, sweatshirts, 1989-1991; banners, 1985, 1989; sound recordings, videotapes, [198-]-1991; conference proceedings, pamphlets, flyers, press releases.

AMOUNT: 4 filing cabinets, 20 boxes, 2 shelves.

CONDITION: Good.

ACCESS: Permission required. Client files closed.

1024. Emily Stowe Shelter for Women

✣ Scarborough, Ont. Formed 1981.

This is an emergency shelter for assaulted women and their children. It provides safe refuge, advocacy, and counselling in various languages (including Cantonese, Punjabi, and Spanish.

LOCATION OF RECORDS: Emily Stowe Shelter for Women. [*Address:* 21 Brimley Rd., Scarborough, Ont. M1M 3H3. *Telephone:* (416) 264-4478. *Fax:* (416) 265-4755.]

RECORDS: Constitution, 1981; minutes, correspondence, log-books, financial records, grant applications, client records, newsletters, 1981-1991; membership lists, mailing lists, briefs, 1984-1991; reports, 1982-1991; conference proceedings, 1985-1991; pamphlets, flyers, 1982; press releases, 1984, 1990; buttons, 1984; T-shirts, 1984, 1986; photographs, 1983-1991.

AMOUNT: Approx. 8 filing cabinets.

CONDITION: Fair.

ACCESS: Permission required. Client files and some financial records closed.

1025. Empathy House of Recovery

✣ Ottawa, Ont. Formed 1978.

This is a residential treatment centre for women with addictions. Its services include counselling, group therapy, and a relapse-prevention programme.

LOCATION OF RECORDS: Empathy House of Recovery. [*Address:* 360 Sunnyside Ave., Ottawa, Ont. K1S 0S4. *Telephone:* (613) 232-7319.]

RECORDS: Constitution, minutes, correspondence, log-books, financial records, grant applications, client records, reports.

AMOUNT: 4 filing cabinets.

CONDITION: Good.

ACCESS: Permission required. Client files closed.

1026. Fédération nationale des femmes canadiennes-françaises d'Oshawa

✣ Oshawa (Ont.). Groupe fondé 1958.

La Fédération nationale des femmes canadiennes-françaises d'Oshawa (FNFCF d'Oshawa) s'est donné pour mission de sauvegarder et de promouvoir la culture et la langue françaises, d'informer la femme sur la façon d'améliorer sa condition sociale et de lui ouvrir la voie à l'autonomie personnelle. La FNFCF d'Oshawa a été constituée en société sous le nom d'Association des femmes canadiennes-françaises d'Oshawa. La FNFCF s'appelait auparavant la Fédération des femmes canadiennes-françaises (FFCF).

LIEU DE CONSULTATION: Fédération nationale des femmes canadiennes-françaises d'Oshawa. [*Adresse:* 671, promenade Greenbriar, Oshawa (Ont.) L1G 7J5. *Téléphone:* (416) 728-5951.]

MATÉRIEL: Statuts et règlements, procès-verbaux, correspondance, documents financiers, demandes de subvention, listes de membres, albums de coupures, mémoires, dépliants, communiqués de presse, affiches, livres, coupures de presse, photographies, enregistrements sonores, vidéocassettes, 1958-1991; bulletins (*Bonjour, puis-je vous aider?*, 1979, 1982-1988).

ÉTAT: Bon.

ACCÈS: Permission requise.

1027. Feminist Faith Concerns

✣ St Catharines, Ont. Formed 1988.

Affiliated with the Niagara Presbytery of the United Church of Canada, this group was formed to support women and gay people (both laity and clergy) in their struggles for acceptance within the church. The group's concerns include women's spirituality and local women's issues.

LOCATION OF RECORDS: Feminist Faith Concerns. [*Address:* c/o United Church of Canada, Niagara Presbytery, 366 St Paul St., St Catharines, Ont. L2R 3N2. *Telephone:* (416) 682-8328.]

RECORDS: Correspondence, membership lists, mailing lists, 1988-1991.

CONDITION: Good.

1028. Groupe féminin pluri-elles

✣ Thunder Bay (Ont.). Groupe fondé 1986.

Le Groupe féminin pluri-elles réunit les femmes francophones de la région en organisant des réunions sur divers thèmes, tels que la condition féminine. Ce groupe était connu sous le nom de Groupe des femmes canadiennes-françaises de 1986 à 1988.

LIEU DE CONSULTATION : Groupe féminin pluri-elles. [*Adresse* : 3135, rue Lloyd, R.R. 2, B.P. 62, Thunder Bay (Ont.) P7C 4V1. *Téléphone* : (807) 939-1270.]

MATÉRIEL : Procès-verbaux, correspondance, documents financiers, demandes de subvention, listes de membres, rapports, 1986-1991.

ÉTAT : Bon.

ACCÈS : Permission requise.

1029. Guelph-Wellington Women in Crisis

✣ Guelph, Ont. Formed 1978.

Guelph-Wellington Women in Crisis (GWWIC) is committed to ending violence against women and children in all its forms: physical, sexual, emotional, and verbal. It operates Marianne's Place, a shelter for abused women and children; the Rural Women's Shelter Program, which provides services to abused women and children in Wellington County; and the Sexual Assault Centre of Guelph.

LOCATION OF RECORDS: Guelph-Wellington Women in Crisis. [*Mailing Address:* Box 1451, Guelph, Ont. N1H 6N9. *Telephone:* (519) 836-1110. *Fax:* (519) 836-1979.]

RECORDS: Constitution, minutes, mailing lists, scrapbooks, reports, clippings, photographs, newsletters, 1978-1991; financial records, 1984-1991; grant applications, membership lists, 1987-1991; buttons, 1983, 1987; banners, [198-]; sound recordings, 1982; videotapes, 1980; correspondence, briefs, pamphlets, press releases, posters, T-shirts.

AMOUNT: Approx. 2 drawers of a filing cabinet.

ACCESS: Permission required.

1030. Half The Sky Feminist Theatre Company

✣ Hamilton, Ont. Formed 1982.

The aim of this community-based women's theatre group is to make theatre a part of the process of freeing women. Working collectively, it strives to create theatre which reflects women's experiences and educates audiences. It was called the Women's Centre Theatre Group until 1985.

LOCATION OF RECORDS: Half the Sky Feminist Theatre Company. [*Address:* 89 Homewood Ave., Hamilton, Ont. L8P 2M3. *Telephone:* (416) 522-3984.]

RECORDS: Flyers, 1985-1991; videotapes, 1990-1991; financial records, mailing lists, scrapbooks, press releases, T-shirts, clippings, photographs.

AMOUNT: 1 filing cabinet.

CONDITION: Good.

ACCESS: Permission required.

1031. Immigrant Women's Health Centre

✣ Toronto, Ont. Formed 1976.

The Immigrant Women's Health Centre (IWHC) provides health and social services to immigrant, refugee, and visible-minority women. The centre's counsellors are members of the ethnic groups served. The organization was called Centro Donne until 1986.

LOCATION OF RECORDS: Immigrant Women's Health Centre. [*Address:* 750 Dundas St. W., Suite 301, Toronto, Ont. M6J 3S3. *Telephone:* (416) 367-1388.]

RECORDS: Minutes, correspondence, log-books, grant applications, client records, membership lists, mailing lists, reports, press releases, 1976-1991; handbook, 1988; photographs, sound recordings, videotapes.

CONDITION: Fair.

ACCESS: Permission required. Most records closed to outside researchers.

1032. Immigrant Women's Job Placement Centre

✣ Toronto, Ont. Formed 1978.

The mandate of the Immigrant Women's Job Placement Centre (IWJPC) is to find meaningful employment for immigrant and refugee women. IWJPC provides vocational counselling and training programmes and promotes awareness of the problems of immigrant women in the labour force. Until 1980 it was called Employment Services for Immigrant Women (ESIW). Its French name is le Centre d'emploi pour les femmes immigrantes.

LOCATION OF RECORDS: Immigrant Women's Job Placement Centre. [*Address:* 546A St Clair Ave. W., Toronto, Ont. M6C 1A5. *Telephone:* (416) 656-8933. *Fax:* (416) 656-6335.]

RECORDS: Constitution, minutes, correspondence, financial records, grant applications, client records, membership lists, mailing lists, reports, pamphlets, flyers, press releases, student projects, handbooks, clippings, videotapes.

ACCESS: Permission required. Client and personnel records, board minutes, and records of executive and staff meetings closed.

1033. Interval House of Ottawa-Carleton

✣ Ottawa, Ont. Formed 1976.

Interval House of Ottawa-Carleton provides shelter and support to battered women and their children, does public education, and advocates social change and an end to violence against women.

LOCATION OF RECORDS: Interval House of Ottawa-Carleton. [*Address:* c/o 755 Somerset St. W., 2nd Floor, Ottawa, Ont. K1R 6R1. *Telephone:* (613) 234-8511/5181/5393. *Fax:* (613) 234-9474.]

RECORDS: Minutes, 1976-1991; log-books, 1988-1991; financial records, 1983-1991; flyers, 1988; buttons, [1986?]; T-shirts, [1987?]; photographs, sound recordings, 1985; by-laws, letters patent, correspondence, grant applications, client records, mailing lists, scrapbooks, reports, banners, newsletters (*Housecall*), clippings, videotapes.

AMOUNT: Approx. 6 filing cabinets.

CONDITION: Good.

ACCESS: Permission required. Client files, log-books, and certain other records closed.

1034. Jewish Women's Federation

✣ Willowdale, Ont. Formed 1985.

The Jewish Women's Federation (JWF) is a department of the Jewish Federation of Greater Toronto (formerly the Toronto Jewish Congress). JWF is an umbrella organization for Jewish women's volunteer groups in Toronto. Its goal is to strengthen the role of Jewish women in the community.

LOCATION OF RECORDS: Jewish Women's Federation. [*Address:* c/o Jewish Federation of Greater Toronto, 4600 Bathurst St., Willowdale, Ont. M2R 3V2. *Telephone:* (416) 635-2883. *Fax:* (416) 635-1408.]

RECORDS: Minutes, correspondence, mailing lists, flyers, posters, 1985-1991; newsletters (*In Touch*, 1986-1991); clippings, 1990-1991; photographs, 1989-1991.

AMOUNT: Approx. 3 filing cabinets.

CONDITION: Good.

ACCESS: Permission required.

1035. Kenora Sexual Assault Centre

✣ Kenora, Ont. Formed 1976.

The Kenora Sexual Assault Centre (KSAC) assists women and children in crisis. It offers counselling, a crisis line, public education on issues of violence, and advocacy. Until 1990 it was part of Women's Place Kenora. [See also Women's Place Kenora (1109).]

LOCATION OF RECORDS: Kenora Sexual Assault Centre. [*Mailing Address:* Box 687, Kenora, Ont. P9N 3X6. *Telephone:* (807) 468-7958. *Fax:* (807) 468-4808.]

RECORDS: Constitution, 1990; minutes, correspondence, telephone logbooks, financial records, grant applications, client records, mailing lists, pamphlets, flyers, press releases, 1990-1991.

CONDITION: Good.

ACCESS: Permission required. Client files closed.

1036. Kitchener-Waterloo Young Women's Christian Association

[See also entry # 414 (in Part I), which lists other records of this organization.]

✣ Kitchener-Waterloo, Ont. Formed 1905.

Originally called the Young Women's Christian Association of Berlin, the Kitchener-Waterloo YWCA provides services for women and children in response to current needs. Its services have included temporary housing, child care, and a physical-education programme.

LOCATION OF RECORDS: Kitchener-Waterloo Young Women's Christian Association. [*Address:* 84 Frederick St., Kitchener, Ont. N2H 2L7. *Telephone:* (519) 744-6507. *Fax:* (519) 747-4475.]

RECORDS: Financial records, 1989-1991; membership lists, photographs, 1980-1991; buttons, 1988; T-shirts, 1990-1991; banners, 1990; clippings, 1987-1991; sound recordings, 1989; videotapes, 1988-1991; newsletters (*Interchange*, 1990-1991; *Hoots from the Y's Owl*; *Behind the Blue Triangle*); constitution, minutes, correspondence, log-books, grant applications, client records, reports, conference proceedings, pamphlets, flyers, press releases.

AMOUNT: 3 filing cabinets.

CONDITION: Good.

ACCESS: Permission required. Client files closed; certain other records confidential.

1037. Korean Canadian Women's Association

✣ Toronto, Ont. Formed 1985.

The chief aims of the Korean Canadian Women's Association (KCWA) are to provide culturally sensitive family and social services and to help Korean-Canadian women and their children to integrate into Canadian society. KCWA operates primarily in Ontario.

LOCATION OF RECORDS: Korean Canadian Women's Association. [*Address:* 593 Yonge St., Suite 302, Toronto, Ont. M4Y 1Z4. *Telephone:* (416) 975-3868. *Fax:* (416) 975-8236.]

RECORDS: Constitution, 1985; minutes, correspondence, 1983-1991; logbooks, financial records, grant applications, client records, membership lists, mailing lists, scrapbooks, reports, conference proceedings, press releases, newsletters, 1985-1991; pamphlets, videotapes, 1986; T-shirts, 1986-1991; banners, 1990; books, 1989; petitions, clippings, photographs.

AMOUNT: 1 filing cabinet.

CONDITION: Good.

ACCESS: Permission required. Client files closed.

1038. Lakehead Social Planning Council. Childcare Committee

✣ Thunder Bay, Ont. Formed 1974. Disbanded 1984.

Before 1985 the Childcare Committee of the Lakehead Social Planning Council (LSPC) was the day-care advocacy voice for the region. In 1985 LSPC began directing day-care concerns to the Northwestern Ontario Regional Day Care Committee. [See also Northwestern Ontario Regional Day Care Committee (1053).]

LOCATION OF RECORDS: Lakehead Social Planning Council. Childcare Committee. [*Address:* 221 Bay St., Thunder Bay, Ont. P7B 1R1. *Telephone:* (807) 345-3631.]

RECORDS: Minutes, correspondence, grant applications, membership lists, mailing lists, reports, briefs, conference proceedings, press releases, 1979-1984.

AMOUNT: Half a drawer of a filing cabinet.

CONDITION: Fair.

1039. Lanark County Interval House and Sexual Assault Centre

✣ Carleton Place, Ont. Formed 1979.

This organization offers shelter and support to abused women and their children and provides sexual-assault services.

LOCATION OF RECORDS: Lanark County Interval House and Sexual Assault Centre. [*Mailing Address:* Box 107, Carleton Place, Ont. K7C 3P3. *Telephone:* (613) 257-3469.]

RECORDS: Minutes, financial records, client records, 1978-1991; newsletters (*Interval*, 1985-1991); constitution, grant applications, membership lists, mailing lists, scrapbooks, reports, briefs, pamphlets, press releases, posters, buttons, T-shirts, banners, clippings, photographs, videotapes.

AMOUNT: 1 filing cabinet.

CONDITION: Good.

ACCESS: Permission required. Client files closed.

1040. Lesbian and Gay Community Appeal of Toronto

[See also entry # 416 (in Part I), which lists other records of this organization.]

✣ Toronto, Ont. Formed 1980.

The Lesbian and Gay Community Appeal of Toronto (LGCA) provides project funding for lesbian and gay groups and individuals in areas such as health, culture, and politics. LGCA produces "Fruit Cocktail," a lesbian and gay musical comedy revue. LGCA was originally called the Gay Community Appeal of Toronto.

LOCATION OF RECORDS: Lesbian and Gay Community Appeal of Toronto. [*Mailing Address:* P.O. Box 2212, Station P, Toronto, Ont. M5S 2T2. *Telephone:* (416) 920-5422.]
RECORDS: Minutes, financial records, 1981-1991; grant applications, 1989-1991; constitution, 1988; newsletters, 1983-1990; membership lists, mailing lists, reports, pamphlets, buttons, banners, books, videotapes.
AMOUNT: 2 storage lockers.
CONDITION: Fair.
ACCESS: Permission required. Membership and mailing lists confidential.

1041. Midwifery Task Force of Ontario

✣ Toronto, Ont. Formed 1983.

The Midwifery Task Force of Ontario (MFTO) does public education and political lobbying on the issue of midwifery.

LOCATION OF RECORDS: Midwifery Task Force of Ontario. [*Mailing Address:* P.O. Box 64, Toronto, Ont. M5A 1N0. (*Street Address:* 260 Adelaide St. E.) *Telephone:* (807) 475-8815.]
RECORDS: Constitution, 1988-1991; minutes, financial records, membership lists, mailing lists, reports, briefs, 1983-1991; grant applications, photographs, sound recordings, videotapes, 1987-1991; conference proceedings, buttons, 1987; pamphlets, flyers, T-shirts, 1991; posters, 1989; newsletters (*Issue*, 1983-1991); correspondence.
AMOUNT: 1 filing cabinet.
CONDITION: Good.
ACCESS: Permission required.

1042. Mothers Are Women

✣ Ottawa, Ont. Formed 1984.

Mothers Are Women (MAW) aims to support and empower women at home by bringing their voices into the feminist movement and into mainstream society. MAW publishes a periodical, *Homebase*.

LOCATION OF RECORDS: Mothers Are Women. [*Mailing Address:* P.O. Box 4104, Station E, Ottawa, Ont. K1S 5B1. *Telephone:* (613) 722-7851.]
RECORDS: Correspondence, scrapbooks, [198-]-1991; financial records, grant applications, clippings, 1984-1991; reports, 1987-1991; newsletters (*Homebase*, 1984-1991); films, 1991; membership lists, mailing lists, pamphlets, flyers, buttons.
CONDITION: Good.
ACCESS: Permission required.

1043. Mrs Dalloway's Books

✣ Kingston, Ont. Formed 1984.

This is a women's bookstore which also serves as an information clearinghouse, an informal meeting place for women, and a lesbian-positive space. Mrs Dalloway's Books occasionally sponsors readings by authors and other events.

LOCATION OF RECORDS: Mrs Dalloway's Books. [*Address:* #1 - 72 Princess St., Kingston, Ont. K7L 1A5. *Telephone:* (613) 544-4243.]
RECORDS: Correspondence, posters, photographs, 1984-1990; financial records, 1984-1991; clippings, 1986.
AMOUNT: 1 filing cabinet.
CONDITION: Good.
ACCESS: Permission required.

1044. Multicultural Council of Professional Women

✣ Ottawa, Ont. Formed 1989.

This council addresses issues facing foreign-trained professional women, especially underemployment and unemployment. It does networking, provides skills training, and operates a resource centre.

LOCATION OF RECORDS: Multicultural Council of Professional Women. [*Address:* c/o Catholic Immigration Centre, 219 Argyle, Ottawa, Ont. *Telephone:* (613) 232-9634, ext. 120.]
RECORDS: Constitution, 1990-1991; minutes, correspondence, financial records, grant applications, membership lists, mailing lists, petitions, briefs, pamphlets, flyers, clippings, photographs, 1989-1991; reports, 1989.
AMOUNT: 1 filing cabinet.
CONDITION: Good.
ACCESS: Permission required.

1045. Multicultural Women's Association

✣ Ottawa, Ont. Formed 1981.

The Multicultural Women's Association (MWA), which has also been called the Multicultural Women's Centre, strives for social justice and equality for immigrant women and women who belong to visible and ethnic minorities. MWA does public education and lobbying and encourages women to explore and respect one another's culture. The association began as the Women's Outreach Program of the Ottawa-Carleton Immigrant Services Organization (OCISO).

LOCATION OF RECORDS: Multicultural Women's Association. [*Mailing Address:* P.O. Box 2866, Ottawa, Ont. K1P 5W8. *Telephone:* (613) 230-4473.]
RECORDS: Constitution, 1989; minutes, correspondence, membership lists, mailing lists, 1980-1991; financial records, grant applications, petitions.
AMOUNT: 1 filing cabinet.
CONDITION: Fair.
ACCESS: Permission required.

1046. National Association of Women in Construction. Ottawa, Ontario Chapter 319

✣ Ottawa, Ont. Formed 1986.

This association, also known as NAWIC, encourages women to pursue careers in construction.

LOCATION OF RECORDS: National Association of Women in Construction. Ottawa, Ontario Chapter 319. [*Address:* 196 Bronson Ave., Ottawa, Ont. K1R 6H4. *Telephone:* (613) 736-7043.]
RECORDS: By-laws, minutes, correspondence, financial records, membership lists, mailing lists, scrapbooks, reports, pamphlets, flyers, posters, T-shirts, sweatshirts, banners, newsletters, clippings, photographs.
AMOUNT: 1 filing cabinet.
CONDITION: Good.
ACCESS: Permission required. Correspondence, financial records closed.

1047. Native Women's Centre (Hamilton, Ont.)

✣ Hamilton, Ont. Formed 1975.

The Native Women's Centre (NWC) provides emergency accommodation and other essential services to women and children. It is a project of the Hamilton-Wentworth Chapter of Native Women (HWCNW).

LOCATION OF RECORDS: Native Women's Centre. [*Address:* 47 East Ave. N., Hamilton, Ont. L8L 5H4. *Telephone:* (416) 522-1501.]

RECORDS: Constitution, 1974-1975, 1983-1984, 1987-1988; minutes, correspondence, log-books, financial records, grant applications, client records, membership lists, mailing lists, reports, 1975-1991; pamphlets, 1991; newsletters, 1975-1980; photographs, 1975; videotapes, 1982.
AMOUNT: 4 filing cabinets, 8 boxes.
CONDITION: Good.
ACCESS: Permission required. Client files and daily log-books closed.

1048. Native Women's Resource Centre (Toronto, Ont.)

✣ Toronto, Ont. Formed 1984.

Operated by and for Native women, the Native Women's Resource Centre (NWRC) provides both emergency and long-term services, including counselling, an information and referral service, housing and employment assistance, provision of food and clothing, workshops, support groups, networking, and lobbying.

LOCATION OF RECORDS: Native Women's Resource Centre. [*Address:* 245 Gerrard St. E., Toronto, Ont. M5A 2G1. *Telephone:* (416) 963-9963. *Fax:* (416) 963-9573.]
RECORDS: Constitution, minutes, log-books, financial records, client records, membership lists, mailing lists, reports, conference proceedings, pamphlets, flyers, buttons, T-shirts, banners, 1986-1991; newsletters (*Women Spirit Newsletter*); photographs, videotapes.
AMOUNT: 10 filing cabinets.
CONDITION: Good.
ACCESS: Permission required. Client files closed.

1049. Nellie Langford Rowell Library

✣ North York, Ont. Formed 1983.

This library, which houses books, periodicals, and other material related to women, has its roots in a collection which the New Feminists began to build in 1969. When the New Feminists disbanded, the collection was passed on to the Women's Place, which later gave it to the YWCA of Metropolitan Toronto. Material was donated by many individuals and groups, including the Lesbian Organization of Toronto. In 1983 the collection was moved to York University on loan as the York-YWCA Women's Collection. In 1985 York University was able to establish the library on a permanent basis, and it was then named the Nellie Langford Rowell Library. [See also Young Women's Christian Association of Metropolitan Toronto (581, 1116).]

LOCATION OF RECORDS: Nellie Langford Rowell Library. [*Address:* 204 Founders College, York University, 4700 Keele St., North York, Ont. M3J 1P3. *Telephone:* (416) 736-2100, ext. 33219.]
RECORDS: Constitution, 1990; minutes, correspondence, 1985-1991; log-books, 1988-1990; financial records, reports, 1987-1991; pamphlets, 1988; flyers, 1989; membership cards, miscellaneous records.
AMOUNT: 2 drawers of a filing cabinet.
CONDITION: Good.
ACCESS: Permission required.

1050. New Experiences for Refugee Women

✣ Toronto, Ont. Formed 1984.

In order to facilitate the social, cultural, and economic integration of Latin American women into Canadian society, New Experiences for Refugee Women (NEW) offers practical programmes which help women develop employment and life skills. The group's Spanish name is Nuevas Experiencias para Mujeres Refugiadas.

LOCATION OF RECORDS: New Experiences for Refugee Women. [*Address:* 815 Danforth Ave., Suite 406, Toronto, Ont. M4J 1L2. *Telephone:* (416) 469-0196.]
RECORDS: Constitution, 1984-1991; newsletters, 1987-1991; minutes, correspondence, financial records, grant applications, client records, membership lists, mailing lists, reports, briefs, conference proceedings, pamphlets, flyers, press releases, books, clippings, photographs, sound recordings, videotapes, testimony.
CONDITION: Good.
ACCESS: Permission required. Client files closed.

1051. Northern Woman Journal

✣ Thunder Bay, Ont. Formed 1973.

The *Northern Woman Journal* promotes a feminist awareness of the situation of women. In addition to covering issues of global and national concern, it features articles of particular relevance to Northwestern Ontario women. [See also Northern Women's Centre (451).]

LOCATION OF RECORDS: Northern Woman Journal. [*Mailing Address:* Box 144, Thunder Bay, Ont. P7C 4V5.]
RECORDS: Periodicals (*Northern Woman Journal*, 1973-1991); publications, [197-]; mailing lists, buttons, photographs.
AMOUNT: Approx. 2 cabinets.
ACCESS: Permission required.

1052. Northern Woman's Bookstore

✣ Thunder Bay, Ont. Formed 1983.

The Northern Woman's Bookstore provides access to feminist literature through a storefront location and a mail order service.

LOCATION OF RECORDS: Northern Woman's Bookstore. [*Address:* 184 Camelot St., Thunder Bay, Ont. P7A 4A9. *Telephone:* (807) 344-7979.]
RECORDS: Correspondence, financial records, flyers, 1983-1991; scrapbooks, 1983-1988; mailing lists, photographs, book lists.
AMOUNT: Approx. 2 cabinets.
CONDITION: Good.
ACCESS: Permission required. Mailing lists would not be provided without individual readers' permission.

1053. Northwestern Ontario Regional Day Care Committee

✣ Thunder Bay, Ont. Formed 1985.

The Northwestern Ontario (NWO) Regional Day Care Committee lobbies for a universal, comprehensive, non-profit, high-quality child-care system. [See also Lakehead Social Planning Council. Childcare Committee (1038).]

LOCATION OF RECORDS: Northwestern Ontario Regional Day Care Committee. [*Mailing Address:* Box 144, Thunder Bay, Ont. P7C 4V5. *Telephone:* (807) 345-8803.]
RECORDS: Minutes, correspondence, financial records, 1985-1991; grant applications, newsletters, 1987-1991; reports, briefs, 1986-1991; membership lists, mailing lists, conference proceedings, pamphlets, flyers, banners, clippings, photographs, sound recordings, videotapes, studies.
AMOUNT: Approx. 2 filing cabinets, 1 bookcase.
CONDITION: Good.
ACCESS: Permission required. The committee reserves the right to limit access.

Flyer / Tract, 1991
New Experiences for Refugee Women
CWMA Collection / Fonds de l'ACMF

1054. Northwestern Ontario Women's Decade Council

✣ Thunder Bay, Ont. Formed 1976.

This is an umbrella organization for groups and individuals working to improve the status of women. Its main activities are lobbying, networking, and providing resources. Until 1982 it was known as the Northwestern Ontario International Women's Decade Co-ordinating Council.

LOCATION OF RECORDS: Northwestern Ontario Women's Decade Council. [*Address:* R.R. #16, Mitchell Rd., Thunder Bay, Ont. P7B 6B3. *Telephone:* (807) 683-5662.]

RECORDS: Constitution, 1986; minutes, correspondence, financial records, grant applications, membership lists, mailing lists, reports, briefs, conference proceedings, pamphlets, flyers, press releases, 1976-1991; books, 1986; posters, buttons, T-shirts, banners, clippings, photographs.

AMOUNT: Approx. 3 filing cabinets.

CONDITION: Good.

ACCESS: Permission required. Some files may be closed.

1055. Northwestern Ontario Women's Health Information Network

✣ Thunder Bay, Ont. Formed 1982.

The Northwestern Ontario Women's Health Information Network (WHIN) works to enable women to take responsibility for their health and to participate actively in their health care. The network grew out of the Northwestern Ontario Women's Health Education Project. WHIN also has a branch in Kenora.

LOCATION OF RECORDS: Northwestern Ontario Women's Health Information Network. [*Address:* 4A South Court St., Suite 17, Thunder Bay, Ont. P7B 2W4. *Telephone:* (807) 345-1410. *Fax:* (807) 343-4236.]

RECORDS: Constitution, minutes, correspondence, financial records, grant applications, membership lists, mailing lists, scrapbooks, reports, 1982-1991; pamphlets, press releases, T-shirts, banners, newsletters, books, clippings, photographs.

CONDITION: Good.

ACCESS: Permission required.

1056. Older Women's Network

✣ Toronto, Ont. Formed 1988.

The Older Women's Network (OWN) helps older women to participate actively in decision making which affects their lives and society in general. OWN's activities include advocacy on behalf of older women and the building of a co-operative residence.

LOCATION OF RECORDS: Older Women's Network. [*Address:* 427 Bloor St., Suite B4, Toronto, Ont. M5S 1X7. *Telephone:* (416) 924-4188.]

RECORDS: Constitution, minutes, correspondence, financial records, grant applications, membership lists, mailing lists, scrapbooks, reports, briefs, conference proceedings, pamphlets, flyers, press releases, banners, clippings, photographs, 1988-1991; newsletters (*Contact*, 1988-1991).

AMOUNT: Approx. 1 filing cabinet.

CONDITION: Good.

ACCESS: Permission required.

1057. Ontario Association of Interval and Transition Houses

✣ Toronto, Ont. Formed 1978.

The Ontario Association of Interval and Transition Houses (OAITH) is a network of houses for abused women and their children. OAITH lobbies all levels of government on issues relating to woman abuse.

LOCATION OF RECORDS: Ontario Association of Interval and Transition Houses. [*Address:* 229 College St., Suite 105, Toronto, Ont. M5T 1R4. *Telephone:* (416) 977-6619. *Fax:* (416) 977-6619.]

RECORDS: Constitution, minutes, correspondence, financial records, 1978-1991; grant applications, reports, 1981-1991; membership lists, 1991; briefs, 1982-1991; conference proceedings, 1985-1991; flyers, 1989; buttons, banners, 1989-1991; T-shirts, videotapes, 1990.

AMOUNT: Approx. 4 filing cabinets.

CONDITION: Fair.

ACCESS: Permission required.

1058. Ontario Farm Women's Network

✣ Iroquois, Ont. Formed 1988.

The Ontario Farm Women's Network (OFWN) works to secure social, legal, and economic equality for farm women in Ontario and to strengthen the family farm.

LOCATION OF RECORDS: Ontario Farm Women's Network. [*Address:* R.R. 1, Iroquois, Ont. K0E 1K0. *Telephone:* (613) 652-2097. *Fax:* (613) 652-2097.]

RECORDS: Minutes, correspondence, financial records, grant applications, membership lists, mailing lists, petitions, scrapbooks, reports, newsletters, 1988-1991; briefs, conference proceedings, pamphlets, flyers, press releases, posters, buttons, 1989-1990; T-shirts, banners, 1990; constitution, clippings, photographs.

AMOUNT: 1 filing cabinet.

CONDITION: Good.

ACCESS: Permission required. Membership and mailing lists closed.

1059. Ontario Liberal Party. Women's Perspective Advisory Committee

✣ Toronto, Ont. Formed 1982.

The Women's Perspective Advisory Committee (WPAC) of the Ontario Liberal Party works to have women in leadership positions in the party, encourages women to become candidates, and prepares policy papers.

LOCATION OF RECORDS: Ontario Liberal Party. Women's Perspective Advisory Committee. [*Address:* 10 St Mary St., Suite 310, Toronto, Ont. M4Y 1P9. *Telephone:* (416) 961-3800.]

RECORDS: Constitution, 1982-1989; correspondence, financial records, petitions, reports, briefs, pamphlets, flyers, press releases, posters.

AMOUNT: 1 cabinet.

CONDITION: Good.

ACCESS: Permission required.

1060. Ontario Native Women's Association

✣ Thunder Bay, Ont. Formed 1971.

The Ontario Native Women's Association (ONWA) represents Native women and their families living on reserves or elsewhere. ONWA's main activities are lobbying, education, and consultation on issues of employment, anti-racism, family violence, self-government, and community and economic development.

LOCATION OF RECORDS: Ontario Native Women's Association. [*Address:* 115 North May St., Thunder Bay, Ont. P7C 3N8. *Fax:* (807) 623-1104.]

RECORDS: Constitution, [1973?]; minutes, correspondence, log-books, financial records, grant applications, membership lists, mailing lists,

reports, briefs, conference proceedings, pamphlets, flyers, press releases, banners, 1971-1991; photographs, sound recordings, videotapes.
CONDITION: Good.
ACCESS: Permission required.

1061. Ottawa Women's Centre

[See also entry # 466 (in Part I), which lists other records of this organization.]

✣ Ottawa, Ont. Formed 1972. Disbanded 1980.

The Ottawa Women's Centre, also known as the Women's Centre of Ottawa-Carleton, was committed to the struggle for the liberation of women. The centre provided various services, resources, and activities in support of this aim. The centre's French name was le Centre des femmes d'Ottawa. [See also Chez nous (1008) and Ottawa Women's Information and Referral Service (1062).]

LOCATION OF RECORDS: Women's Place. [*Address:* 241 Bruyère St., Ottawa, Ont. K1N 5E5. *Telephone:* (613) 789-2155. *Fax:* (613) 789-2745.]

RECORDS: Constitution, 1975; minutes, correspondence, financial records, 1972-1980; log-books, 1975-1978; grant applications, membership lists, flyers, newsletters, 1972-1979; reports, 1973-1975; pamphlets, [197-]; press releases, 1973-1979; books, 1976; clippings, 1972-1978; photographs, [1975?].

AMOUNT: Approx. 1 filing cabinet.
CONDITION: Good.

1062. Ottawa Women's Information and Referral Service

✣ Ottawa, Ont. Formed 1978. Disbanded [1979 or 1980].

The Ottawa Women's Information and Referral Service (OWIRS) provided support, information, and referrals. OWIRS started as a part of the Ottawa Women's Centre. [See also Ottawa Women's Centre (466, 1061).]

LOCATION OF RECORDS: Women's Place. [*Address:* 241 Bruyère St., Ottawa, Ont. K1N 5E5. *Telephone:* (613) 789-2155. *Fax:* (613) 789-2745.]

RECORDS: Minutes, correspondence, financial records, grant applications, 1978-1979; clippings, 1978; manual, 1979.

AMOUNT: Approx. 15 cm.
CONDITION: Good.

1063. Pink Triangle Services / Services du triangle rose

[Renseignements en français, notice 1074.]

✣ Ottawa, Ont. Formed 1983.

Pink Triangle Services (PTS) aims to foster an understanding of homosexuality and promote a gay-positive attitude within the lesbian and gay community and society at large. One service offered by PTS is Gayline, a telephone counselling and information and referral service.

LOCATION OF RECORDS: Pink Triangle Services. [*Mailing Address:* Box 3043, Station D, Ottawa, Ont. K1P 6H8. *Telephone:* (613) 563-4818.]

RECORDS: Constitution, minutes, correspondence, financial records, grant applications, client records, membership lists, mailing lists, reports, pamphlets, banners, 1983-1991; newsletters (*Triangle*, 1989-1991).

CONDITION: Good.
ACCESS: Permission required. Client files and membership lists closed.

1064. Place aux femmes / Women's Place (Ottawa, Ont.)

[For English entry, see # 1110.]

✣ Ottawa (Ont.). Groupe fondé 1984.

Place aux femmes est un centre de femmes qui encourage tous les efforts visant à promouvoir et à garantir la maîtrise totale par la femme de tous les aspects de sa vie en tant que femme. Le centre offre un service d'information et de référence et un lieu de rencontre pour les femmes.

LIEU DE CONSULTATION: Place aux femmes. [*Adresse:* 241, rue Bruyère, Ottawa (Ont.) K1N 5E5. *Téléphone:* (613) 789-2155. *Télécopieur:* (613) 789-2745.]

MATÉRIEL: Statuts et règlements, 1985; procès-verbaux, 1984-1991; correspondance, documents financiers, demandes de subvention, listes de membres, listes d'envoi, tracts, communiqués de presse, 1985-1991; journaux de bord, 1987-1991; rapports, 1988-1991; dépliants, photographies, 1986-1991; calendrier des événements, 1989-1991; macarons, bannières.

QUANTITÉ: Env. 3 classeurs.
ÉTAT: Bon.

1065. Planned Parenthood Ontario

[See also entry # 472 (in Part I), which lists other records of this organization.]

✣ Toronto, Ont. Formed 1972.

Planned Parenthood Ontario (PPO) promotes responsible sexuality and reproductive choice through public education and advocacy.

LOCATION OF RECORDS: Planned Parenthood Ontario. [*Mailing Address:* P.O. Box 953, Station P, Toronto, Ont. M5S 2S2. *Telephone:* (416) 922-9290.]

RECORDS: Constitutions, 1972, 1986; minutes, correspondence, financial records, 1972-1991; grant applications, briefs, 1991; mailing lists, 1989-1991; reports, 1986, 1988; conference proceedings, 1990; newsletters (*Choice Words*, 1989-1991).

AMOUNT: 2 filing cabinets, 1 book shelf.
CONDITION: Good.

1066. Planned Parenthood Society of Hamilton

[See also entry # 473 (in Part I), which lists other records of this organization.]

✣ Hamilton, Ont. Formed 1931.

The Planned Parenthood Society of Hamilton (PPSH) is dedicated to creating a community where responsible and healthy sexual behaviour is practised and supported. PPSH was originally known as the Maternal Health Clinic, and subsequently as the Birth Control Society of Hamilton.

LOCATION OF RECORDS: Planned Parenthood Society of Hamilton. [*Address:* 20 Hughson St. S., #611, Hamilton, Ont. L8N 2A1. *Telephone:* (416) 528-3009.]

RECORDS: Constitution, minutes, correspondence, financial records, grant applications, membership lists, mailing lists, reports, briefs, pamphlets, press releases, 1986-1991; client records, 1977-1991; buttons, 1989; T-shirts, 1990; banner, 1973; newsletters (*For the Public Good*, 1974); books, 1970; photographs, 1932; slides, 1982.

CONDITION: Poor.
ACCESS: Permission required.

1067. Planned Parenthood Waterloo Region

✣ Kitchener, Ont. Formed 1971.

Planned Parenthood Waterloo Region (PPWR) promotes responsible and healthy sexuality and birth planning by providing counselling and information, educational programmes, and a resource library.

LOCATION OF RECORDS: Planned Parenthood Waterloo Region. [*Address:* 119 King St. W., Kitchener, Ont. N2G 1A7. *Telephone:* (519) 743-9360.]
RECORDS: Constitution, 1972-1991; minutes, financial records, reports, 1973-1991; briefs, 1990; client records, membership lists, grant applications, pamphlets, press releases, newsletters (*Happenstance*).
AMOUNT: Approx. 4 filing cabinets.
CONDITION: Good.
ACCESS: Permission required. Client files and membership lists closed.

1068. Project Hostel

✢ Aurora, Ont. Formed 1978.

Project Hostel, also known as Yellow Brick House, offers emergency shelter and crisis intervention to women and children.

LOCATION OF RECORDS: Project Hostel. [*Telephone:* (416) 727-0930. *Fax:* (416) 727-7316.]
RECORDS: Minutes, log-books, client records, 1978-1991; correspondence, grant applications, membership lists, 1982-1991; financial records, 1985-1991; mailing lists, 1987, 1991; scrapbooks, reports, clippings, 1979-1991; T-shirts, 1989; banners, 1984-1991; videotapes, 1990; constitution, posters, photographs.
AMOUNT: 6 filing cabinets, 12 boxes.
CONDITION: Fair.
ACCESS: Permission required. Client files closed.

1069. Provincial Council of Women of Ontario

[See also entry # 476 (in Part I), which lists other records of this organization.]

✢ Formed 1923.

The Provincial Council of Women of Ontario (PCWO) is a network of local councils of women throughout the province.

LOCATION OF RECORDS: Provincial Council of Women of Ontario. [*Address:* 128 Gregory Dr. W., Chatham, Ont. N7L 2L4.]
RECORDS: Constitution, minutes, correspondence, membership lists, mailing lists, reports, 1923-1991; financial records, grant applications.
CONDITION: Good.
ACCESS: Permission required.

1070. Queen's University. Women's Centre

✢ Kingston, Ont. Formed 1976.

The Queen's University Women's Centre provides information and a women-only environment for women at the university and elsewhere in Kingston.

LOCATION OF RECORDS: Queen's University. Women's Centre. [*Address:* 51 Queen's Crescent, Kingston, Ont. K7L 3N6. *Telephone:* (613) 545-2963.]
RECORDS: Newsletters (*Off Limits*, 1988); constitution, minutes, correspondence, financial records, posters, banners.
AMOUNT: 3 filing cabinets.
CONDITION: Good.

1071. Réseau des femmes du Sud de l'Ontario

✢ Toronto (Ont.). Groupe fondé 1982.

Le réseau, appelé aussi le RFSO, vise à coordonner l'action communautaire en vue d'améliorer la prestation de services socio-communautaires en français, à outiller les femmes pour qu'elles prennent le contrôle de leur vie et à amener des changements d'attitudes dans la communauté par rapport aux besoins des femmes. Le Centre de recherches et de ressources pour femmes, au Collège Glendon, est le siège social du réseau.

LIEU DE CONSULTATION : Réseau des femmes du Sud de l'Ontario. [*Adresse :* a/s Collège Glendon, 2275, av. Bayview, Manoir 301, Toronto (Ont.) M4N 3M6. *Téléphone :* (416) 487-6794. *Télécopieur :* (416) 487-6728.]
MATÉRIEL : Statuts et règlements, 1990; procès-verbaux, documents financiers, demandes de subvention, dossiers concernant la clientèle, listes de membres, listes d'envoi, rapports, mémoires, actes de congrès, dépliants, coupures de presse, 1985-1991; bannières, 1991.
QUANTITÉ : 2 rangées.
ÉTAT : Bon.
ACCÈS : Permission requise.

1072. Scarborough Women's Centre

✢ Scarborough, Ont. Formed 1982.

The Scarborough Women's Centre (SWC) helps women equip themselves for full participation in the community, by providing information, education, and support. SWC runs the Scarborough Women's Action Network (SWAN).

LOCATION OF RECORDS: Scarborough Women's Centre. [*Address:* 91 East Park Blvd., Scarborough, Ont. M1H 1C6. *Telephone:* (416) 431-1138. *Fax:* (416) 431-1547.]
RECORDS: Constitution, buttons, 1982; minutes, correspondence, financial records, grant applications, membership lists, pamphlets, 1982-1991; reports, press releases, 1986-1991; banners, 1990; guides, 1989-1990; mailing lists, flyers.
AMOUNT: Approx. 1 filing cabinet, 4 boxes.
CONDITION: Fair.
ACCESS: Permission required.

1073. Service, Office, and Retail Workers' Union of Canada. Local 7

✢ Ottawa, Ont. Formed 1982. Disbanded [198-].

The Service, Office, and Retail Workers' Union of Canada (SORWUC) was a feminist, member-controlled union founded in Vancouver in 1972. Local 7 was chartered for the region of Ontario. Its objective was to organize workers, the unemployed, women on welfare, and women working in the home. SORWUC disbanded in 1986. [See also Service, Office, and Retail Workers' Union of Canada. Local 4 (Bank and Finance Workers) (146).]

LOCATION OF RECORDS: Women's Place. [*Address:* 241 Bruyère St., Ottawa, Ont. K1N 5E5. *Telephone:* (613) 789-2155. *Fax:* (613) 789-2745.]
RECORDS: Constitution, membership lists, 1982; minutes, correspondence, financial records, pamphlets, 1982-1983; mailing lists, [1982 or 1983]; clippings, 1983.
AMOUNT: 1 drawer of a filing cabinet.
CONDITION: Good.

1074. Services du triangle rose / Pink Triangle Services

[For English entry, see # 1063.]

✢ Ottawa (Ont.). Groupe fondé 1983.

L'objectif principal des Services du triangle rose (STR) est de favoriser une meilleure compréhension de l'homosexualité et de promouvoir une attitude plus positive à l'égard des lesbiennes et des hommes gais. L'un des programmes des STR est Télégai, qui dispense des conseils et des services d'information et de références professionnelles.

Flyer / Tract, [1987?]
Sister Vision: Black Women and Women of Colour Press
CWMA Collection / Fonds de l'ACMF

LIEU DE CONSULTATION : Services du triangle rose. [*Adresse postale* : C.P. 3043, Succursale D, Ottawa (Ont.) K1P 6H8. *Téléphone* : (613) 563-4818.]

MATÉRIEL : Statuts et règlements, procès-verbaux, correspondance, documents financiers, demandes de subvention, dossiers concernant la clientèle, listes de membres, listes d'envoi, rapports, dépliants, bannières, 1983-1991; bulletins (*Triangle*, 1989-1991).

ÉTAT : Bon.

ACCÈS : Permission requise. Dossiers concernant la clientèle et listes de membres confidentiels.

1075. Sexual Assault Centre London

✣ London, Ont. Formed [1975?].

The Sexual Assault Centre London (SACL) offers counselling and a crisis line, works to raise awareness of sexual assault, and offers support and training to other organizations and the general public.

LOCATION OF RECORDS: Sexual Assault Centre London. [*Address:* 700 Richmond St., Suite 210, London, Ont. N6A 5C7. *Telephone:* (519) 439-0844. *Fax:* (519) 439-9931.]

RECORDS: Constitution, minutes, correspondence, financial records, pamphlets, flyers, posters.

1076. Sexual Assault Support Centre of Ottawa / Centre d'aide aux agressées sexuelles d'Ottawa

[Renseignements en français, notice 1006.]

✣ Ottawa, Ont. Formed 1983.

The Sexual Assault Support Centre of Ottawa (SASC) provides counselling services to women who have survived sexual violence. It also works to educate the public, schools, universities, and other organizations about sexual assault, incest, and other forms of sexual violence against women.

LOCATION OF RECORDS: Sexual Assault Support Centre of Ottawa. [*Mailing Address:* P.O. Box 4441, Station E, Ottawa, Ont. K1S 5B4. *Telephone:* (613) 725-2160 or 234-2266.]

RECORDS: Minutes, log-books, financial records, grant applications, 1982-1991; miscellaneous records, 1989.

AMOUNT: 3 filing cabinets.

CONDITION: Fair.

ACCESS: Permission required. Log-books and minutes of meetings closed.

1077. Sister Vision: Black Women and Women of Colour Press

✣ Toronto, Ont. Formed 1985.

This community-based press provides a forum for the writing of women of colour and fosters understanding among Canada's diverse cultures by exposing mainstream Canada to true types instead of stereotypes.

LOCATION OF RECORDS: Sister Vision: Black Women and Women of Colour Press. [*Mailing Address:* Box 217, Station E, Toronto, Ont. M6H 4E2. *Telephone:* (416) 533-2184. *Fax:* (416) 536-3383.]

RECORDS: Correspondence, financial records, grant applications, client records, membership lists, pamphlets, flyers, press releases, posters, T-shirts, 1985-1991; constitution, log-books.

AMOUNT: 1 filing cabinet.

CONDITION: Fair.

ACCESS: Permission required.

1078. Sistering: A Drop-in Centre for Transient Women

✣ Toronto, Ont. Formed 1981.

This centre offers assistance and support to socially isolated, low-income, and homeless women.

LOCATION OF RECORDS: Sistering: A Drop-in Centre for Transient Women. [*Address:* 181 Bathurst St., Toronto, Ont. M5T 2R7. *Telephone:* (416) 861-1954. *Fax:* (416) 861-0958.]

RECORDS: Newsletters, 1983-1991; buttons, T-shirts, 1991; constitution, minutes, correspondence, log-books, financial records, grant applications, membership lists, mailing lists, scrapbooks, reports, briefs, pamphlets, flyers, banners, books, clippings, photographs, videotapes, posters.

CONDITION: Good.

ACCESS: Permission required.

1079. Skiltec Association

✣ North Bay, Ont. Formed 1982.

This association trains women in non-traditional trades. It was called Women into Non-traditional Training until 1983.

LOCATION OF RECORDS: Skiltec Association. [*Address:* 755 Wallace Rd., North Bay, Ont. P1B 8G4. *Telephone:* (705) 472-2102. *Fax:* (705) 472-7951.]

RECORDS: Minutes, financial records, grant applications, 1982-1991; client records, 1984-1991; reports, photographs, 1985-1991; pamphlets, 1990.

AMOUNT: 3 filing cabinets.

CONDITION: Good.

ACCESS: Project Manager's permission required for access to client files and financial records.

1080. South Asian Women's Group

✣ Toronto, Ont. Formed 1982.

Through services such as language training, career counselling, and advocacy, this group helps South Asian women to overcome social isolation, gain access to programmes and skills, achieve economic independence, and develop to their full potential.

LOCATION OF RECORDS: South Asian Women's Group. [*Address:* 973 1/2 Bloor St. W., Toronto, Ont. M6H 1L7. *Telephone:* (416) 537-2276.]

RECORDS: Constitution, photographs, 1982; minutes, financial records, 1989-1991; grant applications, 1982-1991; client records, mailing lists, pamphlets, flyers, newsletters, 1989; membership lists, banners, 1987; clippings, 1985.

AMOUNT: 1 filing cabinet.

CONDITION: Fair.

ACCESS: Permission required. Client files closed.

1081. Sudbury Women's Centre / Centre des femmes de Sudbury

[Renseignements en français, notice 1007.]

✣ Sudbury, Ont. Formed 1981.

This bilingual organization is dedicated to improving the status of women in Northern Ontario through public education, advocacy, and political action.

LOCATION OF RECORDS: Sudbury Women's Centre. [*Address:* 258 Victoria St., Sudbury, Ont. P3C 1K4. *Telephone:* (705) 673-1916.]

RECORDS: Constitution, minutes, correspondence, log-books, financial records, grant applications, membership lists, mailing lists, petitions,

PART II: RECORDS HELD BY GROUPS / PARTIE II : FONDS DÉTENUS PAR DES GROUPES

T-shirt, 1983
Sudbury Women's Centre / Centre des femmes de Sudbury
CWMA Collection / Fonds de l'ACMF

scrapbooks, reports, briefs, conference proceedings, pamphlets, flyers, press releases, banners, clippings, photographs, 1981-1991; posters, buttons, T-shirts, 1985-1991; newsletters, 1982-1991.

AMOUNT: 6 filing cabinets.

CONDITION: Fair.

ACCESS: Permission required. Financial records and related documents closed.

1082. Times Change Women's Employment Service

✣ Toronto, Ont. Formed 1974.

Times Change provides employment counselling for women in Metropolitan Toronto.

LOCATION OF RECORDS: Times Change Women's Employment Service. [*Address:* 22 Davisville Ave., Toronto, Ont. M4S 1E8. *Telephone:* (416) 487-2807.]

RECORDS: Minutes, 1982-1991; correspondence, log-books, 1986-1991; financial records, 1984-1991; grant applications, 1972-1991; client records, 1989-1991; membership lists, mailing lists, 1991; reports, briefs, 1981-1991; clippings, slide/tape show, videotapes.

AMOUNT: 20 boxes.

CONDITION: Good.

ACCESS: Permission required. Client files closed.

1083. Toronto Black Women's Collective

✣ Toronto, Ont. Formed [1985?].

The Toronto Black Women's Collective is dedicated to ending oppression against Black women and all other oppressed groups. It does public education and works toward solidarity with other communities in this struggle.

LOCATION OF RECORDS: Toronto Black Women's Collective. [*Mailing Address:* P.O. Box 248, Toronto, Ont. M5T 2W7. *Telephone:* (416) 536-2261.]

RECORDS: Constitution, [after 1985]; minutes, financial records, membership lists, mailing lists, pamphlets, flyers, 1985-1991; periodicals (*Our Lives,* [1987?]-[1990?]); film, 1991; scrapbooks, buttons, T-shirts.

AMOUNT: Approx. 3 boxes.

CONDITION: Good.

ACCESS: Permission required.

1084. Toronto Organization for Domestic Workers' Rights (Intercede)

✣ Toronto, Ont. Formed 1979.

This organization conducts research, does advocacy, and provides services to domestic workers in areas such as immigration, employment, human rights, and social services. The organization used to be called the International Coalition to End Domestic Exploitation (Intercede).

LOCATION OF RECORDS: Toronto Organization for Domestic Workers' Rights (Interecede). [*Address:* 489 College St., Suite 402, Toronto, Ont. M6G 1A5. *Telephone:* (416) 324-8751.]

RECORDS: Minutes, log-books, [1979?]-1991; correspondence, financial records, grant applications, client records, membership lists, mailing lists, petitions, reports, briefs, conference proceedings, pamphlets, flyers, press releases, buttons, T-shirts, banners, clippings, photographs, 1979-1991; newsletters (*Domestics' Cross-Cultural News*).

AMOUNT: 1 filing cabinet.

CONDITION: Good.

ACCESS: Permission required.

1085. Toronto Socialist Feminist Action

[See also entry # 505 (in Part I), which lists other records of this organization.]

✣ Toronto, Ont. Formed 1978.

Toronto Socialist Feminist Action (TSFA) was originally called the International Women's Day Committee (IWDC); it changed its name in 1989. IWDC was formed by women who had taken part in organizing the 1978 International Women's Day events in Toronto; from 1979 to 1984, it played a leadership role in the March 8th Coalition. IWDC made outreach to women in unions a priority. (Source: *Feminist Organizing for Change: The Contemporary Women's Movement in Canada* / Nancy Adamson, Linda Briskin, and Margaret McPhail. — Toronto: Oxford University Press, 1988.) TSFA is now an independent, multi-issue, socialist-feminist organization. It publishes a newsletter, *Rebel Girls' Rag: A Forum of Women's Resistance.* [See also March 8th Coalition (439) and Cayenne: A Socialist Feminist Bulletin (364).]

LOCATION OF RECORDS: Toronto Socialist Feminist Action. [*Mailing Address:* P.O. Box 70, Station F, Toronto, Ont. M4Y 2L4. *Telephone:* (416) 531-2369.]

RECORDS: Minutes, flyers, 1978-1991; financial records, 1980-1991; newsletters (*International Women's Day Committee Newsletter,* 1979-1986; *Rebel Girls' Rag: A Forum of Women's Resistance,* 1987-1991); membership lists, 1991; articles, 1987; T-shirts, 1990; banners, 1989.

AMOUNT: 1 drawer of a filing cabinet.

CONDITION: Good.

1086. Toronto Women in Film and Television

✣ Toronto, Ont. Formed 1984.

Toronto Women in Film and Television (TWIFT) works to improve the status and portrayal of women in film and television and to celebrate women's accomplishments in the field. The organization used to be called Toronto Women in Film and Video.

LOCATION OF RECORDS: Toronto Women in Film and Television. [*Address:* 150 John St., Suite 215, Toronto, Ont. M5V 3C3. *Telephone:* (416) 348-9578/9540. *Fax:* (416) 973-6318.]

RECORDS: Constitution, 1988; minutes, correspondence, financial records, membership lists, 1984-1991; client records, 1985-1991; reports, briefs, press releases, 1990-1991; conference proceedings, study, 1990; buttons, 1989; mailing lists, flyers, newsletters (*Changing Focus*), photographs, sound recordings, videotapes.

AMOUNT: 1 filing cabinet, 16 boxes.

CONDITION: Good.

ACCESS: Permission required. Client files closed.

1087. Trent Lesbian and Gay Collective

[See also entry # 511 (in Part I), which lists other records of this organization.]

✣ Peterborough, Ont. Formed 1972.

The Trent Lesbian and Gay Collective (TLGC) offers support, social events, and political activities to lesbians and gay men at Trent University and elsewhere in Peterborough. Originally known as the Trent Homophile Association (THA), it became Gays of Trent and Peterborough (GTP) and then Gays and Lesbians of Trent and Peterborough (GLTP).

LOCATION OF RECORDS: Trent Lesbian and Gay Collective. [*Address:* 290 Rubidge St., Peterborough, Ont. K9J 3P4. *Telephone:* (705) 743-5414.]

RECORDS: Minutes, 1987; correspondence, 1985-1991; financial records, posters, 1987-1991; pamphlets, buttons, 1991; T-shirts, 1989; newsletters, 1976-1991; clippings, photographs.

AMOUNT: 1 drawer of a filing cabinet.

CONDITION: Fair.

1088. Union culturelle des Franco-Ontariennes

[Voir aussi la notice 512 (dans la partie I) pour autres documents de ce groupe.]

✤ Ottawa (Ont.). Groupe fondé 1936.

Parmi ses objectifs, l'Union culturelle des Franco-Ontariennes (UCFO) vise à améliorer le statut socio-économique des femmes par la formation, l'information et la revendication. Jusqu'en 1969 l'UCFO portait le nom de l'Union catholique des fermières.

LIEU DE CONSULTATION : Union culturelle des Franco-Ontariennes. [*Adresse* : 50, rue Vaughan, salle 6, Ottawa (Ont.) K1M 1X1. *Téléphone* : (613) 741-1334. *Télécopieur* : (613) 741-8577.]

MATÉRIEL : Statuts et règlements, procès-verbaux, correspondance, listes de membres, listes d'envoi, albums de coupures, affiches, bannières, 1936-1991; documents financiers, demandes de subvention, rapports, mémoires, actes de congrès, dépliants, tracts, communiqués de presse, livres, 1982-1991; dossiers concernant la clientèle, photographies, [1936?]-1991; macarons, [1982?]; bulletins (*Communiqué*, 1982-1991).

QUANTITÉ : 5 classeurs, 3 bibliothèques, 3 placards.

ACCÈS : Permission requise.

1089. Union culturelle des Franco-Ontariennes (Sturgeon Falls, Ont.).

✤ Sturgeon Falls (Ont.).

L'Union culturelle des Franco-Ontariennes (UCFO) à Sturgeon Falls est un des soixante-huit cercles de l'UCFO. Parmi ses objectifs, l'UCFO (qui portait le nom de l'Union catholique des fermières jusqu'en 1969) vise à améliorer le statut socio-économique des femmes par la formation, l'information et la revendication.

LIEU DE CONSULTATION : Union culturelle des Franco-Ontariennes. [*Adresse postale* : C.P. 2642, Sturgeon Falls (Ont.).]

MATÉRIEL : Statuts et règlements, procès-verbaux, correspondance, documents financiers, demandes de subvention, dossiers concernant la clientèle, listes de membres, albums de coupures, rapports, actes de congrès, communiqués de presse, affiches, macarons, T-shirts, bannières, livres, coupures de presse, photographies.

QUANTITÉ : 1 classeur.

ÉTAT : Assez bon.

1090. Université d'Ottawa. Programme en études des femmes / University of Ottawa. Women's Studies Programme

[For English entry, see # 1091.]

✤ Ottawa (Ont.). Groupe fondé 1978.

Le Programme en études des femmes à l'Université d'Ottawa offre un baccalauréat ès arts avec concentration en études des femmes. [Voir aussi La Collective (Université d'Ottawa)/The Collective (University of Ottawa) (1014).]

LIEU DE CONSULTATION : Université d'Ottawa. Programme en études des femmes. [*Adresse* : 143 Séraphin-Marion, Ottawa (Ont.) K1N 6N5. *Téléphone* : (613) 564-4019. *Télécopieur* : (613) 564-7461.]

MATÉRIEL : Procès-verbaux, listes de membres, listes d'envoi, dépliants, 1977-1991; correspondance, rapports, livres, 1978-1991; documents financiers, demandes de subvention, tracts, 1983-1991; communiqués de presse, 1990; T-shirts, 1988-1991; coupures de presse, photographies, enregistrements sonores.

ÉTAT : Bon.

ACCÈS : Permission requise.

1091. University of Ottawa. Women's Studies Programme / Université d'Ottawa. Programme en études des femmes

[Renseignements en français, notice 1090.]

✤ Ottawa, Ont. Formed 1978.

The Women's Studies Programme at the University of Ottawa offers a B.A. with concentration in women's studies. [See also The Collective (University of Ottawa)/La Collective (Université d'Ottawa) (1015).]

LOCATION OF RECORDS: University of Ottawa. Women's Studies Programme. [*Address*: 143 Séraphin-Marion, Ottawa, Ont. K1N 6N5. *Telephone*: (613) 564-4019. *Fax*: (613) 564-7461.]

RECORDS: Minutes, membership lists, mailing lists, pamphlets, 1977-1991; correspondence, reports, books, 1978-1991; financial records, grant applications, flyers, 1983-1991; press releases, 1990; T-shirts, 1988-1991; clippings, photographs, sound recordings.

AMOUNT: 3 filing cabinets.

CONDITION: Good.

ACCESS: Permission required.

1092. University of Toronto. Sexual Harassment Education, Counselling, and Complaint Office

✤ Toronto, Ont. Formed 1988.

The Sexual Harassment Education, Counselling, and Complaint Office administers the University of Toronto's sexual-harassment policy and complaints procedure. It also does counselling and public education.

LOCATION OF RECORDS: University of Toronto. Sexual Harassment Education, Counselling, and Complaint Office. [*Address*: Suite 302 - 455 Spadina Ave., Toronto, Ont. M5S 2G8. *Telephone*: (416) 978-3908. *Fax*: (416) 978-7162.]

RECORDS: Correspondence, financial records, client records, mailing lists, reports, pamphlets, posters, clippings, 1988-1991.

AMOUNT: Approx. 2 filing cabinets.

CONDITION: Good.

ACCESS: Permission required. Most records are confidential. Client files, correspondence closed.

1093. University of Western Ontario. University Students' Council. Women's Issues Commission

[See also entry # 524 (in Part I), which lists other records of this organization.]

✤ London, Ont. Formed 1971.

As part of the students' council at the University of Western Ontario, the Women's Issues Commission (WIC) acts as an advocate for women students, operates a women's centre, provides an information and referral service, and organizes discussions, lectures, and film screenings.

LOCATION OF RECORDS: University of Western Ontario. University Students' Council. Women's Issues Commission. [*Address*: 268 UCC Bldg., London, Ont. N6A 3K7. *Telephone*: (519) 679-2111, ext. 2625.]

RECORDS: Correspondence, financial records, membership lists, petitions, pamphlets, flyers, posters, buttons, T-shirts, 1990-1991.

AMOUNT: 1 filing cabinet

CONDITION: Good.

1094. Windsor Feminist Theatre

✤ Windsor, Ont. Formed 1980.

Through performances and workshops, Windsor Feminist Theatre works to improve the status of women.

LOCATION OF RECORDS: Windsor Feminist Theatre. [*Address:* 867 Victoria Ave., Windsor, Ont. N9A 4N5. *Telephone:* (519) 256-1497.]

RECORDS: Constitution, correspondence, financial records, grant applications, membership lists, mailing lists, scrapbooks, reports, briefs, flyers, press releases, posters, T-shirts, books, photographs, videotapes, 1980-1991; sound recordings, 1990; minutes.

AMOUNT: 1 filing cabinet.

CONDITION: Good.

ACCESS: Permission required.

1095. Windsor Women's Incentive Centre

✤ Windsor, Ont. Formed 1981.

Through skills training, counselling, advocacy, and a library, the Windsor Women's Incentive Centre (WIC) works to improve the status of women, especially in terms of employment opportunities.

LOCATION OF RECORDS: Windsor Women's Incentive Centre. [*Address:* 4547 Wyandotte St. E., Windsor, Ont. N8Y 1H4. *Telephone:* (519) 944-8989.]

RECORDS: Minutes, financial records, grant applications, reports, briefs, newsletters, clippings, 1981-1991; correspondence, client records, press releases, photographs, 1986-1991; membership lists, mailing lists, 1990-1991; petitions, 1981; pamphlets, flyers, 1991; T-shirts, 1990; by-laws, 1981, 1991; awards, 1982-1991.

AMOUNT: 11 filing-cabinet drawers, 5 boxes.

CONDITION: Good.

ACCESS: Permission required. Client and personnel records and certain other files closed at discretion of board of directors.

1096. Women and Children's Crisis Centre

✤ Barrie, Ont. Formed 1981.

Through an emergency residence, counselling, education, and an information and referral service, the Women and Children's Crisis Centre works toward the prevention and elimination of violence within the family.

LOCATION OF RECORDS: Women and Children's Crisis Centre. [*Telephone:* (705) 728-6300. *Fax:* (705) 728-1364.]

RECORDS: Constitution, minutes, financial records, scrapbooks, press releases, books, clippings, 1981-1991; correspondence, log-books, grant applications, conference proceedings, T-shirts, sweatshirts, 1989-1991; client records, mailing lists, reports, pamphlets, flyers, posters, photographs, videotapes, 1988-1991; buttons, 1986-1991; newsletters (*The Turning Point*, 1989-1991); films, 1991.

AMOUNT: 1 filing cabinet.

CONDITION: Good.

ACCESS: Permission required. Client files closed.

1097. Women and Environments Education and Development Foundation

✤ Toronto, Ont. Formed 1976.

The Women and Environments Education and Development Foundation (WEED) grew out of *Women and Environments*, a periodical exploring women's relationships with their built, natural, and social environments. While WEED continues to publish the magazine, it is also involved in other activities relating to women and planning, health, design, economics, sociology, and community development.

LOCATION OF RECORDS: Women and Environments Education and Development Foundation. [*Address:* 736 Bathurst St., Toronto, Ont. M5S 2R4. *Telephone:* (416) 516-2379.]

RECORDS: Minutes, 1982-1991; financial records, 1983-1991; membership lists, 1976-1991; conference proceedings, 1989-1990; press releases, posters, sound recordings, videotapes, 1990; constitution, correspondence, grant applications, mailing lists, reports, flyers, photographs.

ACCESS: Permission required.

1098. Women for the Survival of Agriculture — Winchester

✤ Winchester, Ont. Formed 1975.

Women for the Survival of Agriculture (WSA) — Winchester is a farm women's organization which offers a support group, a newsletter, and courses.

LOCATION OF RECORDS: Women for the Survival of Agriculture — Winchester. [*Address:* R.R. #2, Winchester, Ont. K0C 2K0. *Telephone:* (613) 448-3425.]

RECORDS: Correspondence, 1978-1988; membership lists, mailing lists, newsletters, clippings, 1975-1991; slide presentation, 1979-1980; booklets, 1980; research papers, 1980-1985; guides, 1987.

AMOUNT: 1 filing cabinet.

CONDITION: Good.

ACCESS: Permission required.

1099. Women Immigrants of London Resource Service Centre

✤ London, Ont. Formed 1984.

Offering skill training, advocacy, counselling, and referral, this centre (also known as WIL) fosters the economic and social development of immigrant women in London.

LOCATION OF RECORDS: Women Immigrants of London Resource Service Centre. [*Address:* 73 King St., London, Ont. N6A 1C1. *Telephone:* (519) 663-0774.]

RECORDS: Constitution, 1984; minutes, financial records, grant applications, 1984-1991; correspondence, client records, mailing lists, scrapbooks, reports, clippings, photographs, 1987-1991; membership lists, videotapes, 1989; conference proceedings, banners, 1989-1991.

AMOUNT: 4 shelves.

CONDITION: Good.

ACCESS: Permission required. Personnel records and some financial records closed.

1100. Women Today

✤ Clinton, Ont. Formed 1980.

This is a network of women working to change the social structure of Huron County. It promotes a feminist perspective and provides facilitator training to women, in order to promote health awareness, well-being, and life skills. Women Today sponsors the Women Being Well project.

LOCATION OF RECORDS: Women Today. [*Mailing Address:* Box 1405, Clinton, Ont. N0M 1L0. (*Street Address:* 56 Huron St.) *Telephone:* (519) 482-9706.]

RECORDS: Constitution, minutes, correspondence, financial records, grant applications, membership lists, mailing lists, reports, briefs, pamphlets, flyers, press releases, 1980-1991; banners, 1990; books, clippings, photographs, videotapes, manuals.

AMOUNT: 3 filing cabinets.

ACCESS: Permission required.

1101. Women Working with Immigrant Women of Metro Toronto

✤ Toronto, Ont. Formed 1974.

Women Working with Immigrant Women of Metro Toronto (WWIW) provides a forum in which women and agencies working with immigrant women can share ideas and information and promote the development of new skills and programmes. WWIW also lobbies on issues affecting immigrant women. Until 1985 it was called Women Working with Immigrant Women.

LOCATION OF RECORDS: Women Working with Immigrant Women of Metro Toronto. [*Address:* 555 Bloor St. W., Toronto, Ont. M5S 1Y6. *Telephone:* (416) 531-2059. *Fax:* (416) 588-5556.]

RECORDS: Constitution, 1978; minutes, [1974?]-1991; correspondence, financial records, grant applications, speeches, 1978-1991; membership lists, mailing lists, pamphlets, flyers, 1982-1991; reports, briefs, newsletters, clippings, 1980-1991; conference proceedings, sound recordings, videotapes, 1985; posters, 1982; organization history, 1986.

AMOUNT: 10 boxes.

CONDITION: Good.

ACCESS: Permission required.

1102. Women's Centre (Grey Bruce)

✤ Owen Sound, Ont. Formed 1982.

This organization provides shelter, counselling, and support to women and their children who are in crisis as a result of abuse. It also does public education.

LOCATION OF RECORDS: Women's Centre. [*Mailing Address:* Box 905, Owen Sound, Ont. N4K 6H6. *Telephone:* (519) 376-0755.]

RECORDS: Constitution, 1982; correspondence, log-books, financial records, grant applications, client records, membership lists, mailing lists, scrapbooks, reports, pamphlets, flyers, press releases, buttons, clippings, photographs, 1982-1989; newsletters, 1989-1991.

AMOUNT: Approx. 6 filing cabinets.

CONDITION: Good.

ACCESS: Permission required. Client files and personnel records closed.

1103. Women's Community House

✤ London, Ont. Formed 1978.

Women's Community House (WCH) is an emergency shelter for physically, emotionally, and sexually assaulted women and their children. WCH also offers counselling, advocacy, referrals, and public and professional education.

LOCATION OF RECORDS: Women's Community House. [*Mailing Address:* P.O. Box 939, Station B, London, Ont. N6A 5K1. *Telephone:* (519) 439-0755. *Fax:* (519) 439-4252.]

RECORDS: Constitution, 1978; minutes, correspondence, log-books, financial records, grant applications, client records, scrapbooks, reports, briefs, flyers, buttons, banners, clippings, photographs, 1978-1991; mailing lists, 1989; membership lists, conference proceedings, pamphlets, press releases, posters, T-shirts.

AMOUNT: 1 room.

CONDITION: Fair.

ACCESS: Permission required. Client files available only through written consent of client or for court purposes.

1104. Women's Counselling Referral and Education Centre

✤ Toronto, Ont. Formed 1975.

The Women's Counselling Referral and Education Centre (WCREC) promotes the mental well-being of women and works toward the development of affordable and accessible feminist mental-health services. WCREC provides immediate emotional support and referrals and does public education. It used to be called the Women's Counselling Referral Centre.

LOCATION OF RECORDS: Women's Counselling Referral and Education Centre. [*Address:* 525 Bloor St. W., Toronto, Ont. M5S 1Y4. *Telephone:* (416) 534-7501. *Fax:* (416) 534-1704.]

RECORDS: Minutes, correspondence, financial records, grant applications, client records, membership lists, mailing lists, reports, briefs, conference proceedings, pamphlets, flyers, press releases, banners, photographs, [197-?]-1991; constitution, 1975; buttons, 1991; newsletters.

AMOUNT: 6 filing cabinets.

ACCESS: Permission required. Client files, records of complaints, records of personnel-committee meetings closed. Other records may be closed.

1105. Women's Educational Resources Centre (Ontario Institute for Studies in Education)

✤ Toronto, Ont. Formed 1975.

The Women's Educational Resources Centre (WERC) at the Ontario Institute for Studies in Education (OISE) provides material and consultation on women's studies, research, and curriculum development. The library has holdings in both English and French.

LOCATION OF RECORDS: Women's Educational Resources Centre. [*Address:* Ontario Institute for Studies in Education, 252 Bloor St. W., Toronto, Ont. M5S 1V6. *Telephone:* (416) 923-6641. *Fax:* (416) 926-4725.]

RECORDS: Constitution, 1988; minutes, newsletters, 1985-1991; correspondence, financial records, grant applications, reports, 1976-1991; membership lists, petitions, conference proceedings, pamphlets, flyers, clippings, photographs.

AMOUNT: 1 filing cabinet.

CONDITION: Good.

ACCESS: Permission required.

1106. Women's Emergency Centre (Woodstock, Ont.)

[See also entry # 555 (in Part I), which lists other records of this organization.]

✤ Woodstock, Ont. Formed 1976.

The Women's Emergency Centre provides shelter and support to abused women.

LOCATION OF RECORDS: Women's Emergency Centre. [*Mailing Address:* P.O. Box 1207, Woodstock, Ont. N4S 8P6. *Telephone:* (519) 539-4811.]

RECORDS: Minutes, scrapbooks, clippings, 1974; correspondence, grant applications, 1989-1991; log-books, 1990-1991; financial records, 1987-1991.

AMOUNT: 2 filing cabinets.

CONDITION: Good.

ACCESS: Permission required. Client files closed.

1107. Women's Health Interaction

[See also entry # 558 (in Part I), which lists other records of this organization.]

✤ Ottawa, Ont. Formed 1983.

Women's Health Interaction (WHI) does community education on women's health issues, particularly women's reproductive health and women and medicinal drugs. WHI is a partner of Inter Pares, a group working in international development. In 1985, WHI produced *Side Effects: A Play about Women and Pharmaceuticals*. WHI's French name is Interaction femmes-santé.

LOCATION OF RECORDS: Women's Health Interaction. [*Address:* 58 Arthur St., 2nd Floor, Ottawa, Ont. K1R 7B9. *Telephone:* (613) 563-4801. *Fax:* (613) 594-4704.]

RECORDS: Minutes, financial records, 1983-1991; correspondence, 1987-1991; grant applications, 1983-1989; membership lists, 1984-1991; briefs, 1984, 1987, 1990; pamphlets, 1985, 1990; newsletters (*Interaction*, 1986-1988); press releases, 1985-1986; posters, buttons, 1985; banners, 1990; booklets, 1984-1988; videotapes, 1988; clippings, photographs.

AMOUNT: 1 filing cabinet.

CONDITION: Good.

ACCESS: Permission required.

1108. *Women's Information and Support Centre of Halton*

✢ Oakville, Ont. Formed 1989.

This organization, also known as WISCOH, offers information, referrals, counselling, and educational activities to women experiencing emotional distress, family difficulties, or health problems.

LOCATION OF RECORDS: Women's Information and Support Centre of Halton. [*Address:* c/o St. John's United Church, 262 Randall St., Oakville, Ont. L6J 6L6. *Telephone:* (416) 338-1953.]

RECORDS: Minutes, correspondence, log-books, financial records, grant applications, membership lists, scrapbooks, reports, pamphlets, flyers, press releases, newsletters, 1989-1991.

AMOUNT: 1 box.

CONDITION: Good.

ACCESS: Permission required. Some log-books closed.

1109. *Women's Place Kenora*

✢ Kenora, Ont. Formed 1976.

Women's Place Kenora (WPK) is a collectively owned and operated women's centre providing counselling, workshops, discussion groups, educational material, information, and referrals. [See also Kenora Sexual Assault Centre (1035).]

LOCATION OF RECORDS: Women's Place Kenora. [*Mailing Address:* Box 687, Kenora, Ont. P9N 3X6. *Telephone:* (807) 468-9095. *Fax:* (807) 468-4808.]

RECORDS: Minutes, correspondence, telephone log-books, financial records, grant applications, client records, 1976-1991; conference proceedings, T-shirts, 1989; banners, 1990; membership lists, mailing lists, petitions, scrapbooks, reports, briefs, pamphlets, flyers, press releases, posters, newsletters, books, clippings, photographs, sound recordings, videotapes.

AMOUNT: Approx. 3 filing cabinets.

CONDITION: Good.

ACCESS: Permission required. Client files closed.

1110. *Women's Place / Place aux femmes (Ottawa, Ont.)*

[Renseignements en français, notice 1064.]

✢ Ottawa, Ont. Formed 1984.

Women's Place is a women's centre which supports women's efforts to gain control over their own lives. It offers information, counselling, and a space for women.

LOCATION OF RECORDS: Women's Place. [*Address:* 241 Bruyère St., Ottawa, Ont. K1N 5E5. *Telephone:* (613) 789-2155. *Fax:* (613) 789-2745.]

RECORDS: Constitution, 1985; minutes, 1984-1991; correspondence, financial records, grant applications, membership lists, mailing lists, flyers, press releases, 1985-1991; log-books, 1987-1991; reports, 1988-1991; pamphlets, photographs, 1986-1991; events calendar, 1989-1991; buttons, banners.

AMOUNT: Approx. 3 filing cabinets.

CONDITION: Good.

1111. *Women's Place (St Catharines, Ont.)*

✢ St Catharines, Ont. Formed 1977.

Women's Place is a shelter for abused women and their children. It works toward the empowerment of women and the abolition of abuse of all kinds.

LOCATION OF RECORDS: Women's Place. [*Mailing Address:* Box 1265, St Catharines, Ont. L2R 7A7. *Telephone:* (416) 684-4000.]

RECORDS: Constitution, minutes, financial records, grant applications, client records, 1977-1991; pamphlets, T-shirts, 1991.

AMOUNT: 4 filing cabinets.

CONDITION: Fair.

ACCESS: Permission required. Client files closed.

1112. *Women's Place, Welland and District*

✢ Welland, Ont. Formed 1981.

Women's Place, Welland and District provides shelter and crisis counselling to abused women and their children.

LOCATION OF RECORDS: Women's Place, Welland and District. [*Address:* 178 King St., Welland, Ont. L3B 3J5. *Telephone:* (416) 732-4632.]

RECORDS: Constitution, minutes, correspondence, log-books, financial records, grant applications, client records, membership lists, mailing lists, petitions, scrapbooks, reports, briefs, conference proceedings, pamphlets, flyers, press releases, posters, buttons, T-shirts, banners, clippings, sound recordings, 1981-1991.

AMOUNT: 1 room.

CONDITION: Fair.

ACCESS: Permission required. Client records and conference proceedings closed.

1113. *Working Skills Centre of Ontario*

✢ Toronto, Ont. Formed 1978.

The Working Skills Centre of Ontario recognizes the economic, social, and political boundaries faced by immigrant women and helps them gain skills in order to achieve equality and participate fully in Canadian society.

LOCATION OF RECORDS: Working Skills Centre of Ontario. [*Address:* 604 King St. W., 3rd Floor, Toronto, Ont. M5V 1M6. *Telephone:* (416) 868-0770. *Fax:* (416) 868-1805.]

RECORDS: Minutes, log-books, financial records, grant applications, client records, membership lists, mailing lists, reports, briefs, pamphlets, flyers, press releases, 1978-1991; correspondence, 1984-1991; books, 1990; clippings, photographs, sound recordings, videotapes, films.

CONDITION: Fair.

ACCESS: Permission required. Some client files closed.

1114. Working Women Community Centre

✣ Toronto, Ont. Formed 1975.

This centre, also known as WWCC, helps immigrant women to overcome barriers and develop self-sufficiency skills. The centre offers language training, counselling, and support groups.

LOCATION OF RECORDS: Working Women Community Centre. [*Address:* 533A Gladstone Ave., Toronto, Ont. M6H 3J1. *Telephone:* (416) 532-2824. *Fax:* (416) 532-1065.]

RECORDS: Constitutions, 1987, 1991; minutes, correspondence, financial records, grant applications, client records, membership lists, scrapbooks, reports, 1986-1991; briefs, 1987; pamphlets, 1986; manuals, 1979, 1990; flyers, newsletters, books.

AMOUNT: Approx. 7 boxes.

CONDITION: Fair.

ACCESS: Permission required.

1115. York Women's Centre

[See also entry # 580 (in Part I), which lists other records of this organization.]

✣ North York, Ont. Formed 1975.

A centre for women's activities and information at York University, the York Women's Centre offers referral services, peer counselling, and educational forums. The organization has also been referred to as the York Women's Group. [See also York University. Committee on Women's Programmes (575).]

LOCATION OF RECORDS: York Women's Centre. [*Address:* York University, 4700 Keele St., S156 Ross, North York, Ont. M3J 1P3. *Telephone:* (416) 736-2100, ext. 33484.]

RECORDS: Minutes, correspondence, 1986-1991; log-books, conference proceedings, 1987-1988; financial records, 1987-1991; petitions, 1989-1990; reports, 1987-1990; banners, 1990; newsletters (*Breakthrough*, 1975-1977; *York Women's Centre Newsletter*, 1986-1988); pamphlets, buttons, books, clippings, photographs, sound recordings, videotapes, films.

AMOUNT: 2 drawers of a filing cabinet.

CONDITION: Good.

1116. Young Women's Christian Association of Metropolitan Toronto

[See also entry # 581 (in Part I), which lists other records of this organization.]

✣ Toronto, Ont. Formed 1873.

The YWCA of Metropolitan Toronto works to create better lives for women through education, pre-employment counselling, fitness and recreation programmes, affordable housing, crisis shelters, and advocacy. It was once called the Young Women's Christian Guild of Toronto. The YWCA ran Stop 158 (a hostel for young women) and the Women's Resource Centre. [See also Nellie Langford Rowell Library (1049).]

LOCATION OF RECORDS: Young Women's Christian Association of Metropolitan Toronto. [*Address:* 80 Woodlawn Ave. E., Toronto, Ont. M4T 1C1. *Telephone:* (416) 961-8100. *Fax:* (416) 961-7739.]

RECORDS: Correspondence, 1987-1991; financial records, 1981-1991; client records, 1980-1991; membership lists, 1984-1991; reports, 1965-1991; conference proceedings, 1989-1991; newsletters (*Perspectives*, 1990-1991; *Link*, 1989-1991); mailing lists, pamphlets, press releases, posters, buttons, T-shirts.

CONDITION: Good.

ACCESS: Permission required. Client files and confidential minutes closed.

1117. Young Women's Christian Association of Peterborough Victoria and Haliburton

[See also entry # 582 (in Part I), which lists other records of this organization.]

✣ Peterborough, Ont. Formed 1891.

The YWCA of Peterborough Victoria and Haliburton works to improve the status of women, offering shelters for abused women and children, a resource centre for low-income tenants, and a variety of programmes designed to empower women.

LOCATION OF RECORDS: Young Women's Christian Association of Peterborough Victoria and Haliburton. [*Address:* 216 Simcoe St., Peterborough, Ont. K9H 2H7. *Telephone:* (705) 743-3526. *Fax:* (705) 745-4654.]

RECORDS: Constitution, 1897; minutes, correspondence, log-books, financial records, grant applications, client records, membership lists, mailing lists, scrapbooks, reports, briefs, conference proceedings, pamphlets, flyers, press releases, clippings, photographs, 1980-1991; newsletters (*YWCA Voices*, 1980-1991; *Springboard*); books, 1991; films.

AMOUNT: Approx. 12 filing cabinets.

CONDITION: Good.

ACCESS: Permission required. Client files closed.

1118. Young Women's Christian Association of St Thomas-Elgin

[See also entry # 583 (in Part I), which lists other records of this organization.]

✣ St Thomas, Ont. Formed 1902.

The YWCA of St Thomas-Elgin works to improve the status of women. Its services include support groups, a shelter for abused women and children, and a work-orientation programme.

LOCATION OF RECORDS: Young Women's Christian Association of St Thomas-Elgin. [*Address:* 16 Mary St., St Thomas, Ont. N5P 2S3. *Telephone:* (519) 631-9800.]

RECORDS: Minutes, photographs, 1902-1991; correspondence, financial records, grant applications, client records, scrapbooks, reports, press releases, clippings, 1985-1991; log-books, membership lists, mailing lists, pamphlets, flyers.

AMOUNT: Approx. 1 filing cabinet.

CONDITION: Good.

ACCESS: Permission required. Client and personnel files closed.

QUÉBEC

1119. *Accueil du sans-abri*

✣ Valleyfield (Québec). Groupe fondé 1978.

L'Accueil du sans-abri est un centre d'aide et d'hébergement pour femmes et enfants victimes de violence. L'organisme offre des services en français et en anglais.

LIEU DE CONSULTATION : Accueil du sans-abri. [*Adresse postale* : C.P. 644, Valleyfield (Québec) J6S 5N6. *Téléphone* : (514) 371-4618.]

MATÉRIEL : Statuts et règlements, dépliants, procès-verbaux, correspondance, journaux de bord, documents financiers, demandes de subvention, listes de membres.

QUANTITÉ : 1 classeur, 2 armoires.

ÉTAT : Bon.

ACCÈS : Permission requise. Certains dossiers sont confidentiels.

1120. *Action des femmes handicapées (Montréal, Québec)*

[For English entry, see # 1121.]

✣ Montréal (Québec). Groupe fondé 1985.

Action des femmes handicapées regroupe des femmes de cultures différentes issues de toutes les couches de la société et ayant des handicaps divers. Ses membres travaillent pour la défense de leurs droits, l'interaction, l'épanouissement personnel et l'autonomie féminine, tout en demeurant ouvertes aux différences physiques, sexuelles, culturelles ou politiques qui les caractérisent. Cet organisme est un membre du Réseau d'action des femmes handicapées du Canada.

LIEU DE CONSULTATION : Action des femmes handicapées. [*Adresse* : 7785, rue Louis-Hébert, Montréal (Québec) H2E 2Y1. *Téléphone* : (514) 725-4123 ou 633-1616. *Télécopieur* : (514) 725-4123.]

MATÉRIEL : Statuts et règlements, photographies, 1987; procès-verbaux, correspondance, documents financiers, demandes de subvention, listes de membres, listes d'envoi, rapports, mémoires, actes de congrès, dépliants, tracts, communiqués de presse, coupures de presse, discours, 1986-1991; pétitions, affiches, 1987-1991; macarons, T-shirts, enregistrements sonores, 1988; vidéocassettes, 1988-1991.

QUANTITÉ : 1 classeur, 7 boîtes.

ÉTAT : Bon.

ACCÈS : Permission requise.

1121. *Action des femmes handicapées (Montreal, Quebec)*

[Renseignements en français, notice 1120.]

✣ Montreal, Quebec. Formed 1985.

Action des femmes handicapées is a network of women from many cultures and classes, with diverse handicaps. The organization defends the rights of women with disabilities, shares information, promotes personal development and autonomy, and remains open to physical, sexual, cultural, or political differences. The group is a member of the DisAbled Women's Network Canada (DAWN Canada).

LOCATION OF RECORDS: Action des femmes handicapées. [*Address:* 7785 Louis-Hébert, Montreal, Quebec H2E 2Y1. *Telephone:* (514) 725-4123 or 633-1616. *Fax:* (514) 725-4123.]

RECORDS: Constitution, photographs, 1987; minutes, correspondence, financial records, grant applications, membership lists, mailing lists, reports, briefs, conference proceedings, pamphlets, flyers, press releases, clippings, speeches, 1986-1991; petitions, posters, 1987-1991; buttons, T-shirts, sound recordings, 1988; videotapes, 1988-1991.

AMOUNT: 1 filing cabinet, 7 boxes.

CONDITION: Good.

ACCESS: Permission required.

1122. *Action-Info-Femmes*

✣ Rivière-Portneuf (Québec). Groupe fondé 1988.

Cet organisme aide les femmes à sortir de leur isolement et à devenir autonomes. Il organise des cafés-rencontres et des ateliers thématiques; il offre également des services d'aide. Ce groupe s'appellait à ses débuts Action-Information-Femmes; il a changé de nom en 1991.

LIEU DE CONSULTATION : Action-Info-Femmes. [*Adresse postale* : C.P. 310, Rivière-Portneuf, Saguenay (Québec) G0T 1P0. *Téléphone* : (418) 238-2793. *Télécopieur* : (418) 238-5319.]

MATÉRIEL : Statuts et règlements, procès-verbaux, correspondance, documents financiers, demandes de subvention, listes de membres, listes d'envoi, pétitions, albums de coupures, rapports, actes de congrès, communiqués de presse, bannières, coupures de presse, photographies, 1988-1991; bulletins (*Focus sur l'action féminine*, 1989-1990).

QUANTITÉ : 1 classeur.

ÉTAT : Bon.

ACCÈS : Permission requise.

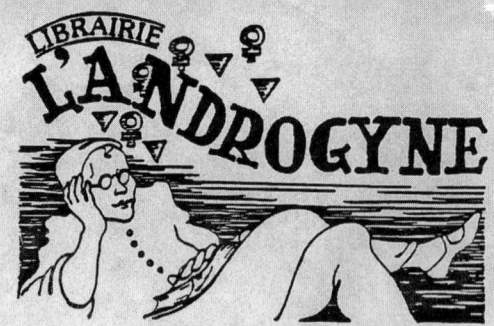

Leonar's New bookstore in Montreal 29 March 82

L'Androgyne, la librarie gaie, lesbienne, et féministe, situeé depuis 1973 sur la rue Crescent a ouvert ses portes sur le boul. St. Laurent le 1er février 1982. Nous vous acceuillerons dans un espace plus spacieux, bien éclairé et mieux localisé.

Pour ceux et celles qui ne nous connaissent pas, voilà une brève description de L'Androgyne: la librarie fonctionne grâce à un collectif à but non-lucratif, composé de femmes et d'hommes travaillant bénévolement à diffuser des écrits féministes, lesbiens, homosexuels et non-sexistes pour enfants. Nos livres et périodiques sont choisis dans la mesure où ils reflètent la lutte commune des mouvements homosexuels et féministes contre l'oppression sexuelle et/ou la culture homosexuelle et lesbienne au passé et au présent.

Le déménagement du centre-ville au boulevard St. Laurent représente la réalisation d'un désiré du collectif d'aller ver un nouvel espace. Il ne s'agit pas seulement d'agrandir notre sélection de livres, de périodiques, de disques et autres, mais surtout d'evoluer d'un lieu de rencontre vers un lieu propice aussi à l'échange; échange entre nos écrivains et nos lecteurs et lectrices (et entre nous). Le nouvel espace, quoique intime, offre la possibilité de réunions, dont nous éspérons profiter au cours de la nouvelle année.

Le collectif de L'Androgyne recherche de nouveaux membres. Chaque membre participe aux opéerations quotidiennes de L'Androgyne en faisant de la permanence $3\frac{1}{2}$ heures par semaine. Il y a aussi la possibilité d'être responsable d'une section en faisant le choix de livres et les commandes. Le collectif se réunit mensuellement. Aucune expérience n'est nécessaire. Il va de soi qu'un tel projet nécessite des resources tant humaines que financières. Tout support sera non seulement apprécié, mais servira une bonne cause, la nôtre.

LA LIBRAIRIE L'ANDROGYNE 3642 boul. St. Laurent 2ième etage, Mtl. 842-4765

Tract / Flyer, 1982
L'Androgyne
Fonds de l'ACMF / CWMA Collection

1123. Action travail des femmes du Québec

✣ Verdun (Québec). Groupe fondé 1976.

Action travail des femmes du Québec (ATF) vise à améliorer l'accès des femmes au marché du travail et les oriente vers des emplois non traditionnels. Il offre des séances d'information, des services de recherche d'emploi et des cours de formation professionnelle.

LIEU DE CONSULTATION : Action travail des femmes du Québec. [*Adresse :* 4706, rue Wellington, Verdun (Québec) H4G 1X3. *Téléphone :* (514) 768-7233.]

MATÉRIEL : Statuts et règlements, procès-verbaux, correspondance, documents financiers, demandes de subvention, dossiers concernant la clientèle, listes de membres, listes d'envoi, pétitions, albums de coupures, rapports, mémoires, dépliants, communiqués de presse, macarons, bannières, coupures de presse, enregistrements sonores, vidéocassettes, 1976-1991.

QUANTITÉ : 25 boîtes.

ÉTAT : Bon.

ACCÈS : Permission requise. Dossiers concernant la clientèle confidentiels.

1124. Aide à la femme pour l'allaitement maternel et la maternité

✣ Plessisville (Québec). Groupe fondé 1983.

L'Aide à la femme pour l'allaitement maternel et la maternité (AFAM) vient en aide aux futures mamans qui désirent allaiter leur bébé de même qu'à celles qui ne désirent pas allaiter.

LIEU DE CONSULTATION : L'aide à la femme pour l'allaitement maternel et la maternité. [*Adresse :* a/s Louise Routhier, CLSC de l'Érable, 1331, rue Saint-Calixte, Plessisville (Québec) G6L 1P4. *Téléphone :* (819) 362-6301.]

MATÉRIEL : Correspondance, journaux de bord, listes de membres, albums de coupures, 1990-1991; dépliants, 1983-1991; affiches, 1984.

QUANTITÉ : 1 boîte.

ÉTAT : Bon.

1125. L'Androgyne

[For English entry, see # 1126.]

✣ Montréal (Québec). Groupe fondé 1973.

L'Androgyne est une librairie qui se spécialise dans les livres lesbiens, féministes et gais. Dans le passé, la librairie a aussi porté le nom d'Androgyny.

LIEU DE CONSULTATION : L'Androgyne. [*Adresse :* 3636, boul. St-Laurent, Montréal (Québec) H2X 2V4. *Téléphone :* (514) 842-4765.]

MATÉRIEL : Statuts et règlements, 1973; procès-verbaux, documents financiers, 1973-1991; dossiers concernant la clientèle, listes d'envoi, 1987-1991; tracts, bannières, catalogues, 1984-1991; photographies.

ÉTAT : Bon.

ACCÈS : Permission requise.

1126. L'Androgyne

[Renseignements en français, notice 1125.]

✣ Montreal, Quebec. Formed 1973.

L'Androgyne is a bookstore specializing in lesbian, feminist, and gay material. It used to have an English name as well: Androgyny.

LOCATION OF RECORDS: L'Androgyne. [*Address:* 3636 St-Laurent Blvd., Montreal, Quebec H2X 2V4. *Telephone:* (514) 842-4765.]

RECORDS: Constitution, 1973; minutes, financial records, 1973-1991; client records, mailing lists, 1987-1991; flyers, banners, catalogues, 1984-1991; photographs.

CONDITION: Good.

ACCESS: Permission required.

1127. Ano-Sep

✣ Montréal (Québec). Groupe fondé 1970.

Ano-Sep offre une aide morale et technique aux femmes qui vivent une séparation de couple. Ses activités sont la consultation en relation d'aide, l'accompagnement pour démarches juridiques, les groupes d'entraide, les cours, les cliniques juridiques et les cafés-rencontres. Ano-Sep est l'abréviation des mots « anonyme » et « séparée ».

LIEU DE CONSULTATION : Ano-Sep. [*Adresse :* 911, rue Jean-Talon est, #132, Montréal (Québec) H2R 1V5. *Téléphone :* (514) 277-9870.]

MATÉRIEL : Statuts et règlements, dépliants, 1973; procès-verbaux, correspondance, documents financiers, 1971-1991; demandes de subvention, 1973-1991; dossiers concernant la clientèle, 1975; listes de membres, listes d'envoi, albums de coupures, rapports, 1970-1991; mémoires, 1970; affiches, 1976; bulletins (*Oasis de bonheur*, 1973-1974; *Ano-Sep en marche*, 1975-1976; *Le Lien*, 1982-1991); coupures de presse, 1970-1990; photographies, 1985, 1990; vidéocassettes, 1985-1986, 1988-1990.

QUANTITÉ : 2 classeurs.

ÉTAT : Bon.

ACCÈS : Permission requise. Les procès-verbaux du conseil d'administration et les renseignements concernant la clientèle sont confidentiels.

1128. Arcade

✣ Montréal (Québec). Groupe fondé 1981.

Arcade est une revue littéraire consacrée à l'écriture des femmes. Elle publie deux ou trois numéros thématiques par année.

LIEU DE CONSULTATION : Arcade. [*Adresse postale :* C.P. 206, Succursale Beaubien, Montréal (Québec) H2G 3C9.]

MATÉRIEL : Revues (*Arcade*, 1981-1991); entrevue, 1991; procès-verbaux, documents financiers, demandes de subvention, dossiers concernant la clientèle, albums de coupures, dépliants, communiqués de presse, T-shirts, coupures de presse, enregistrements sonores.

ÉTAT : Assez bon.

ACCÈS : Permission requise.

1129. Assaut sexuel secours

✣ Val d'Or (Québec). Groupe fondé 1983.

Assaut sexuel secours est un centre d'aide pour victimes d'assaut sexuel. Il offre une aide immédiate, un accueil chaleureux, un service d'écoute téléphonique, un soutien moral, des informations juridiques et médicales et un programme de sensibilisation et de prévention.

LIEU DE CONSULTATION : Assaut sexuel secours. [*Adresse postale :* C.P. 697, Val d'Or (Québec) J9P 4P6. *Téléphone :* (819) 825-6968.]

MATÉRIEL : Statuts et règlements, procès-verbaux, journaux de bord, documents financiers, demandes de subvention, dossiers concernant la clientèle, listes de membres, listes d'envoi, pétitions, albums de coupures, rapports, mémoires, actes de congrès, dépliants, tracts, communiqués de presse, coupures de presse, photographies, enregistrements sonores, vidéocassettes, 1983-1991.

QUANTITÉ : Env. 3 classeurs.

ÉTAT : Bon.

ACCÈS : Permission requise. Dossiers concernant la clientèle confidentiels.

1130. Association des femmes collaboratrices

✣ St-Hubert (Québec). Groupe fondé 1980.

L'Association des femmes collaboratrices (ADFC) vise à faire reconnaître sur le plan économique la valeur distincte du travail de la femme collaboratrice au sein de l'entreprise. De plus, elle sensibilise la population en géneral et les organismes publics à la situation des femmes collaboratrices.

LIEU DE CONSULTATION : Association des femmes collaboratrices. [*Adresse* : 3925, Grande Allée, suite 101, St-Hubert (Québec) J4T 2V8. *Téléphone* : (514) 462-3730.]

MATÉRIEL : Statuts et règlements, procès-verbaux, correspondance, documents financiers, demandes de subvention, listes de membres, rapports, mémoires, actes de congrès, dépliants, publications, photographies, 1980-1991; enregistrements sonores, vidéocassettes, 1985-1991.

ÉTAT : Bon.

ACCÈS : Permission requise. États financiers et liste de membres confidentiels. Évaluation à la pièce pour les procès-verbaux des conseils d'administration.

1131. Association féminine d'éducation et d'action sociale

[Voir aussi la notice 588 (dans la partie I) pour autres documents de ce groupe.]

✣ Montréal (Québec). Groupe fondé 1966.

L'Association féminine d'éducation et d'action sociale (AFÉAS) est un corps intermédiaire de pression qui pilote d'importants dossiers pour l'avancement de la condition féminine. L'AFÉAS représente les intérêts de ses plus de 30,000 membres de toutes les régions du Québec auprès des différents paliers de gouvernements. L'AFÉAS est née du fusionnement de l'Union catholique des femmes rurales et des Cercles d'économie domestique.

LIEU DE CONSULTATION : Association féminine d'éducation et d'action sociale. [*Adresse* : 5999 de Marseilles, Montréal (Québec) H1N 1K6. *Téléphone* : (514) 251-1636. *Télécopieur* : (514) 251-9023.]

MATÉRIEL : Statuts et règlements, procès-verbaux, correspondance, documents financiers, demandes de subvention, listes de membres, listes d'envoi, pétitions, rapports, mémoires, actes de congrès, dépliants, tracts, communiqués de presse, affiches, macarons, livres, coupures de presse, photographies, enregistrements sonores, vidéocassettes, 1976-1991; bulletins (*Femmes d'ici*, 1976-1991).

QUANTITÉ : 8 classeurs.

ÉTAT : Bon.

ACCÈS : Permission requise.

1132. Association internationale des secrétaires professionnelles. Section Ville-Marie / Professional Secretaries International. Ville-Marie Chapter

[For English entry, see # 1240.]

✣ Montréal (Québec). Groupe fondé 1969.

L'Association internationale des secrétaires professionnelles (AISP) a comme principal objectif l'amélioration des connaissances et la promotion du statut professionnel de la secrétaire.

LIEU DE CONSULTATION : Association internationale des secrétaires professionnelles. Section Ville-Marie. [*Adresse postale* : C.P. 847, Succursale Desjardins, Montréal (Québec) H5B 1B9. *Téléphone* : (514) 733-5243.]

MATÉRIEL : Statuts et règlements, procès-verbaux, correspondance, documents financiers, listes de membres, rapports, mémoires, actes de congrès, dépliants, communiqués de presse, bulletins (*Le Trait d'union*, *The Secretary*, *Vision*), livres, coupures de presse, photographies, enregistrements sonores.

QUANTITÉ : 1 classeur.

ÉTAT : Bon.

ACCÈS : Permission requise.

1133. L'Autre Parole

✣ Montréal et Rimouski (Québec). Groupe fondé 1976.

L'Autre Parole est un collectif de femmes chrétiennes et féministes qui interviennent dans le champ religieux contre le sexisme ecclésial, oeuvrant pour la mise en place d'alternatives. Ses activités comprennent un colloque annuel, la publication de la revue *L'Autre Parole* et des rencontres de groupes de réflexion (à Montréal, Sherbrooke, Rimouski et Matane).

LIEU DE CONSULTATION : L'Autre Parole. [*Adresse postale* : C.P. 393, Succursale C, Montréal (Québec) H2L 4K3. *Téléphone* : (418) 724-1739/1986. *Télécopieur* : (418) 724-1525.]

MATÉRIEL : Procès-verbaux, demandes de subvention, albums de coupures, 1976-1990; correspondance, dépliants, 1976-1991; documents financiers, 1976-1980; dossiers concernant la clientèle, 1984-1991; bulletins (*L'Autre Parole*, 1979-1991); pétitions, communiqués de presse, affiches, macarons, foulards, bannières, coupures de presse, photographies.

QUANTITÉ : 5 boîtes.

ÉTAT : Bon.

ACCÈS : Permission requise.

1134. Bouée régionale

✣ Lac-Mégantic (Québec). Groupe fondé 1984.

La Bouée régionale est une maison d'hébergement pour femmes victimes de violence conjugale et leurs enfants. Elle travaille à un changement social pour les droits des femmes.

LIEU DE CONSULTATION : Bouée régionale. [*Adresse* : 4038 Villeneuve, Lac-Mégantic (Québec) G6B 2C1. *Téléphone* : (819) 583-1233.]

MATÉRIEL : Statuts et règlements, procès-verbaux, correspondance, journaux de bord, documents financiers, demandes de subvention, dossiers concernant la clientèle, listes de membres, listes d'envoi, pétitions, albums de coupures, rapports, mémoires, actes de congrès, dépliants, communiqués de presse, affiches, macarons, bannières, livres, coupures de presse, photographies, vidéocassettes, 1984-1991.

ÉTAT : Bon.

ACCÈS : Permission requise. Dossiers concernant la clientèle confidentiels.

1135. Carrefour des femmes de Lachute

✣ Lachute (Québec). Groupe fondé 1983.

Par ses activités éducatives et ses actions collectives, cet organisme vise à permettre aux femmes de se regrouper, d'échanger et de lutter contre tout ce qui les opprime. Il offre un centre de documentation, une halte-garderie, et un café-causerie, entre autres services.

LIEU DE CONSULTATION : Carrefour des femmes de Lachute. [*Adresse* : 310, rue de l'Église, Lachute (Québec) J8H 4A8. *Téléphone* : (514) 562-7122.]

MATÉRIEL : Statuts et règlements, procès-verbaux, correspondance, journaux de bord, documents financiers, demandes de subvention, pétitions, albums de coupures, rapports, actes de congrès, dépliants, tracts, coupures de presse, photographies, 1983-1991; bannières, 1988-1991; bulletins (*Paroles de femmes*, 1988-1991).

QUANTITÉ : 1 classeur.

ÉTAT : Assez bon.

ACCÈS : Permission requise.

1136. Centre Actu-elle

✣ Buckingham (Québec). Groupe fondé 1984.

Le centre Actu-elle vise à améliorer la condition de vie des femmes en favorisant leur autonomie individuelle et leur prise en main. Ses services comprennent : accueil et référence, écoute active, ateliers et cours.

LIEU DE CONSULTATION : Centre actu-elle. [*Adresse* : 290 Principale, Buckingham (Québec) J8L 2G3. *Téléphone* : (819) 986-9713.]

MATÉRIEL : Statuts et règlements, procès-verbaux, correspondance, documents financiers, demandes de subvention, listes d'envoi, pétitions, albums de coupures, rapports, actes de congrès, dépliants, communiqués de presse, affiches, macarons, bannières, 1984-1991; vidéocassettes, 1991; coupures de presse, photographies.

ÉTAT : Bon.

ACCÈS : Permission requise.

1137. Centre Avec des elles

✣ St-Gabriel-de-Brandon (Québec). Groupe fondé 1983.

En offrant des services d'accueil, d'écoute et de support et des activités éducatives, le Centre Avec des elles travaille à briser l'isolement des femmes, à créer des réseaux d'entraide et à favoriser l'autonomie financière et affective des femmes.

LIEU DE CONSULTATION : Centre Avec des elles. [*Adresse postale* : C.P. 95, St-Gabriel-de-Brandon (Québec) J0K 2N0. (*Indication de rue* : 158, rue Marcel.) *Téléphone* : (514) 835-3393.]

MATÉRIEL : Statuts et règlements, procès-verbaux, correspondance, demandes de subvention, dossiers concernant la clientèle, listes de membres, actes de congrès, 1983-1991; journaux de bord, coupures de presse, 1985-1991; documents financiers, 1988-1991; albums de coupures, photographies, 1989-1991; bulletins (*Bulletin des femmes*, 1990-1991); rapports.

QUANTITÉ : 1 classeur.

ÉTAT : Bon.

ACCÈS : Permission requise. Dossiers concernant la clientèle confidentiels.

1138. Centre communautaire des femmes sud-asiatiques / South Asian Women's Community Centre

[For English entry, see # 1255.]

✣ Montréal (Québec). Groupe fondé 1981.

Le Centre communautaire des femmes sud-asiatiques (CCFSA) veut aider les femmes à utiliser pleinement leur potentiel et à acquérir leur autonomie. Le centre offre des cours de langue et de formation professionnelle, entre autres services.

LIEU DE CONSULTATION : Centre communautaire des femmes sud-asiatiques. [*Adresse* : 3600, rue Hôtel de Ville, Montréal (Québec) H2X 3B6. *Téléphone* : (514) 842-2330/9439.]

MATÉRIEL : Statuts et règlements, livres, 1981; procès-verbaux, correspondance, journaux de bord, documents financiers, demandes de subvention, dossiers concernant la clientèle, listes de membres, listes d'envoi, pétitions, rapports, dépliants, tracts, macarons, bannières, photographies, 1981-1991; mémoires, 1987-1989, 1991; actes de congrès, 1983-1991; communiqués de presse, 1991; T-shirts, 1988; bulletins (*Shakti*, 1983; *Bulletin CCFSA/SAWCC Bulletin*, 1981).

QUANTITÉ : 4 classeurs.

ÉTAT : Assez bon.

ACCÈS : Tous les documents de l'organisme et des clientes sont confidentiels.

1139. Centre d'aide et de lutte contre les agressions à caractère sexuel de Rimouski

✣ Rimouski (Québec). Groupe fondé 1988.

Parmi ses objectifs, le Centre d'aide et de lutte contre les agressions à caractère sexuel (CALACS) de Rimouski défend les intérêts des femmes dans la lutte contre les abus et agressions sexuelles, favorise le développement et l'autonomie des femmes et établit et dispense un processus d'intervention auprès des femmes victimes d'agressions à caractère sexuel.

LIEU DE CONSULTATION : Centre d'aide et de lutte contre les agressions à caractère sexuel de Rimouski. [*Adresse* : 99 St-Louis, #18, Rimouski (Québec) G5L 5P6. *Téléphone* : (418) 725-4220.]

MATÉRIEL : Statuts et règlements, 1988; procès-verbaux, documents financiers, demandes de subvention, rapports, communiqués de presse, listes de membres, 1988-1991; correspondance, albums de coupures, dépliants, 1989-1991; pétitions, mémoires, 1989; affiches, 1991; bannières, photographies, 1990; bulletins (*Bloc-notes*, 1990-1991).

QUANTITÉ : 1 classeur.

ÉTAT : Bon.

ACCÈS : Permission requise.

1140. Centre d'aide et de lutte contre les agressions à caractère sexuel (Trois-Rivières, Québec)

✣ Trois-Rivières (Québec). Groupe fondé 1980.

Le centre, appelé aussi le CALACS, offre des services d'aide aux femmes et adolescentes victimes d'agressions à caractère sexuel et travaille au développement de politiques destinées à prévenir et à enrayer les agressions à caractère sexuel.

LIEU DE CONSULTATION : Centre d'aide et de lutte contre les agressions à caractère sexuel. [*Adresse postale* : C.P. 776, Trois-Rivières (Québec) G9A 5J9. *Téléphone* : (819) 373-1232.]

MATÉRIEL : Procès-verbaux, documents financiers, demandes de subvention, dossiers concernant la clientèle, 1980-1991; correspondance, 1990-1991; journaux de bord, 1989-1991; albums de coupures, 1981-1991; vidéocassettes, 1986; statuts et règlements.

QUANTITÉ : Env. 5 boîtes.

ÉTAT : Assez bon.

ACCÈS : Permission requise. Tous les documents confidentiels.

1141. Centre d'aide et de prévention d'assauts sexuels de Châteauguay / Châteauguay Sexual Assault Prevention and Aid Center

[For English entry, see # 1174.]

✣ Châteauguay (Québec). Groupe fondé 1978.

Le Centre d'aide et de prévention d'assauts sexuels (CAPAS) de Châteauguay s'est donné pour mission d'enrayer des agressions sexuelles, d'offrir des services d'aide aux femmes victimes d'agressions sexuelles et d'offrir des activités d'éducation-sensibilisation dans la communauté. Le centre était connu sous le nom de Centre d'aide aux victimes de viol de Châteauguay (CAVV) de 1979 à 1980.

LIEU DE CONSULTATION : Centre d'aide et de prévention d'assauts sexuels de Châteauguay. [*Adresse postale* : C.P. 284, Châteauguay (Québec) J6J 4Z6. *Téléphone* : (514) 699-8258.]

MATÉRIEL : Statuts et règlements, 1978, 1980; procès-verbaux, correspondance, documents financiers, demandes de subventions, dossiers concernant la clientèle, albums de coupures, rapports, communiqués de presse, 1978-1991; listes de membres, 1985; dépliants, 1978, 1985;

affiches, bannières, 1980; macarons, 1980-1983; photographies, 1985-1988.
QUANTITÉ : 2 tiroirs de classeur.
ÉTAT : Assez bon.
ACCÈS : Permission requise. Dossiers concernant la clientèle confidentiels.

1142. *Centre d'animation mère-enfant*

✣ St-Bruno (Québec). Groupe fondé 1981.

Le Centre d'animation mère-enfant (CAME) offre aux mères d'enfants d'âge pré-scolaire des moyens de mieux vivre leur choix d'éducatrices à la maison et, également, des moyens de planifier un éventuel retour aux études ou au travail.

LIEU DE CONSULTATION : Centre d'animation mère-enfant. [*Adresse postale :* C.P. 312, Succursale Saint-Bruno, Saint-Bruno (Québec) J3V 5G8.]
MATÉRIEL : Statuts et règlements, procès-verbaux, documents financiers, 1981-1991; demandes de subvention, 1988-1991; dossiers concernant la clientèle, listes de membres, 1984-1991; correspondance.
QUANTITÉ : Env. 4 boîtes.
ÉTAT : Assez bon.
ACCÈS : Permission requise.

1143. *Centre de documentation sur l'éducation des adultes et la condition féminine*

✣ Montréal (Québec). Groupe fondé 1983.

En 1983, les centres de documentation de Relais-Femmes de Montréal et de l'Institut canadien d'éducation des adultes (ICEA) se sont joints pour donner naissance au Centre de documentation sur l'éducation des adultes et la condition féminine (CDEACF). L'organisme réunit une documentation de base pour l'information, l'intervention et la recherche concernant l'éducation des adultes, spécialement l'alphabétisation, et l'ensemble des domaines relatifs à la condition féminine. (Source : *Guide sommaire : Archives des femmes au Québec*/Madeleine Lamothe, Ghislaine Fecteau et Pierrette Lalancette. — Québec : Archives nationales du Québec, 1990.)

LIEU DE CONSULTATION : Centre de documentation sur l'éducation des adultes et la condition féminine. [*Adresse :* 1265, rue Berri, #340, Montréal (Québec) H2L 4X4. *Téléphone :* (514) 844-3674.]
MATÉRIEL : Lettres patentes, correspondance, documents financiers, contrats, évaluation, album des visiteurs, rapports annuels, procès-verbaux, avis de convocation, demandes de subvention, dépliant, documents divers.
QUANTITÉ : 5 m.
ACCÈS : Accessible.

1144. *Centre de femmes de Shawinigan*

✣ Shawinigan (Québec). Groupe fondé [1980?].

Les objectifs poursuivis sont de briser l'isolement des femmes, d'améliorer les conditions de vie des femmes et de favoriser leur autonomie. Jusqu'en 1987, le centre s'appelait la Maison d'accueil et d'information pour les femmes de la Mauricie (MAIFM).

LIEU DE CONSULTATION : Centre de femmes de Shawinigan. [*Adresse :* 453 5e rue, app. 2, Shawinigan (Québec) G9P 1E4. *Téléphone :* (819) 537-4277.]
MATÉRIEL : Statuts et règlements, 1982, 1987; procès-verbaux, correspondance, documents financiers, rapports, 1982-1991; journaux de bord, 1987-1991; bulletins (*La Causerie*, 1987-1991); demandes de subvention, albums de coupures, 1980-1991; dossiers concernant la clientèle, 1989-1991; actes de congrès, 1990; dépliants, bannières, 1991; affiches, 1985;

macarons, 1984; document de présentation, 1989; coupures de presse, photographies, enregistrements sonores, vidéocassettes.
QUANTITÉ : 1 classeur.
ÉTAT : Bon.
ACCÈS : Permission requise.

1145. *Centre de femmes du pays Maria-Chapdelaine*

✣ Dolbeau (Québec). Groupe fondé 1984.

En tant que ressource en santé mentale, le centre vise à favoriser l'autonomie des femmes. Il offre des services individuels et collectifs et des activités telles que les cafés-rencontres et les ateliers.

LIEU DE CONSULTATION : Centre de femmes du pays Maria-Chapdelaine. [*Adresse postale :* C.P. 233, Dolbeau (Québec) G8L 2R1. (*Indication de rue :* 1201, rue des Pins.) *Téléphone :* (418) 276-8585.]
MATÉRIEL : Statuts et règlements, 1989; procès-verbaux, demandes de subvention, listes de membres, 1988-1991; correspondance, 1990-1991; journaux de bord, 1984-1991; documents financiers, 1989-1990; listes d'envoi, pétitions, albums de coupures, communiqués de presse, photographies, 1989-1991; rapports, 1985-1991; dépliants, 1985-1989; vidéocassettes, 1991.
QUANTITÉ : 1 classeur.
ÉTAT : Bon.
ACCÈS : Permission requise.

1146. *Centre de femmes Espoir pour elles*

✣ Saint-Polycarpe (Québec). Groupe fondé 1989.

Par ses activités, telles que cafés-rencontres, ateliers et cours, le Centre de femmes Espoir pour elles veut promouvoir l'autonomie sociale, affective et financière de la femme.

LIEU DE CONSULTATION : Centre de femmes Espoir pour elles. [*Adresse :* 139, rue Sainte-Catherine, Saint-Polycarpe (Québec) J0P 1X0. *Téléphone :* (514) 265-3877.]
MATÉRIEL : Procès-verbaux, 1986-1991; statuts et règlements, correspondance, journaux de bord, documents financiers, demandes de subvention, dossiers concernant la clientèle, listes de membres, listes d'envoi, pétitions, albums de coupures, rapports, mémoires, actes de congrès, dépliants, communiqués de presse, affiches, livres, coupures de presse, photographies, 1989-1991.
QUANTITÉ : 1 classeur, 1 étagère, 4 boîtes, 1 bibliothèque.
ÉTAT : Bon.

1147. *Centre de femmes La Moisson*

✣ Dorion (Québec). Groupe fondé 1985.

Le centre, né du projet « Alternative-Violence », est un lieu où toutes les femmes peuvent trouver support, information, références et relation d'aide et une ressource pour les femmes qui sont, ou ont été, victimes de violence.

LIEU DE CONSULTATION : Centre de femmes La Moisson. [*Adresse postale :* C.P. 183, Dorion (Québec) J7V 5W1. *Téléphone :* (514) 455-8720.]
MATÉRIEL : Statuts et règlements, procès-verbaux, correspondance, documents financiers, demandes de subvention, dossiers concernant la clientèle, listes de membres, albums de coupures, rapports, dépliants, communiqués de presse, coupures de presse, 1985-1991; macarons, livres, 1990; bulletins, 1990-1991.
QUANTITÉ : 1 classeur.
ÉTAT : Bon.
ACCÈS : Permission requise.

1148. Centre de femmes La Tuque

✣ La Tuque (Québec). Groupe fondé 1988.

Le centre maintient un lieu d'échange, favorise une prise en charge individuelle et informe les femmes des services dont elles peuvent bénéficier.

LIEU DE CONSULTATION : Centre de femmes La Tuque. [*Adresse* : 375, rue St-Joseph, La Tuque (Québec) G9X 3P6. *Téléphone* : (819) 523-2240.]

MATÉRIEL : Statuts et règlements, 1983; procès-verbaux, 1990-1991; correspondance, documents financiers, demandes de subvention, actes de congrès, tracts, communiqués de presse, 1991; listes de membres, 1989-1990; coupures de presse, 1988-1991.

QUANTITÉ : 1 tiroir de classeur.

ÉTAT : Bon.

1149. Centre de femmes L'Éclaircie

✣ Saint-Constant (Québec). Groupe fondé 1980.

Le centre brise l'isolement que vivent les femmes en leur offrant un lieu d'échange en visant : l'autonomie, la valorisation sociale, la défense de leurs droits et surtout la solidarité. À ses débuts, l'organisme s'appelait le Groupe ma'me chose.

LIEU DE CONSULTATION : Centre de femmes L'Éclaircie. [*Adresse* : 97A, montée des Bouleaux, Saint-Constant (Québec) J5A 1A9. *Téléphone* : (514) 638-1301.]

MATÉRIEL : Statuts et règlements, 1982-1991; procès-verbaux, correspondance, documents financiers, listes de membres, albums de coupures, rapports, dépliants, communiqués de presse, coupures de presse, photographies, 1980-1991; demandes de subvention, 1983-1991; macarons, 1988-1991; bulletins (*Journal*, 1984-1988; *Info-Éclair*, 1988-1991); vidéocassettes, 1990; dossiers concernant la clientèle.

QUANTITÉ : 1 classeur.

ÉTAT : Bon.

ACCÈS : Permission requise.

1150. Centre de femmes L'ÉRIGE

✣ La Sarre (Québec). Groupe fondé 1987.

Le centre organise et met à la disposition des femmes d'Abitibi-Ouest, des services d'écoute, d'hébergement dépannage et d'accompagnement. De plus, il vise à sensibiliser la population et les intervenants et intervenantes aux problèmes que vivent certaines femmes. (Le nom du centre vient des mots suivants : écoute, références, information, générateur et emploi.)

LIEU DE CONSULTATION : Centre de femmes L'ÉRIGE. [*Adresse* : 35, 3e av. ouest, La Sarre (Québec) J9Z 1G8. *Téléphone* : (819) 333-9706.]

MATÉRIEL : Statuts et règlements, procès-verbaux, correspondance, documents financiers, demandes de subvention, listes d'envoi, pétitions, albums de coupures, rapports, dépliants, communiqués de presse, coupures de presse, photographies, 1987-1991; listes de membres, 1988-1991; actes de congrès, 1989-1991; bulletins (*Par celles*, 1991); enregistrements sonores, 1990-1991; vidéocassettes, 1990.

QUANTITÉ : 1 classeur.

ÉTAT : Bon.

ACCÈS : Permission requise.

1151. Centre de femmes L'Étincelle

✣ Baie-Comeau (Québec). Groupe fondé 1979.

Le centre était connu sous le nom de la Maison des femmes de la Côte-Nord, secteur ACT, jusqu'en 1989. Il veut trouver des solutions à l'isolement psychosocial des femmes et donner aux femmes des outils d'autodétermination et des moyens de lutter pour l'avancement de la condition féminine.

LIEU DE CONSULTATION : Centre de femmes L'Étincelle. [*Adresse* : 766, rue Bossé, Baie-Comeau (Québec) G5C 1L6. *Téléphone* : (418) 589-9366.]

MATÉRIEL : Statuts et règlements, procès-verbaux, correspondance, documents financiers, demandes de subvention, listes de membres, albums de coupures, rapports, affiches, macarons, coupures de presse, photographies, 1979-1991; mémoires, dépliants, communiqués de presse, 1989-1991; bannières, 1986-1991; bulletins (*Pléiades*, 1990-1991); vidéocassettes, 1990.

QUANTITÉ : 1 classeur.

ÉTAT : Bon.

ACCÈS : Permission requise.

1152. Centre de femmes Parmi elles

✣ St-Pierre-les-Becquets (Québec). Groupe fondé [1988?].

Les objectifs du centre sont d'informer et de sensibiliser les femmes afin d'en arriver à une modification de leurs conditions de vie. De plus, il vise à développer l'égalité entre les hommes et les femmes. Les activités comprennent des services d'écoute, de support et d'accompagnement et un centre de documentation.

LIEU DE CONSULTATION : Centre de femmes Parmi elles. [*Adresse* : 135, rue Lapérade, St-Pierre-les-Becquets (Québec) G0X 2Z0. *Téléphone* : (819) 263-2586.]

MATÉRIEL : Statuts et règlements, procès-verbaux, correspondance, documents financiers, demandes de subvention, dossiers concernant la clientèle, listes de membres, albums de coupures, rapports, dépliants, syllabus cours, comptes rendus d'activités, 1988-1991; communiqués de presse, bannières, 1989-1991; affiches, 1990-1991; photographies, 1988-1990; récits de vie, 1988; bulletins (*Les Elles de l'écriture*, 1989-1991); romans-photos, 1989.

QUANTITÉ : 4 boîtes.

ÉTAT : Bon.

ACCÈS : Permission requise

1153. Centre de prévention et d'intervention pour victimes d'agression sexuelle (Laval, Québec)

✣ Laval (Québec). Groupe fondé 1986.

Le but de l'organisme, appelé aussi le CPIVAS, est de venir en aide aux victimes d'agression sexuelle et à leurs proches.

LIEU DE CONSULTATION : Centre de prévention et d'intervention pour victimes d'agression sexuelle. [*Adresse postale* : C.P. 294, Succursale Vimont, Laval (Québec) H7M 3W9. *Téléphone* : (514) 669-9053.]

MATÉRIEL : Statuts et règlements, 1986; procès-verbaux, correspondance, journaux de bord, documents financiers, demandes de subvention, dossiers concernant la clientèle, listes d'envoi, albums de coupures, communiqués de presse, 1986-1991; mémoires, 1991; dépliants, 1989-1991; vidéocassettes, 1990-1991.

QUANTITÉ : Env. 2 classeurs.

ÉTAT : Bon.

ACCÈS : Dossiers concernant la clientèle confidentiels.

1154. Centre d'éducation et d'action des femmes de Montréal

✥ Montréal (Québec). Groupe fondé 1971.

Le Centre d'education et d'action des femmes de Montréal, connu sous le nom de Services aux familles jusqu'en 1982, a pour objectifs de briser l'isolement des femmes et de promouvoir leur développement.

LIEU DE CONSULTATION : Centre d'éducation et d'action des femmes de Montréal. [*Adresse :* 1468 Fullum, Montréal (Québec) H2K 3M1. *Téléphone :* (514) 524-5656/3901.]

MATÉRIEL : Statuts et règlements, 1984-1985, 1990-1991; procès-verbaux, documents financiers, demandes de subvention, rapports, 1971-1991; affiches, macarons, 1971; bannières, 1982; bulletins (*L'Expressive*, 1988-1991); dossiers concernant la clientèle, listes de membres, listes d'envoi, albums de coupures, actes de congrès, dépliants, tracts, coupures de presse, photographies, enregistrements sonores, vidéocassettes.

QUANTITÉ : 20 boîtes.

ÉTAT : Bon.

ACCÈS : Permission requise.

1155. Centre des femmes de Charlevoix

✥ Baie St-Paul (Québec). Groupe fondé 1988.

Le Centre offre des services d'aide, de référence et d'education pour les femmes.

LIEU DE CONSULTATION : Centre des femmes de Charlevoix. [*Adresse postale :* C.P. 548, Baie St-Paul (Québec) G0A 1B0. (*Indication de rue :* 4, rue Notre-Dame.) *Téléphone :* (418) 435-5752.]

MATÉRIEL : Statuts et règlements, 1988; procès-verbaux, correspondance, documents financiers, demandes de subvention, listes de membres, pétitions, rapports, mémoires, dépliants, livres, enregistrements sonores, vidéocassettes, 1988-1991; communiqués de presse, affiches, macarons, coupures de presse, 1990-1991.

QUANTITÉ : 1 classeur, 1 bibliothèque.

ÉTAT : Assez bon.

1156. Centre des femmes de Laval

✥ Laval (Québec). Groupe fondé 1982.

Le centre oeuvre à briser l'isolement des femmes et à encourager l'entraide et la solidarité. Il favorise le développement de l'autonomie affective et financière, la prise de conscience et la prise en charge.

LIEU DE CONSULTATION : Centre des femmes de Laval. [*Adresse :* 70, rue Lahaie, Pont Viau, Laval (Québec) H7G 3A8. *Téléphone :* (514) 629-1991.]

MATÉRIEL : Statuts et règlements, 1982; procès-verbaux, correspondance, documents financiers, demandes de subvention, listes de membres, rapports, mémoires, dépliants, communiqués de presse, macarons, 1983-1991; listes d'envoi, 1987-1991; albums de coupures, actes de congrès, 1982-1991; bulletins (*Répercussion*, 1983-1991); coupures de presse, photographies.

QUANTITÉ : Env. 3 classeurs.

ÉTAT : Bon.

ACCÈS : Permission requise. Listes de membres confidentielles.

1157. Centre des femmes de Lennoxville et des environs / Lennoxville and District Women's Centre

[For English entry, see # 1217.]

✥ Lennoxville (Québec). Groupe fondé 1981.

Le Centre des femmes de Lennoxville et des environs est un lieu de rencontre et un centre de documentation qui a pour but d'aider les femmes à atteindre leur plein potentiel.

LIEU DE CONSULTATION : Centre des femmes de Lennoxville et des environs. [*Adresse postale :* C.P. 102, Lennoxville (Québec) J1M 1Z3. (*Indication de rue :* 151-A, rue Queen.) *Téléphone :* (819) 564-6626.]

MATÉRIEL : Statuts et règlements, procès-verbaux, correspondance, journaux de bord, documents financiers, listes de membres, listes d'envoi, rapports, dépliants, tracts, communiqués de presse, affiches, coupures de presse, photographies, 1981-1991; demandes de subvention, mémoires, bulletins, 1982-1991; pétitions, 1986-1991; actes de congrès, 1984-1991.

QUANTITÉ : Env. 3 classeurs.

ACCÈS : Permission du conseil d'administration requise.

1158. Centre des femmes de l'Estrie

✥ Sherbrooke (Québec). Groupe fondé 1982.

Le Centre des femmes de l'Estrie (CFE) est un lieu d'accueil et de référence où l'on peut trouver des documents pertinents concernant l'éducation, le travail, les droits des femmes et les services qui leur sont spécialement offerts.

LIEU DE CONSULTATION : Centre des femmes de l'Estrie. [*Adresse :* 111, rue King ouest, bureau 103, Sherbrooke (Québec) J1H 1P5. *Téléphone :* (819) 823-7759.]

MATÉRIEL : Statuts et règlements, demandes de subvention, albums de coupures, actes de congrès, affiches, coupures de presse, 1983-1991; procès-verbaux, correspondance, documents financiers, rapports, photographies, 1982-1991; listes de membres, 1991; dépliants, 1989; bulletins (*Informelles*, 1986-1991).

QUANTITÉ : 2 tiroirs de classeur.

ÉTAT : Bon.

ACCÈS : Permission requise.

1159. Centre des femmes de Verdun

✥ Verdun (Québec). Groupe fondé 1980.

Les objectifs du Centre des femmes de Verdun (CFV) sont de briser l'isolement des femmes et de défendre et promouvoir leurs intérêts et droits. Il offre des services d'information et de références et des cours et ateliers.

LIEU DE CONSULTATION : Centre des femmes de Verdun. [*Adresse :* 3993, rue Wellington, Verdun (Québec) H4G 1V6. *Téléphone :* (514) 767-0384.]

MATÉRIEL : Procès-verbaux, 1984-1991; journaux de bord, documents financiers, listes de membres, rapports, bannières, 1982-1991; journaux (*La Répliquée*, 1982-1991); demandes de subvention, 1980-1991; albums de coupures, dépliants, tracts, 1981; guide d'intervention, 1991; statuts et règlements, listes d'envoi, coupures de presse.

QUANTITÉ : 3 classeurs.

ÉTAT : Bon.

ACCÈS : Permission requise.

1160. Centre des femmes du ô pays

✥ Lac-des-Aigles (Québec). Groupe fondé 1980.

Les principaux objectifs du centre sont d'améliorer les conditions de vie des femmes, d'accroître leur autonomie et de favoriser l'entraide et la solidarité. Cet organisme offre, entre autres, des services d'aide et de documentation et des ateliers.

LIEU DE CONSULTATION : Centre des femmes du ô pays. [*Adresse postale :* C.P. 159, Lac-des-Aigles (Québec) G0K 1V0. (*Indication de rue :* 69, rue Principale.) *Téléphone :* (418) 779-2316.]

QUÉBEC

MATÉRIEL : Statuts et règlements, 1985-1991; procès-verbaux, correspondance, rapports, 1980-1991; documents financiers, 1982-1991; demandes de subvention, 1981-1991; actes de congrès, 1989; dépliants, 1988; affiches, 1990; publications, 1988, 1991.

QUANTITÉ : 1 classeur.

ÉTAT : Bon.

ACCÈS : Permission requise.

1161. Centre des femmes du Témiscouata L'Aurore

✢ Cabano (Québec). Groupe fondé 1981.

Le centre regroupe les femmes de la région de toutes les conditions et de tous les âges. Il vise à accroître leur autonomie aux niveaux économique, affectif et social.

LIEU DE CONSULTATION : Centre des femmes du Témiscouata l'Aurore. [*Adresse postale* : C.P. 427, Cabano (Québec) G0L 1E0. (**Indication de rue** : 32, rue Bérubé.) *Téléphone* : (418) 854-2399.]

MATÉRIEL : Statuts et règlements, 1982, 1985-1991; procès-verbaux, correspondance, journaux de bord, documents financiers, demandes de subvention, listes d'envoi, rapports, dépliants, coupures de presse, 1987-1991; guides d'animation, 1987, 1990; livres, 1984-1985; communiqués de presse, affiches, macarons, photographies.

QUANTITÉ : 2 classeurs.

ÉTAT : Bon.

ACCÈS : Permission requise.

1162. Centre des femmes (Forestville, Québec)

✢ Forestville (Québec). Groupe fondé 1981.

Les objectifs du centre sont de développer la solidarité entre les femmes, de briser l'isolement, de favoriser les contacts et les échanges et de promouvoir chez les femmes une prise de conscience de leur propre condition et de celle des autres femmes. Le centre offre de nombreux services et activités pour répondre aux besoins des femmes.

LIEU DE CONSULTATION : Centre des femmes. [*Adresse* : 13, route 138, Forestville (Québec) G0T 1E0. *Téléphone* : (418) 587-4204.]

MATÉRIEL : Statuts et règlements, procès-verbaux, correspondance, journaux de bord, documents financiers, demandes de subvention, listes de membres, listes d'envoi, pétitions, albums de coupures, rapports, mémoires, actes de congrès, communiqués de presse, affiches, macarons, bannières, bulletins (*Causerie de femmes*), livres, coupures de presse, photographies, vidéocassettes.

QUANTITÉ : 2 classeurs.

1163. Centre émersion manicouagan

✢ Baie-Comeau (Québec). Groupe fondé 1981.

Le Centre émersion manicouagan (CE) travaille à améliorer la condition socio-économique des femmes en favorisant leur intégration ou leur réintégration sur le marché de travail.

LIEU DE CONSULTATION : Centre émersion manicouagan. [*Adresse* : 42, place Lasalle, Baie-Comeau (Québec) G4Z 1K3. *Téléphone* : (418) 296-6388.]

MATÉRIEL : Statuts et règlements, procès-verbaux, correspondance, documents financiers, demandes de subvention, dossiers concernant la clientèle, listes de membres, albums de coupures, rapports, dépliants, communiqués de presse, affiches, [1981?]-1991; vidéocassettes, [1987?].

ÉTAT : Bon.

1164. Centre-Femmes Catherine Leblond

✢ Trois-Pistoles (Québec). Groupe fondé 1980.

Le centre vise à promouvoir le droit des femmes à l'égalité de traitement dans toutes les sphères de l'activité humaine, que ce soit au niveau politique, économique ou social. Le centre s'appelait la Maison Catherine Leblond de 1981 à 1990.

LIEU DE CONSULTATION : Centre-Femmes Catherine Leblond. [*Adresse postale* : C.P. 1798, Trois-Pistoles (Québec) G0L 4K0. (**Indication de rue** : 220, rue Jean-Rioux.) *Téléphone* : (418) 851-3178.]

MATÉRIEL : Statuts et règlements, procès-verbaux, correspondance, journaux de bord, documents financiers, demandes de subvention, dossiers concernant la clientèle, listes de membres, listes d'envoi, rapports, mémoires, actes de congrès, communiqués de presse, coupures de presse, photographies, 1980-1991; pétitions, 1988-1989; albums de coupures, 1981-1991; affiches, bannières, 1990-1991; macarons, 1987-1991; livres, 1990; documents divers.

QUANTITÉ : 2 classeurs.

ÉTAT : Bon.

ACCÈS : Permission requise. Dossiers concernant la clientèle confidentiels.

1165. Centre-Femmes d'aujourd'hui

✢ Québec (Québec). Groupe fondé 1975.

Le but principal du centre est la promotion de la condition féminine. Il offre des services accueil-écoute et référence, et des activités éducatives et politiques.

LIEU DE CONSULTATION : Centre-Femmes d'aujourd'hui. [*Adresse* : 1474, boul. St-Cyrille ouest, Québec (Québec) G1S 1X2. *Téléphone* : (418) 683-2548.]

MATÉRIEL : Statuts et règlements, procès-verbaux, correspondance, journaux de bord, documents financiers, demandes de subvention, listes de membres, albums de coupures, rapports, 1975-1991; bulletins (*Connaissez-vous Centre-Femmes d'aujourd'hui*, 1988; *Reflet*, 1987); mémoires, actes de congrès, dépliants, communiqués de presse, affiches, macarons, coupures de presse, vidéocassettes.

QUANTITÉ : 1 classeur.

ÉTAT : Bon.

ACCÈS : Permission requise.

1166. Centre-Femmes de Lotbinière

✢ St-Flavien (Québec). Groupe fondé 1985.

Par ses activités sociales et éducatives, le centre travaille à briser l'isolement des femmes et à favoriser leur autonomie.

LIEU DE CONSULTATION : Centre-Femmes de Lotbinière. [*Adresse* : 151, rue Principale, St-Flavien (Québec) G0S 2M0. *Téléphone* : (418) 728-4402.]

MATÉRIEL : Statuts et règlements, procès-verbaux, documents financiers, demandes de subvention, listes de membres, albums de coupures, rapports, 1985-1991; dépliants, communiqués de presse, affiches, macarons, livres, photographies.

QUANTITÉ : 2 classeurs.

ÉTAT : Bon.

ACCÈS : Permission requise.

1167. Centre-Femmes La Jardilec

✥ St-Jean-Port-Joli (Québec). Groupe fondé 1979.

Le centre vient en aide aux femmes en détresse en leur offrant les services suivants : accueil, référence, consultation individuelle, écoute active, accompagnement si nécessaire, sensibilisation, suivi individuel et collectif, relation d'aide, intervention de crise, ateliers éducatifs, actions collectives, recherche et expérimentation.

LIEU DE CONSULTATION : Centre-femmes La Jardilec. [*Adresse postale* : C.P. 654, Saint-Jean-Port-Joli (Québec) G0R 3G0. (*Indication de rue* : 25, rue Gérard-Ouellet.) *Téléphone* : (418) 598-9677.]

MATÉRIEL : Statuts et règlements, procès-verbaux, correspondance, documents financiers, demandes de subvention, listes de membres, albums de coupures, rapports, dépliants, tracts, communiqués de presse, affiches, 1979-1991 ; bannières, 1983-1991 ; agenda, 1989 ; pétitions.

ÉTAT : Bon.

ACCÈS : Permission requise.

1168. Centre-Femmes L'Envolée

✥ Cap-à-l'Aigle (Québec). Groupe fondé 1987.

Le centre offre ses services aux femmes qui vivent des situations d'isolement, de violence, de maladie mentale, de pauvreté ou toutes autres situations problématiques nécessitant appui, écoute, information et référence. Il tente également de sensibiliser la population à ces problèmes.

LIEU DE CONSULTATION : Centre-Femmes L'Envolée. [*Adresse* : 62, route du Quai, Cap-à-l'Aigle (Québec) G0T 1B0. *Téléphone* : (418) 665-7459.]

MATÉRIEL : Statuts et règlements, listes d'envoi, albums de coupures, dépliants, 1989-1991 ; procès-verbaux, correspondance, demandes de subvention, 1986-1991 ; documents financiers, listes de membres, 1982-1991 ; dossiers concernant la clientèle, rapports, 1988.

QUANTITÉ : 1 classeur.

ÉTAT : Bon.

ACCÈS : Permission requise. Dossiers concernant la clientèle confidentiels.

1169. Centre Louise-Amélie

✥ Ste-Anne-des-Monts (Québec). Groupe fondé 1982.

Le centre vient en aide aux femmes victimes de violence ou en difficulté et à leurs enfants par des services d'accueil et d'hébergement, de consultation, d'accompagnement et d'orientation.

LIEU DE CONSULTATION : Centre Louise-Amélie. [*Adresse postale* : C.P. 813, Ste-Anne-des-Monts (Québec) G0E 2G0. *Téléphone* : (418) 763-7641.]

MATÉRIEL : Statuts et règlements, procès-verbaux, 1986-1991 ; correspondance, journaux de bord, documents financiers, demandes de subvention, listes de membres, rapports, 1987-1991 ; communiqués de presse, 1986 ; affiches, 1988 ; coupures de presse, 1982-1991 ; dépliants, photographies.

QUANTITÉ : Env. 2 tiroirs de classeur.

ÉTAT : Bon.

ACCÈS : Permission requise.

1170. Centre pour femmes immigrantes (Sherbrooke, Québec)

✥ Sherbrooke (Québec). Groupe fondé 1982.

Le Centre pour femmes immigrantes (CEFI) défend les droits des femmes immigrantes et lutte contre le racisme et le sexisme. Il aide aussi les femmes démunies des communautés culturelles en offrant des cours de français, des ateliers et des services de traduction et d'interprète. Il était connu sous le nom de Nous les femmes immigrantes jusqu'en 1987.

LIEU DE CONSULTATION : Centre pour femmes immigrantes. [*Adresse* : 1838 de Rouville, Sherbrooke (Québec) J1J 1W6. *Téléphone* : (819) 822-2259.]

MATÉRIEL : Statuts et règlements, procès-verbaux, correspondance, journaux de bord, documents financiers, demandes de subvention, dossiers concernant la clientèle, listes de membres, pétitions, albums de coupures, rapports, mémoires, actes de congrès, dépliants, communiqués de presse, coupures de presse, 1987-1991 ; bulletins, 1988-1991 ; livres, 1987 ; photographies, enregistrements sonores, vidéocassettes, films.

ÉTAT : Bon.

ACCÈS : Permission requise.

1171. Centre social des femmes du centre-ville de Montréal

✥ Montréal (Québec). Groupe fondé [1981?].

Le centre social des femmes du centre-ville de Montréal (CSFCVM), appelé aussi Coop lesbienne, offre des prêts et dons à des organismes lesbiens ou à des lesbiennes pour des projets non mixtes.

LIEU DE CONSULTATION : Centre social des femmes du centre-ville de Montréal. [*Adresse postale* : C.P. 62, Succursale Place du Parc, Montréal (Québec) H2W 2M9.]

MATÉRIEL : Statuts et règlements, procès-verbaux, correspondance, journaux de bord, documents financiers, listes d'envoi, 1981-1991.

QUANTITÉ : 1 tiroir de classeur.

ÉTAT : Assez bon.

ACCÈS : Permission requise. Correspondance et demandes de prêts et de dons confidentielles.

1172. Centr'elles, comité d'action des femmes d'Avignon

✥ Carleton (Québec). Groupe fondé 1985.

Ce centre a pour objectifs de permettre aux femmes d'accroître leur autonomie, de développer leur solidarité, d'échanger leurs expériences et de se perfectionner. Ses activités comprennent des colloques, des cafés-rencontres et des activités de la Journée internationale des femmes.

LIEU DE CONSULTATION : Centr'elles, comité d'action des femmes d'Avignon. [*Adresse postale* : C.P. 949, Carleton (Québec) G0C 1J0. (*Indication de rue* : 536A, boul. Perron.) *Téléphone* : (418) 364-3157.]

MATÉRIEL : Statuts et règlements, 1985 ; procès-verbaux, correspondance, journaux de bord, documents financiers, listes de membres, albums de coupures, rapports, 1985-1991 ; demandes de subvention, 1984-1991 ; dépliants, 1985-1990 ; affiches, 1986-1990 ; bulletins (*Info-Centr'Elles*, 1987-1990) ; actes de colloque, 1990.

QUANTITÉ : 1 classeur, 4 boîtes.

ÉTAT : Bon.

ACCÈS : Permission requise.

1173. Cercles de fermières du Québec

✥ Longueuil (Québec). Groupe fondé 1915.

En offrant des activités éducatives et sociales, les Cercles de fermières du Québec (CFQ) vise à défendre les droits de la femme et de la famille.

LIEU DE CONSULTATION : Cercles de fermières du Québec. [*Adresse* : 1043, rue Tiffin, Longueuil (Québec) J4P 3G7. *Téléphone* : (514) 442-3983. *Télécopieur* : (514) 442-4363.]

MATÉRIEL : Statuts et règlements, procès-verbaux, rapports, 1968-1991 ; correspondance, documents financiers, 1974-1991 ; albums de coupures, 1980-1991 ; mémoires, 1949-1991 ; bulletins (*La Revue des fermières*, 1974-1990 ; *L'Actuel*, 1990-1991) ; livres, 1980, 1990 ; enregistrements sonores, 1984 ; photographies.

ÉTAT : Assez bon.
ACCÈS : Permission requise.

CONDITION: Fair.
ACCESS: Permission required. Client files and internal documents closed.

1174. Châteauguay Sexual Assault Prevention and Aid Center / Centre d'aide et de prévention d'assauts sexuels de Châteauguay

[Renseignements en français, notice 1141.]

✣ Châteauguay, Quebec. Formed 1978.

The Châteauguay Sexual Assault Prevention and Aid Center (CSAPAC) works to reduce sexual assault, provides services to women who have been sexually assaulted, and offers educational activities in order to sensitize the community. Until 1980 the centre was called le Centre d'aide aux victimes de viol de Châteauguay.

LOCATION OF RECORDS: Châteauguay Sexual Assault Prevention and Aid Center. [*Mailing Address:* P.O. Box 284, Châteauguay, Quebec J6J 4Z6. *Telephone:* (514) 699-8258.]

RECORDS: Constitutions, 1978, 1980; minutes, correspondence, financial records, grant applications, client records, scrapbooks, reports, press releases, 1978-1991; membership lists, 1985; pamphlets, 1978, 1985; posters, banners, 1980; buttons, 1980-1983; photographs, 1985-1988.

AMOUNT: 1 filing cabinet.
CONDITION: Fair.
ACCESS: Permission required. Client files closed.

1175. Chez Doris, the Women's Shelter Foundation / Fondation du refuge pour femmes Chez Doris

[Renseignements en français, notice 1207.]

✣ Montreal, Quebec. Formed 1977.

Chez Doris is a day shelter offering direct services such as food and clothing to women in need, as well as information and educational activities.

LOCATION OF RECORDS: Chez Doris, the Women's Shelter Foundation. [*Address:* 2196 de Maisonneuve Blvd. W., Montreal, Quebec H3H 1L1. *Telephone:* (514) 937-2341.]

RECORDS: Constitution, 1977; minutes, 1982-1991; log-books, reports, 1986-1991; financial records, 1984-1991; grant applications, mailing lists, 1985-1991; newsletters, 1987-1990; correspondence, scrapbooks, pamphlets, banners, clippings, photographs, sound recordings.

AMOUNT: Approx. 2 filing cabinets.
ACCESS: Permission required.

1176. Chinese Family Service of Greater Montreal. Women's Committee / Service à la famille chinoise du Grand Montréal. Comité des femmes

[Renseignements en français, notice 1251.]

✣ Montreal, Quebec. Formed 1976.

The Women's Committee of the Chinese Family Service of Greater Montreal (CFSGM) works to address issues faced by women of Chinese origin in Quebec and to promote the general welfare of women.

LOCATION OF RECORDS: Chinese Family Service of Greater Montreal. Women's Committee. [*Address:* 987 Côté St., 4th Floor, Montreal, Quebec H2Z 1L1. *Telephone:* (514) 861-5244. *Fax:* (514) 861-9008.]

RECORDS: Minutes, correspondence, financial records, grant applications, client records, membership lists, mailing lists, petitions, reports, briefs, press releases, posters, buttons, photographs, videotapes, 1978-1991.

1177. Le Cinquième Monde

✣ Québec (Québec). Groupe fondé 1981.

Les buts de cet organisme sont de développer des liens de solidarité entre les femmes du Québec et les femmes des pays en voie de développement, de sensibiliser les femmes et la collectivité à la situation des femmes dans ces pays et de susciter un appui à leurs mouvements et à leurs luttes.

LIEU DE CONSULTATION : Cinquième Monde. [*Adresse :* 454 Caron, Québec (Québec) G1K 8K8. *Téléphone :* (418) 647-5855. *Télécopieur :* (418) 647-5719.]

MATÉRIEL : Statuts et règlements, 1982, 1985, 1988; procès-verbaux, 1982-1991; correspondance, 1989-1990; documents financiers, 1985-1991; demandes de subvention, rapports, 1984-1990; dépliants, 1990-1991; bannières, [198-]; bulletins (*Univers'elles*, 1988-1991); coupures de presse, 1984-1985, 1988-1990; photographies, 1985-1987, 1990; listes de membres, pétitions.

QUANTITÉ : Env. 1 classeur.
ÉTAT : Bon.
ACCÈS : Permission requise.

1178. La Citad'elle de Lachute

✣ Lachute (Québec). Groupe fondé 1985.

En offrant des services d'accueil, d'hébergement, d'information et d'écoute, La Citad'elle de Lachute vise à promouvoir l'autonomie de la femme et à venir en aide aux victimes de violence et à leurs enfants. L'organisme offre des services en français et en anglais.

LIEU DE CONSULTATION : Citad'elle de Lachute. [*Adresse postale :* C.P. 602, Lachute (Québec) J8H 4G4. *Téléphone :* (514) 562-7797.]

MATÉRIEL : Statuts et règlements, procès-verbaux, correspondance, journaux de bord, documents financiers, demandes de subvention, dossiers concernant la clientèle, listes de membres, listes d'envoi, pétitions, albums de coupures, rapports, mémoires, dépliants, communiqués de presse, affiches, macarons, bannières, coupures de presse, photographies, enregistrements sonores, 1985-1991; vidéocassettes, 1988-1991.

QUANTITÉ : Env. 2 classeurs, 3 boîtes.
ÉTAT : Bon.
ACCÈS : Permission requise. Dossiers concernant la clientèle confidentiels.

1179. Clinique des femmes de l'Outaouais

✣ Hull (Québec). Groupe fondé 1981.

La clinique dispense des services en contraception et avortement aux femmes de la région et défend leurs droits dans ce domaine. Elle était connue sous le nom du Centre de santé des femmes de l'Outaouais jusqu'en 1985 ou 1986. Actuellement, le nom officiel de l'organisme est le Centre d'information et d'action sociale de l'Outaouais (CIASO).

LIEU DE CONSULTATION : Clinique des femmes de l'Outaouais. [*Adresse :* 44, rue Jeanne d'Arc, Hull (Québec) J8Y 2H2. *Téléphone :* (819) 778-2055. *Télécopieur :* (819) 778-3470.]

MATÉRIEL : Statuts et règlements, 1981; procès-verbaux, 1981-1991; correspondance, journaux de bord, documents financiers, demandes de subvention, dossiers concernant la clientèle, listes de membres, listes d'envoi, albums de coupures, rapports, mémoires, actes de congrès, dépliants, tracts, communiqués de presse, photographies.

QUANTITÉ : 2 classeurs.

ÉTAT : Bon.

ACCÈS : Permission requise. Dossiers concernant la clientèle confidentiels.

1180. Club des femmes d'aujourd'hui de Laval

✤ Laval (Québec). Groupe fondé 1973.

Le Club des femmes d'aujourd'hui de Laval (CFAL) offre des activités qui ont pour but d'informer et de créer des liens entre les femmes pour combler une solitude ou un besoin de compagnie.

LIEU DE CONSULTATION : Club des femmes d'aujourd'hui de Laval. [*Adresse postale* : C.P. 150, Succursale Laval-Ouest, Laval (Québec) H7R 5B8. *Téléphone* : (514) 629-8623.]

MATÉRIEL : Statuts et règlements, procès-verbaux, journaux de bord, documents financiers, photographies, bulletins, 1974-1991; correspondance, 1987-1991; demandes de subvention, dossiers concernant la clientèle, 1990-1991; dépliants, communiqués de presse, 1991; tracts, 1984-1991; livres, 1974; vidéocassettes, 1989-1991.

QUANTITÉ : 2 classeurs.

ÉTAT : Assez bon.

ACCÈS : Permission requise.

1181. Club politique féminin

✤ Rimouski (Québec). Groupe fondé 1988.

Ce club (appelé auparavant le Club politique féminin, région Bas-Saint-Laurent-Gaspésie) vise à démystifier ce qu'est la politique et à augmenter la participation active des femmes en politique.

LIEU DE CONSULTATION : Club politique féminin. [*Adresse postale* : C.P. 224, Rimouski (Québec) G5L 1C1.]

MATÉRIEL : Statuts et règlements, 1991; procès-verbaux, correspondance, documents financiers, demandes de subvention, listes de membres, albums de coupures, rapports, dépliants, communiqués de presse, affiches, coupures de presse, 1988-1991.

QUANTITÉ : 1 classeur.

ÉTAT : Bon.

ACCÈS : Permission requise.

1182. Collectif des femmes immigrantes

✤ Montréal (Québec). Groupe fondé 1983.

Le collectif vise à défendre les femmes immigrantes contre le racisme et le sexisme et à favoriser leur intégration à toutes les sphères de la société québécoise. Ses principales activités sont la formation, l'information et la sensibilisation.

LIEU DE CONSULTATION : Collectif des femmes immigrantes. [*Adresse* : 6865 Christophe Colomb, Montréal (Québec) H2S 2H3. *Téléphone* : (514) 279-4246.]

MATÉRIEL : Statuts et règlements, procès-verbaux, correspondance, documents financiers, demandes de subvention, listes de membres, rapports, mémoires, actes de congrès, dépliants, tracts, communiqués de presse, affiches, 1983-1991; albums de coupures, coupures de presse, 1988-1991; bulletins, photographies, 1990-1991; enregistrements sonores, 1987-1991.

QUANTITÉ : 5 classeurs.

ÉTAT : Bon.

ACCÈS : Permission requise.

1183. Collectif d'intervention auprès des femmes victimes de violence

✤ Cabano (Québec). Groupe fondé 1983.

Le Collectif d'intervention auprès des femmes victimes de violence (CIAFVV) vient en aide aux femmes victimes de violence en leur offrant divers services. De plus, il vise à sensibiliser la population et les institutions à ce phénomène.

LIEU DE CONSULTATION : Collectif d'intervention auprès des femmes victimes de violence. [*Adresse* : 32B, rue Bérubé, Cabano (Québec) G0L 1E9. *Téléphone* : (418) 854-7160.]

MATÉRIEL : Statuts et règlements, pétitions, livres, recueil de témoignage, 1988; procès-verbaux, correspondance, 1984-1991; journaux de bord, 1983-1991; documents financiers, listes de membres, rapports, 1988-1991; demandes de subvention, 1986-1991; actes de congrès, 1986; dépliants, affiches, 1987-1991; vidéocassettes, 1989.

QUANTITÉ : Env. 1 classeur.

ÉTAT : Assez bon.

ACCÈS : Permission requise.

1184. Collectif femmes et justice de Québec

✤ Québec (Québec). Groupe fondé 1984.

Les objectifs poursuivis par le collectif sont de démystifier la loi et de la rendre accessible à toutes les femmes. Il veut aussi dénoncer publiquement le traitement discriminatoire subi par les femmes dans le système judiciare. Il informe gratuitement les femmes sur les questions concernant le droit de la famille, le droit social et le droit du travail.

LIEU DE CONSULTATION : Collectif femmes et justice de Québec. [*Adresse* : 301, rue Carillon, Québec (Québec) G1K 5B3. *Téléphone* : (418) 524-0806.]

MATÉRIEL : Statuts et règlements, 1991; procès-verbaux, correspondance, listes de membres, rapports, 1983-1991; documents financiers, demandes de subvention, dossiers concernant la clientèle, mémoires, dépliants, communiqués de presse, affiches, 1985-1991; listes d'envoi, 1989-1991.

QUANTITÉ : 1 classeur.

ACCÈS : Permission requise. Données sur la clientèle confidentielles.

1185. Collective en santé lesbienne

✤ Montréal (Québec). Groupe fondé 1982.

La collective fait partie du Centre de santé des femmes de Montréal. Son objectif à long terme est de créer un centre lesbien. Ses buts à court terme sont de mettre sur pied des ateliers de sensibilisation et de formation pour les intervenantes hétérosexuelles qui sont suceptibles de travailler auprès des lesbiennes. La collective était connue sous le nom de la Clinique pour lesbiennes jusqu'en 1986.

LIEU DE CONSULTATION : Collective en santé lesbienne. [*Adresse* : a/s Centre de santé des femmes de Montréal, 16, boul. St-Joseph est, Montréal (Québec) H2T 1G8. *Téléphone* : (514) 842-8903/8905.]

MATÉRIEL : Objectifs, 1989-1990; procès-verbaux, 1985, 1988-1991; correspondance, 1989, 1991; demandes de subvention, bannières, 1990; dossiers concernant la clientèle, listes de membres, 1988-1990; mémoires, tracts.

ÉTAT : Assez bon.

ACCÈS : Permission requise. Dossiers concernant la clientèle, listes de membres, listes d'envoi confidentiels.

1186. Collective par et pour elle

✣ Cowansville (Québec). Groupe fondé 1982.

La collective opère un centre de jour dans le but d'aider, d'accueillir et de soutenir les femmes isolées, confrontées seules à un problème de santé mentale ou physique.

LIEU DE CONSULTATION : Collective par et pour elle. [*Adresse* : 213 Oxford, Cowansville (Québec) J2K 2M5. *Téléphone* : (514) 263-1028.]

MATÉRIEL : Statuts et règlements, procès-verbaux, correspondance, documents financiers, demandes de subvention, listes de membres, rapports, 1982-1991; vidéocassettes, 1989; livres.

ÉTAT : Bon.

ACCÈS : Permission requise.

1187. Collège de Maisonneuve. Société générale des étudiantes et des étudiants. Comité-femme de Maisonneuve

✣ Montréal (Québec).

Le Comité-femme de Maisonneuve est marrainé par la Société générale des étudiantes et des étudiants du Collège de Maisonneuve (SOGECOM). Les principaux objectifs du comité sont l'information, la sensibilisation et l'action dans la lutte contre l'oppression des femmes.

LIEU DE CONSULTATION : Collège de Maisonneuve. SOGECOM. Comité-femme de Maisonneuve. [*Adresse* : 3800, rue Sherbrooke est, Montréal (Québec) H1X 2A2. *Téléphone* : (514) 253-9898. *Télécopieur* : (514) 255-9041.]

MATÉRIEL : Statuts et règlements, correspondance, journaux de bord, documents financiers, demandes de subvention, dossiers concernant la clientèle, listes de membres, listes d'envoi, pétitions, albums de coupures, rapports, mémoires, actes de congrès, dépliants, tracts, communiqués de presse, affiches, 1981-1990; procès-verbaux, 1977, 1981-1991; macarons, 1985-1991; bannières, 1986.

QUANTITÉ : 2 classeurs.

ÉTAT : Bon.

ACCÈS : Permission requise.

1188. Concordia University. Office on the Status of Women

✣ Montreal, Quebec. Formed 1985.

The Office on the Status of Women at Concordia University works to improve the status of women on campus, mainly through policy development and evaluation.

LOCATION OF RECORDS: Concordia University. Office on the Status of Women. [*Address*: 1455 de Maisonneuve W., Montreal, Quebec H3G 1M8. *Telephone*: (514) 848-4841. *Fax*: (514) 848-8365.]

RECORDS: Minutes, correspondence, financial records, grant applications, membership lists, mailing lists, reports, pamphlets, clippings, miscellaneous records, 1985-1991; videotapes, manual, 1991; flyers, press releases, posters.

AMOUNT: Approx. 2 filing cabinets.

CONDITION: Good.

ACCESS: Permission required. Records of confidential complaints closed.

1189. Concordia Women's Centre

✣ Montreal, Quebec. Formed 1987.

The Concordia Women's Centre provides information, resources, referrals, support, and a drop-in and meeting space for women at Concordia University. The centre offers services in both English and French; its French name is le Centre des femmes de Concordia.

LOCATION OF RECORDS: Concordia Women's Centre. [*Address*: Concordia University, 1455 de Maisonneuve W., P-03, Montreal, Quebec H3G 1M8. *Telephone*: (514) 848-7431.]

RECORDS: Vision document, minutes, correspondence, log-books, financial records, grant applications, mailing lists, scrapbooks, reports, pamphlets, flyers, press releases, posters, buttons, T-shirts, newsletters (*Women's Agenda des femmes*), papers, clippings, photographs.

AMOUNT: 1 filing cabinet, 2 boxes.

CONDITION: Good.

ACCESS: Permission required.

1190. Confédération des syndicats nationaux. Conseil central de Lanaudière. Comité de condition féminine

✣ Joliette (Québec). Groupe fondé 1978.

Le Comité de condition féminine du Conseil central de Lanaudière de la Confédération des syndicats nationaux (CSN) fait un travail d'information, de sensibilisation et de formation auprès des membres de la CSN de la région concernant les dossiers de condition féminine. Le comité s'appelle aussi le Service à la condition féminine.

LIEU DE CONSULTATION : Confédération des syndicats nationaux. Conseil central de Lanaudière. Comité de condition féminine. [*Adresse* : 190, rue Montcalm, Joliette (Québec) J6E 5G4. *Téléphone* : (514) 759-0762.]

MATÉRIEL : Procès-verbaux, 1981-1991; dossiers concernant la clientèle, listes d'envoi, tracts, 1988; rapports.

QUANTITÉ : 1 classeur.

ÉTAT : Bon.

ACCÈS : Permission requise.

1191. Confédération des syndicats nationaux. Conseil central de Thetford Mines. Comité de la condition féminine

✣ Thetford Mines (Québec).

Le Comité de la condition féminine du Conseil central de Thetford Mines de la Confédération des syndicats nationaux (CSN) coordonne ses activités de façon à faire avancer les revendications des femmes syndiquées et non syndiquées et à améliorer leurs conditions de vie et de travail.

LIEU DE CONSULTATION : Confédération des syndicats nationaux. Conseil central de Thetford Mines. Comité de la condition féminine. [*Adresse* : 908, av. Labbé, Thetford Mines (Québec) G6G 2A8. *Téléphone* : (418) 338-5966. *Télécopieur* : (418) 338-6600.]

MATÉRIEL : Rapports, 1963-1991; statuts et règlements, procès-verbaux.

ÉTAT : Bon.

1192. Conseil d'intervention pour l'accès des femmes au travail du Québec

✣ Montréal (Québec). Groupe fondé [1983?].

Le but du Conseil d'intervention pour l'accès des femmes au travail du Québec (CIAFT) est de promouvoir l'autonomie financière des femmes en favorisant leur accès au travail.

LIEU DE CONSULTATION : Conseil d'intervention pour l'accès des femmes au travail du Québec. [*Adresse* : 1265, rue Berri, bureau 930, Montréal (Québec) H2L 4X4. *Téléphone* : (514) 844-0760. *Télécopieur* : (514) 844-1598.]

MATÉRIEL : Statuts et règlements, 1984; procès-verbaux, correspondance, documents financiers, demandes de subvention, listes de membres, listes d'envoi, rapports, actes de congrès, communiqués de presse, 1984-1991; périodiques (*Bouge*, 1984-1991); mémoires, 1983-1991; affiches, 1991.

QUANTITÉ : 2 classeurs, 13 boîtes.

ÉTAT : Bon.

ACCÈS : Permission requise.

1193. Le Coup d'elle

✢ Saint-Jean-sur-Richelieu (Québec). Groupe fondé 1982.

Le Coup d'elle offre des services telles que l'intervention, l'hébergement et la sensibilisation pour contrer la violence conjugale et pour aider les femmes victimes de violence conjugale et leurs enfants. L'organisme offre des services en français et en anglais.

LIEU DE CONSULTATION : Coup d'elle. [*Adresse postale* : C.P. 368, Saint-Jean-sur-Richelieu (Québec) J3B 6Z5. *Téléphone* : (514) 346-1645.]

MATÉRIEL : Statuts et règlements, 1982-1987; procès-verbaux, documents financiers, demandes de subvention, dossiers concernant la clientèle, listes de membres, rapports, dépliants, affiches, 1982-1991; communiqués de presse, 1990-1991; T-shirts, 1991; correspondance, journaux de bord, macarons.

ÉTAT : Assez bon.

ACCÈS : Permission requise. Dossiers concernant la clientèle confidentiels.

1194. D'main de femmes

✢ Valleyfield (Québec). Groupe fondé 1989.

Par ses cours et ses services de documentation, d'accueil et d'écoute, cet organisme permet aux femmes de reconquérir ou de développer leur autonomie et d'améliorer leur condition de vie.

LIEU DE CONSULTATION : D'main de femmes. [*Adresse* : 98, rue Champlain, Valleyfield (Québec) J6T 1W6. *Téléphone* : (514) 371-1500.]

MATÉRIEL : Statuts et règlements, procès-verbaux, correspondance, documents financiers, demandes de subvention, dossiers concernant la clientèle, listes de membres, listes d'envoi, albums de coupures, rapports, actes de congrès, dépliants, communiqués de presse, affiches, 1989-1991; livres, coupures de presse, photographies.

QUANTITÉ : 1 classeur.

ÉTAT : Bon.

ACCÈS : Permission requise.

1195. Échange entre femmes de Saint-Laurent

✢ Saint-Laurent (Québec). Groupe fondé 1983.

Par ses divers activités, l'organisme favorise la solidarité des femmes, stimule leur autonomie, favorise une prise de conscience individuelle ou collective et incite à l'action communautaire.

LIEU DE CONSULTATION : Échange entre femmes de Saint-Laurent. [*Adresse* : 675, boul. Décarie, Saint-Laurent (Québec) H4L 3L3. *Téléphone* : (514) 744-3513.]

MATÉRIEL : Procès-verbaux, correspondance, demandes de subvention, listes de membres, albums de coupures, dépliants, communiqués de presse, coupures de presse, photographies, 1983-1991; macarons, 1986; bannières, 1985-1990; bulletins (*Vivre plus*, 1985-1991; *Au fil des mots de femmes*, 1990); enregistrements sonores, 1989-1990; journaux de bord, documents financiers, pétitions, rapports, vidéocassettes.

QUANTITÉ : 1 compartiment de classeur.

ÉTAT : Bon.

ACCÈS : Permission requise.

1196. Elizabeth Fry Society of Montreal / Société Elizabeth Fry de Montréal

[Renseignements en français, notice 1253.]

✢ Montreal, Quebec. Formed 1977.

The Elizabeth Fry Society of Montreal assists women in conflict with the law. It operates a transition house as well as other programmes. Until 1985 it was called the Elizabeth Fry Society of Greater Montreal.

LOCATION OF RECORDS: Elizabeth Fry Society of Montreal. [*Address*: 1000 Sherbrooke E., Montreal, Quebec H2L 1L5. *Telephone*: (514) 528-9888. *Fax*: (514) 528-8924.]

RECORDS: Minutes, 1987-1991; newsletters (*Femmes et justice*, 1988-1991); constitution, correspondence, financial records, grant applications, client records, membership lists, mailing lists, reports, briefs, conference proceedings, pamphlets, press releases, posters, books, manuals, publications.

AMOUNT: 4 filing-cabinet drawers.

CONDITION: Fair.

ACCESS: Permission required.

1197. Entraide familiale Outaouais

✢ Gatineau (Québec). Groupe fondé 1982.

Connu sous le nom d'Entraide femmes de Gatineau jusqu'en 1988, Entraide familiale Outaouais vise à développer des moyens de dépannage, d'entraide et de partage pour les personnes démunies.

LIEU DE CONSULTATION : Entraide familiale Outaouais. [*Adresse* : 194 Harold, Gatineau (Québec) J8P 4S4. *Téléphone* : (819) 643-5711.]

MATÉRIEL : Statuts et règlements, documents financiers, 1982-1991; procès-verbaux, journaux de bord, demandes de subvention, dossiers concernant la clientèle, listes de membres, listes d'envoi, albums de coupures, dépliants, communiqués de presse, coupures de presse, photographies, 1988-1991; vidéocassettes, 1990.

QUANTITÉ : 2 tiroirs de classeur.

ÉTAT : Bon.

ACCÈS : Permission requise. Dossiers concernant la clientèle confidentiels.

1198. Espace Val d'Or

✢ Val d'Or (Québec). Groupe fondé 1987.

Les principaux objectifs d'Espace sont l'éducation, la sensibilisation et la prévention des abus commis envers les enfants. Espace Val d'Or fait partie d'un regroupement de neuf groupes Espace au Québec. À partir de 1985, le Regroupement québécois des centres d'aide et de lutte contre les agressions à caractère sexuel, via son comité Espace-Québec, a marrainé le programme Espace au Québec.

LIEU DE CONSULTATION : Espace Val d'Or. [*Adresse postale* : C.P. 697, Val d'Or (Québec) J9P 4P6. *Téléphone* : (819) 824-3572.]

MATÉRIEL : Statuts et règlements, procès-verbaux, correspondance, journaux de bord, documents financiers, demandes de subvention, rapports, dépliants, 1987-1991; vidéocassettes, 1991; communiqués de presse, photographies.

QUANTITÉ : 1 classeur, 2 boîtes.

ÉTAT : Bon.

ACCÈS : Permission requise.

1199. Essor féminin La Tuque

✣ La Tuque (Québec). Groupe fondé 1963.

Essor féminin La Tuque est un mouvement qui permet à un grand nombre de femmes de se réunir dans le but de se cultiver, de se divertir et de s'épanouir.

LIEU DE CONSULTATION : Essor féminin La Tuque. [*Adresse* : 520, rue Bourassa, La Tuque (Québec).]

MATÉRIEL : Statuts et règlements, procès-verbaux, correspondance, documents financiers, listes de membres, coupures de presse, photographies, 1963-1991.

QUANTITÉ : 1 classeur.

ÉTAT : Bon.

ACCÈS : Permission requise.

1200. Évaluation-Médias / MediaWatch (Outremont, Québec)

✣ Outremont (Québec). Groupe fondé 1983.

Il s'agit d'une section de l'organisme national Évaluation-Médias/MediaWatch, connu aussi sous le nom d'Évaluation nationale des images des femmes dans les médias/National Watch on Images of Women in the Media. Cet organisme cherche à améliorer l'image des femmes dans les médias et à dénoncer le sexisme dans la publicité et dans les vidéoclips.

LIEU DE CONSULTATION : Évaluation-Médias. [*Adresse postale* : C.P. 552, Succursale Outremont, Outremont (Québec) H2V 4N4. *Téléphone* : (514) 270-7069.]

MATÉRIEL : Statuts et règlements, 1983; procès-verbaux, correspondance, journaux de bord, enregistrements sonores, 1986-1991; documents financiers, vidéocassettes, 1987-1991; demandes de subvention, albums de coupures, rapports, coupures de presse, 1989-1991; listes de membres, T-shirts, 1990; listes d'envoi, 1988-1991; pétitions, tracts, 1989-1990; mémoires, communiqués de presse, 1985-1991; actes de congrès, affiches, 1987; dépliants, 1989; macarons, 1986; bannières, 1988; photographies, 1985-1990; bulletins (*Petites nouvelles du Québec*, 1991).

QUANTITÉ : 3 tiroirs de classeur.

ÉTAT : Bon.

1201. Expansion-Femmes de Québec

✣ Charlesbourg (Québec). Groupe fondé 1983.

Ce groupe a pour mission de favoriser la réhabilitation et la réinsertion dans la société des femmes qui ont des démêlés avec la justice. Il offre des services tels que des suivis individuels et de groupe axés sur la croissance personnelle.

LIEU DE CONSULTATION : Expansion-Femmes de Québec. [*Adresse* : 2189, Place des Colibris, Charlesbourg (Québec) G1G 2B4. *Téléphone* : (418) 623-3801. *Télécopieur* : (418) 623-9559.]

MATÉRIEL : Statuts et règlements, procès-verbaux, correspondance, journaux de bord, documents financiers, demandes de subvention, dossiers concernant la clientèle, listes de membres, pétitions, albums de coupures, rapports, mémoires, dépliants, communiqués de presse, coupures de presse, photographies, enregistrements sonores, vidéocassettes.

QUANTITÉ : 1 classeur.

ÉTAT : Bon.

ACCÈS : Permission requise. Certains dossiers confidentiels.

1202. Fédération des associations de familles monoparentales du Québec

✣ Montréal (Québec). Groupe fondé 1974.

La fédération, connue aussi sous l'acronyme de FAFMQ, est un réseau des associations dont le but est d'améliorer la situation socio-économique des familles monoparentales. La clientèle de la FAFMQ est composée de plus de quatre-vingt pour cent de femmes dont une grande partie vit en pauvreté. La FAFMQ était d'abord connue sous le nom du Carrefour des associations de familles monoparentales du Québec (CAFMQ).

LIEU DE CONSULTATION : Fédération des associations de familles monoparentales du Québec. [*Adresse* : 890, boul. René-Lévesque est, bureau 2320, Montréal (Québec) H2L 2L4. *Téléphone* : (514) 288-5224. *Télécopieur* : (514) 288-7823.]

MATÉRIEL : Statuts et règlements, procès-verbaux, correspondance, documents financiers, demandes de subvention, listes de membres, listes d'envoi, pétitions, rapports, mémoires, actes de congrès, dépliants, bulletins, 1976-1991; journaux de bord, affiches, macarons, photographies, 1986-1991; communiqués de presse, 1977-1991; livres, 1980, 1983; vidéocassettes, 1975.

ÉTAT : Bon.

ACCÈS : Permission requise.

1203. Fédération des femmes du Québec

[Voir aussi la notice 603 (dans la partie I) pour autres documents de ce groupe.]

✣ Montréal (Québec). Groupe fondé 1966.

La Fédération des femmes du Québec (FFQ) s'est donné pour mission de travailler solidairement, dans une perspective féministe, à l'accès des femmes à l'égalité dans tous les secteurs d'activité : social, politique, économique, juridique, familial et culturel. La Fédération comprend une centaine d'associations membres à travers le Québec.

LIEU DE CONSULTATION : Fédération des femmes du Québec. [*Adresse* : 5225, rue Berri, bureau 100, Montréal (Québec) H2J 2S4. *Téléphone* : (514) 948-3262. *Télécopieur* : (514) 948-2046.]

MATÉRIEL : Statuts et règlements, procès-verbaux, correspondance, documents financiers, demandes de subvention, rapports, communiqués de presse, coupures de presse, photographies, 1966-1991; listes de membres, listes d'envoi, T-shirts, 1991; mémoires, 1971-1990; dépliants, 1990; périodiques (*Bulletin de la FFQ*, 1968-1981; *La Petite Presse*, 1981-1987; *Le Féminisme en revue*, 1987-1991); vidéocassettes, 1988; bannières.

ÉTAT : Assez bon.

ACCÈS : Permission requise.

1204. Félibre

✣ Québec (Québec). Groupe fondé 1984.

Félibre est un collectif d'intervention lesbien dont le but est de témoigner de l'existence d'une communauté lesbienne à Québec. Ce groupement vise à permettre aux lesbiennes de se rassembler et, par ses activités sociales, d'échanger leurs expériences sur différents aspects de leur vie. Finalement, il tâche de permettre à celles qui acceptent mal leur orientation d'avoir une image positive et nuancée des lesbiennes.

LIEU DE CONSULTATION : Félibre. [*Adresse postale* : C.P. 1125, Québec (Québec) G1R 4V2. *Téléphone* : (418) 694-0372.]

MATÉRIEL : Listes d'envoi, 1990-1991; dépliants, 1989-1991; macarons, 1985.

QUANTITÉ : Un quart d'un tiroir de classeur.

ÉTAT : Bon.

ACCÈS : Permission requise. Listes d'envoi confidentielles.

TEXTE DE L'ANNONCE DE LA F.F.Q.

Un électeur sur deux est une femme. Le 15 novembre, ne l'oubliez pas.

Les femmes veulent :

- réseau universel de garderies
- à travail de valeur égale, salaire égal
- des comités d'avortements thérapeutiques multi-disciplinaires
- des congés de maternité avec plein salaire, maintien des avantages sociaux et garantie de l'emploi au retour.
- la participation des femmes au foyer au Régime des rentes du Québec
- un traitement équitable des femmes dans les manuels scolaires, les programmes d'orientation scolaire et professionnelle ainsi que dans les mass-media.
- des femmes à l'Assemblée nationale.

Ce sera le rôle du prochain gouvernement de répondre efficacement à ces demandes.

Femmes du Québec, c'est maintenant qu'il faut agir.

Fédération des Femmes du Québec

Extrait d'un document de 1976 intitulé : / Excerpt from a 1976 document entitled:
« L'Implication des femmes dans la présente campagne électorale »
Fédération des femmes du Québec
Fonds de l'ACMF/ CWMA Collection

1205. Femmes chefs de foyer (Shawinigan, Québec)

✣ Shawinigan (Québec). Groupe fondé 1973.

Le but de l'organisme Femmes chefs de foyer (FCF) est d'aider les femmes séparées, divorcées et veuves par des activités éducatrices et sociales.

LIEU DE CONSULTATION : Femmes chefs de foyer. [*Adresse* : 882, rue Hemlock, Shawinigan (Québec) G9N 1H8. *Téléphone* : (819) 537-1273 ou (819) 536-3350.]

MATÉRIEL : Statuts et règlements, procès-verbaux, correspondance, journaux de bord, documents financiers, demandes de subvention, dossiers concernant la clientèle, liste de membres, listes d'envoi, pétitions, albums de coupures, rapports, mémoires, actes de congrès, dépliants, tracts, communiqués de presse, affiches, macarons, 1973-1991; livres, 1973-1983; photographies.

QUANTITÉ : 1 classeur.

ÉTAT : Bon.

ACCÈS : Permission requise.

1206. Ficelles pour l'accès des femmes au travail

✣ Rimouski (Québec). Groupe fondé 1985.

Ficelles pour l'accès des femmes au travail est un service de formation (de groupe et individuelle) et de placement en emploi pour les femmes.

LIEU DE CONSULTATION : Ficelles pour l'accès des femmes au travail. [*Adresse* : 49, rue Saint-Jean Baptiste, Rimouski (Québec) G5L 4J2. *Téléphone* : (418) 723-2205.]

MATÉRIEL : Statuts et règlements, procès-verbaux, documents financiers, demandes de subvention, dossiers concernant la clientèle, rapports, dépliants, communiqués de presse, coupures de presse, 1985-1991; liste de membres, 1986-1991.

QUANTITÉ : 2 tiroirs de classeur.

ÉTAT : Bon.

ACCÈS : Permission requise.

1207. Fondation du refuge pour femmes Chez Doris / Chez Doris, the Women's Shelter Foundation

[For English entry, see # 1175.]

✣ Montréal (Québec). Groupe fondé 1977.

Chez Doris est un centre de jour qui offre des services matériels (nourriture, vêtements) aux femmes en difficulté aussi bien que des services d'information et des activités éducatives.

LIEU DE CONSULTATION : Fondation du refuge pour femmes Chez Doris. [*Adresse* : 2196, boul. de Maisonneuve ouest, Montréal (Québec) H3H 1L1. *Téléphone* : (514) 937-2341.]

MATÉRIEL : Statuts et règlements, 1977; procès-verbaux, 1982-1991; journaux de bord, rapports, 1986-1991; documents financiers, 1984-1991; demandes de subvention, listes d'envoi, 1985-1991; bulletins, 1987-1990; correspondance, albums de coupures, dépliants, bannières, coupures de presse, photographies, enregistrements sonores.

QUANTITÉ : Env. 2 classeurs.

ACCÈS : Permission requise.

1208. FormOsud

✣ Longueuil (Québec). Groupe fondé 1979.

L'objectif principal de FormOsud est l'intégration et la ré-intégration d'assistées sociales et de femmes non rémunérées au marché du travail.

LIEU DE CONSULTATION : FormOsud. [*Adresse* : 237, rue de Gentilly ouest, Longueuil (Québec) J4H 1Z5. *Téléphone* : (514) 670-4198.]

MATÉRIEL : Statuts et règlements, procès-verbaux, documents financiers, demandes de subvention, listes de membres, 1979-1991; correspondance, dossiers concernant la clientèle, 1987-1991; dépliants, communiqués de presse, coupures de presse.

QUANTITÉ : Env. 3 classeurs, 1 placard.

ÉTAT : Bon.

ACCÈS : Permission requise.

1209. A Friend Indeed Publications / Publications Une Véritable Amie

[Renseignements en français, notice 1242.]

✣ Montreal, Quebec. Formed 1984.

A Friend Indeed is a bilingual periodical which provides information and support for women at menopause or mid-life.

LOCATION OF RECORDS: A Friend Indeed Publications. [*Mailing Address*: Box 515, Station Place du Parc, Montreal, Quebec H2W 2P1. *Telephone*: (514) 843-5730. *Fax*: (514) 843-5681.]

RECORDS: Correspondence, financial records, client records, mailing lists, scrapbooks, flyers, press releases, periodicals, 1984-1991; books, clippings, sound recordings, videotapes, films.

AMOUNT: 2 filing cabinets, 1 cupboard.

CONDITION: Good.

ACCESS: Permission required.

1210. Groupe intervention vidéo

[For English entry, see # 1211.]

✣ Montréal (Québec). Groupe fondé 1976.

Le Groupe intervention vidéo (GIV) produit et distribue des vidéos réalisés par des femmes et des vidéos non sexistes.

LIEU DE CONSULTATION : Groupe intervention vidéo. [*Adresse* : 3575, boul. St-Laurent, #421, Montréal (Québec) H2X 2T7. *Téléphone* : (514) 499-9840. *Télécopieur* : (514) 844-5498.]

MATÉRIEL : Procès-verbaux, correspondance, journaux de bord, documents financiers, demandes de subvention, dossiers concernant la clientèle, listes d'envoi, dépliants, tracts, communiqués de presse, 1976-1991.

QUANTITÉ : 2 classeurs.

ÉTAT : Bon.

ACCÈS : Permission requise.

1211. Groupe intervention vidéo

[Renseignements en français, notice 1210.]

✣ Montreal, Quebec. Formed 1976.

Le Groupe intervention vidéo (GIV) produces and distributes videos by women and non-sexist videos.

LOCATION OF RECORDS: Groupe intervention vidéo. [*Address*: 3575 St-Laurent Blvd., #421, Montreal, Quebec H2X 2T7. *Telephone*: (514) 499-9840. *Fax*: (514) 844-5498.]

RECORDS: Minutes, correspondence, log-books, financial records, grant applications, client records, mailing lists, pamphlets, flyers, press releases, 1976-1991.

AMOUNT: 2 filing cabinets.

CONDITION: Good.

ACCESS: Permission required.

1212. Havre des femmes

✤ L'Islet-sur-Mer (Québec). Groupe fondé 1981.

Le Havre des femmes est une maison d'accueil et d'hébergement pour toute femme (et ses enfants) qui est victime de violence physique ou psychologique de la part de son conjoint.

LIEU DE CONSULTATION : Havre des femmes. [*Adresse postale :* C.P. 52, L'Islet-sur-Mer (Québec) G0R 2B0. *Téléphone :* (418) 247-7622.]

MATÉRIEL : Procès-verbaux, correspondance, journaux de bord, documents financiers, demandes de subvention, 1981-1991; bulletins (*Journal ficelle*, 1989-1991); vidéocassettes, documents de colloque, 1991; statuts et règlements, dossiers concernant la clientèle, listes de membres, rapports, mémoires, actes de congrès, dépliants, tracts, communiqués de presse, bannières.

QUANTITÉ : 3 classeurs.

ÉTAT : Bon.

ACCÈS : Permission requise. Fiches concernant la clientèle confidentielles.

1213. Impulsion-Travail

✤ Montréal-Nord (Québec). Groupe fondé 1984.

L'objectif principal de cet organisme est de développer les possibilités d'emploi des femmes, en particulier, des femmes haïtiennes. Depuis ses débuts en 1984 jusqu'à sa constitution en 1986 sous la désignation Impulsion-Travail, le groupe était connu sous le nom de Projet : Relance sociale, phase II du Centre des femmes de Rivières-des-Prairies.

LIEU DE CONSULTATION : Impulsion-Travail. [*Adresse :* 5403 Charleroi, 3e étage, Montréal-Nord (Québec) H1G 3A6. *Téléphone :* (514) 327-1363.]

MATÉRIEL : Statuts et règlements, 1986; procès-verbaux, correspondance, documents financiers, demandes de subvention, dossiers concernant la clientèle, listes de membres, listes d'envoi, pétitions, rapports, dépliants, communiqués de presse, affiches, 1986-1991.

QUANTITÉ : 2 classeurs.

ÉTAT : Bon.

ACCÈS : Permission requise. Dossiers sur la clientèle confidentiels.

1214. Inform'elle

✤ Saint-Hubert (Québec). Groupe fondé 1978.

Inform'elle a pour objectifs de répondre aux besoins d'information juridique et sociale des femmes démunies et de promouvoir l'autonomie des femmes en leur procurant les outils nécessaires à une prise en charge personnelle. Inform'elle offre un service gratuit d'information juridique.

LIEU DE CONSULTATION : Inform'elle. [*Adresse :* 3757, rue Mackay, Saint-Hubert (Québec) J4T 2P6. *Téléphone :* (514) 443-3442.]

MATÉRIEL : Statuts et règlements, 1982-1991; procès-verbaux, 1981; correspondance, 1978; documents financiers, demandes de subvention, 1982; listes de membres, listes d'envoi, albums de coupures, rapports, dépliants, communiqués de presse, affiches, coupures de presse, photographies, enregistrements sonores, vidéocassettes, documents divers.

QUANTITÉ : 4 classeurs.

ÉTAT : Bon.

ACCÈS : Permission requise.

1215. Institut Simone de Beauvoir / Simone de Beauvoir Institute

[For English entry, see # 1252.]

✤ Montréal (Québec). Groupe fondé 1978.

L'Institut Simone de Beauvoir de l'Université Concordia vise à stimuler la compréhension du rôle historique et contemporain des femmes dans la société. Il offre un diplôme de baccalauréat en études des femmes.

LIEU DE CONSULTATION : Institut Simone de Beauvoir. [*Adresse :* Université Concordia, 1455 de Maisonneuve ouest, Montréal (Québec) H3G 1M8. *Téléphone :* (514) 848-2370. *Télécopieur :* (514) 848-3494.]

MATÉRIEL : Statuts et règlements, 1978, 1985; procès-verbaux, correspondance, bulletins, vidéocassettes, 1978-1991; documents financiers, documents des étudiantes et étudiants, listes de membres, listes d'envoi, tracts, 1991; actes de congrès, 1987; communiqués de presse, 1989-1991; demandes de subvention, rapports, affiches, coupures de presse, photographies.

QUANTITÉ : 2 classeurs, 7 boîtes.

ÉTAT : Bon.

ACCÈS : Permission requise.

1216. Laval au féminin

✤ Laval (Québec). Groupe fondé 1979.

Parmi ses objectifs, l'association offre à la femme des moyens d'accéder à l'autonomie selon son rythme et développe la solidarité entre les femmes par les contacts et les échanges. Elle offre également des activités éducatrices, culturelles et sociales.

LIEU DE CONSULTATION : Laval au féminin. [*Adresse :* 25, rue Saint-Louis, Pont-Viau, Laval (Québec) H7G 4W3. *Téléphone :* (514) 967-8204.]

MATÉRIEL : Statuts et règlements, correspondance, documents financiers, dossiers concernant la clientèle, listes de membres, listes d'envoi, communiqués de presse, coupures de presse, photographies, 1979-1991; procès-verbaux, albums de coupures, livres, 1977-1991; demandes de subvention, rapports, dépliants, macarons, 1985-1991; affiches, 1988-1991; bulletins (*Bulletin d'information*, 1980; *Laval au féminin*, 1981-1983; *Entre-Elles*, 1983-1991).

QUANTITÉ : 1 classeur.

ÉTAT : Bon.

ACCÈS : Permission requise.

1217. Lennoxville and District Women's Centre / Centre des femmes de Lennoxville et des environs

[Renseignements en français, notice 1157.]

✤ Lennoxville, Quebec. Formed 1981.

The Lennoxville and District Women's Centre is a meeting place and resource centre dedicated to helping women reach their full potential.

LOCATION OF RECORDS: Lennoxville and District Women's Centre. [*Mailing Address:* P.O. Box 102, Lennoxville, Quebec J1M 1Z3. (*Street Address:* 151-A Queen St.) *Telephone:* (819) 564-6626.]

RECORDS: Constitution, minutes, correspondence, log-books, financial records, membership lists, mailing lists, reports, pamphlets, flyers, press releases, posters, clippings, photographs, 1981-1991; grant applications, briefs, newsletters, 1982-1991; petitions, 1986-1991; conference proceedings, 1984-1991.

AMOUNT: Approx. 3 filing cabinets.

ACCESS: Permission of board of directors required.

1218. Lesbian Studies Coalition of Concordia

[See also entry # 615 (in Part I), which lists other records of this organization.]

✤ Montreal, Quebec. Formed 1987.

This organization at Concordia University (also known as LSCC or "Lez Studs") opposes heterosexism in education and advocates the establishment of a degree-granting programme in lesbian studies. It is also committed to fighting racism, sexism, classism, and other forms of oppression. The coalition's French name is les Études lesbiennes de Concordia.

LOCATION OF RECORDS: Lesbian Studies Coalition of Concordia. [*Address:* Concordia University, c/o CUSA, 1455 de Maisonneuve Blvd. W., Montreal, Quebec H3G 1M8. *Telephone:* (514) 848-7431/7474.]

RECORDS: Constitution, minutes, correspondence, financial records, reports, posters, photographs, 1987-1991; pamphlets, flyers, 1991; buttons, banners, 1989-1991; videotapes, 1990-1991; publications, 1988-1991.

AMOUNT: 2 drawers of a filing cabinet.

CONDITION: Good.

ACCESS: Permission required.

1219. Lesbo Info

[For English entry, see # 1220.]

✣ Dorval (Québec). Groupe fondé 1986.

Lesbo Info (parfois appelé *Info Lesbo*) est un bulletin d'information bilingue pour les lesbiennes de Montréal. Son objectif est de promouvoir la recherche, l'information, les services et un appui pour les lesbiennes. La publication s'appelait à ses débuts le *Bulletin du Projet lavande*.

LIEU DE CONSULTATION: Lesbo Info. [*Adresse postale* : C.P. 2381, Succursale Dorval, Dorval (Québec) H9S 5N4. (*Indication de rue* : 303, av. Dorval.)]

MATÉRIEL : Statuts et règlements, 1990; procès-verbaux, 1988-1991; correspondance, documents financiers, listes d'envoi, enregistrements sonores, 1990-1991; listes de membres, 1989-1991; dépliants, 1988; bulletins (*Lesbo Info*, 1990-1991; *Bulletin du Projet lavande/Project Lavender Bulletin*, 1986-1990).

QUANTITÉ : 1 tiroir de classeur.

ÉTAT : Bon.

1220. Lesbo Info

[Renseignements en français, notice 1219.]

✣ Dorval, Quebec. Formed 1986.

Lesbo Info (sometimes called *Info Lesbo*) is a bilingual newsletter for the lesbian community in Montreal. Its objective is to promote research, information, services, and support for lesbians. It used to be called the *Project Lavender Bulletin*.

LOCATION OF RECORDS: Lesbo Info. [*Mailing Address:* P.O. Box 2381, Dorval Station, Dorval, Quebec H9S 5N4. (*Street Address:* 303 Dorval Ave.)]

RECORDS: Constitution, 1990; minutes, 1988-1991; correspondence, financial records, mailing lists, sound recordings, 1990-1991; membership lists, 1989-1991; pamphlets, 1988; newsletters (*Lesbo Info*, 1990-1991; *Project Lavender Bulletin/Bulletin du Projet lavande*, 1986-1990); layouts.

AMOUNT: 1 drawer of a filing cabinet.

CONDITION: Good.

1221. Liaison information entraide novatrice

✣ Trois-Rivières-Ouest (Québec). Groupe fondé 1979.

Ce groupe communautaire féministe, connu plus souvent sous l'acronyme LIEN, offre des activités telles que soupers-conférences, cafés-rencontres ou autres dans un but social mais surtout culturel.

LIEU DE CONSULTATION : Liaison information entraide novatrice. [*Adresse* : 735 des Dominicains, Trois-Rivières-Ouest (Québec) G9A 3A5. *Téléphone* : (819) 379-3653.]

MATÉRIEL : Statuts et règlements, procès-verbaux, correspondance, journaux de bord, documents financiers, demandes de subvention, dossiers concernant la clientèle, listes de membres, listes d'envoi, pétitions, albums de coupures, rapports, mémoires, actes de congrès, dépliants, communiqués de presse, livres, coupures de presse, photographies, enregistrements sonores, 1979-1991.

ÉTAT : Bon.

ACCÈS : Permission requise. Certains documents confidentiels.

1222. Maison De Connivence

✣ Trois-Rivières (Québec). Groupe fondé 1985.

La Maison De Connivence est une maison d'aide et d'hébergement pour femmes victimes de violence conjugale ou familiale et pour leurs enfants.

LIEU DE CONSULTATION : Maison De Connivence. [*Adresse postale* : C.P. 424, Trois-Rivières (Québec) G9A 5G4. *Téléphone* : (819) 379-1011.]

MATÉRIEL : Statuts et règlements, procès-verbaux, journaux de bord, documents financiers, demandes de subvention, dossiers concernant la clientèle, albums de coupures, rapports, coupures de presse, 1986-1991; dépliants.

QUANTITÉ : 1 classeur.

ÉTAT : Bon.

ACCÈS : Permission requise. Dossiers concernant la clientèle confidentiels.

1223. Maison des femmes de la région de Rimouski

✣ Rimouski (Québec). Groupe fondé 1979.

La Maison est un centre d'aide pour les femmes éprouvant des difficultés de toutes sortes reliées à des situations de pauvreté, de santé mentale, de monoparentalité, d'isolement, de violence conjugale ou sexuelle. Les services du centre comprennent l'accueil, l'écoute, la relation d'aide, la référence, l'accompagnement, l'information juridique et le dépannage. Jusqu'en 1986, l'organisme s'appelait la Maison des femmes du Bas-St-Laurent.

LIEU DE CONSULTATION : Maison des femmes de la région de Rimouski. [*Adresse* : 78, Ste-Marie, 2e étage, Rimouski (Québec). *Téléphone* : (418) 723-0333.]

MATÉRIEL : Statuts et règlements, 1980-1985; procès-verbaux, 1980-1991; correspondance, documents financiers, demandes de subvention, listes de membres, albums de coupures, rapports, macarons, coupures de presse, photographies, 1989-1991; pétitions, mémoires, actes de congrès, dépliants, communiqués de presse, affiches, enregistrements sonores, 1990-1991.

QUANTITÉ : 3 classeurs.

ÉTAT : Bon.

ACCÈS : Permission requise.

1224. Maison d'hébergement de Pabos

✣ Pabos (Québec). Groupe fondé 1984.

La Maison d'hébergement de Pabos vient en aide aux femmes et enfants victimes de violence conjugale et sensibilise la population en dénonçant la violence sous toutes ses formes. L'organisme offre des services en français et en anglais.

LIEU DE CONSULTATION : Maison d'hébergement de Pabos. [*Adresse postale* : C.P. 347, Pabos (Québec) G0C 2H0. *Téléphone* : (418) 689-6288.]

MATÉRIEL : Albums de coupures, mémoires, coupures de presse, documents divers.

QUANTITÉ : 1 classeur.

ÉTAT : Bon.

ACCÈS : Permission requise.

1225. Maison du réconfort

✣ Verdun (Québec). Groupe fondé 1980.

Cette maison d'hébergement accueille toute femme victime de violence avec ou sans enfants et l'oriente vers les ressources. L'organisme favorise un processus évolutif d'autonomie et cherche à promouvoir et à protéger les droits économiques et sociaux des femmes victimes de violence.

LIEU DE CONSULTATION : Maison du réconfort. [*Adresse postale* : C.P. 295, Succursale Verdun, Verdun (Québec) H4G 3E9. *Téléphone* : (514) 765-9668.]

MATÉRIEL : Statuts et règlements, 1980; procès-verbaux, documents financiers, 1980-1991; correspondance, journaux de bord, demandes de subvention, dossiers concernant la clientèle, 1985-1991; dépliants, photographies, 1985; listes de membres, 1989; T-shirts, 1990; bannières, 1988.

QUANTITÉ : 4 classeurs.

ÉTAT : Bon.

ACCÈS : Permission requise. Dossiers concernant la clientèle confidentiels.

1226. Maison La Source

✣ Sorel (Québec). Groupe fondé 1982.

La Maison La Source est une maison d'hébergement qui vient en aide aux femmes violentées et en difficulté avec ou sans enfants. Jusqu'en 1991, elle s'appelait la Maison Notre-Dame La Source.

LIEU DE CONSULTATION : Maison La Source. [*Adresse postale* : C.P. 585, Sorel (Québec) J3P 5N9. *Téléphone* : (514) 743-2821.]

MATÉRIEL : Statuts et règlements, procès-verbaux, correspondance, documents financiers, demandes de subvention, dossiers concernant la clientèle, albums de coupures, rapports, 1982-1991; listes de membres, 1989-1991; dépliants, communiqués de presse, 1988-1991; vidéocassettes, 1988.

QUANTITÉ : 2 tiroirs de classeur, 1 armoire.

ÉTAT : Bon.

ACCÈS : Permission requise. Dossiers concernant la clientèle confidentiels.

1227. Maison le coin des femmes (Sept-Îles, Québec)

[For English entry, see # 1228.]

✣ Sept-Îles (Québec). Groupe fondé 1983.

Cet organisme offre de l'hébergement, de l'écoute et de l'aide aux femmes victimes de violence et à leurs enfants et vise à sensibiliser le public à la violence conjugale. Il offre des services pour femmes autochtones.

LIEU DE CONSULTATION : Maison le coin des femmes. [*Adresse postale* : C.P. 278, Sept-Îles (Québec) G4R 2S9. *Téléphone* : (418) 968-6446.]

MATÉRIEL : Procès-verbaux, demandes de subvention, 1983-1991; correspondance, documents financiers, dossiers concernant la clientèle, rapports, dépliants, 1985-1991; affiches, 1988-1991; statuts et règlements.

QUANTITÉ : 5 classeurs.

ÉTAT : Bon.

ACCÈS : Permission requise. Dossiers concernant la clientèle confidentiels.

1228. Maison le coin des femmes (Sept-Îles, Quebec)

[Renseignements en français, notice 1227.]

✣ Sept-Îles, Quebec. Formed 1983.

This organization provides shelter, counselling, and assistance to women and their children who have been victims of violence. It also does public education. Services for Native women are available.

LOCATION OF RECORDS: Maison le coin des femmes. [*Mailing Address:* P.O. Box 278, Sept-Îles, Quebec G4R 2S9. *Telephone:* (418) 968-6446.]

RECORDS: Minutes, grant applications, 1983-1991; correspondence, financial records, client records, reports, pamphlets, 1985-1991; posters, 1988-1991; constitution.

AMOUNT: 5 filing cabinets.

CONDITION: Good.

ACCESS: Permission required. Client files closed.

1229. Maison Mikana

✣ Amos (Québec). Groupe fondé 1984.

Ce centre est une maison d'hébergement pour les femmes victimes de violence et pour leurs enfants. Son objectif principal est d'aider les femmes à devenir autonomes et à prendre leur destin en main.

LIEU DE CONSULTATION : Maison Mikana. [*Téléphone* : (819) 732-9161.]

MATÉRIEL : Statuts et règlements, procès-verbaux, correspondance, documents financiers, demandes de subvention, dossiers concernant la clientèle, albums de coupures, rapports, dépliants, macarons, coupures de presse, photographies, 1984-1991; vidéocassettes, 1991; journaux de bord, listes de membres.

ÉTAT : Bon.

ACCÈS : Permission requise.

1230. Maison Unies-Vers-Femmes

✣ Gatineau (Québec). Groupe fondé 1979.

La Maison Unies-Vers-Femmes offre aide et hébergement pour femmes victimes de violence conjugale et pour leurs enfants.

LIEU DE CONSULTATION : Maison Unies-Vers-Femmes. [*Téléphone* : (819) 568-4710.]

MATÉRIEL : Statuts et règlements, procès-verbaux, correspondance, journaux de bord, documents financiers, demandes de subvention, dossiers concernant la clientèle, listes de membres, albums de coupures, rapports, communiqués de presse, coupures de presse, photographies, contrats, 1979-1991; macarons, 1990; bannières, charte, 1989; bulletins, 1990-1991; documents divers, 1991.

QUANTITÉ : 4 classeurs.

ÉTAT : Bon.

ACCÈS : Permission requise. Certains dossiers sont confidentiels.

1231. La Marie Debout, Centre d'éducation des femmes

✣ Montréal (Québec). Groupe fondé 1982.

La Marie Debout offre des services d'accueil, de référence et des cours. Les objectifs du centre sont l'autonomie de la femme et la défense des droits des femmes.

LIEU DE CONSULTATION : Marie Debout, Centre d'éducation des femmes. [*Adresse* : 562, rue Leclaire, Montréal (Québec) H1V 2Z1. *Téléphone* : (514) 255-1304.]

MATÉRIEL : Statuts et règlements, procès-verbaux, correspondance, documents financiers, demandes de subvention, listes de membres, rapports, dépliants, affiches, macarons, coupures de presse, photographies, 1982-1991; albums de coupures, communiqués de presse, 1983-1991; mémoires, 1988; actes de congrès, 1988-1991; tracts, 1985-1989; bannières, 1990-1991; bulletins (*Allô Marie*, 1989; *Bulletin de liaison*, 1991).

QUANTITÉ : 2 classeurs.

ÉTAT : Assez bon.

ACCÈS : Permission requise.

1232. MATCH international (Saguenay-Lac-St-Jean, Québec)

✣ Alma (Québec). Groupe fondé 1978.

MATCH international au Saguenay-Lac-St-Jean veut aider les femmes des pays en voie de développement en reliant leurs besoins avec les ressources des femmes canadiennes par la coopération internationale. Cet organisme marraine des projets soumis et mis en oeuvre par les femmes des pays en voie de développement, et il sensibilise la population aux problèmes des femmes et à leur condition de vie dans ces pays.

LIEU DE CONSULTATION : MATCH international. [*Adresse* : 250, rue Harvey, Alma (Québec) G8B 1N7. *Téléphone* : (418) 662-5577.]

MATÉRIEL : Statuts et règlements, albums de coupures, coupures de presse, 1978-1991; enregistrements sonores, 1986; procès-verbaux, journaux de bord, dépliants, photographies.

QUANTITÉ : 2 boîtes.

ÉTAT : Bon.

1233. Mouvement contre le viol et l'inceste

[For English entry, see # 1234.]

✣ Montréal (Québec). Groupe fondé 1973.

Parmi ses autres services, le Mouvement contre le viol et l'inceste (MCVI) offre l'intervention de crise et la thérapie à long terme aux femmes victimes de viol, d'inceste ou d'abus sexuel sur leur personne ou sur la personne de leurs enfants. À ses débuts, cet organisme s'appelait Rape Crisis Centre. En 1980, il a changé de nom pour devenir le Mouvement contre le viol/Women against Rape. En 1991, il est devenu le Mouvement contre le viol et l'inceste.

LIEU DE CONSULTATION : Mouvement contre le viol et l'inceste. [*Adresse postale* : C.P. 364, Succursale N.-D.-G., Montréal (Québec) H4A 3P7. *Téléphone* : (514) 842-5040.]

MATÉRIEL : Statuts et règlements, 1973-1991; procès-verbaux, correspondance, journaux de bord, documents financiers, demandes de subvention, dossiers concernant la clientèle, rapports, communiqués de presse, 1980-1991; listes d'envoi, pétitions, 1991; dépliants, 1983-1991; albums de coupures, affiches, macarons, coupures de presse, photographies.

ÉTAT : Bon.

ACCÈS : Permission requise.

1234. Mouvement contre le viol et l'inceste

[Renseignements en français, notice 1233.]

✣ Montreal, Quebec. Formed 1973.

Le Mouvement contre le viol et l'inceste (MCVI) provides crisis intervention and long-term therapy to women who have survived rape, incest, sexual abuse, or abuse of their children. The organization was originally called the Rape Crisis Centre. In 1980 the name was changed to Women against Rape/Mouvement contre le viol; the present name was adopted in 1991.

LOCATION OF RECORDS: Mouvement contre le viol et l'inceste. [*Mailing Address*: P.O. Box 364, Station N.D.G., Montreal, Quebec H4A 3P7. *Telephone*: (514) 842-5040.]

RECORDS: Constitution, 1973-1991; minutes, correspondence, log-books, financial records, grant applications, client records, reports, press releases, 1980-1991; mailing lists, petitions, 1991; pamphlets, 1983-1991; scrapbooks, posters, buttons, clippings, photographs.

CONDITION: Good.

ACCESS: Permission required.

1235. Naissance-Renaissance

✣ Montréal (Québec). Groupe fondé 1980.

Le but primaire de Naissance-Renaissance (N-R) est l'humanisation de la naissance et de la périnatalité. N-R veut permettre aux femmes le choix quant au lieu de naissance et quant aux personnes qui les accompagnent (sages-femmes ou médecins).

LIEU DE CONSULTATION : Naissance-Renaissance. [*Adresse* : 530 Cherrier, Montréal (Québec) H2L 1H3. *Téléphone* : (514) 843-9552.]

MATÉRIEL : Statuts et règlements, procès-verbaux, correspondance, journaux de bord, documents financiers, demandes de subvention, listes de membres, listes d'envoi, pétitions, albums de coupures, rapports, mémoires, actes de congrès, dépliants, tracts, communiqués de presse, affiches, macarons, T-shirts, bannières, revues, coupures de presse, photographies, enregistrements sonores, vidéocassettes, films, 1982-1991; périodiques (*L'Une à l'autre*, 1984-1991).

QUANTITÉ : Env. 2 classeurs.

ACCÈS : Permission requise.

1236. Nouveau départ national

✣ Montréal (Québec). Groupe fondé 1977.

Les objectifs principaux de cet organisme sont l'orientation des femmes de trente ans et plus de toute condition socio-économique et la formation des intervenantes. Nouveau départ est devenu Nouveau départ national en 1989.

LIEU DE CONSULTATION : Nouveau départ national. [*Adresse* : 1355, boul. René-Levesque ouest, Montréal (Québec) H3G 1T3. *Téléphone* : (514) 866-0416. *Télécopieur* : (514) 866-4866.]

MATÉRIEL : Statuts et règlements, procès-verbaux, correspondance, documents financiers, demandes de subvention, rapports, 1977-1991; mémoires, 1979-1991; dépliants, communiqués de presse, affiches, livres, coupures de presse, photographies, enregistrements sonores, vidéocassettes, recherches.

QUANTITÉ : 3 classeurs, 1 armoire.

ÉTAT : Bon.

ACCÈS : Listes de participantes confidentielles.

1237. La Passe-r-elle des Hautes-Laurentides

✣ Mont-Laurier (Québec). Groupe fondé 1983.

La Passe-r-elle des Hautes Laurentides offre de l'hébergement et d'autres services aux femmes victimes de violence conjugale et à leurs enfants.

LIEU DE CONSULTATION : Passe-r-elle des Hautes-Laurentides. [*Adresse postale* : C.P. 354, Mont-Laurier (Québec) J9L 3N7. *Téléphone* : (819) 623-1523.]

MATÉRIEL : Statuts et règlements, procès-verbaux, dépliants, communiqués de presse, affiches, 1984-1991; correspondance, 1989-1991; journaux de bord, documents financiers, documents de subvention, 1983-1991; listes d'envoi, 1991; rapports, 1986-1991; vidéocassettes, 1987-1989; dossiers concernant la clientèle, albums de coupures.

QUANTITÉ : 2 classeurs.

ÉTAT : Bon.

ACCÈS : Permission requise. Journaux de bord et dossiers de la clientèle confidentiels.

1238. La Passerelle de Weedon

✣ Weedon (Québec). Groupe fondé 1983.

La Passerelle de Weedon est un centre de femmes qui vise à améliorer la condition de vie des femmes en offrant des services directs, des cours et une action collective.

LIEU DE CONSULTATION : Passerelle de Weedon. [*Adresse* : Local 305, 209, rue des Érables, Weedon (Québec) J0B 3J0. *Téléphone* : (819) 877-3423.]

MATÉRIEL : Statuts et règlements, procès-verbaux, correspondance, documents financiers, demandes de subvention, dossiers concernant la clientèle, listes de membres, listes d'envoi, pétitions, albums de coupures, rapports, mémoires, actes de congrès, dépliants, tracts, communiqués de presse, affiches, macarons, photographies, 1983-1991 ; enregistrements sonores, 1990.

QUANTITÉ : 1 classeur.

ÉTAT : Bon.

ACCÈS : Permission requise. Dossiers concernant la clientèle confidentiels.

1239. Point d'appui, Centre d'aide et de prévention des agressions à caractère sexuel de Rouyn

✣ Rouyn-Noranda (Québec). Groupe fondé 1983.

Le centre vient en aide aux personnes agressées sexuellement en offrant une aide directe et des services d'accompagnement médical, juridique et psychologique. Le centre s'adonne en plus à des activités éducatives.

LIEU DE CONSULTATION : Point d'appui, Centre d'aide et de prévention des agressions à caractère sexuel de Rouyn. [*Adresse postale* : C.P. 1274, Rouyn-Noranda (Québec) J9X 6E4. *Téléphone* : (819) 797-0101.]

MATÉRIEL : Statuts et règlements, 1983 ; procès-verbaux, correspondance, documents financiers, demandes de subvention, listes de membres, rapports, 1983-1991 ; albums de coupures, 1983-1985 ; actes de congrès, 1986 ; bulletins (*Bulletin des militantes*, 1989-1991) ; mémoires, dépliants, communiqués de presse, affiches.

QUANTITÉ : 3 classeurs.

ÉTAT : Assez bon.

ACCÈS : Permission requise.

1240. Professional Secretaries International. Ville-Marie Chapter / Association internationale des secrétaires professionnelles. Section Ville-Marie

[Renseignements en français, notice 1132.]

✣ Montreal, Quebec. Formed 1969.

Professional Secretaries International (PSI) works for the improvement of secretaries' skills and the promotion of their professional status.

LOCATION OF RECORDS: Professional Secretaries International. Ville-Marie Chapter. [*Mailing Address*: P.O. Box 847, Station Desjardins, Montreal, Quebec H5B 1B9. *Telephone*: (514) 733-5243.]

RECORDS: Constitution, 1969-1991 ; minutes, correspondence, financial records, membership lists, reports, briefs, conference proceedings, pamphlets, press releases, newsletters (*Le Trait d'union*, *The Secretary*, *Vision*), books, clippings, photographs, sound recordings.

AMOUNT: 1 filing cabinet.

CONDITION: Good.

1241. Projet intégration des femmes

✣ Hull (Québec). Groupe fondé 1980.

Projet intégration des femmes (PIF) aide les femmes économiquement défavorisées à réintégrer le marché du travail dans le cadre d'une orientation professionnelle. Il offre des programmes d'orientation, de développement personnel et professionel et des ateliers de travail en commun.

LIEU DE CONSULTATION : Projet intégration des femmes. [*Adresse* : 103, rue Montcalm, 1er étage, Hull (Québec) J8X 2L9. *Téléphone* : (819) 771-1725.]

MATÉRIEL : Statuts et règlements, procès-verbaux, correspondance, journaux de bord, documents financiers, demandes de subvention, dossiers concernant la clientèle, listes de membres, listes d'envoi, pétitions, albums de coupures, rapports, mémoires, actes de congrès, dépliants, communiqués de presse, affiches, 1980-1991.

QUANTITÉ : 2 classeurs.

ÉTAT : Bon.

ACCÈS : Permission requise.

1242. Publications Une Véritable Amie / A Friend Indeed Publications

[For English entry, see # 1209.]

✣ Montréal (Québec). Groupe fondé 1984.

Une Véritable Amie est un périodique bilingue qui fournit de l'information et un appui aux femmes aux prises avec la ménopause.

LIEU DE CONSULTATION : Publications Une Véritable Amie. [*Adresse postale* : B.P. 515, Succursale Place du Parc, Montréal (Québec) H2W 2P1. *Téléphone* : (514) 843-5730. *Télécopieur* : (514) 843-5681.]

MATÉRIEL : Correspondance, documents financiers, dossiers concernant la clientèle, listes d'envoi, albums de coupures, tracts, communiqués de presse, périodiques, 1984-1991 ; livres, coupures de presse, enregistrements sonores, vidéocassettes, films.

QUANTITÉ : 2 classeurs, un placard.

ÉTAT : Bon.

ACCÈS : Permission requise.

1243. Re-Nou-Vie

✣ Châteauguay (Québec). Groupe fondé 1984.

Le but de Re-Nou-Vie est de regrouper les femmes séparées, divorcées, en voie de séparation et en prise de décision, les veuves et les mères célibataires du territoire du Grand Châteauguay et des régions environnantes.

LIEU DE CONSULTATION : Re-Nou-Vie. [*Adresse* : 123 St-Jean Baptiste, Châteauguay (Québec) J6K 3B1. *Téléphone* : (514) 692-9805.]

MATÉRIEL : Statuts et règlements, procès-verbaux, documents financiers, demandes de subvention, rapports, 1984-1991 ; correspondance, 1990-1991 ; dossiers concernant la clientèle, listes de membres, 1988-1991 ; communiqués de presse, affiches, 1989-1991.

QUANTITÉ : 1 classeur, 1 bibliothèque.

ÉTAT : Bon.

ACCÈS : Permission requise. Dossiers concernant la clientèle confidentiels.

1244. Refuge pour les femmes de l'Ouest de l'Île / West Island Women's Shelter

[For English entry, see # 1264.]

✣ Roxboro (Québec). Groupe fondé 1979.

En offrant un hébergement et une ligne de crise, le Refuge pour les femmes de l'Ouest de l'Île travaille à réduire la violence conjugale dont les femmes sont victimes.

LIEU DE CONSULTATION : Refuge pour les femmes de l'Ouest de l'Île. [*Adresse postale* : C.P. 203, Roxboro (Québec) H8Y 3E9. *Téléphone* : (514) 620-4845.]

MATÉRIEL : Statuts et règlements, 1979, 1982, 1987 ; procès-verbaux, documents financiers, demandes de subvention, dossiers concernant la clientèle, listes de membres, listes d'envoi, albums de coupures, dépliants, communiqués de presse, macarons, 1979-1991; correspondance, journaux de bord, 1990-1991; mémoires, 1985; bannières, publications, 1986, 1988, 1990; vidéocassettes, 1986; rapports, coupures de presse.

QUANTITÉ : 6 classeurs.

ÉTAT : Bon.

ACCÈS : Permission requise. Dossiers concernant la clientèle confidentiels.

1245. Réseau d'action et d'information pour les femmes

✣ Québec (Québec). Groupe fondé 1973.

Le Réseau d'action et d'information pour les femmes (RAIF) lutte pour les droits des femmes et pour une société plus juste. Cet organisme entreprend des pressions politiques, présente des mémoires pour modifier ou obtenir des lois, sensibilise le public et les médias, coordonne des actions et publie la revue RAIF.

LIEU DE CONSULTATION : Réseau d'action et d'information pour les femmes. [*Adresse postale* : C.P. 5, Sillery (Québec) G1T 2P7. *Téléphone* : (418) 658-1973.]

MATÉRIEL : Statuts et règlements, procès-verbaux, correspondance, journaux de bord, documents financiers, listes de membres, listes d'envoi, pétitions, albums de coupures, rapports, mémoires, actes de congrès, dépliants, tracts, communiqués de presse, affiches, macarons, bannières, revues, livres, coupures de presse, photographies, 1973-1991; enregistrements sonores, 1981; sommaires des revues, 1973-1977.

QUANTITÉ : 30 boîtes.

ÉTAT : Bon.

1246. Réseau féministe populaire

✣ Montréal (Québec). Groupe fondé 1987.

Des femmes du Centre de pastorale en milieu ouvrier (CPMO) et du secteur Promotion communautaire du Centre St-Pierre ont créé le Réseau féministe populaire dont les objectifs sont de constituer un centre de ressources et d'échanges pour les femmes de milieu populaire et les intervenantes; de développer une analyse féministe et socialiste; et de concevoir des outils d'intervention. Jusqu'en 1989, le réseau s'appelait le Réseau populaire des femmes du Québec.

LIEU DE CONSULTATION : Réseau féministe populaire. [*Adresse* : 1212 Panet, local 315, Montréal (Québec) H2L 2Y7. *Téléphone* : (514) 524-3561, poste 301. *Télécopieur* : (514) 524-5663.]

MATÉRIEL : Procès-verbaux, correspondance, documents financiers, demandes de subvention, listes de membres, listes d'envoi, albums de coupures, rapports, 1987-1991; dépliants, 1989-1991; enregistrements sonores, 1983-1987; vidéocassettes, 1983, 1990.

QUANTITÉ : 2 tiroirs de classeur.

ÉTAT : Bon.

ACCÈS : Permission requise.

1247. Réseau vidé-elle

✣ Montréal (Québec). Groupe fondé 1975.

Les objectifs poursuivis par le Réseau sont de produire, réaliser et diffuser des vidéos sur le vécu culturel et politique des lesbiennes et des femmes.

LIEU DE CONSULTATION : Réseau vidé-elle. [*Adresse* : 4013, rue des Érables, Montréal (Québec) H2K 3V7. *Téléphone* : (514) 525-8456.]

MATÉRIEL : Correspondance, tracts, affiches, 1975-1991; vidéocassettes, 1972-1975.

ÉTAT : Bon.

ACCÈS : Permission requise.

1248. Résidence de l'avenue A

✣ Trois-Rivières (Québec). Groupe fondé 1976.

La Résidence de l'avenue A est une maison d'hébergement pour femmes en difficulté avec ou sans enfants. Elle offre des services d'écoute, d'appui, d'orientation et de référence. Elle est marrainée par les Filles de Jésus.

LIEU DE CONSULTATION : Résidence de l'avenue A. [*Téléphone* : (819) 376-8311.]

MATÉRIEL : Statuts et règlements, coupures de presse, 1976; procès-verbaux, correspondance, documents financiers, dossiers concernant la clientèle, listes de membres, albums de coupures, dépliants, communiqués de presse, statistiques, 1976-1991; photographies.

QUANTITÉ : Env. 2 tiroirs de classeur.

ÉTAT : Assez bon.

ACCÈS : Permission requise. Dossiers concernant la clientèle confidentiels.

1249. S.O.S. Grossesse

✣ Limoilou (Québec). Groupe fondé 1974.

S.O.S. Grossesse vient en aide à des personnes vivant de près ou de loin une situation concernant la grossesse. Cet organisme offre un service d'écoute téléphonique, des tests de grossesse et des entrevues de relation d'aide.

LIEU DE CONSULTATION : S.O.S. Grossesse. [*Adresse* : 1000, 3e Avenue, Limoilou (Québec) G1L 2X4. *Téléphone* : (418) 523-9324/9323.]

MATÉRIEL : Statuts et règlements, demandes de subvention, 1975-1991; procès-verbaux, listes de membres, albums de coupures, mémoires, 1974-1991; correspondance, 1988-1991; documents financiers, 1982-1991; listes d'envoi, 1989-1991; rapports, communiqués de presse, 1990-1991; dépliants, tracts, affiches, 1991.

QUANTITÉ : 2 classeurs.

ÉTAT : Bon.

ACCÈS : Permission requise. Dossiers concernant la clientèle confidentiels.

1250. La Séjournelle : Maison d'aide et d'hébergement pour femmes victimes de violence conjugale

✣ Shawinigan (Québec). Groupe fondé 1983.

Cet organisme offre une ressource adaptée aux besoins des femmes victimes de violence et de leurs enfants. Elle vise également à déprivatiser la violence conjugale et à promouvoir et défendre les intérêts des femmes victimes de violence dans l'espoir d'enrayer ce fléau. Jusqu'en 1987, l'organisme était marrainé par la Maison d'accueil et d'information pour les femmes de la Mauricie.

LIEU DE CONSULTATION : Séjournelle : Maison d'aide et d'hébergement pour femmes victimes de violence conjugale. [*Adresse postale* : C.P. 342, Shawinigan (Québec) G9N 6V1. *Téléphone* : (819) 537-8348.]

MATÉRIEL : Statuts et règlements, procès-verbaux, correspondance, documents financiers, demandes de subvention, dossiers concernant la clientèle, listes de membres, albums de coupures, rapports, mémoires, actes de congrès, dépliants, tracts, communiqués de presse, affiches, 1987-1991; journaux de bord, 1983-1991.

QUANTITÉ : 4 classeurs, env. 10 boîtes, 20 cartables à pochettes.

ÉTAT : Bon.

ACCÈS : Permission requise. Dossiers concernant la clientèle confidentiels.

1251. Service à la famille chinoise du Grand Montréal. Comité des femmes / Chinese Family Service of Greater Montreal. Women's Committee

[For English entry, see # 1176.]

✤ Montréal (Québec). Groupe fondé 1976.

Le Comité des femmes du Service à la famille chinoise du Grand Montréal (SFCGM) aborde les questions qui touchent les femmes chinoises-québécoises et oeuvre pour le bien-être des femmes en général.

LIEU DE CONSULTATION : Service à la famille chinoise du Grand Montréal. Comité des femmes. [*Adresse* : 987, rue Côté, 4e étage, Montréal (Québec) H2Z 1L1. *Téléphone* : (514) 861-5244. *Télécopieur* : (514) 861-9008.]

MATÉRIEL : Procès-verbaux, correspondance, documents financiers, demandes de subvention, dossiers concernant la clientèle, listes de membres, listes d'envoi, pétitions, rapports, mémoires, communiqués de presse, affiches, macarons, photographies, vidéocassettes, 1978-1991.

ÉTAT : Assez bon.

ACCÈS : Permission requise. Dossiers concernant la clientèle et documents internes confidentiels.

1252. Simone de Beauvoir Institute / Institut Simone de Beauvoir

[Renseignements en français, notice 1215.]

✤ Montreal, Quebec. Formed 1978.

The Simone de Beauvoir Institute at Concordia University promotes understanding of the historical and contemporary situation of women in society. It offers undergraduate degrees in women's studies.

LOCATION OF RECORDS: Simone de Beauvoir Institute. [*Address:* Concordia University, 1455 de Maisonneuve W., Montreal, Quebec H3G 1M8. *Telephone:* (514) 848-2370. *Fax:* (514) 848-3494.]

RECORDS: Constitution, 1978, 1985; minutes, correspondence, newsletters, videotapes, 1978-1991; financial records, student records, membership lists, mailing lists, flyers, 1991; conference proceedings, 1987; press releases, 1989-1991; grant applications, reports, posters, clippings, photographs.

AMOUNT: 2 filing cabinets, 7 boxes.

CONDITION: Good.

ACCESS: Permission required.

1253. Société Elizabeth Fry de Montréal / Elizabeth Fry Society of Montreal

[For English entry, see # 1196.]

✤ Montréal (Québec). Groupe fondé 1977.

La Société Elizabeth Fry de Montréal vient en aide aux femmes qui ont des démêlés avec la justice. Elle gère une maison de transition aussi bien que d'autres programmes. Jusqu'en 1985, cet organisme s'appelait la Société Elizabeth Fry du Grand Montréal.

LIEU DE CONSULTATION : Société Elizabeth Fry de Montréal. [*Adresse* : 1000, rue Sherbrooke est, Montréal (Québec) H2L 1L5. *Téléphone* : (514) 528-9888. *Télécopieur* : (514) 528-8924.]

MATÉRIEL : Procès-verbaux, 1987-1991; bulletins (*Femmes et justice*, 1988-1991); statuts et règlements, correspondance, documents financiers, demandes de subvention, dossiers concernant la clientèle, listes de membres, listes d'envoi, rapports, mémoires, actes de congrès, dépliants, communiqués de presse, affiches, livres, manuels, publications diverses.

QUANTITÉ : 4 tiroirs de classeur.

ÉTAT : Assez bon.

ACCÈS : Permission requise.

1254. Solidarité post-avortement

✤ Ste-Foy (Québec). Groupe fondé 1987.

Solidarité post-avortement est un service offert par la Clinique de planification des naissances du Centre hospitalier de l'Université Laval (CHUL). En offrant des activités telles que des rencontres thématiques et des groupes ouverts, l'organisme aide la femme à bien ou mieux assumer un avortement lointain ou récent.

LIEU DE CONSULTATION : Solidarité post-avortement. [*Adresse* : Clinique de planification des naissances, Centre hospitalier de l'Université Laval (CHUL), 2705, boul. Laurier, Ste-Foy (Québec) G1V 4G2. *Téléphone* : (418) 654-2167.]

MATÉRIEL : Correspondance, 1987-1991; journaux de bord, 1987; actes de congrès, 1989; communiqués de presse, coupures de presse, 1989-1991; dossiers concernant la clientèle, ressources du milieu.

ÉTAT : Bon.

ACCÈS : Permission requise.

1255. South Asian Women's Community Centre / Centre communautaire des femmes sud-asiatiques

[Renseignements en français, notice 1138.]

✤ Montreal, Quebec. Formed 1981.

The South Asian Women's Community Centre (SAWCC) aims to help women achieve their full potential and become independent. Its services include language courses and vocational training.

LOCATION OF RECORDS: South Asian Women's Community Centre. [*Address:* 3600 Hôtel de Ville, Montreal, Quebec H2X 3B6. *Telephone:* (514) 842-2330/9439.]

RECORDS: Constitution, books, 1981; minutes, correspondence, log-books, financial records, grant applications, client records, membership lists, mailing lists, petitions, reports, pamphlets, flyers, buttons, banners, photographs, 1981-1991; briefs, 1987-1989, 1991; conference proceedings, 1983-1991; press releases, 1991; T-shirts, 1988; newsletters (*Shakti*, 1983; *SAWCC Bulletin/Bulletin CCFSA*, 1981).

AMOUNT: 4 filing cabinets.

CONDITION: Fair.

ACCESS: All records of the organization and its clients are confidential.

1256. Syndicat des agricultrices de la Côte-du-Sud

✤ La Pocatière (Québec).

Le Syndicat des agricultrices de la Côte-du-Sud vise à regrouper toutes les agricultrices de la région de la Côte-du-Sud, à les représenter, à les informer, à développer chez elles une prise de conscience de l'importance de la contribution des femmes à l'agriculture et à participer aux orientations de l'agriculture québécoise en définissant une place aux femmes dans le secteur agricole. L'organisme est affilié à l'Union des producteurs agricoles (UPA) et à la Fédération des agricultrices du Québec (FAQ).

LIEU DE CONSULTATION : Syndicat des agricultrices de la Côte-du-Sud. [*Adresse postale* : C.P. 100, La Pocatière (Québec) G0R 1Z0. (*Indication de rue* : 1120, 6e Avenue.) *Téléphone* : (418) 856-3044. *Télécopieur* : (418) 856-5199.]

MATÉRIEL : Statuts et règlements, 1987; bulletins (*Agri-Culture-Elle*, 1990-1991); procès-verbaux, correspondance, documents financiers, demandes de subvention, listes de membres, rapports, dépliants, macarons, coupures de presse, vidéocassettes.

QUANTITÉ : 1 classeur.

ÉTAT : Bon.

ACCÈS : Permission requise.

1257. Théâtre collectif des femmes de St-Basile

✣ St-Basile-le-Grand (Québec). Groupe fondé 1985.

Le but de ce collectif est de regrouper des femmes afin de les encourager à créer à partir d'un vécu féminin. Il s'intéresse à tous les aspects du théâtre : conception, écriture, mise en scène et production.

LIEU DE CONSULTATION : Théâtre collectif des femmes de St-Basile. [*Adresse* : 7, rue Mont-Bruno, St-Basile-le-Grand (Québec) J3N 1A7.]

MATÉRIEL : Journaux de bord, listes de membres, 1985-1990.

QUANTITÉ : 1 demi-classeur.

1258. Transition'elle

✣ Saint-Romuald (Québec). Groupe fondé 1986.

Transition'elle aide les femmes de la rive-sud du Québec à réintegrer le marché du travail. Cet organisme offre des services qui permettent aux femmes d'acquérir les habitudes de travail et les compétences requises pour trouver, occuper et conserver un emploi.

LIEU DE CONSULTATION : Transition'elle. [*Adresse* : 2220, ch. du Fleuve, Saint-Romuald (Québec) G6W 1Y4. *Téléphone* : (418) 839-3109.]

MATÉRIEL : Statuts et règlements, 1986-1987, 1990-1991; procès-verbaux, correspondance, documents financiers, demandes de subvention, dossiers concernant la clientèle, listes de membres, albums de coupures, rapports, dépliants, communiqués de presse, affiches, coupures de presse, 1986-1991.

QUANTITÉ : 1 classeur.

ÉTAT : Bon.

ACCÈS : Permission requise.

1259. La Traversée : Centre de lutte contre les agressions à caractère sexuel de la Rive-Sud

✣ St-Lambert (Québec). Groupe fondé 1984.

La Traversée fournit de l'aide directe aux femmes et aux jeunes filles victimes d'agression sexuelle, en plus d'offrir des services de prévention et de sensibilisation face à la problématique des agressions sexuelles.

LIEU DE CONSULTATION : Traversée : Centre de lutte contre les agressions à caractère sexuel de la Rive-Sud. [*Adresse postale* : C.P. 512, Saint-Lambert (Québec) J4P 3R8. *Téléphone* : (514) 465-5263.]

MATÉRIEL : Statuts et règlements, procès-verbaux, correspondance, journaux de bord, documents financiers, demandes de subvention, dossiers concernant la clientèle, listes de membres, listes d'envoi, pétitions, albums de coupures, rapports, mémoires, actes de congrès, dépliants, tracts, communiqués de presse, affiches, livres, coupures de presse, photographies, 1984-1991.

QUANTITÉ : 4 boîtes.

ÉTAT : Bon.

ACCÈS : Permission requise.

1260. Trêve pour elles : Centre d'aide et de prévention contre les agressions à caractère sexuel

✣ Montréal (Québec). Groupe fondé 1986.

Le centre offre aux femmes agressées sexuellement des services de soutien, d'accompagnement et d'intervention, aussi bien que des moyens de prévention.

LIEU DE CONSULTATION : Trêve pour elles : Centre d'aide et de prévention contre les agressions à caractère sexuel. [*Adresse postale* : C.P. 51119, Montréal (Québec) H1N 3T8. (*Indication de rue* : 3365 Granby.) *Téléphone* : (514) 251-0323.]

MATÉRIEL : Statuts et règlements, 1988; procès-verbaux, correspondance, demandes de subvention, rapports, 1986-1991; journaux de bord, documents financiers, dossiers concernant la clientèle, listes de membres, listes d'envoi, pétitions, albums de coupures, mémoires, actes de congrès, dépliants, tracts, communiqués de presse, 1988-1991.

QUANTITÉ : 3 classeurs, 4 boîtes.

ÉTAT : Bon.

ACCÈS : Permission requise. Dossiers concernant la clientèle confidentiels.

1261. Université Laval. Groupe de recherche multidisciplinaire féministe

✣ Québec (Québec). Groupe fondé 1983.

Le Groupe de recherche multidisciplinaire féministe (GREMF) à l'Université Laval est un regroupement de chercheuses féministes provenant de diverses facultés et écoles de l'université. Son objectif principal est de contribuer à l'avancement des connaissances sur la condition des femmes en participant aux débats actuels du féminisme et en servant de lieu d'échange pour les chercheuses féministes de l'université. Le GREMF publie la revue *Recherches féministes*.

LIEU DE CONSULTATION : Université Laval. Groupe de recherche multidisciplinaire féministe. [*Adresse* : Faculté des sciences sociales, bureau 3800, Édifice Jean-Durand, Québec (Québec) G1K 7P4. *Téléphone* : (418) 656-5421. *Télécopieur* : (418) 656-3266.]

MATÉRIEL : Statuts et règlements, 1989; procès-verbaux, correspondance, documents financiers, 1985-1991; demandes de subvention, listes de membres, listes d'envoi, rapports, mémoires, dépliants, affiches, publications, revues (*Recherches féministes*).

QUANTITÉ : 2 classeurs.

ÉTAT : Bon.

1262. Vidéo femmes

✣ Québec (Québec). Groupe fondé 1975.

Les activités primaires du groupe sont la production et la distribution de films et de vidéos concernant la condition féminine. À ses débuts, Vidéo femmes s'appelait la Femme et le film.

LIEU DE CONSULTATION : Vidéo femmes. [*Adresse* : 700, rue du Roi, Québec (Québec) G1K 2X7. *Téléphone* : (418) 529-9188. *Télécopieur* : (418) 648-9201.]

MATÉRIEL : Charte, 1975; documents financiers, demandes de subvention, dossiers concernant la clientèle, listes de membres, listes d'envoi, albums de coupures, rapports, mémoires, actes de congrès, dépliants, communiqués de presse, affiches, T-shirts, livres, coupures de presse, photographies, enregistrements sonores, vidéocassettes, films, 1975-1991; catalogues, 1985-1988, 1991; procès-verbaux, correspondance.

QUANTITÉ : 3 classeurs, 2 armoires.

ÉTAT : Bon.

ACCÈS : Permission requise.

1263. La Vigie : Centre d'aide et de prévention des assauts sexuels de Valleyfield

✣ Valleyfield (Québec). Groupe fondé 1984.

Cet organisme vient en aide aux femmes et aux adolescentes agressées sexuellement par l'aide directe et par la prévention et la sensibilisation.

LIEU DE CONSULTATION : Vigie : Centre d'aide et de prévention des assauts sexuels de Valleyfield. [*Adresse postale* : C.P. 295, Valleyfield (Québec) J6S 4V6. *Téléphone* : (514) 371-4222. *Télécopieur* : (514) 373-9919.]

MATÉRIEL : Statuts et règlements, 1987-1990; procès-verbaux, listes de membres, 1983-1991; documents financiers, demandes de subvention, rapports, 1984-1991; dossiers concernant la clientèle, listes d'envoi, dépliants, vidéocassettes, 1988-1991; communiqués de presse, 1985-1991; affiches, 1987-1991; coupures de presse, 1986-1991; photographies, 1989-1991.

QUANTITÉ : Env. 1 classeur.

ÉTAT : Bon.

ACCÈS : Permission requise. Dossiers concernant la clientèle confidentiels.

1264. West Island Women's Shelter / Refuge pour les femmes de l'Ouest de l'Île

[Renseignements en français, notice 1244.]

✣ Roxboro, Quebec. Formed 1979.

Offering shelter and a crisis line, the West Island Women's Shelter works to reduce domestic violence against women.

LOCATION OF RECORDS: West Island Women's Shelter. [*Mailing Address:* P.O. Box 203, Roxboro, Quebec H8Y 3E9. *Telephone:* (514) 620-4845.]

RECORDS: Constitutions, 1979, 1982, 1987; minutes, financial records, grant applications, client records, membership lists, mailing lists, scrapbooks, pamphlets, press releases, buttons, 1979-1991; correspondence, log-books, 1990-1991; briefs, 1985; banners, publications, 1986, 1988, 1990; videotapes, 1986; reports, clippings.

AMOUNT: 6 filing cabinets.

CONDITION: Good.

ACCESS: Permission required. Client files closed.

NEW BRUNSWICK / NOUVEAU-BRUNSWICK

1265. *Accueil Sainte-Famille*

✢ Tracadie (N.-B.). Groupe fondé 1979.

Cet organisme offre un abri sûr à toutes femmes et à leurs enfants, surtout aux victimes de violence physique ou psychologique, et aux femmes en attente d'hébergement permanent. L'accueil offre, de plus, des services d'appui et d'accompagnement.

LIEU DE CONSULTATION : Accueil Sainte-Famille. [*Adresse postale* : C.P. 3001, Tracadie (N.-B.) E0C 2B0. *Téléphone* : (506) 395-2212.]

MATÉRIEL : Statuts et règlements, procès-verbaux, documents financiers, 1987-1991 ; correspondance, dossiers concernant la clientèle, albums de coupures, photographies, 1979-1991 ; mémoires, 1987 ; dépliants, 1985-1991 ; films, 1990.

QUANTITÉ : 1 classeur.

ÉTAT : Bon.

ACCÈS : Permission requise. Dossiers concernant la clientèle confidentiels.

1266. *Action éducation femmes (Nouveau-Brunswick)*

✢ Moncton (N.-B.). Groupe fondé 1987.

Appellée aussi l'AEF (N.-B.), cet organisme vise à promouvoir l'éducation chez les femmes francophones du Nouveau-Brunswick. Ses principales activités sont la recherche, la sensibilisation et l'information.

LIEU DE CONSULTATION : Action éducation femmes. [*Adresse postale* : C.P. 1458, Moncton (N.-B.) E1C 8T6. *Téléphone* : (506) 859-8182. *Télécopieur* : (506) 859-7182.]

MATÉRIEL : Statuts et règlements, 1989-1990 ; procès-verbaux, correspondance, listes de membres, rapports, 1987-1991 ; journaux de bord, documents financiers, demandes de subvention, dépliants, 1989-1991 ; albums de coupures, vidéocassettes, 1990-1991 ; mémoires, 1989 ; actes de congrès, 1988 ; communiqués de presse, T-shirts, dossier statistique, 1990 ; photographies, enregistrements sonores, 1991.

QUANTITÉ : 1 classeur.

ÉTAT : Bon.

1267. *Albert County Women's Outreach Co-op*

✢ Elgin, N.B. Formed 1989.

The Albert County Women's Outreach Co-op (ACWOC) provides women with an outlet for their crafts. Twenty per cent of revenue is used to present educational seminars on subjects concerning women. The organization used to be called the Albert County Women's Network.

LOCATION OF RECORDS: Albert County Women's Outreach Co-op. [*Address:* R.R. #1, Elgin, N.B. E0A 1P0. *Telephone:* (506) 756-2518.]

RECORDS: Minutes, financial records, client records, membership lists, mailing lists, scrapbooks, reports, flyers, press releases, posters, buttons, 1989-1991 ; pamphlets, 1989.

CONDITION: Good.

ACCESS: Permission required.

1268. *Amana House*

✢ Saint John, N.B. Formed 1984.

Amana House offers a long-term, residential recovery programme for chemically dependent women.

LOCATION OF RECORDS: Amana House. [*Address:* 371 Dufferin Row, Saint John, N.B. E2M 2J7. *Telephone:* (506) 635-5735.]

RECORDS: Minutes, correspondence, 1982-1991 ; financial records, 1984-1991 ; grant applications, 1985-1991 ; client records, 1986-1991 ; mailing lists, 1989-1990 ; conference proceedings, 1986-1990 ; briefs, pamphlets, buttons.

CONDITION: Good.

ACCESS: Permission required. Client files and board-meeting minutes closed. Financial statements may be closed.

1269. *Association des enseignantes et des enseignants francophones du Nouveau-Brunswick. Comité sur les valeurs et les droits humains en éducation*

✢ Fredericton (N.-B.). Groupe fondé 1975.

Une partie du mandat du Comité sur les valeurs et les droits humains en éducation est de conseiller l'Association des enseignantes et des enseignants francophones du Nouveau-Brunswick (AEFNB) sur les moyens à prendre pour la promotion de l'égalité des sexes dans la profession enseignante et dans le système d'éducation.

LIEU DE CONSULTATION : Association des enseignantes et des enseignants francophones du Nouveau-Brunswick. Comité sur les valeurs et les droits humains en éducation. [*Adresse postale* : C.P. 712, Fredericton (N.-B.) E3B 5B4. *Téléphone* : (506) 452-8921. *Télécopieur* : (506) 453-9795.]

MATÉRIEL : Procès-verbaux, correspondance, rapports, mémoires, actes de congrès, communiqués de presse, photographies, 1975-1991 ; guide pédagogique, 1984 ; demandes de subvention.

ÉTAT : Bon.

ACCÈS : Permission requise.

1270. Canadian Congress for Learning Opportunities for Women (Fredericton, N.B.)

✤ Fredericton, N.B. Formed 1979.

The Canadian Congress for Learning Opportunities for Women (CCLOW) in Fredericton works to make education accessible to women and to increase women's earning potential in the workplace.

LOCATION OF RECORDS: Canadian Congress for Learning Opportunities for Women. [*Address:* 101 Oakland Ave., Fredericton, N.B. E3A 1W5. *Telephone:* (506) 474-0641.]
RECORDS: Grant applications, membership lists, scrapbooks, pamphlets.
CONDITION: Good.
ACCESS: Permission required.

1271. Carrefour pour femmes / Crossroads for Women

[For English entry, see # 1277.]

✤ Moncton (N.-B.). Groupe fondé 1981.

Le Carrefour pour femmes est un centre de refuge pour femmes victimes d'abus et pour leurs enfants. Il offre hébergement et appui pendant quelques semaines à des femmes qui ont besoin d'une période de réflexion.

LIEU DE CONSULTATION: Carrefour pour femmes. [*Adresse postale:* C.P. 1247, Moncton (N.-B.) E1C 8P9. *Téléphone:* (506) 853-0811.]
MATÉRIEL: Statuts et règlements, 1981; procès-verbaux, correspondance, 1980-1991; journaux de bord, documents financiers, demandes de subvention, dossiers concernant la clientèle, albums de coupures, dépliants, communiqués de presse, 1981-1991; listes de membres, listes d'envoi, 1985-1991; mémoires, actes de congrès, 1989; macarons, 1981-1984; documents divers.
QUANTITÉ: 2 classeurs.
ÉTAT: Bon.
ACCÈS: Permission requise. Dossiers concernant la clientèle confidentiels.

1272. Cercle des dames d'Acadie de Lamèque

✤ Lamèque (N.-B.). Groupe fondé 1978.

Ce groupe se donne pour mission de regrouper les femmes francophones et de promouvoir les intérêts et défendre les droits des femmes et des francophones. Le cercle fait partie de la Fédération des dames d'Acadie.

LIEU DE CONSULTATION: Cercle des dames d'Acadie de Lamèque. [*Adresse postale:* C.P. 655, Lamèque (N.-B.) E0B 1V0. *Téléphone:* (506) 344-7793.]
MATÉRIEL: Statuts et règlements, procès-verbaux, correspondance, journaux de bord, documents financiers, demandes de subvention, dossiers concernant la clientèle, listes de membres, listes d'envoi, pétitions, albums de coupures, rapports, mémoires, actes de congrès, dépliants, communiqués de presse, affiches, bannières, livres, coupures de presse, photographies, enregistrements sonores, vidéocassettes, 1978-1991.
QUANTITÉ: 2 classeurs.
ÉTAT: Bon.
ACCÈS: Permission requise.

1273. Cercle des dames d'Acadie de Shippagan

✤ Shippagan (N.-B.). Groupe fondé 1976.

Ce groupe s'est donné pour mission de promouvoir les intérêts et de défendre les droits des femmes acadiennes et francophones. Ses champs d'action comprennent les droits linguistiques, la valorisation des femmes dans la communauté et la lutte contre la violence faite aux femmes. Le cercle est marrainé par la Fédération des dames d'Acadie.

LIEU DE CONSULTATION: Cercle des dames d'Acadie de Shippagan. [*Adresse postale:* C.P. 871, Shippagan (N.-B.) E0B 2P0. *Téléphone:* (506) 336-8224.]
MATÉRIEL: Statuts et règlements, procès-verbaux, correspondance, documents financiers, listes de membres, albums de coupures, rapports, dépliants, communiqués de presse, photographies, 1976-1991; bulletins (*Le Noyau*, 1976-1991).
QUANTITÉ: 1 classeur.
ÉTAT: Bon.
ACCÈS: Permission requise. Certains documents sont confidentiels.

1274. Cercle des dames d'Acadie (Tracadie, N.-B.)

✤ Tracadie (N.-B.). Groupe fondé 1976.

La mission de ce groupe est de promouvoir et de défendre les droits des femmes et des francophones du Nouveau-Brunswick.

LIEU DE CONSULTATION: Cercle des dames d'Acadie. [*Adresse postale:* C.P. 1305, Tracadie (N.-B.). *Téléphone:* (506) 395-5185.]
MATÉRIEL: Statuts et règlements, 1976; procès-verbaux, correspondance, journaux de bord, documents financiers, listes de membres, listes d'envoi, rapports, actes de congrès, bannières, 1976-1991; demandes de subvention, 1987; bulletins (*Le GAU*, 1976-1991); dossiers concernant la clientèle, mémoires, dépliants, livres, coupures de presse, photographies.
ÉTAT: Bon.
ACCÈS: Permission requise.

1275. Contact: Women's Resource and Information Centre

✤ Sussex, N.B. Formed 1988.

This centre promotes equality for women by providing information and referral services, workshops, seminars, and a meeting space.

LOCATION OF RECORDS: Contact: Women's Resource and Information Centre. [*Mailing Address:* Box 681, Sussex, N.B. E0E 1P0. *Telephone:* (506) 432-6024.]
RECORDS: Minutes, correspondence, log-books, financial records, membership lists, mailing lists, scrapbooks, pamphlets, flyers, press releases, 1988-1991; clippings, sound recordings, videotapes.
AMOUNT: 1 filing cabinet.
CONDITION: Good.
ACCESS: Permission required.

1276. Coverdale Foundation

✤ Saint John, N.B. Formed 1976.

The Coverdale Foundation, also known as the Coverdale Centre, provides rehabilitative services such as counselling and self-help groups to female offenders. The Coverdale Foundation has a connection with an earlier organization, the Interprovincial Home for Women, which operated from 1923 to 1972.

LOCATION OF RECORDS: Coverdale Foundation. [*Address:* 61 Union St., Suite 302, Saint John, N.B. E2L 1A2. *Telephone:* (506) 634-1649.]
RECORDS: Constitution, minutes, financial records, membership lists, reports, pamphlets, 1976-1991; grant applications, 1980-1991; client records, 1987-1991; scrapbooks, press releases, 1989-1991; photographs, 1923, 1989; videotapes, 1990; posters.
AMOUNT: 2 cabinets.
CONDITION: Good.
ACCESS: Permission required. Client files closed.

1277. Crossroads for Women / Carrefour pour femmes

[Renseignements en français, notice 1271.]

✣ Moncton, N.B. Formed 1981.

Crossroads for Women is a shelter for women victims of abuse and their children. It provides refuge and support for a temporary period to women who need time for reflection.

LOCATION OF RECORDS: Crossroads for Women. [*Mailing Address:* P.O. Box 1247, Moncton, N.B. E1C 8P9. *Telephone:* (506) 853-0811.]

RECORDS: Constitution, 1981; minutes, correspondence, 1980-1991; logbooks, financial records, grant applications, client records, scrapbooks, pamphlets, press releases, 1981-1991; membership lists, mailing lists, 1985-1991; briefs, conference proceedings, 1989; buttons, 1981-1984; miscellaneous records.

AMOUNT: 2 filing cabinets.

CONDITION: Good.

ACCESS: Permission required. Client files closed.

1278. Dames d'Acadie de Neguac

✣ Neguac (N.-B.). Groupe fondé 1980.

Les Dames d'Acadie de Neguac fait partie de la Fédération des dames d'Acadie, qui a pour but de regrouper les femmes francophones et de promouvoir les intérêts et défendre les droits des femmes et des francophones.

LIEU DE CONSULTATION : Dames d'Acadie de Neguac. [*Adresse :* Rue Principale, Neguac (N.-B.) E0C 1S0. *Téléphone :* (506) 776-8639.]

MATÉRIEL : Statuts et règlements, procès-verbaux, correspondance, documents financiers, demandes de subvention, albums de coupures, rapports, livres, coupures de presse, photographies, vidéocassettes, 1980-1991.

QUANTITÉ : 1 armoire.

ÉTAT : Bon.

ACCÈS : Permission requise.

1279. Ecumenical Decade of Churches in Solidarity with Women (Hampton, N.B.)

✣ Hampton, N.B. Formed 1989.

The Ecumenical Decade, sponsored by the World Council of Churches, is a ten-year project (from 1988 to 1998) to further the cause of women by celebrating women's gifts and removing obstacles keeping women from their rightful place in the church and in society. This branch of the Ecumenical Decade, affiliated with the United Church of Canada, organizes meetings, conferences, and workshops in the Maritimes.

LOCATION OF RECORDS: Ecumenical Decade of Churches in Solidarity with Women. [*Address:* c/o Joan Colborne, 30 Church Lane, Box 569, Hampton, N.B. E0G 1Z0. *Telephone:* (506) 832-4024.]

RECORDS: Correspondence, mailing lists, 1989-1991; grant applications, 1991; conference proceedings, 1990; terms of reference, minutes, reports, pamphlets, flyers, press releases, clippings, photographs.

AMOUNT: 1 drawer of a filing cabinet.

CONDITION: Good.

1280. Elizabeth Fry Society of New Brunswick

✣ Moncton, N.B. Formed 1957.

The Elizabeth Fry Society of New Brunswick helps women re-integrate into society after prison terms, gives court support to women facing charges, does crime prevention, and assists families of women in conflict with the law. Until 1968 it was known as the Elizabeth Fry Society, Moncton Branch.

LOCATION OF RECORDS: Elizabeth Fry Society of New Brunswick. [*Address:* 18 Botsford St., Moncton, N.B. E1C 4W7. *Telephone:* (506) 855-7781.]

RECORDS: Constitution, reports, minutes, grant applications, correspondence, financial records, membership lists, pamphlets, books.

AMOUNT: 1 filing cabinet.

CONDITION: Good.

ACCESS: Permission required. Client files closed.

1281. Fédération des dames d'Acadie (Bathurst, N.-B.)

✣ Bathurst (N.-B.). Groupe fondé 1978.

La Fédération des dames d'Acadie s'est donné pour mission de regrouper les femmes francophones du Nouveau-Brunswick dans le but de promouvoir les intérêts et défendre les droits des femmes et des francophones.

LIEU DE CONSULTATION : Fédération des dames d'Acadie. [*Adresse :* 1154, av. St-Pierre, Bathurst (N.-B.) E2A 2N7. *Téléphone :* (506) 546-3033. *Télécopieur :* (506) 546-2382.]

MATÉRIEL : Statuts et règlements, procès-verbaux, correspondance, documents financiers, demandes de subvention, listes de membres, listes d'envoi, pétitions, albums de coupures, rapports, mémoires, actes de congrès, communiqués de presse, affiches, macarons, 1978-1991; dépliants, 1980-1984; bannières, 1980; bulletins, 1981-1991.

ÉTAT : Bon.

ACCÈS : Permission requise.

1282. Fédération des dames d'Acadie du Nouveau-Brunswick

✣ Campbellton (N.-B.). Groupe fondé 1976.

La Fédération a pour objectifs d'encourager les femmes à se perfectionner et à jouer un rôle utile dans la société, de promouvoir et de défendre leurs valeurs culturelles et linguistiques et de coopérer à des projets favorisant la cause des femmes et l'amélioration des conditions sociales.

LIEU DE CONSULTATION : Fédération des dames d'Acadie du Nouveau-Brunswick. [*Adresse :* 142, rue Arran, Campbellton (N.-B.).]

MATÉRIEL : Statuts et règlements, bannières, 1982; procès-verbaux, 1982-1991; correspondance, documents financiers, listes de membres, albums de coupures, rapports, communiqués de presse, coupures de presse, photographies, 1976-1991; mémoires, 1985; macarons, 1983; bulletins, 1979-1991; livres, 1977-1987.

QUANTITÉ : 1 classeur.

ÉTAT : Bon.

ACCÈS : Permission requise.

1283. Fondation Muriel McQueen Fergusson / Muriel McQueen Fergusson Foundation

[For English entry, see # 1289.]

✣ Fredericton (N.-B.). Groupe fondé 1985.

La Fondation Muriel McQueen Fergusson (FMMF) est un fiducie de bienfaisance dont les buts sont de subventionner des projets de recherche sur les causes, la fréquence et la nature de la violence sociale et de marrainer des programmes de sensibilisation du public dans ce domaine.

LIEU DE CONSULTATION : Fondation Muriel McQueen Fergusson. [*Adresse postale :* C.P. 50000, Fredericton (N.-B.) E3B 6C2.]

MATÉRIEL : Statuts et règlements, 1985-1986; procès-verbaux, correspondance, documents financiers, 1985-1991; actes de congrès, 1987;

demandes de subvention, rapports, dépliants, tracts, communiqués de presse.
QUANTITÉ : 1 classeur.
ÉTAT : Bon.
ACCÈS : Permission requise.

1284. Fonds d'action et d'éducation juridiques pour les femmes. Section Nouveau-Brunswick / Women's Legal Education and Action Fund. New Brunswick Branch

[For English entry, see # 1301.]

✣ Fredericton (N.-B.). Groupe fondé 1985.

Le Fonds d'action et d'éducation juridiques pour les femmes (FAEJ) soutient la cause de l'égalité pour les femmes du Canada par le biais de poursuites judiciaires et de l'éducation. La Section Nouveau-Brunswick du FAEJ organise des campagnes de souscription de fonds, des campagnes de recrutement et des conférences ouvertes au public.

LIEU DE CONSULTATION : Fonds d'action et d'éducation juridiques pour les femmes. Section Nouveau-Brunswick. [*Adresse postale* : C.P. 1413, Succursale A, Fredericton (N.-B.) E3B 5B3.]

MATÉRIEL : Correspondance, documents financiers, listes de membres, 1985-1991; demandes de subvention, 1988; listes d'envoi, tracts, 1991; affiches, 1985-1989; bannières, 1987; procès-verbaux, photographies.
QUANTITÉ : 3 boîtes.
ÉTAT : Bon.

1285. Fredericton Rape Crisis Centre

✣ Fredericton, N.B. Formed 1975.

The Fredericton Rape Crisis Centre (FRCC) provides information, support, and counselling to survivors of sexual violence and works toward the eradication of sexual violence through education. Prior to 1979, it was called the Rape Crisis Service.

LOCATION OF RECORDS: Fredericton Rape Crisis Centre. [*Mailing Address*: P.O. Box 174, Fredericton, N.B. E3B 4Y9. *Telephone*: (506) 454-0460.]

RECORDS: Constitution, 1979; minutes, correspondence, client records, scrapbooks, pamphlets, flyers, clippings, 1976-1991; log-books, 1980-1990; financial records, 1979-1991; grant applications, 1977-1991; petitions, 1984-1991; briefs, 1985-1986; posters, 1985-1991; books, 1987; sound recordings, 1980-1991; videotapes, 1980; press releases.
AMOUNT: Approx. 6 filing cabinets.
CONDITION: Good.
ACCESS: Permission required. Client files closed.

1286. Hestia House

✣ Saint John, N.B. Formed 1981.

This is a transition house for women and their children who are being physically, emotionally, or sexually abused (or are living in fear of such abuse).

LOCATION OF RECORDS: Hestia House. [*Mailing Address*: P.O. Box 7135, Station A, Saint John, N.B. E2L 4S5. *Telephone*: (506) 634-7570/7571.]

RECORDS: Minutes, correspondence, log-books, financial records, client records, clippings, 1981-1991; grant applications, 1982-1991; briefs, photographs, 1987; pamphlets, flyers, press releases, reports, 1990-1991; newsletters, 1982-1986.

AMOUNT: 7 filing cabinets.
ACCESS: Permission required. Client files, personnel files, and log-books closed.

1287. Maison de Passage House

[For English entry, see # 1288.]

✣ Bathurst (N.-B.). Groupe fondé 1987.

C'est une maison d'hébergement pour femmes et leurs enfants victimes de violence familiale.

LIEU DE CONSULTATION : Maison de Passage House. [*Adresse postale* : C.P. 1284, Bathurst (N.-B.) E2A 4J1.]

MATÉRIEL : Statuts et règlements, 1987-1991; procès-verbaux, correspondance, journaux de bord, documents financiers, demandes de subvention, dossiers concernant la clientèle, listes d'envoi, albums de coupures, rapports, livres, coupures de presse, photographies, 1988-1991; dépliants, communiqués de presse, affiches, 1989-1991.
ÉTAT : Assez bon.
ACCÈS : Permission requise. Dossiers concernant la clientèle confidentiels.

1288. Maison de Passage House

[Renseignements en français, notice 1287.]

✣ Bathurst, N.B. Formed 1987.

This is a shelter for women and their children who are victims of family violence.

LOCATION OF RECORDS: Maison de Passage House. [*Mailing Address*: Box 1284, Bathurst, N.B. E2A 4J1.]

RECORDS: Constitution, 1987-1991; minutes, correspondence, log-books, financial records, grant applications, client records, mailing lists, scrapbooks, reports, books, clippings, photographs, 1988-1991; pamphlets, press releases, posters, 1989-1991.
CONDITION: Fair.
ACCESS: Permission required. Client files closed.

1289. Muriel McQueen Fergusson Foundation / Fondation Muriel McQueen Fergusson

[Renseignements en français, notice 1283.]

✣ Fredericton, N.B. Formed 1985.

The Muriel McQueen Fergusson Foundation (MMFF) is a charitable trust which funds research into the causes, incidence, and forms of family violence and sponsors programmes to sensitize the public to the problem.

LOCATION OF RECORDS: Muriel McQueen Fergusson Foundation. [*Mailing Address*: Box 50000, Fredericton, N.B. E3B 6C2.]

RECORDS: Constitution, 1985-1986; minutes, correspondence, financial records, 1985-1991; conference proceedings, 1987; grant applications, reports, pamphlets, flyers, press releases.
AMOUNT: 1 filing cabinet.
CONDITION: Good.
ACCESS: Permission required.

1290. New Brunswick Coalition of Transition Houses for Abused Women

✢ Saint John, N.B. Formed 1987.

This coalition, known until 1988 as the New Brunswick Coalition for Family Peace, does networking and lobbying.

LOCATION OF RECORDS: New Brunswick Coalition of Transition Houses for Abused Women. [*Mailing Address:* P.O. Box 7135, Saint John, N.B. E2L 4S5. *Telephone:* (506) 634-7571.]

RECORDS: Constitution, 1987; minutes, correspondence, financial records, grant applications, membership lists, press releases, clippings, 1987-1991; newsletters (*Taking Control*, 1991).

AMOUNT: 1 filing cabinet.

CONDITION: Good.

ACCESS: Permission required.

1291. New Brunswick Farm Women's Organization

✢ Moncton, N.B. Formed 1986.

The New Brunswick Farm Women's Organization (NBFWO) works to enhance the quality of life of farm women through education, provides a forum for farm women's concerns, preserves the family farm, and promotes respect for its life style.

LOCATION OF RECORDS: New Brunswick Farm Women's Organization. [*Address:* R.R. #2, Moncton, N.B. E1C 8J6. *Telephone:* (506) 387-8520.]

RECORDS: Constitution, correspondence, financial records, grant applications, 1988-1991; minutes, 1986-1991; membership lists, mailing lists, 1990-1991; briefs, T-shirts, 1991; pamphlets, 1988; newsletters, clippings, 1990.

AMOUNT: 3 filing cabinets.

CONDITION: Good.

ACCESS: Permission required.

1292. Restigouche Family Crisis Interveners / Unité d'intervention pour crises familiales de Restigouche

[Renseignements en français, notice 1298.]

✢ Campbellton, N.B. Formed 1980.

Restigouche Family Crisis Interveners (RFCI) provides support and referrals to people in crisis. The majority of RFCI's clients are women, and domestic violence is a primary concern of the organization.

LOCATION OF RECORDS: Restigouche Family Crisis Interveners. [*Mailing Address:* P.O. Box 355, Campbellton, N.B. E3N 3G7. *Telephone:* (506) 753-6769.]

RECORDS: Minutes, correspondence, financial records, grant applications, client records, 1986-1991; pamphlets, flyers, 1980-1991; posters, 1988; clippings, 1989-1991; videotapes, 1989; reports.

CONDITION: Good.

ACCESS: Permission required. Client files closed.

1293. Second Stage Housing (Saint John, N.B.)

✢ Saint John, N.B. Formed 1986.

Second Stage Housing provides safe, affordable housing and ongoing support to abused women and their children.

LOCATION OF RECORDS: Second Stage Housing. [*Mailing Address:* P.O. Box 3339, Station B, Saint John, N.B. E2M 4X9. *Telephone:* (506) 632-9289.]

RECORDS: Constitution, minutes, correspondence, financial records, grant applications, client records, scrapbooks, pamphlets, photographs, 1986-1991.

AMOUNT: Approx. 2 filing cabinets.

CONDITION: Good.

ACCESS: Permission required. Client files closed.

1294. Single Parent Resource Centre (Saint John, N.B.)

✢ Saint John, N.B. Formed 1983.

The Single Parent Resource Centre provides information and support to single parents (including single pregnant women). The centre's programmes address issues of poverty, isolation, and personal and parental development.

LOCATION OF RECORDS: Single Parent Resource Centre. [*Address:* 39 Cliff St., Saint John, N.B. E2L 3A8. *Telephone:* (506) 633-2182.]

RECORDS: Constitution, 1985-1991; minutes, correspondence, financial records, grant applications, 1983-1991; log-books, client records, press releases, 1986-1991; scrapbooks, 1988-1991; reports, pamphlets, 1987-1991; briefs, 1989-1991; posters, 1990-1991; banners, 1991; newsletters (*The Singles File*, 1988-1991); clippings, photographs.

AMOUNT: 2 filing cabinets.

CONDITION: Good.

ACCESS: Permission required. Client files restricted to staff.

1295. Support aux mères célibataires / Support to Single Mothers

[For English entry, see # 1296.]

✢ Moncton (N.-B.). Groupe fondé 1982.

Support aux mères célibataires travaille à améliorer la qualité de vie des parents uniques et de leurs enfants en les aidant à faire des changements positifs dans leur vie.

LIEU DE CONSULTATION : Support aux mères célibataires. [*Adresse :* 154, rue Queen, Moncton (N.-B.) E1C 1K8. *Téléphone :* (506) 858-1303.]

MATÉRIEL : Statuts et règlements, 1982; procès-verbaux, correspondance, documents financiers, demandes de subvention, dossiers concernant la clientèle, listes de membres, listes d'envoi, albums de coupures, rapports, mémoires, dépliants, tracts, affiches, macarons, T-shirts, 1982-1991; bulletins, 1989-1991.

QUANTITÉ : 2 classeurs.

ÉTAT : Bon.

ACCÈS : Permission requise. Dossiers concernant la clientèle confidentiels.

1296. Support to Single Mothers / Support aux mères célibataires

[Renseignements en français, notice 1295.]

✢ Moncton, N.B. Formed 1982.

Support to Single Mothers works to improve the quality of life for single parents and their children, by helping them to make positive changes in their lives.

LOCATION OF RECORDS: Support to Single Mothers. [*Address:* 154 Queen St., Moncton, N.B. E1C 1K8. *Telephone:* (506) 858-1303.]

RECORDS: Constitution, 1982; minutes, correspondence, financial records, grant applications, client records, membership lists, mailing lists, scrapbooks, reports, briefs, pamphlets, flyers, posters, buttons, T-shirts, 1982-1991; newsletters, 1989-1991.

AMOUNT: 2 filing cabinets.

1297. Sussex Vale Transition House

✣ Sussex, N.B. Formed 1988.

The Sussex Vale Transition House provides emergency shelter to abused women and their children and works toward the elimination of domestic violence.

LOCATION OF RECORDS: Sussex Vale Transition House. [*Mailing Address:* P.O. Box 2184, Sussex, N.B. E0E 1P0. *Telephone:* (506) 432-6999.]

RECORDS: Constitution, 1988; minutes, correspondence, financial records, grant applications, reports, books, clippings, 1988-1991; log-books, client records, pamphlets, posters, 1991; petitions, press releases, [1988?].

AMOUNT: 1 filing cabinet.

CONDITION: Good.

ACCESS: Permission required. Client files closed.

1298. Unité d'intervention pour crises familiales de Restigouche / Restigouche Family Crisis Interveners

[For English entry, see # 1292.]

✣ Campbellton (N.-B.). Groupe fondé 1980.

Cet organisme offre des services d'appui et de référence aux personnes en crise. Un grand nombre des situations de crise dans lesquelles cet organisme intervient sont des situations de violence familiale. Les femmes forment la majorité de la clientèle de l'Unité.

LIEU DE CONSULTATION: Unité d'intervention pour crises familiales de Restigouche. [*Adresse postale :* C.P. 355, Campbellton (N.-B.) E3N 3G7. *Téléphone :* (506) 753-6769.]

MATÉRIEL: Procès-verbaux, correspondance, documents financiers, demandes de subvention, dossiers concernant la clientèle, 1986-1991; dépliants, tracts, 1980-1991; affiches, 1988; coupures de presse, 1989-1991; vidéocassettes, 1989; rapports.

ÉTAT: Bon.

ACCÈS: Permission requise. Dossiers concernant la clientèle confidentiels.

1299. Women in Transition House

✣ Fredericton, N.B. Formed 1980.

Women in Transition House (also known simply as Transition House) provides emergency shelter for abused women and their children and operates a crisis line.

LOCATION OF RECORDS: Women in Transition House. [*Mailing Address:* P.O. Box 1143, Fredericton, N.B. E3B 5C2. *Telephone:* (506) 457-2770.]

RECORDS: Minutes, 1982-1991; client records, 1980-1991; mailing lists, 1989-1991; photographs, sound recordings, 1985; correspondence, log-books, financial records, grant applications, pamphlets.

AMOUNT: 4 filing cabinets.

CONDITION: Good.

ACCESS: Permission required. Client files closed.

1300. Women Working with Immigrant Women (Fredericton, N.B.)

✣ Fredericton, N.B. Formed 1984.

Women Working with Immigrant Women (WWIW) applies a race, gender, and class analysis to the situation of immigrant women in Canada. It offers a resource centre, information sessions, and a news bulletin.

LOCATION OF RECORDS: Women Working with Immigrant Women. [*Address:* 519 Beaverbrook Court, Fredericton, N.B. E3B 1X6. *Telephone:* (506) 458-5708.]

RECORDS: Constitution, 1984; minutes, correspondence, financial records, 1984-1991; grant applications, 1985-1991; conference proceedings, 1985; newsletters (*Women Working with Immigrant Women Newsletter*, 1988-1989; *ImmigrantVoices*, 1990-1991); membership lists, mailing lists, scrapbooks, reports, pamphlets, article, clippings, photographs, sound recordings, guest book.

AMOUNT: 1 filing cabinet.

CONDITION: Good.

ACCESS: Permission required. Client files closed.

1301. Women's Legal Education and Action Fund. New Brunswick Branch / Fonds d'action et d'éducation juridiques pour les femmes. Section Nouveau-Brunswick

[Renseignements en français, notice 1284.]

✣ Fredericton, N.B. Formed 1985.

The Women's Legal Education and Action Fund (LEAF) promotes equality for Canadian women through legal action and public education. The New Brunswick Branch of LEAF organizes fundraising campaigns, membership drives, and public lectures.

LOCATION OF RECORDS: Women's Legal Education and Action Fund. New Brunswick Branch. [*Mailing Address:* P.O. Box 1413, Station A, Fredericton, N.B. E3B 5B3.]

RECORDS: Correspondence, financial records, membership lists, 1985-1991; grant applications, 1988; mailing lists, flyers, 1991; posters, 1985-1989; banners, 1987; minutes, photographs.

AMOUNT: 3 boxes.

CONDITION: Good.

PRINCE EDWARD ISLAND / ÎLE-DU-PRINCE-ÉDOUARD

1302. Canadian Abortion Rights Action League. Prince Edward Island Chapter

✣ Charlottetown, P.E.I. Formed 1984.

Through lobbying, referral, and public education, the P.E.I. chapter of the Canadian Abortion Rights Action League (CARAL) works toward full access to safe, legal abortions in the province.

LOCATION OF RECORDS: Canadian Abortion Rights Action League. Prince Edward Island Chapter. [*Address:* 81 Prince St., Charlottetown, P.E.I. C1A 4R3. *Telephone:* (902) 368-7337.]

RECORDS: Correspondence, membership lists, reports, pamphlets, newsletters, 1984-1991; financial records, briefs, buttons, T-shirts, clippings.

AMOUNT: 3 boxes

CONDITION: Fair.

ACCESS: Permission required.

1303. Canadian Federation of University Women. Charlottetown Branch

[See also entry # 653 (in Part I), which lists other records of this organization.]

✣ Charlottetown, P.E.I. Formed 1955.

The Charlottetown branch of the Canadian Federation of University Women (CFUW) encourages advanced study and research by women and works to improve the status of women. It holds guest lectures and raises funds for scholarships for female students.

LOCATION OF RECORDS: Canadian Federation of University Women. Charlottetown Branch. [*Address:* c/o 30 Oak Dr., Charlottetown, P.E.I. C1A 6T5. *Telephone:* (902) 892-5637.]

RECORDS: Constitution, minutes, correspondence, financial records, membership lists, mailing lists, petitions, scrapbooks, reports, briefs, conference proceedings, pamphlets, banners, books, clippings, photographs, 1985-1991.

CONDITION: Good.

ACCESS: Permission required. All files currently closed.

1304. Canadian Research Institute for the Advancement of Women / Institut canadien de recherches sur les femmes. 1990 Publications Committee

✣ Warren Grove, P.E.I. Formed 1989.

The institute is also known as CRIAW/ICREF. The Conference '90 Committee was formed to organize CRIAW/ICREF's 1990 conference in Charlottetown. The committee was re-formed as the 1990 Publications Committee in order to publish the conference's proceedings.

LOCATION OF RECORDS: Canadian Research Institute for the Advancement of Women/Institut canadien de recherches sur les femmes. 1990 Publications Committee. [*Address:* c/o Houston Stewart, Warren Grove, P.E.I. C0A 1H0. *Telephone:* (902) 628-1438.]

RECORDS: Minutes, grant applications, 1989-1990; correspondence, financial records, membership lists, mailing lists, 1989-1991; scrapbooks, conference proceedings, pamphlets, flyers, press releases, posters, books, clippings, sound recordings, videotapes, 1990.

AMOUNT: 2 boxes.

CONDITION: Good.

1305. Centre d'aide aux victimes de viol et d'agression sexuelle de l'Î.P.É. / P.E.I. Rape and Sexual Assault Crisis Centre

[For English entry, see # 1309.]

✣ Charlottetown (Î.-P.-É.). Groupe fondé 1981.

Le Centre offre un soutien moral et des renseignements aux victimes d'agression et de harcèlement sexuel, et s'occupe également de sensibilisation du public.

LIEU DE CONSULTATION: Centre d'aide aux victimes de viol et d'agression sexuelle de l'Î.P.É. [*Adresse postale:* C.P. 1522, Charlottetown (Î.-P.-É.) C1A 7N3. *Téléphone:* (902) 566-1864.]

MATÉRIEL: Statuts et règlements, 1983; procès-verbaux, correspondance, journaux de bord, documents financiers, demandes de subvention, dossiers concernant la clientèle, listes de membres, listes d'envoi, rapports, 1982-1991; bannières, 1991; mémoires, actes de congrès, dépliants, communiqués de presse, affiches, coupures de presse.

QUANTITÉ: Env. 3 classeurs.
ÉTAT: Bon.
ACCÈS: Tous les documents sont confidentiels.

1306. Charlottetown Business and Professional Women's Club

[See also entry # 654 (in Part I), which lists other records of this organization.]

✣ Charlottetown, P.E.I. Formed 1949.

The Charlottetown Business and Professional Women's Club works for improvement in the status of women in Canada and around the world. The club's activities include fund raising and networking.

LOCATION OF RECORDS: Charlottetown Business and Professional Women's Club. [*Address:* 39 Rochford Sq., Charlottetown, P.E.I. C1A 1P9.]

RECORDS: Minutes, correspondence, membership lists, mailing lists, scrapbooks.

CONDITION: Good.

ACCESS: Permission required.

1307. East Prince Women's Information Committee

✣ Summerside, P.E.I. Formed 1984.

The East Prince Women's Information Committee (EPWIC), which operates a resource centre and other programmes for women, is committed to improving the status of women and encouraging women's full and equal participation in all areas of life. It was called the East Prince Women's Information Centre until 1990.

LOCATION OF RECORDS: East Prince Women's Information Committee. [*Address:* 218 First St., Summerside, P.E.I. C1N 5E6. *Telephone:* (902) 436-9856.]

RECORDS: Minutes, correspondence, financial records, scrapbooks, reports, newsletters, clippings, photographs, 1984-1991; grant applications, membership lists, mailing lists, press releases.

AMOUNT: 2 filing cabinets

CONDITION: Good.

1308. Prince Edward Island New Democratic Party. Standing Committee on Women

✣ Charlottetown, P.E.I. Formed 1991.

This committee promotes the equal representation of women at all levels of the P.E.I. New Democratic Party, makes recommendations regarding the party's policies and programmes, and works to advance the equality of women in P.E.I. generally. The committee was originally called the Advisory Committee on Women's Issues.

LOCATION OF RECORDS: Prince Edward Island New Democratic Party. Standing Committee on Women. [*Address:* c/o 302 Fitzroy St., Charlottetown, P.E.I. C1A 1T1. *Telephone:* (902) 566-5750 or 368-3125. *Fax:* (902) 566-4473.]

RECORDS: Minutes, correspondence, membership lists, 1991.

AMOUNT: 1 file.

CONDITION: Good.

1309. P.E.I. Rape and Sexual Assault Crisis Centre / Centre d'aide aux victimes de viol et d'agression sexuelle de l'Î.-P.-É.

[Renseignements en français, notice 1305.]

✣ Charlottetown, P.E.I. Formed 1981.

The P.E.I. Rape and Sexual Assault Crisis Centre (PEIR/SACC) provides support and information to victims of sexual assault and harassment and does public education.

LOCATION OF RECORDS: P.E.I. Rape and Sexual Assault Crisis Centre. [*Mailing Address:* Box 1522, Charlottetown, P.E.I. C1A 7N3. *Telephone:* (902) 566-1864.]

RECORDS: Constitution, 1983; minutes, correspondence, log-books, financial records, grant applications, client records, membership lists, mailing lists, reports, 1982-1991; banners, 1991; briefs, conference proceedings, pamphlets, press releases, posters, clippings.

AMOUNT: Approx. 3 cabinets.

CONDITION: Good.

ACCESS: All records closed.

1310. Ragweed Press

✣ Charlottetown, P.E.I. Formed 1980.

Ragweed Press publishes children's books, poetry, books of regional interest, and fiction. Ragweed's lesbian-feminist imprint, gynergy books, publishes fiction, poetry, and books about political and social issues.

LOCATION OF RECORDS: Ragweed Press. [*Mailing Address:* P.O. Box 2023, Charlottetown, P.E.I. C1A 7N7. *Telephone:* (902) 566-5750. *Fax:* (902) 566-4473.]

RECORDS: Correspondence, financial records, grant applications, mailing lists, reports, briefs, conference proceedings, pamphlets, flyers, 1980-1990.

CONDITION: Good.

ACCESS: Permission required.

1311. Services for Adult Survivors of Sexual Abuse and Sexual Assault

✣ Charlottetown, P.E.I. Formed 1988.

Services for Adult Survivors of Sexual Abuse and Sexual Assault (SAS) provides a safe and supportive healing environment for women facing the pain of childhood sexual abuse. Services include health maintenance, support groups, and individual counselling. The organization's acronym used to be SASSA.

LOCATION OF RECORDS: Services for Adult Survivors of Sexual Abuse and Sexual Assault. [*Address:* 81 Prince St., Charlottetown, P.E.I. C1A 4R3. *Telephone:* (902) 368-7337. *Fax:* (902) 368-7180.]

RECORDS: Constitution, membership lists, mailing lists, reports, conference proceedings, press releases, 1989; minutes, correspondence, grant applications, briefs, 1989-1991; financial records, clippings, 1990-1991; pamphlets, 1990; videotapes, 1991.

AMOUNT: 1 filing cabinet.

CONDITION: Good.

ACCESS: Permission required.

1312. Transition House Association (Charlottetown, P.E.I.)

✣ Charlottetown, P.E.I. Formed 1981.

This association provides emergency accommodation to physically or emotionally abused women and their children (through its shelter, Anderson House) and works toward the elimination of violence against women and children.

LOCATION OF RECORDS: Transition House Association. [*Address:* 81 Prince St., Charlottetown, P.E.I. C1A 4R3. *Telephone:* (902) 894-3354.]

RECORDS: Minutes, financial records, grant applications, briefs, 1985-1991; client records, 1981-1991; membership lists, mailing lists, conference proceedings, 1991; reports, 1983-1991; pamphlets, 1990-1991; posters, 1990; buttons, books, 1985; newsletters, 1984.

AMOUNT: 3 filing cabinets.

CONDITION: Good.

ACCESS: Permission required. Client files closed.

1313. Women's Network (Charlottetown, P.E.I.)

✣ Charlottetown, P.E.I. Formed 1981.

The Women's Network promotes equality for women and publishes a feminist magazine, *Common Ground*. The organization was called the P.E.I. Women's Network Committee until 1984.

LOCATION OF RECORDS: Women's Network. [*Mailing Address:* Box 233, Charlottetown, P.E.I. C1A 7K4. *Telephone:* (902) 368-5040.]

RECORDS: Minutes, correspondence, financial records, grant applications, 1981-1991; log-books, 1990-1991; membership lists, mailing lists, scrapbooks, clippings, 1984-1991; press releases, 1986-1991; periodicals (*Common Ground*, 1982-1991); videotapes, 1986, 1988, 1990-1991; constitution, reports, briefs, photographs.

AMOUNT: Approx. 2 drawers of a filing cabinet, 2 boxes.

CONDITION: Good.

NOVA SCOTIA / NOUVELLE-ÉCOSSE

1314. Acadia University. Presidential Advisory Committee on the Status of Women

✤ Wolfville, N.S. Formed 1979.

This committee advises the university's president and board of governors on issues relating to women on campus, and it enables women to express their concerns and have them brought before the appropriate administrative personnel.

LOCATION OF RECORDS: Acadia University. Presidential Advisory Committee on the Status of Women. [*Address:* Wolfville, N.S. B0P 1X0. *Telephone:* (902) 542-2201.]
RECORDS: Minutes, correspondence, membership lists, reports, pamphlets.
AMOUNT: Approx. 1 box.
CONDITION: Good.
ACCESS: Permission required.

1315. Antigonish Women's Association

✤ Antigonish, N.S. Formed 1983.

The Antigonish Women's Association (AWA) operates the Antigonish Women's Resource Centre (AWRC), sponsors programmes of interest to women, and promotes public awareness of women's issues.

LOCATION OF RECORDS: Antigonish Women's Association. [*Address:* 219 Main St., Suite 204 B, Antigonish, N.S. B2G 2C1. *Telephone:* (902) 863-6221.]
RECORDS: By-laws, minutes, correspondence, log-books, financial records, grant applications, membership lists, scrapbooks, reports, briefs, conference proceedings, pamphlets, flyers, press releases, posters, T-shirts, banners, books, clippings, photographs, 1983-1991; newsletters (*AWAre*, 1983-1991).
AMOUNT: 3 filing cabinets.
CONDITION: Good.
ACCESS: Permission required. Log-books closed.

1316. Association des Acadiennes de la Nouvelle-Écosse

[Voir aussi la notice 657 (dans la partie I) pour autres documents de ce groupe.]

✤ Halifax (N.-É.). Groupe fondé 1984.

L'Association des Acadiennes de la Nouvelle-Écosse (AANE) vise à regrouper les femmes acadiennes de la Nouvelle-Écosse afin de travailler à leur plein épanouissement. Elle fonctionne au sein de la Fédération acadienne de la Nouvelle-Écosse (FANE), un groupe de pression et de développement communautaire. [Voir aussi Société Madeleine LeBlanc (1341).]

LIEU DE CONSULTATION : Association des Acadiennes de la Nouvelle-Écosse. [*Adresse* : 1106, rue South Park, Halifax (N.-E.) B3H 2W7. *Téléphone* : (902) 421-1772. *Télécopieur* : (902) 422-3942.]
MATÉRIEL : Statuts et règlements, 1984, 1988-1991; procès-verbaux, correspondance, documents financiers, demandes de subvention, listes de membres, rapports, 1984-1991; albums de coupures, 1984-1990; bulletins, 1990-1991; étude, 1981; livres, 1988; mémoires, dépliants, communiqués de presse, macarons, bannières.
QUANTITÉ : 1 classeur, 1 bibliothèque.
ÉTAT : Bon.
ACCÈS : Permission requise.

1317. Canadian Congress for Learning Opportunities for Women — Nova Scotia

✤ Dartmouth, N.S. Formed 1979.

Through research and public education, the Canadian Congress for Learning Opportunities for Women (CCLOW) — Nova Scotia addresses issues of education, training, and literacy from a feminist perspective.

LOCATION OF RECORDS: Canadian Congress for Learning Opportunities for Women — Nova Scotia. [*Address:* c/o L. Randolph, 3 Dillman Place, #127, Dartmouth, N.S. B3A 1A6.]
RECORDS: Minutes, grant applications, 1980-1991; financial records, reports, briefs, 1982-1991; conference proceedings, 1980, 1989; newsletters, 1987-1991; correspondence, mailing lists, press releases, miscellaneous records.
CONDITION: Good.
ACCESS: Permission required.

1318. Canadian Research Institute for the Advancement of Women — Nova Scotia

[See also entry # 661 (in Part I), which lists other records of this organization.]

✤ Halifax, N.S. Formed 1976.

This organization (also known as CRIAW — Nova Scotia) promotes the advancement of women through feminist and woman-centred research. It encourages information exchange among academic women, activists, women's groups, and concerned individuals and disseminates its research results through publications and conferences.

LOCATION OF RECORDS: Canadian Research Institute for the Advancement of Women — Nova Scotia. [*Mailing Address:* Box 8264, Station A, Halifax, N.S. B3K 5L9. *Telephone:* (902) 477-0094.]

RECORDS: Minutes, correspondence, financial records, grant applications, reports, 1987-1991; briefs, conference proceedings, pamphlets, flyers, press releases, banners, newsletters, 1986-1991, membership lists, mailing lists, photographs.

AMOUNT: 2 boxes.

CONDITION: Good.

ACCESS: Permission required. Access would depend on reason required.

1319. Chrysalis House

✣ Kentville, N.S. Formed 1981.

Chrysalis House, which was known as BEKA until 1989, provides shelter, support, and advocacy for abused women and their children and works toward the empowerment of all women.

LOCATION OF RECORDS: Chrysalis House. [*Mailing Address:* P.O. Box 356, Kentville, N.S. B4N 3X1. *Telephone:* (902) 582-7955.]

RECORDS: Constitution, minutes, correspondence, log-books, financial records, grant applications, client records, membership lists, mailing lists, scrapbooks, reports, briefs, conference proceedings, pamphlets, press releases, posters, buttons, T-shirts, banners, clippings, photographs, sound recordings.

AMOUNT: 3 filing cabinets, approx. 10 boxes.

CONDITION: Good.

ACCESS: Permission required. Some files closed.

1320. Committee against Woman Abuse (Mainland South)

✣ Halifax, N.S. Formed 1989.

This committee (also known as CAWA) does public education to address family violence and other issues of woman abuse in the Spryfield area of Halifax.

LOCATION OF RECORDS: Committee against Woman Abuse (Mainland South). [*Address:* c/o Captain William Spry Community Centre, 10 Kidston Rd., Halifax, N.S. B3R 2J7. *Telephone:* (902) 479-1111.]

RECORDS: Minutes, correspondence, 1989-1991; grant applications, membership lists, 1990-1991; reports, 1991; pamphlets, 1990.

AMOUNT: 3 files.

CONDITION: Good.

ACCESS: Permission required.

1321. Cumberland County Family Planning

✣ Amherst, N.S. Formed 1981.

Cumberland County Family Planning (CCFP) disseminates information about sexuality and birth control, in order to encourage informed, responsible attitudes toward healthy sexuality.

LOCATION OF RECORDS: Cumberland County Family Planning. [*Mailing Address:* Box 661, Amherst, N.S. B4H 4B8. *Telephone:* (902) 667-7500.]

RECORDS: Constitution, minutes, correspondence, grant applications, scrapbooks, press releases, newsletters, clippings, photographs, 1981-1991; membership lists, 1986-1991; pamphlets, 1985; posters, sound recordings, 1991; banners, 1989; videotapes, 1989, 1991.

AMOUNT: Approx. 3 filing cabinets.

ACCESS: Permission required. Access restrictions to be determined.

1322. Dalhousie University. Women's Studies Programme

✣ Halifax, N.S. Formed 1988.

The Women's Studies Programme at Dalhousie University offers a B.A. and sponsors seminars and other activities related to feminist research and activism.

LOCATION OF RECORDS: Dalhousie University. Women's Studies Programme. [*Address:* Multidisciplinary Centre, 1444 Seymour St., Halifax, N.S. B3H 3J5. *Telephone:* (902) 494-3814.]

RECORDS: Minutes, financial records, grant applications, membership lists, reports, 1988-1991; correspondence, pamphlets, 1985-1991; seminar records, flyers, course outlines, student records.

AMOUNT: 1 drawer of a filing cabinet.

CONDITION: Good.

ACCESS: Permission required. Student records closed.

1323. Elizabeth Fry Society of Cape Breton

✣ Sydney, N.S. Formed 1973 or 1974.

The Elizabeth Fry Society of Cape Breton works with women in the criminal justice system and women at risk of being in conflict with the law. It was originally called the Unison Society of Cape Breton.

LOCATION OF RECORDS: Elizabeth Fry Society of Cape Breton. [*Address:* 106 Townsend St., Sydney, N.S. B1P 5E1. *Telephone:* (902) 539-6165. *Fax:* (902) 539-1992.]

RECORDS: Minutes, correspondence, financial records, membership lists, reports, pamphlets, 1974-1991; grant applications, 1978-1991; client records, 1986-1991; mailing lists, 1988-1991; flyers, T-shirts, 1990-1991; press releases, 1978-1991.

AMOUNT: 2 filing cabinets.

CONDITION: Good.

ACCESS: Permission required. Client and personnel files closed.

1324. Elizabeth Fry Society of Halifax / Dartmouth

✣ Halifax, N.S. Formed 1982.

This organization works with and for women in conflict with the law. Most of its work is done in the areas of community development and advocacy.

LOCATION OF RECORDS: Elizabeth Fry Society of Halifax/Dartmouth. [*Address:* 2850 Agricola St., Suite 100, Halifax, N.S. B3K 4E4. *Telephone:* (902) 454-5041.]

RECORDS: Constitution, 1990; minutes, financial records, grant applications, 1982-1991; correspondence, membership lists, 1985-1991; client records, reports, 1989-1991; briefs, conference proceedings, 1983-1991; newsletters (*Between the Issues*, 1988-1990; *Inside Out*, 1991); mailing lists, scrapbooks, pamphlets, flyers, press releases, posters, buttons, T-shirts, books, clippings, photographs.

CONDITION: Good.

ACCESS: Permission required. Client files and some correspondence restricted.

1325. Halifax City Regional Library. North Branch Library. Women's Group

✣ Halifax, N.S. Formed [between 1976 and 1979].

The North Branch Library Women's Group, which has also been called the Ward Three Women's Group, provides opportunities for women in the North Branch community to discuss local issues of concern to women and identify relevant information and resources.

LOCATION OF RECORDS: Halifax City Regional Library. North Branch Library. Women's Group. [*Address:* 5381 Spring Garden Rd., Halifax, N.S. B3J 1E9. *Telephone:* (902) 421-7673.]
RECORDS: Guest book, 1989-1991; flyers, photographs.

1326. *Halifax Women's Housing Coop*

✣ Halifax, N.S. Formed 1982.

This organization provides women with affordable housing, security, and a sense of community.

LOCATION OF RECORDS: Halifax Women's Housing Coop. [*Address:* 2040 Creighton St., Halifax, N.S. B3K 3R2. *Telephone:* (902) 422-5987 or 425-1725.]
RECORDS: Constitution, minutes, correspondence, financial records, membership lists, 1982-1991.
AMOUNT: Approx. 2 drawers of a filing cabinet
CONDITION: Good.
ACCESS: Permission required.

1327. *Halifax Young Women's Christian Association*

[See also entry # 667 (in Part I), which lists other records of this organization.]

✣ Halifax, N.S. Formed 1874.

The mandate of the Halifax YWCA is to further the development of women and their families. It offers a residence, child care, employment training, adult education, and physical education. [See A Woman's Place (Halifax, N.S.) (677).]

LOCATION OF RECORDS: Halifax Young Women's Christian Association. [*Address:* 1239 Barrington St., Halifax, N.S. B3J 1Y3. *Telephone:* (902) 423-6162. *Fax:* (902) 423-7761.]
RECORDS: Minutes, 1961-1991; constitution, financial records, grant applications, client records, membership lists, mailing lists, scrapbooks, reports, pamphlets, flyers, T-shirts, newsletters (*Your News*), clippings, photographs, videotapes.
ACCESS: Permission required. Client files, membership and mailing lists, and payroll information closed.

1328. *Jezebel Productions*

✣ Halifax, N.S. Formed 1990.

Jezebel Productions promotes woman-positive performance and music by women.

LOCATION OF RECORDS: Jezebel Productions. [*Address:* 2358 Agricola St., Halifax, N.S. B3K 4B6. *Telephone:* (902) 492-3125.]
RECORDS: Press releases, posters, clippings, photographs, miscellaneous records, 1990-1991.
AMOUNT: Approx. 2 files.
CONDITION: Good.
ACCESS: Permission required.

1329. *Juniper House*

✣ Yarmouth, N.S. Formed 1985.

Juniper House, operated by the South West Nova Transition House Association, provides temporary shelter to abused women and their children in Digby, Yarmouth, and Shelbourne counties. It also provides a crisis line and counselling.

LOCATION OF RECORDS: Juniper House. [*Mailing Address:* Box 842, Yarmouth, N.S. B5A 4K5. *Telephone:* (902) 742-4473.]
RECORDS: Constitution, minutes, correspondence, log-books, financial records, grant applications, client records, membership lists, mailing lists, scrapbooks, reports, pamphlets, posters, clippings, photographs, sound recordings, videotapes, 1985-1991.
AMOUNT: 2 filing cabinets.
CONDITION: Good.
ACCESS: Permission required. All records revealing women's identities confidential.

1330. *Metro Area Family Planning Association*

✣ Halifax, N.S. Formed 1971.

The Metro Area Family Planning Association (MAFPA) offers clinical and educational services relating to birth control and sexuality. From 1977 to 1988 it was called the Planned Parenthood Association of Halifax, Dartmouth, and Halifax County (PPHDHC).

LOCATION OF RECORDS: Metro Area Family Planning Association. [*Address:* 5541 Russell St., Halifax, N.S. B3K 1X1. *Telephone:* (902) 455-9656.]
RECORDS: Constitution, 1971; minutes, financial records, 1970-1991; client records, 1974-1991; newsletters, 1971-1991; correspondence, grant applications, membership lists, mailing lists, pamphlets, press releases, posters.
AMOUNT: 15 filing cabinets, approx. 12 boxes.
CONDITION: Fair.
ACCESS: Permission required. Client files closed.

1331. *Mount Saint Vincent University*

[See also entry # 670 (in Part I), which lists other records of this organization.]

✣ Halifax, N.S. Formed 1873.

Mount Saint Vincent University's primary concern has been the education of women. It began as an academy established by the Sisters of Charity. In 1925 it gained the right to grant its own degrees, making it the only independent women's college in the British Commonwealth. In 1966, Mount Saint Vincent College became Mount Saint Vincent University. Male students have been admitted since 1967, but about 85 per cent of the students are women. The Institute for the Study of Women (ISW) at Mount Saint Vincent University was established in 1981 to do research which aims to improve women's lives and promote equality for women. ISW publishes the journal *Atlantis*.

LOCATION OF RECORDS: Mount Saint Vincent University. Institute for the Study of Women. [*Address:* Halifax, N.S. B3M 2J6. *Telephone:* (902) 443-4450, ext. 568. *Fax:* (902) 443-1352.]
RECORDS: Records of the Institute for the Study of Women (terms of reference, 1981; correspondence, financial records, grant applications, client records, mailing lists, reports, briefs, conference proceedings, pamphlets, 1984-1991; periodicals [*Atlantis*, 1975-1991; *Bulletin*, 1990-1991; *Communiqué*, 1982-1987]).
CONDITION: Good.
ACCESS: Permission required. Files of some projects on women and children closed.

1332. *Naomi Society for Victims of Family Violence*

✣ Antigonish, N.S. Formed 1983.

This organization provides crisis intervention and ongoing support to victims of family violence and promotes public awareness of the issue. It was originally called the Naomi Society for Battered Women.

LOCATION OF RECORDS: Naomi Society for Victims of Family Violence. [*Address:* 220 Main St., #201, Antigonish, N.S. B2G 2C2. *Telephone:* (902) 863-3807/2852.]

RECORDS: Constitution, 1983; minutes, correspondence, log-books, financial records, grant applications, client records, scrapbooks, reports, clippings, photographs, 1984-1991; mailing lists, 1989-1991; conference proceedings, 1988-1989; pamphlets, posters, newsletters, 1984-1985; bookmarks, 1991; membership lists.

AMOUNT: 5 filing cabinets.

CONDITION: Good.

ACCESS: Permission required. Client files, personnel files, and files of executive and personnel committees closed.

1333. Nova Scotia Women Artists' Network

✣ Halifax, N.S. Formed 1989.

Through workshops and discussion groups, the Nova Scotia Women Artists' Network (NSWAN) enables women artists to exchange ideas and information about current art practice and criticism, creative history, and issues of representation.

LOCATION OF RECORDS: Nova Scotia Women Artists' Network. [*Address:* 2182 Gottingen St., Halifax, N.S. B3K 3B4. *Telephone:* (902) 425-6412.]

RECORDS: Constitution, membership lists, mailing lists, 1989; minutes, correspondence, financial records, grant applications, 1989-1991; reports, flyers, press releases, posters, 1990-1991; conference proceedings, photographs, sound recordings, 1990.

AMOUNT: 2 files.

CONDITION: Good.

ACCESS: Permission required.

1334. Pandora Publishing

✣ Halifax, N.S. Formed 1985.

This organization publishes the feminist newspaper *Pandora*.

LOCATION OF RECORDS: Pandora Publishing. [*Mailing Address:* Box 1209 North, Halifax, N.S. B3K 5H4. *Telephone:* (902) 454-4977.]

RECORDS: Minutes, 1985-1989; financial records, 1985-1991; T-shirts, 1989; newspapers (*Pandora*, 1985-1991); grant applications, 1986-1988; guide, 1991; correspondence, mailing lists, clippings.

AMOUNT: 2 filing cabinets.

CONDITION: Good.

ACCESS: Permission required.

1335. Pictou County Women's Centre

✣ New Glasgow, N.S. Formed 1976.

The Pictou County Women's Centre (PCWC) provides information and services related to health, child care, violence against women, and other issues of concern to women.

LOCATION OF RECORDS: Pictou County Women's Centre. [*Mailing Address:* Box 964, New Glasgow, N.S. B2H 5K7. *Telephone:* (902) 755-4647.]

RECORDS: Minutes, clippings, 1976-1991; log-books, 1984-1991; financial records, 1980-1991; grant applications, membership lists, petitions, scrapbooks, reports, pamphlets, flyers, press releases, 1979-1991; newsletters, 1984-1985; photographs, 1983-1991; videotapes, 1980, 1990.

CONDITION: Good.

ACCESS: Permission required.

1336. Planned Parenthood Nova Scotia

✣ Halifax, N.S. Formed 1972.

Through education, advocacy, and an information and referral service, Planned Parenthood Nova Scotia (PPNS) encourages informed, responsible attitudes toward sexuality. Until 1974 it was called the Family Planning Association of Nova Scotia.

LOCATION OF RECORDS: Planned Parenthood Nova Scotia. [*Mailing Address:* P.O. Box 1206, Halifax North, Halifax, N.S. B3K 5H4. *Telephone:* (902) 492-0444.]

RECORDS: Minutes, correspondence, financial records, reports, 1974-1991; membership lists, posters, 1985; briefs, 1982; pamphlets, 1989; clippings, 1974; videotapes, 1986.

AMOUNT: Approx. 8 boxes.

CONDITION: Good.

ACCESS: Permission required.

1337. Public Service Alliance of Canada. Local 80384. Women's Committee

✣ Sydney, N.S. Formed [ca. 1987].

The Women's Committee of Local 80384 of the Public Service Alliance of Canada (PSAC) applies a feminist perspective to issues of concern to women. The committe has organized International Women's Day activities and worked for the development of an on-site child-care facility.

LOCATION OF RECORDS: Public Service Alliance of Canada. Local 80384. Women's Committee. [*Mailing Address:* P.O. Box 1736, Sydney, N.S. B1P 6T7. *Telephone:* (902) 564-7829.]

RECORDS: Minutes, correspondence, financial records, mailing lists, petitions, reports, briefs, posters, buttons, 1987-1991.

AMOUNT: 2 files.

CONDITION: Good.

ACCESS: Permission required.

1338. Second Story Women's Centre

✣ Bridgewater, N.S. Formed 1983.

The Second Story Women's Centre (SSWC) offers information, resources, referrals, and a drop-in space for women. The centre's goal is to raise awareness and support for women's issues.

LOCATION OF RECORDS: Second Story Women's Centre. [*Address:* 99 York St., Bridgewater, N.S. B4V 1R2. *Telephone:* (902) 543-1315.]

RECORDS: Constitution, minutes, correspondence, log-books, financial records, grant applications, membership lists, scrapbooks, reports, briefs, pamphlets, press releases, posters, buttons, T-shirts, banners, clippings, photographs, 1983-1991; newsletters (*Women's Share*, 1983-1991); manuals, 1989; handbooks, 1991.

AMOUNT: 1 filing cabinet.

CONDITION: Good.

ACCESS: Permission required. Log-books and confidential material closed.

1339. The Secret Furies

✣ Halifax, N.S. Formed 1990.

The Secret Furies (also called simply the Furies) is a women's chorus which performs songs of empowerment at marches, benefits, and other feminist events.

LOCATION OF RECORDS: The Secret Furies. [*Address:* 6575 Liverpool St., Halifax, N.S. B3L 1Y6. *Telephone:* (902) 454-6052.]

RECORDS: Constitution, 1991-1992; membership lists, photographs, 1990-1991; T-shirts, videotapes, 1990.
AMOUNT: Approx. 1 file.
CONDITION: Good.
ACCESS: Permission required.

1340. Single Parent Centre (Halifax, N.S.)

✣ Halifax, N.S. Formed 1980.

The Single Parent Centre offers prenatal classes, parenting programmes, advocacy, and other services to single-parent families. The centre is a service of the Home of the Guardian Angel.

LOCATION OF RECORDS: Single Parent Centre. [*Address:* c/o Home of the Guardian Angel, 3 Sylvia Ave., Halifax, N.S. B3R 1J7. *Telephone:* (902) 479-3031. *Fax:* (902) 479-0508.]
RECORDS: Constitution, financial records, grant applications, client records, mailing lists, reports, flyers, posters, 1980-1991; log-books, 1989-1991; minutes, correspondence, clippings, photographs.
AMOUNT: Approx. 1 drawer of a filing cabinet.
CONDITION: Good.
ACCESS: Permission required. Client records closed.

1341. Société Madeleine LeBlanc

✣ Saulnierville (N.-É.). Groupe fondé 1981.

Cette société se donne pour mission de regrouper, d'informer et de former les femmes acadiennes de sa région. La Société est marrainée par l'Association des Acadiennes de la Nouvelle-Écosse (AANE). [Voir aussi Association des Acadiennes de la Nouvelle-Écosse (657, 1316).]

LIEU DE CONSULTATION: Société Madeleine LeBlanc. [*Adresse :* Centre de la Baie, Saulnierville (N.-E.) B0W 2Z0. *Téléphone :* (902) 769-0955.]
MATÉRIEL: Procès-verbaux, correspondance, documents financiers, demandes de subvention, 1982-1991; listes de membres, rapports, mémoires, communiqués de presse, 1988-1991; albums de coupures, 1991; photographies, 1987-1991.
QUANTITÉ: 1 classeur.
ÉTAT: Bon.
ACCÈS: Permission requise.

1342. Soroptimist International of Halifax/Dartmouth

✣ Halifax, N.S. Formed 1938.

This organization of business and professional women supports various community projects, some of which cater specifically to women's needs (for instance, shelters and sexual assault centres).

LOCATION OF RECORDS: Soroptimist International of Halifax/Dartmouth. [*Address:* 5 Laurel Lane, Halifax, N.S. B3M 2P7. *Telephone:* (902) 443-1241.]
RECORDS: Constitution, minutes, correspondence, log-books, financial records, grant applications, membership lists, scrapbooks, reports, conference proceedings, pamphlets, buttons, banners, clippings, photographs, videotapes, 1989-1991.
AMOUNT: 1 filing cabinet.
CONDITION: Good.
ACCESS: Permission required.

1343. South Shore Transition House Association

✣ Bridgewater, N.S. Formed 1987.

This association operates a shelter called Harbour House and offers crisis intervention, support, resources, and information to abused women and their children.

LOCATION OF RECORDS: South Shore Transition House Association. [*Mailing Address:* P.O. Box 355, Bridgewater, N.S. B4V 2W9. *Telephone:* (902) 543-3665/3999.]
RECORDS: Constitution, minutes, 1985; correspondence, 1985-1991; log-books, financial records, grant applications, client records, membership lists, mailing lists, petitions, scrapbooks, reports, clippings, 1987-1991; pamphlets, 1986-1990; flyers, press releases, posters.
AMOUNT: 5 filing cabinets.
ACCESS: Permission required. Client records, logs, case conferences, financial records, and other records specified by the association are closed.

1344. Stepping Stone Program

✣ Halifax, N.S. Formed 1987.

The Stepping Stone Program is a grass-roots, user-directed street outreach programme for women, youth, and men who are involved in street prostitution or are at risk of becoming involved. Stepping Stone provides practical services such as AIDS education and "bad date" lists and speaks out on issues affecting street workers. Until 1991 the organization was called Stepping Stone Street Services for Women and Youth Association.

LOCATION OF RECORDS: Stepping Stone Program. [*Address:* 2224 Maitland St., Halifax, N.S. B4K 2Z9. *Telephone:* (902) 420-0103.]
RECORDS: Constitution, minutes, correspondence, financial records, grant applications, client records, reports, 1987-1991; pamphlets, 1990; T-shirts, clippings, 1991.
AMOUNT: Approx. 3 filing cabinets.
CONDITION: Good.
ACCESS: Permission required. Client files closed. Other records may be restricted.

1345. Transition House Association of Nova Scotia

✣ New Glasgow, N.S. Formed 1985.

The Transition House Association of Nova Scotia (THANS) co-ordinates and consolidates the efforts of transition houses and their clients throughout the province. It does lobbying at the provincial level and serves as a resource clearinghouse.

LOCATION OF RECORDS: Transition House Association of Nova Scotia. [*Mailing Address:* P.O. Box 423, New Glasgow, N.S. B2H 5E2. *Telephone:* (902) 755-4878.]
RECORDS: Constitution, 1985; minutes, correspondence, log-books, financial records, grant applications, mailing lists, scrapbooks, reports, briefs, press releases, 1985-1991.
AMOUNT: 6 filing-cabinet drawers, 2 boxes.
CONDITION: Good.
ACCESS: Permission required. Client files, mailing lists closed.

1346. Victims of Family Violence Association

✣ Truro, N.S. Formed 1983.

This association operates the Third Place, a transition house for abused women and their children. The association also offers counselling, advocacy, and referral.

LOCATION OF RECORDS: Victims of Family Violence Association. [*Mailing Address:* P.O. Box 1681, Truro, N.S. B2N 5Z5. *Telephone:* (902) 893-4844.]

RECORDS: Constitution, 1983; minutes, scrapbooks, reports, briefs, press releases, clippings, photographs, 1988-1991; correspondence, log-books, grant applications, client records, 1989-1991; financial records, 1985-1991; pamphlets, flyers.

AMOUNT: Approx. 1 filing cabinet.

CONDITION: Fair.

ACCESS: Permission required. Many records confidential. Client and personnel files closed.

1347. *Wild Womyn Don't Get the Blues*

✢ Scotsburn, N.S. Formed 1983.

Wild Womyn Don't Get the Blues (WWDGTB) organizes the annual Atlantic Women's Retreat, a four-day event sponsored by lesbians and open to all women.

LOCATION OF RECORDS: Wild Womyn Don't Get the Blues. [*Address:* R.R. 1, Scotsburn, N.S. B0K 1R0. *Telephone:* (902) 485-8202.]

RECORDS: Correspondence, financial records, flyers, T-shirts, 1984-1991; buttons, 1982; photographs, 1984-1990; membership lists, mailing lists.

CONDITION: Good.

ACCESS: Permission required.

1348. Women Aware

✢ Port Hawkesbury, N.S. Formed 1986.

Women Aware promotes the advancement of women through research and other educational projects.

LOCATION OF RECORDS: Women Aware. [*Mailing Address:* P.O. Box 101, Port Hawkesbury, N.S. B0E 2V0.]

RECORDS: Minutes, correspondence, log-books, financial records, grant applications, membership lists, mailing lists, scrapbooks, reports, pamphlets, press releases, clippings, 1986-1991.

AMOUNT: 1 chest of drawers.

CONDITION: Good.

ACCESS: Permission required.

1349. *Women's Action Coalition of Nova Scotia*

✢ Halifax, N.S. Formed 1987.

The Women's Action Coalition of Nova Scotia (WACNS), an umbrella organization of provincial women's groups, lobbies on behalf of women's concerns, mainly at the provincial level.

LOCATION OF RECORDS: Women's Action Coalition of Nova Scotia. [*Mailing Address:* P.O. Box 9436, Station A, Halifax, N.S. B3K 5S3.]

RECORDS: Constitution, minutes, financial records, membership lists, scrapbooks, briefs, press releases, clippings, 1987-1991; newsletters (*WAC Action*, 1990-1991); pamphlets, T-shirts, sweatshirts, banners.

AMOUNT: 2 drawers of a filing cabinet.

CONDITION: Good.

1350. *Women's Centres Connect!*

✢ Bridgewater, N.S. Formed 1988.

Also know simply as Connect!, this organization works to articulate a common vision of the concerns and needs of women's centres in Nova Scotia, enhance the credibility of women's centres, and provide a forum for information exchange and organizational development

LOCATION OF RECORDS: Women's Centres Connect!. [*Address:* 99 York St., Bridgewater, N.S. B4V 1R2. *Telephone:* (902) 543-2932. *Fax:* (902) 543-1985.]

RECORDS: Constitution, 1990; minutes, 1988-1990; correspondence, pamphlets, press releases, clippings, 1989-1991; log-books, financial records, grant applications, scrapbooks, reports, briefs, conference proceedings, flyers, 1990-1991.

AMOUNT: 2 drawers of a filing cabinet.

CONDITION: Good.

ACCESS: Permission required.

NEWFOUNDLAND AND LABRADOR / TERRE-NEUVE ET LABRADOR

1351. 52% Solution: Women for Equality, Justice, and Peace
✣ St John's, Nfld. Formed 1986.

The 52% Solution provides a forum for women to exchange ideas and empower one another. It aims to spread the spirit of feminism and encourage women to work for change.

LOCATION OF RECORDS: 52% Solution: Women for Equality, Justice, and Peace. [*Address:* 6 Duckworth St., St John's, Nfld. A1C 1E4. *Telephone:* (709) 579-4246.]

RECORDS: Minutes, clippings, photographs, 1986-1987; correspondence, 1986-1991; conference proceedings, videotape, 1987; financial records, grant applications, buttons, T-shirts.

CONDITION: Good.

ACCESS: Permission required.

1352. Bay St George Status of Women Council
✣ Stephenville, Nfld. Formed 1985.

Also known as the Bay St George Women's Council, this organization operates the Bay St George (BSG) Women's Centre and other services by and for women. The council is committed to the improvement of women's social, economic, and political condition.

LOCATION OF RECORDS: Bay St George Status of Women Council. [*Mailing Address:* P.O. Box 501, Stephenville, Nfld. A2N 3B4. *Telephone:* (709) 643-4444.]

RECORDS: Constitution, briefs, 1987-1991; minutes, financial records, scrapbooks, reports, pamphlets, flyers, press releases, posters, newsletters, 1985-1991; correspondence, grant applications, membership lists, mailing lists, 1986-1991; conference proceedings, 1989; T-shirts, banners, clippings, photographs, videotapes.

AMOUNT: 2 filing cabinets.

CONDITION: Fair.

ACCESS: Permission required. Client files closed.

1353. Canadian Abortion Rights Action League, St John's
✣ St John's, Nfld.

The St John's chapter of the Canadian Abortion Rights Action League (CARAL) lobbies governments to provide all Canadian women with access to safe abortions.

LOCATION OF RECORDS: Canadian Abortion Rights Action League, St John's. [*Mailing Address:* P.O. Box 6072, St John's, Nfld. A1C 5X8. *Telephone:* (709) 737-4405. *Fax:* (709) 737-4000.]

RECORDS: Financial records, 1984, 1989-1991; membership lists, mailing lists, 1975-1991; petitions, [198-]-1991; reports, flyers, press releases, 1989-1991; banners, 1990; clippings, photographs, videotapes, 1989-1990.

AMOUNT: 2 drawers of a filing cabinet.

CONDITION: Good.

ACCESS: Permission required.

1354. Canadian Research Institute for the Advancement of Women, Newfoundland and Labrador
✣ St John's, Nfld.

This organization, also known as CRIAW Newfoundland, encourages women-centred research, supports community-based researchers, and provides a network for women researchers.

LOCATION OF RECORDS: Canadian Research Institute for the Advancement of Women, Newfoundland and Labrador. [*Address:* 131 LeMarchant Rd., St John's, Nfld. A1C 2H3. *Telephone:* (709) 753-7270.]

RECORDS: Minutes, correspondence, financial records, grant applications, membership lists, reports, briefs, 1987-1991.

AMOUNT: 1 drawer of a filing cabinet, 2 boxes.

CONDITION: Good.

ACCESS: Permission of current local membership required.

1355. Committee on Family Violence
✣ Corner Brook, Nfld. Formed 1980.

This committee offers a transition house for abused women and their children, support groups for survivors of family violence, and educational forums.

LOCATION OF RECORDS: Committee on Family Violence. [*Mailing Address:* P.O. Box 152, Corner Brook, Nfld. A2H 6C9. *Telephone:* (709) 634-8815.]

RECORDS: Constitution, minutes, correspondence, grant applications, membership lists, press releases, clippings, 1980-1991; log-books, client records, mailing lists, scrapbooks, reports, pamphlets, 1983-1991; financial records, 1981-1991; posters, T-shirts, banners, 1989-1991; photographs.

AMOUNT: Approx. 6 filing cabinets.

CONDITION: Good.
ACCESS: Permission required. Client files closed.

1356. Corner Brook Status of Women Council
✤ Corner Brook, Nfld. Formed 1973.

The Corner Brook Status of Women Council oversees the Women's Centre and other projects designed to improve the status of women.

LOCATION OF RECORDS: Corner Brook Status of Women Council. [*Mailing Address*: P.O. Box 373, Corner Brook, Nfld. A2H 6E3. *Telephone*: (709) 639-8522.]

RECORDS: Constitution, minutes, correspondence, financial records, grant applications, membership lists, mailing lists, scrapbooks, reports, briefs, press releases, T-shirts, banners, newsletters (*Women's Forum*), clippings, photographs, 1975-1991.

AMOUNT: Approx. 1 filing cabinet, approx. 21 boxes.
ACCESS: Permission required. Client files and certain current files closed.

1357. Gander Status of Women Council
✤ Gander, Nfld. Formed [1984?].

The Gander Status of Women Council operates the Gander Women's Centre and other services and activities designed to improve the quality of life for women in central Newfoundland.

LOCATION OF RECORDS: Gander Status of Women Council. [*Mailing Address*: P.O. Box 246, Gander, Nfld. A1V 1W6. *Telephone*: (709) 256-4395.]

RECORDS: Constitution, minutes, correspondence, financial records, grant applications, membership lists, reports, press releases, 1984-1991; pamphlets, 1987-1991; buttons, 1991; banners, videotapes, 1986; photographs, 1986-1988; clippings.

AMOUNT: 3 filing cabinets.
CONDITION: Good.
ACCESS: Permission required.

1358. Gateway Status of Women Council
✤ Port aux Basques, Nfld. Formed 1982.

The Gateway Status of Women Council, which operates the Gateway Women's Centre, is committed to improving the status of women.

LOCATION OF RECORDS: Gateway Status of Women Council. [*Mailing Address*: Box 1359, Port aux Basques, Nfld. A0M 1C0. *Telephone*: (709) 695-7505. *Fax*: (709) 695-9691.]

RECORDS: Constitution, minutes, correspondence, log-books, financial records, grant applications, client records, membership lists, mailing lists, petitions, scrapbooks, reports, briefs, conference proceedings, pamphlets, flyers, press releases, posters, buttons, T-shirts, banners, books, clippings, photographs, videotapes, 1982-1991.

AMOUNT: Approx. 3 filing cabinets.
CONDITION: Good.
ACCESS: Permission required.

1359. Labrador West Family Crisis Shelter
✤ Labrador City, Labrador. Formed 1984.

The Labrador West Family Crisis Shelter provides safe refuge, supportive counselling, transportation, referral services, and advocacy to battered women and their children.

LOCATION OF RECORDS: Labrador West Family Crisis Shelter. [*Mailing Address*: P.O. Box 106, Labrador City, Labrador A2V 2K3. *Telephone*: (709) 944-3600.]

RECORDS: Constitution, minutes, correspondence, log-books, financial records, grant applications, client records, scrapbooks, reports, briefs, posters.

CONDITION: Good.
ACCESS: Permission required. Client files, log-books, and some correspondence closed.

1360. Labrador West Status of Women Council
✤ Labrador City, Labrador. Formed 1977.

This council works to end discrimination against women and promote equality of law and opportunity. It operates the Women's Resource and Information Centre (called simply the Women's Centre until 1990).

LOCATION OF RECORDS: Labrador West Status of Women Council. [*Mailing Address*: P.O. Box 171, Labrador City, Labrador A2V 2K5. *Telephone*: (709) 944-6562. *Fax*: (709) 944-8442.]

RECORDS: Constitution, books, 1977; minutes, correspondence, 1977-1991; log-books, newsletters, 1983-1991; financial records, 1980-1991; membership lists, 1982-1991; mailing lists, reports, 1985-1991; scrapbooks, 1979-1991; clippings, [198-]; photographs, [198-]-[199-]; briefs, conference proceedings, pamphlets, press releases.

AMOUNT: 4 filing cabinets.
CONDITION: Good.
ACCESS: Permission required.

1361. Libra House
✤ Happy Valley, Labrador. Formed 1985.

Libra House offers emergency shelter, counselling, and referrals to abused women and their children.

LOCATION OF RECORDS: Libra House. [*Mailing Address*: P.O. Box 449, Happy Valley, Labrador A0P 1E0. *Telephone*: (709) 896-8251.]

RECORDS: Constitution, 1985; minutes, correspondence, log-books, financial records, client records, reports, 1985-1991; grant applications, 1987, 1989.

AMOUNT: Approx. 2 filing cabinets, 1 closet.
CONDITION: Good.
ACCESS: All records closed due to confidential material.

1362. Memorial University of Newfoundland. Women's Studies Programme
✤ St John's, Nfld. Formed 1983.

The Women's Studies Programme offers courses which enable students to examine the contributions of women to society, past and present. The programme also conducts research about women and provides information to the community.

LOCATION OF RECORDS: Memorial University of Newfoundland. Women's Studies Programme. [*Address*: St John's, Nfld. A1C 5S7. *Telephone*: (709) 737-4539. *Fax*: (709) 737-4569.]

RECORDS: Minutes, correspondence, membership lists, mailing lists, scrapbooks, reports, 1983-1991; client records, 1991; financial records, grant applications, briefs, pamphlets, flyers, posters, clippings, course outlines.

AMOUNT: 2 filing cabinets.
CONDITION: Good.

St. John's, Nfld.,
December 1, 1972.

It is good that your magazine is prepared to give publicity to the women's movement in Canada as it is so essential that as many people as possible know about the many aspects of the women's movement which are now being looked at critically.

With regard to your request for a photograph of myself, I'm afraid I will have to be unco-operative. First of all, I really don't consider my role in the women's movement to be of sufficient significance, but more important, the Nfld. Status of Women Council have discussed this area of publicity and came to the conclusion that we wanted and needed as much publicity as possible about the movement but as little as possible about any one individual. As you know, the women's movement represents a wide range of interests from the radical group to conservative groups interested in perhaps only one small area of the women's movement and it is for this reason that we do not want the movement to become identified with a few names. It is our sincere wish to attract as many women as possible to the movement as we feel each and every woman has something to gain.

I am sorry that I feel unable to co-operate with you at this time and can only hope that you will understand and be sympathetic.

Excerpt from a 1972 letter written by a representative of the Newfoundland Status of Women Council to a magazine which was preparing an article on the women's movement /
Extrait d'une lettre écrite en 1972 par une représentante du Newfoundland Status of Women Council à un périodique qui préparait un article sur le mouvement des femmes
CWMA Collection / Fonds de l'ACMF

ACCESS: Permission required. Student transcripts, student papers, recent exams, and personnel records closed.

1363. National Association of Women and the Law. Newfoundland and Labrador Caucus

✣ St John's, Nfld. Formed [1980?].

The Newfoundland and Labrador Caucus of the National Association of Women and the Law (NAWL) promotes women's equality through public education, lobbying, consciousness raising, and networking with other women's groups.

LOCATION OF RECORDS: National Association of Women and the Law. Newfoundland and Labrador Caucus. [*Address:* 744 Water St., St John's, Nfld. A1E 1C2. *Fax:* (709) 754-0915.]

RECORDS: Minutes, membership lists, reports, 1991; correspondence, 1990-1991; financial records, grant applications.

AMOUNT: Approx. 2 files.

CONDITION: Good.

ACCESS: Permission required.

1364. St John's Status of Women Council

[See also entry # 689 (in Part I), which lists other records of this organization.]

✣ St John's, Nfld. Formed 1972.

The St John's Status of Women Council (SJSWC) was originally called the Newfoundland Status of Women Council (NSWC). It was established to improve the status of women and promote the recommendations of the Royal Commission on the Status of Women. SJSWC sponsors the Women's Centre. It also sponsors Iris Kirby House, a battered women's shelter providing crisis intervention, counselling, advocacy, and referral. Iris Kirby House was founded in 1981; until 1983 it was called Transition House. SJSWC co-sponsored the Women's Health Education Project of Newfoundland and Labrador, which operated from 1981 to 1984.

LOCATION OF RECORDS: Iris Kirby House. [*Mailing Address:* P.O. Box 6208, St John's, Nfld. A1C 6J9. *Telephone:* (709) 722-8272. *Fax:* (709) 722-0164.]

RECORDS: Records of Iris Kirby House (constitution, 1981; minutes, logbooks, financial records, 1981-1991; grant applications, client records, posters, buttons, T-shirts, clippings).

AMOUNT: 7 filing cabinets.

CONDITION: Good.

ACCESS: Permission required. Client files closed.

1365. Women and History Group

✣ St John's, Nfld. Formed 1987.

The Women and History Group was formed to produce published material on Newfoundland women's history which would be accessible to general readers, teachers, and university and college students. It was originally called the Ad Hoc Committee on Women's History in Newfoundland and Labrador.

LOCATION OF RECORDS: Women and History Group. [*Address:* c/o L. Kealey, Dept. of History, Memorial University of Newfoundland, St John's, Nfld. A1C 5S7. *Telephone:* (709) 737-8442. *Fax:* (709) 737-4569.]

RECORDS: Minutes, correspondence, 1987-1991; grant applications, 1990-1991; financial records, drafts of articles, research materials.

AMOUNT: Half a drawer of a filing cabinet, approx. 3 boxes.

CONDITION: Good.

1366. Women Interested in Successful Employment

✣ St John's, Nfld. Formed 1987.

Women Interested in Successful Employment (WISE) is a career-exploration programme for women. It encourages skill development, goal setting, problem solving, and decision making.

LOCATION OF RECORDS: Women Interested in Successful Employment. [*Address:* 50 Parade St., St John's, Nfld. A1C 4C7. *Telephone:* (709) 739-1374. *Fax:* (709) 739-6506.]

RECORDS: Minutes, correspondence, financial records, grant applications, mailing lists, 1987-1991; client records, reports, 1988-1991; flyers, 1988; clippings, photographs, 1988-1989; sound recordings, videotapes, 1989.

AMOUNT: 5 filing cabinets.

CONDITION: Good.

ACCESS: Permission required. Client files closed.

1367. Women's Enterprise Bureau

✣ St John's, Nfld. Formed 1990.

The Women's Enterprise Bureau (WEB) promotes women's entrepreneurship and business development in Newfoundland and Labrador. WEB's seven branches offer business counselling, information, referral, training, and research.

LOCATION OF RECORDS: Women's Enterprise Bureau. [*Address:* 85 Water St., St John's, Nfld. A1C 1A5. *Telephone:* (709) 754-5555. *Fax:* (709) 754-0079.]

RECORDS: Minutes, correspondence, financial records, grant applications, client records, membership lists, mailing lists, reports, briefs, conference proceedings, pamphlets, flyers, press releases, posters, T-shirts, banners, clippings, photographs, sound recordings, videotapes, 1990-1991.

AMOUNT: 4 filing cabinets.

CONDITION: Good.

ACCESS: Permission required. Client files closed.

1368. Women's Involvement (Green's Harbour, Nfld.)

✣ Green's Harbour, Nfld. Formed 1982.

Women's Involvement offers women a meeting place and assistance of various forms. Its services include a small library, a thrift shop, and assistance to abused women.

LOCATION OF RECORDS: Women's Involvement. [*Mailing Address:* P.O. Box 163, Green's Harbour, Nfld. A0B 2A0. *Telephone:* (709) 582-3377.]

RECORDS: Constitution, 1984-1991; minutes, correspondence, financial records, grant applications, membership lists, mailing lists, scrapbooks, reports, briefs, press releases, books, clippings, photographs, videotapes, 1982-1991.

AMOUNT: 1 filing cabinet.

CONDITION: Good.

ACCESS: Permission required. Client files closed.

NAME INDEX/INDEX DES NOMS

Use this index to locate entries by:
- groups' names (including earlier and alternate forms)
- acronyms
- titles of periodicals or conferences

The numbers refer to individual entries, not pages.
(Names which are used as headings for entries appear in boldface.)

Cet index permet de retrouver les notices selon :
- noms des groupes (y compris les désignations antérieures ou autres formes des noms)
- sigles
- titres de périodiques ou de congrès

L'index renvoie à des numéros de notices et non à des numéros de pages.
(Les noms qui servent d'entête paraissent en caractères gras.)

❖ ❖ ❖

3 of Cups, 495
52% Solution: Women for Equality, Justice, and Peace, 1351
5ᵉ Monde, 1177
923-GAYS, 394
A Bunch of Feminists, 358
A Fine Kettle of Fish : Lesbians and Feminists in the Women's Movement (1979 : Toronto, Ont.), 424
A Friend Indeed Publications, 1209
À l'action, 44, 720
À propos, 591
A Room of One's Own (Victoria, B.C.), 166
A Woman's Place (Halifax, N.S.), 677
A Woman's Place (Montreal, Quebec), 635
A Woman's Place (Vancouver, B.C.), 168
A Woman's Place (Winnipeg, Man.), 333
A Women's Newsletter, 655
A Women's Place (Montreal, Quebec), 635
A Women's Press, 344
AAAC, 398
AAM, 875
AANE, 657, 1316
AANE. Société Madeleine LeBlanc, 1341
AASUA. Committee on Employment Conditions of Full Time Women Faculty, 223
ABC, 874
Aboriginal Women's Council of Saskatchewan, 918
Abortion Action, 431
Abortion and Contraception Committee of Toronto, 341
Abortion and Contraceptive Committee of Toronto, 341
Abortion by Choice Society of Alberta, 874
Abortion Caravan, 1
Abortion Cavalcade, 1
Abortion Coalition Committee, 304
About Us, 831
Academic Women's Association of the University of British Columbia, 151
Academic Women's Association (University of Alberta), 180
Acadia University. Presidential Advisory Committee on the Status of Women, 1314

ACAFS, 699
ACALA, 5
ACAP, 876
ACCT, 341
Accueil du sans-abri, 1119
Accueil Sainte-Famille, 1265
ACDA, 5
ACE, 398
ACMF, 3
ACO. Women's Project, 993
ACSEF, 697
ACT. Women and AIDS Project, 994
Action (Amalgamated Clothing and Textile Workers Union/Travailleurs amalgamés du vêtement et du textile), 2, 695
Action (Canadian Association for the Advancement of Women and Sport and Physical Activity/Association canadienne pour l'avancement des femmes, du sport et de l'activité physique), 704
Action (Comité canadien d'action sur le statut de la femme/National Action Committee on the Status of Women), 44, 71, 720, 744
Action (Manitoba Action Committee on the Status of Women), 305, 964
Action (Saskatchewan Action Committee, Status of Women), 260, 937
Action Day Care, 342
Action des femmes handicapées (Montréal, Québec), 1120, 1121
Action éducation femmes (Nouveau-Brunswick), 1266
Action éducation femmes. Réseau national, 761
Action féministe, 44, 720
Action for Women's Rights in the U.S.S.R., 343
Action-Info-Femmes, 1122
Action-Information-Femmes, 1122
Action Now, 71, 744
Action on Women's Addictions: Research and Education/AWARE à Kingston, 992
Action travail des femmes du Québec, 1123
Actuel, 1173
ACTWU, 2, 695
ACWC. B.C. Chapter, 868
ACWN, 696
ACWOC, 1267

NAME INDEX

Ad Company, 69
Ad Hoc Committee for a Feminist Information Network, 58
Ad Hoc Committee of Native Indian Women, 846
Ad Hoc Committee on Family Violence, 773
Ad Hoc Committee on the Treatment of Child Sexual Abuse, 773
Ad Hoc Committee on Women's History in Newfoundland and Labrador, 1365
ADFC, 1130
ADGQ, 591
AEF (N.-B.), 1266
AEF. Réseau national, 761
AEFNB. Comité sur les valeurs et les droits humains en éducation, 1269
AFAM, 1124
AFDU, 586
AFÉAS, 588, 1131
AFÉAS. Section Rouyn-Noranda, 589
Affirm (Winnipeg, Man.), 288
AGFFA, 879
Agri-Culture-Elle, 1256
AIC, 8
Aide à la femme pour l'allaitement maternel et la maternité, 1124
AIDS Committee of Ottawa. Women's Project/Comité du SIDA d'Ottawa. Comité ELLES, 993
AIDS Committee of Toronto. Women and AIDS Project, 994
AIDS Network of Edmonton. Edmonton Women and AIDS Project, 890
AIIAC, 700
AISP. Section Ville-Marie, 1132
Albert County Women's Network, 1267
Albert County Women's Outreach Co-op, 1267
Alberta Association of Midwives, 875
Alberta Coalition against Pornography, 876
Alberta Community Health Nurses Society, 181
Alberta Council and Register of Domiciliary Midwives Association, 875
Alberta Farm Women's Network, 877
Alberta Native Women's Conference (1st : 1968 : Edmonton, Alta.). Planning Committee, 182
Alberta Native Women's Conference (2nd : 1969 : Edmonton, Alta.), 231
Alberta Provincial Council of Women, 183
Alberta Status of Women Action Committee, 184, 878
Alberta Women's Association, 230
Alberta Women's Institutes, 185
Alberta Women's Liberal Association, 186
ALGO, 346, 347, 996, 997
Alison McAteer House, 782
Alliance des professeurs de Montréal. Comité de la condition féminine, 584
Alliance des professeurs de Montréal. Comité des droits de la femme, 585
Alliance nationale des lesbiennes/National Lesbian Forum, 694
Alliance of Women against Racism Etcetera, 783
Allô Marie, 1231
Alternative, 986
Alternative-Violence, 1147
Amalgamated Clothing and Textile Workers Union/Travailleurs amalgamés du vêtement et du textile, 2, 695
Amalgamated Clothing and Textile Workers Union. Local 178, 106
Amana House, 1268
Amata Transition House Society, 784
Amazon Community Press, 344
Amazon Press, 344
AMCAL, 11

Amethyst Matters, 995
Amethyst Women's Addiction Centre, 995
Anderson House, 1312
Androgyne, 1125, 1126
Androgyny, 1126
ANFD, 702
ANL, 694
Anna Project, 345
Ano-Sep, 1127
Anonyme-Séparée, 1127
Antigonish Women's Association, 1315
Antigonish Women's Resource Centre, 1315
AOM, 998
APCFV, 773
APEC. Women's Atlantic Council, 652
APPLE, 658
Aquelarre: Latin American Women's Cultural Society, 785
Arab Canadian Women's Network, 696
Arcade, 1128
Archives canadiennes du mouvement des femmes/Canadian Women's Movement Archives, 3
Archives Collective, 107
ASP (Winnipeg, Man.), 317
Assaut sexuel secours, 1129
Association Aid'Elle de Timmins, 570
Association canadienne des sociétés Elizabeth Fry/Canadian Association of Elizabeth Fry Societies, 697
Association canadienne nationale des infirmières diplômées, 8
Association canadienne pour la promotion des services de garde à l'enfance/Canadian Day Care Advocacy Association, 698
Association canadienne pour la santé, l'éducation physique et la récréation. Comité athlétique féminin/Canadian Association for Health, Physical Education, and Recreation. Women's Athletic Committee, 4
Association canadienne pour l'abrogation de la loi sur l'avortement, 5
Association canadienne pour l'avancement des femmes, du sport et de l'activité physique/Canadian Association for the Advancement of Women and Sport and Physical Activity, 699
Association canadienne pour l'avancement des femmes et du sport, 699
Association canadienne pour le droit à l'avortement/Canadian Abortion Rights Action League, 5
Association des Acadiennes de la Nouvelle-Écosse, 657, 1316
Association des Acadiennes de la Nouvelle-Écosse. Société Madeleine LeBlanc, 1341
Association des adjoints administratifs/Association of Administrative Assistants, 6
Association des enseignantes et des enseignants francophones du Nouveau-Brunswick. Comité sur les valeurs et les droits humains en éducation, 1269
Association des femmes canadiennes-françaises d'Oshawa, 1026
Association des femmes chefs de famille (Moncton, N.-B.), 639
Association des femmes collaboratrices, 1130
Association des femmes d'affaires et professionnelles d'Ottawa, 1002
Association des femmes des universités du Québec, 586
Association des femmes diplômées des universités (Montréal, Québec), 586
Association des femmes diplômées des universités (Québec), 587
Association des femmes progressistes conservatrices/Progressive Conservative Women's Association, 7
Association des femmes universitaires du Québec, 586
Association des groupes de femmes francophones de l'Alberta, 879

Association des infirmières canadiennes, 8
Association des infirmières et infirmiers autochtones du Canada/Indian and Inuit Nurses of Canada, 700
Association des infirmières et infirmiers du Canada/Canadian Nurses Association, 8
Association des lesbiennes et des gais de l'Outaouais/Association of Lesbians and Gays of Ottawa, 346, 996
Association des universités et collèges du Canada. Comité spécial sur le rapport de la Commission royale d'enquête sur la situation de la femme/Association of Universities and Colleges of Canada. Special Committee on the Report of the Royal Commission on the Status of Women, 9
Association des universités et collèges du Canada. Comité sur la situation de la femme dans les universités/Association of Universities and Colleges of Canada. Committee on the Status of Women in Universities, 10
Association féminine d'éducation et d'action sociale, 588, 1131
Association féminine d'éducation et d'action sociale. Section Rouyn-Noranda, 589
Association for the Modernization of Canadian Abortion Laws, 11
Association for the Prevention of Community and Family Violence, 773
Association for the Repeal of Canadian Abortion Laws, 11
Association for the Review of Canadian Abortion Laws, 11
Association for the Safety of Prostitutes (Winnipeg, Man.), 317
Association for Women's Equity in the Canadian Forces, 701
Association internationale des secrétaires professionnelles. Section Ville-Marie/Professional Secretaries International. Ville-Marie Chapter, 1132
Association lavande, 1219
Association nationale de la femme et du droit/National Association of Women and the Law, 702
Association of Administrative Assistants/Association des adjoints administratifs, 12
Association of Administrative Assistants or Private Secretaries, 12
Association of Canadian Women Composers. B.C. Chapter, 868
Association of Certified Nursing Assistants, 453
Association of Homemakers' Clubs of Saskatchewan, 267, 941
Association of Lesbians and Gays of Ottawa/Association des lesbiennes et des gais de l'Outaouais, 347, 997
Association of Ontario Midwives, 998
Association of Private Secretaries, 12
Association of the Academic Staff at the University of Alberta. Committee on Employment Conditions of Full Time Women Faculty, 223
Association of Universities and Colleges of Canada. Committee on the Status of Women in Universities/Association des universités et collèges du Canada. Comité sur la situation de la femme dans les universités, 13
Association of Universities and Colleges of Canada. Special Committee on the Report of the Royal Commission on the Status of Women/Association des universités et collèges du Canada. Comité spécial sur le rapport de la Commission royale d'enquête sur la situation de la femme, 14
Association of University and College Employees. Local 1, 108
Association of Women Teaching at Queen's, 348
Association pour la planification familiale de Montréal/Family Planning Association of Montreal, 590
Association pour l'équité à l'égard des femmes dans les forces canadiennes, 701
Association pour les droits des gai(e)s du Québec, 591
ASWAC, 184, 878
Atelier Powerhouse, 592
ATF, 1123

Atira Transition House, 786
Atlantic Provinces Economic Council. Women's Atlantic Council, 652
Atlantic Provinces Political Lesbians for Equality, 658
Atlantic Women's Retreat, 1347
Atlantis, 670, 1331
Au fil des mots de femmes, 1195
AUCC. Comité spécial sur le rapport de la Commission royale d'enquête sur la situation de la femme, 9
AUCC. Comité sur la situation de la femme dans les universités, 10
AUCC. Committee on the Status of Women in Universities, 13
AUCC. Special Committee on the Report of the Royal Commisssion on the Status of Women, 14
AUCE. Local 1, 108
Augustine United Church (Winnipeg, Man.). Herstory, 959
Aurora House (The Pas, Man.), 984
Aurora House (Vancouver, B.C.), 787
Aurora Society, 787
Aurore, 1161
Autre Parole, 1133
Avec des elles, 1137
AWA (Antigonish, N.S.), 1315
AWA (Vancouver, B.C.), 151
AWARE à Kingston/Action on Women's Addictions: Research and Education, 999
AWAre (Antigonish, N.S.), 1315
AWARE (Kingston, Ont.), 992
AWARE (Vancouver, B.C.), 783
AWCS, 918
AWECF, 701
AWLA, 186
AWP, 677
AWRC, 1315
Back Chat, 377
Bande d'anarchistes féministes, 789
Bank and Finance Workers, 146
Barner House, 838
Battered Women's Advocacy Clinic, 349
Battered Women's Support Services, 788
Battlefords' and Area Rape Crisis Centre, 919
Battlefords' and Area Sexual Assault Centre, 919
Bay Centre for Birth Control, 1000
Bay St George Status of Women Council, 1352
Bay St George Women's Centre, 1352
Bay St George Women's Council, 1352
BC & YAWC, 790
B.C. and Yukon Association of Women's Centres, 790
B.C. Committee to Defend Dr Morgentaler, 110
B.C. Electric Employees' Association, 142
B.C. Federation of Women, 111, 791
B.C. Government Employees' Union. Provincial Executive Women's Committee, 792
B.C. NDP. Vancouver Women's Committee, 112
B.C. NDP. Women's Rights Committee, 113, 793
B.C. Nurses' Union, 794
B.C. PIRG (Simon Fraser University), 841
B.C. Protestant Orphanage, 838
B.C. Public Interest Research Group (Simon Fraser University), 841
B.C. Task Force on Immigrant Women, 853
B.C. Voice of Women, 115
B.C. WoHoCo, 795

NAME INDEX

B.C. Women's Abortion Law Repeal Coalition, 122
B.C. Women's Housing Coalition, 795
B.C. Women's Resource Guide, 841
BCBC, 1000
BCFW, 111, 791
BCGEU. Provincial Executive Women's Committee, 792
BCNU, 794
BCSWACC, 158
BCSWC, 158
BEAVER, 350
Behind the Blue Triangle, 414, 1036
BEKA, 1319
Bellyful, 509
Better End All Vicious Erotic Repression, 350
Between the Issues, 1324
Bevy of Anarchist Feminists, 789
Bi-national Lesbian Conference (1979 : Toronto, Ont.), 424
Bi-national Lesbian Conference Committee (Vancouver, B.C.), 67
Birth Control and V.D. Information Centre, 351
Birth Control Centre (Toronto, Ont.), 351
Birth Control Group (London, Ont.), 431
Birth Control Society of Hamilton, 473, 1066
Birth Control/Venereal Disease Information Centre, 351
Bisexual, Lesbian, and Gay Alliance at York, 352, 1001
Bishop Cridge Centre for the Family, 838
Black Gold, 195
Black Women's Collective, 1083
Blackflash, 931
BLGAY, 352, 1001
Bloc-notes, 1139
BOA Magazine and Productions, 789
Body Politic, 15
Body Politic Free the Press Fund, 15
Bonjour, puis-je vous aider?, 1026
Border Cities Local Council of Women, 532
Bouée régionale, 1134
Bouge, 1192
BPWC (Victoria, B.C.), 163, 857
Brampton Women's Centre, 353
Branching Out: Lesbian Culture Resource Centre, 354
Branching Out: Lesbian Productions (Toronto, Ont.), 354
Brandon Council of Women, 289
Brandon University. Status of Women Organization, 955
Bread and Roses (Vancouver, B.C.), 109
Breaking the Silence : A Feminist Newsmagazine on Social Issues, 355
Breaking the Silence : A Feminist Quarterly, 355
Brescia College. Circle, 1010
British Columbia and Yukon Association of Women's Centres, 790
British Columbia Committee to Defend Dr Morgentaler, 110
British Columbia Electric Employees' Association, 142
British Columbia Federation of Women, 111, 791
British Columbia Government Employees' Union. Provincial Executive Women's Committee, 792
British Columbia New Democratic Party. Vancouver Women's Committee, 112
British Columbia New Democratic Party. Women's Rights Committee, 113, 793
British Columbia Nurses' Union, 794
British Columbia Protestant Orphanage, 838
British Columbia Provincial Co-operative Commonwealth Federation. Women's Council. Vancouver Branch, 114
British Columbia Public Interest Research Group (Simon Fraser University), 841
British Columbia Status of Women Action and Coordinating Council, 158
British Columbia Status of Women Council, 158
British Columbia Task Force on Immigrant Women, 853
British Columbia Voice of Women, 115
British Columbia Voice of Women. Nanaimo Branch, 116
British Columbia Voice of Women. North Shore Branch, 117
British Columbia Voice of Women. Parksville-Qualicum Branch, 118
British Columbia Voice of Women. Powell River Branch, 119
British Columbia Voice of Women. Vancouver Branch, 120
British Columbia Voice of Women. Victoria Branch, 121
British Columbia Women's Abortion Law Repeal Coalition, 122
British Columbia Women's Housing Coalition, 795
Broadside, 356
Brown Envelope, 267, 941
Brunswick Four, 357
Brunswick Four Minus One, 357
BSG Women's Centre, 1352
Bulletin des femmes, 1137
Bulletin des militantes, 1239
Bunch of Feminists, 358
Business and Professional Women's Club (Flin Flon, Man.), 290
Business and Professional Women's Club of Moose Jaw, 241
Business and Professional Women's Club of Ottawa, 1002
Business and Professional Women's Club of Regina, 242
Business and Professional Women's Club of Winnipeg, 291
Business and Professional Women's Club (Prince Albert, Sask.), 251
Business and Professional Women's Club (Swift Current, Sask.), 275
Business and Professional Women's Clubs of British Columbia and Yukon, 123
Business and Professional Women's Clubs of Ontario, 359
BUSWO, 955
Busy Women's Bulletin, 654, 1306
BWAC, 349
BWC, 353
CAAWS, 704
CADIW, 374
CAEFS, 705
CAEFS. Cape Breton Branch, 1323
CAEFS. Halifax/Dartmouth Branch, 1324
CAEFS. Hamilton Branch, 1021
CAEFS. Kamloops and District Branch, 818
CAEFS. Kingston Branch, 387, 1022
CAEFS. Moncton Branch, 1280
CAEFS. Toronto Branch, 1023
CAFMQ, 1202
Cahiers de la femme/Canadian Woman Studies, 703
CAHPER. Women's Athletic Committee, 17
CALACS de Rimouski, 1139
CALACS (Trois-Rivières, Québec), 1140
Calgary Abortion Information Centre, 187
Calgary Birth Control Association, 187
Calgary Coalition against Pornography, 876
Calgary Housewives Association, 188
Calgary Local Council of Women, 189
Calgary Society for Women Plus, 880
Calgary Status of Women Action Committee, 190, 881
Calgary Voice of Women, 232, 906

Calgary VOW, 232, 906
Calgary Women's Emergency Shelter Association, 191, 882
Calgary Women's Health Collective, 883
Calgary Women's Newspaper, 190, 881
Calgary YWCA, 238, 914
Cambodian Women's Group of Ontario, 1003
CAME, 1142
Campus and Community Co-operative Day Care Centre, 360
Campus Co-operative Community Day Care Centre, 360
Campus Gay Club (University of Manitoba), 299
Canadian Abortion Rights Action League/Association canadienne pour le droit à l'avortement, 16
Canadian Abortion Rights Action League. Fraser Valley Chapter, 796
Canadian Abortion Rights Action League. Prince Edward Island Chapter, 1302
Canadian Abortion Rights Action League, St John's, 1353
Canadian Association for Health, Physical Education, and Recreation. Women's Athletic Committee/Association canadienne pour la santé, l'éducation physique et la récréation. Comité athlétique féminin, 17
Canadian Association for Repeal of the Abortion Law, 16
Canadian Association for the Advancement of Women and Sport and Physical Activity/Association canadienne pour l'avancement des femmes, du sport et de l'activité physique, 704
Canadian Association of Elizabeth Fry Societies/Association canadienne des sociétés Elizabeth Fry, 705
Canadian Association of Elizabeth Fry Societies. Cape Breton Branch, 1323
Canadian Association of Elizabeth Fry Societies. Halifax/Dartmouth Branch, 1324
Canadian Association of Elizabeth Fry Societies. Hamilton Branch, 1021
Canadian Association of Elizabeth Fry Societies. Kamloops and District Branch, 818
Canadian Association of Elizabeth Fry Societies. Kingston Branch, 387, 1022
Canadian Association of Elizabeth Fry Societies. Moncton Branch, 1280
Canadian Association of Elizabeth Fry Societies. Toronto Branch, 1023
Canadian Association of Social Workers. Manitoba Branch, 307
Canadian Association to Repeal the Abortion Law, 16
Canadian Business Women's Club, 498
Canadian Cambodian Association of Ontario. Cambodian Women's Group of Ontario, 1003
Canadian Child Day Care Federation/Fédération canadienne des services de garde à l'enfance, 706
Canadian Coalition against Media Pornography/Coalition canadienne contre la pornographie dans les médias, 18
Canadian Committee on Learning Opportunities for Women, 21, 707
Canadian Committee on Learning Opportunities for Women (Fort Smith, N.W.T.), 778
Canadian Committee on Learning Opportunities for Women (Fredericton, N.B.), 1270
Canadian Committee on Learning Opportunities for Women — Nova Scotia, 1317
Canadian Committee on Learning Opportunities for Women. Regina Chapter, 243
Canadian Committee on the Status of Women/Comité canadien sur la situation de la femme, 19
Canadian Committee on Women's History/Comité canadien de l'histoire des femmes, 20
Canadian Congress for Learning Opportunities for Women/Congrès canadien pour la promotion des études chez la femme, 21, 707
Canadian Congress for Learning Opportunities for Women (Fort Smith, N.W.T.), 778

Canadian Congress for Learning Opportunities for Women (Fredericton, N.B.), 1270
Canadian Congress for Learning Opportunities for Women — Nova Scotia, 1317
Canadian Congress for Learning Opportunities for Women. Regina Chapter, 243
Canadian Congress on Learning Opportunities for Women. Regina Chapter, 243
Canadian Day Care Advocacy Association/Association canadienne pour la promotion des services de garde à l'enfance, 708
Canadian Ethnocultural Council. Women's Committee/Conseil ethnoculturel du Canada. Comité des femmes, 709
Canadian Farm Women's Network, 710
Canadian Federation of Business and Professional Women's Clubs/Fédération canadienne des clubs de femmes de carrières libérales et commerciales, 22
Canadian Federation of Business and Professional Women's Clubs. Calgary Local, 192
Canadian Federation of University Women/Fédération canadienne des femmes diplômées des universités, 23
Canadian Federation of University Women. Cape Breton Branch, 659
Canadian Federation of University Women. Charlottetown Branch, 653, 1303
Canadian Federation of University Women. Halifax Branch, 660
Canadian Federation of University Women — Kelowna, 797
Canadian Federation of University Women. Nelson Branch, 798
Canadian Federation of University Women. Parksville/Qualicum Beach Club, 799
Canadian Federation of University Women. Port Arthur and Fort William Chapter, 361
Canadian Federation of University Women. Sackville Club, 640
Canadian Federation of University Women. Saskatchewan Provincial Council, 264
Canadian Federation of University Women. Thunder Bay Chapter, 361
Canadian Interuniversity Athletic Union. National Coaching School for Women, 746
Canadian Journal of Women and the Law/Revue Femmes et droit, 711
Canadian Lesbian and Gay Rights Coalition/Coalition canadienne pour les droits des lesbiennes et gais, 24
Canadian Library Association. Gay Interest Group, 25
Canadian Mental Health Association. Women and Mental Health Committee, 26
Canadian National Association of Trained Nurses, 28
Canadian Native Sisterhood Organization, 27
Canadian Newsletter of Research on Women, 85, 762
Canadian Nurse, 28
Canadian Nurses Association/Association des infirmières et infirmiers du Canada, 28
Canadian Organization for the Rights of Prostitutes, 29, 712
Canadian Rape Crisis Centres/Centres canadiens de viol, 30
Canadian Research Institute for the Advancement of Women/Institut canadien de recherches sur les femmes, 31, 713
Canadian Research Institute for the Advancement of Women/Institut canadien de recherches sur les femmes. Conference '90 Committee, 1304
Canadian Research Institute for the Advancement of Women/Institut canadien de recherches sur les femmes. 1990 Publications Committee, 1304
Canadian Research Institute for the Advancement of Women, Newfoundland and Labrador, 1354
Canadian Research Institute for the Advancement of Women — Nova Scotia, 661, 1318
Canadian Teachers' Federation/Fédération canadienne des

enseignantes et des enseignants, 714
Canadian Textile and Chemical Union/Syndicat canadien des travailleurs du textile et de la chimie, 32
Canadian Textile Council/Conseil canadien du textile, 33
Canadian Voice of Women for Peace (Edmonton, Alta.), 233
Canadian Woman Studies/Cahiers de la femme, 715
Canadian Women's Coalition to Repeal the Abortion Laws, 34
Canadian Women's Cooperative Press, 99
Canadian Women's Educational Press, 99
Canadian Women's Festival, 36
Canadian Women's Movement Archives/Archives canadiennes du mouvement des femmes, 35
Canadian Women's Music and Cultural Festival, 36
Canadian Women's Music Festival, 36
Canadian Women's Press, 99
Canadian Women's Press Club, 37
Canadian Women's Press Club. Calgary Branch, 193
Canadian Women's Press Club. Edmonton Branch, 194
Canadian Women's Press Club. Ottawa Branch, 362
Canadian Women's Press Club. Toronto Branch, 363
Canadian Women's Press Club. Vancouver Chapter, 124
Canadian Women's Press Club. Winnipeg Branch, 292
Canadian Women's Studies, 715
Candida Foundation, 716
Candida Research and Information Foundation (Canada), 716
CAPAS, 1141
Cape Breton Transition House, 662
CARAL, 16
CARAL. Fraser Valley Chapter, 796
CARAL. FV Chapter, 796
CARAL. Prince Edward Island Chapter, 1302
CARAL, St John's, 1353
Carleton University. Institute of Women's Studies, 1004
Carleton University. Interfaculty Committee on Women's Studies, 1004
Carleton University. School of Social Work. Feminist Caucus. *Breaking the Silence : A Feminist Newsmagazine on Social Issues*, 355
Carleton University. Status of Women Office, 1005
Carrefour des associations de familles monoparentales du Québec, 1202
Carrefour des femmes de Lachute, 1135
Carrefour pour femmes/Crossroads for Women, 1271
Catalyst Research and Communications. *The Womanist*, 768
Causerie, 1144
Causerie de femmes, 1162
CAVV, 1141
CAWA, 1320
CAWES, 886
Cayenne : A Socialist Feminist Bulletin, 364
CBCA, 187
CBWC, 722
CBWC. Manitoba Chapter, 956
CBWC. Regina Chapter, 920
CCA, 44, 720
CCAMP, 18
CCDCF, 706
CCDLG, 41
CCF (British Columbia). Women's Council. Vancouver Branch, 114
CCF (Moose Jaw, Sask.). Women's Club, 248
CCFP, 1321
CCFSA, 1138

CCHF, 45
CCLOW, 21, 707
CCLOW (Fort Smith, N.W.T.), 778
CCLOW (Fredericton, N.B.), 1270
CCLOW — Nova Scotia, 1317
CCLOW. Regina Chapter, 243
CCNC. Women's Issues Committee, 719
CCPEF, 48, 721
CCSF, 46
CCSW, 19
CCSWD, 293
CCWH, 20
CDCAA, 708
CDEACF, 1143
CE, 1163
CEC. Comité des femmes, 723
CEC. Women's Committee, 709
CEFI, 1170
Celebration of Women in the Arts, 884
Central Alberta Immigrant Women's Association, 885
Central Alberta Women's Emergency Shelter, 886
Central Valley Transition House Society, 800
Centrale, 592, 593
Centrale de l'enseignement du Québec. Comité de la condition féminine, 594
Centrale de l'enseignement du Québec. Comité Laure-Gaudreault, 594
Centre actu-elle, 1136
Centre Avec des elles, 1137
Centre communautaire des femmes sud-asiatiques/South Asian Women's Community Centre, 1138
Centre communautaire sud-asiatique, 1138
Centre d'aide aux agressées sexuelles d'Ottawa/Sexual Assault Support Centre of Ottawa, 1006
Centre d'aide aux victimes de viol de Châteauguay, 1141
Centre d'aide aux victimes de viol et d'agression sexuelle de l'Î.P.É./P.E.I. Rape and Sexual Assault Crisis Centre, 1305
Centre d'aide et de lutte contre les agressions à caractère sexuel de Rimouski, 1139
Centre d'aide et de lutte contre les agressions à caractère sexuel (Trois-Rivières, Québec), 1140
Centre d'aide et de prévention contre les agressions à caractère sexuel (Montréal, Québec), 1260
Centre d'aide et de prévention d'assauts sexuels de Châteauguay/Châteauguay Sexual Assault Prevention and Aid Center, 1141
Centre d'aide et de prévention des agressions à caractère sexuel de Rouyn, 1239
Centre d'aide et de prévention des assauts sexuels de Valleyfield, 1263
Centre d'animation mère-enfant, 1142
Centre de documentation sur l'éducation des adultes et la condition féminine, 1143
Centre de femmes de Shawinigan, 1144
Centre de femmes du pays Maria-Chapdelaine, 1145
Centre de femmes Espoir pour elles, 1146
Centre de femmes L'Éclaircie, 1149
Centre de femmes L'ÉRIGE, 1150
Centre de femmes L'Étincelle, 1151
Centre de femmes La Moisson, 1147
Centre de femmes La Tuque, 1148
Centre de femmes Parmi elles, 1152
Centre de la femme nouvelle/New Woman Centre, 595

Centre de lutte contre les agressions à caractère sexuel de la Rive-Sud, 1259
Centre de planning familial du Québec, 596
Centre de prévention et d'intervention pour victimes d'agression sexuelle (Laval, Québec), 1153
Centre de recherches et de ressources pour femmes (Collège Glendon), 1071
Centre de santé des femmes de l'Outaouais, 1179
Centre de santé des femmes de Montréal. Collective en santé lesbienne, 1185
Centre d'éducation et d'action des femmes de Montréal, 1154
Centre d'emploi pour les femmes immigrantes, 1032
Centre des femmes (Forestville, Québec), 1162
Centre des femmes d'Ottawa, 466, 1061
Centre des femmes d'Ottawa. Chez nous, 1009
Centre des femmes de Charlevoix, 1155
Centre des femmes de Concordia, 1189
Centre des femmes de l'Estrie, 1158
Centre des femmes de Laval, 1156
Centre des femmes de Lennoxville et des environs/Lennoxville and District Women's Centre, 1157
Centre des femmes de Rivières des Prairies. Projet : Relance sociale, phase II, 1213
Centre des femmes de Sudbury/Sudbury Women's Centre, 1007
Centre des femmes de Verdun, 1159
Centre des femmes du ô pays, 1160
Centre des femmes du Témiscouata L'Aurore, 1161
Centre d'information et d'action sociale de l'Outaouais, 1179
Centre émersion, 1163
Centre émersion manicouagan, 1163
Centre Espoir pour elles, 1146
Centre-Femmes Catherine Leblond, 1164
Centre-Femmes d'aujourd'hui, 1165
Centre-Femmes de Lotbinière, 1166
Centre-Femmes La Jardilec, 1167
Centre-Femmes L'Envolée, 1168
centre/fold, 499
Centre for Women (Sheridan College. Brampton Campus), 365
Centre hospitalier de l'Université Laval. Clinique de planification des naissances. Solidarité post-avortement, 1254
Centre international MATCH/MATCH International Centre, 38, 717
Centre Louise-Amélie, 1169
Centre pour femmes immigrantes (Sherbrooke, Québec), 1170
Centre social des femmes du centre-ville de Montréal, 1171
Centrefold, 817
Centr'elles, comité d'action des femmes d'Avignon, 1172
Centres canadiens de viol/Canadian Rape Crisis Centres, 39
Centro Donne (Toronto, Ont.), 1031
CEQ. Comité de la condition féminine, 594
CEQ. Comité Laure-Gaudreault, 594
Cercle des dames d'Acadie de Lamèque, 1272
Cercle des dames d'Acadie de Shippagan, 1273
Cercle des dames d'Acadie (Tracadie, N.-B.), 1274
Cercles de fermières du Québec, 1173
Cercles d'économie domestique, 588, 1131
CFAL, 1180
CFBPWC, 22
CFBPWC. Calgary Local, 192
CFE, 1158
CFO, 370
CFQ, 1173

CFSGM. Women's Committee, 1176
CFUW, 23
CFUW. Cape Breton Branch, 659
CFUW. Charlottetown Branch, 653, 1303
CFUW. Halifax Branch, 660
CFUW — Kelowna, 797
CFUW. Nelson Branch, 798
CFUW. Parksville/Qualicum Beach Club, 799
CFUW. Sackville Club, 640
CFUW. Saskatchewan Provincial Council, 264
CFUW. Thunder Bay Chapter, 361
CFV, 1159
CFWN, 710
CGRO, 371, 1011
Changing Focus, 1086
Changing Together: A Centre for Immigrant Women, 887
Charlottetown Business and Professional Women's Club, 654, 1306
Charter of Rights Coalition (Vancouver, B.C.), 848
CHAT, 377
Châteauguay Sexual Assault Prevention and Aid Center/Centre d'aide et de prévention d'assauts sexuels de Châteauguay, 1174
Chatham Business and Professional Women's Club, 366
Chetwynd Women's Centre, 801
Chetwynd Women's Council, 801
Chetwynd Women's Resource Society, 801
Chez Doris, the Women's Shelter Foundation/Fondation du refuge pour femmes Chez Doris, 1175
Chez nous, 1008, 1009
Child Care Federation, 125
Child Care Focus, 965
Child Care Occupation Forces, 126
Childbirth by Choice Trust, 718
Chilliwack Business and Professional Women's Club, 127
Chilliwack Council of Women, 128
Chimo Personal Distress Intervention Service, 802
Chinese Canadian National Council. Women's Issues Committee, 719
Chinese Family Service of Greater Montreal. Women's Committee/ Service à la famille chinoise du Grand Montréal. Comité des femmes, 1176
ChoiceWords, 472, 1065
Chrysalis House, 1319
CHUL. Clinique de planification des naissances. Solidarité post-avortement, 1254
CIAFT, 1192
CIAFVV, 1183
CIASO, 1179
CIAU. National Coaching School for Women, 746
Cinquième Monde, 1177
Circle, 1010
Circle Resource Centre, 1010
Citad'elle de Lachute, 1178
Citizens' Day Care Action Committee, 663
Citizen's Organization to Repeal Prostitution-Related Laws, 367
CJWL, 711
CLA. Gay Interest Group, 25
Clearinghouse for Feminist Media, 368
Clementyne's Café, 369
ClericalVoice, 866
CLFN, 81, 756
CLGRC, 24
CLGRO, 371, 1011

NAME INDEX

Clinique de planification des naissances. Solidarité post-avortement, 1254
Clinique des femmes de l'Outaouais, 1179
Clinique pour lesbiennes, 1185
Club des femmes d'aujourd'hui de Laval, 1180
Club politique féminin, 1181
Club politique féminin, région Bas-Saint-Laurent-Gaspésie, 1181
CMHA. Women and Mental Health Committee, 26
CNA, 28
CNATN, 28
CNDH, 41
CNFC, 73
CNRW, 85, 762
Co-operative Commonwealth Federation (British Columbia). Women's Council. Vancouver Branch, 114
Co-operative Commonwealth Federation (Moose Jaw, Sask.). Women's Club, 248
Coalition canadienne contre la pornographie dans les médias/ Canadian Coalition against Media Pornography, 40
Coalition canadienne pour les droits des lesbiennes et gais/Canadian Lesbian and Gay Rights Coalition, 41
Coalition des associations de femmes canadiennes : Le Congrès international sur la paix/Coalition of Canadian Women's Groups: International Peace Conference, 42
Coalition des femmes de l'Ontario/Ontario Women's Action Coalition, 370
Coalition for a Women's Centre at U of T, 522
Coalition for Gay Rights in Ontario, 371, 1011
Coalition for International Women's Day (Toronto, Ont.), 439
Coalition for Lesbian and Gay Rights in Ontario, 371, 1011
Coalition for the Week of Survival and Disarmament, 372
Coalition nationale pour les droits des homosexuels, 41
Coalition of Canadian Women's Groups: International Peace Conference/Coalition des associations de femmes canadiennes : Le Congrès international sur la paix, 43
Coalition of Visible Minority Women (Ontario), 1012
Coalition pour la réforme des droits de la personne du Nouveau-Brunswick/New Brunswick Coalition for Human Rights Reform, 641
Coalition pour les droits des lesbiennes et des hommes gais en Ontario, 371, 1011
Coalition to Answer Anita Bryant (Saskatoon, Sask.), 244
Coalition to Stop Anita Bryant (Toronto, Ont.), 373
Collectif de la santé des femmes de Vancouver, 162, 855
Collectif des femmes francophones du nord-est ontarien, 1013
Collectif des femmes immigrantes, 1182
Collectif d'intervention auprès des femmes victimes de violence, 1183
Collectif femmes et justice de Québec, 1184
Collective en santé lesbienne, 1185
Collective par et pour elle, 1186
Collective (Université d'Ottawa)/Collective (University of Ottawa), 1014
Collective (University of Ottawa)/Collective (Université d'Ottawa), 1015
Collège de Maisonneuve. Société générale des étudiantes et des étudiants. Comité-femme de Maisonneuve, 1187
Collège Glendon. Centre de recherches et de ressources pour femmes, 1071
Comité canadien d'action sur le statut de la femme/National Action Committee on the Status of Women, 44, 720
Comité canadien de l'histoire des femmes/Canadian Committee on Women's History, 45
Comité canadien sur la situation de la femme/Canadian Committee on the Status of Women, 46
Comité CEQ de la condition féminine, 594
Comité d'action manitobain sur le statut de la femme, 305, 964
Comité d'étude sur la condition féminine à l'Université Laval, 632
Comité du SIDA d'Ottawa. Comité éducation, liaison, lumière et services, 1016
Comité du SIDA d'Ottawa. Comité ELLES/AIDS Committee of Ottawa. Women's Project, 1016
Comité-femme de Maisonneuve, 1187
Comité national d'action sur le statut de la femme, 44, 720
Comité pour l'Université Laval au féminin, 633
Commission libérale féminine nationale, 81, 756
Committee against the Deportation of Immigrant Women, 374
Committee against Woman Abuse (Mainland South), 1320
Committee for a Socialist Women's Conference, 375
Committee for the Feminist Symposium, Montreal 1973, 597
Committee on Family Violence, 1355
Committee on Sexual Harassment at the University of Toronto, 515
Committee to Establish Ontario Federation of Women, 376
Common Ground, 1313
Communications Union Canada/Syndicat des communications Canada, 47
Communiqué, 512, 1088
Community Homophile Association of Toronto, 377
Community Resources for Women, 378
Community Women's Centre (Regina, Sask.), 245
Company of Sirens, 1017
Concerned Aboriginal Women, 129
Concerned Woman, 379
Concerned Women (Sault Ste Marie, Ont.), 379
Concordia University. Gay Friends of Concordia, 613
Concordia University. Lesbian and Gay Friends of Concordia, 613
Concordia University. Lesbian Studies Coalition, 615, 1218
Concordia University. Office on the Status of Women, 1188
Concordia University. Simone de Beauvoir Institute, 1252
Concordia University. Women's Centre, 1189
Concordia Women's Centre, 1189
Confédération des syndicats nationaux. Conseil central de Lanaudière. Comité de condition féminine, 1190
Confédération des syndicats nationaux. Conseil central de Lanaudière. Service à la condition féminine, 1190
Confédération des syndicats nationaux. Conseil central de Thetford Mines. Comité de la condition féminine, 1191
Conférence de lesbiennes de Montréal (1975 : Montréal, Québec), 616
Conference '80 : Women and the Economy (1980 : Fredericton, N.B.). Provincial Organizing Committee, 642
Conférence lesbienne bi-nationale (1979 : Toronto, Ont.), 424
Conférence nationale de lesbiennes (2e : 1975 : Montréal, Québec), 616
Conférence nationale de lesbiennes (1976 : Ottawa, Ont.), 426
Congrès canadien pour la promotion des études chez la femme/ Canadian Congress for Learning Opportunities for Women, 48, 721
Congrès international sur la paix (1985 : Halifax, N.-É.), 42
Congrès national des femmes noires du Canada (4e : 1977 : Windsor, Ont.), 405
Congress of Black Women of Canada, 722
Congress of Black Women of Canada. Manitoba Chapter, 956
Congress of Black Women of Canada. Regina Chapter, 920
Connect!, 1350
Conseil canadien du textile/Canadian Textile Council, 49
Conseil des femmes de Montréal/Montreal Council of Women, 598
Conseil des femmes juives du Canada, 72, 747

Conseil d'intervention pour l'accès des femmes au travail du Québec, 1192

Conseil ethnoculturel du Canada. Comité des femmes/Canadian Ethnocultural Council. Women's Committee, 723

Conseil national des femmes du Canada, 73

Conseil œcuménique des chrétiennes du Canada/Women's Inter-Church Council of Canada, 724

Constance Hamilton Housing Co-operative, 1018

Consulting Committee on the Status of Women with Disabilities, 293

Contact (Edmonton, Alta.), 239, 915

Contact (Toronto, Ont.), 1056

Contact: Women's Resource and Information Centre, 1275

Coop lesbienne, 1171

Coppermine Women's Group, 779

Cora: The Feminist Bookmobile, 380

CORC, 848

Corner Brook Status of Women Council, 1356

CORP, 29, 712

CORPL, 367

Council of Business and Professional Women's Clubs of Metropolitan Toronto, 381

Council of Women (Alberta), 183

Council of Women (Brandon, Man.), 289

Council of Women (British Columbia), 145

Council of Women (Calgary, Alta.), 189

Council of Women (Chilliwack, B.C.), 128

Council of Women (East Pictou, N.S.), 671

Council of Women (Edmonton, Alta.), 197

Council of Women (Halifax, N.S.), 666

Council of Women (Hamilton, Ont.), 403

Council of Women (London, Ont.), 427

Council of Women (Manitoba), 318

Council of Women (Moncton, N.B.), 647

Council of Women (Montreal, Quebec), 621

Council of Women (Moose Jaw, Sask.), 249

Council of Women (New Brunswick), 651

Council of Women (New Glasgow, N.S.), 671

Council of Women of Winnipeg, 294

Council of Women (Ontario), 476, 1069

Council of Women (Ottawa, Ont.), 465

Council of Women (Red Deer, Alta.), 215

Council of Women (Regina, Sask.), 253

Council of Women (Saskatchewan), 252

Council of Women (Saskatoon, Sask.), 271

Council of Women (St John's, Nfld.), 685

Council of Women (Swift Current, Sask.), 276

Council of Women (Toronto, Ont.), 496

Council of Women (Vancouver, B.C.), 157

Council of Women (Victoria, B.C.), 164

Council of Women (West Algoma, Ont.), 530

Council of Women (Weston, Ont.), 428

Council of Women (Westville, N.S.), 676

Council of Women (Windsor, Ont.), 532

Council of Women (Winnipeg, Man.), 294

Council on Homosexuality and Religion, 295

Councillor, 496

Coup d'elle, 1193

Coverdale Centre, 1276

Coverdale Foundation, 1276

CPIVAS, 1153

CRC, 966

CRIAW, 31, 713

CRIAW. Conference '90 Committee, 1304

CRIAW Newfoundland, 1354

CRIAW. 1990 Publications Committee, 1304

CRIAW — Nova Scotia, 661, 1318

Cridge Centre for the Family, 838

CRIF, 716

Crisis Centre (Barrie, Ont.), 1096

Critical Creations, 909

Cross-Canada Abortion Caravan, 1

Cross-Canada Abortion Conference (1972 : Winnipeg, Man.), 304

Crossroads, 888

Crossroads for Women/Carrefour pour femmes, 1277

Crowsnest Pass Women's Resource Centre, 889

Crowsnest Pass Women's Resources and Crisis Centre Society, 889

CRQ, 604

CRW, 378

CSAPAC, 1174

CSFCVM, 1171

CSN. Conseil central de Lanaudière. Comité de condition féminine, 1190

CSN. Conseil central de Lanaudière. Service à la condition féminine, 1190

CSN. Conseil central de Thetford Mines. Comité de la condition féminine, 1191

CSO. Comité ELLES, 1016

CSWAC, 190, 881

CTC, 33

CTF, 714

Cumberland County Family Planning, 1321

Current Event Club, 192

CVMW (Ontario), 1012

CWA, 884

CWC, 245

CWCRAL, 34

CWES, 191, 882

CWMA, 35

CWPC, 37

CWPC. Calgary Branch, 193

CWPC. Edmonton Branch., 194

CWPC. Vancouver Chapter, 124

CWPC. Winnipeg Branch, 292

CWS/CF, 703, 715

Dalhousie University. Women's Studies Programme, 1322

Dames d'Acadie de Neguac, 1278

Dauphin Crisis Centre, 978

DAWN Canada, 725

DAWN Canada. Action des femmes handicapées (Montreal, Quebec), 1121

DAWN (Fort St John, B.C.), 803

DAWN Toronto, 1019

Dawning, 1019

Dawson Shelter Society, 774

Day Care for Everyone, 382

Day Care Organizing Committee, 382

Day Care Reform Action Alliance, 383

Day Nursery Centre, 296

Daycare and the Union Movement (1980 : Toronto, Ont.), 462

DCOC, 382

De Connivence, 1222

December 6th Women's Memorial Committee, 957

Desk and Derrick Club of Calgary, 195

Deuxième décennie, 577
Dignity Canada Dignité. Toronto Branch, 384
Dignity Toronto Dignité, 384
Digression, 1014, 1015
Diocèse de Sainte-Anne-de-la-Pocatière. Service de la condition des femmes dans l'Église et la société, 600
DisAbled Women's Network Canada/Réseau d'action des femmes handicapées du Canada, 725
DisAbled Women's Network Canada. Action des femmes handicapées (Montreal, Quebec), 1121
DisAbled Women's Network (Fort St John, B.C.), 803
DisAbled Women's Network, Toronto, 1019
D'main de femmes, 1194
Documentation sur la recherche féministe/Resources for Feminist Research, 50, 726
Doing It!: Lesbian and Gay Liberation in the '80s (1982 : Toronto, Ont.), 502
Domestics' Cross-Cultural News, 1084
Douglas College. Women's Centre, 804
Douglas College. Women's Studies Programme, 130
Dovercourt NDP. Women's Action Committee, 385
Downtown Eastside Women's Centre, 131
DRF, 50, 726
Druhyi Vinok, 218
Dryden Aboriginal Women's Resource Centre, 1020
Dryden Native Women's Resource Centre, 1020
Durham International Women's Day Committee, 386
DWA, 861
E-Fry (Calgary, Alta.), 201, 892
E. Fry (Kingston, Ont.), 387, 1022
East Pictou Local Council of Women, 671
East Prince Women's Information Centre, 1307
East Prince Women's Information Committee, 1307
Échange entre femmes de Saint-Laurent, 1195
Éclaircie, 1149
École des hautes études commerciales. Groupe femmes, gestion et entreprises, 599
Ecumenical Decade of Churches in Solidarity with Women (Hampton, N.B.), 1279
Edmonton Business and Professional Women's Club, 196
Edmonton Local Council of Women, 197
Edmonton Women and AIDS Project, 890
Edmonton Women's Centre, 198
Edmonton Women's Coalition, 199
Edmonton Women's Health Collective, 891
Edmonton Women's Liberation, 236
Edmonton Women's Place, 200
Edmonton YWCA, 239, 915
EGALE — Regina, 921
Église catholique. Diocèse de Sainte-Anne-de-la-Pocatière. Service de la condition des femmes dans l'Église et la société, 600
ELCW, 197
Elizabeth Fry Societies, 705
Elizabeth Fry Society. Hamilton Branch, 1021
Elizabeth Fry Society (Kamloops, B.C.), 818
Elizabeth Fry Society. Moncton Branch, 1280
Elizabeth Fry Society of Alberta, 201, 892
Elizabeth Fry Society of British Columbia. Kamloops Branch, 818
Elizabeth Fry Society of Calgary, 201, 892
Elizabeth Fry Society of Cape Breton, 1323
Elizabeth Fry Society of Greater Montreal, 1196
Elizabeth Fry Society of Halifax/Dartmouth, 1324

Elizabeth Fry Society of Kingston, 387, 1022
Elizabeth Fry Society of Montreal/Société Elizabeth Fry de Montréal, 1196
Elizabeth Fry Society of New Brunswick, 1280
Elizabeth Fry Society of Toronto, 1023
Elizabeth Fry Society. Ottawa Branch, 388
Elles de l'écriture, 1152
Emily Stowe Shelter for Women, 1024
Empathy House of Recovery, 1025
Employment Services for Immigrant Women, 1032
En Lutte!. Comité de la condition féminine, 629
Encrelle, 1014
ENF Housing Society, 805
Entraide familiale Outaouais, 1197
Entraide femmes de Gatineau, 1197
Entre-Elles, 1216
Entre Femmes, 207
Entre Nous Femmes Housing Society, 805
Envolée, 1168
EPWIC, 1307
Equal Times, 643
Equality for Gays and Lesbians Everywhere — Regina, 921
Equality of Rights Committee, Health Sciences Association of British Columbia, 813
ERC, 813
ÉRIGE, 1150
ESIW, 1032
Espace Val d'Or, 1198
Espoir pour elles, 1146
Essor féminin La Tuque, 1199
Étincelle, 1151
Études lesbiennes de Concordia, 615, 1218
Évaluation-Médias/MediaWatch, 727
Évaluation-Médias/MediaWatch (Outremont, Québec), 1200
Évaluation nationale des images des femmes dans les médias, 727
Évaluation nationale des images des femmes dans les médias (Outremont, Québec), 1200
Every Woman's Place (Edmonton, Alta.), 202
Every Woman's Place Society of Edmonton, 202
Everywoman, 200
Everywoman's Health Centre Society, 806
EWP ([ca. 1973]-[197-?]), 200
EWP (1981-[198-]), 202
Expansion-Femmes de Québec, 1201
Expressive, 1154
Faculty Women's Association (University of Alberta), 203
Faculty Women's Club (University of Alberta), 203
FAEJ, 733
FAEJ. Section Nouveau-Brunswick, 1284
FAFMQ, 1202
Fairview and District Women's Centre, 888
Family Benefits Work Group, 389
Family Crisis Shelter, 1359
Family Place (Vancouver, B.C.), 851
Family Planning Advisory Service (Pointe-Claire, Quebec), 612
Family Planning Association of B.C., 831
Family Planning Association of Montreal/Association pour la planification familiale de Montréal, 601
Family Planning Association of Nova Scotia, 1336
Family Planning Association of Saskatchewan, 250

Family Planning Association of Winnipeg, 316
Family Planning Federation of Canada, 758
FANE. Association des Acadiennes de la Nouvelle-Écosse, 657, 1316
Farm Women's Union of Alberta. Hillside Local, 204
Farm Women's Union of Alberta. Sunniebend Local, 205
FBWG, 389
FCE, 728
FCF, 1205
Federated Women's Institutes of Canada, 51
Federated Women's Institutes of Ontario, 390
Fédération acadienne de la Nouvelle-Écosse. Association des Acadiennes de la Nouvelle-Écosse, 657, 1316
Fédération canadienne des clubs de femmes de carrières libérales et commerciales/Canadian Federation of Business and Professional Women's Clubs, 52
Fédération canadienne des clubs de femmes de carrières libérales et commerciales. Club de Shawinigan, 602
Fédération canadienne des enseignantes et des enseignants/Canadian Teachers' Federation, 728
Fédération canadienne des femmes diplômées des universités/ Canadian Federation of University Women, 53
Fédération canadienne des services de garde à l'enfance/Canadian Child Day Care Federation, 729
Fédération de la planification familiale du Canada, 731
Fédération des associations de familles monoparentales du Québec, 1202
Fédération des dames d'Acadie du Nouveau-Brunswick, 1282
Fédération des dames d'Acadie (Bathurst, N.-B.), 1281
Fédération des dames d'Acadie (Lamèque, N.-B.), 1272
Fédération des dames d'Acadie (Neguac, N.-B.), 1278
Fédération des dames d'Acadie (Shippagan, N.-B.), 1273
Fédération des dames d'Acadie (Tracadie, N.-B.), 1274
Fédération des femmes canadiennes-françaises, 55
Fédération des femmes canadiennes-françaises (Alberta), 206
Fédération des femmes canadiennes-françaises (Gravelbourg, Sask.), 922
Fédération des femmes canadiennes-françaises (Oshawa, Ont.), 1026
Fédération des femmes canadiennes-françaises. Section Rouyn-Noranda, 605
Fédération des femmes canadiennes-françaises. Section Willow Bunch, 246
Fédération des femmes du Québec, 603, 1203
Fédération des femmes du Québec. Conseil régional de Québec, 604
Fédération des femmes médecins du Canada/Federation of Medical Women of Canada, 54
Fédération nationale des femmes canadiennes-françaises, 55
Fédération nationale des femmes canadiennes-françaises (Alberta), 206
Fédération nationale des femmes canadiennes-françaises d'Oshawa, 1026
Fédération nationale des femmes canadiennes-françaises (Gravelbourg, Sask.), 922
Fédération nationale des femmes canadiennes-françaises. Section Rouyn-Noranda, 605
Fédération nationale des femmes canadiennes-françaises. Section Willow Bunch, 246
Fédération nationale des femmes libérales du Canada/Women's Liberal Federation of Canada, 56
Fédération nationale des syndicats d'infirmières/infirmiers/National Federation of Nurses' Unions, 730
Fédération nationale Saint-Jean-Baptiste, 606
Federation of Medical Women of Canada/Fédération des femmes médecins du Canada, 57

Fédération pour le planning des naissances du Canada/Planned Parenthood Federation of Canada, 731
Félibre, 1204
Féminisme en revue, 603, 1203
Feminist Action, 71, 744
Feminist Bookmobile, 380
Feminist Caucus of the League of Canadian Poets, 66
Feminist Communication Collective, 607
Feminist Faith Concerns, 1027
Feminist Lesbian Action Group, 132
Feminist News Service, 58
Feminist Newspaper, 1015
Feminist Party of Canada, 59
Feminist Print Media Conference (1980 : Ottawa, Ont.), 60, 732
Feminist Publications of Ottawa, 60, 732
Feminist Symposium (1973 : Montreal, Quebec), 597
Féministes lesbiennes de Montréal/Lesbian Feminists of Montreal, 608
Femme et le droit, 763
Femme et le film (Québec, Québec), 1262
Femme et le film (Toronto, Ont.), 95
Femmes chefs de foyer (Shawinigan, Québec), 1205
Femmes d'aujourd'hui, 207
Femmes d'ici, 588, 1131
Femmes et droit, 763
Femmes et justice, 1196, 1253
Femmes et les mots (Vancouver, B.C.), 863
Femmes et sociologie/anthropologie canadiennes, 97
Femmes et sociologie canadiennes, 97
Femmes pour l'action politique, 543
Fernie Women's Resource and Drop-in Centre, 807
Festival culturel des femmes canadiennes, 36
Festival des femmes canadiennes, 36
FFCF, 55
FFCF (Alberta), 206
FFCF d'Oshawa, 1026
FFCF (Gravelbourg, Sask.), 922
FFCF. Section Rouyn-Noranda, 605
FFCF. Section Willow Bunch, 246
FFQ, 603, 1203
FFQ. Conseil régional de Québec, 604
FGWRC, 958
Ficelles pour l'accès des femmes au travail, 1206
Fifty-Two Per Cent Solution: Women for Equality, Justice, and Peace, 1351
Fighting Back (1982 : Toronto, Ont.), 504
Filles de Jésus. Résidence de l'avenue A, 1248
Fine Kettle of Fish : Lesbians and Feminists in the Women's Movement (1979 : Toronto, Ont.), 424
Fireweed : A Quarterly Journal, 61
Fireweed : A Women's Literary and Cultural Journal, 61
First Mature Women's Network Society, 808
First United Church (Kelowna, B.C.). Wednesday Nite Live, 860
FLAG (Fredericton, N.B.), 644
FLAG (Victoria, B.C.), 132
Flaming Apron, 609
FLF, 610, 611
Flin Flon Graduate Nurses Association, 297
Fly by Night Lounge, 391
FMMF, 1283
FNFCF, 55
FNFCF (Alberta), 206

FNFCF (Gravelbourg, Sask.), 922
FNFCF (Oshawa, Ont.), 1026
FNFCF. Section Rouyn-Noranda, 605
FNFCF. Section Willow Bunch, 246
FNFL, 56
FNS, 58
FNSII, 730
Focus sur l'action féminine, 1122
Follow-up Committee, March 8 1984 Coalition, 562
Fondation du refuge pour femmes Chez Doris/Chez Doris, the Women's Shelter Foundation, 1207
Fondation Muriel McQueen Fergusson/Muriel McQueen Fergusson Foundation, 1283
Fonds d'action et d'éducation juridiques pour les femmes/Women's Legal Education and Action Fund, 733
Fonds d'action et d'éducation juridiques pour les femmes. Section Nouveau-Brunswick/Women's Legal Education and Action Fund. New Brunswick Branch, 1284
For the Public Good, 473, 1066
FormOsud, 1208
Forrest House, 677
Fort Garry Women's Resource Centre, 958
Fort McMurray Sexual Assault Centre, 893
Fort St John Women's Resource Centre, 809
Fort St John Women's Resource Society, 809
FPC, 59
FPO, 60, 732
FRCC, 1285
Fredericton Lesbians and Gays, 644
Fredericton Rape Crisis Centre, 1285
Fredericton Women's Centre, 645
Freespace, 836
Friend Indeed Publications/Publications Une Véritable Amie, 1209
Friends of Hagar, 392
Front de libération des femmes du Québec, 610, 611
Front de libération des femmes québécoises, 610, 611
Fruit Cocktail, 416, 1040
Furies, 1339
FWIC, 51
GAE, 664
Gais de l'Outaouais, 346, 996
Galerie La Centrale, 592, 593
Galerie Powerhouse, 592
Gallerie Publications, 734
Gallerie Women's Art, 734
Gallerie : Artists' News, 734
Gallerie : Women Artists, 734
Gander Status of Women Council, 1357
Gander Women's Centre, 1357
GATE (Toronto, Ont.), 393
GATE (Vancouver, B.C.), 133
Gateway Status of Women Council, 1358
Gateway Women's Centre, 1358
GAY, 352, 1001
Gay Academic Union, 519
Gay Alliance at York, 352, 1001
Gay Alliance for Equality (Halifax, N.S.), 664
Gay Alliance toward Equality (Toronto, Ont.), 393
Gay Alliance toward Equality (Vancouver, B.C.), 133
Gay and Lesbian Academics, Students, and Staff (University of Calgary), 894

Gay Archives Collective (Vancouver, B.C.), 107
Gay Christian Week, 298
Gay Community Appeal of Toronto, 416, 1040
Gay Community Calendar, 394
Gay Conference for Lesbians and Gay Men in Canada and Quebec (4th : 1976 : Toronto, Ont.), 393
Gay Friends of Concordia, 613
Gay Interest Group of the Canadian Library Association, 25
Gay/Lesbian Outreach, 810
Gay Religious Group of Regina, 923
Gay Rising, 393
Gay Students Association (University of Calgary), 894
Gay Students Society (University of Calgary), 894
Gay Tide, 133
Gay Week, 298
Gay Women Unlimited, 395
Gayline, 1063
Gays and Lesbians against the Right Everywhere, 396
Gays and Lesbians at the University of Toronto, 516
Gays and Lesbians in Health Care, 397
Gays and Lesbians of Trent and Peterborough, 511, 1087
Gays at the University of Toronto, 517
Gays for Equality (Winnipeg, Man.), 299
Gays in Health Care, 397
Gays of Ottawa, 347, 997
Gays of Trent and Peterborough, 511, 1087
George Brown College. Advisory Committee for Equity, 398
George Brown College. Affirmative Action Advisory Committee, 398
GERM, 399
GFE, 299
GGUL, 634
GIG, 25
GIV, 1210, 1211
GLARE, 396
GLASS, 894
GLAUT, 516
GLHC, 397
GLO, 810
GLTP, 511, 1087
GMR, 62
GO, 346, 347, 996, 997
GO Info, 346, 347, 996, 997
Golden Women's Centre Society, 811
Golden Women's Resource Centre, 811
Good Daycare, 383
Grande Cache Transition House, 895
Grande Prairie Women's Place, 208
Grapevine, 422
Greater Victoria Women's Shelter Society, 812
GREMF, 1261
Group for Equal Rights at McMaster, 399
Groupe de concertation des Franco-Albertaines, 209
Groupe de recherche multidisciplinaire féministe, 1261
Groupe des femmes canadiennes-françaises (Thunder Bay, Ont.), 1028
Groupe féminin pluri-elles, 1028
Groupe femmes, gestion et entreprises, 599
Groupe gai de l'Université Laval, 634
Groupe intervention vidéo, 1210, 1211
Groupe ma'me chose, 1149
Groupe marxiste révolutionnaire/Revolutionary Marxist Group, 62

Growing Pains, 125
Growing Room Collective, 735
GTP, 511, 1087
Guelph Business and Professional Women's Club, 400
Guelph Council for International Women's Year, 401
Guelph International Women's Year Council, 401
Guelph IWY Council, 401
Guelph-Wellington Women in Crisis, 1029
Guelph Women's Centre, 402
GWU, 395
GWWIC, 1029
gynergy books, 1310
Half The Sky Feminist Theatre Company, 1030
Halifax City Regional Library. North Branch Library. Women's Group, 1325
Halifax Club of Business and Professional Women, 665
Halifax Local Council of Women, 666
Halifax Women's Centre, 680
Halifax Women's Housing Coop, 1326
Halifax Young Women's Christian Association, 667, 1327
Halifax YWCA, 667, 1327
Hamilton and District Local Council of Women, 403
Hamilton McMaster Gay Liberation Movement, 434
Hamilton McMaster Homophile Association, 434
Hamilton-Wentworth Chapter of Native Women. Native Women's Centre, 1047
Hamilton-Wentworth Native Women's Centre, 1047
Hamilton Women Back into Stelco Committee, 542
Happenstance, 1067
Harbinger Community Services, 576
Harbour House, 1343
Harpies, 336
Hatch, 689, 1364
Haven House, 849
Havre des femmes, 1212
Hay River Women's Centre, 781
Hay River Women's Coalition, 781
Healing Images, 358
Health Sciences Association of British Columbia, 813
Healthmatters, 162, 855
Healthsharing : A Canadian Women's Health Quarterly, 96
HEC. Groupe femmes, gestion et entreprises., 599
HEIB, 300
HER, 814
HERE. Local 40, 815
Herizons, 736
Herspectives, 814
Herstory, 959
Hestia House, 1286
Hiring Opportunities for Women, 828
Holly Near Concert Organizing Committee, 404
Home Economists in Business — Winnipeg, 300
Home of the Guardian Angel. Single Parent Centre, 1340
Homebase, 1042
Hoots from the Y's Owl, 414, 1036
Hotel, Restaurant, Culinary Employees, and Bartenders Union. Local 40, 815
Hour a Day Study Club, 405
Housecall, 1033
HSA, 813

HWCNW. Native Women's Centre, 1047
ICREF, 64, 739
Identity, 406
IGCC, 817
IGS, 817
IH, 897
IIDOIC, 700
IINC, 737
ILGWU. Local 216, 301
ILGWU. Local 237, 301
ILGWU. Local 286, 301
ILGWU. Local 304, 301
ILGWU. Local 319, 301
ILI, 1219, 1220
Images : West Kootenay Women's Paper, 134, 816
Immigrant Voices, 1300
Immigrant Women's Association of Manitoba, 960
Immigrant Women's Association of Manitoba. Thompson Chapter, 961
Immigrant Women's Health Centre, 1031
Immigrant Women's Job Placement Centre, 1032
Impetus : The Black Woman (1977 : Windsor, Ont.), 405
Impulsion-Travail, 1213
In Touch, 1034
in versions, 970
Incentives, 314
Indian and Inuit Nurses of Canada/Association des infirmières et infirmiers autochtones du Canada, 737
Indian Brook Women's Group, 668
Indian Rights for Indian Women, 63
Indigenous Women's Collective of Manitoba, 962
Indochinese Women's Conference (1971 : Toronto, Ont.), 509
INFACT, 738
Infant Feeding Action Coalition Canada, 738
Infirmière canadienne, 8
Infirmières et infirmiers diplômés d'origine indienne du Canada, 700
Info, 761
Info-Éclair, 1149
Info Lesbo, 1219, 1220
Inform'elle, 1214
Informelles, 1158
Inside Out, 1324
Institut canadien de recherches sur les femmes/Canadian Research Institute for the Advancement of Women, 64, 739
Institut Simone de Beauvoir/Simone de Beauvoir Institute, 1215
Institute for the Study of Women, 670, 1331
Institute of Women's Studies, Carleton University, 1004
Integrity Regina, 923
Inter-Board Committee of the Women's Missionary Societies of Canada, 771
Interaction, 558, 1107
Interaction femmes-santé, 558, 1107
Intercede, 1084
Interchange, 414, 1036
Interim Committee of the Federated Women's Missionary Boards of Canada, 771
International Coalition to End Domestic Exploitation, 1084
International Ladies Garment Workers Union. Local 216, 301
International Ladies Garment Workers Union. Local 237, 301
International Ladies Garment Workers Union. Local 286, 301
International Ladies Garment Workers Union. Local 304, 301

International Ladies Garment Workers Union. Local 319, 301
International Peace Conference (1985 : Halifax, N.S.), 43
International Women's Day Coalition of Marxist-Leninists and Progressives, 135
International Women's Day Coalition (Toronto, Ont.), 439
International Women's Day Committee (Toronto, Ont.), 505, 1085
International Women's Day Committee (Vancouver, B.C.), 136
International Women's Week Coalition (Kingston, Ont.), 407
Interprovincial Home for Women, 1276
Interval Home (Lloydminster, Alta.), 897
Interval House of Ottawa-Carleton, 1033
Interval House (Saskatoon, Sask.), 944
Inuit Women's Association of Canada, 757
Iranian Woman Publications of Canada, 740
Iris Kirby House, 689, 1364
IRIW, 63
Ishtar Women's Centre and Transition House, 137
Iskwew, 924
Iskwew : Saskatchewan Native Women's Movement Newsletter, 263
Island Gay Community Centre Society, 817
Island Gay Society, 817
Isobel Johnson Shelter, 259, 936
Isquway House, 984
Issue (Association of Ontario Midwives), 998
Issue (Midwifery Task Force of Ontario), 1041
ISW, 670, 1331
IWA, 757
IWAM, 960
IWAM. Thompson Chapter, 961
IWD Coalition of Marxist-Leninists and Progressives, 135
IWDC (Toronto, Ont.), 505, 1085
IWHC, 1031
IWJPC, 1032
IWS, 1004
Jane Doe Study Group, 408
Jardilec, 1167
Jewish Federation of Greater Toronto. Jewish Women's Federation, 1034
Jewish Women's Federation, 1034
Jezebel Productions, 1328
Journal féministe, 1014
Journal Ficelle, 1212
Juniper House, 1329
JWF, 1034
K-W Woman's Place, 409
K-W Women's Coalition for Repeal of the Abortion Laws, 413
Kamloops and District Elizabeth Fry Society, 818
Kamloops Sexual Assault Counselling Centre, 819
Kaslo Women's Centre, 138
Kaslo Women's Group, 138
Kate Booth House, 820
KCWA, 1037
Kelowna University Women's Club, 797
Kelowna Women's Resource Centre, 821
Kenora Sexual Assault Centre, 1035
Kincardine Women Alive, 410
Kincardine Women's Study Group, 410
Kinesis, 158
Kingston Women's Centre, 411
Kingston Women's Liberation Movement, 411
Kipichisichakanisik Women's Peace Camp, 247

Kirby House, 689, 1364
Kitchener-Waterloo Business and Professional Women's Club, 412
Kitchener-Waterloo Woman's Place, 409
Kitchener-Waterloo Women's Coalition for Repeal of the Abortion Laws, 413
Kitchener-Waterloo Young Women's Christian Association, 414, 1036
Kitchener-Waterloo YWCA, 414, 1036
Kitimat Business and Professional Women's Club, 139
Knitting Circle of the New Left Caucus, 448
Korean Canadian Women's Association, 1037
KSAC, 1035
KSACC, 819
Kumtuks, 163, 857
L/L, 421
La Centrale, 592, 593
La Leche League Alberta/Northwest Territories, 210
La Leche League International. Calgary Branch, 211
La Ronge Native Women's Council, 925
La Ronge Native Women's Organization, 925
Labor Unity, 2, 695
Labour Centre. Socialist Women's Caucus, 408
Labrador West Family Crisis Shelter, 1359
Labrador West Status of Women Council, 1360
Ladies Coldstorage Workers Union, 684
LAFMPAG, 140
Lake Agazzis Amazon Guild, 302
Lakehead Social Planning Council. Childcare Committee, 1038
Lakeshore Business and Professional Women's Club, 506
Lakeshore Unitarian Church. Family Planning Advisory Service, 612
Lanark County Interval House and Sexual Assault Centre, 1039
Langley Family Services. Gay Lesbian Outreach, 810
Langley Gay/Lesbian Support Group, 810
LAR, 425
Latin American Women's Cultural Society, 785
Laval au féminin, 1216
Lavender Sheets, 424
Lavender Times, 896
LCW (St John's, Nfld.), 685
LDC, 420
LEA Wife Abuse Committee, 963
LEAF, 772
LEAF. New Brunswick Branch, 1301
LEAF (Vancouver, B.C.), 862
Leaflet, 862
League for Socialist Action, 65
League of Canadian Poets. Feminist Caucus, 66
Leche League Alberta/Northwest Territories, 210
Leche League International. Calgary Branch, 211
Leila Khaled Collective, 415
Lennoxville and District Women's Centre/Centre des femmes de Lennoxville et des environs, 1217
LES FAM, 646
Lesbia News, 822
Lesbian and Feminist Mothers Political Action Group, 140
Lesbian and Gay Academic Society at the University of Toronto, 519
Lesbian and Gay Alliance at York, 352, 1001
Lesbian and Gay Community Appeal Foundation, 416, 1040
Lesbian and Gay Community Appeal of Toronto, 416, 1040
Lesbian and Gay Friends of Concordia, 613
Lesbian and Gay History Group of Toronto, 417

Lesbian and Gay Pride Day Committee (Toronto, Ont.), 418
Lesbian Canada Lesbienne, 658
Lesbian Caucus of the Gay Alliance toward Equality Bulletin, 393
Lesbian Collective (Waterloo, Ont.), 419
Lesbian Conference Committee (Vancouver, B.C.), 67
Lesbian Conference (1981 : Vancouver, B.C.). Organizing Committee, 67
Lesbian Dance Committee, 420
Lesbian Dance Council, 420
Lesbian Feminists of Montreal/Féministes lesbiennes de Montréal, 614
Lesbian/Gay Pride Planning Committee (Regina, Sask.), 926
Lesbian Information Line, 896
Lesbian/Lesbienne, 421
Lesbian Mothers' Defence Fund (Toronto, Ont.), 422
Lesbian Mothers Support Group, 303
Lesbian Network (Toronto, Ont.), 503
Lesbian Organization of Kitchener, 423
Lesbian Organization of Toronto, 424
Lesbian Perspective, 424
Lesbian Power : Organizing for the '80s (1981 : Vancouver, B.C.), 67
Lesbian Sexuality Conference (1984 : Toronto, Ont.), 354
Lesbian Studies Coalition of Concordia, 615, 1218
Lesbians against the Right, 425
Lesbians of Ottawa Now, 426
Lesbiennes de Montréal/Montreal Gay Women, 616
Lesbo Info, 1219, 1220
Let Us Out Books, 507
Lethbridge and District YWCA, 916
Lez Studs, 615, 1218
LFS. Gay/Lesbian Outreach, 810
LGAS, 519
LGAY, 352, 1001
LGCA, 416, 1040
Liaison information entraide novatrice, 1221
Liberal Party. Alberta Women's Liberal Association, 186
Liberal Party of Canada. National Federation of Liberal Women, 98
Liberal Party of Canada. National Women's Liberal Commission/Parti libéral du Canada. Commission libérale féminine nationale, 68, 741
Liberal Party of Canada. Women's Liberal Federation of Canada, 98
Liberal Party (Ontario). Women's Perspective Advisory Committee, 1059
Liberation Media, 561
Liberté Égalité Sororité : Femmes acadiennes de Moncton, 646
Libra House, 1361
Lien (Montréal, Québec), 1127
LIEN (Trois-Rivières-Ouest, Québec), 1221
Life Line Society. Marguerite Dixon House, 825
Lifeline Program, 856
Ligue communiste (marxiste-léniniste) du Canada, 630
Ligue des droits et libertés. Office des droits des femmes, 617
Ligue socialiste ouvrière, 65
LIL, 896
Link, 581, 1116
Linkages, 839
LLC, 429
LLLI. Calgary Branch, 211
Lloydminster Interval Home, 897
LMDF, 422
Local Council of Women (Calgary, Alta.), 189

Local Council of Women (Hamilton, Ont.), 403
Local Council of Women (London, Ont.), 427
Local Council of Women of Montreal, 621
Local Council of Women of Regina, 253
Local Council of Women of Toronto, 496
Local Council of Women (Ottawa, Ont.), 465
Local Council of Women (St John's, Nfld.), 685
Local Council of Women (Victoria, B.C.), 164
Local Council of Women (Weston, Ont.), 428
Local Council of Women (Windsor, Ont.), 532
London Lesbian Collective, 429
London Status of Women Action Group, 430
London Women's Liberation, 431
London Women's Resource Centre, 432
Long Time Coming, 618
LOOK, 423
LOON, 426
LOOT, 424
Louis Riel University Family Co-op, 147
Lower Fraser Valley Lesbian Support Network, 810
LRNWC, 925
LSA, 65
LSCC, 615, 1218
LSO, 65
LSPC. Childcare Committee, 1038
LSWAG, 430
Lundar/Eriksdale/Ashern Wife Abuse Committee, 963
LWRC, 432
Lysistrata, 166
Mac *see* Mc
MACSW, 305, 964
MACSW. Parkland Branch, 979
MAFPA, 1330
MAIFM, 1144
Maison Catherine Leblond, 1164
Maison d'accueil et d'information pour les femmes de la Mauricie, 1144
Maison d'accueil et d'information pour les femmes de la Mauricie. Séjournelle : Maison d'aide et d'hébergement pour femmes victimes de violence conjugale, 1250
Maison d'aide et d'hébergement pour femmes victimes de violence conjugale (Shawinigan, Québec), 1250
Maison de Passage House, 1287, 1288
Maison De Connivence, 1222
Maison des femmes de la Côte-Nord, secteur ACT, 1151
Maison des femmes de la région de Rimouski, 1223
Maison des femmes du Bas-St-Laurent, 1223
Maison d'hébergement de Pabos, 1224
Maison du réconfort, 1225
Maison La Source, 1226
Maison le coin des femmes (Sept-Îles, Québec), 1227, 1228
Maison Mikana, 1229
Maison Notre-Dame La Source, 1226
Maison Unies-Vers-Femmes, 1230
Maiya House, 823
Makara, 69
Makara Publishing and Design Co-operative, 69
Making Waves, 958
Malaspina College. Faculty Association. Status of Women Committee, 824
Mama Quilla II, 438

NAME INDEX

Manitoba Abortion Action Coalition, 304
Manitoba Action Committee on the Status of Women, 305, 964
Manitoba Action Committee on the Status of Women. Parkland Branch, 979
Manitoba Artists for Women's Art, 970
Manitoba Association of Home Nurses, 306
Manitoba Association of Licensed Practical Nurses, 306
Manitoba Association of Practical Nurses, 306
Manitoba Association of Social Workers, 307
Manitoba Association of Trained Practical Nurses, 306
Manitoba Child Care Association, 965
Manitoba Coalition for Reproductive Choice, 966
Manitoba Committee on the Status of Women, 305, 964
Manitoba Federation of Labour. Equal Rights and Opportunities Committee, 308, 967
Manitoba Federation of Labour. Women's Committee, 308, 967
Manitoba Gay/Lesbian Archive, 986
Manitoba Homebirth Network, 968
Manitoba Institute on Society and Sexuality. Winnipeg Gay/Lesbian Resource Centre, 986
Manitoba Organization of Nurses' Associations. Local 1, 309
Manitoba Provincial Organization of Business and Professional Women's Clubs, 310
Manitoba Society of Occupational Therapists, 311
Manitoba Teacher, 312, 969
Manitoba Teachers' Federation, 312, 969
Manitoba Teachers' Society, 312, 969
Manitoba Volunteer Committee on the Status of Women, 305, 964
Manitoba Women in Trades Association, 334
Manitoba Women's Institute, 313
Manitoba Women's Newspaper, 736
March 8 1984 Coalition. Follow-up Committee, 562
March 8th Coalition, 439
Margaret Beaton Foundation for Women, 669
Marguerite Dixon House, 825
Marianne's Place, 1029
Marie Debout, Centre d'éducation des femmes, 1231
MASW, 307
MATCH International Centre/Centre international MATCH, 70, 742
MATCH international (Saguenay-Lac-St-Jean, Québec), 1232
Maternal Health Clinic, 473, 1066
Matrix, 430
Mature Women's Network, 808
Maud Bevan Transition House, 835
Mavis McMullen Housing Society, 826
MAW, 1042
MAWA, 970
May 10th March Committee, 452
May 28th Coalition for Abortion Rights, 440
MCC (Toronto, Ont.), 442
MCCA, 965
MCF, 444
MCFA. Status of Women Committee, 824
McGill Committee for Teaching and Research on Women, 619
McGill University. Committee for Teaching and Research on Women, 619
McGill University. Feminist Symposium (1973 : Montreal, Quebec), 597
McGill University. Women's Collective Press, 636
McGill University. Women's Union, 620
McGill Women's Union, 620
McMaster Faculty Association. Committee to Study the Status of Women Faculty at McMaster, 433
McMaster Homophile Association, 434
McMaster Student Social Work Association. Sub-committee to Celebrate International Women's Year, 435
McMaster University. Equal Rights Review and Co-ordinating Committee of Senate., 437
McMaster University. Faculty Association. Committee to Study the Status of Women Faculty at McMaster, 433
McMaster University. Faculty of Humanities Council. Sub-committee to Encourage Qualified Women Students to Proceed to Honours and Graduate Study in the Humanities, 436
McMaster University. Group for Equal Rights, 399
McMaster University. Homophile Association, 434
McMaster University. Senate. Equal Rights Review and Co-ordinating Committee, 437
McMaster University. Student Social Work Association. Sub-committee to Celebrate International Women's Year, 435
MCTRW, 619
MCVI, 1233, 1234
MCW, 621
Media Club of Canada, 37
Media Club of Canada. Calgary Branch, 193
Media Club of Canada. Edmonton Branch, 194
Media Club of Canada. Winnipeg Branch, 292
MediaWatch/Évaluation-Médias, 743
MediaWatch/Évaluation-Médias (Outremont, Québec), 1200
Medicine Hat Women's Shelter, 898
Melfort Sexual Assault and Information Centre, 928
Memorial University of Newfoundland. Women's Association, 686
Memorial University of Newfoundland. Women's Studies Programme, 1362
Mentoring Artists for Women's Art, 970
Metro Area Family Planning Association, 1330
Metro Toronto Women's Credit Union, 441
Metropolitan Community Church of Toronto, 442
MFL. Equal Rights and Opportunities Committee, 308, 967
MFL. Women's Committee, 308, 967
MHA, 434
MHN, 968
Midwifery Task Force of Ontario, 1041
Minerva, 21, 48, 707, 721
Minnedosa and Area Committee on Wife Abuse, 971
MISS. Winnipeg Gay/Lesbian Resource Centre, 986
Mission Transition House Society, 800
Mixer News, 815
Mizpah Transition House, 827
MLU, 443
MMFF, 1289
Moisson, 1147
MONA. Local 1, 309
Moncton Council of Women, 647
Monthly, 681
Montreal Council of Women/Conseil des femmes de Montréal, 621
Montreal Gay Women/Lesbiennes de Montréal, 622
Montreal Lesbian Conference (1975 : Montreal, Quebec), 622
Montreal Women's Liberation, 623
Montreal Young Women's Christian Association, 624
Montreal Young Women's Christian Association. Women's Centre, 638
Montreal YWCA, 624
Montreal YWCA. Women's Centre, 638
Moose Jaw Business and Professional Women's Club, 241

Moose Jaw Co-operative Commonwealth Federation Women's Club, 248

Moose Jaw Council of Women, 249

Moose Jaw Transition House, 927

Mother Led Union, 443

Mother's Allowance Group (Winnipeg, Man.), 314

Mothers Are Women, 1042

Mothers' Association Day Nursery, 296

Mother's Club (Windsor, Ont.), 405

Mothers Organizing Mothers, 389

Mount Saint Vincent College, 670, 1331

Mount Saint Vincent University, 670, 1331

Mouvement contre le viol, 1233

Mouvement contre le viol et l'inceste, 1233, 1234

Movement for Christian Feminism, 444

Mrs Dalloway's Books, 1043

Mrs D's, 1043

MSOT, 311

MTFO, 1041

MTS, 312, 969

Multicultural Council of Professional Women, 1044

Multicultural Women's Association, 1045

Multicultural Women's Centre, 1045

MUN. Women's Association, 686

MUN. Women's Studies Programme, 1362

Munroe House, 179, 873

Muriel McQueen Fergusson Foundation/Fondation Muriel McQueen Fergusson, 1289

MWA, 1045

MWL, 623

MWN, 808

N-R, 1235

NAC, 71, 744

Naches, 625, 626

Naissance-Renaissance, 1235

Nanaimo Voice of Women, 116

Nanaimo Women's Resources Society, 828

Nannies' Voice, 861

Naomi Society for Battered Women, 1332

Naomi Society for Victims of Family Violence, 1332

National Action Committee on the Status of Women/Comité canadien d'action sur le statut de la femme, 71, 744

National Ad Hoc Action Committee on the Status of Women, 71, 744

National Association of Women and the Law/Association nationale de la femme et du droit, 745

National Association of Women and the Law. Newfoundland and Labrador Caucus, 1363

National Association of Women and the Law (Vancouver, B.C.), 847

National Association of Women in Construction. Ottawa, Ontario Chapter 319, 1046

National Coaching School for Women, 746

National Committee on Indian Rights for Indian Women, 63

National Conference of Women in Trades (1980 : Winnipeg, Man.), 334

National Conference of Women's Centres (1st : 1975 : Thunder Bay, Ont.), 451

National Conference on Abortion (1967 : Ottawa, Ont.), 11

National Congress of Black Women of Canada (4th : 1977 : Windsor, Ont.), 405

National Council of Jewish Women of Canada, 72, 747

National Council of Jewish Women of Canada. Calgary Branch, 212

National Council of Jewish Women of Canada. Edmonton Section, 899

National Council of Jewish Women of Canada. Winnipeg Section, 315, 972

National Council of Women of Canada, 73

National Council of Young Men's Christian Associations. Task Force on the Status of Women in the YMCA, 74

National Eating Disorder Information Centre, 748

National Farmers Union. Women's Advisory Committee, 749

National Federation of Liberal Women, 98

National Federation of Nurses' Unions/Fédération nationale des syndicats d'infirmières/infirmiers, 750

National Feminist Print Media Conference (1980 : Ottawa, Ont.), 60, 732

National Gay Rights Coalition, 24

National Lesbian Conference (2nd : 1975 : Montreal, Quebec), 622

National Lesbian Conference (1976 : Ottawa, Ont.), 426

National Lesbian Forum/Alliance nationale des lesbiennes, 751

National Native Women's Conference (1st : 1971 : Edmonton, Alta.), 231

National Organization of Immigrant and Visible Minority Women of Canada/Organisation nationale des femmes immigrantes et des femmes appartenant à une minorité visible du Canada, 752

National Watch on Images of Women in the Media, 743

National Watch on Images of Women in the Media (Outremont, Quebec), 1200

National Women's Liberal Commission, 68, 741

National Women's Press Conference (1974 : Saskatoon, Sask.), 58

Native Nurse, 737

Native Nurses, 737

Native Sisterhood, 27

Native Women's Association of Canada, 753

Native Women's Centre (Hamilton, Ont.), 1047

Native Women's Resource Centre (Toronto, Ont.), 1048

Native Women's Transition Centre (Winnipeg, Man.), 973

Natural Family Planning Centre, 981

NAWIC. Ottawa, Ontario Chapter 319, 1046

NAWL, 745

NAWL. Newfoundland and Labrador Caucus, 1363

NAWL (Vancouver, B.C.), 847

NBFWO, 1291

NBWI, 650

NCJW, 72, 747

NCJW. Calgary Branch, 212

NCJW. Edmonton Section, 899

NCJW. Winnipeg Section, 315, 972

NCSW, 746

NCWC, 73

NDP (British Columbia). Vancouver Women's Committee, 112

NDP (British Columbia). Women's Rights Committee, 113, 793

NDP. Dovercourt NDP Women's Action Committee, 385

NDP. Federal Women's Committee, 75

NDP of Prince Edward Island. Advisory Committee on Women's Issues, 1308

NDP of Prince Edward Island. Standing Committee on Women, 1308

NDP (Ontario). Provincial Committee on Women's Issues, 457

NDP (Ontario). Women's Committee, 457

NDP. Participation of Women Committee. Task Force on Older Women in Canada, 76

NDP (Quebec). Comité féminin, 628

NDP. Rosemary Brown Leadership Campaign Committee, 77

NDP. Waffle. Women's Caucus, 94

NDP. Women's Liberation Caucus, 78

NDP. Women's Liberation Movement, 78

NECIC, 928

NEDIC, 748
Nellie, 141, 829
Nellie Langford Rowell Library, 1049
Nellie McClung Conference (1975 : Guelph, Ont.), 401
Nellie's, 445
Nelson and District Women's Centre, 864
Nelson Women's Centre, 864
Network of Saskatchewan Women, 260, 937
NEW, 1050
New Brunswick Coalition for Family Peace, 1290
New Brunswick Coalition for Human Rights Reform/Coalition pour la réforme des droits de la personne du Nouveau-Brunswick, 648
New Brunswick Coalition of Transition Houses for Abused Women, 1290
New Brunswick Farm Women's Organization, 1291
New Brunswick Native Indian Women's Council, 649
New Brunswick Women's Institutes, 650
New College. Women's Studies Programme, 446
New College. Women's Studies Student Union, 573
New Democratic Party (British Columbia). Vancouver Women's Committee, 112
New Democratic Party (British Columbia). Women's Rights Committee, 113, 793
New Democratic Party. Dovercourt NDP Women's Action Committee, 385
New Democratic Party. Federal Women's Committee/Nouveau Parti démocratique. Comité fédéral féminin, 75
New Democratic Party of Prince Edward Island. Advisory Committee on Women's Issues, 1308
New Democratic Party of Prince Edward Island. Standing Committee on Women, 1308
New Democratic Party (Ontario). Provincial Committee on Women's Issues, 457
New Democratic Party (Ontario). Women's Committee, 457
New Democratic Party. Participation of Women Committee. Task Force on Older Women in Canada, 76
New Democratic Party (Quebec). Comité féminin, 628
New Democratic Party. Rosemary Brown Leadership Campaign Committee, 77
New Democratic Party. Waffle. Women's Caucus, 94
New Democratic Party. Women's Liberation Caucus, 78
New Democratic Party. Women's Liberation Movement, 78
New Experiences for Refugee Women, 1050
New Feminists, 447
New Glasgow Local Council of Women, 671
New Left Caucus. Knitting Circle, 448
New Left Committee. Women's Liberation Front, 449
New Woman Centre/Centre de la femme nouvelle, 627
Newfoundland and Labrador Federation of Labour. Women's Committee, 687
Newfoundland Federation of Labour. Women's Committee, 687
Newfoundland Outport Nursing and Industrial Association, 688
Newfoundland Status of Women Council, 689, 1364
Newsflash, 790
NFNU, 750
NFU. Women's Advisory Committee, 749
NGRC, 24
Niagara Women This Year, 450
Niagara Women's Magazine, 450
Nikamo Ishwewak (Singing Women), 801
NLC. Knitting Circle, 448
NLF, 751

NMAM, 975
NOIVMWC, 752
NONIA, 688
North Branch Library Women's Group, 1325
North East Crisis Intervention Centre, 928
North Shore Voice of Women, 117
North Shore Women's Centre, 141, 829
North Win House, 985
Northern Woman Journal, 1051
Northern Woman's Bookstore, 1052
Northern Women's Centre, 451
Northern Women's Coalition, 105
Northern Women's Resource Service, 974
Northwestern Ontario International Women's Decade Co-ordinating Council, 1054
Northwestern Ontario Regional Day Care Committee, 1053
Northwestern Ontario Women's Centre, 451
Northwestern Ontario Women's Decade Council, 1054
Northwestern Ontario Women's Health Education Project, 1055
Northwestern Ontario Women's Health Information Network, 1055
Not-So-Invisible Woman : Lesbian Perspectives in the Gay Movement (1976 : Kingston, Ont.), 477
Nous les femmes immigrantes, 1170
Nouveau départ, 1236
Nouveau départ national, 1236
Nouveau Parti démocratique. Comité fédéral féminin/New Democratic Party. Federal Women's Committee, 79
Nouveau Parti démocratique du Québec. Comité féminin, 628
Nouveau Parti démocratique Ontario. Comité des femmes, 457
Nouvel essor : La Femme noire (1977 : Windsor, Ont.), 405
Nova House (Richmond, B.C.), 802
Nova House (Selkirk, Man.), 980
Nova Scotia Home Economics Association. Cape Breton Branch, 672
Nova Scotia Voice of Women, 675
Nova Scotia Women Artists' Network, 1333
Nova Scotia Women's Action Committee, 673
Noyau, 1273
NPD. Comité fédéral féminin, 79
NPD (Ontario). Comité des femmes, 457
NPD-Q. Comité féminin, 628
NSWAC, 673
NSWAN, 1333
NSWC, 689, 1364
Nuevas Experiencias para Mujeres Refugiadas, 1050
Nurse-Midwives Association of Manitoba, 975
NWAC, 753
NWC, 1047
NWH, 985
NWLC, 68, 741
NWO Regional Day Care Committee, 1053
NWRC, 1048
NWRS, 974
NWTC, 973
OAITH, 1057
OARNA, 453
Oasis, 191, 882
Oasis de bonheur, 1127
OCA. Women's Art Mobile, 549
OCAC, 454
OCISO. Women's Outreach Program, 1045

OCRC, 464
OCSW, 456
October 25th Women's Action Coalition, 452
OEIU. Local 378, 142
Off Limits, 1070
Office and Professional Employees' Union. Local 378, 142
Office and Technical Employees' Union. Local 378, 142
Office Employees' International Union. Local 378, 142
OFR, 461
OFW, 376
OFWN, 1058
OISE. Women's Educational Resources Centre, 1105
Older Women's Network, 1056
OLP. Women's Perspective Advisory Committee, 1059
On Our Way, 213
ONDP. Provincial Committee on Women's Issues, 457
ONDP. Women's Committee, 457
One Day Awareness Conference (1976 : Hamilton, Ont.), 481
One Sky, 929
ONFIFAMVC, 754
Ontario Association of Interval and Transition Houses, 1057
Ontario Association of Midwives, 998
Ontario Association of Registered Nursing Assistants, 453
Ontario Coalition for Abortion Clinics, 454
Ontario Coalition for Better Child Care, 455
Ontario Coalition for Better Day Care, 455
Ontario College of Art. Women's Art Mobile, 549
Ontario Committee on the Status of Women, 456
Ontario Farm Women's Network, 1058
Ontario Federation of Women, 376
Ontario Institute for Studies in Education. Women's Educational Resources Centre, 1105
Ontario Lesbians' Conference (1978 : Ottawa, Ont.), 426
Ontario Liberal Party. Women's Perspective Advisory Committee, 1059
Ontario Messenger, 359
Ontario Native Women's Association, 1060
Ontario New Democratic Party. Provincial Committee on Women's Issues, 457
Ontario New Democratic Party. Women's Committee, 457
Ontario Nurse-Midwives Association, 998
Ontario Psychological Association. Task Force on the Status of Women in Psychology in Ontario, 458
Ontario Women for an Abortion Law Repeal Coalition, 459
Ontario Women's Abortion Action Conference (1971 : Toronto, Ont.), 459
Ontario Women's Abortion Law Repeal Coalition, 459
Ontario Women's Action Coalition/Coalition des femmes de l'Ontario, 460
ONWA, 1060
Open Women's Group, 408
Operation Family Rights, 461
OptiMSt, 777
Options for Women (Edmonton, Alta.), 214
Orbit, 327
Organisation marxiste-léniniste du Canada En Lutte!. Comité de la condition féminine, 629
Organisation nationale des femmes immigrantes et des femmes appartenant à une minorité visible du Canada/National Organization of Immigrant and Visible Minority Women of Canada, 754
Organizational Society for the Spouses of Military Members, 755
Organized Working Women (Toronto Area), 462
Original Women's Network, 976

Osborne House, 977
OSSOMM, 755
OTEU. Local 378, 142
Other Woman, 80
OtherWise : A Feminist Newspaper at U of T, 463
Ottawa-Carleton Immigrant Services Organization. Women's Outreach Program, 1045
Ottawa Coalition for Reproductive Choice, 464
Ottawa Local Council of Women, 465
Ottawa Women's Centre, 466, 1061
Ottawa Women's Centre. Chez nous, 1008
Ottawa Women's Information and Referral Service, 1062
Ottawa Women's Liberation Committee, 467
Ottawa Women's Liberation Group, 467
Our Lives, 1083
OWAC, 460
OWIRS, 1062
OWN (Toronto, Ont.), 1056
OWN (Winnipeg, Man.), 976
OWW, 462
PACE, 900
Pacific Women's Graphic Arts Co-operative Association, 69
Pandora, 1334
Pandora Publishing, 1334
Par celles, 1150
Parents' Information Bureau, 468
Parkland Crisis Centre, 978
Parkland Status of Women, 979
Parksville-Qualicum Voice of Women, 118
Parmi elles, 1152
Paroles de femmes, 1135
Parti communiste ouvrier. Comité des femmes, 630
Parti féministe du Canada, 59
Parti libéral du Canada. Commission libérale féminine nationale/ Liberal Party of Canada. National Women's Liberal Commission, 81, 756
Parti libéral du Canada. Fédération nationale des femmes libérales du Canada, 56
Parti progressiste conservateur du Canada. Bureau des femmes/ Progressive Conservative Party of Canada. Women's Bureau, 82
Parti progressiste conservatrice du Canada. Association des femmes, 7
Partisan Gallery. Women's Collective, 565
Partisan Gallery. Women's Perspective Collective, 565
Passage House, 1288
Passe-r-elle des Hautes-Laurentides, 1237
Passerelle de Weedon, 1238
PATHS, 934
Pauktuutit: Inuit Women's Association of Canada, 757
Pauline McGibbon Cultural Centre, 469
PAWRS, 832
PC Women's Association, 84
PCC, 978
PCWC, 1335
PCWO, 476, 1069
Pedestal, 161
P.E.I. NDP. Advisory Committee on Women's Issues, 1308
P.E.I. NDP. Standing Committee on Women, 1308
P.E.I. Rape and Sexual Assault Crisis Centre/Centre d'aide aux victimes de viol et d'agression sexuelle de l'Î.P.É., 1309
P.E.I. Women's Network Committee, 1313
PEIR/SACC, 1309

NAME INDEX

Penitentiary for Women (Kingston, Ont.). Canadian Native Sisterhood Organization, 27
Penticton and Area Women's Centre, 830
People for a Sane Society, 431
Perceptions : The Gay and Lesbian Newsmagazine of the Prairies, 930
Perspective : A Women's Journal, 238, 914
Perspectives (Kelowna Women's Resource Centre), 821
Perspectives (Young Women's Christian Association of Metropolitan Toronto), 581, 1116
Peterborough Women's Committee, 470
Peterborough Women's Place, 471
Peterborough Young Women's Christian Association, 582, 1117
Peterborough YWCA, 582, 1117
Petite Presse, 603, 1203
Photographers Gallery, 931
Pictou County Women's Centre, 1335
PIF, 1241
Pink Triangle Press, 15
Pink Triangle Services/Services du triangle rose, 1063
Pink Type, 15
PIRG (Simon Fraser University), 841
Place aux femmes/Women's Place (Ottawa, Ont.), 1064
Planned Parenthood Association of British Columbia, 831
Planned Parenthood Association of Halifax, Dartmouth, and Halifax County, 1330
Planned Parenthood Federation of Canada/Fédération pour le planning des naissances du Canada, 758
Planned Parenthood Manitoba, 316
Planned Parenthood Nova Scotia, 1336
Planned Parenthood Ontario, 472, 1065
Planned Parenthood Regina, 932
Planned Parenthood Saskatchewan, 250
Planned Parenthood Saskatoon Centre, 933
Planned Parenthood Society of Hamilton, 473, 1066
Planned Parenthood Waterloo Region, 1067
Planner, 933
Pléiades, 1151
PLOT, 474
Plug in Gallery. Manitoba Artists for Women's Art, 970
PLUM, 475
Point d'appui, Centre d'aide et de prévention des agressions à caractère sexuel de Rouyn, 1239
Political Lesbians of Toronto, 474
Political Lesbians United about the Media, 475
Politics of Contraception Conference (1976 : Toronto, Ont.), 341
Port Alberni Women's Resources Society, 832
Port Coquitlam Area Women's Centre, 143, 833
Powell River Voice of Women, 119
POWER (Winnipeg, Man.), 317
Powerhouse, 592, 593
Powerhouse Gallery, 593
PPABC, 831
PPFC, 758
PPHDHC, 1330
PPNS, 1336
PPO, 472, 1065
PPR, 932
PPSC, 933
PPSH, 473, 1066
PPWR, 1067
Prairie Woman : A Newsletter of Saskatoon Women's Liberation, 273

Prairie Women's Socialist-Feminist Conference (1978 : Saskatoon, Sask.), 273, 284
Press Gang, 144, 834
Prince Albert Business and Professional Women's Club, 251
Prince Albert Co-operative Health Centre. Iskwew/Women Helping Women, 924
Prince Edward Island New Democratic Party. Advisory Committee on Women's Issues, 1308
Prince Edward Island New Democratic Party. Standing Committee on Women, 1308
Prince Edward Island Rape and Sexual Assault Crisis Centre, 1309
Prince Edward Island Women's Network Committee, 1313
Prince Rupert Transition House, 835
Print Her, 1015
Priorities, 113, 793
Professional and Business Women's Club of Winnipeg, 291
Professional Secretaries International. Ville-Marie Chapter/ Association internationale des secrétaires professionnelles. Section Ville-Marie, 1240
Progressive Conservative Party of Canada. Women's Association, 84
Progressive Conservative Party of Canada. Women's Bureau/Parti progressiste conservateur du Canada. Bureau des femmes, 83
Progressive Conservative Women's Association/Association des femmes progressistes conservatrices, 84
Project Hostel, 1068
Project Lavender, 1220
Projet intégration des femmes, 1241
Projet lavande, 1219
Prostitutes and Other Women for Equal Rights (Winnipeg, Man.), 317
Providing Assistance, Counselling, and Education, 900
Provincial Association of Transition Houses of Saskatchewan, 934
Provincial Council of Women of British Columbia, 145
Provincial Council of Women of Manitoba, 318
Provincial Council of Women of New Brunswick, 651
Provincial Council of Women of Ontario, 476, 1069
Provincial Council of Women of Saskatchewan, 252
PSAC. Local 80384. Women's Committee, 1337
PSAC. Yellowknife Regional Women's Committee, 780
PSI. Ville-Marie Chapter, 1240
PSW, 979
PTS, 1063
Public Interest Research Group (Simon Fraser University), 841
Public Service Alliance of Canada. Local 80384. Women's Committee, 1337
Public Service Alliance of Canada. Yellowknife Regional Women's Committee, 780
Publications Une Véritable Amie/A Friend Indeed Publications, 1242
QHA. Conference Steering Committee, 477
Queen's Homophile Association. Conference Steering Committee, 477
Queen's University. Association of Women Teaching at Queen's, 348
Queen's University. Homophile Association. Conference Steering Committee, 477
Queen's University. Women's Centre, 1070
Queen's University. Women's Studies Programme. Ad Hoc Lesbian Speakers Series Committee, 478
Queen's University. Women's Studies Programme. Lesbian Speakers Series Committee, 478
Queen's University. Women's Study Action Committee, 479
Queen's Women's Centre, 1070
Radio Free Women, 480
Radio Libres Femmes, 480

Ragamuffin, 125
Ragweed Press, 1310
RAIF, 1245
Rainbow Harbour Women's Association, 901
Rape Crisis Centre (Hamilton), 481
Rape Crisis Centre (Montreal, Quebec), 1234
Rape Crisis Service (Fredericton, N.B.), 1285
Rape Relief, 852
Re-Nou-Vie, 1243
Rebel Girls' Rag : A Forum of Women's Resistance, 505, 1085
Recherches féministes, 1261
Recherches sur la femme : Bulletin d'information canadien, 50, 726
Red Deer Local Council of Women, 215
Red Deer University Women's Club, 216
Redlight Theatre, 482
Reel Life, 674
Reflet, 1165
Refuge pour les femmes de l'Ouest de l'Île/West Island Women's Shelter, 1244
Regina CCLOW, 243
Regina Council of Women, 253
Regina Status of Women Co-ordinating Committee, 254
Regina Transition Women's Society, 255
Regina Voice of Women, 256
Regina Women's Community Centre, 935
Regina Women's Community Centre and Rape Crisis Line, 935
Regina Women's Community Centre and Sexual Assault Line, 935
Regina Women's Liberation Movement, 257
Regina Women's Network, 258
Regina Young Women's Christian Association, 259, 936
Regina YWCA, 259, 936
Regional Lesbian Conference (1983 : Toronto, Ont.), 483
Regional Lesbian Conference (Ontario). Coordinating Committee, 483
Regional Women's Health Centre. Bay Centre for Birth Control, 1000
Registered Nurses Association of B.C. Labour Relations Division, 794
Registered Nurses Association of Ontario. Sub-Committee on Nursing Assistants, 453
Registered Nurses of Canadian Indian Ancestry, 737
Regroupement québécois des centres d'aide et de lutte contre les agressions à caractère sexuel. Comité Espace-Québec. Espace Val d'Or, 1198
Remarkable Women of Newfoundland and Labrador, 685
Répercussion, 1156
Répliquée, 1159
Reproductive Health Clinic, 902
Réseau d'action des femmes handicapées du Canada. Action des femmes handicapées (Montréal, Québec), 1120
Réseau d'action des femmes handicapées du Canada/DisAbled Women's Network Canada, 759
Réseau d'action en milieu urbain/Urban Core Support Network, 760
Réseau d'action et d'information pour les femmes, 1245
Réseau des femmes du Sud de l'Ontario, 1071
Réseau féministe populaire, 1246
Réseau national d'Action éducation femmes, 761
Réseau National WITT, 769
Réseau populaire des femmes du Québec, 1246
Réseau vidé-elle, 1247
Résidence de l'avenue A, 1248
Resources for Feminist Research/Documentation sur la recherche féministe, 85, 762
Restigouche Family Crisis Interveners/Unité d'intervention pour crises familiales de Restigouche, 1292

Revolutionary Marxist Group/Groupe marxiste révolutionnaire, 86
Revolutionary Prostitutes League, 484
Revolutionary Workers League, 87
Revue des fermières, 1173
Revue Femmes et droit/Canadian Journal of Women and the Law, 763
Revue juridique La Femme et le droit, 763
Revue Statut de la femme, 44, 720
RFCI, 1292
RFD, 763
RFR/DRF, 50, 85, 726, 762
RFSO, 1071
RFW, 480
RHC, 902
Richmond Crisis Centre, 802
Richmond Women's Resource Centre Association, 836
Rights of Lesbians Subcommittee of the British Columbia Federation of Women, 111, 791
Rites Magazine, 764
Riverside Villa Association, 217
RMG, 86
RMH Women's Committee, 903
RMH Women's Conference Committee, 903
RNAO. Sub-committee on Nursing Assistants, 453
RNCIA, 737
Rocky Mountain House Women's Committee, 903
Rocky Mountain House Women's Conference Committee, 903
Room of One's Own (Vancouver, B.C.), 735
Room of One's Own (Victoria, B.C.), 166
Rosemary Brown Leadership Campaign Committee, 77
Royal Alexandra Hospital. Reproductive Health Clinic, 902
Rural Women's Seminar Society, 837
Rural Women's Shelter Program, 1029
RWHC. Bay Centre for Birth Control, 1000
RWL, 87
RWS, 837
Ryerson Polytechnical Institute. Department of Campus Safety and Security Services. Office of Harassment Prevention Services, 486
Ryerson Polytechnical Institute. Employment and Educational Equity Office, 485
Ryerson Polytechnical Institute. Office of Harassment Prevention Services, 486
Ryerson Polytechnical Institute. Women's Centre, 550
Ryerson Women's Centre, 550
S.O.S. Grossesse, 1249
SAC (Fort McMurray, Alta.), 893
SAC (Regina, Sask.), 260, 937
SAC Women's Commission, 492
SACL, 1075
SAIF, 904
Saint *see* St
Salvation Army. Kate Booth House, 820
Sappho Sound, 487
SARA (Saskatoon, Sask.), 943
SARA (Surrey, B.C.), 839
Sarnia-Lambton Committee on the Status of Women, 488
Sarnia-Lambton Status of Women Committee, 488
Sarnia Women's Centre, 488
SAS, 1311
SASC, 1076
Saskatchewan Action Committee, Status of Women, 260, 937

NAME INDEX

Saskatchewan Business and Professional Women's Clubs, 261
Saskatchewan Cross-Cultural Centre, 929
Saskatchewan Health-Care Auxiliaries Association, 262
Saskatchewan Hospital Auxiliaries Association, 262
Saskatchewan Interfacing Law and Sociology, 938
Saskatchewan Native Women's Movement, 263
Saskatchewan Provincial Council of the Canadian Federation of University Women, 264
Saskatchewan Provincial Council of Women, 252
Saskatchewan Teachers' Federation. Saskatoon Women Teachers' Local, 265
Saskatchewan Teachers' Federation. Women in Education Advisory Committee, 939
Saskatchewan Tradeswomen, 266
Saskatchewan Women's Agricultural Network, 940
Saskatchewan Women's Institutes, 267, 941
Saskatchewan Women's Resources, 942
Saskatchewan Working Women, 268
Saskatchewan Working Women. Regina Chapter, 269
Saskatoon Abortion Rights Association, 943
Saskatoon Business and Professional Women's Club, 270
Saskatoon Interval House, 944
Saskatoon Local Council of Women, 271
Saskatoon Rape Crisis Centre, 945
Saskatoon Sexual Assault and Information Centre, 945
Saskatoon WLM, 273
Saskatoon Women for Abortion Law Repeal, 272
Saskatoon Women Teachers' Association, 265
Saskatoon Women Teachers' Local of the Saskatchewan Teachers' Federation, 265
Saskatoon Women's Centre, 273
Saskatoon Women's Charities, 946
Saskatoon Women's Liberation, 273
Saskatoon Women's Network, 947
Saskatoon Women's Resource Centre, 273
Saskatoon Women's Service Coalition, 946
SASSA, 1311
SAWCC, 1255
Scarborough Women's Action Network, 1072
Scarborough Women's Centre, 1072
SCOAAW, 980
SCWIST, 765
SEC, 520
Second Decade/La Deuxième décennie, 577
Second Mile Club, 321
Second Penny, 267, 941
Second Stage Housing (Saint John, N.B.), 1293
Second Stage Program (Victoria, B.C.), 838
Second Story Women's Centre, 1338
Second Wreath, 218
Second Wreath Conference (1985 : Edmonton, Alta.), 218
Secret Furies, 1339
Secretary, 1240
Sécurité : une question d'urgence : les alternatives des femmes pour négocier la paix (1985 : Halifax, N.-É.), 42
SEIU. Local 268, 489
Séjournelle : Maison d'aide et d'hébergement pour femmes victimes de violence conjugale, 1250
Selkirk Cooperative on Abuse against Women, 980
Senate Task Force on the Status of Women at York University, 579
Senator Patrick Burns Family Shelter, 191, 882

Serena Manitoba, 981
Service à la famille chinoise du Grand Montréal. Comité des femmes/Chinese Family Service of Greater Montreal. Women's Committee, 1251
Service d'information féministe, 58
Service Employees' Union. Local 268, 489
Service, Office, and Retail Workers' Union of Canada. Local 2 (United Bank Workers), 146
Service, Office, and Retail Workers' Union of Canada. Local 4 (Bank and Finance Workers), 146
Service, Office, and Retail Workers' Union of Canada. Local 7, 1073
Services aux familles, 1154
Services du triangle rose/Pink Triangle Services, 1074
Services for Adult Survivors of Sexual Abuse and Sexual Assault, 1311
Sexual Assault Centre London, 1075
Sexual Assault Centre of Guelph, 1029
Sexual Assault Recovery Anonymous, 839
Sexual Assault Support Centre of Ottawa/Centre d'aide aux agressées sexuelles d'Ottawa, 1076
Sexual Education Centre (University of Toronto), 520
Sexual Orientation Lobby, 319
Sexual Orientation Lobby of Manitoba, 320
SFCGM. Comité des femmes, 1251
SFSS. Women's Centre, 842
SFU Co-op Family, 147
SFU. Employment Equity Advisory Committee, 840
SFU. Public Interest Research Group, 841
SFU. Women's Caucus, 161
SFU. Women's Centre, 842
SFU. Women's Studies Program, 148
SFUPIRG, 841
Shakti, 1138, 1255
SHARE, 817
She Ain't Heavy, 208
She Mail, 821
Sheridan College. Brampton Campus. Centre for Women, 365
Side Effects : A Play about Women and Pharmaceuticals, 558, 1107
SILS, 938
Simon Fraser Student Society. Women's Centre, 842
Simon Fraser University. Co-op Family, 147
Simon Fraser University. Employment Equity Advisory Committee, 840
Simon Fraser University. Louis Riel University Family Co-op, 147
Simon Fraser University. Public Interest Research Group, 841
Simon Fraser University. Women's Caucus, 161
Simon Fraser University. Women's Centre, 842
Simon Fraser University. Women's Studies Program, 148
Simon Fraser Women's Caucus, 161
Simone de Beauvoir Institute/Institut Simone de Beauvoir, 1252
Single Moms, 690
Single Moms Centre, 690
Single Parent Centre (Halifax, N.S.), 1340
Single Parent Resource Centre (Saint John, N.B.), 1294
Singles File, 1294
Sioux-Hudson Steering Committee to Examine Violence against Women, 545
Sioux-Hudson Transition House Steering Committee, 545
Sister, 166
Sister Vision: Black Women and Women of Colour Press, 1077
Sistering: A Drop-in Centre for Transient Women, 1078
Sisters, 166
Sisters' Lightship, 658

Sisters of Charity. Mount Saint Vincent College, 670, 1331
SJSWC, 689, 1364
Skid Row National Coalition Committee, 767
Skiltec Association, 1079
Slate, 794
Snow Lake Centre on Family Violence, 982
Snow Lake Crisis and Resource Centre, 982
SNWM, 263
SOAUUW, 491
Socialist Women's Caucus of the Labour Centre, 408
Socialist Women's Group, 408
Société des Canadiennes dans les sciences et les téchnologies, 765
Société Elizabeth Fry de Montréal/Elizabeth Fry Society of Montreal, 1253
Société Elizabeth Fry du Grand Montréal, 1253
Société générale des étudiantes et des étudiants du Collège de Maisonneuve. Comité-femme de Maisonneuve, 1187
Société Madeleine LeBlanc, 1341
Société Saint-Jean-Baptiste de Montréal. Section féminine, 606
Sociétés Elizabeth Fry, 697
Society for Canadian Women in Science and Technology, 765
Society for Homosexual Awareness, Research, and Education, 817
Society for Political Action by Gays, 149
Society for Political Action for Gay People, 149
Society for Women in Music, 868
SOGECOM. Comité-femme de Maisonneuve, 1187
Solidarité post-avortement, 1254
Soroptimist Club of Winnipeg, 321
Soroptimist Federation of the Americas. Western Canada Region, 322
Soroptimist International of Halifax/Dartmouth, 1342
Soroptimist International of Toronto, 490
Soroptimist International of Winnipeg, 321
SORWUC. Local 2 (United Bank Workers), 146
SORWUC. Local 4 (Bank and Finance Workers), 146
SORWUC. Local 7, 1073
Source (Edmonton, Alta.), 219
Source (Fort McMurray, Alta.), 913
Source (Sorel, Québec), 1226
South Asian Community Centre, 1255
South Asian Women's Community Centre/Centre communautaire des femmes sud-asiatiques, 1255
South Asian Women's Group, 1080
South Peace Community Resources. Mizpah Transition House, 827
South Shore Transition House Association, 1343
South Vancouver Family Place, 851
South West Nova Transition House Association. Juniper House, 1329
Southern Ontario Association of Unitarian-Universalist Women, 491
Southern Ontario Coalition to Stop Anita Bryant, 373
Southwest Action Group for Battered Women, 948
Southwest Crisis Services, 948
Spadina Childcare Co-operative Association, 274
SPAG, 149
Spokes/Women, 689, 1364
Spokeswoman, 34
SSWC, 1338
St Albert Prevention of Family Violence Committee, 904
St Albert SAIF Society, 904
St Albert Stop Abuse in Families Society, 904
St John's Council of Women, 685
St John's Status of Women Council, 689, 1364

Standing Committee on Women's Rights of the B.C. New Democratic Party, 113, 793
Starting Line, 704
Status of Women Action and Coordinating Council of B.C., 158
Status of Women Action Committee (Calgary, Alta.), 190, 881
Status of Women Action Group (Victoria, B.C.), 165, 858
Status of Women Council (Vancouver, B.C.), 158
Status of Women News, 71, 744
Status of Women Society (Regina, Sask.), 260, 937
Steering Committee for a Women's Network, 564
Stepping Stone Program, 1344
Stepping Stone Street Services for Women and Youth Association, 1344
STF. Saskatoon Women Teachers' Local, 265
STF. Women in Education Advisory Committee, 939
Stiletto, 29, 712
Stop 158, 581, 1116
Stop Rape Week Committee, 631
STR, 1074
Strength, 409
Students' Administrative Council (University of Toronto). Women's Commission, 492
Sudbury Women's Centre/Centre des femmes de Sudbury, 1081
Superior Woman, 379
Support aux mères célibataires/Support to Single Mothers, 1295
Support to Single Mothers/Support aux mères célibataires, 1296
Surfacing, 166
Survival and Disarmament Week, 372
Sussex-Devonshire Day Care Centres, 360
Sussex Vale Transition House, 1297
Suvaguuq, 757
SWAC, 190, 881
SWACC, 158
SWAG (Victoria, B.C.), 165, 858
SWALR, 272
Swan River Committee on the Abuse of Women, 983
Swan Valley Crisis Centre, 983
SWAN (Saskatoon, Sask.), 940
SWAN (Scarborough, Ont.), 1072
SWC (Saskatoon, Sask.), 946
SWC (Scarborough, Ont.), 1072
SWC (Vancouver, B.C.), 158
SWC (Windsor, Ont.), 408
SWG, 408
SWI, 267, 941
Swift Current Business and Professional Women's Club, 275
Swift Current Council of Women, 276
Swift Current Sexual Assault and Information Centre, 948
SWN, 947
SWTA, 265
SWW, 268
SWW. Regina Chapter, 269
Symposium féministe (1973 : Montréal, Québec), 597
Syndicat canadien des travailleurs du textile et de la chimie/Canadian Textile and Chemical Union, 88
Syndicat des agricultrices de la Côte-du-Sud, 1256
Syndicat des communications Canada/Communications Union Canada, 89
TAG, 497
Take Back the Night Committee (Toronto, Ont.), 493
Taking Control, 1290

NAME INDEX

Tamarack, 844
Tamitik Status of Women, 150
Target, 817
Task Force on Lesbians in Violent Relationships, 494
Task Force on Older Women in British Columbia, 113, 793
Task Force on Older Women in Canada, 76
Task Force on the Status of Women at York University, 579
Task Force on the Status of Women in Psychology in Ontario, 458
Task Force on Violence in Lesbian Relationships, 494
TAVT, 90, 766
TBP, 15
TCC, 985
TCLGS, 499
Technology and the Working Woman (1982 : Toronto, Ont.), 462
Télégai, 1074
Terrace Sexual Assault Centre, 843
Terrace Women's Resource Centre, 844
TGA, 501
TGCC, 502
THA, 511, 1087
THANS, 1345
That Time of the Month, 522
The Pas Committee for Women in Crisis, 984
Théâtre collectif des femmes de St-Basile, 1257
Third Place, 1346
This Is for You Anna, 345
Thompson Crisis Centre, 985
Thompson Nicola Rape Crisis Centre, 819
Thompson Rape Crisis Centre, 985
Thompson Women's Crisis Centre, 985
Three of Cups, 495
Thriving, 725
Times Change Women's Employment Service, 1082
Times Feminist, 165, 858
TLGC, 511, 1087
Toronto Abortion Committee, 572
Toronto and Area Council of Women, 496
Toronto Area Gays, 497
Toronto Black Women's Collective, 1083
Toronto Business and Professional Women's Club, 498
Toronto Centre for Lesbian and Gay Studies, 499
Toronto Committee to Defend Dr Morgentaler, 500
Toronto Feminist Network, 510
Toronto Gay Action, 501
Toronto Gay Community Council, 502
Toronto Jewish Congress. Jewish Women's Federation, 1034
Toronto Lesbian Network, 503
Toronto Lesbian Organization, 424
Toronto Organization for Domestic Workers' Rights (Intercede), 1084
Toronto Rape Crisis Centre, 504
Toronto Socialist Feminist Action, 505, 1085
Toronto Soroptimist Club, 490
Toronto Wages for Housework Committee, 528
Toronto West Business and Professional Women's Club, 506
Toronto Women in Film and Television, 1086
Toronto Women in Film and Video, 1086
Toronto Women's Bookstore, 507
Toronto Women's Caucus, 508
Toronto Women's Liberation Front, 509
Toronto Women's Liberation Group, 509
Toronto Women's Liberation Movement, 509
Toronto Women's Network, 510
Toronto Women's Services Network, 572
Toronto YWCA, 581, 1116
TOW, 80
Traffic Employees Association, 47
Trait d'union, 1132
Transition House Association (Charlottetown, P.E.I.), 1312
Transition House Association of Nova Scotia, 1345
Transition House (Fredericton, N.B.), 1299
Transition House (Regina, Sask.), 255
Transition House (St John's, Nfld.), 689, 1364
Transition'elle, 1258
Travailleurs amalgamés du vêtement et du textile/Amalgamated Clothing and Textile Workers Union, 90, 766
Traversée : Centre de lutte contre les agressions à caractère sexuel de la Rive-Sud, 1259
TRCC, 504
Trent Homophile Association, 511, 1087
Trent Lesbian and Gay Collective, 511, 1087
Trent University. Gays and Lesbians of Trent and Peterborough, 511, 1087
Trent University. Gays of Trent and Peterborough, 511, 1087
Trent University. Homophile Association, 511, 1087
Trent University. Lesbian and Gay Collective, 511, 1087
Trent University. "Women", 547
Trêve pour elles : Centre d'aide et de prévention contre les agressions à caractère sexuel, 1260
Triangle, 1063, 1074
TSFA, 505, 1085
Turning Point (Elizabeth Fry Society. Hamilton Branch), 1021
Turning Point (Women and Children's Crisis Centre), 1096
TWC, 508
TWIFT, 1086
TWLM, 509
U of T. Advisory Committee to the Status of Women Officer, 514
U of T. Campus and Community Co-operative Day Care Centre, 360
U of T. Committee on Sexual Harassment, 515
U of T. Gay Academic Union, 519
U of T. Gays and Lesbians at the University of Toronto, 516
U of T. Gays at the University of Toronto, 517
U of T. Homophile Association, 518
U of T. Lesbian and Gay Academic Society, 519
U of T. New College. Women's Studies Programme, 446
U of T. New College. Women's Studies Student Union, 573
U of T. New Left Caucus. Knitting Circle, 448
U of T. *OtherWise : A Feminist Newspaper at U of T,* 463
U of T. Sexual Education Centre, 520
U of T. Sexual Harassment Education, Counselling, and Complaint Office, 1092
U of T. Status of Women Committee, 521
U of T. Students' Administrative Council. Women's Commission, 492
U of T. Women's Centre, 522
U of T. Women's Coalition, 523
U of T. Women's Liberation Movement, 509
U of T. Women's Studies Programme, 446
UBC. Academic Women's Association, 151
UBC. Association of University and College Employees. Local 1, 108
UBC. Centre for Continuing Education. Women's Resources Centre, 872
UBC. Women's Office, 152
UBC. Women's Resources Centre, 872

UBW, 146
UCFO, 512, 1088
UCFO (Sturgeon Falls, Ont.), 1089
UCSN, 767
UCWNY, 525
UFAWU. Women's Rights Committee, 845
UFWA, 220
UFWA. County of Red Deer Local, 221
UFWA. Horn Hill Local, 222
UFWA. Sunniebend Local, 205
Une à l'autre, 1235
Une Véritable Amie, 1242
Unies-Vers-Femmes, 1230
Unifarm. Women of Unifarm, 911
Union catholique des femmes rurales, 588, 1131
Union culturelle des Franco-Ontariennes, 512, 1088
Union culturelle des Franco-Ontariennes (Sturgeon Falls, Ont.), 1089
Union des producteurs agricoles. Syndicat des agricultrices de la Côte-du-Sud, 1256
Union Woman, 462
Union Women, 308, 967
Unison Society of Cape Breton, 1323
Unitarian Universalist Association. Gay Caucus. Toronto Branch, 513
Unitarian Universalist Gay Caucus. Toronto Branch, 513
Unitarian Universalist Women's Federation. Southern Ontario Branch, 491
Unité d'intervention pour crises familiales de Restigouche/Restigouche Family Crisis Interveners, 1298
United Action Committee for Abortion Reform, 277
United Bank Workers, 146
United Church of Canada. Affirm (Winnipeg, Man.), 288
United Church of Canada. Augustine United Church (Winnipeg, Man.). Herstory, 959
United Church of Canada. Committee to Consider the Report of the Royal Commission on the Status of Women, 91
United Church of Canada. First United Church (Kelowna, B.C.). Wednesday Nite Live, 860
United Church of Canada. Maritime Conference. Ecumenical Decade of Churches in Solidarity with Women (1988-1998) (Hampton, N.B.), 1279
United Church of Canada. Niagara Presbytery. Feminist Faith Concerns, 1027
United Farm Women of Alberta, 220
United Farm Women of Alberta. County of Red Deer Local, 221
United Farm Women of Alberta. Horn Hill Local, 222
United Farm Women of Alberta. Sunniebend Local, 205
United Fishermen and Allied Workers Union. Women's Rights Committee, 845
Univers'elles, 1177
Université Concordia. Institut Simone de Beauvoir, 1215
Université d'Ottawa. Collective des étudiantes en études des femmes, 1014
Université d'Ottawa. Collective en études des femmes, 1014
Université d'Ottawa. Programme en études des femmes/University of Ottawa. Women's Studies Programme, 1090
Université d'Ottawa. Programme en études des femmes. La Collective, 1014
Université Laval au féminin, 632, 633
Université Laval. Comité d'étude sur la condition féminine, 632
Université Laval. Comité pour l'Université Laval au féminin, 633
Université Laval. Groupe de recherche multidisciplinaire féministe, 1261

Université Laval. Groupe gai, 634
University and Community Day Care Society, 224
University of Alberta. Academic Women's Association, 180
University of Alberta. Association of the Academic Staff at the University of Alberta. Committee on Employment Conditions of Full Time Women Faculty, 223
University of Alberta. Campus Day Care Committee, 224
University of Alberta. Day Care Centre Committee, 224
University of Alberta. Faculty of Extension. Women's Program and Resource Centre, 228
University of Alberta. Faculty Women's Association, 203
University of Alberta. Faculty Women's Club, 203
University of Alberta. Office of the Advisor to Women Students, 225
University of Alberta. Office of the Dean of Women, 225
University of Alberta. President's Interim Advisory Committee on Women's Issues, 226
University of Alberta. Senate. Task Force on the Status of Women, 227
University of Alberta. Task Force on Women in Scholarship, Engineering, Science, and Technology, 235, 908
University of Alberta. University and Community Day Care Society, 224
University of Alberta. Women in Scholarship, Engineering, Science, and Technology, 235, 908
University of Alberta. Women's Program and Resource Centre, 228
University of British Columbia. Academic Women's Association, 151
University of British Columbia. Association of University and College Employees. Local 1, 108
University of British Columbia. Centre for Continuing Education. Women's Resources Centre, 872
University of British Columbia. Women's Office, 152
University of British Columbia. Women's Resources Centre, 872
University of Calgary. Gay and Lesbian Academics, Students, and Staff, 894
University of Calgary. Gay Students Association, 894
University of Calgary. Gay Students Society, 894
University of Calgary. Student's Union. Gay and Lesbian Academics, Students, and Staff, 894
University of Calgary. Women's Collective and Resource Centre, 912
University of Calgary. Women's Studies Programme, 905
University of Manitoba. Campus Gay Club, 299
University of Manitoba. Gays for Equality, 299
University of Manitoba. Women's Studies Committee, 323
University of Ottawa. Women's Studies Collective, 1015
University of Ottawa. Women's Studies Programme/Université d'Ottawa. Programme en études des femmes, 1091
University of Ottawa. Women's Studies Programme. The Collective, 1015
University of Ottawa. Women's Studies Student Collective, 1015
University of Saskatchewan. Committee on the Status of Women, 278
University of Saskatchewan. Students' Union. Women's Centre, 949
University of Saskatchewan. Women in Science Network, 951
University of Saskatchewan. Women's Centre, 949
University of Saskatchewan. Women's Directorate, 949
University of Saskatchewan. Women's Studies Research Unit, 950
University of Toronto. Advisory Committee to the Status of Women Officer, 514
University of Toronto. Campus and Community Co-operative Day Care Centre, 360
University of Toronto. Committee on Sexual Harassment, 515
University of Toronto. Gay Academic Union, 519
University of Toronto. Gays and Lesbians at the University of Toronto, 516
University of Toronto. Gays at the University of Toronto, 517
University of Toronto. Homophile Association, 518

NAME INDEX

University of Toronto. Lesbian and Gay Academic Society, 519
University of Toronto. New College. Women's Studies Programme, 446
University of Toronto. New College. Women's Studies Student Union, 573
University of Toronto. New Left Caucus. Knitting Circle, 448
University of Toronto. *OtherWise : A Feminist Newspaper at U of T*, 463
University of Toronto. Sexual Education Centre, 520
University of Toronto. Sexual Harassment Education, Counselling, and Complaint Office, 1092
University of Toronto. Status of Women Committee, 521
University of Toronto. Students' Administrative Council. Women's Commission, 492
University of Toronto. Women's Centre, 522
University of Toronto. Women's Coalition, 523
University of Toronto. Women's Liberation Movement, 509
University of Toronto. Women's Studies Programme, 446
University of Victoria. Faculty Association. Status of Women Committee, 153
University of Victoria. President's Advisory Committee on Equal Rights and Opportunities, 154
University of Victoria. Women's Action Group, 155
University of Waterloo. Federation of Students. Women's Centre, 551
University of Waterloo. Women's Centre, 551
University of Waterloo. Women's Resource Centre, 551
University of Western Ontario. University Students' Council. Women's Issues Commission, 524, 1093
University of Western Ontario. Women's Issues Commission, 524, 1093
University Women's Club (Moose Jaw, Sask.), 279
University Women's Club of Calgary, 229
University Women's Club of Edmonton, 230
University Women's Club of Halifax, 660
University Women's Club of North York, 525
University Women's Club of Ottawa, 526
University Women's Club of Parksville/Qualicum Beach, 799
University Women's Club of Regina, 280
University Women's Club of Winnipeg, 324
University Women's Club (Red Deer, Alta.), 216
University Women's Club (Saskatoon, Sask.), 281
University Women's Club (Swift Current, Sask.), 282
Up, 237
UPA. Syndicat des agricultrices de la Côte-du-Sud, 1256
Update, 312, 969
Upstream : A Canadian Women's Publication, 60, 732
Upstream : An Ottawa Women's Publication, 60, 732
Urban Core Support Network/Réseau d'action en milieu urbain, 767
Urban Images for Native Indian Women, 846
Urgency for True Security : Women's Alternatives for Negotiating Peace (1985 : Halifax, N.S.), 43
USSU. Women's Centre, 949
UTHA, 518
UTSWC, 521
UTWC, 523
UUGC. Toronto Branch, 513
UUWF. Southern Ontario Branch, 491
UVFA. Status of Women Committee, 153
UWC, 229
UWCE, 230
UWO. University Students' Council. Women's Issues Commission, 524, 1093
UWO. Women's Issues Commission, 524, 1093
Vancouver Association of Women and the Law, 847
Vancouver Business and Professional Women's Club, 156

Vancouver Charter of Rights Coalition, 848
Vancouver Council of Women, 157
Vancouver International Women's Day Organizing Committee, 136
Vancouver Island Haven Society, 849
Vancouver Lesbian Centre, 850
Vancouver Lesbian Connection, 850
Vancouver Life Skills Society, 851
Vancouver Rape Relief and Women's Shelter, 852
Vancouver Society on Immigrant Women, 853
Vancouver Status of Women, 158
Vancouver Voice of Women, 120
Vancouver WILPF, 172
Vancouver Women in Focus Society, 159
Vancouver Women's Bookstore, 160, 854
Vancouver Women's Caucus, 161
Vancouver Women's Health Collective, 162, 855
Vancouver Women's Liberation Alliance, 174
Vancouver Young Women's Christian Association, 179, 873
Vancouver YWCA, 179, 873
VANWS, 231
VAWL, 847
VCW, 157
Velvet Fist : A Women's Liberation Newspaper, 508
Venture Club of Toronto, 490
Véritable Amie, 1242
Vernon Women's Forum Society, 856
Vernon Women's Transition House Society, 856
Victims of Family Violence Association, 1346
Victoria and Vancouver Island Local Council of Women, 164
Victoria Business and Professional Women's Club, 163, 857
Victoria Council of Women, 164
Victoria Faulkner Women's Centre, 102
Victoria Status of Women Action Group, 165, 858
Victoria Voice of Women, 121
Victoria Women's Centre, 166
Victoria Women's Sexual Assault Centre, 859
Vidéo femmes, 1262
Vigie : Centre d'aide et de prévention des assauts sexuels de Valleyfield, 1263
Villa Vignettes, 217
Vinok, 218
Violence in Lesbian Relationships Political Action Group, 494
Virago, 402
Vision (Association canadienne pour la promotion des services de garde à l'enfance/Canadian Day Care Advocacy Association), 698
Vision (Professional Secretaries International. Ville-Marie Chapter/Association internationale des secrétaires professionnelles. Section Ville-Marie), 1240
Vitality, 681
Vivre plus, 1195
VLC, 850
Voice of Alberta Native Women's Society, 231
Voice of Women/Voix des femmes, 92
Voice of Women (British Columbia), 115
Voice of Women (Calgary, Alta.), 232, 906
Voice of Women. Edmonton Branch, 233
Voice of Women (Halifax, N.S.), 675
Voice of Women. Manitoba Branch, 325
Voice of Women (Nanaimo, B.C.), 116
Voice of Women. North Shore Branch, 117

Voice of Women Nova Scotia, 675
Voice of Women. Parksville-Qualicum Branch, 118
Voice of Women (Powell River, B.C.), 119
Voice of Women (Regina, Sask.), 256
Voice of Women (Vancouver, B.C.), 120
Voice of Women (Victoria, B.C.), 121
Voices, 179, 873
Voix des femmes / Voice of Women, 93
VOW, 92
VOW (British Columbia), 115
VOW (Calgary, Alta.), 232, 906
VOW. Edmonton Branch, 233
VOW (Halifax, N.S.), 675
VOW. Manitoba Branch, 325
VOW (Nanaimo, B.C.), 116
VOW. North Shore Branch, 117
VOW Nova Scotia, 675
VOW. Parksville-Qualicum Branch, 118
VOW (Powell River, B.C.), 119
VOW (Regina, Sask.), 256
VOW (Vancouver, B.C.), 120
VOW (Victoria, B.C.), 121
VSIW, 853
VSW, 158
VWHC, 162, 855
VWTH, 856
WACH, 284
WACNS, 1349
Waffle. Women's Caucus, 94
WAG, 155
Wages Due, 527
Wages Due Lesbians, 527
Wages for Housework Committee (Toronto, Ont.), 528
Waitresses' Action Committee, 529
WAM, 549
WAMUN, 686
WANT, 539
WANTE, 326
WAP (Victoria, B.C.), 169
WAR, 537
WARC, 770
Ward Three Women's Group, 1325
WAVAW (Toronto, Ont.), 540
Waves, 111, 791
WBCS, 316
WBN, 775
WCDWA, 861
WCH, 1103
WCP, 636
WCRC, 912
WCREC, 1104
WCWN, 167
Web (St John's Status of Women Council), 689, 1364
WEB (Women's Enterprise Bureau), 1367
WECS, 987
Wednesday Night Health Group, 175
Wednesday Nite Live, 860
WEED, 1097
Week on Disarmament and Survival Coalition, 372
Week on Survival and Disarmament Coalition, 372

Wellspring Women's Association, 907
Wen-Do WEST, 867
WERC, 1105
WEST, 867
West Algoma Council of Women, 530
West Coast Domestic Workers Association, 861
West Coast Feminist Literary Magazine Society, 735
West Coast LEAF Association, 862
West Coast Legal Education and Action Fund Association, 862
West Coast Women and Words Society, 863
West Island Women's Shelter / Refuge pour les femmes de l'Ouest de l'Île, 1264
West Kootenay Status of Women Council. *Images : West Kootenay Women's Paper*, 134, 816
West Kootenay Women's Association, 864
West Kootenay Women's Festival, 864
West Kootenay Women's Paper, 134, 816
West Word, 863
Westcoast Women Futures Community Economic Development Society, 865
Western Canadian Women's News Service, 167
Western Nurse Midwives Association, 875
Western Women's Labour History Project of B.C., 173, 871
Weston Business and Professional Women's Club, 531
Weston Council of Women, 428
Westville Local Council of Women, 676
WETC, 870
WFH, 528
WGLRC, 986
WHC (Calgary, Alta.), 883
WHC (Winnipeg, Man.), 988
WHEN, 681
WHI, 558, 1107
WHIN, 1055
Whitehorse Business and Professional Women's Club, 103
WHRF, 989
WIC (London, Ont.), 524, 1093
WIC (Toronto, Ont.), 559
WIC (Windsor, Ont.), 1095
WICC, 771
WICC. Winnipeg Branch, 337
Wicca, 162, 855
WICSHN, 545
WIE, 939
WIL (London, Ont.), 1099
WIL (Toronto, Ont.), 560
Wild Womyn Don't Get the Blues, 1347
WILPF. Vancouver Branch, 172
WIM, 868
Windsor Feminist Theatre, 1094
Windsor Local Council of Women, 532
Windsor Woman, 533
Windsor Women's Incentive Centre, 1095
Winnipeg Association of Non-Teaching Employees, 326
Winnipeg Birth Control Society, 316
Winnipeg Civic Registered Nurses Association, 309
Winnipeg Council of Self-Help, 327
Winnipeg Council of Self-Help Groups, 327
Winnipeg Council of Women, 294
Winnipeg Gay Community Health Centre, 328

Winnipeg Gay/Lesbian Resource Centre, 986
Winnipeg Gay/Lesbian Youth, 329
Winnipeg Gay Media Collective, 298
Winnipeg Gay Youth, 329
Winnipeg Women School Administrators Club, 330
Winnipeg Women's Cultural and Education Centre, 336
Winnipeg Women's Health Collective, 331
Winnipeg Women's Liberation, 332
WINS, 869
WIRRS, 682
WISCOH, 1108
WISE, 1366
WISEST, 235, 908
WISN, 951
WIT (Toronto, Ont.), 546
WIT (Winnipeg, Man.), 334
Witches against Nuclear Technology, 534
Witches ANT, 534
WITT National Network, 769
WKWA, 864
WLA, 174
WLFC, 98
WLHP, 173, 871
WLM (Toronto, Ont.), 509
WMA, 563
WMDP, 564
WMN, 910
Woman Today (1973 : Regina, Sask.), 254
Womanews, 830
Womanist, 768
Womanly Times, 988
Womanpower, Inc., 535
Woman's Place (Halifax, N.S.), 677
Woman's Place (Kitchener-Waterloo, Ont.), 409
Woman's Place (Montreal, Quebec), 635
Woman's Place (Vancouver, B.C.), 168
Woman's Place (Winnipeg, Man.), 333
Womanspirit Art Research and Learning Centre, 536
Womantalk, 570
Women after Rights, 537
Women against Free Trade, 538
Women against Nuclear Technology, 539
Women against Pornography (Victoria, B.C.), 169
Women against Rape, 1234
Women against Violence against Women (Toronto, Ont.), 540
Women Alone Society. Saskatoon Interval House, 944
Women and AIDS Project, 994
Women and Children's Crisis Centre, 1096
Women and Children's Health Centre (Toronto, Ont.), 541
Women and Drug Use Society of Saskatoon, 283
Women and Environments, 1097
Women and Environments Education and Development Foundation, 1097
Women and Film, 95
Women and Health Conference (1975 : Guelph, Ont.), 401
Women and History Group, 1365
Women and the Constitution Conference (1984 : St John's, Nfld.). Organizing Committee, 691
Women and the Economy (1980 : Fredericton, N.B.), 642
Women and Words/Les Femmes et les mots (Vancouver, B.C.), 863

Women and Work Research and Education Society, 866
Women Aware, 1348
Women Back into Stelco Committee, 542
Women Being Well, 1100
Women Can, 161
Women Educating in Self-Defense Training, 867
Women for Political Action (Calgary, Alta.), 234
Women for Political Action (Toronto, Ont.), 543
Women for Survival, 544
Women for the Survival of Agriculture — Winchester, 1098
Women Futures, 865
Women Healthsharing, 96
Women Helping Women, 924
Women Immigrants of London Resource Service Centre, 1099
Women in Action (1983 : Yellowknife, N.W.T.), 105
Women in Canadian Sociology, 97
Women in Canadian Sociology/Anthropology, 97
Women in Crisis — Sioux, Hudson, North, 545
Women in Focus (Vancouver, B.C.), 159
Women in Music, 868
Women in Need Society, 869
Women in Revolution Weekend, 411
Women in Scholarship, Engineering, Science, and Technology (University of Alberta), 235, 908
Women in Science Network (University of Saskatchewan), 951
Women in Trades Association of Toronto, 546
Women in Trades Association (Winnipeg, Man.), 334
Women in Trades News : A Saskatchewan Tradeswomen's Quarterly, 266
Women in Trades, Technology, and Operations — National Network, 769
Women in Transition House, 1299
Women Interested in Successful Employment, 1366
Women into Non-traditional Training, 1079
Women into Rail Committee, 335
Women Now, 678
Women of Colour Collective, 909
Women of the Métis Nation Alliance, 910
Women of Unifarm, 911
Women Plus, 880
Women Principals and Supervisors Club, 330
Women Principals Club, 330
Women Rally for Action, 170
Women Spirit Newsletter, 1048
Women Today (Clinton, Ont.), 1100
Women Today (Port Coquitlam, B.C.), 143, 833
Women (Trent University), 547
Women Unlimited, 679
Women Working Together, 952
Women Working with Immigrant Women (Fredericton, N.B.), 1300
Women Working with Immigrant Women of Metro Toronto, 1101
Women's Action Coalition of Nova Scotia, 1349
Women's Action Collective on Health, 284
Women's Action for Peace, 548
Women's Action Group (University of Victoria), 155
Women's Agenda des femmes, 1189
Women's Art Mobile, 549
Women's Art Resource Centre, 770
Women's Association of Memorial University of Newfoundland, 686
Women's Atlantic Council, 652
Women's Bookmobile, 380

Women's Building (Winnipeg, Man.), 336
Women's Business Network, 775
Women's Caucus (Simon Fraser University), 161
Women's Caucus (Vancouver, B.C.), 161
Women's Centre and Transition House (Victoria, B.C.), 166
Women's Centre at the University of Toronto, 522
Women's Centre (Concordia University), 1189
Women's Centre (Corner Brook, Nfld.), 1356
Women's Centre (Douglas College), 804
Women's Centre (Grey Bruce), 1102
Women's Centre (Halifax, N.S.), 680
Women's Centre (Kingston, Ont.), 411
Women's Centre (Labrador City, Labrador), 1360
Women's Centre (Penticton, B.C.), 830
Women's Centre (Queen's University), 1070
Women's Centre (Ryerson Polytechnical Institute), 550
Women's Centre (Sarnia, Ont.), 488
Women's Centre (Simon Fraser University), 842
Women's Centre (St John's, Nfld.), 689, 1364
Women's Centre (University of Saskatchewan), 949
Women's Centre (University of Waterloo), 551
Women's Centre (Vancouver, B.C.), 171
Women's Centre (Victoria, B.C.), 166
Women's Centre (Whitehorse, Yukon), 102
Women's Centre (York University), 580, 1115
Women's Centre of Ottawa-Carleton, 466, 1061
Women's Centre Review, 432
Women's Centre Theatre Group, 1030
Women's Centres Connect!, 1350
Women's Coalition for Inclusion of the Word "Sex" in the Ontario Human Rights Code, 552
Women's Coalition (Toronto, Ont.), 552
Women's Collective and Resource Centre (University of Calgary), 912
Women's Collective Press, 636
Women's College Hospital. Regional Women's Health Centre. Bay Centre for Birth Control, 1000
Women's Commission (Students' Administrative Council, University of Toronto), 492
Women's Communication Centre, 553
Women's Communications Centre, 553
Women's Community House, 1103
Women's Counselling Referral and Education Centre, 1104
Women's Counselling Referral Centre, 1104
Women's Cultural Building Collective, 554
Women's Cultural Centre (Toronto, Ont.), 469
Women's Directorate (University of Saskatchewan), 949
Women's Economic Agenda, 841
Women's Education des femmes, 21, 48, 707, 721
Women's Education Press, 99
Women's Educational Resources Centre (Ontario Institute for Studies in Education), 1105
Women's Emergency Centre (Woodstock, Ont.), 555, 1106
Women's Employment and Training Coalition, 870
Women's Employment Counselling Service, 987
Women's Enterprise Bureau, 1367
Women's Forum (Corner Brook Status of Women Council), 1356
Women's Forum (Sarnia-Lambton Status of Women Committee), 488
Women's Free Press, 781
Women's Fund, 556
Women's Fund-Raising Coalition, 556

Women's Habitat, 557
Women's Health Centre (Toronto, Ont.), 541
Women's Health Clinic (Winnipeg, Man.), 988
Women's Health Collective (Calgary, Alta.), 883
Women's Health Education Network, 681
Women's Health Education Project of Newfoundland and Labrador, 689, 1364
Women's Health Interaction, 558, 1107
Women's Health Research Foundation of Canada, 989
Women's Health Research Foundation of Manitoba, 989
Women's Hostels Incorporated, 445
Women's Information and Support Centre of Halton, 1108
Women's Information Centre (Montreal, Quebec), 638
Women's Information Centre of Toronto, 559
Women's Information Line, 560
Women's Information, Resource, and Referral Service (Halifax, N.S.), 682
Women's Institutes (Alberta), 185
Women's Institutes (Canada), 51
Women's Institutes (New Brunswick), 650
Women's Institutes (Ontario), 390
Women's Inter-Church Council of Canada/Conseil œcuménique des chrétiennes du Canada, 771
Women's Inter-Church Council of Canada. Winnipeg Branch, 337
Women's International League for Peace and Freedom. Vancouver Branch, 172
Women's International Peace Conference (1985 : Halifax, N.S.), 43
Women's Involvement (Green's Harbour, Nfld.), 1368
Women's Involvement Programme (Toronto, Ont.), 561
Women's Labour History in B.C., 173, 871
Women's Labour History Project, 173, 871
Women's Legal Education and Action Fund/Fonds d'action et d'éducation juridiques pour les femmes, 772
Women's Legal Education and Action Fund. New Brunswick Branch/Fonds d'action et d'éducation juridiques pour les femmes. Section Nouveau-Brunswick, 1301
Women's Legal Education and Action Fund (Vancouver, B.C.), 862
Women's Lib Type Press, 344
Women's Liberal Federation of Canada/Fédération nationale des femmes libérales du Canada, 98
Women's Liberation Abortion and Birth Control Collective, 509
Women's Liberation Alliance (Vancouver, B.C.), 174
Women's Liberation Bookmobile, 380
Women's Liberation Campus Community Cooperative Daycare Centre, 360
Women's Liberation (Edmonton, Alta.), 236
Women's Liberation Front of the New Left Committee, 449
Women's Liberation Group of Regina, 257
Women's Liberation Group (Toronto, Ont.), 509
Women's Liberation Movement (Montreal, Quebec), 623
Women's Liberation Movement of Toronto, 509
Women's Liberation Movement (Saskatoon, Sask.), 273
Women's Liberation Newsletter (Ottawa, Ont.), 467
Women's Liberation Study Group (Montreal, Quebec), 637
Women's Liberation Working Group (Toronto, Ont.), 562
Women's Media Alliance of Toronto, 563
Women's Model Parliament, 338
Women's Movement Development Project Committee, 564
Women's Network (Charlottetown, P.E.I.), 1313
Women's Network Steering Committee (Hamilton, Ont.), 564
Women's Network (Toronto, Ont.), 510

Women's News, 569
Women's Newsletter, 655
Women's Office (University of British Columbia), 152
Women's Peace Camp (Cole Bay, Sask.), 247
Women's Perspective '83, 565
Women's Perspective Collective, 565
Women's Place Kenora, 1109
Women's Place (Kitchener-Waterloo, Ont.), 409
Women's Place (Lethbridge, Alta.), 237
Women's Place (Montreal, Quebec), 635
Women's Place/Place aux femmes (Ottawa, Ont.), 1110
Women's Place (Peterborough, Ont.), 471
Women's Place (St Catharines, Ont.), 1111
Women's Place (Toronto, Ont.), 566
Women's Place, Welland and District, 1112
Women's Place (Windsor, Ont.), 567
Women's Poetry Salon, 574
Women's Post Treatment Centre, 990
Women's Post Treatment Project, 990
Women's Press, 99
Women's Press, A, 344
Women's Press Conference (1974 : Saskatoon, Sask.), 58
Women's Program and Resource Centre (University of Alberta), 228
Women's Recreational, Educational, and Cultural Centre, 680
Women's Regale, 568
Women's Research Centre, 100
Women's Resource and Information Centre (Labrador City, Labrador), 1360
Women's Resource Centre Association of Timmins, 570
Women's Resource Centre (Calgary, Alta.), 238, 914
Women's Resource Centre (Hay River, N.W.T.), 781
Women's Resource Centre (Ontario Institute for Studies in Education), 1105
Women's Resource Centre (St Catharines, Ont.), 569
Women's Resource Centre (Timmins, Ont.), 570
Women's Resource Centre (Toronto, Ont.), 581, 1116
Women's Resource Centre (University of Waterloo), 551
Women's Resource Society of Fort McMurray, 913
Women's Resources Centre (University of British Columbia), 872
Women's Self-Defence Centre, 571
Women's Self-Help Clinic (Vancouver, B.C.), 175
Women's Services Network (Toronto, Ont.), 572
Women's Sexual Assault Centre (Victoria, B.C.), 859
Women's Share, 1338
Women's Socialist-Feminist Study Group, 177
Women's Strength News, 867
Women's Studies Association of British Columbia, 176
Women's Studies Newsletter, 446
Women's Studies Research Unit (University of Saskatchewan), 950
Women's Studies Student Union (New College), 573
Women's Study Action Committee, Queen's University, 479
Women's Study Group (Vancouver, B.C.), 177
Women's Union of McGill University, 620
Women's Writing Collective, 574
Women's Writing Salon, 574
Womynews, 949
Womyn's Action for Peace, 548
Womyn's Collective (Calgary, Alta.), 896
Womyn's Social and Recreational Collective of Calgary, 896
Working for Women, 953

Working Skills Centre of Ontario, 1113
Working Woman, 268
Working Women Community Centre, 1114
Working Women's Association, 178
World Council of Churches. Ecumenical Decade of Churches in Solidarity with Women (1988-1998) (Hampton, N.B.), 1279
WPA (Toronto, Ont.), 543
WPAC, 1059
WPK, 1109
WRA, 170
WRC (British Columbia New Democratic Party), 113, 793
WRC (Timmins, Ont.), 570
WRC (United Fishermen and Allied Workers Union), 845
WRC (University of British Columbia), 872
WSA — Winchester, 1098
WSAC, 859
WSN, 572
WSRU, 950
WSSU, 573
WWA (Vancouver, B.C.), 178
WWA (Whitecourt, Alta.), 907
WWCC, 1114
WWDGTB, 1347
WWIW (Fredericton, N.B.), 1300
WWIW (Toronto, Ont.), 1101
Y des femmes, 624
Yellow Brick House, 1068
Yellowknife Young Women's Christian Association, 782
Yellowknife YWCA, 782
Yeux au coeur, 879
YIWA, 776
YM-YWCA (Winnipeg, Man.). Osborne House, 977
YMCA of Canada. Task Force on the Status of Women, 74
York Committee on Women's Programmes, 575
York University. Bisexual, Lesbian, and Gay Alliance, 352, 1001
York University. Committee on Women's Programmes, 575
York University. Federation of Students. Bisexual, Lesbian, and Gay Alliance, 352, 1001
York University. Harbinger Community Services, 576
York University. Nellie Langford Rowell Library, 1049
York University. Office of the Advisor to the President on the Status of Women, 577
York University. Office of the Advisor to the University on the Status of Women, 577
York University. Presidential Committee to Review the Salaries of Full-Time Faculty Women, 578
York University. Senate Task Force on the Status of Women, 579
York University. Women in Canadian Sociology/Anthropology, 97
York University. Women's Centre, 580, 1115
York University. Women's Studies Committee, 575
York University. York-YWCA Women's Collection, 1049
York Women's Centre, 580, 1115
York Women's Group, 580, 1115
York Women's Studies Committee, 575
York-YWCA Women's Collection, 1049
Yorkton Business and Professional Women's Club, 285
Yorkton Women's Advisory Committee, 286
Young Men's Christian Association of Canada. Task Force on the Status of Women, 74
Young Men's-Young Women's Christian Association (Winnipeg, Man.). Osborne House, 977

Young Women's Christian Association. Banff Community Resource Centre, 917
Young Women's Christian Association (Halifax, N.S.), 667, 1327
Young Women's Christian Association (Montreal, Quebec), 624
Young Women's Christian Association (Montreal, Quebec). Women's Centre, 638
Young Women's Christian Association of Berlin, 414, 1036
Young Women's Christian Association of Calgary, 238, 914
Young Women's Christian Association of Calgary. Women's Resource Centre, 238, 914
Young Women's Christian Association of Canada, 101
Young Women's Christian Association of Edmonton, 239, 915
Young Women's Christian Association of Kitchener-Waterloo, 414, 1036
Young Women's Christian Association of Lethbridge and District, 916
Young Women's Christian Association of Metropolitan Toronto, 581, 1116
Young Women's Christian Association of Peterborough Victoria and Haliburton, 582, 1117
Young Women's Christian Association of Prince Albert, 954
Young Women's Christian Association of Regina, 259, 936
Young Women's Christian Association of St Thomas-Elgin, 583, 1118
Young Women's Christian Association of Thompson, 339, 991
Young Women's Christian Association of Yellowknife, 782
Young Women's Christian Association, Saskatoon, 287
Young Women's Christian Association (St Catharines, Ont.). Women's Resource Centre, 569
Young Women's Christian Association (St John's, Nfld.), 692
Young Women's Christian Association (Vancouver, B.C.), 179, 873
Young Women's Christian Association (Winnipeg, Man.), 340
Young Women's Christian Association (Winnipeg, Man.). Osborne House, 977
Young Women's Christian Guild of Toronto, 581, 1116
Your News, 667, 1327
Yukon Child Care Association, 104
Yukon Indian Women's Association, 776
Yukon Status of Women Council, 777
YWCA Banff Community Resource Centre, 917

YWCA Community Resource Centre (Banff, Alta.), 917
YWCA (Halifax, N.S.), 667, 1327
YWCA (Montreal, Quebec), 624
YWCA (Montreal, Quebec). Women's Centre, 638
YWCA of Berlin, 414, 1036
YWCA of Calgary, 238, 914
YWCA of Calgary. Women's Resource Centre, 238, 914
YWCA of Canada, 101
YWCA of Edmonton, 239, 915
YWCA of Kitchener-Waterloo, 414, 1036
YWCA of Lethbridge and District, 916
YWCA of Metropolitan Toronto, 581, 1116
YWCA of Peterborough Victoria and Haliburton, 582, 1117
YWCA of Prince Albert, 954
YWCA of Regina, 259, 936
YWCA of St Thomas-Elgin, 583, 1118
YWCA of Thompson, 339, 991
YWCA of Yellowknife, 782
YWCA (Saskatoon, Sask.), 287
YWCA (St Catharines, Ont.). Women's Resource Centre, 569
YWCA (St John's, Nfld.), 692
YWCA (Vancouver, B.C.), 179, 873
YWCA (Winnipeg, Man.), 340
YWCA (Winnipeg, Man.). Osborne House, 977
YWCA Women's Centre (Montreal, Quebec), 638
YWCA Women's Resource Centre (Calgary, Alta.), 238, 914
Zonta Club (Charlottetown, P.E.I.), 656
Zonta Club (Halifax, N.S.), 683
Zonta Club of Edmonton, 240
Zonta Club of St John's, 693
Zonta International. Charlottetown Chapter, 656
Zonta International. Edmonton Branch, 240
Zonta International. Halifax Club, 683
Zonta International. St John's Club, 693

SUBJECT INDEX / INDEX DES SUJETS

Use this index to locate entries by subject — for instance, a particular issue (such as sexual assault), type of organization (such as women's centres) or group of women (such as nurses).

This index has two sections: the first section, in French, indexes the French entries; the second, in English, indexes the English entries. (Bilingual collections, which have both French and English entries, appear in both sections of the Subject Index.) To assist readers who wish to consult both sections, each section begins with a list of the terms used and their equivalents in the other language.

Most of the terms used in the subject index were taken from the *Canadian Feminist Thesaurus* (Toronto: Ontario Institute for Studies in Education, 1990).

◆ ◆ ◆

Cet index permet de retrouver toutes les notices traitant d'un même sujet — p. ex. une question particulière (telle que l'agression sexuelle), un type d'organisme (tel que les centres des femmes) ou une catégorie de femmes (telle que les infirmières).

Cet index a deux sections : la première, en français, porte sur les notices françaises et l'autre, en anglais, porte sur les notices anglaises. (Les collections bilingues, dont les entrées sont inscrites en français et en anglais, figurent dans les deux sections de l'Index des sujets.) Pour aider les lectrices et lecteurs qui veulent consulter les deux sections, chacune commence par une liste des expressions employées et leurs équivalents dans l'autre langue.

La plupart des expressions employées dans l'index des sujets ont été empruntées au *Thésaurus féministe du Canada* (Toronto : Institut d'études pédagogiques de l'Ontario, 1990).

Section 1 : Notices en français / French Entries

LIST OF FRENCH TERMS USED, WITH ENGLISH EQUIVALENTS / LISTE D'EXPRESSIONS FRANÇAISES EMPLOYÉES, AVEC ÉQUIVALENTS ANGLAIS

In alphabetical order by the French terms / Classée par ordre alphabétique d'après l'expression française

abus sexuel des enfants • sexual abuse of children
accouchement • childbirth
agression sexuelle • sexual assault
agricultrice • farmers
allaitement maternel • breast feeding
alphabétisation • literacy
archives • archives
assistance sociale • social assistance
avortement • abortion
bar et café • bars and cafés
bibliothèque • libraries
bisexuelle • bisexual women
centre des femmes • women's centres
Chinoise • Chinese women

christianisme • Christianity
coalition • coalitions
collège • colleges
condition féminine • status of women
congrès • conferences
consultation d'orientation • counselling
contrôle des naissances • birth control
corps professoral • faculty
dépendance • addiction
diplômée • alumnae
droit • law
éducation • education
éducation physique • physical education
éducation sexuelle • sex education

SUBJECT INDEX: FRENCH ENTRIES

emploi • employment
employée de bureau • clerical workers
enfance maltraitée • child abuse
enseignante • teachers
études sur les femmes • women's studies
féminisme socialiste • socialist feminism
femme autochtone • Native women
femme battue • battered women
femme de carrières libérales et commerciales • business and professional women
femme de couleur • women of colour
femme de la classe ouvrière • working-class women
femme francophone • francophone women
femme sans abri • homeless women
femme sud-asiatique • South Asian women
film • films
financement • funding
galerie d'art • art galleries
grossesse • pregnancy
groupe de gauche • left-wing organizations
Haïtienne • Haitian women
handicapée • disabled women
histoire • history
immigrante • immigrant women
infirmière • nurses
Journée internationale des femmes, 8 mars • International Women's Day, March 8
Juive • Jewish women
lesbienne • lesbians
librairie • bookstores
littérature • literature

logement temporaire • temporary housing
médecin • physicians
ménopause • menopause
mère • mothers
mère seule • single mothers
paix • peace
parti politique • political parties
pauvreté • poverty
pays en voie de développement • developing countries
périodique • periodicals
politique • politics
pornographie • pornography
représentation médiatique • media portrayal
réseau • networks
sage-femme • midwives
santé • health
santé mentale • mental health
séparation • separation
service de documentation • information services
SIDA • AIDS
soins à l'enfant • child care
syndicat • trade unions
système pénal • criminal justice system
théâtre • theatre
travailleuse du textile • textile workers
université • universities
veuve • widows
vidéo • videos
violence • violence
violence familiale • family violence

In alphabetical order by the English equivalents / Classée par ordre alphabétique d'après l'équivalent anglais

abortion • avortement
addiction • dépendance
AIDS • SIDA
alumnae • diplômée
archives • archives
art galleries • galerie d'art
bars and cafés • bar et café
battered women • femme battue
birth control • contrôle des naissances
bisexual women • bisexuelle
bookstores • librairie
breast feeding • allaitement maternel
business and professional women • femme de carrières libérales et commerciales
child abuse • enfance maltraitée
child care • soins à l'enfant
childbirth • accouchement
Chinese women • Chinoise
Christianity • christianisme
clerical workers • employée de bureau

coalitions • coalition
colleges • collège
conferences • congrès
counselling • consultation d'orientation
criminal justice system • système pénal
developing countries • pays en voie de développement
disabled women • handicapée
education • éducation
employment • emploi
faculty • corps professoral
family violence • violence familiale
farmers • agricultrice
films • film
francophone women • femme francophone
funding • financement
Haitian women • Haïtienne
health • santé
history • histoire
homeless women • femme sans abri
immigrant women • immigrante

INDEX DES SUJETS : NOTICES EN FRANÇAIS

information services • service de documentation
International Women's Day, March 8 • Journée internationale des femmes, 8 mars
Jewish women • Juive
law • droit
left-wing organizations • groupe de gauche
lesbians • lesbienne
libraries • bibliothèque
literacy • alphabétisation
literature • littérature
media portrayal • représentation médiatique
menopause • ménopause
mental health • santé mentale
midwives • sage-femme
mothers • mère
Native women • femme autochtone
networks • réseau
nurses • infirmière
peace • paix
periodicals • périodique
physical education • éducation physique
physicians • médecin
political parties • parti politique
politics • politique
pornography • pornographie
poverty • pauvreté
pregnancy • grossesse
separation • séparation
sex education • éducation sexuelle
sexual abuse of children • abus sexuel des enfants
sexual assault • agression sexuelle
single mothers • mère seule
social assistance • assistance sociale
socialist feminism • féminisme socialiste
South Asian women • femme sud-asiatique
status of women • condition féminine
teachers • enseignante
temporary housing • logement temporaire
textile workers • travailleuse du textile
theatre • théâtre
trade unions • syndicat
universities • université
videos • vidéo
violence • violence
widows • veuve
women of colour • femme de couleur
women's centres • centre des femmes
women's studies • études sur les femmes
working-class women • femme de la classe ouvrière

INDEX DES SUJETS : NOTICES EN FRANÇAIS/
SUBJECT INDEX: FRENCH ENTRIES

abus sexuel des enfants

(*voir aussi* **agression sexuelle, enfance maltraitée, violence, violence familiale**)

Mouvement contre le viol et l'inceste, 1233

Acadienne *voir* **femme francophone**

accouchement

Naissance-Renaissance, 1235

agression sexuelle

(*voir aussi* **violence**)

Assaut sexuel secours, 1129

Centre d'aide aux agressées sexuelles d'Ottawa/Sexual Assault Support Centre of Ottawa, 1006

Centre d'aide aux victimes de viol et d'agression sexuelle de l'Î.P.É./P.E.I. Rape and Sexual Assault Crisis Centre, 1305

Centre d'aide et de lutte contre les agressions à caractère sexuel de Rimouski, 1139

Centre d'aide et de lutte contre les agressions à caractère sexuel (Trois-Rivières, Québec), 1140

Centre d'aide et de prévention d'assauts sexuels de Châteauguay/Châteauguay Sexual Assault Prevention and Aid Center, 1141

Centre de prévention et d'intervention pour victimes d'agression sexuelle (Laval, Québec), 1153

Centres canadiens de viol/Canadian Rape Crisis Centres, 39

Mouvement contre le viol et l'inceste, 1233

Point d'appui, Centre d'aide et de prévention des agressions à caractère sexuel de Rouyn, 1239

Traversée : Centre de lutte contre les agressions à caractère sexuel de la Rive-Sud, 1259

Trêve pour elles : Centre d'aide et de prévention contre les agressions à caractère sexuel, 1260

Vigie : Centre d'aide et de prévention des assauts sexuels de Valleyfield, 1263

agricultrice

Cercles de fermières du Québec, 1173

Syndicat des agricultrices de la Côte-du-Sud, 1256

aide sociale *voir* **assistance sociale**

alcoolisme *voir* **dépendance**

allaitement maternel

Aide à la femme pour l'allaitement maternel et la maternité, 1124

allocation familiale *voir* **assistance sociale**

alphabétisation

(*voir aussi* **éducation**)

Centre de documentation sur l'éducation des adultes et la condition féminine, 1143

Réseau national d'Action éducation femmes, 761

Amérindienne *voir* **femme autochtone**

analphabétisation *voir* **alphabétisation**

apprentissage *voir* **éducation**

archives

(*voir aussi* **bibliothèque**)

Archives canadiennes du mouvement des femmes/Canadian Women's Movement Archives, 3

arts *voir* **film, galerie d'art, littérature, théâtre, vidéo**

assistance sociale

(*voir aussi* **pauvreté**)

FormOsud, 1208

avortement

(*voir aussi* **contrôle des naissances, grossesse**)

Association canadienne pour le droit à l'avortement/Canadian Abortion Rights Action League, 5

Centre de planning familial du Québec, 596

Clinique des femmes de l'Outaouais, 1179

Solidarité post-avortement, 1254

bar et café

Chez nous, 1009

bibliothèque

(*voir aussi* **archives**)

Centre de documentation sur l'éducation des adultes et la condition féminine, 1143

bisexuelle

Coalition pour la réforme des droits de la personne du Nouveau-Brunswick/New Brunswick Coalition for Human Rights Reform, 641

café *voir* **bar et café**

centre contre le viol *voir* **agression sexuelle**

centre contre les agressions sexuelles *voir* **agression sexuelle**

centre de ressources *voir* **centre des femmes**

centre des femmes

Carrefour des femmes de Lachute, 1135

Centre actu-elle, 1136

Centre Avec des elles, 1137

Centre communautaire des femmes sud-asiatiques/South Asian Women's Community Centre, 1138

Centre de femmes de Shawinigan, 1144

Centre de femmes du pays Maria-Chapdelaine, 1145

Centre de femmes Espoir pour elles, 1146

Centre de femmes La Moisson, 1147

Centre de femmes La Tuque, 1148

Centre de femmes L'Éclaircie, 1149

Centre de femmes L'ÉRIGE, 1150

Centre de femmes L'Étincelle, 1151

Centre de femmes Parmi elles, 1152

Centre de la femme nouvelle/New Woman Centre, 595

Centre d'éducation et d'action des femmes de Montréal, 1154

Centre des femmes de Charlevoix, 1155

INDEX DES SUJETS : NOTICES EN FRANÇAIS

Centre des femmes de Laval, 1156

Centre des femmes de Lennoxville et des environs/Lennoxville and District Women's Centre, 1157

Centre des femmes de l'Estrie, 1158

Centre des femmes de Sudbury/Sudbury Women's Centre, 1007

Centre des femmes de Verdun, 1159

Centre des femmes du ô pays, 1160

Centre des femmes du Témiscouata L'Aurore, 1161

Centre des femmes (Forestville, Québec), 1162

Centre-Femmes Catherine Leblond, 1164

Centre-Femmes d'aujourd'hui, 1165

Centre-Femmes de Lotbinière, 1166

Centre-Femmes La Jardilec, 1167

Centre-Femmes L'Envolée, 1168

Centre pour femmes immigrantes (Sherbrooke, Québec), 1170

Centr'elles, comité d'action des femmes d'Avignon, 1172

Chez nous, 1009

Collective par et pour elle, 1186

D'main de femmes, 1194

Fondation du refuge pour femmes Chez Doris/Chez Doris, the Women's Shelter Foundation, 1207

Maison des femmes de la région de Rimouski, 1223

Marie Debout, Centre d'éducation des femmes, 1231

Passerelle de Weedon, 1238

Place aux femmes/Women's Place (Ottawa, Ont.), 1064

Réseau des femmes du Sud de l'Ontario, 1071

centre d'information et de référence *voir* **centre des femmes**

Chinoise

Service à la famille chinoise du Grand Montréal. Comité des femmes/Chinese Family Service of Greater Montreal. Women's Committee, 1251

christianisme

Autre Parole, 1133

Conseil œcuménique des chrétiennes du Canada/Women's Inter-Church Council of Canada, 724

Église catholique. Diocèse de Sainte-Anne-de-la-Pocatière. Service de la condition des femmes dans l'Église et la société, 600

Réseau d'action en milieu urbain/Urban Core Support Network, 760

Résidence de l'avenue A, 1248

cinéma *voir* **film**

coalition

(*voir aussi* **réseau**)

Coalition canadienne contre la pornographie dans les médias/Canadian Coalition against Media Pornography, 40

Coalition canadienne pour les droits des lesbiennes et gais/Canadian Lesbian and Gay Rights Coalition, 41

Coalition des associations de femmes canadiennes : Le Congrès international sur la paix/Coalition of Canadian Women's Groups: International Peace Conference, 42

Coalition des femmes de l'Ontario/Ontario Women's Action Coalition, 370

Coalition pour la réforme des droits de la personne du Nouveau-Brunswick/New Brunswick Coalition for Human Rights Reform, 641

Comité canadien d'action sur le statut de la femme/National Action Committee on the Status of Women, 44, 720

Conseil ethnoculturel du Canada. Comité des femmes/Canadian Ethnocultural Council. Women's Committee, 723

Fédération des femmes du Québec, 603, 1203

Fédération des femmes du Québec. Conseil régional de Québec, 604

collecte de fonds *voir* **financement**

collège

(*voir aussi* **université**)

Association des universités et collèges du Canada. Comité spécial sur le rapport de la Commission royale d'enquête sur la situation de la femme/Association of Universities and Colleges of Canada. Special Committee on the Report of the Royal Commission on the Status of Women, 9

Association des universités et collèges du Canada. Comité sur la situation de la femme dans les universités/Association of Universities and Colleges of Canada. Committee on the Status of Women in Universities, 10

Collège de Maisonneuve. Société générale des étudiantes et des étudiants. Comité-femme de Maisonneuve, 1187

condition féminine

(*N.B. : Cette expression désigne les organisations qui se préoccupent du statut de la femme en général. Des expressions plus spécifiques (p. ex. (université, femme de carrières libérales et commerciales) ont été employées pour décrire les organisations traitant du statut de la femme dans un domaine particulier.*)

Association féminine d'éducation et d'action sociale, 588, 1131

Association féminine d'éducation et d'action sociale. Section Rouyn-Noranda, 589

Coalition des femmes de l'Ontario/Ontario Women's Action Coalition, 370

Comité canadien d'action sur le statut de la femme/National Action Committee on the Status of Women, 44, 720

Comité canadien sur la situation de la femme/Canadian Committee on the Status of Women, 46

Conseil des femmes de Montréal/Montreal Council of Women, 598

Échange entre femmes de Saint-Laurent, 1195

Fédération des femmes du Québec, 603, 1203

Fédération des femmes du Québec. Conseil régional de Québec, 604

Fédération nationale Saint-Jean-Baptiste, 606

Front de libération des femmes québécoises, 610

Ligue des droits et libertés. Office des droits des femmes, 617

Réseau d'action et d'information pour les femmes, 1245

congrès

Coalition canadienne pour les droits des lesbiennes et gais/Canadian Lesbian and Gay Rights Coalition, 41

Coalition des associations de femmes canadiennes : Le Congrès international sur la paix/Coalition of Canadian Women's Groups: International Peace Conference, 42

Institut canadien de recherches sur les femmes/Canadian Research Institute for the Advancement of Women, 64, 739

Lesbiennes de Montréal/Montreal Gay Women, 616

consultation d'orientation

(*voir aussi* **abus sexuel des enfants, agression sexuelle, dépendance, femme battue, santé mentale, violence familiale**)

Nouveau départ national, 1236

contraception *voir* **contrôle des naissances**

contrôle des naissances

Association pour la planification familiale de Montréal/Family Planning Association of Montreal, 590

Centre de planning familial du Québec, 596

Clinique des femmes de l'Outaouais, 1179

Fédération pour le planning des naissances du Canada/Planned Parenthood Federation of Canada, 731

SUBJECT INDEX: FRENCH ENTRIES

corps professoral
  (*voir aussi* **enseignante, université**)
  Alliance des professeurs de Montréal. Comité de la condition féminine, 584
  Alliance des professeurs de Montréal. Comité des droits de la femme, 585

dépendance
  AWARE à Kingston/Action on Women's Addictions: Research and Education, 999

désarmement *voir* **paix**

diplômée
  Association des femmes diplômées des universités (Montréal, Québec), 586
  Association des femmes diplômées des universités (Québec), 587
  Fédération canadienne des femmes diplômées des universités/Canadian Federation of University Women, 53

divorce *voir* **séparation**

docteur *voir* **médecin**

droit
  Association nationale de la femme et du droit/National Association of Women and the Law, 702
  Collectif femmes et justice de Québec, 1184
  Fonds d'action et d'éducation juridiques pour les femmes/ Women's Legal Education and Action Fund, 733
  Fonds d'action et d'éducation juridiques pour les femmes. Section Nouveau-Brunswick/Women's Legal Education and Action Fund. New Brunswick Branch, 1284
  Inform'elle, 1214
  Revue Femmes et droit/Canadian Journal of Women and the Law, 763

écrivaine *voir* **littérature**

éducation
  (*voir aussi* **alphabétisation, collège, corps professoral, diplômée, éducation physique, éducation sexuelle, enseignante, études sur les femmes, université**)
  Action éducation femmes (Nouveau-Brunswick), 1266
  Association des femmes diplômées des universités (Montréal, Québec), 586
  Association des femmes diplômées des universités (Québec), 587
  Association féminine d'éducation et d'action sociale, 588, 1131
  Association féminine d'éducation et d'action sociale. Section Rouyn-Noranda, 589
  Centre de documentation sur l'éducation des adultes et la condition féminine, 1143
  Collectif des femmes francophones du nord-est ontarien, 1013
  Congrès canadien pour la promotion des études chez la femme/Canadian Congress for Learning Opportunities for Women, 48, 721
  Fédération canadienne des femmes diplômées des universités/Canadian Federation of University Women, 53
  Réseau national d'Action éducation femmes, 761

éducation physique
  Association canadienne pour la santé, l'éducation physique et la récréation. Comité athlétique féminin/Canadian Association for Health, Physical Education, and Recreation. Women's Athletic Committee, 4
  Association canadienne pour l'avancement des femmes, du sport et de l'activité physique/Canadian Association for the Advancement of Women and Sport and Physical Activity, 699

éducation sexuelle
  Fédération pour le planning des naissances du Canada/Planned Parenthood Federation of Canada, 731

église *voir* **christianisme**

emploi
  (*voir aussi* **agricultrice, corps professoral, employée de bureau, enseignante, femme de carrières libérales et commerciales, infirmière, médecin, sage-femme, syndicat, travailleuse du textile**)
  Action travail des femmes du Québec, 1123
  Centre émersion manicouagan, 1163
  Conseil d'intervention pour l'accès des femmes au travail du Québec, 1192
  Fédération nationale Saint-Jean-Baptiste, 606
  Ficelles pour l'accès des femmes au travail, 1206
  FormOsud, 1208
  Impulsion-Travail, 1213
  Projet intégration des femmes, 1241
  Transition'elle, 1258

employée de bureau
  Association des adjoints administratifs/Association of Administrative Assistants, 6
  Association internationale des secrétaires professionnelles. Section Ville-Marie/Professional Secretaries International. Ville-Marie Chapter, 1132
  Syndicat des communications Canada/Communications Union Canada, 89

enfance maltraitée
  (*voir aussi* **abus sexuel des enfants, violence familiale**)
  Espace Val d'Or, 1198

enseignante
  (*voir aussi* **corps professoral**)
  Association des enseignantes et des enseignants francophones du Nouveau-Brunswick. Comité sur les valeurs et les droits humains en éducation, 1269
  Centrale de l'enseignement du Québec. Comité de la condition féminine, 594
  Fédération canadienne des enseignantes et des enseignants/Canadian Teachers' Federation, 728

enseignement supérieur *voir* **collège, université**

études sur les femmes
  (*voir aussi* **archives, bibliothèque, histoire, université**)
  Archives canadiennes du mouvement des femmes/Canadian Women's Movement Archives, 3
  Cahiers de la femme/Canadian Woman Studies, 703
  Collective (Université d'Ottawa)/Collective (University of Ottawa), 1014
  Documentation sur la recherche féministe/Resources for Feminist Research, 50, 726
  École des hautes études commerciales. Groupe femmes, gestion et entreprises, 599
  Institut canadien de recherches sur les femmes/Canadian Research Institute for the Advancement of Women, 64, 739
  Institut Simone de Beauvoir/Simone de Beauvoir Institute, 1215
  Université d'Ottawa. Programme en études des femmes/University of Ottawa. Women's Studies Programme, 1090
  Université Laval. Groupe de recherche multidisciplinaire féministe, 1261

étudiante *voir* **collège, université**

famille monoparentale *voir* **mère seule**

féminisme marxiste *voir* **féminisme socialiste**

INDEX DES SUJETS : NOTICES EN FRANÇAIS

féminisme socialiste

(*voir aussi* **groupe de gauche**)

(*N.B. : Cette expression ne désigne que les organisations qui se sont explicitement identifiées comme étant féministes socialistes; il se peut que d'autres organisations partagent cette orientation sans que ce soit mentionné dans la notice.*)

Réseau féministe populaire, 1246

femme aborigène *voir* **femme autochtone**

femme acadienne *voir* **femme francophone**

femme autochtone

Association des infirmières et infirmiers autochtones du Canada/ Indian and Inuit Nurses of Canada, 700

Maison le coin des femmes (Sept-Îles, Québec), 1227

femme battue

(*voir aussi* **logement temporaire**, **violence**, **violence familiale**)

Accueil du sans-abri, 1119

Accueil Sainte-Famille, 1265

Bouée régionale, 1134

Carrefour pour femmes/Crossroads for Women, 1271

Citad'elle de Lachute, 1178

Coup d'elle, 1193

Havre des femmes, 1212

Maison d'hébergement de Pabos, 1224

Maison du réconfort, 1225

Maison La Source, 1226

Maison le coin des femmes (Sept-Îles, Québec), 1227

Maison Unies-Vers-Femmes, 1230

Passe-r-elle des Hautes-Laurentides, 1237

Refuge pour les femmes de l'Ouest de l'Île/West Island Women's Shelter, 1244

Séjournelle : Maison d'aide et d'hébergement pour femmes victimes de violence conjugale, 1250

femme chef de famille *voir* **mère seule**

femme chinoise *voir* **Chinoise**

femme d'affaires *voir* **femme de carrières libérales et commerciales**

femme de carrières libérales ou commerciales

Association des femmes collaboratrices, 1130

École des hautes études commerciales. Groupe femmes, gestion et entreprises, 599

Fédération canadienne des clubs de femmes de carrières libérales et commerciales/Canadian Federation of Business and Professional Women's Clubs, 52

Fédération canadienne des clubs de femmes de carrières libérales et commerciales. Club de Shawinigan, 602

femme de couleur

(*N.B. : Pour une liste d'expressions désignant des groupes spécifiques (p. ex. Chinoise, Haïtienne), voir* **organisme ethnoculturel**.)

Conseil ethnoculturel du Canada. Comité des femmes/Canadian Ethnocultural Council. Women's Committee, 723

Organisation nationale des femmes immigrantes et des femmes appartenant à une minorité visible du Canada/Nationa Organization of Immigrant and Visible Minority Women of Canada, 754

femme de la classe ouvrière

(*voir aussi* **syndicat**)

Réseau féministe populaire, 1246

femme francophone

(*N.B. : Cette expression ne s'applique qu'aux organismes de femmes francophones vivant en milieu minoritaire.*)

Accueil Sainte-Famille, 1265

Action éducation femmes (Nouveau-Brunswick), 1266

Association des Acadiennes de la Nouvelle-Écosse, 657, 1316

Association des enseignantes et des enseignants francophones du Nouveau-Brunswick. Comité sur les valeurs et les droits humains en éducation, 1269

Association des femmes chefs de famille (Moncton, N.-B.), 639

Association des groupes de femmes francophones de l'Alberta, 879

Cercle des dames d'Acadie de Lamèque, 1272

Cercle des dames d'Acadie de Shippagan, 1273

Cercle des dames d'Acadie (Tracadie, N.-B.), 1274

Collectif des femmes francophones du nord-est ontarien, 1013

Dames d'Acadie de Neguac, 1278

Fédération des dames d'Acadie du Nouveau-Brunswick, 1282

Fédération des dames d'Acadie (Bathurst, N.-B.), 1281

Fédération nationale des femmes canadiennes-françaises, 55

Fédération nationale des femmes canadiennes-françaises (Alberta), 206

Fédération nationale des femmes canadiennes-françaises d'Oshawa, 1026

Fédération nationale des femmes canadiennes-françaises (Gravelbourg, Sask.), 922

Fédération nationale des femmes canadiennes-françaises. Section Willow Bunch, 246

Femmes d'aujourd'hui, 207

Groupe de concertation des Franco-Albertaines, 209

Groupe féminin pluri-elles, 1028

Liberté Egalité Sororité : Femmes acadiennes de Moncton, 646

Réseau des femmes du Sud de l'Ontario, 1071

Réseau national d'Action éducation femmes, 761

Société Madeleine LeBlanc, 1341

Union culturelle des Franco-Ontariennes, 512, 1088

Union culturelle des Franco-Ontariennes (Sturgeon Falls, Ont.), 1089

femme gaie *voir* **lesbienne**

femme haïtienne *voir* **Haïtienne**

femme handicapée *voir* **handicapée**

femme immigrée *voir* **immigrante**

femme juive *voir* **Juive**

femme maltraitée *voir* **femme battue**

femme professionnelle *voir* **femme de carrières libérales et commerciales**

femme sans abri

(*voir aussi* **logement temporaire**)

Fondation du refuge pour femmes Chez Doris/Chez Doris, the Women's Shelter Foundation, 1207

femme sud-asiatique

Centre communautaire des femmes sud-asiatiques/South Asian Women's Community Centre, 1138

femme universitaire *voir* **corps professoral**

film

(*voir aussi* **vidéo**)

Vidéo femmes, 1262

financement

Centre social des femmes du centre-ville de Montréal, 1171

Fondation Muriel McQueen Fergusson/Muriel McQueen Fergusson Foundation, 1283

foyer *voir* **logement temporaire**

galerie d'art

Centrale, 592

SUBJECT INDEX: FRENCH ENTRIES

garde de jour voir **soins à l'enfant**

gauchiste voir **groupe de gauche**

grossesse

S.O.S. Grossesse, 1249

groupe de gauche

(voir aussi **féminisme socialiste**)

Front de libération des femmes québécoises, 610

Groupe marxiste révolutionnaire/Revolutionary Marxist Group, 62

Nouveau Parti démocratique. Comité fédéral féminin/New Democratic Party. Federal Women's Committee, 79

Nouveau Parti démocratique du Québec. Comité féminin, 628

Organisation marxiste-léniniste du Canada En Lutte!. Comité de la condition féminine, 629

Parti communiste ouvrier. Comité des femmes, 630

Haïtienne

Impulsion-Travail, 1213

handicapée

Action des femmes handicapées (Montréal, Québec), 1120

Réseau d'action des femmes handicapées du Canada/DisAbled Women's Network Canada, 759

histoire

Comité canadien de l'histoire des femmes/Canadian Committee on Women's History, 45

immigrante

(N.B. : Pour une liste d'expressions désignant des groupes ethniques spécifiques, voir **organisme ethnoculturel**.)

Centre pour femmes immigrantes (Sherbrooke, Québec), 1170

Collectif des femmes immigrantes, 1182

Conseil ethnoculturel du Canada. Comité des femmes/Canadian Ethnocultural Council. Women's Committee, 723

Organisation nationale des femmes immigrantes et des femmes appartenant à une minorité visible du Canada/National Organization of Immigrant and Visible Minority Women of Canada, 754

inceste voir **abus sexuel des enfants**

infirmière

Association des infirmières et infirmiers autochtones du Canada/Indian and Inuit Nurses of Canada, 700

Association des infirmières et infirmiers du Canada/Canadian Nurses Association, 8

Fédération nationale des syndicats d'infirmières/infirmiers/ National Federation of Nurses' Unions, 730

Journée internationale des femmes, 8 mars

Centr'elles, comité d'action des femmes d'Avignon, 1172

judaïsme voir **Juive**

Juive

Naches, 626

lesbienne

Alliance nationale des lesbiennes/National Lesbian Forum, 694

Androgyne, 1125

Association des lesbiennes et des gais de l'Outaouais/Association of Lesbians and Gays of Ottawa, 346, 996

Association pour les droits des gai(e)s du Québec, 591

Centre social des femmes du centre-ville de Montréal, 1171

Coalition canadienne pour les droits des lesbiennes et gais/Canadian Lesbian and Gay Rights Coalition, 41

Coalition pour la réforme des droits de la personne du Nouveau-Brunswick/New Brunswick Coalition for Human Rights Reform, 641

Collective en santé lesbienne, 1185

Documentation sur la recherche féministe/Resources for Feminist Research, 50, 726

Félibre, 1204

Féministes lesbiennes de Montréal/Lesbian Feminists of Montreal, 608

Lesbiennes de Montréal/Montreal Gay Women, 616

Lesbo Info, 1219

Naches, 626

Réseau vidé-elle, 1247

Services du triangle rose/Pink Triangle Services, 1074

Université Laval. Groupe gai, 634

librairie

Androgyne, 1125

littérature

(voir aussi **théâtre**)

Arcade, 1128

logement temporaire

Accueil du sans-abri, 1119

Accueil Sainte-Famille, 1265

Bouée régionale, 1134

Carrefour pour femmes/Crossroads for Women, 1271

Centre Louise-Amélie, 1169

Citad'elle de Lachute, 1178

Coup d'elle, 1193

Havre des femmes, 1212

Maison de Passage House, 1287

Maison De Connivence, 1222

Maison d'hébergement de Pabos, 1224

Maison du réconfort, 1225

Maison La Source, 1226

Maison le coin des femmes (Sept-Îles, Québec), 1227

Maison Mikana, 1229

Maison Unies-Vers-Femmes, 1230

Passe-r-elle des Hautes-Laurentides, 1237

Refuge pour les femmes de l'Ouest de l'Île/West Island Women's Shelter, 1244

Résidence de l'avenue A, 1248

Séjournelle : Maison d'aide et d'hébergement pour femmes victimes de violence conjugale, 1250

maison de transition voir **logement temporaire**

maison d'hébergement voir **logement temporaire**

médecin

Fédération des femmes médecins du Canada/Federation of Medical Women of Canada, 54

ménopause

Publications Une Véritable Amie/A Friend Indeed Publications, 1242

mère

(voir aussi **accouchement**, **mère seule**, **soins à l'enfant**)

Aide à la femme pour l'allaitement maternel et la maternité, 1124

Centre d'animation mère-enfant, 1142

mère seule

Association des femmes chefs de famille (Moncton, N.-B.), 639

Fédération des associations de familles monoparentales du Québec, 1202

Femmes chefs de foyer (Shawinigan, Québec), 1205

Re-Nou-Vie, 1243

Réseau d'action en milieu urbain/Urban Core Support Network, 760

INDEX DES SUJETS : NOTICES EN FRANÇAIS

Support aux mères célibataires/Support to Single Mothers, 1295

Métisse *voir* **femme autochtone**

minorité visible *voir* **femme de couleur**

mouvement ouvrier *voir* **syndicat**

mouvement pour le libre choix *voir* **avortement**

organisme ethnoculturel *voir* **Chinoise, femme autochtone, femme de couleur, femme francophone, femme sud-asiatique, Haïtienne, immigrante, Juive**

pacifisme *voir* **paix**

paix

Coalition des associations de femmes canadiennes : Le Congrès international sur la paix/Coalition of Canadian Women's Groups: International Peace Conference, 42

Voix des femmes/Voice of Women, 93

parent unique *voir* **mère seule**

parti politique

Association des femmes progressistes conservatrices/Progressive Conservative Women's Association, 7

Fédération nationale des femmes libérales du Canada/Women's Liberal Federation of Canada, 56

Nouveau Parti démocratique. Comité fédéral féminin/New Democratic Party. Federal Women's Committee, 79

Nouveau Parti démocratique du Québec. Comité féminin, 628

Parti communiste ouvrier. Comité des femmes, 630

Parti libéral du Canada. Commission libérale féminine nationale/Liberal Party of Canada. National Women's Liberal Commission, 81, 756

Parti progressiste conservateur du Canada. Bureau des femmes/Progressive Conservative Party of Canada. Women's Bureau, 82

pauvreté

(*voir aussi* **assistance sociale**)

Entraide familiale Outaouais, 1197

Fondation du refuge pour femmes Chez Doris/Chez Doris, the Women's Shelter Foundation, 1207

Réseau d'action en milieu urbain/Urban Core Support Network, 760

pays en voie de développement

Centre international MATCH/MATCH International Centre, 38, 717

Cinquième Monde, 1177

MATCH international (Saguenay-Lac-St-Jean, Québec), 1232

périodique

Arcade, 1128

Association des infirmières et infirmiers du Canada/Canadian Nurses Association, 8

Association des lesbiennes et des gais de l'Outaouais/Association of Lesbians and Gays of Ottawa, 346, 996

Autre Parole, 1133

Cahiers de la femme/Canadian Woman Studies, 703

Congrès canadien pour la promotion des études chez la femme/Canadian Congress for Learning Opportunities for Women, 48, 721

Documentation sur la recherche féministe/Resources for Feminist Research, 50, 726

Lesbo Info, 1219

Organisation marxiste-léniniste du Canada En Lutte!. Comité de la condition féminine, 629

Publications Une Véritable Amie/A Friend Indeed Publications, 1242

Réseau d'action et d'information pour les femmes, 1245

Revue Femmes et droit/Canadian Journal of Women and the Law, 763

Université Laval. Groupe de recherche multidisciplinaire féministe, 1261

pièce de théâtre *voir* **théâtre**

planification familiale *voir* **contrôle des naissances**

poésie *voir* **littérature**

politique

(*voir aussi* **parti politique**)

Club politique féminin, 1181

pornographie

Coalition canadienne contre la pornographie dans les médias/Canadian Coalition against Media Pornography, 40

prisonnière *voir* **système pénal**

professeure *voir* **corps professoral**

psychologie *voir* **santé mentale**

psychothérapie *voir* **consultation d'orientation**

religion *voir* **christianisme, Juive**

représentation médiatique

Coalition canadienne contre la pornographie dans les médias/Canadian Coalition against Media Pornography, 40

Évaluation-Médias/MediaWatch, 727

Évaluation-Médias/MediaWatch (Outremont, Québec), 1200

réseau

(*voir aussi* **coalition**)

Action des femmes handicapées (Montréal, Québec), 1120

Association des groupes de femmes francophones de l'Alberta, 879

Centres canadiens de viol/Canadian Rape Crisis Centres, 39

Fédération des associations de familles monoparentales du Québec, 1202

Réseau d'action des femmes handicapées du Canada/DisAbled Women's Network Canada, 759

Réseau d'action en milieu urbain/Urban Core Support Network, 760

Réseau d'action et d'information pour les femmes, 1245

Réseau des femmes du Sud de l'Ontario, 1071

Réseau féministe populaire, 1246

Réseau national d'Action éducation femmes, 761

Réseau vidé-elle, 1247

sage-femme

Naissance-Renaissance, 1235

santé

(*voir aussi* **abus sexuel des enfants, accouchement, agression sexuelle, avortement, consultation d'orientation, contrôle des naissances, dépendance, éducation physique, éducation sexuelle, enfance maltraitée, femme battue, grossesse, handicapée, infirmière, médecin, ménopause, sage-femme, santé mentale, SIDA, violence, violence familiale**)

Association des infirmières et infirmiers autochtones du Canada/Indian and Inuit Nurses of Canada, 700

Collective en santé lesbienne, 1185

santé mentale

(*voir aussi* **consultation d'orientation**)

Centre de femmes du pays Maria-Chapdelaine, 1145

secrétaire *voir* **employée de bureau**

séparation

Ano-Sep, 1127

Femmes chefs de foyer (Shawinigan, Québec), 1205

Re-Nou-Vie, 1243

service de documentation

(*voir aussi* **archives, bibliothèque, centre des femmes**)

Inform'elle, 1214

SUBJECT INDEX: FRENCH ENTRIES

Services du triangle rose/Pink Triangle Services, 1074

SIDA

Comité du SIDA d'Ottawa. Comité ELLES/AIDS Committee of Ottawa. Women's Project, 1016

soins à l'enfant

Association canadienne pour la promotion des services de garde à l'enfance/Canadian Day Care Advocacy Association, 698

Fédération canadienne des services de garde à l'enfance/Canadian Child Day Care Federation, 729

sport voir **éducation physique**

subvention voir **financement**

syndicat

Alliance des professeurs de Montréal. Comité de la condition féminine, 584

Alliance des professeurs de Montréal. Comité des droits de la femme, 585

Association des enseignantes et des enseignants francophones du Nouveau-Brunswick. Comité sur les valeurs et les droits humains en éducation, 1269

Centrale de l'enseignement du Québec. Comité de la condition féminine, 594

Confédération des syndicats nationaux. Conseil central de Lanaudière. Comité de condition féminine, 1190

Confédération des syndicats nationaux. Conseil central de Thetford Mines. Comité de la condition féminine, 1191

Conseil canadien du textile/Canadian Textile Council, 49

Fédération canadienne des enseignantes et des enseignants/ Canadian Teachers' Federation, 728

Fédération nationale des syndicats d'infirmières/infirmiers/ National Federation of Nurses' Unions, 730

Syndicat canadien des travailleurs du textile et de la chimie/ Canadian Textile and Chemical Union, 88

Syndicat des agricultrices de la Côte-du-Sud, 1256

Syndicat des communications Canada/Communications Union Canada, 89

Travailleurs amalgamés du vêtement et du textile/Amalgamated Clothing and Textile Workers Union, 90, 766

syndrome immuno-déficitaire acquis voir **SIDA**

système judiciaire voir **droit, système pénal**

système pénal

Association canadienne des sociétés Elizabeth Fry/Canadian Association of Elizabeth Fry Societies, 697

Expansion-Femmes de Québec, 1201

Société Elizabeth Fry de Montréal/Elizabeth Fry Society of Montreal, 1253

téléphoniste voir **employée de bureau**

théâtre

Théâtre collectif des femmes de St-Basile, 1257

thérapie voir **consultation d'orientation**

Tiers Monde voir **pays en voie de développement**

toxicomanie voir **dépendance**

travail voir **emploi**

travailleuse du textile

Conseil canadien du textile/Canadian Textile Council, 49

Syndicat canadien des travailleurs du textile et de la chimie/ Canadian Textile and Chemical Union, 88

Travailleurs amalgamés du vêtement et du textile/Amalgamated Clothing and Textile Workers Union, 90, 766

travailleuse du vêtement voir **travailleuse du textile**

université

(voir aussi **collège, diplômée**)

Association des universités et collèges du Canada. Comité spécial sur le rapport de la Commission royale d'enquête sur la situation de la femme/Association of Universities and Colleges of Canada. Special Committee on the Report of the Royal Commission on the Status of Women, 9

Association des universités et collèges du Canada. Comité sur la situation de la femme dans les universités/Association of Universities and Colleges of Canada. Committee on the Status of Women in Universities, 10

Collective (Université d'Ottawa)/Collective (University of Ottawa), 1014

École des hautes études commerciales. Groupe femmes, gestion et entreprises, 599

Institut Simone de Beauvoir/Simone de Beauvoir Institute, 1215

Université d'Ottawa. Programme en études des femmes/University of Ottawa. Women's Studies Programme, 1090

Université Laval. Comité d'étude sur la condition féminine, 632

Université Laval. Comité pour l'Université Laval au féminin, 633

Université Laval. Groupe de recherche multidisciplinaire féministe, 1261

Université Laval. Groupe gai, 634

veuve

Femmes chefs de foyer (Shawinigan, Québec), 1205

Re-Nou-Vie, 1243

victime d'inceste voir **abus sexuel des enfants**

vidéo

Groupe intervention vidéo, 1210

Réseau vidé-elle, 1247

Vidéo femmes, 1262

viol voir **agression sexuelle**

violence

(voir aussi **abus sexuel des enfants, agression sexuelle, enfance maltraitée, femme battue, pornographie, violence familiale**)

Centre de femmes La Moisson, 1147

Centre Louise-Amélie, 1169

Cercle des dames d'Acadie de Shippagan, 1273

Collectif d'intervention auprès des femmes victimes de violence, 1183

Conseil œcuménique des chrétiennes du Canada/Women's Inter-Church Council of Canada, 724

Maison Mikana, 1229

violence domestique voir **femme battue, violence familiale**

violence faite aux enfants voir **abus sexuel des enfants, enfance maltraitée**

violence familiale

(voir aussi **abus sexuel des enfants, enfance maltraitée, femme battue**)

Fondation Muriel McQueen Fergusson/Muriel McQueen Fergusson Foundation, 1283

Maison De Connivence, 1222

Maison de Passage House, 1287

Unité d'intervention pour crises familiales de Restigouche/Restigouche Family Crisis Interveners, 1298

Section 2 : English Entries / Notices en anglais

**LISTE D'EXPRESSIONS ANGLAISES EMPLOYÉES, AVEC ÉQUIVALENTS FRANÇAIS/
LIST OF ENGLISH TERMS USED, WITH FRENCH EQUIVALENTS**

Classée par ordre alphabétique d'après l'expression anglaise/In alphabetical order by the English terms

abortion • avortement
addiction • dépendance
AIDS • SIDA
alumnae • diplômée
anarchism • anarchisme
anthropology • anthropologie
anti-racism • anti-racisme
Arab women • femme arabe
archives • archives
art galleries • galerie d'art
arts • arts
bank workers • personnel bancaire
bars and cafés • bar et café
battered women • femme battue
birth control • contrôle des naissances
bisexual women • bisexuelle
Black women • femme noire
bookstores • librairie
breast feeding • allaitement maternel
business and professional women • femme de carrières libérales et commerciales
Cambodian women • Cambodgienne
child care • soins à l'enfant
child custody • garde des enfants
childbirth • accouchement
Chinese women • Chinoise
Christianity • christianisme
clerical workers • employée de bureau
coalitions • coalition
colleges • collège
conferences • congrès
consciousness raising • conscientisation
counselling • consultation d'orientation
craft arts • artisanat
credit unions • caisse d'épargne et de crédit
criminal justice system • système pénal
demonstrations • manifestation
developing countries • pays en voie de développement
disabled women • handicapée
domestic workers • personnel domestique
eating disorders • trouble de l'alimentation
economy • économie
education • éducation
employment • emploi
employment equity • équité d'emploi
engineers • ingénieure
environment • environnement
faculty • corps professoral

family violence • violence familiale
farmers • agricultrice
festivals • festival
films • film
fishing industry • industrie de la pêche
funding • financement
health • santé
health care workers • travailleuse de la santé
history • histoire
home economics • économie domestique
homeless women • femme sans abri
homemakers • femme au foyer
housing • logement
immigrant women • immigrante
information services • service de documentation
International Women's Day, March 8 • Journée internationale de la femme, 8 mars
International Women's Year, 1975 • Année internationale de la femme, 1975
Iranian women • Iranienne
Jewish women • Juive
journalists • journaliste
Korean women • Coréenne
Latin American women • Latino-Américaine
law • droit
left-wing organizations • groupe de gauche
lesbian mothers • mère lesbienne
lesbians • lesbienne
libraries • bibliothèque
literacy • alphabétisation
literature • littérature
media arts • arts médiatiques
media portrayal • représentation médiatique
menopause • ménopause
mental health • santé mentale
midwives • sage-femme
military • armée
mothers • mère
music • musique
Native women • femme autochtone
networks • réseau
nontraditional employment • emploi non traditionnel
nuclear energy • énergie nucléaire
nurses • infirmière
oil industry • industrie pétrolière
older women • femme âgée
oral history • histoire orale
organizational development • développement organisationnel
peace • paix

SUBJECT INDEX: ENGLISH ENTRIES

periodicals • périodique
photography • photographie
physical education • éducation physique
physicians • médecin
political parties • parti politique
political prisoners • prisonnière politique
politics • politique
pornography • pornographie
poverty • pauvreté
printing • imprimerie
prostitutes • prostituée
publishing industry • industrie de l'édition
radio • radio
refugees • réfugiée
religion • religion
rural women • femme rurale
sales workers • vendeuse
sciences • sciences
self-defence • autodéfense
separation • séparation
service occupations • métier de service
services • services
sex education • éducation sexuelle
sexual abuse of children • abus sexuel des enfants
sexual assault • agression sexuelle
sexual harassment • harcèlement sexuel
sexually transmitted diseases • maladie transmise sexuellement
single mothers • mère seule
social assistance • assistance sociale
social workers • travailleuse sociale
socialist feminism • féminisme socialiste
sociology • sociologie
South Asian women • femme sud-asiatique
Soviet women • femme soviétique
spirituality • spiritualité
status of women • condition féminine
teachers • enseignante
technology • technologie
temporary housing • logement temporaire
textile workers • travailleuse du textile
theatre • théâtre
trade unions • syndicat
Ukrainian women • Ukrainienne
universities • université
videos • vidéo
violence • violence
visual arts • arts visuels
waitresses • serveuse de restaurant
women of colour • femme de couleur
women's centres • centre des femmes
women's studies • études sur les femmes
working-class women • femme de la classe ouvrière
young women • jeune femme

Classée par ordre alphabétique d'après l'équivalent français/In alphabetical order by the French equivalents

abus sexuel des enfants • sexual abuse of children
accouchement • childbirth
agression sexuelle • sexual assault
agricultrice • farmers
allaitement maternel • breast feeding
alphabétisation • literacy
anarchisme • anarchism
Année internationale de la femme, 1975 • International Women's Year, 1975
anthropologie • anthropology
anti-racisme • anti-racism
archives • archives
armée • military
artisanat • craft arts
arts • arts
arts médiatiques • media arts
arts visuels • visual arts
assistance sociale • social assistance
autodéfense • self-defence
avortement • abortion
bar et café • bars and cafés
bibliothèque • libraries
bisexuelle • bisexual women
caisse d'épargne et de crédit • credit unions
Cambodgienne • Cambodian women
centre des femmes • women's centres
Chinoise • Chinese women
christianisme • Christianity
coalition • coalitions
collège • colleges
condition féminine • status of women
congrès • conferences
conscientisation • consciousness raising
consultation d'orientation • counselling
contrôle des naissances • birth control
Coréenne • Korean women
corps professoral • faculty
dépendance • addiction
développement organisationnel • organizational development
diplômée • alumnae
droit • law
économie • economy
économie domestique • home economics
éducation • education
éducation physique • physical education
éducation sexuelle • sex education
emploi • employment
emploi non traditionnel • nontraditional employment

INDEX DES SUJETS : NOTICES EN ANGLAIS

employée de bureau • clerical workers
énergie nucléaire • nuclear energy
enseignante • teachers
environnement • environment
équité d'emploi • employment equity
études sur les femmes • women's studies
féminisme socialiste • socialist feminism
femme âgée • older women
femme arabe • Arab women
femme au foyer • homemakers
femme autochtone • Native women
femme battue • battered women
femme de carrières libérales et commerciales • business and professional women
femme de couleur • women of colour
femme de la classe ouvrière • working-class women
femme noire • Black women
femme rurale • rural women
femme sans abri • homeless women
femme soviétique • Soviet women
femme sud-asiatique • South Asian women
festival • festivals
film • films
financement • funding
galerie d'art • art galleries
garde des enfants • child custody
groupe de gauche • left-wing organizations
handicapée • disabled women
harcèlement sexuel • sexual harassment
histoire • history
histoire orale • oral history
immigrante • immigrant women
imprimerie • printing
industrie de la pêche • fishing industry
industrie de l'édition • publishing industry
industrie pétrolière • oil industry
infirmière • nurses
ingénieure • engineers
Iranienne • Iranian women
jeune femme • young women
journaliste • journalists
Journée internationale de la femme, 8 mars • International Women's Day, March 8
Juive • Jewish women
Latino-Américaine • Latin American women
lesbienne • lesbians
librairie • bookstores
littérature • literature
logement • housing
logement temporaire • temporary housing
maladie transmise sexuellement • sexually transmitted diseases
manifestation • demonstrations

médecin • physicians
ménopause • menopause
mère • mothers
mère lesbienne • lesbian mothers
mère seule • single mothers
métier de service • service occupations
musique • music
paix • peace
parti politique • political parties
pauvreté • poverty
pays en voie de développement • developing countries
périodique • periodicals
personnel bancaire • bank workers
personnel domestique • domestic workers
photographie • photography
politique • politics
pornographie • pornography
prisonnière politique • political prisoners
prostituée • prostitutes
radio • radio
réfugiée • refugees
religion • religion
représentation médiatique • media portrayal
réseau • networks
sage-femme • midwives
santé • health
santé mentale • mental health
sciences • sciences
séparation • separation
serveuse de restaurant • waitresses
service de documentation • information services
services • services
SIDA • AIDS
sociologie • sociology
soins à l'enfant • child care
spiritualité • spirituality
syndicat • trade unions
système pénal • criminal justice system
technologie • technology
théâtre • theatre
travailleuse de la santé • health care workers
travailleuse du textile • textile workers
travailleuse sociale • social workers
trouble de l'alimentation • eating disorders
Ukrainienne • Ukrainian women
université • universities
vendeuse • sales workers
vidéo • videos
violence • violence
violence familiale • family violence

SUBJECT INDEX: ENGLISH ENTRIES /
INDEX DES SUJETS : NOTICES EN ANGLAIS

Aboriginal women *see* **Native women**

abortion

(*see also* **birth control**)

Abortion and Contraception Committee of Toronto, 341

Abortion by Choice Society of Alberta, 874

Abortion Caravan, 1

Association for the Review of Canadian Abortion Laws, 11

Bay Centre for Birth Control, 1000

B.C. Committee to Defend Dr Morgentaler, 110

British Columbia Women's Abortion Law Repeal Coalition, 122

Calgary Birth Control Association, 187

Canadian Abortion Rights Action League/Association canadienne pour le droit à l'avortement, 16

Canadian Abortion Rights Action League. Fraser Valley Chapter, 796

Canadian Abortion Rights Action League. Prince Edward Island Chapter, 1302

Canadian Abortion Rights Action League, St John's, 1353

Canadian Women's Coalition to Repeal the Abortion Laws, 34

Childbirth by Choice Trust, 718

Coalition to Answer Anita Bryant (Saskatoon, Sask.), 244

Everywoman's Health Centre Society, 806

Kitchener-Waterloo Women's Coalition for Repeal of the Abortion Laws, 413

Manitoba Abortion Action Coalition, 304

Manitoba Coalition for Reproductive Choice, 966

May 28th Coalition for Abortion Rights, 440

Ontario Coalition for Abortion Clinics, 454

Ontario Women's Abortion Law Repeal Coalition, 459

Ottawa Coalition for Reproductive Choice, 464

Reproductive Health Clinic, 902

Saskatoon Abortion Rights Association, 943

Saskatoon Women for Abortion Law Repeal, 272

Toronto Committee to Defend Dr Morgentaler, 500

Toronto Women's Caucus, 508

United Action Committee for Abortion Reform, 277

University of Toronto. Sexual Education Centre, 520

Women's Action Collective on Health, 284

Women's Services Network (Toronto, Ont.), 572

YWCA Women's Centre (Montreal, Quebec), 638

abuse *see* **battered women, sexual abuse of children**

academic women *see* **faculty**

acquired immune deficiency syndrome *see* **AIDS**

addiction

Action on Women's Addictions: Research and Education/AWARE à Kingston, 992

Amana House, 1268

Amethyst Women's Addiction Centre, 995

Aurora House, 787

Empathy House of Recovery, 1025

Maiya House, 823

Riverside Villa Association, 217

Women and Drug Use Society of Saskatoon, 283

Women's Post Treatment Centre, 990

aging *see* **older women**

AIDS

AIDS Committee of Ottawa. Women's Project/Comité du SIDA d'Ottawa. Comité ELLES, 993

AIDS Committee of Toronto. Women and AIDS Project, 994

Edmonton Women and AIDS Project, 890

alcoholism *see* **addiction**

alumnae

Canadian Federation of University Women/Fédération canadienne des femmes diplômées des universités, 23

Canadian Federation of University Women. Cape Breton Branch, 659

Canadian Federation of University Women. Charlottetown Branch, 653, 1303

Canadian Federation of University Women. Halifax Branch, 660

Canadian Federation of University Women — Kelowna, 797

Canadian Federation of University Women. Nelson Branch, 798

Canadian Federation of University Women. Parksville/ Qualicum Beach Club, 799

Canadian Federation of University Women. Sackville Club, 640

Canadian Federation of University Women. Thunder Bay Chapter, 361

Red Deer University Women's Club, 216

Saskatchewan Provincial Council of the Canadian Federation of University Women, 264

University Women's Club (Moose Jaw, Sask.), 279

University Women's Club of Calgary, 229

University Women's Club of Edmonton, 230

University Women's Club of North York, 525

University Women's Club of Ottawa, 526

University Women's Club of Regina, 280

University Women's Club of Winnipeg, 324

University Women's Club (Saskatoon, Sask.), 281

University Women's Club (Swift Current, Sask.), 282

anarchism

BOA Magazine and Productions, 789

anorexia nervosa *see* **eating disorders**

anthropology

Women in Canadian Sociology/Anthropology, 97

anti-racism

(*see also* **Black women, ethnocultural organizations, immigrant women, Native women, women of colour**)

Alliance of Women against Racism Etcetera, 783

Women of Colour Collective, 909

Arab women

(*see also* **Iranian women**)

Arab Canadian Women's Network, 696

archives
  (*see also* **libraries**)
  Archives Collective, 107
  Canadian Women's Movement Archives/Archives canadiennes du mouvement des femmes, 35
  Winnipeg Gay/Lesbian Resource Centre, 986

art *see* **visual arts**

art galleries
  Centrale, 593
  Mentoring Artists for Women's Art, 970
  Photographers Gallery, 931
  Womanspirit Art Research and Learning Centre, 536
  Women's Perspective Collective, 565

arts
  (*see also* **art galleries, craft arts, films, literature, media arts, music, photography, radio, theatre, videos, visual arts**)
  Celebration of Women in the Arts, 884
  Fireweed: A Quarterly Journal, 61
  Pauline McGibbon Cultural Centre, 469
  Vancouver Women in Focus Society, 159
  Women's Cultural Building Collective, 554
  Women's Media Alliance of Toronto, 563

bank workers
  Service, Office, and Retail Workers' Union of Canada. Local 4 (Bank and Finance Workers), 146
  Service, Office, and Retail Workers' Union of Canada. Local 7, 1073

bars and cafés
  Chez nous, 1008
  Clementyne's Café, 369
  Fly by Night Lounge, 391
  Three of Cups, 495

battered women
  (*see also* **family violence, temporary housing, violence**)
  Atira Transition House, 786
  Battered Women's Advocacy Clinic, 349
  Battered Women's Support Services, 788
  Calgary Society for Women Plus, 880
  Calgary Women's Emergency Shelter Association, 191, 882
  Cape Breton Transition House, 662
  Central Alberta Women's Emergency Shelter, 886
  Central Valley Transition House Society, 800
  Chimo Personal Distress Intervention Service, 802
  Chrysalis House, 1319
  Crossroads for Women/Carrefour pour femmes, 1277
  Emily Stowe Shelter for Women, 1024
  Grande Cache Transition House, 895
  Guelph-Wellington Women in Crisis, 1029
  Hestia House, 1286
  Interval House of Ottawa-Carleton, 1033
  Iskwew, 924
  Juniper House, 1329
  Kate Booth House, 820
  La Ronge Native Women's Council, 925
  Labrador West Family Crisis Shelter, 1359
  Lanark County Interval House and Sexual Assault Centre, 1039
  Libra House, 1361
  Lundar/Eriksdale/Ashern Wife Abuse Committee, 963
  Maison le coin des femmes (Sept-Îles, Quebec), 1228
  Marguerite Dixon House, 825
  Medicine Hat Women's Shelter, 898
  Minnedosa and Area Committee on Wife Abuse, 971
  New Brunswick Coalition of Transition Houses for Abused Women, 1290
  Ontario Association of Interval and Transition Houses, 1057
  Osborne House, 977
  Regina Young Women's Christian Association, 259, 936
  St John's Status of Women Council, 689, 1364
  Saskatchewan Interfacing Law and Sociology, 938
  Saskatoon Interval House, 944
  Second Stage Housing (Saint John, N.B.), 1293
  Selkirk Cooperative on Abuse against Women, 980
  South Shore Transition House Association, 1343
  Sussex Vale Transition House, 1297
  Task Force on Violence in Lesbian Relationships, 494
  Thompson Crisis Centre, 985
  Transition House Association (Charlottetown, P.E.I.), 1312
  Vancouver Island Haven Society, 849
  Wellspring Women's Association, 907
  West Island Women's Shelter/Refuge pour les femmes de l'Ouest de l'Île, 1264
  Women in Crisis — Sioux, Hudson, North, 545
  Women in Need Society, 869
  Women in Transition House, 1299
  Women's Centre (Grey Bruce), 1102
  Women's Community House, 1103
  Women's Emergency Centre (Woodstock, Ont.), 555, 1106
  Women's Habitat, 557
  Women's Place (St Catharines, Ont.), 1111
  Women's Place, Welland and District, 1112
  Women's Resource Centre (Hay River, N.W.T.), 781
  Young Women's Christian Association of Lethbridge and District, 916
  Young Women's Christian Association of Peterborough Victoria and Haliburton, 582, 1117
  Young Women's Christian Association of St Thomas-Elgin, 583, 1118
  Young Women's Christian Association of Yellowknife, 782
  Young Women's Christian Association (Vancouver, B.C.), 179, 873
  Young Women's Christian Association (Winnipeg, Man.), 340

birth *see* **childbirth**

birth control
  Abortion and Contraception Committee of Toronto, 341
  Bay Centre for Birth Control, 1000
  Birth Control and V.D. Information Centre, 351
  Calgary Birth Control Association, 187
  Cumberland County Family Planning, 1321
  Family Planning Association of Montreal/Association pour la planification familiale de Montréal, 601
  Lakeshore Unitarian Church. Family Planning Advisory Service, 612
  Metro Area Family Planning Association, 1330
  Parents' Information Bureau, 468
  Planned Parenthood Association of British Columbia, 831
  Planned Parenthood Federation of Canada/Fédération pour le planning des naissances du Canada, 758

SUBJECT INDEX: ENGLISH ENTRIES

Planned Parenthood Manitoba, 316
Planned Parenthood Nova Scotia, 1336
Planned Parenthood Ontario, 472, 1065
Planned Parenthood Regina, 932
Planned Parenthood Saskatchewan, 250
Planned Parenthood Saskatoon Centre, 933
Planned Parenthood Society of Hamilton, 473, 1066
Planned Parenthood Waterloo Region, 1067
Reproductive Health Clinic, 902
Serena Manitoba, 981
Women Now, 678

bisexual women
Bisexual, Lesbian, and Gay Alliance at York, 352, 1001
Fredericton Lesbians and Gays, 644
Lesbian Information Line, 896
New Brunswick Coalition for Human Rights Reform/Coalition pour la réforme des droits de la personne du Nouveau-Brunswick, 648

Black women
(*see also* **women of colour**)
Committee against the Deportation of Immigrant Women, 374
Congress of Black Women of Canada, 722
Congress of Black Women of Canada. Manitoba Chapter, 956
Congress of Black Women of Canada. Regina Chapter, 920
Hour a Day Study Club, 405
Sister Vision: Black Women and Women of Colour Press, 1077
Toronto Black Women's Collective, 1083

bookstores
Androgyne, 1126
Cora: The Feminist Bookmobile, 380
Mrs Dalloway's Books, 1043
Northern Woman's Bookstore, 1052
One Sky, 929
Toronto Women's Bookstore, 507
Vancouver Women's Bookstore, 160, 854

breast feeding
Infant Feeding Action Coalition Canada, 738
Leche League Alberta/Northwest Territories, 210
Leche League International. Calgary Branch, 211

built environment *see* **environment**

bulimia *see* **eating disorders**

business and professional women
Business and Professional Women's Club (Flin Flon, Man.), 290
Business and Professional Women's Club of Moose Jaw, 241
Business and Professional Women's Club of Ottawa, 1002
Business and Professional Women's Club of Regina, 242
Business and Professional Women's Club of Winnipeg, 291
Business and Professional Women's Clubs of British Columbia and Yukon, 123
Business and Professional Women's Clubs of Ontario, 359
Canadian Federation of Business and Professional Women's Clubs/Fédération canadienne des clubs de femmes de carrières libérales et commerciales, 22
Canadian Federation of Business and Professional Women's Clubs. Calgary Local, 192
Charlottetown Business and Professional Women's Club, 654, 1306
Chatham Business and Professional Women's Club, 366
Chilliwack Business and Professional Women's Club, 127
Council of Business and Professional Women's Clubs of Metropolitan Toronto, 381
Edmonton Business and Professional Women's Club, 196
Guelph Business and Professional Women's Club, 400
Halifax Club of Business and Professional Women, 665
Home Economists in Business — Winnipeg, 300
Kitchener-Waterloo Business and Professional Women's Club, 412
Kitimat Business and Professional Women's Club, 139
Manitoba Provincial Organization of Business and Professional Women's Clubs, 310
Multicultural Council of Professional Women, 1044
Prince Albert Business and Professional Women's Club, 251
Saskatchewan Business and Professional Women's Clubs, 261
Saskatoon Business and Professional Women's Club, 270
Saskatoon Women's Network, 947
Soroptimist Club of Winnipeg, 321
Soroptimist Federation of the Americas. Western Canada Region, 322
Soroptimist International of Halifax/Dartmouth, 1342
Soroptimist International of Toronto, 490
Swift Current Business and Professional Women's Club, 275
Toronto Business and Professional Women's Club, 498
Toronto West Business and Professional Women's Club, 506
Vancouver Business and Professional Women's Club, 156
Victoria Business and Professional Women's Club, 163, 857
Weston Business and Professional Women's Club, 531
Whitehorse Business and Professional Women's Club, 103
Women's Business Network, 775
Women's Enterprise Bureau, 1367
Yorkton Business and Professional Women's Club, 285
Zonta Club (Charlottetown, P.E.I.), 656
Zonta Club (Halifax, N.S.), 683
Zonta Club of Edmonton, 240
Zonta Club of St John's, 693

cafés *see* **bars and cafés**

Cambodian women
Cambodian Women's Group of Ontario, 1003

centres *see* **women's centres**

child abuse *see* **family violence**, **sexual abuse of children**

child birth *see* **childbirth**

child care
Action Day Care, 342
Campus and Community Co-operative Day Care Centre, 360
Canadian Child Day Care Federation/Fédération canadienne des services de garde à l'enfance, 706
Canadian Day Care Advocacy Association/Association canadienne pour la promotion des services de garde à l'enfance, 708
Child Care Federation, 125
Child Care Occupation Forces, 126
Citizens' Day Care Action Committee, 663
Coppermine Women's Group, 779
Day Care Organizing Committee, 382
Day Care Reform Action Alliance, 383
Day Nursery Centre, 296
Halifax Young Women's Christian Association, 667, 1327
Jane Doe Study Group, 408

Kitchener-Waterloo Young Women's Christian Association, 414, 1036
Lakehead Social Planning Council. Childcare Committee, 1038
Manitoba Child Care Association, 965
Northwestern Ontario Regional Day Care Committee, 1053
Ontario Coalition for Better Child Care, 455
Public Service Alliance of Canada. Local 80384. Women's Committee, 1337
Regina Young Women's Christian Association, 259, 936
SFU Co-op Family, 147
Spadina Childcare Co-operative Association, 274
University of Alberta. Campus Day Care Committee, 224
Young Women's Christian Association of Edmonton, 239, 915
Young Women's Christian Association of Lethbridge and District, 916
Young Women's Christian Association of Yellowknife, 782
Yukon Child Care Association, 104

child custody
Lesbian Mothers' Defence Fund (Toronto, Ont.), 422
Lesbian Mothers Support Group, 303

child sexual abuse *see* **sexual abuse of children**

childbirth
(*see also* **midwives**)
Manitoba Homebirth Network, 968

childhood sexual abuse *see* **sexual abuse of children**

Chinese women
Chinese Canadian National Council. Women's Issues Committee, 719
Chinese Family Service of Greater Montreal. Women's Committee/Service à la famille chinoise du Grand Montréal. Comité des femmes, 1176

Christianity
Affirm (Winnipeg, Man.), 288
Dignity Toronto Dignité, 384
Ecumenical Decade of Churches in Solidarity with Women (Hampton, N.B.), 1279
Feminist Faith Concerns, 1027
Friends of Hagar, 392
Gay Christian Week, 298
Halifax Young Women's Christian Association, 667, 1327
Herstory, 959
Integrity Regina, 923
Kate Booth House, 820
Kitchener-Waterloo Young Women's Christian Association, 414, 1036
Metropolitan Community Church of Toronto, 442
Movement for Christian Feminism, 444
National Council of Young Men's Christian Associations. Task Force on the Status of Women in the YMCA, 74
Regina Young Women's Christian Association, 259, 936
United Church of Canada. Committee to Consider the Report of the Royal Commission on the Status of Women, 91
Urban Core Support Network/Réseau d'action en milieu urbain, 767
Wednesday Nite Live, 860
Women's Inter-Church Council of Canada/Conseil œcuménique des chrétiennes du Canada, 771
Women's Inter-Church Council of Canada. Winnipeg Branch, 337
Young Women's Christian Association of Calgary, 238, 914
Young Women's Christian Association of Canada, 101
Young Women's Christian Association of Edmonton, 239, 915
Young Women's Christian Association of Lethbridge and District, 916
Young Women's Christian Association of Metropolitan Toronto, 581, 1116
Young Women's Christian Association of Peterborough Victoria and Haliburton, 582, 1117
Young Women's Christian Association of Prince Albert, 954
Young Women's Christian Association of St Thomas-Elgin, 583, 1118
Young Women's Christian Association of Thompson, 339, 991
Young Women's Christian Association of Yellowknife, 782
Young Women's Christian Association (St John's, Nfld.), 692
Young Women's Christian Association, Saskatoon, 287
Young Women's Christian Association (Vancouver, B.C.), 179, 873
Young Women's Christian Association (Winnipeg, Man.), 340

churches *see* **Christianity**
cinema *see* **films**

clerical workers
Association of Administrative Assistants/Association des adjoints administratifs, 12
Association of University and College Employees. Local 1, 108
Communications Union Canada/Syndicat des communications Canada, 47
Office and Technical Employees' Union. Local 378, 142
Professional Secretaries International. Ville-Marie Chapter/Association internationale des secrétaires professionnelles. Section Ville-Marie, 1240
Service, Office, and Retail Workers' Union of Canada. Local 4 (Bank and Finance Workers), 146
Service, Office, and Retail Workers' Union of Canada. Local 7, 1073
Women and Work Research and Education Society, 866

coalitions
(*see also* **networks**)
Abortion and Contraception Committee of Toronto, 341
Alberta Coalition against Pornography, 876
British Columbia Federation of Women, 111, 791
British Columbia Women's Abortion Law Repeal Coalition, 122
British Columbia Women's Housing Coalition, 795
Canadian Coalition against Media Pornography/Coalition canadienne contre la pornographie dans les médias, 18
Canadian Ethnocultural Council. Women's Committee/Conseil ethnoculturel du Canada. Comité des femmes, 709
Canadian Lesbian and Gay Rights Coalition/Coalition canadienne pour les droits des lesbiennes et gais, 24
Canadian Women's Coalition to Repeal the Abortion Laws, 34
Citizen's Organization to Repeal Prostitution-Related Laws, 367
Coalition for Lesbian and Gay Rights in Ontario, 371, 1011
Coalition for the Week of Survival and Disarmament, 372
Coalition of Canadian Women's Groups: International Peace Conference/Coalition des associations de femmes canadiennes: Le Congrès international sur la paix, 43
Coalition of Visible Minority Women (Ontario), 1012
Coalition to Answer Anita Bryant (Saskatoon, Sask.), 244
Coalition to Stop Anita Bryant (Toronto, Ont.), 373
Edmonton Women's Coalition, 199
Family Benefits Work Group, 389
Infant Feeding Action Coalition Canada, 738
International Women's Day Coalition of Marxist-Leninists and Progressives, 135
International Women's Week Coalition (Kingston, Ont.), 407

SUBJECT INDEX: ENGLISH ENTRIES

Kitchener-Waterloo Women's Coalition for Repeal of the Abortion Laws, 413

Lesbian Studies Coalition of Concordia, 615, 1218

Manitoba Abortion Action Coalition, 304

Manitoba Coalition for Reproductive Choice, 966

March 8th Coalition, 439

May 28th Coalition for Abortion Rights, 440

National Action Committee on the Status of Women/Comité canadien d'action sur le statut de la femme, 71, 744

New Brunswick Coalition for Human Rights Reform/Coalition pour la réforme des droits de la personne du Nouveau-Brunswick, 648

New Brunswick Coalition of Transition Houses for Abused Women, 1290

Northern Women's Coalition, 105

October 25th Women's Action Coalition, 452

Ontario Coalition for Abortion Clinics, 454

Ontario Coalition for Better Child Care, 455

Ontario Women's Abortion Law Repeal Coalition, 459

Ontario Women's Action Coalition/Coalition des femmes de l'Ontario, 460

Ottawa Coalition for Reproductive Choice, 464

Saskatoon Women's Charities, 946

United Action Committee for Abortion Reform, 277

University of Toronto. Women's Coalition, 523

Vancouver Charter of Rights Coalition, 848

Women against Free Trade, 538

Women's Action Coalition of Nova Scotia, 1349

Women's Coalition (Toronto, Ont.), 552

Women's Employment and Training Coalition, 870

Women's Fund, 556

Women's Liberation Working Group (Toronto, Ont.), 562

coffee-houses *see* **bars and cafés**

colleges

(*see also* **universities**)

Association of Universities and Colleges of Canada. Committee on the Status of Women in Universities/Association des universités et collèges du Canada. Comité sur la situation de la femme dans les universités, 13

Association of Universities and Colleges of Canada. Special Committee on the Report of the Royal Commission on the Status of Women/Association des universités et collèges du Canada. Comité spécial sur le rapport de la Commission royale d'enquête sur la situation de la femme, 14

Centre for Women (Sheridan College. Brampton Campus), 365

Circle, 1010

Douglas College. Women's Centre, 804

Douglas College. Women's Studies Programme, 130

George Brown College. Advisory Committee for Equity, 398

Malaspina College. Faculty Association. Status of Women Committee, 824

Women's Art Mobile, 549

conferences

Abortion and Contraception Committee of Toronto, 341

Alberta Native Women's Conference (1st : 1968 : Edmonton, Alta.). Planning Committee, 182

Association for the Review of Canadian Abortion Laws, 11

Branching Out: Lesbian Productions (Toronto, Ont.), 354

Calgary Housewives Association, 188

Canadian Lesbian and Gay Rights Coalition/Coalition canadienne pour les droits des lesbiennes et gais, 24

Canadian Research Institute for the Advancement of Women/Institut canadien de recherches sur les femmes, 31, 713

Canadian Research Institute for the Advancement of Women/Institut canadien de recherches sur les femmes. 1990 Publications Committee, 1304

Celebration of Women in the Arts, 884

Coalition of Canadian Women's Groups: International Peace Conference/Coalition des associations de femmes canadiennes : Le Congrès international sur la paix, 43

Committee for a Socialist Women's Conference, 375

Committee for the Feminist Symposium, Montreal 1973, 597

Conference '80 : Women and the Economy (1980 : Fredericton, N.B.). Provincial Organizing Committee, 642

Congress of Black Women of Canada, 722

Feminist News Service, 58

Feminist Publications of Ottawa, 60, 732

Gay Alliance toward Equality (Toronto, Ont.), 393

Guelph Council for International Women's Year, 401

Hour a Day Study Club, 405

Kingston Women's Centre, 411

Lesbian Conference (1981 : Vancouver, B.C.). Organizing Committee, 67

Lesbian Organization of Toronto, 424

Lesbians of Ottawa Now, 426

Manitoba Abortion Action Coalition, 304

Montreal Gay Women/Lesbiennes de Montréal, 622

Northern Women's Centre, 451

Northern Women's Coalition, 105

Ontario Women's Abortion Law Repeal Coalition, 459

Queen's Homophile Association. Conference Steering Committee, 477

Rape Crisis Centre (Hamilton), 481

Regina Status of Women Co-ordinating Committee, 254

Regional Lesbian Conference (Ontario). Coordinating Committee, 483

Saskatchewan Teachers' Federation. Women in Education Advisory Committee, 939

Saskatoon Women's Liberation, 273

Second Wreath, 218

Toronto Gay Community Council, 502

Toronto Women's Liberation Movement, 509

Voice of Alberta Native Women's Society, 231

West Coast Women and Words Society, 863

Women and the Constitution Conference (1984 : St John's, Nfld.). Organizing Committee, 691

Women in Trades Association (Winnipeg, Man.), 334

Women's Action Collective on Health, 284

consciousness raising

Flaming Apron, 609

Kaslo Women's Group, 138

Kingston Women's Centre, 411

London Women's Liberation, 431

Montreal Women's Liberation, 623

Women's Resource Centre (St Catharines, Ont.), 569

construction workers *see* **nontraditional employment**

contraception *see* **birth control**

INDEX DES SUJETS : NOTICES EN ANGLAIS

counselling
(*see also* **addiction, battered women, family violence, mental health, sexual abuse of children, sexual assault**)
Amata Transition House Society, 784
Battered Women's Advocacy Clinic, 349
Calgary Society for Women Plus, 880
Calgary Women's Health Collective, 883
Chimo Personal Distress Intervention Service, 802
Ishtar Women's Centre and Transition House, 137
Kamloops Sexual Assault Counselling Centre, 819
Providing Assistance, Counselling, and Education, 900
Toronto Area Gays, 497
Womanpower, Inc., 535
Women's Counselling Referral and Education Centre, 1104
Women's Employment Counselling Service, 987
Women's Resources Centre (University of British Columbia), 872

craft arts
Albert County Women's Outreach Co-op, 1267
Flaming Apron, 609
Newfoundland Outport Nursing and Industrial Association, 688

credit unions
Metro Toronto Women's Credit Union, 441

criminal justice system
Brunswick Four, 357
Canadian Association of Elizabeth Fry Societies/Association canadienne des sociétés Elizabeth Fry, 705
Canadian Native Sisterhood Organization, 27
Coverdale Foundation, 1276
Elizabeth Fry Society. Hamilton Branch, 1021
Elizabeth Fry Society of Calgary, 201, 892
Elizabeth Fry Society of Cape Breton, 1323
Elizabeth Fry Society of Halifax/Dartmouth, 1324
Elizabeth Fry Society of Kingston, 387, 1022
Elizabeth Fry Society of Montreal/Société Elizabeth Fry de Montréal, 1196
Elizabeth Fry Society of New Brunswick, 1280
Elizabeth Fry Society of Toronto, 1023
Elizabeth Fry Society. Ottawa Branch, 388
Kamloops and District Elizabeth Fry Society, 818

day care *see* **child care**

demonstrations
(*see also* **International Women's Day, March 8**)
Abortion Caravan, 1
Coalition to Answer Anita Bryant (Saskatoon, Sask.), 244
Coalition to Stop Anita Bryant (Toronto, Ont.), 373
March 8th Coalition, 439
May 28th Coalition for Abortion Rights, 440
October 25th Women's Action Coalition, 452
Take Back the Night Committee (Toronto, Ont.), 493
University of Toronto. Women's Coalition, 523
Women Rally for Action, 170

developing countries
MATCH International Centre/Centre international MATCH, 70, 742
One Sky, 929

disabled women
Action des femmes handicapées (Montreal, Quebec), 1121
Consulting Committee on the Status of Women with Disabilities, 293
DisAbled Women's Network Canada/Réseau d'action des femmes handicapées du Canada, 725
DisAbled Women's Network (Fort St John, B.C.), 803
DisAbled Women's Network, Toronto, 1019

disarmament *see* **peace**

divorce *see* **separation**

doctors *see* **physicians**

domestic violence *see* **battered women, family violence**

domestic workers
Toronto Organization for Domestic Workers' Rights (Intercede), 1084
West Coast Domestic Workers Association, 861

drama *see* **theatre**

drug addiction *see* **addiction**

eating disorders
National Eating Disorder Information Centre, 748

economy
Conference '80 : Women and the Economy (1980 : Fredericton, N.B.). Provincial Organizing Committee, 642
Simon Fraser University. Public Interest Research Group, 841
Westcoast Women Futures Community Economic Development Society, 865
Women against Free Trade, 538
Women's Atlantic Council, 652

education
(*see also* **alumnae, colleges, faculty, physical education, sex education, teachers, universities, women's studies**)
Canadian Congress for Learning Opportunities for Women/Congrès canadien pour la promotion des études chez la femme, 21, 707
Canadian Congress for Learning Opportunities for Women (Fort Smith, N.W.T.), 778
Canadian Congress for Learning Opportunities for Women (Fredericton, N.B.), 1270
Canadian Congress for Learning Opportunities for Women — Nova Scotia, 1317
Canadian Congress for Learning Opportunities for Women. Regina Chapter, 243
Canadian Federation of University Women/Fédération canadienne des femmes diplômées des universités, 23
Canadian Federation of University Women. Cape Breton Branch, 659
Canadian Federation of University Women. Charlottetown Branch, 653, 1303
Canadian Federation of University Women. Halifax Branch, 660
Canadian Federation of University Women — Kelowna, 797
Canadian Federation of University Women. Nelson Branch, 798
Canadian Federation of University Women. Parksville/Qualicum Beach Club, 799
Canadian Federation of University Women. Sackville Club, 640
Canadian Federation of University Women. Thunder Bay Chapter, 361
Red Deer University Women's Club, 216
Saskatchewan Provincial Council of the Canadian Federation of University Women, 264
University Women's Club (Moose Jaw, Sask.), 279
University Women's Club of Calgary, 229
University Women's Club of Edmonton, 230
University Women's Club of North York, 525

University Women's Club of Ottawa, 526
University Women's Club of Regina, 280
University Women's Club of Winnipeg, 324
University Women's Club (Saskatoon, Sask.), 281
University Women's Club (Swift Current, Sask.), 282
Winnipeg Association of Non-Teaching Employees, 326
Winnipeg Women School Administrators Club, 330
Women after Rights, 537
Women's Educational Resources Centre (Ontario Institute for Studies in Education), 1105
Women's Health Education Network, 681

elderly women *see* **older women**

employment

(*see also* **business and professional women, clerical workers, domestic workers, employment equity, engineers, faculty, farmers, fishing industry, health care workers, homemakers, journalists, midwives, nontraditional employment, nurses, oil industry, physicians, prostitutes, service occupations, social workers, teachers, textile workers, trade unions**)

Canadian Congress for Learning Opportunities for Women (Fredericton, N.B.), 1270
Halifax Young Women's Christian Association, 667, 1327
Immigrant Women's Job Placement Centre, 1032
Multicultural Council of Professional Women, 1044
Nanaimo Women's Resources Society, 828
Saskatchewan Working Women, 268
Saskatchewan Working Women. Regina Chapter, 269
Times Change Women's Employment Service, 1082
Urban Images for Native Indian Women, 846
Windsor Women's Incentive Centre, 1095
Womanpower, Inc., 535
Women and Work Research and Education Society, 866
Women Interested in Successful Employment, 1366
Women's Employment and Training Coalition, 870
Women's Employment Counselling Service, 987
Women's Labour History Project, 173, 871
Women's Place (Windsor, Ont.), 567
Working for Women, 953
Working Skills Centre of Ontario, 1113
Working Women Community Centre, 1114

employment equity

Association for Women's Equity in the Canadian Forces, 701
Ryerson Polytechnical Institute. Employment and Educational Equity Office, 485
Simon Fraser University. Employment Equity Advisory Committee, 840

engineers

Society for Canadian Women in Science and Technology, 765
University of Toronto. Status of Women Committee, 521
Women in Scholarship, Engineering, Science, and Technology (University of Alberta), 235, 908

environment

(*see also* **nuclear energy**)

Simon Fraser University. Public Interest Research Group, 841
Women and Environments Education and Development Foundation, 1097

ethnocultural organizations *see* **Arab women, Black women, Cambodian women, Chinese women, Iranian women, Jewish women, Korean women, Latin American women, Native women, South Asian women, Ukrainian women, women of colour**

faculty

(*see also* **colleges, universities**)

Association of Women Teaching at Queen's, 348
Faculty Women's Club (University of Alberta), 203
McMaster Faculty Association. Committee to Study the Status of Women Faculty at McMaster, 433
Malaspina College. Faculty Association. Status of Women Committee, 824
University of Alberta. Association of the Academic Staff at the University of Alberta. Committee on Employment Conditions of Full Time Women Faculty, 223
University of British Columbia. Academic Women's Association, 151
University of Victoria. Faculty Association. Status of Women Committee, 153
York University. Presidential Committee to Review the Salaries of Full-Time Faculty Women, 578

family planning *see* **birth control**

family violence

(*see also* **battered women, sexual abuse of children**)

Association for the Prevention of Community and Family Violence, 773
Committee against Woman Abuse (Mainland South), 1320
Committee on Family Violence, 1355
Lloydminster Interval Home, 897
Maison de Passage House, 1288
Moose Jaw Transition House, 927
Muriel McQueen Fergusson Foundation/Fondation Muriel McQueen Fergusson, 1289
Naomi Society for Victims of Family Violence, 1332
Prince Rupert Transition House, 835
Provincial Association of Transition Houses of Saskatchewan, 934
Restigouche Family Crisis Interveners/Unité d'intervention pour crises familiales de Restigouche, 1292
St Albert Stop Abuse in Families Society, 904
Second Stage Program (Victoria, B.C.), 838
Snow Lake Centre on Family Violence, 982
Swan Valley Crisis Centre, 983
Victims of Family Violence Association, 1346
Women and Children's Crisis Centre, 1096

farm women *see* **farmers, rural women**

farmers

(*see also* **rural women**)

Alberta Farm Women's Network, 877
Canadian Farm Women's Network, 710
Farm Women's Union of Alberta. Hillside Local, 204
Farm Women's Union of Alberta. Sunniebend Local, 205
National Farmers Union. Women's Advisory Committee, 749
New Brunswick Farm Women's Organization, 1291
Ontario Farm Women's Network, 1058
Saskatchewan Women's Agricultural Network, 940
United Farm Women of Alberta, 220
United Farm Women of Alberta. County of Red Deer Local, 221
United Farm Women of Alberta. Horn Hill Local, 222
Women for the Survival of Agriculture — Winchester, 1098

Women of Unifarm, 911

female-headed households *see* **single mothers**

feminist scholarship *see* **women's studies**

festivals
- Canadian Women's Music and Cultural Festival, 36
- West Kootenay Women's Association, 864
- Women and Film, 95

films
(*see also* **media arts**, **videos**)
- Reel Life, 674
- Toronto Women in Film and Television, 1086
- Women and Film, 95

fishing industry
- Ladies Coldstorage Workers Union, 684
- United Fishermen and Allied Workers Union. Women's Rights Committee, 845

funding
- Lesbian and Gay Community Appeal of Toronto, 416, 1040
- Lesbian Dance Committee, 420
- Muriel McQueen Fergusson Foundation/Fondation Muriel McQueen Fergusson, 1289
- Women's Fund, 556

garment workers *see* **textile workers**

gay women *see* **lesbians**

grants *see* **funding**

graphic arts *see* **visual arts**

handicapped women *see* **disabled women**

health
(*see also* **abortion, addiction, AIDS, battered women, birth control, breast feeding, childbirth, counselling, disabled women, eating disorders, family violence, health care workers, menopause, mental health, midwives, nurses, physical education, physicians, sex education, sexual abuse of children, sexual assault, sexually transmitted diseases, violence**)
- Candida Research and Information Foundation (Canada), 716
- Edmonton Women's Health Collective, 891
- Gays and Lesbians in Health Care, 397
- Immigrant Women's Health Centre, 1031
- Indian and Inuit Nurses of Canada/Association des infirmières et infirmiers autochtones du Canada, 737
- Northwestern Ontario Women's Health Information Network, 1055
- St John's Status of Women Council, 689, 1364
- Vancouver Women's Health Collective, 162, 855
- Winnipeg Gay Community Health Centre, 328
- Winnipeg Women's Health Collective, 331
- Woman's Place (Vancouver, B.C.), 168
- Women and Children's Health Centre (Toronto, Ont.), 541
- Women and Work Research and Education Society, 866
- Women Healthsharing, 96
- Women Now, 678
- Women Today, 1100
- Women's Action Collective on Health, 284
- Women's Health Clinic (Winnipeg, Man.), 988
- Women's Health Education Network, 681
- Women's Health Interaction, 558, 1107
- Women's Health Research Foundation of Canada, 989
- Women's Self-Help Clinic (Vancouver, B.C.), 175
- York University. Harbinger Community Services, 576

health care workers
(*see also* **midwives, nurses, physicians**)
- Gays and Lesbians in Health Care, 397
- Health Sciences Association of British Columbia, 813
- Manitoba Society of Occupational Therapists, 311
- Ontario Association of Registered Nursing Assistants, 453
- Saskatchewan Health-Care Auxiliaries Association, 262
- Service Employees' Union. Local 268, 489

higher education *see* **colleges**, **universities**

history
(*see also* **oral history**)
- Canadian Committee on Women's History/Comité canadien de l'histoire des femmes, 20
- Lesbian and Gay History Group of Toronto, 417
- Women and History Group, 1365
- Women's Labour History Project, 173, 871
- Women's Regale, 568

home economics
(*see also* **homemakers**)
- Home Economists in Business — Winnipeg, 300
- Nova Scotia Home Economics Association. Cape Breton Branch, 672

homeless women
(*see also* **temporary housing**)
- Chez Doris, the Women's Shelter Foundation/Fondation du refuge pour femmes Chez Doris, 1175
- Sistering: A Drop-in Centre for Transient Women, 1078

homemakers
(*see also* **home economics**)
- Alberta Women's Institutes, 185
- Calgary Housewives Association, 188
- Federated Women's Institutes of Canada, 51
- Federated Women's Institutes of Ontario, 390
- Manitoba Women's Institute, 313
- Mothers Are Women, 1042
- New Brunswick Women's Institutes, 650
- Saskatchewan Women's Institutes, 267, 941
- Saskatoon Women's Network, 947
- Wages Due Lesbians, 527
- Wages for Housework Committee (Toronto, Ont.), 528

hostels *see* **temporary housing**

household workers *see* **domestic workers**

housing
(*see also* **temporary housing**)
- British Columbia Women's Housing Coalition, 795
- Constance Hamilton Housing Co-operative, 1018
- Entre Nous Femmes Housing Society, 805
- Greater Victoria Women's Shelter Society, 812
- Halifax Women's Housing Coop, 1326
- Mavis McMullen Housing Society, 826
- Older Women's Network, 1056
- Second Stage Housing (Saint John, N.B.), 1293
- Young Women's Christian Association of Calgary, 238, 914

illiteracy *see* **literacy**

SUBJECT INDEX: ENGLISH ENTRIES

immigrant women
   (*see also* **refugees**)
   (*Note: For a list of terms for specific ethnic groups, see* **ethnocultural organizations**.)
   Aquelarre: Latin American Women's Cultural Society, 785
   Cambodian Women's Group of Ontario, 1003
   Canadian Ethnocultural Council. Women's Committee/Conseil ethnoculturel du Canada. Comité des femmes, 709
   Central Alberta Immigrant Women's Association, 885
   Changing Together: A Centre for Immigrant Women, 887
   Coalition of Visible Minority Women (Ontario), 1012
   Committee against the Deportation of Immigrant Women, 374
   Emily Stowe Shelter for Women, 1024
   Immigrant Women's Association of Manitoba, 960
   Immigrant Women's Association of Manitoba. Thompson Chapter, 961
   Immigrant Women's Health Centre, 1031
   Immigrant Women's Job Placement Centre, 1032
   Iranian Woman Publications of Canada, 740
   Korean Canadian Women's Association, 1037
   Multicultural Council of Professional Women, 1044
   Multicultural Women's Association, 1045
   National Organization of Immigrant and Visible Minority Women of Canada/Organisation nationale des femmes immigrantes et des femmes appartenant à une minorité visible du Canada, 752
   South Asian Women's Group, 1080
   Toronto Organization for Domestic Workers' Rights (Intercede), 1084
   Vancouver Society on Immigrant Women, 853
   West Coast Domestic Workers Association, 861
   Womanpower, Inc., 535
   Women Immigrants of London Resource Service Centre, 1099
   Women Working with Immigrant Women (Fredericton, N.B.), 1300
   Women Working with Immigrant Women of Metro Toronto, 1101
   Working Skills Centre of Ontario, 1113
   Working Women Community Centre, 1114

incest *see* **sexual abuse of children**

incest survivors *see* **sexual abuse of children**

Indian women *see* **Native women**, **South Asian women**

information and referral centres *see* **women's centres**

information services
   (*see also* **archives**, **libraries**, **women's centres**)
   East Prince Women's Information Committee, 1307
   Feminist News Service, 58
   Gay Community Calendar, 394
   Lesbian Information Line, 896
   Ottawa Women's Information and Referral Service, 1062
   Pink Triangle Services/Services du triangle rose, 1063
   Western Canadian Women's News Service, 167
   Women's Information Line, 560
   Women's Information, Resource, and Referral Service (Halifax, N.S.), 682

International Women's Day, March 8
   Durham International Women's Day Committee, 386
   Edmonton Women's Coalition, 199
   International Women's Day Coalition of Marxist-Leninists and Progressives, 135
   International Women's Day Committee (Vancouver, B.C.), 136
   International Women's Week Coalition (Kingston, Ont.), 407
   March 8th Coalition, 439
   Public Service Alliance of Canada. Local 80384. Women's Committee, 1337
   Stop Rape Week Committee, 631
   Toronto Socialist Feminist Action, 505, 1085

International Women's Year, 1975
   Committee for a Socialist Women's Conference, 375
   Guelph Council for International Women's Year, 401
   Local Council of Women (St John's, Nfld.), 685
   McMaster Student Social Work Association. Sub-committee to Celebrate International Women's Year, 435
   October 25th Women's Action Coalition, 452

Inuit women *see* **Native women**

Iranian women
   Iranian Woman Publications of Canada, 740

Jewish women
   Jewish Women's Federation, 1034
   Naches, 625
   National Council of Jewish Women of Canada, 72, 747
   National Council of Jewish Women of Canada. Calgary Branch, 212
   National Council of Jewish Women of Canada. Edmonton Section, 899
   National Council of Jewish Women of Canada. Winnipeg Section, 315, 972

journalists
   (*see also* **periodicals**)
   Canadian Women's Press Club, 37
   Canadian Women's Press Club. Calgary Branch, 193
   Canadian Women's Press Club. Edmonton Branch, 194
   Canadian Women's Press Club. Ottawa Branch, 362
   Canadian Women's Press Club. Toronto Branch, 363
   Canadian Women's Press Club. Vancouver Chapter, 124
   Canadian Women's Press Club. Winnipeg Branch, 292
   Clearinghouse for Feminist Media, 368

journals *see* **periodicals**

Judaism *see* **Jewish women**

Kampuchean women *see* **Cambodian women**

Korean women
   Korean Canadian Women's Association, 1037

labour *see* **employment**

labour movement *see* **trade unions**

Latin American women
   Aquelarre: Latin American Women's Cultural Society, 785
   New Experiences for Refugee Women, 1050

law
   Canadian Journal of Women and the Law/Revue Femmes et droit, 711
   National Association of Women and the Law/Association nationale de la femme et du droit, 745
   National Association of Women and the Law. Newfoundland and Labrador Caucus, 1363
   Saskatchewan Interfacing Law and Sociology, 938
   Vancouver Association of Women and the Law, 847
   Vancouver Charter of Rights Coalition, 848
   West Coast LEAF Association, 862
   Women and the Constitution Conference (1984 : St John's, Nfld.). Organizing Committee, 691
   Women's Legal Education and Action Fund/Fonds d'action et d'éducation juridiques pour les femmes, 772

INDEX DES SUJETS : NOTICES EN ANGLAIS

Women's Legal Education and Action Fund. New Brunswick Branch/Fonds d'action et d'éducation juridiques pour les femmes. Section Nouveau-Brunswick, 1301

learning *see* **education**

left-wing organizations

(*see also* **anarchism, socialist feminism**)

British Columbia New Democratic Party. Vancouver Women's Committee, 112

British Columbia New Democratic Party. Women's Rights Committee, 113, 793

British Columbia Provincial Co-operative Commonwealth Federation. Women's Council. Vancouver Branch, 114

Dovercourt NDP. Women's Action Committee, 385

Front de libération des femmes québécoises, 611

International Women's Day Coalition of Marxist-Leninists and Progressives, 135

League for Socialist Action, 65

Leila Khaled Collective, 415

Moose Jaw Co-operative Commonwealth Federation Women's Club, 248

New Democratic Party. Federal Women's Committee/Nouveau Parti démocratique. Comité fédéral féminin, 75

New Democratic Party. Participation of Women Committee. Task Force on Older Women in Canada, 76

New Democratic Party. Rosemary Brown Leadership Campaign Committee, 77

New Democratic Party. Women's Liberation Caucus, 78

New Left Caucus. Knitting Circle, 448

New Left Committee. Women's Liberation Front, 449

Ontario New Democratic Party. Women's Committee, 457

Prince Edward Island New Democratic Party. Standing Committee on Women, 1308

Revolutionary Marxist Group/Groupe marxiste révolutionnaire, 86

Revolutionary Workers League, 87

Toronto Women's Caucus, 508

Toronto Women's Liberation Movement, 509

United Action Committee for Abortion Reform, 277

Waffle. Women's Caucus, 94

legal system *see* **law, criminal justice system**

lesbian mothers

Lesbian and Feminist Mothers Political Action Group, 140

Lesbian Mothers' Defence Fund (Toronto, Ont.), 422

Lesbian Mothers Support Group, 303

Wages Due Lesbians, 527

lesbians

(*see also* **lesbian mothers**)

Affirm (Winnipeg, Man.), 288

Androgyne, 1126

Archives Collective, 107

Association of Lesbians and Gays of Ottawa/Association des lesbiennes et des gais de l'Outaouais, 347, 997

Atlantic Provinces Political Lesbians for Equality, 658

Bisexual, Lesbian, and Gay Alliance at York, 352, 1001

Body Politic, 15

Branching Out: Lesbian Productions (Toronto, Ont.), 354

British Columbia Federation of Women, 111, 791

Brunswick Four, 357

Canadian Lesbian and Gay Rights Coalition/Coalition canadienne pour les droits des lesbiennes et gais, 24

Canadian Library Association. Gay Interest Group, 25

Coalition for Lesbian and Gay Rights in Ontario, 371, 1011

Coalition to Answer Anita Bryant (Saskatoon, Sask.), 244

Coalition to Stop Anita Bryant (Toronto, Ont.), 373

Community Homophile Association of Toronto, 377

Council on Homosexuality and Religion, 295

Dignity Toronto Dignité, 384

Equality for Gays and Lesbians Everywhere — Regina, 921

Feminist Faith Concerns, 1027

Feminist Lesbian Action Group, 132

Fredericton Lesbians and Gays, 644

Gay Alliance for Equality (Halifax, N.S.), 664

Gay Alliance toward Equality (Toronto, Ont.), 393

Gay Alliance toward Equality (Vancouver, B.C.), 133

Gay and Lesbian Academics, Students, and Staff (University of Calgary), 894

Gay Christian Week, 298

Gay Community Calendar, 394

Gay/Lesbian Outreach, 810

Gay Women Unlimited, 395

Gays and Lesbians against the Right Everywhere, 396

Gays and Lesbians in Health Care, 397

Gays for Equality (Winnipeg, Man.), 299

Identity, 406

Integrity Regina, 923

Island Gay Society, 817

Lake Agazzis Amazon Guild, 302

Lesbia News, 822

Lesbian and Gay Community Appeal of Toronto, 416, 1040

Lesbian and Gay Friends of Concordia, 613

Lesbian and Gay History Group of Toronto, 417

Lesbian and Gay Pride Day Committee (Toronto, Ont.), 418

Lesbian Collective (Waterloo, Ont.), 419

Lesbian Conference (1981 : Vancouver, B.C.). Organizing Committee, 67

Lesbian Dance Committee, 420

Lesbian Feminists of Montreal/Féministes lesbiennes de Montréal, 614

Lesbian/Gay Pride Planning Committee (Regina, Sask.), 926

Lesbian Information Line, 896

Lesbian/Lesbienne, 421

Lesbian Organization of Kitchener, 423

Lesbian Organization of Toronto, 424

Lesbian Studies Coalition of Concordia, 615, 1218

Lesbians against the Right, 425

Lesbians of Ottawa Now, 426

Lesbo Info, 1220

London Lesbian Collective, 429

Long Time Coming, 618

McMaster Homophile Association, 434

Mama Quilla II, 438

Metropolitan Community Church of Toronto, 442

Montreal Gay Women/Lesbiennes de Montréal, 622

Mrs Dalloway's Books, 1043

Naches, 625

National Lesbian Forum/Alliance nationale des lesbiennes, 751

New Brunswick Coalition for Human Rights Reform/Coalition pour la réforme des droits de la personne du Nouveau-Brunswick, 648
New Feminists, 447
Perceptions : The Gay and Lesbian Newsmagazine of the Prairies, 930
Pink Triangle Services/Services du triangle rose, 1063
Political Lesbians of Toronto, 474
Political Lesbians United about the Media, 475
Queen's Homophile Association. Conference Steering Committee, 477
Queen's University. Women's Studies Programme. Lesbian Speakers Series Committee, 478
Ragweed Press, 1310
Regional Lesbian Conference (Ontario). Coordinating Committee, 483
Resources for Feminist Research/Documentation sur la recherche féministe, 85, 762
Rites Magazine, 764
Sexual Orientation Lobby, 319
Sexual Orientation Lobby of Manitoba, 320
Society for Political Action by Gays, 149
Task Force on Violence in Lesbian Relationships, 494
Toronto Area Gays, 497
Toronto Centre for Lesbian and Gay Studies, 499
Toronto Gay Action, 501
Toronto Gay Community Council, 502
Toronto Lesbian Network, 503
Trent Lesbian and Gay Collective, 511, 1087
Unitarian Universalist Association. Gay Caucus. Toronto Branch, 513
University of Toronto. Gays and Lesbians at the University of Toronto, 516
University of Toronto. Gays at the University of Toronto, 517
University of Toronto. Homophile Association, 518
University of Toronto. Lesbian and Gay Academic Society, 519
Vancouver Lesbian Centre, 850
Wild Womyn Don't Get the Blues, 1347
Winnipeg Gay Community Health Centre, 328
Winnipeg Gay/Lesbian Resource Centre, 986
Winnipeg Gay/Lesbian Youth, 329
Women (Trent University), 547

libraries
(*see also* **archives**)
Association of University and College Employees. Local 1, 108
Canadian Library Association. Gay Interest Group, 25
Cora: The Feminist Bookmobile, 380
Halifax City Regional Library. North Branch Library. Women's Group, 1325
National Council of Women of Canada, 73
Nellie Langford Rowell Library, 1049
One Sky, 929
Peterborough Women's Committee, 470
University of British Columbia. Women's Office, 152
Vancouver Women in Focus Society, 159
Winnipeg Gay/Lesbian Resource Centre, 986
Women's Educational Resources Centre (Ontario Institute for Studies in Education), 1105

literacy
(*see also* **education**)
Canadian Congress for Learning Opportunities for Women — Nova Scotia, 1317

literature
(*see also* **theatre**)
Growing Room Collective, 735
League of Canadian Poets. Feminist Caucus, 66
West Coast Women and Words Society, 863
Women's Writing Collective, 574

magazines *see* **periodicals**
marches *see* **demonstrations**
martial arts *see* **self-defence**
Marxist feminism *see* **socialist feminism**

media arts
(*see also* **films, media portrayal, photography, radio, videos**)
Clearinghouse for Feminist Media, 368
Vancouver Women in Focus Society, 159
Women's Communications Centre, 553
Women's Media Alliance of Toronto, 563

media portrayal
(*see also* **media arts**)
Canadian Coalition against Media Pornography/Coalition canadienne contre la pornographie dans les médias, 18
MediaWatch/Évaluation-Médias, 743
Political Lesbians United about the Media, 475
University of Toronto. Status of Women Committee, 521

menopause
Friend Indeed Publications/Publications Une Véritable Amie, 1209

mental health
(*see also* **counselling**)
Canadian Mental Health Association. Women and Mental Health Committee, 26
Ontario Psychological Association. Task Force on the Status of Women in Psychology in Ontario, 458

Métis women *see* **Native women**

midwives
Alberta Association of Midwives, 875
Association of Ontario Midwives, 998
Manitoba Homebirth Network, 968
Midwifery Task Force of Ontario, 1041
Nurse-Midwives Association of Manitoba, 975

military
Association for Women's Equity in the Canadian Forces, 701
Organizational Society for the Spouses of Military Members, 755

mothers
(*see also* **breast feeding, child care, childbirth, lesbian mothers, single mothers**)
Lesbian and Feminist Mothers Political Action Group, 140
Mothers Are Women, 1042
Vancouver Life Skills Society, 851

motion pictures *see* **films**
movies *see* **films**

music
Canadian Women's Music and Cultural Festival, 36
Fly by Night Lounge, 391
Holly Near Concert Organizing Committee, 404
Jezebel Productions, 1328
Mama Quilla II, 438
Sappho Sound, 487

Secret Furies, 1339

Three of Cups, 495

Women in Music, 868

Native women

Aboriginal Women's Council of Saskatchewan, 918

Alberta Native Women's Conference (1st : 1968 : Edmonton, Alta.). Planning Committee, 182

Canadian Native Sisterhood Organization, 27

Concerned Aboriginal Women, 129

Dryden Aboriginal Women's Resource Centre, 1020

Indian and Inuit Nurses of Canada/Association des infirmières et infirmiers autochtones du Canada, 737

Indian Rights for Indian Women, 63

Indigenous Women's Collective of Manitoba, 962

Iskwew, 924

Kipichisichakanisik Women's Peace Camp, 247

La Ronge Native Women's Council, 925

Maison le coin des femmes (Sept-Îles, Quebec), 1228

Native Women's Association of Canada, 753

Native Women's Centre (Hamilton, Ont.), 1047

Native Women's Resource Centre (Toronto, Ont.), 1048

Native Women's Transition Centre (Winnipeg, Man.), 973

New Brunswick Native Indian Women's Council, 649

One Sky, 929

Ontario Native Women's Association, 1060

Original Women's Network, 976

Pauktuutit: Inuit Women's Association of Canada, 757

Saskatchewan Native Women's Movement, 263

Urban Images for Native Indian Women, 846

Vancouver Island Haven Society, 849

Voice of Alberta Native Women's Society, 231

Women in Crisis — Sioux, Hudson, North, 545

Women of the Métis Nation Alliance, 910

Yukon Indian Women's Association, 776

networks

(see also **coalitions**)

Action des femmes handicapées (Montreal, Quebec), 1121

Alberta Farm Women's Network, 877

Arab Canadian Women's Network, 696

B.C. and Yukon Association of Women's Centres, 790

Canadian Congress for Learning Opportunities for Women (Fort Smith, N.W.T.), 778

Canadian Congress for Learning Opportunities for Women. Regina Chapter, 243

Canadian Farm Women's Network, 710

Canadian Rape Crisis Centres/Centres canadiens de viol, 30

Committee to Establish Ontario Federation of Women, 376

Community Resources for Women, 378

DisAbled Women's Network Canada/Réseau d'action des femmes handicapées du Canada, 725

DisAbled Women's Network (Fort St John, B.C.), 803

DisAbled Women's Network, Toronto, 1019

First Mature Women's Network Society, 808

Manitoba Homebirth Network, 968

Native Women's Association of Canada, 753

Northwestern Ontario Women's Decade Council, 1054

Northwestern Ontario Women's Health Information Network, 1055

Nova Scotia Women Artists' Network, 1333

Older Women's Network, 1056

Ontario Association of Interval and Transition Houses, 1057

Ontario Farm Women's Network, 1058

Options for Women (Edmonton, Alta.), 214

Original Women's Network, 976

Provincial Association of Transition Houses of Saskatchewan, 934

Regina Women's Network, 258

Saskatchewan Women's Agricultural Network, 940

Saskatoon Women's Network, 947

Toronto Lesbian Network, 503

Toronto Women's Network, 510

Transition House Association of Nova Scotia, 1345

Urban Core Support Network/Réseau d'action en milieu urbain, 767

Winnipeg Council of Self-Help, 327

Women in Science Network (University of Saskatchewan), 951

Women in Trades, Technology, and Operations — National Network, 769

Women Today, 1100

Women Working with Immigrant Women of Metro Toronto, 1101

Women's Business Network, 775

Women's Centres Connect!, 1350

Women's Health Education Network, 681

Women's Network (Charlottetown, P.E.I.), 1313

Women's Network Steering Committee (Hamilton, Ont.), 564

Women's Services Network (Toronto, Ont.), 572

Yukon Child Care Association, 104

newspapers see **periodicals**

nontraditional employment

(see also **employment**)

National Association of Women in Construction. Ottawa, Ontario Chapter 319, 1046

Saskatchewan Tradeswomen, 266

Skiltec Association, 1079

Women Back into Stelco Committee, 542

Women in Trades Association of Toronto, 546

Women in Trades Association (Winnipeg, Man.), 334

Women in Trades, Technology, and Operations — National Network, 769

Women into Rail Committee, 335

nuclear disarmament see **peace**

nuclear energy

Witches against Nuclear Technology, 534

Women against Nuclear Technology, 539

Women for Survival, 544

nurses

Alberta Community Health Nurses Society, 181

Association of Ontario Midwives, 998

British Columbia Nurses' Union, 794

Canadian Nurses Association/Association des infirmières et infirmiers du Canada, 28

Coalition of Visible Minority Women (Ontario), 1012

Flin Flon Graduate Nurses Association, 297

Indian and Inuit Nurses of Canada/Association des infirmières et infirmiers autochtones du Canada, 737

SUBJECT INDEX: ENGLISH ENTRIES

Manitoba Association of Licensed Practical Nurses, 306
Manitoba Organization of Nurses' Associations. Local 1, 309
National Federation of Nurses' Unions/Fédération nationale des syndicats d'infirmières/infirmiers, 750
Newfoundland Outport Nursing and Industrial Association, 688
Nurse-Midwives Association of Manitoba, 975
Ontario Association of Registered Nursing Assistants, 453
Parents' Information Bureau, 468

office workers *see* **clerical workers**

oil industry
Desk and Derrick Club of Calgary, 195

older women
(*see also* **menopause**)
British Columbia New Democratic Party. Women's Rights Committee, 113, 793
First Mature Women's Network Society, 808
Mavis McMullen Housing Society, 826
New Democratic Party. Participation of Women Committee. Task Force on Older Women in Canada, 76
Older Women's Network, 1056
Soroptimist Club of Winnipeg, 321
Womanpower, Inc., 535

oral history
Faculty Women's Club (University of Alberta), 203
Herstory, 959
Lesbian and Gay History Group of Toronto, 417
Women's Labour History Project, 173, 871

organizational development
Saskatchewan Women's Resources, 942

pacifism *see* **peace**

peace
British Columbia Voice of Women, 115
British Columbia Voice of Women. Nanaimo Branch, 116
British Columbia Voice of Women. North Shore Branch, 117
British Columbia Voice of Women. Parksville-Qualicum Branch, 118
British Columbia Voice of Women. Powell River Branch, 119
British Columbia Voice of Women. Vancouver Branch, 120
British Columbia Voice of Women. Victoria Branch, 121
Coalition for the Week of Survival and Disarmament, 372
Coalition of Canadian Women's Groups: International Peace Conference/Coalition des associations de femmes canadiennes : Le Congrès international sur la paix, 43
Kipichisichakanisik Women's Peace Camp, 247
Regina Voice of Women, 256
Voice of Women/Voix des femmes, 92
Voice of Women (Calgary, Alta.), 232, 906
Voice of Women. Edmonton Branch, 233
Voice of Women (Halifax, N.S.), 675
Voice of Women. Manitoba Branch, 325
Witches against Nuclear Technology, 534
Women against Nuclear Technology, 539
Women's Action for Peace, 548
Women's International League for Peace and Freedom. Vancouver Branch, 172

periodicals
Aquelarre: Latin American Women's Cultural Society, 785
Association of Lesbians and Gays of Ottawa/Association des lesbiennes et des gais de l'Outaouais, 347, 997
Body Politic, 15
Breaking the Silence : A Feminist Quarterly, 355
Broadside, 356
Canadian Congress for Learning Opportunities for Women/Congrès canadien pour la promotion des études chez la femme, 21, 707
Canadian Journal of Women and the Law/Revue Femmes et droit, 711
Canadian Native Sisterhood Organization, 27
Canadian Nurses Association/Association des infirmières et infirmiers du Canada, 28
Canadian Woman Studies/Cahiers de la femme, 715
Cayenne : A Socialist Feminist Bulletin, 364
Clearinghouse for Feminist Media, 368
Equal Times, 643
Feminist Communication Collective, 607
Feminist News Service, 58
Feminist Publications of Ottawa, 60, 732
Fireweed : A Quarterly Journal, 61
Friend Indeed Publications/Publications Une Véritable Amie, 1209
Friends of Hagar, 392
Gallerie Publications, 734
Growing Room Collective, 735
Herizons, 736
Herspectives, 814
Identity, 406
Images : West Kootenay Women's Paper, 134, 816
Iranian Woman Publications of Canada, 740
Lesbia News, 822
Lesbian/Lesbienne, 421
Lesbo Info, 1220
Long Time Coming, 618
Makara Publishing and Design Co-operative, 69
Mount Saint Vincent University, 670, 1331
Niagara Women's Magazine, 450
Northern Woman Journal, 1051
On Our Way, 213
Other Woman, 80
OtherWise : A Feminist Newspaper at U of T, 463
Pandora Publishing, 1334
Perceptions : The Gay and Lesbian Newsmagazine of the Prairies, 930
Photographers Gallery, 931
Resources for Feminist Research/Documentation sur la recherche féministe, 85, 762
Rites Magazine, 764
Saskatchewan Tradeswomen, 266
Source, 219
Toronto Women's Caucus, 508
Vancouver Status of Women, 158
Vancouver Women's Caucus, 161
Western Canadian Women's News Service, 167
Windsor Woman, 533
Winnipeg Women's Liberation, 332
Womanist, 768
Women and Environments Education and Development Foundation, 1097
Women Healthsharing, 96

Women's Art Resource Centre, 770
Women's Collective Press, 636
Women's Network (Charlottetown, P.E.I.), 1313
Women's Newsletter, 655
Young Women's Christian Association of Calgary, 238, 914
Yukon Status of Women Council, 777

photography

(*see also* **visual arts**)

Photographers Gallery, 931

physical education

Canadian Association for Health, Physical Education, and Recreation. Women's Athletic Committee/Association canadienne pour la santé, l'éducation physique et la récréation. Comité athlétique féminin, 17

Canadian Association for the Advancement of Women and Sport and Physical Activity/Association canadienne pour l'avancement des femmes, du sport et de l'activité physique, 704

Halifax Young Women's Christian Association, 667, 1327

Kitchener-Waterloo Young Women's Christian Association, 414, 1036

Montreal Young Women's Christian Association, 624

National Coaching School for Women, 746

National Council of Young Men's Christian Associations. Task Force on the Status of Women in the YMCA, 74

Regina Young Women's Christian Association, 259, 936

Young Women's Christian Association of Calgary, 238, 914

Young Women's Christian Association of Canada, 101

Young Women's Christian Association of Edmonton, 239, 915

Young Women's Christian Association of Lethbridge and District, 916

Young Women's Christian Association of Metropolitan Toronto, 581, 1116

Young Women's Christian Association of Peterborough Victoria and Haliburton, 582, 1117

Young Women's Christian Association of Prince Albert, 954

Young Women's Christian Association of St Thomas-Elgin, 583, 1118

Young Women's Christian Association of Thompson, 339, 991

Young Women's Christian Association of Yellowknife, 782

Young Women's Christian Association (St John's, Nfld.), 692

Young Women's Christian Association, Saskatoon, 287

Young Women's Christian Association (Vancouver, B.C.), 179, 873

Young Women's Christian Association (Winnipeg, Man.), 340

physicians

Federation of Medical Women of Canada/Fédération des femmes médecins du Canada, 57

plays *see* **theatre**

poetry *see* **literature**

political parties

Alberta Women's Liberal Association, 186

British Columbia New Democratic Party. Vancouver Women's Committee, 112

British Columbia New Democratic Party. Women's Rights Committee, 113, 793

British Columbia Provincial Co-operative Commonwealth Federation. Women's Council. Vancouver Branch, 114

Dovercourt NDP. Women's Action Committee, 385

Feminist Party of Canada, 59

Liberal Party of Canada. National Women's Liberal Commission/Parti libéral du Canada. Commission libérale féminine nationale, 68, 741

Moose Jaw Co-operative Commonwealth Federation Women's Club, 248

New Democratic Party. Federal Women's Committee/Nouveau Parti démocratique. Comité fédéral féminin, 75

New Democratic Party. Participation of Women Committee. Task Force on Older Women in Canada, 76

New Democratic Party. Rosemary Brown Leadership Campaign Committee, 77

New Democratic Party. Women's Liberation Caucus, 78

Ontario Liberal Party. Women's Perspective Advisory Committee, 1059

Ontario New Democratic Party. Women's Committee, 457

Prince Edward Island New Democratic Party. Standing Committee on Women, 1308

Progressive Conservative Party of Canada. Women's Bureau/Parti progressiste conservateur du Canada. Bureau des femmes, 83

Progressive Conservative Women's Association/Association des femmes progressistes conservatrices, 84

Waffle. Women's Caucus, 94

Women's Liberal Federation of Canada/Fédération nationale des femmes libérales du Canada, 98

political prisoners

Action for Women's Rights in the U.S.S.R., 343

politics

(*see also* **political parties**)

Brandon Council of Women, 289

Women for Political Action (Calgary, Alta.), 234

Women for Political Action (Toronto, Ont.), 543

Women's Model Parliament, 338

pornography

Alberta Coalition against Pornography, 876

Better End All Vicious Erotic Repression, 350

Canadian Coalition against Media Pornography/Coalition canadienne contre la pornographie dans les médias, 18

Women against Pornography (Victoria, B.C.), 169

Women against Violence against Women (Toronto, Ont.), 540

position of women *see* **status of women**

post-secondary education *see* **colleges**, **universities**

poverty

(*see also* **social assistance**)

Chez Doris, the Women's Shelter Foundation/Fondation du refuge pour femmes Chez Doris, 1175

Margaret Beaton Foundation for Women, 669

Sistering: A Drop-in Centre for Transient Women, 1078

Urban Core Support Network/Réseau d'action en milieu urbain, 767

Winnipeg Council of Self-Help, 327

printing

Amazon Press, 344

Press Gang, 144, 834

prisoners *see* **criminal justice system**, **political prisoners**

pro-choice movement *see* **abortion**

professional women *see* **business and professional women**

professors *see* **faculty**

prostitutes

Better End All Vicious Erotic Repression, 350

Canadian Organization for the Rights of Prostitutes, 29, 712

Citizen's Organization to Repeal Prostitution-Related Laws, 367

Prostitutes and Other Women for Equal Rights (Winnipeg, Man.), 317
Revolutionary Prostitutes League, 484
Stepping Stone Program, 1344
Women against Pornography (Victoria, B.C.), 169

psychotherapy *see* **counselling**

publishing industry
(*see also* **periodicals**)
Amazon Press, 344
Body Politic, 15
Clearinghouse for Feminist Media, 368
Press Gang, 144, 834
Ragweed Press, 1310
Sister Vision: Black Women and Women of Colour Press, 1077
Women's Press, 99

racism *see* **anti-racism**

radio
(*see also* **media arts**)
Gay Christian Week, 298
Local Council of Women (St John's, Nfld.), 685
Radio Free Women, 480

rape *see* **sexual assault**

rape crisis centres *see* **sexual assault**

refugees
(*see also* **immigrant women**)
Immigrant Women's Health Centre, 1031
Immigrant Women's Job Placement Centre, 1032
New Experiences for Refugee Women, 1050

religion
(*see also* **Christianity**, **Jewish women**, **spirituality**)
Council on Homosexuality and Religion, 295
Lakeshore Unitarian Church. Family Planning Advisory Service, 612
Southern Ontario Association of Unitarian-Universalist Women, 491
Unitarian Universalist Association. Gay Caucus. Toronto Branch, 513

resource centres *see* **libraries, women's centres**

retail trade *see* **sales workers**

rural women
(*see also* **farmers**)
(*Note: This term has not been used for all groups in rural communities, only for groups which represent rural women as such.*)
Alberta Women's Institutes, 185
Federated Women's Institutes of Canada, 51
Federated Women's Institutes of Ontario, 390
Manitoba Women's Institute, 313
New Brunswick Women's Institutes, 650
Rural Women's Seminar Society, 837
Saskatchewan Women's Institutes, 267, 941

sales workers
Service, Office, and Retail Workers' Union of Canada. Local 4 (Bank and Finance Workers), 146
Service, Office, and Retail Workers' Union of Canada. Local 7, 1073

sciences
Society for Canadian Women in Science and Technology, 765
Women in Scholarship, Engineering, Science, and Technology (University of Alberta), 235, 908
Women in Science Network (University of Saskatchewan), 951

secretaries *see* **clerical workers**

self-defence
Women Educating in Self-Defense Training, 867
Women's Self-Defence Centre, 571

separation
(*see also* **child custody**)
Moose Jaw Transition House, 927

service occupations
(*see also* **domestic workers, prostitutes, waitresses**)
Hotel, Restaurant, Culinary Employees, and Bartenders Union. Local 40, 815
Service, Office, and Retail Workers' Union of Canada. Local 4 (Bank and Finance Workers), 146
Service, Office, and Retail Workers' Union of Canada. Local 7, 1073

services
(*Note: For agencies which provide specific services, see* **health, sexual assault, temporary housing,** *etc.*)
Community Resources for Women, 378
Saskatoon Women's Charities, 946
Women's Services Network (Toronto, Ont.), 572

sex education
Cumberland County Family Planning, 1321
Metro Area Family Planning Association, 1330
Planned Parenthood Association of British Columbia, 831
Planned Parenthood Federation of Canada/Fédération pour le planning des naissances du Canada, 758
Planned Parenthood Nova Scotia, 1336
Planned Parenthood Ontario, 472, 1065
Planned Parenthood Regina, 932
Planned Parenthood Saskatoon Centre, 933
Planned Parenthood Society of Hamilton, 473, 1066
Planned Parenthood Waterloo Region, 1067
Reproductive Health Clinic, 902
University of Toronto. Sexual Education Centre, 520

sexual abuse of children
(*see also* **family violence, sexual assault, violence**)
Fort McMurray Sexual Assault Centre, 893
Mouvement contre le viol et l'inceste, 1234
Providing Assistance, Counselling, and Education, 900
Services for Adult Survivors of Sexual Abuse and Sexual Assault, 1311
Sexual Assault Recovery Anonymous, 839
Women's Post Treatment Centre, 990

sexual assault
(*see also* **violence**)
Battlefords' and Area Sexual Assault Centre, 919
Canadian Rape Crisis Centres/Centres canadiens de viol, 30
Châteauguay Sexual Assault Prevention and Aid Center/Centre d'aide et de prévention d'assauts sexuels de Châteauguay, 1174
Fort McMurray Sexual Assault Centre, 893
Fredericton Rape Crisis Centre, 1285
Guelph-Wellington Women in Crisis, 1029
Kamloops Sexual Assault Counselling Centre, 819
Kenora Sexual Assault Centre, 1035
Lanark County Interval House and Sexual Assault Centre, 1039
Mouvement contre le viol et l'inceste, 1234
North East Crisis Intervention Centre, 928

P.E.I. Rape and Sexual Assault Crisis Centre/Centre d'aide aux victimes de viol et d'agression sexuelle de l'Î.P.É., 1309
Rape Crisis Centre (Hamilton), 481
Regina Women's Community Centre and Sexual Assault Line, 935
Saskatoon Sexual Assault and Information Centre, 945
Sexual Assault Centre London, 1075
Sexual Assault Support Centre of Ottawa/Centre d'aide aux agressées sexuelles d'Ottawa, 1076
Stop Rape Week Committee, 631
Terrace Sexual Assault Centre, 843
Thompson Crisis Centre, 985
Toronto Rape Crisis Centre, 504
Vancouver Rape Relief and Women's Shelter, 852
Victoria Women's Sexual Assault Centre, 859

sexual assault centres *see* **sexual assault**

sexual harassment

Ryerson Polytechnical Institute. Office of Harassment Prevention Services, 486
University of Toronto. Committee on Sexual Harassment, 515
University of Toronto. Sexual Harassment Education, Counselling, and Complaint Office, 1092

sexually transmitted diseases

(*see also* **AIDS**)
Birth Control and V.D. Information Centre, 351
Reproductive Health Clinic, 902

shelters *see* **temporary housing**

single mothers

Entre Nous Femmes Housing Society, 805
Family Benefits Work Group, 389
Mavis McMullen Housing Society, 826
Mother Led Union, 443
Mother's Allowance Group (Winnipeg, Man.), 314
Single Moms Centre, 690
Single Parent Centre (Halifax, N.S.), 1340
Single Parent Resource Centre (Saint John, N.B.), 1294
Support to Single Mothers/Support aux mères célibataires, 1296
Urban Core Support Network/Réseau d'action en milieu urbain, 767
Vernon Women's Transition House Society, 856
Womanpower, Inc., 535
Women after Rights, 537
Young Women's Christian Association of Calgary, 238, 914

single-parent families *see* **single mothers**

social assistance

Family Benefits Work Group, 389
Mother Led Union, 443
Mother's Allowance Group (Winnipeg, Man.), 314
Operation Family Rights, 461
Service, Office, and Retail Workers' Union of Canada. Local 7, 1073
Winnipeg Council of Self-Help, 327

social services *see* **services**

social workers

Breaking the Silence: A Feminist Quarterly, 355
McMaster Student Social Work Association. Sub-committee to Celebrate International Women's Year, 435
Manitoba Association of Social Workers, 307

socialist feminism

(*see also* **left-wing organizations**)
(Note: This term has been used only for entries which specifically mention socialist feminism; other organizations may be socialist feminist without this fact being mentioned in the entry.)
Bread and Roses (Vancouver, B.C.), 109
Cayenne : A Socialist Feminist Bulletin, 364
Committee for a Socialist Women's Conference, 375
Jane Doe Study Group, 408
Kingston Women's Centre, 411
Saskatoon Women's Liberation, 273
Toronto Socialist Feminist Action, 505, 1085
Women's Action Collective on Health, 284
Women's Press, 99
Women's Study Group (Vancouver, B.C.), 177

sociology

Saskatchewan Interfacing Law and Sociology, 938
Women in Canadian Sociology/Anthropology, 97

sole-support mothers *see* **single mothers**

South Asian women

South Asian Women's Community Centre/Centre communautaire des femmes sud-asiatiques, 1255
South Asian Women's Group, 1080

Soviet women

Action for Women's Rights in the U.S.S.R., 343

spirituality

(*see also* **religion**)
Circle, 1010

sports *see* **physical education**

spouse abuse *see* **battered women**

status of women

(Note: This term has been used for groups dealing with the status of women in general. More specific terms (e.g., **universities, business and professional women**) have been used for groups dealing with the status of women in a particular field.)
52% Solution: Women for Equality, Justice, and Peace, 1351
Alberta Provincial Council of Women, 183
Alberta Status of Women Action Committee, 184, 878
Antigonish Women's Association, 1315
Bay St George Status of Women Council, 1352
Brandon Council of Women, 289
Bread and Roses (Vancouver, B.C.), 109
British Columbia Federation of Women, 111, 791
Calgary Local Council of Women, 189
Calgary Status of Women Action Committee, 190, 881
Canadian Committee on the Status of Women/Comité canadien sur la situation de la femme, 19
Chilliwack Council of Women, 128
Committee to Establish Ontario Federation of Women, 376
Concerned Women (Sault Ste Marie, Ont.), 379
Coppermine Women's Group, 779
Corner Brook Status of Women Council, 1356
Council of Women of Winnipeg, 294
Edmonton Local Council of Women, 197
Edmonton Women's Coalition, 199
Front de libération des femmes québécoises, 611
Gander Status of Women Council, 1357

SUBJECT INDEX: ENGLISH ENTRIES

Gateway Status of Women Council, 1358
Halifax Local Council of Women, 666
Halifax Young Women's Christian Association, 667, 1327
Hamilton and District Local Council of Women, 403
Kincardine Women's Study Group, 410
Kitchener-Waterloo Young Women's Christian Association, 414, 1036
Labrador West Status of Women Council, 1360
Local Council of Women (London, Ont.), 427
Local Council of Women (St John's, Nfld.), 685
Local Council of Women (Weston, Ont.), 428
London Status of Women Action Group, 430
London Women's Liberation, 431
Manitoba Action Committee on the Status of Women, 305, 964
Moncton Council of Women, 647
Montreal Council of Women/Conseil des femmes de Montréal, 621
Montreal Women's Liberation, 623
Montreal Young Women's Christian Association, 624
Moose Jaw Council of Women, 249
National Action Committee on the Status of Women/Comité canadien d'action sur le statut de la femme, 71, 744
National Council of Women of Canada, 73
New Feminists, 447
New Glasgow Local Council of Women, 671
Northern Women's Resource Service, 974
Northwestern Ontario Women's Decade Council, 1054
Nova Scotia Women's Action Committee, 673
Ontario Committee on the Status of Women, 456
Ontario Women's Action Coalition/Coalition des femmes de l'Ontario, 460
Options for Women (Edmonton, Alta.), 214
Ottawa Local Council of Women, 465
Ottawa Women's Liberation Committee, 467
Parkland Status of Women, 979
Provincial Council of Women of British Columbia, 145
Provincial Council of Women of Manitoba, 318
Provincial Council of Women of New Brunswick, 651
Provincial Council of Women of Ontario, 476, 1069
Provincial Council of Women of Saskatchewan, 252
Rainbow Harbour Women's Association, 901
Red Deer Local Council of Women, 215
Regina Council of Women, 253
Regina Status of Women Co-ordinating Committee, 254
Regina Women's Liberation Movement, 257
Regina Young Women's Christian Association, 259, 936
Rocky Mountain House Women's Committee, 903
St John's Status of Women Council, 689, 1364
Sarnia-Lambton Status of Women Committee, 488
Saskatchewan Action Committee, Status of Women, 260, 937
Saskatoon Local Council of Women, 271
Saskatoon Women's Liberation, 273
Swift Current Council of Women, 276
Tamitik Status of Women, 150
Toronto and Area Council of Women, 496
Toronto Women's Liberation Movement, 509
Toronto Women's Network, 510
Vancouver Council of Women, 157
Vancouver Status of Women, 158
Vancouver Women's Caucus, 161
Victoria Council of Women, 164
Victoria Status of Women Action Group, 165, 858
West Algoma Council of Women, 530
Westville Local Council of Women, 676
Windsor Local Council of Women, 532
Winnipeg Women's Liberation, 332
Women Aware, 1348
Women Rally for Action, 170
Women Today, 1100
Women Unlimited, 679
Women Working Together, 952
Women's Action Coalition of Nova Scotia, 1349
Women's Coalition (Toronto, Ont.), 552
Women's Involvement (Green's Harbour, Nfld.), 1368
Women's Liberation Alliance (Vancouver, B.C.), 174
Women's Liberation (Edmonton, Alta.), 236
Women's Liberation Study Group (Montreal, Quebec), 637
Women's Liberation Working Group (Toronto, Ont.), 562
Women's Network (Charlottetown, P.E.I.), 1313
Women's Network Steering Committee (Hamilton, Ont.), 564
Young Women's Christian Association of Calgary, 238, 914
Young Women's Christian Association of Canada, 101
Young Women's Christian Association of Edmonton, 239, 915
Young Women's Christian Association of Lethbridge and District, 916
Young Women's Christian Association of Metropolitan Toronto, 581, 1116
Young Women's Christian Association of Peterborough Victoria and Haliburton, 582, 1117
Young Women's Christian Association of Prince Albert, 954
Young Women's Christian Association of St Thomas-Elgin, 583, 1118
Young Women's Christian Association of Thompson, 339, 991
Young Women's Christian Association of Yellowknife, 782
Young Women's Christian Association (St John's, Nfld.), 692
Young Women's Christian Association, Saskatoon, 287
Young Women's Christian Association (Vancouver, B.C.), 179, 873
Young Women's Christian Association (Winnipeg, Man.), 340
Yukon Status of Women Council, 777

students *see* colleges, universities

substance abuse *see* **addiction**

teachers

(*see also* **faculty**)

Canadian Teachers' Federation/Fédération canadienne des enseignantes et des enseignants, 714
Manitoba Teachers' Society, 312, 969
Saskatchewan Teachers' Federation. Saskatoon Women Teachers' Local, 265
Saskatchewan Teachers' Federation. Women in Education Advisory Committee, 939

technology

Society for Canadian Women in Science and Technology, 765
Women in Scholarship, Engineering, Science, and Technology (University of Alberta), 235, 908

telephone operators *see* **clerical workers**

INDEX DES SUJETS : NOTICES EN ANGLAIS

temporary housing
- Amana House, 1268
- Amata Transition House Society, 784
- Atira Transition House, 786
- Aurora House, 787
- Calgary Women's Emergency Shelter Association, 191, 882
- Cape Breton Transition House, 662
- Central Alberta Women's Emergency Shelter, 886
- Central Valley Transition House Society, 800
- Chimo Personal Distress Intervention Service, 802
- Chrysalis House, 1319
- Committee on Family Violence, 1355
- Crossroads, 888
- Crossroads for Women/Carrefour pour femmes, 1277
- Dawson Shelter Society, 774
- Emily Stowe Shelter for Women, 1024
- Empathy House of Recovery, 1025
- Golden Women's Resource Centre, 811
- Grande Cache Transition House, 895
- Guelph-Wellington Women in Crisis, 1029
- Halifax Young Women's Christian Association, 667, 1327
- Hestia House, 1286
- Interval House of Ottawa-Carleton, 1033
- Ishtar Women's Centre and Transition House, 137
- Juniper House, 1329
- Kate Booth House, 820
- Kitchener-Waterloo Young Women's Christian Association, 414, 1036
- La Ronge Native Women's Council, 925
- Labrador West Family Crisis Shelter, 1359
- Lanark County Interval House and Sexual Assault Centre, 1039
- Libra House, 1361
- Lloydminster Interval Home, 897
- Maison de Passage House, 1288
- Maison le coin des femmes (Sept-Îles, Quebec), 1228
- Maiya House, 823
- Marguerite Dixon House, 825
- Medicine Hat Women's Shelter, 898
- Minnedosa and Area Committee on Wife Abuse, 971
- Mizpah Transition House, 827
- Montreal Young Women's Christian Association, 624
- Moose Jaw Transition House, 927
- Native Women's Centre (Hamilton, Ont.), 1047
- Native Women's Transition Centre (Winnipeg, Man.), 973
- Nellie's, 445
- New Brunswick Coalition of Transition Houses for Abused Women, 1290
- Ontario Association of Interval and Transition Houses, 1057
- Osborne House, 977
- Parkland Crisis Centre, 978
- Port Alberni Women's Resources Society, 832
- Prince Rupert Transition House, 835
- Project Hostel, 1068
- Provincial Association of Transition Houses of Saskatchewan, 934
- Regina Transition Women's Society, 255
- Regina Young Women's Christian Association, 259, 936
- Riverside Villa Association, 217
- St John's Status of Women Council, 689, 1364
- Saskatoon Interval House, 944
- Second Stage Program (Victoria, B.C.), 838
- Selkirk Cooperative on Abuse against Women, 980
- South Shore Transition House Association, 1343
- Southwest Crisis Services, 948
- Sussex Vale Transition House, 1297
- Swan Valley Crisis Centre, 983
- The Pas Committee for Women in Crisis, 984
- Thompson Crisis Centre, 985
- Transition House Association (Charlottetown, P.E.I.), 1312
- Transition House Association of Nova Scotia, 1345
- Vancouver Island Haven Society, 849
- Vancouver Rape Relief and Women's Shelter, 852
- Vernon Women's Transition House Society, 856
- Victims of Family Violence Association, 1346
- Wellspring Women's Association, 907
- West Island Women's Shelter/Refuge pour les femmes de l'Ouest de l'Île, 1264
- Women and Children's Crisis Centre, 1096
- Women in Crisis — Sioux, Hudson, North, 545
- Women in Need Society, 869
- Women in Transition House, 1299
- Women's Centre (Grey Bruce), 1102
- Women's Community House, 1103
- Women's Emergency Centre (Woodstock, Ont.), 555, 1106
- Women's Habitat, 557
- Women's Place (St Catharines, Ont.), 1111
- Women's Place, Welland and District, 1112
- Women's Resource Centre (Hay River, N.W.T.), 781
- Young Women's Christian Association of Calgary, 238, 914
- Young Women's Christian Association of Canada, 101
- Young Women's Christian Association of Edmonton, 239, 915
- Young Women's Christian Association of Lethbridge and District, 916
- Young Women's Christian Association of Metropolitan Toronto, 581, 1116
- Young Women's Christian Association of Peterborough Victoria and Haliburton, 582, 1117
- Young Women's Christian Association of Prince Albert, 954
- Young Women's Christian Association of St Thomas-Elgin, 583, 1118
- Young Women's Christian Association of Thompson, 339, 991
- Young Women's Christian Association of Yellowknife, 782
- Young Women's Christian Association, Saskatoon, 287
- Young Women's Christian Association (Vancouver, B.C.), 179, 873
- Young Women's Christian Association (Winnipeg, Man.), 340

textile workers
- Amalgamated Clothing and Textile Workers Union/Travailleurs amalgamés du vêtement et du textile, 2, 695
- Amalgamated Clothing and Textile Workers Union. Local 178, 106
- Canadian Textile and Chemical Union/Syndicat canadien des travailleurs du textile et de la chimie, 32
- Canadian Textile Council/Conseil canadien du textile, 33
- International Ladies Garment Workers Union. Local 286, 301
- Newfoundland Outport Nursing and Industrial Association, 688

theatre
- Anna Project, 345

Company of Sirens, 1017
Half The Sky Feminist Theatre Company, 1030
Jezebel Productions, 1328
Lesbian and Gay Community Appeal of Toronto, 416, 1040
Redlight Theatre, 482
Windsor Feminist Theatre, 1094
Witches against Nuclear Technology, 534
Women's Health Interaction, 558, 1107

therapy *see* **counselling**

Third World *see* **developing countries**

trade unions

Amalgamated Clothing and Textile Workers Union/Travailleurs amalgamés du vêtement et du textile, 2, 695
Amalgamated Clothing and Textile Workers Union. Local 178, 106
Association of University and College Employees. Local 1, 108
British Columbia Government Employees' Union. Provincial Executive Women's Committee, 792
British Columbia Nurses' Union, 794
Canadian Teachers' Federation/Fédération canadienne des enseignantes et des enseignants, 714
Canadian Textile and Chemical Union/Syndicat canadien des travailleurs du textile et de la chimie, 32
Canadian Textile Council/Conseil canadien du textile, 33
Communications Union Canada/Syndicat des communications Canada, 47
Health Sciences Association of British Columbia, 813
Hotel, Restaurant, Culinary Employees, and Bartenders Union. Local 40, 815
International Ladies Garment Workers Union. Local 286, 301
Ladies Coldstorage Workers Union, 684
Manitoba Association of Licensed Practical Nurses, 306
Manitoba Federation of Labour. Women's Committee, 308, 967
Manitoba Organization of Nurses' Associations. Local 1, 309
Manitoba Teachers' Society, 312, 969
National Federation of Nurses' Unions/Fédération nationale des syndicats d'infirmières/infirmiers, 750
Newfoundland and Labrador Federation of Labour. Women's Committee, 687
Office and Technical Employees' Union. Local 378, 142
Organized Working Women (Toronto Area), 462
Public Service Alliance of Canada. Local 80384. Women's Committee, 1337
Public Service Alliance of Canada. Yellowknife Regional Women's Committee, 780
Saskatchewan Teachers' Federation. Saskatoon Women Teachers' Local, 265
Saskatchewan Teachers' Federation. Women in Education Advisory Committee, 939
Saskatchewan Working Women, 268
Saskatchewan Working Women. Regina Chapter, 269
Service Employees' Union. Local 268, 489
Service, Office, and Retail Workers' Union of Canada. Local 4 (Bank and Finance Workers), 146
Service, Office, and Retail Workers' Union of Canada. Local 7, 1073
Toronto Socialist Feminist Action, 505, 1085
United Fishermen and Allied Workers Union. Women's Rights Committee, 845
Winnipeg Association of Non-Teaching Employees, 326
Working Women's Association, 178

trades *see* **nontraditional employment**

transition houses *see* **temporary housing**

Ukrainian women

Second Wreath, 218

unions *see* **trade unions**

universities

(*see also* **alumnae, colleges**)

Academic Women's Association (University of Alberta), 180
Acadia University. Presidential Advisory Committee on the Status of Women, 1314
Association of Universities and Colleges of Canada. Committee on the Status of Women in Universities/Association des universités et collèges du Canada. Comité sur la situation de la femme dans les universités, 13
Association of Universities and Colleges of Canada. Special Committee on the Report of the Royal Commission on the Status of Women/Association des universités et collèges du Canada. Comité spécial sur le rapport de la Commission royale d'enquête sur la situation de la femme, 14
Association of University and College Employees. Local 1, 108
Bisexual, Lesbian, and Gay Alliance at York, 352, 1001
Brandon University. Status of Women Organization, 955
Breaking the Silence: A Feminist Quarterly, 355
Campus and Community Co-operative Day Care Centre, 360
Carleton University. Institute of Women's Studies, 1004
Carleton University. Status of Women Office, 1005
Collective (University of Ottawa)/Collective (Université d'Ottawa), 1015
Concordia University. Office on the Status of Women, 1188
Concordia Women's Centre, 1189
Dalhousie University. Women's Studies Programme, 1322
Gay and Lesbian Academics, Students, and Staff (University of Calgary), 894
Gays for Equality (Winnipeg, Man.), 299
Group for Equal Rights at McMaster, 399
Lesbian and Gay Friends of Concordia, 613
Lesbian Studies Coalition of Concordia, 615, 1218
McGill University. Committee for Teaching and Research on Women, 619
McGill Women's Union, 620
McMaster Homophile Association, 434
McMaster Student Social Work Association. Sub-committee to Celebrate International Women's Year, 435
McMaster University. Faculty of Humanities Council. Sub-committee to Encourage Qualified Women Students to Proceed to Honours and Graduate Study in the Humanities, 436
McMaster University. Senate. Equal Rights Review and Co-ordinating Committee, 437
Memorial University of Newfoundland. Women's Association, 686
Memorial University of Newfoundland. Women's Studies Programme, 1362
Mount Saint Vincent University, 670, 1331
Nellie Langford Rowell Library, 1049
New College. Women's Studies Programme, 446
New Left Caucus. Knitting Circle, 448
OtherWise: A Feminist Newspaper at U of T, 463
Queen's Homophile Association. Conference Steering Committee, 477

INDEX DES SUJETS : NOTICES EN ANGLAIS

Queen's University. Women's Centre, 1070

Queen's University. Women's Studies Programme. Lesbian Speakers Series Committee, 478

Queen's University. Women's Study Action Committee, 479

Ryerson Polytechnical Institute. Employment and Educational Equity Office, 485

Ryerson Polytechnical Institute. Office of Harassment Prevention Services, 486

SFU Co-op Family, 147

Simon Fraser University. Employment Equity Advisory Committee, 840

Simon Fraser University. Public Interest Research Group, 841

Simon Fraser University. Women's Centre, 842

Simon Fraser University. Women's Studies Program, 148

Simone de Beauvoir Institute/Institut Simone de Beauvoir, 1252

Stop Rape Week Committee, 631

Students' Administrative Council (University of Toronto). Women's Commission, 492

Toronto Women's Liberation Movement, 509

Trent Lesbian and Gay Collective, 511, 1087

University of Alberta. Campus Day Care Committee, 224

University of Alberta. Office of the Dean of Women, 225

University of Alberta. President's Interim Advisory Committee on Women's Issues, 226

University of Alberta. Senate. Task Force on the Status of Women, 227

University of Alberta. Women's Program and Resource Centre, 228

University of British Columbia. Women's Office, 152

University of Calgary. Women's Studies Programme, 905

University of Manitoba. Women's Studies Committee, 323

University of Ottawa. Women's Studies Programme/Université d'Ottawa. Programme en études des femmes, 1091

University of Saskatchewan. Committee on the Status of Women, 278

University of Saskatchewan. Women's Centre, 949

University of Saskatchewan. Women's Studies Research Unit, 950

University of Toronto. Advisory Committee to the Status of Women Officer, 514

University of Toronto. Committee on Sexual Harassment, 515

University of Toronto. Gays and Lesbians at the University of Toronto, 516

University of Toronto. Gays at the University of Toronto, 517

University of Toronto. Homophile Association, 518

University of Toronto. Lesbian and Gay Academic Society, 519

University of Toronto. Sexual Education Centre, 520

University of Toronto. Sexual Harassment Education, Counselling, and Complaint Office, 1092

University of Toronto. Status of Women Committee, 521

University of Toronto. Women's Centre, 522

University of Toronto. Women's Coalition, 523

University of Victoria. President's Advisory Committee on Equal Rights and Opportunities, 154

University of Victoria. Women's Action Group, 155

University of Western Ontario. University Students' Council. Women's Issues Commission, 524, 1093

Vancouver Women's Caucus, 161

Women in Scholarship, Engineering, Science, and Technology (University of Alberta), 235, 908

Women in Science Network (University of Saskatchewan), 951

Women (Trent University), 547

Women's Centre (Ryerson Polytechnical Institute), 550

Women's Centre (University of Waterloo), 551

Women's Collective and Resource Centre (University of Calgary), 912

Women's Collective Press, 636

Women's Resources Centre (University of British Columbia), 872

Women's Studies Student Union (New College), 573

York University. Committee on Women's Programmes, 575

York University. Harbinger Community Services, 576

York University. Office of the Advisor to the University on the Status of Women, 577

York University. Senate Task Force on the Status of Women, 579

York Women's Centre, 580, 1115

university graduates *see* **alumnae**

urban environment *see* **environment**

venereal diseases *see* **sexually transmitted diseases**

videos

(*see also* **films**)

Groupe intervention vidéo, 1211

Toronto Women in Film and Television, 1086

Women's Involvement Programme (Toronto, Ont.), 561

violence

(*see also* **battered women, family violence, pornography, self-defence, sexual abuse of children, sexual assault, sexual harassment**)

Anna Project, 345

Association for the Prevention of Community and Family Violence, 773

Bunch of Feminists, 358

Coppermine Women's Group, 779

December 6th Women's Memorial Committee, 957

Kamloops Sexual Assault Counselling Centre, 819

North East Crisis Intervention Centre, 928

Parkland Crisis Centre, 978

Southwest Crisis Services, 948

Stop Rape Week Committee, 631

Take Back the Night Committee (Toronto, Ont.), 493

University of Toronto. Women's Coalition, 523

Vancouver Rape Relief and Women's Shelter, 852

Women against Violence against Women (Toronto, Ont.), 540

Women's Inter-Church Council of Canada/Conseil œcuménique des chrétiennes du Canada, 771

visible minorities *see* **women of colour**

visual arts

(*see also* **art galleries, craft arts, films, photography, videos**)

Bunch of Feminists, 358

Gallerie Publications, 734

Makara Publishing and Design Co-operative, 69

Mentoring Artists for Women's Art, 970

Nova Scotia Women Artists' Network, 1333

Womanspirit Art Research and Learning Centre, 536

Women's Art Mobile, 549

Women's Art Resource Centre, 770

Women's Perspective Collective, 565

waitresses

Hotel, Restaurant, Culinary Employees, and Bartenders Union. Local 40, 815

Waitresses' Action Committee, 529

welfare *see* **social assistance**

wife abuse *see* **battered women**

women of colour

(Note: *For a list of terms for specific groups (e.g.,* **Black women, Chinese women**) *see ethnocultural organizations.*)

Canadian Ethnocultural Council. Women's Committee/Conseil ethnoculturel du Canada. Comité des femmes, 709

Coalition of Visible Minority Women (Ontario), 1012

Immigrant Women's Health Centre, 1031

Multicultural Women's Association, 1045

National Organization of Immigrant and Visible Minority Women of Canada/Organisation nationale des femmes immigrantes et des femmes appartenant à une minorité visible du Canada, 752

Sister Vision: Black Women and Women of Colour Press, 1077

Women of Colour Collective, 909

women's centres

Antigonish Women's Association, 1315

Bay St George Status of Women Council, 1352

Brampton Women's Centre, 353

B.C. and Yukon Association of Women's Centres, 790

Centre for Women (Sheridan College. Brampton Campus), 365

Changing Together: A Centre for Immigrant Women, 887

Chetwynd Women's Resource Society, 801

Chez nous, 1008

Circle, 1010

Community Women's Centre (Regina, Sask.), 245

Concordia Women's Centre, 1189

Contact: Women's Resource and Information Centre, 1275

Corner Brook Status of Women Council, 1356

Crossroads, 888

Crowsnest Pass Women's Resources and Crisis Centre Society, 889

Douglas College. Women's Centre, 804

Downtown Eastside Women's Centre, 131

Dryden Aboriginal Women's Resource Centre, 1020

East Prince Women's Information Committee, 1307

Edmonton Women's Centre, 198

Edmonton Women's Place, 200

Every Woman's Place (Edmonton, Alta.), 202

Fernie Women's Resource and Drop-in Centre, 807

Fort Garry Women's Resource Centre, 958

Fort St John Women's Resource Centre, 809

Fredericton Women's Centre, 645

Gander Status of Women Council, 1357

Gateway Status of Women Council, 1358

Golden Women's Resource Centre, 811

Grande Prairie Women's Place, 208

Guelph Women's Centre, 402

Ishtar Women's Centre and Transition House, 137

K-W Woman's Place, 409

Kaslo Women's Group, 138

Kelowna Women's Resource Centre, 821

Kingston Women's Centre, 411

Labrador West Status of Women Council, 1360

Lennoxville and District Women's Centre/Centre des femmes de Lennoxville et des environs, 1217

London Women's Resource Centre, 432

McGill Women's Union, 620

Multicultural Council of Professional Women, 1044

Nanaimo Women's Resources Society, 828

Native Women's Centre (Hamilton, Ont.), 1047

Native Women's Resource Centre (Toronto, Ont.), 1048

New Woman Centre/Centre de la femme nouvelle, 627

North Shore Women's Centre, 141, 829

Northern Women's Centre, 451

Original Women's Network, 976

Ottawa Women's Centre, 466, 1061

Pauline McGibbon Cultural Centre, 469

Penticton and Area Women's Centre, 830

Peterborough Women's Committee, 470

Peterborough Women's Place, 471

Pictou County Women's Centre, 1335

Port Alberni Women's Resources Society, 832

Port Coquitlam Area Women's Centre, 143, 833

Queen's University. Women's Centre, 1070

Regina Women's Community Centre and Sexual Assault Line, 935

Richmond Women's Resource Centre Association, 836

St John's Status of Women Council, 689, 1364

Sarnia-Lambton Status of Women Committee, 488

Saskatoon Women's Liberation, 273

Scarborough Women's Centre, 1072

Second Story Women's Centre, 1338

Simon Fraser University. Women's Centre, 842

Single Moms Centre, 690

Single Parent Centre (Halifax, N.S.), 1340

Single Parent Resource Centre (Saint John, N.B.), 1294

Sistering: A Drop-in Centre for Transient Women, 1078

South Asian Women's Community Centre/Centre communautaire des femmes sud-asiatiques, 1255

Sudbury Women's Centre/Centre des femmes de Sudbury, 1081

Tamitik Status of Women, 150

Terrace Women's Resource Centre, 844

University of Alberta. Women's Program and Resource Centre, 228

University of British Columbia. Women's Office, 152

University of Saskatchewan. Women's Centre, 949

University of Toronto. Women's Centre, 522

University of Western Ontario. University Students' Council. Women's Issues Commission, 524, 1093

Vancouver Lesbian Centre, 850

Vancouver Life Skills Society, 851

Vancouver Women's Health Collective, 162, 855

Victoria Faulkner Women's Centre, 102

Victoria Status of Women Action Group, 165, 858

Victoria Women's Centre, 166

West Kootenay Women's Association, 864

Windsor Women's Incentive Centre, 1095

Woman's Place (Halifax, N.S.), 677

Woman's Place (Montreal, Quebec), 635

Woman's Place (Vancouver, B.C.), 168

Woman's Place (Winnipeg, Man.), 333

Womanspirit Art Research and Learning Centre, 536

Women Immigrants of London Resource Service Centre, 1099

Women's Art Resource Centre, 770

Women's Centre (Halifax, N.S.), 680
Women's Centre (Ryerson Polytechnical Institute), 550
Women's Centre (University of Waterloo), 551
Women's Centre (Vancouver, B.C.), 171
Women's Centres Connect!, 1350
Women's Collective and Resource Centre (University of Calgary), 912
Women's Communications Centre, 553
Women's Information and Support Centre of Halton, 1108
Women's Place Kenora, 1109
Women's Place (Lethbridge, Alta.), 237
Women's Place/Place aux femmes (Ottawa, Ont.), 1110
Women's Place (Toronto, Ont.), 566
Women's Place (Windsor, Ont.), 567
Women's Resource Centre (Hay River, N.W.T.), 781
Women's Resource Centre (St Catharines, Ont.), 569
Women's Resource Centre (Timmins, Ont.), 570
Women's Resource Society of Fort McMurray, 913
Women's Resources Centre (University of British Columbia), 872
Working Women Community Centre, 1114
York University. Committee on Women's Programmes, 575
York Women's Centre, 580, 1115
Yorkton Women's Advisory Committee, 286
Young Women's Christian Association of Calgary, 238, 914
Young Women's Christian Association of Metropolitan Toronto, 581, 1116
Young Women's Christian Association of Yellowknife, 782
YWCA Banff Community Resource Centre, 917
YWCA Women's Centre (Montreal, Quebec), 638

women's studies

(*see also* **archives**, **history**, **libraries**, **universities**)

Canadian Research Institute for the Advancement of Women/Institut canadien de recherches sur les femmes, 31, 713
Canadian Research Institute for the Advancement of Women/Institut canadien de recherches sur les femmes. 1990 Publications Committee, 1304
Canadian Research Institute for the Advancement of Women, Newfoundland and Labrador, 1354
Canadian Research Institute for the Advancement of Women — Nova Scotia, 661, 1318
Canadian Woman Studies/Cahiers de la femme, 715
Canadian Women's Movement Archives/Archives canadiennes du mouvement des femmes, 35
Carleton University. Institute of Women's Studies, 1004
Collective (University of Ottawa)/Collective (Université d'Ottawa), 1015
Dalhousie University. Women's Studies Programme, 1322
Douglas College. Women's Studies Programme, 130
Lesbian Studies Coalition of Concordia, 615, 1218
McGill University. Committee for Teaching and Research on Women, 619
Memorial University of Newfoundland. Women's Studies Programme, 1362
Mount Saint Vincent University, 670, 1331
National Council of Women of Canada, 73
Nellie Langford Rowell Library, 1049

New College. Women's Studies Programme, 446
Queen's University. Women's Studies Programme. Lesbian Speakers Series Committee, 478
Resources for Feminist Research/Documentation sur la recherche féministe, 85, 762
Simon Fraser University. Women's Studies Program, 148
Simone de Beauvoir Institute/Institut Simone de Beauvoir, 1252
Toronto Centre for Lesbian and Gay Studies, 499
University of Alberta. Women's Program and Resource Centre, 228
University of Calgary. Women's Studies Programme, 905
University of Manitoba. Women's Studies Committee, 323
University of Ottawa. Women's Studies Programme/Université d'Ottawa. Programme en études des femmes, 1091
University of Saskatchewan. Women's Studies Research Unit, 950
University of Victoria. Faculty Association. Status of Women Committee, 153
University of Victoria. Women's Action Group, 155
Women's Educational Resources Centre (Ontario Institute for Studies in Education), 1105
Women's Research Centre, 100
Women's Studies Association of British Columbia, 176
Women's Studies Student Union (New College), 573
York University. Committee on Women's Programmes, 575
Young Women's Christian Association (St John's, Nfld.), 692

work *see* **employment**, **homemakers**

working-class women

(*see also* **trade unions**)

Women's Labour History Project, 173, 871

writers *see* **journalists**, **literature**

young women

Halifax Young Women's Christian Association, 667, 1327
Kitchener-Waterloo Young Women's Christian Association, 414, 1036
National Council of Young Men's Christian Associations. Task Force on the Status of Women in the YMCA, 74
Regina Young Women's Christian Association, 259, 936
Stepping Stone Program, 1344
Winnipeg Gay/Lesbian Youth, 329
Young Women's Christian Association of Calgary, 238, 914
Young Women's Christian Association of Canada, 101
Young Women's Christian Association of Edmonton, 239, 915
Young Women's Christian Association of Lethbridge and District, 916
Young Women's Christian Association of Metropolitan Toronto, 581, 1116
Young Women's Christian Association of Peterborough Victoria and Haliburton, 582, 1117
Young Women's Christian Association of Prince Albert, 954
Young Women's Christian Association of St Thomas-Elgin, 583, 1118
Young Women's Christian Association of Thompson, 339, 991
Young Women's Christian Association of Yellowknife, 782
Young Women's Christian Association (St John's, Nfld.), 692
Young Women's Christian Association, Saskatoon, 287
Young Women's Christian Association (Vancouver, B.C.), 179, 873
Young Women's Christian Association (Winnipeg, Man.), 340

APPENDIX: ADDRESSES AND ENTRY NUMBERS FOR ARCHIVES
ANNEXE : ADRESSES ET NUMÉROS DE NOTICES DES ARCHIVES

Anglican Church of Canada, General Synod Archives
600 Jarvis St.
Toronto, Ont.
M4Y 2J6
Telephone/Téléphone : (416) 924-9192, ext. 278
Entries/Notices : 392, 444

Archives de l'Association des infirmières et infirmiers du Canada voir **Canadian Nurses Association Archives / Archives de l'Association des infirmières et infirmiers du Canada**

Archives de l'Évêché de Sainte-Anne-de-la-Pocatière
C.P. 430
La Pocatière (Québec)
G0R 1Z0
Téléphone/Telephone: (418) 856-1811
Télécopieur/Fax: (418) 856-5513
Notices/Entries: 600

Archives nationales du Canada / National Archives of Canada
395 Wellington
Ottawa (Ont.)
K1A 0N3
Téléphone/Telephone: (613) 995-5138
Télécopieur/Fax: (613) 995-6274
Notices/Entries: 2, 4-5, 7-8, 11, 16-20, 22-23, 28, 32-33, 37-38, 40, 44-47, 49, 51-57, 68, 70-71, 73-75, 79, 81-84, 88-90, 92-93, 98, 101, 146, 252, 256, 359, 362-363, 387-388, 445, 465, 490, 498, 526, 598, 603, 606, 621, 624

Archives nationales du Québec, Centre d'archives de la Mauricie et des Bois-Francs
225, rue des Forges, suite 208
Trois-Rivières (Québec)
G9A 2G7
Téléphone/Telephone: (819) 371-6015
Notices/Entries: 602

Archives nationales du Québec, Centre d'archives de l'Abitibi-Témiscamingue
27, rue du Terminus ouest
Rouyn-Noranda (Québec)
J9X 2P3
Téléphone/Telephone: (819) 762-4484
Notices/Entries: 589, 605

Archives nationales du Québec, Centre d'archives de Montréal
1945, rue Mullins
Montréal (Québec)
H3K 1N9
Téléphone/Telephone: (514) 873-3064
Télécopieur/Fax: (514) 873-2980
Notices/Entries: 588, 590, 601, 606, 612

Archives nationales du Québec, Centre d'archives de Québec et de Chaudière-Appalaches
1210, av. du Séminaire, C.P. 10450
Sainte-Foy (Québec)
G1V 4N1
Téléphone/Telephone: (418) 643-8904
Télécopieur/Fax: (418) 646-0868
Notices/Entries: 604

APPENDIX: ADDRESSES AND ENTRY NUMBERS FOR ARCHIVES

Archives of Ontario / Archives publiques de l'Ontario

77 Grenville St.

Toronto, Ont.

M7A 2R9

Telephone/Téléphone : (416) 965-4039

Fax/Télécopieur : (416) 324-3600

Entries/Notices : 6, 12, 359, 366, 381, 390, 400, 403, 428, 453, 458, 468, 472, 476, 490, 496, 498, 506, 525, 531, 581

Archives provinciales du Manitoba voir **Provincial Archives of Manitoba / Archives provinciales du Manitoba**

Archives provinciales du Nouveau-Brunswick / Provincial Archives of New Brunswick

C.P. 6000/P.O. Box 6000

Fredericton (N.-B.)

E3B 5H1

Téléphone/Telephone: (506) 453-2122

Télécopieur/Fax : (506) 453-3288

Notices/Entries: 73, 647, 650-652

Archives publiques de l'Ontario voir **Archives of Ontario / Archives publiques de l'Ontario**

Beaton Institute, University College of Cape Breton

P.O. Box 5300

Sydney, N.S.

B1P 6L2

Telephone/Téléphone : (902) 539-5300

Entries/Notices : 659, 662, 668-669, 672, 678-679

Brampton Public Library, Local History Collection, Chinguacousy Resource Branch

150 Central Park Dr.

Brampton, Ont.

L6T 1B4

Telephone/Téléphone : (416) 793-4636

Fax/Télécopieur : (416) 793-0506

Entries/Notices : 353

Brandon University Archives

Umphrey Centre, Victoria Avenue & 20th St.

Brandon, Man.

R7A 6A9

Telephone/Téléphone : (204) 727-9628

Entries/Notices : 289

British Columbia Archives and Records Service

655 Belleville St.

Victoria, B.C.

V8V 1X4

Telephone/Téléphone : (604) 387-5885/1321

Fax/Télécopieur : (604) 387-2072

Entries/Notices : 92-93, 115, 123, 145, 163-164, 173

Canadian Gay Archives

P.O. Box 639, Station A

Toronto, Ont.

M5W 1G2

Telephone/Téléphone : (416) 777-2755

Entries/Notices : 15, 24-25, 41, 65, 67, 80, 111, 133, 149, 299, 346-347, 352, 357, 367, 371, 373, 377, 384, 393-394, 396-397, 416-419, 424, 426, 429, 434, 442, 475, 477, 495, 497, 501-502, 511, 513, 516-519, 527-528, 547, 591, 608, 613-615, 618, 625-626, 641, 644, 648, 658, 664

Canadian Jewish Congress, National Archives

1590 Docteur Penfield

Montreal, Quebec

H3G 1C5

Telephone/Téléphone : (514) 931-7531

Fax/Télécopieur : (514) 931-0548

Entries/Notices : 72

Canadian Nurses Association Archives / Archives de l'Association des infirmières et infirmiers du Canada

50 The Driveway

Ottawa, Ont.

K2P 1E2

Telephone/Téléphone : (613) 237-2133

Fax/Télécopieur : (613) 237-3520

Entries/Notices : 8, 28

Canadian Women's Movement Archives Collection, Morisset Library Special Collections, University of Ottawa / Fonds des Archives canadiennes du mouvement des femmes, Collections spéciales de la Bibliothèque Morisset, Université d'Ottawa

65 University/Université

Ottawa, Ont.

K1N 9A5

Telephone/Téléphone : (613) 564-8130

Fax/Télécopieur : (613) 564-9886

Entries/Notices : 1, 3, 5, 9-10, 13-16, 21, 24, 27, 29-30, 34-36, 39, 41, 44, 48, 50, 58-63, 65-67, 69, 71, 78, 80, 85-87, 91, 94-97, 99-100, 105, 109-111, 122, 125-126, 129, 132, 135-137, 140, 144, 147, 150, 152, 158, 160-162, 165-171, 174-175, 177-178, 182, 184, 199-200,

202, 208, 213, 218-219, 231, 236-237, 244-245, 247, 254, 257, 263, 266, 268, 272-273, 277, 284, 286, 304, 317, 323, 332-336, 341-345, 348, 350-351, 353-358, 360, 364-365, 368-370, 372-377, 379-380, 382-383, 385-386, 389, 391-393, 395, 399, 401-402, 404, 406-411, 413, 415, 419-426, 429-433, 435-441, 443-452, 454-456, 458-464, 466-467, 469, 471, 474, 477-484, 487-489, 491-495, 499-500, 502-505, 507-510, 514-515, 519-523, 527-529, 533-534, 537-546, 548-549, 551-554, 556-574, 576, 581, 592-593, 595, 597, 607, 609-611, 616, 618, 620, 622-623, 627, 631, 635-638, 642-643, 645-646, 649, 655, 658, 663, 673-674, 680-681, 685, 689-691

Centrale de l'enseignement du Québec, Centre de documentation

1170, boul. Lebourgneuf, bureau 300
Québec (Québec)
G2K 2G1
Téléphone/Telephone: (418) 627-8888
Télécopieur/Fax: (418) 627-9999
Notices/Entries: 594

Centre acadien de l'Université Sainte-Anne

Pointe-de-l'Église (N.-É.)
B0W 1M0
Téléphone/Telephone: (902) 769-2114, 769-0909
Notices/Entries: 657

Centre de recherche en civilisation canadienne-française, Université d'Ottawa

145, Jean-Jacques Lussier
Ottawa (Ont.)
K1N 6N5
Téléphone/Telephone: (613) 564-6847/8
Notices/Entries: 55, 512

Centre d'études acadiennes, Université de Moncton

Moncton (N.-B.)
E1A 3E9
Téléphone/Telephone: (506) 858-4085
Télécopieur/Fax: (506) 858-4585
Notices/Entries: 639

Centre for Newfoundland Studies Archives, Memorial University of Newfoundland

Queen Elizabeth II Library, Memorial University of Newfoundland
St John's, Nfld.
A1B 3Y1
Telephone/Téléphone : (709) 737-4349
Entries/Notices : 684, 686, 692-693

Chancellor Paterson Library Archives, Lakehead University

Oliver Rd.
Thunder Bay, Ont.
P7B 5E1
Telephone/Téléphone : (807) 343-8110
Entries/Notices : 361

Chilliwack Archives, Chilliwack Museum and Historical Society

9291 Corbould St.
Chilliwack, B.C.
V2P 4A6
Telephone/Téléphone : (604) 795-9255
Entries/Notices : 127-128

City of Red Deer Archives

P.O. Box 800
Red Deer, Alta.
T4N 5H2
Telephone/Téléphone : (403) 343-6842
Fax/Télécopieur : (403) 346-6195
Entries/Notices : 183, 215-216

City of Vancouver Archives

1150 Chestnut St.
Vancouver, B.C.
V6J 3J9
Telephone/Téléphone : (604) 736-8561
Entries/Notices : 124, 131, 156-157

D.B. Weldon Library — Regional Collection, University of Western Ontario

London, Ont.
N6A 3K7
Telephone/Téléphone : (519) 679-2111, ext. 4813
Entries/Notices : 349, 427, 524, 535-536

Dalhousie University Archives

University Library, Dalhousie University
Halifax, N.S.
B3H 4H8
Telephone/Téléphone : (902) 494-6490
Entries/Notices : 673

APPENDIX: ADDRESSES AND ENTRY NUMBERS FOR ARCHIVES

Doris Lewis Rare Book Room, University of Waterloo Library
Waterloo, Ont.
N2L 3G1
Telephone/Téléphone : (519) 885-1211, ext. 3122
Fax/Télécopieur : (519) 747-4606
Entries/Notices : 73, 92-93, 414, 465, 468

Douglas College Archives
P.O. Box 2503
New Westminster, B.C.
V3L 5B2
Telephone/Téléphone : (604) 527-5181
Fax/Télécopieur : (604) 527-5095
Entries/Notices : 130

École des hautes études commerciales, Service des archives
5255, av. Decelles
Montréal (Québec)
H3T 1V6
Téléphone/Telephone: (514) 340-6207
Télécopieur/Fax: (514) 340-5639
Notices/Entries: 599

Flin Flon Community Archives
58 Main St.
Flin Flon, Man.
R8A 1J8
Telephone/Téléphone : (204) 687-3397
Entries/Notices : 290, 297

Fonds des Archives canadiennes du mouvement des femmes, Collections spéciales de la Bibliothèque Morisset, Université d'Ottawa voir **Canadian Women's Movement Archives Collection, Morisset Library Special Collections, University of Ottawa / Fonds des Archives canadiennes du mouvement des femmes, Collections spéciales de la Bibliothèque Morisset, Université d'Ottawa**

George Brown College Archives
P.O. Box 1015, Station B
Toronto, Ont.
M5T 2T9
Telephone/Téléphone : (416) 867-2416
Fax/Télécopieur : (416) 867-2298
Entries/Notices : 398

Glenbow Museum Archives
130 9th Ave. S.E.
Calgary, Alta.
T2G 0P3
Telephone/Téléphone : (403) 264-8300
Fax/Télécopieur : (403) 265-9769
Entries/Notices : 73, 183-184, 186-193, 195, 201, 205, 209-212, 217, 229, 232, 234, 238

Grace Schmidt Room of Local History, Kitchener Public Library
85 Queen St. N.
Kitchener, Ont.
N2H 2H1
Telephone/Téléphone : (519) 743-0271
Fax/Télécopieur : (519) 743-1261
Entries/Notices : 378, 412

Griffin-Greenland Collection on the History of Canadian Psychiatry, Queen Street Mental Health Centre
1001 Queen St. W.
Toronto, Ont.
M6J 1H4
Telephone/Téléphone : (416) 535-8501, ext. 294
Entries/Notices : 26

Hamilton Public Library, Special Collections
P.O. Box 2700, Station A
Hamilton, Ont.
L8N 4E4
(Street Address: 55 York Blvd.)
Telephone/Téléphone : (416) 529-8111
Fax/Télécopieur : (416) 529-5326
Entries/Notices : 403, 473

Jewish Historical Society of Western Canada
Suite 404-365 Hargrave St.
Winnipeg, Man.
R3B 2K3
Telephone/Téléphone : (204) 942-4822
Entries/Notices : 315

Kitchener Public Library see **Grace Schmidt Room of Local History, Kitchener Public Library**

Kitimat Centennial Museum
293 City Centre
Kitimat, B.C.
V8C 1T6
Telephone/Téléphone : (604) 632-7022
Entries/Notices : 139, 150

ANNEXE : ADRESSES ET NUMÉROS DE NOTICES DES ARCHIVES

Kootenay Lake Archives
Box 537
Kaslo, B.C.
V0G 1M0
Entries/Notices : 138

Lakehead University *see* **Chancellor Paterson Library Archives, Lakehead University**

Legislative Library of Manitoba
200 Vaughan St.
Winnipeg, Man.
R3C 1T5
Telephone/Téléphone : (204) 945-4330
Entries/Notices : 338

McGill University Archives
3459 McTavish St.
Montreal, Quebec
H3A 1Y1
Telephone/Téléphone : (514) 398-3772
Fax/Télécopieur : (514) 398-8456
Entries/Notices : 619

McMaster University Library, William Ready Division of Archives and Research Collections
1280 Main St. W.
Hamilton, Ont.
L8S 4L6
Telephone/Téléphone : (416) 525-9140, ext. 4737
Entries/Notices : 92-93, 111

Manitoba Gay/Lesbian Archive
Winnipeg Gay/Lesbian Resource Centre, Box 1661
Winnipeg, Man.
R3C 2Z6
Telephone/Téléphone : (204) 284-5208, 474-0212
Entries/Notices : 288, 295, 298-299, 302-303, 319-320, 328-329

Memorial University of Newfoundland *see* **Centre for Newfoundland Studies Archives, Memorial University of Newfoundland**

Moose Jaw Public Library, Archives Department
461 Langdon Crescent
Moose Jaw, Sask.
S6H 0X0
Telephone/Téléphone : (306) 692-2787
Entries/Notices : 241, 249, 279

Mount Allison University Archives
Ralph Pickard Bell Library, Mount Allison University
Sackville, N.B.
E0A 3C0
Telephone/Téléphone : (506) 364-2563
Entries/Notices : 640

Mount Saint Vincent University Archives
E. Margaret Fulton Centre, 166 Bedford Highway
Halifax, N.S.
B3M 2J6
Telephone/Téléphone : (902) 443-4450
Entries/Notices : 670

Municipal Archives — Windsor Public Library
850 Ouellette Ave.
Windsor, Ont.
N9A 4N9
Telephone/Téléphone : (519) 255-6782
Fax/Télécopieur : (519) 255-7207
Entries/Notices : 532

National Archives of Canada *see* **Archives nationales du Canada/National Archives of Canada**

Nellie Langford Rowell Library, York University
202C Founders College, 4700 Keele St.
North York, Ont.
M3J 1P3
Telephone/Téléphone : (416) 736-2100, ext. 33219
Entries/Notices : 447, 575, 577-580

Newfoundland Historical Society
Room 15, Colonial Bldg., Military Rd.
St John's, Nfld.
A1C 2C9
Telephone/Téléphone : (709) 722-3191
Entries/Notices : 688

North American Black Historical Museum
P.O. Box 12
Amherstburg, Ont.
N9V 2Z2
(Street Address: 277 King St.)
Telephone/Téléphone : (519) 736-5433
Entries/Notices : 405

APPENDIX: ADDRESSES AND ENTRY NUMBERS FOR ARCHIVES

Northwest Territories Archives
Northern Heritage Centre
Yellowknife, N.W.T.
X1A 2L9
Telephone/Téléphone : (403) 873-7698
Fax/Télécopieur : (403) 873-0205
Entries/Notices : 31, 64

Provincial Archives of Alberta
12845 102nd Ave.
Edmonton, Alta.
T5N 0M6
Telephone/Téléphone : (403) 427-1750
Fax/Télécopieur : (403) 454-6629
Entries/Notices : 63, 181, 185, 194, 196-198, 204, 206-207, 214, 220-222, 230, 233, 239-240

Provincial Archives of Manitoba / Archives provinciales du Manitoba
200 Vaughan St.
Winnipeg, Man.
R3C 1T5
Telephone/Téléphone : (204) 945-3971
Fax/Télécopieur : (204) 948-2008
Entries/Notices : 291-294, 296, 300-301, 304-314, 316, 318, 321-322, 324-327, 330-333, 337, 339-340

Provincial Archives of New Brunswick *see* **Archives provinciales du Nouveau-Brunswick / Provincial Archives of New Brunswick**

Provincial Archives of Newfoundland and Labrador
Colonial Bldg., Military Rd.
St John's, Nfld.
A1C 2C9
Telephone/Téléphone : (709) 753-9380/9390/9398
Entries/Notices : 685, 687

Public Archives of Nova Scotia
6016 University Ave.
Halifax, N.S.
B3H 1W4
Telephone/Téléphone : (902) 424-6060
Fax/Télécopieur : (902) 424-0516
Entries/Notices : 31, 42-43, 64, 92-93, 115, 660-661, 665-667, 671, 673, 675-677, 682-683

Public Archives of Prince Edward Island
Box 1000
Charlottetown, P.E.I.
C1A 7M4
Telephone/Téléphone : (902) 368-4290
Entries/Notices : 653-654, 656

Queen Street Mental Health Centre *see* **Griffin-Greenland Collection on the History of Canadian Psychiatry, Queen Street Mental Health Centre**

Queen's University Archives
Kathleen Ryan Hall, Queen's University
Kingston, Ont.
K7L 3N6
Telephone/Téléphone : (613) 545-2378
Entries/Notices : 457

Region of Peel Archives
Peel Heritage Complex, 9 Wellington St. E.
Brampton, Ont.
L6W 1Y1
Telephone/Téléphone : (416) 457-3948
Entries/Notices : 44, 71, 92-93

Ryerson Polytechnical Institute Archives
350 Victoria St.
Toronto, Ont.
M5B 2K3
Telephone/Téléphone : (416) 979-5000, ext. 7027
Fax/Télécopieur : (416) 979-5155
Entries/Notices : 485-486, 550

St Thomas-Elgin Public Library, Local History Section (George Thorman Room)
153 Curtis St.
St Thomas, Ont.
N5P 3Z7
Telephone/Téléphone : (519) 631-6050
Entries/Notices : 583

Saskatchewan Archives Board, Regina
University of Regina
Regina, Sask.
S4S 0A2
(Street Address: 3303 Hillsdale St.)
Telephone/Téléphone : (306) 787-4068
Fax/Télécopieur : (306) 787-1975
Entries/Notices : 21-22, 48, 52, 241-243, 245-246, 250-253, 255-261, 264, 267, 269-270, 273, 275-276, 280, 282, 285

ANNEXE : ADRESSES ET NUMÉROS DE NOTICES DES ARCHIVES

Saskatchewan Archives Board, Saskatoon
University of Saskatchewan
Saskatoon, Sask.
S7N 0W0
Telephone/Téléphone : (306) 933-5832
Entries/Notices : 248, 252, 260, 262, 265, 270-271, 273-274, 281, 283, 287

Selkirk College Library, Archives and Local History Collection
Box 1200
Castlegar, B.C.
V1N 3J1
Telephone/Téléphone : (604) 365-7292
Fax/Télécopieur : (604) 365-6568
Entries/Notices : 134

Simon Fraser University Archives
Burnaby, B.C.
V5A 1S6
Telephone/Téléphone : (604) 291-3261
Fax/Télécopieur : (604) 291-4908
Entries/Notices : 141, 143, 148, 176

Thomas Fisher Rare Book Library, University of Toronto
120 St George St.
Toronto, Ont.
M5S 1A5
Telephone/Téléphone : (416) 978-5285
Fax/Télécopieur : (416) 978-1667
Entries/Notices : 80, 167, 447, 496, 508-509, 607

Thunder Bay Historical Museum Society
219 South May St.
Thunder Bay, Ont.
P7E 1B5
Telephone/Téléphone : (807) 623-0801
Entries/Notices : 530

Trent University Archives
Bata Library, Trent University
Peterborough, Ont.
K9J 7B8
Telephone/Téléphone : (705) 748-1413
Entries/Notices : 470, 582

Université de Moncton voir **Centre d'études acadiennes, Université de Moncton**

Université de Montréal, Service des archives
C.P. 6128, Succursale A
Montréal (Québec)
H3C 3J7
Téléphone/Telephone: (514) 343-6021
Télécopieur/Fax: (514) 343-2239
Notices/Entries: 586

Université d'Ottawa, Centre de recherche en civilisation canadienne-française voir **Centre de recherche en civilisation canadienne-française, Université d'Ottawa**

Université d'Ottawa, Collections spéciales de la Bibliothèque Morisset voir **Canadian Women's Movement Archives Collection, Morisset Library Special Collections, University of Ottawa / Fonds des Archives canadiennes du mouvement des femmes, Collections spéciales de la Bibliothèque Morisset, Université d'Ottawa**

Université du Québec à Montréal, Service des archives
C.P. 8888, Succursale A
Montréal (Québec)
H3C 3P8
Téléphone/Telephone: (514) 987-6130
Télécopieur/Fax: (514) 987-8487
Notices/Entries: 596, 617, 628-630

Université Laval, Division des archives
Pavillon Jean-Charles-Bonenfant, bureau 5470
Sainte-Foy (Québec)
G1K 7P4
Téléphone/Telephone: (418) 656-3722
Télécopieur/Fax: (418) 651-3419
Notices/Entries: 584-585, 587, 632-634

University College of Cape Breton see **Beaton Institute, University College of Cape Breton**

University of Alberta Archives
1-19 Rutherford (South)
Edmonton, Alta.
T6G 2E1
Telephone/Téléphone : (403) 432-5146
Fax/Télécopieur : (403) 492-4327
Entries/Notices : 180, 203, 223-228, 230, 235

APPENDIX: ADDRESSES AND ENTRY NUMBERS FOR ARCHIVES

University of British Columbia Library, Special Collections–Manuscripts
1956 Main Mall
Vancouver, B.C.
V6T 1Y3
Telephone/Téléphone : (604) 228-2521
Fax/Télécopieur : (604) 228-6465
Entries/Notices : 92-93, 106-108, 111-121, 142, 145-146, 157-159, 172, 174, 179

University of British Columbia Library, University Archives
1956 Main Mall
Vancouver, B.C.
V6T 1Y3
Telephone/Téléphone : (604) 228-2521
Fax/Télécopieur : (604) 228-6465
Entries/Notices : 151

University of Guelph Library, Archives and Special Collections
Guelph, Ont.
N1G 2W1
Telephone/Téléphone : (519) 824-4120, ext. 3413
Fax/Télécopieur : (519) 824-6931
Entries/Notices : 73

University of Manitoba Libraries, Department of Archives and Special Collections
Winnipeg, Man.
R3T 2N2
Telephone/Téléphone : (204) 474-6350
Entries/Notices : 291

University of Ottawa, Morisset Library Special Collections see **Canadian Women's Movement Archives Collection, Morisset Library Special Collections, University of Ottawa / Fonds des Archives canadiennes du mouvement des femmes, Collections spéciales de la Bibliothèque Morisset, Université d'Ottawa**

University of Saskatchewan Archives
Saskatoon, Sask.
S7N 0W0
Telephone/Téléphone : (306) 966-6028
Entries/Notices : 267, 278

University of Toronto Archives
120 St George St.
Toronto, Ont.
M5S 1A5
Telephone/Téléphone : (416) 978-5344
Entries/Notices : 34, 76-77, 457, 525

University of Toronto, Thomas Fisher Rare Book Library see **Thomas Fisher Rare Book Library, University of Toronto**

University of Victoria Archives
P.O. Box 1800
Victoria, B.C.
V8W 3H5
Telephone/Téléphone : (604) 721-8258
Entries/Notices : 153-155

University of Waterloo Library see **Doris Lewis Rare Book Room, University of Waterloo Library**

University of Western Ontario see **D.B. Weldon Library — Regional Collection, University of Western Ontario**

Windsor Public Library see **Municipal Archives — Windsor Public Library**

Winnipeg Gay/Lesbian Resource Centre see **Manitoba Gay/Lesbian Archive**

Woodstock Public Library, Local History Collection
445 Hunter St.
Woodstock, Ont.
N4S 4G7
Telephone/Téléphone : (519) 539-4801
Entries/Notices : 555

York University see **Nellie Langford Rowell Library, York University**

Yukon Archives
Box 2703, 2071 - 2nd Ave.
Whitehorse, Yukon
Y1A 2C6
Telephone/Téléphone : (403) 667-5321
Fax/Télécopieur : (403) 667-4253
Entries/Notices : 102-104

LIST OF ILLUSTRATIONS
LISTE DES REPRODUCTIONS

Excerpt from a 1970 brief entitled: / extrait d'un mémoire de 1970 intitulé: "Abortion Caravan Demands"	34
Buttons / macarons	44
Newspaper / journal, 1972 — *The Other Woman*	52
International Women's Day march / manifestation de la Journée internationale des femmes, Toronto, 1987	56
Excerpt from minutes / extrait de procès-verbaux, 1980 — Bread and Roses	62
Demonstration to protest discrimination against women in the Indian Act / manifestation contre la discrimination envers les femmes dans la Loi sur les Indiens, 1973	67
Excerpts from a 1972 document entitled: / extrait d'un document de 1972 intitulé: "Lesbians Belong in the Women's Movement" [Vancouver Women's Caucus]	74
"We Want Equal Pay for Work of Equal Value"	84
Flyer / tract, 1979 — Saskatoon Women's Liberation	96
Flyer / tract, 1972 — Cross-Canada Abortion Conference [Manitoba Abortion Action Coalition]	102
"Sisters Pick Up Sisters"	110
Photo — *Breaking the Silence*	114
Flyer, [1977 or 1978] / tract, [1977 ou 1978] — Committee against the Deportation of Immigrant Women	118
Excerpts from a 1974 document entitled / extraits d'un document de 1974 intitulé: "The Adventures of Cora, the Bookmobile" [Cora: The Feminist Bookmobile]	120
International Women's Day march / manifestation de la Journée internationale des femmes, Toronto, 1982	136
Excerpt from a 1975 document entitled: / extrait d'un document de 1975 intitulé: "Notes on Consciousness-Raising" [Women's Resource Centre (St Catharines, Ont.)]	152
Excerpt from a personal account of a conference / extrait d'un compte rendu personnel — National Lesbian Conference / Conférence nationale de lesbiennes, 1975 [Montreal Gay Women/Lesbiennes de Montréal]	162
Bulletin / newsletter, 1975 — Liberté Égalité Sororité: Femmes acadiennes de Moncton	168
Newsletter / bulletin, 1978 — Atlantic Provinces Political Lesbians for Equality	172
Victoria Status of Women Action Group, [197-?]	208
Demonstration on child care / manifestation concernant la garde d'enfants, Toronto, 1980	220
Demonstration, Parliament Hill / manifestation, Colline du parlement, [197-]	234
Flyer / tract, 1991 — New Experiences for Refugee Women	244
Flyer / tract, [1987?] — Sister Vision: Black Women and Women of Colour Press	248
T-shirt, 1983 — Sudbury Women's Centre / Centre des femmes de Sudbury	250
Tract / flyer, 1982 — L'Androgyne	258

LIST OF ILLUSTRATIONS / LISTE DES REPRODUCTIONS

Extrait d'un document de 1976 intitulé: / excerpt from a 1976 document entitled:
« L'Implication des femmes dans la présente campagne électorale » [Fédération des femmes du Québec] 272

Excerpt from a 1972 letter written by a representative of the Newfoundland Status of Women Council to a magazine which was preparing an article on the women's movement / extrait d'une lettre écrite en 1972 par une représentante du Newfoundland Status of Women Council à un périodique qui préparait un article sur le mouvement des femmes 300